THE DEVIL HAS SLIPPERY SHOES, **written in the 1960s and reprinted** here with new opening and ending material, and a new foreword by Sheldon H. White of Harvard University, is of inestimable value as an inspiration, blueprint, and mind-blowingly insightful guide for today's professionals in Head Start and other programs for low-income young children and their families, as well as for faculty and students in early childhood education, social work and public health; grassroots project specialists; and indeed all citizens who sincerely want to play an active part in helping our troubled country get at the roots of its greatest domestic problem—its greatest shame—poverty.

This glorious ''story'' has more drama, emotion, suspense, excitement, plot, fascinating analysis, sharp social commentary, and magnificent characters than most prize-winning novels. It can be read as

- a seminal report on a successful model for the development of poor children and their parents,
- the ignored chapter in sixties Mississippi civil rights history when protest became program and black people were finally freed from a form of financial slavery, or
- an enormously stirring personal document of inner and professional growth.

Read this dramatic documentation of the next step in rapid social reform toward democratization of the old slave-holding South. This is the next chapter in a centuries' long story—when the life-risking protest of the 1950s and early 1960s became, in 1965, federally funded program—CDGM's unique HEAD START—economically releasing black people from an entrenched peonage system, thus forging the link to the future.

SLIPPERY SHOES presents a major missing piece of 1960s MISSISSIPPI HISTORY.

THE DEVIL HAS SLIPPERY SHOES

A Biased Biography of the Child Development Group of Mississippi

A Story of
Maximum Feasible Poor Parent Participation

POLLY GREENBERG

Youth Policy Institute
P.O. Box 40132
Washington, D.C. 20016

Originally published (1969) by the MacMillan Company
Collier-Macmillan Canada Ltd., Toronto, Ontario
printed in the United States of America, as
THE DEVIL HAS SLIPPERY SHOES:
A Biased Biography of the Child Development Group of Mississippi

Paperback reprint
with new beginning and ending material,
published (1990), by

Youth Policy Institute
David L. Hackett, Executive Director

P.O. Box 40132
Washington, D.C. 20016

Library of Congress Catalog Card Number: 90-071769
(previously Catalog Card Number 68-26430)
ISBN: 0-9628441-0-1

In memory of
Robert F. Kennedy
who cared about people
struggling to unstrangle themselves from poverty,
and worked to make
opportunities *truly* available to them.

When he met people in need,
he didn't write a paper,
he took *action.*

When he heard folks saying that changes
in their neighborhoods, or lives, or children's lives should be made,
he didn't get professionals to execute the changes *for* them
(thus executing initiative and budding leadership skills as well).
Instead he worked to ensure that
opportunities were created
so people could come together
and do their *own* planning:
and take it from there.

Under Robert F. Kennedy,
Chairman of the President's
Committee Against Juvenile Delinquency,
understanding the twin needs for opportunity
and maximum feasible participation
was discovered, developed,
and promoted until many
of us 1960s Poverty Warriors became infused
with the concepts.

Robert F. Kennedy
visited the Child Development Group of Mississippi (CDGM)
and understood it:
He saw people pulling themselves up by the bootstraps,
even though they were barefoot, and
were being stomped on by
"the American way of life."

ACKNOWLEDGMENTS

1990

With super thanks to R. Sargent Shriver, the founding father of Head Start. Sargent Shriver signed off on every cent CDGM ever had from the federal government.

With great gratitude to Richard Boone, Director of the Office of Economic Opportunity's Division of Policy and Development. Dick was the individual most responsible for writing the all-important "maximum feasible participation of the poor" concept into law; the person from whom I learned this pivotal principle while working as an OEO staff member during the hatching of the national Community Action and Head Start programs in 1964; and the person responsible for the 1990 reprinting of this book—with the new accompanying assessment section at the end.

With apologies to Jule Sugarman, whose life CDGM made miserable, and without whose superb administrative gifts there would have been no Head Start program in the first place. From Jule I learned that huge, wonderful things can happen overnight if we stop talking and take action.

With unending admiration for Tom Levin, Ph.D., creator of the brilliant, inadequately recognized, never replicated CDGM concept, and for the Reverend Arthur Thomas, superb community organizer, deceased and much missed, without whose Delta Ministry volunteers there would have been no CDGM, and therefore none of its amazing ramifications ever since.

With cheers and accolades for world-class children's crusader Marian Wright Edelman, key CDGM Board member, its general counsel, and one of its major saviors (in a transformed sort of way) mid-summer 1965 when the federal axe fell; later the founder and President of the Children's Defense Fund.

With much affection and respect for John Mudd, brought in by Marian to pick up the financial pieces in the fall of 1965; till two a.m. most nights all during the winter of 1965–66 he and I labored, trying together, and almost alone, to keep the unfunded communities connected and hopeful. Thank you, John, for many times saying that SLIPPERY SHOES has always been the definitive book about CDGM.

With gratitude and love to my original editor at Macmillan, Alan Rinzler, a true and rare sponsor of creativity. The longer I live, the more remarkable an editor I realize Alan was.

With thanks to two individuals at the National Council of Churches, which helped me financially for four of the eighteen fundless months it took in 1966 and 1967 to digest and document CDGM; and with thanks to the bank and loan companies that financed the other fourteen months at exorbitant interest rates (better that than eviction and starvation). At the time, there were five young children, but there was no job, husband, investment, inheritance, or other source of income, so doing the DEVIL was a bit of an economic feat, not unlike the feats accomplished by poor people every day.

For the funding required to reprint SLIPPERY SHOES as a paperback (with an entirely new section at the end on assessment) twenty-five years later in honor of the marvelous Head Start program's twenty-fifth birthday, Youth Policy Institute and I warmly thank (in addition to Dick Boone) the Tides and Delta Foundations, and John Mudd, each for a small, short-term loan at a critical moment. I thank, also, from the bottom of my heart, an abundantly generous entity that works in strange and mysterious ways. In spite of the rhetoric around us, for some puzzling reason there are few foundations these days that are interested in disseminating successful strategies and models for providing comprehensive services to low-income minority children on a large scale, and for involving parents in significant ways in these programs.

For her voluntary bookkeeping chores, we thank Judith Hackett.

With high regard for Sheldon H. White and many, many thanks to him for taking time from his overflowing schedule to write a foreword for the 1990 edition.

With appreciation of Stan Salett who, as a Youth Policy Institute board member, interested David L. Hackett, Executive Director of the Youth Policy Institute, in reissuing THE DEVIL HAS SLIPPERY SHOES: A Biased Biography of the Child Development Group of Mississippi (CDGM)—a Story of Maximum Feasible Poor Parent Participation.

I am very grateful to Youth Policy Institute for sponsoring this project. YPI is a nonpartisan, interracial, intergenerational, nonprofit research organization interested in America's children, youth, and families. Its goal is to create a data base of information about programs that already exist to enable planners to integrate the best components in order to achieve stronger, more lasting results. YPI is attempting to establish a partnership between experienced professionals, scholars and college students, so that appropriate wisdom may be shared and improved upon, while reinventing the wheel can be avoided.

Now a few words about the extraordinary Dave Hackett, for many years Robert F. Kennedy's best friend, formerly Executive Director of the President's Committee on Juvenile Delinquency, currently Executive Director of Youth Policy Institute. My five children, now adults, have always said that I'm the most optimistic person they know, with a philosophy of, "Do what feels right and everything will fall in place." Well, I've certainly met my match in Dave Hackett! Never has there been a more optimistic person. Flying resolutely in the face of fundlessness,

Dave has many times said of this DEVIL reissuing project, "We're going to do it because it should be done." And he did do it. And it is done.

Most of all, I want to acknowledge the contributions made by Margaret Pollitzer (my mentor in democratic childrearing, democratic education, and social change toward a more democratic America) to my life, to CDGM, to the DEVIL book, and to better lives for poor children and their families. She has always believed that actions speak louder than words.

ABOUT CDGM, ABOUT THIS BOOK

THE DEVIL HAS SLIPPERY SHOES is an epic testament to the efforts of thousands of dirt poor African American Mississippians, known in the 1960s as "Negroes," many of them sharecroppers and maids scattered across dozens of counties, *to change their society for themselves and their children.* Lunch-counter sit-ins, freedom rides and marches, integration summers, voter registration blitzes, all had had their invaluable day, but now in 1965, Movement leaders knew something new was needed. SLIPPERY SHOES shows in depth and detail how *poor black parents organized and operated a huge, state-wide network of Head Start centers* **themselves.** The idea, needless to say, and the multi-million dollar Head Start it almost instantly became, met with considerable opposition and harassment from the Ku Klux Klan (which had, mere months before, murdered Chaney, Goodman, and Schwerner and buried their bodies in a hastily built dam)—opposition and harassment from the local press, the Mississippi state government, Southern senators and congress people, the Office of Economic Opportunity *itself,* and many newly militant young, black people, mostly SNCC workers from out-of-state.

Nevertheless, CDGM survived and continues to survive—under a variety of different grantees and names—both as a HEAD START program; and in the memory and confidence of many individuals as proof that social change *can* be made to happen, that individuals *do* make a difference, and that progress is a rung-by-rung happening in which each rung is essential in reaching the next.

CDGM has achieved and continues decades later to achieve many of its goals:

- generating other indigenous projects which have brought a new era to Mississippi,
- affecting governmental policies regarding the role of poor people and parents in social action and education programs across the country, and
- demonstrating what the currently popular concept of low income "parent empowerment" can really be.

The three people who created the HEAD START-funded Child Development Group of Mississippi—CDGM—realized that four of the most promising arenas, four of the most crucial instruments for potential democratic reform in our time **are childrearing, education, community organizing, and political empowerment.**

It is here that society can be revolutionized *within* existing social and political institutions.

In the 1990s we see ever more evidence that if as a society we choose *not* to permit and provide opportunities and supports for the families and their children who are in desperate need of opportunities and supports, the whole society, as well as the individuals we leave stranded, suffers—through substance abuse, child abuse, crime, illiteracy, unemployability, racial warfare, class warfare, rage, and whatever is destined to come next while the rest of us enjoy our trivial pursuits. For some of us this is self-pampering; middle- and upper-class Americans are developing reputations as the greatest consumers and materialists the world has ever known. For others, the chief trivial pursuit is theorizing, writing, lecturing, and presenting at symposiums about whether poverty is best approached this way or that way; excessive analysis precludes action of *any* sort, and becomes an end in itself. Meanwhile, regardless of what others are doing while neglecting to take significant action to reduce poverty, reality in our great nation sinks farther and farther from the ideals it was created to strive for.

CDGM began, on the other hand, in a period of great national optimism (spring 1965) as a junction between the passionate civil rights movement (left after the sensational summer of 1964 without a next step to take, without wind in its sails), and the exhilarating creation in Washington, D.C. of multiple War on Poverty Programs (Job Corps, VISTA Volunteers, Community Action Program, and HEAD START).

CDGM was conceptualized by three non-Mississippians, each with a different agenda. *Polly Greenberg* was senior Program Analyst for HEAD START's Southeast Region at its Washington headquarters. She was responsible for soliciting the first grant applications the new Project Head Start would receive from North and South Carolina, Tennessee, Georgia, Florida, Alabama, and Mississippi. She was under strict orders from Sargent Shriver's office not to work with blatant racists, and to seek out liberal groups.

Tom Levin, Ph.D. a New York City psychoanalyst who had organized the Medical Committee for Human Rights as the medical wing for Mississippi civil rights workers the previous summer; and the *Reverend Arthur Thomas*—Director of the Delta Ministry, a Mississippi ministry that played a major role in voter registration, running a freedom information service, distributing tons of food, clothing, and books collected by church groups in the North, and many other projects—were planning a new project for the summer of '65: five to ten day care centers for civil rights workers' children. Levin had been organizing people since as a teenager, he had been a union organizer. He believed that helping people organize around issues of great concern to them was the way to help them gain, realize, and use power to make their lives better. Thomas believed that working for justice, a traditional goal of the church, is only meaningful when new concepts of ministry and new action methods responsive to the real issues in individuals' lives are invented. He also believed in the power of the vote.

Greenberg (from the viewpoint of a child, parent, and staff development specialist) and Levin (from the perspective of a psychoanalyst) understood the power of positive childrearing and education in developing free people. Thomas and Levin understood the power of community organizing and political representation in developing free people. Polly knew of the new federal funding program, HEAD START, which Art and Tom had never heard of. Moreover, she knew the program's technicalities—including how to by-pass the inevitable governor's veto and get HEAD START money directly to the poor if Art and Tom could find an institution of higher education *on their side,* the side of the civil rights movement, willing to be the grantee.

Because they had been working closely with their liaison group, the Student Nonviolent Coordinating Committee (SNCC), which was vehemently against accepting federal money with all its strings, Art Thomas and Tom Levin were very reluctant to consider the HEAD START idea. Polly Greenberg persuaded them to pass the information about this new health and education program for young children along to poor black community people, and let them decide for themselves if they wanted to form a coalition and apply for a grant. They did. The Child Development Group of Mississippi (CDGM) was formed.

All over the state, poor black people who had risked their lives to register to vote or run a freedom school in their home the summer before (1964) mobilized to create HEAD START programs for their own children (1965). These adults formed committees similar to "school boards" from among themselves, found and repaired available buildings (typically Delta churches owned by the black community like the one shown on the cover of this book), recruited 13,000 poorest-of-the-poor children, selected and hired (sometimes fired) "teachers," health and social service workers, cooks, etc. all from within their own dusty hamlets. Then *they* learned how to write proposals to Head Start and other Washington agencies, and how to be leaders. Three thousand, two hundred seventeen people learned to be HEAD START teachers, activist health and social service coordinators, advocates, and administrators within a year.

THE DEVIL HAS SLIPPERY SHOES, a magnificently moving documentation of the Child Development Group of Mississippi, has much of value to share with those involved in HEAD START, family resource and support programs, and many other model projects around the United States in which people struggle daily with most of the same painful issues examined here with astonishing honesty.

FOREWORD

by
Sheldon H. White

Harvard University
(1990)

A tide has turned and once again we address the task of providing more early care and education for American children. Budget realities being what they are, we will mostly support poor families and, poverty being what it is, we will offer early education connected to family support, health care, and community action. Head Start has offered just this mix of services since 1965 and now we are going to have more Head Start—either an expansion of Head Start itself or new Head-Start-like programs under other auspices.

All of this is well justified. Statistics say that more women work, more children are poor, more children need care. Experts say that Head Start works. All's right with Reason and the numbers augur well for the future. Yet every once in a while the political ground shifts for an instant, something glows, something glimpsed out of the corner of the eye evokes pain, menace, confusion, compassion, yearning...

Bureaucracies, Isaiah Berlin has remarked, turn moral problems into technical problems and Head Start, let it be remembered, was born in the fires of searing social problems. If we are going to build Head Start once more, some of us are going to have to go back to the dream-time and re-experience and re-understand the work and passion and idealism and confusions and frustrations and desperate commitments that burn still today at the heart of the program. This book takes one into the heart of Head Start; nothing else I have ever seen comes close to it in that regard. It is a remarkable story of the time when Head Start began and of the beginning of Isaiah Berlin's process, a "biased biography," telling how the Child Development Group of Mississippi (CDGM) began Head Start programs in that state in 1965 in spite of the fact that the governor was proclaiming that no War on Poverty programs would be permitted in the Magnolia State.

> *The story of CDGM,* Polly Greenberg says, *seems to me to be a fairy tale, complete with all the blood, magic, shining beauty, and repeated themes characteristic of fairy tales. It's a simple narrative dealing with such supernatural beings as fairies, magicians, and dragons who are typically of folk origin and are written or told about for the amusement of children. It's also a more sophisticated narrative, containing supernatural or obviously improbable events, scenes, persons; and having a whimsical, satirical, and moralistic character. A fairy tale, like certain facets of CDGM's history, is an improbable, incredible, or lying story, a story designed to delude or mislead.* (p. 625)

Polly Greenberg was a War on Poverty staff member at OEO's Washington, D.C., headquarters' serving as Senior Head Start program analyst for the Office of Economic Opportunity's Southeast region. Like many bureaucrats, she was driven by a mixture of cynical realism and high idealism. Politics is about managing human affairs, and it inevitably contains elements of manipulation, lying, deluding, and misleading, and she understood that:

I understood that Head Start was a wedge made of appealing little children which would help the Administration wiggle itself into the hearts of the poor, minority groups and liberals; that the purpose was more to win votes than to eliminate poverty. (p. 14)

But politics is also about faith, hope, and love. What surprises visitors to Washington are the occasional glimpses of deep, selfless moral commitment that motivates many bureaucrats. The Office of Economic Opportunity had people who believed in the possibilities of human development and who unabashedly wanted to help other people; Polly Greenberg was one of them.

My background and particular interest was in early education and community development, in human development, not in politics. But it was clear that these things are not separable, and to be effective in the content, one must be at least cognizant of the political underpinnings, framework, pressures, and likelihoods in the location of which one is speaking. We know it's possible for a handful of men to seclude themselves as monks and yogis in monasteries and on mountaintops and to develop themselves extraordinarily. But what I wondered was how much can we do about human development under normal (including political) conditions? (p. 15)

As an OEO official, Polly dealt with seven states. Her job was to encourage and assist potential Head Start applicants in Southern cities and hamlets everywhere. Because she was receiving *no* applications from Mississippi that would meet OEO standards regarding racial integration and maximum feasible participation of the poor, she actively sought out progressive groups in the South. Innumerable investigative phone calls eventually led her to Tom Levin, a practicing New York City psychoanalyst, who had been a strategist for some of the preceding summer's civil rights activities in Mississippi.

Tom invited Polly to a meeting with the Reverend Arthur Thomas, Director of the Delta Ministry, and a handful of Northern professionals and academics who were about to plan five or ten freedom preschools in Mississippi for the summer of '65. Polly would be allowed to present the new federal Head Start program to the group and suggest ways that an organization could be formed to serve as recipient of a Head Start grant that would be exempt from the governor's veto. These origins of CDGM are detailed in the book. (pp. 3–14)

Art Thomas, who lived in Mississippi, agreed to carry the news of the new Head Start program to the tiny impoverished black Delta communities with which he and his team of out-of-state community organizer volunteers worked every day. What extraordinarily poor people did next to organize *their own* Head Start centers is thoroughly explained in *The Devil Has Slippery Shoes.* Several representatives, most of them people who earned less than $1,000 a year, would be on an overall governing board of this new network of Head Start communities, named by Tom Levin The Child Development Group of Mississippi. Additionally, Marian Wright, a young lawyer living in Mississippi in order to be actively involved in civil rights cases and a rising star in the civil rights movement, and Dr. Dan Beittel, President of Tougaloo College, joined the board.

Separately, each member of this group had waged war in the hard civil rights battles of that time, sometimes risking their lives.

Any Head Start program the group created would do more than offer services *to* the poor. This group would involve the poor in their own programs to very significant degree, stimulate community action, and seek through the vehicle of Head Start to empower people in a *real* way. CDGM received its first grant from OEO in May of 1965—when the first Head Start group of grants in the nation were given. Greenberg resigned in June and went to work for CDGM, arriving in Mississippi on the one year anniversary of the murders of civil rights workers Chaney, Goodman, and Schwerner.

Polly Greenberg was one of two program coordinators helping poor people establish their own Head Start centers the first summer. She worked under very difficult circumstances. There was a $1.3 million grant, a large one. Tom Levin had set aside his psychoanalytic practice for the summer and came down in June to manage a set of sixty-four Head Start centers that were to open in early July. CDGM had no administrative and managerial history; it had a central staff of forty, under contract just for the summer and divided, Greenberg says, into thirty-five who attacked each other and five or six who attacked the problems. There was much administrative confusion, which may or may not have been Levin's fault. OEO took the position that it was, and began making peremptory demands for administrative reform, the demands largely serving to increase the confusion. Tom Levin was forced to depart before the end of the first summer and a new Director, John Mudd, came in.

We are, of course, not talking about any old set of Head Start Centers in 1965. We are talking about Head Start in Mississippi, with political menace all around. CDGM played out overtly the social pressures and tensions confronting Head Start centers in many ostensibly quieter places. From Washington and from the Mississippi state house, Southern politicians protested CDGM's sponsorship of Head Start programs. . . seeing CDGM as a stalking horse for the civil rights movement, which in truth it was. OEO seems to have been at first proud of its pet dragon but then more and more apprehensive as CDGM's provocative mobilization of community action and its political and administrative vulnerability cast a shadow over the national effort of which it was a part. Locally, all across Mississippi, there were incidents of menace and harassment. The blacks themselves were not without menace: some were profoundly skeptical and distrustful. Was CDGM a sop? Greenberg quotes a long conversation with a black co-worker:

They tell us that the reason we're in poverty is that we're dumb niggers, and if we will sub-

mit ourselves to a white head shrinker named Tom Levin, and a white lady who calls herself an "expert" in education named Polly Greenberg, and a rich white boy from the Philadelphia suburbs named John Mudd who wants to study us niggers so he can get his Ph.D. from Harvard, we won't be poor anymore... Lots of us ignorant niggers have fallen for all this: especially the Poverty Program. They don't understand. It isn't changing anything, except for the words—quieting the burning baby so his screams won't save him from death. How're you going to improve a worm-ridden putrid maggot-writhing pot of food by adding vitamins? How're you going to revive a stinking corpse by sprinking perfume on it? (pp. 513–514)

This is the fairy tale told in this book, not pretty-pretty, not a simple kind of fairy tale about a hero and a sword and a dragon, good here, evil there, but a fairy tale no less, one for an age of bureaucracy. It is told by a master storyteller, a tale rich in anecdote and color. At the center of the story, there is a tempestuous program for little children, born in the civil rights wars of the 1960s, animated by the deepest kinds of commitments to and feelings for human development, surviving and growing amidst perils on all sides. There are nests of heroes and nests of villains, often played by the very same people. Sometime during her life in CDGM, Greenberg made a self-conscious decision to write about the reality of the program in just this way. She quotes from her diary:

If I ever write the book about CDGM that I'd like to write, I won't know how to handle all the petty, personal, negative, nasty things. It isn't proper to put them in a book. I should just write about our great ideas and the wonderful poor people. The ugly stuff is our family skeleton. But then, what would be the point of writing such a book?... CDGM is a perfect example of the struggle between our destructive parts (evil) and our capacities for greatness (good). (pp. 295–296)

In time, Isaiah Berlin's process was completed. The turbulent, stormy set of Mississippi programs set in train by CDGM was tamed, cooled out, made orderly, managed, subdued, squelched, defused, brought within the compass of the system. An all-out, merciless idealist such as Polly Greenberg had to feel that something was lost:

The kaleidoscopic thing that Tom had kindled had become well ordered by OEO nonentities. The creativity had somewhere, slowly, seeped out of CDGM. The many experimental elements had become as many mere routines. The diagnosis and the dialogue of departures from the norm had dwindled to the level of dull, diluted, and diffuse declarations, put forth by discussants who hadn't the smallest notion of the deep significance of the subject on which they spoke. (p. 657)

Why, then, should we walk with Polly Greenberg through the birth of CDGM in 1965? This is not simply a story about the past, something done and finished with. The chemistry of Isaiah Berlin's process isn't complete and can never be so. We can't turn moral problems into technical problems. We can build political structures to contend with moral problems. We can, as it were, provide political figures and symbols to personify and express those moral problems in public discussion—this is, I suspect, one of the fundamental meanings of political discourse in contemporary society. We can work within the operational structures of programs like Head Start to grapple with the conditions that lead to outrage and injustice. But I don't believe anyone can fully understand programs like Head Start without coming to terms with the realities set forth in Polly Greenberg's book.

CONTENTS

NOTE: The following pages from here through page 705—
are reprinted exactly as they were published in 1969.

BOOK ONE: GENESIS

Part I: From Dream to Dragon in Sixty-Eight Days

Before the first grant announcement: before May 18, 1965; the origins of CDGM

Part II: Why and How Poor People Planned a School System

Between the grant announcement, May 18, 1965, and the opening of centers, July 12; the psychological and educational rationale for CDGM's approach; forming a framework for them; concepts.

Part III: The First Summer

July–September, 1965; samples and examples of how CDGM worked and did not work at first, with resulting plans for a future program and a little federal intervention

Part IV: Gone with the Political Wind (Almost)

August, 1965: How a triangular spasm of CDGM-Mississippi-Administration politics brought thinking about the children of poverty to a grinding halt and placed thinking about the politics of poverty in the fore.

BOOK TWO: SISYPHUS

Part V: Nothing Left but a Flock of Wild Turkeys

The unfunded period in the long, cold winter of 1965–1966. How CDGM survived and grew in the communities without government funds. How poor people began to bud as spirited teacher supervisors, community organizers, and administrators. How a skeleton Central Staff held things together, and how the whole of CDGM wrung water from a rock to get re-funded.

Part VI: Toward Autonomy

February 23, 1966—August 30, 1966: How CDGM improved and institutionalized, went more professional and went to pieces, lost its soul, splintered, almost committed suicide in a collision of white and black power, created and destroyed, and thanks to John Mudd, grew more mature.

Part VII: Doing Good

September 30, 1966–January, 1967: According to whom? Is it possible?

NOTE: The following section of this book was not in the original 1969 edition; the index does not include the new pages.

New in 1990

BOOK THREE: ASSESSMENT
(longitudinal)
AFTER WORDS (1990)

Part VIII: Social Progress Occurs Inch by Inch, One by One (If Individuals Work at It)

1965–1990: Childrearing, education, economics, politics—it's all entwined, it's all the child's environment; "providing an optimal environment for the low-income minority child's development" means dealing with all this racism, classism, and politicking wherever we are; it means having great patience; it means (to quote former farmer and CDGM Area Teacher Guide Hattie Saffold, who is now, thanks to Head Start, a public school kindergarten teacher), "Keeping on keeping on."

DEDICATION

This book is dedicated to all the people in the Child Development Group of Mississippi: to the 13,000 little children who will one day make Mississippi a state fit for black folks to live in, and to their hard-working parents, who often risked danger and loss of jobs to send their children to CDGM for kindergarten; to the 2,272 employees in Child Development centers, in area offices, and on Central Staff, most of them very, very poor, many of whom have worked night and day to bring subjugation to an end; to the 945 unpaid, bitterly poor citizens who served on community committees, and whose earnest efforts made this project "run by the poor" as much as the poor wished to run it; to the seventeen board members, mostly poor people too, who had the strength, vision, and faith to withstand the federal government and all its wondrous weapons; to the friends of the children of Mississippi, wherever they are, with gratitude for all they did to "keep the project keeping on"; and especially to Tom Levin, and Art Thomas.

Tom brought most of the ideas and features of CDGM into being with several grand sweeps of his imagination. He was right when he said that if he could design this thing well enough, individuals would become expendable. It would be bigger and have more momentum than its individual friends and enemies, in it and around it. And Art made the incredible thing possible with his access to these communities and his faith in them.

This book is also dedicated to John Mudd, without whom CDGM would certainly have sunk after its first breathless summer, and without whose extraordinary patience it would never have achieved whatever human-to-human honesty and day-to-day democracy it had; and with very special love to the area teacher guides, many of whom were fifteen-dollar-a-week maids just prior to being the spirit and hope and the instigators of progressive actions, which more than anything else kept the program for children going and the confederation of isolated poor black communities hanging together during the long, cold winter of 1965, when the government couldn't afford us.

I heard you, Charles, and I learned a great deal from what you said. You told me, "Some of us love you, and many of us know what you have done for us, and most of us agree with your ideas. *But you have got to learn,* we can't let love and appreciation get in the way of *us* doing for us, and *us* having ideas. It's not that we're against *you.* It's that we've got to do this thing for *ourselves.* It's the only way we'll ever *feel* our freedom." I hope you'll understand that this book isn't an effort to be an "expert" about you. It's just what I saw, or thought I saw, and what I felt, and knew I felt, written with awe and admiration for your desolate fight to be free people. This book is an effort to follow Stokely's advice: Whites work on the white side of the problem.

The white side of the problem: lack of acquaintance with all of you and your point of view; comfortableness with the conventional ways in which we're used to working and thinking; insufficient concern about you to wage more than a gentle, gentleman's War on Poverty; willingness to feel that fate is unalterable, and because politics have always come before or been incompatible with human solutions, this must always remain true; a basic complacence caused by the feeling that, after all is said and done, it's true that we are, and very anxious to stay, superior to you; so we'll take better care of you than we have in the past, partly because our consciences have been stirred, and partly so you who are pressing your noses so hard against the window pane won't break the glass and burst in and take what we've so piously got.

Last but not least, this book is dedicated to R. Sargent Shriver, who, because history placed him in the position of representing views on poor people and Negroes held by the American public, the Congress, the White House, and the OEO, had to bear the brunt of the battle in CDGM's struggle with the "white side of the problem."

This is intended to be the biography of the beginning of one group's search for a way to overcome the discouragingly formidable weave of economic, educational, psychological, racial, social, and political obstacles that lurk between people and their modest dream. Many kinds of people participated in CDGM's initial explorations—poor Negroes, civil rights workers, nursery school teachers, community development specialists, psychologists, politicians, and others.

Different participants had different interests. The book is a study of how these interests coincided and clashed; and evolved. Experimenting includes deadends and details, too. So does the book. The story of CDGM is a story of loss and gain, beauty and bitterness, protest and program, defiance and determination.

The book is neither a comprehensive nor a neutral biography. The subject is too big and will never end, so it can't be comprehensive. The subject is too controversial, and everyone in and out of CDGM developed a point of view about different facets of it as soon as he acquired enough information to write about it, so it can't be neutral.

Besides, it isn't necessary to be neutral about the misery of others and about injustice. Neutrality is just a spiritually slothful habit we have. Poverty isn't insoluble in America, and if fewer of us were neutral, we would eliminate this national disgrace. If I haven't been thorough and unbiased, at least I was in the middle of CDGM from the moment of its conception, and have tried as honestly as I could to present the representative events and thinking that seem to be important themes of this complex story. Whether CDGM has proven a triumph or a sellout depends upon one's ideas of good, bad, and possible.

POLLY GREENBERG
1968

A poor black man who lives on a plantation in Issaquena County, Mississippi, said: "We pray together. We used to dream someday we would act together. For our children. For justice. For decency. One day, God heard all that weeping and hollering and praying and then he came to Mississippi. He gave us CDGM. They knew we couldn't run a school system. Let's face one thing right now. Through all the obstacles, and believe me, we'll meet up with all *the obstacles, let's remember this one thing: God is here, now, and if there is no way, we'll find a way anyway."*

"'Course CDGM's good," said a large lady from Lauderdale County. "'Cept the things about it that's bad. There's a lotta good folks come here to help us. 'Course, there's a lot just come to cause a fuss too. And the federal government's finally recognized us down here—'course sometimes that ain't so good, 'cause for every smile it gives us, it gives us a kick too. Well, at least it's got us colored peoples workin' for 'oursel's. 'Cept the ones that won't. One thing, though, it's great for the kids. On'y thing, it's kinda hard on 'em when they get to real school and it ain't like our school. God's helpin' us, ain't no doubt. It's just that the Devil keeps skippin' in and outa things so's we won't get spoilt. He really keeps you guessin'! Each thing, you gotta study it to see if it's God in the disguise of difficulty, or the Devil in the disguise of somebody good. This whole thing really keep us workin' our mind."

BOOK ONE:
Genesis

PART I

From Dream to Dragon in Sixty-Eight Days

BEFORE THE FIRST GRANT ANNOUNCEMENT:
BEFORE MAY 18, 1965: THE ORIGINS OF CDGM

CHAPTER 1

THE CHALLENGING QUESTION

Did maximum participation of the poor and total development of the child mean maximum participation of the poor and total development of the child?

A HANDFUL OF us had a belief—just a belief, nothing more than a belief—that the poor, we were thinking particularly of the Negro poor in Mississippi, knew enough about their lack of skills in a twentieth-century world and their lack of rights in "free" America; and knew enough about their need for skills and their right to have rights. We believed that they were ripe and restless to *do* something about it, *themselves,* with technical assistance from friends and financial assistance from "their" government.

On the night of March 11, 1965, the night that Reverend James Reeb died of murderous bludgeonings administered by a law enforcement officer in Selma, Alabama, six of us had a meeting in New York City. The meeting had been arranged several days before by Dr. Tom Levin, a New York psychoanalyst who was very active in trying to get social scientists and appropriate professionals involved in the bloody freedom battles of the South. He had worked in Mississippi the previous summer, and was close to what was happening. The meeting was intended to explore the possibility of establishing from five to ten day care centers in Mississippi, with a total budget of about $65,000. The centers would be staffed by volunteers from the freedom fighting elements of poor communities, and professional consultants from the Committee of Conscience (a group of eminent social scientists). They would serve the children of Movement workers and sympathizers.

The purpose of the proposed project was to create a program that would build the iron egos needed by children growing up to be future leaders of social change in a semifeudal state. Perhaps fifty to one hundred children would be given care.

It was hoped that with the day care centers as a nucleus, parents and volunteers would build an experimental "private" school system, because they have a hopeless time trying to influence state schools in even the smallest ways, and because this state system is one of the major instruments that perpetuates "slavery" in Mississippi. In this way it was hoped that at least a small group of Negro children, who already had the tremendous advantage of having parents who were engaged in changing things, could get a psychologically strengthening, thought provoking, reality oriented education, rather than the psychologically crushing, thought controlled, mythically oriented, education currently available to them in public school. As a by-product, the project might serve as an exciting example of what could be done in both Negro and white schools in the state, something to guide Southern radicals, and be a stimulating base for parents, from which they could chide the public schools into doing some of the things that should be done. The project was seen as part of a total effort to involve poor Negroes in pushing progress on all fronts.

Three people other than Dr. Levin were especially interested in the idea. Jeannine Herron was a young mother with cooperative nursery school experience, and with commitment to Mississippi's Freedom Movement deep enough that the year before she and her husband had moved to Jackson with their two children, to become active participants in all that was happening. All that was going on was so dangerous to civil rights workers, and so repressive to noisy children with thoughts of their own, that the Herrons thought it unwise to put their children in school. They tutored them at home throughout the school year. There is no compulsory school law in Mississippi. It was wiped out after the 1954 Supreme Court school desegregation decision. Better total ignorance than token integration.

The Herrons were feeling their way to see how they could best serve the Movement. Matt, a free-lance photographer, took pictures of Movement events and personalities, which have appeared in many national magazines and several books. Jeannine wrote a piece for *The Nation* about the movement, and another about the Beckwith trial. The idea of getting some cooperative nursery schools going, with the poor doing the cooperating, began growing in her mind. Before Christmas she went to a few COFO [see Appendix A] meetings to discuss the possibility with potential fellow workers. It was there that she had run into Art Thomas, whom she had known for some time, and discovered that he too was thinking about Freedom Schools at the nursery level.

At the time of our meeting, Reverend Arthur Thomas, the creative and courageous thirty-three-year-old director of the Delta Ministry, was in the midst of marches, demonstrations, jailings, boycotts, bombings, burnings, beatings, and other typical early 1960's occurrences in the Negro 40 percent of the mild and lovely Magnolia state. Art never talked of Christian principles, but with the ingenuity of a five-star general, the diplomacy of a master politician, and the sensitivity of an extraordinary human being, he quietly helped people put these principles into practice. He was searching for ways that the Delta Ministry, the Southern branch of the National Council of Churches, which actively engaged in social change, could begin to establish solid programs financed by the federal government, to follow Mississippi Negroes' growing awareness that they deserved some. He hoped that ministers and other volunteers in his group would endorse the day care centers, and would aid people who trusted them in setting them up and operating them *themselves.*

The third party interested in the day care project was Dr. Sol Gordon, a psychologist then working in New Jersey. I learned of the meeting through Dr. Gordon, who telephoned me at OEO. I knew of Reverend Arthur Thomas and the Delta Ministry, and knew of Dr. Levin's work. I had met him thirteen years before, when he was a student at the National Psychological Association for Psychoanalysis, and I was a part-time record keeper, allowed to sit in on classes.

Dr. Gordon wanted to try several approaches to teaching reading in a few Delta counties where conditions in homes and schools are such that learning to read by any approach constitutes a small miracle. He had worked briefly in Mississippi. He believed that older children and cotton picking parents would be far better teachers for spirited little children than the bored, hostile, and remote public school teachers the children were often forced to face from their first day on as captives of the consolidated school system.

The older children and parents were determined to make a brighter future for their children. They knew the ways of the children and the whys of their people. They knew, and were dramatically dealing with, the context in which the children are raised. Many of them had a natural flair for working warmly and humorously with young children. Many regarded changing life for the children a twenty-four-hour-a-day job, requiring no pay, necessitating putting up with wrath and frequent physical outbursts of violence from former white "friends," and often the loss of whatever meager jobs they could get. Most were eager to discover what education really is.

These three people and an observer from the National Council of Churches were at Tom's New York meeting. The sixth person was an uninvited but passively tolerated guest: me. At that time I was the senior Head Start program analyst for the Southeast Region at the Office of Economic Opportunity in Washington. It was before OEO had divided into regional offices. We had only regional individuals. In spite of official expectations, we were getting many hundreds of applications from the Deep South. But they were all from school superintendents. This was true across the country, but it was the South with which I was concerned.

It had been with reluctance that the experts had declared school systems eligible to run Head Start programs at all. Head Start was supposed to be a preschool-medical-community-action program, not a downward extension of public schools. Only a few proposals I received bore close resemblance to Head Start as it had originally been conceived during the four months before. The others had many disappointing features.

Head Start was designed to offer poor people unlimited opportunities to participate in the *initial planning* and in all other phases of operating projects concerning their own children; in this sense, projects concerning their own future. I didn't feel that scores of Southern school superintendents and "their best Negroes" (as the superintendents themselves frequently described their safest principals and most dutiful teachers to me) represented anybody's idea of maximum participation of the poor in *originating and running* Head Starts. That there were many brave and well-intentioned people in this group, who were sticking their necks way, way out, considering the communities surrounding them, was neither deniable nor relevant.

Of course the mounting applications for Head Start projects included countless names of excellent people who had long been forward-looking leaders of their areas. Overnight OEO had established a vast and impressive network to alert governors, mayors, state departments of health, education and welfare, school superintendents in even the most remote rural counties, business and industrial leaders, college and university faculty members, professional associations of all kinds, and every type of civic group or prominent individual.

It was an intention of Head Start designers that liberal leaders and professionals would be encouraged to continue and expand their efforts through this new program, and that moderates would be offered opportunities to become interested in problems of poverty "in their back yards." Strengthening these individuals and their communities was considered very important because their backing, skills, articulateness, political connections, etc., were required in a total attempt to create a climate in which the poor could help themselves. Head Start *was* reaching for these people, and they were responding in great numbers (as were some of their more questionably motivated neighbors).

But where were the poor? and leaders the poor had selected? No equal effort was apparently being made by OEO to contact and excite *them.* It seemed urgently important to search them out, along with the others. I didn't know more than a few "indigenous" leaders myself. Since the Levin group included many such leaders, I asked to come to its meeting.

Head Start was designed to promote and develop mass production, ACTION TODAY versions of early childhood education, nursery education, and research-based programs for children who typically have trouble in school when they officially begin. It was known that not nearly enough professionals in these fields existed, because these had never been large-scale fields before. But it was assumed that those there *were* would be heavily involved in Head Start; that they would be the valued ones. Head Start's widely distributed pamphlet from "The Rainbow Series" titled "The Staff" thoroughly and vehemently stressed the need for each community to vigorously recruit trained active or out-of-service nursery education specialists. OEO didn't name elementary school teachers as first priority, or mention, among professional associations to contact, the elementary school teachers' biggest professional associations (National Education Association and American Federation of Teachers) because it was seeking *nursery* teachers, *not elementary* teachers. Instead, prevailing hiring practices stated in Head Start proposals flying across my desk *required* teachers to have teaching certificates and licenses, for public school teaching! This virtually guaranteed that they wouldn't be preschool teachers, because preschool teachers usually don't have public school teaching credentials—they don't aspire to teach in public schools, as they are a beast of another color.

These precautions were put in so we would get "qualified" Head Start teachers, the applicants explained. But in none of the Head Start planning had elementary and secondary qualifications (if certificates make a person of quality even at *those* levels) been equated with qualifications for a new kind of early childhood education. Head Start was not to be elementary or secondary school. Interests and abilities needed by a "good" teacher of small children are quite different from those needed by a "good" teacher of older children or adolescents or typing, not to mention those possessed by a "good" teacher as judged by a dull and mediocre small town Southern school administrator.

Many individuals are such basically excellent teachers that they can readily adapt to teaching at any level, but much-mocked training in sixty-years-out-of-date schools of education, and much-criticized experience in a hundred-years-out-of-date classrooms does not necessarily make a teacher "qualified" to teach in a new, experimental type of community center, with a group of children whose age makes them closer to the crib than the formal classroom.

Many outstanding early childhood educators had taken part in planning educational standards for Head Start. Most of them had insisted that nursery school or kindergarten teachers with experience in *research* projects for "disadvantaged" children were to be given first priority as Head Start teachers. Second best, they unhappily agreed, because of the shortage in this rapidly expanding field, would be straight, ordinary, routine nursery school and kindergarten teachers. And they sadly admitted that, third choice, would have to be "other people who have worked with children" (among whom can be included librarians, nurses, social workers, people in nonteaching middle-class jobs, the elderly and retired, the poor with potential, and elementary and secondary school teachers).

Hardly any Head Start I saw from the South listed a full staff of talented nursery educators with experience in poor community neighborhood work. So I was very concerned at this time with teacher development programs for whoever taught Head Start.

Another defect of most of the Head Start proposals being submitted from the Southern region was that they contained either no teacher development component, or one that was shallow and public-school oriented. Their emphasis gave the impression that the major aim was to press children into shapes convenient for the public school. Much stress was placed on teaching children to behave in a subdued and conforming manner, and on the acquisition of a string of skills such as using scissors, knowing colors, memorizing meaningless songs, sitting quietly at story time, and learning to follow directions. These programs were geared, whether intentionally or unintentionally, to giving children a head start in the most superficial immediate demands of the public schools. There are more important skills and achievements children need to master if our goal is to develop mature human beings, rather than easy-to-handle first graders.

I needed to find a group somewhere in the South that really believed in human potential (of all colors); a group that wanted to experiment with unique ways of releasing and channeling this potential into a current area of great need and of great vacuum: preschool teaching. I knew of no group more dedicated to the development of human potential—in the social, economic, and political context in which these humans find themselves, rather than in the usual educational thermos bottle—dedicated even to the point of death, than Freedom Movement workers in Mississippi.

My fourth disappointment with Head Start (even before its first summer!) was that it was designed to create new careers for the poor, yet in the thousands of applications I was receiving, the only jobs for poor people were as maids in classrooms. It didn't seem like a new career to shuffle out of Miss Ann's kitchen and into Miss Teacher's classroom, even though these "teachers' aides," as Head Start center maids were euphemistically titled (but recognizably treated), would earn $1.25 an hour; considerably more than the $10 a week a maid in Mississippi generally gets.

I thought it possible for concerned teachers who came to Head Start only half-equipped, because they had had only teaching experience and no neighborhood development experience, to learn how to do the latter if creative training programs were initiated for this purpose. Conversely, I thought it possible for concerned poor people who came to Head Start only half-equipped, because they had had only neighborhood experience and no nursery school teaching experience, to learn how to do the latter if creative training programs were initiated for *that* purpose.

It seemed that teachers and poor people alike were inexperienced and untrained in Head Start teaching, and while many members of both groups would prove too rigid, stupid, or bored to learn, other members of both groups would love to apply themselves to learning in this new field—not "subprofessionals," not "aides." We shouldn't perpetuate patterns of dependency and second-best.

We could assume that all people are equally eligible (if equally enthusiastic) for an equally unlimited amount of growth in a newly emerging career, now filled by practically no one. It seemed prejudiced for us to assume that a whole vast varied mass of people couldn't do a job before we even knew yet what this new job was. It seemed presumptuous to assume that God gave growth capacity only to a chosen few.

And finally, though the federal government accepts the fact that skin color, and the spider web of reactions to it resulting in laws, customs, and behaviors on the part of whites, and the reaction to these discriminations on the part of blacks, has much to do with continuing poverty; and though OEO had decided that racial integration would be a strongly emphasized and mandatory requirement for Head Start projects, applications poured in from the South with obvious violations intended. The inspection office, the section of OEO specially focused on integration, discovered, one by one, the infinitely clever ways intelligent and diligent Southerners could segregate after signing compliances that their programs would be "open."

Techniques included, for example: choosing facilities traditionally attended only by one race or another, facilities buried deep in the heart of ghetto neighborhoods, and inviting (or one might more accurately say, daring) members of the excluded race to come; hiring several Negro teachers for white Head Starts and using them as receptionists or in other ways not directly working with children; hiring white teachers for Negro Head Starts and placing them in top positions so they wouldn't have to suffer the indignity of working under Negroes; routing "integrated" school buses so they only pick up children of one color; officially recruiting both black and white children, but unofficially spreading the word along the grape vine that this is "a nigger program" to assure that poor whites wouldn't come and upset the safely segregated apple cart. These things didn't occur in all cases. There were examples of astonishing and unbelievable integration in Southern Head Starts. But one only had to look at the majority of programs to see how often these or other subtle methods were used to prevent anything drastic from happening. Especially, of course, in Mississippi.

OEO people were doing their frantic and understaffed level best to correct these violations, and many moderate Southern groups were being very honorable in their efforts and honest in their statements that they would go no further in their context. But *little effort was being made by OEO to find and boost groups committed to aggressive compliance with the Civil Rights Act.* Such groups would not only refrain from remarkable forms of deceipt and deviousness, or would not only move quietly ahead as far as they could without causing turmoil in a middle-class milieu, they would actively surge forward, using every weapon at their disposal, to obey the nation's law.

Integrating a few classrooms in a token, or better yet, in a real way, is unquestionably a step ahead for Negroes in a Jim Crow community. But it is not nearly as meaningful as integrating the community itself. Since a child doesn't live and learn exclusively in a classroom, I was worried about OEO's nervousness in urging change of attitudes and behavior of the child's entire community. We couldn't claim to be concerned with child development and yet ignore the terrible indignities and dangers this child would suffer in his devoutly segregated community. We couldn't be devoted child development workers, especially in such a state as Mississippi, and not be bothered into significant action in human and community development too.

Even courageous moderates in the South, because their middle-class status and important positions were at stake, could only go so far in driving toward real change. Therefore, even in cases involving very honest men, Head Start policy and planning boards were usually, on their own initiative or after succumbing to OEO's demands, black and white numbers games and balancing acts which schemed to represent both races without representing articulate poor Negroes of radical persuasions (or at least, without including them in effective majorities).

Along with everyone who had recently worked toward and written about social change in the South, I felt that it was extremely important for the government to take a stronger position on integration than mere tokenism. It used to be that a token was a promise of more to come in the near future. But by 1965 it began to look as if tokens were the total of all that Negroes would ever be given unless the government took a more strenuous stand. Martin Luther King said:

> Those who argue in favor of tokenism point out that we must begin somewhere; that it is unwise to spurn any breakthrough, no matter how limited. This position has a certain validity, and the Negro freedom movement has more often than not attained broad victories which had small beginnings. There is a critical distinction, however, between a modest start and tokenism. The tokenism Negroes condemn is recognizable because it is an end in itself. Its purpose is not to begin a process, but instead to end the process of protest and pressure. It is a hypocritical gesture, not a constructive first step.[1]

It seemed clear that the government was obliged to do more than talk a good line, and that it was in a position of great influence from which it could, realistically, move into the leadership role in race relations which it had long avoided.

Since the government is only as good as the individuals who work for

[1] King, Martin Luther, Jr., *Why We Can't Wait.* New York: Harper & Row, 1963, pp. 20–21.

it, it seemed urgent that ordinary OEO staff members such as I persuade "radical" leaders to get into the Head Start business, to join their conservative, liberal, and reactionary brothers. Only they would strive unadulteratedly toward the not so radical, but really rather modest and moral goal, of developing programs for children and their families which consciously and in detail would encourage curiosity, questioning, challenging, thinking, deciding, and acting according to conscience (about art work, about free play activities, about segregation, about the beautiful "American way of life" rather than programs in which children and parents alike were taught what somebody else thought "is good for them." (In Southern Head Starts it looked like "what is good for them" and "what's right" included "not being a troublemaker" and "not going too fast," and avoiding the issues of integration, power, and other fundamentals of poverty as completely as possible.) If OEO was to be given an opportunity to turn speeches into actions, we would have to find for it some groups, such as Dr. Levin's, that would struggle to achieve real integration by attacking each obstacle preventing it.

The six of us met that night in March and talked till dawn. Jeannine Herron admitted that turning the day care project into a Head Start would add much needed medical and food programs. But she was afraid that governmental regulations would replace initiative and creativity on the part of the poor, that paychecks for eight weeks would distract people from their more long-range and important goals—such as acquiring liberties and opportunities natural to other citizens—and that intricate federal restrictions would prevent centers from forging full steam ahead toward their goal—freeing children, freeing parents, and forcing Mississippi to face the facts of FREEDOM NOW. She saw this thing as a choice between nonviolent civil war and noneffective civil service.

Sol Gordon would give his consent to anything reasonable, as long as he was allowed to do his reading research in several spots, CDGM or otherwise. Art Thomas and Tom Levin were torn. They wanted to see the Mississippi movement toward twentieth-century America gain, through federal funding and endorsement, the economic and political strength it so desperately needed. Yet they wanted to protect a strong spiritual movement from intolerable tangles of federal caution and bureaucratic nonsense. They wanted to bring a part of the poverty program to struggling Negroes of the state.

No one more richly deserved a big slice of the political pork pie than these heroic soldiers of the Constitution (a slice containing a bit of education, a little milk, and some medicine for their five-year-olds). But these men also knew that blood-won leadership and decision-making powers had to stay in the hands of the poor, and could not be surrendered to what they believed to be the omnipotent, manipulative, string-pulling, slippery, invisible hands of OEO.

There was another very serious consideration. A primary problem in abolishing peonage was lack of political power for the poor. For the Negro, the Student Non-Violent Coordinating Committee (SNCC), the Freedom Democratic party (FDP: see Appendix A), CORE, the Delta Ministry (see Appendix B), and other freedom-seeking forces were concentrating on developing political awareness, understanding of the tie between personal injustices and the ballot, and the importance of a vote as a voice in crushing out criminal unfairness. Up and down rows of lush crops in huge plantation fields, door to door in shabby shack towns, and in dimly lit one-room churches, everybody was working on voter registration. Art and Tom hesitated to shift the focus from this critical front.

I was as persuasive as possible. I was with *all* groups in the South that couldn't decide whether to take the plunge. I urged this group to allow the government to back all its semimeaningless recent laws about black and white with green. A large part of the solution to black and white *is* green. Money seems to act like magic in producing respect. Besides, the people needed money. Anybody can do more for their children if they have a pocket full of cash to do it with, I argued. Must the people have fighting spirit, and Christian principles *only?* Can't they have some income too? Besides, with independent incomes people can have more security to engage in what they wish to, because they don't need to live in terror of eviction and loss of job for participating in things that don't suit "the man."

I begged the group to consider other rights in addition to voting rights. The right to quality education, for example, and the right to run programs for themselves. Must we pass up programs in other core areas of need? Wouldn't it be better to take advantage of all available programs? Why not launch companion campaigns?—one during the eight-hour government-paid day, one during other hours? It was true, I acknowledged, that if these tiny hamlets used their one meeting place, the church, for Head Start schools, they couldn't have political activities going on in there at the same time; but *after* hours. Never having received an OEO memo saying that Head Start staff members across the nation must give up being active Republicans or Democrats in their spare time, I saw no reason why this staff couldn't be strenuous in the Freedom Democratic party during its spare time.

Tom reminded us that politics isn't only partisan. The word describes what happens when people directly engage themselves with the structures of their society in an attempt to alter them. In this sense the project could and *should* be highly political. It's the failure of the poor to engage in this way that is called passivity. It's the building of thought and action in these directions that is called involvement of the poor.

I thought this group, which believed so passionately that the poor should make decisions and take action regarding their own destiny, should at least announce the existence of this new federal program to leaders in poverty-ridden communities. They had access and I didn't. They could explain all the implications, complications, and uncertainties of communicating with Washington, and could ask the poor thmselves to decide whether or not to apply for Child Development centers. There was no need, I said, for these leaders to risk betraying the trusting people. They didn't have to promise anything. They could simply carry the word, talk the matter over with people, and assist with procedures should the poor want to go ahead with this. They could help community people understand all along the way that applying for something isn't a guarantee you will get the thing. If the people decided not to get involved, OK. If they wanted it and took all the required steps to get it, and OEO didn't give the grant, it would be bad, but not betrayal. Nobody had promised. At least the poor would get practice in dealing with iron-faced, stone-hearted Uncle Sam. At most they would get one of their first chances to run something in Mississippi and to help their children get first-rate educational experiences.

I insisted that it wasn't fair for Art and Tom to say that OEO didn't intend to go for the high ideals it was stating and writing, if they, who stood for every one of these ideals, were unwilling to get into the act. I protested that this was a new federal program, with exceptional people in all relevant fields serving as policy-making consultants. The staff was more alive than staffs in established government agencies. People were more willing to stick out their necks; take a chance. You owe it to the government to give it an opportunity to make its fabulous words into a model Head Start; to create a project with which OEO experts can compare other Head Starts not able to so completely comprehend and comply with the real meanings of the program. I believed in OEO. You owe it to your constitutents in Mississippi to spread the word and go along with whatever decision they make. If OEO means what it says, marvelous. If not, let's show that *we* mean it. Let's prove that the poor need us only as catalysts, connections, and consultants, not as benefactors, missionaries, and controllers. Let's demonstrate that the role of the white liberal is to *listen* to the poor and *hear* them; to *look* at the poor and *see* them; to try to let the messages penetrate; and to help work out structures and politics that put this message into productive action.

I promised to help interpret the guidelines and translate their ideas into federal jargon—something I did for all applicants in the seven Southern states in my region who wanted this service. I promised to see that the proposal was handled tenderly, so it wouldn't get the guts cut out of it by low level budget slashers and anxiously conventional judges, before it reached higher levels, where its value would be instantly recognized.

Art and Tom said they would think about the idea and let me know. A few days later Tom telephoned and said they had to come to the conclusion that it couldn't work. It would be selling the desperate poor to the discouraging government.

Meanwhile, in Washington, Jule Sugarman, deputy director and chief administrator of Head Start, acting according to a policy from Mr. Shriver, had appointed a specialist for starting projects in the South. Dudley Morris was instructed to look for liberal groups as well as others. From his days as Southern civil rights reporter for *Time* magazine, Dudley was well acquainted with the Delta Ministry. He shared the opinion of many that the Delta Ministry was the most effective organization working for social change in Mississippi. He found it to be capable without manipulating. Without knowing that I had done so already, for such is the way of huge government agencies, he contacted Art Thomas. Probably this double reassurance of OEO's sincere interest in involving real community action specialists in Head Start was the determining factor in Art's decision to bring the news of the program to the shabby shacks and valiant leaders of black Mississippi.

The spirit at OEO that spring of its youth, its first spring, was idealistic and vigorous. At staff meetings we were urged to aim high and work hard. We were praised when we did so. We were praised particularly when we used our own judgment, showed initiative, and seemed to be implementing to the greatest possible degree, considering the ferocious pressure of time and "case load," the standards of content quality being set by some of the nation's foremost experts in the collection of fields coordinated by Head Start; experts who served as planning consultants for OEO. This explained why I was seeking groups like the Levin group all over the South.

Later, when CDGM became OEO's perhaps most controversial Head Start project, and greatest Head Start headache, friends at OEO forgave me for having been involved in its initiation by explaining that I'd been politically naïve, and didn't realize the political implications of what I was getting into. The rationalization they made to excuse me was that I'd been hoodwinked into a liaison with some dubious and disastrous politicians. On the contrary, I knew exactly the political implications of what I was becoming involved in—and I thought they were the political implications with which the War on Poverty was intended to get involved. I understood that Head Start was a wedge made of appealing little children which would help the Administration wiggle itself into the hearts of the poor, minority groups, and liberals; that the purpose was more to win votes than to eliminate poverty. I understood that the poverty program as a whole was intended to reduce the restlessness and mounting anger of civil rights militants, partly by throwing them something to assuage the keenest edge of their hunger, partly by taking the wind out of their sails. I thought the Levin group fit into this picture in a positive way.

I also knew that the politicians and administrators making policies and decisions at the White House, in Congress, and in OEO its limited self, were on the whole the "good people," temporarily in ascendance over more selfish people, and that they genuinely wanted to make use of the American public's temporarily "generous" feeling in 1965 to engage the nation in domestic "good works."

My background and particular interest was in early education and community development, in human development, not in politics. But it was clear that these things are not separable, and to be effective in the content, one must be at least cognizant of the political underpinnings, framework, pressures, and likelihoods in the location of which one is speaking. We know it's possible for a handful of men to seclude themselves as monks and yogis in monasteries and on mountaintops and to develop themselves extraordinarily. But what I wondered was how much can we do about human development under normal (including political) conditions? I believed that the combination of professionally original and dazzlingly effective Dr. Tom Levin, with the solidity, courage, entré, respectability, and power of the National Council of Churches, was well worth encouraging. I thought this team might provide OEO with a model Head Start in the South, of which it could be proud.

And both more important and more interesting, I thought this group might, due to its sophistication and determination, help explore the answers to some challenging questions. How far was OEO, as an agent of American public opinion, going to be willing to go in experimenting with methods that would really be successful with the children and their "apathetic" families? How much would OEO promote the poor in their effort to get "in"? How far in did the American public feel safe allowing the poor, and the Negro especially, to push? To what degree was a "solution" to poverty problems yearned for by the public and sought by OEO, and to what degree was a pacifier preferred? How deep would the Administration feel it had to penetrate the hearts of the poor and their allies to win their allegiance, and at what point would allegiance to or dependence upon politicians of other persuasions and interests interfere? To what extent would the goal of a national advertising campaign to alert the middle-class to the needs of the poor overwhelm and halt the goal of mobilizing the poor in their own behalf —the goals were not compatible. How far would OEO, representing Americans everywhere, side with those willing and eager to honor civil rights laws, even in rough country? And at what point would cautiousness, fear of rocking the boat, and political bartering, cause OEO to take the part of those desirous of defying these laws? How much influence would the prominent professional consultants swarming around the OEO office be granted, and where was the cut-off line, where hidden political considerations would take precedence? Did anyone seriously believe in human growth and development?

I was a midlevel government employee. I didn't know the subtleties of the community organization and Movement profession, but I knew that the Levin-Thomas group did. I didn't know much about Mississippi, except that there was only one side for the federal government to be on, the questions being to what extent and through what means middle-ground Mississippians could be moved onto that side, and to what degree OEO was planning to move them there.

I knew very little about White House politics, but no one working at OEO could avoid knowing that strong undercurrents swirled beneath all our talk of little children, and that strong counter currents would be necessary to prevent the former from swirling any truly meaningful project program work down the political drain—especially in Mississippi. I didn't have the authority to decide if church and state (the National Council of Churches was interested in this) and political parties (were civil rights workers political parties?) were eligible for a Head Start grant, but it seemed necessary at this junction of civil rights with federal program, and mission work with federal program, to encourage all knowledgeable parties to join in the shaping of the junction.

I didn't have the authority to *decide* on these questions, or to approve a proposal, but I did have the authority, and I thought in the flush of the idealism the OEO staff then had, the obligation to get this Levin group's capabilities into proposal form so that someone else could decide if they could don the uniform of the Poverty War troops. In my exuberant enthusiasm and unlimited faith in the potential of the War on Poverty, I was convinced that one role day-to-day OEO staff should play was that of hunting for the forces most likely to make the War effective; forces on the operational local project level, and forces on the level of rallying political support for the poor, to offset that which has always existed to keep them from acquiring power; thus keeping the poor from feeling able and being able to change their lot. So I worked closely with those able to build the necessary invisible underwater pressure in behalf of this intriguing project. After my groundwork on content and strategy, the fate of this project, like the fate of all other projects in "my" Southern region, would be determined by routine conveyor belt bureaucratic processes, or if the propressure groups were successful enough, would be determined by special senior staff action.

I tried to protect all the proposals in the region I worked, but unfortunately axes and hack saws were plentiful at OEO that spring, and few applications made it to the end of the interdepartmental conveyor belt with all the worthwhile features we labored so hard to devise still in them. It became clear by May that administrative determinations had been made, not to push the ceiling to encompass all that communities *could do,* but instead to lower it for governmental convenience and speed.

In small part, CDGM came to be an albatross hanging at the neck of OEO, instead of becoming a small church-funded or volunteer free-lance day care project, because one girl believed that the poverty program was an experiment—and believed it to be a responsibility of ordinary staff members to sponsor a liaison between the dedicated doers and the still ubiquitous OEO, in order to establish just how far all the above questions were negotiable. To what extent could OEO administrators, political strategists, the Administration, and the American people to whom they all responded, be influenced in the direction of what the poor want and need, and which the rhetoric of the poverty program was telling us they must have? And to what extent would all of us naïve but well-intentioned citizens and poverty warriors prove to be educable—open to experimental evidence as to the possible nature and potential solutions of poverty?

In the spring of 1965 many sophisticated people were already somewhat cynical about how much really meaningful work could be done within the political limitations of a federal program. The same people were often hopeful that this new federal gray area would prove productive on a human rather than exclusively political level. We were doubtful, but hopeful, as Art Thomas set his Mississippi machinery in motion.

CHAPTER 2

THE DREAM BEGINS TO MOVE AND BREATHE

SIX DELTA MINISTRY volunteers, spurred on by a gentle young girl from Idaho named Karen Shillington, and some independent SNCC and FDP workers, whose primary loyalty had shifted from their respective organizations to progress and programs in individual communities, started quietly talking about day care projects with poor friends in Mississippi's "pockets of poverty." Karen's role can't be overestimated. Whenever I asked people in the first summer communities and on the first summer staff where they first heard of CDGM, they were apt to reply with Karen's name. Karen became the second district coordinator, but due to health problems, was forced to leave before the end of the summer. The grapevine connecting rickety shacks perched ever-precariously on the endless land began reverberating. Excitement generated among sharecroppers, cotton choppers, fishermen, maids, and laborers, far and wide. Do something for the children! Do something for themselves! The enthusiasm that leaped from village to village had nothing to do with money, as Head Start had not yet been mentioned. The topic was day care and an educational program for little children which people would, if interested, set up and manage for themselves. Most of the volunteers tried poor *white* communities, but their friendly offers were met with slammed doors and a bit of buckshot.

On April 3, three weeks after the original New York meeting, representatives from approximately twenty tiny poor black communities came together at the Delta Ministry's conference center, an abandoned Negro junior college campus called Mount Beulah. Several had day care programs already. Some came bearing problems, some came bearing hopes. During this meeting they heard for the first time about the alternative to volunteer day care centers: Head Start. (I had sent an assistant to the meeting, who described the details of the Head Start program.)

The people asked careful questions. They considered. They ended up even more enthusiastic than when they had started, and left the meeting with hastily duplicated sheets for signing up children by name, and for signing up sponsoring committee members in each locality, from among the poor themselves, and for describing the specific facilities available to them for their Child Development centers. They arranged that if they had good luck and others were interested, they could come back in a few weeks, just before OEO's deadline for Head Start applications, to plan some more. Between the first meeting and the proposed second meeting, this confederation of poor communities from many counties began to call itself the Child Development Group of Mississippi. The Child Development Group of Mississippi was described from the outset as a project of Mississippi Action for Community Education—MACE. Tom selected this name for the meaning of its initials, as well as its direct meaning. A mace is a club, a weapon, used for breaking armor. It's a staff carried by a dignitary to show authority. It's a fragrant and highly aromatic raw spice. Tom thought this a perfect summary of what CDGM sought to be.

At OEO I turned my attention back to my many other applicants. I remember a Mississippi school superintendent from one of the Delta counties explaining to me on the phone, quite sincerely and as a friend, that I didn't understand the poor "down here," because they would never sign their children up for Head Start. They didn't grasp the value of preschool experience, he said, and wouldn't bother to enroll their children. Furthermore, he told me, the government expectation that Head Start groups would establish adult education programs for parents, and get these dawn-to-dusk cotton choppers stumbling in exhausted of an evening "to hear lectures," was based on ridiculous ivory tower views. "These people will never come in. We'll be doing well if we can pull them out for one PTA meeting. They never do come. They are too tired, and besides, they don't care that much about education," he said.

Yet at this time in sunny spring-filled Mississippi, CDGM people, as poor as the superintendent's, but evidently more motivated by doing for themselves than by his well-meant fatherly attempt to do for them, were trudging through clouds of enveloping, suffocating dust, from church to church, from cabin to cabin, to find facilities available to them to house their program when summer and the grant came. They trudged before they went to work in the fields at 6 A.M., and they trudged again after dark, searching, searching, asking, inquiring, explaining, looking for a place and a way to give their children something they had never, in their wildest dreams, anticipated they would ever be in a position to give them. The superintendent was right. Poor people, like other people, don't respond to many goodies that are doled out to them. He was right that they "don't appreciate things like that." His failure was not a failure of goodwill or of effort. It was the failure we all make—

the failure to understand fully and act upon the fact that people prefer to be given the wherewithal to do things for themselves, rather than to have things done for them.

Later, local people told of some of the troubles they had getting started. These are some examples, taken off tapes of the discussions: "Our community was frightened because they knew there was going to be some whites in this. They know the officials will say any white people who are involved working with us Negroes in Mississippi are civil rights workers. Up North if teachers work with Negroes they are good people. Down here they are called civil rights workers, and that means subversive. People stay away from them. We are talking in our community about only a few white teachers, but our people were afraid this means loss of jobs . . . that the white people would take the good jobs, like they always do . . . that they would decide how everything would be . . . like they always do.

"Then they were also afraid if they work with white people *they* will be called civil rights workers, and won't ever to able to get a job again after this ends. Our people don't want to get involved with whites. I mean, they are not against whites, but they don't want whites getting into their affairs and taking them over, and they don't want to be called agitators. But I said, how can we improve things for our children if we try to keep segregated? How can we integrate their places if we won't let them in ours? How can we say it's the whites won't mix if we won't mix with them? I'm for getting in all the whites we can, side by side, not on top of us. It's hard to teach white people side by side and not on top, but we are patient people, we can teach them if we try hard enough. You know something funny? (That's what I said to my community . . .)

"Even if we don't get a single white child or a single white person at all, they're going to call us civil rights. You can't get away from it. Whenever we look up from the land and move a muscle for improvement they say that. You can't get away from it, so you may as well go all the way and come with us. (That's what I told my community. I didn't have no trouble getting people interested after I explained it.)"

This was an elderly man talking. He was credited with having found a delapidated building, doing most of the plumbing, wiring, and carpentry renovations himself, and rallying the community behind the establishment of this new school. A young preacher said, "I think people must first understand what this program is. They ain't afraid when they understand this. This is going to be a school. To teach their child things. Jail? Why are they afraid of jail? Why are they afraid to be locked up? If we been in Mississippi all our life, we *been* locked up all our life. What is such civil rights about this program? I told the parents we're going to have a Head Start school that teaches the alphabet and has hot dinner. That's civil rights? Only in Mississippi! We are getting active in the education of our little children. Is that bad? Only in Mississippi! Because if we begin to get good education, it may change a lot of things around here, that's why they calls it civil rights. They makes civil rights sound like a terrible thing to get near. Civil rights happens to be the federal law from Washington. You *are* involved in them one way or another, fair side or unfair side, if you're alive. So I'll be involved by doing the best for my children the best way I know how. I told parents these things when I canvassed."

First Person: "I saw the parents was scared. So I said they could visit one day."

Second Person: "One day, you said? I don't think it should be one day. I told our parents any day, all day. Get in there and help teach. It's the parents' program. That's how we overcome fear in our community. We say, you don't have to give up your kids to nobody. Come, too."

A father, who never had earned more than $550 a year, said, "In our county we got bothered from everywhere. The plantation owners threatened us with being throwed off the land. Throwed out of the house we was borned in. They said they'd fire you if you was their maid or worked in their gas station. The crackers don't mind usin' their guns and matches. Mysterious lots of fires happens to colored peoples in Mississippi. An' they disappear. Whole families of 'em. Usually families that voted, or put up some white civil rights worker. I'd hate to drain these mucky murky black rivers down here and look at the sawed up black bodies on the bottom. That's why peoples was afraid to send their childrens. But they did. They did. Nowadays peoples doesn't mind these things they do because freedom's comin'. They just about runnin' off them plantations to our Head Start schools in our county."

A lady from Rolling Fork said, "Some families I went to see said they didn't want their children to come to our school because the principal said they wouldn't get into real school if they didn't go to his Head Start. But mostly they come to our Head Start anyway. Because it belongs to the people."

A lady from Indianola said, "We had gone out to tell our families in April. The teachers in the school system didn't do nothing then. No canvassing. Then the teachers got the idea of Head Start. They came back and told our families they'd go to jail if they sent their children to us; that we were Communist. So we had to go out all over again and tell the people it wasn't so. Then we were turned down at many a nervous Negro church before we found one that would allow us in there with the children. Then the church deacons chickened out, and we had to haul the children to Leland. That's eighteen miles away."

And a young woman in her late teens or early twenties told the group: "Talk about a problem! I'm telling you, we had one. We walked and we walked. We had a nice school building in our town, but they wouldn't let us have it. Because they said we wanted to do something for the community in it. It's a school, they said, not for the community. We told them helping the community people helps the school. Then they said, *yes,* well, *we* will do something for the community. But naturally not let us, who *is* the community, do it for ourself. You know why, though, you have to be patient with them people. They know we could get them people up and out better than them and they're ashamed because it would make liars out of them when they say niggers won't do nuthin'. Anyway, they's scared of us . . . we're a whole lot smarter than them. So we have seven colored churches. We just walked and walked till we found one that would let us locate. We fixed it up real good. It looked like a one-room rural church, you know, empty. Now it look like children."

The people had their second meeting at Mount Beulah in mid-April, as they had planned. But instead of the straggling remains of the first group, which was all that might have been expected to survive the organizational ordeal, sixty-four communities showed up at that meeting—approximately forty-four more than came the first time. They had the names of 4,200 real live children; not statistical children, which the school system Head Starts were submitting in forty-some counties. Sixty buildings had been pinned down, and many of them were already being renovated. This, of course, was with no promise of a grant, and with only the materials and labor the poorest people in one of the South's poorest states could furnish. Contributions of time, cash, and services were not pouring forth from the white communities. I'm not aware of *any.*

At this meeting a wizened old man shuffled across the floor of the auditorium, wending his way through stifling crowds. He had on socks that didn't match and bedraggled bedroom slippers. His pants bagged and sagged and were held up by one crisscross suspender. He grinned a great black gap-toothed grin as he shook hands with a white volunteer. Nodding his head repeatedly up and down in proud affirmation of himself, he said, "Ah done sahned up a hunert 'n' sev'n chillens. Yessir. Yes indeed ah did. Ah done it mahsel." Chuckling with secret pleasure he began to turn away. Suddenly he gave a loud cackle of laughter, and called triumphantly over his shoulder, "Ah is the apathetic poor!"

CHAPTER 3

THE "FUNNY-NAMED PSYCHOLOGIST" AND THE "WELL-KNOWN COMMUNIST"

WHILE HE AND hundreds of other "apathetic" people scuttled around the state's unheard-of nooks and crannies, starting a vast school from nothing but earth and determination, Dr. Tom Levin was busy in related arenas. He attended both Mississippi meetings, but otherwise was still a full-time practicing psychoanalyst in New York. Around the edges he worked furiously hard to slap bricks and mortar onto our incredible castle in the air.

A first summer resource teacher described Tom: "He has an interesting sculptured-looking face, such a short crew cut that it's more fuzz than hair, and you can't see what color it is, and a lithe muscular figure for a man in his forties. He is short and solid. When he walked, he strutted, but he never strutted because he always loped—he was always in a great tense hurry except with community people. For them he always had time. He has a very nice persuasive voice. He either wooed us with it, or cut us to ribbons, apparently depending upon mood."

An immediate need was to neutralize influential freedom-seeking activists in Mississippi who considered the entire poverty program a fraud and a menace to the people's deep yearning and bursting readiness to move forward rapidly toward rights that people of a paler hue are wrapped in from birth. They felt the poverty program was designed to delude and detour the determined freedom-seeking poor with bit jobs and foolish repressive kindergartens.

Tom went to see Jim Forman, executive director of SNCC, who had already heard of CDGM and was hostile to the idea of people selling their souls and futures for a temporary bone. Tom explained CDGM's intents to Jim, and expressed his view that the Movement was falling apart because it had had no thriving, driving program since the COFO Summer Project almost a year before. This would be a good and meaningful project to pull people together again. Besides, he said, why should everybody get a share of this blood-building medicine except "the good guys"? The loyal Democrats (see Appendix A) were getting some through the Corinth Project (the director of this Northeastern Mississippi project was the nephew of Senator Sparkman) and the Catholic-Church-sponsored STAR literacy project. The liberal Reform Democrats (Labor and NAACP) were piecing together the Coahoma project in the Clarkesdale part of the state.

Tom Levin and Art Thomas understood the tremendous political implication of CDGM long before either civil rights groups or OEO itself did. They were both brilliant political strategists and tacticians. Jim Foreman agreed that it was important for poor people and their representatives to benefit in this political parceling out of power, too. He said that he wanted no part of it, but wouldn't fight it. He invited Tom to a regional SNCC staff meeting at Waveland, Mississippi, to present the case for CDGM.

At the Waveland meeting Jim talked a little about CDGM and then retreated. Tom found the group generally not interested in CDGM one way or the other, with a small group at each extreme of emotion. Frank Smith, a strong leader of the no-compromises faction, was ardently against it, because he claimed to be interested in organizing communities. Tom said, "Great, so is CDGM, come and organize with us." Frank agreed to do so.

Later there was a great deal of criticism of Tom for hiring Frank, particularly from board member Marian Wright, because Frank appeared to do more attacking than organizing during the following summer. While it was true that credit unions, cooperatives, and other evidences of good organizing did not spring up in Frank's footsteps, and that many CDGM staff members got more blasts from him than helpful hints, it was also true that by joining CDGM, Frank probably prevented the total destruction of this prenatal organization by his admirers, who remained hostile throughout his tenure, but who did not attempt to tear CDGM down completely. At that delicate point they could have done just that, by turning community people's happiness into suspicion, and efforts into rejections.

Sad to say, many people in Mississippi could still be swayed by leaders in whom they had faith, even if the leaders were not leading them where they wanted to go. Perhaps Frank Smith's greatest message to CDGM staff and constituents, which proved all too true later in the grotesque game, was: "Don't trust the government. They don't know you, they don't like you, they are using you to gain prestige for themselves. Be independent. Use *them* while you can, but don't swallow the bait and forget where you're going."

The SNCC executive committee never took an official position on CDGM, though individual workers in some cases came to our staff. In other cases they fought us tooth and nail. Occasionally individuals joined our staff *and* fought us, simultaneously. They said they were infiltrating our "bureaucracy" to keep us honest. They said they were with us to keep reminding the poor not to become too dependent on *any* organization, but to continue thinking for themselves, because in this world of political pressures and deals you can never tell when a "good" organization will become a bad one. The devil is a slick fellow, they said.

During the frantic spring, while everyone was trying to lay the groundwork for CDGM, Tom Levin also contacted the Medical Committee for Human Rights, and what was left of the Committee of Conscience, to see if he could get their support for the new venture. These groups had come into existence the year before, and were both originated by Tom.

As a result of the hoses and dogs to which Negroes and sympathizers were treated during the spring of 1963 in Birmingham, Dr. Levin had thought it would be nice if some eminent social scientists substituted their "square" heads for those less erudite ones being billy-clubbed. He felt that Ph.D. professors could demonstrate deep commitment to the doctrines of their disciplines by carrying them to the battlefronts of the civil rights movement, and exposing their bodies as well as their ideas to the risk of beatings and insults. Tom saw that news reporters were getting weary of mere routine violence, and hoped that some scholarly disasters would reawaken their tired typewriters. He felt that medical presence would be supportive to the Movement, as well as the dignity and respectability these professionals would lend it. He had recruited about twenty distinguished sociologists, psychologists, anthropologists, economists, etc.

The group named itself the Committee of Conscience, and offered its services to Reverend Martin Luther King. The committee was active at Selma, and was a co-sponsor of the 1964 March on Washington. It supported the COFO Summer Project of 1964 by organizing teams of more than two hundred social workers, public health people, psychiatrists, and others to go into Mississippi and assist in organizing community action projects. (Tom himself has seen over five hundred civil rights workers in private consultation, at no charge, of course; civil rights workers don't have any money.)

Tom Levin, first coordinator of the Medical Committee for Human Rights, conceptualized, organized, and activated the first teams in Mississippi in a seven day period! Those who knew him had confidence that he could do the same kind of things with this new Head Start project. He could follow the precedent he had set for mixing quantities of professionals with Movement activity, design a unique project, and act effectively and rapidly.

By the time Tom contacted the Medical Committee, a year after its birth, regarding possible services to CDGM, it had become dominated by medical politics, with resulting anxiety about nonprofessionalism and professional status, and fear of treading on the toes of antagonistic

Mississippi colleagues. The immense value of the Medical Committee was dwarfed only by the opportunities for social action programs and new careers for subprofessional health workers that it did not utilize, one of which was CDGM. Medical Committee workers told Tom that they didn't believe in CDGM's community health workers. Though individual members of the Committee helped CDGM, the organization didn't help us with the doctors and nurses it could have supplied, had it chosen to do so. The Medical Committee continued to exist, but was not a dynamic, limelight organization during CDGM's era.

Only a person with Tom Levin's grandiosity, imaginative ideas, capacity for enduring and dismissing the doubts of reasonable people who said it couldn't be done, ability to plunge into action as fast as action was called for, hell-or-high-water perseverance (considered ruthlessness or deviousness by some), and need for no sleep, could have concocted and carried out efforts as enormous and significant as the Medical Committee for Human Rights so quickly, and could have hatched the even more extraordinary CDGM ten months later. Tom had been a child of poverty and a ghetto resident himself, so his feelings were in this as well as his mind.

Tom spent what was left of the rapidly evaporating spring of 1965 working with a small group of volunteers in New York, recruiting and orienting people for the summer project. Leaflets describing CDGM were sent to schools of education, social work, psychology, etc.; even to the New York Employment Bureau! Tom was very concerned about integrating the summer experiment because of OEO's insistence that each center be integrated, combined with the strong feeling of the people that they wanted their children to get to know "ordinary" people of "the other color."

There was also quite a bit of talk about mixing local nonteachers, local teachers, other professionals, and future-professional students. As best as could be determined under the difficult circumstances, a majority of community members and leaders wanted a program in which professionals were included, but in which poor people predominated. Out-of-state professionals and students were contacted because, coming on the heels of the warlike summer before, it didn't seem that we would have much luck with native white Mississippians and local college students. One of Tom's strongest interests of the summer was to find new ways to use professionals in poverty projects. He thought that the poor benefited from the professionals' experience, connections, and support. The group had two meetings a week: one to explain the program and its background to recruits, and one to develop philosophy and structure. Art was doing the same thing in Mississippi with local Negroes.

Tom says of this period: "I felt like a juggler on a tightrope, whose feet were being burned, his eyes blindfolded, his hands in bandages, juggling the red hot canon balls of OEO, Aaron Henry [head of the

Mississippi NAACP, a more conservative group], the communities, the Delta Ministry, the Freedom Democratic party, the Mississippi politicians and press, SNCC, administrative systems, white professional staff with strong opinions, and the Mississippi professional teachers, who were in an uproar. It was quite an unusual spring for a quiet psychoanalyst."

Just as Dr. Tom Levin was a full-time professional in another field and in another state while directing the assemblage of CDGM long distance, so the Reverend Arthur Thomas was full-time busy with the direction of the vigorous Delta Ministry, while getting CDGM mobilized in scores of communities. Art, the cornerstone of CDGM, first got into this kind of work when he and a group made up predominantly of Methodists (he was ordained as a Methodist minister) started an interracial church in Durham, North Carolina, in 1960. Art said the Methodists did not refuse to recognize this church because of its black and white composition; they just simply refused to discuss it at all.

So it was not only interracial, but also interdenominational. The congregation, with Art as pastor, was involved in many important social problems, such as North Carolina lunchroom sit-ins, employment of Negroes in downtown stores, dealings with the garbage workers' union, and a battle with the telephone company for better service in Negro neighborhoods. Many members of the congregation were at the Raleigh meeting at which SNCC was formed. One member was the later famous national chairman of CORE: Floyd McKissick. When the National Council of Churches formed its Commission on Religion and Race, Art was asked to work with it. He worked in many Southern states.

In September, 1964, he wound up in Mississippi as the first director of the newly established Delta Ministry, administered through the National Council of Churches Division of Home Missions, and supported by contributions from five continents as well as some domestic churches. Not all, Art hastened to point out, felt that applying Christian codes in communities where Christians object is Christian.

In its brief, brisk, and busy ten months of life before the birth of sister CDGM, and during the first year and a half of CDGM's existence, the Delta Ministry did an immeasurable amount of good in Mississippi. Delta Ministry staff and budget were completely separate from CDGM. The only connections were mutual goals, the fact that Delta Ministry (church) volunteers told communities about Head Start, and until he left the state, Art Thomas served as director of one, and board member of the other. Dr. Beittel and Marian Wright were on the boards of both.

It was in the rich soils the Delta Ministry had plowed that CDGM seeds were able to take root and sprout. Therefore, many poor people were active in both organizations. Perhaps its greatest achievement was the "presence" of a Christian view actively applied to modern Mississippi realities. A Negro sharecropper referred to it as "that justice place." It's impossible to understand how revolutionary and fundamental a change it is in the lives of many Mississippi Negroes to know that there is a justice place and a group of just people. Under Art's visionary direction the Delta Ministry had many solid programs in addition to presence (see Appendix B).

Largely because of Art Thomas, CDGM stood on the shoulders of COFO and its companion projects which were active the preceding summer. CDGM was a link between volunteer efforts that had been gaining strength during the past few years *to stir Negroes into motion* in Mississippi—efforts which culminated in the COFO project of 1964—and *funded* efforts to encourage Negroes *to develop* skills—initiated in a massive and systematic way by the 1965 War Against Poverty.

Tom Levin, Art Thomas, Marian Wright, and others involved felt that it was extremely important not to lose new, hard-won Negro momentum—brought to a climax by COFO—by planting the first federal programs in soils of white benevolence, rather than soils of Negro enthusiasm. Most federal programs in Mississippi occurred in white territory, in white terms, and under white control, even when they were "for" Negroes. They didn't take place in the heart of intricately structured Negro communities, they strictly ruled out strivings for rights, and they ignored budding Negro initiative.

CDGM wasn't intended to be an unbridled anarchic movement. It was intended to follow government rules. But neither was it to be the tightly reigned state-controlled type of government program typical in this state. It was meant to take all the nonadrenaline, old fashioned, respectable implications of the term *civil rights,* and put them to work in advance Movement form: federal programs. Federal programs were not new, but the poverty program was, and the thought behind CDGM was that poverty program projects could be a junction between old-style donor-donee government programs and real meaty community action.

For four days during that mad rush, Tom, Art, Jeannine, and Karen locked themselves up in a Washington hotel room, and scrambled together a proposal. It was thought by many OEO higher-ups to be the most interesting structure and description received from any part of the nation. Karen stayed on the phone to Mississippi much of the time, steadily collecting up-to-the-minute statistics and suggestions from volunteers and community people. The proposal was technically placed on paper by a few white folks, but it condensed and articulated more of the views of strong Negro spokesmen from poor communities than any proposal I saw from hundreds of Negro school principals. It was easy to understand this. The proposals I had read were from Negro principals. A Negro school principal in Mississippi belongs to a white school superintendent, who belongs to a white board of education, which is part and parcel of a white supremacist society.

CHAPTER 4

THE LAST MINUTE RUSH

TWO LAST MINUTE crises occurred in the spring of 1965 during the organizing of CDGM.

The first was the discovery that the Council of Neighborhood Centers, a body made up only of elected representatives from those communities in the confederation proposed by Tom for the day care project, did not constitute a suitable Head Start board of directors in the eyes of OEO. OEO wanted some "responsible," "respectable" citizens, which left us with the distinct feeling that OEO considered poor leaders and their allies irresponsible and unrespectable.

So everybody was detailed to hustle out and search for responsible citizens who were not too responsible to the system and who might be irresponsible enough to allow the poor to be responsible for their own program, and yet who were at the same time respectable enough to impress OEO with their respectability but not respectable enough to consider us too unrespectable to work with, given the fact that outsiders and Negroes were pretty unrespectable in Mississippi.

The pressure of time was terrible. A small group that satisfied everyone, at least for a beginning, was quickly selected (not elected) from available sources, with the understanding that each member would have to be either ratified or dropped at the first opportunity for community meetings, and that a larger number of poor people would be added from each local district by popular vote. There would also be established in the near future a Council of Neighborhood Centers, which would consist exclusively of poor elected delegates and would balance the board and Central Staff as policy making groups. The council and the board were written into the proposal. Poor people would be in the majority on the board. The board members seemed distinguished enough to OEO.

Our prize find was a Mississippi mayor. OEO was very proud of him.

I don't know whether officials there knew he was around eighty years old, black, hard of hearing, the mayor of a bitterly poor all-Negro town, and that he slept through many board meetings. He was from Mound Bayou, where it was said that the county superintendent of schools had decreed that Civics and American History between 1860–1875 would not be taught in Negro schools.

Though many a well-meaning white Mississippian assured us that our board was composed of "well-known Communists and Communist dupes"—such as Dr. Beittel, the elderly white ex-president of Tougaloo, an integrated college—they seemed to others a nucleus of devoted, hard-working, intelligent men and women.

Marian Wright was a member of this original board, a pivotal person in formulating CDGM, and a CDGM backbone thereafter. Although she was not at the first New York meeting, was not involved in the OEO negotiations for the first grant, and was not a key concept planner, as she put it, "I heard of CDGM long before there was one." A Southern Negro herself, she had gone to Yale Law School for the express purpose of returning to the South as a lawyer, because of the shocking lack of lawyers willing to involve themselves in civil rights cases, and the enormous need for them. In the spring of 1964, operating out of the New York Inc. Fund office, she had worked in Tennessee and Mississippi, establishing INC Fund offices in Memphis and Jackson. She moved to Jackson before the summer of 1964 to head this office.

Marian was vitally concerned with all forms of social change as well as with "the legal approach to human relations." She said, "I'm not a great advocate of the law as a means of rapid social change. It helps though. It provides the underpinnings—the framework. Everybody today sort of cavalierly ignores the huge impact of the 1954 school desegregation decision, but if it weren't for that, we wouldn't have a framework to work in. I wanted to work through the law, but also to back it up with all kinds of other things—mainly community organization." As early as the fall of 1964 she and Art Thomas had talked with friends at the Merrill Foundation about developing programs in Mississippi to help children prepare for public school. She, Art, and others had had many discussions of how to bring OEO to the state. "I never envisaged what CDGM soon became though. I didn't have a concrete plan. Actually, I had in mind one or two communities. I was so interested because the kids always seem to just wander around in Mississippi—wasted; unoccupied. I was terribly concerned about the failure and the difficulty Negro kids have keeping up in previously white schools. I thought prior preparation might help them cope better. My major concern was decent education for these kids."

Marian had had more experience with the Mississippi school situation for Negro children than some of the others. She remembers a six-hour session at her house sometime in April with Art, Tom, Jeannine, and others battling over the educational program for CDGM—what approaches, methods, etc. "We were listeners, but the others fought over all kind of plans!" She was also involved with Art in urging Delta Ministry volunteers to spread the word about Head Start in outlying rural communities. She knew many local poor leaders in these communities and helped think of people who might be interested candidates for the first board.

Official board meeting minutes begin May 16, 1965. At this meeting Tom Levin was elected project director, and Dr. Beittel was elected chairman of the board. Dr. Beittel said of Tom's election: "Tom was elected the same way John was the next year: John became the second director in February, 1966, when we secured the second grant, because he was there, the moving spirit, the sole survivor. Who else would be the logical person? He had the whole program and its goals in his head. In Tom's case, he was the moving spirit, the organizer, the originator. No one thought of looking for anyone else."

Board members mostly agreed that Dr. Beittel be elected chairman because, to get off the ground, the project needed the man with the most board experience in the lead. Dr. Beittel told me: "I had a general idea that here was a group wanting to start a Head Start program. I knew about Head Start, of course, from the time the bill was passed. I had been trying to start something like it in Jackson since the previous December [Dec. 1964]. I was already on the steering committee of the Jackson Head Start, which is a completely separate project. Art Thomas, I believe it was, invited me to become a member of this board. I didn't realize the implications of CDGM at first. But in board meetings there was always this emphasis that the poor people committees were so important. Tom was responsible for this point of view. Art backed him up in this regard, but Tom talked more about it. I began to think that CDGM had really far-reaching implications: if poor people really got interested in education, think what that would mean politically, socially, and economically!"

Reverend James McCree, a tall, handsome Negro pastor in Canton, Mississippi, said: "I believe it is a part of my work as a minister to respond to the needs of my people. Education is one of them. Learning to run their own organizations is another. I stay close to my people. When the Commission on Religion and Race offered me a car to get our work done faster, I kept it one week, and then turned it back in. I wasn't afraid that people would think less of me, those that want to call me a Tom and say they don't like me will anyway—but I was afraid I would think about the people less often. If they were out there walking around in their head rags, with nothing to ride on but their feet, how could I ride around in a fancy air-conditioned car? But even though I stay close, live right in with them, live like they do, still I try to lead them. People have to stand on their own feet, but they don't always know what they want. We haven't had much experience with being asked what we want. I was interested in CDGM because it was going to struggle to get people standing on their own feet. If necessary it would force them to their feet.

"Art Thomas mentioned Head Start to me and George Raymond. I first met George when he came here as a CORE worker from New Orleans in 1963. We had been working together. We were interested in Head Start. I felt I'll do what I have to do, let the chips fall where they may. Lots of people in my congregation didn't want us to get into this. I heard of Head Start from other people too: Al Ulmer of the Southern Regional Council told us about it. Then Mrs. Ritter from OEO came and begged us to do it alone, not to do it with the Delta Ministry and CDGM. We refused, and she asked what it was we wanted. I said, 'To get out of the kitchens, independent incomes, to develop strong community spirit, to develop our own ideas, to express ourselves, to start a network for reaching smaller communities—things we need to join together to get, and not things we can develop through a little Head Start here and there.' Mrs. Ritter wasn't pleased.

"We talked it over with Art in Stevens Kitchen. I went to meetings at Mount Beulah. We had one meeting that Karen Shillington was supposed to be at to give people from eight communities more information. She didn't come, we didn't have enough information, and we were embarrassed. We had another meeting. She came, but four out of eight communities left when they thought it had something to do with Freedom Schools. People from all over the state began coming to see me. They thought I had all the information, but I never had enough. We collected enrollment for eighteen units, door-to-door. The whole thing got lost, and we did it all again the night before deadline.

"I met Tom in May when I was elected to the board."

The second organizational crisis was that the president of Tougaloo College, who had promised all along that his institution would serve as applicant agent for us to OEO, panicked twenty-four hours before OEO deadline for Head Start applications. Tougaloo College, under the presidency of Dr. Beittel, had been a leader in Mississippi civil rights activities, but had become, under the guidance of the new president, very concerned with its academic image as the protégé of Brown University in a new "big brother" program. President Owens said things about his board not being able to meet in time.

Dr. Beittel says, "It is my opinion that Tougaloo College should have done this, because of its reputation in the past, and in the few years just before, too. But CDGM came during the year President Owens was serving as acting president. He was insecure. He told me he felt it wouldn't be wise to undertake anything of this kind. If I had still been president, I think I could have done it. If Mr. Owens had been there longer, he probably would have been willing to have

Tougaloo College assume this responsibility. Mr. Owens said he just couldn't do it without assuming responsibility, and he said he didn't have the staff to do that. I could understand that."

In order to be out of reach of the governor's veto, we had to have as applicant agent an institution of higher education. No white colleges, of course, could be considered, because they wouldn't consider us. Neither could we consider state-controlled colleges (which, for fear of losing their funding, looked on us as the plague itself), thus eliminating most of the Negro colleges and junior colleges. Rust College was not a possibility because it is controlled by the Methodists, a very conservative group in Mississippi and not likely to favor our mission. The Unitarian Church was so liberal (*i.e.*, integrated) that later in the summer one of its ministers was ambushed by night riders and confined to the hospital for some time in critical condition because of bullets in the shoulder and lungs, but unfortunately the Unitarians didn't control a college we could approach.

The best bet looked like Mary Holmes Junior College, an obscure little school up in a remote corner of the state. It was sponsored by the Presbyterian Church, which had ordered all its institutions open to both races. The Presbyterians were moving to strengthen their schools and bring them in line with changing times.

Art Thomas flew to see the president of Mary Holmes, Mr. D. I. Horne. Mr. Horne seemed interested. He had never been active in civil rights work, but he saw this as a way of building his school. He would be on an important board of directors, he would get a center in his town, he would get a twenty-thousand-dollar administrative fee for being willing to make the project possible, but for very little additional work, and his institution would be put "on the map."

He said he would consult, consider, and notify Art next week. We had six hours until OEO Head Start deadline, and no applicant agency. CDGM could not apply directly, because it was not an organization with one year's prior concern with poverty, though its members had had a lifetime of nothing but concern with poverty. Art said he was so glad that Mr. Horne wanted to do it, and would be happy to leave the room for several minutes while Horne consulted and considered, and would return then to be notified. He had to have an answer instantly.

President Horne gulped, said *all right,* and flew to New York the next day to finalize the arrangement with some of the sensible members of the Board of Presbyterian Missions, who wanted to see Mary Holmes move into "mission with a vision." Progressive thinkers at the Board of Missions were in the minority and had a hard time working around their colleagues, as do progressive workers everywhere. But they were strategists, and they succeeded. One month later President Horne found his institution the recipient of a million and a quarter dollar Head Start grant, one of the biggest in the nation.

CHAPTER 5

OEO IS PROUD OF ITS PET DRAGON

THROUGHOUT THE FIVE weeks it took to organize CDGM, OEO officials were in constant touch, and knew just what was brewing. I remember a day when I asked Head Start's chief administrator, Jule Sugarman, about the wisdom of going along with CDGM's decision to locate at Mount Beulah. I mentioned its "reputation," as the hornet's nest of civil rights activities in Mississippi, and said that this might cause OEO undue embarrassment and difficulties later on when the powers that be in Mississippi realized the full scope and implications of this project. The administrator said that OEO doesn't tell other local projects where to locate their headquarters, and he didn't see why it should interfere in this case either. A reasonable point of view, but one which he was forced to change dramatically three months later.

Mr. Sugarman was kindly enough inclined toward CDGM that he persuaded the newly forming Citizen's Crusade Against Poverty (The AFL-CIO's poverty program) to contribute four thousand dollars to it, so it would have a little organizational money for airplane tickets, telephone bills, and postage stamps.

Mr. Sugarman admired CDGM's community action aspects. He thought that most Head Start aplications sounded too much like traditional schools, and not enough like action of the community. The OEO hierarchy was happy enough about the project to up funding from the requested three quarters of a million dollars to the granted $1,263,480.

There is no evidence that the Board of Missions, or any of the other powerful liberal groups which later helped CDGM fight for grants, put any pressure on OEO at this time. The proposal looked good, and OEO was naïve. Our plans were greeted with excitement, but were treated rather routinely.

Mr. Shriver himself was sympathetic. In May 1965 during a congratulatory cocktail party for exhausted Head Start staff given on his luscious, gracious green lawn, Governor Johnson of Mississippi called to say (it is alleged), "You have funded mah political enemies. Blood will flow all over the steps of the Mississippi State Capitol, and it will be on the hands of OEO, not the state of Mississippi." Mr. Shriver (it was reported) came out of the house saying to his Congressional relations deputy, "Tell him to keep his big, fat mouth shut."

The inspection office, then headed by William Haddad, with whom Dr. Levin, Reverend Arthur Thomas, and I had worked closely on this delicate affair, was proud enough of the CDGM project that one of its staffers said, "My, God, look at that beautiful dragon!" But that was in the days when OEO was still blushing with childlike excitement about what Congress and the American public would allow it to accomplish.

Judging by later events, the dragon was only beautiful as long as it was *in utero* and OEO had full control of its parents. By the time it had emerged, and worse yet, slithered through the hands of OEO so that they didn't even have it by the tail, it was no longer beautiful, but was instead, in the notable words of one of the high level political appointees in OEO's Atlanta Office, "Nuthin but a mob of Negras."

PART II

Why and How Poor People Planned a School System

BETWEEN THE GRANT ANNOUNCEMENT, MAY 18, 1965, AND THE OPENING OF CENTERS, JULY 12; THE PSYCHOLOGICAL AND EDUCATIONAL RATIONALE FOR CDGM'S APPROACH; FORMING A FRAMEWORK FOR THEM; CONCEPTS.

CHAPTER 6

CLIMATE AND CONCEPTS COME BEFORE CLASSROOM—FORMING A FRAMEWORK FOR FREEDOM

The improvement of the institution is better than adjustment of the individual

BY EARLY JULY, just before our five-day Head Start teacher orientation, CDGM had pulled together its Central Staff of forty people. It was composed of Movement leaders and workers with experience working for the real goals of real educational thinkers. There were old and young, well-known and soon-to-be-known "experts" from several disciplines who were also eager to work toward these goals; in unorthodox fashion, if necessary (the first time something new is tried, it is by definition, unorthodox), and local Negroes with some training in needed areas, or as "trainees" for all positions, including director (our application form reflected our values—see Appendix C).

I was one of the forty, because one day in May—which should be the title of a whole other book—of 1965, OEO and Head Start higher-ups gave us the first clue in a long series, about the answer to our original question: How far will the poverty program go in tolerating community development and children's program quality before political considerations arise? It was announced that quantity and quickness were more important than quality. Through those exhausting eighteen-hour-a-day winter and spring months we had striven so hard for quality—and so successfully. Many Head Start applicants *wanted* to do well. Quality was tossed blithely out the window of the old New Colonial Hotel, Head Start headquarters on Fifteenth Street, in Washington.

That was the day they brought in the time and motion experts and had them shadow the seven senior program analysts. We tried to hang on to some of the essence of Head Start proposals. The newly established conveyor belt, designed by a man from the Civil Service Commission and another from the Post Office, rushed applications from one department to another. One cut the budget regardless of what was in it (orders from the Bureau of the Budget, always interested in economy, and, many critics think, unaware of much else). Usually what was cut was carefully worked in educational "frills" like psychological services and teacher development work. One was to rewrite the educational program to make sure it conformed perfectly to the formula all analysts were given in memo form and required to use. One was to write the "highlights" of projects the previous department had just leveled so that they had neither highs nor lights. (It was easier for newcomers on the staff. They were hired at that time from the roles of D.C. substitute teachers and the lists of the unemployed at a furious rate. They could judge proposals only if they all fit a pattern.) It was decided that, for the time being, "open" (but segregated) Head Starts were integrated enough; that the statement "only licensed teachers in our public schools will be hired" represented maximum effort to comb the community for teachers trained in nursery education; and that a telephone acquiescence from an applying school superintendent that he would "involve the poor" at some vague future time equaled "maximum participation of the poor in all phases of planning." It was necessary "to cut these corners," they said, because the President wanted thousands of Head Starts to announce in the Rose Garden on Thursday.

Part of the policy priorities shift naturally included liquidating those who would be likely to interfere with the new twist of the thing. Consequently, like so many major and minor staff members before me in the short life of the President's Task Force on Poverty, beginning with Adam Yarmolinsky and not ended yet, I was "instantly eliminated." The task force was set up in the spring of 1964 to start creating a War on Poverty, and it became the Office of Economic Opportunity in the fall of 1964, when Congress gave it its authorization and appropriation. I was a staff worker on the task force, too.

One of the working assumptions of the Poverty Tsar, Mr. Shriver, well known to a cemetery full of unfortunates, was that those who started things were not those to maintain them. Those who were good at something might be in the way precisely because they were good. Sometimes they even had principles. He had political considerations to deal with, too. They generally took precedence.

Other victims in much higher positions than mine have described the procedure as luring distinguished experts in or wearing faithful staff members ragged, wringing them dry, and then dropping their lifelessly mangled minds out the wringer at the other end of their usefulness, without so much as a word of explanation.

To quote a senior staff victim's description of Mr. Shriver's operational style: "He's got a perfect system. He's a human meat grinder. In the process, all the bits of quality meat end up in one big tasteless political hamburger, with a little horse meat and bullshit thrown in for the consumption of the poor. But he gets away with it—probably the bullshit is the flavor that puts it over well." The form of each liquidation was different, but the basic intention was the same: to get people interested in program content out of the way of political factors not known to them, and suspected not to be important to them if they *were* known to them.

In my case "they" sent me to Atlanta one Friday night with a fever of 102° and three hours of notice in which to arrange weekend baby sitting for my little girls. I was to take care of the mission a co-worker had forgotten. During the eighteen hours I was gone, my desk was moved from the first to the third floor, my pictures and Southern regional decorations were taken off the wall, my precious files on many Southern Head Start projects were thrown away or mislaid, my job was changed to one *they* "thought I'd like," a woman with no sensitivity to the South or to nursery education or to poor people was put in charge of the delicately flowering projects I'd gently been tending, and "a friend" was instructed to call me on Saturday night to tell me how nice it would all be.

Three statements of explanation were made to me by prominent OEO officials. They illustrated basic government thinking: First was this statement by the Post Office official who had come in to take over processing Head Start proposals: "You are expendable, young lady, you idealistic ones are all expendable, and you just remember that." A kindly superior responsible for the action said, "I know it isn't fair. We can't afford to be fair. We have more important things to worry about than justice." (The Rose Garden?) A close "friend" and immediate supervisor said, "I know it's hard on you. But to lots of the staff you are the symbol of quality, and we have to hang you publicly so everyone will see that quality is passé and quickness is the rule of the day."

I never sat at my new desk or did my new nice-sounding job. I believed in Head Start on the literal level of experimental early education for children of poverty and maximum involvement of their parents. If we were going to be forbidden to work on these goals in the office, I wanted to see if we could move toward them in a specific project. The only Head Start I could think of in the South that was really going to forge ahead in these directions was embryonic CDGM. I resigned in protest from OEO. We piled into our station wagon—the daughters, the pets, the houshold possessions for a summer—and drove to Mississippi. We arrived at Mount Beulah on June 20, the one-year anniversary of the murder of Schwerner, Goodman, and Chaney. We were assigned two rooms in Chaney Hall, and I joined Jeannine Herron at work that night as "co-coordinator" of the program.

Our "ends" at CDGM were those of educators everywhere at every level. It was our "means" that were different, and our determination, to quote a man from Meridian, "to reach them as well as to speech them." Thirty of the original summer Central Staff of forty were Northerners, intrigued by the idea of spending a summer manning a chaotically cheerful office, which would attempt to set up massive instant bookkeeping, purchasing, filing, and procedural systems to serve a reality of local community semiautonomy, and which would not attempt to "run" the sprawling statewide project. Another one hundred people had been recruited from the North, to act as "resource teachers" in each local Child Development center, as five district coordinators, and as members of special projects, such as a roving group of singing, dancing, costume and scenery making actors, and carpenters for an equipment-making project. Tom wanted to keep the great feature of 1964: cross-fertilization from around the nation—blending Southern Negro talents and needs with those of college students and professionals, screened for psychological and/or skill suitability.

A hoped-for by-product was "new careers for the college student," too. Vivid personal experiences "convert" the passive poor into participants or even leaders. Vivid personal experiences also "convert" passive liberals into active liberals, or condescending professionals into professionals with greater respect for humans, and therefore, with greater human relations skills. Those Negro leaders not yet planning revolution needed the right kind of professionals to help in the general reform of American society and resurrection of two races. CDGM was interested in helping develop this new breed of professionals, *i.e.*, sensitive, imaginative, concerned, and effectively energetic human beings, just in case it was not too late for conscious people to keep civilization from ending. We tried to attract promising students from Berkeley and Bennington, New York University, and Yale, to enrich the program and themselves, for improved service in the future.

Creative citizens of the future, who would be able to solve social problems the rest of us had not been creative enough to solve, would grow from creative children in classrooms. Creativity in children is either suppressed or stressed, depending upon the degree of creativity and the value placed on it by adults in the classroom, in the home, and in the immediate community. The degree of creativity and value placed on creativity by adults around a child depends on the degree of creativity and value placed on creativity by those having influence upon the adults around the children. Our Northerners would sponsor local creativity.

> . . . almost always wherever independence and creativity occur and persist, there is some other individual or agent who plays the role of "sponsor" or "patron." This role is played by someone who is not a member of the . . . group, but who possesses prestige and power in the same social system. He does several things. Regardless of his own views, the sponsor encourages and supports the other in expressing and testing his ideas and in thinking through things for himself. He protects the individual from the reactions of his peers long enough for him to try out some of his ideas and modify them. He can keep the structure of the situation open enough so that originality *can* occur.[2]

[2] Torrance, E. Paul, *Guiding Creative Talent*. Englewood Cliffs, New Jersey: Prentice-Hall, 1962, pp. 8–9.

There are few text books on education that fail to mention the importance of creativity in the curriculum. Yet, historically, creative people have been frowned upon in educational institutions.

It's all the more true in Mississippi that creativity is one of the parts of personality that has been most paralyzed.

Creativity is inventiveness, imaginativeness, ability to cope in new ways with given factors. *It's a process.* It can only be "taught" to children by people who have it, and people who have it, have it because they have experienced the process themselves while growing up or while in one program or another.

Better kinds of education are slower in coming than they should be or need to be because those creative enough to conceive and implement them are excluded from opportunities to do so. We felt that establishing an environment conducive to creative thought and letting the hot sparks fly would be a good way of attacking this frontier of education—a better way than would be putting out some pamphlets on "the way we do things in a nursery school" and dropping them from the professional air onto the heads of unimpressed farmers, busy in their fields. So CDGM would need a staff that wouldn't perpetuate paralysis—risk-taking problem-solvers, rather than "reputable" pedagogical conformists.

Many hundreds of pieces of research on the subject of creativity agree in defining creative thinking as producing something new as a result of finding something wrong or lacking. Researchers have never found that creative thinking is a result of achieving a teacher's license. CDGM sought the person with the flare of ideas and the passion or self-discipline to pursue meaningful paths, not the one with the certificate in routine teaching and "experience" in repetitiously performing the ordinary.

In *Growing Up Absurd,* Paul Goodman says:

> Timid supervisors, bigoted clerics, and ignorant school boards forbid real teaching . . . . A commercially debauched popular culture makes learning disesteemed. The academic curriculum is mangled by the demands of reactionaries, liberals, and demented warriors. Progressive methods are emasculated. Attention to each case is out of the question, and all the children—the bright, the average, and the dull—are systematically retarded one way or another, while the teacher's hands are tied. Naturally the pay is low—for the work is hard, useful, and of public concern, all three of which qualities tend to bring lower pay. It is alleged that the low pay is why there is a shortage of teachers and why the best do not choose the profession. My guess is that the best avoid it because of the certainty of miseducating. Nor are the best *wanted* by the system, for they are not safe.[3]

We accidentally hired some out-of-staters who had more commitment or curiosity than creativity about specific tasks and obstacles. And we

[3] Goodman, Paul, *Growing Up Absurd.* New York: Random House, Inc., 1956, pp. 24–25.

accidentally hired some with more conversational creativity than ability to get out there and put it into action. We hired many with creativity *and* credentials, but largely because of Tom Levin's Central Staff hiring policies, which set the tone for the project, CDGM had more creative people than most Head Starts—and probably fewer accredited ones. We determined our standards of "qualified" by referring to our common sense.

We were happy with the wonderful surprise we imagined we were brewing. CDGM: a living proof that many obvious knowledges could be put together in surprisingly sensible ways to form something new and useful, if we were not afraid to rearrange them.

> An act that produces *effective surprise*—this I shall take as the hallmark of a creative enterprise. The content of the surprise can be as various as the enterprises in which men are engaged. It may express itself in one's dealing with children, in making love, in carrying on a business, in formulating physical theory, in painting a picture. I could not care less about the person's intention, whether or not he intended to create. The road to banality is paved with creative intentions. Surprise is not easily defined. It is the unexpected that strikes one with wonder or astonishment. What is curious about effective surprise is that it need not be rare or infrequent or bizarre and is often none of these things. Effective surprises . . . seem rather to have the quality of obviousness about them when they occur, producing a shock of recognition following which there is no longer astonishment.[4]

A young physician who came to direct the medical program described this unusual staff in a fall 1965 issue of *Key List Mailing:*

> The Northerners were a motley crew: older professional people, and semi-hippy students, liberals and radicals, New Yorkers and Californians, but the sense of uniting for a common cause in a hostile land quickly brought us together. We spent much of our free time at orientation singing folk and freedom songs. Orientation culminated in one wild morning session that began as a class in children's games and wound up in a foot-stomping, snake-dancing freedom-singing hootenany. Freedom was acoming, and we were to be part of it.

Poor people were demanding more than an opportunity to announce their againstness. They deserved more than that. However, the programs they wanted required outlining a procedure, proposing a scheme, making a comprehensive schedule in order to pursue this goal.

Freedom requires a framework. Many of the poor of course are able to discuss and decide what programs they want—a fact overlooked by most professionals "planning for the poor," and one that lessens the "success" of "their" programs. But many of the poor have not evidenced the ability yet, for reasons which must be corrected, to outline the

[4] Bruner, Jerome S., *On Knowing*. Cambridge: The Belknap Press of Harvard University Press, 1963, p. 18.

procedures, propose the schemes, and make the comprehensive schedules that will free them to pursue their goal; and *this* is a fact frequently skirted by Movement workers. We who wanted so much for CDGM to be what it was because of the poor alone, sometimes let our prejudices and needs edit our perceptions and memories so that we quite sincerely believed that the poor alone *did* create CDGM. This was not true. Somebody had to think about these administrative things for CDGM, because government grants don't fall from heaven. Paychecks to give people independence from "the man," so they can act freely, don't come regularly unless some system has been designed and implemented to gather the necessary information to get them. Children don't get education consistent with freedom goals unless adults get together and work out details of what that is. And communities that have been skillfully alerted and organized don't get any further than that good beginning, toward that for which they were alerted and organized. The somebody to whom this organizational task fell—because no one else offered to do it—was Tom Levin.

Tom believed that just because the poor don't exhibit the ability to program their programs themselves today is no reason to leave them out of such programing so they'll be equally unable to do so tomorrow. It's not enough to leave them out because of tight deadlines or because cursory inquiry produces little response among poor people. Tom felt that all efforts needed to be made to urge people to participate. They would learn how to run their own programs through participating in the running of every step and phase of the program. If efforts weren't made to find out who had interest in this, and efforts weren't made to be patient with that mild interest and fan it, the usual thing would happen. Because poor people were *not* making decisions, other people *would be* making decisions. We would have missed the essence of the poverty program: to reduce the helplessness people feel about their own fate. Helplessness is resignation. Resignation is inability to take advantage of opportunity. Helplessness is caused by a feeling that fate is too great, and that all is uncontrollable anyway, so why try and take the guaranteed risk of failing? There would be some people who would refuse to participate, or who would participate only negatively. But Tom was interested in those who had never had the opportunity and the welcome, and who would participate in planning if sought. The following are some of the mechanics that were worked out so the poor could plan their schools:

1. *Forming Business Arrangements That Would Blend OEO and Project Goal Requirements:* In early June, Tom Levin moved to Mississippi for the summer, to be project director. He made arrangements with the accounting firm of Spokney, Gersten and Company in New York. It had a history of interest in social action in Mississippi. CDGM came on the heels of the "invasion" of 1964. Local politicians and press had

already started their attack on CDGM. Tom was not sure that local white Mississippi accounting firms had this interest in social change. Nor could he, at that prenatal stage, take the risk of learning for certain. Representatives of the firm had an office in our farmhouse headquarters on the Mount Beulah campus. Tom made arrangements, also, with the tiny nonpar Bank of Edwards, near Mount Beulah. This afforded us a small amount of protection from police and Klan marauders, because the bank president spoke to the town police officer and told him it was good for the bank to handle over a million dollars in a few months.

The month of June, when he was finally "on location," was frantic for Tom. Tom tried to set up a complete business department, without assistance from management consultants, which he frequently begged OEO to send on a temporary basis to help design administrative procedures.

The business side included a payroll officer, a paycheck writing and distribution plan, and a system for discovering *who* the eleven hundred suddenly hired community staff members *were*. They were being hired daily in eighty-four different distant rural places through eighty-four hiring committees composed of poor people unaccustomed to handling application forms in triplicate. (Five thousand applications were received in June alone!) There was a personnel officer who tried to keep some kind of track of records, resumés, reports, etc., revolving around all these scattered persons.

Many Head Starts would have minimized what looked, at best, as if it would be an exasperating administrative undertaking by doing all hiring centrally. This would have eliminated situations in which committees forgot to mail in names and full information on employees, such as Social Security numbers and W-4 information. It would also have avoided the problem of the unreliability of the postal system in small towns where Post Office employees didn't feel kindly toward their newly awakening Negro clients. It would have given CDGM administrators a feeling of "being on top" of hiring, and OEO administrators the security that this was so. But of course no one considered doing this. One of CDGM's biggest purposes was to eliminate or reduce the concept of authorities and powers on top and people at the bottom being administered. The very opposite is true for government employees, so conflict later arose in this area.

Local hiring produced considerable confusion, and therefore bitterness. But though this was so in the case of a wrong or a late paycheck to an employee, there would probably have been much more bitterness, as well as perpetuation of disastrous patterns, had communities *not* hired, and had a magical administration manipulated jobs. If people had trouble learning about requesting receipts and the like, the answer didn't seem to be to remove the urgent opportunity to learn. It would have been ideal if communities could have hired autonomously *and* central systems could have flowed perfectly. But we had another problem: Not every crisply adroit businessman was willing to come to murderous Mississippi for the uncertainty of a seven-week job in a maybe-funded project, and not every Movement and local poor Negro was a crisply adroit businessman. Tom did the best he could to combine principle, purpose, and practicality.

A number of local Negroes with various stages and quality of business training or experience were in a kind of a minute-by-minute, emergency-to-emergency payroll, personnel, and finance "on the job" training. They would have learned more, and the business end of the operation would have been more efficient, if CDGM had had skilled people above them. But the facts of life were that none were available to us. It wasn't a question of being against qualified people, or taking administration cavalierly. No qualified applicants were rejected. No qualified applicants appeared, and none were sent by OEO.

There was Jim Monsonis, with a ridiculous list of tasks to perform. He was responsible for renting, regulating, and keeping detailed records on cars, which were the only means of *communication* as well as of transportation with some of the remote communities. There were no telephones for miles around, and people often didn't read well enough to make written communication reliable. There weren't enough cars permitted in the budget for staff members, all of whom were grounded and unable to get to work in the local areas without them. Jim was also responsible for ordering and arranging trucking and distribution and keeping all records about equipment and supplies for 6,400 children in widely dispersed places.

Among his duties were repairing and running the constantly whirring mimeograph machine, which reeled out every kind of form and memo for our soon-to-be staff of fourteen hundred and for the federal government's infinite requirements for reports. He also was in charge of preventing penniless civil rights workers, with whom we shared Mount Beulah, from making *their* business calls to communities on *our* phones. The government auditors wouldn't have regarded that kindly. His other duties involved such things as trying to keep a semblance of sanitation in the communal kitchen. This was difficult with all of us sloppy youngsters, staff members, small children, and unhousebroken cats.

Tom's "instant business office," scraped, hung, and smacked together in three weeks, was cemented into functioning by two moody young ladies of talent and temper. There was the irascible, barefooted unforgettable finance coordinator, Lenore Monsonis (Jim's wife), whose "volunteer 10 percent" duty (required of every CDGM employee out-of-state or local) was answering the all-night office phone. And there was the irascible, barefooted, red-headed Frankie Stein, twenty-four-hour-a-day administrative assistant, who did most of the out-of-state hiring, and who answered the daily questions of fourteen-hundred confused people regarding the program, which as the reader knows but the inquirers did not, there would be none of, until the poor people and staff planned it together at Orientation.

Only top administrators in OEO itself, who were in the midst of doing it themselves, can appreciate the difficulties of flinging together the intricacies of a massive administrative structure where there has been no administrative structure before, and simultaneously trying to operate it at a furious speed. Only OEO could have appreciated our difficulties, made worse than theirs by the fact that we had none of the excellent consultants from around the country that they did to call upon, and in fact were in very hostile territory.

Most Head Starts had a wild time getting launched even though they had the distinct advantage, administratively speaking, of being able to build from existing structures, such as school system administrative systems, or agency or college business offices. We started from scratch. We needed our own independent administration. It gave us many painful headaches, but our experiment would not have been possible if we had tried to conceive CDGM under the most liberally lenient of school systems—not to mention those in Mississippi. Most Head Starts had the second advantage of being confined to a compact area. See the map and see the problem. We could have confined ourselves to a manageable amount of territory. But the idea of the project was community initiative. We couldn't turn down communities. The purpose of the project had to come before administrative convenience.

In a sense, then, we *chose* an unmanageable administrative task. Most Head Starts were in urban areas or had access to county organizations. Human services to ease the load and add to quality were present to some degree. We were not so fortunate in Mississippi. Tom had ascertained that at this time too.

2. *Forming an Unusual Staff That Could Work in a Hostile Environment:* Head Start administrators in all states know the difficulty of finding capable staff members, even in their own home towns, on four weeks' last minute notice. All CDGM staff members, in addition to their paid eight hours a day, had to contribute 10 percent again as much time on a volunteer basis to make up our 10 percent nonfederal share. The usual kinds of middle-class community volunteers were not, at that time, willing to affiliate with us. Then, too, they had to be willing to live in isolated hot towns in the crowded homes of CDGM families, which automatically placed them in considerable physical danger. They had to put up with treatment from whites that made them feel deeply guilty and very much hated. Tom convinced OEO to let the community committees of poor people hire poor people to do the teaching. He slithered and insisted to get Movement workers we needed but whom

OEO feared as though they were dangerous carriers of the bubonic plague instead of applauded carriers of last summer's freedom banner. He convinced OEO to grant permissions for unusual things, such as our film-making project, and he convinced non-civil rights people to come to Mississippi—neither of which was a minor job.

3. *Forming the District Coordinator System:* Five of the volunteers who had carried the word of the original day care project to the communities became district coordinators for our five districts. They were the connection between communities and Central Staff, and vice versa. Four had come from SNCC, and one from the Delta Ministry. It was their work, and almost theirs exclusively, that altered community attitudes toward the program, and helped them organize committees and do their hiring, find facilities, and get whatever information they could get about the project prior to Orientation. There surely could have been no CDGM without them.

At this stage OEO was talking about trained social workers to perform the district coordinators' job. The term "community organizer" wasn't yet part of its everyday vocabulary. Tom was talking double-talk to keep the key feature of achieving an organization of the poor: leaders the poor trusted. OEO's inability to understand why Movement workers were more "trained" for *this* kind of work than any number of social workers became so staggering that we stopped trying to explain. I was an advocate throughout for more medical and psychiatric social workers. But this community organizing job was just not for social workers. It was a different kind of job altogether. Tom didn't *do* the job of organizing communities, but he protected the right of others to do it. One of the most important things an administrator can do is protect the right of those who have specialized knowledge and abilities to put them into practice for the good of the goal of the project.

4. *Forming Special Projects:* Tom planned a number of special projects, set them up, more or less staffed them with a Central Staff coordinator and roving field workers, and tried to get them to form themselves clearly enough so they could describe themselves to the poor people at Orientation, and function in the field shortly thereafter.

The purpose of the special projects was to add services and stimulating enrichment to isolated, partially autonomous Child Development centers, in a state in which both services and stimulation are scarce as hen's teeth, and as inaccessible to Negroes as the Golden Fleece was to Jason. Negroes now, like Jason then, must conquer the cast-iron, cruel, crushing God with the vulnerable ankles; the clashing rocks; the hundred-headed Hydra; and the warrior skeletons that rise up from the dead past of the earth to keep them from getting the fleece: peace, health, happiness, all that is good.

The special projects were community organization and development; equipment-making; health and medical; living arts (drama, puppetry, costume and scenery making, dance, music, etc.); making films for later use in teacher development, community organization, and dissemination purposes; printing our own books for children; developing a program with community teachers for children; psychological counseling; reading readiness; research on reading in three counties (Dr. Sol Gordon); sewing clothes for project children; social services. All projects were equal, and all reported back to CDGM's Central Staff as a whole.

The intention was that members of each *service*—program for children, social services, health, reading readiness, and community development—would work directly with community committees and staffs. They would work in conjunction with the district coordinator in situations where he recommended something extra. Each of the other *nonservice* enrichment projects would work as seemed suitable. They would not necessarily organize themselves within districts and try to get to every center. For example, equipment would be made at Mount Beulah and distributed as samples, which community people could copy or use as inspiration for making their own tables, rocking boats, etc. The film team would hunt for a center that seemed appropriate and would settle in for six weeks to shoot. In the fall we would select footage, give it our message, a script, and a shape. The little reading project which Dr. Sol Gordon had been interested in from the beginning would take place in two out of eighty-four centers, of Dr. Gordon's choice. He wouldn't live in the state in people's homes during the summer as others would, but would fly in at intervals to check in at a motel and make rounds to evaluate his sliver of the project. A local Negro printer, Mr. Kirksey, would move his printing plant from Jackson to Mount Beulah and would print books in color for the children. Poor Negroes in Canton who had previously organized a sewing cooperative would make clothes for project children. We would be distributing them as necessary. Our order would give the cooperative a boost, and the cooperative's help would give us very low-priced clothes.

5. *Forming an Office and Office Procedures:* Mount Beulah was a seedy looking twenty-three-acre abandoned Negro junior college campus twenty-six miles out of Jackson toward Vicksburg. The Delta Ministry had recently rented it from the Church of Christ and was beginning to repair it as they used it for a conference center for social activist groups. Tom rented a house on the campus from the Delta Ministry, to serve as the CDGM central office. He also rented warehouse space, a place for our printing plant, a carpentry shop, and the auditorium when needed, all for six hundred dollars for the summer. We thought that a pretty fair price.

Many of the forty Central Staff members paid sixty dollars a month room and board individually to the Delta Ministry (more for families who had more than one room). This entitled them to live in the crowded dormitories, eat in the community dining room, and "be at the office" around the clock. Some had their rooms in the same house the office was in, and a few actually had to use their bedroom as an office. I did, and so did Tom. Central Staff members who were local people lived at home and commuted. Other out-of-state staff members worked in the communities and made their own arrangements to live with poor families in the project. It was important that CDGM be headquartered at a place known for activity toward freedom, rather than at a place which intimidated poor people by its traditional white-world appearance.

We didn't feel entirely at ease with the idea of Jackson, for example, because of only twelve-month-old memories such as the one this girl had: "In Jackson, fifteen hundred people were out. Fifteen hundred! Police had guns and billies. They were herding people into garbage trucks. You could see the girls with their little overnight cases, ready to go to jail for wanting to be people. They took us to the fair grounds and locked us up—one huge prison for the human race."

We also needed a place that would rent to an integrated group, and that could house, at times, hundreds; feed them, park dozens of cars, provide classroom space for training, provide work space for special projects, store truckloads of supplies, etc.

Various buildings on the campus, excluding CDGM's office, were rented from the Delta Ministry by various groups at various times. Out of the confusion of coming and going in clouds of red dust, and of brakes screeching to avoid small children playing in pondlike puddles, and of "rival" groups circling and snarling at each other, and of the screaming power saw in the carpentry shop where drying preschool furniture was strewn everywhere, and of the drama team practicing and clowning with purple-painted faces on the lawn, and of truck loads of incoming shipments of newsprint, picture books, and Cuisenaire rods for teaching mathematical concepts, and of Spanish moss hanging languidly on the lovely old live oak trees, and of bewildered newcomers in search of answers and order, and of wandering hostile newsmen, and of the scorching sweating humid heat of a Mississippi June, and of endless food and housing complaints, and of the most amazingly outsized bugs of every sort, and of tensely typing staff sitting under ancient trees with typewriters in their laps for lack of desks, and of groups singing freedom songs to the strumming of somebody's guitar, and of groups clustered here and there heatedly forming plans, Tom cleared and equipped a functioning office.

He thought of everything that had to be done. A Watts line was installed so we could call communities (if they had phones) for less than the long distance rate. Regular telephone lines were put in too. The girls assembled the worn furniture and made themselves little cages of privacy out of desks and shelves, so they could concentrate through the chaos. Filing systems and an interdepartmental-memo-in-triplicate system were organized. Supplies were picked up and stacked in cupboards and on shelves. Every staff member, including the director, was assigned to telephone answering duty until Lenore took over at midnight, while she slept. Forms flew, workers pursued, policies grew, and without an office manager, because we couldn't get one, with only two qualified secretaries, Duff and Carol, and an assortment of search-and-peck typists, an office began.

6. *Forming Plans for Orientation:* The night and day, scattered, scurrying, and angry debates of many came together in an orderly fifty-page notebook, one copy for each person at Orientation (over eight-hundred people).

There were diagrams of the campus, parking instructions, different schedules for each group, outlines of each workshop for teachers, paragraphs on general meetings for out-of-staters and different meetings for local people, descriptions of the administration and lists of which individual to go to for each type of question. There were lists of all participating communities giving the name and address of the local chairman, maps of districts and centers, a list of board members, and a list of Central Staff members. There was a lengthy description of each special service and special project, discussions of differences between the job of aide, trainee teacher, and resource teacher, pointers on special features of the sample classroom Diane Feeley had fully set up for people to browse in, a discussion of the sample playground Naomi and her group of local Edwards poor people had cleared out of a bramble patch, recipes for dough and finger paint, and an invitation to use the teachers' resource library, which Harriet had put together upstairs in the office house.

7. *Forming Security Plans for a Summer in Mississippi:* This *was* Mississippi, and federally backed or not, CDGM was a group of outlaws by the nature of the fact that: We had an interracial staff that even lived and socialized together, and seemed to like it; and on which whites often worked beneath Negroes; we were a phase of a many-faceted movement toward full citizenship for Negroes, and therefore socialized more with members of the other groups so interested than with white Mississippians, who would not have socialized with us anyway; we intended to obey the compliance forms we had signed with OEO that said it was illegal to use segregated services or facilities. This resulted in us integrating many a horrified public place; many whites had told "their" Negroes not to come near us, and the Negroes had done so anyway, and this was dangerous defiance.

Other Head Starts in Mississippi didn't have as much trouble as we anticipated we would have (and did), because in each of these ways they were different from CDGM:

Staff, if integrated at all, was usually integrated with an occasional white volunteer in an all-Negro situation, or Negro aides in a white situation. There was neither socialization nor equality of position.

They were a new arm of the power structure trying to capitalize on federal monies and summer jobs for underpaid teachers, often, and in occasional cases they were really trying to crawl toward progress within the framework of Mississippi acceptability. In both cases they considered the groups we were friends with irresponsible, agitators, etc.

They got around compliance intentions as deftly and quietly as they could. For example, a top man in the Jackson Head Start (*not* part of CDGM) was overheard telling the Jackson superintendent of schools that he promised "there will be no civil rights in this." They did what they had to, but they didn't go around looking for segregation and challenging it, like CDGM did.

Negroes didn't defy whites to send their children to the other Head Starts. If whites told them not to go, they generally didn't. More often whites didn't mind if Negroes sent their children, because the Head Start was "well under control." It was only an extension of the "safe," vacuous colored school system.

Because we expected troubles all summer, and had had some already, Tom hired a legal and security officer. Gordon Wilcox's job was to insure that CDGM staff engaged only in CDGM business during paid working hours, and also to "rescue" staff members who got into legal difficulties through no fault of their own, but because they were being harassed by police or others. Gordie wrote pages of instructions into the Orientation Notebook, including ferocious passages such as:

"Under the terms of our grant, CDGM, its staff, or its committees, may not participate in political activities on CDGM business, or during working hours. As a citizen, your right and privilege to pursue political activities outside your working hours will not be restricted. CDGM employees who engage in political activities during their working hours, or present themselves as CDGM representatives in political activities, will have their employment terminated."

And there were oddly appropriate words of paternalistic protectiveness such as: "In the event that you are detained, arrested, and/or fined, you should . . . report the incident to Gordon Wilcox," followed with detailed instructions about how to avoid getting arrested and what to do if arrested, and informing CDGM employees that they were expected to fill out bail forms before going to work.

The memorandum on how not to get arrested specified strict uses of CDGM cars. This document made many Freedom Democratic party co-tenant workers absolutely apoplectic. Most of them passed us without speaking. They thought this was extraordinarily selfish and that it was inexcusable for us to exempt ourselves from the Movement's traditional understanding that what is available to anybody must be made available to everybody, so that survival might be possible.

Tom even had an alarm system installed. It was a siren that screamed if the night guard activated it. We usually had shifts of unarmed young men standing guard all night. No arms were allowed.

Our Head Start grant began in May and ended in August, 1965. It included two five-day orientations for two separate groups, and seven weeks of operation. It was just as short and temporary as all other Head Starts that first summer. But to us, it was a continuation of the progression from what scholars consider to have been the most debilitating version of slavery devised by any civilization in the world, through the relenting Reconstruction years, through the lynching and Jim Crow years, and into the massive movement toward freedom of recent years. It was a factor in the opening of "the closed society" of Mississippi. It was a piece of "action research" in the effort of social scientists and educators to recognize education of the poor as a specialized kind of education. It was a merger of movements: nursery education, civil rights, community development, new careers for the poor.

To those interested in position descriptions and organizational charts, we had to keep explaining that we had none. Tom's reason for this was that until the staff assembled at least into one state, and hopefully into one room—until members of this new heterogeneous staff began to talk about their ideas and reveal their abilities through a few weeks of work—it was impossible to know who would come and stay, and who would fail to show up or decide it was not for them and go home; who were the leaders and who the negativists (we had no followers); who were the gifted and who the routine; who were the persevering and who the lazy; which jobs needed to be done and which were white elephants. It was impossible to know how the group would wish to organize (into divisions? and if so which divisions? or some other way? and if so, how?) until it had had a brief chance to function.

This group couldn't have come into being had the Movement not paved the way: with local whites, who were now expecting social change; with Negroes who were ready to produce certain kinds of change; with Northerners who were used to the idea of coming in to help temporarily; with OEO officials who felt a little bit guilty and romantic about helping the heroes in Mississippi. CDGM grew out of the Movement, as well as out of other things. It had many Movement people in it, as well as many other kinds of people. The Movement people were used to working in an unstructured manner. CDGM would have been blown to bits by the indignant rage of these people, had structure been thrust upon them.

Tom hoped that many molten ideas and feelings would flow and semisolidify into something workable by the end of July. There was no precedent to guess from. Tom was anxious not to make the mistake so many administrators make, which is to suffocate the talented by letting them find themselves under the mediocre. People would shake down into place as some began to produce and some didn't. In any organization there is always a natural "in group," a natural alignment of skilled people, different from the names in charted and plotted boxes. Tom would let the natural situation function till the corks and the rocks separated themselves automatically.

CDGM was the beginning of many federally financed community "growth and development" projects in Mississippi, and hopefully, the first of many grants for CDGM itself. We regarded the whole first summer as our orientation. The second step would start and follow in the fall. We didn't expect that we would get very far in all these areas of activity, but a variety of seeds for the future might be planted, some of which might eventually bear fruit. And if no further grants came to us, as an organization, then to quote a sentence Tom Levin wrote in our first proposal to OEO: "A primary purpose of the summer is to stimulate communities to function autonomously so that the program can continue permanently with or without outside help."

We were given a boost in stimulating communities by other groups, which were busy putting out literature, too. A stack of papers was found under a tree on the campus around this time: "Here are twenty reasons WHY you should, if qualified, join, aid and support the White Knights of the KU KLUX KLAN of Mississippi:

". . . Because it is a democratic organization, governed by its members. . . . Because it is an organization that is sworn to uphold the lawful Constitution of the United States of America. . . . Because there comes a time in the life of every man when he has to choose between the right or wrong side of life. . . .

"We are looking for, and enlisting ONLY: Sober, Intelligent, Courageous, Christian, American, White men who are consciously and fully aware of the basic FACT that their physical life and earthly destiny are absolutely bound up with the Survival of this Nation, under God. Our governmental principles are precisely those of the ORIGINAL U.S. Constitution. Our members are Christians who are anxious to preserve not only their souls for all eternity, but who are MILITANTLY DETERMINED, God willing, to save their lives, and the Life of this Nation, in order that their descendants shall enjoy the same, full, God-given blessings of True liberty that we have been permitted to enjoy up to now.

"We do not accept Jews, because . . . through the machinations of their International Banking Cartel, are at the root-center of what we call "communism" today.

"We do not accept Papists, because . . ."

And the following Jack Ward editorial from the May 21, 1965 Jackson *Daily News*, showed that if we weren't getting outside help, we were, at least, getting the attention of the local press:

There is a disquieting aura, almost terrifying in its ultimate projection, hovering wraith-like above the Head Start phase of the federal government's poverty program.

Head Start is specifically designed to include children, of all races and both sexes, from one to six years of age, considered underprivileged and in need of guidance and direction in preschool preparation.

On the face of this undertaking, it appears to be most wholesome and humane, appealing to the most tender senses in assisting infant youngsters who otherwise might be relegated to slum dwelling influence, undesirable home background and lack of basic necessities.

However, as all federal programs are now designed, here is one of the most subtle mediums for instilling the acceptance of racial integration and ultimate mongrelization ever perpetuated in this country.

The most formative years of a child's life are in this particular area, from 1 to 6, and the mixing of children of both races, and both sexes, will be of paramount importance in this program, with the children subconsciously registering such associations as natural and an indelible way of life in future years.

Naturally, the do-gooders and racists will immediately raise the loudest screams and sanctimonious objections to any such advanced objections, because such a program fits into the scheme of total integration and overlapping of the races which is being preached and taught throughout the United States today.

The most frightening parallel to these so-called Head Start programs, and they certainly are a head start toward a thorough conditioning of the young to the new race-thinking endorsed and encouraged by the federal government, are some similar programs which have been a part of some anti-American countries for years.

Soviet Russia has operated a children's commune for years, this as a part of the education of both the pre-school child and the family, conditioning them to total Communism and dedication to the State.

Red China takes the young child, separating parent and children, for their peculiar brand of schooling, utilizing the early and impressionable years to instill the doctrine of blind obedience to designated leaders.

Hitler's Germany built its most infamous Youth Corps and Nazi bullies from the children's camps and goose-stepping schools of rigid political doctrine, and a constantly-taught regimentation.

Somewhere, in this Head Start program, affecting the precious lives and minds of the most impressionable youth of this country, there is an ugliness which keeps making itself felt, well over the sound of crisp dollars being rustled as a conscience-appeaser.

The character of those officials designated to administer these projects, from the highest-placed post to the local day-to-day teacher, and their background should be of the highest, unquestioned dedication to the best interests of the children.

The summer was punctuated and footnoted with plenty of fright and excitement. For example, the week before Orientation, a white man drove into Mount Beulah, fired bursts from a .45 pistol at a group of staff members, and fled. Tom and ten or twelve staff members jumped behind some boxes of play equipment, and others, after some confusion, ran inside the office as the man opened fire from about seventy-five feet away. They would certainly have been killed, had the boxes not luckily been there to serve as a fortress. One shot smashed a porch ceiling light, which was so close to Tom's head that his hair was filled with bits of glass. Other bullets shattered Vari-Play sets and other toys. (My four little girls witnessed the shooting. Their reaction was annoyance that staff prevented them from leaving for a swimming expedition until the bullets stopped flying.)

Another night, near midnight, the siren screamed, and every able-bodied male on the campus ran toward the driveway, well-weaponed with rocks, pipes, and soft drink bottles. It turned out that a flood had short-circuited the siren wires. There was no enemy.

I kept a sporadic diary, which brings back so many warm memories: "Did some instant homemaking for my four bunnies today. All went to Edwards general store, and bought an ironing board; yards of dime-store quality orange and pink flower print material to use as 5 strips of cloth on top of each bunk bed (bedspreads, you might say, but unsewn) and a dab of color nailed at each window; a can of pink paint to paint M's table; and a sack full of "hungries" to keep in the closet for the children to nibble on at bedtime—juice, paper cups, crackers, fruit—they hate the dining room food but are very obliging about it. They've made a hall-wall long mural with magic markers on yellow shelf paper, showing a Negro nursery school. So that's it, so now we have a three room and a hall and a shared bath home, in a cottage with the Herrons and some miscellaneous others. Very cozy and gay! And hot! This one story cottage, evidently made entirely of fiber board, sits in the middle of the sun near a cornfield and the r.r. tracks at the end of the campus. The train whistle echoing off into the night seems very symbolic . . . alone, going somewhere in the dark."

CHAPTER 7

ORIENTATION*

First group July 3-July 7;
second group July 7-July 11, 1965

IN SPITE OF the best intentions and a double registration system in which the Delta Ministry (DM) registered everyone for rooms and CDGM registered everyone who came to the Orientation classes, the exact number who came, as opposed to the number invited and expected, was never clearly determined. It was later a reason for endless squabble between OEO, CDGM, and DM. Art Thomas and Tom Levin had made an agreement about this, which neither of them ever disputed, but unfortunately, being close friends and not realizing that there was any likelihood of institutional dissension, failed to put in writing. There were approximately eight hundred people there, half in the first group and half in the second.

Governor Paul B. Johnson and Marshall Fraley, state poverty coordinator, were sent formal personal invitations by Tom, to be key speakers at Orientation. They neither came, nor, to my knowledge, responded in any way. State superintendent of schools, Mr. Tubb, was invited, too. He politely declined.

A young girl who lived in a tiny house in the Delta under weeping willow trees that trailed their mournful branches in the serene Sunflower River, and who had been hired by me to be my assistant children's program trainee, wrote this about her orientation experience: "As I began my journey to Head Start which I attended at Mount Beulah thinking that it would be just like any other program or camp in Mississippi, I thought they would tell me what to teach the children, when and how to teach it. After a two hours' drive from Rolling Fork, I surprisingly opened my eyes to the Mount Beulah Center. Everything seemed to be full of life. The big healthy trees, green grass, even the buildings seemed alive. Not from the construction work which had been

* Quotes in this chapter are taken from tapes. Interruptions are omitted, but nothing else.

done. No, not at all, it was all the friendly attitudes of the fine people of both races living together as a big family. They laughed and sang and had fights. They wore old clothes. Nobody was pretending to be polite friends hiding under fancy clothes. They were just people living and feeling and thinking. It was a feeling of real respect because no one had to act politely respectful because everyone respected each other enough to be themself. Breathing fresh air and feeling free. It was a footloose and fancy free feeling. In the classrooms most problems were asked and answered by mothers, aides, and trainees from the poor communities. The resource people were mostly in the background, sometimes asking a question to keep us on our toes thinking. Most classes were led by us. The idea is to think what you want yourself and what you want for children. There is no way to do it right. It depends on what feels right to you. And that they expect us to decide for ourselves. They say they will help us do it after we decide what makes sense. The old as well as the young children and teenagers took part in all the activities. We played the roles of children in plays, played childrens' games, used blocks, cut, pasted, painted pictures, and did many things we had never done before. We shared our own ideas to carry home to our Centers. All of us were so enthusiastic about it because we knew that we were doing the work for ourselves and by our own free will. For selfish reasons I sort of wish I could remain within this small world that we have created. But I realize that this is simply too much for such a few people to experience alone. We must go back into that hustle outside world and work and fight for the *real free feel of freedom* in more places than just on one wonderful campus. Our preschool program will be just the beginning. We hope that we will let the small children taste from this cup of freedom this summer. We hope that they will grow thirsty for more. We hope that they will be so thirsty that they will never settle for anything less than the real free feeling of freedom everywhere."

Much of this "real free feel of freedom" and the feeling that this Head Start was another surge forward in a continuing stream of progress for Negroes in Mississippi, was generated by Frank Smith. Many professional members of the first summer's staff were angry with Frank for his denigrating attitude toward the role of professionals, his laziness, and his oft-made remarks about not caring about this one project as much as he cared about local people getting on their feet. Yet it's generally agreed by those who were there that he was largely responsible for getting them on their feet in this particular project. At his General Problems sessions at the Orientation, he led the auditorium packed with coming and going shabbily dressed people, fanning the sweltering July heat off themselves with funeral parlor fans, and eating the food they had brought in paper sacks, in daring to challenge the Mississippi they had always known. They gave endless impassioned testimonials about their new efforts. They sang spirituals, slave songs, and freedom songs, and chorused *Amen* to speakers' inspiring personal statements.

* * *

Throughout Orientation the Mississippi Highway Patrol gave us the extra attention they were known to give to integrated groups. For example:

On July 2, the head of the psychological counseling Project, a middle-aged lady psychologist from New York who looked less like a proverbial Beatnik civil rights worker than like Eleanor Roosevelt, was stopped on Highway 80. She was driving to the airport to pick up an OEO worker who was coming to Orientation. The group was ostensibly stopped for speeding. Other cars were stopped, given tickets, and released, but the psychologist was told to follow the policeman. "He did not take us to Jackson where the incident occurred, but to Brandon," many miles away. "At times the police officer drove so fast it was impossible to keep up with him.

"The Justice of the Peace offered us the opportunity of a trial, but since we did not have enough money for bail, we chose to settle the matter then and there. The fine was twenty-seven dollars for going five miles over the speed limit. When the officer was asked for his name, he said it was on the ticket he had given us, but he had actually never given us a ticket. He insisted he had, and that it was on the front seat of the car. We went with him to the car, but there was no ticket there. He then told the Justice of the Peace to give us nothing; no receipt, no name, because we had thrown the ticket out of the car window. His manner was most hostile, as it had been when we explained to him that we were on our way to the airport to pick up a worker. Our statement that we worked for the federal government was greeted with "I don't care who you work for, and I sure don't care for the federal government!"

* * *

Frank Smith was director of the community staff. It was widely felt, unanimously felt, I believe it is safe to say, including by Frank himself, that he did little or nothing to organize his resource staff, to assign specific tasks and beats to them, and to produce tangible community development results. In addition, he made CDGM's nursery school teachers furious, because he didn't work with hiring committees in the communities to talk about what kind of people they might want to hire, and he didn't help these communities develop judgment. On the contrary, he kept telling people that anyone can teach, parents know best, etc. Several members of the board of directors wanted to have him fired. Most of the professionals felt that they could have done much better community development work had Frank promoted it. Many of the professionals felt baffled, frustrated, insulted, and overwhelmed. However, the things he didn't do that he should have done were balanced by the things he did do that were not official assignments. Many local people remember that it was Frank who first gave them the courage to integrate previously segregated places in their own communities. It was Frank who, as one local man expressed it, "made me ask myself, you don't plant cotton and reap peas; what are we planting in our childrens? Well, what is it we want to reap?"

Frank's lack of interest in the professionals and lack of effort expended for CDGM was doubtless detrimental to a maximally effective summer. But his great interest in community people doing something for themselves was equally doubtless a determining factor in the extraordinary involvement of the poor in CDGM's program. It was also a turning point in the lives of many future professionals. A college girl from Colorado, who says she came to Mount Beulah, "with long hair, a pair of sandals, and a religious zeal to set up a school for poor children," said later, "I never hated anybody in my life as I hated Frank Smith. He made me feel like a pompous pretender and an obnoxious Lady Bountiful. But it was at his mass meetings with the swaying, hugging, soul singing, that I underwent a conversion that will influence the rest of my life. I learned what it means to be humble. I learned respect for people. I learned what it is to be a powerful group instead of a lone individual—to feel there is something bigger and more pure than everything. I'll never forget what Frank Smith did for me."

A male graduate student from New York wrote: "Frank was a very insubordinate staff member. He wouldn't cooperate with anybody about anything. He was the Monarch of Mississippi. I couldn't see why Tom Levin let him be such a tyrant. But he mobilized many hundreds of poor people into feeling themselves as a force. He attacked the educators on the staff endlessly. But I never saw poor people so feverishly interested in education, as Frank stirred them to be. He drove the professionals wild and he didn't work himself, but I bet every professional there learned a new attitude from Frank that will increase their value through their careers. I discovered that there are some things more important than orderly procedure and controlled staff. Making dull, dragging, defenseless, defeated masses come alive and flare into action as Frank did at Mount Beulah and re-orienting professionals' view of their value is more important. Tom knew that, I guess, and it's a tribute to him that he could put up with it because of the long-range importance. Frank kept shouting, 'We ain't gonna have no more second-class citizens!' and he made every person in that auditorium feel he was a first class citizen. If you can do that, you're gifted first, and insubordinate becomes unimportant."

We wanted to honor the conviction of most articulate Negroes that what poor Negroes need today is to carry the burden of their own programs. It was necessary that CDGM poor people not languish in the second-rate roles of parents and aides, but find themselves in the first-rate roles of teachers and policy-making committee members and directors on the board. No matter how democratically a program functions, parents and aides are dependent upon the will of teachers, hiring bodies, and board members.

These are the dominant groups. The role of parent or aide is a lesser one. While most educational programs would lose richness if parents and aides disappeared, the programs would still continue functioning in much the same manner as before. On the other hand, if the teachers and planners disappeared, the programs would collapse. These are the vital positions, and no amount of fancy terminology can make it otherwise. So in CDGM we would explore the effects of these positions being held by the poor.

> The evil of slavery (and to some degree Negroes are still enslaved) is in the way it permitted white men to *handle* Negroes—their bodies, their actions, their opportunities, their very minds and thoughts. To the depths of their souls Negroes feel handled, dealt with, ordered about, manipulated—by white men. I cannot overemphasize the tenacity and intensity of this feeling among Negroes and I believe any fair-minded person pondering the history of the Negro's enforced posture in a world of white power would concede the justice of the feeling. So, as Negroes began to sense that the civil rights movement was *their* movement, an instrument for *their* self-expression, *their* freedom (in addition to being a vehicle for universal ideals), it became difficult to convince them that once again they must be led by whites.[5]

We wanted to experiment with continuing where protest left off, with a program based on the same principle: that "Men must act on their own behalf; they must aim to move the world and sense its movement under their impact"; that if you "Do it for them . . . you extinguish the spark which makes freedom possible and glorious."[6]

We wanted to experiment with practical application of the idea that "*Potency* . . . is the same as virtue; *impotence*, the same as vice.[7] . . . *good in humanistic ethics is the affirmation of life, the unfolding of man's powers. Virtue is responsibility toward his own existence.* Evil constitutes the crippling of man's powers; *vice is irresponsibility toward himself.*"[8]

* * *

Harassment continued. July 2: The driver of a carload of CDGM staff, including a male social worker and the middle-aged director of professional staff, among others, was arrested just outside Mount Beulah. They were not told the charge.

Two visitors from OEO had comments. One of the Head Start deputy

[5] Farmer, James, *Freedom When?* New York: Random House, Inc., 1965, p. 89.
[6] *Ibid.*, p. 80.
[7] Fromm, Erich, *Man for Himself*. New York: Rinehart & Company Inc., 1947, p. 27.
[8] *Ibid.*, p. 20.

director's special assistants said, "It was a refreshing reversal of what you usually see—which is everybody trying to put on a professional façade. Here the professionals are all trying to see who's more indigenous than who."

Dave Walls, training director for Head Start came to see our training. He went away to tell Mr. Sugarman that now he really understood for the first time what participation of the poor really means.

* * *

A third incident on July 2: a man from Laurel was detained by the sheriff of Rankin County on his way home from taking some people to Orientation. The sheriff said he knew the man had been to Edwards. He was therefore going to throw the book at him. He arrested the driver for drunken driving. Throughout the driver's protestations that he was not drunk, but instead was suffering from a heart condition for which he was under a doctor's care, the sheriff told him not to talk "biggity." The sheriff took the driver to jail. He left him there all night, allowing another man to bring him his heart pills, but refusing him his legal right to make one phone call. The sheriff said the charge would be $110. The man kept telling the sheriff he was very sick. In the morning, the sheriff finally took him to a doctor, who said, "he might have been drunk, but not from whiskey, he has high blood pressure." The sheriff examined the contents of the driver's wallet, and changed the fine to the exact amount the man had with him, which was $15 "plus $2 federal tax."

* * *

We sang. A lady stood, came to the front, spontaneously sat down at a piano, and led the audience in singing:

Ride on, King Jesus, no man can-a hinder me.
Ride on, King Jesus, no man can-a hinder me.
I was but young when I begun, no man can-a hinder me.
But now my race is almost run, no man can-a hinder me.
King Jesus rides a milk white horse, no man can-a hinder me.
The river of Jordan he did cross, no man can-a hinder me.
Ride on, Jesus, Ride on, Jesus, Ride on, Jesus,
No man can-a hinder me.

Another lady led:

Go tell it on the mountain,
Over the hills and everywhere—
Go tell it on the mountain,
To let my people go.

We sang:

Oh-h freedom!
Oh-h freedom!
Oh-o-o freedom over me-e!
And before I be a slave,

I'll be buried in my grave,
And go home to my Lord and be free.

* * *

The next day, July 3, the out-of-state New York Museum of Modern Art teacher from our Edwards center and a CDGM roving program development teacher were stopped.

* * *

The Lord is my light and my salvation,
whom, then, shall I fear?
The Lord is the strength of my life,
of whom shall I be afraid?
Though an host of men shall rise
against me,
Yet shall not my heart be afraid.

And, of course, in a spiritually cemented circle of hundreds, swaying and holding firmly to each other:

We'll walk hand in ha-a-and,
We'll walk hand in ha-a-and,
We'll walk hand in hand toda-a-aay,
Oh-o-, deep in my hear-r-rt
I do believe,
We'll walk hand in hand, to-day.
We shall overco-o-me,
We shall overco-me
We shall overcome some da-a-ay, oh-o.

God is on our si-i-ide,
God is on our si-i-ide,
God is on our si-i-ide toda-a-ay,
Oh-o, deep in my hear-r-rt
I do belie-ieve,
God is on our side today.

* * *

On the last day of Orientation, July 11, a Delta Ministry volunteer from Iowa, who had graciously contributed a great deal of time driving CDGM people back and forth to Orientation, was stopped in Flora for allegedly "running a stop sign."

* * *

On the same day, a local man was detained while carrying an open truckload of integrated employees home from Orientation. He was charged with "wobbling all over the road."

* * *

After the general sessions for everybody, Frank led some three-hour sessions for trainees, aides, and community committee chairmen listed on the schedule as: "What Are Some of the Things Kids Ought to Know?" People talked.

"When the schools were taken from the community, an emptiness was left. The schools were our own. Now they consolidated them. They belong to the system, far away from us. We had only our church left. Head Start is to put life back in the community, to give us something to run for our children the way we want it run. We will not teach the children to hate themselves and their people as the schools do. We will teach the children to be proud. Nothing you know is worth anything if you don't first know to be proud of yourself."

"Kids ought to learn parents wants to do fer em, that's what kids ought to know. These new consolidated schools cut the parent right out. He can't go across the ocean to a place what don't want him, and sometime he ain't even got no transportation. We're puttin' the school right next to him. We need him. Head Start is to give back doin' for the child to his parent instead of makin' the parent feel helpless and unwanted and far far away. How can a parent help a child if he feel like a fool?"

"Head Start is to teach the childrens one thing. There's only one thing I wants them to know after this school. To respect their parents. History has never let our chilrens respect us. They see us bein' nuthin'. They respec' peoples with all the good English you could want but they got no fight in'em. I don't want my chilrens to respec' that. I want the chilrens to respec' their parents proud and strong. Then they'll do like us, and we'll inerest 'em in education."

The basic ambivalences of feelings and directions that poor people and Negro people have, have been ignored in most educational projects. So we would begin with them in CDGM. We believed that "great is the truth and mighty above all things. [Apocrypha, Douay Bible]." It is accepted by the various depth psychologies, and perhaps someday will be accepted by more than the exceptional educator, that until a person has himself uncovered, discovered, and unraveled his complex feelings, and until he has sorted them out sufficiently thoroughly to know his own priorities, he probably won't be able to move very consistently and constructively in any direction whatsoever. He may unconsciously undo much of what he consciously does. A poor Negro may be full of desire to have the abilities, privileges, status, and possessions whites have, but he may at the same time hate whites for keeping these things from him so much that he has trouble "copying" characteristics associated with them, such as efficiency, coping skills, responsibility for follow-up details, etc.—the very skills he needs to get what he thinks he wants. Helping a child who hasn't yet had opportunities to figure himself out and route himself in personally profitable directions is one of the specialties of nursery educators. Similarly, on the adult and race relations level, engaging groups in discussions of every issue, including whether to aim at assimilation or separatism is one of the specialities of the many factions of sophisticated civil rights leaders. In fact, everywhere except in Mississippi and in the typical public school program around the country, discussion of important issues is considered fundamental to man's earthly progress.

In CDGM we all felt that this poverty program should utilize the wisdom of psychology and the Movement. It should encourage each person to confront and clarify his issues. We thought that many OEO and non-OEO programs feared the issues burning in their constituents. They therefore went to great lengths to evade them. Playing ostrich doesn't make feelings evaporate. Unresolved issues that smolder within may block much of the value a program might otherwise have. Avoiding issues may reduce staff trauma, but CDGM wasn't designed to protect staff. It may avert a collision with conventions of the greater community, but CDGM was not designed to avert collisions of this kind. It will not, however, help teachers or teaching parents deal with their lives. And so, it won't help teachers and teaching parents help children deal with their lives. We thought Head Start was intended to help teachers and parents help children deal with their lives.

CDGM searched for professionals who had skill in reaching and releasing poor people's feelings. We found them in a mixture of psychologists, educators, artists of many kinds, college students, social workers, and social action workers, heavily weighted in the direction of social action workers. Many of them had been Freedom Movement workers in Mississippi. Most poor people are highly reluctant to express any feelings except feelings of profound gratitude, stemming not from real gratitude but from helplessness and dependency.

It was important for us to find leaders who could be trusted by the people, as much as they can trust, so we could try to begin talking without the masks. Some of these professionals were professional community organizers with a knack for working delicately and nondirectively with frightened people on and off of plantations. Others were various kinds of people who could engage in honest and deep dialogue without being too greatly threatened when they learned that they were not loved, respected, nor in many cases, needed. The purpose of the discussions was not that superiors with cleverly extracted "insights" could write secret case histories. It was that we could get people figuring out what they would do and what directions they wanted Central Staff to take.

We operated on the assumption that school, home, and community adults immediately surrounding the child (not the mailman, and those other traditionally curriculumed community people) have some influence on him. We thought that uncrippling crippled communities, and unparalyzing paralyzed adults, would help children grow up uncrippled and unparalyzed.

FIRST PERSON (*Confidently*): I think he should learn discipline.

SECOND PERSON (*Angrily*): I think if there's one thing we colored people got enough of, prob'ly the *onliest* thing we got enough of, it's discipline. I think our children should learn self-respect first, 'cause that's what he don't have right now.

THIRD PERSON (*Excitedly*): That's right. We shouldn't try to teach our kids what they already got: to be afraid of people. To follow orders. Let's teach them what they ain't got: dignity.

SECOND PERSON (*Indignant*): That's right, that's right. He can wipe his nose. He can choose a toy. He can think. What he needs to practice is to do for hisself.

FIRST PERSON (*Pouting*): He should learn to respect adults.

SECOND PERSON (*Positively*): If the adults that teaches him is any good, he *will* respec' them, you don't have to teach him that unless he can't see it for hisself cause they ain't worth respectin'. Then you gotta teach him to *pretend* to respec' them. Respec' jus comes natural if peoples ac' right.

THIRD PERSON (*Laughing*): What I want to know is, do the adults respect *the children?* I seen a lot of adults push a lot of children around in my time. I say, let's quit pushing the children around.

AUDIENCE: Amen, Amen, Amen.

RESOURCE STAFF MEMBER FROM FLOOR: *How* do you *teach* a lesson in self-respect?

TEACHER'S AIDE IN AUDIENCE: You don't teach a lesson in self-respect. Talk sweet and nice and you are respecting him. Listen to him, that's respecting him too. Say whatever he does is good. Hang it up. Tell the others, "Look! Look! Look what Leroy done!" That's respect. Because you must be respecting his idea or you wouldn't be letting him do it. That's how we're going to be different from public school. They talks about respect all the time, but we're not going to talk about it, we're just going to respect everybody.

In this long, general discussion, parents and neighbors discussed what *they* wanted the Head Start experience to be. Because the concerns and abilities of the poor are generally ignored in educational programs, we began with them. We didn't develop guidelines and notebooks full of recommended procedures, patterns, recipes, and games *ahead* of our Head Start "teacher" orientation. We first formally considered these things *at* the orientation with the poor people hiring committees, "school boards" from each of the sixty-four communities, and with the poor people who would be there. (During May and June communities had elected their committee members, and the committees had selected members of their own poverty-stricken communities to teach.)

We created guidelines for center teaching and gathered as many specifics as possible *at* the orientation by using it as an opportunity to draw upon the experiences, wisdom, talents, and goals of the people whose Head Start this was. This is a very old concept in educational circles, but it is one which seems to have trouble getting practiced.

We used as many professionals as we could get, to encourage each person to dip into his or her self and come up with unnoticed resources, rather than to intimidate and further alienate people with an exhibition of imperialism by experts. We didn't hire professionals whose only working method was to shower instructions on captive and cowed listeners.

Supporting those who have never been supported in realizing their potential is one of the primary objectives of the nursery education movement, the civil rights movement in Mississippi, the Negro movement in America, and so, it is said, of the public school system and the War on Poverty. We wondered if whites and professionals have any role in this exciting junction of movements. We believed they have a vital one: to assist, not dominate, those who have been deprived of self-realization in achieving the feeling that they are capable and worthwhile people now. This can't be done most effectively by "providing" programs for them and discussing self-image at professional conferences. It can only really be done by trusting that the poor have the ability and the will to operate programs for themselves and to learn. I guess what we were really trying to do in these sessions was convey Buddha's message:

"Be ye lamps unto yourselfs. Be your own reliance. Hold to the truth within yourself as to the only lamp."

* * *

"In our school, we really going to see what this child is inerested in. When I went to school, I wasn't inerested in nuthin', but in this school every little child going to be inerested because we going to have so many inerestin' things and *let* him be inerested. How can somebody be inerested if there ain't anything inerestin' going on? That's what's wrong in Mississippi. Nothin's goin' on in them schools. We going to have aplenty going on! 'English at 9; Arithmetic at 9:45.' Like you're teaching them to be a grammar book or a adding machine. Our first job is to make them feel at home. You can't give a person too much friendliness. Seems like school teachers is afraid to be loving. Love never killed nobody, but hate sure do. Nobody gonna die of getting hugged."

* * *

The average educational program in the United States, and all the educational programs in Mississippi, capitalize on the human child's infinite ability to adjust. The poor Negro child has, like his family, for immediate survival, already learned the art of adjustment, to a self-destructive degree. We would begin from our first Head Start orientation session together to stress the sadly neglected skills of inquiry, rational thinking, creativity, and independence. Graduates of white universities and colleges in Mississippi, graduates of Negro colleges in Mississippi, and poor parents in Mississippi, have all suffered equally from the tragedy of thought-control.

The very presence of white people, even gentle kindly white people, makes many Negroes feel inadequate, overwhelmed, and that "somebody else" is responsible for thinking and deciding. We knew that it was critical from the start that most figures of authority, such as discussion leaders, be Negro, and as often as possible, be members of those poor communities linked together in the project. There was a good deal of question in CDGM whether *any* leaders working directly in the communities should be white. Some whites were tolerated, but only those who had an unusual degree of honesty, disgust for even subtle manipulation, and trust in the judgment of the project participants.

We thought it important to plan into our project design the fact that Negroes are *not* "just like everybody." People who have for centuries been shamed, squashed, disparaged, and destroyed, cannot, conceivably, be "just like everybody." The principles upon which their psychology operates are the same. But they are very different from people who haven't expected to be trampled, and who have not formed defenses to protect themselves from pain while they're being trampled.

Children of local and national leaders probably have a better chance of becoming independent than do the children of "the passive poor." We wanted our CDGM children to be the children of leaders too. No longer would they know their parents as the bypassed belittled refuse of a bustling community. These children would know their parents as pioneers on America's new frontier: not clearing away forests and planting seeds for food, but clearing away unfairness and planting seeds of fulfillment—from forming their own centers to leading their own discussions.

There were special sessions for resource teachers *not* from Mississippi. These emphasized the nature of Negro and integrated Mississippi. They stressed the idea that resource teachers had *not* been hired to run or lead children's classes, but to be in the background. One local person explained the role of the resource teacher to the assemblage: "A resource person is a well, not a firehose. A firehose is for putting down demonstrations. We don't want to put down poor people. Poor people need to be seen and heard. But the water in a well don't do any good unless we haul it out, either. Haul out the resources without blasting the people's ways."

People who attended these gatherings reported that they were, for the most part, taken aback to find that they had not come to Mississippi to rescue people. They weren't needed to bring light to the wilderness, but just to act as catalysts and boosters to local people. Many were critical of Tom Levin for not letting them be in charge of classrooms. However, equally many *local* people and Movement people were angry at Tom for bringing in outsiders at all, because of the effect they might have on local people (through no fault of their own) of letting them slip out of a feeling of responsibility and pass it to the out-of-staters.

He was, on this matter, as on many others, in a vise, squeezing from each side. He thought he was doing the right thing, regardless of *everyone's* disapproval. And he was, on this matter, as on many others, several years ahead of most of us, as subsequent civil rights history has shown. Resourceful and talented people *should* be available, but should *not* be put in dominating positions. He thought that each center should have at least one such person, but they could choose which person. Orientation was like a backwards slave market. Communities looked over the imported goods, and when they left, took home the one they wanted for the summer.

Almost all the out-of-state resource teachers were enraged that it was made painfully clear what resource staff was *not* to do, but what they *should* do was vague and unclear. Tom said there was no way to make exact duties clear. This would vary from center to center, as individuals and social structure in each locale would be different. And the resource staff members in question were each different. It would just have to be worked out on location. Tom's frequently uttered statement, "We don't care very much about what *you* want," made him many enemies. It was exactly what he meant. His major interest was in what the *communities* wanted, and about that he did care. He had considerable contempt for resource people who were so resourceless that they couldn't even work out a job for themselves when they saw and sized up the situation.

A member of the first summer's professional staff told me: "At the time, I thought Tom was insane. All these people brought in with no guidance as to what to do. Only the poor people seemed to be plodding on with great confidence. But in retrospect, I'm convinced there was method to his madness. He didn't want to begin with the usual type organization, or we would have ended up with the usual type program. As it was, some people quit, or rambled on in disgust and disorder, but Tom's dizzy idea gave us a nationally distinguished program. Actually, he had more confidence in each of us than anyone I've ever worked for. The only thing I still don't understand is why he didn't explain his ideas to all of us? It seems only the 'in group' understood the theories, and the rest of us just understood the hopeless frustration. We would all have been more patient with him if he had included us in the theory."

I repeated this to Tom. He looked surprised, and asked, "Who would have listened? Each person had his own thing—no one was interested in mine." But I think perhaps something else Tom said on another occasion answers the lady's question, too: "When I'm giving birth, *I'm* giving birth, and everyone better help or get out of the way."

There were also special sessions for local public school teachers. Committees believing in credentials as ardently as much of the rest of the world had hired teachers, often regardless of their suitability. Many were willing to take the risk of going with CDGM because they had no chance with the school system anyway. They had been shed as unacceptable even to the Negro schools of Mississippi. These individuals became the communities' biggest handicap. They "knew how to teach." They would not learn. They kept trainees from learning. The subject they taught was the ABC's and the method was the switch. When I joined CDGM, I discovered some other OEO staff member had given Tom Levin and Jeannine Herron to understand that there would have to be a licensed teacher for each unit of fifteen, regardless of her duties. This was not unnegotiable, and I was disappointed that so many useless teachers had been hired because of this misunderstanding. We did not insist on licensed teachers in the future. The same misunderstanding caused us to call some people "aides" the first summer. In later grants we had no aides, and twice as many trainees.

CDGM didn't especially seek teachers, because expanding the horizons of teachers wasn't its focus. We were against glorifying teachers from the lowest quality colleges in a state with the lowest quality education, solely on the grounds that they had certificates and licenses. They had neither educations as the truly educated know education, nor certificates and licenses in what CDGM was trying to learn to do.

We didn't, of course, deny that there were some exceptional Negro teachers in Mississippi. We indulged in pirating them whenever we came upon a gifted teacher who was willing to work in CDGM's own inimitable way. However, we did question the wisdom of pulling them out of the school system, where they were so sorely needed, to use them in Head Start. Head Start should have been using some of its energies to attract and develop new talent to a new kind of community early childhood education. "Job development and training comprise two essential elements for a comprehensive attack on poverty. If either is lacking it is difficult to conceive of an effective result."[9]

We didn't question the assumption that almost all teachers can grow a great deal if given the right kind of chance, though a limiting kind of chance is all they are usually offered. Many public school teachers come back from Head Start summers greatly enriched, even in Mississippi. But our job did not include enriching the school system. However, we were lucky enough to get some people from the public schools who were daring and excellent teachers. They saw CDGM as the kind of school in which they had always dreamed they could teach. Some of the latter group said during Orientation discussions:

"The purpose of Head Start is to show the school system in Mississippi a good school, a school made for children to learn instead of for teachers to teach out what the top people give her—white people—and for them to earn their paycheck."

"These schools will make the children feel they are equal with any race. The public schools do not make them feel this way. It will also let them know they have more to think about than playing."

[9] Pearl, Arthur and Riessman, Frank, *New Careers for the Poor.* New York: The Free Press, 1965, p. 184.

"Sometimes the children I get in public school cry for two, three months, and while they cry they can't learn. When they stop crying the fear remains. They have just learned not to show it. By then they're so far behind they can't catch up. Then most teachers don't like them because they're so 'stupid' and 'foolish.' In our Head Start school we will consider each child intelligent. We will try to make them happy. I am different from most of the teachers where I teach. That is why I've come here."

"I am from the public school. I had a job there, in the schools, till yesterday. I was a teacher there for thirteen years. I have come here to work with this group because I feel inspired to go in with this group to help prepare the children for a new life we never could give them in Mississippi before. And I don't expect them to give me my job back in September. The schools aren't likely to hire me back after I went with the people. The principal asked me to work for *his* Head Start. I said, 'No, I'd rather work with CDGM because the parents can help plan it.' The principal said, 'It's Communist.' I said, 'Well, in your Head Start will you teach the children to be free-thinkers?' The principal said, 'Oh, no, we'll teach them to be obedient. You can't do nuthin' in school later with wild children.' I said to the principal, 'I thought education was to teach children to think?' The principal said, 'Oh, no, education is to teach children discipline.' You all can see why the power structure doesn't mind our principal's Head Start as much as they mind ours."

Besides the general meetings and the separate meetings for in-state resource teachers and for out-of-state resource teachers, there were workshops in medical services, social services, civil rights compliance, in the special two-county reading project, administration, supplies, and petty cash—each of the special projects listed before—plus nine required workshops in teaching for all aides, trainees, and resource teachers present (about one third of those who would be teaching). These were in science, arithmetic, children's work, language, freedom to move and play, freedom of expression, limits of freedom, sample classroom, and living arts. The classes were scheduled from 9 A.M. to 9 P.M. for groups of thirty. Each group had its own printed schedule. All groups were discussions. Some had children doing the thing being discussed, and most were both informal and active. Almost all, depending upon the staff member responsible, began with the participants' interests, and moved to the topic from there and treated it from that angle.

We thought it would be difficult for teachers to teach children how to think and how to be creative if they had never experienced these things themselves. We thought it wise for every minute of our teacher development work to promote the ability and absolute necessity of each teacher thinking out what she wanted eventually for the children. What would she do now in this Head Start to help children get to be the kinds of people the poor community dreamed that they could be? In many teacher training classes teachers are told that children should seek. We believe that "told" teachers would not be able to "teach" seeking.

We bent exaggeratedly backward at our first Head Start five-day orientation to avoid "giving answers." We aggravated everybody by leaving them dangling, continually asking provoking questions, until they, as a group, came up with teaching policies and procedures in line with their own community change goals. They would have preferred to have had our predigested thoughts, or better yet, thoughts we had predigested from the experts. It's so difficult to think! But we were convinced that real education is a process of personal discovery through which a person can "organize what he is encountering in a manner not only designed to discover regularity and relatedness, but also to avoid the kind of information drift that fails to keep account of the uses to which information might have to be put."[10]

We didn't do this as a gimmicky way of "getting" people to think our thoughts. We did it for the reason that in all the varied experiences of the "educator types" among us, experiences in psychological clinics, lab nurseries, slum kindergartens, social work agencies, and early childhood education courses, we'd never been confronted with the task of analyzing whether or not educational technique was in any way appropriate to the grim and locked context in which these people were trapped—and if it turned out to be appropriate, how to use it.

We did it because the Movement members of the staff, with all their experience contacting timid people and making them alert and aware—and being shot at, run off the road at high speed, carrying on voter education and registration projects, working in nonmanipulatory ways with people, and striving day and night for community development—had never been confronted with the task of considering how to handle every interaction *with a child* in the same exact ways they knew were so important in interactions with poor adults. They wanted grown-ups to feel "unhandled," unmanipulated, free to choose, free to decide, free to challenge, learning where to get information relevant to their lives, strong enough to speak out and act on their convictions. But they hadn't yet been in a position to think of these goals in relation to three, four, and five year olds. You have to *do* something with little children. How do you take them to the bathroom without yanking them silently by the arm? (Adults don't want to be yanked around.) How do you use art materials in a way that brings out the child's gift of imagination and true feelings and makes him proud? (Adults don't want to be told to "keep in the lines" and "color it red.")

It would have been impossible for professionals to have established a program "for" these people, though we could have done a fine job for middle-class children in Minnesota. It would have been impossible

[10] Bruner, Jerome S., *On Knowing*. Cambridge: The Belknap Press of Harvard University Press, 1963, p. 87.

for Movement leaders to have established a program for children that was as sound as the program they established for adults, because they had never worked in those terms. Principles of adult and child growth and development are the same; activities and techniques are not. Together with the technical assistance provided by professionals in the field of early education and with technical assistance provided by professionals in the field of community organization (Movement workers) people could plan a program which meant something vital to them. It was their problem—a problem they would be left to live with when some of us went home to central heat, a cocktail party, and graduate school; and while others of us went off to do the spade work in new communities, to be salesmen for lack of "bread," to college, or to rest in Greenwich Village and indulge in fantasies of revolution. All we could do as visitors from another planet was try to share with the poor what we might have, as they worked to free themselves.

The goal of the educator, the literature repeatedly tells us, is to turn out mature citizens. But neither maturity nor its cousin freedom can be bestowed by well-meaning whites or well-meaning experts. Freedom and maturity are things one can't learn through the most scientifically based and professionally polished indoctrinations. They are not academic, they are spiritual. We have to struggle with ourselves until we slowly find them and can make them work for us.

The workshop called "Limits of Freedom," went as follows:

A local person with a seventh grade education was asked to lead the discussion. The Central Staff member assigned to be responsible for the workshop was one of a group of thirty—*a resource,* welcome to talk at any time. The local person was given a question to ask the group. In this case her question was, "What does freedom for children *mean* at this age, and are there ever limits to it?"

The group began responding with vehemence. The lady moderator directed the traffic: "When I say free, I mean powerful and sunny. Make a kid feel important, and he'll feel big and strong. Like he can do things. Like he's good. Let him help you in every way and tell him 'thank you.'

"Let him choose what song you sing when you sing a song. Ask him to choose. Freedom is when you get to choose.

"A free child is a contented child. A contented child is a child with time on his mind to learn. He's not so swallowed with problems that he can't think. In seven weeks time we can't do too much, but we can give him a taste of freedom. Maybe the only one he'll get, in this state! Let him alone to play like he wants. No switching in this school. I'm sick and tired of my child coming home half switched to death, too scared to learn. This school is to have fun and learn school ain't something awful."

An old man in the group said, "I hear everybody talkin' bout free childrens, but I'm a-thinkin', what're you ladies gonna *do* with these little uns all day long? Seems like you better talk 'bout *that* some, gotta, do somethin' with em."

A teen-ager replied heatedly, "Yeah, sure you gotta do something with them, can't just have them running around, but you can do it *nice;* not like the school teachers do it. If he wishes to play puzzles when you're tellin' a story, won't nobody die if you lets him."

And other people broke in with their ideas: "At lunch time, don't shame him into eatin'. Leave his food lay on the plate if he don't want it. You don't have to boss him ever' way. How'd you like someone to push the food down your throat and tell you 'be a good girl'?"

"Don't correct his grammar every time he open up his mouth. Let him tell you things without that you hear only the grammar. Grammar don't say nuthin', but words says a whole lot."

"If I'm readin him a story, say, an he breaks in an' talks, say, I'd let him tell. Maybe that ain't the right thing to do, but say he has somethin' to tell. Maybe, say, the story has reminded him of somethin'. I mean we ain't readin' to him to keep him still, see what I mean, we's reading to him to in'rest his mind. If he breaks in, say, then you knows you has in'rested his mind, do you see what I mean?"

Another older man snorted at the speakers, waved his arms erasingly at them, and said indignantly, "I don't know why you is all talkin' so much! Ain't gonna be no trouble gettin' no freedom for chillens if we jes all feels free to do it like we wants it, and if we jes all asked 'bout it oursel. We is on our way to freedom right here settin' up this school, an they ain't no chile too dumb to see that."

After uproarious laughter from the group, the staff member in the group, slumped in her seat, said, "Well, I think that's the absolute truth, and the most important truth! Sounds like everybody agrees with Mr. —— about it, too! But what I'm wondering is, do you think there is *ever* a time when there have to be limits to freedom for small children?"

At first the members of the group loudly and positively asserted that there should never be limits. This would make it another public school, etc. Then a middle-aged mother sounded hesitant and asked, "Well, I'd like to ask this young lady what she means. What kind of limits do you have in mind?"

The staff member repeated (she didn't want to suggest "the answer" to the lively group), "I'm just wondering if in your opinion there should *ever* be *any* limits?"

The lady pressed on. "You mean, should you *ever* stop him from what he's doing?"

"Yes, that's what I mean."

The leader of the group with the seventh grade education rephrased, "These two ladies is axin' the rest of you ladies, and these here three gentlemen too, if you'd care to answer, should you ever stop a child from what's he doin'."

The persistent lady was not yet at ease. "Well, I know this is the wrong answer, but I'll be honest with you. I have eight children of my own . . . and if he's about to get hurt, you should. Then you should grab him or whatever you need to do to keep him safe."

There was unanimous agreement to this, much to the lady's relief, it appeared. Some people added that you should "give him a good whuppin" to keep him from the fire, highway, sharp knife, high place, or dangerous farm machinery in the future. Many personal examples were described. A young man suggested: "You also might have to stop his freedom if he's tryin' to hurt another child. You can't let a children free to hurt someone else. Freedom doesn't mean that, but kids do."

Lots of laughter. "Before you control a child, make sure its necessary. Sometimes we control him just to feel useful and important. I've seen that with my sister-in-law. Seems like whenever things ain't goin' so good between her 'n' her husband, why she's ordering them children every way. You don't really have to do all that bossing unless they're real mean and ugly or breakin' things or getting too dirty or getting in danger. Even then—you can usually interest his attention in something else."

The discussion leader aimed the discussion in a new direction, when she said, "Sometime you get a real bad child. Real bad! You don't hardly know what to do with him. What would you do with him in the Head Star' School?"

A trained kindergarten teacher who had been hired by a committee on the more middle-class Gulf Coast answered, "I'm a trained licensed kindergarten teacher, and I have some suggestions in a case like this. You could call his mother in for a conference and give her instructions to improve his behavior at home. Discipline him a little more. Home and school are connected you know. And you could also have a special chair in the room. We had one one place I taught—we called it 'the bad boy chair'—the children were very ashamed to sit in it. Of course, if you are firm enough, you won't have many of these situations; the children wouldn't dare. After you teach them to be obedient, most of these things won't come up."

No one answered, but the room was suddenly filled with whispering and buzzing behind pieces of paper and schedules. The discussion leader asked several people if they wanted to comment out loud. They did not. Nobody was ready to publicly challenge this blond white girl, who had the extra authority of a teacher's license.

The staff person said, "Not everyone seems to agree with this teacher. You're all teachers starting day after tomorrow, so if you have other ideas, feel free to say them so we can all hear."

People giggled, and an ancient lady stood up and said with toothless passion, "We Negroes in Mississippi have a mental block. We have been so conditioned that we feel wrong when we speak up. If we don't teach the children anathing else, I say let's teach them to speak their mind. Sometimes children speak by acting, doing things. Let them. This is their freedom of speech. Never mind obedience. They'll fit in as they grow. I wouldn't want anyone shaming my grandchildren in no chair."

The blond kindergarten teacher became flustered and angry. "I've had training, I've taught for several years. When you people begin teaching, you'll see you need discipline. You have to do *something* with these children, you can't just let them do whatever they want."

"Why can't you?" shouted the discussion leader, leaning forward aggressively.

"You'd have chaos! You couldn't teach them anything like that!"

"Well, what are you trying to teach them, that you can't teach it if they choose what they want to do?" the discussion leader insisted.

"You have to teach them their numbers and colors and alphabet and to have good manners, and how to sit quietly in class and how to eat properly—lots of things."

"I think you're talkin about nice things," shouted the discussion leader with the seventh grade education, "but you is missin' the point altogether. First we want to teach the child *never* to feel ashamed, always to decide for hisself, always to speak up like we is doin right here in this room. Then we'll teach all them other things you is talkin' 'bout too."

There was a chorus of *Amens* and *That's right!* and *Tell it! Tell it, sister!* Then everybody clamored at once about freedom and our own school to raise the right kind of children and that's what's wrong with the public schools, just look at that smart girl . . .

The staff member in the group said, "OK, then, we're mostly agreed that the school doesn't want to shame children, and that you don't want many limits to freedom except in the case of danger and things like that. But we didn't settle this other question that was raised—what about a child who just seems bad, difficult, a troublemaker? What will you do? We've had suggestions from the kindergarten teacher, and not everybody agreed. Who else has suggestions?"

"Who else have suggestions?" repeated the discussion leader, keeping the reins.

A lady stood up: "I think in a case like that, you could offer him something special to do. I have always found with my children at home that they act up when they're bored. You could play a game with him, or even give him a little job to do, like wipe the table."

"You could let him sweep up . . ."

"Little chillen *love* to hep! When they's climbin' the walls they's glad to hep you do sunthin'."

"But if you give them all this extry attention when they's bad, don't that make them want to be bad to git the attention?"

"The thing to do in a case like this is to give him this extra attention when he's *good,* or you might say *normal,* in between his badness. Then you're not treatin' him when he's bad, yet you're *preventin'* it."

"I think it helps to tell him the polices will get him. I have always found this to be helpful."

"I don't want to frighten him bout the p'lices, so I tells him his parents is going to whup him when he gits home."

"I don't think you should do either one of those things. We ain't tryin' to scare him of school, we wants him to *like* it. I just talk to them real nice, and I tells them to be sweet. If I has to, I has them sit in a chair, any chair, not a bad boy chair, a little while by theirself to think about bein' sweet, but I tells them to come back as soon as they feels nice."

Many people thought that was a good idea. One lady added, "I always tells my childrens that I'm very disappointed in them. I tell them I knows they can be gooder than that. I begs them to be nize. I says, 'I know pretty soon you is going to be the best girls and boys in the world again.'"

"I agree with that lady. They want to please. If you ac' disappointed they'll come around real quick."

"And, you know, sometimes when they're fighting, they have a reason. I usually ask the children in my neighborhood, 'What're you all fighting fer?' They tell me. Then I can han'l' it fairly. I try to be fair. Children have reasons too, I know that. I have thirteen of them."

"That's the truth! That's the truth! You can help them take turns, that's half what they fight about. They can't wait. You tell them they'll get turns and they'll hush."

"My kids jes gits nasty sometime. Jes fer no reason, jes gits so ugly you jes can't har'ly stan' it. Then what would you do?"

"Well, I gits nasty sometimes too! Sometimes I have a headache, or something on my mind. I figure a chil' might get ornery and ugly like that too. If it don't happen too often, I jes lets him be nasty once in a while. Can't be nice all the time!"

"I ben teach Sunday School for twenty-four years, and I find the worser they is, the sooner I make them the leader and that works. When children are the leader, they're proud, and they don't want to cause trouble no more."

"I think this is wonderful! I really do! This is a kindergarten, but the school people don't like it because they can't tell us what to do. Maybe they don't like us even a little worse because, maybe, we're going to do our kindergarten even a little better than them, since they never did one neither, and that's embarrassing to them. Besides, they're jealous. They think they owns the childrens, and they hates to see the government admit we owns a piece of them too! They has never done very well raising citizens, look at our people in the past, have they been good citizens? We are going to do much better raising good citizens, I can tell just by listening to his talk here today. That's what the schools is jealous about."

This discussion will be familiar to readers knowledgeable about teachers' discussions. I record it faithfully here not because it's unusual, but because it's usual—yet poor people, not teachers, were having it. Our aim in preparing written materials and "guidelines" for teachers was to take tapes or notes of discussions like this one, to edit and duplicate them, and to distribute them. This way, we didn't send instructions from experts, but digested suggestions from one local group to another.

It was very important, we thought, to puncture the myth of the teacher's mysterious magic, omnipotence, and omniscience, to make the foreign building and trappings of education familiar. This could best be done, we guessed, by opening wide the doors so poor people could see and learn the secrets of teaching by themselves becoming teachers and could themselves create the building and trappings. Poor people are said not to "care" about the education of their children. In those cases where this appears to be true, it's because they have been forced by circumstances to reject as dangerous a "thrusting" orientation to life, to accept what the distinguished psychoanalyst Erich Fromm describes as the "receptive" orientation:

> The receptive orientation is often to be found in societies in which the right of one group to exploit another is firmly established. Since the exploited group has no power to change, or any idea of changing, its situation, it will tend to look up to its masters as to its providers, as to those from whom one receives everything life can give. No matter how little the slave receives, he feels that by his own effort he could have acquired even less, since the structure of his society impresses him with the fact that he is unable to organize it and to rely on his own activity and reason. . . . It appears particularly in the attitude toward the "expert" and public opinion. People expect that in every field there is an expert who can tell them how things are and how they ought to be done, and that all they ought to do is listen to him and swallow his ideas.[11]

We believed that until members of Mississippi's poor Negro communities began organizing some part of society that affected them, such as the education of their children, and began relying on their own activity and reason, using "experts" as they were useful in this endeavor, they would remain receptive and their children would remain receptive. One can't "receive" an education, but must engage in it actively. Our aim, then, was not to "sell" society, including the school system, to the poor. It wasn't to pour selected and possibly irrelevant pieces of information on the passive children of passive parents. It was to work together to alter a situation, common to all states, but exaggerated in Mississippi, a situation in which "the right of one group to exploit another is firmly established" and to alter a situation in which "the exploited group has no power to change, or any idea of changing."

Educators Arthur Pearl and Frank Riessman say:

> The school is often seen as an authoritarian institution, walled off from the slum community, incommunicative except when it chooses not to be, and aloof

[11] Fromm, Erich, *Man for Himself*. New York: Rinehart & Company, Inc., 1947, pp. 79–80.

from the lives of people to the point where its attitude is often interpreted as unsympathetic and disapproving of slum people. A school which does not secure the trust and confidence of its community has failed. Therefore, many school systems have undertaken much more aggressive school-community relations programs in an effort to narrow the social distance which exists between the educated work-secure faculties and their less educated insecure communities. Often these programs take the form of community school programs, and the hiring of special personnel—as "bridge" people who work between the school and the neighborhood, interpreting the school to the community and the community to the school.[12]

In Mississippi, the Negro school was not only "seen as an authoritarian institution," it *was* an authoritarian institution. There were many adults throughout the school system hierarchy who acted in an authoritarian manner only because they had been raised and educated that way and through no conscious purpose of their own making. But there were those above the school system to whom the school had to stay responsive to stay in existence, who still operated on the philosophy so aptly stated by Mississippi's Governor Vardaman (1904–1908) who said of the Negro, he is "a lazy, lying, lustful animal, which no amount of training can transform into a tolerable citizen." The governor, therefore, recommended: "Education would be a positive unkindness to him," as "It simply renders him unfit for the work he will be forced to perform."[13]

That was in 1904. In 1963, Mississippi's Governor Paul B. Johnson was saying, ". . . in the past few years we lost 270,000 good-for-nothing lazy Negroes . . ."[14] and was explaining the kind of educational program Mississippi needed: ". . . an education program to teach some of our Negroes that they are wasting their time staying in Mississippi."[15]

To be honest and fair to the poor, at least in Mississippi, one would have to make the Riessman statement read: "the school's attitude *is* unsympathetic and disapproving of poor people." There were no school systems undertaking "much more aggressive school-community relations programs in an effort to narrow the social distance." If schools were undertaking any new programs regarding parents, these were to promote the school as it was, which was a sham and a farce and something very very far from true education. The schools *weren't* working with parents in evolving educational programs of meaning to them and their children. Schools there weren't hiring "bridge" people. If we were interested in this bridge, convinced that we had to have it, our whole Head Start program, not just occasional personnel, had to be the bridge.

[12] Pearl, Arthur and Riessman, Frank, *New Careers for the Poor.* New York: The Free Press, 1965, p. 45.

[13] McCord, William, *Mississippi: The Long Hot Summer.* New York: W. W. Norton & Co., Inc., 1965.

[14] Jackson *Clarion-Ledger,* July 9, 1963, p. 10.

[15] *Ibid.,* July 27, 1963, p. 6.

Nor could it be a bridge which simply landed and ended when it reached the dismal school. It would have to be a bridge that carried resurrected people, armed with new, exciting knowledge, because they had *experienced* it, of what education can and ought to be, and armed with new audacity to challenge the absurdity that education is in Mississippi; people who would gallop en masse off that bridge and into the school on the other end, to try to effect some positive twentieth-century change. As long as Head Start perpetuated the attitude in the minds of the poor Negro that he was, as in slave days, to be grinningly grateful for the miserable scrap of learning tossed carelessly his way, it would be one additional fraud in several centuries of fraud concerning how well he "is cared for" by his benevolent white benefactors.

In the arithmetic workshop teachers and campus children played with Cuisenaire rods (sticks of different colors and sizes, which children use to discover mathematical relationships), did mathematical experiments, and collected items from around the grounds that could be used on "counting tables" in centers: bottle caps, sticks, pebbles, milk cartons, and so on.

In the science workshop the "class" went for a walk, gathering beautiful and interesting "gifts of Mother Nature" that could make a center full of wonderful natural living surprises and lovely natural beauty.

The children's work workshop took place in the sample classroom Diane Feeley, our Montessori-Deutsch teacher, had organized. It concerned the earnestness with which children play. To them play is work, and is just as important as work is for adults. The adults played all the homemade number, color, matching, and grouping games we had made. They talked about possibilities in the housekeeping corner, and with dress-up clothes, horse-head broom sticks, toy telephones, mirrors, washing and scrubbing, and so forth.

In the language workshop we talked about grammar over content or content over grammar, and how to make books from the children's own sayings and ideas. We practiced conversing with children and keeping the conversation going when it seemed to come to an end. We discussed why this was important in enriching the children's confidence as well as their vocabulary, and in experiencing communicating through language as well as in the many other ways they do.

In the workshop on freedom to move and play, everyone sang and played circle games. The discussion which emerged from these activities stressed that these are *little* children who are normally very active. Therefore, at this level, school shouldn't be a sitting down school. Freedom of expression was led by the psychology staff. It was child development as stimulated and interpreted from some children who painted and romped through the classes.

Living arts was puppet making, acting out the part of a tree, frog, a bad girl, and happy person.

There was a tremendous variation of quality from one workshop to another. Some got better after several reruns, and others got drier, drabber—and in a few instances, disintegrated altogether. It was clear that we had a long way to go to develop our "working style."

Some resource staffs were too scattered to get their groups focused. The participants felt that they did not accomplish anything. This was the case in workshops of staff members who felt the local person discussion leader should do the job alone, and who did not help from the floor.

Some resource staffs did not know how to guide and stimulate a discussion. To get the most out of the time alloted to them, they succumbed to lecturing. The participants felt "talked at" and were resentful.

None of the workshops had as many actual materials as would have been desirable. We felt strongly that talk should come out of doing. This was not always the case.

Twelve hours a day is much too much for people accustomed to a very slow pace of life. Many people drifted away. Also, many people couldn't read their schedules, and were very confused about what they were to do. In the future we would have better organized, shorter sessions.

Yet we felt that we were on the right track emphasizing through informal discussion the concerns of the poor, the urgent all-consuming concerns, and the past experience of group members—*their* talent, *their* wisdom—to concentrate on concept development and working techniques rather than on separate segments of "knowledge"; to be content for this first time with exposure, friendliness, a warm and positive introduction; and to make use of the learning style of most people (and more so the poor): practical experience, creative exploration, and the careful analysis of it, rather than reading, memorizing, sitting through lectures and carrying on theoretical discussions not based on immediate specific situations. We were operating on Dr. Jerome Bruner's premise that: "Practice in inquiry, in trying to figure out things for oneself is indeed what is needed—but in what form? Of only one thing I am convinced: I have never seen anybody improve in the art and technique of inquiry by any means other than engaging in inquiry."[16]

At the Orientation nondenominational service in the auditorium on Sunday, Reverend Willie Brown of Laurel, later the director in training, said, "Men all over the world are crying for freedom and justice. Ever since the world began, men have been oppressed. We're tired of being oppressed. We're tired of being the lowest man on the totem pole. The Bible tells us that if we act, God will come and help us. But He won't come first. He won't act first. And nothing will happen till He does. This CDGM gives many of us our first chance, God will help us."

[16] Bruner, Jerome S., *On Knowing*. Cambridge: The Belknap Press of Harvard University Press, 1963, p. 94.

PART III

The First Summer

JULY-SEPTEMBER, 1965; SAMPLES AND EXAMPLES OF HOW CDGM WORKED AND DID NOT WORK AT FIRST, WITH RESULTING PLANS FOR A FUTURE PROGRAM AND A LITTLE FEDERAL INTERVENTION

CHAPTER 8

HUMAN GROWTH AND DEVELOPMENT

Of poor people and of professional staff (Hattiesburg and Quitman)

ON THE NIGHT of July 2, eighty-three crosses were burned throughout Mississippi to celebrate the Civil Rights Bill, which was to be implemented on that date. The same week, several days before the centers opened, I was fortunate enough to be taken on a day's rambling ride from community to community in the fourth district by the district coordinator, Lou Grant. I learned a lot that day. Louie, for all his theatrical lethargy and incessant overalls, was a master of informative, supportive, nondirective, slow motion work in communities of emerging poor people.

We streaked down several hours of rapidly unfurling highway, through lovely hilly red clay country, covered with feathery pine trees and tall grasses. We went first to a meeting in the back of a dark, empty store on the hot, dusty, unpaved main street of Hattiesburg, a small town in Forest County, in the southern section of the state. A large group of perspiring ladies was stuffed into the small room, seated on up-ended packing crates, an assortment of straight-backed wooden chairs, and a bench borrowed from next door. There was no air-conditioning. The temperature was 92° and humid. The ladies talked of their plans for the children. These included large doses of ABCs and rote counting. They spoke excitedly of the artwork the children would do. This, as it turned out in the discussion, was to be coloring one duck red, two ducks blue, etc. Louie made several comments about letting the kids play some, but essentially endorsed their excellent start at planning for themselves and not waiting for "they" to do everything.

After the meeting Mrs. Earlene Beard dictated an article to me to put in a CDGM newsletter I was about to start issuing. She said of Kelly Settlement, the tiny Negro community she lives in near Hattiesburg, "This is a community that's been here more than a hundred years. I'm told that my grandfather was a man who couldn't read and write, but he had foresight and great vision of the future. . . . I am one of twelve children born and reared in this community. My mother and father were some of the first students at Jackson State College. . . . Many people were like them that had put forth great effort to do something about the potential that went many times underdeveloped. It is a constant thought how that before this time many of the people with talent were in a state of deterioration from lack of use. Having a chance to be registered and to be counted it gives such a different feeling. A very great anxiety among the people for a better life. Now with Head Start we have a chance to develop the potential that lies within our immediate community of a few people. We are happy for those who have come and made themselves a part of us and to help show the way. This will give the children a better chance than we've had. We are glad to make the sacrifice of time and of putting up with the opposition to make the world a better place."

While some people were "inarticulate," or possessive about the only thing in the world that was purely theirs—their particular way of life and local knowledge—most were more than eager to talk about an area of knowledge in which *they* were the experts. People came in and went out as we visited several homes. Most of the homes were gray, unpainted, and unlikely from the outside, but tidy, trim, and attractive on the inside. Lou came and went about his business, and people kept me company, talking to me and to each other.

"I don't know why these whites are so mean and ugly. Most of us are more white than we are Negro. Take me. My mother's father was half white, the child of a slave owner and his Negro mistress. Mother's mother was an all white child, born out of wedlock and given to a Negro woman to raise to hide her shame. My father is white—a Mississippi white. He had Negro half-brothers, though, because his mother remarried a Negro man. Even the ex-mayor of Hattiesburg has half-Negro children. Everybody knows about his colored lady friend and his colored children. He even put them through school. Most of them don't take care of the lady friend and the children, though. You know how they are: They'll kill to keep segregation by day, but they sure don't believe in it by night!"

Another lady said, "I don't know where we'll get the strength to start these CDGM schools. We will though, but sometimes I get to feeling a little weather-beaten. Eight or nine years ago we lost everything we had through fire. It was a big place. We were accustomed to just throwing open the doors to everybody. We were overshadowed by many debts. Then my husband and I both had to be hospitalized. I lost a baby boy. It was lack of prenatal knowledge. I know now. I was timid about doctors going under my clothes, so I didn't go to one till the very end. I acted like a cowboy: chasing cows and everything. I fell in a hole one evening, and threw the baby out of position. I carried him in pain till the very end, but at birth, as a result of the fall, he was buttocks-first, and the doctor had to choose between him and me. My husband told him, 'Save her.' They damaged his head so bad at birth, he died. I had a midwife to deliver the next one. Then I lost a baby girl. I had toxemia, they said. And the baby was born strangled with the cord tight around her neck three times. Most of my family left Mississippi. Then my brother, the only one that stayed, we were very close, he was taken from me by night-riding Klansmen . . . they murdered him. My relatives started dying and they all just died in a pile. They didn't have enough health to fight it or money to pay the doctoring bills. I hardly have any relatives left now. But I still have roots . . . that's why I stay . . . what else would I do at my age? Where would I go? I don't know anybody. I don't have a home in the North. I still have roots and a determination to make it better for all the children. . . . We *have* to get these CDGM schools going, and we will."

I asked, "How can you stay so fair and friendly toward whites after all those bitter experiences you've had?"

She replied, "I guess I just don't have the foundations for too much nastiness in my nature. You be fair and frank with me; I'll be fair and frank with you—whatever color you are."

A man explained, "It's a different environment here from some places. There's a tree in my neighbor's field here in Forest County where there was a lynching a while back. You just live with it. Don't let it get you. But we don't let them get away with it anymore."

A lady laughed at herself and said, "I'm the cautious type. I never got involved in civil rights activities. I was fearful. You know. But I'm active in church, and one night last year there were some white visiting ministers here, so we took this integrated group to our church where we could all use the organ and the piano and sing. When we came out, we heard shots. Since this is Mississippi and it was the middle of midnight, the minister said, 'Ladies, take to the dust!' My friend I was with took to the dust. I took to a nearby graveyard. My Daddy is dead, so I said, 'Daddy, here I come!' But CDGM's different. It's not civil rights, it's education. So I got involved."

I asked who in the community had brought in the news of Head Start, and who had organized the five centers. (The first summer centers in the Hattiesburg vicinity were Library, Eaton, Kelly Settlement, Walthall, and Palmer's Crossing. The next year, Springfield, Myers, and Brooklyn joined them.) I asked *why* people organized them.

"Well, some of the Delta Ministry workers who work here to bring us information from what you might call 'the outside world,' which the officials here keep from us, they told us about it. Then we local people sat down and thought, 'Who are the key people, you might call them, in each community and neighborhood?' Then we called all them that had telephones, and asked them to go walk out, or drive if they had cars, to tell the news to others without phones. That way, you might fairly say one person in each community has done all the work, but others join. You have to rely on the ones willing to do. Not all will go first, you might say."

"Yes," another person added, "we surely cooled the potato of those who say we can't organize anything. But, of course, many of us can't. We have to poke the devil outa them to get them up on their slippery shoes. And they'll usually set right back down again if you don't keep poking. I don't know what it is. Something just keeps some people scared."

And someone said, "Yes, when white people bring me information on something new to me, my attitude is, 'I don't feel inferior to you, but I feel my *experience* has been inferior to yours. Tell me, what it is you know, don't be scared to do that, and then I'll take care of it, you don't have to do it for me like a baby.' "

A man broke in good-naturedly with, "I'll tell you who didn't *organize* CDGM, young lady. The ministers in this area around Hattiesburg. You couldn't exactly call them courageous and forward-looking. Just upward looking: at heaven. Many people have left their congregations in disgust. The preachers just get left behind preaching on and on at the old folks. The really forward-looking preachers, even, they don't exactly go first, but at least they'll follow after their congregations. I guess there might be an exception. I can't think of one. Except that Bob Beech, he's a preacher you know, but he's white and here from the Delta Ministry. He's not from Mississippi. He gives us a lot of comfort. Doesn't lead, but he tries to give us patience to work out the changes in things. He talks to whites and us. He's like a management-labor middleman. We are management."

A mother said, "I'm interested in CDGM schools because I have never been to a school where I was treated nice, and my child was not treated nice in school, but I still have the crazy idea that maybe there could be a school that treats children nice. We have PTAs around Hattiesburg, but they're not too well attended. Parents don't have time to take off work to go to PTA and to visit classes. We would probably get fired if we missed work. When you do go, they don't give what you would call a welcome. I'll tell you what I mean.

"One day when my daughter was twelve years old, a man teacher beat her with a strap so she came home black and raised up all over her side. I went to see the principal because this had happened just too much for me, and I couldn't stand it no more. I hate to complain, but she was coming into womanhood, you know, and I thought . . . but anyway, the principal called the teacher in, and the teacher said, 'Well, I figured if you take care of the home end, we'll take care of this end up here.' The principal heard that, but he didn't do anything. It doesn't make you want to go to school much, if you understand what I mean.

"Then let me tell you another time, earlier. Her grades weren't better than they were because the teachers in grade school just cleaned the confidence right out of her. They beat her for everything. One day the teacher beat her for looking out the window. They were having a quiz, and she had finished. She had gotten them all right. The teacher beat her till the blood came, and kept hollering all the while, 'if you think you're better than I am because your face is lighter, I'll just show you what I think of your light face. It was hell if she worked and hell if she didn't. I don't believe our superintendent puts forth every effort he could, either. If he limits what he gives to the colored schools, he can keep us down for his friends to use better."

A large, very black lady came swooping in from the yard and told everyone else to "hush and be quiet," she was going to "give this little white girl a good transexplanation of every rotten thing down here":

"I'll tell you how it is in Forest County. Before '63, we just had a few NAACP voter registration lawsuits, but nothing was really rollin'. Then Hollis an Curtis come in here. You know them? Well, when they came, people had nothin' against them—except members of the NAACP. NAACP members didn't want them around. They were SNCC. These two ragged little boys! I remember them well. They were something else! All they wanted was to set up a small group of paid workers, because they felt we had to speed up registerin' voters. Vernon was the only one of that NAACP bunch that wanted 'em. He said, 'Look, those boys can afford to talk with folks to get them to register, because they'll be paid a little of subsistence by their organizations. They can go door to door to get people out. We should be doin' this ourself, but we got no subsistence, we can only do a little around the edges, we gotta work. We gotta make a livin', they don't, let 'em help us.' The rest of the NAACP people blackballed Vernon for talking like that. NAACP was jealous of these kids, if you can believe it! NAACP is very cautious; very conservative. They don't know what's happenin' anymore than a monkey with a yo-yo, but they want to be sure to run it, whatever it is, or run away from it, they don't know, but they put up a lot of fuss.

"OK, so Hollis and Curtis took the risks and then they got things rolling. We took to them jes' fine. Put them up, worked hard helpin' them register people, like that. We wanted it done.

"Then in the summer of '64, last summer, all these kids came down from up North. Some of these kids were so innocent! We were too! We all honestly believed that just one year a trouble, just gettin' everybody registered, and then everything is going to be changed. These kids thought people was people and they could just talk to them and they would straighten out. They never lied to us. They just didn't know these whites we've got down here! These kids had faith in people. We had faith in *them.* They had good will. They believed it would work. When we saw what it was still like in the fall of '64 after that summer a work, they was broke-hearted, like us. A forty-seven-year-old man from Harvard broke down on my lap and cried, he surely did!

"Now let me tell you what happened next. The last part of '64, let me tell you, we was on the critical list! So this began stage two. We began to get sure-enough political minded. We started learnin' about unfair elections, lawsuits, Congressional districts, challenges; all that stuff I never heard of before. We really got busy. We saw we really had to get tough with these crackers. I told a white lady I know, 'You crackers all settin' there on the one side, and all them borgeouis niggers settin' there on the other side drinkin' coffee so pretty with your feets crossed real nice . . . and us folks out here doing the federal government's work without gettin' paid for it, while the FBI sets with you crackers and niggers taking notes real nice.' I told her that! I surely did, I was wisin' up how you have to handle these folks.

"We formed FDP and got real busy. NAACP had given money, but at this time they denied us. They withdrew from COFO. You know what it is, white girl? COFO? All the good groups hooked together last summer and called theirself Confederated Organization of Federated Organizations, or something like that. Well, NAACP withdrew itself. It was because they wanted to control and we wouldn't let them. They served us a good purpose here in Forest County years ago when nobody else wouldn't do nothin', but their time is past. They won't move with the progress. They're still carryin' on like cars ain't been invented. They won't do the dirty work and the groundwork. We did, with Curtis and Hollis. But then they want the credit. Uncle Roy Wilkins had the squeeze on Medgar. Medgar was the field secretary, I think, for the NAACP. Means he worked in the fields with us instead of like them other stay-at-home NAACPers. Medgar wanted to organize and demonstrate like we did. But Medgar felt Uncle Roy's squeeze so much he tried to hold us back. We told him, 'Medgar, we're goin' ahead, rain, shine, NAACP, or sleet!' So Medgar, he came along with us. Three days before the crackers killed him, he had been fired by Uncle Roy or someone, or so they say, for not obeyin' orders to stay outa our mess. Then the NAACP did everything they could to claim the credit when he was killed. Suddenly he was their big hero. They're good at mobilizin' . . . the dead!"

(Medgar Evers was murdered, shot in the back, in June, 1963, only two springs before CDGM. It is well known that almost everybody in NAACP was more cautious than Mr. Evers. For example, they did not want children exposed. They did not think, they say, that it was "dignified" to "exploit" children. It was too daring, too dangerous. Medgar Evers believed that it was precisely the children who must be involved, as the older people were too set in their ways and fears to do much. People who knew him well say he died an isolated and lonely man.)

"So this was stage two, see. First registerin', then politics. Now we saw stage three comin'. We heard of all these federal programs from Marian Wright and people who came around. She's a lawyer—colored. We were tryin' to learn about these programs in workshops. At that time we could've controlled the whole Poverty Program in Mississippi, because we knew all about all the parts of it, and the whites didn't. But we couldn't get our own people together. You know, they was scared it was civil rights. I felt the CDGM was good, and we had to organize it. I worked hard at organizing it. I thought we should get Movement people in so they could eat for a spell while they worked for their rights. I don't care how hard we're trying to overthrow the devil, we got to eat while we do it. We took the risks that made this federal program possible, and then local committees is leavin' us out now that they're hiring, because they say OEO says this ain't civil rights. I wanted CDGM committees to hire the scared naked ones too, the ones that didn't ever have anything to do with the Movement, because we wanted to get them civicly active, but I felt we should hire those who had paid the big price first.

"Now take me. I don't want to be no teacher. It was a problem raising my own children, why would I want to raise somebody else's? But I wanted to be a cook. They haven't hired me. They say they ain't gonna. We don't want mean ones like me with the children, but we ain't too mean to be janitors. I call myself an unfinished product of the Movement. I'm all stirred up, broke with my past way of life, learned a lot, grew a lot with knowledge, and still I'm as poor as I was an' in the same ol' bag. I had more security then than I do now. Those cats in the government ain't ever been hungry. There are some good ones, thinkin' the same things we do, but there are many thousands more in government an' in the worl' don' even know we azist. They're not against us, they're jes *so* busy with their personal selfish concerns we can jes all get shot to death an starve as long as things are comfy for the fellow Americans. So while there there they are, here I am, tryin' to make things work in a pennyanny place like Hattiesburg.

"So let me tell you what the Movement and CDGM have done for me. When I was little, I desperately wanted to take music lessons. I loved music! Oh, I loved it. I still love music. Mama, she couldn't afford no music lessons. Then my little girl got big and she wanted piano lessons. And I told her, 'Honey, you'll *have* piano lessons. And a piano. The best piano in the world!' I bought one. I paid seven hundred dollars for it over a long, long time, and had only two hundred and forty dollars left to pay. I was makin' thirty-five dollars a week at that time. Then I registered to vote. The man I worked for, he asked me did I register to vote. I didn't want to lose that little job. It was small, it was wrong to lie, but it was all I had. I wanted that piano for my little girl, so bad! So I said, 'Oh, no. Wasn't *I* registered!' He said, 'How come I seen a woman named your name on your street listed in the paper for registerin'?' I said, 'Must be someone else. Or maybe a mistake.' He said, 'Girl, you lyin' to me. Get gone from here and don't you never come back. We don't want the likes a you here!' Then I had no job, and they took my piano from my little girl. Now I've revaluated my life, and I've changed my standpoint of view. I was makin' sixty dollars a week as a chef cook. Then forty dollars a week as a presser in the dry-cleaner. Since my Movement work, I can only get twenty-five dollars *a month* ADC. Now what can I do with that? An' CDGM says, 'This ain't the Movement,' they says."

People told me proudly of the Freedom School in Hattiesburg the summer before this one: "There was this Negro man and his wife from Deetroit. They was plannin' a high school for fifty kids. The first day five hun'red and fifty people come, eight years to eighty years. That school went mornin', noon, and night with volunteers and real teachers. There's one teacher, told me he never seen high school kids before that hadn't heard of the Desegregation School Law exactly ten years before. We told this teacher, 'Why are you surprised? These kids only learn Mississippi laws in school, not Communist *federal* laws."

"I've learned since we started CDGM that there's a library in Hattiesburg. I've learned because CDGM is talking about getting books to read the children. Before this, I s'pose there must've been one, they didn't just build it, but the only library I ever heard of was our library at the Freedom School last summer. We had books and books and books! They kept it open whenever we could come."

"At Palmer's Crossing Freedom School, the teacher said to a lady, 'I know that education is supposed to teach people about the world.' Did you ever hear that? Even said Negroes and whites were supposed to learn about each other. Also we had a debate: whether nonviolence is possible. We agreed it doesn't work. If it worked, we would have some freedom now, just a spoonful, don't you think? What do you think?"

And they talked of other things that had happened in Hattiesburg that summer: "Did you ever hear what happened in Hattiesburg last summer to some of the COFOs? There were these five, one was a rabbi from Ohio—that's a Jewish preacher—and two white boys and two were girls. They were on their way home to dinner from registering people. They was walking along the railroad tracks. A pickup stopped and some whites come running and jumped them and cursed at them and kept beating on their heads with iron rods. They kicked them with work boots, and they beat on them and stuffed registration papers in their mouths. They just set there, nonviolent. I'd a killed them, I wouldn'ta just set there loving everybody. They had to get a lotta stitches in their head and Larry had a broke arm. They had a trial, but all they asked this rabbi, who nearly bled to death and was so weak he could hardly walk, was how many nigger girls he slept with! The one who did it, well the Grand Jury didn't make him pay or go to jail. They didn't even write it in the newspaper. You know, they hardly ever do, it was only niggers and agitators nearly got killed, not people."

"And a different day these other COFOs, they didn't know you ain't supposed to call the polices in Mississippi if you're in a integrated group and if whites is after you. They was walking along together downtown when this white man started kicking this white boy, Peter. They hollered for the polices and they come, but then they arrested *Peter* for assault and battery for fighting in the street. Then they had a trial, too. There's always a trial. If you care to call it that. They asked them questions if they ever were a Communist. The white man had to pay $20 and they lectured this white kid about destroying gradualism in Mississippi and ruining our wonderful race relations. In the Hattiesburg Courthouse they got white and colored signs still. That's the wonderful race relations COFO is rapidly trying to ruin."

Lou and I had a hamburger in a colored cafe before driving to the next CDGM community in another county. Integrated groups in Mississippi, especially a black man and a white girl as we were, didn't go into white eating places in unfamiliar territory, or usually, even in familiar territory, other than in Jackson and a few chain motels. This was partly because it was an extremely dangerous and foolhardy thing to do. It was also because you felt so hate-stared and tense that you couldn't possibly eat, relax, and enjoy a little refreshing conversation before continuing work. It was, too, because whenever possible, we tried to give our two cents worth to strengthening the Negro economy by "buying black." But finally, I suppose, we stayed completely in the black community because it was too horribly embarrassing to show our true color in this context.

With a few exceptions, all the Negro cafes I ate in from one end of the state to the other looked approximately the same. They were made of gray cement and colorless plaster. There were eight to twenty battered brown chairs and tables, and usually a counter with stools. Except at dinner time, when two or three complete meals were offered for eighty-eight cents to one dollar, and at breakfast time when you could get eggs, meat, grits, preserves, biscuits, etc., very little was served other than soft drinks, hamburgers, coffee, and several other such items. There were no long lists of sandwiches, soups, and elaborate ice cream dishes. Cafes usually had something of an intimate, informal family spirit, as if you were eating in the cook's home kitchen, or in the camaraderie of a cozy club in which everyone knows everyone else very well.

Often the only decor was a jarringly out-of-place beige-colored couple in dinner clothes laughing suavely from a patio on a poster advertising beer or something to their less elegant brothers.

At our next destination, forty miles down lonely, two-lane rural blacktops from Hattiesburg, the lady who was expecting us for a community meeting was not at home. A relative invited us to sit in the living room to wait. As was frequently the case in CDGM, we waited two hours.

People in these communities generally have a relaxing and refreshing unawareness of time. Perhaps it's an unconscious feeling that they can't control their lives because of such things as frequent flat tires due to buying used tires and putting butane in them, jobs which come and go quite arbitrarily, education in which they're totally at the mercy of the system, fate. Perhaps it's this that makes them innocent of effort to control time. Time, like everything else, just happens to them. Or maybe it's that, having accustomed themselves to dawdling their lives away at a sluggish pace because it is forbidden to them to fill their long years with activity, intellectual pursuits, and progress, they are so in the habit of *killing* time that they lack experience in *filling* it instead. I think there is quite a bit of survival value in being timeless, aimless, and lethargic. If they didn't cope and adjust in this manner of pace expectation, they would all have nervous breakdowns from forced idleness. The absence of books, zoos, museums, parks, recreation centers, after school activities, hobbies, civic projects, color, records, and in short, anything whatsoever to do, is beyond imagination.

Making people wait for them could be, in addition to these other things, a subtle way of controlling those whom they feel control them. I've found that the more silently angry people are, the later they are.

Inability to organize time is doubtless one facet of lack of experience in organizing anything. Poor people, confined to overcrowded homes and unequipped schools, haven't had much practice in sorting, grouping, and categorizing. CDGM people gradually became more punctual and organized, but it was hard. Everybody had to yield a little on the time matter. They regarded our gentle "wishing" in this direction as authoritarian, demanding, and superfluous rigidity, which it often was. It seems that the more "sophisticated" we get, the more we become the slaves of mere notions, man-made notions, such as time.

This waiting time was never wasted time for CDGM professionals. It was extra working time. It could always be used for talking to people directly or indirectly connected with CDGM, or not connected at all, but still related, in that they too, being poor, black, and Mississippians, were part of the CDGM context. The more we asked and the more we listened, the more our theoretical ideas wove themselves into and out of the woof and warp of people's perceptions and realities. The timelessness was hard for prompt professionals to adapt to, but when we learned to take it easy, we had greatly extended our value. Then we went to the field not to instruct or supervise or research specific interests of *ours,* but to learn what *others* had to give and *then* to share through friendly informal conversation what we had to give. Oddly enough, much less of our so-called "knowledge" seemed appropriate after we listened.

While Lou and I waited for everyone "in the rurals" to be contacted and collected for the meeting, I began to feel a little of the flavor of life in Quitman, a tiny town in Clarke County, next to the Alabama line.

I asked the chairman, Mrs. Jumana Sumrall, how she got interested in CDGM.

"My son went to Greenville about some other business. He and his friends were sitting in a cafe eating, and this girl Karen Shillington from the Delta Ministry, a volunteer, came in and asked them if they knew about Head Start back home in Clarke County. So my son asked a lot of questions, and came home and told me. I told the others here in Quitman. It's been very hard to get committee members to serve. They're afraid they'll be cut off welfare for stepping out like that. Some people here told some people in Stonewall. We're going to have two centers for children in this county.

"I've followed civil rights in the past, and I've let civil rights workers sleep here, but I had read a lot about being nonviolent and getting knocked around in a march, or something. I wasn't interested in that. I'm an older woman, I'll leave that to my sons. But when I had a chance to do something peaceful for progress, this Head Start thing, I was pleased to take the risk.

"They asked the superintendent here in the county if he wanted a Head Start, but he said *no.* They say we're not good for much, but we're good for taking risks when they won't. We decided if there's going to be a Head Start here for the little children, we'll have to organize it. My husband is economically independent enough so I could risk it. What? Yes, oh, well he belongs to the Cement Masons Union. He takes jobs out of the state, mostly. Some whites here asked where he worked, I suppose to fire him for my goings on. But nobody seemed to know where he worked." (The lady chuckled.)

I asked the group what people were afraid of, other than being cut off welfare, which is quite a legitimate fear for civically active Negroes in Mississippi; why was it hard to get committee members to hire for the center and run it?

"Oh, you know how they is. They remembers things. In the forties they hung two little boys nine and eleven years old in this county. For molesting an older white lady, they said. The lady said it was two colored boys. The sheriff went out and picked up these two colored babies, only babies they were. Little, little boys. They had them in jail. They say the people stormed the jail and took them out, but the truth is the sheriff was there helping them lynch them. Then they showed them to the white lady, and she said it was the wrong ones, and they said, 'Don't worry, we'll run right out and get the right ones.' They still call that place in Shubuta the hanging bridge."

"Yes, and tell her that other thing. There was two women and two men they hung here in the county. The two women was pregnant. People says they went down there to look at the bodies and they could still see those babies wiggling around in the bellies after those mothers was dead. They were strangulating too. Their air was gone."

One by one, in clumps and clusters, various community-elected committee members and the poor people they had hired began collecting. When enough seemed to have gathered and settled themselves like nesting hens in sofas and armchairs, the district coordinator, Lou Grant, asked in his soft low voice if any plans had yet been made for what they were going to do with those little kids Monday. There was a comfortable but apparently permanent silence in the sweltering room, while twenty-three people sat squeezed together smiling faintly and fanning the sticky ninety degrees of evening heat off their streaming faces with their transportation contracts.

Silences in community meetings were frequent and not a strain if the community people felt at home with the visitors present, as they did with Lou; if staff refrained from rushing in with embarrassed talk to crowd the quiet with answers, instead of letting the questions seep and soak through several hundred years of never having been offered these administrative, information, content, procedural, and policy questions to think about; if staff was patient and had faith, good thinking was often the outcome of the silences. We professionals are so used to glib clichés and jargon-coated platitudes, that we tend to provoke them, forgetting that silence is necessary for thinking, and that thinking is, after all, more desirable than automatic answers. The less said is the more heard.

Eventually, if pertinent questions had been asked by the discussion leader, someone would always speak. A few more comments would be contributed from around the room. And you would have had your discussion, without much fanfare but with much fruitfulness. Many people with valid ideas and information offered them in few words. As professional meetings and conferences prove, verbosity isn't necessarily either profundity or effectively creative thinking or action. CDGM poor people didn't always speak much, but it was the *opportunity* to speak, then being consulted, and the *knowing that ideas would be heeded,* that was critical. The length of the discussion might range from all day to five minutes and wasn't an important consideration.

After a while Mrs. Sumerall, the community committee chairman, spoke in her whispery scarcely audible voice. "Well, I don't guess we've thought about *that* yet. What we'll do with the kids Monday." Her eyes moved slowly from face to face in the room ringed with dark faces, gathering people's wordless opinions as she did so. Then she added, "See, we don't got the children yet. We'll tell you next week what we'll do with them after we get 'em." Louie smiled his winning smile and said that that was OK. He would ask them after their first day, then.

Later, in the car, speeding through the strikingly, starkly dark black two hours of isolated night to Mount Beulah, I confess that I suffered last minute pangs of doubt. Though it was not fashionable in CDGM to admit any doubt regarding the competence of the poor in professional endeavors, nevertheless, in the name of truthful recollection, I recall and confess that for a few fleeting moments I doubted. Pictures of the poor program we were about to produce for children rose up before my distressed eyes. I saw flashing glimpses of quality nursery schools I attended as a two year old, and nursery schools I'd visited or practice taught in, or taught in, or read about, or heard about, or seen films about: the vibrant and vital all around activity of the Bank Street nursery school in New York; the rich experience of Pacific Oaks children in California; the enriched warmth and supermothering of Dr. Hess's program in Chicago; the scientifically detailed additions to standard contemporary preschool curriculum of Dr. Deutsch's classes; the sophisticated and subtle personality and interpersonal insights and techniques of the National Children Research Center in Washington, and of Sarah Lawrence's lab nursery in Bronxville; the beautiful equipment and quietly sequentialed order of Montessori programs, stressing the importance of the child's work and tangible success experiences; the thrilling bursts of internal powers of Dr. Gattegno's students. I thought of all the carefully conceived cooperatives and day care centers here and there. I thought of early childhood art teachers and art therapists I have known, and of creative dance and drama specialists. I thought of reading specialists of ten types. I thought, with horror, of what Drs. Bruner, Piaget, Erikson, Josselyn, Fraiburg, Isaacs, Klein, and company would shudderingly think. And I felt grim.

I swallowed my fears and climbed back on top of my theories.

The hardest thing in the world that summer was to withhold and watch and "let" human beings develop. It's so much easier, if you believe certain things violently, and time is short, to do them to people. Luckily, Lou had had far more experience than I in the working ways of rural Negro Mississippians. He had focused people's attention on the fact that it would be *them*, not "they," who would need to plan for the children. But he didn't force plan-making prematurely, or make their plans for them because they were so slow doing it. He knew what I did not know until the second day of center operation in this community, when I dropped in for a few minutes. That many people in these communities don't think abstractly. They think when the need arises.

The need didn't arise in advance. It arose concretely and specifically.

On the second day of conducting a preschool, never having seen one of any shape or size before, this staff of male and female maids and field hands was playing with the children, singing with them, telling them stories, grouping and scheduling after a fashion, and had, with no *pre*-arranging, arranged a creditable beginning.

The moral of my day as I felt it, was *not* that nothing further could be developed in the way of first-rate nursery technique and programming. It was *not* that "anyone can do it." It was that a trusting and noninterfering person, who leaves communities free to work in their own style until problems crop up, and who does not assume and anticipate disaster and incompetence, does more for the child's eventual growth and development than any amount of advice on these subjects from an "expert" would be able to do. I learned that a glossy veneer of scientific principles painted on a project to make it look satisfactorily professional, may actually retard the growth of rooted principles by hiding the fact that they're missing. I learned that we professionals have a tendency, in contrast to community development workers, to supersaturate a poor child with highly active nutrients, seeing only his immediate radical response, but failing to observe that the upward spurting child is enclosed in a case of steel, which will shortly stunt the growth completely, and may even turn the newly budded sensitivities ricocheting back downward to destroy with frustrated bitterness the very child we think we're "saving." Cracking the steel case of parental futility feelings comes before "fertilizing" the child.

Foot-stamping, snake-dancing, and other demonstrations of vibrant life there were in CDGM, and also many sound principles not found in most educational programs designed for poor people. Tom Levin wanted to change, not just the image of school, as were other Head Starts with varying degrees of success, but the very nature of the school. He knew that if, following the lead of Freud, Erikson, and others, psychoanalytic wisdom could be built into a social action project, the result would be a powerful organization. So he started there.

The children who were about to enter our CDGM centers tended toward passivity and individual resignation. The economic reality of their families played the major part in this. Mothers were forced to leave babies alone, or with older brothers and sisters who were busy about their own affairs. They had to work in the field or in the white lady's kitchen. Passiveness and limited aspirations were appropriate adaptations to the frustration and deprivation imposed on children by mothers who had no other choice. Mothers were also being frustrated and deprived, and also had developed passive qualities and limited aspirations. Thus the children's passivity was expected and encouraged by adults.

It was Tom's professional psychoanalytic opinion that no factor intervened, during the stage of development in which children usually become assertive, to alter these earlier adaptations, because toilet training was late, sporadic, and mild. The children had little about which to assert themselves. They didn't develop a streak of struggling for autonomy as middle-class children generally do. Passiveness was once again reinforced.

A factor further curtailing the development of little boys' aggressive, thrusting drives, and preventing these drives from evolving into initiative, the ability to plan, attack problems, and learn, as is usually the case with middle-class preschool boys, was that in most homes there were no strong men with whom little boys could identify, from whom little boys could learn how to be men, and who could prevent little boys from getting too wrapped up in relationships with their mothers. Potent men of this kind were not in most homes to block infantile fantasies, the search for magical fulfillment through a powerful mother, waves of rage at frustration and disappointment, and unlikely aspirations that resulted in feelings of complete inadequacy and inaction. Therefore, childlike feelings remained childlike, instead of being channeled in directions that were useful to adults. The cycle perpetuated itself. Passive men produced passive little boys who sought powerful mothers and wives, who married passive men and produced passive little boys. So poor Negro family structure and its products were different from middle-class family structure and products.

But there were other differences, too—differences that have been overlooked by people trying to coax the children into more assertive behavior—differences Tom felt could form the foundation for a program that would create real change in children. Within the same pattern of infant handling, strengths were developed as well as problems. Babies were taken care of by a wide variety of older children and adults. Children looked to this whole extended family and trusted it to take care of them. Adults were comfortable entrusting the care of their children to many members of the community. This reliance on community, was reinforced by absence of drive toward autonomy, and absence of strong feelings of shame, so while confidence in self and individual hope lay dormant, children grew to adulthood counting heavily on the community. Children tended to invest in the whole community for security. One of the most profound strengths in the Negro community was that, while there was reluctance to engage in individual activity, many people would readily join in community activity—especially, because of the already established pattern, if it revolved around children.

And children looked to their whole community for adults to emulate. Potent men didn't need to be in the homes, as long as they were in the children's immediate, trusted community. Nonmatriarchal women interacting productively with men of strong character didn't need to be in the home, as long as they were in the children's immediate, trusted community. Therefore, concluded Tom, it was neither stimulation nor male teachers CDGM most needed, but opportunities for children to see virile male members of *their* communities functioning in significant roles, and women from *their* communities working creatively instead of dominatingly with these men. Because children had so much invested in their community, they would admire and identify with these "new" kinds of men and women in the centers in the same way that they would have admired and identified with them had they been in their homes instead. Children's personal aspirations would rise. However, these adults couldn't be from the school system: That's not part of the child's extended family. The effect would be lost. We would take education out of isolation, and experiment with it in a context.

It was Tom's plan that children would attend CDGM schools in their own community. This was a big issue in rural areas having far away consolidated schools. Children would go to a school their families were building, even if in shabbier facilities. They would feel the excitement and pride of their parents. We hoped not to reproduce the public school situation so aptly described by this Sharkey County subsistence farmer: "They leaves me out; so I stays out, all the way out. They got no use fer me cause they says I ain't got sense. I got no use fer them, neither, cause they ain't got sense enough to treat peoples human."

Children would go to people selected from their families by committee members elected by their families, where they would find reinforcement of the potential and worth of their people. CDGM children wouldn't leave homes in which parents had no opportunity for planning about the lives of their children, and no opportunities to learn and grow themselves; and go to "ideal" classrooms; and return to homes where they found parents as excluded as ever from the educational process. Instead, CDGM children would go to less "ideal" classrooms in which their parents were working out educational philosophies and techniques appropriate for changing their total lives. They would return to homes where families were involved to the core in planning, learning, growing. *The classroom would be less ideal, but the climate would be an educator's dream.*

It's the consensus of articulate spokesmen from among the poor, as well as of other "poverty experts" and "education experts" everywhere, that the American system of education at all levels has somehow thus far not been able to effectively educate most poor people, especially Negroes. Negroes often drop out of educational institutions in a vague cloud of embarrassed failure feelings; or in disgust and hostility; or they docilely allow themselves to be "passed along" in the system, learning nothing of meaning to them, and learning a lot about "faking it"; or they adapt themselves to another man's values and come out doing well in his world, abandoning their own, which cries for their leadership.

Those who fade out of school before they are finished often feel mildly ashamed and confused, because they have failed at something in which there's no clear reason why they should succeed, and yet there is every manner of harsh indication that they should want to succeed. People know, of course, that education is the road out of poverty, and therefore, out of political and social helplessness. But they also know that it's frequently a dead-end road, leading nowhere, while demanding a high toll. They see their friends yielding to pressures to turn against their origins, their language, their values, their habits, their ability to think, their right to act in accordance with their beliefs, and toppling off the assembly line of the educational system perfect "white men's niggers."

These people are now middle-class Negroes, who sneer at old friends and keep clean of them, or maybe poor niggers, because after all is said and done, after all the sacrifice of soul, society, especially in Mississippi, still doesn't usually permit escape. There are no jobs. There is no social acceptance. Black people are still niggers, not men for themselves. So people are understandably ambivalent about education. They know it's the only possible way out, but they know that more often than not it is not a way out.

Therefore, when these deceived people become parents, they pay lip service to the value of education. They wish they could have faith in it. There's nothing else, but God, in which to have faith. They're expected to believe in education, and are skilled at doing what's expected. But simultaneously they convey to their children a great and entirely realistic distrust of education and teachers; an uncertainty. Because, though it may be Negro teachers and principals with whom they come in contact, the teachers and principals are products of the castrating education they endured. They are the people whom the system succeeded in forcing to renounce and deny their background and their right to work openly for a future featuring potency.

Recently there has been a tremendous focus of interest from many disciplines on this problem of Negro lack of success in school. Much exciting and promising work is being done by researchers and innovative educators. They are experimenting with how children learn, training them in listening and perceiving, creating more appropriate learning materials, machines, and gadgets, developing enrichment curricula for minority groups and nonmiddle-class groups, strengthening self-image, intervening early, working with parents, perfecting "reward" systems, emphasizing language growth, and training teachers to work with "the disadvantaged." Almost everything of an experimental nature that's being done concerning this problem revolves around processes, procedures, and programs for the classroom—*in* the classroom—in a prefabricated system; including how to interest parents. Ours was an experiment in reversing the usual Head Start procedure in an effort to reach Head Start's goal. Instead of beginning with classroom quality and atttempting to work toward "involving" parents and the community, we were going to try beginning with parents and the community—and then work toward quality in the classroom.

CDGM's "revolutionary" educational belief was that while all the other avenues of exploration are critical, they all fit into stage two of "solving the problem." Stage one of solving the problem is to direct experimental work at the process through which, and the people through whom, the classroom and the system even come into existence. As a lady from Laurel explained, "It ain't gonna get you there no quicker no matter how beautiful you drives if you is drivin' in the wrong direction. Better jes go back and start all over, or you kin talk all day 'bout the little things and you ain't never gonna get no place you wants to go."

We wanted to see if poor people and minority groups could develop their own educational systems and classrooms. We guessed they needed their own elected school boards, which would hire their brands of specialists and supervisors who would specialize and supervise according to *their* goals, exactly as middle-class people and the majority group now do. Until this had happened, we felt it mattered relatively little what kinds of ultrasubtle and superaccurate, sophisticated things went on in the classroom. These come later, these come in stage two, and at that time are vitally important. But until their school system reflected them as much as the middle-class school system reflects the middle-class, we thought poor people would consciously or unconsciously sabotage many of the gains that we made for them in our ivory tower. In this thought as in so many others, history soon testified to Tom's sensitivity.

The public school system "works" and is so hard to change because it comes out of the middle-class, is for the middle-class, and it suits the middle-class. This is true from kindergarten to college. It does not suit the poor. But they cannot change it much because it is entrenched in the satisfaction of those to whom it "belongs." Since the poor don't like the educational situation, and cannot affect it, they leave it alone.

The poor may not be "qualified" to design and staff a school system, but then of course the middle-class isn't qualified either. Seldom is a person who is brilliantly distinguished in a field taught in the schools, or is a talented and renowned educator elected to a local school board. Middle-class citizens who haven't the least idea how to teach or what is worth teaching from any particular field of knowledge or how education has varied historically and internationally, or about the lives of those for whom they plan, elect each other to school boards. They control. It doesn't seem odd to us that they, knowing nothing of education and still less about creating new kinds of dynamic education based on research and invention, should control. We don't think it strange that they, eminently prepared to conform to the status quo and to pass it down as sanctified "heritage," rather than individuals who are gifted creative thinkers and could possibly begin to deal with the problems confronting education today, should control. We feel that these people are "qualified" as superintendents, principals, teachers, specialists, and supervisors because they *do* have the qualifications that really matter to the middle-class public: They will use their judgment in hiring people who will look out for their interests and promote their values; they will see to it that no great changes occur which might seriously jeopardize their children's future occupational, social, economic, political, psychological, and status level; and they will move slowly and cautiously.

The poor, if they ran schools for their children, would they do the same thing? Would they use their judgment in hiring people who would look out for their interests and promote their values (which might be the same as the values of the middle-class or might be less superficial)? Would they see to it that very great changes were made which might seriously enhance their children's future chances economically, occupationally, socially, politically, psychologically, and in status terms? We guessed *yes*. We would experiment.

CHAPTER 9

BEGINNING TO BLEND DIVERSE INGREDIENTS ON LOCATION

(Holly Springs, Marshall County)

ANOTHER DAY, BEFORE we began center operation, Diane Feeley, the Central Staff nursery school teacher with a Montessori-Deutsch background, and I drove four and a half night hours "after work" up to Marshall County at the top of the state, just under Tennessee. We wanted to visit centers the next day. Due to the stimulus of two district co-coordinators in that remote part of the state, four centers had been organized and had started running four weeks before CDGM Orientation—completely on their own. "Allowing" for irregularity and individuality produced astonishing confusion, but also remarkable initiative. Tom Levin preferred to take a risk and gamble on initiative, since that, more than orderly regulations, has been the missing ingredient in poor communities. Diane went to learn at two centers, and I went off with the car to see the other two.

Many of our centers were not exactly a snap to find the first time. It was dangerous to ask about them in the white community, and difficult to get anywhere asking in the Negro community. I did find the Credit Union in Holly Springs, which was a gathering point and crossroads for CDGM staff in the county. Someone told me to "go on up number 7, then you'll get to town and go on a gravel road one or two miles and there'll be a white church on your left." I went up the road. It was a narrow blacktop running ribbonlike through flat, wooded country bathed in a billow of serenely swooping ground cover.

After many miles, I turned off on a still smaller blacktop, which ended in a hollow at a railroad track. A thin thread of a single-track public dirt road went winding peacefully through the lush summer greenery. Most of the time there was not a sign of human beings or their buildings. Every few miles I passed an 8-by-10-foot "house" with a sagging, rusted, hole-ridden tin roof and a few chairs on the tilting porch. The porches held either very young or very old inhabitants who were beginning or ending lives of waiting, in which there would be little more than this porch sitting to do. The houses were set way back from the road in fields that reached beyond the eye. It was desolately beautiful. I thought how this rural Mississippi tranquility contrasted with racial Mississippi warfare.

After many more miles I came to a battered once-white church. The glass was out of the windows, and the door was tied with a string. It had a vacant, gaping look, and appeared quite deserted. But so does much of occupied Negro Mississippi—so did many of our centers in the beginning. I pulled the car into a rutted lane of unkempt weeds and mud holes. I got out, waded through tall field grasses, wondered warily as to the whereabouts of the rattlesnakes and water moccasins which thrive in Mississippi, and stood on tip-toe to peep and peer into a high window. This didn't seem to be a Head Start center.

I drove on to a tattered shack and asked an ancient old man if he knew where the Child Development Group had its program for little kids. The man appeared bewildered. I asked if he knew where there was a kindergarten for the summer in a church. He answered that he did not, in that mumbly dialect, liberally sprinkled with many murmured "ma'ms," that visitors claim not to be able to understand, but which is very constant, and can be linguistically unlocked, decoded as it were, by a simple flick of the ear. I asked if he knew where colored people had made themselves a baby school. Oh, yes, he stood, beamed, he became animated. He gave me directions.

I learned, after a number of similar encounters, that doing things *very* locally, instead of conveniently centrally, and that forever getting lost in the backwoods, was terribly important for professional desk staff's concept development. We tended to fret over methods of concept development for children, and neglect our own. Every time I got lost, my understanding of people's environment got a thin layer deeper. I also learned that many Negroes didn't realize what we were asking for when we asked directions. They expected we were asking for something white. When we referred to Head Start as "the school Negroes are making for themselves," it quickly fell into a realm of interest to them, and they knew where it was—unless they were acting cleverly stupid and intentionally giving wrong directions to mislead us, like a bird protects her nest by fluttering in false directions, so that we who were white, and could therefore have only bad intentions, would not find their private world.

In this case, the directions were accurate, but I failed to recognize one caving-in unpainted building as "town," a landmark the man had mentioned. I went scuttling off another wrong ten miles on a wider mud road. By this time I was so coated with dust I was a healthy American Indian color. I had to ask at several more sharecropper shacks before I found a white, one-room, mason block, plank floored CME church;

the Head Start center. The bottom panel of each window had been painted a vivid teel blue. The panels were the gayest, liveliest things I'd seen all day. No other building could be seen in any direction. Just red erosion and scrub greenery with kudzu swarming its huge leaves and tough vines up every tree and bush and over stretches of scruffy dust flats. There weren't even telephone poles. The nearest phone to this CDGM center was three miles away. The staff used to have "telephone drills." They practiced simultaneously running the three miles to various phones, just in case an emergency should arise.

That afternoon Mr. Quintell Gipson, a Holly Springs Negro high school teacher, who was the resourceful resource teacher at this Hudsonville center, wrote a piece for the first issue of the newsletter, which was distributed at the Mount Beulah Orientation.

I felt that one of the most useful services I could render this first summer as a children's program coordinator would be to put out a newsletter concerned with the children's program. For community people it would have two purposes. The first would be to coordinate and to cross-pollinate from center to center by requesting local or nonlocal in-center staff to write or dictate special things that could be of practical use or inspirational value to other centers. This way, people who were so inclined could have access to new ideas. They could learn from peers instead of from prescriptions. Resourcefulness would be reinforced. Good ideas separated by huge distances could be spread and shared. There would be no danger of overawed people being intimidated by professionalism, for these were, after all, only the enthusiastic reports of their fellows in far-flung spots. Besides, they could always throw the newsletter away, disregarding its contents.

The second purpose of the newsletter for community readers was to create a vehicle for stimulating discussion of preschool and Head Start program standards for children among center staffs. There *were* standards, after all, and although CDGM didn't want to ram them down the throats of newly sprouting teachers, some of us thought it both desirable and honest to share knowledge of what OEO and early childhood experts had in mind as a general framework for further local initiative elaboration. Again, it was assumed that readers opposed to information and exchange of ideas would throw the newsletter away, but it would be an attempt to clarify and share with those who wanted to be "on the in," and with those wishing to expand their educational thinking.

I had a third *non*community purpose in mind for the newsletter, too. It was urgently important to build national interest in CDGM, among people in related professions, Northern liberals, foundation and government officials, congressmen and senators, etc. We would need public support to help us promote funding for future programs. We would need, also, to disseminate some of our exciting, "successful," new-style community action and Head Start learnings. Joan Bowman, the project historian, was sending out press releases and general information to a large mailing list. The newsletter and other papers Tom Levin and I wrote were sent to another mailing list of over two thousand names, and were our major out-of-state printed effort at "winning friends and influencing people," until the second grant in the spring of 1966, nearly a year later.

Since participatory democracy in CDGM meant not only the inclusion of the poor in sophisticated areas of work, but also the inclusion of the professionals in simple areas of work, and I thus had no secretary, I gathered material, edited, typed, collated, enveloped, and addressed five issues of the newsletter, each about twenty pages in length. These were printed by our printing project the first summer, all in all about 2,500 copies of each issue. I got tired of the taste of glue, but the effort paid off in full in the fall when we sorely needed friends.

The reasons for the newsletter were more elaborate than its content. The first issue invites resourcefulness in the use of available materials, too. There is a page titled: "LIST OF COMMON ITEMS WHICH THOSE OF YOU WHO WILL BE AT HOME DURING ORIENTATION MIGHT FIND OF USE IN YOUR CENTERS: boxes of all sizes, such as shoe boxes, cartons, crates, cigar boxes, cardboard, bottle caps. . . .

Mr. Gipson's piece described what his Child Development center *had already done* before CDGM officially opened: while Central Staff was still in the midst of considerable pre-opening administrative chaos:

HUDSONVILLE'S HEAD-START CENTER

A REPORT WRITTEN BY THE
HUDSONVILLE CENTER STAFF

(Quintell Gipson)

On the first day, the center opened with eighteen children and a staff of nine in a one room rural church filled with benches. Now we have forty-seven children divided into three groups, four, five, and six year olds, with three separate play areas, sets of pre-school toys, tables and chairs, charts and pictures on the walls, and a brightly colored playground.

On the first day, many of the children were very upset, and some of them cried for their parents, but now many of them enjoy the Center so well that they forget to go home. They run to the car that picks them up in the morning.

We believe we are on our way to meeting our goal, which is primarily to prepare the children for school.

Our program for a day begins with opening attendance circles where we sing, do exercises, talk, and tell stories. Then after a milk break and a trip to the bathroom, the children play on the outside playground and do circle games. After this, *the children choose the toys they wish to play with:* puzzles, trains, clay, tinker toys, and others. *The staff talks with them and helps them play.* Next there is an arts and crafts period. The children paint, make things, draw, or crayon. Since there are three groups and our space is small we take turns doing these activities. Then all three groups clean up and have a hot lunch together. After lunch we have a quiet period. The four year olds sleep on blankets under the trees outside. The five and six year olds play quiet games, look at books, and rest on their quilts on the floor of their corner. This is a usual day at Hudsonville Center.

We have taken one field trip to Holly Springs on a big blue bus and visited both the post office and the fire station. We are planning another trip for next week to the zoo in Memphis.

Problems and how we solved or tried to solve them:

1. The place for the Center was gotten by coordinators Shelby and Bobby. They contacted the Deacons of the church for us. We use the benches for tables until we go to our own tables. The benches were also used to divide the church into sections.

2. Transportation was our greatest problem. We had to use makeshift transportation for the first week. Even then we had too many routes for the amount of money that was available. After discussing the problem with the community and the drivers, the difficulty was overcome by one of the drivers volunteering to drive two routes for the same rate. We had competition from the County that had buses and well established transportation. This factor took many of our students. *Transportation can mean the difference between success and defeat.*

3. Food is another critical problem. At the beginning we didn't have any money for food so we had to pay for it out of our pockets and we were reimbursed. For the first week we used milk, fruit, and sandwiches which the children enjoyed. After many proposals, we found a place that the Health Department OKed for us to use to prepare hot food. In this cafe, all our cooks come together and prepare the food. Each center has three gallon pots that the food is cooked in. The food is transported hot in these containers to Centers and is served hot. The menu is planned for two weeks. The menu is well balanced. Our cook, Mrs. Jeffries, transports the food, too. Each person that works with the food must have a health card. Mrs. Modena Malone is in charge of the cooking. Our food is ordered and paid for by invoice. Milk is given twice a day.

4. The water has to be chlorinated, so we transport it from Holly Springs.

5. Our playground was made by all of the community. Mr. William H. Murle built the sandbox. Mr. Bryson brought a big load of sand for it. Mrs. Young brought a tire and a barrel which we painted and use for a swing and a rolling barrel. Mr. Dortch painted Tarzan ropes. Miss Jordon and Mr. A. Gipson painted the pull-up bars. These bars were the bottoms of picnic tables. Mr. Jordon painted the big wire spool which the children use to pull, roll, jump off of and sit on. Miss Levine painted the sandbox and many other things too. Mr. Q. Gipson painted the Clorox bottles and made a "Mobile sign" to attract attention. Miss Bean, Miss Dortch, Miss Jordon made the sign for our school. We feel that every school should have a sign. Mr. W. C. Rainey cut the grass off the playground. Mr. T. C. Young, Jim Dortch, and S. P. Gipson helped dig the hole for the outhouse. Mr. Briggs supervised some of the work. There were many others who helped to make our playground a place that children love.

6. Inside facilities were bought and made by people of the community. Miss Bean made the supply boxes. Miss Levine painted crates to store the toys and books in. Mrs. Woodson helped with the decoration. Mrs. Saunders has been very helpful in making things, painting, and bringing needed materials. Mr. Russel donated a long table to our Center. *The whole community helped.*

7. We have a P.T.A. meeting every other Thursday night and at the last meeting forty-five persons were present. *All of the parents who have been talked to would like to see the program continue. But most of all the little children would like to see it continue. We are ready to continue.*

8. Health is a very critical point. Our Center is kept as clean as possible. We believe that our Center is a very healthy place.[17]

This work was accomplished by the poor Negro communities in spite of the white middle-class community. In Marshall County, for example, there were no whites offering better facilities or offering to help dig outhouse pits. The Negro "library" was several shelves of books, accessible only a few hours a week, and seemingly a thousand miles from scattered rural families without transportation. Only two or three books in it were ideal for Head Start children anyway. Since the "library" was walk-in closet size in the basement of a church, we were not able to consider recommended trips there. Town efforts to help relieve this shortage of reading material included jailing COFO workers the summer before for bringing in truckloads of books. Some of these "inflammatory" books, I saw for myself, were high school chemistry texts dated 1935. Nevertheless, workers were forced to descend a ladder into the dark underground pit which serves as the Holly Springs jail and kept there for hours to pay for their treasonous interest in books. This is also the town where the superintendent of schools said, the year before, that he would burn down the school if a meeting to "enlighten" Negroes with information on federal programs was held in it. Police surrounded the school.

It was interesting and significant that whenever we asked a community to report about itself, many individual names of poor people were mentioned, alongside their contributions of services and goods. One of the reasons that CDGM streaked like a flash of flame from nothing to national recognition was that it was a program of *individuals,* not of "the teachers," "the parents," and "the administration."

My perspective contrasted with Mr. Gipson's. Notes from that June 23, 1965, visit to this center say, in part: "Very pleasant, relaxed, laissez-faire, gentle, vague, silent program . . . a far cry from any nursery school of good standing, and a farther cry from anything these children have ever known, or ever will if we wait for the whites or the Northerners. . . . If the Center closed tomorrow it would have been a raging success for what it has already done: 3 cartons of milk, a huge man-size daily

[17] CDGM *Newsletter,* No. 1.

dinner, some toys, some books, informal social experiences with other children for children who live literally miles apart. . . . I hear the critical comments of the experts, but where are they? I don't see them in the kudzu vines, they'll have to let us do the best we can. . . . How artificial it would be to "plant" an ideal nursery school here, plunk, in this other worldly world. It would be like jabbing one cut flower in the mud and taking pride in having cultivated a thriving garden. Maybe they will work toward something that challenges children as *they* would be challenged. That lets children have important jobs and make important decisions as *they* would do. That works, tediously, to help children interact democratically, as they struggle to understand democracy for themselves. If so, it will be invaluable when it gets closer to done . . . it will be rooted in sturdy reality, with soils fertilized and ploughed and killing weeds hacked away by the back-breaking, heart-breaking efforts of the people. . . . Any suggestion Program makes should be in this context. Perhaps we could talk to the staff about concentrating on individual children . . . there is a tendency to "serve out" activities and then either to stand gazing between children or to do housework . . . tendency to move children by arm or herd them en masse instead of to talk with them about everything . . . more personal contact might be a reasonable thing to work on. . . . But it would be better to do nothing than to spoil this lovely thing, if that should be the choice. . . . I don't see that it *is* the choice. Teachers, enough of them, seem terribly eager to try, to think."

Mrs. Rebecca Myers, director of CDGM's professional staff and a life-long supervisor of special education in the Philadelphia, Pennsylvania, public schools wrote in early July of the other Marshall County centers (Newell Chapel at Victoria, and Mount Peel at Chulahoma, each of which had approximately eighty-five children): "These Centers were all very clean, brightly decorated, work of children dated and displayed. The climate was warm, relaxed, friendly. Resource Teachers prepared materials, worked with the children that are special cases, held staff meetings, and in general give the trainees and aides a feeling of support if needed. Teachers seem well informed with a deep feeling for humanity. . . . The growth of the trainees is great. Not only do they run these centers but have developed a sense of security that they can tell the aides and teachers what they need to be done. The parents show a deep sense of concern and attend P.T.A. meetings regularly. . . . Program Schedules: well planned, allowing for short attention span, free expression, creativity, directed and indirected work."

And during the same week the director of the psychological counseling staff, a New York psychologist of note, wrote, "The Center at Mount Peel was seen as functioning in a creative fashion. The children were given every opportunity for spontaneous expression but at the same time there was structure and limits were set. There was generally a fluid but nevertheless organized atmosphere. Without directly supervising the children the teachers were always available when their help was needed."

We didn't make written reports as a form of spy system related to promoting and firing. Local committees of poor people held these powers, anyway, not Central Staff. It was as a form of "written photography," so we could see the baby giant grow, and see what he looked like. It was a form of gathering data from many people's points of view, so we could figure out a way to measure—so we could plan.

During this visit to Holly Springs I also visited several Head Start centers run by county officials in public school classrooms. I did this in as many communities as I could, where CDGM and the county both operated. I wanted to know our competition, and also to do a little liaison work with the frightened "enemy." In Holly Springs the Negro supervisory staff was very, very nice to me. They were typical "black bourgeoisie," neither *poor* black nor Northern intellectual, nor professional early educators. They ran watered-down versions of Mississippi first grade. I saw staring immobile children, sitting at desks with their hands folded. They sat thus for all the hours I visited. I saw formal Negro public school teachers sitting at desks looking busy with record-keeping. I saw Negro mothers sitting in classroom corners ready to jump up when chores and errands were requested by the teachers. The rooms were completely empty except for an array of brand new Little Golden Books arranged attractively on window sills high above the children's reach. They told me they did not want the children to "mess up" the books. They said that the parents had not been in yet, but that they were "planning a program" soon. I was impressed by the antiseptic appearance of the buildings. We could not claim to have that in our centers.

There are other Central Staff notes, reminding us that CDGM professional staff always expected to be versatile: "Picked up Ken Scudder, excellent Resource Teacher from Milwaukee and COFO. On way to Newell, stopped at Miss Modena's to pick up heavy cases of day's milk for children. Then stopped at a teacher's house to carry her out to Center, but she had left on children's bus. (Center unique! Has bus!) Arrived half hour later at Center in rurals. Heard that bus had broken down somewhere along road. I was sent out like a lifeboat to find it along a ten mile route, and to retrieve the hot, restless children. Found them all standing at edge of road eating popsicles share-cropper teachers had trudged down road and bought for them with the only nonfarm income they've ever received. Which they haven't yet. Payroll is late."

Individual out-of-state resource teachers, as well as local poor people and several local teachers, were making important contributions, too. They did this in as many ways as there were out-of-state resource teachers, because their role had intentionally not been defined narrowly. Miss Levine, mentioned in passing in Mr. Gipson's report of the Hudsonville center, was a social work student from New York. As can be sensed from references to her among references to many other people, she didn't dominate the staff. Mr. Gipson was the center leader, and Miss Levine did her share quietly and well by teaching one unit of children in the one-room church with many other teachers and units, where all could see, hear, and pick up or not pick up any parts of her "method" that made sense to them.

At Mount Peel Mrs. Patricia Scudder, an artist, and Miss Phyllis McNeil, a nursery school teacher from the North who later went on to Bank Street College for further nursery education training, taught and planned actively along with the others. At Newell Chapel, Miss Doris Derby, a first-grade teacher from Yonkers, acted as center director, and took a lead role in organizing a fine program. After Newell Chapel closed late in the summer, Doris spent two weeks at the Second Pilgrim's Rest Center in Holmes County. She is the visiting teacher in CDGM's film *Chance for Change*. She also visited several other centers for short spells. A function of the two children's program coordinators, me and Jeannine, was to spot the best human resources we had, local or otherwise, and arrange with centers having difficulty functioning productively for these booster resources to work for a few days with them.

Miss Doris Copek, a physical education teacher from a college in the Midwest, used herself at the Ashbury center in quite a different way: She worked on specific aspects of the program, such as physical education and conversational development. Doris wrote these teaching episodes so we could share them with far-away centers through the newsletter:

AN EXAMPLE OF GETTING THE CHILD TO THINK

(ALSO GOOD PHYSICAL EDUCATION)
(ALSO LANGUAGE DEVELOPMENT)

. . . by Doris Copek
Rust College Child
Development Center

TEACHER: How many ways can you find to go from this tree to that one?
CHILD: Walk.
TEACHER: OK., good, let's all walk to that tree. Let's see how fast we can walk. How else can we get there?
ANOTHER CHILD: Run.
TEACHER: Let's run! Can anyone think of another way?
CHILD: Skip.
(*We skipped. I noticed many skip only on one foot.*)
CHILD: Let's jump!
(*We jumped.*)
CHILD: Hop.
(*We hopped.*)
TEACHER: Now let's all hop on the other foot.
(*This they found more difficult. This should help them learn how to skip with both feet.*)

TEACHER: Any other good ways to get from this tree to that?
(*Soon they were down on all fours.*)

THIS IS NOT JUST "FOOLING AROUND." IT IS ENCOURAGING THE CHILD TO STRETCH HIS MIND AND THINK, AND THINK AGAIN, AND THINK MORE.

Frequently discussion is opened with the question from the teacher (aide, trainee, resource person): "What did you do when you left school yesterday?" At first there were few answers other than, "Nothing." Now they are much freer to talk about what they did. On this particular morning, Patricia answered quickly:

"I made a blackberry pie."
"Where did you get the blackberries?"
"I picked them."
"Did anyone else pick blackberries yesterday?"
"I did." "I did." "I did."
"I like pumpkin pie."
"What is in pumpkin pie?"
"Some flour." "Some salt." "Some milk."
"What makes a pumpkin pie brown?"
"The oven." "When you bake it."
"Don't you put pumpkin in a pumpkin pie?"
"Yes." "I have a pumpkin pie at home."
"Do you remember what we did yesterday that was different from other days?"
"Played."
"Don't we do that every day?"
"Yes."
"Remember we took a walk? What did we see?"
"Leaves. With seeds in them."
"What do you do with seeds?"
"Plant them."
"Then what grows?"
"Flowers."
"What else did we see?"
"Sand."
"What were they doing with the sand?"
"Making mud."
"What kind of mud?"
"Cement."
"What do you do with cement?"
"Make bricks."
"What did the men do with the bricks?"
"Took them up on the new building."
"How did he get up there?"
"That thing that went up."
"What do you call that thing that goes up?"
"A elevator."
(We all worked on the word elevator.)
"What does an elevator do besides go up?"
"Come down."[18]

[18] CDGM *Newsletter,* No. 2.

Sophisticated readers may find these episodes rather trite. They don't reveal exceptional subtlety in teaching, creative experimentation, interpersonal democratic relations, child development theory, or inventiveness in using the beautiful language of the child. We couldn't teach any of these things through a newsletter to a semiliterate group unfamiliar with all of these concepts.

We hoped that the newsletter would give creditability to forms of teaching neither the parent "teachers" nor the public school teachers in our centers had ever been allowed to let creep into the classroom: encouraging children to talk, even if only in a structured conversation, instead of to sit quietly in their places; doing moving activities instead of paper and pencil activities; practicing remembering; offering ideas, even if only one-word ideas; involving teachers *with* the children, looking at them, listening to them, valuing the answers; being physically active, instead of gazing over children's heads from behind a desk; filling the day instead of waiting for it to evaporate. We were trying to tackle a reality: eleven hundred center teachers, almost a thousand of whom had never worked in an educational program, and almost all of whom had neved worked in a nursery school, including the large majority of adaptable but not "trained" resource teachers from out-of-state. There were five people working in the area of children's program on Central Staff, 6,400 children, eighty-four child development centers, and twenty-eight counties.

When children's program workers went to centers we tried to work through demonstration and discussion. The newsletter was clearly a case of tossing sailing seeds in the wind and praying some would land safely, seed side down, in friendly soil. We guessed that we lost 60 percent of what we wrote and probably 40 percent got used. That was a large rate of change for black folks in Mississippi. One of the lively local resource teachers at the other end of the state, in McComb, wrote: "It's great to get the newsletter. Many don't read it. Others read but don't use it. I get many ideas from it on the nature of this new program. The thing I like about it is you can't feel anyone taking your right to plan away from you, with only these few scraps of ideas. It isn't that you never happened to think. I have taught public school for nine years. They tell us everything to do. CDGM just gives general flavorings. I especially liked the game ideas Miss Copek gave last issue. Send more like that!"

As the lady said, many people didn't read it. I used short sentences, clear simple words, and brief ideas, but even at that, the reading level was far too hard. I used pieces the people themselves wrote, in their own exact way of putting it on paper, and spaced the pieces with lots of margin. But even though it came from them, it was difficult to read. Most people couldn't, for all intents and purposes, read.

Delivery was also a problem. I mailed it to each center chairman, each issue, and sent enough copies for every teacher in the center, resource and trainee, and for many parents. But the chairman didn't always get the packet to the center. When the brown envelope *did* get there, it was often two or more weeks late. Frequently it was stuffed on a shelf or under heaps of things on a table, and its usefulness died there. A flyer was stapled to each front page saying in huge magic marker letters: PLEASE READ AND DISCUSS AT YOUR NEXT COMMUNITY MEETING. Many didn't. They had other things on their minds. They didn't have orderly desks and orderly filing systems and orderly minds experienced in planning and paper work. There was also the perpetual matter of hostility and ambivalence toward "they." One lady summed up a pretty general attitude toward everything in these people's experience with print when she said, "Huh! White man's books is full of lies!" Diane and I were very impressed by the great efforts being made by the Holly Springs out-of-staters. They seemed able to introduce educational ideas unheard of by the people, and at the same time, bring out local resources and talents the people never suspected they had. Things I had "known" were true when we were *talking* about centers, I new began to *feel* were true as I *looked* at them. Without Tom's "local responsibility" invention, the children's program would have been a stiffly plastic import; without the new input of ideas about early education, it would have been a dreary repetition of that dismal phenomena in rural Negro Mississippi that sags along under the deceptive flag of education.

The resource teachers from the North also impressed me with their ability to adjust to poverty housing conditions, and to central office's confusion. The four girls, two Negro and two white, shared a little half-built house buried in the Negro section of Holly Springs. They had a landlord who kept promising to finish their kitchen so they could cook, but never did. Other than this, they had little in the way of homemaking gear except pretty burlap curtains, and a steady stream of central and roving CDGM staff visitors who slept on various mattresses on various parts of the crowded floor. We didn't patronize segregated motels, nor did we have the budget to do so had we so chosen. But the main thing was to get to know each other. "Non-working" hours were coordinating hours.

Dr. Marv Hoffman, then a psychology teacher at Tougaloo College and starting a summer job with CDGM, remembers that the whole counseling staff drove up to Holly Springs a week or two after Orientation to see what operating centers were like. He says he "found all the resource teachers sitting glumly on their beds with their heads in their hands muttering that they couldn't possibly keep the centers open a day longer because there was no gas money to get the kids there, no food money, and not enough supplies."

Marshall County's problems with central office services were worse than most, because they began spontaneously before there *was* a functioning central office. But the problems were indicators of similar ones that we were to come up against all around the state.

Marv and "the two Florences," both older Northern lady psychologists who amazed everybody by their cheerful willingness to put up with bug-bitten legs, a shambles of an office at Mount Beulah, thousands of highway miles to cover between testing children, and sleeping on floor mattresses such as those in Holly Springs, spent the night with the girls. Marv recalls that he was exhausted because, while the two Florences stayed at the house agreeing that most CDGM staff members were paranoid from being in Mississippi too long, he and someone else had been chased round and round Holly Springs town square by a carload of "rednecks" and the highway patrol. They finally pretended to leave town, and then circled and dodged back to the house.

After eventually calming down and falling asleep, Marv was awakened in the wee hours by the arrival of the CDGM doctor. Dr. Gerry Rosenfield had just driven across the state from Mount Beulah with armfuls of the fourth version of the medical forms, just sent from OEO. He had to climb gingerly over Marv's mattress to get into the house.

The doctor and those with him were somewhat upset because on the way up they had somehow driven off an embankment and fallen twenty feet into a white man's cotton field. The man wasn't too keen on this integrated interlude, and came after them with a gun, causing them to drive madly through the cotton blossoms to safety. This new group slept fitfully for a few hours on some more mattresses, but soon became guiltily restless about all the work they weren't doing and got up at 3 A.M. to drive six and a half hours to McComb to deliver some more forms, which it was feared, at the rate OEO was revising forms, would be obsolete if not delivered immediately.

Marv was very impressed not only by the doctor's dedication, but also, the next day, by the beautifully painted playgrounds and outhouses he saw at centers, by the good food and pleasant children's programs in their surprising settings, and by some excellent, packed parents' meetings he attended.

He remembers how enthusiastic he felt about the weaving of special projects into the community context of these meetings. Teachers brought out children's artwork and explained it proudly. Everyone sang children's songs. A Movement worker talked about forthcoming ASCS [Agricultural Stabilization and Conservation Service] elections, which were of vital interest to these farming parents. Everybody sang more children's songs and some freedom songs of deep meaning to them. At another meeting Mary Varella of CDGM's reading readiness staff talked with parents and teachers about making their own children's readers from folklore, songs, and experience.

CDGM's chief psychologist, Dr. Halpern, talked of her experiences as a mother and the mothers' experiences as mothers. Howard Croft, a New York CDGM social worker, talked about welfare programs, and all this was mixed in with prayers and songs and community members' discussion and announcements. Marv was amazed at this staff saturation.

Unfortunately, it was a freak situation. Everyone was in the Holly Springs area during those first few weeks to get some experience to use in their dispersed and *under*saturated, scarcely touched districts during the remaining weeks of the brief summer. A note I wrote to Tom later in the month says: "Marshall County is beautifully important, not because it is typical, but because it is a demonstration of more to come in future programs. Your ideas work!"

CHAPTER 10

NEW FORMS FOR AN OLD FIELD?

The psychological counseling project

IN TERMS OF how the psychologists could best use their profession to the project's best advantage, Marv Hoffman was less happy than he was about what CDGM meant to communities. Like everyone else, the psychologists had come to Mississippi not knowing exactly what they would do.

Marv, who had rarely left the Tougaloo College campus during his year in the state, had heard of the germinating project in the spring through Karen Shillington. He had thought it sounded interesting. In June he had found himself in New York for other reasons. He had gone to one of Tom Levin's recruiting-orienting sessions. When he asked what his job would be if he joined CDGM, Tom had said, "I don't know. We'll have to get down there and see how we can use professional skills in some new kind of way with community workers and in a freedom school setting."

The psychologists had come through Orientation with the same feeling of awe and bewilderment that everyone remembers, and with a dim plan of skipping around the state doing testing and referrals of children. But now, as they visited Marshall County centers, trying to spot children with severe problems and do something constructive about them, things began to look overwhelming.

They found some extremely withdrawn children sitting in the background at centers, a schizophrenic child, some children who seemed desperately in need of contact and kept climbing all over the visitors, some overaggressive acting-out children, and a little Mongoloid boy of nine. Our centers usually had a number of retarded children who were older than preschool age, because there are no special schools for them in the state. Their alternative was to stay home as they always have. They seemed to benefit a great deal from CDGM.

Marv went to the Mongoloid child's home after center hours to test him. The home was a barren, desolate place. A large family sat around intently watching the testing. They practically applauded when the child successfully completed the simplest three-year level tasks, and made excuses for him when he failed.

In contrast to the protective pride the family showed toward the little boy, Marv thought of Whitfield, the state mental institution he had visited with his college students the previous month. At Whitfield there were 4,400 patients, 27 nurses, and 4 part-time psychiatrists. There was drug therapy, but no psychotherapy. The grounds were beautiful and immaculate, and the patients were strictly segregated. The white patients wore their own clothes, the Negro patients wore prisonlike uniforms.

It seemed impossible for a handful of scorned CDGM psychologists to revamp the entire power structure's provisions for mental care in a state in a few weeks. It seemed pointless to test children when nothing could be done about the results. So Marv recommended that the child remain in his CDGM setting. What was done to help the child was what is generally donc in Mississippi with the special problems of Negro children: nothing. Marv wrote a report recommending that the counseling staff concentrate on working with teachers, and in occasional cases, with parents.

He was distressed by one psychologists's desire to repeat the Kenneth Clark doll test (a tool to discern children's social attitudes), which he felt represented a sloppy rehashing of something already well done, instead of the new, carefully conceived and controlled productive research which he felt should be done, but couldn't be done in our crash program.

He was equally distressed by another member of the team, who he described as "a perfect New York Jewish lady liberal . . . . a big talker with no sensitivity, who analyzed everything in psychological jargon and didn't understand anything outside the clinic. . . . She kept talking about sibling rivalry, concept formation, and rejecting mothers, when the problems are economics, politics, race, social psychology, and lack of a plentiful number of a new kind of community-oriented psychologists."

He was also unimpressed by the fourth member of the team, a white Mississippian willing to work with us, at least, but who "always seemed to be driving up eagerly in his Cadillac, looking like an overblown insurance salesman and inquiring about good motels."

The fifth member of the psychological counseling project staff was the only one who Marv thought was very useful to CDGM, "probably because he was only a student and was trying to learn something."

There were five psychologists and five CDGM districts in the state, so they agreed to work one per district for the rest of the summer. This meant that a psychologist could visit each center approximately twice.

Marv says: "I wasn't aware that this was a continuing program. I wasn't in the 'in group.' I kept thinking, 'Only three weeks left, and this or that isn't done. Those staff meetings at Mount Beulah were horrors!

Big uproars over minor matters! Endless votes, countervotes, everyone chewing everyone else out about letting the communities down. And I remember those two junior accountants sitting on beds in their bedroom-office, desperately punching adding-machine buttons and wildly trying to invent a system for keeping out the constant hordes of paycheck malcontents. I didn't begin to see a way clear to straightening out the muddle of CDGM, and I felt I had a long-term commitment in Mississippi. Other things seemed more meaningful to me. I wanted to find a niche for myself doing something manageable. I had gotten interested in the community problems around the Tougaloo center. After three weeks I quit to work as a volunteer in that center and in several Canton centers."

The young man with humility whom Marv admired also left in the middle of the summer.

The three psychologists who were left went to work amidst administrative hardships and impossibilities. One of them said, "It's fine to be critical, but unless you plan to stick around to help, criticism is more self-righteous and self-ventilating than productive. Sure we 'should do that' and we 'should do this.' The question is, 'what *can* we do'? And who has the stamina and stomach to stick around and do it?"

I think without exception those who followed the psychological project were disappointed that it didn't come up with some creative experiments, or at least creative suggestions for the future. However, Dr. Halpern, director of the counseling project, did something that all our angry internal criticizers rarely did. She surveyed the scene, made a manageable plan, and carried it out, as her contribution to the total task.

One California member of the first summer's staff, when asked to consider in retrospect the major Central Staff factions he remembered from that period, replied, "those who attacked *each other,* and those who attacked *the problems.* There were thirty-five of the former, and five or six of the latter."

A psychiatrist who observed the project said, "A project like this will always attract scores of people who can't perform. So to save face, they naturally have to castrate the few who *do* perform. If they 'prove' that the capable ones aren't performing either, they come out of the fray feeling more adequate."

At the end of the summer Dr. Halpern submitted a report describing the activities of the counseling staff. Where the emphasis was placed depended on the nature and needs of the community, and on the special skill of the counselor working in a given district. In several districts, observation, testing, and discussion with Center Staff was the typical technique used. In others, a member of the psychology team talked with individual parents or groups of them.

Dr. Halpern reported that the majority of children referred to the counseling service suffered from serious lack of emotional satisfaction, as well as from severe economic and cultural deprivation. Of those children referred as retarded or deviant, most reacted to their feelings of deprivation by withdrawing and becoming depressed. As they were unable to involve themselves with others or to respond to the stimulation offered by the center, social and intellectual development was hampered. Others relied on unrealistic fantasies and aggressive acting-out behavior to cope with their feelings.

Dr. Halpern's team found that the children referred as retarded showed a greater tendency to act out sexual preoccupations. The team found that the majority of *all* CDGM children showed verbal retardation in contrast to relatively good ability in manual and motor areas. The psychologists "examined" most of the "deviant" children, and urged center staff to give depressed children as much individual attention and mothering as possible. They found that some children markedly improved in their attitudes toward the whole center situation after half an hour with a psychologist.

Dr. Halpern then gave the names of individual poor people in three parts of the state whom she felt had unusual wisdom, intelligence, interest, ability to work well with fellow community members, and common sense about children. She also gave a brief report on each child examined, including rough diagnosis and action taken or recommended.

In retrospect we saw, a year and a half later, that many of these children improved considerably in health and happiness. This was doubtless due to the discussions the counseling staff had with the adults surrounding each child; discussions which aroused hope and unlocked alternatives for adults unsatisfied with the way their handling had worked; discussions which reduced guilt and offered reassurance to adults who felt that they were at fault. The number of children thus helped was important in itself, but more important was the discovery that so little professional time at such a superficial level can make so much difference in apparently deadlocked situations.

A twelve-dollar-a-week maid in Gulfport, newly a trainee in a CDGM center, said, "I don't remember the lady's name, but she was from Edwards. She was the smartest lady I ever met because she seemed to know things about my child *I* never thought of, and she hadn't never seen him before, and yet when she asked me if this could be something or the other might be the matter, I could tell like lightening she had the right thought. She didn't *tell* me anything, she just kept wondering with me for a while, and ever since then it's been working better with him."

Community staff members, district staff members, and Central Staff members alike were each encouraged by Tom Levin in his anarchic administrative system to develop our own jobs as we saw what the many strands of need and talent available were, and as we saw them in new relations to one another in the total context of rural Negro Mississippi.

My job was to act as one of the two program coordinators. Tom had told me much the same thing that he had told Marv Hoffman regarding what my duties would be if I stopped being the senior program analyst for the Southeast Region of Head Start at OEO and came to CDGM. "You and Jeannine will coordinate whatever needs to be coordinated—the children's program, teachers, plans for the future about program and teachers. We'll have all these separate projects coming in and the thing will need to be coordinated. We'll know by the middle of the summer."

What the phrase "program coordinator" meant to Tom kept shifting in a manner which didn't dismay him at all. He had planned and predicted this kind of role experimentation and emergence over and over again from the beginning. Tom called it "creative administration." Marian Wright, our lawyer and a member of the board of directors, called it "chaotic administration." It drove Jeannine and me mad.

We thought we were to coordinate the *children's program.* We knew we were expected to study and keep track of strengths and weaknesses in the children's program, *i.e.*, in the teaching and in the coming together of all the splintered special projects coming at the children. We knew we were responsible for this area to Tom, the CDGM board of directors, and OEO Head Start. We knew we were responsible, since this was only a summer short-term trial run, for developing the information we gathered into a creative solution plan for the future. We knew that coordinating the children's program would involve making supply choices, knowing the general daily program in each center, gathering data on which personnel would still be available to continue the program in the fall, pulling together the reading readiness, equipment making, living arts, and other projects affecting the children directly. We knew that we were responsible for getting across minimum Head Start program requirements to the community teachers, and planning for much deeper teacher development in the fall, based on our summer's learnings.

We had immediately discovered that Tom meant, also, when he said "program coordinators," that we would coordinate (design, recruit, write, invite, duplicate, implement, teach much of) the *orientation program* for eight hundred people. This we had done, with more surprise than skill. It seemed relevant, as orientation was about the children's program.

We quickly learned, Jeannine and I, that "program coordination" required us to take on the responsibilities left undone by other staff members who had "chosen" duties which removed them from the areas that rough preplanning had tentatively projected for them. For example, as director of community staff, we thought Frank Smith and his department would help local committees with hiring problems and judgment in guiding teachers. Since he didn't, Jeannine and I had a lot of work of this kind. We met and talked with many committees and community meetings.

We thought Joan Bowman, project historian, would be collecting and keeping reports, but by this time she had decided the medical project was desperately short-handed and very important, and had gone into the field leaving the recording untended. There would be no organized record of this extravagant ideological experiment.

We thought that the director of professional staff, Mrs. Rebecca Myers, would be responsible for the problems and growth of the in-state and out-of-state resource teachers, but instead she visited *every single one of the eighty-four widely spread centers,* a feat of no mean proportions, and was a marvelous whirlwind motivator. But no one was working with the resource teachers to help them release or research resources. Jeannine and I tried to pitch into the gap, but did not have time to succeed. I remember saying that I thought that Tom and Mrs. Myers should work out this problem. Tom's answer was a perfect example of his "staff-management" philosophy, which made CDGM what it is, and Marian Wright furious. He replied, "Why? Mrs. Myers is an instant abrupt inspiration to community teachers. She has the personality and the skin color to get away with violent appreciation and criticism. You are a compulsive creative planner. You have a vision of the over-all picture and the ability to invent. Besides, you're the wrong color. Why should I call her out of the field to fulfill some preconceived notion of "director of professional staff," when she's great at what she's doing? It's too late to do much about *present* resource teachers anyway, and you can plan for *future* professional teaching staff."

And finally, after we had been operating for two or three weeks, when the field confusion became clear, the job of the program coordinators, Tom assumed, was to coordinate *all the services and subjects affecting the children.* In other words, medical services, social services, psychological services, etc., in so far as they touched the children and teachers. This was, in fact, every content area! Everything in CDGM except the many business, administrative, and technical support services.

Jeannine and I pestered Tom for a job definition. The more we tried to pin him down, the more he tore into us. He told us he didn't care about job *definitions,* he cared about jobs *done.* We staunchly maintained that we couldn't tell if we were doing a job, shirking a job, or doing somebody *else's* job in an encroaching way unless he gave us a clue to boundaries and expectations. He kept tormenting us and making us feel uncomfortably rigid. We cried a lot, and argued. He would say, "If it hasn't been done, and no one's doing it, do it. You've had lots of experience in early education, administering big projects, grant programs, and innovational educational planning: If you think it should be done, do it, damn it."

We thought this was flattering, but very undemocratic. Where were the community people? Where were the other Central Staff people? Tom maintained that it wasn't the least bit undemocratic to develop an impromptu "data bank." We weren't deciding anything, or even doing anything. We were just coordinating and collecting from this ocean of information. He felt that while much of the staff was busy shouting at each other, and the rest of it was busy performing its functions, it was important for us to shadow people and ponder and draw up tentative conclusions and recommendations showing all we had learned from this first rushing summer. Later, community people and other staff could think about what to do with this material. There would be community and noncommunity evaluations too.

Tom pointed out that I was apparently the only member of the central, district, or out-of-state resource staff that even *might* stay in the fall. All the others had committed themselves only for a summer of service before returning, for the most part, to their professional and college careers. He himself, of course, was planning to return to psychoanalytic practice in September in New York. And it was highly unlikely that I would stay, because my four children were expected back in Washington in their school. So, in the end, Jeannine and I were forced to deal with this: If we didn't pull things together, think about them all, make recommendations, write all of it down, nobody would, and all this exciting beginning could not be capitalized upon for future planning. We would have to begin all over fresh.

Jeannine and I each reacted to this frustrating situation in our own way. Jeannine despaired of ever being able to grab hold of anything in this statewide wallow of activity. She was still really interested in her original demonstration-day-care-center-run-by-the-poor idea. She didn't want to bring cold administration to many, but rather warm soul to a few. Whatever soul the quarreling Central Staff had, was centered in Jeannine. Therefore, she withdrew from the overwhelming larger situation and set herself certain things to do in certain centers. This left the coordination to me.

I agreed completely with Jeannine that we had a massive amount of disjointed activity, but instead of making me despair, it thrilled me with its tremendous implications and possibilities. It appeared that besides trying to pull together the general tone and progress through the Newsletter, I could perform a useful service by chasing around the state after members of the various projects, community spokesmen, district coordinators, and others with ideas, and eliciting written or taped reports, which I would type up and file. We could examine the mass of conflicting opinions, the wealth of experience, and the many suggestions flowing unchanneled in communities and in every special project. If this was the beginning of a continuing program, then we urgently needed to gather the steaming pieces and get some kind of a sensible picture for future planning. CDGM was teaming with dissenters and condemners, but we badly lacked constructive planners.

Therefore, when we received Dr. Halpern's psychological services report, it seemed important to extrapolate from it, blend extrapolations together with my own ideas from other projects in the country, such as Frank Reissman's new-careers-for-the-poor ideas, and have the results available for consideration by fall staff. A paper in the files, signed P. G., begins: "*Psych Services: Suggestions*—CDGM's major task is to confront massive problems in Negro Mississippi that have previously been tackled by no one, because they are too big for those interested, and just fine for those wishing to maintain the "Southern way of life." Therefore, in thinking of psychological services, we will have to *give priority to large experimental projects that might help a great number of people,* rather than to in-depth demonstration projects of a "reasonable" size that can only hope to reach a few individuals. In other words, considering our primary goal, it will be *less significant* to give significant amounts of help to individuals, and *more significant* to develop a system for giving people help that are presently, and in the foreseeable future, getting none at all. We know that saturation of high quality services and ideal conditions 'work.' *What we need to know is whether there is any way to use psychological services effectively when we do not have the number and quality of personnel to saturate, and conditions are the opposite of ideal.*"

The first half of the report discussed seven implications for CDGM's future psychological services. First, the immediate need to recruit for a psychologist with early childhood experience, who had faith in our "new careers" concept, and who could design and implement programs for "natural psychological counselors" (poor people in our communities now serving this role) to increase their skills. The potentially talented person could bring problems they found with children, teachers, parents, and other CDGM staff to regular workshops, and could go back to his or her community better able to help. This person could train others. We could begin a radiating type of program right away. The community child development specialist (CCDS) could do everything the summer counseling staff recommended, especially giving "impact" attention to disturbed children, *except* testing, and under the circumstances in the state, that seemed low in priority anyway.

The report recommended looking for more psychologists, so we could, again, provide direct service of some sort to communities, in addition to the exciting idea of new psychology careers for the poor. And looking for psychologists who, while unable to work in the overwhelming vastness of CDGM's over-all needs, could work in a small, intense area as demonstrators of what can be done. It suggested that we continue to try to uncover and entice local Mississippi persons, services, agencies, etc., if indeed any existed, to work with us, but that we not let this effort overshadow the primary focus of HELP NOW.

It talked about trying to attract more good professional psychologists to work in existing and sadly lacking Mississippi clinics and so forth, and recruiting innovational and sensitive researchers to come and help us in our search for knowledge. The report ends with a caution about "the average haughty, smug, rigid, brainless research psychologist" . . . who very likely would soon be down wanting to prick "his foolish little elaborately ordinary thermometer one inch into the ocean of a project, and run pompously off to all the journals as the pedantic, pedagogical expert on everything." Before discussing Dr. Halpern's "implications for community development, reading readiness, and program for children services," the first half of the paper concludes gloomily: "Knowing psychological researchers, however, I imagine they will swarm in in a year or two and 'discover' because of their own wondrous sleuthing brilliance, the things Tom Levin purposely did."

We were able to implement some of the suggestions and not others; not the most important ones.

CHAPTER 11

"LAMING LOTSA BIRDS WID A ROCK"

The equipment project

EARLY IN THE summer, a letter, signed by the seven members of the equipment project at Mount Beulah (six of whom were local young Negro men from poor communities and one of whom was a white Dartmouth student of considerable carpentry skill and of great understanding of the goals of the program) was sent to "All Project Head Start Community Centers." The letter explained that to decide what the children need and enjoy, to design it or select designs from catalogues, and to order things in terms of priorities, summer temporary resource staff and local people would need to work together. Together, everybody would have to decide if the shop at Beulah should be a small factory for turning out quantities of priority items, or a place where models of individual designs were made as samples, for communities to copy. The letter said that the equipment team would be traveling around to communities to collect ideas and to deliver things. It urged that as much as possible be made in communities, both so children and other people could participate, and to reduce cost. The letter concluded: "Finally, the equipment project will be busy trying to plan a year-round project which could produce equipment for a more permanent development program. This cooperative workshop could supply toys and playground equipment for many more children and centers than the number that will be in the program this summer. This shop could sell toys and equipment in Mississippi and other states that need them, and keep itself going for a long time. Cooperatives mean community participation, and this workshop would not only replace the things that get broken, but would keep us working together."

Many patterns were mailed to centers during the summer. Many others were collected from them. It was important to involve the men, women, and teen-agers in our communities in doing the new, stimulating things they could for their children. They often had time on their hands. They welcomed a chance to be usefully busy. It was important to lead up to a cooperative workshop business to help provide jobs to help the economy in CDGM communities. We were starting in most places with barren frame churches sitting in the middle of overgrown fields. Before the children's program staff could develop much of a program, we needed the kind of equipment with which teachers could develop a program. A good program can be worked out with nothing, but it takes teachers with a great deal of ingenuity to do it. Equipment makes it easier. We couldn't buy all the equipment we would need. No Head Start in the country was given a big enough budget to do this, even if it started with more than we had as a base.

We couldn't buy all we needed for another reason. If CDGM was to differ from other Head Starts by being a new-careers-for-the-poor teaching program, and by helping parents help their children because they were earning decent salaries, much of our grant money would be put into paychecks for the poor. We would have to be resourceful if we were to acquire enough equipment.

Then there was our idea of helping communities mobilize for a continuing program, future grant or not. If we simply bought fancy equipment and stocked classrooms to the rafters with the latest commercial items, we would be doing nothing permanent. If we could manage to interest families in why and how these things could be done with their own materials and know-how, we would leave something lasting in Mississippi, if only beautiful playgrounds for idle children and pride in parents, because *they* could offer their children something more than they had had as children.

Another important reason for the equipment project, educationally speaking, was that we very much wanted to get *men* into the centers. We thought it urgently important to prevent this from becoming one more matriarchal experience for children. A good way to interest men in our schools was to put stress on tasks natural for men to do. We considered carpentry, building, etc., a critical part of the educational program. It would be hard for children to fail to see that their families were earnestly concerned with their education if they saw them constantly around the centers improving them. It would be hard for families to continue to feel unneeded by schools, if these schools put such emphasis on actual, visible, immediately gratifying things they not only could but virtually *had to* do.

Last, but not least, it would be hard for the teachers to turn these into the kinds of sitting down drill-drill-drill schools they had a tendency to turn toward, with all those men circulating busily about, and all that carpentry noise in the midst of the program. We felt that the commotion and excitement would lend a good deal of informality, friendship with men, and projects for individual or small groups of children. Specific, tangible details, rather than verbal generalities, were the essence of CDGM. The equipment project produced many broadsides and patterns of swings, slides, and many unorthodox varieties of equipment.

CDGM EQUIPMENT PROJECT

Playground equipment; "stairs" and "special places"

Plan of how sections of steel drums might be arranged. This plan is for sections cut from barrels with one plank used for a bridge.

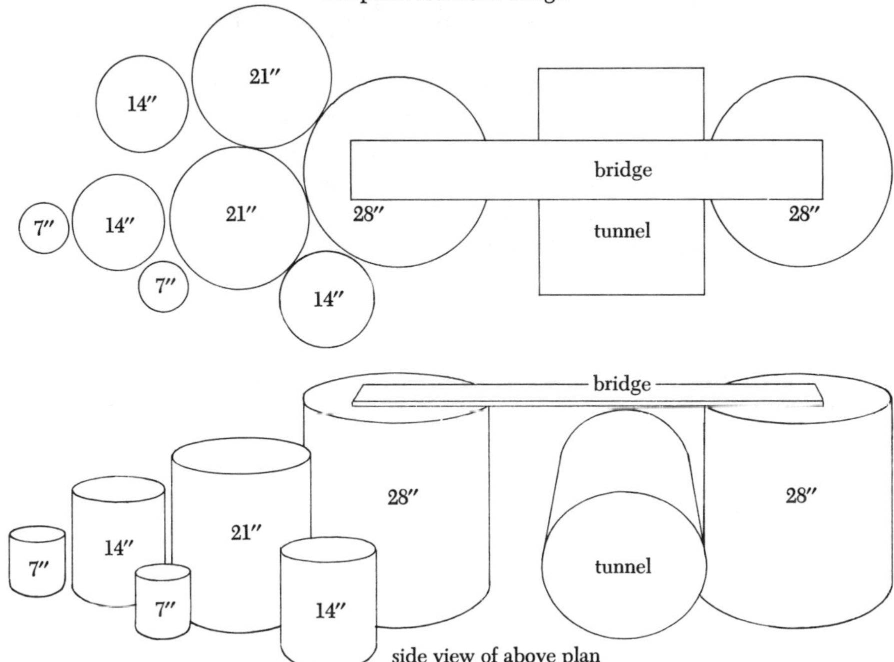

side view of above plan

Some patterns were original, some were "borrowed." The aim wasn't so much originality on the part of the equipment project staff, though that was desirable, too. The important thing was stimulation by the team and originality of action on the part of *community people*. The patterns suffered the fate of all CDGM's printed materials. People can't read. It isn't possible to indicate the extent of the implications that semiliteracy has for poor people. Many many of the resources they could theoretically use to pull themselves out of poverty are useless to them—might as well not exist. They can't read what the health departments post, or the FHA rules and regulations that would make home improvement loans available to them. They can't read welfare laws to know that they're being cheated and to know they can take action. They can't read the books the plantation owners keep of what they owe, which tends to be enough to keep them virtually in slavery, due to "miskept" records. They can't read for vocational improvement, or to their children.

Yet playgrounds sprung up everywhere overnight like brilliant mushrooms. We read the patterns out loud and discussed them. The grapevine spread them in one form or another; frequently unique variations on the theme. We make a mistake in thinking that because people can't read things, they can't deal with things. Literally, I went to many centers where there was only a field to play in, discussed item by item playground ideas they might get their community to build, and came back, unexpected, in the morning, to find a fabulous fairyland of pink and yellow and white and blue, and whatever other colors people had in paint cans in the shed. Playgrounds popped out of the earth due to research, ideas, visits, and discussions on the part of the equipment staff and the rest of us.

The alacrity with which the poor jumped to playground building when someone came to inspire and launch them, and the amazing imaginativeness with which they *kept* building their playgrounds for months after the inspiring visitor left, convinced me that ambivalent as these people might have been about "advice" from whites, they more *wanted* to do things for their children than they wanted not to accept suggestions from whites. The lack of response to written patterns indicated that print, at any level, was not as effective as a person, who could bring more than patterns. A person could bring enthusiasm for the task, appreciation of what the people had already done and had the potential to do, confidence in their capacity for change, and help with the tiny, specific barriers that had prevented them from getting going.

These barriers can seem insurmountable to people not accustomed to surmounting, but can be as small as, "Muh son has muh saw, 'n he's over to Rolling Fork, now he stays over there." Or, "The Methodists won't help because this is a Baptist Church we have our center in." Problems of time, with everybody out in the cotton fields, could be overcome, with questions whether people could come from six to eight one morning, just *one* morning of their lives, before they went to the fields, or if they could come on Sunday afternoon, just *one* Sunday, to build a playground. Often the offer to come, too, to help, got the group over the hurdle of beginning. After that, things went fairly smoothly.

I'd never been much of one for climbing trees to hang tires at five in the Delta morning. I was not big on using a saw at any time of day. But I learned that the effect of my willingness and exuberance on the people far outweighed the effort and wearing exhaustion of the heavy work and scorching sun on me. A visiting Mississippi State Welfare Department white kindergarten "expert" that summer said with undisguised disapproval that she thought it was a waste of my professional time to be clearing brush from a bramble patch behind the cabin, or painting a tire tangerine orange at ten at night. I said I thought we'd have better luck in this whole field of community education if we *didn't* think such use of time a waste of time.

We knew people couldn't read much, but we tried to reinforce the aspirations of the equipment project through the Newsletter. The hope was that those roving central and district staff members who hand-delivered the Newsletters would read them with community teachers and parents. Also, we had an out-of-state student or professional in almost all centers that summer to serve as back-of-the-room resources. *They* could read. Many helped people follow through to get started on some of

SUNNY MOUNT CENTER DESIGNS AND BUILDS A SLIDE
Designed by Mr. Eugene Montgomery. Built by Mr. Montgomery and Mr. G. Wright.

(The newsletter printed proud items Centers mailed in.)

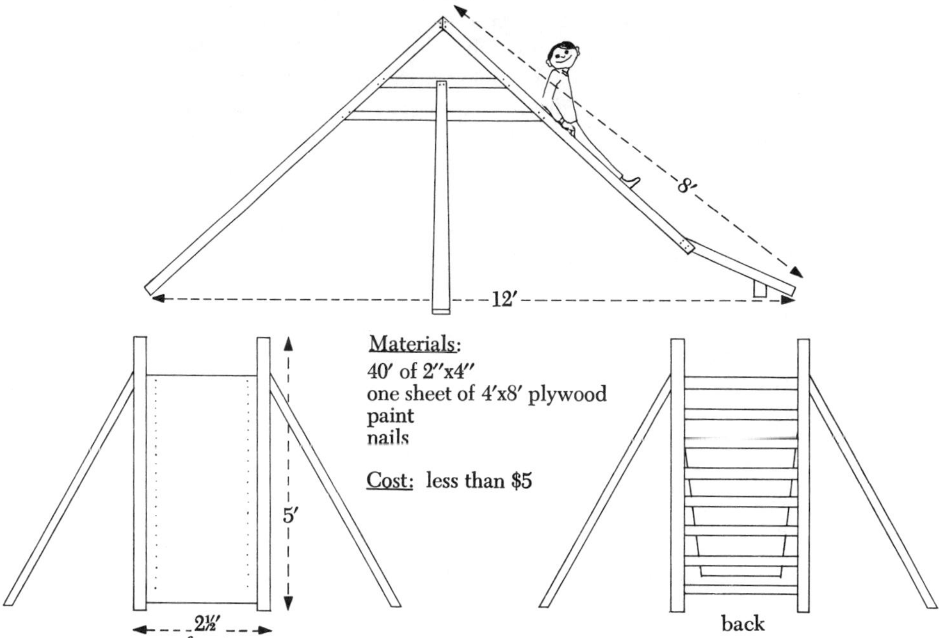

the suggestions. Many ideas suggested nowhere but in the Newsletter appeared on playgrounds. Evidently the information filtered through somehow in some cases. The Newsletter printed proud items mailed in from various centers:

Issue Number Three of the newsletter carried a long hopeful section on playgrounds:

QUESTIONS

QUESTIONS

QUESTIONS

QUESTIONS

QUESTIONS? ? ? ? ? ? ? ?

Has your community built you a playground yet? Some of our Centers have these things ready for the children now:

2 × 4s nailed together and painted for children to climb on. Some have plywood platforms at different heights for children to play house or airplane on. Some climbing bars are shaped like a horse, a tent, a giraffe, ladders, etc.

Swings made of rope and a board.

Tires painted and lying in heaps for children to walk on or roll or stand up and climb through. [We stressed uses of tires so much, and have many on our playgrounds, because everyone seemed to have innumerable old tires lying around their yard.]

Tractor tires or cement blocks or boards fixed like a sandbox with sand in them. Or gravel. Buckets and scoops to use in them made by cutting plastic Clorox bottles into shapes that will work. Big cooking spoons and all kinds

of cartons and boxes to put the sand or gravel in to play cooking, or whatever.
Huge cement pipes for children to sit in and crawl through.
Wash tubs filled with water for children to float chips of wood in (maybe painted like boats or fish), or for children to wash doll dishes in (foil dishes or jar tops or real doll dishes), or doll clothes (sewed up by mothers in your community or by teen-age girls). Children can bring extra things.
Hoses and sprinklers for children to squirt each other to get cool, to be gay, and to have something fun to talk and tell about that you can write down into a book for them. [We had astonishingly little response to suggestions about water play. This seemed incredible to us, considering the impossible heat of these crowded sweat boxes soaking in the sun, considering the ease and inexpensiveness of water play at Centers that had running water, and considering how universal is a child's joy in water play. Teachers said they feared the children would "take cold."]
Four foot long brightly painted boards of not-too-heavy wood and painted soft drink crates or hollow wooden blocks of about 14″ × 14″ × 8″ to carry and build with.
Steps going up to a wooden platform for children to climb up and play—it's a boat, house, anything.
A steering wheel from an old car fastened to a stump or block of wood for children to play driving.
An old car body, completely stripped and checked for sharp or dangerous things for children to play inside.
A super large packing box, painted and carried in out of the damp at night for children to play inside.
Merry-go-rounds made by fastening two boards across each other like a cross and attaching them loosely to a post sunk in cement in the ground.
A tall sliding board, a large see-saw, two ladders with a platform across the top.
A railroad tie or something like it for children to see if they can walk across, hop across, etc.

The white lady kindergarten expert from the state said, "There's nothing in the least unique about these playground equipment suggestions. We've been advocating such usages of simple materials for years, long before you people came into our state."

I agreed that there was nothing new to nursery-kindergarten teachers about using everyday things in educational ways, but ventured the opinion that some of these things were new to some of these *parents,* judging by the fact that we never saw sprawling wonderlands of play things surrounding Negro houses in the fields.

She said, "There's nothing in the least unique about having a group of totally untrained people pretending to be teachers. It's a skilled profession."

I agreed that there was nothing new about bad teachers, but tried to explain the difference between ordinary bad teachers who were neither especially important people in the children's lives, nor submerged in development programs, and CDGM "bad" teachers, who were the rapidly learning, awakening, mobilizing *parents* of the children, learning new things within them and learning a new career in a manner guaranteed to alter the children's entire environment significantly.

She became very angry. She said Mississippians were taking care of their Negroes, and there was no need for us "fly-by-night" transients.

I said that I could see she and her department were working terribly hard to bring standards to the state's day care and kindergarten programs. But since, no matter how much work they *had* already done, they had not yet had the time, staff, budget, etc., to reach all these rural counties and all the Negroes in them, I was sure she would appreciate our effort simply to extend the type of service she was offering elsewhere, "until such time as you all get time for this too."

The lady did *not,* however, appreciate our effort to extend the services her department could offer. So we went and had a Coke. She did not visit again, nor did she answer my letters and phone calls.

It was hard to know where facilities, equipment, and program began and ended, but the equipment project was tied to all three, and the Newsletter attempted to promote imaginative use of all three, too. This issue continues with "Questions":

Has your center made something to divide up your groups into fifteen or fewer if you have more than one set of fifteen in a room?
Some of the centers are using church benches as partitions.
Some centers are arranging low shelves of crates or boards and bricks to be low walls, dividers.
Some centers are using masonite or wallboard with metal brackets or legs as low screens to divide their space.
Itta Bena has hung sheets of plastic foam by shower hooks from a wire around each group's area. Special feature: absorbs some of the sound, pictures can be hung on it, gives a lot of privacy.
Some centers are dividing space by stringing a high string or wire from one side of the room to the other and hanging huge paintings on it to hang down all across except where one "door" space is left. Shelf paper or brown wrapping paper comes big enough to do this. Many children with many colors of paint can make beautiful "wall paper" for this. Or stamp it with sponges and spools dipped in paint.
Have your parents and community older boys and girls and grandparents and church people and skilled workers made you "boy toys" out of wood and items from the used car parts place or the junk yard or the hardware store or the lumber yard? A three foot truck or wagon or scooter car or something that rolls and maybe carries blocks? Little boys are sure to love something that looks like a car or boat or plane or rocket or fire engine or truck.
Have your ladies found a corner of your room to screen off and fix up like a playhouse for little girls? With crates or cardboard cartons painted to look like a stove (with spool knobs to turn it "on") and a shelf with a dishpan of water and detergent sunk in it for a sink, and a mirror to primp and prink and preen in and a dolly cradle and shelves with empty grocery boxes and cans and bottles for kitchen play? And high heels and hats and purses and

lady dresses? And cowboy hats and daddy hats and old boots and huge jackets or trousers? And a necktie? And a wallet? And a telephone made out of two tin cans tied together with a string? And what else could be in it? What's in your home that you could make a small copy of out of odds and ends?
What else special have you made for the children? A telephone booth out of cartons or partitions with a toy telephone in it? A grocery store? A gas station with cartons or wood with hoses? Rag dolls with pretty dresses that come off? Puppets out of stuffed paper bags and scraps of cloth with magic markered faces?

When we began, we had almost nothing except tiny rooms, really cubicles, and church benches. Tables were a first priority item for the children to eat dinner, work puzzles, etc. Due to some of the teachers' passion for seating children at tables and keeping them there all day, I soon decided that a table *burning* project would have had more educational value than a table *building* project. The equipment staff sent out a pattern for a multipurpose table. It came apart and could readily be rearranged into a small playhouse or a room divider. There were no legs, only detachable supports. The tables were easy to take apart for shipping. As many a distressed child soon found out, they also tipped over easily. The equipment project not only sent patterns of tables, but sent one to every center, so community people could copy them to make enough for all the children in every center.

The equipment project also made a large number of rocking boats and inset form boards of geometric shapes, letters, and numbers. Project staff had many items in mind, but the summer was too short, and the handicaps too great.

Rick Dodge, coordinator of the equipment project, wrote this final report: "The immediate and tangible successes of this 'special project' are to be questioned. Planning of the articles to be produced will be completed at the close of the project. Projected planning of the operation of the project given various developments in the CDGM program will be completed. Models of several articles to be distributed to the centers will be completed, and a smaller number of articles which should be produced in quantity will be completed. But the goals of the summer's project will not have been reached. All the articles which might have been supplied to the centers as models will not have been produced."

Rick felt that this project should have been in operation for at least two months before the opening of any centers; a reasonable, but under the circumstances, an impossible suggestion. One of Rick's major complaints was that his staff had to waste a good deal of time because it was forced to handle all the particulars relating to their jobs, such as deliveries and maintenance of vehicles, which could better have been dealt with by others. All efficient CDGM Central Staff complained of this. Why the doctor should hand-deliver medical forms, and I should hand-address eighty-four envelopes once a week, and the director should type his own professional papers, and Jeannine should struggle with trucking for her classroom supplies, and Mrs. Myers should have to wait half a day at a garage to get her office car repaired, etc., no one could understand. Others labeled the complainers snobbish, and undemocratic, and so forth. On the whole, the sanctimonious were not the people that did the work, so they did not have to cry for help, and could afford to be "democratic."

Rick's recommendations for a future equipment project called for:

1. A shop director, coordinator and twelve trainees to work in a large central plant.

2. A project in the field composed of skilled community people, which would work in conjunction with the central project, and which might further mobilize members of local communities toward equipment-making in specific and toward community action in general.

3. A centrally located cooperative which could produce toys and teaching aids to be marketed throughout Mississippi and the South.

Rick concluded his report: "In some areas there is no community participation, or participation is limited to segments of the community which should be in a less important position in the program. The Central Staff is being reorganized, but what is to be done through the state where the program is to have value and where it is to be beneficial to the POOR people, not the middle class who will step forward?

"The poor people must be brought into the program where at present they seem to be on the periphery. Centers where this is the case should have the power shifted. In centers where everything that is accomplished is accomplished by a small group, the power must be removed. Before what has been spawned by this inefficient bureaucracy is allowed to enlarge itself, there must be a return to the foundations of the program. This summer's program should certainly not have been sacrificed in order that the time be spent organizing a more perfect program, but this summer's program must not be allowed to become too firmly established so as to set itself as the norm for the future."

Rick's report was well taken by those who read it. In my opinion, equipment-building, facilities improvement, putting more burden on committees, setting higher standards of community-nursery education with them through committee education work, and working toward certain shifts in committee membership (and thus in teaching staff), should be major thrusts of the early fall. We needed to stimulate bored poor people with few outlets to use their need for activity in behalf of the children, through equipment-making; developing a money-making cooperative; providing teachers and children with wonderfully educational equipment to stir dormant imaginations, blunted curiosity, and stunted vocabularies; stretching the budget to provide for more paychecks to the poor and professional career development services; mobilizing communities on a continuing basis to use untapped resources for the children; attracting men; encouraging informal programs full of "boy" activities and community projects, as well as standard preschool curriculum.

In addition, I had two things in mind, about which I wrote this note to myself in the equipment project files:

"(a) Poor people in Mississippi have been protesting, demonstrating, singing, marching, risk-taking for FREEDOM.

"Haven't yet started on their own planning, programming, projecting for FREEDOM. It won't come by itself. It can't always come from outsiders.

"How do we help them move from the invisible, untouchable SOMEDAY of freedom into immediate signs of it? Encouragement to continue?

"Equipment Project is a great link. People see their own hands, heads, backs, transforming settings that have been bleak, gray, unpainted, emptier than a vacuum as far as toys and ed equipment go, have been this way all their lives, into gorgeous dazzling structures, games, colors, and so forth. What is more visible, touchable, a sign of changing times for children, than a beautiful hand-made playground and playroom made by themselves?

"Should stress this very much in fall because is positive, immediate gratification. Reinforcement of theoretical social change for parents, teachers. Can see what they are doing for chil.

"(b) Must be practical, too. Stupid as it may be, gov't inspectors and the mediocre early childhood types they hire to look us over, JUDGE BY APPEARANCES, NOT ESSENCE. They don't understand what we're doing. Can't hear when we eagerly explain. Can't be converted. ALL THEY KNOW IS IF IT LOOKS RIGHT.

"So it is urgent we make Centers 'look right.' Must look at them not only as poor do (great improvement over past, thrilling, satisfactory), but also as outsiders do (dingy, shabby, crowded, inadequately equipped, etc.).

"First priority: put high-gloss paint in lovely colors on everything. Make toys, make equip, paint, paint, paint, on top of everything. For children and for grant-getting.

"Cheap P.R. attitude? Perhaps, but jobs in the grant-giving industry taught me: WHEN IN THE GRANTSMANSHIP GAME, SATISFY THE GRANT-GIVER ON SURFACE MATTERS, AND SMUGGLE YOUR IDEALS, UNIQUE FEATURES AND PRINCIPLES THROUGH BY HOLDING THEM SO HIGH AND PROUD THEY ARE HIDDEN FROM THOSE WHO CAN ONLY SEE ONE DIMENSIONALLY; ON THE SURFACE DIMENSION.

"What is a more surface matter than paint? And what more principled than CDGM?"

Rick's observations on community committee weaknesses and potential were of core importance. The poor-people-committee system was the heart of Tom Levin's CDGM inspiration. The committees were to CDGM as his hair was to Samson.

CHAPTER 12

SAMSON'S HAIR

Potentially powerful poor people community committees

WHILE CENTRAL AND roving staff struggled to figure out what to do with themselves, community committees jockeyed and juggled and suffered, too. New steps are exhilarating, but aren't without pain. There was Pineville.[19] One dark night at a community meeting in this hill country rural area, the chairman, Mrs. Reed, pulled the district coordinator aside, and whispered, "Now advise me what I should do. When we hired the janitor, we told him his duty was to clean the center daily. But he refuses to mop. He won't mop. We *didn't* say he had to mop. We said *clean.* Do you think cleaning includes mopping?"

The district coordinator said it wasn't so much what *he* thought, as it was what the chairman and the others on the CDGM committee who *hired* the janitor thought.

"Well, we all agree that cleaning means mopping, too," said the chairman in some distress.

The district coordinator assured her that the committee was the equivalent of the school board in this program, and that *it,* therefore, was the employer. He pointed out that employers are not under any compulsion to keep employees who refuse to cooperate in making the job run smoothly. He said that only she and her committee were in a position to know if these duties had or had not been clearly spelled out to the recalitrant janitor, and if all means had been used to help him understand the purposes and requirements of the job.

The district coordinator helped clarify the rights and responsibilities of the committee, but didn't "tell" it what to do. He didn't assume that her request for advice meant "tell me the answer." He assumed, instead, that her request meant "help me solve this problem." As a matter of fact, she probably *did* mean, with part of her intentions at least, for him

[19] All places in this chapter have been given pseudonyms, so as to embarrass no one.

to relieve her of the burden of making a decision in this sticky social situation. But had he chosen to handle her problem, she would have resented his usurpation of her authority, and she would not have begun learning to deal with new kinds of difficulties.

A few minutes later, several teachers in this center called *me* aside—it was one of my two visits to this community during the summer—and said they thought their chairman was a bully, a dictator, and monstrously unfair. They said she had hired herself as a resource teacher, telling everyone that "Edwards" (Central Staff) appointed her. Ever since, they accused, she had spent the summer doing paper work at a desk in the corner of the center, or doing errands for the kitchen. They wanted me to fire her, since "you are in charge of teachers."

I explained that my job was to help teachers with new program ideas, but that I was not in charge of teachers, and had no authority to hire and fire. I explained that whoever hired her was the only one who could fire her. They said that no one hired her. I asked who hired others. They said she did. I asked if they had a community committee as per prescription. *Yes.* They named the members. Then I described the authority and privileges of the community committee. I repeatedly pointed out that this was a local problem and had to be solved locally. They asked if the committee could fire people. I said *yes,* regardless of what contrary information the chairman may have given them, the committee *can* hire and fire resource teachers, as long as fair hearings and fair employment practices are used.

When it was my turn to talk as a "guest speaker" at the meeting, I decided to talk about these problems. They were on everyone's mind to the exclusion of other problems. It seemed unthinkable to ramble on about reading readiness in a climate so tense about personnel and patronage. I thanked them for inviting me, said I had heard from many sources that they were operating a lovely loose program for children in contrast to many of the rigidly public-school programs many communities were running.

Then I talked about conflict. I said that disagreeing and arguing aren't bad, it isn't failure, if it's because people inexperienced in doing something, like running something, like running a center, are beginning, finally, to have chances to plan, make decisions, get into the business of being an employer. I said that even fancy offices, industries, and government agencies contain plenty of conflict within their creamy walls, and carpeted conference rooms.

We discussed, back and forth, the importance of people seeing these things through for themselves: trying, revising where appropriate, acting, reacting, considering, reconsidering, and responding to each new problem as it arose. We stressed the point that hypocritical compliance with CDGM's "rules" wasn't valued as much by CDGM leadership as open and productive conflict. We worked toward the idea that it's not avoiding or hiding problems that helps people or communities, nor is shipping the problem to higher levels for arbitrary or autocratic "solution" (or, more accurately, suppression) a *real* help. We said an honest attempt to learn to solve problems is worth more than any of these things; that it's to be expected that people who had never been "allowed" to be employers before will have some initial difficulties ironing things out, but that of course they can do so when they get together to straighten out their situation.

A phone call the next week said that the community had had a meeting and had "unelected" some committee members "because they wouldn't do nothin." They had elected others.

"Now the kitchen helpers stay past their four hours and volunteer work till the kitchen is done, so five of us teachers don't have to spend a hour a day doing dishes and leaving the childrens alone. Also the janitor is mopping in the morning, after dinner, and at four o'clock."

I asked how all this had come about.

"The new committee talked to everybody. They said, 'This is a program for your children's future. How come you are selfish and thinks only of you?' Then everybody started doing different."

The following week, a delegation from Pineville came to Mount Beulah to hunt for me.

"We ben thinkin since you come up. How come our district coordinator never told us all these thing a committee could do? He never came to see us before, that was the first time. He came 'cause you were there. He wanted to impress you. He likes Mrs. Reed and he don't care about us. That's why he didn't tell us we could let her go. We feel he has let us down. If you don't have information how can you think? We want a different district coordinator who plays fair."

This, along with numerous other similar community complaints, was sent through appropriate channels, and Pineville got a different district coordinator. The first one's approach with community people was excellent. But part of doing a good job was getting to work each day. This person, unfortunately, because he was a fine worker when he did work, seldom worked and had a hard time accounting for his CDGM time. Regardless of his talent, he was not of help to all those communities counting on him for information, but to which he never got. People all over the state were beginning to believe that authorities might, on a rare occasion at least, listen to the voices of the poor and act in accordance.

A letter arrived from Pineville. It said:

"To whom it May Concern:

"This is to inform you of the results of a meeting held August 17, 1965 by the Pineville Community. A partial set of minutes . . . is enclosed. The Community has elected a new . . . committee chairman to represent Pineville to the Child Development Group and the Head Start Program. We would therefore appreciate it if further correspondence. . . .

". . . and the community discussed whether we would have enough people available to run a fall program for the children, once picking begins [cotton].

"The new chairman agreed to take the job only if the committee will share the work with him. He said he doesn't have time to be fussing around the Center all the time, and will resign if the committee doesn't do their share. He said he is busy driving a tractor twelve hours a day, and can only do committee work two days and several nights a week."

All Head Starts were supposed to include poor people in planning and governing. All were supposed to involve poor people in teacher's aide or volunteer work, and in parent education. Most did. Even in Mississippi a few of the forty-nine Head Starts operating during the summer of 1965 did. But the poor were peripheral. They came *after* the fact. They were *included,* but they didn't *initiate.* They "advised," at best, and audited more typically. They didn't carry the burden of problem solving, professional planning, administering, and hiring staff. They were in nonessential positions. They were in the minority. They learned, but they learned to attend programs featuring child care films and how to sew better. They didn't learn how to be administrators, what early education can be, how to hire fairly, the intricacies of project policies and politics, how to develop and express their *own* ideas and desires, sources of help in the "outside world," how to change their communities for their children. They learned to accept something new and better. They didn't learn how to *produce* something new and better. They learned that fate could be kind to them. They didn't learn to force fate. The goals and efforts of most Head Starts did not appear to be concerned with these facts. These, too, were peripheral, if considered at all.

In CDGM the goal and efforts were primarily directed toward lifting the lid off children by prodding their parents and others in the poor communities toward recognizing and developing the latent power they have, to cope with ceilings cramping their children, not by adjusting to them, as they always skillfully have, but by cutting into them so as to provide the children with a "place in the sun."

These ceilings are sometimes kept in place by white communities who refuse to allow Negroes to come up from their world below opportunity level. The ceilings are sometimes kept in place by poor Negroes' own inability to turn wish into action. CDGM was equally concerned with destroying both kinds of ceilings.

There was no chance that the poor would be dominated by others on committees. There were no others. The poor, exclusively the poor, *were* the committees. From initiating the organization of a center through problems of recruiting, hiring, expenses, agendas, and getting a grant again, the people had to learn how to carve a program out of the granite walls of Mississippi and of Washington.

All CDGM communities were ashamed to admit weaknesses. They

tried hard to hide them from Central Staff. They had been considered failures for too many centuries to desire further exposure. This was CDGM's single greatest problem, because until individuals and groups can bring themselves to face what's wrong, they're unable to get at the roots of it and begin replanting what they feel is right.

Democratic processes, smoothly efficient administration, and educational understanding were at a minimum in community committees the first summer. To Tom, that was the simplest and clearest imaginable explanation of their *raison d'être*. Tom spent a great deal of time in communities and in centers to prevent theoreticians from getting out of touch with reality, In its infancy, CDGM was a very person-to-person project.

Committee problems in Rollingdale came to Central Staff's attention on the first day of center operation, when Tom went there to pay his respects.

During organizational stages, this center had been run by a powerful matriarch, who assigned all jobs and made all decisions without sharing a morsel with community members. During our intervening orientation we had stressed that centers should be run with full community participation.

Tom arrived at 10:45 A.M. to find the children being sent home! The community people had refused to participate in the transportation and food preparation because they had never been consulted in the planning of either. The center had not succeeded in reaching its proposed enrollment the first day because of the inefficiency of a boss system with these people, who had too long been bossed to take it easily. The aides, trainees, and resource teachers knew they couldn't keep their jobs or service their children unless they were willing to sacrifice their aspiration for real participation in order to hold on to their jobs. These were their idealistic feelings. With their realistic feelings they were starting to suspect that there were new authorities on their scene who would back them up in their new daring in defying the dominating lady.

In the ensuing discussion Tom refused to resolve the conflict between chairman, staff, and puppet committee. He stated that everyone was allowed to make mistakes, and if this center was a mistake because people couldn't get together and make it work, we would use the funds allocated for it to open a center that had people with greater ability to solve problems in order to serve the children. The following morning committees had been elected, food and transportation problems had been worked out, and the center was in business.

Several Central Staff people were shocked at this harsh treatment. Tom said it was just truthfulness instead of condescending "tolerance" of the "poor helpless poor." It was said that Tom was threatening the community. Tom said he was forcing the community to confront itself. People would have to "stop playing around with pleasant habits of submission" and "quickly start ordering their values"—complain and not gain, or act with some pain and perhaps gain a grain. Tom often said, "Confrontation is the key to change." Some said Tom was putting people "right back under Mabel Ann's thumb in order to get that money." Tom said he was forcing them to put up or shut up.

A project psychologist said, "I can't agree with Movement workers who consider outside intervention criminal encroachment. The only thing that will break the circle of community ambivalence, which keeps their tongues wagging and their actions lagging, is the new factor of an outsider. This person introduces a new element: people feel free to complain, and foolish when they realize how their idle complaining looks to others they admire. It makes them feel uneasy; that maybe they should take the bulls by the horns."

However, human relations aren't simple, nor are they permanently cured by quick shock treatments, regardless of whether or not shock treatments are a wise beginning. This type of problem is so tough to untangle that most projects avoid getting into them. But undiagnosed and untreated physical disease doesn't disappear, and neither does undiagnosed and untreated community pathology. There were many Central Staff members in CDGM who denied that communities had pathological features. We were supposed to say that communities were beautiful, wise, full of simplicity, courage, and humor not found widely elsewhere. While these things are true, they're misleadingly not the whole truth. Poor communities also—not surprisingly considering their depressing history—are full of pathology.

Staff fought a lot about this: Those who clung to the myth that all is lovely in poor communities and who condemned those who didn't mouth the myths as they might an oath of commitment, angrily accused the others of "trying to play God—you think you know everything about the people better than the people know about themselves." And the others answered miserably that on the contrary they were quite disturbed over their own lack of total understanding and over their own inability to help distressed, diseased communities.

CDGM seldom solved problems. But some staff members tried to open problems for examination. In personal pathology, "experts" can help the patient pinpoint and pull apart the problem. They can help the patient interpret and reconstruct. But the patient must *solve* the problem himself. Central Staff and district coordinators, when they were working according to Tom's theory, didn't tell communities *how* to solve problems, but they did pressure for problems to be solved.

This problem in Rollingdale didn't go away. In the fall the local young lady who had replaced the out-of-state district coordinator for the second district wrote: "Chairman is Mabel Ann Smith who is very difficult because she wants to be the over-all boss. She is a Trainee, but sits at a desk all day and accuses people of stealing the food out of the kitchen. Wants to tell the entire staff what to do. . . . The community people felt obligated to her because she was the chairman. The community elected her because she is the loudest in the community. They are afraid of her. The two out-of-state Resource Teachers have been cut off from the Trainees by Mrs. Smith who talked to them against the Resource Teachers because they are threatening to her, though not threatening. Both RTs had good ideas . . . and worked well with staff when Mrs. S. wasn't around. . . . Mr. Samson, a lazy RT fanned in a chair all day. Local man . . . from public school . . . His two comments all summer were 'My, my it's hot today,' and 'Come here, little boy, have a drink of water.' Mrs. Smith threatened to fire people, but not him, he was her friend. She said she would just call Tom Levin. Food problem: Mrs. Smith never bought enough food. She and Mr. Samson ate first, served mostly starch, then ran out of food two-thirds through feeding the children. Some got none. One day she served rotten fish and several children's stomachs tore up. I worked with the staff about a balanced diet, but they said Mrs. Smith would run things her own way. Community is active. . . ."

Needless to say, but worth saying anyway because of certain criticisms of CDGM, a situation of this sort required immediate Central Staff intervention. We argued all night as to where to let standards for the children's program sag in order to allow communities to develop their own common sense standards, but no one condoned poisoning children. The trouble was, we occasionally didn't learn of cases like this until later. CDGM was very big, and communications were not all they should have been.

This new coordinator worked intensively with the community to try to get them to take some stand against this tyrannization. She reported, "They seem afraid to go against her. She's always run things up there. They think they won't know how to do anything, or get any information, if they throw her out. She has all the good ideas. They fear CDGM will end and leave them with her. So they try to win her."

This was hitting several of the key factors blocking the solution to many of these matters right on the head. The people lacked confidence in their ability to cope effectively. The Rollingdale group wasn't coping with this as well as they could have. The tyrant usually *did* have superior skills. That's why she rose to the throne. Rollingdale was one of our top twenty centers as far as the children's program went. And once in a top position in the community, a dictator *did* have access to information and opportunities the others didn't have, so she simultaneously kept others from gaining skills and developed her own much further. As an active member of FDP, as an active CDGM chairman, and as an active teacher in CDGM, Mrs. Smith learned much more than the others about political shenanigans, federal programs, Head Start regulations, and nursery education.

In all communities where a tyrant reigned, there was a great deal of rumbling, uproar, and reporting behind the scenes. People might have allowed themselves to be dependent and externally passive toward the tyrant, but they didn't allow themselves to be grateful or tranquil. There were complaints behind backs and over heads. In a few communities there was someone strong enough to stand up and speak for more democratic processes. Those lone individuals didn't generally fare well.

Here are excerpts from a letter written to an out-of-state COFO friend from the previous summer by the only person in Rollingdale willing to take public exception to the totalitarian performances of Mrs. Smith: "I enjoyed talking with you Sunday night and I am working hard for Head Start, and it's just as I told you; Mabel Ann is ploting and planning just about all the time. . . . It makes it very, very hard for me to get an idea over when people are use to being told what to do and bossed around, so they feel that she is boss and will not cooperate with me.

"So I went to the meeting that she set for the next night at the Center and tryed to get the point over about the school situation. . . .

"I hate to say that we just can't make it, but I am afraid something is going to happen that is not good for us. . . . I did get up and let the people know how I felt toward the way Mabel Ann has been treating me lately but they preferred to let everything remain as she has it, but I am going to have to try to find time to get some other people out in the community to help me.

"I am going to do all I can to stick with Head Start but things are not good at all for the two of us.

"I have been doing as you suggested when something come up I go to her and try to settle it but the last time I went to her home I was not invited in by her, but I went in anyway and tryed to talk to her but she said there was nothing I could do or say that would make her feel any better.

"Now I am not asking that you defend me in this because there are two sides to any given situation, she has her side, I only mention how things are so if and when something does come that is drastic, you will have one general idea. . . .

"The resource teacher we had during the summer was not treated very good, but I am praying that when the young lady get here she will not be treated like they are treating me. This is the only thing I fear."

It didn't seem surprising that "the system" had produced some Mrs. Smiths. It appeared miraculous, however, that any Lorettas had survived. These interpersonal problems, and others like them in most CDGM communities, were never solved any better than are more sophisticated but similar ones at levels all the way to the White House, but many of their symptoms improved.

This report came from the third district coordinator as one part of his total impressions of one of his centers. It's a center in an extraordinarily poor Delta rural area. ". . . Mrs. Gray was the first one who heard of Head Start at a meeting at Edwards in the spring. She came back and told a community meeting that Edwards had chosen her to be the chairman 'to run this.' She 'chose' a committee composed of three members of her family and her next door neighbor. When it came time to 'give out the jobs,' the lion's share seemed to go to her family and neighbors. Mrs. Gray has been denounced by her community, but no one seemed willing to take steps. I encouraged people who complained to me to have a meeting and an election for a committee and chairman of their choice. Three weeks after opening they had a meeting and an election. They told me the next day that they had elected exactly the same committee members again! They said it was because Mrs. Gray and the old committee were present and they were embarrassed to vote against them. Complaints and anger continued. I suggested that they try again and vote as they really wanted to. They did. They enlarged the committee and elected Mrs. Kingman chairman. Mrs. Gray did not accept this. She said it was an illegal election because she was not present. People say she was not present because just before the vote she and all her family excused themselves 'to take care of some other business,' and filed out of the house. Mrs. Gray tried to overthrow this development by coming to me. Central Staff and I were pleased at the development, because nepotism is not one of our creeds. Mrs. Gray kept trying during the seventh week of the program to get herself re-elected. She did this by accusing Mrs. Kingman of embezzling money. This charge was investigated and was not true, but she had already convinced five members of the new committee: enough to make a revolution possible. This was not hard, as even with the new election they all turned out to be members of her extended family! People kept continuously asking me to straighten this out and I continuously told *them* to straighten it out. I told them to settle it or live with it, but not to keep running to Daddy. A community meeting was then held at which they threw out the whole committee and put in a whole new committee with Mrs. Kingman as chairman. Plotting and politicking still go on. Attendance drops with each factional explosion, but builds up when things are calm."

A VIP visitor murmured that this was all very interesting but he didn't see what it had to do with the children. What good does it do the children for staff to spend time sorting out puzzles like this? I thought it had a fair amount to do with the children, and was better than staff sorting out children's jigsaw puzzle pieces. Parents can't find energy to concentrate on social change and children's education until they stop stewing over these interpersonal learning processes and procedures for overcoming individual struggles to succeed instead. Children couldn't learn anything about democratic processes and effective group action when they grow up in communities where the one who kills best is king. And communities writhing in the wreckage of what Mississippi history has done to them couldn't begin salvaging themselves without intervention. CDGM raised innumerable questions and produced no recommendations except one: We couldn't solve a problem if we didn't begin trying.

This is a memo written by a Central Staff children's program worker after she visited Bridgeton:

BRIDGETON

Problem: Rebellious staff, weak committee, nobody with ideas.

Committee Says: "We are in charge" (therefore, committee members spend most of their days in center "supervising").

Staff Says: "This drives us batty."

Committee Says: "This is a daycare program to help parents who are in the fields. Therefore the hours will be 8–4."

Staff Says: "That's much too long, we can't 'teach' children this age that long."

Committee Says: "Don't teach them. Take care of them. Have a nice time singing, outdoors, eating, sleeping."

Staff Says: "We only have eight weeks with them and we must teach them to read or they will never learn."

Staff went over committee's head to Polly, D.C., and Levin. All three supported committee's authority to plan for center. Tom suggested committee, staff, D.C. and people from Polly's-Jeannine's staff have a meeting and try to work out a mutually satisfactory plan. Then stick to it.

Had meeting. D.C. didn't show. Polly suggested more organized program of music, art, stories in morning. (Is now nothing but racing and screaming), and more home-style program of individual conversations and free play in P.M. P. also suggested staff take shifts on duty in P.M. supervising free play, while "off" shift prepares for next day and gets breath away from children. Says this might make whole program fuller: time to prepare.

I say we may want to teach reading in eight weeks in the future, but now we're not ready, so read to them.

Later D.C. came around bringing several neighboring chairmen to discuss this with Bridgeton committee. Neighbors urged committee to hold reins tighter and fire insurgents.

Regarding another center, the district coordinator tape-recorded: "Mr. Peterson is an excellent chairman in one sense: tremendous energy. Does more work than ten mules all by himself. Also tremendous courage. White principal in county told families that the inspector was going to close this center and our staff would be clomped in jail. Mr. Peterson went from door to door telling them it's a lie. In another sense he's not a good chairman: dominates completely. Center is his little kingdom, and he is the dictator. He is responsible for getting this center going in the face of terrible intimidation and for all the physical work. Also guards it every night with shotguns due to several shooting incidents by night-riders. Yet he is also responsible for keeping it a one-man show. Watch him: he has figured out the flaws in CDGM's accounting system and takes full advantage in behalf of food and toys for the children of his community. A worthy aim, but . . ."

The community view of things was not always the same as the outside appraiser's view of the same things. The committee chairman at Magnoliaville wrote to central office: "As chairman of the Magnoliaville child's development center I have very little oppersition at present. The committee and the intire staff work with me splendidly." The staff of the center wrote: "To whome it may concern: We the staff of the Magnoliaville, child development center strongly recomment, and request that Mr.——, our faithful, and profound chairman be placed on the yearly payroll. . . . He is hindered by not being self employed."

But the local Negro district coordinator (from another part of the state) wrote of the same man: "Chrmn Mr.——is a weak leader. Does all he can and community likes him moderately for it. . . . Has a job and is never around Center." She added, "This is a terrible Center."

Frequently these community problems were very complex. It was hard to know what to do. The only guaranteed thing was that any "outsider" who did anything would be greatly hated by one faction or another, and of course by much of the Movement contingent on our staff, which resented most of what others than themselves did. Man is a territorial creature, and this was their turf.

The case of Kawaha is a good example of the fact that whatever we did was wrong. On several occasions the district coordinator told me that this center was in extremely bad shape. The only activity he had ever seen the one hundred children engaged in, other than in the class of one outside resource teacher, was coloring in coloring books. No CDGM supplies were in evidence. The medical program was in a shambles. Teachers walked around with long switches, and children were regularly whipped for not falling asleep at nap time. One Trainee made a child stand in the corner and wouldn't let her have breakfast until she said the ABCs correctly from A to Z. There were two men on the payroll as teachers, but they were allowed only to do janitorial work.

All the teachers seemed in great fear of the "director," Mrs. Sandstrom, an elderly woman who was the principal of a private Negro church school during the year, and in Head Start never left her desk in the "office." The district coordinator had visited a number of times, and the only contact he had seen the "director" make with the children was to sit in a chair issuing commands such as, "Boy, get me that pencil. Hurry, hurry, I don't know what's the matter with children nowadays, they don't obey their elders at all!" The district coordinator said he had a whole district to cover, and a lot of payroll problems to sort out, so he would not have time to work with the individual parents and community people on this.

The out-of-state resource teacher was unhappy. She felt that Mrs. Sandstrom was keeping teachers in line by letting them know that they would not have jobs in her school in the fall if they did anything to disobey her in Head Start. The resource teacher said she couldn't make any headway at all in introducing enthusiasm or new kindergarten ideas, because Mrs. Sandstrom "knew all about education." The resource teacher said "parents are not interested, but the police are. They keep coming around." The resource teacher felt that parents weren't interested, there had never been a PTA meeting, the community had made nothing and done no volunteering whatsoever, because Mrs. Sandstrom did everything in her power to prevent them from knowing that Head Start was supposed to be a community venture.

Both the district coordinator and the resource teacher were angry at "Edwards," because they said we were shirking our responsibility to the children and the community by not stepping into this situation.

So I drove several hours to Kawaha. I spent a full day talking with Mrs. Sandstrom. I assumed this was just a misunderstanding of the nature of Head Start and of the duties of a teacher (Mrs. Sandstrom was getting paid as a resource teacher). I tried to get her fullest views on what she was supposed to do, what she was doing, why, what obstacles she saw, etc.

She talked a good CDGM line, but when we got to specifics, she dodged questions such as: Had teachers ever visited children's homes? Had there ever been regular community meetings? If they were planned, how were they announced? Who elected the committee? Did they use any of the program ideas from Orientation or others of their own creation? Had they visited any other CDGM centers or would they like to, just to see what others were doing? Did parents serve as volunteers?

I was friendly and spoke out of a sincere certainty that she wanted to run a good program, but that Head Start's particular peculiarities had never clearly been explained to her. I felt that CDGM often was at fault for not explaining things clearly, yet expecting people to do them. However, it quickly became clear that Mrs. Sandstrom's concern was keeping control, and program was not a matter on her mind.

I talked with teachers, each of whom proudly confirmed that "the director *never* came into classrooms, she wouldn't do *that*," but sat at her desk as a director should. They seemed utterly intimidated. Their entire day-long conversation included almost nothing other than "Yes ma'm" to me, or "Yes ma'm" to Mrs. Sandstrom, who I noticed winced when a teacher, who quickly corrected herself, just said "Uh huh," and who, I noticed, sharply undid a number of children who failed to show her the expected courtesy of "ma'm."

I talked with Mrs. Sandstrom privately for some time. I didn't want to embarrass her, and did want her to feel we were working confidentially together on a matter of mutual professional concern, which was what it seemed to me. I explained that anyone receiving teacher's pay was expected by OEO and CDGM to be with the children almost all the time doing art work, music, games, etc. She agreed in stifled cynicism for a while. Then she blurted out, "Well what do you think I am! I'm seventy years old. I can't stand the noise they make. I don't know how to do all that nonsense. I'm a school principal not a recreation leader!"

I genuinely sympathized with the difficulties of teaching small children at her age, and said I was sure I wouldn't want to by the time I reached her age. I said that therefore she might prefer to keep the job of chairman, and let someone younger take the teaching job. She was furious. She accused me of trying to underhandedly fire her, trying to take her income, and being "a rich girl who don't understand what it is to be poor."

I did understand about needing income and what it is to be poor, a little at least, but I also understood what it is to be a nursery school teacher, which *two* understandings always put CDGM staff in conflict within themselves. I then suggested that she keep the teaching job and get someone else from the community, through elections, to be chairman. I said I didn't see how she could do a full-time paper work job *and* a full-time teaching job, both requiring around eight hours a day, and besides, I thought the community was taking advantage of her making her do all that work. This conversation resulted in a rumor later that "Mrs. Greenberg told me we shouldn't even answer our telephone, just let it ring. She won't let anyone in the office during school hours."

I asked if we could have a staff meeting after the children left to discuss CDGM requirements as established by OEO for all Head Starts. I was trying to avoid making her feel that I was picking only on her by bringing out standards *OEO* sets, not CDGM, not me, for *all* Head Starts, not just for Kawaha, not just for Mrs. Sandstrom. We had the staff meeting. Mrs. Sandstrom used it to deliver a eulogy about herself, and then said, "We thank our visitor for coming, and now we are dismissed." The same technique public schools sometimes use to get rid of dissatisfied and dissenting parents.

She and I prepared some notes to parents afterward, inviting them to a meeting and center tour on a night she reluctantly named. We worked out a list of step-by-step plans for involving the community in spite of their real fear of white retaliation for introducing preschool to this building. This we did by me pushing her to think. I did push, but I didn't come up with the statements and plans. I couldn't visit parents myself at this time, as there were eighty-three centers to think of, records to keep on each, program ideas and Newsletters to get out, plans for fall to make, etc.

Members of the roving staff kept coming back to Mount Beulah during the next few weeks bitterly complaining about Central Staff not backing them up in "doing something about the old witch with the switch." Far from feeling like God, I felt like a begrudging interloper, not at all sure what I should do.

I called Mrs. Sandstrom and asked if I could come to the community meeting. I hoped perhaps we could discuss community elections, government by group, etc. Sensing that this was my interest in the meeting, Mrs. Sandstrom told me the meeting had been canceled. How come? Mrs. Sandstrom had a headache. She had had a headache since she had last seen me. She supposed she would still have the headache on the day of the proposed meeting. She strongly hinted that I had given it to her. Probably I did. Surely she had given me one.

Word filtered in that the resource teacher was spending a lot of time off the job, because Mrs. Sandstrom had launched a turn-your-back-on-that-tattle-tale campaign against her. Meanwhile the children were having a bleak experience.

I didn't want to be "bossy," or appear to be taking the side of the white resource teacher. But this was a preschool program, and the children had to come first, at least up to a minimal point. It *was* a new careers program, and poor people learning to be teachers had to come ahead of one negative woman. It *was* a community growth program, and the community was being systematically excluded.

There were Central Staff members who claimed not to be in conflict in these CDGM community problems. They seemed to me to be either insensitive to the complexities and multiple truths of situations from the community viewpoint; or uncommitted to the preschool, new careers, community development triple goals of our project; or lying to allow themselves the easy way out: See nothing, do nothing, solve nothing, and everyone will like you fine.

Then I learned of an interesting new twist to the thing. Mrs. Myers, director of professional staff, came back from a visit to Kawaha. Mrs. Sandstrom had told her that I said that she, Mrs. Sandstrom, had no right to tell her staff what to do, and that I said Mrs. Sandstrom's staff could do whatever they wanted to! She also told Mrs. Myers that Tom Levin said the community is to run things, and now Mrs. Greenberg is "coming in trying to run things her way." Mrs. Myers was mad at me, which she should have been, had I done this.

The resource teacher appeared at Mount Beulah. She had been fired for "refusing to cooperate." A white man took her place. I visited *again*. Things were even worse for the children, now that the only teacher with any program had been forced out of the center. This time I met with the committee. Members were Mrs. Sandstrom's friends. They were heavily indebted to her for other affairs. They nodded agreement to whatever I said, while silently supporting her. I spent another whole day working hopefully with her. As a result I got this letter from her: "Dear Mrs. Greenberg, Very sorry of the misunderstand of my staying in the office. You only heard what one person said, and that person didn't know whether I stayed in the office or not, for they were absent quite a bit. I thought you should have talked with me and others and not decided with one person. I am helping in the classroom all that I can. When the children take their nap and rest why I go to the office. And too the Sec'y take care of the office now. I am known to do my duty at any place and at any time. . . ."

Thus, though I had talked with many people, not one, who had sought *me*, not I them, and though I had worked lengthily with her in private, not behind her back, toward helping her stay, not leave the program, I cemented my "reputation" for doing-in community people "in favor of" out-of-staters, though the out-of-stater was fired, and I at no time spoke in her behalf.

Two community delegations came to Edwards due to alerting work done by an FDP worker as to what CDGM should be. They were deeply chagrined to confess that they had "let" Mrs. Sandstrom get away with this, and hurried home, after a long discussion of Head Start's goals and aproaches, to "set up a real one." I visited Mrs. Sandstrom one last time, found her stubbornly sticking to the thesis that Edwards was "trying to ruin me by making me work with these uneducated people who will ruin this fine children's program," came home, and wrote this letter. I hoped it would help her save face, but at the same time provide an opportunity for someone else to get a toe in the door. "Dear Mrs. Sandstrom, It is the consensus of opinion at Edwards that the Kawaha community did not really rally and run its own community program as strongly as our other communities did. The government tells us that the only reason they give us money instead of (or in addition to) the school superintendent, is that our program is not run *for* poor people by educators, it is run *by* poor people.

"We now have about 10,000 children registered for CDGM Head Start for this fall. The government says it will probably give us money for 5,000. They told us to recommend NOT ONLY THE BEST CENTERS, AND YOURS *WAS* A GOOD ONE, BUT ALSO THE COMMUNITIES THAT WERE THE MOST ACTIVE IN SHARING AND INITIATING THE WORK.

"We are wondering if you would be willing to resign as committee chairman, and as resource teacher, because you have worked very hard and run things very efficiently, and now it is time to see if the community can or will do the job themselves. The point of the poverty program is to encourage people who are *not* . . . good administrators and teachers to learn how to be.

"You brought the CDGM program to Kawaha, you offered your building, you held staff meetings, you invited the community.[20] And they relied on your skill and let you lead. We feel that now is the time for

[20] She finally did, once, and delivered a lecture on religion. But she kept bringing this meeting up to me as proof of her interest in community action, so I had to acknowledge it.

you to lead them to stand on their own feet by telling them that you will no longer take a central position: it is up to them whether the program stands or falls.

"Will you be so good as to bring the matter to the attention of the entire community of parents, staff, committee, and friends, and see what they wish to do? We will need to know your decision by Friday morning, in a letter.

"As it is, there is very little chance that we can prove to Washington that this is a community action program, and therefore there is very little chance we will get more money for it. Sincerely yours, hope to see you at the Thursday meeting at Edwards, Polly Greenberg."

I felt very badly about playing this horrid role. She saw it that way too. I received this reply. I was no longer called "Dear." The letter just commenced: "I am sorry that Central staff believe that I ran the school alone and had all the say so.

"I admit that the community didn't do as it should. We called several meetings. The people were afraid to come on account of others in the town talked against it.

"We had to send a committee to the board to explain about the school.

"I've had quite a bit to go through with. But if you think that I am the cause of the community not doing its duty, why I will not have anything to do with it. We appreciate everything you did for us. Also thank you, after all I've done I don't feel supposed to offer my resignation, as chairman I am willing to work as sec'y. and resign as resource teacher.

"I've done too much for the school to give up everything. In fact we believe it's personal—may be we will try to get something else—probably every thing might be for the better. G. S. Sandstrom.

"P.S. I am sorry the committee don't have the privelege to get who they want.

"I guess the building is still available."

Mrs. Sandstrom *did* "try to get something else." She wrote to Washington and denounced me as a "dictator." I was questioned by OEO officials as to why I treated this poor struggling woman so meanly. Such is the price one pays for crossing an entrenched Mississippi matriarch.

Erik H. Erikson tells us that whatever deep psychic stimulus may be present in the life of a young child, it is identical with his mother's most neurotic conflict. If this is true, thought Tom, then we needed to consider what his mother's greatest conflict was.

In our situation this conflict was between shame-doubt-guilt and autonomy-initiative-free choice-action. Adults were ashamed of their poverty and of their race. They *acted* small, dependent, unable to do for themselves. They doubted that they could be different. They doubted that they could take on powerful rivals: the white community, white out-of-staters, even the dictators among themselves.

All their lives they had been taught not to show initiative. A small child is taught "not to get into things" around the house and yard. A bigger child is taught "not to get into things" at school—not to think or question. An adult is taught "not to get into things" affecting his life—white things, decision-making, the greater society, social change.

So if adults *did* express their unfulfilled wishes to have the initiative whites have, and the initiative they once had themselves when they learned to walk, talk, etc., they felt guilty. Thus the children of these adults came to school caught in this conflict. They came with a strong psychic stimulus to fail. Short of starting all over again in the neonatal period with both parents and children, there was probably nothing that could be done to eradicate such conflict.

But could anything be done to reduce it in both parents and children, so children could have a head start on the psychic stimulus toward initiative required for success? Tom thought the committee system a worthwhile experimental beginning in this direction. Initiative was rewarded: Adults got a center; it worked well, paid well; they got admiration. Therefore, feelings of self-doubt were lessened. Adults were making it, yet not being punished by harsh judges; mothers, Mississippi whites, the Negro power structure. Therefore, they felt less guilty about the risks they were taking and the authorities they were displeasing. Because they felt less ashamed of being themselves—poor, Negro, and all—they could be more themselves; could be more autonomous. And their children began to be freed to do the same.

The committees were *not* powerful the first summer. They were *potentially* powerful as a force in children's education and as a force for social change.

CHAPTER 13

READING: A KEY TO THEIR FUTURE: A FREEDOM

TODD'S STORY ABOUT HIS BIKE

When I ride my bicycle I fall and I get back up and start riding again. And I let my brother ride. I pulled my sister and brother down to the school. I like to share rides with my brother. I all the time let my big brother ride. I put the bicycle up and play a little while. Some of those old dogs get after me and I ride my bicycle fast. Some children throw them dogs and the dogs run back home. The dogs bite them children and they run home crying. The children start fighting and go home. That boy fell off that bicycle and broke his arm. He was a white boy. And that boy's Mama dreamed about him. That boy's Dad jumped off in that ditch and come and got him.[21]

* * *

IN THE COURSE of the summer I visited more than half of the eighty-four centers. Other members of the children's program staff of five visited also. The purpose of the visits was to show Central Staff appreciation and enthusiasm for the wonderful things local staff was doing with children—to provide a bit of yeast for further growth in all aspects of the program, regardless of which project they "belonged to." We were coordinating. I observed and participated all in the same breath.

I found staff generally proud and happy to be given a chance to "show off" their new accomplishments, and eager for suggestions. (Of course, there were also many who very much resented Central Staff and did their sullen best to turn to stone. Their suspicious certainty that the visitor had come to spy, supervise, and "report them" was immovable. But most were friendly toward help.)

As they moved from activity to activity, it was always possible to add some whimsey and playfulness. Many of the centers suffered from the formality of the public school in which adults had learned. Between activities there was usually a period of emptiness. They hadn't learned yet to make smooth transitions from one thing to the next, and tended to leave chasms of vacant sitting between things. It was often easy to

[21] Stories are reproduced here as recorded by the children's teachers.

introduce a new form of the last thing they were doing during the void. Regardless of what they were doing, I could chat and converse with the children, always wringing a little more language development from any activity. By the time the children went home, typically at about two o'clock, the grown-ups could sit down and find a lot to talk about from our joint morning experiences.

What we talked about varied from center to center, depending upon what seemed to be most critical. We ranged from exchanging ideas on ways to develop the housekeeping corner, to new ways of using the art materials they had had out in the morning. We went from putting puzzles together before shelving them instead of pouring all the boards and pieces into a carton at clean-up time, to painting the furniture with community donated paint to liven up this new world for the young.

But whatever else we discussed, two subjects were generally brought up by teachers: *discipline* and *reading readiness*. It was not hard to lead from the former to the latter, and to tie the two together, because before long, in our back-and-forth talk about specific examples of discipline problems they had encountered, and our mutual brain-picking to find alternative ways of handling them, someone would always say that children are "bad" when they are bored.

In talking of ways in which teachers might want to experiment with tightening up the lag time between activities (when many of the "discipline" problems were reported to crop up), and ways in which they might want to experiment with brightening up their "lessons" (the other major occasion they mentioned when the children were so "bad"), it was almost always appropriate to discuss and demonstrate many reading readiness ideas.

There were many complaints that the children wriggled and squirmed and had to be whipped at story time. So we would play a game in which I would scrunch the teachers all up on top of each other, and then drone at great length in an inaudible mumble, usually from an intermediate grade arithmetic. There were frequently many lying around. Then I would read a lovely piece of preschool literature to a group of four or five "children" using a lot of expression and dramatic action, and encouraging much interaction between reader and listeners. "Children" would take turns acting out the parts afterward. We would make word cards of one or two or three words that the "children" agreed were their favorites from the book: the scariest, the best, the sweetest, etc.

When we were through, with everyone hilariously laughing, I would ask them which way they thought would interest children the most, and therefore, which way would produce the fewest "discipline" problems?

There is a realm of classical adult literature, and of quality current literature, and so it is also in children's books. Great books for children like great books for grown-ups, deal with fairly universal human feelings and problems, and are full of insights. They may be presented through cats and ducks and simple plots, but the themes and human truths are there. Great books for children, like great books for grown-ups, are written in wonderful language. For children the language will be patterned in pretty ways, often repetitiously, often playfully, but it will be pleasing to the ear.

Mary Varella, "chief" of the reading readiness project, thought, and I agreed, that there was much danger in reading to our children about middle-class children, and teaching them thoroughly that *they* were not in books. But it's possible to select books that show animals, not people at all, and are still significant literature. It's possible to find a few books that have both quality story and Negro illustrations, and more than a few that show children of other minority groups or stylized people that are of no group: stick figures, abstract shapes, etc. If the themes are human, and middle-class themes are screened out, they will be classless, and equally applicable to any child. I thought we should buy some of the best literature suitable for our group: rural, Negro, age level four, five, and six, but listening level, two, three, and four, due to the newness of the story-listening experience.

Whatever the special problems that would require a careful selection of books, these were, after all, children, not just Negroes, and they should not be deprived of things children love in an overboard effort to consider their specialness, any more than they should be deprived, as they are usually, of consideration for their special situation.

When teachers began reading with children, with the goal of helping children love and enjoy books instead of the goal of "getting them to sit through the story," both the reading readiness and the discipline parts of the program improved noticeably.

* * *

BOUGAR MAN

by Shirley

The Bougar Man scared the children.
And the children ran away . . .
And they run home and told they Mama.
They told they Mama they saw the Bougar Man.
The children say that they were tired.
They went to bed, and went to sleep. . . .

* * *

Arrival, departure, and waiting for dinner times also upset the teachers. The children "kept getting into everything" and were so wild. We talked about these times as being ideal times to work with individual or small groups of children on story-telling and book-making. We discussed all the many things children might have seen or done or said to their friends or heard or felt or dreamt at home before coming in; and the great number of things they had thought and done at school in the block area and the garden, in the tub of water and the doll corner; and the pets and family members and activities and naughty things and happy things they might get involved with when they got home.

Wild times would be good times to direct children's energies into drawing from within themselves, and writing stories from within.

* * *

. . . The children woke up, and looked through the window.
Then they saw the Bougar Man again.
They saw their Mama, and say Mama what you brought me.
Mama went back to town and came back at night time.
Their Mama brought some potato chips and ice cream.
The Bougar Man came back and burst the wind pane out.
And said I am going to get you.
And he got all the children.

* * *

We thought that since the whole program was to be geared toward discovering (and helping the *children* discover) their qualities, characteristics, interests, and powers, it would be quite appropriate to begin building a reading program out of the resources, experiences, living techniques, friendships, interests, standards, thoughts, dreams, language, and wealth of "material" inside a child. Whatever else we would or wouldn't eventually do in reading readiness, welcoming the child's world in our reading program would help each child unfold and dip inward and stretch out and reach around and continue becoming a person; for himself, for *his* sub-community. Using the material each child brought to the center with him, by making it into books for him to learn to read from, could help us work *with* him—not *on* him—toward evolving a strong self that could cope and contribute in a manner that brought him satisfaction.

Another reason for making learning-to-read books from the children's conversation was that there is little a child is more interested in than himself. During the first summer and subsequent year we got some very fine books in many centers. The other children were fond of them, too, but especially their proud authors, who, even though they couldn't read, could often read their own books quite admirably. The books were overwhelmingly often about fear, punishment, violence, death, food, and sex. They tended to be more associative than the "neat," trite stories of middle-class children:

I DREAMED SAMMIE WAS DEAD

by Jackie

Last night I dreamed Sammie was dead.
Sammie just died, and I went to bed.
In the morning, Mama gave me a banana and I ate the banana.
I didn't even cry when Sammie died.
My Daddy cry, and my sister cry too.

I cried last night when Sammie was dead.
My uncle brought my brother some skates.
My Mama brought some Coca Cola, and she cooked . . .
Some soup, cabbage, greens, some potatoes,
She buy some potato.
It made my tummy hurt.
I saw a cowboy picture, Superman, Batman, and Robin Hood.
Sammie was alive, and my Grandmama died.

BIG FAT JELLYMAN

by Charles

Once upon a time there was a big fat jellyman, and he said I ate peas and drank some water and I will eat you all up. Then Petty went to the store, and if I catch you I will eat you all up. Mama say where Petty at and she had never come back from the store. Sister I say sent Petty to the store for some salt. My brother say don't pull my sister hair. I chop off my head. Sister say Mama come back home and throwed Petty's head out in the garden, and throwed Petty's body out in the field. Mama come home and ask Petty and she say I killed Petty. Mama say hold your neck down and let me kill you.

Frank Smith's wife Jean, a brilliant young woman with years of Movement experience and a groping eagerness to use freedom theory in new programs, was a member of the reading readiness staff who did considerable work in this area.

With the reading material they gathered at centers, Mary Varella, Jean Smith, and others working in the reading readiness project prepared three books, which we thought of general enough interest for CDGM's printing project to print. The printing project was headed by a native Negro Mississippi printer named Mr. Kirksey. Three more were planned but not finished. *Pond* was a simple collection of sentences about experiences our children related concerning ponds: fish, "toad-frogs," snakes, etc. It was illustrated in clumsily beautiful childlike outlines of green tempera paint and was printed on lemon yellow paper. *Today* was a book of photographs taken by project photographers. They showed center children doing center things, including snoozing on a church bench and trudging to the outhouse. Descriptive captions went with most pictures.

We did not agree on spelling and punctuation. I felt that while we should be sticklers in recording exact ideas, language, idiomatic and dialectic grammar and flavor, we should generally use correct spelling. First, because people dictating are not misspelling, and it is a bit "cute" and even a little condescending, to misspell for them. Secondly, because I do not think it is relevant, and I do think it puts up artificial difficulties later, to teach children to read in a misspelled version of what they said; a rendition of the words that they will never run into again.

Some of Mary Varella's staff tramped through the back country, collecting the stories and memories of the old people. From this material Mary planned to make a rhymes book, a folk stories book, and a book of games to help parents teach their children reading. These were the three that were not printed, whether because of lack of time or funds to print I do not know. In addition to these, I worked with eleven community teachers compiling and illustrating a book for teachers called *Poor People Plan a School.* OEO cut off funds as this went to print.

* * *

MY BABY BROTHER

by Darlene

I gotta baby brother. My Mama say I'm gonna get him. She say I'm gonna get it. I say where? She say from D. Diddley Little. I say you ain't gonna get no baby from D. Diddley Little. You gonna get that baby out you stomach. My mama say that ain't true I'm gonna get that baby from Babyland. I say that ain't true Mama. You gonna get that baby from out you stomach. You fat. My Mama she say well how you think a baby get in my stomach. I say the midwife lady.

* * *

Many groups in many states have requested copies of these books. It was my feeling that *the product,* the book, was not valuable. We should probably send no more than one copy to requesting groups, as a sample of the loveliness that can be captured. It's *the process,* the active instead of passive process, children telling stories and making books from them, and children learning to read first from their own creations, that's important. We would make little contribution if we disseminated our finished material, even though it's nicer than much available material. We might make a sizable contribution if we disseminated our process of preparing materials and teaching reading from them.

At our meetings teachers, one by one, told something they remembered from when they were little—an escapade or an old tale their grandmother told them. We made them into books then and there.

How well society and the schools have succeeded in downgrading the worth of these people is indicated in the fact that whenever one of us came upon a gem of a little anecdote or adventure, so rhythmically told, and got very excited, the group would say, "Oh, that," with some embarrassment and face-covering, "That's nothing, we *all* got that!"

We envisioned this not only as another facet of our emphasis on "drawing out and extending" instead of "pouring in and suppressing" what is already in there. It would also be a bridge between the child's real world and the world of print he would shortly enter in public school. We wanted to see if we could draw out and extend each child into print, complete with all his culture and idiomatic expression. We thought this a good way to affirm the fact, unfamiliar to the children of the poor and to the Negro first-grader in general, that print is no more than thoughts, experiences, humor, etc., written down. This method might help us get across the point that books aren't foreign, frightening, and irrelevant to real life. They are only a reflection of people you know and your own life in another form. And reading is not an impossibly elaborate external code. It is just the easy continued flow of the same internal growth powers that enabled babies to learn to coo and roll over, sit, crawl, stand, walk, run, and talk.

We were trying to separate two giant steps these children are expected to take. One is learning to read, a great step in anyone's life. The other is learning a whole other world, the world of the middle class, which is as far from these children's world as is the world of the Chinese child from the world of a typical middle-class American white child. This is merely a logical adaptation of what we do with middle-class children. We teach them to read in a classroom that reflects their middle-class world. We teach them to read from books filled with their middle-class world. We don't expect a middle-class child to learn to read in a Chinese classroom and from books written in Chinese. If he is going to learn a foreign language and read in it and understand the culture it is based upon, he usually does it in a later grade. He first learns to read in a familiar milieu and in a "friendly" language, the one he has always spoken. This is one of Sylvia Ashton-Warner's key themes, as well as obvious.

* * *

. . . she put it in there. I say don't let that lady come here any more. Mama say that ain't true, the mailman brought me. The mailman is going to bring my brother. I said no. Mama say no the truth is I'm going to get it from the doctor. In his bag. I say you lying. You fat. I know. Aunt Fannie Lou told me that. Mama said well she is wrong. I am going to get that baby out from a hollow stump. But you know what? That baby here now. He was buck naked. He got a weiner on. He got a little tiny coofanny. I heard my Mama say death going to pass over her nine times. I seen the mid wife brought Christine's baby. He didn't have no weiner. He was a girl. My Mama said no a little bird brought this brother. But it ain't true. And he drinks milk from her nanyjugs whenever he ain't sleeping.

* * *

CDGM's approach to the language of the community was not without opposition. As Tom Levin later wrote:

An investigator (an accountant by trade) for Senator John Stennis of Mississippi testified disparagingly concerning CDGM pre-primers. Among our own staff there were some who objected as well. Many of the middle class Negro teachers reacted with strong feelings of shame to the appearance of POND. One center, which at the beginning of the program had to be directed to alter its restrictive recruitment policy (*i.e.,* avoiding poor children to recruit from middle class homes), passed a resolution requesting CDGM not to publish books unless they were in "good English." The second significant resolution offered by this group was a strong assertion that only "qualified" teachers be used.[22]

At most centers teachers were still doing a great deal of ABC writing. They were generally pleased with the children's progress in the ABCs, though I saw few children who could get past D, and none who knew what sounds the letters made. But teachers were also impressed by the theme of orientation: Do it your own way, but taste, test, before you decide what that is.

When I visited centers, many teachers asked more about "the things you girls were doing at Orientation." I felt strongly that the thrust of our first summer should *not* be to install a particular method or sequence, but should be to instill a feeling that you can be experimental and exploring without losing control and without losing the power to decide what you will eventually do. I didn't think we should put teachers in a position where they either had to succumb to an endorsed method, thus relinquishing their new power to pick and choose, or had to dig their heels into history and refuse to budge for fear of being threatened with superior "technology." Therefore, I responded to requests of this kind *not* by endorsing a particular method, but by mentioning the existence and highlights of several major approaches to early reading. Then I demonstrated a few games, which seemed practical in a touch-and-go situation with no continued contact, through a series of workshops. I thought we would have better opportunities in the future to figure out what methods were most ideal for our mass and primitive circumstances, and to work on them with teachers in an on-going deep-reaching manner. At this point, my purpose was to pave the way for that.

* * *

ROGER: "Ah gotta wor', Ah gotta wor'!"
LISA: "Teacha, ah gotta wor', too, teacha? Teacha?
When you gonna lemme say mah wor', teacha?"
THIRD CHILD: "Ah got me one too, teacha, ah wanna say *mah* wor'."
ROGER: "Nah, ah gotta fa'rit wor' teacha, lemme be firs'."
TEACHER: "O.K., chilrens, now hush, we gonna go one atta ti'.
We gonna ta' terms. Roga, wha's yo wor'?"
ROGER: "I's drank bahl."
TEACHER: "O.K., Roga, yo wor's drank bahl, raht?"
ROGER: "Yeah, drank bahl, tha's *mah* wor'."
TEACHER: "Roga, yo's a funni boa, tha's a nize wor', bu' why you choose drank bahl?"
ROGER: "Cus Ah wanna choo' dat wor'."
TEACHER: "Ahright, Roga, das a fahn wor'. Yo gotta stori 'bout dat drank bahl? Yo gonna tell us?"
ROGER: "Yeah, I'z gonna tell i', here's my stoh: . . ."

22 Levin, Tom, "Preschool Education and the Communities of the Poor," in Hellmuth, Jerome, ed., *Disadvantaged Child,* Vol. I. Seattle: Special Child Publications, 1967, pp. 361, 362.

I would demonstrate several auditory discrimination games about rhyming words and words that start or end with the same or different sounds. We would talk about making large lettered signs to place over each interesting object in the room. We showed how to give a child a twin to it, while making a jolly game of seeing if he could find the partner. I didn't think of this as the definitive way of teaching reading, but as a way to move from letters to whole words, and from dull learning to game-type learning—a new concept to most of our teachers. We played a version of the Sylvia Ashton-Warner word elicitation game:

Da mouse eat pāpa. Den he cut Juni's Sundi cō', and Mama ta' da cō' 'way fru behime da mouze, an take i' behime da dō' an fiss it widda trea'. Den Pa kill one mouze wit a broke drank bahl, and den Mama seen a rĕ' snā, an kiil im wit dat drank bahl, an Mama she saw a rabbi, an she gotim and putim ina bō', Mama. Den, mah Daddi wen' to huntin' las nigh' and kill him fī' rabbis, and dressem, and we eatem an dey was goo', an we ha' ahcecrea'n'cā'."

TEACHER: "O.K., Roga, das a nize wor', drank bahl.
Now Āhm gonna wrī' drank bahl on dis peice ta' boar'.
See dat? Nah *you* rea' dat to me, Roga."

ROGER: "Dat say: 'drank bahl.'

TEACHER: "Das righ', you's learnin' da' rea' real well.
Nah, you jes ta' dis ho' ta you Mama, an' read it real nize ta her tonigh', O.K., Roga?"

LISA: "Ah gotta wor', teacha, ah go' one too!"

TEACHER: "O.K., Lisa, wha's dis wor' you got?"

LISA: "Ah go' ki' an kill."

TEACHER: "No, Lisa, you can't on'y ha' but *one*. Which one?"

LISA: "Ah wan' ki'."

TEACHER: "O.K., tell us 'bout kick, den."

* * *

Generally, parents considered the CDGM program's major possible contribution to their children teaching them to read. The only method of learning to read they knew was the rote memorization ABC method. So they pressed hard for it. They felt that they did not read well enough, so naturally assumed it was because they had had too little ABC drill. Therefore they wanted their children to have more of it than they had had.

We had to interpret parents' insistence on having the children learn *ABCs* to mean they were insisting that the children learn *reading*. We had to interest them in trying alternative methods of teaching reading in the hope that they would soon come to see that there might be some that would work better for them than ABCs. If CDGM planners were going to claim to be deeply concerned with community values and parents' ideas, we could not stoically resist parental conviction that reading is critically important.

Furthermore, parents were by no means being "pushy" when they worried that their children wouldn't learn to read unless CDGM taught them. Most CDGM Head Start graduates would never learn to read adequately if we left the matter entirely to the public school system. Statistics and thousands of adults in our project proved this. Therefore we felt we had to engage in a quest for ways and means to teach reading. We couldn't indulge in the luxury of smug membership in a well-established pedagogic rigidity that said, in 1965, teaching reading to the preschool-age child is somehow repressive to the child and a denial of other important parts of programming.

Of course, the best-known early childhood educators were in much greater sympathy with our problem and proposed emphasis on early reading than the run-of-the-mill early educators. It is usually true that leaders in a field are more open to special problems and new solutions than are followers. The latter seem to have to cling desperately to conventions for fear they will otherwise not "pass." Deviation is dangerous to them, but is creative to the leaders. OEO insisted that Head Start was not supposed to "teach by lessons" or do anything with "formal subjects." No one could have been more sympathetic to OEO's emphasis on a program full of varieties of relaxed yet stimulating rich experiences, rather than a narrow schedule of prepared lessons and seated paper work, than were members of CDGM's reading readiness and children's program staff. We had no quarrel with this general approach. However, besides wanting to inspire a generally full contemporary lab school type atmosphere with all the attendant activities, we were confronted with a reality.

We couldn't plummet our graduates, innocent of what it takes to learn to read, into a wasted first grade year and a fall into the fatal finality of academic failure in a system with no remedial services. But of course we would use methods essentially consistent with our determination to capitalize upon growth from within children and their adults, and methods stressing the democratic *process.*

There is no *subject* that should be taboo for little children, from sex to space science, and from higher mathematics to reading. What should be forbidden is starting with the subject at this young age, and hoping the child can latch on and hang on for the rough, rigorous ride through senseless formulas. Rigid scheduling instead of excitingly full, fluid classroom living and learning, drill and rote coming from above rather than self-expression and a personal evolution into sequentialled skills from this, and emphasis of one subject to the exclusion of others in a stylishly faddish way are all a denial of the many-facetedness of the child and what is within and what is valuable. But *any* curiosity and talent for *any* subject can come from inside out to where it can be enriched and extended. Teachers who have sensitivity and skill in helping a child discover what he has and what kind of "who" he is, can channel this into reading as well as into good dramatic play, good art, good project work—and with the same techniques. One need not replace the other. A variety of subjects can all give body and detail to the spirit and ideology of personal and democratic child and group development.

So I made up a game called "The Sound Table Game." This game had the advantage of focusing the teachers' interest on teaching the *sound* of an initial consonant or consonant blend, instead of teaching only its *name*. It moved from teaching through sitting and copying to teaching through movement and active involvement in learning. The idea was for the children to study one sound for a whole week, which seemed better than the habit teachers in many centers had of teaching strings of letters all at once: "Make an A. Make a B." The children went treasure hunting around the room for things starting with the designated sound. They were urged to bring things from home starting with the sound. All items were displayed on the Sound Table. The sound itself was stenciled in four-inch black letters over the table.

This, it seemed to me, added several dimensions to the letter-copying technique being practiced by the teachers. First, it encouraged relating familiar objects to reading. Second, it began the notion of building printed vocabulary around things the children dealt with daily. Third, it gave children chances for personal pride in showing off their contributions to the collection. Fourth, it might intrigue parents with a hint of the new things their children would be getting at the centers; convince them that though they saw fewer papers coming home strewn with littered letters and slanting rows of crooked ABCs, the school was still "teaching" something of value to *them* as parents, and give them a tangible way to help their own children with "homework." Compared to the ABC writing, which was the only thing on the scene to compare it to at the time, it seemed a way of giving the child a more playful active role in the learning process. Activities starting with the sound of the week were planned to get the children out of those well-worn chairs, and to give teachers a chance to draw upon their resourcefulness. Children and teachers chanted the names of the collected items.

After all the children knew them, each child got a chance to do it himself. This was an improvement over the many failures children experienced in making their As and Bs wrong and being chastised for it. They went from the security of acting as a group and the familiar techniques of chanting a response widely used in their churches and community meetings, to the proud independence of doing it alone; *right.* At the end of the week, since parents and children alike so badly wanted children to learn to write letters, each child got a sandpaper letter to feel, and a crayon to use in making the strokes of the letter on a large scale. Each day the child could help himself to a snack off the Sound Table, the name of which started with the letter of the week.

In devising this game, I was trying to include a similar but improved substitute for each detrimental thing the teachers were doing, and draw from ideas found in successful methods. From the Phono-Visual method I took the idea of a table of sounds, children gathering objects to put on it, activities starting with the letter, and sticking to the sound long enough to master it thoroughly. From the Furnald method I took the idea of tracing the letter and making learning kinesthetic, rather than copying it. From Montessori I took the idea of a letter each child could manipulate and feel the shape of and have for himself. And from Peabody I borrowed the touch of a culminating edible reinforcement reward. [See Appendix D.]

Perhaps one of the most important ideas I worked on with teachers during these one-day visits was the reasons and techniques for talking with children. I had a tape recorder of my own, as the project had none. During the morning I taped children and teachers talking, or not talking, as was more often the case, and me conversing with the children as they went about their business. In the afternoon at staff meeting we replayed the tapes, concentrating on the questions: "As we listen to these tapes, can we find any missed opportunities for showing interest in the individual child? Developing vocabulary? Building informal friendship between teacher and child? Encouraging children to develop verbal relationships with each other? Can we make suggestions for how, exactly, we might do more of these things?"

Teachers thought it very funny to hear themselves recorded. They were clever at picking out places where budding conversations dead-ended and dropped into silence. We often acted out the scene, taking turns being the teacher, and seeing how many ways we could think of to draw a child further into talk, and to extend a possible chat rather than letting it fall at an apparent stopping place. *Talking* about talking with children didn't work. If people don't habitually talk lengthily with children, they don't know *how* to talk lengthily with children. So we actually practiced it:

Tape Plays:
TEACHER: Oh, you tease Tom, what you telling Winston?
TOM: I tellin' him my brother Gary a bad bad boy.
TEACHER: Oh, now, that ain't nice.

The group analyzes and discusses this. Then the same teacher goes to find Tom, who is waiting for our staff meeting to be over so one of the teachers will drive him home. The same teacher runs through the same conversation. I tape this conversation too, and afterward we discuss it to see if and how the teacher prolonged and enriched the verbal exchange.

TEACHER: Tom, what was you tellin' Winston this mornin' when you was playin' with the ball?
TOM: I tole him Gary my brother.
TEACHER: You like Gary?
TOM: Yeah, I lahk him, but he bad.
TEACHER: What's he do that's bad?

TOM: Oh, he let down the gears and the truck went down, down, and it go fast, and it smash into a tree.

TEACHER: Yeah? What your Mama say 'bout that?

TOM: She give him a good whuppin . . . with a switch.

TEACHER: Then what Gary do?

TOM: He hollered, dat what he do. He get a whuppin' alla time. Then we go in the church and he sat and he got *so* tired just settin' and he got a whuppin'.

TEACHER: Why's dat?

TOM: Cause he walked up and set with his friend when they was singing 'bout Jesus and the preacher was preachin'.

TEACHER: Who whipped him?

TOM: Daddy . . . he tuk him outside an whupped him with a red belt.

TEACHER: Did Gary cry?

TOM: Oh, yeah! He got tears in his eyes. Mama wiped his eyes with a rag when he come back in. Then he popped his fingers. That boy can't *never* be quiet.

TEACHER: What else did he do one day?

TOM: Oh, he took Daddy's bolts and screws when he was fixin' his truck. Then he got a lickin' with a shoe.

TEACHER: Ain't he *ever* a good boy? You're a good boy, aint you?

TOM: I cried because I had a sore throat, and I wanted to sleep with Mama, and Mama shook her finger at me, and she said, "When you gonna behave?" And I said, "When I'm big," and then Daddy moved on the floor and I got in with Mama and my sore throat got better. Gary was in there awready.

TEACHER: What else did Gary do?"

TOM: Gary took da money out Daddy's pocket. He run, run, run, all the way to the store, and he buy cherry ice cream and he eat it all up. When Daddy woke up, he say, "Gary, where's my money at?" And Gary was scared, so he didn't say nuthin', but he got a whippin'. . . with a belt.

TEACHER: Don't Gary never be good? Sometimes he must be good. Ain't he only four years old?

TOM: I'm five.

TEACHER: You're five. Gary's four. Was he ever a good little boy?

TOM: Yeah, he's good once. He went to get the cows once, and once he took Daddy a sandwich in the field when he was choppin' cotton. But then he was hittin' some girls and fighting them. He was fightin' Hannah. They was fussin'. He threw down Hannah. He picked up a King snake and put it down her neck. Mama tole him, "You better ac' right, Gary, you better not meddle like that!" Then Gary threw a rock at a bottle and it broke glass all on the grass, and it got in the girl's foot, and the girl screamed, and Mama beat Gary with a batman belt.

We loved the children's language, and we wanted them to love it. The children would need another language, "English," as a second language, later. They would need to be bilingual. There would be plenty of time later. Let them just learn to enjoy themselves first, all the parts of them. Let them learn to enjoy themselves in print first. Let them learn to read in an atmosphere of acceptance, not condemnation. We could not imagine how we would be helping a child love to communicate verbally, supposedly a goal of language arts programs in the early grades, if we shot him down with grammatical bullets and threw pronunciation grenades at him every time he eagerly opened his mouth to share with us.

The first summer our reading readiness program hardly made a dent. At the beginning of the summer Mary Varella, a girl who had had some experience in sensitively developing reading materials with poor Southern Negroes, and had also had some Movement experience, had written her goals for the Head Start reading program to Tom. She hoped that our preschoolers would start reading. She hoped that a few parents in each community could be trained by interested CDGM personnel to teach their children to read. This training program would lead to a longer range winter program. She proposed that we modify some of Dr. Doman's ideas to incorporate Sylvia Ashton-Warner's ideas of using the child's own culture.

Tom had agreed to the plan. He didn't see how Mary's group was going to get to each community, as Mary planned. He favored training interested community people for readiness to begin teaching in the fall, and preparing a plan for us all to follow, whether modified Doman or something else.

We all agreed who should teach the children in these ways. Who else but the parents? They were the people who believed in the children as they were, and valued the community as it actually was. They knew local folklore, songs, and other raw material from which "bridge readers" could be shaped, as well as the children from whose minds readers could be shaped. They lived with the children and could teach them at opportune moments every day, not just during the arbitrary school day and the arbitrary length of a federal grant.

If it were parents who caused children to perceive the printed word as foreign because printed words were not part of the parents' lives, then it would be parents who could spark a reading interest in their little children by beginning themselves to have warm and happy feelings about stories. It was these parents who had deep concern that their children read. To most others it was either of no consequence, considered an inherited impossibility, or at best, a professional challenge. So we were unanimously anxious to start working with a few parents in each community as a core of reading teachers.

In the fall, when he found that not a single community person had been prepared to spark a home reading teaching program, no center yet had a really strong reading program that could be demonstrated to others, no booklet for parents to teach from had been prepared, and there was not yet even an over-all plan, Tom felt that the reading readiness staff had been somewhat more eager to keep the professionals they so dreaded from doing anything about reading than it was to do something effective itself.

Tom didn't have much use for the generally negative, cantankercus behavior of some of the most creative members of the group. Unfortunately CDGM, like the Movement, attracted at least as many nihilistic and belligerent young people as it attracted idealists and social reformers. I guess the only really meaningful difference between the two types, since both were likely to be bright, was that the former were there to express againstness and use their imagination to tear everything and everybody down in the socially heroic name of speaking for Negroes, and the latter was there to build something better *with* Negroes.

In spite of what was not done and the perhaps immature and unattractive reasons why it wasn't, we came out of the summer knowing more than when we started. We had known to begin with that, theoretically, teaching would work best with the kids if poor parents did it. But now we knew that these parents *would* do it, that they would respond eagerly to bringing the best in education to their long-starved children. We now knew they regarded CDGM as a pipeline under the wall to sources of information and choice. We knew for a fact that what we had assumed at the beginning of the summer—that our uncredentialed *and* credentialed teachers alike could scarcely read, write, and spell was true.

Jean Smith wrote of a Greenwood mother with whom she was demonstrating home reading teaching technique: "Although she was enthusiastic, she could not do much with her child because she was unable to make letters uniformly or to spell simple words."

Since these were the people who had all the hard-to-get qualifications we wanted in order to do the job, and were lacking only the easily obtainable 3 Rs skills, this would be the group we would work with in the future. But we would need to design something so that parents who were not teaching in centers, thus attending teachers' workshops, would have regular adult education programs, where they would learn to write and read around folklore, current events, and community concerns.

These findings implied that teachers and parents were ready to move from our summer-style teacher *exposure* new horizons program, into a new careers for the poor-style teacher *development* program. The seriously disturbing question in my mind was, were *we*? I had had superficial experience on other jobs with some of the new work of the avant-garde group in the National Council of Teachers of English, psycho-linguists, the cognitive psychologists (particularly Jerome Bruner, Benjamin Bloom, and J. McV. Hunt), and the many many new approaches to teaching reading, writing, and spelling much earlier to children and much better to grown-ups, such as Myron Wohlman's approach, Caleb Cattegno's *Words in Color*, Laubach's *Each One Teach One*, and so on. Knowledge of all this made me feel very *un*ready to start a real reading program in the fall.

Strongly as I agreed with Mary about using material from the people as a beginning, I felt, alone I think as far as CDGM staff went, that there was a lot more to excellent reading than a beginning. It is of no use to read unless one can read well enough to sort, discard, extend, adapt, and fit what one wants into self. If a person reads only well enough to swallow the distortions others find it convenient to give him, he would be better off isolated from print (knowledge) altogether. Reading is one of the vital features of real personal freedom. It is a power only if the reader can select and *use* his material, fitting it to, blending it with, what his inner self tells him are his needs, directions, and beliefs. A bridge, yes, and that would be CDGM's unique contribution. But a bridge to what?

I thought it was high priority to preserve people as they were, language and all, in reading and writing as well as in ideas and styles. But English as it is written and spoken in books and classrooms *is* the language of our country, whether CDGM approved of it or not. I didn't think it did people any favor to protect their picturesque provincialism to the degree of preventing them from gaining fluency in thinking and living in this national language. I didn't see the need to choose between the people's language and the national language.

There was bitter disagreement between me and most of the staff on this, especially with many of the Movement workers. They were violently, silently, sullenly, against teaching *anything*. Because their own experiences had shown them that education was imposition, domination, straitjacketing, and they were unable to envision it as consistent with the development goals they spoke of as the expansion of powers and resources within people.

I felt that we should try to budget (and *get*—an equally difficult problem in rural Mississippi) a researcher with enough background in the field that we wouldn't have to wait for him to start from scratch. He should be an inventive enough person to be able to adapt his findings to our overpopulated, underbudgeted project. He should be given free reign to study both popular and off-beat approaches, and to make up new methods if necessary.

But since this was first and foremost an action project, we should not sit twiddling our thumbs while a researcher researched and children failed in first grade. There were a number of things we could do immediately. We could develop our bridge readers with guidelines and lesson plans to help teachers and parents get the meat out of them. We could write a digest of the most important early childhood reading before they could read well enough to do it from original sources. Whatever adult reading plan a researcher eventually worked out could be based from the beginning on this vocational, educational, child-raising interest.

We could begin emphasizing orderliness, sequence, and accurate perception in classrooms of sights, sounds, and also, specifically, phonics. A great trouble CDGM people had with reading was that they didn't have much logic in their lives, and they had refined the ability to shut *out* sights and sounds rather than the ability to notice them precisely. Logic and precision are important ingredients of reading.

Instead of trying to teach temporarily by *one* method, which would make teachers and parents rely on experts instead of on their own resourcefulness and judgment, and which would dig our own grave for the future, when researchers might have come up with better methods and our people would still be clinging loyally to the one we had taught them, we could stress *an experimental attitude,* not a method. We could try to lure and use the best of the best consultants, who themselves *are* innovative and experimental, and who could fire people with the excitement of trying new things, rather than rope them with the imprisoning conviction that there is only one method by which to do a thing. Our teachers needed this oportunity to work with inspired teachers more than they needed to learn a "method." I think that is true of all learning-to-be teachers. It has always saddened me that colleges and school systems give methods instead of inspiring sponsors, and the "best ways" instead of a curious approach.

At the end of the summer the only person who seemed to me to consider a research-based reading program good, rather than an insult to the poor, was our project printer, Mr. Kirksey. Mr. Kirksey had been very active in the Movement in Mississippi. He had been in it since it got started. He had come into it with Medgar Evers in 1962, but he found himself less and less in agreement with his friends, as they began advocating black separatism and down with education. He was all for freedom, and took great economic risks to show it, but he was also for reading—a key to the future—a freedom, too.

While Central Staff wrangled interminably with theoretical and personality conflicts, centers continued spinning along as cool as tops in the communities—at least compared to Central Staff. Central Staff was concerned with important concepts and their implementation. Community people were concerned only with the essence of what CDGM was doing for people. Mrs. Pinky Hall, committee chairman from the Hattiesburg Eaton center wrote: "This letter is to let you all know. Since we open up on the 12 of July how much we have enjoyed it. How great attendances we have had, the childrens have enjoyed it so much they love to play with their games, like to paint and they ask for their second helping eat all their food.

"Oh at milk break is the thrill of their life. Those that was crying didn't want to go, on the first day. Now they is crying wanting to stay. On Saturday morning they think it is a day to go to school. They look like flower blooming in early Spring time they be so happy and gay.

"They enjoy playing lady the boys enjoy playing mens. They dress up in look their best. They like to play cooking we went on a tour on the street the childrens saw the road men working on the road they did enjoy they had never seen the road mechine before."

CHAPTER 14

COME ALIVE! YOU'RE IN THE JOYFUL GENERATION!

The living arts project

IF IN THE eyes of many participants and observers massive confusion was the most outstanding feature of CDGM's first summer, the living arts project should have been their best example.

Tom Levin originally conceived of this project as a team of talented young people who would move from center to center bringing a thrilling taste of theatrical entertainment to isolated communities which had never had the pleasure. They would create with local people in each place a repertory of "indigenous arts" which would be more valued by local citizens, and more organized for them than before, for greater joy in the future.

The idea was once again to initiate the feeling that education need not be a deadly dull, droning ordeal. It can be alive and exciting. It can be filled with singing known songs and new ones; imitating animals and people and feeling what it feels like to be someone else through role playing; enjoying the new delight of expressing emotions that are usually supposed to be suppressed because it's "permissible" to enjoy them "when you are only making believe"; putting vivid color into familiar children's stories by reading them dramatically, telling them with fresh expression, and by making masks, costumes, scenery, and props for acting them out; making puppets with children and teachers and putting on experience-rooted puppet shows; making instruments; listening and moving to a great variety of records from African folk songs to modern jazz and engaging in rhythmic exercises and creative dances. The project was included in CDGM's summer program as one more way of reinforcing and extending the meaning of CDGM's goals.

This would give teachers another opportunity to see people working in informal ways with children in which the children's feelings and ideas were noticed and considered very important. This would be offered as another alternative to stiff, cold "subject" teaching. It could provide casual, happy occasions for black and white to work together on matters of mutual interest and pleasure. Perhaps it would reach children and teachers who hadn't responded to the regular program and pull them into the flavor of it. It might give a few local people "trainee" experiences—a chance to see if the arts might interest them for future study.

The living arts project would hopefully enrich empty programs and some of the beginnings being made by other special project groups—to all of which elements of living arts would be centrally relevant. Jeanine and I regarded every day that the living arts staff spent at a center as a wonderful workshop for the teachers at that center, as well as an eye-widening adventure for the children.

* * *

EVELYN: Ah'm fishin' an I catched a crawfish an a goggle-eyes an a yella trout an a catfish.

ROBERT: Ah'm a shad, Ah'm a skinny boney shad, an you gonna haffa ea' me!

EVELYN: Ah ain' gonna ea' no sha'! Ah'm catchin a skipper an a grinner an a butterfish.

ROBERT: Ah'm a shark an Ah'm eatin' you! Yump! You in mah bellyache now!

* * *

There was nothing wrong with the concept, but there were serious deficiencies in its implementation. Artistically talented as they were, the codirectors of the living arts project, Tom Griffin and Alan Pearlman, had absolutely no organizational ability whatsoever. Lovely as they were with an individual child, they didn't seem to have the dimmest glimmers of either the total nature or any of the simplest techniques of nursery education. Therefore, after contributing some lively but bewildering episodes to Orientation, and after spending two weeks vaguely developing a collection of initial activities with which to approach children, they set out in a station wagon full of spasmodically used equipment and staff members unsure of what to do with themselves, to ramble around the state for the summer.

Unlike the other projects, they didn't study the map of districts and centers before departure, decide whether to concentrate on several areas or try to briefly touch them all, and work through district coordinators to give advance notification of their anticipated arrival dates in specific places. The result was that this marvelously spirited caravan of chaos just descended from time to time on schedule-addicted teachers, asking them to throw aside their routine plans, and turn themselves over to a day of what seemed to many teachers to be utterly bizarre behavior and more than mild madness.

Community comments on this effort ranged from, "Oh, you mean the one with the bare feet who told us to guess what he was—a forest in a windstorm?" to "Those guys helped a lot. They dug us a pit for our outhouse." The team left a great giraffelike climbing thing made out of lumber and wild-colored paint on the playground at one spot, and glowing memories of "Beauty and the Beast" at another. They left a huge wire mesh creature at one place, and children acting out each story the teacher haltingly read them at another. They left teachers at many centers agreeing that it was wonderful for the children to have ridden on white men's shoulders and galloped like a horse, because it made the frightened children a little less frightened of whites. They left the teachers at other centers agreeing angrily that it was a wasted day, because the polaroid camera, tape recorder, and well-practiced performances about enchanted princesses seemed so remote from what *they* were equipped to follow up for the children.

A few teachers reported that the troupe gave them new ideas of what was "allowed" in the program. It stimulated them to build much stronger arts programs and fantasy activities with the children. But more said that they were overwhelmed by the furiously paced rush from a spurt of puppeting over here to a whirl of dancing over there, with a camera clicking and distracting the children from either of the other two activities, and uproars of singing on top of all the rest to "get the group together," while people dashed outside to "get a game going" and burst back in on the on-going other activities when the game came to an abrupt, unexplained halt, with long milling spaces of unannounced nothing while staff fell to the grass gasping for breath, and overstimulated children ran in circles shouting.

One teacher said, "It was confusing. All summer people came from Edwards and encouraged us to handle children quietly in small groups for individual attention, and then these people swooped in and got seventy children together, where they couldn't hear or see, and had everybody whooping it up. We were trying to go by a loose schedule like the program teachers suggested, so the children could get in the habit of planning with us, knowing what was coming. Then these people came crashing in, never telling us what was coming next, and went through all this wildness. The children were excited, but it wasn't the right kind of excited. It would have been nice for them to look forward to each part of the program, and know when each thing was ending, and say goodbye and know if the people were ever coming again. It was nice and lively, but it was so sudden and confusing to us. Program people wanted us to excite the children and act enthusiastic, but it was different—I don't know, not so crazy."

Had the coordinators of the living arts project been more skilled in administrative talents, center teachers could have been in on planning and understanding the reason for these fabulous activities, and could have had aid in developing follow-up programs. A few members of the children's program staff and myself tried to brief teachers on the possible arrival of the living arts group whenever we had a clue that they might be in the vicinity. We tried to help teachers sort out what had been done and think up similar things to do with the children, when we found ourselves at centers the team had just left. But the project was badly coordinated, even allowing for the difficulties the whole CDGM project had had coordinating and getting cars and petty cash when needed to function—all due to the bigness and newness.

Living arts trainees whom I ran into from time to time during the summer seemed half enthusiastic about their vibrating summer, and half frustrated that no one helped them learn skills in their special interests.

For example, Jewel and Beatrice, both with budding talents, were never given definite projects of their own for which to be responsible (a violation of CDGM carry-a-complete-burden-even-if-a-small-one policy). They were never given help developing a particular skill past the point at which it was when they came. This made them angry. Jewel taught games and songs most of the summer, but the group never got together and shared the many songs and games they knew, so her collection was small. Beatrice helped make books from pictures of the children taken by Joe, but the codirectors apparently did not help her make the necessary connections with the book-makers in the reading readiness project. This was too bad, as she could have gained a great deal of insight about learning to read from homespun materials if she had worked with the talented Mary Varella.

Joe struggled with the technical aspects of his polaroid camera, and was never given adequate help by either Matt Herron, the CDGM photographer, or Adam Giffard, the CDGM film maker, or several photographer friends-of-the-project, who would gladly have helped if they had been asked by the living arts codirectors. Modena told me she "did puppets," but apparently with some reluctance, as the codirectors regarded puppetry more as a filler than as a full-blown project. Modena felt she was getting the remnants of an interesting program.

Part of the problem with the training of the trainees in living arts was that the personnel people on Central Staff "didn't have time" to tell Alan Pearlman or Tom Griffin that they were supposed to recruit and train trainees. Therefore, the codirectors didn't do this until after Orientation. By then the Trainees had missed the extensive discussions about CDGM's implications, scope, etc. They were unaware till the end of the summer that it was more than the living arts project. Had Alan and Tom understood the "new careers for the poor" side of their responsibilities, they would perhaps have talked with the trainees about these things. They were busy enjoying performing and didn't organize their "department." By the end of the summer Alan realized this. He recommended in his final report that CDGM work out a training procedure with the Free Southern Theater, a foundation-supported group interested in community theater and the use of the Arts in education:

"As we see it, a group of people paid out of the living arts budget could travel with the Free Southern Theater and receive on-the-job training in the use of the performing arts in education. Kate Pearl, who is in charge of Community Theater Workshops for FST . . . is willing to conduct workshops. These workshops would deal mainly with the arts as tools in education—how they can be used to broaden the young child's comprehension of the world around him and to strengthen and create a sense of individual value and worth through imaginative expression and perception. Techniques of improvised theatre, dance, space design, movement, rhythm, sense perception, and telling and creation would also be taught. Finally, traditional stories and music of the South would be used as basic material. These last, of course, would be collected in their travels and later drawn upon for dramatic activities. Out of this would come local personnel trained to carry on a living arts project. At the same time a local audience and, ideally, local theaters would be created which would further the use of the performing arts in the education of a whole people. What could be done in this way is unlimited and a very important help to the kind of educational atmosphere a program like CDGM is trying to create. That great and important part of childhood experience which is not used in ordinary education would be drawn on to enrich the growing up of children."

The living arts project picked up considerably in organization, and thus in effectiveness, with the arrival of a gifted young girl named Marilyn Lowen. Due to a serious car accident en route to Mississippi, Marilyn didn't join CDGM until three weeks before the end of the summer project. Marilyn was the only member of the group who had previously taught at the preschool level. She had worked in creative movement with children in Detroit, New York, and Bennington. She had also worked with SNCC. It was a pity for the project that Marilyn couldn't come sooner.

As one of the two program coordinators trying to appraise each part of the program for children, I had come to the conclusion that Alan Pearlman and Tom Griffin were not at all hostile to the idea of organization, as many of CDGM's first summer's staff were, but that organization was simply not part of their charming natures. They added zest, vivacity, a wonderfully free, childlike spontaneity, and many other needed ingredients to the tensely tight and nervously narrow program we had in so many places—and they added hysteria. I could see no way to pull the project together from the outside. I felt that someone with nursery education skills and organizational skills, as well as creative arts skills, working from within the project could do so. It wasn't until later, after many roving staff members told us of the improvements they saw in the living arts project as they happened upon them at centers, that I realized Marilyn had all these missing skills.

After the summer was over, Marilyn wrote a report in which she commented formally, as others had informally, on the negative effects such amorphous structure, boundlessness in terms of time, space, and activity, disorder of events, procedures, and materials, etc., must have had on the preschool principles we were trying to inculcate. Marilyn wrote: "Children need to be informed about what is going to happen to them, what they are going to do. They need smooth transitions between activities so that they feel *part* of those activities and can therefore join freely in them. When a group of strangers, some of whom are white, makes extraordinary demands on the children's flexibility and stamina, I wonder if we are truly widening their horizons or whether we make them passive and confused in the sheer effort they must exert to keep up with the directions they are supposed to follow."

Marilyn pressured for changes, and created some. Her report discussed in detail recommendations for better training for trainees and better coordination with center teachers showing greater respect for their programs and enabling them to get more out of a living arts visit. She came back again to the necessity for staff to have experience in preschool work.

Before Marilyn came, and before she handed in her report in the fall, it had become clear to the program coordination staff and the CDGM director that psychological services, equipment-making, reading readiness, children's program, and living arts were intimately involved splinter parts of the total program for teachers and children. Everybody was feeling very frustrated at not being able to get to the heart of the project and program at all. We had a heap of programmatic splinters. In the end we thought that a more manageable, coordinatable working pattern for the future would be to tie these separate segments all into one division, called, Teacher Development and Program for Children.

Doubtless we would have difficulty getting anyone to staff any of the "departments" in the division. Insofar as possible we would plan to have crack specialists with total commitment to the new careers for the poor concept at the head of each department. That person would be responsible for planning first-rate experiences and responsibilities for the Central Staff trainees *in* the department as well as much more in-depth work in workshops, on location, for center staffs. These would occasionally be done by the whole department, including the expert, but would more often be done by the Central Staff trainees.

We could use the same pattern here as the one described in the chapter on the psychological counseling project.

A few living arts people, with *early education experience,* working from within the division of Teacher Development and Program for Children could hunt for talented local people. They could design training programs for them, carry on some training in a block and once-a-week workshops thereafter to help trainees with problems as they encountered them in the field, and to strengthen their skills and repertory. If the Free Southern Theater stayed funded and operative, perhaps Kate Pearl might be this person.

The trainee in the psychology program, we thought, could be considered a Community Child Development Specialist (CCDS). Similarly this trainee could be considered Community Living Arts Specialist (CLAS). He or she could do a great deal of enrichment work with center teachers and children. The same would apply to the equipment-making trainee: Community Equipment-Making Specialist (CEMS). It would also apply to the Community Reading Readiness Specialist (CRRS).

These would all be manageable new careers for the poor. Any one of them could later go on to special schools for "real" further training. We could probably find scholarships because of all their CDGM experience and natural inclination, or they could branch out into the broader field of early childhood or primary education. At the same time, we would be giving immediate first-aid help to communities in a variety of areas before we had the national prestige to get the numbers of magnificent specialists we could probably profitably use. We would be gradually building toward readiness for specialists *after* people had felt themselves, instead of starting with them and overshadowing people before they were on their teaching feet.

As in the psychological counseling project, *if* we could by any miracle get more than one or two living arts specialists during the winter in Mississippi, we could use them one per district to hold continuous workshops for groups of representatives from centers. They could also help community living arts specialists in the field. If we could get *still more* "living artists," we could have demonstration and dissemination centers as described for psychologists.

Local hiring was the responsibility of locally elected *poor* people committees, untampered with by local whites or middle-class Negroes unless elected by the poor (and I don't remember that any were). The controlling board of directors included a majority of representatives elected from the districts by the poor. Still, the point of view during the first summer was strongly that professionals were to provide knowledge, skills, and ideas *as a contribution of technical assistance in order to make new careers possible.*

At that time we were receiving many community complaints that people weren't getting enough workshops and guidance. They felt letdown that the new careers idea was getting lost. Decision-making was largely in their hands, and one of the decisions they were making was that they wanted opportunities which they knew were available in other states, to other "classes" of people. There was never the thought that the poor would "have to" do any of these suggested things. However, there was definitely the idea, unashamedly held by many CDGM professional employees, that we were expected to produce recommendations and services desired by the people. They would decide if these recommendations went into the next proposal to OEO as specific budgeted plans.

But the best laid plans of mice and men . . . So we didn't put these plans into effect during the second year of CDGM. No one from the living arts project stayed on after summer. No one else could be found to come aboard in this capacity. Marilyn would have been the ideal one to do it, but even she was not available to us until late February. She couldn't return to Mississippi for financial reasons until she knew we could provide her with some kind of modest salary. We couldn't do this until we had a second OEO grant. This we didn't have until late February. By the time she did return, "divisions" and "departments" were so far gone along altogether different structural lines that there was no way to work in the above plans. Marilyn didn't begin doing creative movement in a concentrated way until the following summer. Her talents were used in other ways, but I think not as effectively as they should have been. Periodic unfunded episodes caused CDGM much talent loss of this type.

The remainder of Marilyn's first summer report confirmed Jeannine's and my feeling that if living arts was the most tumultuous part of the CDGM program, other than the payroll section, it was also the part with the most soul, spirit, and the flavor of freedom and imagination we were seeking. We thought that in its own disheveled and offbeat way, it had given many centers a shot in the arm. Marilyn wrote: "children saw live plays. They had seen only TV before. Children acted out stories. They learned to concentrate on a plot from beginning to end and to speak and move uninhibitedly in front of others. Children saw Negro actors and actresses. They saw only white people in plays before. Children made puppets themselves. They made their puppets talk to each other. They learned how to create a toy out of cloth and yarn and staples and glue that they could keep for their own, could make again, could play with in a variety of ways.

"Through dance classes children learned to use their bodies in ways they had never done before. They memorized sequences of movement and began to make discoveries about space, tempo, dynamics, rhythm, characterization. They responded to images through sound and movement such as moving and sounding like a variety of animals, which they first had to identify by name from small models of animals. They did dances to African records. They also responded to rhythms on a drum by changing their locomotor movement (run, skip, jump, etc.) as the drum rhythms changed. The children were given opportunities to beat out their own rhythms on the drum while the rest of the class clapped these out. Through new songs and games, they developed their listening skills and verbal acuity.

"Living arts brought other experiences than those described here to the children. The most valuable cumulative effect of all these was to give the children a taste of the joy of learning and sharing new experiences. The whole educational process, even if they don't meet it in public schools for a long time, will now have exciting possibilities. Education can be seen as something that one does with a group, by expressing his own ideas, rather than as a form of discipline to be mutely or loudly suffered.

"Negro children came back from their first day at the integrated schools saying, 'No, we wasn't afraid. They was afraid, though. They wouldn't say nothin' to us. But I'd speak if they would.' As Mrs. Saffold in Durant said: 'They learned that not all white people were their enemies.'

"Living arts put on plays so that children could be involved in the action. They learned not to be afraid of white people, even those disguised as ghosts, or giants, or cows. They were encouraged to enter into the plays and often literally attacked the monsters and giants and ghosts.

"Daily contact with white staff members of community centers taught the children some trust of white people. But through plays the children had a chance to express fear and anger *at* white actors and then to play with them when they took their costumes off. I think this kind of free expression is very valuable.

"When you walk into a preschool center, you can immediately sense whether it is 'alive' or 'dead,' passive or participating. In live centers the children come up and say, 'what's your name,' they sing songs, build blocks, and generally keep busy in activities of their own choosing. There is laughter and movement. In dead centers, teachers sometimes carry sticks and paddles to shock children back to their seat, back to silence. There children look down and whisper when you ask their names. They are quiet and afraid. They don't initiate activities but wait to be told what to do.

"Living arts made every center a live center, at least for moments while they watched a play, or learned a new song. Through the kinds of group activities living arts initiated, all the children had some opportunity for self-expression and making a little noise and moving fast and then moving slow.

"It seems clear that a living arts program, perhaps in a different form, should be part of any preschool program that is concerned with developing the whole child. Acting, dance, music, games, puppetry, are valuable educational media at the preliterate level. Through widening the child's experience and giving him opportunities to learn about his own potential for achievement, he is prepared for all kinds of learning experiences that will come in elementary school, and on his own."

JEROME: Ah'm a big ol' snā'. Ah keel, Ah'm gonna bī you! You day-ud! See de bleud!"

RODNEY: Ah ain' day-ud! You crazi? Ah'm 'lahv! Ah'm gonna cook you an ea'ch you jus' lahk dey do in de junga. Ah'm gonna cŭ' you ŭ' an' putchoo inna pŏ'. Den Ah'm gonna putchoo onna plā' an ea' chou.

JEROME: Oh no you isn'! Oh no! Ah'm gonna pawzen you, an you cain' li' trew mah pawzen! Ah gotta keen mouf, an you betta watchou'!

RODNEY: You cain' keel me! Ah'm a princess! You cain' keel no princess, J'rō'!

JEROME: Man, you ain' no princess! You is too black to be a princess!

RODNEY: Boi, you lyin', teach' say Ah's de princess when dat beas' come. Da' whi' ladi, she say Ah's de princess. An cain't no snā' kēel no princess!

JEROME: Dat raht?

RODNEY: Das de trufe, don' gi' me no mō' you lyin', cain't no snā' keel no princess!

JEROME: Oh, ah din' know da'. I din' know no snā' coultn' keel no princess . . . well, das awrah', Ah'll keel Glori', she ain' no princess, she jus' a whī' ladi!

CHAPTER 15

MEDICAL AND SOCIAL SERVICES PROGRAMS: CDGM VS. MISSISSIPPI

WHEN SARGENT SHRIVER first began talking at the end of the summer of 1964 about a summer pre-first grade program for the children of poverty, he talked of a medical and nutritional program. We added the educational and the community action components in the fall, before Head Start came to be called Head Start, and before it was announced. This was one reason that Tom strongly emphasized the medical side of CDGM.

Another reason for this emphasis was the health scene among Mississippi Negroes. In 1964 nonwhite infant mortality in Mississippi was the highest in the nation. White infant mortality in Mississippi was higher than the national average, but not extremely so. 1965 statistics show that in Mississippi 23,238 white babies were born in hospitals, and 16,341 nonwhite babies born in hospitals. Fifty-two white babies were born in doctors' offices, and 740 nonwhite babies were born in doctors' offices. Seventy-nine white babies were born with the aid of only midwives, and 10,721 nonwhite babies were born with midwives.

One cause for the apparent "retardation" of poor children is birth damage caused by improper prenatal, delivery, and pediatric care. In 1965 the median death rate age for Mississippi whites was 70.4. For nonwhites it was 63.5. Nor was there an observable rush to remedy these things. In 1967 an honest Mississippi medical official told me that Mississippi was "about the lowest state in the nation on the Medicare participation totem pole." And in January, 1967, only 68 out of 138 hospitals had signed their 441 forms, the integration compliances that would make them eligible for federal funds. They preferred to let the badly needed money go rather than integrate.

Statistics for 1967 show that there were 1,073 licensed doctors in Mississippi. This is one physician for every 1,053 people. The average in the nation is one physician for 742 people, which is generally considered to be a shortage. In Mississippi there was one nurse for every 571 people. In the nation, the average was one nurse for every 291 people, and this is not considered enough.

These statistics, of course, do not indicate the quality of training and experience of the doctors and nurses, or indicate their willingness to serve the poor, to give equal medical treatment to Negroes, and to treat Negroes as equals, socially, in waiting rooms, etc. Nor do the statistics reveal the location of doctors in relation to the location of patients, how far a patient must go to get medical attention, or who will provide his transportation to get it.

Tom Levin had worked with the Medical Committee for Human Rights in Mississippi the previous summer. He harbored no illusions regarding discrepancies between health services claimed and health services offered, or about discrepancies between health services offered and health services *received* by poor Negroes. But he wanted the best medical care we could get for CDGM children. Cooperation from county clinics and doctors in the state was essential. He also wanted to see if it was possible for CDGM to be viewed by state officials as the federal program it was, as the Head Start it was, instead of the second installment of the guerilla COFO war of the summer before.

In order to try to reach an understanding, Tom Levin, (CDGM director), Helen Bass Williams (CDGM health director), and a local Negro doctor who was advisor to Mrs. Williams, made a proper appointment, through proper letters and proper confirming telephone calls, to see the proper person: Dr. A. L. Gray, commissioner of the Mississippi State Board of Public Health. The last of the letters from Dr. Gray to Tom regarding the imminent discussion expressed wonder at Tom's concern about the summer's health services for CDGM preschoolers. Dr. Gray asserted that Mississippi has long provided all services specified by Head Start and always will, without outside aid.

On what Dr. Gray based this assertion, CDGM was unclear. Head Start required thorough individual physical examinations, medical histories, and medically determined developmental assessments. We didn't find evidence of thorough work and records of this nature kept on each child by county clinics. Head Start required vision, hearing, speech, and tuberculin screening tests. We didn't find that clinics went into these things with preschool children, except tuberculin tests in some instances. Lack of records at clinics on these topics, plus the number of cases of impaired sight, hearing, or speech found in CDGM's medical work, were an indication that clinics probably had not yet done these things. Head Start required urine tests for albumin and sugar, and blood tests for anemia. Clinics didn't regularly do this work. Many protested that it wasn't a regular service when CDGM asked if they could help with it. Head Start required dental examinations. Not 5 percent of our CDGM children had ever been to a dentist, so it was doubtful that Dr. Gray was accurate when he said Mississippi Public Health provided *all* Head Start medical care.

Well over half the CDGM children had had *no* immunizations, and even fewer had had their full compliment. Head Start required the "completion of immunizations." Head Start required gross psychological screening of the children. There was no evidence that any CDGM child had ever been seen by a psychologist in a county clinic, or referred to one by the county clinic. Head Start urged follow-up treatment. Clinics didn't claim to offer this. Head Start requested home visits to discuss health with parents. Home visits to track down VD or TB were common, but no one knew of any general visits to discuss a child's health with parents. Head Start strongly recommended the use of specialists as consultants in the childrens' medical program. We were unable to unearth many instances in which the Mississippi Department of Public Health provided orthopedists, psychiatrists, audiologists, etc., to every five-year-old who lived in poverty. Specialists just weren't abundant in rural Mississippi, and it was highly problematic if they would have voluntarily served little black youngsters if they were.

The delegation that went to call on Dr. Gray reported the first thing the doctor did was deliver a soliloquy about "you people" who come in and launch medical programs without having the courtesy to come to the "authorities."

It was pointed out to Dr. Gray that the group *was* coming to him: that was why it was presently sitting in his office. He smirked a "you can't fool me" smirk. He indicated that "the big people" in the project didn't consider it worth their time to come to see him. Group members reviewed their various titles again, to reassure Dr. Gray that "the biggest people" in CDGM and its proposed medical programs were indeed in front of his desk. He accused them of coming "long after" medical work had started. They patiently explained that there were no *plans* yet, much less accomplished medical facts. They had come to see if a cooperative medical plan could be conceived.

Dr. Gray said this simply wasn't true. CDGM, Head Start in general, had been planned without him. Tom replied that the federal government had planned it, and had, true, planned a specifically outlined medical component, and that, yes, CDGM had already been planned by Mississippi Negroes and their Northern friends, but CDGM was now seeking Dr. Gray's advice as to how it could support, promote, and extend *his* services to the poor.

Tom said he understood that health clinics were available in every county. He wondered if advance arrangements could be made to guarantee the greatest convenience to clinic staffs and the greatest service for children. Dr. Gray refused to give Tom a list of clinic locations and hours. Tom said politely that that was all right, he wouldn't trouble Dr. Gray's busy staff further for the list, as it could easily be obtained.

Tom asked if the group could get Dr. Gray's endorsement for CDGM to use the clinics. Would Dr. Gray write to clinics and ask them to serve CDGM? *No,* Dr. Gray said, he would not do that, because his doctors were overworked as it was. Tom said it was possible that he could get local Negro doctors to help out at the clinics, under the direction of clinic staff of course, to stretch services. Dr. Gray became angry, saying that these matters were entirely up to local officials, and he would certainly not "force" doctors on them. He became very excited about "unlicensed" out-of-state doctors and "quacks"—evidently a reference to Harvard medical school graduates licensed in other states, and other assorted licensed doctors from the Medical Committee for Human Rights.

Tom repeated wearily that he was speaking of local Mississippi doctors. At this point, Dr. Gray whirled upon the local Mississippi Negro doctor in the delegation and offered the information that he, Dr. Gray, was the chief health officer in the state, and as such had the power to license and *de*license physicians in Mississippi if he "was not satisfied" with their professional behavior. The Negro doctor received the ominously issued threat with deferential humility and grace.

This was the auspicious beginning of CDGM's health program. Dr. Gray then said he thought it was a good thing CDGM was going to have a medical program for five-year-olds "because those Negroes need birth and VD control." Tom felt sure these would be suitable programs for CDGM to get into, although he was more doubtful than Dr. Gray that this would take care of all the health needs of a preschool group.

However, Tom was delighted that he had somehow pleased Dr. Gray. Tom later reported: "After this meeting and several other experiences with the "state," I made a tactical decision. Those against us had a hardened line. Those *for* us prayed we would leave them alone and not put them on the spot. *We* prayed everybody would leave us alone and not stamp us out. If they'd had anything to do with us, that's what they would've had to do, since we were the dreaded 'Summer Project' coming after the terrifying 'Summer Project of 1964.' Under the circumstances, our goal was to avoid being stamped out till we got roots. We couldn't have a goal of cooperation with the state. It was entirely unrealistic. If we had tried to cooperate with the state to the extent of waiting till it was converted and condoned us, we would have gotten nothing done on the Negro side of the fence for the next ten years. The tactical decision was that we would have to forget about doing more than lightly tapping the possibility of obtaining state agency services. We would have to make out the best we could."

In spite of his conclusion, however, Tom continued to urge community people to take advantage of available health opportunities. A letter from Tom to CDGM committee chairmen, dated June 28, quoted Dr. Gray's statement that services are offered and advised people to "properly use these facilities within the framework of the total objectives of the war on poverty and the civil rights compliance."

When Helen Bass Williams, a large light-middle-aged Negro lady from South Carolina, a child of poverty herself, began working in CDGM communities the next week, she began to discover for herself the full implications of Dr. Gray's statement that his clinics ran autonomously. Not only did clinics differ in services they could offer (what was a matter of routine in one county, you couldn't even ask for in the next), but very few doctors in the state felt free to do anything that wouldn't suit the State Board of Public Health.

It appeared to Helen that counties were autonomous in *not* offering services, but they weren't autonomous in freedom to offer what was required to reach and meet the needs of the poor. So Helen went ahead and prepared her own program. She wrote a "job description" for local poor person health aides, who would be working in each center when centers opened. It appeared as a page in the loose-leaf notebook guidelines that were given to each person attending Orientation. It was also given to each health aide separately, and was the basis of discussion at Helen's Orientation workshops with them.

The printed guidelines, which were clearly and simply expressed step-by-step instructions, and the spirited discussions Helen led, emphasized three categories. The first was service. This outlined details: arranging a physical examination for each child enrolled in CDGM, completing the health history form, calling the CDGM health coordinator if the Health Department said it couldn't help, arranging for transportation for the children, what to do with completed health forms, helping parents understand the meaning of their child's physical condition, keeping a file of health booklets for parents to browse in, keeping a record of CDGM lunches eaten by each child, and checking and recording the weight of each child every two weeks.

The second category stressed health education and community organization. Helen helped people learn how to form health committees of interested persons in each community. She elicted from them topics to be discussed with this committee, and if possible with a local physician: avoiding diseases, improving the health of the mother, care of the sick in the home, what foods are healthy, and how does a child grow healthfully. She showed health aides how to write to the State Board of Health for films and booklets.

Helen's third category was fact finding. This included how to discover and list every health organization in each health aide's area, and how to communicate with them in an effort to get their ideas on what could be done for the improvement of the children's health. And it included stress on the importance of trying to work with Health Department personnel, and keeping documented notes on cases in which service was not all that could be expected.

As was often the case with CDGM, the plans were sound, and the print was clear, but putting ideas and words into *effective* use by means of people who have no habits in the least of these suggestions, and who have as much unconscious negative reaction to the tasks as they do conscious positive reaction, will take many years and many skilled workers.

Subsequent CDGMians had a nihilistic way of denying the efforts of their predecessors by implying, if forced to acknowledge them at all, that they were either lazy, poorly endowed with imagination, or badly organized. They seldom, even if pressed, admitted that the whole new careers thing was a discouragingly difficult job, and the best we could do was build on each others' shoulders.

Disorder in the 1965 medical program could be attributed to factors readily visible from an analysis of the tasks that needed to be done. Community people in CDGM communities weren't used to arranging *anything*. Things just happened to them from on high. They didn't know how to make arrangements involving time, place, and elaborate cross-scheduling. Yet they needed to begin learning how, through this practical opportunity for doing so. If they didn't, they would continue to miss available services because they couldn't cope with the details of using them.

Cars were very scarce, so people needed this chance to try to figure out ways to utilize those they had. People were afraid to approach clinic personnel as fellow arrangers—they had not traditionally been received in that role. It was time to begin offering clinic personnel chances to perceive poor people in this new capable role.

In many cases clinics put people off about proposed services. Poor people haven't been trained in perseverance. It has not paid off in the past. So they tended not to follow up on things clinics vaguely postponed. Now they could begin to grapple with techniques for getting around this detour too. Often, local doctors contacted in lieu of the clinics didn't readily respond to the proposition of becoming involved in what many termed a "civil rights program." CDGM people insisted on using nonsegregated facilities and usually appeared in cozily integrated groups. Nevertheless, it was important for CDGM people to surround local doctors with their new expectations of them or the status quo would never change.

Rural doctors didn't have secretaries, usually, and didn't write up full records, so these weren't available to CDGM health aides. This, also, health aides needed to protest. Families were reluctant to give complete medical history information because they didn't know where it would go and who would use it against them. They were accustomed, of course, to "authorities" using their own confidences against them. "Name the child's father" caused severe problems in many communities, as naming him might lead to social disaster for the namer, or people feared they would be dropped from welfare. In fact, they would have been, if the confidential information had inadvertently got to the welfare people. Then, too, parents didn't remember much of the information requested. They had many children, and with the press of things like staying alive, the date one of the children learned to walk or creep wasn't terribly important. No one had had experience in keeping records.

Reading what was being asked for, and spelling the answers, was frequently an obstacle. This would have been true had the OEO medical form been simple. But, as Head Starts everywhere affirmed, this wasn't the way it was. It seemed to Helen, and to Dr. Gerald Rosenfield who later replaced her, that OEO was more concerned with standardized administrative procedures than with unique medical problems in Mississippi. That pink, white, and green medical form, for instance, was designed for easy sorting by an IBM machine and for esoteric research purposes, but not for collecting useful information from *people.*

Communications with Central Office for help were enormously difficult, because we didn't have easily accessible phones in many communities, and we didn't have enough lines or receptionists at Mount Beulah. To complicate communications still further, those members of Central Staff needed to answer the health aide's question were sometimes in the field solving problems in person, so messages didn't always get delivered. As medical workers didn't understand the meaning of the child's physical condition, and as, again, transportation to go forty miles or so was virtually impossible for a plantation family to secure, it was hard for health aides to help parents understand their children's medical problems.

Poor people are accustomed to seeing "the children" rather than "a child." Therefore, reports on food consumed by an individual turned out to be reports on food cooked in the kitchen. There were no scales to weigh children every two weeks—or ever. A few doctors were very generous about attending community meetings to discuss ways of improving health conditions. Most looked at CDGM as a hot potato. Besides, they were overloaded.

There were no projectors and few capable readers in our communities, so ordering films and booklets was regarded as low priority. There were few health organizations in remote, rural areas, and they were more likely to procrastinate than to rush to the education and service of the "niggers." People did make some documentations of agencies that didn't cooperate with them, but it was hard for them to write explicit essays, as their schools hadn't taught them to express themselves in print, and neither paper nor pencils were common household items. Filing systems weren't a familiarity. But all these things were important things for community people to start thinking about. Placing the burden on them promoted thinking.

The local community *was* concerned about health. But without further specifics, and services and solutions, getting the community together to nod and agree about the importance of health, was, though a shocking revelation of existing conditions, not a catalyst for change.

All these problems had been predicted, but there was no one else to do the job. And as our original proposal to OEO made clear, we were interested in developing at least the embryonic stage of new medical careers for the poor.

Helen Bass Williams felt violently that there were deeper reasons underlying poor people's failure in all states to use existing health services to the fullest. She felt that these were exaggerated to the point of absurdity in Mississippi. She said that poor people would be clean and healthy when they wanted to be, when they felt important in shaping their families' lives and health, not when sweet neat little middle-class health nurses told them to do so. The major message Helen tried to convey at her well-attended Orientation sessions was that mothers had the key role in bringing health to their children.

Wherever she went, Helen stormily informed her audiences that health clinics have services all right, but that not enough people realize *what else* they give *besides* services. In addition to such piecemeal bits of service as an inoculation here and a vitamin there, she explained, they give each mother the distinct and undeniable impression that she is inferior, that her child is inferior, and that they, the superior clinic personnel, will "provide" any "health" the heathen children will get, by smugly "getting around" his resistant, superstition-ridden mother, who persists in her ignorant conviction that health is irrelevant. Each child might leave the clinic with an inoculation, but also with the impression that his mother, who has been called by her first name throughout the transaction, and who has been made to enter the clinic through a side door, sit in a segregated waiting room, and wait God knows how long, is a useless blob in the mass of dirty and shiftless people who make up the masses of blacks.

When clinic personnel served out what Helen called the "sweet evilness" of calling her (with two masters degrees and well-shined shoes) by her first name when she accompanied community groups to get their shots, she retaliated by calling the nurse "Sally Lou," and by pursuing a conversation in this vein until it was obvious to her community friends that she had put the "professionals" under her heel and pulverized them. Helen admitted that children didn't often get what they came for as a result of this routine, but she knew they got something just as important: a chance to see a member of their race stand up for herself and refuse to tolerate traditional forms of humiliation.

When Helen's groups walked out of the clinic, they kicked up their heels with pride and laughter.

Some community people reported less ecstatically on their experiences with the health program. The chairman of one center wrote: "On August 25, 1965 I took eight (8) children to the County Health Department for immunizations. I reported at the desk who I was and that I had brought children from the Child Development Center for immunizations. After giving the clerk the names of the children and parents I sat waiting for the clerk to bring the cards. While waiting the nurse from the immunization room came to the door and asked was there anyone in the room to take shots. I replied, 'We Are.' She said rudely, 'Come on back.' We proceeded to go to the immunization room. Then she asked, 'Do you have your cards?' I said 'no.' She replied, 'you know you can't get any shots without cards.' I said, 'We are waiting for our cards to be pulled.'

"After the clerk returned with the cards, the nurse apeared again and said roughly 'Y'all come on if you want to take shots.' I took two children by the hands and started in the door and she said again 'Y'all come on. I don't have time to fool around.' Since I was going in the door with two children I thought and the children thought too she was talking to them, so the aid and the other six children came in the room behind me. And she said rudely, 'Where all of "y'all" going?'

"I spoke and said, 'you told them to come in here.' She said, 'I didn't because I had two (2) children bringing them in and you said, "Yall come on."' She said for me not to talk to her like that. I said, 'Well, don't you talk to me like that either.'

"I again went to the waiting room and got two (2) more children which didn't have anything on their cards but their name and birth dates. Then she asked if I had permission from the parents to give these children shots. I told her I had. Then she replied we are supposed to have proof. So I returned to the waiting room again and got the paper the mother had signed and returned to the immunization room to show her. She refused to look at the papers and said, 'If you want these children to have shots you better bring them on in here for I don't have time for all this.' I said, 'I can't do but one thing at a time. You asked for proof and I brought it for you to see.' By this time she was furious.

"So I went out and got three (3) children and placed their cards in their hands. When they got into the room she snatched the cards out of their hands and threw them in a box without writing on them the shots she had given. She didn't write on but one of the eight cards.

"After she had given the fifth child shots and turned and filled the needle she reached for the fifth child again to give her another shot. And I snatched the child away from her and told her she had given this child a shot. Then she asked me where was her card? I told her, 'You took their cards and threw them in the box without writing anything on them.' She didn't know who had been given shots and who hadn't and I don't want the shots if there was no record kept. I took the children and walked out.

'When I got in the waiting room she came back to the door and said 'Come on if you want these children to have shots.' I said again, 'If I don't know and you don't know what they are taking and not keeping a record of it I would rather for them not to have it. Then she asked me the name of the child that took the last shot. I told her, 'If you had been writing it down like you were suppose to you would know. You won't get it by me telling you.' I walked out with the children."

Helen was furious with the U.S. Public Health Service for sponsoring and promoting this approach. She wanted to know why it was that clinics were allowed to get more and more federal millions, and yet were allowed to shut down at the hours when poor people could get to them, and in some cases be open as infrequently as once every four weeks—a fact in some of the outlying clinics in Mississippi. She wanted to know why clinics were allowed to advertise their services merely by posting their hours on their own doors, miles from the people, and by giving notices to those *they* consider "Negro leaders," often individuals who don't see a poor person from one month to the next.

Why weren't they required to consult with their constituents as to when they could come? Why weren't they required to go to churches to promote their services? Why weren't they required to make sure that services were *used*, instead of just offered? And above all else, why weren't they required to gain the confidence of mothers instead of being ignored while they condescendingly continued their long-practiced patterns of insulting these mothers?

Helen had it in for the Medical Committee for Human Rights, too. She acknowledged that they were doctors, and that all doctors do good. But she felt it was an indictment of the MCHR as well as of *all* doctors in all states that they weren't teachers and motivators. Nobody will ask for things about which they don't know. The poor won't ask for health services of which they have never heard.

Thus, Helen felt, it's incumbent upon health people to teach poor people what to request. Poor people won't get better health service and better social treatment from public health personnel until they press for it, And they won't press for it until medical people help them. And the Medical Committee on Human Rights would seem to be the group to do that.

Helen was head of the medical program for three weeks. After two of these weeks Dr. Gerald Rosenfield arrived from California to join the CDGM medical project. Helen said she was leaving because she couldn't stand all the frustrations inherent in trying to accomplish anything with Negroes in Mississippi, and because of the frustrations of working in the religious cult that CDGM was that summer. She described herself as the most religious, down by the water, and there were the converts, and we were ready. She felt CDGM was the first thing in the state that was interested in developing *people*—not only leading them forward and organizing them, but *developing* them. She thought we had a wonderful program, but she felt we brought our own barriers by being *so* committed, so exclusively committed. Each of us was sure we alone were concerned and were right. We wouldn't listen to each other.

Like many other professionals that summer, Helen didn't know anything about COFO. She didn't know we were working with the remains of a great thing. She wasn't able to deify any group. She just wanted to meet her coworkers on equal terms and get to work. She didn't have the slant. She didn't know we were supposed to give a testimonial about how terrible the middle class is before we could prove ourselves. She got sick and tired of throwing everything professional out the window and denouncing people who combed their hair and took baths. She got a reputation for fighting the Movement because she insisted on her right to judge people as individuals, and because she didn't swallow the idea that she, and all others who are trying to find ways to help people, are bad.

She suffered many indignities and indecencies. For example, one day she'd been working with mothers in Indianola. On her way back to Mount Beulah, near Isola, a 1957 Chevy pulled in front of her and pushed her car off the road. Four young men opened all her car doors and cursed at her. One spat in her face. She started to wipe off the spittle. He told her if she wanted to wipe it off, she had better open her mouth first. It was dark. She was alone. So she opened her mouth. He spat into her mouth. From that night on she decided that there had to be a CDGM to fight for human dignity, but that she couldn't work in a context where people of her degree of commitment were so scornfully condemned.

Gerry Rosenfield had completed his residency in California. He was going on to a fellowship in psychiatry in the fall. He brought a point of view that was rare among us that summer. He felt that overwhelming pressures were upon him to get the work done—to see that 6,400 children got the inoculations, tests, examinations, and recommended treatments expected in the government contract under which we were operating. He didn't approve of the way it was done, but felt that any way possible was the *only* way possible for such a short-handed staff to do such a huge job. He agreed with Helen Bass Williams. But he had to do a job.

Gerry and his staff, largely local poor people trainees, one per district, got the prescribed medical work done. Both Gerry and the local Negro doctor who served as a consultant wrote to all doctors in CDGM areas explaining our health program, follow-up plans, billing procedures, and antisegregation policy, and asked for cooperation.

Many subsequent staff members virtually erased Gerry's efforts and tenure with the statement: "There *was* no health program the first summer." Perhaps if these latter-day saints had made arrangements for 6,400 children, had kept records on each, had done much of the doctor recruiting and bill figuring, they would have found it less easy to wipe out the work with a sweep of the hand. It is true that there was highly insufficient work done in training community health aides. Nor did center teachers and parents experience the renaissance Helen had hoped for them. The children were rarely checked at the door each morning, nutrition and variety were less abundant than food in center meal planning, and the children didn't learn to find the doctor an interesting friendly personality.

But judging by the thousands of parents and teachers who extolled the health program to the fullest, perhaps more than other parts of CDGM's multifaceted program, and the pride with which they showed off their nutrition and sanitation to visitors, the health situation was evidently enough superior to the usual one they experienced that it far surpassed their health aspiration level. Even the ridiculously superficial physicals and absurdly gross developmental assessment CDGM whizzed the children through, were fabulous by parents' standards. A sad commentary on CDGM's medical program, and a sadder one on Mississippi's.

Snatches out of reports in the first summer files paint the picture. A visiting resource teacher writes of a center at which she spent a few days: ". . . a pleasant area where the earth has cracks all over it, and the sun dries the soil out so much that they can't plant fruits or vegetables and expect them to last. The general store is the same as the post office, and that's about it. . . . the health problem is one which is concerned with very many runny noses, and an abundance of sores on the arms, legs, and faces of several children, the source of which is not known. We talked about this and the teachers plan to take the children to the Rolling Fork Public Health Center. . . . The problem of . . . buying fresh fruit and vegetables for the children . . . . there is no place, so they decided they would go to . . . whenever they could buy these things . . . The science table presents a few problems in as much as the local rats come in at night and eat up their sweet potatoes and other similar exhibits. . . . They decided to move these things at night."

People in the country usually have gardens, hence fresh vegetables. Mississippi is known for its rural nature and its lack of urbanization and culture, but it has enough urbanization to have mud-road town slums galore. People residing there do not grow a substantial amount of vegetables. And they have other problems.

A poor person resource teacher wrote: "This week we are putting emphasis on personal hygiene, and have declared this as 'Health Week' in our Center. With this in mind, the children were ready for the doctor early Monday morning. The children have all been examined by Dr. and now look forward to the preschool inoculations. . . .

"Mrs. —, our parent president, had thirty one mothers with her on Wednesday night. [She] and a committee of people will have a neighborhood bazaar to supplement the staff members' contributions. This money will get . . . underpants . . . and other needed articles.

"In the area of this school, there is a city dump and near-by is the cities sewer lagoon. The children therefore are a mass of sores. . . . With green soap, PhisoHex and the first aids kit, we are fighting a winning battle against infected mosquito and spider bites."

Mrs. Winson Hudson, chairman of the Harmony center, wrote: "Because of the thorough medical examinations our children received we can honestly say two or three lives have been saved, which wouldn't have been otherwise."

While the "thorough examinations" were a possible three minutes in length in many places, they were the first that most CDGM children had ever received. It's doubtful that CDGM saved any lives, but it is important that it was *perceived* as having saved lives.

Medical and health problems are intertwined with all the other terrible problems involved in being poor. The local resource teacher wrote in a voluntary report on her center: "Much poverty exists such as need for jobs to support large families. There are large numbers of seven, eight, and nine year olders who have never been to school because of poverty and negligence on the part of the parents. Some unwedded mothers have been taken from the Welfare list as punishment for immoral living, etc.: however, those children are suffering . . ."

Mississippi wasn't entirely sympathetic to problems of this sort. For example, a law required the State Health Department to supply the names and addresses of unwed mothers monthly to county district attornies. Most officials were evidently not in agreement with this law. They didn't do anything about it. However, some did. A lady from Clarksdale in Coahoma County brought us this letter from the county prosecuting attorney: "Vergie Mae: Please make arrangements for the care of your children so that you can report for trial on the charge of having an illegitimate child on Monday, August 2, 1965. I will recommend to the Court that you be sentenced to thirty days in the county jail, but the court has the power to sentence you up to 90 days in jail or a $250.00 fine.

"I will expect to see you in my office on that morning." Many such letters appeared.

Our health program revealed that many problems communities considered mental were physical, and vice versa:

A staff psychologist wrote: "A 5½ year old boy was examined because of some noted difficulties in learning. The boy . . . was found to have a serious visual difficulty that made it necessary for him to place his head on the surface of the table in order to attempt some of the tasks asked of him by the counselor. However, for tasks that did not require drawing, he adequately handled certain materials and he also was found to be fairly high level in his verbal abilities. Mrs. — will attempt to have this boy seen by an eye specialist."

Several centers for which out-of-staters the summer before had helped raise money and which had been constructed as community centers, had their own "clinics." Mileston had a clinic which a public nurse visited on her regular beat. Winstonville had a clinic where staff treated an epidemic of impetigo with Dial soap baths, and gave head treatments to those who needed them.

A mother in Laurel wrote to Central Staff (the newsletter); "The program of headstart was a very nice one. It helped the children. . . . It learned children how to eat there food, where at home they probly didn't get milk. It helped them get there food they didn't get a home because there parents didn't have no job to get it. I think if this program will continue we will have strong girls and boys of tomorrow and girls and boys for a higher education they won't be so tird and hongry for there studys."

An aide wrote a long letter to Mr. Shriver, which included this paragraph: "There are children who come to this center in the morning without breakfast. No doubt if they were home there would be no lunch. Here in this program these Children found what we all need. Learning and food to eat. You might ask why they didn't get breakfast or lunch. Well, that's easy, these parents are out early trying to work to support their children. That leaves no one to care for these 3-4-5-6 year olds. So to me this Causes Crime. Anyone hungry will do anything for food. I believe this American government can stop Juvenile Delinquency if we get food . . ."

The health aide in the Kingston center wrote: "This program has helped expose the many public health facilities to the families who have not made previous use of them."

Glen Allen community people laughed for months about the day they suddenly, in mid-operation, got sixty new center applicants—it was the day teachers paraded through town all the children who had got Head Start eyeglasses.

In August, Joan Bowman, a white Southerner, former SNCC worker, and CDGM historian, dropped her historian responsibilities to become coordinator of the medical program in the Delta. "I commuted almost daily to the Head Start centers in my district, seeing that the Health Aide . . . roughly equivalent to a practical nurse . . . was surveying the health resources of her area, and prying benefits from the fist of the dominant white community. . . .

"Since medical technology has reduced some complicated laboratory techniques to simple steps, we were able to do much of the laboratory work ourselves. We detached some staff from the centers and trained them to do urinalysis, to administer tests for tuberculosis, and collect blood samples for anemia. Daily the laboratory team would travel to a center where we had arranged with teachers to test the children. We draped sheets around furniture arranged so that we could simulate the conditions of a 'laboratory.'

"Poor rural children are terribly frightened by needles. Heartbreaking scenes occurred, where the children lined up apprehensively to face our table of sanitized cotton, alcohol, tines, lancers, apparatus. They had been promised by their teachers that it would not hurt, and sometimes even the teachers themselves would take the tests to offer an example for the children. Frequently, however, the first child would yelp when his finger was jabbed for blood, and the whole lot of children would set up such a howl that an observer happening along might have thought we were slaughtering them.

"Afterwards, the team would hold the children, play with them, offer them balloons, and try to undo the havoc they had wreaked. They would pick up a shabby waif and be overcome with guilt and remorse, as if what they had done symbolized what white technology had done to colored peoples throughout the world."[23]

By the end of the summer I had come to the conclusion that what we were doing psychologically to the children through our medical program was probably so ghastly that it negated any physical good we might have done. I thought in the future we should pay all doctors for half an hour of their time *before* examinations and inoculations—unless they would volunteer their time—to play with the children. We could make our torture chamber a little more human with balloons and lollipops, romping and wrestling, lap-sitting, and completely honest explanations of what was going to happen and why. Children could be promised and given the non-needle part of plastic disposable hypodermics and a peek at their blood under a microscope, even if this was a little bit of "unnecessary" work.

I thought we should make the long trip to the clinic a center event, an outing. Parents could be specially invited, and given transportation, to come. Picnics could be served in a wooded spot en route. Or plantation people, to whom a trip to the distant hamlet was a rarity, could sightsee. The jaunt could be joined by a field trip to the fire station or to the park for a boat ride. The program department could emphasize a medical doll corner: a toy clinic with pillow cases for nurse and doctor costumes, real nurse hats, donated stethoscopes, popsicle sticks for tongue depressors, dolls and each other for patients, and medical pictures to page through. I thought that if we ever got to the point of sophistication where resource teachers or center health aides were tak-

[23] From Joan Bowman's book on the South, unpublished as of this date.

ing temperatures and checking throats each morning, these things could be done in the make-believe "clinic."

Tom's biggest concern about the medical program was, as in all areas of the program, how to combine new careers *for* the poor with the great need for better services *to* the poor. He had an elaborate plan for training community medical workers. Some people would be community psychiatric counselors. As they would be friends and neighbors of the families, they would not be regarded as "foreigners" from another walk of life appearing out of the blue in what were seen as critical roles. They could, with training, "counsel in a context."

Those wishing to do so, would go on through training, advancing to center health aide, practical nurse, registered nurse, and in rare cases, doctors. Training would utilize special initial training under the auspices of programs to be developed under Mississippi Action for Communty Education (MACE: Tom's original name for the umbrella including CDGM and all sister projects to be brought into existence with other federal and foundation funding), and professional training programs for orthodox medical personnel in and out of Mississippi, scholarships, and so forth. Tom has since refined this plan in New York. He wrote a proposal describing it in detail from his position as assistant professor of Psychiatry at the Albert Einstein College of Medicine.

Neither my plan nor Tom's proved practical during CDGM's second year, though I did go and talk to Dr. Gray about possible ways to bridge the gap between health services offered in Mississippi and the poor who don't get them. I began by expressing admiration for the Public Health Department's triumphs over hookworm, malaria, pellagra, and venereal disease, and the great increase of services offered by clinics in recent years. Then I outlined the medical messenger idea; not the medical training part.

Dr. Gray responded that of course poor people never use available health services in any state, and it wasn't necessary for quacks to come in behind the backs of officials prying into the communities when they were all perfectly happy and in good enough health anyway, because his staff had managed to handle everything satisfactorily "before all these other groups discovered health." If poor people didn't go to clinics it was their own fault, they had a lot of health problems, but they evidently didn't care, or they would go to clinics, which were "open all the time." His staff was overloaded and couldn't take care of all these demands. He wanted no more projects and programs pressed on his staff members; they were overworked and he did not like to hear them criticized. The government was pouring money for health programs into the state "by the bucketfull" and didn't even care how it was spent, or it would give it to his department, not to "the meddlers and fly-by-nights."

He did not believe his staff should train and supervise medical messengers because poor people only care about the money anyway, and besides, his staff members would have to be stopping their work and running out all the time to see if the poor people were doing anything. He would certainly not use medical messengers unless his staff trained them.

You can't change health habits overnight. No, he did not have a plan for changing health habits. He didn't believe in untrained people running around without scientific information spreading misinterpretations and inserting intrauterine tubes. He would not sponsor any program in which birth control pills were handed out to every ten- and twelve-year-old girl—he did not want to condone this kind of sexual behavior. Some of his best friends were Negroes and he never knowingly mistreated a Negro.

I had the feeling that the will to progress in their field is sometimes, for some professionals, overshadowed by their will to possess it. The health picture looked quite different from Dr. Gray's floor-to-ceiling wood-paneled and wall-to-wall carpeted office in the modern urban State Board of Health Building than it did from hovels and huts balanced on bricks all around the remote rural regions of the state. After an hour and a half of trying to detect *his* plans for progress, I left, feeling very weary.

An equally great problem we faced was developing a realistic social service program. Social service components in most Head Starts were based on the assumption that existing agencies wished to offer all the services they could—that the agencies were handicapped only by lack of quantity and lack of quality in the personnel area, and by lack of funds. CDGM questioned the orientation of these services, which was in all but exceptional cities and counties, 'to take care of people," instead of to equip and organize people to take care of themselves.

The usual aftereffects of such services are that a "problem," or in usual situations, "multiproblems" are temporarily settled. But the individuals involved are no more on top of the situation than they were before. They don't have the breadth of information the social workers have. No program has tried to give it to them. They do not have the determination to solve problems that come only from feeling responsible for the solution, and from knowing that technical assistance is available for self-solving them.

Most CDGM thinkers didn't quarrel with the good intentions of the workers engaged in rendering these helpful services, though in welfare work, perhaps more than in many kinds of work, the cliché applies about the road to hell being paved with good intentions. (Subsequent to the summer of 1965, welfare policies and practices have become a subject of national focus. However, when we were setting up CDGM's social service program, we were atypical in our approach.) In Greenwood, Mississippi, known as one of the cruelest and most vicious cities in the South, CDGM couldn't assume the good intentions of social agencies, in spite of an isolated and super-silent worker here or there who was an exception.

Marian Wright, CDGM board member, remembers Greenwood in its pre-CDGM days. She had flown down from Yale Law School several months before she graduated in June, 1963. She came in the early spring to get acquainted, because she intended, soon, to take the Mississippi bar exam and open an NAACP Legal Defense and Education Inc. Fund office in Jackson. She went to Greenwood.

The night before she was introduced to Mississippi, the Greenwood Freedom House had been burned to the ground. The Welfare Department had just cut off commodities, and those hungry Delta folks were in long lines waiting, waiting, to be given some of the food SNCC was dispensing. SNCC was bringing in truckloads from the North. After all the burning and shooting the night before, people were afraid to come for their free food. They stood across the dirt street from it in nervous little groups, silent, watching, wanting the food, needing it, but afraid to cross the street because the police kept cruising menacingly. Several SNCC workers began singing "We Are Climbing Jacob's Ladder." Slowly, people took courage and crossed the invisible line to the Movement; to a new attitude of daring.

After a while they decided to walk uptown to the police station. Marian, who had promised her mama she would be a good girl, was so moved that she set down her suitcase and walked too.

The police responded by reeling out snarling, growling dogs, a little closer to the people, a little more leash, till one ripped out the seat of Bob Moses's pants, and the people panicked. People ran in terror, fell all over each other, were trampled. An old white lady in a car kept backing up and going forward to knock down old people and children. Marian was horrified. It was the ugliest thing she'd ever seen in her life. On impulse, she ran to the nearest phone and called John Doar at the Justice Department in Washington. Ten minutes later you couldn't make a call out of Greenwood to save your life; literally.

"When I hung up I ran back, just in time to see Moses being dragged off to jail. SNCC kids had decided if they wouldn't let them walk to the Courthouse, they would drive to the Courthouse. They were trying to load people into station wagons and cars. I remember an old woman not knowing what to do. The SNCC kids kept telling her to get in a car, and the cops kept telling her to get out. She got in, she got out—several times—looking so confused. Finally, I stepped up to her and said, 'You know, you don't have to do what *any* of them tell you. You can decide for yourself.' I remember, it was lovely. She just stood quietly in the midst of this madness, these hooting whites, milling and jeering, and she thought. Then she said, 'Yeah, that's right, ain't it? I can decide for *myself*.' Then she squared her shoulders and got into that car and went to the Courthouse to register.

"This solidified, to say the least, my decision to come to Mississippi as a lawyer."

The coming of the COFO Summer Project of 1964 caused Mississippi to make many changes due to people's dread of the deluge of freedom workers they anticipated. Laws were made to make life difficult for incoming civil rights workers and local Negroes alike.

House Bill 180 illustrated the concern, love, care, and protection the state legislature felt for the burdened Negro. Civil rights workers commonly nicknamed this bill "The Genocide Bill." It was passed by the Mississippi Senate in May, 1964. It provided the choice of a steep fine or a prison term for anyone giving birth to a second illegitimate baby, and steeper fines or steeper prison terms for anyone having a third. Earlier in the year the Senate Health and Welfare Committee had done away with a plan for these same ladies to attend compulsory planned parenthood clinics. Such persons aren't allowed to benefit from Welfare assistance in Mississippi. The intent of this was to get rid of excess Negroes, no longer needed because of automation, and a new threat because of the possibility that they might vote.

This was in contrast to the fact that not long before, white Mississippi *bred* its Negroes like animals, to produce workers. The bill that passed was extraordinarily mild compared to the bill as originally proposed and as actually passed in the House. This version offered a prison sentence of from one to three years for having a second illegitimate baby—or *sterilization!* Probably the only factor that prevented the first version from getting the seal of the Senate was the delicate nature of the feelings of state officials regarding state image. The national press picked up the story and howled. Mississippi politicians laughed, but altered the bill somewhat.

Another law reflecting official Mississippi's tender concern for black children was the one called "the war on orphans law." Mississippi has a very high Negro migration rate because of conditions and automation-caused unemployment. Therefore, there are many migration-broken homes. Children are frequently left behind while parents establish themselves in Chicago or other Northern points. This law required children whose parents weren't residents of Mississippi to pay as much as $360 a year tuition to go to public school. This might be related to the fact that so many Negro children don't ever go to school.

Many changes came to Greenwood with the COFO Summer Project. COFO caused citizenship clubs to be initiated, children crowded the Freedom Schools, the new Negro Community Center was very popular, and people poured to the Courthouse to register. SNCC was there with a network of carpools to carry those without transportation, and with legal aid for those taking the registering risk. The national press and the FBI watched while Greenwood responded gracefully—with electric cattle prods and billy clubs.

Authorities managed to arrest and carry 115 would-be voters off to jail in their van—also called by officials the "nigger bus." One was a pregnant woman, arrested for carrying a picket sign, and dragged down the street by a policeman with a stick at her neck.

Later, white Greenwoodians could readily be induced to discuss with pride how well they suppressed the uprising of indecent "Communists" who "didn't really want to vote, they just wanted to create a riot It's the riff-raff. You can't believe the Northern newspapers." And Greenwoodians of the other color tell with equal pride how they tore up the jail on this occasion, to "teach 'em a lesson." They ripped boards off the jail walls and flung them out windows, set a number of small fires, flooded floors by stopping drains, clapped, sang, stamped, shouted, cheered, and "hollered up a storm."

The Greenwood Commonwealth was on hand, in fact, on hand and under foot, on the first day we opened CDGM centers the next summer. When both the Greenwood center and the nearby Leflore County Itta Bena center were still registering children and were doing well in the confusion to have some sandwiches available for them as they ran around getting used to things, reporters from the *Commonwealth* "visited." A story appeared the next day giving the "facts" about the two centers. These "facts" were selected to give readers the right prejudice from the start. We read that centers were sponsored by the Delta Ministry (not OEO!), in contrast to county Head Starts also in operation in Leflore; that CDGM did not serve hot lunch (actually, all centers in this district served a daily hot dinner *and breakfast* from the second day on); and that CDGM teachers smashed the photographer's camera (a lie).

The staff of the Greenwood CDGM center wrote a very literate reply. The author of the letter and several others hand-carried it to the newspaper. They were told that since it was untrue it would not be run. Evidently it was cricket to run false stories but not honest corrections:

535 Avenue H
Greenwood, Miss.
July 15, 1965

The Editor
Greenwood Commonwealth
Greenwood, Miss.

Dear Editor:

On behalf of the Greenwood Child Development Center we would like to correct the errors which were written in the article on Monday, July 12.
Our center is not sponsored by the Delta Ministry; we are part of the Child Development Group of Mississippi, which received a grant of $1½ million under Project HEAD START from the federal government.
You implied that we do not serve hot meals, and misquoted two of our teachers on this subject. We serve 2 hot meals a day, even though sandwiches were served on opening day.

Your article stated some of the staff tried to break a camera. The cameraman was told by a teacher not to take pictures without presenting press credentials or asking permission.

Your article completely missed the point of our program. We are preparing our 60 children, ages 4–6, for entrance into the public schools. We are involving their parents and the poor people of the community, who planned the center and are building playground equipment and shelves. They are donating toys and clothing.

Our center is working with the children in the following ways: we are teaching the alphabet, numbers, colors, stories, and dramatics. They are painting, learning indoor and outdoor games, and are learning to cooperate with each other and to express themselves well. Our program will offer medical examinations for the children and counseling services for them and their parents.

In the spirit of the war on poverty, our program allows poor people to help themselves.

Sincerely yours,

Eddye Lane, for the
Child Development Center
Greenwood Community

There were also middle-class and professional Negroes in Greenwood. We thought they might feel strongly for their less lucky brothers, and might want to help:

"Oh, really?" said a very nice middle-aged Negro lady who has been prominent enough in Leflore County Negro education to have a Negro school named after her. "Oh, really? I wasn't aware that anything like that had happened." This was in reference to a question from me regarding how she felt about all the atrocities during the past few years. She was very uncomfortable and continuously tried to distract me by explaining about the County Head Start, which I was visiting at the time. It was very nice. No parents had seen it, but it was pleasant. "I think it would be better," she said genially, "if the other Head Start could get some real teachers."

If we had been unfortunate enough to have appealed to "real teachers," we would surely have reproduced the reprehensible Leflore County colored school system, well known in the area for its suddenly constructed Negro school buildings—since the 1954 school desegregation decision—and its punitive suppression of issues of interest and concern to its constituents.

In another city, in another state, one might safely have assumed that welfare department personnel were different from atrocity-committing white citizens; that welfare people were struggling in behalf of the poor, to whom their hearts went out, over the obstacles and in a climate created by their more reactionary fellows. There are no records in the CDGM social service project files documenting the atitudes and statements of workers in the Leflore County Department of Public Welfare. However, in my diary I come upon this entry:

"So many families complained to me about welfare problems while I was here working with Center staff this week (they do not discriminate between staff members and categorize our fields of expertise, so no matter what you're in the Center or homes for, you get whatever is on people's mind), and so many Movement people I meet at Blood's cafe insist that Welfare workers are heartless, that I decided to cross the town square to the welfare dep't after leaving Supt. Allen's office and see if the case workers are really being misjudged.

"A lady named Miss Conklin (I think) talked to me. She did not know I was connected with CDGM. I didn't tell her. I said Negroes seem to have great hostility toward welfare, and numerous complaints. She said that's true, but it's because they're very ungrateful, 'especially since the agitators came,' and 'don't appreciate all we're doing for them.' I said they especially seem to resent the white workers 'inspecting' them. I asked her if using poor people, Negroes, in these 'home visiting' jobs would be useful because of the hostility. Trained, of course, by welfare staff. She became very upset, and said you 'couldn't trust them,' since all the poor Negroes try to 'get as much out of' welfare as they can, and you have to have workers who can 'keep them straight.' I asked if shortage of budget was a problem in meeting the great financial needs of all these people. She said not really, the biggest problem is that they don't understand anything, and are always pressing 'for more than they deserve.'

"Perhaps they press for more than they deserve according to arithmetic computations or laws, but from *their* point of view, the whole welfare thing looks somewhat different. For example, here are things people told me: . . .

"1. 'I'm 83. I ain't got no wefae. Jes say dey can' pu' me on a dis tim'. Das aw dey says.'

"2. 'I have this one girl Betty Jo, she stay wit me. She ain't really mine. Her mother was took to Whitfield many years ago. She never comin' back, look like. They won't give me no help for Betty Jo acause they say I ain't a relative. I says to them, if a person done raised up a person for 13 years, is you saying the person should go hunt up some kinda kin the person don' even know and separate the person from the person and that's the onliest way to git welfare? The welfare lady, she done told me said there's nuthin' she can do lessn I gives up the chile to kin.'

"3. 'I ben trying to git on for disability. They told me to come back. I did. They told me to come back wifha doctor certifica. I did. They said they didn't see nuthin' wrong with me. The doctor lied on it. He's a colored doctor, but he's a racketeer in with the whites. He told me I was a disability, but he wouldn't write it on the certifica when he seen welfare didn't wanta give me nothin'. I have two to take care of excusin' myself. I can't live. I can't live no kinda way nohow.'

"4. 'I started with forty-eight dollars a month ADC for seven children. Then they cut it to thirty-one dollars. I don't know why. Then they cut it to twenty-three dollars. I dont know why. I axed her, but she said she don't have time to be 'splainin' to peoples all day, just take it and be glad you gets it. If you had any sense you wouldn't have all them childrens, that's what she said. I gets commodities, but I'd almost rather not. When you go in their shed to git em, they shouts at you, like this: "get that mess outa here, girl! Hurry up, I ain't got time to mess with you!" When she collects the facts from me, seems like she puts words in my mouth why she should cut me, an' then she cuts me and says I tole her information that that's why she cut me.'

"5. 'I went to Greenwood. I lives in Itta Bena. I had to pay $2 for someone to drive me. The one I talk with, she was real nice. She told me there was a lot of help ahead for me, she's gonna let me know in 'bout two months. Then Miss Bingham come 'round the corner. She know'd me. I was on welfare before they took me off when I was carryin' this baby. She said, "Ain't that Nola Lou?" I said, "Sho is." She turned her head up and walked away. I seen her car in Itta Bena next week, and I smiled and waved, but she wouldn't pay me no mind. She turned her head up and drove away. Why this was? I don't know, alls I know is last time Miss Bingham was here she was inquirin' my children's Daddy. That's all I know's the holdup.'

"6. 'I'm from Itta Bena. I was getting ADC for eight children. There was meeting at the church one night. Four my children went. Somebody threw something in the church, a bomb or something. They ran out. All fifty-eight of 'em, or so. They marched on up over to the polices to get help. People threw rocks, bricks, bottles, cans, everything at 'em. One boy caught a bottle. So when they arrested ever'body, they arrested him for throwing bottles. They charged them all with disturbing the peace. They kept two of mine, turned the ones underage loose.

'The next week the home visitor came by. She said she seen in the paper that they was in there. She said didn't I know better. I said I didn't see no harm in them going to their own church. She said this is just about going to get your check. That's the exact words she said. I only got one more check. She came back. She said this will be your last check. I asked why. She said if they want to tell you why they will, go up and ask them. I didn't go up. I didn't see what good it would do.'

"7. 'I never seen the home visitor go in nobody's house. She sets in the car, blowin' on her horn, and you're supposed to go out. If you don't hurry on and go out she drives off. Reach out a helping hand? There ain't none of that in *her!* She just comes to check on us. She mostly wants to know if anybody seen a man come in there. Might be your uncle, she don't care. She'll ask all your neighbors. Most of them will protect you, but sometimes there's a mean one. They'll do anything to see you suffer.'

"8. 'The home visitor, Miss. — come in. This time she come in. She made me get out all my papers. I keep them in this can. I have some land, eleven lots here on both sides of my house. It's town, in the city limits, but they let you have a little land. She asked me how much we got for the cotton this year. I told her three bales. Three hundred and thirty dollars. But my husband is disabled, so we has to pay for all the work going into these bales. She had me get out all my bills. I told her, I paid Oscar fourteen dollars and four cents for pickin'. Lula thirty-two dollars. She said didn't you have to pay nuthin' before that. I said yes, ten dollars to George for breaking ground. Twelve dollars for plantin'. Twenty-four dollars for soda. Then I paid Ray one dollar and fifty cents for the first plowin', Sam eleven dollars for the second plowin', Ray one dollar and fifty cents for the third plowin', and Ray one dollar and fifty cents for the fourth plowin'. She couldn't understand the one dollar and fifty cents. She kept saying how come so little. I told her because my husband is disabled. Ray is our friend. He done it for a favor. He almost done it free, but my husband is a proud man, so he charged to make him feel like a man. A man who could pay. He was doing a kindness. She couldn't understand that. Thought there was something suspicious. I guess where she come from they don't do no kindnesses.'

"9. 'The lady set in her car. I stood outside it. It was rainin'. She axed me if I had any chickens. I says no'm. She axed me if I had any gooses. I says no'm. She axed me if I had any cows. I says no'm. She axed me if I had any furniture, any TV. I says yes'm. Then she says I'm not eligible, I should sell them. I says but I bought them when I was workin', before I was too old. I'm seventy. She says you ain't poor if you has a TV. I *is* poor, my TV is old and it's broke. Anyway, I ain't got nothin' else. How long could I live if I did sell the TV? An then what would I do? Ain't nothin' else to do but the TV when it works.'"

We didn't know if the welfare workers were heartless or not. We didn't know where the agents were discriminating and negligent and where it was the welfare laws that were at fault. We didn't know where the clients were eligible and where not, and whether the problem was real ineligibility or that they couldn't fill out the application properly and communicate thoroughly in welfare workers' language. We tried to find out in each case. But however this may be, people perceived all these happenings as coming at them in a completely understandable and uncontrollable way. It appeared to CDGM that one essential way to begin was to bring all available information to the people and then place the burden of understanding and pursuing on them.

In the past no progress had been made in reducing the suspiciousness of workers toward applicants, or of applicants toward workers. No progress had been made in helping people judge their eligibility. No progress had been made in pressing for more adequate provisions under the Mississippi law under the present system. Therefore, we needed a new system. All these things are popular topics now. In 1965 they were not. Tom Levin wasn't merely an *implementer* of social development programs as thousands of new arrivals to this sphere of action (and money!) are now. He was a *definer* and *designer* of such programs.

It was with his concepts and this environment in mind that the CDGM Social Service Project Director Jeannette King, Field Social Service Director Howard Croft, and volunteer Rosemary Bacon, were trying to work out a meaningful social service pilot project for further expansion in the fall.

Jeannette King was a white lady with a Master's degree in Social Work from Boston University. At this time she taught social science at Tougaloo College, where her husband, Ed King, was chaplain. Ed King was one of the rare white native Mississippians who decided to go all the way with poor Negroes in their struggle for rights. He was a key organizer of the Freedom Democratic Party in the summer of 1964, and ran as a Congressional candidate for FDP. He was nearly killed in a serious automobile accident caused by whites who did not like his activities. He still bears the scars, and still continues to be active.

Howard Croft was a Negro social worker from New York, who spent the summer with CDGM and then went to Washington, D.C., to do social work with the Urban League.

Rosemary Bacon was a white lady from San Francisco, a doctor's wife, mother of teen-age children, who helped as a volunteer for a number of weeks.

In any endeavor, especially in social services, those agencies interested and having something constructive to offer, should be coordinated. In Greenwood, Mississippi, in 1965, the only groups that had worked hard to bring information to Negroes so they could organize wisely to solve their own problems, groups with a record of interest in the welfare, social security, and medical problems of Negroes, were FDP and SNCC. The welfare workers were not trying to bring information to Negroes so they could organize wisely, regardless of whatever else they were doing.

In fact, in 1966 when I asked the director of the Leflore County Public Welfare Department if she could tell me about CDGM and Welfare work, she snapped, "We do not work with CDGM." I asked in surprise why not? She said, "Because we have the interests of the people in mind, and CDGM is a very irresponsible group with no interest in the people." I asked if she had talked with CDGM welfare workers.

She said she had, and had found that they were outsiders only interested in stirring up the people. I asked if the workers were trying to stir them up in order to interest them in knowing more about welfare. She said the people already knew quite too much about welfare, and seemed to have but one goal in life: to get on welfare.

In 1967, when I asked about CDGM and welfare, I was told that no county agents were authorized to speak for themselves and I should see Mrs. Gandy in the State Office Building. The lady added, "We do as they say."

It was therefore important for CDGM to work closely with FDP and SNCC on welfare. We were new, and they were experienced in Leflore County with welfare complaints and personages. The social service project was in accord with CDGM's conviction that because projects come and go, but people and problems stay, it's top priority that local people learn how to run their own civic projects which can continue when other projects are not fortunate enough to have federal funds and be operative.

On the night of August 5, at a mass meeting at Elk's Hall (black), the Greenwood Welfare Rights Committee was organized. The Committee was organized by three SNCC and FDP long-time staff and volunteer workers with special knowledge of welfare and medical problems. They canvassed neighborhoods to get a good number of people out. From this group of neighborhood residents a steering committee was chosen. The steering committee was composed of seventeen poor Negroes from Greenwood itself, or from adjoining Baptist Town, with the workers as consultants. A Negro doctor and a Negro minister also offered to act as consultants. Howard Croft was at the organizational meeting and gave CDGM's support. He explained that CDGM could help with information and suggestions, but as headquarters were not located in Greenwood, and as we could only guarantee to be around till the end of the month when federal funds were due to expire, it was important for Greenwood Negroes and resident staff of other organizations to keep the ball rolling.

Mrs. Bacon stayed in Greenwood for several weeks, sleeping in the prettily decorated but crowded cardboard and glue home of Mrs. Lula Bell Johnson on Noel Street. In spite of large numbers of children and a shortage of beds, Mrs. Johnson always managed to have room for workers from any project she felt would be useful to her people. Rosemary spent her days gathering information for signed affidavits regarding welfare, social security, and medical injustices. The steering committee decided to contact the NAACP Legal Defense Fund in New York to press the Department of Health, Education and Welfare to cut off federal funds for welfare in Leflore County, pending a complete investigation of the county department for violation of Title VI of the 1964 Civil Rights Act.

The Greenwood Welfare Rights Committee also collected affidavits concerning possible excess charges and arbitrary discriminatory treatment of Negroes by utility companies. On the basis of complaints from local residents, the committee planned an investigation of the Greenwood office of the Social Security Administration. They didn't plan to demonstrate or picket, but to take their case politely and firmly to the officials involved. The delegation detailed to do this was prevented from doing so, because it had to investigate a murder in the area. The steering committee requested the local Freedom Democratic party hold a rally to raise funds so the Welfare Rights Committee could pay rent for an office. This was not an allowable item in the CDGM budget. The committee cooperated with Congressman Phil Burton of San Francisco and Congressman William Fitz Ryan of New York, who asked for information on welfare discrimination in Mississippi. The Greenwood Welfare Rights Commttee had many meetings, and also attended CDGM workshops to help other communities organize similar projects.

Jeannette King tried to work with county welfare departments, the Farmers' Home Administration, and the Mississippi State Department of Public Welfare, particularly with regard to individual cases. The results were not spectacular.

"I think we needed a little more structure. Everybody on Central Staff was given a completely blank check to plan whatever kind of project they wanted to have. Each Project Director was supposed to work this out with his or her project staff. This was the way it should be, and it's *very* untypical. But we needed more structure *in* each project.

"That summer, and afterwards too, there was a mystique. 'The peoples know everything. Professionalism is corroding. Professional people do not really understand the common people, and never can. We should use what people have.'

"There's some truth in this, and I acted on it. But I realized later that I was very dishonest, too. Common people know a great deal, which is often overlooked in programs, and shouldn't be. But they don't know everything. . . . By the end of the summer . . . I thought there was no chance of a continuing program and spreading what we learned. That's why I didn't even write a summary or projection paper for the future."

Tom Levin was, as always, interested in changing the whole position of the poor in relation to services and institutions. He later wrote a chapter for *Special Child* pointing out that the *quality* of service offered to the poor would need to be altered as well as the quantity, if real results were expected from service agencies.

Traditional concepts of service (in or outside of Mississippi), rooted in the donor-donee relationship traditionally espoused by service agencies, emphasize service *to* the communities of the poor. Service agencies are traditionally directed by, and staffed with, personnel whose roots, social, economic, and educational, are outside the community. The communities of the poor exist separately from the services directed at them; service functions are experienced as coming from the outside and controlled by the outside. For the disadvantaged, there exist two communities; a palpable and understandable inner community of deprivation and constriction, of common problems and common limitations; and an external community, vaguely understood, remote and unreachable. Services are traditionally rendered by representatives of the external donor community. The disadvantaged community remains a recipient donee.

Significant alteration of the communities of the disadvantaged will require a significant alteration in their relationship to services. The qualitative alteration will require a revision from services *to* the communities of the disadvantaged to services *as a community function.* Both quantitative and qualitative changes in services can be met by drawing upon the resources of the communities of the disadvantaged themselves.[24]

* * *

"She said I should'n' whip LisaMae so much. I says I have to. I have to discipline her. If I don', she'll grow up wantin' things she can't have. Things that'll get her in trobble. What else can I do? If I want education for her, they tells me I'll go to jail. There ain't no education in the colored school, and the white one won't take her. If I wants welfare for her so's I can feed her decent they tells me there ain't nuthin' wrong with me I should work. When I works the teacher says why ain't I home bein' a good mother, I don' love my kids. If I wants to git her a doctor when she's sick, I got no money to pay him and he says, Beulah, call me when you kin pay me. She sees all them pretty things on TV and I can't buy any of 'em. I works, but I can't hardly keep beans in their belly with my two dollars and fifty cents a day I gets for workin' in the lady's kitcha. The welfare lady talks 'bout the womens that don' have no husba's, you shouldn't have babies with no husba. I gotta husba, but he can't get no work. On this plantation they laid off ever'body and says we's lucky they lets us stay in the house. If they wouldn't all do me like that, I would'n' have to do her like that, but like it is, the bes' thing I can teach her is to shet her mouth and set still. So I does. I tear her up terr'ble if she don't jus' set. I really dresses her up terr'ble and I whup her fum here to dat fence. All I wants is for her to not git into nothin'. We is livin in the days of evil. Satan's on the loose *these* days! Temptin' us alla time to want, want, want some freedom. They says if you takes one step the Lord'll take two. They says it means if you trys to change things the Lord'll he'p you. That ain't what it means, it don't work that way. Means you train your childrens to be good and the Lord'll see you don' meet no harm. I got no power to he'p my daughter LisaMae 'cept that way. So I trust to the Lor'."

[24] Levin, Tom, "Pre-School Education and the Communities of the Poor," in Hellmuth, Jerome, ed., *Disadvantaged Child,* Vol. I. Seattle: Special Child Publications, 1967, p. 386.

CHAPTER 16

TOM LEVIN, DIRECTOR AND SIMULTANEOUS TRANSLATOR

TOM LEVIN WAS not interested in CDGM as an *institution*. This was perhaps one of the most important factors in understanding the model of administrative confusion, the model of community action, the model of experimental education, and the model of psychoanalysis in the field of social change that he created.

He was infinitely curious about the interpersonal and the inner personal dynamics that might produce action on the part of the poor.

We wanted to experiment with professionals and community organizers to discover new ways they might act to inspire the poor to win themselves personal and collective (political) potency, which would eventually transform their lives and the lives of their children.

So Tom specialized in continuously placing people—from board and Central Staff to community and kitchen staff, from Movement activists to professional educators—in new roles and relationships, rather than in achieving administrative order. In this sense, he was a master manipulator. He wanted to see what would happen. For this same reason, his last desire was to control people.

He controlled nobody, and we had chaos. Also for this reason he spent a great deal of time in communities and in centers instead of in the office. He wanted to watch.

Dr. Beittel, chairman of the first CDGM board, said to me: "Tom was not very willing to manage the staff. I don't know how much experience he had with managing people or funds. The staff didn't seem to understand that the board was the policy-making group, legally responsible, and that each person couldn't go off in his own direction. Some of the staff members seemed to think they *were* the board. We couldn't get anything done that way. It was Tom's job to keep the staff in line. Everything is in a state of flux and chaos unless a board has some powers. Some of the staff seemed to think the board was an unnecessary appendage." All evidence indicates that Dr. Beittel's comments were entirely accurate.

But this truth stemmed from the fact that Tom's chief goal was to preserve flux; to prevent hardening of the administrative arteries. And far from regarding his task as managing people and keeping Central Staff in line, he saw it as urging them on to ever more proficient creative enterprise.

Jim Monsonis, Tom's top administrative assistant, said: "They say Tom was a terrible administrator, and couldn't run an organization. It depends upon what you mean by these terms. Tom was clearly opposed to bureaucratic organizations. He was definitely for giving each person a job to do, and letting him do it on his own. He wanted people who could function this way—creatively, competently. He had little patience with those who needed rules and precedents and checking up in order to perform. It was probably because *he's* not that way. He was very hard on those who couldn't come through that summer. They resented him for letting them show up their incompetence.

"But there is one irreducible factor of bureaucracy: accounting for money. Any organization that's ever tried to run humanely instead of bureaucratically has run into this problem. I don't know if this type of organization is ever successful, but probably in its *un*success, a project like CDGM does more good for *people and ideas* than all the "successful" organizations you can name."

Most key staff members agreed that Marian Wright didn't seem to understand this type of organization, and did not like it. As the summer progressed, she became angrier and angrier.

Most people felt that Marian was a brilliant girl and a brilliant civil rights lawyer. She had total commitment to improving things, *all* things, for her people. She went to Mississippi when there was still great physical danger in doing what she did, and she never hesitated to expose herself. She was a very brave young woman. But people felt that two other things were important also, in explaining Marian—particularly in relation to Tom. First, most people felt that she wasn't at all on the same wave length with Tom's extraordinarily intricate and radical psychological and political thinking and their sweeping implications. Therefore, at this stage, when she was still spending very little time on CDGM because she was extended in so many directions, she didn't much value Tom's contributions to it—those features that made it unique. The second thing most people agreed on was that Marian was highly competitive, and didn't like it that Tom had come into her terrain, yet had refused to come under her spell. The more she realized that he didn't even consider her very important in "his" brain-child, the angrier she seemed to get.

Marian, who was shortly to become one of the most important persons in CDGM, attended almost every board meeting and was active.

She knew most of the Central Staff and was conversant with the program. She thought that Tom was right to start building a federal program from the accomplishments of the Movement. She knew only too well that the Movement was interested neither in educational nor federal programs, and it would take another group, such as CDGM, to push them through.

She thought Tom was wise to include Movement individuals in this new program, but that he should have been more selective in *which* individuals. However, everything went so fast during the first spring that, before she realized who he was getting, they were at work; or on the payroll but *not* at work, which was a problem. She knew some of the staff wasn't working. She thought, quite correctly, that the staff was largely irresponsible and lazy.

Marian agreed to delegate decision-making to Tom, and acknowledged that he was invaluable in that he conceived the program and made it happen. She separated his ability in this area from his ability in the administrative area. She felt, more and more, that administratively Tom was manipulating and misinforming the board by presenting everything rosily. "Tom was withholding information from us. He didn't want to face problems and cope with them. He was too independent and defensive about 'his' program."

She knew, more than any other board member, the real extent of CDGM's administrative problems. She knew, because she had grown up with the young people on the staff. They were her friends. They complained to her. She knew because her other projects often carried her into communities, and people there complained to her. She sensed that the project was in serious trouble, and thought this was because Tom couldn't delegate. She tried to talk with him, but felt he pooh-poohed her. She wanted some of the administrative and mechanical staff members to come in and give reports to the board, because she thought Tom was editing. She favored open board meetings, and resented the possessiveness of some of the board members who insisted on their prerogatives and didn't want staff members at board meetings.

Marian shared the opinion of Central Staff that the board was administration-oriented not program-oriented. However, she believed that this was because the board understood the program end of things, and besides, that was not where the trouble was.

"None of the board members looked into things as thoroughly as we should have," Marian told me, "because most of the board members were inexperienced, and some of us who knew better were terribly busy with other things. I sometimes took Tom's word for things because I was too busy to dig into them. Later I was mad at myself for doing this. We didn't have any administrative systems. We were to blame for not having designed any. Or if Tom had them, which I wasn't aware he did if he did, then he was to blame for not firing people who ignored them or thumbed their noses at them. Part of my rage at Tom was just that the whole situation was very frustrating, and I went around mad at everyone."

Like Marian, but from an entirely different point of view Jake Ayers, a poor board member from Glen Allen, Mississippi, had both credit and criticism to give Tom: "Tom knew Mississippi Negroes better than I did, even though I was one of them. I was so used to the way things are for us that I didn't pay any attention to it. I didn't know till Tom told us that things could be different. He had a good civil rights background, so he understood that even when we know there is something more to be desired, we don't always know what it is or how to go about getting it. I just thought, 'Why bother if you can't change it?'

"I think Tom is a wonderful person. To this day, when he's around I feel everything is going to look up. But he made serious mistakes. One mistake was that he didn't give all the information to the board members, because he didn't think we community people had the ability to consider these complicated things. For example, only D.I., Tom, and Art had copies of the proposal. I never asked for it, just like I never did a lot of things on that board, because I didn't yet know enough to know what I didn't know.

"Because we were from poor communities, we left it all up to Tom. We shouldn't have done that, but then, too, I think Tom is very persuasive and manipulative. Tom gave me the feeling that the board was responsible to Tom, not Tom to the board. The district coordinators were not controlled. Nobody was controlled. Tom had too many responsibilities, he was too busy to do everything well. In spite of all the things that went wrong, it was worth it. If I stack up all the things that were good on one side, and all the things that were bad on the other, it's very easy for me to see which stack is higher."

Yet board minutes show that Tom held two half-day board meetings in May which he had to fly down from New York to attend, two more in June as the project was shifting into high gear, and four in July, the only month while Tom was director that CDGM was actually operating centers (one meeting a week, usually a whole day on the weekend).

The problem wasn't that the director was concealing information by preventing meetings from occurring. Dr. Beittel thought that the quantity of board meetings was adequate, but not the quality. This is the case in many organizations. Dr. Beittel was the only member of the board who had had experience in being a board member. He had had a great deal of it from all points of view. Dr. Beittel was director of the Mississippi Program of the American Friends Service Committee, and has been a member of the following boards of directors in addition to CDGM: Mississippi Council on Human Relations, Southern Regional Council, National Citizens' Committee for Community Relations, the

Commission on the Delta Ministry of the National Council of Churches, and secretary of the Mississippi Advisory Committee of the United States Commission on Civil Rights.

He was an ordained minister of the United Church of Christ (Congregational). He received an A.B. degree from Findlay College (Ohio), A.M. degree from Oberlin College (Ohio), D.B. and Ph.D. degrees from the University of Chicago. He had received honorary LL.D. degrees from Findlay College and Beloit College (Wisconsin). He had served in a number of institutions of higher education. He was professor of Religion at Earlham College (Indiana), professor of Sociology and Dean at Guilford College (North Carolina), president of Talladega College (Alabama), dean of the Chapel and professor of Religion at Beloit College, and President of Tougaloo College. Dr. Beittel was orderly, sensible, and a gentleman, in a project in which the former two characteristics were uncommon, and the third was an absolute rarity. His perceptions always reflected these qualities.

Dr. Beittel was in accord with the consensus that the board itself had problems of immaturity and busy members, and that giving community people their first opportunity to serve on a policy-making body was a point of the project, regardless of how bungling a board resulted. He thought that though there are many times when an administrator must make quick decisions alone, Tom decided some issues that should have been decided by the board. He felt that had Tom come better prepared to board meetings, and had he presented a number of sharpened up issues, a greater number of things could have been considered and decided by the board in a shorter time. Dr. Beittel, a generous man, guessed that Tom would have learned how to work more effectively had he stayed longer.

Many Central Staff members felt very violently about the board, and were all too glad to discuss its closeted skeletons. A young lady from Central Staff, who asked that her name be withheld because "I don't want to hurt the poor people's feelings, and I'd rather have Marian for a friend than an enemy," told me: "It was only a paper-and-pencil board thrown together for a deadline to get a grant anyway. Tom never considered it the real board—it wasn't elected. He didn't believe in phony front groups. He'd been counting on the neighborhood councils. He was just being polite to this one till it passed. When you realize he thought of it as a temporary 'pretender to the throne,' you realize how much time he took with it.

How could Tom be honest with a board that was run exclusively by two people, neither of whom were Negro Mississippians, though Marian at least was a Negro, even if she came from another class and state? Those two managed the project politics under the table and over the telephone. Tom was honest enough to try to get them all to consider things, but they were all bored to death, except Marian, who was always arriving when the meeting was half over, and Art, who was very taciturn and aloof. How could Tom discuss his delicate theories and daily dilemmas with a group that didn't give a damn? All they wanted was to be on a big board and have Tom do the work, except Art and Marian, and they were too jealous of Tom even to talk to him—just to each other by phone.

"Except for Art, that board didn't know or understand one thing about this project."

Jim Monsonis agreed, and added: "It seemed to me that Art and Marian had a clear agreement all summer. Tom was running the program, and they didn't like that. I guess they forgot that he started it, he didn't take it from them. Art had a good understanding of what we were doing, which grew out of his work in the communities. Marian was never around. I don't think anybody ever saw her even at board meetings. The only time she came to Beulah at all, they met up in the Big House. She didn't talk to us. She was in her office in Jackson twenty-six miles away if we wanted her. It was only after the OEO blowup that she took an active part. Even then, it was an administrative interest.

"Art was very active the first summer, much more than Marian. But it's hard to tell: neither of them ever came out from behind the scenes, though they talked a lot about poor people running everything. It seemed to me that Art was a great manipulator. It was for the sake of the project, I think, yet Art had direct conversations with OEO . . . we wondered if this was to get the Delta Ministry to take over CDGM . . . or for Art to take over personally as director. . . . No one understood it, there was a lot of suspicion, nothing was ever explained, we were all very upset about the mysteries. Certainly they seemed to be working behind Tom's back. They said he ignored them. Well *they* didn't need the board either, and they managed everything all summer. They were very politically oriented. What they did seems a good deal more dishonest than what Tom did."

Doubtless it's neither pretty nor proper to document the details of this kind of internecine wrangling, be they petty personality and rivalry disputes, or fundamental conflicts of philosophy. To expand upon such unsavory goings on cheapens both CDGM and a biography of it. Yet clearly it's impossible to describe the many slippery facets of the devil's shoes without mentioning one of the slipperiest. To do a depth study of good and evil, and creativity and destructiveness, which only reveals the good and the creative, would be self-defeating indeed!

Lenore Monsonis was CDGM's chief fiscal officer. She thought Tom tried hard to have control in administrative matters. In fact, the primary reason communities didn't get their various monies when they should have was that Tom insisted everybody obey OEO and follow "sound fiscal practices," as elaborately detailed in its publication *Instructions for*

Financial Management of Community Action Program Funds. A community wanting reimbursement for a budgeted, allotted item had to submit a voucher with receipts. The chairman had to sign it and mail it. Then Lenore had to sign that it was made out correctly and was budgetarily allowable. Then it went upstairs for the accountants to doublecheck. They OK'd it and wrote a check. It came back to Tom, unsigned. He signed it, and it was mailed back to the community, unless it was a routine thing; then Lenore signed it with Tom's name, which she had on a signature machine.

Lenore was convinced, "Community people would have learned much more if it hadn't been such a complicated process. Less should have gone through Central. The procedures shouldn't have been so complicated. I got a lot of pressure on me from Tom to do it this way, but I definitely thought more should have been done in communities.

"I was very firm with people. If I didn't have sufficient receipts to match somebody's voucher, I only reimbursed for what I had receipts for. People had a hard time learning all this—they had never had experience with these tight controls or with so much money before, but they were very good about it, considering their background with it—*very* good. I was surprised how quickly they learned. I had explained all this at Orientation, and so I thought it was fair to expect them to do it.

"If they did it wrong or incompletely, I would write little notes to them, or if they dropped in, I would explain it. It was an educational thing as well as a financial bookkeeping matter. It took lots of time, but it was worth it. One of our big problems was that Tom and I thought there was no point in *us* learning to be good bookkeepers just so OEO could come out fiscally soundly: the point was for community people to learn all this. Of course in spite of its high sounding words, OEO didn't care at all if community people were learning these things. In fact, it annoyed them very much that we placed value on this human side of what they just saw as big business.

"I gave food advances, because poor people don't have money to lay out to feed a hundred children a day. They never see a hundred dollars in ten weeks. If they had all this extra cash for running a school lunch program, they wouldn't need a poverty program. And they couldn't get credit."

Tom and Lenore handled rent, transportation, and all other matters according to Head Start guidelines. Lenore never gave money for rent or repairs until a facilities contract was completed. As OEO didn't have money available for repairing collapsing buildings, it authorized us to allow repairs to be made with money subtracted from that particular building's allotted rent money.

There were three big problems. The first was personnel. All paychecks were supposed to be done by a computer in New York through the accountants. That was one reason Tom hadn't been too upset about not having been able to get a personnel officer. But people didn't understand about W-4's and Social Security numbers, or they forgot to fill them in, or they had none, or they didn't sign some form. Lenore spent a lot of time straightening out these things.

Because of all these difficulties and the brief time span in question, the accountants didn't get around to getting the computer going. When Tom realized the load the accountants were carrying, he hired a personnel officer. It was too late, and he was not considered competent, but was all Tom could get on the spur of the moment for a month-long job in rural Mississippi.

Lenore and Tom worked together closely. Lenore knew he was upset: "Tom knew we were having trouble. He was worried about it. He was very frustrated about it. Finally, he called Neil (the head of the accountants in New York) and told him he just *had* to come down. He and his partner came and worked to straighten things out. They worked solidly for a week to catch up.

The accountants didn't do anything wrong except not send enough staff. Tom told the board we didn't have enough accountants and that the agreement with the accountants called for more people. All we had was those two kids up there! They couldn't handle it alone! Tom also asked OEO for business help.

"I remember he asked Bob Clampitt, and others too. They answered that they'd see what they could do. He also begged OEO to send us some secretaries. No one here would work with us. They were afraid. We didn't have good contacts. There aren't a surplus of them anyway, especially out in the country miles from town. OEO said they didn't have any secretaries, didn't know any secretaries, they would try. Lack of secretaries to get business done was one of the worst problems! No one in that place could type, hardly."

The second problem was that nobody realized how crazily the project was going to grow. We had 4,200 children, and three weeks later we had 6,400 children. Many Head Starts didn't even have the 2,200 difference, and they had a huge task, even in cities with expert administrators and a going organization onto which they could tack Head Start.

When Jim and Lenore came to Mississippi in May, Frankie Stein was the only one in the office. She, as Tom's administrative assistant, was administering everything. Joan Bowman and Karen Shillington were in the field, organizing communities. And that was it. At first Lenore's job was transportation, communications, and legal services. In a few weeks we had three full-time people on these jobs, and even then we couldn't keep up with any one of them. We put everybody on the phones in round-the-clock shifts, but community people still could never get through, and we still couldn't return all those calls.

The third problem was OEO inspectors. Lenore bore the brunt of them: "Every few days, it seems like, teams of them would come in. Auditors and people like that poured in. They pestered the life out of me on things that weren't problems, and never had a suggestion or helped us plan at all on things that *were* problems.

"They bugged me about little things. Sometimes they kept me tied up all day. Other days they interrupted every few minutes. They would ask me a question. I would take time to answer it. Two hours or two days later, they'd be back with the same question. I remember, one of their favorite questions was, 'Who's Mr. Parker?' I'd explain that he was the carpenter who repaired a center. Then a few minutes later, 'Who's Mr. Parker?'

"Tom told the board we had administrative problems. But he said we were handling them. Later it turned out the board thought he was hiding something. Do you know why he said we were handling them? *Because we were.* We were grabbing problems and solving them one after another. If they had left us alone, we would have had a smooth running machine in a few more weeks. There's no doubt of it. *They only gave us a little over three weeks of center operation in this huge project to create problems, discover problems, and solve problems before they jumped on us.*"

The worm at the core of our administrative problems wasn't Tom. It was as project doctor and political analyst Gerry Rosenfield stated in a series he wrote for *Key List Mailing*, entitled "What Happened to the Mississippi Child Development Group":

> The essence of "sound fiscal practice" is undemocratic and systematic; the complete control of money from above. Sound fiscal practice is based on the axiom "Don't trust anybody," that is "Don't give money to anyone unless they show you proof it is being spent for the purposes the rules say it is supposed to be spent for." The alternative—giving a lump sum to each center to spend as it sees fit, with the main proof of the proper expenditure of funds depending on the success or spirit of the center—was of course out of the question in a program run on government money. . . . The muddling through—and learning by experience which may be so rewarding in a democratic experience—can be disastrous for a fiscal office.

Another commentator said, "Thank God we weren't administrators! No sane administrator would ever have undertaken to set up this project. And the orderly businesslike mind of the administrator is not likely to include the fantasies, passionate determination, and revolutionary dreams we had, especially Tom. I'm tired of being told we're not administrators. Of course! What an insult if we were. We could administer after a fashion. But administrators could never have had the ideas, round-the-clock energy, and guts we did."

The fact that Central and district staff hassled and wrangled long into each night, each accusing the other of being the enemy of community people, carelessly withholding their money or carelessly not keeping track of it, and the fact that many members of both groups anxiously tried to do a good job, didn't erase this basic dichotomy.

Jim Monsonis was in a better position to judge Tom's attitude and efforts toward "sound fiscal management" and staff performance than anyone else. "Tom delegated an increasing amount to me all the time. I was assistant to Tom in charge of troubles. Tom isn't an administrator, and I've never heard him pretend to be one. In fact, a trained group of a dozen or so administrators, who had been working together for a long time, still would have had trouble with this. For someone who was quite open about admitting that he wasn't an administrator, he managed to administer a great thing into happening. It was his concept and his drive that created it and pulled it through. We were getting more organized all the time; rapidly.

"Actually, one of the biggest problems we had was Tom's relations with the Central Staff. For some reason, they seemed to hate him. Many of them came into CDGM because of their interest in community people's growth. They couldn't stand his emphasis on administrative order. They resented the government. They didn't like obeying all the inappropriate regulations. They didn't like Tom because he stood for all that—insisted on it. He was always trying to translate this to them; *why* they had to do these things. Others were only interested in the education aspects for the children. They were angry at Tom about all this 'poor people must make decisions and plan their own programs' stuff.

"I talked to Tom one night very strongly. I told Tom he had to stop relating directly to the staff. He was very open about it. He suggested that I be the buffer and handle staff meetings. I agreed to do it. After I took over as intermediary with the staff, things got much better. I get along with everybody, and they trusted my background. We began getting away from those nightly staff meetings at Mount Beulah—we began having Sunday night staff meetings in Vicksburg and Jackson at the Holiday Inn. Key people in all the projects were supposed to make it, and all the district coordinators. We brought out problems and made plans to solve them. It was improving rapidly."

With program coordination essentially turned over to me, and administrative coordination largely delegated to Jim, systems beginning to unsnarl, community people beginning to work cohesively, and the personnel committee beginning to consider several cases of hopeless Central Staff members for dismissal, Tom began getting into Central Staff position career training.

Jim worked with Tom on preparations for staffing an office in the fall when we all were to leave: "Tom was very worried about what would happen to CDGM in the fall. He meant what he said all the time about us replacing ourselves with local Negroes. He felt strongly that we were there only to establish the program, funds, directions, and train people to take over. At first he hoped Frank Smith would take over, but that obviously wasn't going to work. Tom didn't know many Mississippi Negroes who could be future federal project directors. It was pretty hard for even *him* to do it. He looked around. There wasn't much choice. He was sincere.

"Tom had met Reverend Willy Brown from Laurel before. He was impressed with him. We all liked him. After things had gotten going, Tom asked him to be the assistant director trainee. In other words, he would be like a shadow to Tom and me—would go to every meeting with us, meet the OEO officials, see how all the projects work and how problems are solved. We hoped he could take over when Tom and I left at the end of August. Willy was a hell of a nice guy, but he just didn't take over. I don't know what it was, maybe he wasn't up to it . . . nothing happened. Tom was very disappointed.

"Tom was really intending to develop this Negro staff. He couldn't start with the poorest rural people because it was too far to go too quickly to be able to handle the conference table, the books and all. So he got the weak but somewhat trained Jackson Negro middle class. Mr. Tate was supposed to take over my job of supplies and transportation. Mr. Sanders was to replace Lenore as financial officer. He knew it. He worked with her. Tom Moore was supposed to become the personnel officer. Each of them had had some training in the field he put them in, but for various reasons they didn't work out very well."

Tom was in very close touch with Washington. He spoke at least once a day to either Dave Walls, assistant to the chief administrator of Head Start (Jule Sugarman) or to a member of the inspection office, often Bob Clampitt. He constantly sought the most reasonable interpretation of OEO regulations and demands to suit our circumstances.

He spent a great deal of time explaining our philosophy and interpreting our actions to OEO, on the phone, in person, to seemingly endless teams of OEO visitors, and in written reports. Far from trying to do things behind OEO's back, he was forever trying to "educate" it as to the novel and necessary factors in CDGM making it real community action. No matter how OEO tried to steer his head toward administrative detail, Tom tried to steer OEO to consider what the poverty war was all about—or should have been. I remember several times when Joan Bowman as historian and I as program coordinator were told by Tom to prepare reports on the nature and status of "subject matter" areas.

While our reports were regular "progress reports," even if perhaps fresher than the usual kind, Tom's were profound, pungent, beautifully written professional papers, delving into the essence of poor people's psychological problems, and showing how a War on Poverty that detoured the problems couldn't be effective. One such paper was called "The Pacifist Poor in the War on Poverty." It began: "The war on poverty is being fought using the poor. It is not being fought by the poor. The poor largely remain pacifists. . . . The magnificent concepts of a drive toward a great society leave them untouched and disinterested. The older poor compare the war on poverty with the WPA; the younger people talk about welfare and charity."

The paper went on to explain that "the poor have too many needs to be met through the constricted funnel of present poverty program positions." It outlined four confrontation positions. First: "The poor are not motivated by self-help. The poor are not motivated by tomorrow. The poor are not motivated by abstractions. They are motivated by that beautiful fundamental drive of the 'have nots' to 'have.'"

The poor want money, and will be creatively activated if they have a real part in decision-making and the resulting consequences.

The second position Tom outlined was that the concept of a community action program is as sound as the concept of a "community" on which it's based. Community, defined as a political subdivision, results in a "sociological monstrosity" in which the poor are disenfranchised. To make the community action idea work, community must be defined as a group of people who are held together by common reality interests. We need to work with currently bypassed vital Negro communities. To inject the white power structure "into this new political womb would bring immediate abortion."

The third position was that Negroes want equal power socially, economically, and politically. They want *not* to be excluded. But they don't want to be integrated through the presently popular process "reminiscent of the ingestion of the lamb by the wolf. An integration program which denies their legitimate aspirations for power is viewed as, at the best, misguided; and, at the worst, and more commonly, betrayal." All these points have become infamous by now, but were scarcely suggested in 1965 when Tom was writing.

And finally, Tom marveled at the "strangely nefarious" situation that had developed: "OEO, an agency of the federal government pledged, committed, and bound by the principles of the Civil Rights Compliance Act is able to bargain, compromise, and justify its dealings with a Mississippi power structure equally committed and dedicated to evade, destroy, and subvert these very principles; while at the same time they tremble apologetically at the constructive efforts of the law-abiders otherwise known as 'the movement.' The movement has come to be defined out of context as bearded beatniks dedicated to overthrow the government. This is not 'the movement.' . . . The activists of the movement are those who bring to people . . . the message that President Johnson says they can vote.

"In summary we must re-examine our position."

Tom talked with any OEO officials who would listen (but few "had time") about Head Start.

Dave Walls was very interested in the "meat" of CDGM, but he said he practically had to tackle Jule to get his ear on any of this because he was so busy with administrative things. Anyone who knew Jule Sugarman would testify that he worked more than a twenty-four hour day more than seven days a week. He was a very intelligent and liberal sort of man. Surely he had never had a selfish or frivolous moment in his life. But sometimes we questioned a system of government programs which is devised in such a manner as to prevent top decision-makers from having time to learn and consider the professional quality of a program and its social, human, and historical significance, as well as its administrative and political facets.

Dudley Morris, Jule's other administrative assistant at this time, was sincerely interested in CDGM, but there wasn't much he could do about it. A lady with whom we had to have many dealings told a number of people that Tom Levin was the head of the Freedom Democratic party, that CDGM employees engaged in drunken brawls, and other similarly inaccurate tidbits of information. Those who had contact with her felt her to be singularly unsympathetic, and generally confined further contacts to higher levels of authority, sensitivity, and commitment to the meanings of the Head Start concept.

Brushes with OEO employees like this lady caused many in CDGM to wish the government could hire people with commitment to and understanding of the field and human beings they were administering, instead of limiting itself to lists of credentials qualifying applicants at the desired GS level.

Tom found Bob Clampitt in the inspection office always accessible to CDGM. This wasn't so much because Bob understood or sided with CDGM, but because "We viewed ourselves as a safety valve to OEO. Any civil rights worker, any mayor, any concerned person, could always get through to us to discuss their point of view, their problems. We tried to develop a maximum sensitivity through extensive contacts. Newspaper reporters, for example, often called us to tell of problems about to erupt. Sarge Shriver often said that this 'early warning system' kept him informed about major problems affecting the agency before he read about them in the national press or heard about them from the Congress. This gave him critical lead time within which to act."

During this period something happened which I think bore serious consequences for CDGM the next year. While at OEO, I had been good friends with Jack Gonzales, who was head of the inspection office's Head Start in the South division. Since we were both Head Start and both South and both responsible for our area, we worked closely together. Jack was working night and day to foil segregationist attempts to evade OEO civil rights compliance policies. Partly because CDGM had such good civil rights intentions, partly because Jack was a liberal interested in helping the poor, and partly because he admired me and I was so enthusiastic about CDGM, Jack was a CDGM proponent at OEO. (This was in the days when only eight or ten OEO people had even *heard* of CDGM.) He was nervous about its connections to FDP from the outset. He questioned me closely and often as to whether CDGM was sponsored by FDP. I told him it was *not*. It *was* not. He never quite believed me.

When I left OEO, I got a letter from the legal department, pertaining to the possible conflict of interest involved in my going from OEO to CDGM. It said that there would be no problem, as I'd never been in on actually processing the CDGM grant, provided that my work at CDGM concerned program coordination, teacher development, program for children, etc., and provided that I neither became an agent for future granting, nor used close friendships at OEO for the benefit of CDGM.

During July Jack Gonzales called me several times asking for the "truth" about what was happening. I always told him. He became more and more sure that I was hiding something from him as I talked exuberantly about the living arts project, the book-making, the poor people teachers, the program for children, and about all the parts of CDGM that excited me.

He kept asking about our political activities. I told him repeatedly that I didn't know of any, other than the obvious fact that the state didn't like us because we were integrated and bringing education of all kinds to poor Negroes. He asked about our wild parties. I said I knew of none, and if there were any, I hadn't had the privilege of an invitation. I explained that we all worked much too hard to be interested in parties, wild or tame. Jack was hurt. He was convinced that I was betraying him by not sharing secrets. He thought I had used our friendship to push through a "political" project under the guise of a nursery school, and that I was dropping him now that I no longer needed him.

I, in turn, was hurt by his extreme suspiciousness of me and CDGM. I was trying as earnestly as I could to convey to him the nature of our exciting educational experiment. I was describing in the fullest detail our social action and community development theory and practice, and its connection to the children. It all seemed to me completely consistent with poverty program rhetoric. What, I wondered, could I possibly want to hide? I didn't call or write to Jack because I was fearful that my actions would be misinterpreted by those looking for conflict of interest. I told him everything when he asked, and initiated no contact.

He became angry because I didn't correspond and because I wouldn't "admit" his charges. I became angry because I thought he was so busy looking for dirt that he couldn't see a "pure" project when he had one. After July Jack was *not* a CDGM proponent. In fact, his somewhat hysterical exaggeration of our suspected sins was contagious, and many OEOians, who knew nothing about CDGM, knew from Jack that it was suspect.

Later, Jack Gonzales became chief of all Head Start inspecting and, we unanimously felt, inspected us (though he didn't come to Mississippi) with the lurking intention of uncovering some evil of which he was sure we were guilty. Very often, everywhere, things of political import stem from personal relationships and particular personalities. To look only at politics in interpreting political situations is to look only at the surface.

To Tom's dismay OEO brass never seemed as interested in our significant positions as in our alleged politics and our administrative practices. Officials insisted that this was because they considered us their national model for involvement of the poor, and didn't need to be "sold" on our extraordinary accomplishments. Because we had turned out to be a demonstration model, they said, they wanted us to be administratively perfect. They wanted to help us achieve this condition, they assured us. They acknowledged that they were under some attack from Mississippi's Senator Stennis regarding us, but claimed that this in no way prejudiced them against us or weakened their preference for us. But they would, they told us, inspect us carefully in order to be extra-informed about CDGM ins and outs so that they could protect us against Stennis's insinuations and blasts.

One of the chores that kept Tom busy was receiving segregationist investigators who were preparing to hang us, and receiving OEO investigators who we thought were preparing to protect us, but who, as it turned out, were also preparing to hang us. Early in the summer Congressman Long of Louisiana came down to check out some complaints of Mississippi Negro school teachers, who told OEO that we were hiring only people with civil rights backgrounds. Their proof of this was that our application inquired about the applicant's civil rights activities. (The question *could* have served to screen *out* those with civil rights backgrounds, and actually served, with a host of other relevant questions, to determine the degree of exposure to community organization the applicant had had.) The congressman was honest and decent. After taking considerable staff time, he departed, reporting to Washington, we were told, that he was "satisfied" as to CDGM's nondiscriminatory hiring practices.

Then came a Republican ex-Marine from OEO's office, who arrived just in time to help me move from one building to another and to keep Lenore from two days' work on fiscal matters while he learned the system. He visited centers and liked them. To our surprise, we liked him. You never know! Dave Walls came to study the training program for teachers. He understood.

There was a tight-lipped rather negative young man who criticized everything, saw nothing important, and filed a dreadfully bad report in the OEO inspection office. Tom said it didn't matter much, as he was only a minor person and the major people were inspecting for major things. We had faith. An unfortunate accident had occurred, and caused two VIP teams of investigators to set up camp on our doorstep and take a week's time, each of them, totaling two weeks, from key staff members, thus making them even more inefficient than they were anyway, and even more frustrated.

The FDP had had meetings at Mount Beulah in June, out of which grew the impromptu idea of demonstrating at the state Capitol in Jackson. An anonymous friend of the FDP gave a large sum of money to cover inevitable bail costs. CDGM had no part in planning or protesting, except for three employees who participated *before they came to work for CDGM,* three more who were on an officially requested leave of absence because they had worked from two to four straight weeks, including weekends, without a day off, and had accumulated time with which they could do as they liked.

A seventh person involved had *not* been granted permission to leave work, and therefore the CDGM personnel committee put her on suspension until it could study her case. (The committee decided that since she was a roving staff member, and had left no class or group in the lurch, and since there were other extenuating circumstances, they would reinstate her to active service provided she would not expect reimbursement for this week.) She was charged with "parading without a permit."

The Lawyers' Constitutional Defense Committee supplied the one hundred dollars bail for the last-mentioned young lady, and CDGM provided one hundred dollars salary advances for each of the other six, with a deduction-a-week plan worked out so they could reimburse CDGM. Catastrophically, these advances were listed as "bail fund" in our books. All this was dutifully reported by us to the OEO inspection office. We felt legitimate; Jule Sugarman had written to Tom Levin on June 29, 1965, authorizing Tom to reallocate funds within the budget "to provide for necessary legal services . . . up to $2,500."

Senator Stennis decided that CDGM had subsidized the FDP demonstrations, or at least he decided to say we had. He sent the chief legal man for the Senate Appropriations Committee, "his" committee, and a team to investigate CDGM. The team was known at CDGM as "the Cotter boys." Mr. Cotter was an affable, graying, grandfatherly gentleman. Tom described him as "warm, kind, courteous, thorough, and completely unable to comprehend the project. He is one of the most competent investigators of our times—I wish he had been on our side."

The second team came with an introduction from OEO, saying that it had come to help design systems, etc. The head of the team was a man named Cutler, who as someone said, "came on like a bookkeeper from Dickens." The team was immediately nick-named The Cutler Cutthroats. Those who had dealings with them thought they made pompous pronouncements and offered gratuitous opinions way beyond their area of authority or competence. Mr. Cutler asked Tom if he would like help. Tom was very grateful. He threw open the books and gave Mr. Cutler a week of his precious time.

The result was, in Tom's words: "They spent an immense amount of our time investigating with the only improvement being that, because they themselves were fainting from the 102° heat in my office, they granted our previously ignored request for a room or two of air-conditioning. Other than that the only result of their offer to help was that they misquoted, distorted, repealed resolutions they had previously agreed to by phone and we had already used.

"From the moment of the misfortune of FDP using Mount Beulah as a staging ground for the demonstrations, when the deluge of phone calls from OEO began asking menacingly why we had chosen Mount Beulah as our site, our happy engagement to OEO grew into a festering contested divorce. As in a typical marital battle, one partner, in this case OEO, began a series of behind the scenes 'let's-get-the-filth' searches. But we didn't realize till later that this was happening. We thought we were the golden-haired boy. They said so."

Senator Stennis's research culminated in a massive attack, which gave the Jackson press new ammunition to use in their summer-long demolition job on CDGM:

> Stennis Asks Halt to Funds at Mt. Beulah
> Says Federal Money Being Used to Subsidize CR Activities
> . . . Sen. John Stennis said today he has asked Office of Economic Opportunity director Sargent Shriver to withhold funds from the largest Operation Head Start program in Mississippi.
> . . . evidence of irregular handling of funds . . . freedom marchers occupied common facilities . . . daily rate paid for the Head Start personnel was at least four times the rate charged the marchers and was paid two weeks in advance . . .[25]

On the same day, July 27, Dr. Julius B. Richmond, director of Head Start at OEO, and a team of distinguished early childhood educators, visited CDGM centers. All sources agree that Dr. Richmond, well-known pediatrician, was excited by what he saw. Tom was reassured by this, as he was sure that criticisms from auditors would bear less weight with Mr. Shriver than would endorsements from OEO's own honored professionals. I was very uneasy. My experience at OEO had convinced me that "experts" were listened to only when politically convenient for decision-makers; who were administrators, not professionals in appropriate fields.

[25] Jackson *Daily News,* July 27, 1965.

Dr. Richmond was a wonderful man, but appeared to view himself as a consultant. He either did not know or did not expect to exert his authority as director. Day-to-day Head Start decisions were made by Deputy Director Jule Sugarman. Major matters were settled by Sargent Shriver and his superiors. Dr. Richmond expressed opinions, but didn't seem to take sides in disputes. Therefore, it did not seem likely to me that the quality of our program for children or for involvement of their parents would enter into an OEO decision concerning what action to take, if any, in response to Senator Stennis's opposition to CDGM.

In the chapter on CDGM in Joan Bowman's unpublished book on the South, she wrote: "In fairness to it, OEO defended the program against assaults of the crude variety, against those attacks which were random and lacking organization or allies. A disgruntled black school teacher in Hattiesburg could have her feathers smoothed by an official letter from Washington. Charges from the Mississippi press that CDGM was giving aid and support to civil rights workers did not seem such a handicap in the North, and were good public relations for the agency. It was when the program began to receive systematic assault by the organized forces of racism, institutionalized in congressional committees, and able to enlist powerful allies, that OEO began to cave."

Besides these sophisticated attacks, Tom Levin continued to have to deal with the rougher kinds of Mississippi attacks. For example, on July 22, Tom left an evening PTA meeting at our Rolling Fork center. He saw a police car parked with its lights off across from the meeting place. A policeman was in it.

As Tom got half way to Hollandale on Highway 61, he noticed that he was being followed by a light blue pick-up truck with a two-way radio. This was a truck which had frequently followed CDGM personnel. The truck zoomed up to Tom's rear bumper, slammed on its brakes, and continued to do this for two or three minutes. Suddenly, the truck swept past Tom, and then swerved violently to the right, forcing him off the road and into a 360° spin.

Tom's car was smashed enough to indicate that the driver might be dead or unconscious. He took advantage of this. He didn't move for a few minutes. The truck stopped abruptly. A passenger peered out the window at the wreckage, apparently trying to assess the damage. When the truck left, Tom walked to a Southland gas station, which fortunately, considering the isolated rural area in which the "accident" occurred, was not far away. As no one knew where he was except his attackers, who knew he was disabled, he was in great danger.

He called me, because I was in Greenville, and was the nearest staff member he could bring to mind. We were afraid to let Tom wait the length of time it would have taken me to find a car and drive the twenty miles to the Southland station. I called all the center families I could recall who had phones in the Hollandale area, until I found one who had a car and was brave enough to risk going out on the lonely roads to rescue Tom. After thirty minutes this couple picked Tom up and drove him to Greenville. We reimbursed them for their gas. The car required several days worth of major repairs before it could be driven back to Mount Beulah.

We assumed that there was a connection between the police car whose driver saw Tom leave the meeting and the truck with the two-way radio.

In late July, Tom was informed by the Jackson bureau of the FBI that Mount Beulah was scheduled to be bombed shortly. The plan was reported to be steadily gaining support at Klan meetings, during the second half of the month, and in fact seemed so imminent that the local FBI had notified the Washington Bureau. CDGM staff was expecting to be bombed momentarily. Extra night guards were put on, and most staff members were sent out to the field on one mission or another, without being told that evacuation was the real reason.

At 1:30 A.M. on July 26 a light green four-door Rambler was seen driving extremely slowly past the Mount Beulah driveway. It stopped. Four men were in it. The car started again and proceeded at an unusually slow speed for a public road. The speed was estimated to be about ten miles per hour. It paused for several minutes about a quarter of a mile up the road. It turned around, returned, and came into the Mount Beulah driveway. At this time, witnesses saw only one man in the car. Upon closer observation, they detected a second man crouching in the rear of the car looking out the window. The car drove past the back of Freedom Manor, across the lawn to Jacob's Mess, and then left the campus. It halted on the main road. Though it had come from Edwards, it went away in the Vicksburg direction. There was no light over the license plate, so the tag number couldn't be read.

It was the impression of observers that the car let the two men out when it paused the first time, and that these two men walked up a road on the property adjacent to the campus that comes out near the back of the Herbert Lee center, CDGM headquarters. This was the only way one could get to Herbert Lee without driving down the main driveway and being very visible. The car probably picked up the two assigned to look over the situation when it stopped the second time. This would explain why it left in the Vicksburg direction. We were never bombed, nor were we relieved, as we couldn't know our luck except in retrospect.

The Klan type was not the only type of white Mississippian with whom Tom had dealings. A situation in Vicksburg, which occurred earlier in the summer, illustrated another typical kind of transaction that was a continuous threat throughout Tom's days as director. A contract was signed with the Vicksburg YMCA for the use of certain of its facilities for CDGM Head Start. This contract was signed with knowledge that the center would be integrated, since there would be at least one white teacher on the staff.

On July 10 the chairman of the local poor people's committee, who had signed the contract with the *Negro* board of directors, was called and told that the contract had been voided by the entirely white board, which was above Negro and white YMCAs. The Negro Y had "Colored YMCA" carved above the door. The cause of the cancellation was that the white teacher had notified the white board that she planned to canvass for poor white children, in compliance with OEO's regulations, and that she planned for her own daughter to attend the center.

Tom Levin, Jim Dann (district coordinator), Gordon Wilcox (legal officer), and a member of the local CDGM committee went to call on the colored executive director of the colored Y. The latter said that the trouble did, indeed, seem to be the proposed integration. Gordon said CDGM had been advised that the contract was binding. Tom said that CDGM was willing to use other means of pressure to affect the action of the white board if necessary. Such means could include pressure by the national YMCA office, by the national press, and by OEO itself. Jack Gonzales from OEO had already called the white board to express his "concern."

The meeting resolved nothing. The CDGM group, minus Tom, went to see the general secretary of the over-all white board that night. The general secretary was very pleasant and helpful, but he said that his board didn't consider the contract legal. Later, the general secretary telephoned Tom at Edwards. He said the police had already been notified. They were ready to lock up anyone who came into the building the next day, opening day. Tom said, "OK, but at opening time tomorrow every single child and staff member will be outside your Y, and I personally will lead them in. Arrest me if you want. But let me warn you, I'll have TV cameras there."

The man called back later, and said that the staff member's child was ineligible anyway, because she was too old for Head Start, but that CDGM could have the space and could have its two anticipated white staff members. Tom's tactics worked. Confrontation *is* the key to change. They withdrew. They feared a big scene and bad publicity more than they feared integration and violating community mores. In these situations people always said they would hold out against integration "till the end," or "all the way," but we had to test and threaten each time to see exactly where "the end" and "all the way" were. Evidently not as far as they at first wanted us to believe; and no doubt believed themselves.

As this incident illustrated, Negro big shots had no authority. That is, they could always be reversed by whites above them, on whom they had to rely for any phony authority and funds they had. And whites were far from secure, too. The white board had called Gordon on Sunday to say it was all right, but when the children arrived Monday morning, the space had been so severely limited that the local chairman called and said half the children had to be sent to a staff member's house for school.

On Tuesday, the head of the Vicksburg School Board called Tom. He stated his concern that CDGM was having trouble getting enough space, and offered to help. He said we could use public school facilities, providing that the School Board be in control. Tom said that Head Start regulations required members of the children's families to be in control. The man said this could not be arranged. Meanwhile, the Y indicated that no more space was to be forthcoming. It wanted to force us into giving over to School Board control. Tom preferred to remain crowded and with the local committees acting as the CDGM school board for this center.

In between all these other happenings, one of Tom Levin's major concerns continued to be translating psychoanalytic theory into social action processes, and considering social action in terms of psychoanalytic thinking. While over their heads sophisticated psychoanalytic discussions were held and political storm clouds gathered, community people, relatively insulated from all this, continued to wallow through their *own* discussions and politics to evolve their children's programs.

CHAPTER 17

TEACHER DEVELOPMENT AND PROGRAM FOR CHILDREN

AND THROUGH IT all, centers happened. For better or for worse, they happened. That was the astonishing thing. Maids, mothers, and field workers developed into beginning nursery school teachers. Programs for children came about where there had been nothing but emptiness, boredom, and often hunger for the children. The number one goal for the children's program Central Staff workers was to encourage people in this historic effort. We weren't primarily trying to train teachers toward professionalism and polish, but were trying to inspire poor people toward aspiration and action. Respect for *any* effort, no matter how small or poorly done, that community people "could" have made before, but never had, and which represented a giant step simply because they were now making the effort, and the ability to convey this respect in warm, informal, human ways as a booster to the people's own authority position, and as an introduction to a new kind of authorities, was the most valued quality for children's program Central Staff workers.

* * *

". . . This is the Bourbon-Tribbet children: the plantation the strikers came from. A good PTA. Good staff."

". . . strikers' children. Need clothes badly . . . living in tents . . . have a qualified music person who has done much in this line. There is a lot of response from teen-agers who volunteer. . . . They tell stories to the children, clean up, do individual work with the very slow children. . . ."

* * *

Another major goal resulted from our interest in "new careers for the poor." We tried to observe and analyze problems and strengths of teachers, children, special services and projects, and central office, in order to plan the first phase of a teacher development program for fall.

Our next goal was much more difficult than the others. We were attempting to orient everybody to the skeletal and spiritual minimum requirements of Head Start—after all, we *had* signed a contract to do a certain program—without imposing specifics. We were largely successful with two major types of troubles. The first was that when we worked from the community's idea of a children's program toward OEO's idea, we tried so hard not to be imperialistic that our suggestions often didn't "take." In these instances we left very popular but with few "improvements" in our wake. The second was that when we worked with a little more insistence on minimum standards because of distress we felt for the children suffering through the program or because of anxiety we felt lest OEO shut down the sad center, we left visible "improvements" and visible hostility toward us for being so domineering.

Our final goal was to offer first aid where radical rescue was sought by a distraught staff feeling overwhelmed and beyond their depth. Or, in extreme and rare cases, where help was felt by us to be necessary, whether it was sought or resented.

* * *

Dear Teacher,

Here are two reading readiness games:

1. Hang up the flannel, or spread it on the floor. Place one of each of the twin shapes on the flannel. Gather a group of 5, 6, or 7 children around you. Let each take a turn finding the partner to each shape and placing it on the flannel, or else put nothing on the flannel, and let the child find both partners and place them together on the flannel. Talk to the child and encourage him as he works. Give him time. Praise him.
2. Make large signs like these for every shelf, piece of furniture, or special area of your room. Put them up. Go around and read them and talk about them. Take about 6 children with you. Give one child the loose twin card and help him find where it goes. It goes with the other word you put up somewhere. Never scold him while playing this game. Talk with him if necessary. Tell him he's smart. Tell him the answer if necessary. But first give him lots of time to hunt. If you have to find it for him, SMILE AND TELL him you know he'll be able to do it next time. Then let another child have a turn. KEEP YOUR EYES AND ATTENTION ON THE GAME. MAKE IT HAPPY. TALK TO HIM."

(Here is your flannel, some shapes, the printed cards labeling TRAIN, BLOCKS, etc. You have $25 per unit now to spend as you like for the children. You had petty cash to spend yourselves on the children's play program two weeks ago. Any of this maney can be spent on books, records, blankets or mats for resting, more materials for games like those above if you need more, things for doll play–whatever you need for the children. You can plan on $6 per unit twice again during the summer for this type of expense. GIVE ALL RECEIPTS TO DISTRICT COORDINATOR.

We had a map of the state and a general plan. Mrs. Myers would make a rush visit to every center (eighty-four in twenty some counties) to do the general things a skilled person can do in that kind of a visit. Either Jeannine or I would spend a whole day at each center, concentrating with local staff on the biggest bottlenecks and greatest weaknesses preventing "good" program; given community goals, judgements, and context, as well as Head Start guidelines. Barbara Rosen, Naomi Long, and occasionally a resource teacher "borrowed" from another center would make a follow-up visit, if in our first visit we had jointly worked out a plan that needed outside help to see it through. All of us would consider attending a community, PTA, or committee meeting a necessity, if there was any possible way to arrange it, so we could discuss program and teaching standards together. We always had a staff meeting too. These direct discussions occurring in the actual center and community were the most successful way of

REPORT FORM FOR CENTERS

Date____________________ Name________________________

Center____

I. General Group Impressions
   A. Resource Teacher
   B. Children
   C. Growth of parents-trainees-aides
II. Supplies (administrative problems)
III. Program Schedules (timing-safety-overall)
IV. Administrative Problems (resource teachers, paper work, payroll, etc.; other than supplies)
V. Community Problems
   A. What plans for continuation
      1. Building available
      2. Supplies left over
      3. Personnel available in fall
VI. Food-clothing-shelter Situation
VII. District Co-ordinator
VIII. Recommendations
   A. People to be re-employed
   B. Type of people in area who could work a center alone
IX. Special Activities
   A. Activities (art-music-three R's)
   B. Adult Education
   C. Health
   D. Social Services
   E. Counseling
X. Personal Comments

This form was given to every local staff to fill in together, as well as to committee chairmen, and Children's Program staff. Out-of-state Resource Teachers were urged to write letters if they wanted to, as was everyone else, but we felt it would be hard on their local relations if they were formally reporting to Central Staff.

combining reality with "technique" and ensuring that all of us would learn together.

Each of us would fill in a check sheet we had made to give us gross information. I was to keep a file on each center, containing letters or reports from parents, aides, trainees, local or out-of-state resource teachers, district coordinators, roving special project people, and children's program staff. We actively solicited this information, even to the point of taking dictation from people who felt embarrassed to write for us but who were eager to share their thoughts. The Newsletter constantly begged for letters, and got over two thousand. I was also to keep a wall-sized logistics chart covering all centers and summarizing all information.

We tried to reinforce direct work done at Orientation by children's program staff, and by special project staff, in three ways. We worked through informal discussion and printed guidelines with district coordinators to develop concepts of what Head Start is supposed to be for children.

Early in the summer I got a packet of fifty pages full of suggestions and patterns for songs, arts and crafts, and children's games from the Day Care Division of the State Department of Public Welfare. I sent a packet of these to each chairman, to help fill the gap till we could prepare materials that were more suitable: *i.e.*, materials coming out of CDGM teachers' experiences and at a much lower reading level. I also made sample reading readiness games and mailed them to each chairman. The third reinforcement was the Newsletter.

* * *

St. Peter Center
1014 Goodrich St.
Greenville, Miss.
Mrs. Jane Chandler, RT

"The very first week of our CDGM Headstart program was an exciting one. One of our TT's was walking down the hall. One of the student, Sandra Faye, said teacher, where is the bathroom? The teacher replied "Come on I'll show you."

Sandra Faye ! ! ! ! ! ! ! ! ! ! ! ! ! Oh no you don't have to go just tell me where it is I can go there all by myself.

(Sandra Faye showed a mind of her own and a independent mind)

Timothy ! I'm first

Calvin ! I'm first

Calvin ! ! ! ! ! ! Let the teacher drink water first. I don't want no water nohow.

The fact is neither one wanted to drink, but neither one wanted to give over. Benjamin–and Bernice–they like to do things all by them self.

We also have the shy type of children, we have one who always like to hide her face with her hands, or hide behind other children so she would not be seen.

Teacher: ! ! !—Valerie, here is my handchief, we are going to play Charlie Brown.
So at the end of the day, she ask may I keep your handchief? I don't have one of my own. The teacher replied, yes, you may have my handchief, and she smile the next day she brought the teacher a piece of ribbon, and the teacher won her in one week.

* * *

This summer is the first time I have eber had the experience to work with the other race. I am a Trainee to the center working with Mr. Pete . . . one of our white teachers and I have enjoyed every moment of it. . . .

* * *

Within this general framework, we did the best we could on an impromptu basis. We responded first to those who asked for us. For example, we heard a number of rumors that Batesville was in great trouble and crying for aid. I drove to Batesville. It was about four hours from Mount Beulah.

The Batesville center was located in a solid brick building, looking something like a small elementary school building. It was situated in a field of mud and knee-deep puddles. A Freedom School had been housed there the summer before. Many things were left over for the people to use, including a large library of sorted and shelved books.

The first problem in the children's program became clear instantly. The center was budgeted for sixty-five children and had a daily attendance of one hundred and sixty-nine. Mrs. Glover's room, for instance, too small for the fifteen budgeted children, contained fifty-nine children. Mrs. Glover was a widow with ten children. She was one of the few Panola County Negro teachers who took the great risk the summer before and registered to vote. She was not afraid to teach with CDGM.

CDGM workers always slept in community homes. I slept that night in the home of the Batesville chairman, Mr. Robert Miles. His wife put up a steady flow of people who came to help in the community. The Miles family has slept and fed as many as thirteen workers at once, and was rarely without at least one. Their house has frequently been fired on by people who don't fancy Negro hospitality to whites.

I asked Mr. Miles about this marvelous surplus of children. This was a typical problem for children's program workers because it happened so often. It created difficulty in maintaining small groups and in having enough toys, food, etc., per child. But it was the happiest problem we could wish for, and one we applauded. Mr. Miles explained that he thought the community child-scavengers would be doing well to get sixty-five children with a county Head Start acting as a rival. So he requested money for sixty-five children. When people were gathering children, they went to the plantations. They had no way of knowing ahead of time how many children were there. Plantations have many secrets. When there turned out to be more than had been expected, well, neighbors couldn't turn away neighbors in need.

I spent some time phoning neighboring centers and Mount Beulah to see if we could reallocate staff in such a way as to stretch a little more staff for Batesville. We tried to get resource teachers, rovers, and trainees from elsewhere to stay in Batesville for a few weeks. But this couldn't solve the gas problem, which was also critical. Staff had a fifty-six-mile area in which to pick up children. Some of the teachers tried to help by bringing as many as twelve children with them. One member of the staff went eight miles out of her way each morning to get two children.

The trainee for program coordination was a teen-age girl from a poor Sunflower County family. She spent two weeks at Batesville to help with the staff shortage and to practice problem-spotting skills. She wrote this report:

"On Tuesday of the last week of the program we took all the children to the zoo in Memphis, Tennessee. The children just loved it. We were all tired at the end of the day, but it was worth it. Many parents volunteered a day to go with us to help take care of the children at the zoo. There were enough volunteers to divide the group of 165 children into groups of five.

"We wanted to make sure that all of our children looked presentable at the zoo. We were sure that the parents had done their best, but many of the children that were from large families parents' could hardly buy food for the family, besides clothes. So early Tuesday morning we loaded the very, very needy children in two cars and carried them to a dry-goods store and really decorated our children, at least they acted as if we had. We bought underwears, pairs of tennis, pants and tops for this group and distributed them as to need. The expression of some of their little faces were really one of happiness. They were very proud of themselves and their new clothes. BECAUSE THEY WERE DRESSED IN CLEAN clothes and they really looked great! They were really happy and excited even before going to the zoo.

"A check was given to us from the Living Arts people to use for the children in the Batesville Center. When I went to Batesville I also had the materials to make variety puppets, but when I got to Batesville, I realized that the idea of puppets had been great . . . but not for these children and especially making them out of new cloth. So I said to myself, 'We must find other materials to make puppets and use the material for clothing for our children,' and so we did. We organized a sewing group and made dresses and saved the scraps. We made the puppets from paper bags, construction paper, and the scraps from the dresses.

"We also organized a committee to help get a few children in school this fall that had not gone before. There was one family that lived on a plantation that sent their children to our Head Start program this summer, the boy was seven, and his sister was eight. They had never been to school a day in their life before this summer. The mother said that she had not been able to buy clothing for them. So we began to contact people in the community for help and clothes donations to try to get these children in school." (This trainee later applied to work in the Peace Corps.)

In this example lay a basic conflict CDGM staff encountered every day in every dealing; a conflict to which OEO was notably unresponsive. It was a problem of ranking values, coming up with meaningful moral hierarchy, and then bending it and the OEO budget to match what was needed with what was allowed in the budget. The government did not allow its grant money to be used for making clothes. Any preschool teachers consider puppets important for dramatic play. But we couldn't insist with vigor and conviction that puppet production was more important than getting two children in school who had never gone and evidently were never going to go, but whose age indicated that they should have finished second and third grade.

And who can say it was wrong to value beaming faces which have never beamed with pride before more than to value the literal budgetary allocations OEO set, as long as the spirit and intention were the same: to bring good care and new attitudes to little children? We saw that my trainee had neglected to fulfill her puppet-making mission and had violated the terms of our grant. We also saw wonderful initiative and common sense in a girl of poverty, which we could fan into leadership or squelch with bureaucratic restrictions.

I saw bleakness, barrenness, and great confusion in the packed and steaming school building. And I saw two old geezers squatting in a doorway talking about the "shade harbor" they were making for the children, and speaking of how wonderful this great modern educational experience was. They compared it to their ditch-jumping days of hiking ten miles to school to build the fire for the teacher. I saw that the community hadn't yet built beautiful toy shelves and work tables for children, and not even toys. Children had no order and little to do. I also saw the glorious pride of two hundred people at a PTA meeting as they touted "their" school.

* * *

We felt this conflict everywhere. It is clearly reflected in this diary excerpt about a different center:

The center is light and spacious. The walls are of "unlined" wood: the bare backside of the boards that are the outer walls. To cheer up what might otherwise be dreary, they have covered the dark unfinished wood with decorations. There is a poster showing groups of foods in vivid color. Next to it is a crooked collection of children's paintings, tacked partially on top of each other. Next comes a poster picturing three Negroes kneeling in prayer with a caption: "come let us build a new world together," and then a picture of Kennedy and a huge paper clock with movable hands. (They took down their pictures and plaques of Jesus because they were told to, but still have lots of prayers in the Head Start program. I've explained about church and state, but they insist, with an incredulous look, that public schools receive government funds and they say prayers, do devotionals, etc., all the time, which of course is true, it is the core of the public school curriculum.) Then comes another poster with an old man saying, "One Man One Vote." There is a list of every child's name, printed in large black letters, a first aid shelf, a bookshelf filled with donated adult books, shelves full of CDGM toys and art supplies, and a bulletin board of FDP.

There was an FDP meeting here last night, and they went and talked at it. I told them about not getting involved in politics. This lady Mrs.——said, "I wanted to reach the community about making equipment for the children, and one hundred fifty were at this FDP meeting, so I told them about CDGM and the equipment. Was that wrong? . . . "

Then the week before this, a lady made a school integration announcement at the regular Tuesday night CDGM parents' meeting. The chairman told her "this is no place to discuss civil rights, you should have taken that up at the FDP meeting last night." The lady said. "There wasn't no audience last night at the FDP meeting, there was only seven people there, and here at this CDGM meeting you got seventy-five peoples. Besides, first grade is a matter of concern for CDGM parents, and I think this is a good place to announce it." She turned to me and she said, "I don't think this is something I could only speak of at FDP, do you?" I don't know what to say in these cases . . . it all seems so absurd, these distinctions. . . .

* * *

And in all the shabbiness and hubbub at Batesville there were individual children. Mrs. Myers wrote: "This Center is crowded but through the confusion there seemed to be a system and the children showed growth. They seemed to play well together with blocks and knew definitely what they were doing. One child explained he was building a big store where you could use a wagon. . . . I was told that he had been a problem and they had worked very hard to get him to respond to anything."

OEO found this center appalling. I did too, as I tried to evaluate it, but less so when I regarded its relevance to Negro history in this neighborhood. A while back in Charleston, a tiny town in neighboring Tallahatchie County where a CDGM center sprang up during the second grant, a Negro worker was hanged for talking back to his boss. In 1964 residents of the Rabbit Ridge Plantation, also in Tallahatchie County, were told by the manager and by the owner that a certain young man would work there no longer because he had had the audacity to register to vote. Negroes had not done so since Reconstruction days. Shortly after the warning, brothers from Charleston registered, and hours later, at a neighborhood grocery store, were beaten unconscious, one sustaining a broken jaw, broken nose, burst eyeball, and fractured skull.

In Batesville itself, only two Negroes had been able to register in the last seventy years, until the COFO Summer Project got five hundred registrants in a few months time. Prior to COFO, the climate was such that out of five colored high schools, with over one hundred teachers in them there wasn't one registered voter. COFO managed to convince five teachers and one reluctant principal to register. In spite of threats and fears, finding their courage didn't result in losing their jobs. Success was contagious, and as slow as progress will be, a barrier was broken. But it was true that from many points of conventional reference, our center was appalling.

We had many alarmingly "poor" centers. In August Tom and I concentrated on working with communities on future planning. One day we went to First Pilgrim's Rest, where no children's program worker had yet been. We followed our directions: "Go to Lexington, an hour and a half north of Beulah, North on #17 about ten miles. Be sure to go over two unnoticeable white bridges, built into the road—not with railings. To top of second rise after second 'bridge.' Right on dirt road, mile and a half to CDGM Sunny Mount Center, then seven miles. Make right at sign saying "end District One." Left at white gate. Right at a store a few miles on. See brown church on left and center is white church opposite."

We did this, but the white building seemed to be deserted. There were no cars outside. No children. No noise. We climbed a red clay embankment and approached, calling, "Hel-l-o!" No answer. We peeped in a slightly ajar door. No one. We decided they were either all off on a trip, or had moved to another location, as centers often independently did. We went in to see if CDGM supplies were there, that would be proof. Nothing. An empty room, large, spacious, light, and devoid of decoration or inhabitant. A second equally big room adjoined this one. We stuck our heads in the door. And lo! There, silent as church mice, sat thirty solemn children on thirty straight-backed children's chairs arranged in rows of ten. The children were staring mindlessly at a lady who was droning at them out of a discarded third grade science text. She told us she was the bookkeeper, newly hired, and that she had been told to "watch the children."

Polite inquiry revealed that the rest of the staff had gone to Mount Beulah to "sit-in" until they got their overdue paychecks. The local staff returned shortly, but the out-of-state resource teacher, previously an FDP worker, remained at Mount Beulah for several days. In the subsequent staff meeting, the community expressed considerable resentment against this girl who wanted them to believe she was in the state to help them, but whom they saw merely as a money-grabber.

They said she was seldom at the center, and when she was, didn't do anything. The local staff seemed good natured and well meaning, but utterly bewildered as to the basic requirements and creative intentions of Head Start. We asked them if their community was helping them. We saw no toys, no playground equipment, and even the outhouse was outlandish—it was just a reeking cement-covered hole with a bunch of sagging boards standing askew over it to offer partial protection from the weather. They said the community was very proud of its center, but didn't know it was supposed to do anything about it. They scurried out and brought people in for a community meeting then and there. We wondered what the resource teacher saw her function to be. It would have been somewhat forgivable if she had neglected the children's program in favor of good community work, but there was evidence of neither.

We talked in detail about the kinds of things they could do with these wonderfully big rooms. We emphasized what other equally bereft communities were doing with their far less large buildings. They pulled ideas out of their heads and TV sets as we sat together. Almost everybody in Mississippi was familiar with such teaching as one sees on *Captain Kangaroo* and *Romper Room,* and while these might have left something to be desired from a sophisticated vantage point, they had much to add to the resources of the open-minded parent in remote rural areas like these.

One lady asked "if we have to keep on keeping on a resource teacher who ain't got no resources." We agreed they didn't. Others raised the point that they had never seen their district coordinator, and had only once had a visit from a substitute coordinator. We agreed that this was much of the reason for their lack of knowledge of the nature of the program. They said that they had not been at Orientation "except for one lady, and she didn't tell us nothin'."

We openly discussed the fact that OEO would close them down if it discovered them (which it hadn't yet), and that from this practical point of view alone, something should be done. We discussed what the Movement was talking about for adults and how this related to what OEO and CDGM were talking about for children. The group felt that the entire situation was a grievous misunderstanding. A man said, "Now we knows this progum is for us to do, so we's gonna stop waitin' for somebody to do it and *we's* gonna do it right."

We believed in our idea, "failures" and all (one of the fundamental freedoms the poor are usually denied is the freedom of trial and error, and thus growth). Subsequent history of First Pilgrim's Rest explains why. This situation was typical of what poor people can do if they understand the alternatives, are given encouragement, and are exposed to appealing ideas. Mrs. Virgie Saffold, a trainee who took over the resource teacher's job at the end of the summer, did an extraordinary thing with this deserted-looking place. Under her leadership the community unpacked the CDGM supplies, which had been put aside in a locked closet, and activities became a central part of the day. The walls were hung with gay paintings. Shelves were made and filled with bright toys. Men turned two closets into perfectly appointed playhouses for little girls, complete with a freshly painted real wood stove. Everyone hammered, sawed, and painted until the desolate yard was a fairyland playground.

On November 3, months after our first grant had ended, the community opened the center "on voluntur basic. The peoples of this community who have cars and trucks is taken terms getting the children to school. Without any coast. The staff brings food among their self every day. Also have partys to help buy food. We open at 8:30 close at noon. we have 1 trainee 2 jaitor 1 cook who worked this summer is now working on volentur basic we also have 3 other peoples who is working where they may be needed."

After March the center was back on the payroll with our second grant. The area teacher guide, whose area included this center, wrote: ". . . gentle and kind as can be . . . extra good. . . . They have plenty of games, reading readiness games, dolls, dress up clothes, so many activities, extra good school. . . . Beautiful playground . . . they have a loving group."

This center ran again on "volentur basic" for many months the following winter while the OEO refunding battle raged around the state.

One day I took an OEO early childhood education expert to this center. Later she expressed serious disapproval of this teacher's English; particularly of her spelling and punctuation in written reports. I asked her if she knew of eight people who spelled and punctuated better who would be willing to spend two six-month winters in rural Mississippi, seventeen miles from the nearest phone, being "gentle and kind as can be" for no salary, and who would also transport all the children "without any coast" over the winding back dirt roads while being shot at by Klansmen, and supply groceries for the daily dinner out of their own pockets. She didn't know of eight such people. I suggested that some accomplishments were more important than other accomplishments, and asked if she recommended teaching spelling and punctuation to four-year-olds anyway? She was unmoved and unimpressed by these teachers and their lack of credentials. I was unmoved and unimpressed by her credentials, if these were her value priorities.

* * *

We do not find that public school teachers are as reliable as are we poor people. I say this because of things like this in the district where I work. When the Clarkesdale police stopped a CDGM car taking teachers and children from one of our many Greenville centers to the Memphis zoo, the resource teacher, a young man who teaches in public schools during the year, ran away, leaving the children and the trainee teachers. He explained to me later that he feared to jeopardize his position for the fall by letting officials see him with CDGM. However, one can sympathize, but one cannot find him or his type too reliable as compared to the poor who do not mind if they are seen doing things.

* * *

"Jack and Jill went up the hill, to fetch a pail of water. . . ."

* * *

There is a old blue Ford car spends about equal time parked in front of the police office and parked in front of our center. When they cruise past here they usually shoot. The polices says they don't know anything about anything. They killed a dog twenty feet in front of him, and many of us witnesses know it. They was aiming at our chairman, he was carpantering on the front porch of our center. They guard it all night now, and in the day too if they is going to town . . . we have many guns here, we sleep in the center with some guns and others set on the porch all night with a gun. . . . We are protecting the school so the little children will get their necessary education. . . .

* * *

By the end of the summer we had found nineteen out of eighty-four centers that were pretty terrible. In contrast to these, there were twenty-two centers which were generally felt to be excellent, with the other forty-one falling in the middle. Holly Grove, nestled in the hills of Holmes County, was an example of an excellent center.

Central Staff had agreed somewhat vaguely that someone from one project or another would get to each center within the first few days of operation to wave hello and bring encouragement from Beulah. But the days rolled on, and no one seemed to have been at Holly Grove. A staff member was dispatched to go there with greetings and goodwill. At the end of a gruelingly hot day, he came back, limp and wet as a rag. He said defeatedly that he had hunted all day on the snaking red dust roads of backwoods Holmes County, but couldn't find the center.

The next day a girl from the social service project made the attempt. She, too, returned after a ten-hour hunt, baffled and exhausted. We couldn't call the center for directions. There was no phone closer than sixteen miles. These frustratingly futile expeditions went on for close to three weeks, when I finally got tree by tree directions from a neighboring center (thirteen miles distant, and also without a telephone), and wound my way there. ("Turn right at the puddle"—but it had dried up—"turn left at the dairy farm"—it was a weathered heap of gray boards without visible cows, and I didn't know it was a dairy farm—"go aways"—it was ten miles—"and left at the high embankment where the hogs are"—the whole road was beautiful, high, wild, vine-swarming embankments and the hogs weren't there that day.)

When I finally bumped through the pits and potholes and pulled into the dusty parking patch next to the old church, I found all the children outside playing in the pine woods. Sad piano music floated out the church windows, and a hearse was drawn up to the door. The resource teacher, a vivacious and marvelous local teacher named Mrs. Clarke, hurried over, motioning me to hush, and whispered that a funeral was in progress. It was for a baby girl who had starved to death that morning. She said it was "recess" anyway, and "class" would resume momentarily. Meanwhile, the children romped and frisked on a lovely playground which they called "the park." The community had made it in a pine forest. They then had a hearty "lunch" consisting of corn bread and fried chicken, peas, beans, salad, mashed potatoes, canned peaches, all the milk they could drink, and cake, at a table built between big shady trees with benches on each side.

There were a number of men around. One of them told me: "We're building a kitchen. Earl, Mattie, Josephine, and myself started talking about we need one. Mattie is the chairman of the CDGM committee here, and also a trainee. Josephine is the cook and my wife. Earl is a member of this community. We and some of the others went to get an estimate on lumber, of how much it would take and how much it would cost to build a kitchen on 14 feet by 14 feet. Then we called a meeting together of the community to see if we could build a kitchen on church property. We agreed to build it. The first day, Thursday, twelve men helped build. Friday nine came. Monday six came, and to-day five. We're nearly finished. It's gotta be wired. We have a stove available, but we still have to buy it and haul it. We have two tables. We need a sink and refrigerator, we'll get to it when we get money."

CDGM poor people were often unable to cope with many kinds of administrative follow-up and planning because these were new arenas of competence for them, but they managed to cope with other kinds of problems that would horrify the middle-class professional into paralysis and into the statement, "It just can't be done under these conditions." Many CDGM poor people felt that these *were* the conditions. If any change was going to occur, it would just have to occur, conditions not-withstanding.

"The Holly Grove Team," as they signed themselves, wrote: "At first it seemed as if we'd have nothing but children and a church house. (Our supplies were roaming around in Holmes County someplace.) But just as we were about to despair, our Veteran Resource Teacher Mrs. Doris Clarke drove up with Construction paper, toys, Crayola, Tempera, pencils, paper, books, paper clips, tacks, Cardboard, etc., and in a few moments the church was transformed into a classroom for curious four, five, and six year olds. . . . We were as excited as the children when the packages were opened. Some had never handled puzzles, rods, blocks, and many other devices that were sent. . . .

"On Tuesday, Mr. Tracy Whittaker came. . . .

"On Wednesday we'd grouped our children into fives which is a workable number for young children. . . ."

A later letter from "the team" concluded: "We have ice water too. Mr. Earl Thomas brings a cooler each day. So we have safe drinking water.

"We are way, way out and not on the map, but I assure you we're in the hearts of these little children entrusted to our care. We must not, we cannot, fail them."

A Holly Grove parent wrote: "this letter is to say how Much we appreciate haveing the Head Start Program in Our Community. I think it is Very find to have this progrom here at Holly Grove. because it is very helping to the childer as will as the olds peoples in our community thay come out to the center some of the peoples here in our community Every day. and thay ingay see the Childer play and I think is the mose wonderful thong that Every happen to the Negro Peoples here in Mississippi to have a program like is this one."

Reports from other staff members included remarks illustrating the climate of many of our centers: "They couldn't cash their food check in Lexington bank."; "They said they had asked for surplus food at the Welfare office and were unable to get it."; "They are dissatisfied that they were paying eight and one half cents a carton for milk. This was harassment because it was above the public school rate."

Mr. Tracy Whittaker, mentioned above, was a young man from Yale. He and the local Mrs. Clarke were the two resource teachers. This letter from Tracy appears in the fifth CDGM Newsletter:

Holly Grove, Mississippi
August 18, 1965

Dear Dr. Levin,

This letter is written in response to your request for an evaluation of our experience at the Holly Grove Head Start Center with a view to extending the program into the fall.

Any analysis of our center must consider what we started with—which was nothing. We held classes in the community church which had to be constantly converted to serve its dual role. We had no kitchen, no playground, no running water, and no telephone (in a very rural area that is difficult to find). The local staff was totally untrained in the operation and administration of a kindergarten.

At this writing we have a smoothly running preschool, with a capable teaching staff and a more than adequate physical plant. A kitchen and a playground was constructed entirely by volunteer workers. As the kitchen materials and its lack in the beginning absorbed about all of our petty cash and facilities money, we were thrown back on our own resources for any supplementary school supplies. While the men contributed their labor, the women made rag dolls and donated old clothes for the children's "dress-up" play. [A lady at another center said, "We can't have 'dress-up' clothes. People need those clothes. When they're old enough to give up, they're dish rags, not glad rags for dress-up."] Running out of facilities money, we had to ask for contributions to outfit the kitchen with utensils. The response was overwhelming—pots, large spoons, towels, etc., were freely given (from people in one of the lowest income areas in the country). It was no trip to the State Park without donations of transportation and extra help. The trip is on.

To a degree the enthusiastic community response is a reflection of gratitude for the social services provided by CDGM in the form of sorely needed welfare materials and the medical attention given their children. However, the response of the community is more than just gratitude, but instead the reaction of a people that have so long felt that any efforts to improve their lot were futile—doomed to failure and reprisals by an unsympathetic, hostile local autocracy. If for no other reason, Head Start would be money well spent because it serves as tangible evidence that their government in Washington is conscious of their oppressed condition and sympathetic to their advancement.

However, as important as the community unity fostered by Head Start is, it is a mere product of the larger aim of the project here at Holly Grove. The children's advancement is the standard by which this program must ultimately be evaluated. Although eight weeks is, in fact, too short a period for any accurate conclusions, I cannot but feel that we have made great progress in the development of our children. From a mass of withdrawn, repressed pre-schoolers who had never ridden a seesaw, worked a puzzle, drawn a picture, we have, with few exceptions, a happy, cohesive group of kids full of vitality (and now, at last, food) who spend their day creating, pretending, playing, singing, looking, listening, and wondering. We don't pretend to be a super educational machine at Holly Grove—the children didn't learn to read and write in our eight weeks. However, we did expand their limited view of life; we did provide a chance to test their intellectual and physical muscles; we did provide a transition between mother and school as the children learned to work and play with others.

Finally, and perhaps the most important of all, we tried to show these children that they were important—that we cared about what they had to say, what they did, what they made. Some of our kids can't read a word—some can't count to ten—but almost all have a measure of human dignity that they didn't have before. It is for this reason I must conclude we have succeeded admirably at Holly Grove, and it would be a sad mistake if it be denied to their successors.

If my evaluation sounds too glowing, I cannot pretend to be an uninterested observor. However, I hasten to point out that, when you start at the bottom, you can only go up. Indeed, it seems that our success at Holly Grove came almost as a matter of course. For people who have been held in semi-knowledge for so long, the progress must be rapid at the beginning. And at Holly Grove, progress is our most important product. . . .

Not all resource teachers viewed the educational situation as Tracy did. Some communities did not receive outsiders as graciously as did Holly Grove. This was occasionally due to the personality of the outsider, but more often because of the nature of hostility toward anyone community people considered "above" them. In these places, not even an angel could have succeeded in spurring on and developing local people. Also every local climate was influenced by the over-all CDGM climate, which blew hot and cold as the people concerned mostly with conventional preschool education vied with the people concerned mostly with community development, who struggled to establish a balance with those concerned mostly with political implications, all of whom had to maneuver through those concerned mostly with developing their own personal followings.

One of our best professional nursery educators wrote:

Dear Tom Levin,

This is to inform you that I must leave my job as resource teacher in the Sandy Flat [falsename] Operation Headstart after July 21st. I must return to my job in New York City. I am exhausted from the many pressures that have been brought to bear on me in the month I have been here.

Here in Sandy Flat it is impossible to get away and lick one's wounds. One is constantly being involved in the needs of the others. Without even a room to call my own, or a door I can shut against others for just a few minutes, I find that I must leave. . . . This way I can have a chance to restore my inner balance before returning to my job. . . .

As for the general nature of the program, it seems to me that the CDGM made several mistakes. Perhaps you are well aware of them. . . . I have never found it easy to compromise—I always want the ideal. I say this as a preface to my remarks on the program so that you recognize my bias, and understand that I am painfully aware of it too.

Overestimating the abilities of the people.

The people have not had to plan this kind of program before. Calculating the kind of facilities they need, the dishes and pots they need, the kind of glasses (or the fact that paper cups would be better than glasses) they need, the kind of food the children need and would eat, are major areas where the people have received little or no help. They are told to do it themselves, and we expect them to learn from their mistakes. But how? The vitamin deficiencies are still there, it still takes an enormous amount of time to prepare the food (in our center two part time cooks and two other people—either resource teachers or aides—I particularly put my foot down that no trainee could work in the kitchen, that her job was in the classroom). So instead of buying fruit and vegetables with the money, we buy grease and starches and lollipops. Instead of buying a can of tunafish, we buy 3 or 4 cans. Instead of buying milk by the gallon we buy by the quart. Since I live in a slum section of New York, I'm well aware that this is the way many of the poor buy and fix food. But the poor are just being kept poor this way. Why is it that the middle class tend to buy more wisely. Because they have a certain amount of informative sources. I've learned how to shop for my family from publications such as *Consumer Reports* and cookbooks such as Adel[l]e Davis' [*Let's*] *Cook It Right*. In other words, what has made me an intelligent shopper is the availability of information—information that the poor do not have. Is it a lack of confidence in the poor people to provide this? Is there something that can be done, even at this point, which could provide help in planning meals and in shopping?

I deal in this area at length because the poor are concerned about meeting the physical needs of their children. This seems as typical in Harlem as it is in Sandy Flat, Mississippi. The children come to school well dressed in their Sunday type of clothes. (Middle class children are dressed more informally, in clothes that do not need much ironing, and in clothes that are suitable for climbing, sitting on the floor, etc.) Children in Sandy Flat are dressed up, then told they are "nasty" for sitting on the floor or ground. (If I had to work and iron those clothes I'd become a nag too.) Some mothers change their children's clothes at the school before taking them home.[26] One can understand these things. People who have done without, want to have these things for their children. Further, this is what they *can* do for their children. They can, through much sacrifice, feed and clothe their children. This also helps to explain why poor people's expectations for our school is so academically oriented.

They want the children to know their ABC's, to print their names. These are *goals* for a semi-literate society. Even when poor people talk about children sharing[27] they are speaking differently than when the middle class people speak of "sharing"—on one hand, the children have had nothing to handle in their environment (what is within the environment is off limits), on the other, almost everything has been available, and much of what is available personally "belongs" to the child.

Well, I've gone on and on just on this one point. Really, all I'm trying to say is that poor people need help in planning for programs. This is a logical result of oppression, and it is a fact that CDGM and the Movement will have to face. Poor people need help in planning, in teaching and in being kind to children. Perhaps all this is being "middle class." But without this, the poor will generally plan a school structure like the only one they know (as we generally create a family structure like the ones we've known)—and that structure is authoritarian, skill-centered rather than knowledge-centered; obsolete. I understand that the Sandy Flat Center wants to have information for the entire staff. Perhaps this image explains what I mean more than whatever I say. The local staff call the children "babe," rather than a specific name. They use learning by rote, various forms of humiliation, punishment—"candy" rewards as discipline, they ask for little response or involvement from the children other than passivity or repeating things, and there is a heavy emphasis on forms of addressing adults and on manners. They ape the worst of all public school traditions. They tell (command) children to do something, never showing *how* to do it, or helping the children by doing it with them.

[26] Another resource teacher, trying to reduce a mother's anxiety over securing staff approval for her child, revealed her lack of understanding of what it is to be a poor black person when she said to the mother, "You don't have to change your child's clothes when you leave. I never change my child." And the mother replied, "Yes, but if your kid is dirty with school paint, ain't nobody gonna say, 'oh, there goes another dirty nigger.' "

[27] In our centers "sharing" a toy meant "yielding" it—it didn't mean, as it would in a good laboratory contemporary nursery, one child having a full and complete turn and then another child having a full and complete turn. I think this is partly because no one has considered children's activity as purposeful or as work, so the idea of completing a project before "sharing" would naturally not occur.

That's what it means to be poor—to be oppressed, overwhelmed, impatient, tired, resentful. It often means that church is your only outlet, so you scream hysterically to the Lord.

What I'm saying sounds terribly negative. And believe me, that's hard for me. I want so for men to be free, for us to be non-violent towards each other. I don't want to have the *power* to decide whether I should use the colored side of the laundromat or to live in a Sandy Flat. I want more than the right to vote (for I know how deceiving that can be) and the ability to read.

So I am more the dreamer than the doer, though I do try hard to act. If I had the power to decide how CDGM might run, I would vote to concentrate energy in a few centers, to enable them to survive. I would make such a decision on the basis of community involvement and on the abilities of the staff. I would change resource teachers around so that I had the strongest possible forces in those areas.

It's a hot Sunday afternoon. I hope this letter will have some use. I hope this letter is not saying that the poor are nothing—quite the contrary. But the Negro poor has been *oppressed*, with all the implications that word has. We must face this fact. And when we hear the poor telling us—"I want my child to know the ABC's"—we must *understand* the significance of their statement. Perhaps you will show this letter to Jeannine Heron and Polly Greenberg; it might interest them for planning. . . .

This view interested us very much for planning. We couldn't consider the recommendation to concentrate on a few able centers, because this bypassed the whole point of CDGM. Subsequent good nursery teachers on our staff also made this recommendation.

It was the only reasonable recommendation to have made if one's goal was quality nursery education in the standard sense. But if the goal was to involve the parents in changing many aspects of their oppressed lives so their children could freely grow, it would have been suicidal to have eliminated the bulk of them. If the goal was to alter the role model parents offered children by putting them in active positions, it would not have been wise to have kept them in passive positions of observation once again while a few taught. If the goal was to show children and parents that they were part of a potentially powerful group, it wouldn't have been reasonable to have created the usual picture of a few "elite" teachers and a mass of excluded parents. If the goal was new careers for the poor, those who were not able at the outset could not be ruled out of the program. And if the goal was to prove that meaningful education conceptualized differently from currently standard preschool education can be created on a mass scale in depressed areas where there won't be enough "qualified" teachers for many years, a small demonstration model is useless and irrelevant.

Our problem was to plan ways of expanding horizons and therefore of raising standards from a mass base. This resource teacher, it seemed to me, raised two vitally important points in her defeated finale. The first was a question of basic belief from which all one's further thinking and acting in this area flows: Is it lack of confidence in the poor to provide information? Is it an insult to admit that the poor don't know everything *yet*? Is it condescending to *teach* as well as to be friends and co-equals? Is it intimidating to introduce new choices and to discuss alternatives?

Most of the CDGM Central and midlevel staff answered *yes* to this cluster of questions. I answered *no* with qualifications, on the same grounds that the majority answered *yes*.

I thought it was a great lack of confidence, insult, and condescension to assume that the tragically limited amount of information poor people have had access to is all they need to know, or all they can handle. I thought it was a great pessimism and a very conservative position to fail to see that people can grow infinitely; that poor people don't have to continue forever in the information backwater, and therefore, in the power backwater, into which they have been damned. I thought it was myopic to emphasize the possibility of intimidation to the point of locking people into permanent psychic invalidism by protecting their areas of ignorance, weakness, and acknowledged inability to stand up with other people they perceive as overwhelming experts.

My qualification was the fundamental assumption and the human manner in which new ideas are introduced. I agreed with the Movement rather than with most professionals that our manner of "giving" information is usually authoritative rather than cooperative. The assumption is "since you can't do it, leave it to us and we'll do it the right way for you," rather than "since you have certain kinds of expertise we don't have and we have certain expertise you don't have, let's work out a new way together." But I by no means agreed with the Movement that problems of the poor must be protected and glorified as well as previously unrecognized talents.

In her second point, I think the resource teacher suggested the road leading to this exciting new middle area betwen preserving ignorance and intimidating with knowledge. She said: "And when we hear the poor telling us—"I want my child to learn the ABC's"—we must understand the significance of their statement."

We had to "listen with a third ear," as a well-known psychoanalyst put it. We had to interpret the symbolic meaning, not the literal. When the poor said they want ABCs they were saying they wanted their children to have the power of discovery and judgment to which those who can read competently have access. When they said they wanted manners, nice clothes, and good English, they were saying they want what those who are "in" have—doors open to them.

If we interpret this way, it becomes more clear why our customary efforts to paint on these veneers fail. The poor are getting only the veneer and not what they really want. They can't articulate this, so they reject what we offer. If we discuss with poor people what it is they really want, we can, together, work out ways of achieving the whole, not just the husk.

In this way, we can avoid the traditional professional error, which I think comes from an unrecognized but nevertheless real feeling of superiority, of denying the poor their right to their own goals by belittling these goals and labeling them "backward." And we can avoid the jelling Movement error, which I think comes from an unrecognized but nevertheless real immaturity, and bellicosity, of denying the poor their right to their own goals by belittling these goals and labeling them "middle class." In either case, we have been deciding for poor people what they should have. I think it's time we start lending support to them as they unravel figurative and literal meanings and as they decide what they want. If they literally want ABCs, manners, nice clothes, and good English, in addition to what these things stand for, they are entitled to that too, regardless of what Movement rulers ruthlessly try to ram into their heads.

* * *

Dear Central,

We would like to share with you this book our childrens has made. Each child has explained his expression and we have wrote it here under the picture each child has made:

"I saw a monkey climber on my trip and a German Shepherd. They is to eat colored peoples up."

"This is a house. Nobody lives in this house. They went to New York."

"This is a picture of a woman. Her don't have no where to live at. She has eyes and teeth in her head, see, and she can't half talk. This is the man. He told her to let's go somewheres. She likes to watch TV and she doesn't like to go out with her husband. When she doesn't like to watch TV she go out with her husband. They met this hog. He told the man and the woman that he wanted to go live with all the other peoples. A man live in that house, but he come from outer space. He say, no this house just for me. . . ."

* * *

All summer we learned. By late August we thought these were important considerations for fall:

We would need a *functioning* community development division (there was unanimous agreement that Frank Smith didn't function in this capacity) to work with local commitees on developing judgement in hiring poor people known to have a flare for working with young children and in *not* hiring those known to be bristlingly hostile or sullenly bored; in building necessary equipment, developing community projects around the center, making the centers clean and attractive; in determining ways of handling the excess children problem without turning them away, and without crowding classrooms.

Communities could find volunteers to teach extra children at the regular two-to-fifteen Head Start ratio, and volunteers to offer the use of, or build, rent-free rooms or buildings to house extra children; volunteers to donate food, make toys, etc., for unbudgeted children; run split shift sessions—one group in the morning with dinner at the end, and another group in the afternoon with dinner at the beginning; take one group of children for the first half of the new grant and another group for the second half, offer a shorter session to twice as many children; take the extra children on "outdoor" days and keep them home on days when outdoor space could not be used for almost all activities, and so forth. We needed to take *all* children, but we also needed to provide for them.

We needed special orientation sessions for Central and district Staff in early education. We should keep our unique feature of hiring many professional Movement workers, and we should continue with them as the chief people working directly with poor people because of their excellence in doing so, but they would need more familiarity with Head Start. Those not interested shouldn't be hired, as this was a Head Start program.

We would need better selection of out-of-state resource teachers and special project workers to ensure that we got fewer who had little to offer or little intention of offering it. We needed special workshops for them so they got more support in developing useful nonauthoritarian nonoveridentifying roles in center evolution, so that they would neither be rejected because they were "trying to put something over on the poor," or absorbed because they were paralyzed by not wanting to seem different from the poor. Workshops should include sessions on the nature of Mississippi and the Negro poor, specific nursery education skills, and how to try putting the two together.

* * *

In my diary I found these notes: "Getting the work done is not accomplished without distractions. Today I stopped for gas in the Delta before continuing eighty miles to the Center expecting me to work on number concepts. I stupidly went into the gas station to get a candy bar, forgetting that I had piles of Newsletters in the station wagon with integrated sketches in full view. Sure enough, when I came out, the collection of idling cowboy-hatted, cowboy-booted, thug-type, pug-faced whites usually lounging outside gas stations was whispering, laughing, and staring at me. When I drove off, two cars of them drove off behind me! Not being given to hysterics, I was only a little nervous.

"However, after ten miles of driving, with them slowing down every time I did, instead of passing where they could, and them getting so close to my rear bumper that I was afraid to slow down, I thought I better get rid of them. I sped up enough to create enough distance between us so I could safely stop, and then screeched to a halt on the strip of shoulder. Looking very interested in something in the bordering cotton field, I jumped out, bulging with my movie camera and all its paraphernalia, and clambered through the lovely warm rich earth to the middle of the vast field. I pretended to take movies of cotton blossoms. For ten minutes I adjusted the pretty pink flowers and, squinting and focusing more than was necessary considering that I had no film, appeared to be deeply engrossed in my project. Both cars of Klan types parked behind my car. Eight or ten men peered out at me, exchanging many lively remarks about the condition of my sanity.

"I hurried back to the car, and after dawdling over the re-loading process, started up again. Every few miles for twenty minutes I stopped, ran into the fields, and 'took pictures.' Finally, disgusted at the kook they had mistakenly trailed, the men made a U turn and headed disappointedly back to their spider web, probably to wait for their next potential victim. The name of my movie will be 'Who's Afraid of the Big Bad Wolf.'"

". . . Today something funny happened. I had [my two littlest daughters] with me for a day of work in three Holmes County Centers. At sunset, we were just starting out for a night PTA meeting at —. They were hungry, and I knew we wouldn't be back where there was sure food until 11 P.M. or so, so I did something I rarely do: went into a white restaurant. It was that cafe on the square in ——. Katie was next to me, and Biffie farther down on her counter stool.

God help us if the sheriff, distinguished for his cruel physical treatment of Negroes, didn't come in and take the stool next to Biffie. It would have been alright if it had been the big two girls—they know how to wear protective coloring. But this was Biffie, only four, very friendly. . . . She started chatting with the sheriff. I offered her a barrage of help; ketsup, mustard, relish, cut her meat, share my French Fries, anything to get her next to me where I could control the conversation. But Biffie, always fond of men, found the sheriff quite charming, and assured me that he would help her.

"'Where are you going?' He asked the little 'tourist.'

"'We're going to the CDGM center where my mother works,' she replied maturely. I choked on my grits.

"'Oh?' said the sheriff, taking a long look at me over the two innocent little heads. 'And what will you do there?'

"'Well, it's in a Negro church, and we like to sing, so we'll prob'ly sing first. Want to hear a song we might sing?' And before my pounding heart could be heard by astonished guests at the cafe, Biffie drowned it in loud song:

'And before I be a slave,
I'll be buried in my grave,
And go home to my Lord,
And be free—ee-ee-ee-ee ! ! '

"The sheriff broke into hilarious laughter, stood, patted her on the curly head, and walked out.

"I was actually shaking as we paid and left. The sheriff, sitting slouched in his car in the town square, as these rural sheriffs seem always to do, watched us get into the car, which at that time still had Washington tags. Doubtless he had the number. Dark was falling. I was too afraid to set out on lonely roads for the twenty mile hitch to the meeting. And I didn't want to lead him to the people, just in case he didn't yet know who, specifically, they were. I drove up to the motel nearby and went into the phone booth to call Beulah for advice. The sheriff sat in his car behind mine, doing pantomime finger plays through the car windows with the girls. Beulah told me to 'drive around the back roads till you lose him.'

"I did. For two hours! Finally he gave up. I got to the meeting in time to hear: 'An' who will donate a potholder? Miz Green? Fine, fine, an' who will donate a mixin' spoon? Oh, that's jes fine, Miz Mason, an' who will give us a pan, a small pan . . . Oh, here's Polly! Polly [hugs, handshakes, more hugs, laughter] everythins goin jes wonerful, we don hardly have a problem!' "

* * *

We needed to select a small regionally distributed group of poor individuals recommended by district coordinators, chairmen, other community staff, resource teachers, and other staff, as particularly good with children—bright, eager and able to work with others in their communities—and work intensively with them on early education skills. They could, in turn, work with center teachers, committees, parents, and community toward development of early education community school concepts.

This could be the beginning of serious "new careers for the poor" work, and of building a "qualified" quality group of indigenous experts to expand CDGM's permanent effectiveness—*i.e.*, its effectiveness as a continuing community process, even when in later days there might be no organization called CDGM. We might work with this group as much as once a week, after an initial workshop of several weeks duration. Emphasis at first would have to be working up to minimum standards of space, equipment, etc. Soon we should be able to get into democratic processes in the classroom, child development theory, and creative teaching in all "subjects."

We were ready for regularly scheduled regional workshops for center teachers, led by CDGM staff or selected visiting consultants, to add to in-center work done by briefly visiting "impact" early education workers.

We would need a much better system of supply distribution. This could either be a well-organized, well-followed-up, purchaser-district-coordinator-center chairman system with budgeted truck drivers and a salaried inventory-taker, or we could order prepackaged units of supplies and have them drop-shipped to centers and inventoried by a roving person. The latter was Tom's original plan, but it was vetoed. Children's program staff selected supplies this time, but since we were not allowed to see that they got distributed, and no one else really did either, we ran into frequent problems of trying to build programs with no materials.

We stewed and planned, centers struggled and ran.

* * *

At first our centers went raggedy. Also we couldn't get community help. We said we would get them out if we had to drag them out. One morning at five A.M. we *did* drag them out. We picked them up at their door and they came out and they built us tables."

* * *

. . . The strict trainee improved greatly. The community was very responsive to suggestions for improvement. Do matching games, quite a bit of art, loved to sing. Hot breakfast is carried to center, though children go to nearby Negro restaurant for their hot dinner. . . .

* * *

On Saturday, July 17, overt (as opposed to covert, which has been going on all along) harassment began at the Rosedale center. A number of cars loaded with whites and bulging with weapons circled the center chairman's house. Mr. Frank Davis, chairman, is known to have used his house as a meeting place for the Freedom Democratic Party in the past, and is known to use his house now as an office for the CDGM center. Mr. Davis feels that this outbreak of harassment is due to the fact that CDGM is the most concrete program Rosedale Negroes have had, and also due to the presence of two white resource teachers.

* * *

On July 19 at about 11 P.M., two Negro employees of the center were attacked and beaten by five whites. About twenty minutes later a shot was fired from a car in front of the house, and an hour later, after midnight, another shot was fired. Mr. Davis reported the events to both the Rosedale police and the Bolivar County sheriff. The policeman said he would investigate. The sheriff said he should not be disturbed at that hour.

Gordon Wilcox was notified and notified the FBI. Mr. Morris of the FBI assured Gordon that the trouble was only firecrackers set off by Negro children (at midnight). This conflicted with information of witnesses, who saw a blue four-door Oldsmobile going past the center several times at the time of the shooting, and who identified the sound as being caused by "a .22 caliber short rifle bullet."

* * *

Everything else comes after the children. Program is mostly activities. Use record player. Take field trips and picnics. . . . Have parents in daily to supervise outside activities. Purchased gym set, swimming pool (play in water every day), 2 large wagons. . . . Good art classes done by Bunny and Georgie, both women, former local and latter white RT. Good number classes done by Bunny. They have clay classes in which they make objects and let it harden and then paint it. . . .

* * *

He was just settin' there ten miles west of nowheres in Holmes County here on this here back dirt road in the cab of his truck with the parkin' lights on pulled off on the side of the road in a area with no posted parking regulations and they charged him with improper parking and they told him to pay $24 within half'n'hour or go to jail. . . . We knows it's because he works hard at the center and even helped put in new glass. . . .

* * *

Mrs. —— rented a piano so the children could have better music. . . . Tremendous PTA. Contributed clothes and eight hours a day.

* * *

Did welfare investigations and turned their information over to the welfare department for action. They have kept a chart on health and weight records. Mixed parents, members, and teen-age volunteers. The children have been trained to clean off tables when meal time is over. Plan a closing giving each parent a folder of child's work with growth evaluation chart included. Very nice rhythm band. . . .

* * *

In late July, Tom, I, and a few others took three distinguished visitors to see centers here and there, up and down the state. Dr. Keith Osborne, director, Merrill Palmer Institute and Early Childhood Education Consultant for OEO, wrote: "Speaking as an educator with a lifetime of experience in this field, while the training was not as much as we would like, the quality of the program was good for the children. The parents were involved in a very creative fashion."

Dr. George Gardner, recently director of the Judge Parker Guidance Clinic, a widely known and recognized authority on child development, said: ". . . my impression on visiting these programs, and I visited seven of them in (CDGM), when they were about halfway through the summer sessions, was that they were doing an excellent job, a good job in preschool education, getting children ready for the first grade work, and many of the children were well into the first grade in their schoolwork with regard to letters, numbers, reading, arithmetic, and so forth. I thought that the students themselves seemed to be alert, attentive, and eager to get all of the advantages they could out of this program. I would say, too, that the teachers I talked with seemed to me to be highly efficient and well-trained teachers. Many of them had not taught at the preschool level before they came in but they oriented themselves to the tasks peculiar to this particular age level and were doing an excellent job.

"They also had with them a core, at each of these installations, of hard-working student teachers, trainees, volunteers from the community. I would say, too, that they were giving special and individualized education to children who were too far behind for regular classroom, taking them aside and giving them individual instruction in groups of two, three, or four, or even one, and finally getting them back into their regular classroom. . . .

"In conclusion, I would say that they were a group of hard-working youngsters. I have never seen children act so well. They had their cut-ups like any 5 or 6 year old children would, which is much to the good, I thought. They were not subdued, as I thought they might be, but they were happy and alert youngsters. Certainly the Negro parents in [those] communit[ies] are highly dedicated and they are devoted to this chance that they have had at last handed to them for the children."

Dr. Julius Richmond, director, Project Head Start, OEO: "The program . . . was first of all a medical program to try to improve the health of these children. They all had physical examinations, and we followed through to see that they received appropriate care. There is a nutritional program that brought to these children hot meals. We had occasion to inspect these and found their quality to be excellent. Then there was a very important educational program, designed to bring these children the kind of stimulation they don't receive, particularly in the use of language and their ability to develop reading and language readiness for schoolwork that they would be facing in the fall. Then, in addition, we brought to them programs in social service, trying to bring these children to the services that might be able to help them and their families function more effectively."

* * *

Peoples say, "My friends and my relatives makes it so hard for me." That's true. But there is a time you have to chose your path. No one said it was a path of roses. There's bullets on that path and blood. But it's the path to justice. To comply with the federal government you come in direct conflict with Mississippi state law and hundreds of years of habits. The federal government says you can't take the children in Head Start any place segregated. Local law and people say you can't take them anywhere integrated. So man, whose law you gonna break?

* * *

Lots of harassing by community whites. Two RTs, three other staff members were locked up. Because they were protesting that they weren't allowed to vote on a Saturday. They were forced to drink a great deal of milk of magnesia in jail, which made the white girl too ill to teach all week.

* * *

Jeannine Herron . . . Herbert Lee center . . . Greenville . . . Cages of frogs on front porch. Paintings made from dipping string in paint hanging on line. . . .

They're singing their own adaptation of Kumbaya:

> Come by here, my Lord, come by here,
> Come by here, my Lordy, come by here,

Come by here, my Lord, come by here,
Oh, Lo-ord, come by here!

The black folks needs you, won't you come by here?
The black folks needs you, won't you come by here?
The black folks needs you, won't you come by here?
Oh, Lordy, won't you come by here!

* * *

I am George Stephens from Middletown, Mississippi [*false name and town*]. I want to tell you something. When Head Start first came in, to tell the truth, many people were afraid to work with them, because the white folks were so devilish mean, we didn't know. But then we saw how it was, and the new whites would lay down their lives for us, and I say we will lie down and die with them if they will for us. They have done so much for us. With us, so I tell my people to learn, learn, that's the trouble with us, we don't know, we must learn about things, how to do things.

I have lived in Mississippi ninety-three years. Things were dark, dark, I've had every trial a man could have but death, but now things are coming splendid. Whites in Mississippi know it's changing, some of them will talk to us now, some are changing, things are changing—the federal government is helping us now, that's why things are changing. . . .

PART IV

Gone with the Political Wind (Almost)

AUGUST, 1965: HOW A TRIANGULAR SPASM OF CDGM-MISSISSIPPI-ADMINISTRATION POLITICS BROUGHT THINKING ABOUT THE CHILDREN OF POVERTY TO A GRINDING HALT AND PLACED THINKING ABOUT THE POLITICS OF POVERTY IN THE FORE.

CHAPTER 18

AND THEN THE AX FELL

The midnight ride of OEO

INDEED, THE FEDERAL government was noticing us. On Sunday, July 31, so late in the day that it was necessary to charter a plane to get there, OEO summarily ordered CDGM's top staff and board to appear two hundred miles away at Mary Holmes Junior College at nine o'clock that night. The command appearance quality of the appointment was made clear, but no hint of the topic was given. Chairman of the Board Beittel remembers: "I had no idea what the meeting was about. We knew we were having problems—every board has problems—and we had extra problems because of the nature of our community involvement goals. However, at this surprise meeting we quickly learned that we had more serious problems than we had imagined."

Mr. Heller of the OEO legal staff was there, and Mr. Cassidy of the accounting department, and a Mr. Dowdy. Mr. Heller was the spokesman. He said the group was there at the orders of the OEO office. He said all agree that CDGM is a good program and should be saved. But, he said, OEO is a new agency, and must sometimes step on people's toes in order to keep its projects clean enough not to jeopardize its future. He spoke of new projects in the works at OEO, and of possible new OEO programs for CDGM in the future.

Then he handed out a letter of demands—signed by Mr. Jule Sugarman from OEO. There were a great many demands. Some were quite reasonable, and of course no one objected. Others were very vague, almost afterthoughts, in spite of the crispness with which Mr. Heller presented them. There was just one demand that was painfully clear. People got the impression that most of the others were really to cloak this one: CDGM's central office was to be moved from Mount Beulah to Mary Holmes, which was in an isolated place way up in a corner of the state. We were to do this within six days or our entire project funds would be cut off! Mr. Heller spoke with determination. He assured us that all the demands, including the unreasonable move, were completely nonnegotiable. He made it clear that he wasn't there to bargain, but to deliver orders from OEO.

There was no question that even if we threw expense to the wind, and stopped all other activities, we probably couldn't have accomplished the move. Even a program that was compact and running smoothly would have difficulty moving two hundred miles in the middle of an eight-week operation, but we were having significant difficulty already.

While we were in the midst of moving in this abrupt way, we were to make fourteen or fifteen other rather elaborate administrative changes. Some of these changes puzzled the group considerably, as they were things we were already doing. The board was to do all hiring, staff review, and firing, and should notify Mary Holmes of such action. As board minutes show, the wisdom of this had already been realized, and it was being done. It wasn't very tuned in or tactful of OEO to demand that which we were already doing. Tom was to submit program reports to the board. The medical program was to be bolstered. Car and telephone logs were to be more strictly kept. There were to be "corrections" of fiscal policy and control with a clear settlement of expenditures. Control of basic policy and fiscal policy was to be increased, too, but OEO didn't say if this was to be by the board or who—or how.

Then, *for the first time*, a question was raised about payments made to the Delta Ministry for Orientation room and board, the printing project, legal costs, and accounting costs. Dr. Beittel and the others were amazed to see OEO raising a fuss about these things at this late date. They thought Tom, Mr. Horn, OEO, everyone who should have been involved in these matters *had* been involved. All these things were in the original grant, and in none of these cases had we exceeded what was in the OEO approved budget. OEO should have raised these questions when it signed the grant, or at least earlier in the summer; and perhaps in a more friendly manner.

It was unusual for OEO to expect so much control from a board. This doesn't happen in big business, or at colleges—the board meets four to six times a year, approves the budget, approves new building, makes major policy decisions, but boards hire directors, and expect them to take responsibility. This was a way out for OEO. Senator Stennis attacked OEO, so OEO attacked us. It was scapegoating.

They seemed to be blaming Mary Holmes, too. CDGM was carrying out the agreement we had in our contract with OEO regarding MHJC's overseeing of the project. The president, Mr. Horn, was on the CDGM Board, and was in on everything. We had no idea we were violating anything. That night Mr. Heller said OEO would require an increase of control over details by Mary Holmes. Every check was to be countersigned by the chairman of the board, or Mr. Horn. Horn could always have assigned a staff member to Mount Beulah, but he didn't. He probably didn't have a staff member to spare. Advance approval was to be given by Mary Holmes on each purchase of goods, services, petty cash, staff advances, etc., over twenty-five dollars. This would have been absurdly cumbersome in a project that was spending a quarter of a million dollars a week. Mary Holmes was to attend all major staff meetings and get minutes of all staff meetings. This would have kept them quite busy—there were staff meetings nightly!

We felt that OEO wasn't entirely familiar with the situation at Mary Holmes. Mary Holmes was a tiny place, with a handful of staff members in a few buildings way out in the country. In reality, it simply wasn't in a position to take over the administrative details of a project of this size. It would have been no improvement at all. Mary Holmes's role had been a major problem for the board all summer. The board's position was that Mary Holmes could just accept the check from OEO and pass it along. The general feeling was that MHJC was just going to be used as a channel to avoid the governor's veto.

As it developed, Mr. Horn was under a lot of pressure from OEO to do more than act as a vehicle. There were a number of issues and arguments confronting the board, which was trying to thrash out what the CDGM-MHJC-OEO relationship was to be. This was mostly between Tom and Mr. Horn. The rest of the board didn't know exactly what arrangements had been made. It was thought that Mr. Horn was doing this to build his college's reputation. Strategists in the Presbyterian Board of Missions, to whom Mr. Horn reported, were always very cooperative. They wanted Mary Holmes to become more actively involved in CDGM, but Mary Holmes just wasn't a very thriving institution. It reminded some people of a mediocre elementary school, in size and in academic level. CDGM put it on the map.

While the board was wondering *who* at Mary Holmes was going to do all this CDGM administrative work, they learned that it really wouldn't be Mary Holmes at all—an OEO man was to be assigned to Mary Holmes to be responsible for all MHJC-CDGM affairs. It was to be Mr. Dowdy, the unexplained OEO man at this meeting. So it wasn't just more board and MHJC control they were after! It seemed to be more OEO control. This was very unusual. There aren't many OEO projects in which OEO places a resident overseer of this sort.

The ultimatum did seem pretty harsh. Particularly because the second perennial problem confronting the board that summer was OEO. We did talk with OEO representatives when they came down, but we didn't always find these visits altogether helpful, because the representatives didn't always agree with each other. It was very difficult to deal with them. You never quite knew what they wanted. OEO personnel gave contradictory advice. In that sense the charges were as much a criticism of OEO as they were of CDGM staff, board, or Mary

Holmes. OEO representatives were in on all these things—they knew of our problem. Why did they choose to attack us instead of advise us?

Dr. Beittel thought OEO's pressure that the board take more control of the program was not very helpful. The move to Mary Holmes was the urgent issue that night. He told them they should have given us ample warning if they expected us to go through an upheaval such as this. He led a long discussion on this subject at the meeting.

Mr. Jake Ayers, a poor man on the board, was from Glen Allen, Mississippi. Glen Allen was in Washington County, where, when the Delta Ministry tried to work cooperatively with the Washington County Welfare Department in distributing food and clothes, the head of the department is said to have announced that anyone helping Delta Ministry do this would lose his welfare check. Mr. Ayers was for doing anything OEO asked.

"Of course OEO did not treat us fairly. Why does that surprise you? Whites, especially as represented in the government, have *never* treated us fairly—why should they begin now? But we have to have these federal programs, or we'll never get out of this. We'll do anything to get them.

"Most of the people on Central Staff are out-of-staters whose whole lives don't depend on this decision. CDGM whites *can't* be working for the same goals we local Negroes are. The whites aren't working for their lives—they are working for something they find a challenge, or interesting, or adventurous, or moral. But they are not working for their *lives,* and we are. Out-of-staters can leave, and their rights are sitting there in the suburbs waiting for them. Whites in CDGM will risk more, because if their gamble doesn't pay off, they can leave. Whites have put all the brain work into CDGM, but poor Negroes have put in all the blood and sweat and tears. Whites only risked getting killed or losing a tug-of-war with OEO, but we are risking a lifetime of reprisal and suffering for ourselves, our children, and *their* children. We lost what security we had when we suited Mr. Charlie, no matter how grubby that was—and now we *have to have* these new programs to make up for what we lost: good favor, jobs, all. We will always compromise more quickly than CDGM whites. We have no choice."

Lenore Monsonis, CDGM finance officer, was at the meeting. She was shocked at the way OEO officials dealt with CDGM representatives.

"I'm sure they don't talk that way to Mayor Lindsay and Mayor Daley. It was terrible the way they threatened those community people! They put that board in an impossible position: 'Do all these things right this minute, or you'll lose all that money!' They got frightened. Joe Edmunson said it was time the board faced its responsibility. We should do whatever OEO said, and if necessary begin moving to Mary Holmes in the morning. Everyone on the Board seemed to agree, or if not they didn't say anything. Mr. Horn was the only one who actually favored the move, but of course, it was to his great advantage. Oh, no, that's wrong, there *was* one lone voice of protest on the board: Reverend McCree. He said, 'No! We're just doing the same thing we've always done—let the white people push us around even when we will be ruined by it.' But when he realized he was the *only* one, he stopped fighting it.

"Marian said, 'You gotta do what the government says, it's their money.' I was furious. Furious! That they would all back down from their beliefs like that! Marian said we had to move. We were just getting the financial side to work with the accountants upstairs and the finance department downstairs in the same little house. Imagine trying to make it work with one in Edwards, one in West Point, and all the books in cartons in a station wagon in the middle!

"It was only the staff who stood up: me, Jim, and Tom Levin."

Afterward, Central Staff was angry with Marian. Most people understood that community members of the board were intimidated into mental paralysis. Not being easy in their new role of conference table dickerers anyway, they felt they had to capitulate instantly. But why couldn't sophisticated, persuasive Marian convince OEO representatives of the fatal calamity such a move would create? Marian had good reasons for deciding to take the position she did:

"I thought OEO was totally unreasonable to demand all this. We couldn't possibly do it in the designated number of days, and I hated this High Prince of Potentate attitude. I didn't feel things were so non-negotiable, but I knew the rest of the board did. I wanted to stall for time and lobby with each member of the board. I believed Tom and the Monsonises to some extent when they said they thought the Central Staff would resign if we agreed to the move. We had to cool OEO at that moment, so I didn't fight the move, I abstained from voting. We had to handle this right or the whole project might collapse. And Art wasn't at the meeting. . . ."

"Art wasn't there," said Tom, "or the history of CDGM would have been different. Art was very capable and always tried to expedite the project. And he knew what it *was*—he didn't think saving the money was saving the project. We had to save the right of the people to have some decision-making powers, and not have this kind of dictation from Washington. Of course, we all wanted more efficient administration. We didn't object to that at all. We had been begging OEO for administrative help all along; though one might question whether or not what they were 'offering' now was help. . . .

"I was terribly upset, so were Jim and Lenore, because we knew much better than the others did what a terrible strain Central Staff was under, trying to keep things above water, as it was. Those who were hard workers were nearly at the breaking point already; we just didn't think they *could* move without killing the project, and we didn't think, because of their deep commitment to it, that they *would* do that. The choice didn't seem to be 'move and continue the project' or 'refuse to move and lose the funds'—it was 'refuse to move and let OEO kill it,' or 'try to move and murder it ourselves in the confusion.' We had to find a third alternative. I tried to explain this at the meeting. I explained that I wasn't very happy with Mount Beulah—we were having some friction with the Delta Ministry, and activities of other groups sharing the campus with us were distracting to our staff. We would be perfectly willing to move in a month or so; *after* the summer project. I tried to negotiate. I said this would tear up the program. I said a move now would be CDGM's funeral, and I didn't want to be a funeral director, so I might not be able to continue being the director if a move was forced."

A community board member and others heard these points differently. The community man remembers: "Tom began to threaten OEO. He said he would tear up the program. He threatened to resign. He turned it into a power issue. The more he fought, the harder Mr. Heller rammed it down our throats. Mr. Heller said OEO had a full stand-by staff ready to come down and take over the operation of the project if CDGM staff walked out. Mr. Heller promised unlimited financial assistance in moving."

Tom was desperate. "It wasn't a matter of money or principle. It was a matter of mechanics, morale, and practicality. It couldn't be done without causing serious loss of time, *fatal* loss of time, no matter who paid for it."

Marian was desperate. "Tom and the Monsonises were putting their own principle ahead of the children's program. It was crucial that Tom present this issue to Central Staff in an unbiased way. I had no confidence that he would do that. If anything, I felt he would instigate an insurrection—a mass resignation. Tom was using this threat of staff resignation partly because it was true, but at least 50 percent as a political ploy to bend the board. I was appalled at Heller's harshness, but equally appalled at Tom's incredible performance. You just don't threaten the government. I wanted the same thing he did, but he antagonized everyone by fighting OEO openly. The issue for me was *how* to fight, which demanded for me more thought and time."

Dr. Beittel was distressed as much by the open split between staff and board, and by the staff's failure to cover it up, as by the startling orders from OEO: "We were trying to save the program. The staff didn't seem to think the board had any right to make a decision. They expected staff supremacy."

Tom remembers: "The OEO group left the room at one point. Staff implored the board to hold ground and refuse to move. We agreed to everything else in the Sugarman document. The other items in it resembled a series of minor, ineffectual exercises in foreplay, consummated in the rape represented by the move. It was only the move we beseeched the board not to give in on. We tried to convince them that they could yield on this later if necessary.

"The board didn't even know it *had* a unique program, so it wasn't worried about saving it. People say I talked about 'my program' that night. If I did, I meant in the sense of experimenting with my theories. I don't know that the board knew I had any, they were always so busy with superficial things. We begged the board not to be frightened by Mr. Heller's imperious tone in conducting this inquisition, but to request twenty-four hours for us to try to find an alternate location. A move would be devastatingly disruptive under any circumstances, but a move to West Point, Mississippi!

"Mary Holmes was two hundred miles away from the only city in the state—supplies, the airport—and one hundred miles from the nearest Child Development Center, other than Mr. Horn's center! It was six and a half hours from all the Gulfport centers! Clay County was one of the most dangerous outposts of the state. Staff would be in great danger, and harassment of an even greater intensity would seriously hamper their work. We could try Jackson first, or somewhere centrally located.

"When we asked Heller about the twenty-four hour cease-fire so we could set all staff to finding a site that would satisfy him, he seemed to waver momentarily. He went out and conferred with his colleagues. His two henchmen, incidentally, let Heller do the hatchet job, though he didn't seem to have much stomach for this assignment.

"When the delegation reappeared, Heller repeated what he had said before. There had been too much involvement in civil rights activity at Beulah. Head Start is not a civil rights project. Due to untidy surroundings and careless conduct Mount Beulah had received too much publicity and had acquired a bad reputation. OEO wanted Mary Holmes, as applicant agency for CDGM, to take more of a part. Thus, we were to move, and move to Mary Holmes, and as there was no alternative, further discussion was pointless.

"It was obvious to board and staff that this was in response to pressure from Senator Stennis. The problem was not that we were bad administrators—it was that we had administered into existence a beast he feared, and feared was unslaughterable by the usual means. The problem was not that we were untidy—it was that we were effecting social change quite well. Of course we had a bad reputation, but it was because of our aggressive civil rights and civil liberties activities, not because of personal conduct and alleged wild parties.

"It was extraordinarily disturbing to us that night to learn that OEO had felt it necessary to give in to the forces of racist Southern politicians. We had hoped that hard as it would be for the Administration and its poverty arm, OEO, to maneuver through these enemies of the poor in behalf of the poor, that they would manage to hold out a little longer—Head Start had only been operating in the South for a month—we were hoping that the Poverty War could stay useful for at least it's first *few* months. Suddenly we were guilty because we were obeying federal civil rights law. Projects hooked up with the system, over forty other totally Jim Crow Mississippi Head Starts, were 'legitimate'—at least there was no attempt to disrupt them into their death throes or humiliate them in the press. The Klan could harass us and the FBI 'couldn't' do anything about it. We had hoped the FBI, a federal agency, might support our efforts to obey the law and help suppress the Klansmen who were breaking it. Stennis could attack us, and OEO 'could not' even once explain our program and its worth—it could only parrot Stennis's points of attack. We had anticipated that OEO would not be likely to wage a war on the established state of Mississippi, but we had not anticipated that it would fold this near the starting line.

"We were not disturbed by Senator Stennis. He showed good judgment in considering us a danger to the status quo in Mississippi. We *were* a danger. His actions had roots in the rage of his constituency. White Mississippians find it literally sickening to see Negroes managing their own affairs. Integrated groups are bad enough, but when they seem socially at ease, it actually nauseates white onlookers. They see it as a symbol of the changing era they know is coming—an era bringing inevitable pressures to bear against the monopoly their interests have had.

"We were not so foolhardy as to anticipate that the struggle for poverty funds and control of poverty programs would be without casualties, but this flash revelation of OEO's suddenly lowered aspiration level of what they could hope to do when the Southern forces brought out the heavy artillery—well, it put us into the same kind of shock experienced by accident victims. We were numb."

* * *

Rock a bye baby,
In the tree top,
When the wind blows,
The cradle will rock,
When the bough breaks,
The cradle will fall,
And down will come baby
Bough, cradle, and all.

* * *

The board unhappily voted to move the CDGM central office to Mary Holmes. Tom amicably agreed to everything, including the move, if the board insisted, but made a final plea for more time to accomplish these multiple major surgeries. Mr. Heller said that financial "and all possible kinds of help" would be given by OEO, and "past sins would be forgiven" (!), but the time deadline was unalterable. He gave the group to believe that the White House was somehow in on this. The move *must* be finished within six days.

The board urged Tom to place the welfare of the children ahead of "personal feelings and inconveniences" in trying to keep the staff with the program. The board expressly requested him to continue as director of CDGM. Tom agreed sincerely if pessimistically to stay on and do what he could to salvage something worthwhile from the wreckage. The minutes of this notorious meeting end with rather an understatement, considering that the beautiful dragon, which had been lumbering skyward only six hours before, lay in a crumpled heap at the feet of its apparently unmoved slayers, mortally wounded: "At 3:00 A.M., with no further immediate business facing them, it was voted that the Board adjourn."

Several hours later, as the dawn of a new day broke pale faded blue over the cotton fields, Tom, in a dazed condition and in tears, told several of us: "Then Mr. Heller said, 'Now that you've agreed to the move, forget all the other requirements, they don't matter.' It then became clear how they could be enraged at my 'defiance' in objecting to *one* point, *though I had agreed to more than a dozen*—none of the points counted except the one I resisted. The nightmarish quality of it was that we thought OEO people were our friends. We were trying so hard to be their best program. It was Kafkaesque: 'Now that you've signed a suicide pact, nothing else matters.'"

CHAPTER 19

THE LILLIPUTIANS GO INTO ACTION

IT WAS FOUR-THIRTY in the morning when the staff delegation returned from what came to be called the Star Chamber Proceedings in West Point, Mississippi. Because most Central Staff "left for work" at dawn, Tom immediately planted word at several strategic points around Mount Beulah that no one was to go out to the communities that day.

There would be a total staff emergency meeting later in the morning. He assigned several people to conduct a telephone search for the five district coordinators to see if they could be located and gotten to the meeting.

It was agreed by a small group of us that since Tom was so emotionally involved in the situation, and since anything he said to the staff would surely be misconstrued by both hostile board and hostile OEO, Jim Monsonis would present a calm, factual, general account of the midnight meeting. Open discussion would follow.

It was anticipated that staff would erupt in fury and resign at once. However, all efforts would be made to keep the project afloat, regardless of how badly crippled by the move and how badly demoralized by what board and staff alike felt to be a smashing blow beneath the belt. There were only three weeks of center operation remaining. If we could hold the staff, we could limp to the finish line.

At our midday meeting, a tense staff listened in incredulous horror as Jim gave a brief, neutral summary of events occurring during the past hours. Members of the CDGM faction of people with strong civil rights backgrounds, mostly from out-of-state, to whom the project's importance wasn't its nursery school activities but rather its long range political significance, triumphantly announced that they had been right all along. They said the government doesn't give a damn about poor people, and anyone who thinks it does is politically naïve. This "execution" was proof for slow-learning loyalists. The poverty program was only set up as a clever strategy for killing the Movement anyway; by "buying off" civil rights workers and poor people by offering them badly needed money.

Frank Smith, leader of this faction, had been silent, grinning in the corner because things were going "so well" without him. There was a time, he told the group, when committed political personnel had to be bred—but now you could just buy them. He said that OEO didn't care if the program folded up and died, regardless of what it had meant to the poor, as long as OEO could save face and make it look like an inept Central Staff was to blame. In the name of improving the administration of CDGM, said Frank, OEO was in fact annihilating the administration by yielding to pressure from Southern politicians. Frank was pleased that his cynicism regarding the possibility of building any powerful kind of social force within the restricting framework of a federal grant was proving valid. He had been heavily criticized by CDGM "liberals" all summer for his negative attitude toward the government.

Frank felt that there is no way to make needed, basic, radical change in the structure of this country, within the structure of the government. And that there is a real question if this kind of change can be effected in this country *outside* the government. Frank said he wouldn't consider helping OEO get credit for sponsoring a program it had actually murdered or maimed. He wouldn't be party to making this castration appear to "work" to OEO's Northern liberal audiences. If the government was going to play this dirty game, let it fall on its red face in doing so. None of us should help it. All of us should quit. He himself was doing so at that moment.

The majority of the staff broke into excited support of Frank's position. They felt that the government was behaving scandalously. While it preached the Poverty War gospel in the North, it was betraying the poor blacks in Mississippi. Many said that they would quit too. But being veteran fighters as well as idealists, they wouldn't leave the state until they had shown OEO up for what it was, a sanctimonious farce, and until they had rubbed its self-righteous beaurocratic nose in its own filth. There was delighted discussion of picketing Head Start centers, of undermining OEO projects everywhere, and even of urging all 1,100 CDGM community staff members to return their paychecks with letters of protest to President Johnson or Sargent Shriver. Many contacts and ideas were tossed around for getting national publicity on this grim affair. There is little doubt we could have done it.

Tom requested that the staff continue the discussion in an attempt to find a solution more compatible to the immediate interests of the poor people depending on us. He then slipped out and called the OEO inspection office. He told Bob Clampitt that the staff attitude was dangerously negative and what had been said. Bob cautioned Tom that "striking" would be very unwise, that Mr. Shriver does not like to be crossed, and that the decision was irreversible. Tom ran back to the meeting.

Another major faction had the floor. The professional educators and child-oriented college students from the North were heatedly expressing their deep hurt about this whole mess. They had come to Mississippi for the summer to work with children. They had worked hard. They weren't interested in all these political lunacies. Moving would make work so difficult that it didn't seem possible to continue. They were going to resign too, and leave the Machiavellis to their maudlin maneuvers.

Tom ran to the phone and telephoned Bob Clampitt again. This time Mr. Shriver's special assistant for civil rights, Mr. Sam Yette, listened to the conversation on the loudspeaker. Bob said he had been trying to reach Mr. Shriver to find out just how irreversible irreversible was, but with no luck. Bob said there was nothing that could be done, but to call back when a decision had been reached. Again he urged a conservative position. Tom begged for a stay of execution to enable us to find an alternate location. Bob repeated that nothing could be done. (We discovered months later that the inspection office, for all its amateur gumshoe reputation, had not known of the midnight descent until Tom reported it to them! It is said that Mr. Heller had requested that they not be informed in advance, as they were suspected of being pro-CDGM.)

Tom dashed back across the dusty Mount Beulah driveway to the hot room in which the crowded meeting continued. I was talking. My feeling was that gloating about the devils in the federal government wasn't enough, though admittedly at that point of bitter hurt and outraged indignation it was very satisfying. I thought we should consider what we had to work with and form a strategy *to reach our goals,* not to reach a successful kind of revenge on OEO.

First of all, what would the poor people, counting on us and unaware of this new catastrophe, want us to do? Most of them believed in the government as in God. Most of them, having no experience with big business, didn't realize the enormity of Central Staff's task. They were quite angry at us for failing to have a perfectly oiled system of supplies, paychecks, etc. They would be more likely to think OEO was right than to think we were. All of them thought this was the greatest program that had ever been available to them. If consulted, they would have accepted any terms and any orders if doing so would have enabled them to keep the education for their children and the paychecks in their communities.

I said I thought that we, as out-of-staters who could go home to our "rights" on any airplane, had no right to defy the government to the extent of losing the poor people their future in federal programs, and also no right, having encouraged them into this grant, to walk out leaving them just as powerless to hold their own against federal injustice as they had always been. I said I thought we had an obligation to help people see how these things work. Most OEO officials *did* care about the poor, but not enough to defy orders from the eighth floor. Eighth floor officials, including Mr. Shriver, *did* care about the poor too, but not enough to defy Congress, from which they get their funds.

We were being liquidated by OEO, not out of malevolence, but because of pressure from Southern politicians. The only way to avoid being liquidated was to create an equal amount of counterpressure. The only way to fulfill our obligation to our communities was to find a way, God only knew what way, to show them how this could be done. I said that we shouldn't be surprised that OEO was acting dictatorially. It has never acted any other way, except when there was equal power on the other side. That, I thought, was the clue to what we should do.

Tom took over the meeting at this point. He informed the staff of OEO's telephone insistence that we shouldn't attempt to negotiate. He said: "We are left with a number of alternatives. We can do what OEO says do—move. We can strike." (Staff chorused that that was their choice.) "We can resign and leave CDGM. Or we can resign from OEO and the payroll, but continue to serve the communities and their centers on a volunteer basis."

Tom said the last one was what he intended to do. He asked us to record on secret "ballots" which each of us would do. Jeannette King, director of the social services project, a shy and gentle social worker, said: "It was an extraordinary moment. I think everybody grew a great deal when each one had to face the personal crisis of choosing between an ideal and the practical thing to do. We all had these jobs, we needed our pay like anybody else. Reason and the lawyer, Mr. Heller, indicated that the sensible and 'right' thing to do was accept the orders. Besides these things, all the Central Staff members had been tearing each other up all summer, warring; the fighting and turmoil were so terrible that we couldn't possibly have plotted anything—we just weren't that organized.

"Yet at the moment when Tom said 'decide what *you* will do,' each person had to put the value-shifting and inner change that had been twisting him in new directions all summer to the test. The move to Mary Holmes pulled everything together. We had to answer the question: 'Which side are you on, boys?' I felt transformed, cleansed—it was like a spiritual conversion."

Three staff members wanted to accept the move and stay with the program. Two people were undecided, and five said they would resign and leave CDGM. Most of these ten were Edwards residents who were trainee secretaries, and who couldn't leave their families. This had been another of Tom's reasons for not wanting to move: If we couldn't get secretaries near the biggest city in the state, we would never get them in a rural area, when these ladies got left behind.

Twenty-five indicated they would resign from OEO and work full time without pay at their CDGM assignment. The meeting broke up in a mixture of anguish and exhilaration.

Tom called the OEO inspection office once more, and read off the "votes." There was dead silence at the other end of the phone, and then instructions not to say anything, or do anything—"I'll get back to you as soon as I can." As no board members were at this staff meeting, Tom called Dr. Beittel and explained what had happened. Dr. Beittel did not like the news. "When we were told that many members of Central and District Staff would not be remaining with the program, we thought they were willing to sacrifice the project for their own feelings. We thought it was a very irresponsible thing to do."

Marian said she was "enraged at Tom because of his emotionalism. I blamed Tom for presenting the OEO mandate slantedly—in a way calculated to make the staff resign. I heard that the whole staff was quitting the project. I never heard that part about working volunteer. It just proved what I had suspected all along about the irresponsibility of some of the staff."

OEO called back, still sounding shocked, and announced that there had been a grievous "misunderstanding. The team" would be sent back to talk things over with the staff; a formality for which OEO had never found time before. The nonnegotiable had suddenly become negotiable. We thought it curious how quickly those who can talk only with sledgehammers in their hands learn to talk more humbly of ideas, when they discover sledgehammers on the other side too. Of course, in our case, we didn't have sledgehammers on the other side, but our slingshots were in good shape, and our aim was good. To its distress, hulking OEO was beginning to detect them, though it was far from a David and Goliath situation. The weapons of the little Lilliputians were causing soreness to Gulliver's vulnerable skin.

Mr. Heller and escorts appeared at Mount Beulah in a matter of hours, and were forced by CDGM staff to undergo an inquisition in reverse.

* * *

Taffy was a Welshman, Taffy was a thief;
Taffy came to my house and stole a piece of beef.

I went to Taffy's house, Taffy was not home;
Taffy came to my house and stole a marrow bone.

I went to Taffy's house, Taffy wasn't in;
Taffy came to my house, and stole a silver pin.

I went to Taffy's house. Taffy was in bed;
I took up the marrow bone, and hit him on the head.

Before joining CDGM in June, I had had dinner with a long-time friend, Andy Kopkind, in Washington and had enthused so ebulliently about this unusual project that was perking, I think he thought I was somewhat manic. As one of Andy's specialties was social change in the

South, I urged him to come down during the summer and pay us a visit. He did, and was our earliest press understander and promoter. He came in late July, and by chance was present for the week of fireworks. The first of many articles he wrote about CDGM appeared in the August 21, 1965, issue of *New Republic,* titled "Mississippi, too Heady a Start?" he wrote: "Through a long night session, the staff battered the Poverty men: How could CDGM maintain its credibility as champion of poor Mississippi Negroes if it gave in to 'Mister Charlie,' in this case Senator Stennis, at the first attack."

How could OEO pretend to be helping and advising "a good project," when it spoke in these threatening tones, demanded a seething group. Mr. Heller replied, shaken and pale, but surely and prosaicly, that if his "tone" was wrong, he apologized. He had been dealing with a formal meeting at Mary Holmes, at which minutes were being taken; he had not known the board members or their factions, he had not known that "tone" was so important to us, and perhaps we'd better turn to some more urgent problems, such as our "defiantly casual" attitude toward neat administration.

He said that the program was in a sensitive spot and was being scrutinized more than a less sensitive Head Start would be, and whether we liked it or not, we'd been inexcusably sloppy. He said he didn't know he would be the spokesman for the OEO group that came down until he was on the plane to Mississippi, so he didn't have time to rehearse his tone, but he was convinced that whether he liked this assignment or not, which he did not, this clean-up had to occur.

He said he was being perfectly candid with us. The last thing he wanted to do was shear our locks, but he would just have to speak honestly, there was no sense in coating it in sugar. He said he knew about all our orgies. Every time staff asked for proof of this or that, or detailed "charges," he told us he had very little information about CDGM. He was just doing a job that had to be done . . . he didn't know . . . no, he couldn't because he hadn't been informed of the . . . no . . . yes . . . he didn't know much about the project, he believed we should obey orders, OEO cannot tolerate any abuses, etc.

This caused me to write in my diary that night (it was the second consecutive night that many of us had not been to bed, and we were all more punchy than professional): "4 A.M.: . . . so of course he can't see that we are mad at him for anything worse than his tone. If you've made a decision somewhere along the line to give up your human obligation to use your own judgment, gather information before you take action that will seriously affect others, think critically, be moral; if you've yielded all these capabilities to '*the agency*' and henceforth see yourself only as a tool for a nameless, faceless, mechanical monster, then naturally you have nothing more serious to consider than your *tone*. . . . I'm sure he's a 'liberal' . . . he told us that often enough, and

I know it to be true from my OEO era. Most of them are liberals. It doesn't seem relevant whether or not someone is a liberal. What is a liberal? It's what a person *does* each time, each incident . . . that counts —not what a person thinks in sort of a general tomorrow and yesterday but never in the fray today way. Besides, it's all relative. It's which choices you have and, even more complicated, which choices you *think* you have, depending upon your attitude toward what is possible (before you lose your job, embarrass your boss, displease your wife, have a nervous breakdown, or 'can't live with it' or whatever else denotes 'possible' for you). I suppose that whether a position is good, bad, brave, cowardly, etc., depends upon so many factors."

A local Edwards teen-age Negro girl, who sat silently through the distraught proceedings, said on the way out: "He seems like a nice man. What I wanna know is, if the bad ones like the white lady I works for does good things like she done when she give me clothes for the center kids, and the good ones like this here man does bad things like he done when he axed our pogrum, then how kin you all tell where the devil's at anymore?"

At the Mary Holmes meeting, Mr. Heller had suggested that several board members, with Mr. Horn's permission, write a press release announcing the move. A group was at Dr. Beittel's house in Jackson working on the wording of this release, when it got word that the move was canceled. Dr. Beittel was very happy that the move was off, but was perplexed—it seemed an amazing change of position. Twelve hours before, the same individuals had been instructed not even to question the decision, and now OEO had made a 180° turn.

The Reverend Arthur Thomas flew back to Mississippi at once. He was very disturbed to have missed the historic meeting, due to Delta Ministry business in New York. The Delta Ministry itself was in serious trouble, and Art, its director, was desperate, because both his projects were being derailed at once.

Art thought that OEO reversed itself because *Mr. Heller* reversed himself. *He* reversed himself because he was convinced by all of us after he got here that it wasn't the way they had told him it was. He didn't like Tom, Art thought, so nothing Tom said could have mattered much. But he thought Marian was cooler, more professional, more permanent—and she was a lawyer like himself. He seemed to admire Reverend James McCree's toughness, even though he didn't agree with him.

We got the impression that he actually admired the dissenters more than the submitters, but it wasn't a question of whom he admired. He had a job to do, thought Art. After we had convinced him of the danger, the disruption, he agreed that we shouldn't move, and told Mr. Sugarman so at OEO. Art got the impression that Jim Heller still favored the clean-up—he didn't feel "soft" toward CDGM or upset by OEO.

Mr. Heller, who didn't care for people with ideology up to their eyes, was a reasonable and practical man. When he saw, after this battering in the all night session, that it would be impossible for *practical* rather than ideological reasons for us to move, he called Jule Sugarman at OEO and strongly recommended that we be allowed to stay at Beulah for the remaining few weeks of the summer. In a flurry of excitement, OEO not only allowed us to stay, but seemed to forget all the other "nonnegotiable" points too, including separating us from individuals and activities they menacingly labeled "civil rights," which they now estimated to be an "unfeasible" separation.

Meanwhile, we worked [Diary]: "Last night me and the kids had a work hazzard happening. We left the community meeting at . . . at five to midnight. There wasn't any moon, and I was trying to remember all the black lefts and rights. After while, I thought I had made a wrong turn, and backed up into the brush to turn around and try again. Next thing I knew, we were at the jungled bottom of a deep ravine . . . had dropped about eight feet.

"The kids were scared, started whimpering, wanting to know how we would ever get out. Kept asking me if I had a map. I assured them that some one would come along shortly and tow us out. I couldn't decide which was more dangerous—to stay hidden in the bottom of the forest, or to stand on the road and risk being found by an un-friend. We stayed in the thicket, feeling a good deal like B'r Rabbit who felt so safe in the brambles and briars, cheering ourselves up by playing Freedom songs on the tape recorder. Fortunately, one of the songs on the tape was the verse of 'We Shall Overcome' that says, 'We are not afrai-ai-d, We are not afrai-ai-d. . . .'

"It was really quite private and cozy as long as we just huddled and cuddled and I listened to myself telling the girls what fun it was!

"After a while I heard the scrunch of gravel, indicating a car coming. No one but Negroes travel this remote dirt road, I said stalwartly to me. I scrambled up the embankment, gashing my legs on thorns not visible in the pitch dark as I ascended, and stood, half-hidden in the foliage, as ready to hide as to emerge, waiting for the ever-nearing rumbling to come round the bend. It came. I couldn't make out the color of the driver. I took a chance and flagged him. He stopped, got out, and was obviously much more afraid of this midnight 'kidnap' than I could ever have been of him. Ha! It turned out to be one of the few people I know in that whole area, Mr. Thomas, husband of a center chairman! He went away, came back with his son and his tractor, and pulled us out, with much chuckling. (They still tell the story around there, with much amusement and many embellishments.)

" 'See?' I told my daughters. 'Never be afraid. Something good always happens after a while.' (?)"

CHAPTER 20

TOM AND GERRY GO INTO THE MEANING OF THIS FOR THE MOVEMENT

THE FOLLOWING WEEK was a cacophonous, kaleidoscopic collage of explanations, emotions, pledges, rages, apologies, undercuttings, sinuosity, and spuriously specious situations, of which no one, least of all anyone at OEO, had an overview and thus of which no one has complete recollections.

The mysterious wishes of the White House in this curious affair of state, which Mr. Heller had hinted at, but when questioned had said were "classified information," seemed to melt into the total mirage. Staff wondered cynically why, if this could happen as the result of one man's judgment and forceful recommendation, when he decided to get these instruments out of hibernation, he hadn't chosen to use them earlier, in finding out some facts about us before assuming us to be guilty. We hadn't yet been convinced, and this strange incident gave strength to our dissenting opinion, that individuals are impotent and that bureaucracies must blunder on without the aid of intelligent individual action.

Mr. Kirksey, CDGM printer and Movement man, told Tom that he thought people were used to seeing things in traditional ways. America and federal projects just aren't the places for Tom-type revolutionary innovation. There are too many forces against that kind of change. Mr. Kirksey considered Tom's ideas dynamic, unique, and important. But, he said, Tom hadn't been given time to see if his ideas would work because nobody wanted to know if they would work. They upset people. They were different.

Medical project director, Dr. Gerry Rosenfield, said then and later wrote in a SNCC newsletter that this revolt was "our one beautiful moment of the summer." He said this gave Central Staff our chance to show whose side we were on in the battle for the South, and to assert ourselves against the deadly flow of directives from Washington. Gerry felt the crisis proved that the board accepted the premise that

CDGM belonged to Washington more than to the poor of Mississippi. What kind of independent Negro political power could we develop, Gerry demanded to know, if we had to function within the confines of Senator Stennis's politics?

* * *

An the govermin' bothers us too, because they axes us for forms and ways and rules we can't do. Sometimes I wonder if they is tryin' to help us with what we really need, or jes help theirselfs get a good thing going in the newspapers.

* * *

I am the substitute cook. We of this center have made up a school song, to which this is the chorus.

Come on come on come on
Come on and go with us
Come on come on come on
Come and go with us
Come on come on come on
Come and go with us
To the Freedom land.

Tell Senitor Stines come and go with us
Tell Senitor Stines come and go with us.

* * *

The Frank Smith faction agreed with Gerry's thinking, but most of us did not—certainly not with the first idea stated. Though Tom was considered by OEO and the CDGM board to be an unbridled radical, a leader of revolutionary rebellion, he was, in fact, not revolutionary at all in terms of the means. He *was* in terms of the *ends; i.e.*, he really meant what he said about eliminating poverty, when for most people the phrase was a pleasant platitude.

In terms of the *means* of creating social change, however, Tom was CDGM's chief advocate of working through federal programs and federal agencies. Revolutionaries seldom operate on government funds. Tom's attitude toward the "beautiful revolt" concept, verbalized by Gerry and sensed by OEO, was expressed clearly in the reply he wrote to Gerry's articles. It is not known whether his piece was printed in an informal internal SNCC publication or not.

During this paralyzed week, when all productive activity ground to a halt as a result of OEO's "help," many of us had many discussions, in which Tom said these things.

He thought that both the original OEO grant to CDGM and the dramatic OEO about face after the so-called staff revolt, represented significant victories for the Movement, for a heretofore unheard-of segment of the Mississippi poor, and for those in Washington who heartily endorsed them in their growth toward political potency. He believed we should maintain ourselves in this new political arena:

We should hold to our ideas and our programs and if and when we are tossed out we should exit protesting and make a beeline for the next program.

I believe that the American economic, social and political institutions owe a profound debt to the disenfranchised and exploited poor, both black and white. This debt cannot be renounced; either by the American government, local social and economic hierarchies, or by advocates of nihilistic parallelism. I also do not believe that the poor will collect their long overdue economic, social and political compensation by subservience, submissiveness or resignation to powerlessness. The note due must be presented with forcefulness and imaginative political tactic.

The movement has contributed toward establishing the political climate necessary to make the collection of this debt a reality. I believe that now is the time for the movement to provide both the ideas and the personnel to establish peoples' programs to receive the payment due while at the same time continuing pressures to extract every cent of the debt owed. I believe that now is the appropriate historical time to make the claim because of a number of factors.

First, the American economy has more than adequate economic and technical capability to provide the 100 billion dollars required as a significant down payment toward its social obligation to the black and white poor of America.

Secondly, I believe it is possible for the poor, particularly the black poor, through honorable alliances with labor, liberals, reformers and other men of good will to develop the political power necessary to implement the fulfillment of our country's profound social obligation to its poor.

Thirdly, I believe we should not discount the widespread and growing national recognition of America's responsibility toward all segments of society. There are those in government, industry, labor and the professions who are prepared to work toward a realistic and full program to meet the needs of the poor and disenfranchised.

Finally, I believe historically, we have an obligation to do everything within our power to effect a reappraisal of the American national goals. One way to press for a revocation of an American foreign policy which supports despots and corrupt puppet regimes and thereby dissipates a large part of our gross national product is to forcefully press our claims to make the primary national goal a full and meaningful life for all Americans—and then for all citizens of the world.

From these premises it seems to me that every effort toward engagement of the poor with the structures of our society in the pursuit of their economic, social and political rights is a meaningful step toward altering our total society. Conversely, I believe that every step toward disengagement, isolation, renunciation and nihilism is a failure to utilize and respond to social, historical and political reality. We must fight for every penny of poverty money to be placed in the hands of the poor—and for every bit of power and control to be invested in the poor themselves.

I take the position that we should not renounce the politics of poverty, the politics of welfare, the politics of education, the politics of health, the politics of housing or the politics of jobs. I believe that movement people are capable of providing the initiative and creativity necessary to establish programs that truly reflect the needs and skills of the poor. I believe those on the far right are bankrupt of ideas and corrupted of vitality. I believe that those in the middle ground are influenceable and can and will be responsive to our sustained pressures.

There may be those who served with CDGM who felt themselves as agents of an external malevolent federal government. I hope that these people will find more sympathetic and constructive work in the future. I do feel it would be gross calumny to a dedicated civil rights oriented staff to intimate that they were either consciously or unconsciously used as agents against the movement. While I do not regret dialogue I would regret internecine struggle between two groups of sincere movement people choosing different areas of activity.

Tom talked and tried to calm semihysterical Central Staff members all that week. But unbeknownst to him, he would not have many more opportunities to do so. Curious undercurrents were swirling him ever closer to the eclipsing center of the whirlpool.

CHAPTER 21

TOM GOES DOWN THE DRAIN, TWO TOP ADMINISTRATORS GO, JOHN MUDD COMES

To CAST A glimmer of light on this interesting (inadvertent?) intrigue, it will be necessary to take a few steps backward. When Mr. Heller reappeared on Monday night to face the staff for the first time, there arrived with him a new figure in the cast of federal characters. This was Dr. Robert Coles, distinguished psychiatrist and specialist in the relationship between race and mental health, from the Harvard University Medical School faculty. He was greeted in stunned bewilderment, for he was known to us as a longtime friend of the Movement. He had been involved in pre-1964 early Movement activities, as well as in the calamity of McComb, Mississippi, the summer before this.

How could he possibly take his place in the firing squad sent to shoot us down? Had he come with full knowledge of what he was to be involved in and of what his presence on "the team" would mean to us? Dr. Coles seemed to us dazzled and confused by the melee in which he found himself deposited.

Later we found out that Dr. Julius Richmond had telephoned him in Boston. Dr. Coles knew him, of course. They were colleagues. Now he was calling as the director of Project Head Start for OEO. Dr. Richmond said they were having serious difficulties with the medical program in one of their projects, CDGM, and he wanted Dr. Coles to go down to Mississippi to evaluate this part of the program. Dr. Coles was tied up with a commitment to the Appalachian Volunteers. He couldn't possibly fit CDGM into his schedule. Dr. Richmond told him the matter was very urgent; the children weren't getting adequate medical care. He begged Dr. Coles to break his commitment to the Volunteers. If necessary, Sargent Shriver would call them for a release.

When it was suggested that he go to Washington to discuss it, he went immediately.

This was midweek, before the famous Mary Holmes meeting. Dr.

Richmond had lunch with him. At the end Mr. Sugarman joined them for a few hurried minutes. We were told that Dr. Richmond said Tom wasn't paying enough attention to CDGM's medical component. He said that he and Dr. George Gardner, head of the Judge Baker Clinic, had squeezed in a quick trip. So Bob Coles found time. They mentioned in passing that there was to be a meeting of OEO and CDGM at West Point the following weekend, and inquired if Dr. Coles could make it. He said he didn't know, he would try.

Though OEO evidently already knew that the Sunday meeting was planned, it didn't elect to so notify CDGM board or staff. Staff wondered if, in spite of the heavily honied public relations story OEO put out about coming as allies to aid us, officials well understood what this would mean to CDGM, and therefore did not give us advance warning, on which they feared we would capitalize, by summoning national support. It also occurred to us that this might have been a typical OEO matter of "forgetting": in the hubbub, perhaps no one had been assigned to let us know.

When Bob arrived in West Point, Mississippi, Monday instead of Sunday night, Mr. Heller and his companions greeted him with questions about why he hadn't been there for a major meeting the night before. They were very distraught.

When the delegation got to Mount Beulah, Mr. Heller kept referring excitedly to what he called the "civil rights people" who had to be moved out, and the impossible defiance of Tom Levin, and financial irregularities, which we gathered from him were very vast and serious; Tom's terrible judgment and casual nose-thumbing attitude toward OEO. Mr. Heller kept saying that Tom had to go. He said over and over that OEO was caught between Senator Stennis and the "civil rights types." We got the impression that the latter were the greater of the two evils.

We wondered what Bob, an involved Movement person who thought that was what the poverty program was all about, thought of all this. There was no doubt that the whole OEO group thought "civil rights types" were pretty unsavory.

Art Thomas and some other Delta Ministry brass surrounded Bob Coles when he got to the Sun and Sands Motel in Jackson. There was a terrible scene around and around the swimming pool, with the group strafing at Bob: What was he doing here? Did he know what he was doing to CDGM? He must be unhinged to be allowing himself to be used like this. They tried to make him feel guilty for not finding out more about what he was getting into before coming. He must have felt like a turncoat. However, most of us knew he had worked with this same group the summer before in places like McComb, and would never knowingly have done a thing like this.

Mr. Heller was visibly shaken after the night staff meeting, and Bob seemed to encourage him in it. He was wavering, Heller was. Friends in

OEO kept us posted: Jule Sugarman kept calling Coles and asking if it was true that there was all this civil rights in CDGM? How could the program shape up? Who should replace Tom?

It was obvious that Mr. Cassidy and Mr. Heller considered Tom the enemy of what they were trying to do—whatever that was. They seemed to think he was a leftist, not very amenable, recalcitrant, sloppy. One of the strangest "charges" that they kept making against him was that he was "abrasive to the Mississippi power structure." It would be hard to see how the Mississippi power structure could find any director of such a project unabrasive, or how OEO could consider it *good* to be smiled upon by the Mississippi power structure.

Bob told us that he was going to tell Jule that it was his "medical recommendation" that the project not move; that the medical program was good, and moving would slow it down. Even after he caught on to the political intrigue into which he'd naïvely been sent, he tried to be as medical as possible. Throughout his visit he sprinkled medical activities into his agenda. He actually examined children in Vicksburg and sent the reports to OEO. He had been told to get the health picture, he had honestly believed that that was what he was being sent to do, and he had set out to do just that. He talked at length with Gerry, and found him a very capable physician as well as an extremely interesting and politically aware young man. He talked to Tom about the medical program. Bob told the staff that of course Tom wasn't treating it casually. He took it very seriously, and was doing a good job. The whole thing appeared to be a huge hoax to get Bob to Mississippi.

As the week progressed, a possible reason for getting him down began to emerge. OEO seemed to want Bob Coles to replace Tom Levin as director! They thought once they had him there, it would be easy to pressure him into slipping into the directorship. Tom and Bob talked in Tom's room about who should be the director when Tom returned to New York and his practice, as scheduled, in a few weeks. He was anxious to get this happily settled. The matter of knowing that someone strong would take over was very much on Tom's mind. Bob had never met Tom before, though they had talked on the phone the year before about the Medical Committee for Human Rights, which Tom was organizing. Bob had heard good things about his ability and dedication, and thought he was doing an excellent job with CDGM. But Bob had to find someone to take over from Tom in September. So Bob talked this over with Art and Marian a good bit. He didn't know that Tom wasn't in on it—or that Tom meant at the end of the summer, at the end of his "tenure," whereas Art and Marian meant *now*.

At first Art and Marian tried to urge Bob to take the job himself. Marian then suggested a young fellow, a friend of hers, who was in Mississippi, John Mudd. Bob thought it was a good idea. He'd known John well at Harvard, when John was a student. He thought John a very unusual person. Art wasn't sure John was a good idea. He didn't know him, John was only twenty-six years old, and he was white, whereas a local Negro had been slated to take over the job. But Art, too, had great respect for Marian's judgment, which, as it turned out, was excellent.

Marian pushed hard for John. Bob had great respect for Marian's opinion. He found her a shrewd and sophisticated person. He thought both she and Art had amazing antennae in liberal circles around the country. They were both very much connected to the right parts of the establishment—much more so than Tom. There weren't many candidates for the job available, to say the least. Bob recommended John for the job to Jule Sugarman.

Tom was fond of John, though he didn't know him very well. But he was afraid it would be a little like putting a baby in the lion's jaws. He just thought John wouldn't have the political or Movement sophistication to cope with OEO. He thought John was smart, but just the ivy-league type with whom OEO could play, as it evidently had played with Bob Coles in using him as the devil's emissary.

It was said that Mr. Heller spent a busy few days reminding CDGM board members of Tom's "offer to resign": Mr. Heller's memory of Tom's Mary Holmes statement about not wishing to be the director of CDGM's funeral, and preferring to resign rather than stand by for *that.* Heller reportedly said on several occasions that it seemed like a gift when Tom offered to resign from active duty and confine himself to planning for the future. Mr. Heller said that OEO recognized Tom's genius, but that Tom was rapidly becoming a handicap. Some people said they heard Mr. Heller say that Tom would just have to go if we wanted further funds from OEO.

There's no proof that the White House asked OEO to remove Tom Levin from the directorship of CDGM. Top OEO officials denied that the White House ordered OEO to do anything in the CDGM case. If such instructions were issued, they were well kept secrets. There is also no reason to think that top OEO personages gave Mr. Heller orders to remove Tom. They were nervous about what, to them, seemed unfathomable qualities in him, and what, to anyone, were unquenchable qualities. But they claim not to have given Mr. Heller directions to get rid of Tom. Art and Marian said that Mr. Heller didn't "absolutely insist" on the removal of Tom at any point, and "didn't mention getting rid of him right away." Dr. Beittel, as chairman of the board, would appear to have been a reasonable source of information as to where the decision to move Tom aside immediately was hatched, but he didn't know either.

Marian said, "I don't know, Tom had lost the confidence of the board. Art and I talked a lot, and on the telephone; we thought a great deal was at stake and we couldn't take too many risks at this point. We thought it would be better for the program, considering the administrative situation and the way OEO felt, not to wait till Tom left in September."

Tom remembers, "Sometime in the middle of that week, Art brought a news release to me and told me that I had been 'promoted' to planning for the fall and writing a new proposal, which of course, as Jim, Lenore, Polly, and the other key staff know, I was doing anyway, and *had* been since mid-July, as scheduled; these others were doing the day-to-day work.

"Of course I offered to resign if it was necessary to save the program, but one would have thought they could have stood me for three more weeks, or if not, it would have been considerably politer to have discussed it with me, to include me in the decision, not to do it so highhandedly behind my back. Art said to me that night, 'We did everything we could to keep them from bouncing you completely. This is our compromise, the best we could do.' I'm not sure if that's true. And if my removal was purely to satisfy OEO, why did they banish me so completely from 'the inner circle'? Surely OEO didn't require that I be ignored from that point on.

"Probably my greatest quarrel with CDGM and Movement leadership in many situations is that they are singularly inconsiderate, rude, and unprofessional in the *way* they handle things. It's more than lack of time or 'middle-class' amenities—there's a great deal of hostility shining through—I have no quarrel with what they do. Moving me was very likely a wise political decision. I might have decided so myself, had they had the courtesy to consult me. Marian told quite a few people on the staff, so they reported to me, that she didn't think 'it would look good' and 'might be bad for staff morale' if 'we threw him out altogether,' so the story they put out was that I was more or less 'reassigned' to 'things I was so good at.'

"From then on, I was treated like a side of beef in cold storage, exiled to St. Helena's island—that little overflowing cottage in the cornfield down at the end of the campus where I slept. My things were moved there from the director's office. I was never invited to a board meeting again. They were so interested in understanding business arrangements and administrative problems that they forgot the program. I was never asked for information of any sort, or help, in straightening out the administrative problems. Naturally, these problems became much worse when there was no continuity of systems, unraveling, etc."

The next board meeting was the following weekend, August 7. The only reference made to Tom's "dismissal," was: "A reading of the new staff responsibilities of CDGM was given by Doctor Beittel from the minutes of the August 4 telephone meeting. These changes were ratified by the board. . . . A motion was carried that Dr. Tom Levin be invited into the meeting. Doctor Levin could not be found on the campus."

Though OEO and CDGM both valiantly stuck to their stories about

Tom Levin's shift of activity not representing his removal from the position of director, and about OEO not attacking CDGM but "assisting it," the press didn't miss the meaning of this federal-state (Stennis)-CDGM eruption.

One newspaper reported that Dr. Tom Levin had "surrendered" actual operation of CDGM "to be an assistant." The paper explained that Tom would devote his time to proposal writing and "curriculum planning," and that the Reverend Willie Brown would be "in charge of operations."

The New Orleans *Times-Picayune* of August 5, 1965 said:

Project Gets Reform Order
Mt. Beulah Operation Chief Removed

A statewide Headstart project based at nearby Mt. Beulah which has been under fire by a Mississippi senator, has been ordered by the Office of Economic Opportunity to make immediate reforms in administration and fiscal control.

As a result of the reforms, Dr. Tom Levin, a New York child psychologist who has been director of the controversial project . . . will be removed from that post and put in charge of curriculum planning. . . .

* * *

The nature and form of Central Staff protest were misunderstood by the press, but that was only because the board, various members of which had been explained to by Tom Levin, Jeannette King, and me, for sure—and probably by a number of others—"misunderstood" and relayed the misunderstood version to the press. Consequently, one paper announced that federal poverty program officials "faced a revolt of personnel of the nation's biggest Operation Head Start program in protest of government attempts to revise their operation." The same article went on to say that "the entire headquarters staff" of CDGM "threatened to walk off their jobs if . . ."

At the same board meeting, Jim Monsonis agreed to be acting director. He refused to accept this kind of title, out of concern for trainee director Reverend Willy Brown, whom he felt should be kept in the limelight amidst all the white fighting.

Twenty-four hours later Jim and Lenore Monsonis resigned from CDGM and took a plane to New York, never to return.

Dr. Beittel said: "It was very irresponsible to leave without warning when everybody was counting on them. Even if the board was wrong about Tom, Jim shouldn't have promised and then walked out."

Jim Monsonis left because of many things that depressed him. After the board meeting he realized for the first time how remorseless certain board members were about pushing out Tom. He wasn't surprised that the middle-class Negro board members were glad to see him go—that was the struggle that had been going on all summer between the Negro middle-class and the more radical white Northerners. The middle-class Negroes felt more comfortable with middle-class OEO officials than with off-beat Northern youngsters. It just seemed extraordinary to Jim that the board seemed not to count the great thing Tom had done. Jim suddenly realized also that OEO didn't *want* us to get CDGM straight. He didn't want to be responsible for a situation like that.

Then there was the question of his wife's ill health, resulting from total frustration with the government. She wanted to help CDGM function; she felt that the government, with its endless fumblings and interferences, wouldn't let her. Jim said: "Then there was one more very important reason I left: John Mudd. He was at that board meeting. I began to think about the full implications of John Mudd's role. What was it? Art and Marian had introduced me to him during this critical week. He seemed like a very nice kid. They said he was going 'to do something.' *What?* It was never explained.

"During that week they presented John at a staff meeting. They said he was someone to take over field operations. Staff jumped on Art and said, 'Whose job? Frank Smith's? There *is* no such job. What will he do? Who said? We've never heard of this Mudd before. Where did *he* come from to suddenly be stepping into such an important position?'

"Then Art quickly backed down and said John had 'just been asked to help out where he could, no special position.' I was very confused about this at the time. It was kind of ambiguous. *John* didn't say anything, *he* seemed all right, but we've seen people used before—and he was Marian's friend and no one trusted her at this point—and Art made me very uncomfortable—the whole thing seemed sort of sneaky—board maneuvering around central without teamwork.

"Then when they had John at this board meeting; well that seemed even more strange to me. All summer we had been trying to get in to see the board to explain our work, our problems, to build better communications and a closer relationship, and they only replied by sending us messages that they would only deal with the director (while not believing a word the director said, apparently). Why was this John Mudd invited to the board, then? What did this mean about what John was going to do? I came out of that board meeting very fed up with all the infighting, everything.

"But it didn't settle in on me till that night that John had probably been brought in to spy on me, report to the board about my work, take over from me, check me; I didn't want to work with this type of employee-employer relations. I have always trusted people and expected them to trust me.

"We had dinner that night in Jackson with Tom, Polly, several people. Tom had this appealing look on his face. It was clear he needed us to stay. Polly thought we should stay because we were the only ones that could hold things together administratively. She was trying to make the program end hold.

"If I had thought my staying would have made any difference, I would have stayed. I thought everything was lost anyway. . . ."

John Mudd's projected role wasn't only unclear and peculiar to the Monsonises—it was, even to John Mudd.

Most people's first impressions of John were that he was a friendly, fair-minded, affable youth; lithe and athletic looking; amiable and "possessed of a charming humility"; with "marvelous magnetic blue eyes, made sober only by heavily rimmed glasses, through which the sparkle shone gaily"; a "warm and easy smile that revealed teeth stained from four packs of Pall Mall a day"; hair that tumbled in a tousled shock into his eyes; corduroy pants which "fitted his slim figure very attractively," Nigerian shirts, and cowboy boots; "and don't forget that white German Shepherd—you can't describe the early days of the *enfant terrible* without describing the way that wild, unmannerly dog galloped after him everywhere he went, inside as well as out, often knocking staff members down when he suddenly greeted them by placing his huge paws playfully on their unsuspecting shoulders"; "he struck me as the ideal image of an intellectual Harvard boy, which is not odd, as that is exactly what he was."

John was in Mississippi doing research for his Harvard dissertation and working with the Batesville cooperative to get it funded. He had, he said, only the most haphazard knowledge of CDGM. He'd met Tom once in the spring, but all he claimed to know of CDGM was what he read in the papers, what he gathered from friends who were on the staff or board, and from Marian. John said that Marian had never explained the concepts to him—he had heard nothing of the philosophy, committees of poor people deciding things, training and new careers for people, the vital political implications involved, and so on.

He was contemptuous of "OEO types." He didn't know much about little children, and said it all seemed quite foreign to him. He didn't like what he'd heard about Tom's behavior. He saw a few Movement kids taking the project for a ride and so thought everyone was taking the government for a ride. Mostly he saw incredible confusion and lack of information in Batesville—and he heard of all the quarreling.

John said he only came into CDGM because his good friend Marian was being carried away with anger, and he wanted to help her out; calm her down. He respected her and Bob Coles, and they both said CDGM was *a good thing.* John said he would come if he could be of any help in preserving something that was important to community people; and if he didn't have to be placed, but could just look around and work as needed. He felt that he could be most helpful if he was free to appraise the difficulties and concentrate on trouble areas. His situation *was* ambiguous, but not, John felt, because of sinister thinking.

John knew that many staff people resented and distrusted him. He understood that that was because he *had,* indeed, been told to report directly to the board. But he looked at this as a short-term thing. He was just getting going with what he wanted to do with the Batesville cooperative. It was in a very crude stage. He felt it might not be carried on in the direction people wanted it to go. He felt guilty about leaving it. He was willing to give a few short months of his life to CDGM, no matter how grubby they might be.

And grubby they were. As it turned out, John did nothing but payroll and more payroll for days and days and nights and nights, trying to clear up back problems and sort out a system. Though Central Staff's views of John at this time were best summed up by a resource teacher who said, "he was cordial to everybody, but responsive to the pressures to treat us skeptically," he was obviously the bookkeeper for whom we had been waiting. In its typically negative way, the section of the Movement faction that wasn't out in the communities working hard, spent August hanging around Mount Beulah, complaining disgustedly about the payroll problem, but refusing to help John when he asked for volunteers to set the checks straight. The out-of-state teachers had mostly drifted off to their homes in the North. With the exception of two or three hard-working helpers, who only remained for a week or two more themselves, John Mudd had most of the mop-up to do alone. Community people never saw him. Staff rarely acknowledged him. Nobody guessed that humble and unassuming John, coming into CDGM with such simple goals in mind, would shortly show himself to be the popular hero and invaluable asset he did.

In the community, people were only peripherally concerned about all our headaches. They had their own problems:

We only missed one day, though. They burned the center down Sunday night and we skipped Monday because we had to meet all day to make arrangements to continue, but Tuesday we had our classes under the trees, and then in a tent, but it blew away. The sheriff said it was lightning. But the thunder storm ended at 10 P.M. Clarence drove by at 11 P.M. The sky was clear. There was no fire. We found it at 3:30 A.M. That's five hours after any lightning could have hit. If lightning done it, it was mysterious lightning. They said in the newspaper there was no sign of arson. The same night they burned a cross nearby here in Sharkey County.

CHAPTER 22

THE DECLINE AND FALL OF PRACTICALLY EVERYBODY

But at this point in time, *nobody* was a hero, and everybody was a villain to somebody. The board's personnel committee, which had finally started functioning at the board meeting the day before the Mary Holmes meeting, was replaced by the board executive committee. Staff snickered at this and considered it par for the new course: out of four people on it, only one was a community person.

At a staff meeting on August 8, staff disconsolately elected Rev. Willie Brown of Laurel, Mississippi, Tom's trainee director, to be acting administrator. We all knew Willie had long since resigned himself to the hopelessness of the overwhelming situation and would do nothing but slouch on the office couch and mope. There was nothing else he could do "with OEO's Mr. Dowdy on his right hand, and Marian's John Mudd on his left," as a community man sized up the situation. Most other people were just moping and griping too. There was no one else available who had any more ideas either of what over-all program directions were, or of what administrative systems were than Willie did. Willie wanted it. And few people cared any more anyway what Central Staff administration did, because it was viewed as merely a puppet of despotic OEO and the "toady" board. John Mudd was elected as Willie's assistant.

The minutes of this meeting say that Tom Levin backed John as an "active worker and participant in CDGM." In spite of bitterly hurt feelings and a deep sense of insult at what he felt was the board's denigrating rather than constructive criticism of his creation, Tom maintained a professional attitude toward the delapidated administration and busy board. He didn't leave, interfere, criticize, or even express cynicism. Saving and improving his creation was, even at this time, the main thing on his mind.

At this same meeting Tom made a strong plea for staff to give all possible help to communities in organizing people's planning committees to do as much evaluating and recommending as possible for the future proposal. He hoped that before sending their reports in to Edwards, people would begin to experience critical thinking about their own centers and community needs, and would work out some positive suggestions for changing structure, personnel, systems, or whatever was advisable, for improving the service they were (or more often, were not) getting from Central Staff. Tom suggested that district staff stir and organize its communities so they would be able to get some valuable recommendations, instead of the testimonials they were inclined toward from the habit of trying to please those with power over them. The recommendations were to be brought to the final community meeting, scheduled in our original OEO proposal to be held at Mount Beulah for evaluation and future planning purposes.

Tom also talked at this meeting of something some of the staff claimed never to have heard of, and others felt they knew too much about—so much that they were disappointed that it hadn't been established, as it might have saved the day on July 31: a Council of Neighborhood Centers. Our grant proposal, Tom and Art Thomas told the group, included a decision-making triumvirate. Only two parts had thus far been established. The board of directors and the Central Staff existed. It had been Frank Smith's assignment to help communities set up the third body. This would have been composed of strong, elected representatives from each center. The Council was to have had regular meetings and served to balance the board in authority. Since Frank was not only director of community staff, but was also the most vocal advocate of poor people control, Tom had assumed that he would take to this task with alacrity. However, Frank did nothing about this council. Judging by the surprise with which his own staff reacted to discussion of it, he hadn't even discussed it with his division—on purpose. He felt it would have been a powerless advisory board, a bogey man from the beginning, a rubber stamp. Frank didn't go for things like that.

The neighborhood council had been discussed with community people at the original organizational meeting at Mount Beulah in the spring. In the confusion of newness, they had naturally not elected such a council without district coordinators, spurred on by Frank Smith, helping them understand the meaning of electing representatives, delegating power, etc. Tom had been increasingly disturbed over Frank's refusal to function for CDGM. In the course of August, had Central Staff's personnel committee—which found it had difficulty meeting because members were always in the field—and/or the board's personnel committee—which started staff review the day before the Mary Holmes meeting—been left alone to begin reprimanding or weeding out recalcitrant staff, this problem might have been solved. However, the detonation set off by the OEO descent was strong enough to explode any "control" of staff that any group might have been beginning to have.

Some thought that the district staff would react to knowledge of the neighborhood council plan by quickly trying to create as much strength in communities as possible. It was plain that no one else was going to do so. But district staff was thoroughly disenchanted with CDGM. Their frustrations caused them to withdraw from any attempt to make "a real CDGM." They felt it was impossible. They had lost faith in Tom partly because of paycheck problems, which made them look like fools and manipulators to their community constituents, partly because, having an "all or nothing" philosophy themselves, they interpreted Tom's willingness to consider moving to an alternate location a semi-sellout, and partly because they had never had faith in the whole idea of CDGM in the first place. Factors combined to make them unwilling to support Tom or CDGM.

Frank Smith explained that his faction couldn't support anyone in CDGM at that point. The only thing Movement people could do was leave. They knew from the beginning they'd have to leave. It was just a question of how long they could hold on before they either pulled out or got thrown out of the program. It wouldn't have helped Tom even if they had supported him. He was fighting on too many fronts. Tom represented the professional people, and Frank represented the poor people, but they were friends. They used to talk a lot in Tom's office. Frank felt that it wasn't any great feat to get that grant in the aftermath of the 1964 summer—the government was feeling guilty and under a lot of pressure. But still he thought Tom pushed very hard for getting the things he believed in and the realities together and happening. He admired him for fighting a good fight "even if he was bound to get his ass kicked in." He saw CDGM as a by-product of the Movement. He felt that he had discovered these people. He had inspired their confidence. Tom, he correctly surmised, put Frank and his friends on the staff because he had to have them. He could never have gotten the people without them. Frank didn't want the spirit and goal subverted by professionalism—but he wasn't against Tom. He liked his ideas. The fact that Tom "got fired," Frank saw as a tribute to him, because when he was forced to fight, he did. Frank respected Tom. "He died with his guns in his hands."

Frank's friends began talking of making one last splash before pulling out of the project—maybe they could overthrow the board, to dramatize their dissatisfaction with what they thought to be its unabashed unctuousness.

During the ten days before the long-planned August 28 wrap-up and planning meeting for as many community people as could fit into the Mount Beulah auditorium, Frank got together "a committee" of his followers on CDGM staff. They "alerted the poor people." Rumors began to flow to Beulah that the committee wasn't only alerting the poor to come with written criticisms and evaluations, but to come "to elect a new board of directors." Board members got wind of the imminent *coup d'etat*. They were furious. Art Thomas spoke to Frank Smith privately. They weren't prepared to elect a new board so suddenly. Frank said he had been hired as a hoax. He had been hired to get local people elected to decision-making positions. Now nobody would authorize him to do so. Art asked why the "alerting committee" was getting so many *non*-CDGMians to the meeting. Frank replied that he understood CDGM was a community project. He thought the broader the base the better for healthy criticism and for better future planning. Art said things were very tense and this kind of meeting would end up in a fight. Frank said he wasn't looking for a fight, he would be quiet the whole meeting, even relinquish the role of moderator at the meeting, if Art promised that no one would get up there and tell those people they had to know how to read and write to be on the board.

Willie Brown wanted to chair the meeting as his last gesture before going to Syracuse to school. Frank thought happily that this was going to be a tough one. He didn't think Willie could handle it. He didn't think anybody could handle it. He was right. The meeting was out of control from the word go. The "committee" had managed to pack the room with FDP and SNCC workers of the most negative ilk, far more negative than the most negative of the CDGM staff. Their only interest at the meeting was alarming or lynching the board (they hadn't decided which yet) and making them squirm and protest their loyalty. They urged the bewildered poor not to be bought off with the government's greenbacks, produced "witnesses" who were poorer than the poor who had some CDGM jobs, and shouted accusations, sometimes at CDGM in general, more often at the board.

Since the group's purpose was to disrupt and create discontent, members made no effort to help people come up with a plan more satisfactory than CDGM in terms of Movement goals, or with a method of maintaining CDGM which would seem more legitimate to them than the board's "let's play along with OEO temporarily" method. The split which had always run right down the middle of CDGM between those who were jockeying factors to work out the most palatable plan within the framework of a federal program, and those who couldn't conceive of doing anything "real" within such a framework, and therefore saw their mission work as protecting the tempted poor people from "falling for" beguilingly glittering false hopes, was never more violent. We had seen nothing yet. Black Power hadn't yet become an everyday consideration.

There were others at this meeting who were under the impression that they had come to the founding meeting of the Council of Neighborhood Centers. Dr. Gerry Rosenfield had felt that finally forming this body would be our answer. He and other staff members had hurriedly tried to educate the communities as to what was really at stake in our dispute with OEO and with the board. They had asked as many centers as they had been able to reach, to send two delegates to the meeting. Still others came to *discuss* holding a founding meeting for the Council of Neighborhood Centers.

Some of us, including Tom and myself, had felt that rushing communities into electing and sending delegates in time for this meeting would be premature. It would result in a shallow level of community comprehension about what was happening. We had stimulated discussion in each community in which we were working on routine business, about the possibility of setting up such a Council. We also instigated discussions about adding community representatives to the existing board of directors. This would be a way of balancing the pressures the board felt from OEO with counterpressures from the communities. It would also serve as a way of putting more poor people in policy-pondering positions.

Frank Smith said his clique could have got rid of them that day. Dr. Beittel said they could take over, but if they did, there wouldn't be anything to take over, because the government wouldn't give them any more money. Mr. Kirksey said he admired Marian and Dr. Beittel very much. He didn't believe they would do anything against CDGM. Black SNCC workers went after white Delta Ministry workers. Art told Tom to get up and *do* something, he was the only one who could save the day.

Tom said, "The purpose of this meeting is not to overthrow the board; it's to activate the Neighborhood Council."

Frank cried out, "Don't do that to us, Tom, you're selling us out."

Tom urged the SNCCs to let community people make their own decisions. Through the confusion of shouting and accusing, poor person after poor person stood up and testified about the wonderful change CDGM had brought into the lives of the children. Many read stiff criticisms of the bungling Central Staff from documents their committees had prepared back home. Others reeled off programs they wanted to add to Head Start to help others in the community. Each member of the Board was forced to "walk the plank," as one man described it, to "defend" his actions and reveal his role. It turned out that neither community nor Central Staff had any notion of what the board had been doing all summer.

The board was struggling for control of the project. Staff felt that the board attempted to assume command in an abrupt and authoritarian manner. Perhaps it did, and perhaps this was directly related to the degree to which it felt frightenedly *out* of control—which it certainly was. This was partly due to its own immaturity as a board, and to the busyness of some of the key members. It was partly due to Tom's failure to take it seriously and educate it.

There was unanimous agreement, from the communities in Mississippi to the conference rooms in Washington, that the board was justified in being as alarmed as it was about the condition of the project's administrative side. This alarm was another cause of the board's clutch at command. The board was afraid of losing OEO's favor for future funding. It thought it politically wise to follow a temporary strategy of docility until CDGM was funded again and fairer weather appeared. The board realistically felt that many staff members were uncompromising, unreasonable, and were endangering this grant and future grants for the poor people.

The board thought that the refusal of relentless Movement purists to modify their original style Movement and their insistence on running rampant over the concern of the poor for government programs and over the concern of the government for regulations ran counter to its new lie low policy. That was true. But a few of the rest of us were deeply hurt to be crudely lumped in the same category as those who wanted to rip up CDGM. We resented being called irresponsible by the board. We felt that the board, in its panic, was failing to distinguish between destructive negative emotion, and dissenting productive conviction. The board could see the nihilists. But could it see, we wondered, that there were many notches on the continuum and that Tom's faction represented a notch way to the right of our Movement extremists, yet way to the daring side of the board? Could it see the issues we were fighting for, beyond the mere bread and butter matter of funding? The clues we had in answer to our questions were not auspicious.

The most glaring clue was the board's treatment of Tom Levin. Had the board considered and valued the extraordinary number of major and minor administrative achievements Tom brought about in the first three weeks of a functioning program, it might have predicted that within the next three weeks his regime would have brought the bucking bronc under control. It's also possible, since Tom admittedly had considerably more administrative confidence than he had administrative skill, he instead might have run the whole project irretrievably into the ground. In the eyes of expert administrators, perhaps he should have been able to settle all the problems we had in three weeks. But to a nonadministrator like myself, three weeks seemed rather a short time in which to expect anyone, even a cadre of slick management consultants, to solve all the unforeseen problems we had in our raw community context. Therefore, the board's readiness to assume that the clean-up couldn't be entrusted to Tom, and its willingness to dethrone him without a battle, rather than to bolster him with the aid in administrative staff and systems he had been requesting all summer and which OEO now seemed prepared to shower on us, appeared at best a belittling lack of respect for and interest in what Tom had contributed to CDGM.

The board, it must be said, didn't intend to replace Tom as chief administrator quite as completely as it would appear that it did. It fully intended that Jim Monsonis, a strong backer of Tom's and the man on the staff most knowledgeable about administrative matters, would take over the job. John Mudd and the OEO representatives would lend a badly needed hand and John would step into the director's office when Tom left. It's also true that the board once looked for Tom to attend part of a board meeting, and that it asked him to work on future planning. Yet Tom was never again consulted on any policy or practical matter. He was not part of the group that planned for *his* future. He was never asked to other board meetings. No member of his substantive staff was ever asked to describe the program's accomplishments or needs. Tom was neither bid good-bye, nor even, long after the dust settled, sent a thank-you note for his services. In fact, he wasn't even put on the routine mailing list.

Staff was nearly unanimous in feeling that the board exhibited an uncontrollable impulse (recognized off the record by one board member) to put Tom in his place for the egomania that even his close friends felt he displayed during the summer, and was influenced also by the internecine rivalry between organizations and individuals agreed by most observers to have been in existence. Some staff members, realizing the feverish pace and feverish setting in which board members were functioning, in which it would have been impossible for even the most seasoned executive war-horses to have remained maturely professional and reflectively clinical, were willing to wave aside as "unfortunate" the fact that in the confusion the board "overlooked" Tom.

My diary says: "It's sad. I feel so depressed and saddened that in the rush, when many things must be forgotten, overlooked, and sacrificed, the thing the board has chosen to yield is all that we believe in, and all we have done, and worst of all, our fountain of ideas for doing more of the same: Tom. I think these midsummer night's choices mark a point of no return for CDGM. A little clump of us kids defied the mighty government for the sake of "our principles"; and we won. But I don't feel proud. For though we won a minor skirmish with OEO, I believe we've lost our greater battle: the privilege of searching for human solutions to human problems. If I ever write the book about CDGM that I'd like to write, I won't know how to handle all the petty, personal, negative, nasty things. It isn't proper to put them in a book. I should just write about our great ideas and the wonderful poor people. The ugly stuff is our family skeleton. But then, what would be the point of writing such a book? It would avoid the basic tragedy of man, as reflected in CDGM. It *is* precisely these ugly littlenesses in us that always triumph and destroy what's good in us. To write of CDGM as if it were a struggle between this social action method or that, between the good guys and the bad guys, would be absurd. CDGM is a perfect example of the struggle between our destructive parts (evil) and our capabilities for greatness (good)."

All of this raised complex thoughts and conflicting feelings in some of us. What does it mean to believe in what has come to be called "resident participation"?

If the new thrust of the poor Negro was to fight for social change, beginning with protest and in 1965 moving into self-run program, it had to be prime policy in CDGM to welcome this fight and to work with it. Many programs keep the fight quiet by not taking in those who have the most of it, or by insisting that it be kept outside the program's jurisdiction. We wanted to use every ounce of fight, because it's the opposite of detachment, apathy, withdrawal, and acceptance of desperately unfair living. We had to spend lots of energy talking with people about how they would like to direct this fight.

For example, one could fight organizations, including one's "own" CDGM, or one could fight to develop an organization that would do what the people want done. One could fight educators, or one could learn about many kinds of education and fight to make the selected and adapted, or newly created, kind happen. One could fight the federal government for its past neglect and indifference in refusing federal programs, or one could fight to form the kind of program poor people desire and then fight for funds and to force the government to learn to heed and support, if not value, the voice of the poor man.

In this regard we needed a staff that could see hostility and aggression as an excellent beginning in the long process of awakening from soul slavery, rather than as a petulant interference to smooth running programs, or as a personal attack. Early childhood educators and psychologists know that raising hell may be healthier than withdrawal into isolation and defeat. They know that combating hostility with counter-hostility may be healthier (and more likely to be effective) than is submitting to unmerciful and debilitating unfairness. Movement leaders know that the greatest strength their people are gaining is the will to "stop taking it," the courage to challenge, and the spine to speak out against injustice. In this regard CDGM proudly joined other groups in piercing the pus-filled infection of racism and all its ugly results.

We were, thus, a challenge to the supersegregationist, the lazy liberal, the idle moderate, and the status-quo educator, whether they were in Mississippi, OEO, or other parts of the nation. But not because we were hilariously rebellious, obstinately ornery, damnably defiant, or adolescently antisocial. It was because we weren't awed by leaders who won't lead to their utmost limits for fear of losing that precious thing called peace in the community; even at the expense of freedom. We didn't admire either the quietly humming program or the quietly humming community, as long as it concealed the buzzing hornets beneath. We weren't enamored of false tranquility.

Yet though we wanted to include anger, for many reasons it was impossible to determine just how much anger and hate existed in the hearts of CDGM participants. What should we include? What was real? *Who* should we include? Who spoke for the Negro? Surely not most of the members of the poor communities themselves—not on this subject. There was too much to lose. Some people denied that they hate whites at all. They knew fully consciously or at some level of consciousness that they did. But they also knew that they were dependent on the benevolence of whites, at least on the commitment of white civil rights workers, to attain enough of a toehold in the world of skills to be able to risk kicking these whites into places of "mere equality" from places of uncontested superiority. It was too soon, it was too dangerous, they couldn't afford, yet, to speak of their hate and anger. They could speak for themselves on all sorts of other subjects with conviction and accuracy, but they couldn't speak of how much they hated "the good whites" who had made their project possible. However, did our knowledge of this make it right for us to *assume* anger, even when people denied they felt it?

There were others who said they didn't hate whites because, in fact, they didn't know it was whites they should hate. They were still too deep in displaced hate that had turned inward. It hasn't been safe in Mississippi until recently to turn it outward where it belongs. They were still too deep in diffuse, nameless self-hate that comes from hating others but becomes hating self.

It came, also, from absorbing the hate whites around them had for them. This complicated the matter still more, because except in the case of the Ku Klux Klan and other overtly hating groups, it was not obvious hate. It was hate hidden in disguises like lack of respect, a belief that Negroes could never achieve and should be cared for, the notion that the Negro was a delightful joke, and other forms harder to deal with than straight hate. This fanned out within them into worse things, such as self-doubt, dependency on those who would not help or would not be able to help, and a self-destructive inability to do the detailed things that had to be done to achieve enough of whatever it was they had to achieve to like themselves better. This had to happen before they could set higher goals to which to aspire. And *this* had to happen before they could mobilize themselves toward freedom.

Someday these hate-damaged people may be able to tell how much they hate and may be able to direct the energy now gnawing at *them* to gnaw at their world of problems instead. But during CDGM's first summer, they were not yet speaking for themselves about their hate. Were we, then, to ignore their anger at us?

A few of the community people could tell truthfully how they felt about whites in their project. This may have been possible because they knew they hated *all* whites, as each white represents all whites. What was originally legitimate reaction had merged into prejudgment and finally into generalized prejudice. Or it might have been because they distinguished between *most* white people, whom they hated, and *several* white people, whom they found decent—whom they found willing to work in the muck and in ostracism for them. Some said they loved individual white people, but that, in the process of shedding the habit of counting on whites in any way, they had to shed these personal friends too. Others found it possible to work with whites and have white friends and still hold their own.

In taking offense at Negro prejudice against whites, we don't usually admit the extent to which most whites generalize about Negroes all the time. Whites don't make distinctions. We can't assume that Negroes can make these distinctions better than we can. Black prejudice can't be called evil unless white prejudice is called evil, and black prejudice will exist as long as white prejudice does.

And all of this is further complicated by projections and distorted perceptions. But who was so wise that he could sort it all out and find the truth beneath? Many white Southerners maintained that they "know their Negroes" well, and that these Negroes loved them. This was partly a myth they wished to believe so they wouldn't have to shoot themselves upon realizing fully the immoralities and cruelties of which they were guilty. It was a myth that could flourish in all its cherished beauty because its makers remained so far removed from the world of "their Negroes" that they truly, truly didn't know the whole other life that went on there.

It's a lovely, loving myth they can cling to, because all contrary evidence can be attributed to Northern newspapers that "have it in for them" and to "outside agitators," who are un-Americanly stirring up the devoted and innocently childlike "darkies." When evidence can't be explained any other way, it can be called "an exception." Seldom does evidence erase prejudice. It's a myth many Southerners can maintain, in large part because many Negroes help perpetuate it. Some, in their brainwashed way, "believe" it. Others, as seems to be the case much more often, aid and abet the myth-makers because it serves them well to do so. It's a means of remaining eligible for benevolence, which they can't retain, of course, if they utter even the smallest declaration of independence. It is also a means of feeling superior—they have tricked the white man into believing they love him and love the old Southern way of life and have smirked at their success in fooling, thus foiling, the fool.

But in addition to being a myth the whites were fond of, it was a truth about which the whites were right. Some Negroes *did* love some whites in the South, as some whites *did* love some Negroes—a logical result of the fact that all people aren't alike and don't fit any generalization. And as has often been said, the whole thing is more personal in the South, more intimate, and love sometimes is there—not love for the system, but love for a family one has worked for for generations, or love for a man who is a secret love, or love for white children raised as if one were their mother. The white Mississippian either knows more about the truth of the racial situation than anyone else, or he knows less than anyone else, depending upon which aspects. He, of all people, does not speak for the Negro about Negro-white hate. How could we heed (or ignore) his views on this?

Many Movement workers claimed they, and they alone, knew the truth about the poor Negro's feelings toward whites. Many Movement workers were *not* residents. But if they spoke for residents where residents feared to tread, shouldn't we listen? Here again we had the tangle of underground truths and untruths and semitruths, demitruths and sometimes truths and projections and distorted perceptions. On the one hand Movement workers *were* often closer to sensing the feelings of their population than were those with more academic degrees. They went into communities specifically to dig out feelings, rather than to develop programs. They went with sensitivity focused on this thing, allowing "bad" feelings, talking about them, approving of them, repudiating the entrenched idea of inferiority by denying the superiority of the white man. They didn't go to impart information or distribute regulations or try to produce something tangible. They had more success "getting next to" poor Negroes because they went with fewer competencies of the white man's kind with which to intimidate people; and because they went in the uniform of the nonenemy—a working man's clothes instead of a middle-class business suit, a working man's earthiness instead of the slickness and supercleanliness symbolic of middle-class "success." They spoke simply. They had more years of experience in working this unpretentious way in the communities.

But on the other hand, some of these workers went into communities carrying not only sensitivity but hypersensitivity to hostile feelings toward whites. They carried their own problems of negativism, nihilism, and relationships with authority figures, which made it impossible for them to hear positive feelings people offered toward whites and limited their hearing to what *they* wanted to hear, what they themselves thought: antiwhite things. They may have failed to hear nonhostile feelings, or they may have labeled the man who expressed these nonhostile feelings an "Uncle Tom" (a greatly overused term). Most frequently they insisted that hostile feelings were there, visible only to the workers because so hidden from whites. They projected their own antiwhite feelings, legitimate as these may have been, onto their constituents, and then brought them in as "the real story," which nobody else had the "sensitivity" to get.

The positive factor that Movement workers might have been less bristling with awing competencies that tended to overwhelm people and tended to make them hide their feelings than were professionals in other fields than community organization were balanced by another factor. In some instances their very lack of specialized competencies made them feel threatened by those who had them, and therefore possessive about this one realm of personal relations which they felt they "discovered," and in which they felt that they alone excelled.

Because they felt inadequate themselves, they overreacted to the adequateness of out-of-state or white workers by denying that the latter had anything useful to offer at all, by loudly proclaiming that they did more harm than good by overshadowing poor people, and by sincerely thinking that these outsiders could never really "know" the people. Any evidence from a non-Movement staff member that local Negroes, in this or that instance, might have liked him, was immediately thrown out by the statement that the Negro only *said* he liked the white staff member because he felt expected to say so. This was often true, but the difficult part was that the Negro who told the Movement worker that he did *not* like white staff members was *also* working in terms of what he was expected to say. Contrary to the certainty of the workers that they were substituting nonauthority for authority, they were, of course, substituting an authority which *valued* poor people for an authority which did *not*. Workers were seen as authorities as much as "the man" or the white Central Staff member was—a much more desirable kind of authority, and one that made few decisions, but still an authority, whom a poor man wanted to please. So while one couldn't count on the accuracy of a poor Negro's vow to a white man that he liked him, didn't resent or hate him, didn't fear him or feel anger toward him, one could *also* not count on the accuracy of a poor Negro's vow to a Movement worker that he *did* fear and respect whites. In both cases, the overadaptive Negro in the community was trying to appease and to do what was expected, though in either case what the person said, of course, might have been true. To whom, we agonized, should we listen?

"Anger *is* one of the sinews of the soul; he that wants it hath a maimed mind." But could we identify that which was useful and that which was self-destructive, and gradually pare the latter away? Could we find out how much anger there really was? And how much it was interfering with education and other "progress" for which poor people yearn? CDGM couldn't know, its first summer, the answers to these questions. Of course we never learned how much anger there was in communities, or toward whom it was directed. Our determining devices were very human, thus not very "scientific." But we knew, at least, that the best way to help the helpless children of helpless adults was to free the adults to capture the powerful feelings in themselves, be these love or anger, to become conscious of themselves as they really were, and to channel their feelings toward their goals. That CDGM seethed with internal anger and heaved with highly combustible hate was evidence that we were dealing with reality.

Things went from "worse to worser," as an elderly gentleman from Rosedale aptly expressed it. The accountants felt that OEO, the board, the staff, everyone, was using them as scapegoats. The project had mushroomed so uncontrollably that nothing could have prevented payroll problems. And like the administrative staff, they felt that things were getting straightened out, but they were frustrated and overwhelmed like everyone else. The straw that broke their back was OEO announcing that it would not honor the grant agreement approved by it earlier, and would not pay the accountants the fee they anticipated. Our financial flounderings had always received more attention than our content contributions. This period proved no exception. Some Head Starts envied us the ease with which we often made front page news. We were never too pleased:

BOOKS MISSING AT MOUNT BEULAH
Fed Auditors Can't Locate the Record

Financial records of the controversial Operation Head Start center near Edwards have disappeared as they were being checked by investigators for a U.S. Senate Committee.

Sen. John Stennis said Senate Appropriations Committee auditor William Miller discovered the records were missing when he went to the Child Development Group of Mississippi headquarters Monday to resume a check he had started last week.

'Every scratch of financial records was gone,' a spokesman for Stennis said.

HAYDEN PROTESTS

Stennis and Sen. Carl Hayden of Arizona, the committee chairman, protested the disappearance to Poverty Program director Sargent Shriver.

In a telegram to Shriver Monday, Stennis said he was 'deeply and greatly concerned' by the disappearance. He told Shriver he considered a probe into the disappearance 'a matter of the greatest importance.'

Stennis asked Hayden to take action to see that the records were returned. . . .[28]

The matter was resolved, as we read a few days later:

HEAD START ACCOUNTANTS ARE FIRED
New Group Named to Keep Books at Edwards

. . . A controversial Head Start project at Edwards, Miss., has a new accounting firm today—apparently a result of the brief disappearance last week of the project's financial records.

James F. Kelleher, an assistant to Poverty Program Director Sargent Shriver,

[28] Jackson *Daily News,* August 31, 1965.

said here that the firm of Spokney-Gersten Co., of New York, has been dismissed as accountants for the. . . .[29]

Another limb had fallen off CDGM's suffering body.

The board supported the accountants in demanding the fee promised them, but didn't agree to an extra five thousand dollars, which they wanted to cover their costs for additional unbudgeted centers.

The board was now actually only the executive committee, as in its attempt to "strengthen" the board OEO had effected community members like a bolt of lightning, and had electrocuted them into speechless paralysis. They supported Art Thomas and the Delta Ministry in insisting that the eight dollars per day per person paid by CDGM to the Delta Ministry for all Orientation expenses was reasonable (as well as agreed to by OEO in the grant).

When I was still at OEO, and CDGM was writing its original proposal, I remember a phone call in which CDGM asked for the Head Start formula for budgeting Orientation costs per teacher. I told them sixteen dollars a day, the rate that we were told to quote to all institutions and universities holding these Head Start five-day Orientations. Art Thomas, the voice at the other end of the phone, said, "Well, we ought to be able to do it for less than that; Mount Beulah doesn't have as much overhead as a university." Though the Delta Ministry charged exactly half as much as almost every other Orientation "landlord" in the country, the controversy arose. Wrangling over it lasted well into the winter. This was because Senator Stennis had decided to say that the Delta Ministry and CDGM paid for the Jackson FDP demonstrations by charging CDGM "so much" that FDP did not have to pay more than a token for *its* room and board. OEO's reaction to any charge the senator made against CDGM was routinely to throw judgment to the wind and other factors in the files, and to treat CDGM with the same kind of morally superior condescension with which one might treat a guilty party whom one has, out of pure kindness of heart, decided to defend.

"That wasn't the only bewildering charge," said Tom Levin, "The OEO accountants accused us of buying chairs for the children, because capital investments are disallowable, and they also charged us with buying materials to *make* chairs, though we had Jule Sugarman's telephone permission to do both—but at the same time, the inspectors from OEO objected that in some centers children sat on the floor because there were no chairs."

Mary Holmes President D. I. Horne reacted to OEO's pressure for his institution to take more control over CDGM. He asserted himself unequivocally. Many staff members remember his "claiming" items that

[29] Jackson *Daily News*, September 3, 1965.

were claimed by OEO as its property, and also by CDGM as its private nongovernment property, "by going around, raising his arm and saying, 'I claim this printing press in the name of the government of the United States,' the way an explorer would claim newly discovered territory in the name of his queen."

And so, in a thicket of thorny problems, "fiscal amateurism," and tension, the long hot summer ended. In early September I saw two old men standing in the driveway at Mount Beulah surveying the scene. One said, "It look like the devil done foreclosed, and he's finished havin' his auction."

And the other man said, "I thought we poor peoples was doin' real good—I wonder what we done wrong why Mr. Shriver want to snuff this ray of sunshine from our lives?"

In my diary I wrote: "It's easy to blame others, as others can always be found somewhat to blame. It's easy to feel pure, and that others are despicably sinful. But the root of this ruination of CDGM is within *us* as much as within *them*. Whatever *they* did or didn't do to our project, we would have done it in ourselves sooner or later. It's in our nature to break as much as we make: to foul up and fail at everything good we set out to do. We would have slaughtered the project anyway, with our overreaching of ability, overspending of passion, and overrating of selves. With egotistical striving and conniving and competitive possessiveness, we would have stabbed it to death, and snarled it up past untangling. With energies warped into petty personal antagonisms and hateful bitterness we would have strangled the good there was in it. It's comfortable to see ourselves as the virtuous ones, motivated only by the beautiful, but we are so dishonest. On both sides, OEO and CDGM, we're self-indulgent, self-important, very small people, with a long way to go to be wise."

CHAPTER 23

WHAT LOOSED THE FATEFUL LIGHTNING OF HIS TERRIBLE SWIFT SWORD?

IN ADDITION TO limping, disintegrating, dispersing northward, and schizophrenically planning "for the future," depending upon the individual, Central and out-of-state field staff spent the rest of August trying to fathom what had happened to cause Mr. Shriver to "loose the fateful lightning of his terrible swift sword." These are some of the facts and thoughts we collected.

United States Representative John Bell Williams, a typical Mississippi Goldwater Democrat, was displeased to find inflammatory CDGM suddenly nesting in his district. Responsible sources say that he asked Senator Stennis, a conservative but not fanatic man as Mississippi top officials go, to use his influence on OEO to exterminate the pest. Senator Stennis had considerable influence with OEO. He was the head of the Senate Appropriations Committee, from which OEO got its funds. At that time, OEO senior staff was preparing for the imminent and hostile committee, which could decide the unlikely fate of the entire marginally popular poverty program. Senator Stennis responded by sending the committee's chief investigator, Paul J. Cotter, to interrogate us. He extensively investigated our books, cupboards, and file cabinets. He appeared at the National Council of Churches in New York with questions that spokesmen refused to answer. He even appeared early one morning at the New York home of Tom Levin's family.

OEO accountants told us at the time that they could protect us from any charges the senator might make. The worst *their* inspection had turned up was "fiscal amateurism." But other top OEO personnel said that while our administration was no worse than most Head Starts in the country and maybe a little better than most—certainly considering what we started with—we were such a sensitive project that we would have to be perfect to pass. And this we surely weren't. A deputy director of OEO and Mr. Shriver's right hand man, said that funding CDGM *at all* was breaking ground in *that* territory. All evidence indicated that OEO higher-ups *wanted* to protect us, and therefore, as this was the only condition under which they could get away with protecting us, wanted us to be perfect.

The July 31 clamp-down was partially an attempt to placate Senator Stennis by offering him a token of retreat, without, OEO mistakenly thought, seriously impairing CDGM's program. This would have been a clever compromise, and one more in a string of examples of Mr. Shriver's superb political judgment, except that, not having many correct facts about CDGM, and having superb political judgment only from A to M (for mayors), Mr. Shriver weighed his watermelons wrong. Moving *would* destroy the project. The poor and their daring advisers *would* fight back. Decision-makers at OEO evidently weren't aware that this wasn't the average independent small town Head Start run by a group of apolitical little old ladies and wholesome young nursery school teachers, which could be mutilated without much protest or bad publicity, if politically necessary.

The clamp-down was also an attempt to gain more control over roily renegade CDGM, so OEO could protect it better in the future. There's reason to believe that at that time OEO still had a future in mind for CDGM. And so OEO could feel more comfortable with its black sheep. *New Republic*'s social commentator, Andrew Kopkind, said in conversation: "People, including OEO people and John and Marian, didn't understand what was happening the first summer. It was too frightening. It didn't fit with what they could imagine or imagine managing, so they tried to change it and forget what it had been. The rhetoric is the same, but the style of operating and the meaning is entirely different. Tom had an intensely curious experimental attitude and radical instincts. He wanted change in a very big way, explosively, inside poor people and everything they touched. He was concerned with the psychodynamics and the enormous political implications. He spent a lot of time in communities and in centers. He basically did not want to be an elitist, though his professional training pushed him there, but his inclination was with the people. He was extremely intuitive and insightful. He understood the change in people much better than John. And Marian, well, of course that's not her bag at all. She doesn't see that.

"The fact that OEO shifted from relying on Tom to relying on Marian and John is not just a matter of individuals—it represented a basic shift toward conservatism. OEO was much more at ease with Marian, because she had a very definite, closed, rather narrow idea of what should happen in Mississippi. She couldn't stand the uncontrolled sweeping approach Tom had any more than OEO could. She wanted things to move through ordinary channels, as OEO did, and she wanted tight control, like OEO. Marian knew that anything that throws millions of dollars and the national liberal coalition into Negro communities is worth fighting for—and compromising for—she has no greater understanding of CDGM than that.

"John and Marian didn't begin acknowledging CDGM till *after* that wild period—they denied Tom and that summer. John and Marian were more elitists. They felt most comfortable around intellectuals. It was no accident John was never in communities. It wasn't that he was so busy in the office. It was the opposite of that—the reason he was so busy in the office was that he didn't communicate well or feel at ease in the communities. John was more concerned with the orderly development of group processes and the relation of individuals to their institutions. He wanted poor people to develop a full personal feeling that they could make CDGM work for them if they learned to understand the workings of it intimately.

"Of course, it's a good thing John and Marian came in—if Tom had stayed, more of the poor might have become political animals instead of bureaucrats, and it might have kept its wild wonderful qualities, but there probably would have *been* no CDGM. It undoubtedly would not have been re-funded by OEO without the calming and tightening done by Marian and John. Marian was very, very astute politically—but of course Tom's was the exciting period. . . ."

Obviously, then, gaining control over CDGM for OEO meant taking control from Tom Levin. This, OEO estimated, could best and most quickly be done by placing control in the hands of the more governable board and the still more governable Mary Holmes Junior College (MHJC), with an OEO representative, the most governable of the lot, on top of the heap. "We knew Mary Holmes was a front to escape the governor's veto," said an eighth-floor decision maker, "but for God's sake, you can't run around advertising *that!* Besides, you needed professional administrative help."

OEO had to appear to be keeping its commitment to liberals and civil rights leaders nationally, and to act in a manner consistent with its own image of itself as the defender of the poor. Yet at the same time it had to appear to Senator Stennis, avowed enemy of liberals, civil rights, and OEO, to be showing sufficient deference to his demands. OEO brass had to invent a myth explaining what was wrong with CDGM, based on some truth (Tom's administration); invent a second myth of what would cure CDGM, also based on some truth, if the problem was seen strictly in administrative terms (board and MHJC administrative efforts); prepare a cover story that would convince liberals that this was all to improve the program for the poor and prevent them from ferreting out the vandalizing view of it. And all of this was really to curtail the activities and dilute the essence of CDGM so that the senator would be satisfied.

OEO staff members didn't regard their actions as destructive. They didn't see their job as fighting tooth and nail for deeply meaningful community development and child development programs. They didn't see it as awakening sparks of action in poor communities. Their task was to maneuver through political glue and fireworks to leave a little something for the poor as often as possible and to awaken guilt feelings in a somnolent middle-class citizenry. They anticipated much shrinkage. Thus, they weren't distressed at a loss here and there. They had little sophisticated knowledge of real human or community development, so were satisfied with superficial and low level achievements.

Because the dominant tone of the American public, President Johnson's Administration, Congress, and OEO was one of gradualism rather than one of rapid reform, OEO was organized by and for "gradualist liberals" rather than "rapid reform" liberals. Rapid reformers weren't sought, or were limited to the role of consultants, whose services could be, and often were, terminated on twenty-four-hour notice. In the event that rapid reformers got into staff positions by mistake, or in the event that staff members slowly evolved from gradualist liberals into rapid reformers—or, in other words, evolved from willingness to put "orders," administrative considerations, and political practicalities ahead of independent judgment, quality considerations, and project ideologies to an insistence on doing the reverse—there were bureaucratic ways of controlling them, and keeping their committment from interfering with the OEO operation.

The first way was to keep staff from acquiring too much knowledge of a project. Too much knowledge leads to identification, and therefore to a conflict of loyalties. OEO was structured so that each proposal and project was handled in a splintered way by many divisions and departments. This guaranteed wire-crossing, too many cooks, shallow understanding of the project, the left hand (the dreamer) not knowing what the right hand (the politician and the administrator) was doing, duplication of effort, occasional accidental skipping of stages of "treatment" (for example, CDGM's first grant missed legal review and was never signed off as satisfactory); but it *wasn't* sloppy administration. It served a valuable, intentional purpose. It increased the chances of preventing OEO staff members from becoming overinvolved in and overemotional about any one project.

If, by accident, an OEO staffer became knowledgeable about a particular project, he was generally considered to be "prejudiced," thus contaminated. He was artfully kept from being consulted or from being in a position of decision-making regarding this project. This was all the more true if the person was favorably impressed with the project, though it seems not to have been the case if the person was *un*favorably impressed by the project. For example, throughout the commotion concerning CDGM in late July and August, Dudley Morris, who of all OEO people had known the most, with the exception of myself, about

CDGM in its early days, was "isolated from the case," to quote him, and was "kept busy with lots of things," but was never allowed "to comment or shed light on CDGM."

Dave Walls, Mr. Sugarman's other special assistant, was likewise kept busy, for he, too, liked what CDGM was trying to do. On the other hand, Jack Gonzales, of the inspection office, felt to be deeply suspicious of CDGM, was considered safe, and continued to have quite a bit to do with factors totaling the abortive assassination of the project, as were the Cutler, Cassidy accountant crowd.

If top officials expected ahead of time that an individual or division would favor a project, that person or division was prevented from more than minimal exposure to the project. Thus, Sam Yette, special assistant to Mr. Shriver, director of the civil rights division, and Negro, who should logically have had a great deal to do with a project accused of overinvolvement in civil rights, hardly knew anything about CDGM at all. His office was seriously underinvolved in each event that transpired in the drama.

Sam constantly urged that his staff be allowed to be more involved in cases suspected of civil rights violations, either one way or the other, but of course his requests weren't heeded. Insistence on civil rights compliance didn't come from the aroused hearts of OEO leadership or from a White House group dedicated to achieving justice in the United States. It came from a good feel for public relations, the tune of the times, political pressure, and self-image as an institution representing social change. So why would decision-makers give much power to a civil rights division? CDGM was never brought to Sam Yette's division as a violation case! Maybe because CDGM *wasn't* a violations case, and that excuse was a trumped up one, or maybe because it was anticipated that Mr. Yette's staff would interfere with the smoothly billowing assumption that civil rights was bad. Mr. Yette was suspected of being pro-CDGM, though he cautiously and carefully never said so. He had to be kept out of the arena.

Efforts to preserve the party line and to punish those who deviated from it were carried so far that if an OEO staff member predicted that a given project staff would do something that didn't sit well with the "Poverty Tsar," the OEO staff member who made the prediction was considered the *cause* of project staff's "insubordination," once it occurred. As often happens in the jurisdiction of a tsar, the guilty party (project director) was beheaded. So also were those affiliated with him to the extent of thinking about him and predicting about him, and those who were in easy reach. Because Bill Haddad and Bob Clampitt of the OEO inspection office continually advised Mr. Shriver that the "senior staff" of CDGM would probably resign if OEO forced the impossible move, it is thought that they were seen by top-of-the-agency officials as the cause of the ensuing insurrection. Bob Clampitt, because he had often talked directly with Tom Levin, was accused of conspiring with Levin to go around Shriver. He eventually left OEO.

Those who were left handling the project after this conscious or unconscious, organized or impromptu screening, were the reliable gradualists who, pro or con, could be counted on to keep political and administrative thoughts crisply uppermost in their thinking and behavior. As one observer explained, "they're liberal schmiberal, as long as they do the conservative thing. They fancy themselves as liberals, and *are* next to the racists and routines they come in contact with, but just put them next to people who know what they're doing and look how they look!"

They knew far less about any of their projects, even their famous and controversial ones, than oversaturated project participants assumed they did. Therefore, much of what Mr. Shriver, as director of OEO, and Mr. Sugarman, as deputy director of Head Start, were given credit for astutely conceiving of, or were disliked for subterraneanly conniving about, was actually done by them quite accidentally, and with the clear conscience that ignorance can provide.

Much that was perceived by Negroes to be intentional insult on the part of whites was in reality caused by the even more insulting fact that whites were simply unaware of them or their probable reactions. Similarly, much that was perceived by CDGM as intentional destructiveness on the part of OEO was in reality caused by the even more disturbing fact that OEO simply didn't consider CDGM very significant. This was caused by the still more alarming fact that OEO didn't understand the nature or importance of the factors that made CDGM unique. And *this* was because OEO, as a body, didn't understand the essence of community action. Mr. Gonzales of the inspection office told us he was just doing a routine first stage review. "We treated CDGM just like any other project," said many people. CDGM wondered why. Since OEO knew CDGM was a radical departure from the orthodox Southern program and politics, and that it would run into ogres of every sort, why did it not do more than wait for the attacks and then cope with them? Why didn't it prepare, *not* just to defend the points under attack, but to defend qualities of the program skipped over by the attackers? *They* were the qualities that would have made the project appeal to liberal groups.

"There are many conservative forces bearing down on us," said OEO staff members at all levels of the organization. CDGM wondered why, then, didn't OEO, not in regard to CDGM, alone, but in regard to all its good projects, in order to survive at all, concentrate on imaginative ally-building among the poor, minority groups, and liberals, instead of aiming all their wooing and public relations work at conservative audiences? We felt that OEO's condescending attitude toward the poor caused it to fail to develop what could have been a valuable alliance in times of political stress.

"We can't challenge the assumptions and actions of the agency," said many of the underlings and middlings, who knew most about CDGM. Why? wondered CDGM. The world only has the assumptions it has today because somebody challenged the assumptions that surrounded him yesterday. We only have actions because individuals make decisions leading to them. We were depressed by OEO's small-minded view of personal effectiveness.

"We cannot tolerate any abuses," said the accountants. "There's no excuse for that kind of sloppiness," said Mr. Heller of the legal division. Joan Bowman, CDGM historian, wrote: ". . . traditionally, where southern Negroes have rubbed up against the federal bureaucracy, it has been at the intercession of whites who have assisted in filling out forms for social security benefits, or public assistance. The experience of southern Negroes administering their own federal programs was unique, and that experience as profoundly radical and revolutionary as planning and implementing ideals of community education. But to see that it works requires a level of patience and indulgence which flies in the face of 'fiscal responsibility.' It would require blowing a little money on people who have never been considered responsible enough to be trusted in these areas.

"For all the radical tone and quality of the Washington rhetoric about HEAD START and the war on poverty, the humane perspective is lacking; indeed the very imagination to conceive ways to instill these training methods in common people has never emerged. There are a myriad of demands upon any organization which accepts federal funds; one of the most difficult to implement is organizational practices to insure sound fiscal management. There is nothing discriminatory or irrational about these demands: in effect they insist that the taxpayers' funds shall be dispensed with integrity and honesty that can be demonstrated. 'Fiscal responsibility,' however, has become a weapon in the hands of the cynical, those who applaud our spending $1 million per day to wage destruction upon a Southeast Asian countryside and whine about pilferage of toys from a HEAD START center. And the federal government can afford to tolerate no instances of irresponsibility or mismanagement, especially where it embarks upon the sensitive or controversial."[30]

There were important men at OEO who intended to be helpful, but there were a lot of troops, lieutenants, and captains in the field. OEO was coming up before the Appropriations Committee in the fall, and there was a lot of pressure from Senator Stennis. CDGM thought that

[30] From Joan Bowman's as yet unpublished book on the South.

OEO should get its own infamously disordered house straightened out before it landed so hard on ours, but of course, this had nothing to do with the issue.

The issue was that OEO's short-term goal for the poverty program in Mississippi (a preschool program) had collided resoundingly with its long-term goal for the poverty program in Mississippi, and with the goal of CDGM leaders. The Administration's long-term goal was to strengthen moderate leaders and force a change of leadership in the state. The Mississippi Democrats were of little use to President Johnson. In the 1964 election they had voted 80 percent for Goldwater. There was no clash as long as the government mistook CDGM for moderates, and for Movement people who would move right toward moderation, and who would accept leadership from the moderates if put under enough pressure. But when the Administration discovered that the goals and values of those running CDGM were different from its own unrevealed but real goals for this large poverty project, an explosion occurred. There was no inconsistency in OEO's behavior in terms of its own long-term goal. There was only inconsistency in terms of the government's short-term goal and our goal: OEO was placed in the absurd and embarrassing position of shooting down its best Head Start, in order to wrest power from the poor and the rapid reformers, and try to get it into the hands of moderate Mississippi whites. Besides, something dramatic had to be done to placate Senator Stennis. He controlled the committee through which emergency appropriations for the war in Vietnam had to pass. Two days after the Mary Holmes midnight ultimatum, an emergency appropriation, which had been lodged in the senator's committee for weeks, was released. This confirmed staff suspicions that the fortunes of the war and of CDGM were intricately linked through the senator.

The Administration decided to throw bones to the no-change, minimal-implementation-of-mandates programs run by status quo Mississippians, and to keep the spectacular-change, maximum-things CDGMians at bay for as long as possible, while it hurriedly worked on a third, "final solution" alternative.

On July 18, moderate whites and Negroes, with the blessing of the Democratic National Committee, held a meeting to form a statewide middle-of-the-road political force in Mississippi. They called themselves the Mississippi Democratic Congress. The Democratic National Committee sent one of its staff, Don Ellinger, to the meeting to promise the group support and assistance from the national Democratic Party. Among those attending the meeting were moderate regular Mississippi Democratic Party electors and NAACP leaders Aaron Henry and Charles Evers. The Congress elected a wealthy Negro businessman, Charles Young, and a white chairman of the state AFL-CIO, Claude Ramsay, to be co-chairmen. The Jackson *Daily News* noted that "no bids (to attend the meeting) went to "never-never" segregationists or to hard-line integrationist organizations—FDP, SNCC, and COFO." In Mississippi, the Administration was attempting to build a "third force" between two "unacceptable" alternatives.[31]

The poverty program, specifically about twenty million dollars for needy Mississippi, was to be a major tool in building the third force. CDGM was a temporary detention home for militant civil rights groups and movement Negroes, to keep them from feeling frozen out and from causing trouble, while the final solution was brought to fruition. As soon as possible, all poverty monies would go to the white moderates and moderate, middle class, NAACP Negroes. The long-term goal of building a base for a moderate Democratic party, including newly enfranchised Negro voters, a meeting place for the gradualist reformers, had become an immediate goal. The goal of "eradicating poverty," along with the rapid reformers who believed in it, would be fitted in or left out, to whatever degree was compatible with the development of the cautious moderate Democratic party.

* * *

Head Start and the rest of the community action programs *are not* political, Mr. Shriver asserted.

[31] Rosenfield, Gerry, "What Happened to the Mississippi Child Development Group?" *The Movement*, Vol. 2, No. 4, June 1966.

CHAPTER 24

DREAMS AND DRAGONS DIE HARD

IN SPITE OF the antagonisms OEO so effectively polarized and the disillusionment OEO so poignantly produced, it never occurred to most CDGM community people or planning staff that CDGM would not be funded again. Our pecadillos and OEO's pallid palaver about them only caused reanimation and recrudescence on our part. There was a wide range of thought as to when, how easily, and in how significant a form we would be able to continue, but that we *would* continue we never doubted.

Marian Wright said: "It never occurred to me that in spite of all these administrative problems anyone could stop giving us grants. It was unquestionably a wonderful program."

And Dr. Beittel remembers that in addition to clearing up back business, the board's major concern was: "When and how do we get refunded?"

In the same way that the primitive brains of two turtles whose heads have been hacked off cause them to continue to roll their eyes and gulp worms long after the axing has occurred, Tom and I continued to "plan." In doing this, we were unwittingly prejudicing the decision poor people were making as to whether or not to continue—*we* were continuing to think of continuing. So community people thought that CDGM was continuing—that *they* were continuing. We were also taking a huge gamble. It might well have turned out to be leading the people on into a blind alley. *We* weren't planning to stay in Mississippi personally in the fall. Could other instigators be found? Or would the poor people be left in the lurch with plans and no technical assistance? We had no right to proceed. But we did, because the only alternative was to make, unwittingly again, the *opposite* decision for people. By *not* planning we would have been influencing the people *not* to plan: to let the project die in its tracks.

As Tom Levin had been "relieved" of all other duties, he was free to spend most days and evenings at community meetings, community committee meetings, and center staff meetings, discussing problems and plans with local people. August was the month I did most of the planning reported earlier. I chased district coordinators for reports on each center and general ideas of how to improve and add to the program. I "pumped" most traveling staff either by talking with them, or by studying reports they were writing on special projects or individual centers, and extracting clues for the future from them. I finished the huge chart I had sprawled all over my bedroom wall, which compiled all information we had on any community and which made some kind of over-all view possible. Through the Newsletter I conducted a massive campaign to elicit the thinking of community people, and of noncommunity people who had been working full time in centers. The material gathered in these various ways, combined with the hundreds of verbal and written community reports we collected at the August 28 statewide meeting, and the material gathered through a letter sent from John Mudd and Gordon Wilcox to communities, formed the basis of the preliminary proposal Tom wrote for communities to criticize, amend, rewrite, or ratify at a later date, before it was redone by John and me and submitted to OEO later in the fall for a second grant.

The majority of the Movement leaders and their morose, monosyllabic minions and myrmidons, in or outside CDGM, had little to offer during this period except mordant criticism, curses, and condemnations about the way in which poor people were being manipulated and ignored by OEO, the board, and Central Staff. However, I believe we did more to comb communities for facts, dreams, and directions than was generally done in "community action" programs—including in the Movement itself. In the Movement, workers made plans pretty independently from the communities in which they worked. They held innumerable meetings in which poor people were pushed to talk interminably. But the views they were urged to voice were those prefavored by meeting planners. Once they had found local voices to serve as a vehicle for their will, and had encouraged a lot of ventilation to cover their own point of view with a palatable crust of "democratic" appearances, they enforced their preconclusions somewhat tyrannically—a phenomenon with which the nation, a few years later, became familiar.

At no point did CDGM deceive communities about the political perils we faced, though the wishes of some poor people clouded their ability to see the perils and caused them to deceive themselves about how easy it would be to get refunded. We tried to explain the situation as it evolved. We talked in simple terms. We tried to start people acknowledging, pinpointing, and planning out problems. Newsletter number three, which came out before the Mary Holmes meeting, carried a front page piece summarizing why Senator Stennis didn't care for CDGM, and why OEO did. It also urged community people to plan:

WHAT DO YOU WANT TO DO WITH
YOUR CENTER
IN SEPTEMBER?????

We only have money from Washington till the end of August. Head-Start was planned in Washington only for the summer. No Head-Start will have money to continue in the fall. But there are many other Federal programs that give money for educational projects.
Some of the programs are new. We are trying to find out as fast as the Government announces them what they are. Others are going on now, and we are trying to find out as fast as possible if we are eligible: if they will allow us to apply.
What would you like best to do if we could do it? While Edwards is busy trying to find out what the choices are, it is very, very important that you in the communities find out from each other what you would like to do.

Run Centers as they are now with as many resource people as will stay?
Run them without resource people?
Take younger children also?
Take older children after school to help them study and do extra activities?
Have adult education classes?

PLEASE THINK ABOUT WHAT YOU WILL DO WITH YOUR CENTER IF WE DO GET MORE MONEY FROM WASHINGTON

Will you have volunteer adults supervise them so mothers can bring young children to play?
Will you run like you do now but only on Saturday and for free?
Will you close it?

IF WE GET MONEY FROM WASHINGTON, BUT IT TAKES A FEW MONTHS TO COME THROUGH, WHAT WILL YOU DO WHILE YOU ARE WAITING? KEEP IT OPEN? CLOSE DOWN AND RE-OPEN? WILL YOU HAVE TO MOVE?

PROBLEMS IN RUNNING CENTERS: CENTRAL STAFF

Running this project is new for all of us. It is hard for the staff at Edwards. We are just learning how to do it. Payroll has been hard to work out for more than a thousand people. Many checks have gone out on time. Some have not. This should be all straightened out by now too. It seems like it has been forever that we have been trying to solve these big problems, but we should remember that it has been less than a month, really. Even with the things that have gone wrong, we have gotten many supplies to many people in many places in that first month. We have gotten paychecks to many people. We have gotten facilities money and petty cash and transportation money and food money to many people and many places.

Central staff is learning fast and making good progress. Apologies for the trouble. We hope we can serve you better from now on. Because there is only one reason for Central staff to exist: and that is to serve the communities. To serve you in your very fine work.

PROBLEMS IN RUNNING CENTERS: COMMUNITY STAFF

Running this project is new for all of us. It is hard for community staff and community committees. There are many difficult problems. It is hard for a new Committee that has never worked together before to know how much they are right in doing and how much they should leave for the staff at the Center to do. It is hard for a Committee to know how to handle it if one of their friends or neighbors or relatives who is working in the Center is not doing a good job. The most important thing is that none of us hide the problems and the troubles. We can't be too polite and hide the difficulties. We need to face problems, talk them out, make a plan and take action.

If you
like your
center write
a letter and
tell what it
means to you.
Tell us special
things you do good.
Write it to:
Newsletter
Child Development Group
Edwards, Mississippi
We will print it or send a copy to Washington.

Issue number 4 of the Newsletter went out with this flyer stapled to the front of it.

Today! Today! Today!

Send News & Evaluations
to:
Polly Greenberg
Box 348
Edwards, Mississippi

I'd learned some things in nineteen years of sporadic or intensive partnership with poor people in one project or another. Perhaps the most valuable was: If at first you don't succeed in getting genuine participation on basic parts of the program, try, try again. The task may seem onerous and the obstacles obdurate, but lapidaries can't be laggards, and lapidaries of human beings we were.

Evaluations began pouring in, hundreds each day, flooding our constantly diminishing staff. Tom and I read them all, and were excited:

"We are concerned with a Child's Care Program and an Adult Education Class."

* * *

"We badly need a medical center."

* * *

"I have a small amount of land (50 ft. wide 40 ft. long) that I would let the children play on free of charge. Yours truly, Gartha L. Lodge."

* * *

"I am an Aide and my name is Shirley Williams. I am employed at the Kingston Center in Laurel. . . .

"Our only problem is our health-aide have so much work to do and she is suppose to work as a trainee also. We would like to have another trainee and let her work only as a Health-Aide.

"We would also like to have all full-time cooks. because after they finish cooking it is time to leave and they don't have time to show you where the food belongs and they don't have time to put it where it belongs.

"We are planning to get a secretary but up until now Mrs. Gore have worked as a trainee, and she have been the secretary too, and I think she have done a very good job.

"Mr. Gore our chairman have done a wonderful job and has been very patient.

"P. S. I don't know whether the things Stennis said about Head Start is true but I know he don't want to see our children progress."

* * *

The most touching response to the 1965 evaluation was this one. In a packet of stapled-together letters from parents collected by teachers, came a blank piece of paper from Pascagoula, with this note paper-clipped to it from one of the teachers: "Ann Lisa's mother handed in this empty paper for her evaluation at our meeting. I asked her didn't she want to write on it. She whispered in my ear: 'I can't write, but I want my paper to go in because I want Mr. Shriver to know I am evaluating.' So I send it along to you, Mrs. Polly Green, so you will know that the parents are with us all the way, to the best they can. We know you being you you will appreciate."

* * *

To me the most discouraging feature of the summer, except for OEO's position, was the helplessness, the narrowness, the resourcelessness of many of the out-of-state resource teachers. What a sad, silent commentary on the "successful" portions of "the system" it was, that a person with "good" education and enough concern to spend a summer in a small sweltering Mississippi town felt as unable to help with the problems he accurately noted, as did, for example, the young man excerpts of whose letter appear below. Our world, when it manages to produce people who care even enough to make themselves present at all, which is rarely, seems to turn out a high percentage of cynics who have very little inner strength to draw upon.

"*Evaluation of CDGM* (1) There are various fictions which embarrass me and kinder honest communication. I am a 'resource teacher,' although I'm experienced neither in teaching nor in dealing with preschool children. . . .

"Several times this summer I've been on the verge of quitting—not because of other people's shortcomings, but because I lack the skills required to fulfill the role of 'resource teacher' as defined by CDGM. . . .

"One question I face is why *I* should be here, rather than a local person who could do what I'm doing. It's hard to answer. I'm white, and that in itself is important for the children. In addition, I'm more receptive to progressive ideas than the average local person, and can therefore help my trainee and center to adjust to certain foreign concepts. And my commitment is not diluted by monetary considerations, something which sours some of our local people.

"Nevertheless, I feel that the structured roles of 'resource teacher' and 'trainee,' with their salary differential, smack of hypocrisy when I consider the real situation.

"(2) When we first got supplies they came too fast for teachers and children to absorb. . . .

"(3) Our center has very little parent support. They seem quite passive about the whole thing.

"(4) Money is one of the big corrupters. I feel that salaries should be lowered to the point where the job would not be very attractive financially, and that the difference between that salary and the present one should be paid to any charities (*e.g.*, NAACP) which the employee wishes, in his name. In this way he would enjoy the community prestige coming from being a philanthropist, the community would get some help, and the personnel would not be corrupted so much. . . .

"(5) The outside teachers (mostly white) have had very little social interaction with the local people. We come from different backgrounds and different generations, but it would be nice if a local teacher could invite 1 or 2 of us home to dinner sometimes. I wonder whether local people know that some of us outsiders would like to get to know them, but we don't know how. It's a shame that we outsiders (mainly white) form a little clique of our own. . . ."

Luckily, many of the out-of-state resource teachers apparently could make more satisfactory contributions toward alleviating the overwhelming needs around them. A local trainee reported on *her* out-of-state resource teacher:

"I am Mrs. Susan E. Stokes. I am a Trainee at the Palmers Crossing Center. I begin work at the center on July 12, 1965. I was acquainted with my Resource Teacher about two days after. Mr. Willie W. Pritchett of Brooklyn, New York. He is experienced Musician and public school teacher. I enjoyed working with him very much. He had very much to offer. . . . He taught the children songs and never was to buisy to take out time with them. He was always buisy even when the children was out for lunch or snack or rest period. Cleaning around the class room, or emptying paper waste baskets or doing something on playground. He would always give me ideas about different children personalities how to work with the particular to get him acquainted with the others children. We work together and kids would draw and cut out different thing paste and paint on other sheets we tacked on the wall of our class room. Seem like he worked just as hard or harder, because as he played the piano he never refuse not to play some of the children's request even how wet with perspiration, and how closely they was cuddled around him and the piano. He was always pleasent in entering the class room. That is at all times. You can enjoy people with such personality."

We pulled ideas out of people, and we developed our own in response to those of the people. Tom Levin wrote outlines for many proposals.

One such proposal outlined Tom's recommendations for three modes of operation in forthcoming CDGM grants. He described one kind of community commonly found in CDGM, which had enough organic integrity, natural leadership, and skills to organize, obtain approval, and operate a regular Community Action Program (CAP). He wrote of autonomy for those naturally affiliated communities ready for it.

The second mode of operation he suggested applied to those communities with some satisfactory CDGM experience, but without enough skills and leadership to sustain preschool projects entirely autonomously. He recommended that they take over fiscal and administrative responsibilities, but continue to draw on some sort of a central CDGM for certain technical skills in teaching and special projects. He wrote that these centers would proceed as very well run nursery school cooperatives. They would be semiautonomous.

The third mode would encompass a small group of "old" centers banding together to keep a small scale centralized CDGM going. It could continue to pick up raw new communities from among the many requests we'd received since summer began.

Another purpose of keeping a small, new-membered CDGM alive would be to develop special projects. The first would be an extended health program to follow up CDGM children. Tom detailed a plan in which CDGM would contract with the University of Mississippi Medical Center, in consultation with U.S. Public Health Service personnel. The latter would provide five mobile vans, especially adapted to preschool work. The former would staff them with licensed physicians. They would have a regular itinerary and a regular program of follow-up for former CDGM children. They would be required to abide by the full meaning of the civil rights compliance agreement.

A second project Tom suggested was a statewide tutorial service for our graduates. He thought this would provide very important research on the effect of continued stimulation and advanced program material.

The third project orbiting around CDGM would be an adult education program. It would be centered around those services important to a community education concept.

Tom outlined in his proposal a tripartite structure to carry out these ideas. A Mississippi college would be adequately funded to set up a Department of Community Education. Teachers for the various projects described above, and for others described by Tom verbally, would be trained and educated to the point of acquiring college degrees at this Community Education Extension. Courses would be given for a full eight hours a day every third week, so people could work and learn "on-the-job," yet could get a degree in three years time. Various affiliated Northern and Western colleges would encourage instructors, professors, department heads, etc., to serve at least one year in the central Mississippi teacher training program, on pay of course.

Another of Tom's proposals, each of which was fully spelled out and beautifully written, was an outline for a training program in early childhood education. This proposal grew out of two concurrent historical problems: first, the shrinkage of jobs, the displacement of teachers due to integration, and the need for new career opportunities for Negroes in the South; and second, the paucity in the South of either nursery or kindergarten systems and teachers to man them.

Tom wrote that a program could be developed that would combine on-the-job training, service to the community, and academic upgrading. It would be divided into two parts. First, people could receive supervision as they functioned in Head Start teaching positions, and could accumulate both experience and academic credit. This would be like traditional "practice teaching."

Second, every third week, program participants would attend a five-day training seminar. This seminar, requiring forty hours of participation, would be the equivalent of the completion of one three-credit course. These in-residence seminars would be conducted in cooperation with an institution of higher education chartered to give either Bachelors or Masters degrees in education.

The program could be undertaken with joint sponsorship and funding. A group of Negro colleges could act as the host colleges for the seminars, providing facilities and some instructors. A group of national colleges with departments of early childhood education could supply specialized educators. This would have the advantage of bringing new ideas and techniques to both participants and host colleges. The U.S. Office of Education could provide the funds, direction, and supervision for instructors, transportation, and salaries. OEO could provide salaries for participants. Further funds might be available through the Manpower Retraining Act.

Issue five of the Newsletter was put out at the end of August. It was a summary of the summer—an encouragement for the future:

CHILD DEVELOPMENT GROUP
of
MISSISSIPPI
NEWSLETTER
issue #5

A LETTER TO YOU FROM TOM LEVIN:

A letter to all those who have made CDGM possible—

Dear Friends,

This summer in Mississippi we have built upon the struggles of past years. We built CDGM upon the ashes of churches where poor people spoke out for equality. We built CDGM upon the bodies of Negro and white workers for the poor who were killed because they would not stay quietly at home to live in peace with injustice. We built CDGM upon the hunger and humiliation of men and women who were not allowed to work at a decent job because they would not give up being free. We built upon hundreds of years of the suffering and courage of mothers and fathers throughout the state of Mississippi who wanted something human and decent for their children and themselves. If we are proud of what we have done we must remember that we could not have schools run by the poor people, schools with black and white working together, if a place in history had not been won for us by brave men and women before this summer—men and women who said loudly and clearly "All Men Must Be Free." We have a large debt to these brave people of the "Movement." We can only pay it by never being satisfied until all men in Mississippi have political, social, and economic freedom. This summer in Mississippi we took on new debts as well. We worked hard to give over six thousand children a headstart toward being proud and free. We owe them our hand from now on. The children have started but we must go with them into their new schools and we must say, "These are free children of free people. Treat them with respect and they will learn and grow to make a better world for us all." In our homes we must treat each child with dignity and respect so he will learn from his parents how free people are treated. How we treat our children will help them know how the world should treat them.

We showed the whole country this summer that poor people could plan and run their own schools. People talked a lot about poor people running their own centers but they didn't trust the poor. In CDGM we did what others talked about but were afraid to do—every center was run by its own community committee! This summer in a few short weeks, 86 centers were organized, committees chosen, buildings found and repaired, community staff recruited and selected, transportation and meals arranged, and hundreds of problems solved by the communities themselves. From this work we have come to another debt. We must keep our community committees representative of the poor, and we must all take responsibility to see that the committees are not taken away from us by tyrants of the outside or the inside.

Over 1200 people worked for CDGM this summer. Those who have worked cannot feel their job is over. All the staff must think now how they can learn to work better for the communities in the future. We must learn from our mistakes so that we have better ways to be educators, administrators, and specialists. We must always remember we worked for the poor. The jobs must go first to the poor. We cannot settle for the easy way of hiring people who are not poor because they have had more of a chance for more education and work experience. We also cannot reject help from specialists who we need because they are not poor. That is false pride. We have to balance out what will be the most help for the most poor over the long term.

The Office of Economic Opportunity acted with courage and understanding when they gave CDGM the money to run this summer program. If we want a government, and government programs like OEO to keep courage, we must work to make the government truly our government. We must register and then vote with care and thought, always thinking, "Who will help the people most? Who has listened to us in the past? Who will listen to our needs in the future?" If we expect them to listen we must tell them. We must write and tell the representatives in Washington, the President, and the government departments what we want. We have to sit down together and talk about how we can make them hear us and do things we want them to do.

Our Board and the Council of Neighborhood Centers must learn from the mistakes and victories of this summer how a long term program for the poor can best be run. They must listen to the people in the communities and the people must not let things be run for them. If we want our program to stay a program of the poor then the representatives we have chosen must hear from us regularly and we must know what they are doing—and be ready to help with our work whenever we can.

To those of you I will not see before I leave for my home, I must say goodbye with this letter. To all of you I give my thanks for the opportunity to do work in a cause that has given me a feeling of deep pride, for I have worked with free men toward building a free society.

(signed)

Tom Levin
Director CDGM

This newsletter tried to urge and goad people into *thinking:*

Which adults in your community do you admire most? What kind of people are they?
Are they active in community affairs?
Or do they sit home and refuse to participate?
Are they daring and brave and willing to try something new?
Or do they prefer to do as they have always done?
Do they ask questions and think and arrive at their own decisions?
Or do they believe whatever the man says and accept it as the unalterable truth?
Do they have imaginative suggestions for solutions to problems and constructive actions to take?

Or do they feel that they haven't enough brains and imagination to try? If the grownups you admire are active in community affairs, you may want to have children that are active in Center, school, and home affairs. An active, interested child grows into an active, interested adult. This means lots to do. Lots of stories, games, trips, kinds of food, an ever changing number and kind of things to keep a child's body and mind occupied.

If the grownups you admire sit home and refuse to participate you may want to have children sit at the Center or school or home not participating. Waiting. Killing time. A passive, bored, accepting child grows into a passive, bored, accepting grownup. A beaten child grows into a beaten adult. Which kind of adult do you want? So which kind of child? So what will you do with him every day, many hours?

If the grownups you admire are daring and brave and willing to try something new, you may want to give children opportunities to be daring, brave, and try something new. For a child, being daring may mean talking in front of a group about something he is interested in. Being brave may mean leaving his mother to go to your program. Trying something new may mean finger painting for the first time, or swimming, or trying, nervously, to learn to read. A child who is offered help with things that to him, at his age level, seem brave and daring and new, will grow into a grownup who takes chances and tries new things, new ideas, new ways of life, also.

If the grownups you admire prefer to do as they have always done, you may want to have children do as they have always done: romp and wrestle, sit and doodle. You may want to teach them to behave quietly, do as you say immediately or get a whipping, follow orders instead of choose and think for themselves. A child who is taught all his childhood to do nothing special, nothing different, to feel that life is too much for him, will grow up to be a grownup who thinks and feels that he can't do anything special, can't do anything different than it is, that life and the man are too much for him. What do you want? Raise your children as you wish, but think about what you want. Think about if you are doing things with your children, daily, yourself, to get what you want.

If the grownups you admire ask questions and think and arrive at their own decisions, you may want to talk with your children a great deal as they eat and play and wash, and dress, and come home from school. You may wish to ask them questions and give them interesting answers. You may want to give them a choice of two activities, or two ideas, or two kinds of food, or two places to go, or two sets of clothes to put on, and let them decide for themselves. Children who get talked to and respected and who are encouraged to think their own answers, grow into adults who talk up and are respected and think their own answers.

If the grownups you admire believe whatever someone says and accept it as the permanent, definite truth, you may want to cut your children off and tell them, "Because I told you so." You may want to put them down. You may want to use your switch. Children who are made to feel small, will grow up to be adults who feel small. Small feeling adults don't change the world; they bow to it in fear. What kind of grownups do you want? Then what will you do with your children every day, every way, to make them feel important and big? What can he do that you can praise him for? Set the table? Wash out something? Sweep? Carry wood? Bring you field flowers? Make you something pretty at the Center or school? Take care of a littler one? Sing a cute song? What can he do that you can tell him you're proud of him for? What can he say that you can talk with him about and draw him out?

If the grownups you admire have imaginative suggestions for solutions to problems and constructive actions to take, you may want to have children with a lot of imagination and chance to solve problems of their own. This might mean dress-up play, or making puppets, or playing dolls, or playing with toy trucks, or making something fancy with the Tinker Toys, or other imaginative play. Imaginative play is different from running around play. You may want to help him solve his problems wisely. For a small child these problems might be things like someone taking his puzzle. (What can he do? Hit? Let the other child take it? Ask you to get it back? Tell the other child he can have a turn later? Which would be the wise solution?) A child who gets help and encouragement in using his imagination really settling down and using his imagination fully, and a child who gets help in settling his own problems of being a small child in a Center or school or home, will grow up to be an adult who also shows imagination and wisdom when troubles come.

The way you live
with your child today,
determines the way
he will live his life
tomorrow.

The newsletter included several letters from community people to President Johnson like this one:

people community center
Rt 1 Box 56
Durant, Miss.
August 16/65

Dear President Johnson

We the poor negro people in Mississippi, need your support. The negro people need jobs and better education. Mr. Stennis does not represent us. he knows we never had the opportunity to lives in decent homes or educate our children. We don't believe that Mr. Stennis, neither his children, would like to live in Mississippi under conditions that we have to live. We would like for him to think about if he were a poor negro and live under these conditions not being allowed to have freedom of speech. We do not feel that Mr. Stennis should try to take away the Headstart opportunities from our children because it is the best and only program that has ever been in Mississippi to educate negro children and train the adults. This Headstart program has taken the little children out of the shade trees in the cotton fields where they sit all day long, the parents work from sunup to sun down, and half fed. And this is why we feel that CDGM project Headstart is one of the best things that could happen to poor people. Mr. Stennis knows that this type of problem exists, but he is trying to block every opportunity for our race to educate our children. So they may grow up able to make a better life for themselves we feel like we need a poor man to serve Mississippi someone who knows the needs of poor people. The rich man don't work for no one but the rich man.

The newsletter included comments made in letters by several distinguished visitors. From a banker and economist:

> . . . I visited a number of the school centers, spending time not only in the centers but with the parents and staff people during the evenings, in an attempt to appraise their work and attitudes. . . .
> It seems to me that the accomplishments already made by the program in terms of the philosophy of Operation Headstart and the President's program against poverty set an example of what can be done. . . .

From a doctor who visited, and who had worked in Mississippi the previous summer:

> I am convinced that the program you developed is nothing short of miraculous— Remember I was in Mississippi last year and am in a position to compare what I saw this year with the horrors last time. . . .
> Congratulations on your superhuman accomplishment!

We printed a letter from Sargent Shriver to Tom announcing OEO's intention of sending a Head Start flag to the CDGM Valewood center as a tribute to the poor people of the area who lost only one day of operation after "the disgraceful burning of the Head Start Center."

The newsletter concluded:

> WILL WASHINGTON ALLOW THIS TO CONTINUE BEING A PROGRAM RUN BY POOR PEOPLE? OR WILL THEY FORCE US TO PUT IN MIDDLE CLASS NEGROES AND TOMS AND MORE OUT-OF-STATE PEOPLE? WE PRAY THAT THEY WILL RECOGNIZE THE BEAUTIFUL AND MORE EXCELLENT, RATHER THAN WEAKER AND MORE FALSE. IT WILL NOT BE A TRULY PEOPLE'S PROJECT IF THE PEOPLE IT IS FOR DO NOT RUN IT. WE HAVE FAITH THAT WASHINGTON, WITH ALL THE PRESSURES IT HAS FROM THE OTHER DIRECTION, WILL KNOW THIS.
> WILL OUR OWN BOARD OF DIRECTORS LEARN TO BECOME STRONG AND KNOWLEDGEABLE ABOUT THIS PROJECT AND ABOUT THE COMMUNITIES IT REPRESENTS? WILL THEY GIVE WISE DIRECTION AND FIRM LIAISON WITH WASHINGTON? WE PRAY THAT OUR BOARD WILL BE A PEOPLE'S BOARD AND THAT IT WILL DO WHAT IS BEST FOR COMMUNITY PROGRESS. WE HAVE FAITH THAT OUR BOARD WILL WORK GRACIOULY AND REASONABLY WITH WASHINGTON, BUT WILL NOT YIELD IN FEAR TO DESTRUCTIVE (BECAUSE NAIVE) REQUIREMENTS.
> WILL OUR CENTRAL STAFF BE ABLE TO DO SOMETHING SENSIBLE AND EFFECTIVE ABOUT ITS WEAKNESSES SO IT CAN SERVE THE COMMUNITIES MORE RICHLY, MORE DEEPLY, MORE PROMPTLY, AND MORE GRACIOUSLY IN THE FUTURE? WE PRAY THAT THEY WILL BE ABLE TO OVERCOME PERSONAL AND ADMINISTRATIVE PROBLEMS SO THEY CAN ACHIEVE THIS GOAL, FOR THE PEOPLE OF MISSISSIPPI NEED ALL THE FRIENDS AND TECHNICAL ASSISTANCE THEY CAN GET IF THEY ARE TO RUN TRULY EXCELLENT PROGRAMS FOR THEMSELVES.

This is the end of the first baby steps of this program. Let's make it the beginning of the second step. Let's get rid of lazy aides and keep the active, kind aides. Let's get rid of trainees who are not working well with children, and replace them with other community people who have the ability to learn to teach these very little children. Let's have only resource people who work hard and have good ideas for bringing out the children and bringing out the community people. Let's get rid of local chairmen who run the show by themselves, and elect chairmen, like most of those we now have, who want to work with staff, parents, committee members, and community. Let's get rid of committee members who do not take a busy part in the work to be done. Let's not allow any Central or District staff who think more of their own comfort or "principles" than of the needs and wishes of the community people. Let's have administrators and accountants and secretaries who understand the vital importance of them following up on little necessary things. Let's get rid of any Board member who isn't trying hard to keep up with what is going on across the state using his best judgment in big matters. If we don't get more money from Washington, let's run anyway!

Dear Lord,
Please give us strength not to attack each other. Strength to do the hard work, even if we have to do it free. Strength to bear the state and Washington politics. Strength against those who wish to see us fail in the communities. If we continue to help ourselves as we have this summer of 1965, please help us go on with our struggles to be free.

The Jackson *Daily News* continued to shout encouragement. In September, as I drove my packed station wagon full of girls and possessions through town on my way northward, the headline caught my eyes:

MISUSE OF FEDERAL FUNDS IS REPORTED
Mt. Beulah Total May Hit $300,000

. . . *those who wish to see us fail.*

BOOK TWO:

Sisyphus

PART V

Nothing Left But a Flock of Wild Turkeys

THE UNFUNDED PERIOD IN THE LONG, COLD WINTER OF 1965-1966. HOW CDGM SURVIVED AND GREW IN THE COMMUNITIES WITHOUT GOVERNMENT FUNDS. HOW POOR PEOPLE BEGAN TO BUD AS SPIRITED TEACHER SUPERVISORS, COMMUNITY ORGANIZERS, AND ADMINISTRATORS. HOW A SKELETON CENTRAL STAFF HELD THINGS TOGETHER, AND HOW THE WHOLE OF CDGM WRUNG WATER FROM A ROCK TO GET RE-FUNDED.

CHAPTER 25

WRAP-UP AND BUILDUP

John Mudd, acting director

CDGM WAS A rather different animal in September, with no federal grant (endorsement, resources); the resource teacher in most centers missing (the out-of-state element); all five district staff members gone (the SNCC tie to recent history and to community people); the entire Central Staff of forty (Movement, professional, and intellectual influences) gone, except for four or five local middle-class trainees and a few local poor people who clung to their paying jobs till such time as OEO should close them out; and a new acting director whose huge dogs chased each other round and round through our circular office rooms. OEO was paying six Central Staff members and three secretaries to wrap up CDGM. No one in communities was any longer on payroll.

John Mudd signed his letters "Acting Director" until the second grant months later. In the fall he hesitantly considered himself a very tentative, temporary administrative street sweeper, left holding the broom after the curious circus left town. He had an exceedingly different task before him from the one Tom Levin had faced as founding director five or six months earlier. Tom had been free to create, out of his own fertile imagination and extraordinary skill, a fantastic bridge between the best of the Movement and a new, flexible federal program, with lots of freedom-high participants breathing life into his plans. John Mudd was condemned to unscrambling a fantastic administrative mess with lots of disapproving OEO officials breathing down his neck. Tom had given birth to a beautiful nation-shaking creature, and was terribly proud of himself. John suddenly found himself wondering warily what kind of an ugly duckling had been dropped at his doorstep. He was unsure of what Tom had done, and of what he himself could do with what Tom had done.

During his first two months in CDGM John's two chief advisers were his sponsors Art Thomas and Marian Wright of the board of directors.

At that time they gave the impression of being relieved to get rid of Tom and not interested in fanning lingering memories of him. Their attention was focused on consolidating CDGM's political holdings and establishing CDGM's credit with liberals in OEO, foundations, and other Northern circles in order to get a new grant, rather than on capitalizing on the summer's discoveries to develop ideas and techniques for more effectively working with community people. Without a grant, they reasoned, there would be no vehicle through which anyone could develop the ideas and techniques for effectively working with poor people. Whether it was because of his insecurity and respect for Art and Marian, with their resulting influence on him, or because of personal feelings of dislike or competition toward Tom, or for altogether different reasons, there is little evidence that John tried to get to know and appreciate Tom and his accomplishments.

Certainly part of John's tendency to let Tom's CDGM rapidly recede into seldom-mentioned graveyard status with an unpleasant aura was his unusual sense of "being democratic." It was vitally important to John to be open to everybody. But in fact he was necessarily very busy with ledgers and budget sheets in the director's office at Mt. Beulah. The "everybody" he was open to was those individuals who happened to be around on the semiabandoned campus. These tended not to be people from CDGM's poor communities, but either the abovementioned remnants of the summer staff, a few shiftless Movement hangers-on who were not busy working in communities as more productive Movement workers were, irrelevant passers-through who had had a dim, distorted, and desultory peripheral view of CDGM during the summer, and newcomers joining the project. John made an effort to "be democratic," listen to these least of views, and in a "democratic" manner, give them equal weight with views from more informed authentic sources. He wound up in the modestly humble passive position of listening receptively to every kind of criticism of Tom's effort, and withholding comment. Thus, John's perspective of the summer CDGM was lopsided, and much of the heritage that could have been salvaged and passed on from the original dynamic experiment was neither sought nor kept alive through his positive support of it.

John acknowledged that Tom shot off brilliant ideas and was wonderfully creative, but also seemed to accept the Stennis-OEO accusation that Tom had no judgment about administrative systems, overextended the project, was inexperienced in coordination and management, and didn't give much of a damn about that side of CDGM. He was willing to admit that he himself was more skilled in the world of ideas than in the realm of administration, and that every earnest effort he made administratively at this time, and also throughout the second and third grants notwithstanding, he still sometimes gave priority to ideas and their development rather than to mere mindless "efficient administration."

But he was not so willing to credit Tom with equally honest and legitimate choices. He felt that Tom was manipulative and arbitrary, but did not see, as most observers and participants saw, that he too—necessarily and wisely or *un*necessarily and *un*wisely, depending upon the opinion of the individual assessing him—was often manipulative and arbitrary, though in a more modest and offstage manner. Both Tom and John made some critical unilateral decisions, but paradoxically, always for the purpose *and with the effect* of creating *more* opportunities for their clientele to make decisions. John didn't denigrate Tom; he simply avoided mentioning him.

John didn't trust Tom, and said that one big handicap Tom had was that people didn't trust him. If he meant, by "people," Art and Marian, he was making an accurate observation, for surely their lack of trust in him, probably resulting from their frustrated desire to have him under their thumbs, *was* a handicap. If John meant "Movement people," he was also correct. Mississippi Movement people didn't trust "outsiders," and less so whites, as John was soon to find out in a very painful personal way.

However, many of the Movement people did trust Tom—probably because of his background on the Mississippi battlefronts the summer before, and because of his forthright personality—*more* than they ever trusted John, even after two grants full of the latter's hair-raisingly self-sacrificing service. He hadn't "proved" himself at Selma, Philadelphia, and McComb. He came from academia. And he was a person almost everyone at all levels agreed was difficult or impossible to get close to, though it was remarkably easy to get along with him. If John meant "poor people" when he said that people didn't trust Tom, he was pointing to a problem of major and discouraging proportions to all of us who have made the effort to work out something honest together. The people have intelligently and self-preservingly learned to trust no one, and it will take many, many years and many, many positive, varied, human, cheek-to-cheek contacts, before their healthy instincts will allow them to alter this legitimate libidinal learning.

CDGM community people "loved" and "appreciated" Tom as long as their astonishing manna fell through his miraculous hands. For the most part they forgot him the moment he left, though an occasional individual asked fondly after him from time to time. He did not have time to develop deep man-to-man relationships with many community people. When John became the miracle maker, they "loved" and "appreciated" him, in a suitably opportunistic way. John, also, didn't have time to develop real relationships with many individuals in communities. And so it will be with the rest of us, except insofar as we have managed to break through the barrier of boss and employee, white and black, and become just human friends, with warm breath and other bonds between us. The people didn't trust. The victims were not personally loyal to the allies. They *used* us, and so I believe they should have, until many more of us have proved ourselves worthy of long-term trust, loyalty, and true friendship. But I think John *expected* this trust and worked to earn it in a way that Tom did not, because Tom thought trust an unlikely product of the project. Though personally gratifying, he felt it was really not as important as structuring a situation in which people would be stimulated to become engaged with the obstacles confronting them and therefore confronting their young ones. Had Tom been as concerned with what the Movement and Negroes thought of him as John was, it's not likely CDGM would ever have started—launching it required someone to step callously over many bodies.

Not only were the two directors' points of entry and environment in CDGM so different, but they were of two very different backgrounds. Tom was the son of working class Jewish refugees in Brooklyn. He had had an active leadership role in many "radical" labor and political movements before he became prominent in psychoanalysis and in pioneering in the exploration of the role of psychoanalysis in social change. He was a forty-year-old established professional man.

John was the baby of a main-line Philadelphia family; the twenty-six-year-old son of well-to-do and well-known professional parents. He came to CDGM with a BA in political science from Harvard and a great love of classical music. He had been a student in Europe, and was in the process of doing research for a joint Ph.D. degree in political economy and government, for which he had already done two years of graduate work and passed his preliminary exams at Harvard.

In the fall of 1963 John met Bob Moses through his Harvard roommate. John and the roommate were fascinated by some of Bob's ideas, and went to Mississippi in the fall of 1963 to see for themselves what was happening. They went to a Johnson rally in Jackson in which people wandered around in the audience with Kennedy masks on for people to mock. It struck them as a little incongruous. Then they went to Greenwood to the mayor's office. After he had ascertained that they hadn't been "across town," he was very hospitable. He talked to them for days. They were very meek, trying to find out if he and his staff had any positive ideas about social change. Their psychology couldn't admit the possibility of change, so they couldn't consider which paths of change seemed better or worse to them. John, his roommate, and Marian Wright, who was also visiting the state at that time, made contacts at the SNCC office, and spent five days driving around the state, to McComb and elsewhere. John was convinced that he wanted to participate. But how? He didn't think he could add much to the protest efforts—he couldn't march much better than anyone else—but he *had* had a lot of academic training, and he thought maybe he could help out with teaching.

John wrote to Dr. Beittel, who was at that time still president of

Tougaloo College. Tougaloo was still doing a great deal in the race relations field. John proposed that he develop a summer project for students. Dr. Beittel encouraged him. John conceived and directed what turned out to be an extraordinarily exciting project. By word of mouth, John recruited some twenty-five top Harvard professors and graduate students, including Zacharias and Reissman.

At first John thought great teachers, living with the students and surrounding them with their own libraries, music, slews of paperbacks, and overpowering excitement about the intellectual universe, could crack the delusions the students had been learning before. They hadn't mastered what they'd already "had." They didn't read rigorously, or distinguish between academic argument and personal opinion. A lot of confusion and uncertainty stayed hidden under their flippant use of jargon and stock clichés. They retreated before novel insights. Their narrow lives caused them to parrot instead of probe, and blithely accept the views of the instructor without analyzing them.

A lot of the students had never heard of Hitler, and now a professor came down and discussed Potëmkin with them. They read Plato and Kierkegaard. They talked and read about Marx and Weber, Dollard, Bell, John Stuart Mill, Erikson, and Myrdal. They used *Killers of the Dream*. They went into Rousseau and the Russian Revolution. They had a film series with Harvard professor of Philosophy Stanley Cavell leading the discussion, and ten live concerts ranging from Bach to Schönberg. Yosal Rogat, professor of Political Science at Chicago, presented theories of legal decision-making to a seminar on constitutional law. They read plays in the evening—scenes from Brecht and Sartre—everything to excite minds.

By the end of the summer John had made a significant shift. He realized that learning had to be tied in with social action. He saw that the façade of false learning was much more than that; that it was made possible by what society had done to these students. It had made them feel that they couldn't do anything of value, and that academic learning never had any relationship to solving their real life problems, so they accepted irrelevant, memorized things as learning. Why not? So in the spring of 1965, when Tom, Art, I, and others were formulating CDGM, John wrote a research and demonstration training proposal with Marv Hoffman, who had just come to teach at Tougaloo for the spring semester. The proposal was designed to get students involved in community work, train people for new careers, and study what happened to them as they did this.

As is usually the way with imaginatively important progressive ideas, John's proposal was *not* congenial with the goals of the college, which under the new leadership of President Owens, was busily trying to create itself into a baby Brown University. Rather than doing exciting things toward implementing its image as a college connected to its community, the powers and pressures that controlled it had already made a decision to change the image to a more conventional one of academic "excellence." Therefore, this proposal never left the campus, but John Mudd, in disgusted frustration, did.

He went to Batesville to help some Negro farmers run a vegetable cooperative. His chief interest in it was to work with people as they came to grips with an institution—their own institution. He brought the same interest to CDGM. His major interest differed from Tom's. It wasn't the general dynamics of poor people engaging in change. It was people learning to understand and operate the government of their own institution: CDGM. Therefore, CDGM's course veered sharply. After the advent of John, there was far less emphasis on education, child raising, and confrontation between the poor and their present problems. There was far greater emphasis on participating in the running of CDGM, from the ground up to Washington.

From OEO's point of view, CDGM in the fall of 1965 was supposed to be doing two things and was being financially supported to do *only* these two things: wrapping up the summer's administrative leftovers, and wrapping up the children's follow-up medical treatment recommended by doctors during the summer examinations. John Mudd was preoccupied with the former, and paid minimal attention to the latter.

Probably another explanation of why John placed the medical program on the low priority list, besides his administrative busyness, was that it represented people engaging in the problems of their lives, and didn't represent people engaging in CDGM, with the goal of increasing their understanding of governing institutions.

Much of our medical planning seems to have fallen through the wide cracks in the floor boards of CDGM's transitional period. It was never retrieved and expanded during the second grant, and was not picked up again until the third grant in 1967—and then in a more standard manner. Dr. Rosenfield left his directorship of the summer medical program thinking that for all meaningful intents and purposes CDGM had ended. He left two and a half weeks later than he had intended, broke instead of carrying a little needed cash back to California to continue his medical training, and with nothing to show for his summer's efforts but a bad case of bronchitis. He took most of the medical records with him, intending to write final reports. But he got busy, wrote to John, never heard from John, and decided that the medical program must be OK without him.

When Gerry left, the medical program was dumped on a recent college graduate named Dave Fleming. Dave had come to Mississippi during August with a fairly conservative group of Delta Ministry volunteers from Claremont, California. They stayed a month and built a swimming pool. Dave had planned to go to New York "to bum around," but he got interested in CDGM and saw no particular reason to leave.

Gerry left adequate low-scale plans for tying off loose threads. Just before he left, Gerry had hired community people as health coordinators to work for two weeks seeing that recommended treatments were carried out. He hired them for about half of the centers and left a list of others to be hired. There wasn't any clear plan for them. Everything was left up in the air. Nobody told Dave anything about the summer health aides, or that there had been training workshops for them, or even that CDGM was a training program and that workshops were the training method. He was just groping his way around, trying to help. Some of the health coordinators were the summer health aides, but centers had closed and their staffs had disbanded, and some health aides couldn't continue, so some health coordinators were completely new to CDGM. Some were paid for not doing anything but sit around for two weeks, and others did a lot and never got paid at all.

The only two people available to help Dave were two people who hadn't done much in the summer program. One would take a car and tear off someplace and say he was taking people to the doctor. Then the other would get into a car and tear off after the first one. The second would come back saying the first one wasn't doing anything.

After Dave had been doing things for a few days, and had asked for a secretary to help, a lady was sent up with the information that she was Mrs. Mason. Dave assumed that she was his secretary. A few days later he discovered in some roundabout way that she was a local Mississippi R.N., and that John was considering her as the future over-all health coordinator for CDGM. Typical CDGM communication! There weren't more than a dozen people in a farmhouse out in the country, but we still couldn't get a message through! They got some kind of system going. About three-quarters of the 6,400 children who had been diagnosed during the summer were treated now. Despite our failures the children got a lot compared to what they would have received without us.

Mrs. Mason didn't appear to the rest of the staff during this autumn interim, or during the entire second CDGM grant, to have much appetite for her job. One of her coworkers summed up what many others muttered when she said, "Mrs. Mason seemed to be a very socially oriented middle-class Negro lady—things like going out to lunch and leaving at five were a normal part of her life. That seemed very out of place in that environment. I thought she was purely an adornment."

Mrs. Mason, too, felt very out of place. When she first came, she felt that she got the runaround. She had to get a baby-sitter for her baby, drive thirty-six miles several times over to see about the job, and sit around all day before she got any consideration. She thought that Dr. Rosenfield didn't think a nurse could handle the job, and that Rev. Willy Brown and John Mudd didn't know if they had the authority to hire her. During the year she was with CDGM, she didn't think the medical program got the support it should have. She did the best she could without support, and without experience in what she needed now: ability to create the guidelines, make all the plans and decisions, get massive amounts of work done, and create important innovations in the budding new fields of new medical careers for the poor, new health services for the poor, etc. Previously she'd been a pediatric hospital nurse, an OB-GYN nurse, and a nurse on the surgical floor. Then she worked in the non-CDGM Jackson Head Start for eight weeks, but this was getting records to the chief doctor and notifying parents of appointments. She had had some administrative work, but there were always rules and regulations and immediate persons right there to whom to refer. She felt now that being a Negro and a nurse somehow wasn't quite enough.

Mrs. Mason took care of the 60 percent of our 6,400 summer children who had been referred for further work—75 percent of which was dental work. During the second grant she took care of 14,000 children, though she only had a budget to take care of 9,000. She asked area administrators and community organizers (new positions for local people put in during the second grant) to help her, but they didn't consider this their job, and few cooperated. John asked them to a few times, but didn't insist. There was a secretary-health coordinator in each center, but this person's duties were never clearly defined either, and there was no training for them, so Mrs. Mason didn't get much accomplished through this potential source of help.

She tried many times to interest Helen Bass Williams in returning as a staff member or consultant, but Mrs. Williams thought the job was too big, and didn't want to get involved again. She talked to John about getting out-of-state medical health education, and community health consultants, but John was too busy to see about it. Mrs. Mason didn't push it because she didn't see how they would get paid anyway. She found the business office a definite hindrance to the medical program because it couldn't seem to work out smooth arrangements for paying consultants or doctors.

Mrs. Mason had trouble getting local doctors to help us because of all the constant bad publicity about us, and because they didn't need us —they made a very satisfactory living without our dollars. When she *did* convince a doctor to take care of our children or talk at community meetings, she felt that the business office didn't always treat him very well. She also tried to get in-state people to do health education, but they didn't want to risk their lifetime jobs just to be associated with risky CDGM for a guarantee of only six months.

Mrs. Mason said that the job increasingly lost interest for her, because John and the board seemed to have so little interest in this component of CDGM. The board never asked her for a report. John was out of town a lot, and when he was back, he was so busy Mrs. Mason hesitated to bother him. She liked John very much, as did everyone. But when another job came along, she left CDGM and took it because she thought that that outfit cared more about medical matters.

The CDGM board didn't take a deep interest in the medical program at this time, or through most of the second grant, because it always had its eyes on the prize that OEO dangled just out of reach, or benevolently granted and then hoveringly threatened to snatch back again.

Dr. Beittel was still chairman of the board at this time, because we were too much in limbo to have board elections. We didn't even know yet which communities OEO would allow us to include in the next grant. We planned to have new board members elected from the communities as soon as we got the new grant.

The only thing the board was concerned with during the fall of 1965 was, How do we get another grant? It supported Art Thomas and the Delta Ministry about the orientation charges and the accountants' fee, except that the accountants wanted an extra five thousand dollars for the centers added during the summer, and the board said *no* to that. There was some problem about the Vogue Travel Service. There was trouble about who donated the sewing equipment that the National Council of Churches donated, and to whom: CDGM, or OEO via Head Start? We never did get settled who owned the printing press.

Because they were nice people, and sincerely interested in CDGM's work, CDGM accountants Spokney and Gersten had donated printing equipment worth three to four thousand dollars. OEO's assistant general counsel, Jim Heller, approved this gift in writing. He said it didn't represent conflict of interest. A second-hand Multilith and Thermofax worth $1,250 were purchased from Yale University and shipped down to Mississippi. A Justowriter, which was supposed to cost about $3,000 but ended up costing $4,500, was purchased in Jackson. All this was a gift except for $1,500. Tom had promised that CDGM would pay this balance, and it was up to the board to decide how to raise the funds to do so. Tom had started a fund-raising campaign before his eviction from the directorship, but without him it fell through. OEO later claimed the equipment had been donated to Head Start, and thus belonged to the government. Tom denied this and said the equipment had been given to CDGM "as an independent body of project Head Start, having a prior interest in a preschool project and general community education and therefore should be expected to acquire, maintain, and keep various pieces of equipment as part of its long-term program." Much of the huge sum of money the newspapers labeled "misused" was involved in situations such as this one. Much staff energy was sapped in absurd wrangles and efforts to untangle.

The board was trying to inventory every item from the summer. It was willing to meet all OEO's reasonable demands, but so many of them were unreasonable. For example, as Dr. Beittel often pointed out, it was somewhat inconsistent for OEO to expect us to get local white people added to our board in the midst of all the attacks OEO made on us. OEO called us almost criminally negligent and dangerously SNCC oriented, and at the same time expected us to win over scared white Mississippians—and all in one day. They were not only arbitrary in their demands, but also expected instantaneous compliance. We could have got more whites, but *in spite of* OEO, not thanks to it.

The board continuously prepared for another grant. It never gave up hope. And because of its extraordinary tenacity, whether or not it spent much time trying to understand and develop programs, it was the spine of CDGM.

In late August OEO's Mr. Sugarman had assured us that it would only take a week or ten days to process our proposal. On September 11 the board decided to submit a proposal of three or four million dollars. Marian was to write it and to recruit administrative personnel. John was authorized to prepare rent contracts and forms to recruit children, and to keep up the dialogue with communities. I was rehired as director of teacher development and program for children, though no one remembered to call me in Washington to notify me for several more weeks.

I was in Washington sorting, xeroxing, and double-filing all the summer's records on project content, one set to be mailed to John and one set to Marian—there were absolutely no other records on the substantive aspects of CDGM other than those I'd kept and had with me. I was also supposedly conditioning myself to go to another job in the government. I *did* do the CDGM paper work. I *didn't* manage to condition myself to the new job. CDGM felt so tenuous to me. I didn't feel ready to do something else yet. I longed to go back. But I needed some guarantee that if I pulled my four children out of school, piled the household into the station wagon again, and moved back down to Mississippi, the grantless board would arrange for me to subsist. They said they would, but as they had no funds with which to finance the promise, a friend, determined that the project should go, said he would. (OEO said we should have money by the end of the month. "Any day now," said Dave Walls, Mr. Sugarman's assistant, and CDGM's friend.)

My diary for September (in Washington) says, ". . . am having a marvelous mothery good time making pink corduroy dresses with a fringe at the bottom and buying shiney saddle shoes and pasting pictures of the summer in the album and re-arranging my recklessly bright-painted furniture in my recklessly bright-painted house. I cherish the children and smile like the Cheshire cat with happy thoughts about our return to our "homestead." But something's in my blood, bothering me the while—something's in my stomach, whirling around and making me feel unsettled—I'm trying to decide on a good, stable, substantial, respectable job, but I see me procrastinating, stalling, growing daily more miserable.

". . . don't know that it's 'right' to raise my children in an isolated corner of living . . . this is a pluralistic society, and now that I've begun to get a sliver of the disquieting truth of how one-way I see the world, how can I help my children be able to communicate better than I can, and see the world more multipley than I do, if I don't let them learn it in more ways than my comfortable middle-class way? Flexibility is one of the most important things to help children learn. . . ."

For October (in Mississippi) my diary said ". . . I walked round and round the purple floor of the playroom, chatting with Julie and Miggie as they painted pictures, and Julie said, without ever looking up from her absorbing work:

"'Mama, why don't you solve your problems?'

"'My problems! What problems!' I sputtered.

"'Yes, why don't you solve your problems? You're grown-up, you're not supposed to sulk. You're dying to go back to Mississippi, anyone can see that. All you do is walk around wringing your hands, and wishing, and talking to people down there on the telephone. Why don't you just take us and go back?'

"I was stunned. Shocked. Impossible. 'Impossible!' I exploded. 'It isn't at all possible. You have to go to school.'

"'Of course we have to go to school,' said Julie, and then, as if reasoning with a lunatic, 'but you're very rigid. Don't you realize there are schools in Mississippi? We can perfickly well go to school there this year.'

"I must say, this idea had not really occurred to me. I had to stick up for middle-class mores.

"'We can't,' I maintained staunchly. 'I'm a mother. I have to be responsible. I have to earn a paycheck. Our project doesn't have any funds right now. I can't take a chance.'

"'Mama,' said Julie, chastising, 'I'm ashamed of you. You don't do what you think is right. Don't you know there are some things more important than money?'

"'That's ridiculous,' I defended. 'Besides,' I said, grasping at straws in the face of this so, so sensible eight-year-old child, 'Besides, Miggie is having her eight-year-old birthday party in several days.'

"Miggie piped up, in a voice of patronizing patience, 'Mamoo, y'wanna know something? They even have birthdays in Mississippi? I'll have my birthday there.'

"'Well,' I mumbled, trying to recover the more dignified of the positions in the playroom that afternoon, but realizing full well that I'd been defeated by my down-to-earth daughters, 'We would be in the middle of moving on your birthday. We'd be in a motel.'

"'What's so bad about that?' challenged Miggie. 'I'll have a birthday party of some of my Washington friends here, and I'll wake up with my presents on my bed like we do it down there. And we can have a cake *anywhere.*'

"And so, in a trance, knowing that of course this was all true and exactly the solution I'd been yearning for, I re-rented the house in the midst of an improvised birthday party two days later, notified the kids' school, packed once again, and off we went, with me full of admiration for the amazing flexibility of my sugar bunnies. P.S.: We *did* have the second stage of the birthday in a motel room, and the third stage in a house in Jackson when we got one; complete with a hampster and a third birthday cake. So here we are in Mississippi for the year."

In October the board perhaps paid more attention to substantive content considerations in CDGM than it did at any time before or in the year following. Members discussed qualifications of a resource teacher—OEO and CDGM interpretations of qualification. They discussed the eagerness of Dr. Sol Gordon and consultants from Yeshiva University to do a reading readiness research project. No one seemed clear on what his summer research project had discovered. (I'd never received a report.) The board agreed that Dr. Gordon should finance this himself, and not expect it to be funded with money meant for the poor. As it was, nothing came of the idea anyway, and Dr. Gordon wasn't involved in CDGM any more. The board was interested in my discussion with Dr. Martin Deutsch, and in the fact that Deutsch's Institute for Developmental Studies was considering conducting a demonstration center in a CDGM community. Nothing came of this either.

The board asked many questions about the nature of the teacher training workshops I was about to start. It agreed that I was to come and report directly. This never happened. In my time at CDGM I was asked to only one board meeting seven months after this, to outline, in five minutes, my record album project. (The board was, however, too busy to listen to the tapes of songs and chants from old people, teachers, and children, which I'd collected, and organized two local people to collect, and recorded three times to edit and put in an impactful order, and listened to many times so I could write down the words to each song on four potential sides for an accompanying sheet, and negotiated with Folkways to record. The board signed a contract with Folkways anyway.)

John Mudd presented the board with our new area staff idea: replacing the five out-of-state district coordinators with teams of local people in eight area offices. This would be an effort to decentralize and develop the beginnings of local autonomy. There would be, hired *from* the community *by* the community, a community organizer, an area teacher guide, an area administrator, and a secretary in each office. Most of these individuals would be new to CDGM, and would need training immediately. John urged that the board contact foundations for funds to start training, so that the local people could be of service at once when we received a grant.

It was understood that OEO required us to move to a respectable Jackson office building before it would consider re-funding. The board began negotiations with the management of the integrated Milner Building. Dr. Beittel insisted on the importance of making sure poor people were in on the decision regarding our new office location. "They had to feel comfortable in the headquarters' facilities, no matter where we were. OEO said we should be funded in a few weeks. A commitment had not yet been put in writing. ("Any day now," Dave Walls said, and did everything he could to egg Jule Sugarman on to make it true.)

Tension with Mary Holmes Junior College continued. The board decided to approach MHJC requesting that it again be the grantee for the 1965–1966 session. It hoped Mary Holmes would be agreeable to: the instigation of teacher training sessions on campus; participating in a student work program; participating in in-service training; seeing to it that there was a person responsible for the CDGM's interests.

Mary Holmes did nothing about a student work program or a person to work for CDGM's interests. It responded, as previously, with demands relating to control rather than help: All CDGM personnel would be responsible to MHJC; the operation must be closer, geographically, to MHJC; all OEO contact will be done through MHJC. Board minutes say, "The Executive Board unanimously found these conditions unacceptable."

On October 16 John told the board that applications had already been received from fifty-four centers, both old and new, with 5,200 children registered. *Poor people in more than forty new areas had requested Head Start programs.* He reminded the board that the application must be submitted to OEO by the end of the next week. Marian suggested and the board determined that priority be given to the following categories of centers: poorest, most rural, least likely to be reached by the establishment's Community Action Programs (CAP) or in counties where it could be proved that working with CAP wouldn't be possible or effective.

John suggested that the board also give consideration to cases where continued support would help communities become sufficiently strong and independent to organize separate projects, even though they might not qualify under the suggested criteria. It was further determined that the board couldn't make any evaluation until more communities submitted their applications, but that it could rely somewhat on summer experience. Statements would be needed from communities saying they were having intolerable trouble working with the existing CAP.

It was also determined that the above criteria would not eliminate large cities. The board agreed that a member of the board should help

John Mudd with the evaluation decisions. No one was chosen. John stated that CDGM itself shouldn't deny the right of any community to apply for a Head Start program. If any community were to be denied assistance, this should be OEO's responsibility.

Charles Mosely, the OEO man in Mississippi, supported John in this. He counseled the board that it *should* apply according to people's real need, and let OEO face the difficult task of saying no to the yearning human beings out there in these isolated poor communities.

* * *

Dear Government
I have been a citizen of Winstonville 40 some years I have no suport. I have a little house it broke down and it rainy over me. I have no learning. we want a aldult school that will be good. we dont have nothing to do, we will be glad of a aldult school

this is all
Wester
Dodson

* * *

Sargent Shriver
O.E.O.
Washington, D.C.
Dear Sir,

My name is Mrs. Alma Ree Pope. I am writing to you in support of the Operation Head Start Center. I have been working with the children since the center opened. It has been a great inspiration to me and quite impressive in the children's eagerness to learn.

I think this is the greatest move that could have been made in the interest and for the benefit of our children.

If this project does not continue; I feel that it will be a great off set to our children in their development and preparedness to further their education in the future.

I am quite complacent with the outcome and progress of the C.D.G.M. It has helped the children a great deal in the short time it has been under way. I might add to that Mr. Alvin Gore, Chairman of the Committee, has done and is doing a tremendous job. He has worked hard, dilligently, and sufficiently as well as all the others on the Committee.

To conclude my correspondence to you: I hope you will share our points of view and try to comprehend what I have been trying to relay to you as best I can. So on behalf of the committee and myself, please take what I have said under consideration, and give us your full support of Operation Head Start Center. Thank you kindly for your time and patience.

Cordially yours,

CHAPTER 26

BUT THE PEOPLE; THERE *ARE* THE PEOPLE

FROM OEO'S POINT of view, the chief problem in CDGM preventing smoothly flowing administration and maximum acceptance of all governmental directives was that there were *people* in the project. People with needs, people with yearnings. People, to OEO's annoyance, were usually so insufferably human—especially poor people.

During this unfunded interim period, while others negotiated with Washington and accountants, it fell primarily to me and a neophyte twenty-one-year-old University of Chicago graduate student volunteer named Mary Emmons to do the daily negotiations with thousands of CDGM community people. The external political effects of CDGM in Mississippi and in national liberal and Democratic politics, and the individuals associated with this side (chiefly Art Thomas, Marian Wright, and John Mudd), were the side of CDGM that received publicity.

But CDGM's internal people, problems, dynamics, and directions were what produced the strength that made external things of significance happen. Mary and I were interested in working individually with people toward solving specific problems concerning the democratic process, the educational process, and other related parts of their lives.

Poor people all over the state had been having severe problems setting up their committees to suit them, and they were still having them now:

Laurel, Mississippi
August 1965

Dear Sir:

I would like information on how this center is really supposed to be run.

There is a great deal of confusion at this particular center and I think I, as a volunteer, should do my part by writing to find out what can be done about this situation.

I don't show favortism toward no one in particular, but a great deal of wrong doing has taken place at the Community Center.

I will began to tell you my exact feeling toward the events that has taken place during my time working there as a volunteer. I have great interest in this project and would like to see it succeed. So I am taking it on myself to express my views.

The first incident which occurred was the resignation of the chairman. It wasn't done through proper source it was done through *force*. Mrs. ———, and I impersonate, because I feels it is necessary, has worked much too hard to establish this center, and for her long hours spent in doing this task her reward is to have to offer up her resination as chairman. Believe me I can't see why the *officials* there in Edwards could sit and let something of this nature take place. The Co-Ordinator is not of the quality you might presume he is, I had the opportunity to sit in on one of the meetings held by him, and from his talkings he isn't in favor of Mrs. ——— being the chairman, I can't put in words exactly how I feel he treated her, but believe me he didn't treat her with the respect a woman of her dexterity should have been treated.

The community is deeply disturbed about this incident and as one of the community leader I felt obligated to write and let you know that this was a tradgedy event to let happen. As a whole, we know how Mrs. ——— has worked, because she began working on this project in April, taking prospective names of children who might have been eligible to attend the center. And I can tell you the people that are working now weren't in the making at the begining. I felt that after they found out that Mrs. —— weren't going to get bombed for during this type of work they then decided to step into the picture. From this letter I guess you can sense my tenses about Mrs. ——— having to offer up her resination of being chairman, if anyone deserve to be the chairman it is her.

If someone from Edwards could just walk in on some of the meetings without letting them know you could get a whole picture of who is right for the center and who isn't.

This community is behind Mrs. ——— one hundred per cent.

With consideration
of the center.
A volunteer worker,
Mrs. A———

The granting delay caused misunderstandings to mushroom, and resentment to rise: "Dear Mrs. Greenberg, We are having trouble getting the information we need. Our chairman has reserved a great deal of mail but we were still not getting the information. I am speaking for myself and the community people. We haven reseeved any information since the 12 September. I am the Resource Teacher so I feel it is my responsibility to get the information, encourage the mothers, Church people, and community People.

"Did I understand you to say that Community people can not fire a chairman but they can elect a vice chairman? Will you give me more information about getting rid of a chairman. I am unsertin why it is you haven seen fit to send us our grant, Mrs. Greenberg. We are woring hard to keep our school open voluntur and can see no reason for you to not send us our money. Yours Truly,"

People who had had no experience with institutions saw everything very personally—*Mrs. Greenberg* had not given these ladies their grants. "Dear Polly, We would appreciate it if you would take our request unto consideration and send us some money. Volunteering with the 108 children is at our wits end without money, as we have put forth every effort and more available to this community. . . ."

"Dear Headquarters, We are not aware that you know how difficult it is for the peoples to continue this on and on with no help from you. Some of the teachers are the soul supporters of their family and cannot go on forever without support. CDGM has help us mingle and unite the races. Parents can get more rest so be nicer to their children. They can buy more food for them because they can earn more money. Adults are learning to get better personalities to each other and the children learn from this example. Parents and children are more closer than ever before in history. This is all day care and advanced education over what we have had. Most of all, children are learning God is alive. . . ."

But when I wrote to a man in another community, in response to a report that there was dissension there, and that he was unhappy with the commotion CDGM was causing, he replied:

"Dear Mrs. Greenbird, I have concluded. Of my opinin there is no doubts. You ask for it and with your request in my heart I write to you of mine. There have been no major problem here comparing to the problem before. That is the problems of fights and argueings are truely, but we are healing them and this comparing to when we were unable to healing them due to no oppertuntie is as the difference between death illness with no mediecin and light illness with mediecin. Am I clearly? My opinin is as I say all the dirt you see now with fights and argueings where no doubt we should be greatful is because Jesus is cleaning us out of our past.

"I am willing to work with you in any way to make our community convenient for our children. Thanking you for your concern in my problem. Yours for Freedom,"

When people are poor, and a plum is proffered only long enough for a tiny taste, they are pushed to repeat the experience in an urgent way not felt by those with more than one avenue of opportunity. For example:

In October I was deep in the middle of a long-distance telephone call from one of the country's best known activists. It was long distance, Mississippi to New York. The operator abruptly interrupted to say she had an emergency call for me from Mrs. Tuttle of Tadpoletown (fictitious names). I was frightened that Mrs. Tuttle, a plantation sharecropper, was in desperate trouble. Heart pounding, I shouted good-bye to the distinguished New Yorker, and took the call immediately.

"Listen, Polly," she said tensely, "Last week I wrote some names on a slip of paper and stuffed it into your pocketbook for you to read. Now listen, hurry and hunt it up. I need the names." I scrambled through the crowded pocketbook for the piece of paper and read her the names. "Thanks," she said hastily, "I have to go in a hurry. Those are kids' names I want to add to our application for a Head Start before the community chairman mails it in to the office this afternoon."

On the Sidon plantation, a man explained a public temper tantrum his wife had had, by saying, "She's so flusterated about this Head Start thing she fell out and foamed. Its those little slaying things Stennis says about us—she was so mad she just jarred the floors loose. If Stennis was smart, he'd know kindness will make a bad dog lie down, but the way they're laying it on us with that OEO hogwash, we'll *all* flusterate out soon."

Many parents were going through other patience and stamina-straining ordeals at this season, too. They were allowing their children to integrate previously segregated white schools for the first time, although the United States Supreme Court school desegregation decision of 1954 had been around for eleven years by this fall of 1965.

Mrs. Flora Beech (fictitious name) was grateful to CDGM for giving her child Solinda what she called an "integrated happiness" before Solinda became the first colored child in a Delta white school. The principal called Mrs. Beech in for a conference. He said, "Let me just tell you something before we begin, Flora. I hate your people. I hate you. I hate your child. I will not do anything to give her a good time in this school. But I'm an educator. I will see that she's not harmed."

The principal was a man of his word. He had one drinking fountain marked off for Solinda. No other child was permitted to drink from it. On the playground the teacher stood as a silent dividing line so that Solinda would remember to play alone. Solinda ate in the school cafeteria, alone, one hour after the other children had eaten.

Mrs. Beech was *not* an educator. She was only a maid. So she could only handle this educational situation in her own simple way. She said to Solinda, "Listen to me. Many, many years ago there was a job to do. People needed a chance to make a good life for themself. So they took their little children out to wild woods where they might be hungry for food, and Indians might kill them. They loved their children, but they had to, to get a better life for everybody. Now it's the turn for our people. Black people need to make a good life for ourself. So we're putting our little children in white schools where you might be hungry for friends and white folks might kill your spirit—don't be afraid, they won't *all* the way kill you. But its our job to do, and can't anybody do it but you. Be a brave little girl, baby, and no matter what they say or do, remember, you're carrying your people to freedom."

In another county I asked one of a trio of Negro elementary-age children who had just "crashed the white school," as he put the matter of integration, how he was getting along with the white children. He replied: "White children thinks they is more than we is. White children *ain't* more than we is. One white boy called me nigger. I said, 'You better shut up talkin' to me, peckerwood.' Quentin say, 'Don't fool with them white children. If you do what they don' like, they'll beat you, kill you.' So I say, 'Quentin, if we knows they ain't more than we is, we can make 'em step down real nice.'"

The children: To OEO they were statistics and budgetarily allowable, or more often disallowable, items. To their families and to Mary and me as we worked among them, they were children:

Six or eight of them were playing a ring game in the muddy road:

"Aunt Jemima had a baby
Pitza, pitza
Daddy-O!

How you know? How you know?
Pitza, pitza
Daddy-O!

Because you tol' me
Pitza, pitza
Daddy-O!

Do the jerk
Jerk -y, jerk -y
Daddy-O!

Can you twista
Twista, twista,
Daddy-O!

Can you shake it,
Shake it, shake it
Daddy-O?"

A dark little girl darted out of the circle and grabbed my hand. "Lady," she said, "we learn dat song in our school. When Mis' Shiber gonna give us back our school?"

In Madison County I talked with a five-year-old boy and girl, who were racing around a muddy yard, grinning, panting, and whacking each other on the back between bits of conversation. They weren't in their center because it wasn't operating on a volunteer basis:

BRUCE: I know how to catch a little biddy snake!
MICHELE: No you don't!
BRUCE: Yessiree I do, I do too, under my house.
MICHELE: An' at the center I had paper. I can write. I had a Easter basket.
BRUCE: At school I had a playhouse. A policeman made it for us.
MICHELE: That ain't no policeman: that's that white man at the center.

BRUCE: Yeah. We played making a lemon cake in the playhouse.

MICHELE: Boys ain't no mother—you ain't s'posed to cook no lemon cake.

BRUCE: Well I did. At the center.

MICHELE: I can sing "Mary Had a Little Lamb." Listen at me sing it . . . [sings it and three other songs] I sung these at my center.

BRUCE: At the center they give me a shot. I'm going to be a doctor when I'm big. Because they give shots. I like to hurt people. I'm going to lay them on a bed and give them a shot in their butt. I take a shot with no crying at the center. What you going to do when you grown up, Michele?

MICHELE: I'm already grown up.

(An old lady wearing a shiny black straw hat, and a housedress hanging down to the tops of green galoshes joined our conversation. She was Michele's grandmother.)

GRANDMOTHER: See? They got nuthin' to do. The best thing about CDGM was the children got something new each day: a song, a kind of art, a walk, a talk, something new to eat. I've never seen a time in Mississippi when poverty children of our race were daily offered a new something to develop his mind. You wouldn't believe it, lady, but Michele used to be so shy . . . She'd hang back, move off if you'd come up to her . . . If you put your hand on her she'd pull loose of you. She used to murmur, but she didn't talk at all. One day at the center when she thought the children and teachers wasn't paying her no mind, she was murmuring, murmuring . . . They all went over, and they saw she was trying to sing. They actually heard her sing words! That was this summer, and she's five years old, but that's the first time we knew she could talk.

This information made me even more curious about Michele than I had been before. I asked her again what she wanted to be when she grew up.

"A mother . . . No, a meteorologist." The grandmother explained that she had heard about meteorologists on TV.

The children's stated aspirations were fascinating, but tended to be random and unrelated to real thought about the subject or what they saw around them. The *adult's* aspirations *for* the children, on the other hand, consistently from community to community, were very much a product of their own limited luck and were measured from that vantage point, not in reference to a sky-high dream.

Michele's grandmother answered: "Well, I hope she'll do as well as *my* children. I'm done with my children. They come up real nice. I'm proud of 'm. I have six. My baby's twenty-one. They're in Chicago, Michele's mother too. They all have good jobs. They can get *any* job, they're just real fortunate. One is a nurse's aide. One can build roads, dig, *anything*. One's in the union office; I don't know what he does there, but he's very fortunate. He's been there for four years. He's doing very well. One is thirty-two years old, and he's been bagging in a grocery store since he was twelve. My oldest daughter has a night job cleaning a office building so she can be home with her children. Michele's mother, she's in domestic work. She gets fifteen dollars a day! A day! That's what we get for a week! I hope Michele gets something like that when she's grown. I pay a lady eight dollars a week to keep Michele and the baby . . . I only make twenty dollars . . . I'll be so glad when the Head Start school opens up again . . ."

We had sauntered into the house while the grandmother was talking. It was the home of a "prosperous poor" Mississippi Negro. It was decorated like many homes in that category. Flowered linoleum lay on a painted brown rough plank floor, with two small red scatter rugs on top of that. The walls were rough planks painted light green. There was a green plastic-covered sofa with a yellow towel spread over it, and two brown plastic chairs with hand-crocheted antimacassars on the arms. The TV held a collection of ornate dime-store china figurines, a dog made out of a yard-goods-and-ribbon bedecked Coke bottle, and a purple elephant made from a bleach bottle. A coffee table which appeared to be a sawed off taller table also held decorative items: a pink and white mat crocheted of string, a papier mâché vase of crepe paper flowers, and many stiffly formal pictures of family members in cap and gown on high school graduation day. On the wall was the inevitable color picture of JFK, and in this house, in addition, a lacily brass-framed color picture of Jackie. There was a calendar from Johnson's Grocery with a sprig of red artificial roses tacked to the corner and a white plaster of Paris wall plaque of Jesus on the cross. Also a large framed picture of Jesus on the cross, and a large framed picture of a country road. Though interest and ability in home decorating vary among the poor as they do among the nonpoor and are not necessarily related to income, it was typically true that most women did as much as possible to make their homes pretty according to a certain cluttered kind of taste.

"Bitterly poor" people's homes had a different decor, and their inhabitants correspondingly often had their own lowered aspirations for the children. I met a family in Clark County who wouldn't send their children to CDGM. Residents were grandparents, who were in their eighties, a sixty-year-old deaf and dumb sister of the grandmother, the retarded forty-year-old daughter of the grandparents, the grandparents' thirty-year-old granddaughter who was a permanent invalid with heart trouble, and a twenty-year-old relative of some sort who lived there with three small children.

There were none of the traditional chairs and rocking chairs on the porch, and none in the two-room house either. The front room contained three double beds covered with dark quilts and no sheets, and two wardrobes. The windowless, smoke-blackened wooden walls were papered with yellowed newspapers to keep the chill winds from coming through the cracks. Hooks held neatly ironed clothes on every part of the walls. There was nothing else. The back room, which you had to walk outside and around into the back door to get into, looked the same, but instead of containing beds, it was furnished with tables: tables full of buckets and basins to serve as a sink, tables full of jars to drink out of and pans to eat from, tables holding jugs of syrup, preserved foods, commodity foods, and meal. A huge wood-burning stove dominated the room.

During my visit I asked each of the adults what their dreams for the three little children were. The grandmother gazed into space dreamily and said, in a tone that conveyed she hardly dared hope for such a blessing to befall her grandbabies, that she hoped someday they would have electricity, so when they took in washing and ironing for a living, as she did, they would not have to walk half a mile through the fields to the woods for firewood, kindle a fire outside, and beat the wash in a black boiling pot, heat the irons in the fire, and then press the clothes with them. She hoped, also, that the grandchildren would not have to burn roots for illumination, but could afford oil and kerosene for lamps. With a humble dream such as this, it was easy to see why the lady considered kindergarten attendance and public school success irrelevant.

Mrs. Rosie Maria Bradley (fictitious name) of Vossburg said to me: "Let me tell you about a miracle I really saw with my own eyes! My granddaughter is six years old. She attends CDGM Head Start this summer. Now she's in public school. She started reading the little primer and only stayed in it a week! That's the truth—after a week she was promoted to the big primer! She stayed in that two weeks and then went into the hardback book. She can count to one hundred, draw you like you look, write her name and family members' names. Now, you know that's a miracle!"

OEO saw CDGM as alive or dead according to whether its government funds were switched on or switched off at the time. But the life of a poverty community, like the life of any community, is not contingent upon money. The *quality* of that life, undoubtedly, is—and the rate of progress—but not the existence of a social structure, personal relationships, beliefs, and directions of movement.

One autumn evening I was in an impoverished Delta townlet several hundred miles from our headquarters. People begged me to come to their "CDGM community meeting." I went and found that this meeting, like most CDGM community meetings, was in a barren one-room plank church, dimly lit by a single forty-watt bulb suspended six feet or so from the ceiling by a wire. I found that this community meeting, like most CDGM community meetings, was a mixture of things that OEO didn't want mixed:

A poor man on the dais opened the meeting with the customary devotionals:

MAN: I'm reading from Revelation, Chapter One, verses one, two, and three: [*reads haltingly*]

The Revelation of Jesus Christ, which God gave unto him, *to show unto his servants things which must shortly come to pass;* and he sent and signified it by his angel unto his servant John:

Who bare record of the word of God, and of the testimony of Jesus Christ, and of all things that he saw.

Blessed is he that readeth, and they that *hear the words of this prophecy,* and keep those things which are written therein: for the time *is* at hand!

AUDIENCE: Amen, Amen!

MAN: And St. Luke, Chapter Four, tells us that the devil took Jesus into the wilderness for forty days and tempted him. He told Jesus to turn a stone into bread. Jesus said, "Man shall not live by bread alone!" And the devil showed Jesus all the kingdoms of the earth and told him he'd give him all this power if he would worship him. And Jesus said, "Get thee behind me, Satan!"

AUDIENCE: That's right!

MAN: And here's Romans, Chapter Thirteen, verses eleven and twelve: 'Love worketh no ill to his neighbor: therefore love is the fulfilling of the law.

And that, knowing the time, that now it is high time to awake out of sleep: for now is our salvation nearer than we believed.

The night is far spent, the day is at hand: let us therefore cast off the works of darkness, and let us put on the armour of light.'

AUDIENCE: Tell it, brother! Tell it.

MAN: Now you tell me, was Moses a great leader?

AUDIENCE: Um, hum, tell the *truth!*

MAN: But it take a good follower to make a great leader.

AUDIENCE: Tell it! Tell it! Go on, boy!

MAN: [*pulse in neck throbbing*]: Satan tried to lead Christ one day, but Christ had to say, "Get behind me!"

AUDIENCE: [*silence*]

MAN [*Sweating*]: Do you hear me? [*Shouting*] Do you *hear* me?

AUDIENCE: We hear you, brother, we hear you!

MAN: [*Rolling eyes wildly*]: Get this! Listen to me!

AUDIENCE: Yes, boy, talk, talk!

MAN: I want you to hear me!

AUDIENCE: We hear you, brother!

MAN: You ain't doing no service if you ain't gonna listen! They trying to carry you back! Listen! [*Whispering*] Listen! [*jumping up and down*] These sons of Satan been lyin' all these hundred years!

AUDIENCE: [*Shouts, laughter*]

MAN: [*Making mock whipping and chopping sweeping gestures with his arms*]: Have mercy, Lord!

AUDIENCE: [*Applause*] "That's alright!"

MAN: Don't y'all hear me?

AUDIENCE: We hear you, yeah, yeah, we know where you're at.

MAN: [*On his hands and knees, crouched as if for the hundred yard dash*] Outa one blood sprang one nation!

AUDIENCE: Ah, ah, ah!

MAN: So follow your leaders!

AUDIENCE: Yeah, yeah, that's right!

MAN: D'you know what I'm talkin' 'bout? D'y'all know what I'm sayin'? I'm sayin' CDGM! Can y'all hear me?

AUDIENCE: Tell it, tell the truth, tha's right. CDGM!

MAN: Tha's right! I'm saying, the time *is* at hand!

AUDIENCE: Sho is!

MAN: I'm saying CDGM is at *hand!*

AUDIENCE: More! More, preach it, brother!

MAN: [*Hopping*] I'm saying, If you're not goin' to send your chilrens to Head Start, Get thee behind me, Satan!

AUDIENCE: [*Laughter, foot thumping, head wagging, rocking*]

MAN: I'm sayin', the law! cast off the works of darkness! put on the armour of light! CDGM!

AUDIENCE: Yes, sir! Take your time! Say it again!

MAN: Mothers can do more than anyone in the world, because they rocks the cradle.

AUDIENCE: You doin' alright, brother!

MAN: So spend some time with your childrens, I know you're busy, but give them some time, and above all, teach 'em about God!

AUDIENCE: You couldn't do no better, say it again!

MAN: All that whoopin' and hollerin' you gonna do at the cemetary when your child's in that casket ain't gonna do no good!

AUDIENCE: Sho ain't.

MAN: So do a little cryin' now while it's do some good!

AUDIENCE: Tell it, tell it, pour it to us!"

MAN: I knowd a man, stopped on the way to his child's grave to buy some flowers. He met another man. Th'other man say, "you buyin' flowers? I'll buy some soup." First man, he say, "Soup! Why you gonna take soup to a grave?" Secon' man say, "Well, you takin' flowers to a grave, aincha? Anybody alive enough to smell flowers, is alive enough to eat a bowl of soup!"

AUDIENCE: [*Uproarious laughter*]

MAN: D'y'all get my meanin'?

AUDIENCE: You right, so right, sho is!

MAN: Are you listening?

AUDIENCE: Sho is, sho is, that's right, tell it more!

MAN: So don't wait till your childrens is dead an' gone to carry flowers to 'em! Carry 'em to the CDGM!

AUDIENCE: Lay it on 'em!

MAN: 'Cause Jesus said: "Having eyes they see not."

AUDIENCE: We hear you, brother!

MAN: And I say, quit your ways, that's not what'll do it, it ain't too much work if it helps the peoples!

AUDIENCE: Yeah, yeah!

MAN: There's those who will betray you. There's those who will let you down. There's those who will cut your throat for a nickle. But we got to trust someone!

AUDIENCE: Yeah, yeah! Tell the truth!

MAN: If you can't play in the big leagues, get out!

AUDIENCE: Yes, Lord!

MAN: And we colored people needs the little leagues 'bout as much as a hog needs a side saddle!

AUDIENCE: Right, right, tha's right!

MAN: [*Wiping the sweat that pours from his brow*] God bless you sweet people—God bless your heart. Miz Nelson, will you . . .

[*Mrs. Nelson sings a solo; and people keep time with their feet*]

MRS. NELSON: Jesus hold my hand,
Hold my hand . . .

CHORUS: While I run this race,
'Cause I don't want to run this race in vain!

The race does seem to some to be in vain. The same meeting continued, now with a different leader: "Miss Polly, we're having a time now, losing people for progress that we couldn't get out nohow for the Movement, but they came out for CDGM. They don't want to vote; scared. They want to help the children. I can see why they don't care about politics. They don't see it's important. I can see why Stennis doesn't want them to vote. He sees it *is* important. But why does Stennis mind if the children go to kindergarten?"

FDP WORKER: Why haven't you registered yet?

FARMER: I'm going to, I ben busy.

WORKER: Well, even when they had the dogs on us, *I* registered. I was afraid, but I did it.

FARMER: Well, like I said, I'm fixing to go.

WORKER: You are not a law abiding citizen, is that right? You don't vote?

FARMER: I didn't say that. Don't do me like that.

WORKER: Well, why didn't you register?

FARMER: I've neglected to do it. But like I say, I'm going to do it.

WORKER: It's Thursday after next we're going over to the Courthouse. Will you go?

FARMER: Yes, I'll go.

WORKER: Do you mean it?

FARMER: Yes, I'll go. But what I *really* want to know is, when is the CDGM going to open? I've got three grandbaby boys was going . . .

If a *new* value, such as CDGM or voting, can be attached to an *old* value, such as religion, new behavior can often ride through relatively unresisted, on the coattail, as it were, of existing behavior.

After the meeting, a teacher said that this unre-funding was "wasting" all the children, and ruining Curtis. "Curtis is a stout little boy. He fights all the time. He doesn't think anything of cracking a chair over anybody's head. When we were still operating our center, I went around to see his mother. She said she knowed he was bad, but she wouldn't talk any more. I felt she wouldn't talk because she didn't want to admit; because we might not take him in the center. We might make her take him out. I said, 'You won't have to take him out, just tell me so I can help him.' She said, 'Just whip him. I just have to get me a switch and burn him out. I have to work and I just can't be there with him to do it some other way.'

"He climbs on top of the car, up trees, up walls, When you try to get him, he's all down through the bushes. I put my hands on him one day and he was in a moisture of sweat, he was vicious in a manner of speaking. The grandmother says he takes it from his Grand Uncle Old Sam. I don't believe it's inherited. I think its from his parents, Bob and Pearl, and the company they keep. It's not such an intelligent way of life they lead. They're drunk, men and women come in and out all day, they even get the gun on each other. Just last week a man was killed in there. But I wouldn't fault them; both of them are what you would call retarded. The grandfather is a Church deacon, but he can't get Bob and Pearl even to send those children to Sunday School. I'm working with the mother to let him go to live with the grandmother. Everybody in a family is not the same nature, you know; I think a change of home would do him good, but what did him the best good was me taing care of him in Head Start all day. Now with no grant, I only see him when I can—I'm working temporarily in a white lady's kitchen till I can go back to teaching."

In the winter, the agricultural population suffered for lack of jobs, income. Some of the poor could "afford" to teach voluntarily all day long, and some could not.

Mrs. Fair said: "Before the summer I was working for twenty dollars a week sewing part time at a man's tailor shop. When he got caught up with his work he really didn't have anything for me to do, that was true. I didn't have nothing to do. Then CDGM came, and I earned sixty dollars a week as trainee teacher. I paid my debts and fixed up the children for school—but I have seven, it didn't go far, it was only a six-week-long job. I went to welfare. The welfare lady told me to go to the employment service. I did, about a factory job, but they said I needed ninth grade education, and I only had seventh, and they didn't offer any education or training. The employment man said he had some maid jobs, but they wanted full-time permanent maids, paying fifteen dollars a week, and I told him I couldn't work full-time, because we were trying to work volunteer to keep our center open for children till the grant. I didn't want to lie to them and take no job and then quit when my CDGM job came through. The welfare lady told me, 'People who want welfare checks can't afford to do no volunteer work, you just forget that center.' So she put me on welfare, after I quit my volunteer teaching. The other volunteer workers were mad at me—said I didn't care about CDGM, and maybe they wouldn't hire me back when the grant came if I was going to do like that. But I'm in debt again now. Welfare mothers only get free lunch at the public school for one child, so I spend twenty cents a day for six of the seven; that's a dollar twenty a day, six dollars a week, out of such a few dollars a week! Then I have to buy the *Weekly Reader* and *Current Science,* one or the other, for each of them, and paper, pencils. We have to pay ten cents each semester for each child to take exams, and March of Dime money. The ones graduating from sixth grade pay one dollar, and they have to have black shoes, black suit, white sox. When I don't have it, I borrow it. Otherwise the teachers punish the children by taking off their grades. I would rather go in debt than see my children punished and shamed for something they didn't do."

John Mudd was feeling terribly pressured by OEO officials and red tape. Mary and I were feeling terribly pressured by individual people in trouble. The phone summoned us to face the troubles of individuals till 8 or 9 P.M. at "the office," our exhausted, furnitureless farmhouse, and all night at home. Trouble was relentless. People who had trouble and who saw us as a way out of it were relentless, too. I was besieged, beleaguered, beseeched, and beside myself preaching patience to people whose impatience gladdened my heart.

Mrs. Marks called to say: "My sister died. I have to go to Chicago to see about the children. She has five. I said I'd take them, but my older sister said that's be too much for me with my own seven children, so we'll prob'ly divide them. I'm wondering, will CDGM be having a job for me as trainee teacher soon? The committee hired me, but they can't pay me with no grant?"

* * *

Route 2 Box _____
Rolling Fork, Miss.

Mrs. Greenberg:

I have eight small children between the ages of 11, 10, 9, 7, 6, 4, 2, 9 mo. they are in need of food clothes and I don't have no job and my husband doesn't have no job. Also.

If you have any chance of having any clothes please give me a chance to get some, because I havent ever gotton any for them.

In the summer Head Start had three children in school and it was so much help to me and also children, and also help them to study and count, and read much better so I thank that the Head Start has been a fine ideal for children now. I wish that it could have been here for a number of years.

I also went to Walefare department for help because. My husband has no work, and I had a hemerge six times in one week with my leg and they still woulden help.

I asked them to please give me something to buy the baby some milk but they refuses to do so, if you can give, or fine any person that have small children please ask them to send, give this my address. Thank you . . .

Sign
Lelar Mae N______________

CHAPTER 27

FANNING THE WANING FLAMES OF SELF-CONFIDENCE

. . . One of our resource teachers has really gone out of her way for us. She has to support twelve head of her own and she didn't have money to pay her light bill this month, her lights were cut off for a few days, but she never stopped picking up the kids and going out of her way to get them.

We don't know how long we can keep this up, but we have managed thus far.

Mr. Robert Miles
Chairman

Batesville Center
Batesville, Miss.

* * *

OVER FIFTY COMMUNITIES operated their centers on a volunteer basis for many difficult months. For some, the motivation was caring deeply that this good thing not be taken from their children. For more, the motivation was to be on hand to prevent anyone else from elbowing into the slots when the second grant and the paychecks finally came through. This wasn't a ridiculous reason for anyone who lives in a country where money provides so many kinds of freedoms.

I wasn't, as a good professional community organizer should have been, neutral in this matter of whether a community should stay open or should close up till re-funding. My only excuse for the very strong and solitary position I took at this time in behalf of staying open, though I realized the sacrifice and effort this meant to people, was that I've never claimed I was a good professional community organizer—or even a community organizer at all. I'm a professional believer in: there are lots of ways to seek the really important things in life, all of which require faith that you can move toward them, all of which require inner growth, and most of which require self-discipline and sacrifice; not just on the part of the rich or the poor.

There was a vital need in CDGM for organizers who had the art necessary to wheedle people out of hiding, to focus them on issues, and to nondirectively support them as they worked out all the details at their own pace. Most programs don't have this kind of organizer at all. CDGM didn't have enough of them. But, in sharp contrast to many of CDGM's leaders, I also felt that there was a vital need for leaders of another variety: those with exuberance, personal influence, persuasiveness—those able to help people determine what they wanted and *propel* them (in contrast to being patient with them) into strategies and behaviors that might lead them in the directions they wanted to go. Though opportunity to do for self has been lacking in the lives of society's victims, so has percussion and percolation, vitality, dynamism, and excitement about controlling the physical, material, and social flow around them, at least to the limited extent that less victimized people do.

Probably my biggest contribution to CDGM was vividly conveying my own faith in the infinite flexibility of fate and in the power of the flame within each person to rise and shine and illuminate the way. I felt that one specific form of technical assistance we were there to offer, was to help fan the waning flames of the feeling "we can do things for ourselves of which we never dreamed." So I fanned them manicly.

In early October this letter went out:

Dear Chairman,
We still do not know about a grant from Washington to continue our Centers. However, many people have said they would like to open their Centers right now, anyway, money or no money. WE CANNOT PAY FACILITIES MONEY, SALARIES, FOOD, OR SUPPLIES AT THIS TIME. WE HAVE NO MONEY YET.
You could charge 5¢ or 10¢ a week per child to buy gas to get children to you. You could do the same to pay for a snack of juice or milk and a cracker if you wanted to serve some small thing. Do you have someone willing to drive? Do you have some of your summer staff, at least one for every twenty children, who would be willing to teach? Can you ask each mother to come as aide on a certain day of each week?
For example:

**Teacher every day.
Manny's mother as aide every Monday.
John Isaac's mother as aide every Tuesday.
Michael's mother as aide every Wednesday.
Annie Ellen's mother as aide every Thursday.
Jim's mother as aide every Friday.

You could be open every morning for a few hours and take the children home before dinner. Or you could be open three mornings a week. Or you could be open after school when some of the teen-agers that were with you this summer might be able to help out.
If you are opening again now, please let me know immediately and I will be glad to help you with ideas of things to do with the children.

There will be an Oct. 21 meeting at Edwards to talk about volunteer Centers next Thursday at 10 a.m. We cannot pay for gas to get here, but I will be here waiting for you if you can make it. Anyone who was on your committee or staff this summer is welcome. You can do so tremendously, wonderfully much for your children yourselves, while we wait and pray for outside help. Whether or not you come to the meeting, please let me know if you are now open or if you plan to open in the next week.

WRITE TO:
POLLY GREENBERG
CHILD DEVELOPMENT GROUP
BOX 338
EDWARDS, MISSISSIPPI

I'll be seeing or hearing from you soon, I hope!

(signed) Polly Greenberg

Newsletter number six, which I put out in October, 1965, was intended to keep CDGM's processes, procedures, and preparations alive, though the feeble effort had to be made through a high-shrinkage correspondence course, for lack of available staff and funds to do better. Pages and pages stressed the importance and details of holding democratic elections *now* for committee members and chairmen. It included questions people had asked us, and answers, on hiring practices committees should consider. It talked about whites we didn't want in the program, and whites people might consider. (They weren't considering *any* local whites, for the most part, because they weren't discriminating between Klansmen and kindly folks. It mentioned the possibility of splitting jobs and paychecks, and of sharing places for children between two half-day or half-session children. It outlined five ways to make teaching better. It ran many, many community reports, giving ideas relevant to keeping centers running with no money:

ENTERPRISE

Mrs. Lena B. Jordan writes: "We began our Volunteer work at the Enterprise Center, October 29, 1965. We work every Monday and Friday. Every one seems to enjoy there work."

HOLLY GROVE

Mrs. Mattie Thomas says: "Yes we would like very much to open our Center and we have plan to open our Center the first week in Nov. 3 money or no money and we will have 3 days or maybe 4 days a week. We to are praying that we will get some help. I will be righting and let you know about the Center."

HARMONY

"The Harmony Community Center will open on Nov. 1, on a volunteer base. Living in the rural it is much harder to arrange the transportation than in the city, so we wont be able to have school but two days out of a week.

Some parents will bring Childrens in as they come to the Center, others have agreed to give money or gas to help get other childrens to the center. Each child will bring a lunch. Parents will also bring lunches to help out school will turn out at 12."

SUNNY MOUNT

"We are running our school at the Sunny Mount Center on the non-pay term. There are one resource teacher, two trainees, three aides, and four ladies to prepare and serve lunch at noon.

We asked each child to pay fifty cents each per week and each worker pay something to help with the expensives. Such as transportation and food. There are 25 children enrolled in our Center at the present and we are looking for more. We are planning to make the best of our Center."

Sincerely yours.
Equilla H. Taylor
Willie Mae Wright

LIBRARY CENTER

Mrs. Vassie Patton writes: "Library Center—never closed. Moved from church to house. 8:00–2:30. Parents fix lunches and bring them by. Some bring own lunch. They pay 25¢ week to keep up gas bill. Have a kitchen but no stove. About 35–40 children. Agreed to keep open because so many women only earn $18–$20 a week. Some have to pay $7–$9 to somebody to keep their children. 7 teachers during summer—5 of trainees stayed on now."

* * *

The north wind doth blow,
And we shall have snow,
And what will the robin do then,
Poor thing?

CHAPTER 28

INVOLVEMENT OF THE POOR: BEFORE OR AFTER THE FACT?

THOUGH JOHN SPENT the bulk of his time in repartee with OEO, writing and rewriting budgets and administrative plans, overseeing the mechanics of child recruitment, hiring format, committee election procedures, constantly learning from OEO how resplendently remiss CDGM had been, and responding to OEO's ever-escalating denuding demands, his major interest was in the tedious and detailed human area of working with CDGM's community people toward developing an understanding of the words they stated were their goals (freedom) and of their institution designed to work toward these goals. Had he saved the time he spent on efforts to involve community people in beginning to comprehend the difficulties and details of working with OEO and in putting their freedom words into programmatic form, he would doubtless have had more time to "be a good administrator"—but not of CDGM; there wouldn't *have been* a CDGM. CDGM was synonymous with these very efforts to involve community people in concept formation and implementation as well as in routine "parent participation." If people learn through experience, they learn through immersion in the total experience, not just through exposure to a selected segment of it.

As Mr. Sugarman's promise for a new grant "within ten days time" slid vaguely into a promise for a grant "by the end of September" and then into a certainty that CDGM would be refunded "by the middle of October, at the latest," John tried to keep communities informed of progress. He mailed several letters to local committee chairmen during September and October.

One such letter summarized the information we had received from Washington—that Jule Sugarman said we would know about a grant during October—that no decision had yet been made as to whether or not we could spend the $100,000 remaining from the summer—that we had proposed using it for teacher training unless community people had other ideas. The letter also outlined what needed to be done in communities: "To apply for money from the Poverty Program, we must have the following detailed information from each community. A COMMUNITY PREPAREDNESS FORM is enclosed on which you can enter the information. PLEASE FILL OUT AND RETURN THESE FORMS TO EDWARDS AS SOON AS POSSIBLE. When you register children or ask about renting a building, be sure to tell people that you are not making a definite commitment, but that you are simply getting information which is necessary in order to apply for the money from the federal government."

The second CDGM proposal, prepared in October, 1965, was, like the first proposal in the spring of 1965, written by a handful of Northern good guys. However, John exerted much effort to develop Tom Levin's original theme of increasingly involving the poor in this type of planning. The first proposal had been written according to OEO guidelines, plus Tom's innovative ideas, which went way beyond OEO Head Start requirements, plus comments from the poor to organizers in communities and telephone comments, which were worked into the application by its four Movement-graduate writers.

The second proposal was written according to OEO guidelines, plus Tom's, John's, and Polly's summer learnings, plus the extensive numbers of ideas we gathered during our August evaluation and suggestion period via Newsletter, the Mudd-Wilcox letter, and the late August statewide evaluation meeting. Tom (as a parting gift prepared in New York) wrote it. John and I rewrote it, but we were moving gradually in the right direction—more from the poor than the first go-around. This proposal has been termed "a major document" in sophisticated social action circles.

John sent another letter to community and center chairmen on October 25. The significant factor differentiating John's mailings to poor people from most other poverty project's letters to poor people was that John's letters didn't announce, notify, or sell—they shared and asked. This letter outlined significant new features of the proposal, explained to chairmen how to get and write down community reactions to it during the week, and invited them to come Saturday, October 30, at twelve noon, to a statewide planning meeting:

1. Administration

   We have tried to cut down the size of the staff located at a central office, and to increase the responsibility and authority of local areas by establishing a regional office for every eight centers. This regional office would have one area administrator (like the old district coordinator), one person who would work with the local teachers to help improve the program for the children, and one person to work with the parents and the community as a whole in spreading information about social welfare services or other programs which could help the community improve itself. Because these regional offices will be closer to the local communities, the administrator should be able to make sure checks and vouchers are handled more rapidly; the program advisor should visit and hold workshops in each center once every two weeks; and the information about welfare, etc., should reach more people in the communities. We hope that each of these positions will be filled by someone from the surrounding local communities. Each person would have a car so that they could go to the different centers rapidly and often, and the office would have a telephone with someone to take massages at least eight hours a day. Hopefully, in this way, most of the problems which arise could be handled locally.

DO YOU THINK THIS IDEA OF REGIONAL OFFICES IS A GOOD ONE?

2. Center Staff
There have been many suggestions about how to modify the salaries and positions of the community staff working with each unit of 15 children. The present proposal makes the following suggestions:
   a. *One* resource teacher with special responsibility for improving the program in the center for every *four* units, at a salary of $90 or $100. (We have received information from Washington which states that the resource teacher should be the best person available in working with children and in learning new kinds of activities to organize in the center. The resource teacher does *not* necessarily have to have college training or a teaching certificate.)
   b. Two teacher-trainees at a salary of $60 per week. This means ending the distinction between trainees and aides.
   c. One part-time employee at $25 per unit.
   d. One administrator and health coordinator paid $10 per unit with a maximum salary of $50 per week.

DO YOU THINK THESE POSITIONS AND SALARIES WOULD BE GOOD, OR DO YOU HAVE OTHER SUGGESTIONS? (Remember when you make other suggestions, that the total salaries per unit under this proposal add up to $180 per week. If we included all the centers and units which have applied for this winter, a change, in any salary, of $10 would change the total budget by over $170,000.00)

3. Community Services: The present budget provides for the following amounts per unit:
   a. Facility rental and utilities—$40 per month
   b. Transportation—$30 per week
   c. Food—$45 per week

DO YOU THINK EACH OF THESE AMOUNTS WOULD BE ADEQUATE?

4. In kind contribution
The present proposal commits each center to provide at least two volunteer workers for 20 hours each per week for every unit. We are also asking Washington to count the volunteer labor of those who work less than 20 hours.

IS THIS COMMITMENT REASONABLE?

5. Central office—The staff has been considering for some time the possibility of moving to a more central location, probably in Jackson. How would you feel if we moved into a downtown office building?
   Another suggestion is that we move to West Point. What do you think of that?
6. Total budget—The total budget to pay for this proposal would cost over $6 million ($6,200,000). If we do not receive all this from the government, how do you think we should divide the money we do get among all the people who want to participate? (Which of the budgeted items could communities volunteer themselves? Or, which could we cut? Should we accept only children 4 years and older? Should we not accept new centers, or should we try to spread the money as far as possible to all who want to work with us?)

WHAT SUGGESTIONS DO YOU HAVE?

The meeting was held as announced, and went very well. Hundreds of people came.

Marian Wright, as billed, discussed the recent history and present status of negotiations, including the crux of our problems: the Senate Appropriations hearings, in which CDGM was proving to be the featured topic. Marian was a popular speaker amongst the poor because she always had so much to say of vital interest to them, and was so comfortably natural in spilling it out to them. It has been said that Marian talks faster than any female in the world. She dressed informally but beautifully at all times, and explained this by saying (with silent reference to the SNCC chicks), "I don't wear my ideologies in my overalls." Marian no longer thought we shouldn't fight the government. She, too, had emphatically grown through CDGM.

Marian said, "One thing I want to do, before I start telling you about what has happened, is to thank you all for staying with the project. I know it's been awfully hard because every week we have been thinking in terms of next week. And then this week we still haven't heard anything. It is awfully good of you because I know it has been hard, a lot of people haven't had jobs, and yet they cared enough about this program to stay with it, and we are grateful.

"I don't think it's any secret that Senators Stennis and Eastland and the rest of them didn't like this program. And it so happens that we were able to get this program in the first place because they didn't quite know what was going on. They learned about our application a little late to fight it. . . ."

Marian explained, politically, why Senator Stennis had looked for our weakest point, administration, and screamed about it, and why Mr. Shriver was "sort of buckeling in to them," and about the Board's negotiations with OEO. ". . . White people were scared by this program. They know that they have a right to be scared of this program, because this is the first time that Negroes have had this much money to run their own program. The white folks don't want you to run your own program. They don't like that. So all the OEO people spent most of the last two months preparing to answer some of Stennis's attack. Now Senator Stennis had a hearing. He brought out all that stuff about why we don't have any more money and why this program is a bad program. That hearing lasted about four hours, and I think that it is interesting to note the hearing on CDGM took twice as long as the hearing on the whole poverty budget of a billion dollars for next year. As soon as this hearing was over the whole budget was approved. Now Senator Stennis came out with what he thought he wanted. He hemmed and he hawed, and finally he asked Mr. Shriver at that hearing, would you have another poverty program at Mount Beulah? People in Mississippi don't like the Delta Ministry, people don't like Mount Beulah, and Senator Stennis wanted to know whether or not Shriver would refund another project here. Shriver said no he would not refund another project here at Mount Beulah. But that is the only thing that Senator Stennis wanted. Now Stennis didn't ask OEO whether or not he would refund CDGM. He didn't have enough nerve to do that publicly. . . ."

She explained that other politicians didn't know what was going on, and why the board began getting Senator Douglas and others to send telegrams to Mr. Shriver in our behalf.

"And we told him that we made mistakes last summer. We admit that we made mistakes. Y'all made mistakes in most of the poverty programs last summer. But the fact is that we ran one of the largest Head Start programs in this nation, and it was a good program. And now Stennis said that it wasn't a good program.

"So the important thing that I think we must realize is that, one, we have to run the very best program that we can run. Secondly, we've got to be aware that people are always there to take advantage of every mistake we make, therefore it is important for us to keep on, because we can work as hard as we worked last year but one man in Washington can change everything we want in five minutes. What we have got to do is to continue to build up support for this program in Washington so that people can know what we are doing." [From tapes.]

At this meeting, people brought up the fact that CAPs were suddenly being organized in a number of their communities, and expressed unhappiness about the way in which they were being systematically excluded. Marian and John both spoke to this point, interspersed with long "I was kept from information by those forming the CAP in my community" testimonials on the part of group participants.

Marian said, "I think we beat Senator Stennis for the time being, but I think we are going to have a lot of problems because the white folks are going to try to develop Community Action Programs now, and OEO is going to pin it to us that you are going to have to prove that you can't work with white folks and they have implied that where there is a Community Action Program in your county, that CDGM cannot exist. But we are going to have to fight that, because I think that this program is important. And we can justify that we have a right to exist regardless of whether any other program exists. And one thing I think we convinced them of in Washington that remains this way is that they have got the money, we have got the people. And this is a program that people have got to stick with. We got to run this thing well."

John predicted that strong pressures against CDGM as a separate program would make it necessary in the future for community people to work with local school people, CAP people, etc.: ". . . And one of our jobs this year is to prepare ourselves to work with them. So that we know how to do it. So that we can do it without having somebody fool us. So that we can recognize that they need us too. . . ."

Marian urged people to find out about power structure programs in their communities, and complain to Washington about them: ". . . You can now file a notice appeals to OEO about any Community Action Program in your community that you don't think is serving the people. Now, they take those "Toms" and put them on these committees and think that we are going to sit back. We are going to have to start complaining about these other programs and you better start insisting to your local government that you have a chance to choose your own representatives, that they can't take Negroes and put them on these committees. Now you got to get these things. . . ."

Mrs. Summerall; Quitman: ". . . We have something concerning the poverty program has began in Quitman, but it's run by the white people. And Mrs. Jones and I went to Meridian, and we looked and found out how we could get a program started, and we would have to work with the white people there, such as the mayor, or the board of supervisors, and all of those supervisors are white. We don't have any colored. We need something to combine it all and everybody's white on the board of supervisors. We were supposed to come back and talk to the lawyers who were supposed to be representing the group. We went and talked to him, and he tells us who to go to talk to. He said they did have a community poverty program. We asked him what did it consist of. He said it was for road building, and highways, and 'big intentions.' I said anybody can dig a ditch, I told the lady with me that all the money that would be gotten there for that program would go into that white man's pocket. We asked him is it nondiscriminatory. He said it was. I said well they already got Negroes digging ditches, you know doing that kind of work and not getting anything. See where they can make big money in this program, they will hire a few colored people on it. We wrote a letter to Atlanta, but we didn't get an answer, but I did get one back from ———. I understand that a program is being started. The head of this program is Mr. ———. I called him and talked with him about he said he didn't know what the program had for the ladies, but he did say he knew it was for building parks and highways. Which the bulk of the money he said will go in their pockets, and the Negroes who will get seventy or seventy-five cents, just some kind of "hush mouth" money, and that's what we do not want. And to make sure that we wouldn't kick about it, they decided that they would go and put some Negroes on it, and these people we didn't know anything about. I know one of the men. All of his best stuff he gives it to the white people, and his other stuff, little bones for greens, we buy for a quarter. And this other man he don't know anything. He told us that he would have a meeting with us when the charter finally gets signed. But we are not satisfied with that. We want to have another meeting to tell our people. When we get to talking about it, to our people, we got to look at it as long as you stay down and the white man keep you right where he want you. And if you don't holler he going to make you stay there. So it's time for we to get up, and I want to tell my people when I go back, what Mr. ——— told me. He said that any time we want to talk to him, we are free to come to his office, and I am going back to his office and sit down and talk to him and let him know that we aren't satisfied with these two colored men; they are the "Yassa" men to these white people. We will have to do something to get to tell them that we are not going to have that, and you can't put anything over on us."

John urged people to find out, to write to Atlanta and Washington, to run a quality program that could compare favorably to any other.

Many things pertaining to the proposal were discussed, including resource teachers' salaries, whether or not center committee chairmen could be employed by CDGM (OEO had not yet issued a decree on this), whether dinner could be carried in if the center had no kitchen, how the new area staff would work—all important things, things not brought to the attention of the poor in most OEO poverty programs.

But in the tape recorded account of this all-day Head Start meeting, and in the recollections of participants, there were few references to the children's program and to the need to improve it. I was a little startled at this new turn of events. However, this *was* a meeting concerning CDGM *vs.* the federal government, and CDGM *vs.* Mississippi CAPs, and it was understandable that these things were on people's minds more than were the pros and cons of the Montessori method. Both the grant delays and the stacked CAPs were caused by OEO, intentionally or to its horror, and so OEO could not justifiably complain if we had to dwell on these aspects of the operation. After all, it was not our fault that demented dervishes were dancing and practicing necromancy on the Senate floor.

Both John and Marian, I thought, did the best they could, John as honestly and profoundly, and Marian as honestly and eloquently as always. But I was disappointed that, child raising and education in Mississippi being what they are, and being on-going phenomena systematically ruining the next generation while we sat and talked politics, John and Marian didn't squeeze in and steer toward more talk of those parts of the proposal we were purportedly discussing. I didn't feel that they were as interested in educational philosophy and relating it to social philosophy as they were in the politics of grantsmanship and in the administrative technicalities of the program. Very likely I was putting the cart before the horse.

On November third the proposal went off to Washington with the following cover note:

> The proposal presented here was discussed in detail by the communities throughout Mississippi who are applying for funds to operate 138 Head Start Centers within the Child Development Group of Mississippi.
> On 30 October, 1965, representatives of these 138 centers voted their approval of this proposal as it now stands.

It would be months before we would receive a satisfactory reply, though our friend Dave Walls called weekly (and ever more weakly) to say, "I'm sure it'll be any day now." If wishes were horses . . .

The board and Central Staff made every effort to include everybody in this, but made no pretense that they had succeeded. First of all, we didn't have the necessary number of workers, or workers with adequate skill in community organizing, to make sure that every one of these 138 scattered communities actually announced in a manner that would be heard, and held in a manner that would be meaningful, the recommended community discussions of the items listed in the October 25 letter. Therefore, many members of communities didn't consider or ever hear of this letter, though their center chairmen may have. Second, many chairmen didn't read well enough to understand all the points. Third, since only *representatives* of communities came to the meeting, and since people didn't fully understand the concept of a representative, many people never heard about the business and decisions of the meeting even after their representatives had come home. Fourth, when at the meeting, since people were not in the habit of criticizing publicly, but only in private, much criticism probably didn't come out in the open.

Nevertheless, John Mudd made more effort than Head Start and CAP directors generally make not to "include people out," as one community man expressed his feelings about the way another Head Start was "including" him.

* * *

Dear Kind friend:

I am writing on the occasion of CDGM. I think that CDGM is one of the best plans that the Negroes ever had. . . . I have to say that we are in a mean world down here . . . I have seen some bad things done . . . such as a man . . . (who wouldn't sell his timber to some white folks). They went to his home one sunday morning, six of them. They stuck a knife in his jaw and led him to the car, and put him and his son in the car and they drove down the road toward the church and got out the car to get a switch to whip him but he got out of the car and ran and they shot him down with buckshots. . . . All of them had guns of all kind and we didn't have no protection at all, and when he picked him up the blood ran out of him like water through screens. Another man . . . was shot down at the cotton gin by one of the Representatives of Amite County and he laid their about four hours before any one paid any attention to him. But yet and still the cotton gin kept on working. There were four in the gin, they made three of the Negroes who witness forget what they saw but when they made Louis Allen say he didn't see anything he wouldn't. Later he was killed because he going to testify against the sheriff. He was shot with buckshots at his gate three times. His brain was piled up under the truck.

So I think that CDGM should keep operating the Headstart for Negroes.

Yours truly,

CHAPTER 29

PREVIOUSLY WASTED AMERICANS: THE AREA TEACHER GUIDES

CIRCUMSTANCES MADE IT impossible for us to implement Tom's three suggested "modes"—the autonomous, semiautonomous, and new community core CDGM with new satellite special projects. It was also impossible to implement the community child development specialist and the community living arts specialist ideas outlined in section three, or to go any further with the ideas about community health workers, equipment project specialists drawn and trained from poor communities, etc.

But we were able to carry through the idea in three areas: poor people, chosen from among themselves by members of their own subcommunities, started becoming area administrators, community organizers (social services), and area teacher guides. There were sixteen teams serving eight centers in two or three adjacent counties. Every team was made up of these three positions and included an assistant community organizer and a secretary, all from the poor community. *Nobody else was included in the teams.* We were convinced that talented and eager people, regardless of previous education or professional experience, could become experts in these areas. It might be a long and rocky road, but it could be done.

We knew that individuals strategically located among their people, bound to them by shared realities and perceptions, rather than individuals with radically different realities and perceptions caused by the fact that they are sociologically located in another group (public school teachers, for example) have the greatest prestige, therefore the greatest influence, with their peers. We knew that if these "in-group" opinion molders "went abroad," they would begin trying to bring their thinking in line with that of the new group, CDGM, and in spite of the confusion into which this contrast would plunge them, would take important new ideas home. The trend was for these new leaders to bypass traditional leaders, preachers for example, in poor communities.

There had been no such positions in CDGM during the summer. There were neither precedents for selecting individuals to fill the positions nor funds with which to have meetings so people could invent selection systems. It was left to me to find some likely candidates for the area teacher guide role. I studied the reports from the summer, and set about telephoning or driving to the four corners of the state to locate those who had been cross-recommended the most as having good natural ways with children, being dedicated to the task of creating community preschools, eager to learn, possessed of unusual initiative, and having some influence in their home locations.

* * *

My diary says, "Bad gas station near Laurel, known to be run by murderers, never go there. But it was night, I was running out of gas, had to get some urgently, so went there. Figured they'd never guess my affiliations. Did it again! Saw integrated brochures heaped in back of station wagon, and stuff I was delivering for children with CDGM address labels on it. I only asked for $2 worth; that's all I had. He was rather nasty till he learned that—then became very protective, explaining he felt compelled to fill tank, I could mail him money tomorrow, because, 'You'll never make it back to Jackson with two dollars' worth, and I don't want you running out of gas on *these* roads: they're very dangerous at night, you know!'

"Thought of Emerson: 'The world advances by impossibilities achieved!' "

* * *

Frank Glover, a member of the Delta Ministry's California swimming pool digging project, volunteered to work for CDGM and try to recruit the other two categories of area staff members. It was the area teacher guides I came to know best. This group was widely considered the most successful of the three "new careers" groups. The remainder of this chapter will be devoted to a description of what "kind of people" we were able to find, buried in squalor and what had appeared to be dead-end lives.

The following biographies were told to me a year later. I quote: "My name is Beverly Knowles. I was born in Cougar Rush, Mississippi; that is a plantation. My parents were rental farmers, living on the plantation. I lived in a three-room farmhouse: two rooms and a plank annex. The two rooms were bedrooms for the thirteen of us. There were the seven of us children, my parents, my grandmother, and unfortunately, my mother had to raise three of her sister's children, because her sister died.

"She died of pneumonia. She and her husband had had a misunderstanding in Detroit, and she attempted to hitchhike home with the children in the wintertime. The postman found her walking on the highway in Mississippi, ill. There was no hospital in the area at the time, so she died.

"There were two double beds in the back room that took care of three children each, and two beds in the front room. The others slept on the floor on pads and quilts. We took turns. We never suffered for food, because we raised everything, including meal and syrup. The only things we had to buy were salt, flour, soda, sugar.

"My father had control of the boys. He didn't want to put his interest in education; he pushed them to learn to be the best possible farmers—even the girls: I plowed, pulled corn, everything, all day. I wondered as a child why we had to be so far behind everybody else when we worked so hard; all day, every day. And the housework after the field work. They say if you work hard . . . but I didn't see that. My ambition always was to be my own employer, so I decided not to farm when I grew up. I also knew I couldn't work for white ladies and take orders. So school was very important to me.

"At first I went to a Rosenwald school on the plantation; later it became a public school. Then I went to high school in Tom's River. To do that, I had to board with a lady who kept other girls from Cougar Rush. They gave me a cot, and we paid four dollars a week for that. My mother brought me a box of food and a box of firewood every week from the plantation, and I was allowed to cook my meals in the lady's cook stove. Mother hardly ever brought a piece of fresh meat, but she brought preserved things. At school I had to buy all my books: It's only been since the 1940's that textbooks have been free in Mississippi. I had to pay a one dollar entry fee, and of course for pencils, paper, everything. It was very hard for me to pay for a robe and all the other graduation expenses. Since I was the oldest girl, my mother was able to do all this for me. She sold eggs, chickens, milk, and butter; she sewed and washed people's clothes for my high school education. She was not able to do this for all the children. She had many conferences with the teachers, and was the PTA president. She had a high determination for me to get an education.

"I was valedictorian in my class, which made me eligible for college. I was also the best on the basketball team. But neither afforded a scholarship, and my parents couldn't afford it.

"A doctor observed me on the road each day, and he asked my mother what I planned to do. He said, 'Well, I'll see if I can get her in the WACS.' He got an application and helped me get ready for the exam, but when I took it, the time was all up before I got to the literary exam. I guess I was slow. I missed by three points. They told me to come back, but the neighbors at the plantation poisoned my mother's mind against the WACS. They made her feel she was sending her daughter off to be a prostitute for the soldiers. I have always thought it was a wonderful opportunity missed.

"So I went to Birmingham to observe city life, and I convinced my mother to let me get a job there. I didn't know *how* to get a job. That was not taught in the Tom's River High School. So it took me three weeks to find anything. I got a job in a laundry at seventeen dollars a week. I started at the shakeout table separating clothes for the mangle. In the course of three weeks I moved up three positions. I moved to mangle operator, roller machine operator, and another one. But I didn't feel these jobs were my line.

"I wanted a better job so I could save for college. I kept in touch with the unemployment office. He carried me to a school cafeteria where I was supposed to assist an Italian lady. Due to the fact that I couldn't interpret her language, I complained, and he decided to move me to another place; a white school. I was given the task of cleaning half the cafeteria by 10 A.M. My next responsibility was to help at the sandwich table; make sandwiches. My next responsibility was to wash dishes. I worked there for a week. The girl who was supposed to clean the other half of the cafeteria didn't show up one day, and when the students were ready to eat, the place wasn't clean. The white lady I worked for asked me why hadn't I cleaned it? I said, 'I didn't have orders to clean it; had you asked me, I would have been happy to, but I didn't feel I should step into someone's territory and do their work without being asked.' She thought I was resentful, and I guess she complained to the employment man. He came out and said he heard I wasn't working out. He heard I was having some difficulty with my boss. I said I didn't know she was upset, she hadn't told me. I said I thought if she was upset she should tell *me*, not the man. He moved me to be the chef cook's assistant. He was a Negro. I got along well. I learned to do things on a large scale. It was just doing something, though, it wasn't anything I wanted to do. It wasn't self-fulfillment. I wasn't impressed. I did it for a month and then my mother became ill.

"I went home to be of service to her. After three months of talking all the time about wanting to go to college, the principal of the elementary school brought the principal of the Manasquan School to our house to talk to me about carrying out a school term for a school teacher who had to be absent for pregnancy. Did I want to teach? I said I didn't feel qualified. He said I could try, and this would help me save for college. I got forty dollars a month and had to pay room and board at a place near the school out of that. I liked teaching very much. I wanted to go to college very much.

"Then my cousin came from New Orleans, wearing diamond rings, and told me to marry a friend I was writing to while he was in the service, so he would send me an allotment and I could go to college. I said, 'Why? What will I do when he comes home?' She convinced me to do it. I wanted to go to college very much. This made it possible for me to go to college for one semester. Then I taught a second year to save more money to go back to college. The house I boarded in burned, and I lost everything. Then my husband was discharged.

"I had saved two hundred dollars out of the allotment, so we built an L-shaped, three room house in Toms River: no bath, no closets, no shelves—just a small shell. It cost two thousand dollars. We discussed greatly, since he needed one more year to finish high school, whether we should send him to high school or me to college. We naturally decided that he needed high school more that I needed school. He had to prepare to be the head of the household.

"So he went. We had our first child, and it would have been very hard for us both to go to school, so I taught again, but this time closer to Toms River, a mile and a half and across a creek, which I walked. The salary had increased to sixty-five dollars a month. They took out teacher retirement, insurance, and taxes. My husband borrowed two hundred dollars from his grandfather to enter Tuskegee Institute in Alabama, on the agreement that when the GI Bill came through, he would send the extra money home to me for me and the child. I taught at still another school, the only one with a position. I had to pay a taxi to take me twenty miles to work each day.

"Then the same doctor who had taken an interest in getting me into the WACS took an interest in me again, and offered me a job in his office at fifteen dollars a week. By this time I had had a second child. I tried to weigh the advantages of teaching against the advantages of making people feel better. Yet I couldn't afford it unless he paid me twenty dollars a week. He really wanted me. He agreed. I went with him. After I left teaching, the superintendent of education in another county told me I was one of her better teachers, and she would give me a contract, but I did the other because I needed the money, and because I was able to go home at noon to do my housework and feed my little boy.

"My husband came home from his year at Tuskegee empty handed. From that time on I lost confidence in him, because I didn't believe he had received his whole GI Bill in a lump sum and been robbed, as he said. There were numerous bills pending this money, which I had to take care of from my money. He started working in a life insurance company, and earned twelve dollars a week. We began to argue, dispute, disagree. And I couldn't pay all his bills. He decided to go to Yellowstone National Park to work for the summer. That gave us a little relief. But when he came back, he didn't bring enough of his money to go back to Tuskegee for another year. *Now* I see how depressed he must have been that no one would give him any money to go to school, but at that time I could only see that if you work hard and deprive yourself now, you can save for the next thing. I couldn't support my children, myself, and him. He became terribly upset, and began breaking our own property.

"The time had come to decide if we should separate. We had a terrible fight, and I went home to Cougar Rush to my parents. This imposed an awful burden on my family. They all moved into half the house, two rooms, and gave me and my children a whole room. I had a third one by this time. I was still working in the doctor's office. I had never stopped.

"I presured the doctor for more money, but he said he knew of many girls that said they would do the work for *less* than twenty dollars a week, so he got bored with me. He was right: Money is hard to come by, and lots of girls *would* have done it for less. Yet I had done a great deal for him that they might not have done. I was his janitor, bookkeeper, and his practical nurse. I set up machines for treatments; did all the lab work; measured, mixed, and labeled all his medicines (he did his own pharmacy work because he said poor people couldn't pay the price drugstores charge for it); and I did his minor surgery, such as I amputated a lady's finger, I punctured a cyst on a lady's breast, I gave shots. He did a lot of work with midwives, which I helped with, such as teaching them sterilization, danger signals, etc. I delivered most of the babies in our office.

"He was white, but his business was primarily Negro, because he had discovered that it was easier to treat Negroes. He said this was because whites ask so many questions, and he didn't want to have to explain everything he did. Also he said he didn't have to work so hard with Negroes. He had two waiting rooms, but only one examining room, so whites stopped coming. He was exceptionally nice with Negroes. He dealt with them long enough to know the struggles, depressions, desires—long enough to know that people didn't *want* to be the way they are, but had a hard time being anything else. Many plantation owners would come to him and say, 'Take care of this person up to — price, but not over that price, because he isn't worth it to me.' The doctor helped many people get off the plantation and onto the FHA project. I feel I owe him a lot because of the opportunity he gave me, and the time he took to train me in so many areas.

"I finally was doing everything he did. I also took a correspondence course in practical nursing through the Chicago School of Nursing and had my fourth child. I asked him to give me a raise.

"He said he would get in trouble with the other doctors in town if he raised me to thirty dollars a week. So one Monday morning, I went to work and found another girl doing my work. I worked next to her, nicely, all day long. Finally I went to see him, and said, 'I've got to talk with you a little.' He said, 'I have nothing to say to you today.' I said, 'How can we work all day together and you have nothing to say to me? What does that mean? Are you firing me?' He couldn't answer. I could see he was upset. So I said, 'Four years ago when you wanted me to work here, you didn't do it this way. You talked to me. I think you could use the same technique now: You could talk to me like a person and tell me you want to fire me. Is that what you want to tell me?' He couldn't answer. I believe he was very ashamed. So I went home to Cougar Rush to my mother.

"This brought tears to me, because in the course of it, I couldn't picture him as the very strong, stern, considerate, wonderful person I had always known him to be. Fortunately, it was the cotton picking season, so I picked to make a living. I could pick two hundred and fifty pounds a day. I was unemployed for three months from his office, and it became filthy. Patients dropped off. His business became bad. People didn't like what he had done to me, though I didn't discuss it with them.

"One day his wife came around, and said, 'Dr. says he needs you.' I said, 'I can't work for someone who doesn't respect me. The way he treated me was not with dignity. I would rather clean a chicken house if I could be respected, than work for him in that manner.' His wife couldn't believe me, but she went back to him. Three weeks later, *he* came to me. He flatly said, 'I've got to have you back.'

I returned to work for him, and worked as usual. I gave no criticisms. He wanted to explore, to say a lot of things about the past, but I realized that he realized that he *had* to come back to me to make his business a success, so I didn't want to hurt his pride.

"He fell ill. He had to remain at home for many months. I kept the office open for him, doing all the usual treatments, deliveries, minor surgeries, and pharmacy work. Every evening I went around to his house and gave him a report. I was pregnant with my fifth child at this time. During the few days I was in the hospital having this child, they carried the doctor to the sanitarium, and there he stayed until he died of lung cancer or TB. It's a TB sanitarium, but I believe he died of lung cancer.

"His wife asked me to explain the business to her, so she could sell out. I did, and then I asked her if I could have a few of the beds from the clinic. I had not had enough beds for the children since moving home to my mother. But she sold them all, and said nothing.

"So there I was, without a husband, without my own home, and without a job. I decided to go into hair styling. I had been doing it during my spare time through all the jobs. I had been doing it since I was ten. People liked the way I groomed their hair without burning their heads. I charged what people could pay: usually seventy-five cents for a press, and a dollar fifty for a style and a press. Out of that I had to buy a kerosene heater and kerosene to heat the curling iron, a curling iron, pressing oils, combs, brushes, bobby pins, shears to cut, clippers to edge—equipment. I did my younger sisters and sent them off to school with their hair well done. That was how I advertised. I did this and field work every day. With this I was able to buy food for my five children. We were still hauling water from five miles away for drinking and washing every day, as we had through my childhood. This lasted from June to November.

"Then the father of the last two children was instrumental in helping me move to Toms River. I couldn't move back into my own house because my husband had control of it, and he had broken or sold all my furniture, and wouldn't let me live in it. A lady I had treated at the clinic suggested that I sue him to save the house and get alimony.

"I had fifty dollars, so I went to see a lawyer, who took my case for that. It took many years, but I finally got the house and custody of the children, but no alimony or support money. But he threatened to burn it down if I moved into it, so it was mine, but I didn't live in it. Yet I wanted to be in Toms River, because I felt that if I could be there, where people live close together, I could make it on the beauty business.

I was doing all right, but someone reported me to the State Board for practicing without a license. They sent me a letter saying that I would have to go to Beautician's School and get a license, or close up. So I started searching for a means to get the beauty culture training for the most economical price. I was successful in contacting a person at a beauty school in Greenville who would allow me to pay the required $150 as I earned it. The others all charged $250 and required eleven months training. The lady let me take the State Board exam in Meridian after three months. I had been a fast learner. I passed and was granted permission to get a license. It cost twenty-two dollars a year.

"Then I had to spend $450 to buy a shampoo bowl, a dryer, two operator's chairs, a gas jet, a dresserette, cabinets, a sterilizer, to put in running water, to put linoleum on the floor, to put in gas, and to install the shampoo bowl, and to cut a door to the bathroom and a door directly to the outside from the room in the house that I would use as a beauty shop. This was all required to keep the license. It was worth it to do the work, for money, and because there is a serious side to the beauty business.

"I speak words of comfort to people who come and pour their troubles on me. They cry out their troubles. They come to me with three dollars that took a day's work in the fields from sunup to sundown to earn. They come because people *have* to have a change from their world of struggle. That's why they spend their money on hair. And because I need the money, I take it. But in return, I give them beauty, and I give them words of encouragement. I say, 'This is not right. It will not always be like this. We are going to change this.'

"I started talking to people about starting a kindergarten for them. I started talking to the church deacons about forming a community center. People started contributing pennies, nickels, dimes, and dollars, and we bought a piece of land. We made it into a playground for our children. We got the school principal involved, and he helped us build the community center, but then he took control of it. People realized they had contributed to something they didn't control, and they became angry.

"I had a very earnest desire to help people, so when the Masons asked me to be the Mother Mary for a group of theirs called the Herrons of Jerico, I took on the responsibility. I trained young people in civic service. We renovated old furniture and old clothes and sold it to the needy and used the money to help the needy. We also had a talent scout program. Meanwhile, I had written several articles for a Negro paper in Greenville about the standstill our community center had come to, and a young man from CORE read them and came around to talk to me about some of my views. This was 1964.

"He came to Toms River and attempted to help us straighten this control question out. He also got us started meeting at night to discuss different rights we didn't know we had, facilities we knew we needed, and programs we were entitled to have access to. Others came. I openly accepted all who came. I allowed them to meet on my lawn. I wasn't affiliated with any group, and I didn't know under whose auspices they came. I didn't care: I thought it was a way of Providence answering the cries of the people in the wilderness. I felt that this was an opportunity to apply my knowledge of the Bible and the minister's words to our real living situation. If you can't do that, what's the use of the knowledge and the words?

"We began trying to get the Negro leaders in our community, the ministers, and the principals, to find out about all these things and lead us, but we found that they were weaker than we, and we went on without them.

"A CORE man came and told us about Head Start. It was the spring of 1965. How to sign up children, find a building, form a committee. I suggested a lady as chairman because I was so busy with my beauty business.

"Over half the Negroes failed to participate in CDGM the first summer because they feared civil rights. I thought that CDGM was the beginning of the fruits of the labor so many of us had given—something, finally, which we could touch, feel, see, show to others. When I got to Beulah, it was my first time to see whites with Negroes working together on a large scale on a real program. I said, 'Now I know what I want to do with my life. I see now how I can use myself to make certain things work that my heart has always been telling me to do. My so-called friends urged me not to do it. They told me I was risking everything. They told me I could make a living other ways. I said, 'It's not a question, only, of earning a living.' In the course of their lifetime, my children will look back and say, 'My mother helped break down the barriers to a better life. That's part of the question, too.'

"The first summer I was health coordinator. During the volunteer period I was a resource teacher. When you called and asked me to accept the position of area teacher guide, or ATG as we began calling it, I felt very inefficient. But I decided to try, and if I failed I had done my best, and if I succeeded I had helped. I learned how to go into the centers in my area without too much criticism, yet how to offer to leave behind something to lift some of the burden from their brows. Since then, CDGM has made me find my purpose in life. It has helped me communicate in new ways with people who need me. It has helped me blend a little education with my own plentiful experience to help me use myself more. I am telling you this story in 1967. I am no longer with CDGM. But CDGM is still with me. It was the period in my life when I grew most."

"I am Gaynette Flowers, the baby girl out of seven children. My mother died when I was four years old. We had been living in Grovehill, Alabama, but we moved to Selma, where I had my first stepmother. She had three children of her own, and she showed partiality to them. There wasn't enough food, and they got theirs first. If there were treats, a banana or something, she gave it to them sneakily when we were outside. We had to do the chores. They didn't. Her children were always right if there were arguments between us. I learned from her how children feel about partial adults. I resolved never to show partiality. I was very unhappy with her.

"A year later they were divorced. I don't know why, we were never told why. We returned to our grandparents' house in Grovehill. Daddy married again. I had been so happy with my grandparents; I thought I was back home to stay. Then I was hauled off again, against my will.

"This woman was a good but cruel stepmother. That's hard to explain, but it's true: she was good in her way, but unconsciously cruel. She believed punishment would make us good. Punishment was the cure for everything. Such lashings she gave me that my skin was cut for two weeks. She didn't even give me time to open my mouth to say I didn't even do it. I got whippings when I 'let' a hawk sweep down out of the air and grab a biddie. She counted the chicks every night, and if one was missing I got a beating. I was supposed to guard the chicks. Often I got terribly beaten for running off in wonder after an owl in a tree when I was supposed to be getting water at the spring, or for following a red squirrel and coming home five minutes late, or for tearing my dress, like kids sometimes do. Once I got whipped till I was bruised and cut for shaving a bar of soap with a knife. She could have thrown it in the boiling pot and beat it with the battling stick and used it anyway—I didn't really waste it. She placed too much responsibility on children in the first place. She had one hundred dollars in greenbacks tied up in a money sack under her dress; she should have spent some of it to buy wire to protect those chicks. She made me nervous for life. I haven't come out of it yet.

"This type of cruelty kept our house in confusion. My Daddy loved us so much and couldn't stand this. I didn't understand till years later why he would start ruckuses over little or nothing with my stepmother, and take the shotgun to her and beat her. Later I learned it was probably caused by his furious hurt over the way she treated his children. But he didn't want to tell her he knew about it, because he knew she would beat us to death next time he was away. I'll give you an example of his feelings on this.

"One day this stepmother made John eat some peas he didn't want. My father came in, and he was enraged. Some weeks later, when all the children were out, she served him some peas with ham and gravy and corn bread on top, the same way he always liked but didn't like this time. He made *her* eat a huge bowl full, while he held his shotgun on her. It seemed terrible to me at the time that he would do such an unreasonable thing, but later I realized that it was because he was so furious about what she had done to John. John was the baby boy. He got a whipping whether he did anything or not, if she couldn't find anyone else to blame it on. Many times John went out and picked every growing thing he could find that she had told him not to touch because it was poison, and he would put them in water and give it to her hoping she'd die. But she just got fatter.

"I'll give you another example of Daddy's feelings on this. One day I was with Daddy, playing and fooling, with his hair. He said, 'Baby, what's this sore on your wrist?' I told him, just told him, 'Mama beat me and cut me up all over.' He was very upset. He said, 'Would you tell me this in front of her?' I said, 'Sure.' He said, 'I'll ask you all over again when she's here, so she won't know you told me.' She came up from the spring with her big sunbonnet on from doing the wash. She came up and flopped down on the porch. He said, 'Baby, what's this sore on your wrist?' I said, 'Mama whipped me the other day, and cut into my skin.' He said, 'Mama, what's this? What's this?' She swole up with rage, and said, 'I didn't do it, I didn't do no such thing! It's a lie! It's a lie!' Daddy said, 'Well, let me tell you one damn thing! Don't you do any damn thing like this again to my children! I trust you with them. I put you in complete charge. But let me tell you one damn thing: If I'm home or away, don't you dare give them one damn beating again. Just tell me what they do wrong, and I'll take care of it.'

"One day we children got together and decided since Daddy wasn't going to quit this woman, we would have to organize to beat her up. One brother hit her with a hoe in the field, but the others didn't do the part they'd agreed to, so she beat him terribly. If they had come in, there might have been a case of mother murder.

"I've always wondered: if John *had* poisoned her, or we had killed her, who would be guilty? Here was a little boy just trying to get out of a cruel situation he felt he couldn't stand anymore. I learned then that we'll never get anywhere without sticking together—if one of us rises up, they'll beat him back down. But *organized!*

"When my father was mad enough about the way she treated us, he would tell us, 'You can move back in with your grandparents.' We would be *so* happy; just go to bed so happy with our heels clicking in the air! But then they always got back together before daylight, everytime, and in the morning he would say, 'You can stay here.' Our hearts would break. We kept this stuff going till my grandparents persuaded my daddy to let them legally adopt us to end the whole confusion.

"Yet, this stepmother would tell everyone in town how much she loved us! How we were just like her own to her. I thought bitterly of her—so bitterly. I thought, 'Gaynette, you better not open your mouth, but why don't this woman quit lying!' How I got to understand her was when I got grown, and she would sit by the fire and tell me things. Then I realized that she did this way because *she* was raised this way. Her only memory of her father was of him being thrown from a horse and killed. Her granddaddy raised her, and always beat *her* half to death. He was a slave, and his master beat *him* that way. That's all any of them knew. And each was raised to think that none of the others could do wrong, so they followed the same pattern. Yet when she was picking our backs for red bugs, and she found all the scabs and scars from the beatings she had given us, she told us how she beat her own son and how sorry she was when she saw the scars on his back. She really didn't know she had hurt us so bad, but she continued, because she believed it was right. Her motto was 'Spare the rod and spoil the child.' I learned from this that we have to break these two habits: half killing our children, and training them to respect *anything* an adult does, even if they're half killing them. When I got grown, and had my own children, I said they were not going to get all those beatings. I would take away something they liked, or give some other small punishment, but I would not take a limb off a hickory or a chincopin tree and make them lumpy and covered with blue marks and filled with fear. When my name was called as a child, I was just like a little scared rabbit: I ran to her for fear she would slap me down.

"I was happy there with my grandparents, but there was still one problem: I wanted an education so badly, but there was no way out. There was a high school in Grovehill, but it was for whites only. The only way a Negro could go to high school was to pay tuition at a boarding school and send his children to the next county. My daddy *did* do this for the older children. I was with my grandparents by the time of Junior High School. Then my grandmother got sick, and I had to stay out of school for three years to take care of her. Then my grandmother passed, and I went to live with my father's sister. I went back to school then, in the ninth grade. Even when I was little, I always wanted to be a school teacher. I think it was because that's all I'd ever seen an educated Negro be. I had never been inspired that I could be a doctor or something else. I went to school for two more years. Then I went to visit some other relatives, and ended up in Gulfport, Mississippi, married.

"And what do you guess! After going into this to find some peace, I ended up with a man who played the role of a part-time husband; played dictator, beat me, came in at 4 A.M. and called me a nagging wife when I argued. But by that time, nobody could beat Gaynette Flowers anymore! I'm a strong-willed person, and I will not tolerate cruelty, unfairness, and hiding the truth. My children came first, and I would not have them raised that way. So we divorced.

"One thing that appealed to me about CDGM from the start was that nothing was to be hidden. You and Mary and John didn't just give instructions, and you didn't just ask our opinion and hope we would give you your answers; you really wanted to know. I thought you and Mary worked together beautifully—I thought you respected each other, and consulted with each other, and both of you with us. I've never hauled my ideas to workshop and hauled them home again. If I have something to say, there's always some way to get it in. I always admired the way you could listen to two or three people at the same time, and always have time for one more problem. The first few months in area teacher guide workshop, we just talked about how we felt about children, which were good and bad teachers, whether we should teach through cruelty—I thought these were exactly the things I had always felt so strongly about, more important than anything else you can talk about having to do with teaching. I felt that now I could put into practice all I feel so strongly about: people being kind and fair to each other.

"Another thing that appealed to me about CDGM was the new opportunity for the races to get to know each other by working in a program where we have control, so we can bring in whites that have the right attitude and can learn; where we can work in equal positions and *really* start getting to know each other as equal human beings. I have always worked with whites; but not as an equal. I have always been a maid or a seamstress. These positions are not equal. We *have* to have whites in the program: Northern whites, Southern whites—as long as they have the ability to learn about each other. Once I felt that I wanted to leave the South, but now I've learned that there are many wonderful Southern whites, and that we are beginning to build a new South—together. I definitely do not think all white Southerners are killers. We have to work together, that's the only way. How can Negroes and whites stop being so fearful and suspicious of each other unless they start working together as equals? As a maid, I have worked for some nice white folk that I like very much. But it's not equal if we segregate whites out of our program. It's no different than if *they* segregate us out, but the races are still separate, and can't get to know each other's feelings, opinions, and work.

"The first experience I remember with whites was when I was about six years old. My aunt sent me to the commodity store to get some syrup on credit. While I was waiting, I just naturally sat down in a living room chair in the white store lady's house—it was all together, the house and the store. When she came in with the syrup, her eyes were flashing and she went wild. She screamed at me for sitting in her chair. When I got home, all upset, my aunt said, 'Well, white people are just like that.' I have never believed that, and CDGM is proof."

* * *

On October 12, 1965, the Jackson *Daily News* announced on page one:

SMELL OF SCANDAL HANGS OVER MOUNT BEULAH PROJECT

An odious air with the smell of scandal, mismanagement and irregularity still permeates the Mt. Beulah Conference grounds at Edwards, despite the fact the Child Development Group of Mississippi has completed its controversial Head Start program there.

Spotted throughout the almost deserted conference center are project staffers who have remained to clear the books and tie up loose ends. . . . The mystery of the entire operation and the irregularities with which it functioned hopefully will be cleared up and brought further to light when a Senate Appropriations subcommittee Thursday delves into CDGM's misuse of federal funds. Stennis asked for and received a special hearing to present the investigators' findings on the Mt. Beulah project. . . . All board members of the Child Development Group are colored except Beittel and Thomas, the investigators said.

* * *

During the summer of 1966 Mrs. Flowers attended a special six week course for Head Start teachers at Peabody College. She did very well. Dr. Susan W. Gray, director of the Demonstration and Research Center for Early Education at George Peabody College for Teachers had come to make a half-day visit to us earlier, and later encouraged several of her staff members to give us occasional consultant help. In August she wrote: ". . . We have all been amazed at what your group has been able to accomplish in terms of bringing a large group of Child Development Centers into reality. We've also been impressed by the motivation and amazing ingenuity shown by the persons who work in these centers.

"To our way of thinking, the Child Development Group of Mississippi has shown great accomplishments and great potential in terms of improving the educability of the extremely deprived rural children of Mississippi. . . ."

CHAPTER 30

A NEW CAREER FOR THE POOR

Supervisor of social change through early education —area teacher guides in workshop

FROM THE FIRST day the area teacher guides (ATGs), each from a different part of the state, and most unacquainted with each other, were a tightly knit, spirited team. They were cemented together by the fact that as individuals, with few exceptions, they were intelligent, brave, fair, eager, stretching, and deeply concerned people. It wasn't that they were interested; it was that they were *deeply concerned*, and in their own individual ways, were seeking a vehicle through which they could, at last, *do* something with their concern.

John and I had agreed that money or no money we had to go on building local talent to serve as teaching supervisors for the second grant when we finally landed one. I was therefore recruiting ATGs, and Mary and I were preparing educational materials for teachers. Yet we actually had no way of financially supporting this venture in faith. After seventeen- or eighteen-hour days of slaving for CDGM, John and I would sometimes get the early A.M. giggles: It was quite possible that there *was* no CDGM, except in our two obstinately envisioning minds. John was the only person who was making an attempt to get us temporary relief and subsistence funds. Throughout October he talked with his friend Judge Justine Polier, Children's Court judge in New York City and a member of the board of directors of the Field Foundation. On October 26 he wrote to Mrs. Marshall Field, giving a short summary of the summer project, describing its present potentialities for development in the forthcoming year. The letter's outline of the great number of things we planned to do with very little money is an interesting contrast to the exorbitant budgets and tiny tasks proposals these days are prone to propose.

"The requested interim grant would allow CDGM to begin to hire these individuals, to offer them training sessions, and to pay them at least a partial salary to cover living and travel expenses. Specifically, this sum would provide:

"(A) Educational Training—Estimated cost: $16,400.

"(1) Salaries for the top (educational) program staff

"(2) A three-week intensive training session for 15 area education advisors beginning November first

"(3) Educational consultants (from Pacific Oaks and other nationally known child development institutes)

"(4) A one-week training session for 200 resource teachers drawn from every center that wishes to participate in the future program

"(5) Materials and expenses for a demonstration class of 15 children to be used in the training period.

"(B) Administrative and Community Organization staff—$13,150.

"(1) Staff recruitment

"(2) Ten organizers (plus transportation) for community work during the interim, pregnant period

"(3) Two one-week training sessions for the full area administrative and community organization staff of 30

"(4) An orientation for 100 chairmen of community committees for each center in administrative procedures."

Both John and I had family and friendship connections with the Field Foundation, but the fact that it gave us a grant was doubtless due to the efforts of Judge Polier to persuade her board and it's new Executive Director Leslie W. Dunbar, formerly executive director of the Southern Regional Council, that it was urgent to do so. Once again an individual played a key role in CDGM's fortunes. A letter dated November 1, 1965, from Mr. Dunbar to the American Friends Service Committee in Philadelphia, which was to be the administrator of the grant, includes this paragraph: "Because the Field Foundation is mindful of the extraordinary work of the Child Development Group and because, furthermore, our own inquiries have led us to believe the Office of Economic Opportunity shares our high regard and is likely to act favorably on the new program, we have taken the unusual step of agreeing to this emergency request and granting, as per the revised budget, $17,975."

This was half the absurdly small sum we minimally hoped for, but we did everything we'd planned anyway. This involvement set a precedent for Field's great financial and other supporting help later, when CDGM was even more desperate. I believe it also set a precedent for "responsible" liberal organizations, such as the American Friends Service Committee, to consider CDGM important. Thus, CDGM began it's ascension to national significance. John gave Field a financial accounting, and I wrote them a seventeen-page thanking report documenting what we did in the workshops. During this peripatetic season, we continued to encounter dampening happenings daily. My diary notes: "Stopped at the store that sells gas, groceries, and bait between Vicksburg and Redwood on Highway #61 this morning to get some cookies.

Hadn't eaten since lunch yesterday; too busy. Klansman heckled. I said, 'I'll be glad to talk about that with you, just wait a minute till I get some crickets for my little girl Katie.' Then I concentrated hard on crickets, peering into the screen tank they keep them in all the time asking the Klansman's advice on which he thought looked healthiest, fattest, what do you feed crickets? Etc. When through with my purchase, and munching on some chocolate Oreos, which I offered him, I looked fully and with trusting friendship into his eyes and said, 'Now, is there something you wanted to talk about?' He looked utterly taken aback, and said, 'Aw, hell, never mind.' You can't out-evil them, we're no competition in that sphere: but on the heart-to-heart level we're equal, so I try to keep it there."

While John was making his plead-and-pray financial stabs, Mary Emmons and I had already plunged ahead with our ATG workshop and a sample Head Start center. Mary was a bit taken aback when I said something about getting money, maybe, for a workshop, and asked her to run a short sample classroom every day for a week. She was pleased, but a little nervous. She'd never run a demonstration class before, and in both undergraduate and graduate school she was a political science major; international relations. She had done remedial work with older children at the Woodlawn Tutoring Organization in Chicago and had been an assistant teacher at a Montessori school for a year. But it was different. They had an in-service training program with Montessori teachers imported from Holland. They discussed each child intensively and extensively and analyzed every aspect of his learning.

Mary was used to workshops where every detail was agonized over for weeks, and now I expected her to recruit a class, produce a program, even paint the tables, by herself, in less than a week. She still had very little sense of the atmosphere in CDGM communities. She had no idea how many centers there were, or a feeling of the distances involved. She had visited the Tougaloo center and could feel gears shifting in her head—beginning to view the class as coming from nothing, instead of coming well-heeled like the Chicago Montessori.

Mary said: "I was very impressed by the ATGs. They told wonderful stories, said such interesting things about whatever we were talking about. And there was such a feeling of companionship. I learned a lot about what got them going. I kept contrasting it to the CO and AA workshops that were running at the same time. They seemed so half-formed; full of lectures. They were almost all new to the program, but the ATGs were leaders. They had been active in the summer. They knew some of the things they wanted to know. They were ripe to learn. And they got something when they came to workshop. They were the privileged ones working in communities at that time, so they were able to do something immediately with what they were learning. They could go back with new information, ideas, spirit, hope. I think lots of volunteer centers started because of the ATGs. People were on pins and needles about what they could do while waiting. We kept saying, 'Well, you could open your center.' I didn't realize the sacrifices they were making to do it, and the community conflicts. But I think it was good for morale. At that time I wasn't critical of what we were doing. I was very naïve about the whole grant-getting procedure—I thought OEO was our friend—I thought we were quite productive. It wasn't till later in the winter that I got cynical."

My feeling was that sensing and doing come before knowing and managing, and if you do what seems to have to be done, Providence will see to it that the other pieces fall into place. The ATGs knew that John was negotiating for money, but didn't yet have it. They, too, were willing to take a risk.

They voted to come to Mount Beulah to "class" daily from 10:30 to 4:00. These hours gave those who had a three or four-hour drive each day time to make it during daylight hours. Mississippi Negro women are, on the whole, for historically valid reasons, terrified to drive at night. The theme of the two-week workshop was: In two weeks, each ATG would be solely responsible for conducting a four-day orientation session at Mount Beulah for thirty resource teachers apiece. Whether the resource teachers got a wonderful, useful orientation or a weak and boring one was entirely up to each ATG. The credit would go to the individual ATG if she could come up with four days that intrigued her constituency. The burden of responsibility would be the ATG's alone if she failed to impress her group with creative teaching, ability to lead a tangy discussion, and the solid information people craved. Because they felt that such an appalling responsibility would momentarily be upon their shoulders, the ATGs contributed from the depths of their latent wisdom and with more energy than they had probably ever given anything.

* * *

". . . and I was putting up molasses meal. It was about 8 o'clock in the evening. . . . (My wife) said, 'There's a car out there. There go that car again. It went on up, turned around, and it went up to the store and stopped. Then when it stopped, well I opened the door, and just as I opened the door something caught on fire on the hill, and a flame. And it burst, and then right behind that another burst. . . . I shot three times over the head of the car—just to scare him, and let him get away, you know. He came back, made one trip up there, turn around, came back, drove slow, went up to my daddy's fork, turn around, came back, and he stopped. I had got myself on the east side of the house . . . and the car turned there where he stopped, and he fired. . . . Then they went on, and that's when I went on and called the sheriff. Then they told me that my wife was shot . . . One of my kids told me. . . ."[32]

* * *

During our two weeks, we used essentially two methods: demonstration and the Socratic question-and-answer approach. Mary set up her instant Head Start center. ATGs visited this center in teams of two and three for several half days each. They took notes on specific aspects we had agreed upon in advance, besides soaking in the general style of the thing.

All the rest of the time, except for an hour out for dinner in the campus community dining room, ATGs spent with me, the twenty of them and me, in a barren classroom, digesting and defining the pliantly provocative basic living and learning questions I tossed at them; dredging answers from their experience. ATGs stopped being exclusively vassals under the numbing yoke of the orthodox, and began their slow transmutation into conscious people.

ATGs are slumped in old schoolhouse desk chairs. I am pacing and prancing around the barren room. We do not have grand facilities.

ME: What do you guys want for your community? I mean, what do you *really* want?

CHORUS OF ATGS: Freedom! ! !

ME: OK, well I'm not even going to ask you what you mean by that right now. Let's just start with this question: Do you know anybody in your community who you think is working for freedom?

[Appreciative laughter]

Yeah me! Mrs. Robins. Jake Ayers. Reverend McCree.

ME: What do they do that's different from people in your community that *aren't* working for freedom? I mean, what kind of personalities are they? What type of qualities do they have that makes you say they're working for freedom?

ATG #1: Well, this one man, he's a real leader in. . . . He's a leader because he really has guts. He'll stand up to anybody if he thinks he's right.

ME: Does everybody agree that guts to stand up for what you believe in is an important quality in freedom workers?

[Unanimous agreement]

ME: OK, guts, who's taking notes? Have you got guts? [Great laughter]

OTHERS: Yeah, I got plenty guts.

ME: What else? Who else knows a leader? What is special about him or her?

ATG #2: The ones I knows, they'll work. They'll do it when the others'll jes' say it.

ME: Hard workers at this particular thing. Willing to work.

NOTE-TAKER: I put "follow up." That means they won't let you down and be busy when the time comes.

ME: Hard workers, follow up reliably.

[32] Goodman, Mississippi, Oct. 29, 1965 (Excerpts from a tape made by CDGM staff member Frank Glover).

OTHERS: Put "reliable." Reliable about freedom work.
Whatever the dirty work is they'll do it.
They'll stick to a tough job.

ME: What else? Anything else?

ATG #3: That's all.

ME: I don't believe it.

ATG #4: That ain't all—takes a person who wants to know the truth. Some peoples, they don't ask no questions. They takes anything The Man says. But they's some peoples, jes' keeps on axin' questions till they gets to the truth.

ME: Seek information. Want the whole story. Got that?

NOTE-TAKER: I ain't got the whole story yet, Polly, but I sure will when us girls gits through. When us lady peoples gets together, anything can happen!

[Chaos]

ME: Any more? Anybody got anything to say?

ATG #5: I do: When's dinner time?

ME: When we finish figuring out what it takes to be a freedom worker. Think fast, eat soon.

ATG #1: Good sense of humor. The stuff you gotta take in freedom work, you gotta be able to take it light.

ME: That's the truth! More?

ATG #6: Person got to espress hisself. Some folks gets scared and can't say nuthin'. Some folks knows what they wants to say, but it jus' don't come out straight so the others gets an understandin'.

ME: Can you write this fast? What did you say?

ATG #7: I said a person like that has to be friendly, have a lot of influence. Nobody's gon' maybe mind to somebody they don't respect.

ATG #2: Has to be clever like a fox: lots of ideas. White man's got 'em, our leaders have to have 'em too.

ME: Could you read back the list?

NOTE-TAKER: We wants peoples with: guts, do what believe in, follow up, reliable, hard workers, seeks truth by asking questions, good sense of humor, express self in conversation, friendly and able to pull influence, apt at ideas.

ME: Did we get everything? Anyone want to add?

[Satisfaction]

ME: Then let me ask you this question: If that's the kind of grown-ups you want, what do we want to teach children in our centers?

ATG #1: The alphabet. Manners.

ATG #8: Numbers. To play nice with the children.

ME: That's *some* of the things, I'll agree with that, but what kind of qualities?

CHORUS: To be obedient. To be quiet. To behave.

ME: Aw, come on ladies, you're kidding me! You're not making a bit of sense in the world. You just got through telling me you want adults who have guts, ask questions, express what they want to—and now you tell me you want the opposite in children. Do quiet, obedient, well-behaved children who know their colors grow into freedom workers?

ATG #3: That kinda' chile grows into that kinda' grown-up. I know. They lives all over our town.

[Laughter of recognition: They live all over everybody's town.]

ME: If you appreciate and admire the kinds of adults you just told me about, then what kind of children would it make sense to appreciate and admire?

[Ten minutes of cacaphonic babble about "as the twig is bent . . ."; "once I knew a little boy who . . ."; "we have an old-fashioned kindergarten teacher in our town. . . ."; "some children are definitely more curious than others. . . "; "We want all these things we're talking about in children: talk out, not afraid . . ."]

ME: OK, ladies, I gotchou . . . in different ways you're all saying that you want children that are the same kinds of people you admire when they get grown. Now, here's the hard question: If that's what you want, what are we going to do in the centers to promote that? What will we *do*, each minute, each activity, that builds those characteristics in children?

[Confusion: a repetition of the usual kindergarten activities.]

ME: Yes, well, those are the usual activities. That's fine. Those are fun for children. But how will you handle those activities, and each word you have with each child, so you are teaching *those* characteristics instead of teaching him just to obey, follow directions . . . ?

In another long burst of understandings, ATGs verbally milled around the point that the mere presence of activities and materials usually found in a well-planned preschool program, and a speaking acquaintance with child development theory, don't guarantee a good child development program. It's the way in which *every* activity, material, and social situation is used *every* time with *each* child that determines whether he will learn: to follow directions blindly, or to question, think, and decide; to sit still and look attentive, or to become deeply curious and concerned; that adults are abrupt, thoughtless, unfair, and not interested in his feelings or thoughts, or that adults are patient, considerate, fair, and interested above all else in the expression and maturing growth of his feelings and thoughts; that school is boring and restricting, or exciting and challenging and something in which he can feel proud. We emphasized and re-emphasized that activities, materials, and social situations in centers shouldn't be goals. They should be vehicles for developing and stretching the characteristics, qualities, and strengths we valued, because they correlate positively with our community change goals. Our slogan became: "Unless *you* see how the activity you are using with the children relates in the way you want it to to social action, *don't do it.* Have faith in nothing. Find out."

ATG #9: [generally cynical] Is that the way we're supposed to teach?

ME: I don't give a hoot how you teach. You can prepare a bunch of zombies as far as I'm concerned. They're you're children and your communities, not mine. It's not my problem. I'm only interested in helping you determine what *you* as educational leaders value, and connecting up in your minds how *you're* going to get that. *You* set the goal—*you* determine the means of arriving at it. I just want you to feel how much power you have to set the goal and work out techniques that will move you there.

ATG #10: You tell her, honey. We're with you all the way. Let's go eat.

Arm in arm we sauntered across the dirt driveway to the dining room. All we had left to do now was spend the rest of our lives learning how to apply these easy words.

And out of all that we developed a product not in the least extraordinary. But it was *ours,* born of us. We developed a guide to help ATGs lead discussions with their resource teachers at the impending Orientation, and guides to help ATGs work, immediately thereafter, with resource teachers in their own scattered home centers. In a mere three weeks we developed a notebook of 239 pages, mostly single-spaced typing, with many illustrative sketches, plus all the Newsletters and letters from our division to committee chairman to date. It had the not notable title *The Blue Book,* because it was assembled between two blue tagboard covers.

At every session an ATG took blackboard notes on what we were talking about, and another ATG copied these onto paper. Each night I typed what we had, duplicated it, and the next day we added the previous day's discussion to our rapidly, fatly growing personal notebooks. It was the process we were interested in promoting, though the product was temporarily needed too. Our guidebook was not remarkable, though it won much enthusiastic praise from OEO, other Head Start staffs, and distinguished early educators who came to visit, or with whom we corresponded. I hoped that the ATGs would go through a similar process with their teachers, and end up with whatever came out of so doing.

Area teacher guides were disturbed over the demarcation between what OEO insisted on and what was up to communities to decide. So our discussions and our guidebook began with the cold facts of life. We stressed Mary's and my responsibility to bring facts and theories of early education to ATGs, and *their* responsibility to convey them to communities. We itemized OEO's minimum standards for the educational component in one column, and specifics that were up to communities in another. We spelled out steps ATGs could take to become accepted in communities in their new role. Role definition was perhaps the biggest difficulty ATGs had during their first year: From a poor peer to an educational supervisor—how do you handle it?

The same "chapter" that dealt with rules and roles devoted a page or so to each of the ATG's responsibilities, as we evolved them in discussion, through my questions as to how *they* would have liked to have been helped as teachers during the previous summer, always in terms of their community growth goals, and therefore, how they felt *they* could now help as ATGs.

We included literally the words ATGs could say to stimulate discussions on the following topics with their Center staffs: setting up classrooms and playgrounds; planning a balanced day; helping teachers spot and help all kinds of children with all kinds of special problems; becoming familiar with children's games, reading to them, music, art, etc.; taking trips; integrating the medical and health programs with the children's program; using material in the Newsletter; conducting staff meetings with a positive tone, yet a constructive outcome; helping each staff make their center truly a community project; taking on the additional and delicate burden of being a public relations department for CDGM. We encouraged ATGs to take notes on problems, to keep careful records of every kind, to bring them to workshop for us all to hash over, and *please* not to hesitate to ask for help. The notebook included a sheet of questions an ATG could ask herself to determine if she was doing a good job.

We had a vivacious good time, liberally sprinkled with the ATGs' wry humor and whimsey. We *did* things. Since the ATGs had never seen the wealth of distinguished children's literature that exists, we went to the library twenty-six miles away in Jackson. Though we integrated it, we were, to the ATGs proud astonishment, welcomed warmly. We read children's books. I carried another two hundred children's books to Mount Beulah and put them in a room for ATGs to browse through. A disaster befell me, however. I didn't see that the Freedom Information Service, a group which shared Mount Beulah with us, had posted a sign on the door, referring to books sent from the North, saying, "Help Yourself to Free Books." So most of the Jackson library's two hundred children's books were eagerly taken home and distributed to the delighted communities. This didn't seem to be CDGM's responsibility, so I paid for them personally, but the librarians never forgave me. For another year and a half every time I was in the library for my own children or myself, there went up a whispering about infamous me.

Each ATG did a research project in the library. All but three indicated that it was the first time they had known you could find out "all those things you might want to know" in a *library*, of all places! Mrs. Beard and Mrs. Backstrom made lists of all congressmen and senators to whom we might want to send programmatic public relations material and our Newsletter for support. Valentine Blue made a list of publishers we might contact about the adult and children's books we proposed to produce. Others made lists of libraries in the state, names and addresses of home demonstration workers, newspaper and TV stations, junior and senior colleges, parks, businesses, industries, and other field trip possibilities.

We practiced making large labels and labeling things in our room. We practiced the Sound Table Game outlined in Chapter 14. We practiced carrying on conversations with children, role-playing, demonstrating how a chat can drop, or with the teacher's imagination, can be prolonged. Adults who haven't chatted extensively with children as a way of life, don't understand how to do it, and no amount of guidebook instruction, telling them it's important to build children's vocabularies and concepts, helps them do it better. Practice makes closer to perfect. We practiced the Sylvia Ashton-Warner game: making tagboard word cards of each child's special words and a keeping place for them. We practiced the word-matching game, and discussed the ways in which rich experiences relate to learning to read. Mary Emmons prepared a lot of material on reading readiness games. She wrote up simple, clear, illustrated descriptions of how and why to act out stories, to play the color squares game, to play sorting games, to play grouping games (categorizing vegetables, furniture, etc.), to play concentration (a game in which the child lifts and names objects, when his back is turned someone hides one of the objects, and the child has to determine what's missing), to play number and color lotto, to play picture matching games, and to use flannel boards creatively. In all these game descriptions Mary stressed using the *children's* ideas, stretching the *teacher's* ideas—not just copying the instructions she wrote.

We had a harder time with science. We gathered many children's science books, and the ATGs immersed themselves for several days in all kinds of information about plants, animals, birth, rocks, sky, sea, water, electricity, chemicals, and so on; from books written for primary age children, so ATGs wouldn't have too much difficulty reading the material—from books with exciting illustrations so ATGs could see the vividness and excitement of the subject. We didn't administer reading tests, but with few exceptions the ATGs could read at approximately the second to fourth grade level. We would spend a morning outside really *seeing* the multitude of beauties and the thrilling things out there. One purpose of this was to interest them, almost unanimously for the first time, in noticing the wealth of simple things around them. So seldom do any of us take time to love the obviously lovable, and to ponder on the glorious world around us.

Another purpose was to provide them with more resources for responding to the thousands of wondering questions little children ask about these familiar yet infinitely mysterious phenomena. Each ATG was responsible for preparing several science ideas, preferably little experiments, for the science section of the Blue Book. Between us, we wound up with pages listing every kind of food likely to be found in poor Negro Mississippi homes, grouped according to the seven basic food groups, and accompanied by a discussion of balanced meals; a group of questions children often ask about birth, and suggested replies;

a cluster of illustrated experiments with water; a group of experiments with plants and some interesting facts about roots; ideas for collecting shells, twigs, leaves, nuts, etc., and labeling them; "all about bees"; how to make a terrarium; comparative turtles; experiments with air, with sound, and with magnets; and some interesting things to do to cause thinking about what makes the lights light. We mightily urged that each center have a science table; a bright beautiful place for all kinds of things the children might bring in, from nature most likely.

The hard part was patiently containing the knowledge that this is not science. Science is an inquiring mind, curiosity about why and how. Science is wanting to find out seriously enough to explore, experiment, and prove it. My thought was that doing everything we could in *every* area of our work to develop in ATGs and teachers a questioning mode of living, to develop an experimental approach to problems of *all* kinds, was the best we could do at this beginning stage. CDGM wasn't a specially, narrowly defined scientific program: We had a million other facets to our prism. We couldn't afford the time to putter and potter and mess with materials and see what happened, as one must do to really get into experimental science. Because science was an almost totally unvalued interest area in our communities, I felt we would be doing well, as a first step, to bring *anything* into *any* center.

A second step would be to make some kind of science, even a superficial kind, a daily part of *every* center. And then, after that, God and the government willing, we might, through visiting experts and workshops, be lucky enough to get near a real scientific spirit. At this point the best I could do was stress the connection between science and community social action goals. Page 106 of the Blue Book, the cover page for the collection of experiments, stresses specific things to do to develop an inquiring attitude in children.

With art, for a start, we were confined by time to talking about its relation to our real goals with the Negroes in Mississippi, and to writing up specific examples of art activities to offer children.

We talked and wrote of all the standard preschool art experiences, acquaintance with which poor Mississippi Negroes have never had the pleasure. Again the great lack in our work was that we weren't able to provide ample opportunities for the ATGs to *do* these things. As with science, we hoped to overcome initial resistance to "all that senseless mess," and to promote the daily use of these kinds of art in centers. Later, we hoped, people would learn to love it themselves.

We played games. We capered, cavorted, crawled, and giggled, and came up with a Blue Book section of directions for all the games any of us could remember from our childhoods: Crows and Cranes, Statue Maker, Cowboy and Bronco, Hide the Rock, Crawling Under, Barking Dogs, Wheelbarrows, Kick the Stick, Many Ways of Getting There, Fishing Game, Tractor, Obstacle Course, Toss the Clothespins in the

Bucket, Tug of War, High Jump, Broad Jump, Fruit Basket, Simon Says, Tag, Hide and Go Seek, Conga Line, Follow the Leader, Looby Loo, Did You Ever See a Lassie, the Farmer in the Dell, the Farm Game, My Grandmother's Trunk, Button-Button Who's Got the Button, Guessing Game, Mulberry Bush, and two local games that go like this:

Who Stole the Cookies From the Cookie Jar?

(The children stand in a circle with their hands on their hips, and they all chorus together with a syncopated beat, rocking back and forth in a rhythmic twist motion):
Who stole the cookies from the cookie jar?
Teacher stole the cookies from the cookie jar.
[Teacher, solo, looking very surprised]:
Mean *I* stole the cookies from the cookie jar?
[Everybody, pointing at her, triumphantly]:
Yeah, *you* stole the cookies from the cookie jar.
[Teacher]:
No I didn't steal the cookies from the cookie jar!
[Everybody]:
Then, who stole the cookies from the cookie jar?
[Teacher names a child, and the game is repeated until each player has had a turn to shine.]

Here Comes Charlie Brown

Children make a circle and clap while they sing.
One child is Charlie. He has a square of cloth, the *coffin*.

Here comes Charlie Brown,
Little Charlie Brown.
Lay that coffin down.
Fold up a corner, Charlie Brown.
Fold up a corner, Charlie Brown.
Fold another corner, Charlie Brown.
Fold the other corner, Charlie Brown.

Take it to your lover, Charlie Brown.
Show us your motion, Charlie Brown.
Fly like a buzzard, Charlie Brown.

As the group sings, "Fold up the corner," *Charlie* skips at a half-time pace around the cloth, folding each corner as directed. He takes it to a *lover* of his selection, makes any motion of his choice, flaps his wings, and takes the *lover's* place. The *lover* now becomes *Charlie Brown*.

As we played the latter game, ATG Hattie Belle Saffold seemed a bit distracted. Yes, she reluctantly admitted, she was, she *did* have her mind elsewhere . . . yesterday when she had gone home from our workshop, she shyly disclosed, she had found her children huddled under the beds—whites had been shooting into her home.

We talked about weaving number and size understandings into all the other activities in which children engage. We stressed counting real things, taking away, adding, on the playground, at snack time, at the bathroom, in the block corner, etc. The Blue Book contains a number of such games as the flannel board game in which a child puts the correct number of cut-out ducks in the column under the correct numeral; patterns for making graduated "longer and longer" sticks with broomstick bits and paint; directions for making and playing "Spin a Number" games and counting boxes with acorns, buttons, or whatever; the Bigger and Bigger Houses game; how to make clocks and teach telling time; how to make and play number lotto.

Mary demonstrated many other educational things to do in her sample center, and we popped a section into the Blue Book called Other Educational Things To Do. It described the Mystery Bag Game, in which each child gets to reach into the mystery bag and try to identify the objects he feels in there without looking. It described several activities for the housekeeping corner, such as peeling real carrots and polishing real shoes, and how, exactly, one could set up stimulating situations to promote these activities. It illustrated and described a washing table, complete with dishpan, water, soap shaker, sponges, rags, jar lids, doll clothes, and a dolly clothes line with pins. There were illustrated directions for making tying, buttoning, and zipping frames, so children could practice these skills. There were descriptions of a doctor/nurse play area, and how to make a toy telephone that "really works." How to make a workbench and what tools to get was discussed, always with a statement of the educational value:

1. Self help, small muscle skills needed later for writing.
2. Independence.
3. Appreciate workmanship and hard work; good work habits.
4. Self pride; make own tops, value them more than bought ones.
5. Fun; another reason to love school, especially little boys.

Another page bore the headline: BE LIKE DADDY! PAINT THE WALLS AND FURNITURE! (with water); and explained how this could be done. There were descriptions for making a TV set and letting children act, making peg boards of clothespins and plywood, how to make a spool winding game, how to give shadow plays on a sheet screen, and even: "What to do with coats and boots?" There was also a section on playgrounds.

Though much more could have been done with music than we were able to do, it was one of our strongest areas. We encouraged teachers to use all their resources in this area: to bring on all the freedom songs, nursery songs, religious songs, spirituals, work songs, cute children's songs, folk songs, action songs, singing circle games, popular songs, instruments, local talent, and homemade instruments; all they could recall, cajole, or invent. One way to get the flavor of CDGM's music program is to listen to the record album an ATG, and I, and a summer roving folk singer made: Asch Recordings, #701, Head Start with the Child Development Group of Mississippi.

We went into Jackson again in small groups to do research on places around the state, to go on field trips with the children, and to compile lists of agencies and institutions, toy companies, and publishers to write to for printed information. Everyone participated in everything.

But the part of our two weeks that the ATGs liked best was observing children, writing down the details of what they saw, and speculating on the children about whom they were writing. One ATG said, "The most funniest thing is I have seven children, but till today, I never saw a child before." In the Blue Book, we included some of these embryonic "case histories," along with a summary of the discussion we had on each one. Once again our intention was to encourage ATGs to begin helping center teachers begin to look at *a* child, and to think about *him*. The sophisticated reader will see what a long way the ATGs still had to go. And which of us humans has any *less* work, till we have fully developed physically, intellectually, emotionally, and spiritually, instead of being satisfied with using the mere surface skimmings of ourselves for which most of us, "professionals" included, settle.

Of course the essence of the Blue Book was children—the relation of each activity to children. But one section focused just on the child. It suggested questions ATGs could present to resource teachers for discussion:

A teacher said she didn't have time to worry about each of Albert's little problems, because she was too busy teaching. What do you think about that? . . .

Which do you admire more, the adult who relies on other people to do the job, or the one who tries to do as much as he can? Is it sensible to do everything for a child, or should we allow him to do as much as he can for himself? . . .

Talk about things in each Center that the children could do for themselves if you gave them the opportunity and lots of practice . . .

Is it wrong to insist that a child leave the group for a few minutes (five at the most) if he cannot stop hurting or bothering other people? . . .

A teacher was playing a game with her group. One child couldn't do what the game called for, though he was trying to do it. The teacher said, "You can't play, you're not good enough." Do you think this is the right thing to do if we are trying to make each child at our Centers feel big and successful? . . .

Observation of Patricia

A teacher watches one little girl named Patricia in the Center. At this time, other teachers were handling the children, and, by previous plan, this particular teacher was asked to observe only Patricia. She wanted to get to know Patricia a little better than you can when you are trying to handle the whole class. The teacher did not want to forget each detail of what she saw, so she took notes.

The teacher wrote:
"It's 3 minutes till 2 o'clock. Patricia is sitting at the head of the table just observing her surroundings. Now, with both hands, under her chin, she rests her elbows on the table. She raises her body up and down on her seat a few times, then leaves her seat and returns in the same minute. She seats herself to take her turn at stirring the chocolate pudding. She is now spooning it out into separate bowls, where everyone will share eating it. There are two adults sitting near to whom she offers her pudding. When they politely refuse her, she returns to her seat to eat. Patricia is very actively moving from place to place, then decides to seat herself at a different table and proceeds to eat all her chocolate pudding. It's now 10 after 2 o'clock. She squirms, eats, and talks with companions. She lays her hand on a pencil and starts a search for its owner. She returns to eat again, runs out the door to see what her teacher is doing, comes back, sets her bowl on the table, and takes off to the wash room and washes her hands. Then she starts out and thoughtfully returns to dry them.
"Patricia very briskly runs back and forth from washroom to class room and up a stairway and back again, then out the door to the swing area and back again to the washroom. Now, she is gathering up the soiled pudding bowls, when suddenly it occurs to her to drag the toy telephone system out the door. She decides to return through a different entrance and then out again. She misses her teacher and asks for her. She seems perfectly satisfied by the sight of her, then proceeds to fight with another child over a broom. She wins out and goes about sweeping the floor in a spasmodic manner. She now drags the broom and goes out and in the door. With broom in one hand and a wet rag in the other, she rubs it back and forth over one corner of the table alternating a whisk from the broom. About now she leaves the wet rag and, taking her broom, works in spots, but very happily moves around. It's 2:30 P.M. She throws her broom down and runs to the car which will take her home."

What Did You Learn about Patricia by Looking at Her so Closely?

She was playing? Yes, she was. But what else did you learn?
She was happy? But what about the kind of person she is. What did you learn about what kind of person she is?

1. Patricia is a busy child. She is not a child who just sits and lets life go on around her. She lives every minute, and participates.
2. Patricia is a thinker, a child with something in her head. (Evidence: at first she is studying her surroundings thinking what she will do. Then, though she forgets to dry her hands, she stops, thinks, and remembers. So we know she has ideas.)
3. Patricia enjoys activities offered to her, and even helps herself to more activities. She is eager to do things, and takes the initiative. (Evidence:

goes to wash when she feels the need, decides to sweep, although no one told her to, decides to scrub the table, although no one told her to. Knows when it's time to go home, too, and takes herself to the car.)

4. Patricia is a generous child. (Evidence: she offered the ladies some of her pudding, and she tried to give the pencil back to its owner.)
5. Patricia has a will of her own, and definitely pursues her own ideas. (Evidence: she wants the broom, so gets it away from another child because she "needs" it.)
6. Patricia is friendly and has formed a relationship with her teacher. (Evidence: she wanted to please the visiting adults, and offered them pudding. She chatted with her companions. She checked where her teacher was twice, and was happy when she knew where she was.)
7. Patricia is a responsible child. She washes after she gets messy, she dries after she washes, she makes an effort to clean up after she is finished, she goes home voluntarily when she sees it is time.
8. Patricia is an independent child. She does things on her own and does not require a lot of babying.
9. Patricia is restless and has a great deal of energy. Unles she is kept very busy at purposeful activities this energy seems to spill over into rather unconstructive and aimless movement.

The teacher who will help Patricia most will plan daily ways of keeping her attention until she *completes* something. Patricia is far from lazy, and is certainly not bored, but she will have trouble in first grade unless she develops a longer attention span. A sharp CDGM teacher can help Patricia.

Films were a very successful part of ATG Orientation. We showed and discussed *Little World, A Chance at the Beginning, The Child Development Center, Adapting the Curriculum to the Child, Vassar College Nursery School,* and *Los Nietos Kindergarten.*

After the area teacher guides had had only two weeks of specific preparation, two hundred resource teachers came to Mount Beulah for five days of Orientation. In teams of two or three, the ATGs taught groups of thirty their own inimitable version of our two-week workshop.

They used everybody's ideas on how to make the resource teacher Orientation livelier than the summer orientation. One ATG, playing with the words "teaching demonstration," in contrast to the usual kind of civil rights demonstration that was so much a part of her life, suggested that we have a parade-type demonstration with picket signs carrying educational slogans. So one morning everyone driving onto the Mount Beulah campus was startled to see herds of large black ladies picketing our classroom building with signs bearing many slogans such as:

ENCOURAGE ME.

ENCOURAGE ME TO EXPLORE NEW THINGS.

*

SHOW ME NEW THINGS.

*

ASK ME QUESTIONS
RESPECT MY ANSWERS.

*

DEVELOP MY CURIOSITY SO I'LL BE CURIOUS TO LEARN LATER IN SCHOOL.

*

DON'T TEACH CHILDREN,
TEACH A CHILD.
TEACH ME.

*

DEVELOP MY OPINION OF MYSELF.

*

PRAISE ME.

*

LOVE ME.
HAVE FUN WITH ME.

*

LET ME LEARN TO BE PROUD OF MYSELF;
THAT WAY I WILL EXPECT MORE OF MYSELF,
AND I'LL WORK HARDER IN SCHOOL LATER.

*

NOTICE ME!

*

NOTICE *ME!*
I'M NOT ANYONE ELSE. I'M ME.

*

DO YOU KNOW WHO MY FRIENDS ARE?
DO YOU KNOW WHAT I'M AFRAID OF?
WATCH ME, ASK ME, AND YOU'LL FIND OUT! !

* * *

Issue number seven of the Newsletter, a twenty-four-page, largely single-spaced bulletin that I was still compiling, typing, and distributing myself, both in-state and to our public relations mailing list, such as it was, much of which I'd made myself; again stressed raising our standards. There were pages urging planning about the specifics (itemized) of safety, health, kindness, attractive, *clean* rooms, and *planned* programs for children; do-it-yourself, but with constantly rising aspirations of what "it" *is*. Most of this Newsletter was devoted to people's evaluations and comments about resource teacher Orientation, like these:

There is an Ancient proverb saying, 'Know thyself first; above all else.' After several discussions on What a R.T. is, and what the duties are in a Child Development program, I gave myself over to a scientific study and an experimental interview. Here I've dissected my personal characteristics; my attitudes, my enthusiasm and my qualifications as to how I am fitting myself into this Child Development program.

I've learned that the child is my scientific world to explore, and to dissect him bit by bit, understanding him, learning his very being in order that I may help him develop toward the whole part of society. His problems is my job. His attitudes, his questions, and his social welfare is my care. . . .

When I think of (what some people, communities, and children) are doing it gives me a great deal of courage to keep on keeping to make a better person in my community in the center in the Church and any place I go. You have given me that impression.

The person that thinks he can't, then it's a cinch he won't, but if he thinks he can then he will.

You are great, have done a wonder job in getting the things over to us. I shall never forget you, may God forever bless you to live on and do much more good work which is so very important is my prayer.

CHAPTER 31

AREA TEACHER GUIDES IN ACTION

MY DIARY FOR the period has this to say about area teacher guides in action: "I have driven to Canton, and am spending the day with ATG Clarice Coney. Mary and I are trying to spend as much time as it takes to visit each ATG and at least briefly visit each Center (138). The purposes: to give each ATG the boost of companionship and an enthusiastic appreciator during this difficult period for them of adjusting to their new role; to see each particular ATG's strengths and weaknesses in action so we can tilt our future work with her appropriately—structure situations in which she can share her strengths with others, and be sure not to overlook the areas where she will misinterpret or misapply what we do in workshop; to give each Center the feeling of belonging to an alive network—they feel so isolated; to admire whatever a Center Staff is doing to keep alive in this bleak, long unfunded winter, regardless of how small that may be.

"The teachers at Valley View see us do some pretty courageous things on the curves, and screech to a halt at their door in Mrs. Coney's CDGM car (rented with Field Foundation money). 'Here comes Coney, we're going to hear a lecture about CDGM again! I hope they'll get that grant soon so she'll shut up!' . . . hugs, laughter. Coney shouts at them: 'Yeah, I ain't a great speaker but I sure am a great talker!'

"Mrs. Coney is saying: 'You know why I work without a cent? My gas bill is $52.75. I owe it. I don't know if the man is crazy or generous. I can get in the public schools to work anytime I want. I don't, because I *believes* in this. The other day when I was going door to door collecting things for the Centers, a lady said, "I ain't got nuthin' to give you." But when I left, my truck was full of collard greens. I told her, "You don't have to give me nuthin' you ain't got . . . give me what you *do* have, look at all those acres of collard greens, and we have to feed hundreds of children in those Centers without a dime." The lady said,

"Oh, that? I didn't think you'd want *that.* Do me the honor of taking them greens." I said, "Thank you, I'll be proud to take that."'

"When inside the center, Coney assembles the group, leads introductions and devotionals, and we all sit down to a chicken dinner staff has prepared. For an hour Coney inspires them: '. . . There are no little people in Area Seven. . . . Everyone is important. We believe in what we're doing. All you need is a little hard work and faith. That's contagious. I like anything with a challenge, don't you? I like to find a channel, you too? You can live with the devil for many years if you try to get a mutual understanding—you just gotta outwit him with patience, tact, hard work . . . What you ladies need is to pull out your ideas out of storage . . . cigar boxes to put crayons in . . . sand table for indoors for the winter we've got coming . . . get ribbons from a florist for your scrap box . . . cartons make great building blocks . . . you all have magazines around, make a collection of pictures out of them for children to paste . . .'

"We get back in her car and race back to Canton. She hurries me into a store. The man sees us coming and says, 'Ah, Coney, what you need now?' She wheedles armloads of miscellany from him telling me, 'People *are* willing to help, you just have to go after them.'

"As we drive the thirty miles or so to her next Center she chatters."

Mrs. Coney was born in Bogue Chitto, Mississippi, Lincoln County. She grew up in Canton, Mississippi, and completed her elementary and secondary education in the public schools of Lincoln County Training School and Cameron Street High School in Canton, Mississippi. She attended Alcorn A & M College, Lorman, Mississippi, and Jackson State College, Jackson, Mississippi, completing three years, Another day a conversation with Mrs. Coney went like this: "I'm a good wife still, but a new style wife. Most of my children help with the house now. I used to do everything for them—fix their bath, cook their dinner, wash their clothes. Now the big ones are more considerate of me. They take care of the little ones. My eleven-year-old is something of a bookworm, but the seven-year-old cooks breakfast, toast, scrambled eggs, and the five-year-old sweeps the walks, waters the puppy. I have six children. The bookworm daughter lives halfway between my house and my sister's. If there's work to be done, she finds herself over there. My sister believes if a child is reading, just let her alone, let her enjoy herself. She loves to use this reading readiness material I bring home. She gets groups of children all around her, and reads and reads to the children. I test out a lot of material on my children at home. The entire family is involved in CDGM ideas and activities. It's all caught on with all of them—we just all live and breathe CDGM. I don't know what we'll do when it ends—maybe something else will come along. It's changed my home life a great deal.

"We have an old Pontiac. It broke down, but I was so excited about this new thing that my husband decided to go along with this experiment to see what I would do with it—so he got a bank loan and fixed the car for me to get around in the rurals. I go around from house to house, knocking on doors and trying to get people to understand that they can do all these things they've always wanted to do, and they can ask questions; anyone who has a question can ask it and get a decent answer. Hundreds of people keep showing up at my volunteer Centers; they just show up. It makes me feel like back in pioneer days, when everyone got all excited about getting out to settle the land. It's not like a job because I've always had a job—it's like lighting a light and we just want so bad to keep pushing the fuel to keep it burning brighter and brighter. . . .

"I used to take people pretty much the way they are. Now I understand people much more. I don't understand them all—I'm not a psychiatrist—and I *have* come to the conclusion that some people need psychiatric help. This is the first job I've had where I could really choose my own thoughts, do the kind of research I wanted to do, present my ideas better, be freer. I can create more. I worked in the public school off and on as a substitute teacher after I had children—before that I taught full time, first through sixth grade. First was my favorite. But I couldn't develop myself because of all the restrictions. You can't go off on your own and do things without asking the principal, who asks the superintendent, who sends back down the word. Everybody thinks you're a little nutty if you don't just sit back and be a classroom teacher. In CDGM everybody thinks you're nutty if you *don't* try out things. In public school you're supposed to maintain all the graces of a teacher —you can't sit on the ground with the children, it wouldn't look like a teacher is supposed to look. You're not supposed to go bare-legged, it wouldn't be sophisticated like a teacher is supposed to be. Sometimes I wonder if dignity is no deeper than stockings. One kind of dignity you get through learning the graces. The other kind, the CDGM kind, is dignity that is always in any person, and it comes out when they're given an opportunity to bring out and prove all that's in them.

"In public school teaching I came home and was free evenings, nights, holidays. In CDGM I check in every day, but I never check out. I never feel finished. There's always more to do. I take more pride in it. In school, they don't expect teachers to do all that community work. CDGM expects it, and once you begin to do it, it's so creative, you get to love it. Public school expects the parents to come, do everything. There's an invisible line between teachers and parents. CDGM expects teachers to go, get out, there's a mixing between teachers and parents. CDGM is something like a religion—happy exciting. . . .

"You know how I got into this ATG work? I was going to be a Resources Teacher. I went to the Resource Teacher Orientation at Beulah, and Valentine Blue, one of my ATG teaching team, said, 'Ooh! Polly should see this!' I guess she told you about me. Later, Reverend McCree asked me a lot of special questions. At first I felt funny calling Polly *Polly* and John *John*. We had always been used to Mr. and Mrs. for our employers.

"Coming home from that Orientation, I remember, it was awful. We came by Flora. It was night, very very dark. They said this was bad Klan territory. Just then we got a flat! Just a bunch of us women! People started gathering at a house up on a hill and hundreds and hundreds of dogs started barking. At least, it seemed like that many, but you know how it is. They turned on all these lights and shined them on us. After a minute a white man pulled up in his car. We were scared to death. He said, 'Oh, you're having trouble, how can I help you?' We were too frightened to think how he could. So he just rolled up his sleeves, took out a jack, and changed our tire for us! We got to talking. Finally we felt safe enough to ask him why he had stopped for *us*? He said, 'Well, I'm on my way home from the service. I haven't been home yet. My wife is in the hospital having our first child. She was notified that I was killed in action, so I'm hurrying to tell her it isn't true.' 'And you stopped to help *us*?' 'Yes, well, when I was in the service, a Negro saved my life. I had never been out of Mississippi. Here was a man whose race I had always cursed. He saved *my* life! I determined that when I got back to Mississippi I would change myself.' That was the only thing that'd happened though. When we were coming up, I'm the seventh of twelve kids, I remember hearing my parents talk of night-riders—it makes me angry to think about things like that, so I just don't. Never did."

My diary tells of an incident with Mrs. Coney: "Coney slows down, dust billowing behind us, leans out the car window, and shouts to a young man, 'What you doin' outa school?' 'I'm goin',' he says hastily. 'You bet you are!' roars Coney menacingly. 'Is that your son?' I ask. 'Heck no,' Coney replies, 'I don't even know him. I just believe in education.'"

In the files there are pages and pages of activity sheets in Clarice Coney's bold black handwriting, giving the details of what she did that winter.

December 7, 1965

At the Harmony C.D.G.M. Center in Carthage, Mississippi, I conducted a question and answer period with some of the children about Thunder and Lightning. One child had this to say by the name of Jeanette Ashwood.

Q. Hello! What's your name?
A. Jeanette
Q. Do you know what lightning is?
A. Yes
Q. What is it?
A. Rain falling.

Q. What color is it?
A. Blue
Q. Who made it?
A. The weather man and God.
Q. Where is it?
A. In the sky."

December 9th and 10th, 1965

AGENDA
Area Teacher Guide, Mrs. Coney
Workshop for Resource Teachers and Trainees
Ashbury Center

Thursday:
9:00 A.M. Registration
9:15–9:30 Devotion . . .
December 12th—I visited the Community and found that there were many pre-school children in dire need of clothing in the Farmhaven Area.
50 Children size 4
60 Children size 5
40 Children size 6 . . .

December 13th

I visited the communities in the surrounding areas.
This happened at my Ofahoma Center:
CONEY: Men, will you help build your Center?
MEN: No, we don't have any materials, any money, nothing to work with.
CONEY: Men, will you please help the ladies build a Center?
MEN: No, we will not. The women can't do it. OEO haven't given us any money and we won't.
CONEY: Well, the ladies will.
So the ladies started building.
MEN: You ladies are doing it all wrong. Wait, we will show you how. Put this piece here and that piece there. Oh, shucks, you women go cook, *we* will finish the Center.
They did. The men took over. They hammered and nailed and painted and built tables, benches, added on rooms, and showed off all their skills and talents. Ofahoma Center, I love you, you are great!

December 17, 1965

An Area Teacher Guide Workshop and Pre-Christmas Banquet was held at Mt. Beulah in Edwards, Miss., and I attended both. Mrs. Margret Hoben shared our day and enlightened us with many helpful pointers. Mrs. Hoben is a kindergarten teacher from Wisconsin.

This was a cooperative picnic the ATG group, Mary, and I made ourselves, complete with the little red cakes Lillie Ayers made, and the rock 'n' roll on Frances Alexander's transistor. Mary and I had ransacked the warehouse, rummaging among the remnants and remains of the summer program's supplies, to find a few Christmas presents for each

ATG to take to each of her centers. Mary stayed up late into several nights using leftover red and green tempera to block print designs on leftover yellowing newsprint for gift wrap. She wrapped more than three hundred packages—packages of twenty-nine-cent books or a half-empty pack of construction paper, packages of modeling clay or pipe cleaners for the children to make shapes. No doubt we created havoc among the inventory staff and OEO auditors, but I confess, giving two jump ropes to a bitterly poor community running a large school on nothing but devotion, when the government should have given it two jillion dollars, didn't give me a moment's loss of sleep.

Mrs. Lindsay Hoben, full-time educational consultant for the Milwaukee, Wisconsin, Northcott House Head Start during the summer of 1965, a member of the board of the National Child Welfare League, former director of the experimental Walden School in New York City, a former teacher and supervisor of teachers at Milwaukee State Teachers College, and a life-long nursery school teacher herself, wrote: "When I spent a day with the Area Teacher Guides at their workshop I was tremendously impressed. I have never met with a group that was more alert and ready to learn, in a lifetime of varied teaching experiences. It was really exciting. These women brought up many pertinent questions in relation to their challenging job of helping set up and guide the preschool centers. They carried on an excellent discussion of many key problems.

"I myself have always believed that early childhood education required a high degree of professionalism—very different from classroom teaching of older children. But my own experience as consultant to a Head Start program last summer convinced me that a real liking for children, concern for bettering their lives, and eagerness to make the project a success, more than made up for more formal training, when combined with able and imaginative professional leadership."

Through the "Christmas holidays," Mrs. Coney whirled on:

December 18, 1965–I distributed some used clothing . . .
December 29, 1965–I held classes in the parsonage of . . .
Purpose of Workshop–Clarence D. Coney, Area Teacher Guide 1–10–66

This is the second of a series of workshops for Resource Teachers, Trainees, Chairmen, Part-time helpers, Bus Drivers, Health Co-ordinators, Volunteers, Substitutes and other interested people from all Centers. First of all . . .
. . . Mrs. Polly Greenberg, along with Mrs. Ayers A.T.G., Mrs. Alexander, A.T.G., Mrs. Fleming, A.T.G. Mr. Hamblin, A.A. . . . visited with me at the Valley View Center, where we met Texas students who was volunteering their services and had luncheon.

We visited the McNeal Elementary School to see the work of the preschool children from last summer's headstart program.

Mrs. Coney was doing door-to-door child recruiting in an isolated rural area. She discovered eight-year-old Floyd Pierce. He had never been to school because he couldn't talk. His grandmother was reluctant to let Mrs. Coney enroll him at the Hopewell center. She said nothing could be done with him. She even doubted if he could hear. No one had ever heard him speak a word. Mrs. Coney didn't know what could be done either, but she had great confidence in what CDGM did for children. She convinced the grandmother to let Floyd attend. Floyd's teacher spent a great deal of time with him. It was true, he didn't utter a sound. But he watched intently. One day on a routine visit to Hopewell center, Mrs. Coney was demonstrating the use of the newly arrived modeling clay. She had made a cow and molded tits underneath it. To Mrs. Coney's stunned disbelief, Floyd suddenly laughed.

A few weeks later, Mrs. Coney returned for another visit. A little boy rushed up and greeted her with the excitedly spoken words: "Teacher! Teacher!" It was Floyd. Mrs. Coney was so moved that tears flowed down her cheeks. Floyd looked dismayed and said, "What's the matter, am I being bad?" Mrs. Coney wept in earnest now, and pulled the little boy into her arms. When she had composed herself enough to trust her voice, she said, "No, you're not bad, I'm just so happy to see that you can talk, and hear too." Floyd said, "I love you, I love you."

The last two jobs held by another of the ATGs were church correspondent ($35 a month) and occasional daywork, got through an employment agency (maximum $5 a day). Another dynamo was one of twelve children, and a former farm girl, hat trimmer, power machine operator, and part-time insurance lady. Lilly Ayers taught until the day she gave birth to twins (her sixth and seventh children), and returned to work a few days later. Frances Alexander was surrounded by Head Start children in her home one winter Saturday. When I asked what was up, she explained that she and her family were now living in the former center, and the children often stayed overnight because they didn't understand, or weren't willing to accept, that Head Start was defunct. Mrs. Backstrom, previously a maid, was ATG in the least convenient CDGM area. She had to drive hundreds of miles to work. She was much loved and admired by the people at her many centers because of her solid, sensible, constructive attitude and comments. She wrote in a report on her most dilapidated program: ". . . I explained my duties very gently and ask if I could be of any help? There was no response. . . .

"In the kitchen on the sink sat three or four jars of paint and flowers made from egg cartons and pipe cleaners. This was something I had never seen. I complimented this for it goes to prove there is always something to learn even in a most despairing situation. . . ."

We had two male ATGs: Mr. Cusic and Reverend Martin. Mr. Cusic was a hard-working down-to-earth young man who criticized his centers keenly, and at the same time supported them heartily through their travails. Of Reverend Martin, who kept us all laughing in ATG workshop as well as kept his Gulf Coast center staff's spirits up through hell and high water, a Head Start child said: "He a nize man. Ah climb on him an' he wrestle me. When he come to mah center, it's a holler day."

There was the indomitable Flora Brooks. Flora explained the difference she considered the fundamental one between other federal programs and CDGM. In the other programs, she said, whites allowed selected Negroes some small, controlled right to participate in certain segments of the program. In CDGM poor Negroes allowed selected whites to participate in constantly supervised and limited ways.

Flora kept up a regular schedule of center visitation in her huge rural area throughout the unfunded winter. She made about three community meetings each week in the evening, too. When asked how she managed to do it, she shrugged; then added that she'd had some help—since November, Mary had once given her $25. When OEO collected every book and glass of paint and put them in a warehouse, Flora called it "misappropriation of funds," and kept her centers operating anyway. She boldly dealt with local whites in her Laurel area and said she felt good about herself—she wasn't getting pushed around anymore. When a snack bar told her it didn't serve niggers, she replied that was OK, as she didn't *eat* them. She sent her daughter to the white school.

Flora attributed her fighting spirit to her mother, who, she said, talked back to whites whenever the need arose, Mississippi mores notwithstanding. She was considered a bad and unmanageable child, she said, and as an adult was felt to be a difficult, dissatisfied person. She quickly agreed with her critics, saying that she *is* horribly dissatisfied with the condition of Negro communities in Mississippi. Negroes have nothing and control nothing but their churches and their bowels, and spend their whole lives in little power struggles, she commented cynically; why should she be satisfied?

Before CDGM came along, she told us, she was sick all the time with ulcers and migraines and had nothing to do all day but sit home, eat, and read voraciously, because she had given up on the white folks' kitchen; she just didn't want that three dollars a day all that much. She felt that she had no outlets for her intelligence and her emotions. But CDGM seemed to her an opportunity to learn a great deal about federal programs. She felt that with all that was wrong with CDGM (and she was one of its most stringent critics), it had given her a whole new life, and she would never go back to any other kind, regardless of what became of CDGM itself.

And there was the lovely Leola Downs, who attended a number of small Negro grammar schools in rural Walthall and Pike counties, completed tenth grade at a vocational high school, did domestic work in New Orleans, picked up tung nuts, kept books for a Negro farmer, picked cotton, and was the mother of six children. Throughout her life of hard work Leola did whatever "social work" she could through her church. She concluded her "brief autobiography" for CDGM and OEO by writing: ". . . I am well known in my Community and Community near me. All that no me and will be truthful give me a good name. To me a good name is better than preshous gems. I am striving to do more for my family, my community and my state. So help me God."

What course in teachers college teaches the kind of concern, compassion, commitment, and courage these people exhibited?

By January we still had no Head Start grant. Dave Walls had stopped believing it would be "any day now." He was becoming ensnared in the hopeless feeling OEO "good guys" shared. The area teacher guides (ATG), Mary, and I were doing everything we could think of to get centers ready. So that when (if?) we ever did get a grant, we could open the doors officially, not have to begin to begin putting in the facilities and educational basics. We talked a great deal in our sporadic workshops. There was no money left to rent cars to get ATGs to Mount Beulah, so workshops were really a question of when one of us could afford to rent $120 worth of cars out of our paycheckless pocketbook.

We talked a great deal about what "ready" meant when referring to Head Start. It soon became clear that most ATGs measured readiness in terms of physical and facility readiness. If a shack now had a new stove and screens had been put in, regardless of the fact that it did not yet have a single toy or anything to do, it would likely be classed as "ready." I'd run into this "fine facilities" concept of educational quality with taxpayers, in licensed day care centers, nursery schools, and most of all in public schools throughout the states. I wasn't surprised that ATGs tended to think of a good bathroom and roof as a good educational program.

Together we worked out a simple but thorough check sheet, which ATGs agreed to fill out with each center staff (see Appendix E). More often than not an ATG would visit a center and then hitchhike, bum a ride with a friend, or drive to the nearest telephone to phone in a report to me or Mary. We would sit far into the night with the receiver tucked between bent neck and hunched shoulder, rapidly scribbling notes on check sheets. When asked what major impression she had of our work that winter of 1965–1966, Mary said that it was memories of an aching ear from all those readiness reports. A time-consuming but invaluable by-product of this method was that we learned fresh tidbits about persons and situations as fast as they happened. So we continued to build our budding acquaintance with the minds and mechanics of many scattered small black Mississippi communities.

Deciding whether a center was adequate enough to open by CDGM standards, by much more conventional and arbitrary OEO standards, and by altogether different community criteria, was no easy chore. With the best intentions and the greatest flexibility of assessment, it often led to explosions. I find this memo in the files from Mary Emmons to John Mudd, a board member, and me: "There were a lot of bad feelings generated around the opening requirements at the . . . Center in . . . and about the ATG's handling of the situation. This report is to let you know that the central Teacher Development and Program for Children Staff is very sensitive to how these "requirements" for opening were interpreted by the Area Staff to the centers. . . .

"While the center is far from ideal in its location, the real problem in this situation is one of personalities. In the rush of opening centers this problem was overlooked. When the AA took up the problem and when it became apparent to me from other events that the ATG disliked Mrs.——— and was hostile to the ——— Center, I tried to work out a friendly and immediate solution. The ATG was applying the opening requirements unusually severely with [this Center] and I talked with her as soon as the problem became clear about what we can expect from a new center as opposed to an old center and how much people can do without any funds, etc.

"It is unfortunate that this situation held up the opening of ——— by a few days and we are very sorry about it. We know that the central and area staffs have a lot to learn about dealing with communities in a democratic and fair manner. We are not brushing over what happened . . . ; we hope we have learned something from the problem there. . . ." [See Appendix E.]

The biggest problem we had in ATG sessions was that ATGs had no reference point for judging centers except what the community had had *before* CDGM—what the children would get if they were *not* getting CDGM. We worked hard to develop another reference point at the other end of the pole; not necessarily a guide for ATGs to follow, but another magnet, so their minds would be pulled two ways, and they would have to evaluate and judge somewhere on the continuum. The new reference point was what high quality conventional nurseries and kindergartens do. We worked out a center evaluation form to be filled out twice during the forthcoming grant. We presumed the grant would be six to nine months. (*If* we could beat one of Uncle Sam's hands at all, which we were now beginning to doubt we could do. We had long ago given up believing that OEO was going to *give* a grant.)

The form was cumbersome and immense. It was much more than an evaluation sheet. It was a teaching tool. It served as a link between the actual center as it was, and nationwide Head Start expectations. None of the things on the huge form had to be a certain way. The thorough questions simply helped the ATG see each of her eight to ten centers from new, explicit angles. Gradually during the following months the ATG's perceptions became more and more acute and detailed. Probably all the slivers of techniques we used, cemented together by the peoples' determination to help their communities, made this true. (See Appendix F.)

In the field, Mary and I tried to help teachers spot and solve educational problems impromptu:

POLLY: Have you ladies noticed that the children fall down a lot between nap time and transportation home time?

TEACHER #1: Oh, ain't it the truth, they falls down like rain!

POLLY: Why do you think they fall so much at *that* time? I mean, I saw a little girl today who bumped her knee and cried so sadly, I wonder if there's any way they could be kept from falling so much?

TEACHER #2: Oh, they falls because we lifts 'em off the quilts by the arm when they's still fas' asleep, tha's why they drop like that: they still sleepin'.

TEACHER #1: They wouldn't fall if we got 'em up a little sooner. We does it that way because they sleeps till the las' minute and then the transportations is there.

TEACHER #2: Well, sure, we can get 'em up fi' minutes before the transportations comes. Then they can stretch 'n yawn before they has to stan' up.

The ATG whose center this was, was now focusing on nap time. She told me many naptime incidents, defects, good points, jokes—the ATG had added to her repertoire of things to look for at centers.

We were standing in the sun on the grass near the Center, a cluster of us, chatting.

RESOURCE TEACHER: Hey, Pol, since you're here, maybe you can help us with Russell. He has these terrible tantrums.

POLLY: When does he have them?

RESOURCE: Oh, just anytime! Anytime at all! From time to time throughout the day.

POLLY: When somebody has something he wants?

RESOURCE: Anytime.

POLLY: Is he hungry?

RESOURCE: He has them anytime.

POLLY: Well what do you all do, all of you, when Russell throws a fit?

TEACHER #1: I think he's tired and upset if he throws a tantrum, so I put him on my lap and go off in a corner and just talk like, real quiet, to him.

TEACHER #2: Well, I told Miss——I don't think that's right. She's giving him sugar for doing wrong.

TEACHER #1: He *needs* a little sugar. That's what he's lacking at home.

TEACHER #2: Well, I don't do that, that's not what I do. I tell him he's going to get a good whipping if he don't stop.

POLLY: Does hugging him help? Does whipping him help?

[*Both teachers collide in saying with conviction, "Yes!"*]

POLLY: Both whipping and hugging help cure the tantrums?

BOTH TEACHERS: Yes.

POLLY: He doesn't have tantrums anymore then?

BOTH TEACHERS: Oh, yes, he had one this morning.

POLLY: Then whipping and hugging, neither, cured him.

[We all laugh. The ATG has been listening intently.]

TEACHER #3: I recommend taking him home to his mother when he does that, and tell him he can't stay in school when he acts that way, so nasty.

TEACHER #1: I don't think so. We're the teachers. We should be able to help. If his mother could've helped, she would have, long before this.

POLLY: Oh, he has these tantrums at home, too?

[*Mumbling, small verbal exchanges around the circle of teachers.*]

POLLY: What? Does he?

RESOURCE: Nobody knows. We haven't been to see his mother yet. I'm sure he has tantrums at home too.

POLLY: Well, it sounds like it would be a good idea to find out. Maybe he doesn't. Then you'd know it's something special to do with the center. Or maybe he does. Then you'd know to begin looking at home for clues.

TEACHER #3: Well, what would you suggest doing?

POLLY: Looking.

TEACHER #4: Oh, honey, he ain't much to look at when he's hollering like that!

TEACHER #3: Hush! What do you mean, look?

POLLY: I mean, you ladies said he has tantrums *all* the time, *any*time, but there must be some cause. So I'd like play detective and see if you can find the thing that sets him off each time. Could someone follow him around and make a note of exactly what happens each time before he falls apart?

TEACHER #1: Yes, we could do that.

TEACHER #3: You know, when he isn't throwing a tantrum, he still don't seem happy. He has this confused look on his face.

TEACHER #4: [*later turned out to be the cook*] When a child from a home like where he stays at acts up, you have to feed him first, 'fore you can tell what's the matter with him, don't you think Miss Polly?

POLLY: Well, I think each idea you've mentioned sounds reasonable, but maybe it would be best if you could have a staff meeting, sit down, and each tell every single thing you know or think about this little boy. Maybe you could agree on *one* way to handle him for a few weeks, like an experiment, to see what happens. I think I'd have a confused look on my face, too, if four people treated me four totally different ways all in the same morning.

[Laughter, general discussion, resolving into agreement that a staff meeting would be a good idea. Teachers tentatively agreed that they would feed Russell first thing every morning *before* he had a tantrum in case that was the problem; would love and tend him a great deal *when he wasn't having a tantrum* and would see where to go from there.]

TEACHER #1: But what should we do if he has tantrums anyway, while we're doing all this? This will take awhile. I think we should be nice to Russell.

POLLY: What do you teachers think would be best to do if something like this comes up?

[*Circular discussion*]

POLLY: Does it disturb the other children when he flips out like this?

[*Chorus of yeses*]

POLLY: Then it would seem sensible to remove him.

TEACHER #1: Remove him. OK, take him out of class, but not whip him.

TEACHER #2: I'd be willing to not whip him till we study him better. But what should we do with him when we take him out of class?

TEACHER #4: Just don't do nothing with him. Just tell him, 'Russell, honey, you can't act like that in school.' Just take him outside and let him be alone.

RESOURCE: I think that's a good idea. Just let him work it off alone. He'll get tired of that. And it'd keep him from disturbing and upsetting the other children.

POLLY: Let me know how it works out, will you?

Two weeks later the ATG and I were invited to hear the notes that had been taken on Russell. In discussion, with no trained teacher present, the ladies had discovered that: (a) Russell did not have tantrums at home; (b) Russell did not have tantrums for the first month he attended the center; they began on a particular day that the teachers clearly remembered; (c) Russell's first tantrum occurred at nap time when teacher #2 was lying on a quilt near him.

The teachers had piles of notes about tantrums since my other visit, but saw no similarity between the situations. I asked that the notes be read again, with each teacher listening specifically for what thread ran throughout the collection of incidents.

RESOURCE: Hey! They all have something to do with the bathroom, or something like that! Listen! This one says Russell burst out screaming when his teacher took the class to the bathroom. This one says Russell kicked and yelled when Denise wet herself. Here! Russell howled and hollered when he had to change his pants because they got in a puddle. It's all got to do with the bathroom!

TEACHER #4, THE COOK: One day he said to me, 'Teacher, I drew a jay bird!' I thought he meant a bird. But lots of little boys calls their weenie a jaybird . . . you know, 'cause the way it flutters.

[*Scandalized tittering*]

TEACHER #2: Oh my God! That day on the quilt, the first day he had a tantrum, he was playing with hisself, and I said, 'Russell, don't do that, we'll have to cut off your jay bird!' Oh, no, no, do you think he thought I meant that? Oh, no, Lordie, I didn't mean to scare him that much, just a little bit so he would quit.

[*The meeting broke up in an uproar of excitement: the teachers had solved the mystery.*]

TEACHER #1: It all is like I said: You have to be sweet with these children. They *do* need sugar. We should never say mean things to them. They'll believe anything!

RESOURCE: [*thrilled*] That's why he never had tantrums at home!

TEACHER #2: Wait till Russell comes in the morning: I'm going to apologize to him so fast for this misunderstanding, he'll never have anything but sunshine on his pretty little face again!

THE COOK: Ain't it wonderful? I never knew it was so much fun to be a teacher!

ATG [*in an aside to me*] I see how you do this detective work. No need for *you* anymore: I'll take it over.

Besides visiting the 138 centers, meeting with the ATGs as often as possible, keeping records, and setting up files, Mary and I had many other irons in the fire. I was writing long reports for several foundations: one to Field to summarize the brief November developmental program for which we used their money, and one to Ford to summarize the developmental program for which we would *like* to use *their* money. Strike City had asked for help in working out an early education program. Mid-State Opportunities, Inc. (a non-CDGM program) wanted to coordinate Head Starts. The Jackson Head Start (non-CDGM) was seeking ideas. We thought it important to cooperate wherever we could. We spent a fair bit of time at it, considering how little we had. Meanwhile we were trying desperately to get publicity. Several times a week I was on the phone or the typewriter to *Ramparts*, or the Washington *Star*, the Washington *Post*, *Newsweek*, *The New York Times*. An editor at *Look* said, "We had a story on Head Start already."

None of them thought us newsworthy, but my phone bill grew and grew. I wrote a three-page description of CDGM and sent it with a form or personal cover letter to fifteen hundred likely recipients on campuses, in government, and in liberal groups. My hand ached from addressing all those envelopes. The typewriter ribbon wore out. I was so pinched for cash that a friend mailed me a ribbon from New York. My tongue tasted of glue for weeks. We gave occasional lectures in nearby states. I remember driving alone late into the night through rural Mississippi and Alabama to talk with a group affiliated with the Alabama State Teachers' Association (Negro, of course). I belted out a good number of letters to churches and girl scout troops in the North, begging them to send us boxes of good clothing, children's books, and toys. Bulky cartons began arriving in the mail at my house and we drove them up to ATGs in the Delta. We seldom appeared in a community without carloads of miscellany to hand over to the committee chairman or resource teacher. Then I wrote thank-you letters.

I was at this point in the winter answering 75 to 100 letters to *community* people each day. Mary was answering many too. At least fifty more each day went unanswered for lack of time. In addition we sent a steady flow of form letters to community chairmen: in October a letter stating the qualities a Resource Teacher should have; in November a letter urging chairmen to read all mail at meetings and to post it on the wall, and another on the *duties* of the Resource Teacher; in December, a letter stating that we were getting many applications from out-of-state students, and asking if anybody wanted one; in January an "are you ready to open" letter was sent, and a discussion of the duties of trainee teachers, and a letter explaining the Tuskegee course. There were the newsletters from us, too, and letters and announcements from other "departments." It was crucial at this critical stage to keep every remote place involved.

Mary and I flew to New York to view footage for the film that had been shot in the summer. One of Tom Levin's projects had been to get Adam and Ellen Giffard, talented film makers, and their sound man, to come down from New York for part of the first summer, to live at Mount Beulah. They had visited centers for a few weeks, looking for one that seemed just right. They'd settled on Second Pilgrim's Rest, and had begun shooting, when they realized how little time they had left, and how little the program was growing. The point of the film was growth. They asked if there was anything I could do. I "borrowed" Doris Derby, one of our best resource teachers from Holly Springs, and asked her to do her normal work, but at Second Pilgrim's Rest. She did. The program grew. The film makers, filming randomly in terms of their own free judgment, captured the growth exquisitely. In New York Mary and I hashed over CDGM's philosophy with Adam and Ellen, and rearranged some of their beautiful sequences to bring out our points better. Back in Mississippi I wrote the narrative script for the thirty-eight-minute film. The point was not to give the lovely visuals a trite nursery-school message, but instead, in a minimum of well-chosen words, to make each of CDGM's special points. I drove to Holly Springs to make a test tape of a local man speaking it.

Our film, *Chance for Change,* was finished in March. We compiled a guest list of "stars" from appropriate disciplines and fields, and flew to New York again for a Broadway preview. We received many comments such as this one from Dr. Susan Gray, director of the Demonstration and Research Center for Early Education at Peabody College: "I have seldom been so moved by any film as I was by *Chance for Change*. There was an authenticity about it so different from the slick productions we often see. I could really feel the heat and the rough boards under my feet as I watched the film. Most of all, the film leaves me with a hope that through the efforts of the many people working with the Child Development Group of Mississippi and through the children who learn from them, the future of Mississippi's children, and indeed all of us, will be far brighter."

There was a constant flow of VIPs to take on tours: the concerned and the curious; many who wanted to help us; a few who actually did.

The Citizens Crusade Against Poverty started talking about raising funds to finance the construction of some multipurpose community centers, in which Head Start could be housed, too. They sent an architect down. I was asked to take him touring in Delta communities. He was an architect who was especially interested in making buildings fit local conditions. He asked me to describe our urgent needs. It didn't bother him much when I spoke of planning bunkrooms in the back of each

Head Start center in which to put up families evicted from plantations for sending their children to our preschool program, but he blanched as I chattered on about designing roofs that bombs could roll off before exploding, and bulletproof walls of fireproof materials. His tour was abruptly cut off when he was recalled to Washington. I'm not sure what happened to the project—but we didn't get any of it.

We spent a lot of time phoning, writing, and negotiating with OEO and institutions of higher education that specialized in outstanding early education. We were trying to hack open wider opportunities for our eager teachers. We kept in close touch with Drs. Martin and Cynthia Deutsch of the Institute for Developmental Studies in New York, who thought they might run a sample CDGM center for us in Mississippi; and with Pacific Oaks College in California. We had a fat correspondence with Dr. Keith Osborne of the Merrill-Palmer Institute. We tried to get Mrs. Jackie Marlon, director of the National Child Research Center in Washington, Miss Judith Cauman of the Philadelphia Welfare Council and later of OEO, Evelyn Beyer, director of the Sarah Lawrence College (my alma mater) Nursery School, and of course, people from the Day Care Division of the Mississippi Department of Public Welfare. None of these materialized during that winter or the following year—not even a one-day consultant visit, except six months later, after a good bit of negotiating, Dr. Gattegno, director of Schools for the Future, and inventor of Words in Color and Cuissinaire Rod teaching, did give us a few days of help. So did a team from Peabody. But lack of consultants wasn't due to lack of effort, or lack of mutual respect, except possibly in two cases. Time and funds were always the problem.

However, if I failed in my attempt to get consultants to work with the ATGs, I succeeded in a submerged but by no means unconscious part of the effort: to make CDGM known and uniquely interesting to distinguished early educators. This was an investment for CDGM's future. So far, except for occasional piecemeal bits of volunteer help from Mary Emmons' husband, there was no one else to do this sort of dissemination but me and John.

We had good luck with the Bank Street College of Education in New York. Dr. Claudia Lewis held a wonderful workshop on children's literature and storytelling. The ATGs were inspired by her, and she with them: "What you are doing really excited me. It was a heartwarming experience to be with you all. I have never enjoyed working with any group of people more."

We could have rounded up a slew of self-styled experts. But, rightly or wrongly, I was fiercely protective of the ATG's right to have the best. Or, lacking that, to have freedom from the rigidifying mediocre. I couldn't bear to see them battered at by people trying to make them into proper preschool puppets. I wanted them to be influenced by gifted people, who could gently appreciate potential, and could respectfully help it become actual skills.

We worried OEO to death about sending us some of the hundreds of early education consultants they had on contract to sprint around the country helping Head Starts. Eventually we succeeded in getting Dr. Flemmie Kittrell from Howard University for two days with the ATGs. We hounded OEO some more. I continued to develop my reputation for being relentless and impossible. We needed OEO to make some places available for our teachers in the eight-week Head Start teacher development courses it was setting up on various college campuses. Finally, after much backing and filling about "qualified," and with less than seventy-two hours between the time OEO notified us that we could send teachers and the time we were supposed to have completed inviting, screening, picking, packing, and shopping for twenty-two of them, they had left, without money for bus tickets, and with none till some vague future reimbursement date, for Tuskegee Institute in Alabama. We had routed John out of bed, and he had paid for all the tickets with a personal check.

As in all our endeavors, Mary and I tried whenever possible to limit our work to setting others in motion. We helped the ATGs organize a system of contacting and selecting candidates for the course, and a system of recording exactly what transpired in each acceptable and unacceptable case. We notified community committee chairmen by means of one of our frequent letters to them that the candidate they recommended should be evaluated by the whole committee and the whole staff, and should be the best person they had. We specified that the candidate had to be someone to whom the committee had promised a position as resource teacher when the grant came. In spite of elaborate precautions, the usual misunderstandings and mass confusion prevailed. One lady who wasn't chosen called to report bitterly that she had borrowed money from the bank and had purchased two hundred dollars worth of clothing to go to college in, including a winter coat. Now "they" hadn't let her go. Another committee sent a woman they hadn't hired and quite a fight (fist fight) ensued when she returned eight weeks later and demanded to teach. We hoped that someday our institutionally naïve people would be enough accustomed to procedures, that some might go smoothly.

Fan mail poured in from excited teachers off on the greatest adventure and ego boost of their lives.

Mrs. Joyce Jean Stewart of Hollandale wrote: "My trip to Tuskegee has been exciting so far. It has been a great adventure for me.

"My main points are the great lectures by many good speakers and one of the greatest teachers is Mrs. Elsie Smith in Social Services.

"Of course there has been a little mix up here due to teachers that have certificates and others don't. They don't think we are qualified. Well, I can say it's not a certificate you have to become a Head Start teacher, but a dedicated mind.

"I hope I learn a lot and bring it home to my center and help my community be a better place in which to live and help our children to become better men and women of tomorrow."

Mrs. Essie Chaney of Glen Allen wrote: "We have BS degree teachers who think we are not qualify, but we have the answers to the questions and they don't."

Mrs. Lola M. Anderson from Stonewall said: "We were taught that Project Head Start is an attempt to save a child from failure (and thanks to C.D.G.M. for the opportunity of teaching these children). We can give them a sense of hope and a taste of success.

"In the social services studies we discussed how to help troubled people find this way.

"Mrs. Poole lectured us on Activation, Awareness, Clarification, Classification, Enrichment, and Diversification. The course here is fine, *BUT* I like Edwards."

Mrs. Elsie M. Smith, a faculty member for the Tuskegee Head Start Training Program, responded warmly to CDGM's "unqualified" teachers: "After scanning the list (of teachers from many Head Starts, many not from CDGM), we discovered that (CDGM teachers) were leaders in discussion, raised thoughtful questions, and shared very meaningful experiences with the total class.

"This does not represent my personal opinion . . . but rather, it is the consensus of the faculty. We find the CDGM students adequate in all respects and bringing a superior attitude and quest for information."

Another massive task was studying catalogues, figuring quantities, distribution systems, and budgets, and preparing orders for that great (and by now not really counted on at all) day when the grant might be announced. Then we could phone in orders immediately. I worked on children's books, records, and professional materials for ATGs. Mary worked on art materials, toys, games, and everything else. As much as we could, considering that they were scuttling around in the communities most of the time, and we were still camping at Mount Beulah, we talked over ideas with the ATGs. We would get twenty little battery tape recorders so ATGs could record songs and descriptions of things people had done at one center and carry them "live" to the next; and so ATGs could record interesting portions of workshops to pipe them directly into their centers. We would get twenty Instamatic cameras, so ATGs could make picture collections of unique things teachers and community members were making to be used at area workshops and displayed centrally. We would need a simple phonograph for each center and all kinds of music: Cajun music of Louisiana, jazz, easy square dance records, bird calls, Indian dances and music, jump rope rhymes, domestic and international folk dances, Kentucky mountain folk songs, blues and spirituals, standard well-sung children's songs, African folk tales and rhythms, work songs, party songs and games, Mother Goose songs and games, ABC and counting songs, nicely done lullabies, a few classical things, calypso, animal songs and sounds, rhythm records, Negro poetry, records illustrating various instruments—many of which should feature talented Negroes. If we were ever graced with the luxury of music and movement specialists, they could order more as they saw fit.

We would probably need 19,560 quarts of liquid tempera (ten quarts for fifteen children for three months), 3,912 reams of 18 x 24 newsprint, the same amount of 12 x 18 manilla drawing paper, and half as much 12 x 18 construction paper. Certainly between teachers and children we would use up 9,780 markers, 5,868 quarts of paste (only three quarts per unit of fifteen children for three months), 5,216 boxes of crayons, 655 boxes of colored drawing chalk, 1,240 pounds of clay ("and don't forget 5,868 rolls of masking tape, 4,160 large paint brushes for new centers only, 130 staplers, and 125 dozen scissors"). Then there were train sets and Tinkertoys, giant dominoes, magnets, and magnifying glasses to remember. ("Did we remember to budget the cost of printing and mailing the Newsletter? It'll be around $4,500." "How about materials for making books from children's stories and reading readiness games; the printer, remember, and all that tagboard, better guess $76,000 . . . we can always reallocate it if necessary." "What about money for developing film and buying tapes? That'll be in our division, too, won't it?" "Did you add up all those fifteen dollarses a month for resource teacher's petty cash? String, sponges, special art materials, etc.? What does it come to? *What?* $15,000! My God!") More could be ordered as we learned our rate of consumption and areas of demand.

Though I knew we badly needed toys and equipment for teachers to tack their teaching onto, I felt that we should avoid the traditional error of coating classrooms with so much gear and veneer that the absence of relationships, insight, personal growth, and resourcefulness become indiscernible. I felt we should order very few things like dolls, stuffed animals, housekeeping details, blocks—standard preschool items we would need—for another reason too. The secret of feeling successful and productive is accomplishment, and the keys to accomplishment are need, skill, aspiration, and ideas. Need and skills were plentiful in CDGM communities; aspiration and ideas Mary and I could generate. We would see how far we could get with this, reserving some of our budget till this was determined, and then order whatever else was top priority.

I tried to make arrangements with local poor people's cooperatives to make us things, but due to lack of organization and business skills on their part, promises and plans flowed more plentifully than goods. The Delta Woodworkers Cooperative did make us thirty tables, but two men left because of family troubles, one went to bed with bad legs from a previous injury, leaving the ladies, who preferred lamp-making to woodwork. We had to cancel our order for benches and puzzles.

We tried to make arrangements with the Poor People's Corporation. This was an amazing business venture run out of the back of a frame house. Director Jesse Morris visited his two hundred employees (who worked with obsolete equipment scattered around the state, often taking home no more than five to twenty dollars a week, but not complaining because they felt free from dependence on whites) on a motorcycle. Our arrangements, mostly made in a local cafe, never got off the ground, because people were busy with quilting, sewing, and suede for the Northern liberal market. Strike City said it would make something, but its Freedom Crafts was busy making nativity sets, also for the North.

At this point, we would invest in a collection of printed material offering the possibility of new aspirations and full of inspiring helpful hints for teachers. ATGs could dole them out in the manner of a portable lending library. It was hard to find pamphlets and brochures that were not discouragingly complex in composition, sentence structure, vocabulary, and meaningless generalities, but we managed to make lists of some on many subjects: preparing teachers for working with disadvantaged children, teaching creative music, the meaning of free play, discipline, blocks, woodworking with little children, child development principles, reading readiness charts and sets to study, children's fears, the facts of life for preschoolers, picture books of children in nursery schools, beginning science, and so forth.

We needed to order long on children's books. One of the things that was scarcer in Mississippi than libraries for Negroes was preschool books for anybody. We planned a list of some of the books most literarily beautiful and appropriate to our clientele. We arranged for them to be packaged for individual centers and drop-shipped to each area office, with copies of packing slips sent to us for our records, and copies to be signed by recipients for inventory purposes. Oh, we were so thorough! . . . and so tired.

Our major occupation was not this hodgepodge of developmental and dissemination activities, and the holding and hanging on activities. These we fit in around the edges. Our big thrust was to help the ATGs gain sturdiness, and watch their new strengths cause rippling effects in centers and communities. Spurred on by the exuberant ATGs, more and more and more centers opened without funds.

The eighth issue of my Newsletter gleefully reported new volunteer openings, and preparations, and goaded others into the stimulating flow of things. Nichols Chapel in Byhalia made a beautiful dressing room with housekeeping equipment for children to use. Pleasant Grove, near McComb, was buying building materials and saving receipts, hopefully for reimbursement if we ever got a grant. Decell Center in Greenwood and Magnolia in McComb were meeting with their respective ATGs and planning program ideas in advance. Three Rivers staff outside Pascagoula and Stonewall staff in Clarke County were building furniture and dividing themselves into "specialty" teachers. Quitman, Shubuta, Enterprise, and Tougaloo were arranging teaching areas in their classrooms. Richmond Grove, Choctaw, and Shaw were at work, literally day and night. Sacred Heart, Greenville Industrial, and St. Matthews were holding "teachers' workshops" and "practice teaching" on their own. Glen Allen, Hollandale, Harmony, and Fitler were trying out new program ideas. Ofahoma was installing new gas, water, lights, windows, and flooring. Old Pilgrim's Rest, Sunnymount, Holly Grove, Second Pilgrim's Rest, and Hopedale were holding regular community meetings and holding discussions on "educational philosophy." Longbranch was constructing a community center to house their Head Start. The Laurel centers, Queensboro, KC, Kingston, Central, and Wesley were repairing playground equipment and making games for the children. Asbury, Newell Chapel, and other Marshall County centers were reorganizing their area. Most Canton centers were open for children daily. Philadelphia women raised money for a new commode and for kitchen equipment. They worked till midnight for two weeks to get the building in shape.

Oxford, a new Center at Oxford, Mississippi, was open on a volunteer basis. They had seventy-seven children the first day and one hundred the second. All the people who would be the staff when we got the money were present doing volunteer work. Good transportation had been arranged. The center was open from 7 A.M. till 4 P.M.

A report about Quitman opening for children was written by the area administrator, Mrs. Mamie H. Jones (Area 11): "On December 13th, the Quitman Center opened on volunteer basis. The attendance the first day was only 29. The number increased to 46. Many children were unable to attend for different reasons.

1. Due to sickness
2. Unfavorable weather
3. Bad roads
4. Lack of transportation

"Despite the many difficulties, we feel that we have accomplished something. At least the Center was open, the children who attended were comfortable, happy, and filled with excitement. A number of more than 20 adults came to the Center and gave volunteer service.

"The community people gave a donation (from 25¢ to $1) to buy food and milk for the children. No charges were made for those of us who carried children to the Center. And I am happy to say that among those who attended were 15 children riding in the car with me. How did we manage? Fine. (With locked doors.) It's a two door car. All the kids are small, see.

"And we have agreed if the government isn't ready in January, we will be willing to continue on a volunteer basis.

"The program is for the children, and we, the community people, are concerned about them.

"Thanks to Operation Head Start for such a meaningful program. Trusting that it can forever continue."

Quitman Chairman Mrs. Jimana Sumerall wrote a report also. Here is part of it: "Our attendance grew day by day during the week to 187 kids. With the wonderful help of the community and a united staff of teachers and volunteer workers who gave their time and service to make our school run this week without an error. . . . Though the weather was rainy and a bit cold, but our spirits weren't dampened at all, we've a faithful janitor, Mr. Ben Morgan, who had the classrooms warm and ready every morning when we got to school. . . . We have a wonderful attendance of people to come out when our community meetings are called, and everyone is eager to help in any way she or he can. They're always asking is there anything they can do. . . ."

* * *

CHILD DEVELOPMENT
GROUP
OF
MISSISSIPPI
ISSUE #8

ACT
NOW!

Do you know who your Area Administrator is? He can help you find a building, learn about rent money, learn about making repairs, and learn what kinds of jobs pay. He can help you form a committee. If you do not know your AA or are still mixed up, call 852–2491 and ask for help!
No Center will open until it has a busy committee, busy parents, a fixed-up room and playground.
No Center will open until the RTs have talked with the Trainees and the community about all we talked about at Orientation.
Ask your Resource Teacher to bring all the newsletters to a community meeting. Read each one out loud. Talk about it.
Do you think colored public schools in Mississippi are good?
Are you opening a Center that is *better* than public school, or *worse?* Public schools plan ahead. Are you? Some are. Some are not. Don't be an "are not."

* * *

But there was still no government money, and this was still Mississippi. A note lay on the bed that served as my desk in the upstairs bedroom, empty except for stacks and heaps of half-collated papers for teachers. That was Mary's and my office.

"Mrs. Beard (an ATG) will not be at workshop. Klan murdered her brother, Vernon Dahmer. Night-riders set fire to house, fire-bombed him, early this morning. She is keeping his children, except one child, badly burned. Send telegram to funeral."

One of the twelve men later indicted for conspiring to intimidate, threaten, and coerce Mr. Dahmer on account of his race and color and for urging and aiding other Negro citizens to vote, was Sam Bowers, Jr., identified by the FBI as the imperial wizard of the White Knights of the Ku Klux Klan—the most violent and clandestine of the Klans. Mr. Bowers was also involved in the 1964 slayings of three civil rights workers near Philadelphia, Mississippi, but was still at large. On the day that Dahmer's death was grieving Negroes throughout the state, and was headline news in the Jackson papers, I asked my fourth grade daughter what she learned in school that day. She said, "We talked a lot about how important it is to wash your feet before you go to bed at night." "Did they mention the Klan murder?" "No, you wouldn't expect them to, would you? He's a Negro. They don't count them as murders."

Many CDGMians went downstate to the funeral, and I did send the telegram: "Twelve thousand children, citizens, teachers, and staff members of the Child Development Group of Mississippi, offer their deepest sympathy to the loved ones of Vernon Dahmer, who died a cruel death because he lived what he believed, and he believed all men are equal. Improved educational programs, farm programs, and other social changes, come about only because of the votes, efforts, and sometimes the deaths of the courageous. All twelve thousand CDGM people owe their program and their paychecks to brave men like Mr. Dahmer. He is more than equal. His is the flesh of which freedom has for centuries been made."

ATG Mrs. Beard received many telegrams. Many were from national civil rights organizations. The NAACP was very kind. Mrs. Beard, a very poor and semieducated woman, wrote to Roy Wilkins, executive director of the NAACP, to express her feelings: "Let me begin with my sincere thanks to you and our fellow NAACP-ers all over the country, for the many kindnesses shown our family during our most trying hours. The comforting words, the presense of understanding and the prayers of our friends have played a most vital part in our sustenance.

"I was especially glad to have you come to our home for here has been a welcome spot to all civil rights workers from all over the country, regardless of race, religion, creed or organizational affiliation, whose chief objective has been 'freedom.'

"One thinks in terms of civil liberties when speaking of freedom, but to me there is a more supreme meaning or application before we can truly be free, it lies within the soul and is implemented in the spirit of man toward his fellowman. Here are the grass roots of an approach toward the more simplified freedoms or liberties.

"Here in our local chapter, there was a negative assessment of the human interest Vernon had shown in the human being, and it was not until he had died that he was able to strike a responsive chord, and I'm sure he would have been happy to know his brothers at least would stick by him in death.

". . . in his death they sought to redeem themselves by standing arrayed in the glory of his sacrifice. . . . Please let me state here that the work of the Delta Ministry has been most effective here. . . . Anyone can readily recognize the person's objective when the person clearly demonstrates he is willing to push or pull to get the job done. Many people regret the action of the NAACP constituents here in this regard, and have expressed it in their feeling, that an apology evidenced in action and deed must be manifested before there can be any growth realized in the strength of the organization. . . . If you by any means have received information piercing our loyalty toward the organization, you will find upon investigation he, Vernon, was one of the organization's strongest supporters financially. For his pocket book was never ostracised. He did steer clear of the *Power Steering* so as not to prove a threat to anyone's position or image. It is not easy to work with people with small minds whose blinded eyes refuse to see that the road to success and happiness is paved by the deeds we do in our body toward our fellowman: The jealousy and prejudice exhibited by our brothers here cannot superside the hazards that beset us today. The desire to lay hold of personal prestige should not fall short of its content."

In this biblically ornate and oblique way, Mrs. Beard expressed the feelings of many CDGM community people toward the cautious NAACP.

CHAPTER 32

OUT OF STEP WITH THE TUNE OF THE TIMES

Area administrators and community organizers

WHILE MARY, THE area teacher guides, and I tried to work out goals and details for the educational side of CDGM, John Mudd, Frank Glover, and Jesse Paris tried to help area community organizers (CO) and area administrators (AA) work out all other parts of the program. No Movement people were left from the summer program. In spite of frantic recruiting, we were unable to attract a skilled community organizer to come to Mississippi in midwinter with only the merest murmurings about maybe a paying job "someday, if we ever get a grant."

Frank Glover, the white high school civics teacher from California and member of the Delta Ministry volunteer group that built the Beulah swimming pool, was still around helping out with this and that. He was enthusiastic enough to take on the great and difficult responsibility of trying to "train" community organizers. Most of them were poor people. This was part of our new careers for the poor. Only a handful had been with CDGM in any capacity during the summer. Both the leader and the learners in this division were coming entirely cold to CDGM's approach and stormy background.

The same was true regarding area administrators. We had never had skilled administrators, much less skilled administrators who were also teachers of business and administration. The only people still on board from the summer program in the administrative line were trainees themselves. Jesse Paris was a Pennsylvania Negro who had served as a resource teacher in Hattiesburg during the summer. He agreed to take a crack at helping poor people, again most of them new to CDGM, become competent business men and administrators of eight centers and an area staff (including the area teacher guides) for each.

A week-long workshop was held of area administrators and community organizers. It was supported with the remains of the Field Foundation's $17,975. Toward the end of the week area administrators were introduced to administrative procedures pertaining to payroll, supplies, facilities rental, transportation contracts, food vouchers, volunteer time records, and all the vouchers and forms that would be required by OEO—and how to break bottlenecks and unboggle administrative boggles in communities. Community organizers "specialized" in organizing problems and making plans for further research and action on subjects such as cooperatives, credit unions, nursing homes, neighborhood youth corps, legal aid, federal funds for after school enrichment programs, welfare laws, FHA loans, health clinic services, library services, and all things preventing communities from growing, or possibly available to aid them in doing so. The concept of the community organizer position, not yet in vogue all around the U.S.A. horrified OEO. It resisted heroically.

The whole group studied the proposal CDGM had sent to Washington. It was agreed that COs should learn how to write proposals themselves for their own areas of the state, "for next time." General trends in OEO projects across the country were discussed—trends toward complying with swelling demands from mayors and others in the power complex who were becoming increasingly unhappy as the poor gained power. This is old hat now, but was something new to notice in the winter of 1965. The group agreed that it needed to start its own planning and organizations, so it could counteract these forces. People talked about how CDGM community organizers could help do this. They could alert people to OEO appeal procedures in case they felt they were being bypassed in planning for themselves and their poor neighbors. They could collect complaints and double check and verify them. They could call Washington (collect), and could report how poor people felt, and facts about what was going on down there in faraway, castaway mysterious Mississippi. They could form area and state pressure groups. In short, they could teach poor people how to make their needs and strengths felt by their government in a way it had never felt them before. The advocacy approach is popular now, but then it was "radical."

These were the things that interested John Mudd profoundly. He corresponded with many such well-known people in the field as Warren Haggstrom in Syracuse University's Social Action Program. John worked with the Citizens Crusade Against Poverty to see if CDGM could plug in to its proposed leadership training program. He found a section of OEO that was interested in helping us expand this aspect of our work. John investigated many things. He worked through Dr. Alvin Poussaint of the Medical Committee on Human Rights to see about initiating a pilot planned parenthood educational program. He looked into Manpower Development and Training Act (MDTA) training for CDGM secretaries. A bricklayer was located who was willing to teach bricklaying in CDGM communities. Ideas filled John's keen, highly informed mind, while his calendar filled with a clutter of prosaic chores.

Wrangling continued about the summer Orientation fee. John worked with the National Council of Churches (NCC) to prepare new cost material, and participated in discussions between CDGM, NCC, and OEO. OEO audit had challenged part of the accounting fee contracted with Spokney, Gersten Company. John had joined in two Washington negotiating meetings between counsel for Spokney, Gersten, and counsel for OEO, Mr. Jim Heller. OEO had questioned the relationship between the grantee and the delegate agency. On December 15, with the help of Mary Holmes's sponsor, the powerful and excellent Board of Presbyterian Missions, Mary Holmes and CDGM signed a contract specifying the responsibilities of each. The OEO's final audit, in preparation for which John had done a massive amount of midnight work, found CDGM records in good order, but requested a more detailed inventory; in the preparation of which John did *another* massive amount of midnight work. The audit meetings occurred from December 13 to December 23, but fortunately terminated in time for John to indulge in a hurried Christmas dinner.

OEO insisted that adequate fiscal control had not been maintained during the summer. John Mudd, Mary Holmes, and the accounting firm of Garlick and Hoffman, in consultation with OEO and Automatic Data Processing Company, designed new systems for personnel and fiscal control. OEO requested that CDGM contact school officials to explore the possibility of coordinating preschool programs funded under the Elementary and Secondary School Act. John and Dr. Beittel did this. State Superintendent Tubb supported the importance of preschool programs, but we didn't succeed in developing any more intense relationship than that.

At the Senate Appropriations Committee Hearings, Mr. Shriver had promised not to fund a statewide Head Start again at Mount Beulah. But he had *not* promised not to refund CDGM. In fact, he had spoken in support of CDGM:

> During the summer, the grantee operated eighty-three child development centers in forty different communities and twenty-one different counties. Because of this program, 5,820 Mississippi children received the education, the medical care, the social welfare services, and in some cases even the clothes, the like of which they had never before enjoyed. Without this Head Start program, these children would have been denied these elementary necessities due to the absence of Head Start programs in many sections of the State . . . The child development experts and the educational authorities who investigated this program claim that it was a success in fulfilling the purpose of the program, which is what Congress asked us to do.

Dr. Julius Richmond, director of Project Head Start nationally, had also spoken in defense of CDGM, as had many of the authorities mentioned earlier.

But because it had been made clear that Mount Beulah could no longer be CDGM's headquarters, John had sent a delegation to shop office buildings. He had reserved space at the Milner Building in Jackson. OEO had demanded that CDGM contact every funded or pending Community Action Program (CAP) in those areas where it expected to operate, in order to determine possibilities for coordination of programs and to offer the opportunity for any objections to CDGM to be raised. John had contacted all the CAPs on a list provided by OEO. He had discovered only one funded CAP in proposed CDGM territory. He had ascertained that the same children would not be covered by the two parallel organizations, one of which would be controlled by the power structure, and ours by the poor. Reverend James McCree, the black preacher from Canton who was the newly elected chairman of the CDGM board, had contacted STAR, a poverty program intended to train community action technicians chosen from the poor, to see if our community organizers and their technicians could work together, especially regarding CAPs.

For a January 5–6 meeting in Atlanta John prepared a county by county analysis of the CDGM proposal and budget and a listing of other funded or expected CAP programs in the thirty-two counties represented by CDGM. The funding for CDGM was analyzed in terms of the CAP allocations for the thirty-two county group. At another Atlanta meeting, held January 12 through 14, OEO had proposed immediate funding of thirteen CDGM counties that were under guideline budget quotas, nineteen counties that were up to guideline quotas, all administrative costs for the entire project prorated on a county basis, and deferred supplemental funding of all remaining costs of the proposal. It had been determined by those at the meeting (John, board members McCree and Ayers, ATG Coney, and OEO officials) that in the thirty-two county group, the total CAP allocation was four million dollars in excess of the total CDGM application and all other proposals expected by OEO. At this meeting an explicit agreement had been made that CDGM could begin operation at full level. OEO insisted that four counties in which we had had CDGM centers during the summer (Panola, Tallahatchie, Sunflower, and Bolivar) be left out of the grant, pending written affirmative support of CDGM from proposed CAP directors there. We weren't eager to accept that divisive decision: a typical white tactic toward Negroes through the years.

By the end of January John had spent an average of fourteen hours a day, including weekends and holidays, for six straight months on these matters, all of which were to him, as to the rest of us, merely means to the end of getting a grant and going to work on the heart of the problem: community change and growth. He was weary, frustrated, missing most meals, getting very little sleep, living on cigarettes, coffee, and pep pills, and was so ill that the staff was convinced he had TB (not true). Marian, Mary, Lois (a magnificently efficient young woman with great awareness of the feelings and needs of poor people, whom Frank Glover had brought from California in late September to become our office manager and "new careers" for the local clerical staff leader), and I developed a great mother hen yen to take care of him; which, of course, annoyed him.

The difference between OEO's conception of what were critical issues for CDGM and John Mudd's concept were evident from the first. Though John was driven by an unrelenting Calvinistic determination to become an ace administrator and to learn to do all these required things well, so the people could have their grant, CDGM's real meaning and human problems remained uppermost in his mind and in his efforts to communicate with OEO staff people. Therefore he rapidly earned a reputation at OEO, as had Tom Levin, and for the same reason, of being defiant. We, in turn, found discussions with Atlanta OEO somewhat discouraging.

The major problem was that as soon as John complied with required conditions, new, apparently arbitrary conditions, increasing in difficulty, were artfully, startlingly introduced—as if John was the handsomely gallant young hero, and OEO was the wicked fairy-tale king, who didn't want the prince to marry his daughter. There were petty discouraging factors, too, like the older man, a long-term government employee, who always swung conversations of CDGM to his major concerns: whether he could arrange for OEO to continue paying him per diem in Atlanta, though he had bought a house and was "permanently" on the Atlanta staff, and whether he could get a second-hand Peugeot he had bought to run.

On the whole, most people in OEO Atlanta, and OEO Washington, seemed generally "for CDGM," whatever that may have meant to them. There were only three people in important positions who seemed less than hopped up about our goals. But John Mudd was a strong and dedicated young man. He endured. With grace becoming the gentleman that he was, he endured. I began to think of him as Mithridates: the king who became immune to poison by taking gradually increasing doses. I'm afraid that during this period we became a bit self-pitying and conceited. A note in my diary says: "Edmund [Burke], we think of you often: 'Those who would carry on the great public schemes must be proof against the most fatiguing delays, the most mortifying disappointments, the most shocking insults, and worst of all the presumptuous judgment of the ignorant upon their designs.' "

Mary Emmons recalls that this period marked the beginning of her shift from "naïve trust in my government" to cynicism. For John and me, who had been more sophisticatedly cynical to begin with, it was something else. We felt that we had somehow drifted into a strangely lonely position; that when we dealt with OEO, we were in another country, on another continent maybe, where we felt amiable but alien. It was as if we were silently, politely imploring the officials to understand our intentions; to pierce this whole pious but shallow game and see the real business beneath. We were not disagreeable. We did everything that was demanded. But we began to feel slovenly and eccentric in contrast to OEO's well-scrubbed, tidy, administrative view of the orderliness with which we were to proceed. In fact, we felt almost afflicted with our own beliefs—as if we had inadvertently stumbled into the wrong arena. We complied, yet we felt outside it all. At times, I confess, it even seemed comic, occupied as we were with quite other concerns.

In the crevices, between all these necessities, John found brief times to get to these other concerns, to do what he loved to do and was so gifted at doing. He participated in discussions of the fundamentals of our program, and how they related to the daily details of what we would be doing.

The following are excerpts from tapes of a November 30 discussion held during the week-long workshop. Participants were COs, AAs, ATGs, a few board members, and several community friends of the project. John Mudd said, "We're discussing the goals and structure of CDGM . . . forget that there is a fairly detailed proposal that has already been written, and raise the most fundamental goals that you have and see how CDGM can support these, and work towards them."

Jake Ayers [local Negro Board member] said, ". . . if someone came up and said, 'well, you can have whatever you want,' . . . we don't know what it is. . . . We don't know how welfare works, how FHA and a lot of other things work, and we're afraid . . . we're wrong in taking off on these programs. Well, we're going to have to be taught . . . how you get all these programs, and how those people get in those offices and who supervises those programs, and means of getting them out if they don't do the things they're supposed to do."

John Mudd said, "Now . . . I wish that we could start with that question. . . . What do we want? When we talk about that for a little bit, perhaps we can start being aware of where . . . specific programs might fit in. Or where our over-all program working with the kids fits in—what we are after? What are we sitting here struggling for? And why do we hope to work with CDGM? What kind of life are we trying to create? I think we have to consider this at a general level for a while to see where we are headed. . . . What are we after in terms of the development in this state and our community? . . . What do you want?"

The group responded. Many said "Freedom."

John Mudd continued, "Okay, freedom, lets talk a little bit about freedom. We've heard a lot about freedom in the past years in this state, and I don't think there is probably one person here who is against freedom, but what does it mean? What goes into making up freedom? . . ."

Charles Hamberlin [local Negro area administrator] started, ". . . more activities with the parents and I consider it being free to have community organizers working with the community making the grown communities more aware of federal programs that could help them on the farm. . . . I feel that money makes one free. If you can get these people on a better economic basis, then in a sense they will be free."

John Mudd asked, ". . . What is it about money that makes it connected with freedom?"

Charles Hamberlin answered, "Well, mostly I would consider that with money comes power. With money comes influence. And also with money you are not as dependent. . . ."

Jake Ayers countered, "I hate to disagree with the man, but in my way of seeing, money does not make you free. I've seen many many rich Negroes in Mississippi who are still slaves. I want to speak from experience that CDGM has given us the best program that I've seen in Mississippi compared to any other program . . . I've seen the child gain confidence in himself, feel that somebody does care. . . . It gave him better facts, it gave him food to eat. It gave him clothes to wear. It gave him better health. With this I think we gave him freedom."

Mrs. Johnson from Quitman had *her* idea of freedom: "Talking about freedom and money, I think that when our men folk will be able to get jobs along beside the white man and get their money just like they are, that give us more freedom. . . ."

A lady from Canton said, ". . . if we could ever get the feeling into our people that we are just as good as white people. . . . Our self-dignity means more than money or power. This is what I am trying to say . . . to try to get this slaveism and Tomism out of our people. . . ."

Rev. Martin of Pascagoula [an ATG] said, "I do think while we are discussing freedom that I might point out things that I think will help even if it doesn't make us altogether free . . . like . . . being able to vote. People are interested in voters. I know in the community where I preach they always stop the blacktop road at the last voter's house; that happens to be a white person's house. But I notice now that since people in that community have started registering to vote, the blacktop has moved a little further, because they know that they are going to need him at election time. And then I think money, too, if you are dependent upon a man . . . if you are all tied up in debt with him, he can control you. He can tell you how to vote, he can tell you what you better not do. . . . And then holding some land, you see when you own your own place, can't nobody put you off it. But if you rent or are living on somebody else's place, he can easily get you off. And that's some of the trouble we have been having here in Mississippi, even though a person do have a privilege to do things, he is afraid to do it. Now he is not physically afraid that the man is going to do anything to him. But he is afraid that he might get up one morning and lose his job. Some kind of economic [reprisal] like that. And then I think that you ought to have some religion too. I think that goes with it.

A male speaker said, ". . . If I was going to attempt to describe a free man, I would say a man that [has] convictions, he has something, because if he has his self-respect and he is free to do what he pleases in the realm of the law. Now not all laws, because you see he gets tied up there . . . there are some laws that I can't obey, you see. . . . Really, I think that this whole society that we live in has got to be transformed."

Tom Harris from McComb interjected, ". . . I think that freedom comes from within. That's where I think it comes from. Can we ever be free?"

Jake Ayers commented, ". . . to me freedom is the right to assume responsibility. No person, and I hope this is not shocking, but I am convinced that no person will ever be completely free, and no person want to be completely free. Because if you are completely free you have no responsibilities. But to me freedom is the right to make a choice. "I merely want to be free from intimidation, or reach the place where I can ignore intimidation, because I'm not actually going to be free from every criticism. But when I reach a certain level, these things won't tend to bother me. We can have as much freedom as possible when we can . . . not send our children to a white school for the sake of integrating the school, but for the sake of getting a better education. . . ."

Reverend Appleberry said, "*Freedom* is a word to me just like *love*. It has no bounds, you know. . . . This idea of freedom depends upon ability. . . ."

Mrs. Travillion reminded, "We are speaking of freedom for Negroes. . . . Well, first, we have to think about what determines freedom and what determines success. Now we have to think, if we are thinking about the ideas and concepts of our society, the society in which we live of the Western hemisphere. What determines what we call success and freedom here might mean something totally different someplace else.

". . . when we think of becoming totally American, we have to think of getting into . . . the mainstream of society, and what does that consist of, and what it takes to become completely acceptable in this society. Will money do it? Yes ma'am, in our society, here in America, one of the greatest capitalist countries in the world, money rules the world. Now if we are talking about Negroes being acceptable in America, then we must get money. . . . We are called a minority people, but the Jews are more minority than we are, and they are acceptable in America—anywhere—they have money. . . . Money . . . rules all of Europe. We are called the greatest people in the world, because we have money. It isn't knowledge, because we import knowledge to America. We have Russians who run our missile bases. Our mathematicians are foreign. The people with knowledge are foreign. But America is still called the greatest country in the world. And I maintain that until the Negro does something about getting money we will be less free, because that is the way we are going to be decided. . . ."

Jesse Paris said, "I think that the word *freedom* doesn't express itself. We should add two letters to it. *T O:* Freedom *to*. . . . Freedom to what?

Now you can get some answers. Some people will say that they are free to vote, or to go to a restaurant. To me, also, freedom means to me peace of mind."

Cora Fleming from Indianola [an ATG] challenged, "I want to ask a question. Here in Mississippi, are you free to go to the courthouse and vote?"

"Are you free, and your fellow man can't go? . . . Are you free when you have a meeting in your own neighborhood? . . . As long as one person feel like he is free and the rest of us [are] slaves, we are not yet free. And I feel within myself that we are now beginning working with freedom through the children. That's where our freedom begins with, these young children. . . ."

A man said, "We talking about the word *freedom,* which as Jesse said a few minutes ago 'freedom to'; freedom to what? . . . I am free to move until I bump Matthew over here, then my freedom stops. You are free to do what ever you want to do as long as you don't infringe upon the rights of someone else. . . . I would like to have the same privilege as the next person has. . . ."

Another man said, "I feel that if we were to educate people so as to free their minds. . . . We all express our ideas here because our mind is free to function as we want it to. And once we get our people to this stage that they can think for themselves. . . . I think we will have a better knowledge of what the word freedom means. It will mean something different to all of us. . . ."

John Mudd asked what the speaker meant by freeing minds, education, and whether this is really the goal, or if acceptance into the existing society, as Mrs. Travillion stated, was the goal.

Rev. Martin spoke, and concluded: ". . . No, I just really don't like this here society like it is now. I don't, especially here in Mississippi. I sure wish I could bring about a better place in which to live. That means that I am asking for more than accepting me. . . ."

Rev. James McRee said, ". . . Society has kept us down. Not only kept . . . the Negro down, it has kept the white down. . . . I think there needs to be a radical change in this system in which we are living. People sure are going to say we are crazy, communist-inspired, and all that. But there have never been a revolution or changes made that people were [not] called fools. . . . I think in a large measure these so-called fools have been the ones that have transformed our society to where it is today. And they are going to continue to transform it. To change it from the system in which that exist now, in which we live, to a different kind of system. I am bitterly opposed to black supremacy just as well as I am to white supremacy. I am opposed to Negro dictating to Negroes, just as much as I am to white dictating to Negroes. . . . I think we should ask ourselves this question: 'Do I want to follow the norm just to be accepted? Or do I want to go further?' "

Grace Travillion answered, "Well, now . . . I brought the question up about being accepted, in our society. . . . It is wrong, true democracy is right. But we in all our organizations are looking for acceptability, and I come back to that, else why do we say we want to be free. . . . Now I'm not saying that our society is right, it needs changing, yes, but all of our organizations are asking that we be accepted. And I still say that the only way to become accepted in this society is to have money, and . . . when I say money I don't mean individually—I don't mean people here in Mississippi—I mean Negroes must add to the mainstream of this society, the American society, some industry. We've got to get together and put our pennies together and come up with some shipyards, some paper mills, some something. Now I don't mean just for us, but to just add it to America. . . ."

John Mudd interjected, "Let me just make one comment. The question was really not what do the organizations say we want. I think we should be open enough here to say what *we* want, you know. And also to bear in mind that we are a group here, which is and will be an organization. We should try to have more resources behind it, for the next few months, than any of these other groups you are referring to. And the reason that I think this discussion is so significant is that what we do in the next nine months will color how these resources are used and what [impact] they have in terms of the over-all development of the children, the parents, and the communities they work with. That's why I think we have to be very open to say really what we want. A second kind of question is, can we get there, and how do we start getting there? OK, I'm sorry . . ."

A person in the audience said, ". . . I've always faced the word *acceptance, liberal, moderate,* and *tolerant,* all in the same category. I don't feel for people who say they are liberal: liberal with what? Giving what justice demands: they are moderate? How? They tolerate Negroes, tolerate the people in lower income brackets. . . . And be accepted. . . . And who is there to accept me? I am already a part of America. They are not supposed to have to accept me in any society I was born in. . . . Now the things that I think we have to do is like Rev. McRee said, reorganize. . . ."

A man asked, ". . . Would you care if you were accepted by the white race, if you have everything you want—factories, jobs, big executives, etc.? Would you rather be *accepted* by the white man, or *respected* by the white man? Or would you be at the point where you don't want anything from him? . . . Is freedom most important or . . . cutting down on the poverty structure? Are they synonymous terms? . . ."

Another man said, "I don't think that we want to create a black society . . . I don't appreciate the power structure being white, and I would fear the power structure being black. I don't want the black man to dominate the white man, but I certainly am tired of being dominated."

Another speaker said, "We say we are living in a free democracy. I don't say it because I don't believe it. Sure, there are certain freedoms that I have . . . but to give an example, I'm not free to sit on a jury. It just so happens everytime that they get to my name they are through . . . to me they are merely empty words that have no meaning."

A lady remarked, "Well, it was asked how the two words [freedom and democracy] were related. Well, actually, democracy is supposed to mean freedom."

John Mudd asked, "Why is it supposed to mean freedom?"

She answered "Because our country was founded on those facts . . . a country was taken away from the type of government where you had a monarchy type of ruler. . . . They had no freedom of worship, they had a totalitarian type of government, where one person ran it. . . . They came here and set up a government. It was supposed to be set up where people ran their government. . . . Where people would have a freedom of choice, a freedom of worship, freedom of the type of government they would have. So they chose the democratic type of government which meant I am supposed to be free to say what I want, within the realm of as long as I don't hurt you. . . . So actually, democracy and freedom are supposed to mean the same thing. But when we came over here, that kind of changed. We came when they came, but we came in chains. But we are talking about what we want for our children. I said freedom. And we got to talking about how we were going to teach our children freedom. Well now, that is a pretty big thing to say."

John Mudd said ". . . There are some people saying that freedom is an internal thing, any man can be free. And other people are saying that you have to change the system. Now, what about this, what is the connection between the larger social systems and individual freedom?"

A lady answered, ". . . We aren't talking about personal freedom, we are talking about political freedom. . . ."

John Mudd asked, "Aren't they connected?"

The lady answered, "Not necessarily. It is a personal thing what I deem freedom. It could be different from what you deem freedom. But we are thinking about under the law, political. Under the law what am I entitled to get? Freedom? If we talk about individuals, everyone of us here has a different idea of freedom. So I think that we are talking about twenty million people rather than one."

John Mudd questioned, "Do you mean that if you talked about freedom for a while, everybody in this room, that no similarities would come up? Everybody would have a different idea? Aren't there certain things about freedom which you might be able to discuss with people and perhaps agree upon with people? And then the second point, why do we have to, when we talk about broader social institutions and their relation to individual freedom, why do we have to limit it to the political? After all, we have an organization right here, Child Development Group. Are you free in that? You aren't, not completely, no. Are there ways in which this organization could run which would make you freer?"

And so the discussion went on, people trying to tie these general ideas to the specifics of their new roles as CDGM area staff members, people trying—

At another session during the same week-long CO and AA preparatory workshop, I tried to tie together this general freedom kind of discussion with what would be going on in the classrooms with the children in each of the centers where the AAs and COs would be working. So far, though COs and AAs seemed to have some awareness of the connection between freedom, democracy, and their new jobs, there was little evidence that they saw any sense linking these interests with a kindergarten program. Those that didn't consider the Head Start altogether irrelevant to their purposes saw it as "a good thing"; primarily because of the food, and secondarily because it would be sort of fun for the children.

None of us succeeded in doing what we were trying to do that week, of course. John, who tried so hard to keep people thinking of their jobs in an intellectual, significant context, tended to pull them from their personal need to define their new roles, from their eagerness to get into solid bits of the whole. He was a permissive discussion leader, and the discussion wandered. He left some people stronger, and many feeling that the day missed the point of what they needed urgently to know. He saw this kind of a day as the beginning of many days, during which more of the nitty-gritty would be reached. He didn't know that he would soon be so consumed with finance and administration that this day's discussion was not a start, but an isolated fragment.

Frank was perceived as too bossy, Jesse as not knowing enough, and I, who was told that I had an hour to discuss the program for children with this group, and would then be separated from them to work with ATGs and teachers for the year while AAs and COs went into their specialties, was wild to convey to them in this brief moment the exhilaration I felt about the miracle people could bring about if they once, in a flash, realized the power they had in their hands to transform a generation of children by applying their own freedom spirit and techniques on a child-appropriate level. So I was too intense. I raced. I rushed them. I bowled them over with my excitement. I left a few people with a new vision of what Head Start was all about, and many more feeling that I was too forceful, and that they were, in contrast, helpless. In our efforts to do good, we probably did a lot of harm. We didn't succeed, John and I, but we were true believers in the trial.

CHAPTER 33

CHILDREN'S CRUSADE TO WASHINGTON

WHILE ONE PART of each person pondered the nuances of freedom, equality, respect, and responsibility, other parts were preoccupied with weather, winter joblessness for farmers, starvation, and disappointment in federal promises. By late January things were in pretty bad shape. On January 22 the temperature dropped to 18°, and it snowed for the third time in a week. Backyards of houses, which sometimes dated back to slave days, were a mire of mud, which 90 percent of the Delta families had to wade through to get to their outhouses. They had no indoor plumbing facilities. Most houses leaked, and people woke up in the morning with piles of snow and pools of melted snow on their quilts and floors.

People were receiving writs of garnishment against their wages, and the few who had managed to purchase something during the summer were seeing it repossessed now. An elderly couple was found frozen to death in a Delta plantation shack. Many people couldn't sustain their spirits by dreaming of spring, when there would be, again, as annually, a six month season of work. Because of mechanization and a one-third reduction in crop allotments, the state employment service had estimated that 6,500 of the 26,000 tractor drivers living with their families on plantations—approximately 30,000 people altogether—would no longer be needed to work. After this idle winter of being permitted to stay on in The Man's shack, for lack of anywhere else to go, they would join the flow of the displaced and homeless families migrating northward to nothing. For those who would work again come spring, the situation was only a little less desperate. Their median annual income, according to the U. S. Agriculture Department, was $456. In the winter commodity foods meant the difference between life and death. Only about half of the 600,000 people who depended on commodities were receiving them, because commodities were used to reward docile nonregistering adults, and refusal of commodities was used to induce others to leave the state.

The Delta Ministry had begun negotiating with the Department of Agriculture to increase the availability of commodities in December, 1964, but though meetings had gone on through winter, spring, summer, and fall, there were few visible results. In September, 1965, an assistant to Agriculture Secretary Orville Freeman had written: "The OEO assistance which will soon become available will help to get foods to an additional 500,000 needy in the state, and on a year-round basis."

But nothing had happened. In October an OEO spokesman told a Washington *Post* reporter that there was no discrimination in commodity distribution, and that he had never heard of any charges of Negroes not getting food. On November 23 Mississippi state officials had signed a contract with OEO and USDA for a six-month "Operation Help" experimental commodities program. The Welfare Department was to get 24 million dollars worth of commodities from USDA, and one to six million dollars from OEO to help distribute the food. The contract said that the program would be implemented within sixty days. The plan included a biracial committee to supervise the program, and hiring nearly five hundred poor people to help give out the food. Two months later the food was not being distributed, no biracial committee had been set up, and no Negro hiring had been done. Nor had the situation been alleviated by the arrival of Head Start salaries, with which people could have bought food. CDGM didn't have its grant either.

On January 24 the Freedom Democratic party, the Mississippi Freedom Labor Union, and the Delta Ministry, invited "all the poor people in the state" to come to a planning conference at Mount Beulah to decide what action to take. On January 29 seven hundred people met, discussed, expressed disillusionment with federal programs in a telegram to President Johnson, decided to call themselves the Poor Peoples Conference, and agreed to a new tactic for dramatizing their plight:

"There's this Air Force base at Greenville. They got over two thousand acres and three hundred empty buildings, and all they do with it is mow them lawns. So we figured, why not jus' go live in them barrackses? Beats our houses any ways you looks at it. Sewers and water wasn't jus' right, 'cause it was abandoned propity, but that wouldn't matter, we ain't got sewer an water anyways, and there at least we'd have a roof wouldn't leak. So we went. At six-thirty in the morning on January 31, 'bout fifty of us, four cars full of us, went.

"We jus' smiled at the gate guard and waved and rode right in. He was so unexpectin' of us, he jus' smiled and waved us right by. We drove 'round, gettin' the lay of the lan', and then we stopped at a barracks and quick's a Klansman'll kill a nigger, we jumped out, run in with our suitcases an pasteboard boxes, an our mattresses and quilts, an stoves and kerosene lamps, sandwiches, can goods . . . all day long peoples joined us to protes' our living conditions. We wanted from them to put in training programs at the base an' let people being thrown off the land live in it. They could use it for a place to give out the food. To make the government notice us. We organized us some housekeeping committees, and after midnight we laid down and slep'.

"While we was sleepin', the county sheriff and the Greenville polices was runnin' around a lot, scratchin' their heads in confusion as to who should do what about us niggers in there, an the Air Forces didn't know what to do or who should either, 'cause they'd leased the base to Greenville, and they didn't know if it was their authority to deal with us.

"Fin'lly they decided what to do was fly in a hundred forty air polices from Denver and two majors, two lieutenant colonels, three colonels, and a general to show us their strategic air power which was to drag us out. Firs' the general speeched us about we was a fire hazard and a health hazard an' then they shot the lock and carried us out the barracks drug us out. It was sunthin' else to see all them big brasses evictin' li'l black babies an black ladies. We walked back to town fi' miles in the mud, but the newspapers up North kicked up a lotta sand, and the government got inerested, so maybe sunthin' might come of it, maybe."

As a response, possibly to head off further demonstrations, previously unmovable federal and state agencies launched Mississippi's most massive food distribution program since depression days. And later, the Hunger U.S.A. campaign was launched by FCM, a CDGM "child."

But effects weren't felt for the first few weeks in February, and people were furious—at everything federal. Floods of indignant letters flowed to Washington:

Dear Sir,

This come to say we are organized Head Start workers, and have been working every since we closed the summer program, which proved very helpful and successful.

I am a widow not old enough for pension, they won't give me any kind of help from the welfare, not even commodity. I have an Industrial Sewing Certificate, they won't let me work in the Garment Factory, we or scream in against every thing.

We have been promised the Grant for four or five months, how *long*, how long are big polititition going to refuse to sign the grant. We have been doing voluteer work for three months, having work shop, making stuffed dolls, animals, erecting swings with tires, chains and boards, alone with merry go-rounds on the playground.

We are willing and ready to continue but without the aid and support of you we cannot go any farther. So stop think for a few minuts is it I who is depriving poor innocent children from being trained educationally, morally and even food, and even the parents of these children from making an honest and just living by not signing the grant that doesn't come directly out of your pocket. Yet you are one hundred percent for spending millions and millions of dollars sending rockets to the moon, and other projects not near as important, as developing children lives.

I wish you would imagine yourself in our position for a moment. Then maybe you will give this matter careful and quick consideration.

How *long*, How much *longer* will we have to wait.

Yours truly,
(Mrs.) Anna Ashley" (An ATG)

By February poor people had donated free labor valued in excess of $190,000 in terms of prospective pay scales under the new program. They had contributed more than $60,000 in materials, gas, and food toward the operation of volunteer centers. They had physically improved over 90 percent of the centers, with repairs and renovations ranging from the installation of wells and septic tanks, to remodeling homes into schools, and the construction of tables and benches.

As if in demonically ironic response to this historically unheard of effort, at four o'clock in the afternoon on Friday February fourth, CDGM received a telegram from OEO administrator Jule Sugarman, stating that as of nine o'clock Monday morning, as part of sealing off the summer project in anticipation of a new grant, we were not authorized to spend another penny. This meant that after the weekend we couldn't call or communicate with our constituents in any way, shape, or form. We couldn't continue to rent a few typewriters, buy paper, etc. It meant that our five or six paid wrap-up people would no longer receive salaries, which they had been splitting and sharing with all the other volunteer workers for months, so that we could keep our skeleton Central Staff from starving and being forced off to "real" jobs. The only money we had had was a tiny amount supplied by OEO for the central wrap-up operation, and the $17,000 from Field for buildup (the training workshops for area staff). The latter had by now expired. Neither kind of money had been allocated to communities anyway.

At the January 16 board meeting John had formally been asked to become CDGM project director. He had replied that he would rather be considered for the coordinator of community organizers position, but would temporarily accept the directorship if the board would promise to keep looking for a Negro director. Perhaps John, I, and the board members whom we quickly contacted for opinions were paranoid. However that may have been, we didn't receive the news as a harbinger of grant imminency. Rather, we thought it was a politically clever way for OEO to get rid of the pestering poor people altogether—by dissolving their communications system, thus their cohesiveness, thus their confidence, thus the painful pressure they were exerting on plagued OEO—and so to extinction.

Feeling more inflamed than defeated, we hastily, a mite hysterically, assigned every person in sight, including friendly passers-by and nearest relatives, to man the phones. All Friday evening and Saturday morning we dialed chairmen, teachers, parents—notifying them of OEO's action, explaining that if they never heard from us again it wasn't because we had abandoned them, but because we were no longer authorized to telephone or mail; and asking them what they thought we should do. People greeted our news with plucky exasperation, and commented on their government's relationship to them with rather unrancorous raillery, considering the circumstances.

My diary records: " 'They is pure perfidious, that's what they is!'
" 'If you ask me, this ain't no war on poverty; 'ts a war *over* poverty, to see who's gonna git the prize: all of us poor peoples.'
" 'We're doin' a scrimmage to get rid of the OEOses schism. What I want t'know is, when will we get on to get rid of our scourge?'
" 'Ah, yeah, the govmin's alus been a day late an a dollar short 'th us. They don' ever give us nuthin' but dust.'
" 'If they don' give us our grant *now,* after *this* trick, I'm gonna write them this:

Spring is sprung,
The grass is riz,
Where last year's
Hopeful dreamers is.'

" 'These OEO mens, they say they want to help us. They have our ideology. But I'd say, their ideology don't run very deep. In fact, you might say they're crass opportunists—it's stylish to talk nice about the poor these days.'
" 'To me, those mens in Washington are parvenus about the poor, and recoilsome rookies in Mississippi history.'
" 'The idea! Why, the way those OEOs talk to us, why, they jus' thinks they can ride a bulldozer to community change!'
" 'Hah-hah! Ain't that the funniest one they've pulled yet! They thinks just because we're niggers, they can treat us niggardly! Ah, hah! That's a good one!'
" 'Well, what'd'y' expec? Mr. Shriver is a great man. He let's us know *that* everytime we hafta go see 'im. He un'erstans evrathin' down here from A to B. But the Bible say: "Great men are not always wise." I don't bow to no one jus' cause he's great. What we gonna do now to show who's the wise ones.'
" 'Las' summer they gave us a milligramme to mollify our miseries, but they di'n' really mean it, so they let a lotta time ride so the maggots has got into our gains.'
" '*Now* what's OEO sparrin' and spattin' 'bout? We don' take voters to the polls—jes' children to the toilet.'
" 'They're plannin' to drop us quiet! Oh, man, Lucifer's on the launchin' pad now!' "

The overwhelming reply was that we should have an emergency statewide meeting at Beulah the next day, Sunday, at which community representatives could map a strategy before the curtain fell Monday morning. From then until Sunday, staff called wildly in all directions, calling for help, calling congressmen in California and the Ford Foundation, calling major liberal organizations, calling *The New York Times* and New York *Post*, calling strategic friends, calling, calling, calling for somebody sane to do something to save the poor from what we saw as silent suffocation.

The labor unions' poverty organization, Citizens Crusade Against Poverty, had helped us with postage stamp money before we existed. John and I had kept them posted. We had not heard from them since then, but now John called and asked them to publicize our problem through their channels. They responded with strategy and alacrity. And wc wrote. Mary Emmons' husband was summoned in from his thesis writing and commanded to become chief public relations man. He whipped up a dramatic release identifying CDGM and outlining its accomplishments. It ended: "Financial help is also badly needed. OEO has cut off our funds completely, and we are operating on borrowed money. We have enough to last for about a week, but no longer.

"Please Help! We need you so desperately!"

Sunday came, and carloads of incensed representatives from communities. By grand and glorious coincidence, Tom Levin, who had neither been in the picture nor in Mississippi on other business at all since his long ago departure to New York, was at Mount Beulah that day at CORE's invitation. It was in regard to another group's entirely unrelated workshop for CORE leaders working in Southern states. He said little, but his presence was a momentous good omen to many community people.

During the first part of the meeting people kept popping up with indignant and outraged discussion of what they had done—of what we should do, and others shot the ideas down as insufficient. We should write to Washington, Mr. Shriver, President Johnson—a flood of letters. We've done that already. We should send ten telegrams from each center. We've already spent more money than we've got on telegrams. They didn't do any good. We should bombard Shriver's office with phone calls. We did. But some of the calls didn't get through—we seemed to keep getting the U.S. Post Office, and other times we got Shriver's or Sugarman's assistants, but we *have* called. A delegation should go to see Mr. Shriver personally. We've sent delegation after delegation. They *have* seen Mr. Shriver personally. A lady pledged fifteen dollars from the "Tougaloo . . . children on some means to get us to Washington." Someone suggested that Washington was not the only "persons that has been slapping us around," and that if we were going to demonstrate in Washington, we should demonstrate in Mississippi too, "because our state government has slapped us around too." Someone else thought we should gather five thousand children together somewhere in Mississippi and let TV show Washington that the children would be on their way soon. We should send Mr. Sugarman a telegram asking for a deadline: When would we get our grant? We've asked him for deadlines many times. That's the problem, they won't give us a date. We could wait if we just had a date. No date means . . . well, what does it mean? Bad faith? Promises, promises, but never a date. Let's send a telegram with many of us signing it. One more time. Asking for a deadline. Then, if no action, we'll march.

"Look, this is what I'm thinking, how many times are we going to stand up and try 'one more time,' one more time, over and over and over again, and it hasn't done any good. Now what we need to do is demand and put pressure on. That's the only thing Washington and the white Mississippi power structure understands is pressure. So let's do it as a whole right now." [The following comments are from tapes.]

"Which should we talk about . . . adults going to Washington or carrying the children to Washington? Now this is two things you have to take into consideration: How many parents are going to let you carry them away from home? You have to think of that thing, too. And the other point is: How much money would it cost to carry seven, eight or ten buses from here to Washington? Where will that money come from?"

"I think the people that have children would like for their children to go, but I really don't think too many children should go. I think if the parent would go, we could put enough distress on Sargent Shriver. . . . We know we need money, we can work. We can do something and raise money, and pool cars and things like that; or buses, to go to Washington. And just go to Sargent Shriver's office and stay there until he consents [to] give us some kind of consideration. And I am willing to go back and work and we all send, maybe six people from each center can go, or maybe five people from each center can go. Maybe the other people can work and donate food and money, and I think we can make it like that."

". . . the base of propaganda is a lot of . . . so we can just *say* how many are going . . . we can put a thousand or five thousand. . . . We don't have to march. . . . We would use that, that they are going to march, and then take what we can."

". . . about what I said about the telegram, it was a misunderstanding that I said we send telegrams and not go to Washington, but I was thinking when they are going to Washington, we send telegrams in support of this delegation to let them know that these 143 centers are supporting them. And at the same time we have this group of Head Start people and children somewhere where we can get good news coverage. I don't know how we'll get it, because I don't know about those kind of thing, T.V. . . ."

"I believe there's enough parents that's interested enough for this Head Start program, that we could get some parents that will send their kids to Washington. There we can show them we are not interested in politics. We could get out there, maybe in the Lincoln Memorial Park or in Sargent Shriver's office if the weather is bad, to set up *classrooms.* I mean, teachers, let them know that we are interested in *education.* . . . [Polly]"

". . . we are trying to prove to these people that we are trying to help children. I don't think, now this is my personal feeling, I don't think we can prove to anybody in Washington that we are interested in these children if we suggest . . . a long bus ride without proper food, and it's subject to God knows what if we are going to get there."

". . . have nurses on that bus, we can get those to go along with the children . . . have people in Washington . . . working on places to put these people. . . . All these should be done before we leave [Polly]."

I was strongly for the idea of a Childrens' Crusade to Washington—a tactic we hadn't tried; a novelty to worldly politicians—with the inherent appeal of all those charming, heart-winning children. A *teaching* demonstration, showing the dedication of the poor to solving their own problem, showing the humorous ease with which teachers lived with the children. A demonstration to delight and amuse, not to threaten; but with the implicit threat of invisible angry numbers behind it. This was *it* for us, the critical moment. We had to be daring, to go all out to make the national scene, or CDGM would soon sink into anonymity. We had done public relations work all along with "the good guys"; but this should be a thrust at the hearts of the general public as well—our public relations *piece de resistance* in behalf of the poor.

The discussion went on, it went on all day, with considerations of what it was, exactly, that people hoped to achieve through these various moves they had mentioned. John Mudd was to go to Atlanta Monday a week for "terminal discussions." "Terminal discussions," however, had been going on for months. They meant less to us than a bean would mean to feed all the hungry in Mississippi. What people wanted, it emerged, was advance assurance from OEO that a grant would be signed the day John went.

It was decided to send a telegram to Washington OEO insisting that OEO give us a date and give us a promise in writing. There was a discussion of several hours duration as to the wording. Should we "urgently demand" or "urgently request"? Which was more becoming? Which was more honest? We urgently requested, but included the fact that if we weren't given immediate interim funding for central staff expenses by noon the next day, and written confirmation that our proposal would be funded by February 18, we would stop at nothing. Mr. Sugarman replied that he would leave Washington right away, and meet John and the others in Atlanta in the morning. Jule Sugarman was in a bind. He was in favor of our program. But he had a job to do, and orders to obey. At the same time that a community man said of Mr. Sugarman, "Save a little hate for him," Mr. Sugarman was telling people in a New York City Head Start to look at CDGM for inspiration!

Community people decided to wait and see how things went. They would meet again Wednesday to make the decision about whether or not the children were to go to Washington. Several OEO officials were in Jackson that day, trying to straighten out the commodities program. Runners from our meeting kept them informed, and they were in close touch with OEO. Washington and Atlanta OEO were nervous.

Meanwhile the poor people instructed Dave Fleming (the medical program volunteer coordinator) and me to prepare, "just in case." I was to somehow acquire money to rent buses, should they be needed, to recruit and select children and escorts, to plan a "program" to entertain and educate the children on the buses so no one could accuse us of harshly "using" the children, and to make housing arrangements for all in Washington. Dave was to charter buses, and have them waiting at Beulah at one o'clock Wednesday. If the group Wednesday decided the deal was off, because a grant had been signed in Atlanta, well, we would just cancel everything. During the next three days, with Mary Emmons's help, we did it all. I called an aunt in New York and she telegramed nearly four thousand dollars for chartering two buses. (On February 24, 1966, the Jackson *Daily News* carried an article telling us that Representative John Bell Williams said: ". . . a mysterious source financed the cost of two bus loads of Negro children . . .")

I called my cousin Peter Weiss in Washington, and John called his sister-in-law, Marion Mudd, and they made lovely instant housing arrangements for sixty of us, including meals and entertainment. Lots of liberals would like to do something. Seldom are they offered a specific job to do. We invited our best teachers to come and each bring five or six children whose families they knew well, with signed parental releases. We also kept up the image of statewide tension that we had begun when the funds were cut off.

While our delegation was negotiating in Atlanta, hundreds of community people called in with "an emergency, get him out of the meeting, I've got to speak to John Mudd." OEO became more nervous. In fact, on Tuesday, while John was gone, I received thirteen "off the record" phone calls from various "important" people at OEO, imploring me not to "let them do it." I explained each time that whatever the people decided to do, the people would do. That we neither controlled them, nor aspired to control them. OEO feared bricks. I told them about a teaching demonstration. They asked how the people were feeling. Were they really sizzling? Was it dangerous? Was Dave Fleming, who described himself quite accurately as "a nice quiet withdrawn middle-class Protestant recent college graduate," actually a member of the armed black insurrectionist group "Deacons for Defense?" It could be proven, our callers claimed, that the money for the buses had been donated by the Deacons. What would people do? I said I didn't know, and advised them to consult the people directly. (One of the callers, or his boss, made an attempt to do this, within the limitations of his understanding of the suggestion. He called a Negro man prominent in the moderate group, and quite opposed to our rapid reform approach. The man had never had anything to do with CDGM. Moreover, the OEO man didn't *ask* this Negro how people were feeling, but told him how they *should* be feeling—that they should calm down and contemplate all the good deeds OEO had done in the past and in other states.)

I felt that I was lying. I could well guess what the people would do: nothing. They were afraid of scaring off OEO and getting no grant. They were in the habit of being polite, no matter how furious they were inside, and no matter how little reward they got for their good manners. But I thought, just this once, it would be just as well if OEO misinterpreted Mississippians. This time it might work to the people's advantage by giving them some leverage. When he came back, John was bombarded with these OEO calls too. He also bluffed. I suppose he could've kept people from going. Instead, he sent telegrams like this to many key government people:

THE ATTORNEY GENERAL NICHOLAS KATZENBACH
JUSTICE DEPARTMENT
SITUATION IN MISSISSIPPI BECOMING CRITICALLY EXPLOSIVE. 20,000 DESPERATELY POOR PARENTS AND 3,500 POTENTIAL EMPLOYEES HAVE BEEN PROMISED A HEAD START PROGRAM UNDER THE CHILD DEVELOPMENT GROUP OF MISSISSIPPI SINCE SEPTEMBER. THIS PROJECT HAS BEEN WIDELY ACKNOWLEDGED BY NATIONALLY KNOWN EDUCATORS AND GOVERNMENT OFFICIALS AS THE ONLY PROJECT FUNDED BY OEO THAT HAS SIGNIFICANTLY AND HONESTLY INVOLVED THE POOR ON THE BOARD OF DIRECTORS CENTRAL STAFF TEACHERS AND AT ALL OTHER LEVELS OF DESIGNING AND IMPLEMENTING A POVERTY PROGRAM. EDUCATIONAL MATERIALS DEVELOPED BY THE PEOPLE ARE BEING REQUESTED BY OTHER PROGRAMS, PUBLISHERS AND OEO. IN OVER FIFTY COMMUNITIES PEOPLE GAVE UP JOBS AND HAVE SACRIFICED TO ORGANIZE PRE-SCHOOL CENTERS FOR THEIR CHILDREN ON A VOLUNTEER BASIS. THERE HAVE BEEN PROMISES FROM OEO FOR MONTHS BUT NO ACTION. THE SITUATION IS RAPIDLY BECOMING UNCONTROLLABLE. THE MISSISSIPPI POOR FEEL BETRAYED AND WILL WAIT NO LONGER. THEIR GOVERNMENT AND THEIR POVERTY PROGRAM MUST ACT IMMEDIATELY TO AVERT AN IMMINENT EXPLOSION.

Officials were adamant: John and I were to crush this outrageous uprising. OEO executives weren't practicing Lao Tzu's *Way of Life:* they didn't "handle a large kingdom with as gentle a touch as if you were cooking small fish."

Seven hundred poor people showed up at Wednesday's meeting at

Mount Beulah. John began [from a tape]: ". . . The problem we've been facing the past few days is that some people simply cannot seem to respond to the needs and feelings of others. People don't understand each other. They don't sympathize, or seem capable of feeling what life means to others: what it has meant to you to run the volunteer centers; your need for jobs and money; your commitment; the dangers you expose yourself to, to do this. Washington has tried to put me in the position of translating its attitudes to you. I've said that this was not enough. All I can try to do is tell you what has happened, what people have said to me, and what I think it means."

John was very fair. He explained that OEO isn't just one person; that we have both friends and enemies at OEO; that OEO is inefficient. It does this to everybody; it's not especially against us. OEO feels it has made concessions and commitments to us, way past what political wisdom tells it it should. Etc. OEO had sent along a letter that made the entire audience roar with laughter. It said, in elaborate language, that in about ten days OEO would make a decision as to whether to give us a grant. Probably it would be *yes*. A man called it "Sugarman's extemporizing letter."

People again discussed all the pros and cons of sending the children to Washington. Only this time, fifty children and twenty-three adults were dawdling around beyond the doors of the meeting hall, suitcases in hand, looking at two chartered buses, whose drivers paced up and down our driveway. John and I were for people making their own decisions, but hoped it would be *yes*. Silent hoping is different from influencing.

Mary Emmons had butterflies in her stomach, and was afraid going would backfire and cause OEO to be even more punitive toward us. "I wasn't against going to D.C. as a strategy, I was just scared it wouldn't work. If it had been my decision to make, I don't know what I would have done. I didn't know much about the government then, in fact this was going to be my first trip to Washington. I didn't know how the government *or* community people would respond—if community people could come through. As for my husband and me, we were so low on cash and so high on bills, we would have to leave in a month."

Late in the day, the group voted unanimously, though as always, ambivalently, to send the children. John, Mary, and I suddenly felt exhilarated. The tide had turned. We were no longer backed into a corner playing a protective, defensive role. We had the ball, and we were going to run with it.

John sent another telegram to the Justice Department, this time advising them of our imminent departure, giving our buses' tag numbers and route, and concluding "We request your office to take every measure to ensure their safe arrival."

At 6 P.M., after a huge spaghetti dinner and lots of gleefully merry singing and circle games in the dining hall, we loaded the children into the buses, put Mary and a nurse from the Medical Committee in one, me with a sackful of John's cash for seventy-three people's expenses in the other, and drove our surprising cargo off in the drizzle to the nation's capital, eleven hundred miles away.

Youthful Area Teacher Guide Valentine Blue, who had a reputation among the ATGs for being "the life of the party," led us all in song for the greater part of the endless trip. She improvised on old spirituals, popular freedom songs; and children's songs:

Ain't gonna let nobody
Turn me 'round, turn me 'round, turn me 'round,
Ain't gonna let nobody
Turn me 'round
I'm gonna keep on a-walkin', keep on a-talkin',
Marchin' up to freedom land.

Ain't gonna let OEO
Turn me 'round, turn me 'round, turn me 'round,
Ain't gonna let OEO
Turn me 'round
I'm gonna keep on a-ridin', keep on a-singin'
Drivin' up to Washington.

Ain't gonna let lack of funds, Lord,
Turn me 'round, turn me 'round, turn me 'round,
Ain't gonna let lack of funds
Turn me 'round
I'm gonna keep on tryin', keep on crying,
Goin' up to see Sargeant Shriver.

While we sang our way to Washington, tense and tedious negotiations continued. A telegram from OEO's Fred Hayes, deputy director of the Community Action Program (CAP) to John Mudd and the Mary Holmes president began: "The review of your Head Start application continues and we wish for you to be jointly aware of the special grant conditions which we are recommending to the OEO director. These special conditions will include: A. That no CDGM offices or officer may be housed in Edwards, Mississippi. . . ."

There were many more special conditions than those to which any other Head Start in the country was subjected. On this first one we took rather violent exception, saying we would have the American Civil Liberties Union sue OEO for interfering with individual rights. OEO dropped the condition.

* * *

We're coming through the green grass,
green grass, green grass.
We're coming through the green grass.
Happy happy days.

Oh, what you coming here for?
Here for? Here for?
Oh, what you coming here for?
Happy, happy days.

We're coming to get money,
money, money,
We're coming to get money
To run our Head Start school.

Oh, we won't let you have it,
have it, have it,
Oh, we won't let you have it.
Stingy, stingy days.

We're going to get it anyhow,
anyhow, anyhow,
We're going to get it anyhow,
Oh, happy, happy days.

* * *

Now get on board, li'l children,
Get on board, li'l children,
Get on board, li'l children,
We're goin' for our Head Start grant.

* * *

The children slept all over each other under mountains of quilts. To the astonishment of other diners, they trooped into roadside restaurants and ate finer food than they'd ever had. They had a complete kindergarten curriculum on wheels. We arrived at the Bethesda Unitarian Church, which was to be our central meeting point, at midnight. Waiting families came out at dawn and drove small groups of children to their suburban homes, each with a teacher, as scheduled.

The children went happily to bed at 2 A.M., and I began looking for a live mouse. We needed one for the science class that would be part of the next day's demonstration nursery school. We had arranged to conduct it in Representative Adam Clayton Powell's Hearing Room. Representative Powell (Dem., N.Y.) was chairman of the House Education and Labor Committee, which was overseer to the Poverty Program. We thought this a good place to illustrate our point.

I asked my hostess if she had any pet mice. *No,* she said, but added obligingly, "I'll go in the kitchen and catch you a *real* one." To my delight, she returned in five minutes, at 3 A.M., with a fresh mouse in a Have-A-Heart mousetrap. "Anything to help the cause," she said.

In the morning, we set about following the schedule the Citizens Crusade Against Poverty (CCAP) and we had devised. First we loaded everybody into the buses, got a traffic ticket because buses weren't supposed to be on that part of MacArthur Boulevard and the officer wasn't moved by my beseeching that we were late to open school in the

House Office Building, and trailed up those elegant governmental steps past the statue of sober Sam Rayburn, past gaping guards, dragging children, diminutive chairs, teddy bears, quilts, carrots and juice (for morning snack time), clay, crayons, newsprint, homemade dolls, and other paraphernalia appropriate to a preschool. Tourists stared. CCAP and several CDGMians had arranged the best press and TV coverage we could get for this occasion. In a front page story with a picture, the Washington *Evening Star* of February 11, 1966, reported:

> . . . while five members of the House Education and Labor Committee looked on with amazement, the youngsters unloaded crayons, toys, drawing paper, pastepots, and a live mouse in a cage and proceeded to demonstrate the preschool program now being conducted on a voluntary basis in Mississippi. . . .
>
> Rep. Joseph Y. Resnick, D-N.Y., one of the committee members present, told the Mississippians:
>
> "I'm very sorry that members of your congressional delegation are not here to greet you. Your state representatives, congressmen and senators, instead of cooperating with you and working with the OEO, have thrown up blockades and roadblocks and done everything they could to stop the program. . . ."

The Washington *Post* of February 12 also ran a front page picture of our young lobbyists, and an Eve Edstrom story starting:

> If ever Chairman Adam Clayton Powell had a good reason to be absent from the ornate hearing room of his House Education and Labor Committee, it was yesterday.
>
> The swinging Harlem Democrat could not have stopped the show.
>
> The hijinks were really something, what with one young man wheeling a quacking Donald Duck, another taking dead aim on Congressmen with a cap pistol, and the entire group of 48 pre-schoolers chanting to "Who Stole the Cookie from the Cookie Jar." . . .
>
> . . . Theodore M. Berry, director of the Federal poverty war's community action programs, told them that their completed application had just arrived in Washington, and would get speedy attention. . . . a Shriver aide [said] Shriver indicated that a pared-down $3 million grant would be forthcoming next week.

Even *The New York Times,* which we had had considerable difficulty interesting in our plight because we were "just another Head Start," had a piece about our "romper lobby" petitioning Congress for "a redress of grievances."

After being treated to lunch and lots of ice cream by Representative Resnick in the House Office Building cafeteria, we took the children on a tour of the White House. We had intended to give homemade toys to Mrs. Johnson, as she was nationally billed as "the mother of Head Start." She was unavailable. She was making America beautiful they told us. We were disappointed.

The condition of OEO's blood pressure regarding CDGM can be

guessed by the fact that, though I didn't even sit a tired child down to tie a shoelace, our "guide" (a self-proclaimed OEO staff "friend" of CDGM) phoned the OEO inspector general to tell him "Greenberg is leading a sit-down strike at the White House," and the inspection office phoned the director of CCAP in the midst of an important conference with a famous senator to inform him of this emergency and to ask that I be immediately kept from implementing a national disaster.

While we were thus stirring up a storm of excitement, which we further stimulated by singing "Before I Be a Slave, I'll Be Buried in My Grave," etc., on the front steps of the White House, and by killing time on the sidewalk outside later (they thought we were plotting something), others from our group were in conference with Mr. Shriver. "Mr. Shriver is so uncomfortable with us poor people, that he always walks right past us and shakes hands with the others first. Then he looks at them while he 'makes arrangements for us,'" observed a poor black member of the delegation. They received no satisfaction.

The next day, the Washington *Post* said in a story entitled

TRIBUTE TO LINCOLN IS PAID BY JOHNSONS:

Official Washington paid solemn tribute to Abraham Lincoln at the Lincoln Memorial yesterday on the 157th anniversary of his birth.

But perhaps the most touching tribute was an unofficial one from 48 preschool Negro youngsters here from Mississippi to plead for funds for their Head Start program.

They climbed the long steps yesterday morning to stand before his statue in the Memorial, then burst into song—"We Shall Overcome."

Undaunted by a guard who said no singing was allowed in the shrine, they started back down the steps quietly, then paused midway to offer—"Happy Birthday to You."

Later President and Mrs. Johnson and others came to lay wreaths at the Memorial.

We played at the Kennedy playground, paid a visit to President Kennedy's grave, and enjoyed entertainments generously provided by several churches. Then the children clambered raucously back into their buses and rolled "down home."

Meanwhile, in addition to welcoming us to use their offices as our "campaign headquarters," the Citizens' Crusade Against Poverty had done a giant job of getting selected people to send telegrams to the President and to the director of the Office of Economic Opportunity, and of circulating their statements:

The poor of Mississippi need their faith in the Federal Government restored by immediate and vigorous Federal action. The months of delay in establishing the food distribution program and the current delay in funding the preschool program sponsored by the Child Development Group of Mississippi have produced great frustration and a lack of faith in the intentions of the

Federal Government. Poor children should not be made to pay the price of administrative delay. We urge you to take whatever measures may be necessary to expedite anti-poverty programs in Mississippi.

Walter P. Reuther, Chairman
Citizens' Crusade Against Poverty
Rabbi Richard G. Hirsch, Secretary
Citizens' Crusade Against Poverty

I am distressed by the news that has come to me today indicating the fact that the central office of the Child Development Group for Mississippi has been closed. I am further advised that responsible citizens of that community feel that an in-Washington demonstration is a desirable and justified course of action to pursue. The dreams and aspirations of these deserving people must not go unattended. I urge you to supply whatever approvals are necessary to immediately provide funds for this worthwhile project.

Martin Luther King

The poor children of Mississippi need your help now. Your closing of the CDGM offices on Friday and apparent delay in negotiating a new grant has produced great concern throughout the country. As you well know, the great enemy of the poor is bureaucratic delay. The hope you have given to the poor in Missisippi is turning into frustration. I urge you to immediately provide interim administrative funds and speedy approval of the CDGM Headstart proposal.

A. Philip Randolph

Suavely smiling OEO top executives scornfully asked CDGM poor people representatives why they were carrying on so, when OEO was promising three million dollars. One of the poor men said, "Sir, *promising:* that is one problem. Promising and not making available. And sir, let me get you correctly, did you say you were promising us three million dollars?" "Certainly," replied the OEO top executive (later described by the poor man as "a chillingly cool cat"). "That's what I thought you said," replied the poor man. "Well, I just want to say that that's far less than the six to seven million dollars we've been negotiating for all this time; about half of what we've been promised. If that's the best the U. S. government can do for us after all we've done for ourselves, you just keep it, and carry it right straight to hell."

For the next week, there were a lot of private conferences between me and leading liberal congressmen and senators, between John and CCAP and OEO, and between CCAP and NCC and many of their distinguished and powerful patrons, some of whom were in as high places as the White House. There were a lot of hectic plane trips and bus trips up and down to Mississippi, and a lot of community meetings there. Top officials from the Board of Presbyterian Missions and other allied organizations had to fly all night, as Mardi Gras guests had daytime air spaces filled.

There was a board meeting with Mr. Heller, Mr. Sugarman, and others in Jackson, Mississippi, February 18, during which Mr. Shriver upped the ante again. Now OEO wanted an escrow account to post a guarantee on a balance of a still unaccounted for $35,000, though it was agreed by all that 90 percent of this had been substantiated, and receipts would soon be in. John, numb by now, put up the $35,000 from personal sources.

OEO always wanted to cut the number of children. We were only serving 10 percent of the Negro children in the state as it was, not to mention white children, and OEO wanted to cut us to 5 percent. We felt our children's futures were being traded for bombers to kill Vietnamese children. One bomber cost eight million dollars—enough to finance our whole project. OEO made new demands, too, but everyone was too despondent to feel the keener pain of despair.

After some more scurrying, disputing, and obeying—concerning three new "established" Mississippians for the board (a psychiatrist, a child welfare supervisor, and a pediatrician were enrolled), a deputy director for Business and Administration (the executive director of the Jewish Welfare Fund and Associated Jewish Agencies of Cincinnati, Ohio, was good enough to move down on loan for three or four months), a business manager (a principle administrative officer of the National Council of Churches was borrowed), accountants (the local Office of Ernst and Ernst, a leading nationwide public accounting firm accepted the challenge)—and accepting OEO's selection of management consultants to start us off right (we were pleased), a grant of 5.6 million dollars for 9,135 children in twenty-eight counties was announced.

The three million mentioned during the week had scandalized our friends. OEO had never said there was any possibility of so little. So our friendly pressure groups had got busy again (Eugene Carson Blake had intervened at the White House level) and boosted us to 5.6 million dollars. John was in Washington at the time, too busy and disgusted to call us. We read of the news in the Jackson papers.

* * *

Pussy Cat, Pussy Cat,
Where have you been?
I've been to London
To look at the Queen.

Pussy Cat, Pussy Cat,
What did you there?
I frightened a little mouse
Under a chair.

* * *

The office had been moved, carton by carton in cars, from Mount Beulah to the Milner Building, while I was away with the Children's Crusade, and I couldn't find most of our records and all our supply orders now that we were ready to order. Moving was one of those Here-We-Go-'Round-the-Mulberry-Bush issues. OEO wouldn't give us a grant till we got into the respectable Milner Building. The Justice Department was there. OEO liked that. But OEO wouldn't give us rent money to move into the Milner Building till after we had a grant. On January 26 John wrote a $796.25 check of his own for a month's rent. Sometimes we felt OEO expected a lot.

Everybody was dismally depressed. Events of the month evidenced the fact, fatal to our efforts, that impetus and decision-making were increasingly in the hands of other people—powerful, liberal, forward-thinking groups such as the National Board of Presbyterian Missions and the Citizens Crusade Against Poverty—but nonetheless, other people—not the poor. The strategists were doing brilliantly. The poor were being *done to* once again, though benevolently this time.

The Jackson press greeted the news of our grant with its customary grace. The Jackson *Daily News* of February 24, 1966, said:

> Eastland, speaking on the Senate floor, said the matter is particularly shocking to Mississippi because this is the same organization, the same personnel that so thoroughly discredited the poverty programs over the nation in 1965.
> Senator John Stennis Wednesday asserted that leaders of the Child Development Group of Mississippi lack the ability and character to conduct classes for "pre-school children, or children, or adults of any age."
> Representative Williams branded the award as "inconceivable," and charged that . . . "These leaders attempted to undermine the laws of Mississippi and of the United States through civil disobedience, by sit-ins, walk-ins and lie-ins."

OEO's Public Affairs office sent a release to all the major newspapers in the country; the usual defensive approach they had adopted toward CDGM: a list of answers to Stennis's charges. Never anything about what we stood for or had accomplished, or that we were the epitome of what the poverty program was intended to be.

Even the Washington *Star*, so recently our friend, for some reason now took a few pot shots at us—actually, at our allies the Citizens' Crusade Against Poverty. I had to write a reply to the editor, for John's and the board chairman's signatures. More and more I resented the amount of time public relations and press relations took from my work.

> Editor
> The Washington Star
> Washington, D.C.
> Dear Sir:
> The Citizen's Crusade Against Poverty has been accused by the Washington Star's special writer Leslie Carpenter of "militance," "bad manners," and "acting like the poverty program's worst enemy." CCAP is organized labor's new million dollar program designed to consolidate the influence and commitment of more than 125 national liberal organizations and outstanding citizens in behalf of the original and best intentions of President Johnson's poverty program. The accusation results from the fact that when the Child

Development Group of Mississippi made a desperate appeal to CCAP to help it dislodge its five-month promised 6.2 million dollar Head Start application from the mountains of pressures being exerted against it, CCAP responded by doing so. . . .

In spite of this remarkable degree of significant and dedicated involvement of the poor in the destinies of their own children, a grant for CDGM, which was constantly assured, never materialized. Patience became frustration, and frustration became desperation.

The Citizen's Crusade Against Poverty made known both publicly and privately that OEO's actions in the face of furious political opposition were becoming further and further removed from its oft-stated determination to help the poor help themselves. The case of CDGM, which had captured the excitement of nationally renowned early childhood educators, poverty project leaders, and Civil Rights people and had been publicly endorsed by them as one of the best examples of what the War Against Poverty can do, provided the critical test for OEO to overcome its legitimate fears and act in accordance with its birth announcement.

CCAP made no financial contribution to CDGM whatsoever, but it did alert its friends and members of CDGM's urgent situation, and asked them to send telegrams to President Johnson and Sargent Shriver, requesting immediate funding of the program. When frantic CDGM constituents sent two bus loads of little children and their proud teachers to Washington to beg for their grant, CCAP made available its phones and duplicating facilities and several helpful staff members. CCAP neither conceived nor financed the trip, which was made possible by the vigorous determination of poor people to continue the children's program, the generous contributions of several Northern individuals who gave cash to pay for the buses, and a number of Washington families who were kind enough to open their homes to the group. Nor did a CCAP staff member named Ralph Caprio threaten to picket the White House, as charged by the Star's Mr. Carpenter. The Mississippi group took normal brief tours through the White House. It is doubtful that Mr. Carpenter's further statement that Shriver "reacted to the picket threat as a form of blackmail" is true; forty-seven small brown children wandering through a palace are not really much of a threat.

CDGM would like to thank CCAP for having the courage of its convictions and for having helped, which it definitely did, to win us our critically needed grant. If advertising the plight of thousands of hungry and hard-working people and promoting action to help them is "bad manners," "militance," and "acting like the poverty program's worst enemy," may the Citizen's Crusade Against Poverty be guilty soon again.

Very truly yours,

John wrote to CCAP.

March 8, 1966

Members of the Board
Citizens Crusade Against Poverty
2027 Massachusetts Avenue, N. W.
Washington, D. C.

Gentlemen:

As the poor, the disenfranchised, the socially isolated, creatively participate in new organizations to improve their lives, they must inevitably clash with the forces of the established social structure which molded the conditions for their poverty. In this, the poor are crippled by their lack of political voice, and by the inability of those who occupy positions of power and prestige to understand their feelings, expressions, and actions. Too often the creative potential of the disadvantaged will be perverted and crushed in this process, *unless* effective institutions are developed which can come to the aid of the impoverished in this positive struggle for a new society.

To over 20,000 parents of 11,000 children and 3,000 employees, the Citizens Crusade Against Poverty is *the* institution which provided the understanding and support necessary at a critical time in the consideration of their year-long Head Start Proposal under the Child Development Group of Mississippi. Without the immediate responsiveness, energy, effectiveness of Mr. Boone, his staff, especially Mr. Caprio, Mr. Kurland, and Mr. Brown, and members of the Board of Directors, the full CDGM program might not have been funded, and OEO might have passed a critical moment in its history, having failed to confront the deepest issues involved in supporting programs which truly implement the directive for "maximum feasible participation." The most fundamental features of the Community Action Programs for the Southern Negro and the poor across the nation hinged in the balance. Due to the Citizens Crusade Against Poverty's actions, OEO was strengthened in its determination to side with those who believe that *all* individuals are entitled to participate in the opportunity of America.

For this, Citizens Crusade Against Poverty and those who responded to its appeal deserve profound thanks and profound respect.

My diary from that time records only dreary feelings: "I re-read a poem tonight that W—'s brother C— wrote for him when W— was a big man at OEO: before they liquidated him for being a man of dedication to the poor, and of imagination in helping them:

Those blue dots moving on the horizon
Are nothing you can understand;
Neither whiskey nor child,
Not the free torn limbs of savages
Which you might look at
Without judgment, the pain and the
horror stopping criticism!
No. Not at all. Not at all.

They, the dots, are the evidence
of civilization; men are building
things there and shouting encouragement
to each other, Oh yes.
Until they finish the product
I shall peek through binoculars
and wish them luck and send
them long distance love and
Blessings, Blessings on those blue dots.

"Yeah, and now all us blue dots are building a hideous bureaucracy, that's what we're building. I hope anybody peeking through binoculars at us now can't see that as painfully clearly as we suddenly can. But somebody said, I seem to recall, 'History is a cemetary of human hopes.'

"Today Jack Ward wrote an editorial in the Daily News [March 5, 1966, Jackson *Daily News*] that started 'More Bad Apple Money.' That's what I feel like—a rotten apple. That's what we get for being so presumptuous as trying to improve the world. How dare we want to do good? But what else can you do? But it always backfires. We wanted to give birth to something beautiful, but you always have to compromise so much during confinement that what you deliver isn't worth the agony. Here, look, we've given birth to nothing but a big hulking bureaucracy."

PART VI

Toward Autonomy

FEBRUARY 23, 1966–AUGUST 30, 1966:
HOW CDGM IMPROVED AND INSTITUTIONALIZED, WENT MORE PROFESSIONAL AND WENT TO PIECES, LOST ITS SOUL, SPLINTERED, ALMOST COMMITTED SUICIDE IN A COLLISION OF WHITE AND BLACK POWER, CREATED AND DESTROYED, AND THANKS TO JOHN MUDD, GREW MORE MATURE.

CHAPTER 34

BIRTH OF A BUREAUCRACY

THE FIRST THING that was wrong was our new physical environment: a high-rise office building on a downtown street with a waiting room, a receptionist, and a lot of too-little cubicles for various formidably labeled departments and divisions, filled with decent office furniture instead of homely, battered second-hand junk and the cots and sleeping bags of roaming field workers. It just didn't look comfortable to our constituents. The percentage of poor people who came to visit us dropped drastically. There were no mowed fields and mud driveways for parking. There was no community dining room that served cheap familiar food in an intimate family setting. There was nowhere to put the children that accompanied parents. There were white Mississippi faces, that seemed to be solid eyes, ranging from the curious to the outraged, following them as they entered and exited.

There had been enough of a gap between Central Staff and community people before. The distance between "management and labor," black and white, is impossibly unbreachable at best. Now Central Staff members put on the clothes and behavior befitting city office workers. Regardless of continued hectic chaos and warm intentions, our "new look" reduced relations to something frighteningly businesslike.

The second thing that was wrong was staff itself. Gone, with only a few exceptions, were the committed, the creative, the deviants, and rebels, the thinkers, the doers come hell or high water, the professional "enlightened" educators and psychologists, and the professional Movement workers. Gone were those with a vision, and the true believers. We staffed up as quickly as possible, for there was much to be done. Most new staff members (there were only five or six low-level old ones) had heard dimly of Tom Levin. He was that wild man who had created such administrative havoc.

We were not as closely affiliated with the Movement now, in chronology or geography, so we were not terrifying to the Negro middle class. And we were conveniently in the city. So we attracted many young Negro college graduates who could type a little, or who had had a few courses in business administration. They were quickly learning to be middle class. They generously wanted to help the poor become middle class. That was, on the whole, the extent of their ideology, and even this was seldom thought out and expressed, unless John extracted it from them in a rare staff meeting. We were too busy for staff meetings. Our insane, nightly, impassioned screaming at Mount Beulah, which every senior staff member and cleaning lady attended, had been replaced by very infrequent division meetings, or three of four times during the second grant, meetings for everyone working on the second or third floor. It was as Sylvia Ashton-Warner said of her situation:

> A woman said to me once so proudly, "My family never quarrels." I was young at the time and our children were young and I thought 'How wonderful! If only I could say that.' But I'm not young now and I know better. When I look back on that family who never quarreled I remember their passivity; the slow eyes that did not flash; on the parents' faces, no grooves that tears had scoured. I know now that it takes passion and energy to make a quarrel . . . of the magnificent sort. Magnificent rows, magnificent reconciliations; the surging and soaring of magnificent feeling.
>
> We quarrel. . . . Take that straight. We quarrel morning and afternoon, day and night. We quarrel from left to right and from right to left; from front to back and from back to front; from top to bottom, from bottom to top; from side to side and corner to corner . . . an highly complex intricate, sparking, perorating, exhausting network of the most accomplished, nonstop cross-quarelling that ever fired the blood. . . . And that's how it will continue to be until our red-hot, bright-eyed, pioneer corpuscles achieve some kind of dilution. For there is passion and energy here, brilliances and heroisms . . . (as regularly as the morning paper) challenging and piercing the alarmed mediocrities; generating all manner of sensational ideas that collide and explode like astral galaxies . . . like galaxies of southern stars. . . .[33]

Now, we behaved more maturely, and were nicer; at least on the surface. That was good. Underneath, extreme passive aggressive sorts of back-stabbing went on—the kind that people do when they don't dare confront each other and have "magnificent rows and magnificent reconciliations." Only I for one preferred what we traded for superficial niceness, which was priceless.

The third thing that was wrong were our new administrative systems, procedures, and personnel. They were, if not in OEO's view, then at least in contrast to our previous setup, terribly, terrifyingly proper and thorough. They guaranteed that less mess would result, and less creativity would leak through, and community people would have even less feeling than they already did that this thing was theirs to steer and to

[33] Ashton-Warner, Sylvia, *Teacher*. New York: Bantam Books, 1964, pp. 19–20.

comprehend. John's door was kept shut much of the time. The management consultants were in there helping John devise ways of managing things. We needed them. They were very helpful. They were designing systems and advising half-grateful, half-resentful John. The poor people were seldom in there. Neither were the rest of us, except after the others had gone at eleven or midnight and after. The consultants were in there for months.

By force of circumstance, there had been so much focus on politics that John had not yet been able to concentrate on tooling the project up internally. The consultants would help with that. The chief of the consultants was a wonderfully helpful man named Jack Wiersma.

Jack first heard of CDGM on February 15, 1966, when Jule Sugarman called him and asked him to be CDGM's deputy director, so *that* obstacle could be hurdled and the grant could be announced. Jack didn't want to be CDGM's deputy director. He lived in Washington's northern Virginia suburbs with his family, and was in the midst of many projects. On February 19 Mr. Shriver called him to be CDGM's deputy director. Many people at OEO tried to help CDGM. Jack still didn't want the job. He offered to be a consultant to us to determine needs, and to bring in people to help meet these needs. He first met CDGM's leadership during that wakelike week when they were sitting around at OEO, like a bunch of expectant fathers, waiting for the settlement of a satisfactory grant.

Jack spent a great deal of time in Mississippi, in John's office, planning administratively. He was very helpful because he had intelligence, connections, a broader, less provincial view than ours, and a detached approach. He could flick out ideas and not feel destroyed if they were shot down. He wore immaculate dark suits and stayed at a downtown hotel. He was competent and cool. One of the first things he worked on was improving our image with OEO. This included bringing in a girl who prepared a huge report on us, composed of things we had already mailed to OEO, but now authentically compiled so maybe someone would read, and look look see see what we were doing. It also included making up a slew of organization charts. Jack was a sensitive, cooperative man. Realizing that as John's confidante I was feeling very threatened by his endless secret conferences with John, and by all the people he was putting in little black boxes on little white papers, he demonstrated his psychologist's skills by asking *me* to draw my version of organization charts. Mine were upside down from his. I put the poor people at the top and the board of directors, Mary Holmes, and OEO in the bottom corner. My boxes were hearts, and they weren't black, but were drawn with pink magic marker. This chart was shown around in Washington along with the others, but I was told it annoyed officials.

One of the consultants that Mr. Wiersma found and OEO paid was Mr. Ashley, who spent a week with us and immediately sensed and admired the uniqueness of CDGM. His report said: ". . . The Child Development Group of Mississippi is not a conventional project. Few organizations have ever been created under the objectives, restrictions and complex concepts of CDGM. (In a very short time) a statewide organization with a $5.6 million budget was devised, staffed and made operational to involve 10,000 people and children. Furthermore, the essential work skills required at all levels were absent from the environment. The field staff was developed under severe personal harassment in some cases. This feat was accomplished on a crash basis without regard to normal organizational procedures being contained by a plan. . . ." With John Mudd, Mr. Ashley made recommendations for developing an organizational structure analysis and a communications systems design that would generate and distribute information for project management, control and review work not completed on schedule, point out under- or overstaffing, keep track of the under- and overapproved budget status of current commitments and expenditures, etc. He also made many beautifully neat charts, such as one showing the tentative schematic outline of flow of responsibility of various CDGM positions.

Jack Wiersma and the others helped John make charts showing monetary comparisons of line items between the original grant and actual need, such as more money for personnel and less for travel, more for space and equipment and less for rental of office furniture, more for telephone and telegraph, more for transferring record-keeping functions to electronic data processing, and so on. Jack helped John decide what new kinds of personnel would be needed for our new automated system: We would need tab supervisors, key punch operators, key verifiers, and many other kinds of specialists. There was dickering to do with the telephone company to ascertain and install the least expensive system the phone company could offer to meet our needs. We needed thirty-five call director instruments, eleven intercom phones, eight outgoing lines, three Watts lines, and two local lines containing six intercom lines. Any kind of a switchboard system cost much more, and required a three-thousand-dollar deposit plus a guarantee of five years usage.

There was so much for John to learn. Consultants helped him compile up-to-date listings of personnel for center opening, which centers had bank accounts, the condition of food checks, details of facilities and transportation contracts, including licenses and insurance, monthly records on in-kind contributions coming in from communities, pregrant costs, cut-off lines for travel below which no authorization was required, and mileage charts for reimbursement for use of personal cars.

Together with several insurance companies (to be responsibly comparative) they worked out personal and bodily liability insurance. With the Internal Revenue Service they established CDGM's tax status and how much taxes we owed. Using the government guideline, they found that we would save money if we purchased much of the equipment we had planned to rent, and that other things we had planned to rent, such as the mailing machine, could only be bought. Only thirty office staff personnel had originally been budgeted. We soon had seventy-seven. The extras had to be provided. We needed twenty-five more secretary's chairs, twenty 6-foot tables, twenty folding chairs, eleven file cabinets, and sixty wastebaskets. They purchased the second-lowest brand of office furniture available, and decided whether or not we should have bright colors in a children's program office. They took on a leading Jackson attorney as CDGM counsel.

They prepared a financial and accounting manual spelling out internal procedures and controls, which they did in consultation with OEO officials. They carefully made it fully consistent with OEO's procedures for all grantees. It was reviewed by Ernst and Ernst, our new leading nationwide accounting firm with offices in Jackson—in fact, with offices upstairs in our Milner Building. Ernst and Ernst was available for auditing counsel, day-to-day advice, and periodic review of CDGM's financial procedures and internal controls. John and the consultants tried to straighten out deficiencies in applications and confusion in submitting time and attendance sheets that still occasionally caused some workers' paychecks not to appear. They discussed whether or not we should all have plastic ID cards. They worried about supply distribution systems and inventory systems, and ended up with procedures for getting a copy of each purchase order to the organization, a memo regarding the receipt of goods to the right persons, and a copy of reimbursement checks to the area administrators. They struggled with car logs: procedures for keeping, collecting, reviewing, controlling, the use of CDGM rented cars. They designed a system of gas reimbursements.

It was indicative of OEO's values that it paid for management consultants, but "couldn't afford" consultants to help us with early education, community organizing, and various other aspects of the content of our program.

John also worked far into the night with new business and administration Central Staff members. Herman Ellis, the business manager borrowed for six weeks from his job as a principal administrative officer for major activities of the National Council of Churches in New York, helped John process contracts for payment, reimburse a hundred and forty centers from an Impressed Fund Account, process accounts payable and vendor billings, process petty cash expenses pertaining to Central Staff, operate the personnel and payroll end of the thing, supervise our business office of approximately twenty-five people, control purchasing, ordering, bidding, and recording regarding supplies for nearly ten thousand children, control the functioning of the mail room, and control the functioning of the Xerox and duplicating room, which was using approximately twenty cases of paper per week—mostly for my division: teacher development and program for children.

John and the new deputy director Martin Cohn, an enthusiastic middle-aged executive who generously lent himself to CDGM for four months before returning to Cincinnati, labored together, trying to solve administrative problems. Mr. Cohn had quite a sizable range of duties, running from developing an adequate staff in number and competency, by effective recruiting and training, to clarifying responsibility, relationship, and authority of staff; from preliminary planning and negotation for setting up partitions on the third floor to sorting all administrative problems any division had.

Mr. Cohn worked with John and Mississippi's leading "liberal" newspaper woman Hazel Brannon Smith about a possible public relations program. Arranging with Mrs. Smith to prepare weekly press releases bringing out the good points and current events of CDGM's sprawling program for in-state and major nearby newspapers was discussed. This did not materialize. The usual releases were sent out in crises, but this nondefensive tack was not taken. The need for the project was acute. Our image, based as it was exclusively on the wild words of local politicians, was dreadful. People were willing to listen to us, but we had no mechanism for talking to them.

Another plan was proposed. We would hire a white Mississippi public relations consultant to visit mayors, county officials, members of the state legislature, and various such state conventions as the Mississippi Education Association, the Mississippi Press Asociation, the Mississippi Economic Council, and so forth. This was not accomplished, either. It was determined that such a program was outside the authorized budget, and OEO, which seemed to us always more ready to join in the bad image-building than in the good, decided that we could not have any supplementary money to do this.

From my diary comes the following: "As far as I know, except for accidental local encounters in remote communities and John's occasional official dealings with Important People, I'm still the main in-state public relations section of CDGM. Especially with senators in the state legislature. It's still as I described here last fall: They call me at home on the phone for vague and ill-defined reasons, usually ending that we should have a drink and talk. As we have prohibition in Missippi, have a drink generally ends us up in a half-lit basement den somewhere, one of these private drinking clubs the 'elite' have, or in a parked car in the dark at one of these roadside drive-ins that put trays of glasses and icecubes on your windowsill instead of hamburgers and ice cream sodas. Then we sit in the protective night; the senators are afraid to be seen with a CDGMian in the day; and for hours we discuss dangerous things like nursery school.

"Sometimes the brave ones invite me out for dinner. They daringly introduce me to their friends, kind of in a stage whisper, with a lot of flourish, no doubt feeling very risqué to be seen with what is in their minds a beatnik chick. B— invited me to breakfast at the Benbow

Motel and then hinted to his colegislators that I had been there with him all night. I thought it was pretty funny: Catting around is so accepted, admired in fact, that they are eager to show off the female implications of the same person whose politics they dread. The only deep difference I've seen so far between Northerners and Southerners is that Northern men have mistresses and work hard to hide them, and Southern men have mistresses and go to great lengths to show them off.

"I've come to the conclusion that the best p.r. CDGM could possibly have would be a fleet of high-class prostitutes, call girls I guess they should be. After all, if we could favorably influence the state legislature, we'd have it made. Wonder if OEO would consider such an expense legitimate—they're always talking about we should improve our public image. . . . R— invited me to share his hotel suite with him next August for some convention or something. I graciously declined, thinking to myself that this was farther than I was obliged to carry my public relations efforts and general goodwill toward suffering white Southerners, who actually I like quite as much as anyone else. They say the chief difference between the North and the South is the weather. I concur—except to add that Southerners allow themselves more direct acting out of the Negro hostility that most Americans hold dear to their hearts."

Mr. Cohn also proposed a house organ for the same audiences and purposes at which I had aimed my Newsletter. After issue nine I didn't put it out anymore. There was growing underground feeling against whites; especially against whites who were active; especially at active whites who were women. So I gave up the Newsletter for fear it would infuriate someone. However, though Mr. Cohn even did some preliminary research on independent Northern fund-raising to finance such a house organ, it didn't occur. CDGM had no further publications until the third grant, a year and a half later, when a young man from the North was hired and a simple tabloid was started. Nor did it have fund-raising projects for internal extra programs, other than the clothes, books, toys, and occasional petty cash checks my schoolgirlish church and civic group pleas elicited.

And John was, apparently eternally, still working with OEO auditors to clear up a few remaining details from the last grant. Specifically, *where were* ninety-five first aid kits, seventy-five paper cutters, 185 chairs, 345 sleeping pads, $123.25 worth of cooking utensils, and a $13.26 pistol grip? With the help of consultants and new kinds of staff members we were in much better shape than we had been.

When uncertain business department staff members couldn't perform well enough under their incredible loads, John—who most staff agreed had difficulty communicating comfortably with nonintellectuals, and who considered dismissing even the most incompetent undemocratic, and who was acting on the one hand in reference to his own uncommunicated inner vision and on the other hand in reference to inhuman pressure from OEO—tended not to help top level technicians, but to let consultants do their work; or much more often, to wearily, cynically do it himself at one in the morning.

Many thought that because John himself was brilliant, perceptive, committed and inexhaustible, he didn't have an entirely accurate concept of the limits of other workers' intelligence, comprehension, commitment or working hours. It was thought by many that he misjudged what others could do. Because he would go to any lengths to avoid hurting the feelings of Negroes, many staff members felt that even in the case of such extremely able learning-to-be administrators and businessmen as Matt Thomas and Matt King, John had a habit of doing for instead of activating and advising them so they could do themselves. This added intolerably to John's own unheard-of work load. All this kept him too busy to get out into communities. He went very infrequently to a community meeting. He didn't see his first classroom or center until May, and it was his last for many more months. Whenever I urged him, he commented despondently that he'd like to, but he had more urgent things to do.

Indeed it was true. He was inundated with things all so urgent that the only way he could make a priorities list was to determine which task, left undone till dawn, would cause the project to disintegrate. He was disconcertingly disciplined. He was as unable to be derelict as he was to delegate. He demanded unearthly amounts of himself. The more he deserved a day off, the more he seemed driven to do. He seemed to many either destined or determined to destroy himself.

My diary comments: "It seems as if John has Calvin at his elbow, and Clay at his ear, telling him: 'Government is a trust, and the officers of the government are trustees; and both the trust and the trustees are created for the benefit of the people, (and you, John, are the only officer of this trust called CDGM. It is you the people trust, and you must remember that you are created only for the benefit of the people).'

"He certainly hates all this, and longs to get out in the communities and work with people, but in another way he seems to get some kind of strange self-punitive satisfaction out of beating himself to death in behalf of Negroes. It's important that they're Negroes, I think.

"He seems gnawed at by the Goddess of Vengeance, who forces him to concur in offering ever greater oblations to OEO and ever-changing kinds of obloquies before CDGM will be allowed into the nirvana of community action respectability. Whatever makes John go seems entirely occult.

"The whole thing is a giant challenge to him, but there's more to it than that . . . why isn't he as compelled by the content side of it as he is by the administrative side, when he himself considers content the real challenge? Of course, he devotes a great deal of his remarkable self to the *planning* end of the content side; just not to the knots we need untangled in practicing the content part *now*. But on planning, well, I never have known anyone as versatile as John, he's quite an extraordinary person. . . . And marvelously well organized. He has little notebooks of every kind in every drawer and pocket, filled with headings and ideas in every conceivable category."

John investigated more possibilities than I knew existed for expanding and enriching CDGM's services to the poor. He was less innovative and inventive than Tom Levin, and less inclined to develop CDGM's inner content areas, but he was equally as informed about existing programs, and as eager to weave them all together with the Child Development Group of Mississippi as the vehicle.

He read rapidly and widely: books, articles, periodicals, professional pieces—and clipped relevant things for follow-up. He kept in contact with government and Mississippi officials on the progress of Medicare Alert in the state, and Manpower Development and Training Act (MDTA) programs.

He and Dave Fleming, now one of John's two administrative assistants, checked into Title I of the Elementary and Secondary Education Act of 1965 to see what we could do with that. All projecsts had to be approved by state educational agencies, a severe handicap to us. John spoke to the director of the Department of Elementary Education in Mississippi in regard to this. He learned that though $30,905,000 had been granted to Mississippi, most of it under Title I, and though schools had the application forms, the department had not yet received any applications. Officials claimed they did not have adequate information from the government about the program.

So John wrote to the superintendent of Documents in Washington for more information, and for a catalogue of brochures and pamphlets on other government programs. He wrote to several sources for information on integrated material for our children, and suitable materials on Negro history. He gathered information on the Farmer's Home Administration programs. He got lists of jobs available in various districts from the State Employment Security Commission. He had dealings with Claude Ramsay, a powerful man in Mississippi's AFL-CIO. He studied the new housing act. He contacted the Foundation for Cooperative Housing in Washington to see if they meant poor people. He wrote to the Bureau of Indian Affairs in the Department of Interior about equipment for prefab housing. He wrote to Housing and Urban Development (HUD) about building materials. He got in touch with the Public Health Service in regard to digging wells and outdoor toilets. He looked into health grants for preschool children through the Department of Health, Education, and Welfare's (HEW) Children's Bureau, and also into their material and child health services. He studied the Kerr-Mills amendments to the Social Security Act to help with medical programs for the poor. And he examined the Migrant Health section of the Public Health Service's health training programs. He and his assistant wrote for information on HEW's Crippled Children's Services, and on the U.S. Office of Education's programs for mentally and physically handicapped children.

Through the Food Distribution Division of the Department of Agriculture, John found out about free milk, free school lunches, and commodity foods: who was eligible, and how. He learned about HEW aid through state public welfare agencies for general programs, day care services, research, training, and demonstration projects.

John and CDGM's lawyer Henry Aronson worked with OEO's Legal Aid division on possible ideas. John wanted to establish neighborhood law firms, to avoid the psychological barrier people ran into when they had to go to distant downtown to pursue their legal rights. He also discussed neighborhood substations, circuit-riding lawyers, and mobile law offices for rural areas in vans or trailers. He checked into legal services offered at prisons and detention homes and into ways of improving these services. He inquired as to the chances of developing a legal aid program through Mary Holmes Junior College with a poor people board. He suggested local "ombudsmen" to specialize in alleged abuses, malpractice, etc., in systems and services affecting the impoverished. He talked about adding a program of nonprofessional legal aides, who could investigate, educate, do intake, legal research, and clerical work regarding legal difficulties in communities.

John and those so instructed by him learned about the U.S. Department of Agriculture Extension Service's out-of-school agricultural program, their home economics program, and their youth work programs. He explored the Work-Study Program under the Economic Opportunity Act of 1965: grants to institutions of higher education to assist students from low-income families by providing part-time and summer employment to supplement their incomes. He also collected material on the Work-Experience Program, Title V of the same act of Congress. He discovered that 100 percent federal financing was available for applications which had been approved by the state and HEW, for mothers, fathers, and other needy persons who were present or potential recipients of public aid to learn new job skills on the job.

He inquired as to whether a Head Start could sponsor a Neighborhood Youth Corps project, and if we were eligible to get VISTA Volunteers. We pursued the VISTA matter for months, but it never seemed to click. He talked at length with Aaron Schmais and Eric Tolmach of the OEO-CAP Demonstration Program, and with Len Stern of the Office of Juvenile Delinquency and Youth Development in HEW. He had me take them on community and center tours, so we could all see if there was anything we could work out to develop and boost the leadership competencies of our community organizers, particularly in negotiating with CAPs.

John corresponded with Dr. Allen Guttmacher, Kenneth Clark, S. M. Miller, Frank Riessman, the Institute for Policy Studies, and others, about ideas in this area. Through Jack Wiersma, he became more knowledgeable about VITA, Volunteers for International Technical Assistance, Inc. This was a group of a thousand scientists, engineers, etc., who worked without pay in their spare time to solve technical problems submitted from underdeveloped areas. John's investment of energy ranged from studying some rather routine proposals submitted by groups close to our project for training CDGM employees in secretarial skills, business, and accounting, to checking into an interesting sounding organization called SWING, which was a professional cooperative of group psychotherapists who had developed a new technique for accelerated interaction, which could be learned quickly and thoroughly by people not trained in group therapy, and seemed to have implications for CDGM.

John, Marian, and Henry Aronson, a New York Legal Defense and Education Fund (INC Fund) lawyer working in Jackson who helped CDGM consistently, wrote a proposal for a kibbutz in Mississippi, which was printed in *New South*.

John and I talked extensively with Mr. Robert Barrie, an imaginative man newly in charge of health and education for the Board of Presbyterian Missions. We offered many ideas for making Mary Holmes Junior College into something of national significance in the field of community education. Mr. Barrie was already thinking along those lines. His directions and our specifics seemed to mesh well.

One of the most interesting projects John worked to bring into CDGM was with the Peace Corps. Representatives came to Jackson to work out plans. It was proposed that sixty-two Peace Corps volunteers, as part of their three-month training to teach health and nutrition to teachers in Mysore, India, work in CDGM Delta communities for a week. Two weeks of their training would be coordinated by the University of Southern Mississippi (USM) in Hattiesburg. The volunteers would work under USM in county health clinics. The purpose of the CDGM week would be to expose volunteers to poverty, and to place them in teaching positions with our area and community staff. They would study families' health needs and try to determine with which existing services families were not familiar. Jeanette King and Helen Bass Williams, neither of whom had been with CDGM since the end of the first summer, but who both taught nearby at Tougaloo College, coordinated needs and plans with communities. After a considerable amount of conferencing all around, the proposal fell through because State Health Commissioner Dr. Gray and State Welfare Director Miss Evelyn Gandy didn't approve of it. As long as laws insist that so many federal funds for progressive programs must be routed through state agencies staffed with those most likely to stifle such programs, much will not happen in states that need many things to happen.

John sorted and filed all these pieces of information and projects, so he could stress the substantive ones and sit on the others. Also in his files could be found unopened personal mail, unpaid personal bills, neckties, one sock, an old pair of shoes, and a camera he had forgotten he had. His personal life was as lost in the shuffle as were these items in the files. He rarely got to dinner (a hamburger or steak and a Coke at an all-night roadside place or a hurried downtown cafe) or home to his two German Shepherds and unpretentious shack in the Negro community, until long after the middle of the night. When he did, he found it so disheveled and dirty that there was nothing to do but put some of the classical music he loved so much on the record player, put out the lights, and fall asleep in the dark listening to it. A few hours later, it was time to get up, shave, take a pep pill, drink some more black coffee, be sure to have several more packs of Pall Mall in a pocket, and speed back to the office in his Pontiac GTO.

Perhaps once a month he swung by the downtown post office on the way home from work, and picked up a cardboard container into which post office clerks had dumped his month's accumulation of mail after it would no longer fit in his P.O. box. Usually included in the carton were several warning and cut-off notices from the utility companies. Whenever she could, his secretary rescued him before he lost his phone or electricity, but she didn't always catch the notices in time. John didn't care. He was too absorbed with important things.

There were few exceptions to this pattern, except when he had out-of-town visitors and we accompanied them to a nice restaurant for a business dinner—or when he dropped in at my house at 3 A.M. almost every night to coordinate on some critical piece of project planning and had a beer. Or when he was on the milk plane to Atlanta or Washington to make 9 A.M. meetings without missing any time in the office.

In contrast to Tom, whom very few people liked, though many admired, there were many utterly endearing things about John. Almost everybody liked him, from his loud boyish laugh to his big generous heart. I liked him greatly. I liked what he wanted to do with CDGM. But I didn't like what OEO was doing to it. Where once our dragon had proudly preened rough, colorful scales and shimmering wings, he now dolefully licked wounds and newly sprouting flow charts, vouchers, IBM cards, accountants payable, and vendor billings. He listened no longer to rambling discussions engaged in by spontaneous groups of poor people, but was surrounded instead by the humming and clicking, spinning, purring, and whirring of our huge well-oiled gleaming machine, jerking in patterns, flicking with precision along its web of wires, manned by persons with plastic and porcelain faces, apparently with ammonia in their veins. Or so it seemed compared to our earlier creative chaos. I knew it was all necessary, and it was all to be expected, and the dragon wept a little and kicked fitfully as he dreamt fragmentarily of the devil riding astride his back wielding a whip of CAP memos and accountants' ledgers, and fell into a drugged slumber. It was the taxpayers' money—no matter what they didn't get for it.

CHAPTER 35

WHAT THE WHITE LADIES WERE DOING

Trouble-shooting and brewing trouble

IN INCREASINGLY INCONGRUOUS contrast to these important things, Mary Emmons and I intensified our efforts to develop a self-propelled, self-sufficient statewide preschool and teacher development program. Our experiment had produced such unbelievable initial results. I wanted achingly to explore the extraordinary extent to which what was happening might work; and to reveal to relevant leaders around the country its invaluable implications for underdeveloped areas. I felt that while everyone else fought politics, or pettiness, I had suddenly, all alone, fallen into a diamond mine. Mary's major goal was to improve the quality of our classrooms without violating our approach, and without to too great an extent angering a swelling group of antiwhite out-of-state Negro "organizers," soon to become a group painfully well known to the nation.

Basically, my plan was to concentrate on launching a number of projects for the first four and a half months of the new grant, till mid-June probably. Then, to make thorough plans with the teacher development and program for children staffs for building quality till the grant expired at the end of August. It was anticipated that after the planning, on approximately July first, I would leave for Washington. I would stay for six weeks. My children would be in their home in the city with their Daddy. I would start a biography of the project.

John and I thought that after helping to design and implement the educational aspects of CDGM, the next way I could be useful would be to disseminate them. I was also to plan for the future of the educational element of CDGM, go down to Mississippi occasionally during the six weeks to consult with our division's staff, and hopefully, allow a local person, with Mary's help, to try out as my eventual replacement. I had Tom Levin's goal firmly in mind that within a year each of us would've replaced ourselves with a local Negro, or would've failed at our purpose.

In August I was to go back to Mississippi. John and I were to decide what I should do next. It might be to follow Tom's original idea of establishing a parallel and correlated but separate Teacher Development Institute for CDGM and other teachers. This would be one segment of Tom's Community College idea—the one for which we were ripest. It might be to act as a consultant to my replacement until she felt secure. It might be to resume my job, if we didn't have luck in finding a local person capable of being a competent division director.

My future with CDGM was fluid, but I was dealing with the present in terms of building foundations and a framework for my own imminent extinction. Mary would continue to be deputy director of our division, or acting director, depending on my replacement's preference, and would probably leave CDGM in the fall to accompany her husband back to Chicago and graduate school.

So, as soon as the second grant had been obtained, Mary and I increased our insane tempo a little more. We made an "impact" visit to almost every one of the 138 centers, and six others that were operating CDGM centers, but had not been refunded by OEO. Some of the purposes were as before: to show personal appreciation for local efforts, regardless of how small; to discuss specific realizable programmatic and personnel goals with each specific center and to cement these in a thank-you letter; to compare our written views with the ATG's written views for the enrichment of both sets of views and so we could see ATG trends and plan ATG workshops more realistically; and to make both appraisals of progress, and future planning, in individual centers and in general, possible.

We now had a new thought in mind, too. I hoped that one of our major techniques for building quality during the summer could be helping ATGs arrange it so that better teachers and centers worked with less alive ones. If we could identify one outstanding center in each of the sixteen areas, we would have a reasonably accessible more or less "model" center for others to spend time in, observing and "practice teaching." Similarly, we were looking for outstanding individuals. These we would invite to visit weaker centers as temporary consultants, or to accept practice teachers to work with them in their home centers. Thus we would capitalize on our natural strengths.

By the third grant, if there was going to be one, this system might evolve into the core of Tom's Teacher Development Institute. We could concentrate our consultants in these typical, yet unusually good, community contexts.

I resisted the idea of importing "good teachers" and spending extra money on "ideal" equipment and supplies for demonstration centers. One of the biggest flaws in traditional teacher training, and one that weakens the value of much that is learned, is that settings and conditions in lab schools are so ideal that the average teacher-to-be finds little that is transferable to "real life" teaching. I wanted to use the best of our own teachers, buildings typical of our own facilities but used more imaginatively, and amounts and types of supplies and equipment available to all our centers. The point then would not be what we all know, that more money helps make better schools, but more importantly, that more *ideas* make better schools.

I found that because of slight experience in some cases, and experience shared by fellow community people in other cases, most of our first summer's good centers were now excellent, most of the average centers were now good, and most of the beginning centers were beginning at an appreciably higher level than in the summer program.

Stonewall center in Clarke County was an example of this growth. The first summer Mrs. Myers had written: "This center has a long way to go. I told them that they would be closed if they did not get a better understanding of the preschool child and his needs. They definitely must clean up around the center, make it safe by removing any lumber or other pitfalls. Louie has stated he would keep a close watch for improvements. Please keep check on this center and give all help. I will re-check. The minister chairman has declared his support."

In February Mary Emmons wrote: ". . . visit to center by V. Blue, ATG, Mary Emmons, C. Davis, ATG, Mrs. Jones, AA. Rev. K was there and a few men doing repair work . . . center is in house with kitchen and indoor bathroom and heat. It is all set up and very nicely arranged. Mrs. Lela Anderson (RT now at Tuskegee) really put into practice what she learned at orientation. . . . They have a very large space adjacent to house for playground but no one has made playground equipment. . . ."

Mary and I were writing three things after each impact visit: a report according to our undiluted, unadjusted preschool standards (for our files); a report to the center's ATG saying almost the same thing, but adding specific things for her to think about to help in her concept and skill development; and a thank-you letter to the center staff itself.

Of Stonewall, I wrote in April: "Outstanding; ATG Davis and I visited briefly just after the children had left, and found a wonderful staff and a beautiful Center, indoors and out. There is a huge play area, with every kind of equipment, including a tugboat! Inside, there is a large room with a divider which houses two units, and another room with one unit. They are preparing for a fourth unit on the porch. The whole place is beautifully painted and furnished in a trim orderly way with warmth and ideas. They have really used the ideas in our printed material called 'Setting Up the Empty Classroom.' I won't list everything, but I can safely say, if we talked about it or wrote about it, it's there plus twenty per cent!

"I think this Center is ready for advanced work in such things as special study projects for the children and a high quality reading readiness program.

"I hope the ATG can make sure *every staff member in her AREA* goes to visit this Center. I think they will be inspired by it."

Many of the remarkable things that happened in Clarke County, then and later, could be attributed to the remarkable spurt of energy of its ungrammatical ATG, Carrie Davis.

Even some of our sadder-seeming centers sometimes represented enormous growth in their given contexts. Holy Light—later denounced by the OEO—was a case like this. My personal notes say: ". . . horrible Center, though I won't tell them so. Rooms are perhaps five feet by five feet, fifteen children each. They are made of raw gray cement. No decorations. Have made no toys. Playground in a pine woods, nice, have made equip. Nothing doing with children. Adults sit and look at children, smiling. Kind. Have to consider context before condemning. Chairman, Mr. G. spent all afternoon with me. Thrilled over this Center. Told me the following which I've written down to keep myself evaluating fairly . . . I find I'm tending to be too harsh these days . . . to expect more than I should. I forget, just because *I've* been looking at Centers for nearly a year, doesn't mean every community has . . . this one is pretty new at it. Mary tends to vacillate between expecting high quality and being disappointed when she doesn't find it, and being elated when she finds anything at all in our unlikely communities. I used to be more steady. Find I'm vacillating more too, now. Maybe I'm getting too tired to be good at this job. So the following time-consuming hand-recorded 'report' from Mr. G is to 'keep me in my place'—to keep me humble: [Names have been changed. Mr. G feared to be identified.]

" 'Mrs. Greenberg, I am a very wealthy farmer. I have twelve children. We have always believed very strongly in the Lord and education. My first son got his education right here, in this building we now use for our Head Start Center. There were seventy children in this room. The teacher had completed eighth grade. The college was SCI and it used to be at Mount Beulah.

" 'Farm wages were 50¢ a day. We went $3000 into debt and saved and were buying a home and payed his tuition: $65. He got up 3 or 4 times a night to fire this smutty boiler to help with this large $65 expense. When we taken him so far from home, way over there to Mount Beulah, we was so hurt and so choked up we cried all the way home. He made good grades each year. His teachers would write us each year to tell us what a good child he was, and so apt.

" 'The whole family went to see him graduate from twelfth grade on the lawn in front of the President's mansion. My wife were so proud we couldn't do nuthin' but sit and smile and smile and sit.'

"(I recall: my comments on the Center: 'Adults sit and look at the children, smiling . . . a bell rings in my thick head.)

" 'Mrs. Greenberg, this first son of mine has made me very proud, since. He went to Korea, did twenty-four months serving his country and he has been in Chicago ever since in a high position in the post office. What? Yes, ma'm, he carries mail.

" 'My second child finished elementary school in the same little building that her brother did. All the while she was steady asking, "Dad, will I be able to finish high school and go to college?" She always wanted to do what her brother did. I was still earning 50¢ a day. It didn't look possible, but I had to say yes; you can't hurt a child. This girl and I would be in the field chopping, and the white school bus would go by. She would cry and ask, "Dad, why do we have to be here like this and them there like that?" I'd have to find words to consolate these children. *That* a man has to do for his children.

" ' "Margie," I'd tell her, "Things won't always be this way. Probably you'll ride that bus when you're a larger girl. Perhaps you'll be able to enjoy things all Negroes should enjoy. Just do as your mother and father tell you." So in the morning she would chop cotton and at night she would milk the cow. But I made a sacrifice. I *never* kept her out during the day, though I lost a lot of money because of what she could have earned.

" 'I sent her to college. Campbell College, a Methodist College. I paid $65 to get her in, I believe, and then I paid a cousin to let her live there. I didn't pay money; I paid him in vegetables. Marge was always smart. She said, "Dad, I have my high school and college now, so I'll work and give the others a chance to go." Marge is married today and she is assistant teacher in a Head Start in Chicago. Her husband is a switchman at the railroad. She didn't finish college, but she wanted to give the others a chance. She says she'll finish some day.

" 'My third child, Lillian, had very bad health after she was eight years old. Something like arthritis in her legs. Her legs would burn her and hurt her and she would cry out. She never did grow like the other children. She never could work in the fields. But she did little chores, and I saved and saved, and with Marge's help, we got Lillian to Piney Woods. She worked in the library there to help out. One night Piney Woods called me in the middle of the night, she was crying with the pain. I had a little A model Ford. I went and got her. I carried her to the car like a baby. It hurt me so bad to see her hurting so bad. I carried her from doctor to doctor. They all said it was in her head.

" 'Our neighbors criticized my wife and I for working ourselves to death to send the children to school when they were never going to amount to anything in Mississippi anyway, but we felt it was important enough to do to spite the neighbors, and we sent the fourth child.

" 'The fourth child was Ellen. She took a year at Jackson State. I knew it was the finest school when I sent my boy to SCI, but I couldn't afford it then. By the time Ellen went, the price of cotton had gone up. I was making fine money: $3 a day. And my herd had gotten up to 15 cattle. We were still paying to buy our home. The total was $3000 and we had a long way to go on it. My oldest boy paid for my fifth boy to go to college and learn to make cabinets. He's in Chicago making them. He went to college in Mississippi.

" 'Then came my twins, Alex and Ann. Ann took a year at Jackson State. The crippled girl, Lillian, paid for it. She works in a library. Alex cut pulp wood to pay for college. He almost finished. All of us tried to help him. Donald wouldn't finish high school. He worried me and worried his mother, wanting us to sign for him to get his marriage license. His mother couldn't take it, so finally she signed. Donald was married two years, and had a daughter. Then he came home, and he said, "Dad, I was stupid, I want to finish high school." So I said, "I'll do whatever I can." I keep chickens up to a capacity of 400. I turned all that money over to the care of Donald's family. Now he's back in 12th grade.

" 'My others are younger. Alice is in 11th grade in white school. Two boys threw a rock at her. The principal beat them over a barrel. He said he wants integration to work. We are looking for federal aid to get her to college. Hank is in 9th grade at Negro school. He will go to white next year. The baby, Dale, is at white school with Alice. They are the only two at the white school. I knew it was a better school, and Mrs. Greenberg, I *do* believe in education. Though on the bus, they are forced to sit only on the front seat. At least it isn't the back seat. Many things have changed. I'm embarrassed to tell you some of the things that used to be here, but I'll tell you, so you'll see why the front seat and two colored in the white school is an improvement.

" 'When I was a boy, in the 1920's, a white man came to the house of a man I know to buy pigs. He approached my friend's wife. When the husband came in from the field, the wife told him she had been approached, but had refused. The white man came again another day to take the pig. The Negro husband was in the other room. He heard the white man curse his wife because she wouldn't go with him. The white man went away and came back with his brother. They started to shove into the house. The Negro was inside with a gun. He shot the first white man, and killed him. The brother ran away and returned while it was still light with a mob of men. The Negro husband had fled into the woods. They set up road blocks all over the county. For a week, he would slip into Negro people's houses at night and take food.

" 'They saw him slip into one man's house. They didn't catch him, but they took the man out into the woods and whipped him nearly to death for letting the husband steal food from him. No Negroes were allowed out after dark. At night whites came around and checked. The husband swum the creek and made it to some of his relatives. It was known to the whites that he was there. They took his Daddy out and whipped him where he couldn't walk. They caught the wife's mother at her own home. She was so brave, she fought so hard they couldn't whip her, so they gashed her with knives till she bled so much she was so weak that they could tie her up with a grapevine around her neck till she choked to death. They made another Negro dig the grave and roll her in. It wasn't deep enough. Dogs dug her up. So the whites hung her gray hair along the road on a wire fence to scare us.

" 'The man who was running away was still running. But with the road blocks and the rivers swoll too bad to swim, he couldn't get out of the county, and he went home, because he couldn't get nothing to eat, had nowhere to go. When he was crossing the road, they shot his leg. He drug into the brush and hid in a tree top. They found him near morning. A dog smelled the blood from his leg running down the tree. They shot many shots into the air, notifying each other where he was.

" 'They brought a horse and made the first Negro they had whipped so bad ride the horse under a post oak tree. They made the caught husband Negro straddle his shoulder and tie the rope around a limb and had him loop it around his own neck. Then they made his friend ride out from under him and he choked to death and swung and swung and swung till they had his Daddy come and take him down. Then they hung his brother and whipped and shot him till he was dead and threw him in a briar patch. They had his wife in the jail. They let her out. She ran eight miles to where the body was hung, to see him covered in the cemetary. She died from shock.

" 'So did the courage of our whole neighborhood. The post oak I just spoke of is this one here you're leaning on, Miss Greenberg. That's why they told me to lay low, and not fuss with educating all my children. That's why they didn't want to mess with all this Head Start mess. Well, I'm a God-fearing man, a mild-mannered man, and I have never done anything before I talked with the Lord. So I went out in my cow pasture, and I asked the Lord should I undertake to organize this Head Start. Suddenly something came upon me, and a voice said, "You're not doing anything wrong!" So I knew if I was killed for this school, I would at least be killed for *something*. I went to tell my mother and others in our community. They were so happy they grabbed me. Together we walked out and cleared the land around our new school.'

"So now I will record some more criticisms of this Center, but don't believe I have my heart in these oh-so-accurate statements about the low quality of their educational program and the fact that it took them three months to get a water loan so they could put in running water so they could wash the kids' dinner dishes."

Unfortunately, due to uncorrectable degrees of damage earlier in their lives, there were some teachers who were incorrigibly cruel, dull, or selfish. We spent a lot of time in our continuing, cozy, all-day-Wednesday ATG workshops, working out standards and methods for detecting and expelling such people. We agreed that if an ATG found such a person, she would urge her teammates, the area administrator, and the two community organizers to accompany her to the center to observe and evaluate. If all agreed, they would meet with the local committee and lay their opinions on the table. The committee could switch personnel, fire if legitimate and necessary, or ignore the team. We thought this system would reduce the risk of one ATG going after a foe of hers. It would strengthen the authority of the AA and COs, which was shaky in all but rare situations. And it would expand the horizons of committee members regarding education administration. Time and time again I asked John Mudd if he would authorize this procedure or another, and since things were constantly tenser and tenser between out-of-staters and board members, if the board would ratify the procedure. John was always busy.

Especially after John, Oscar Lott, a personnel management consultant Jack Wiersma brought in, and an ad hoc committee representing all levels and positions worked out a personnel plan specifically calling for a six to eight-week probationary period for each of us, I hounded John for support in using this or other procedures for weeding out our worst teachers. Where one stands on any position in relation to one's coworkers is, of course, as much a matter of where the *coworkers* stand on the continuum, as it is a matter of one's own views. To my credentials-conscious fellow early childhood educators, who had pioneered for generations in worrying about the acquisition and maintenance of subtly sophisticated standards, I was a dangerous extremist because I favored giving the least "qualified" maximum policy planning and supervising opportunities. To the experts it seemed as though I was advocating the traditional scornful snort of the uninformed: "Little kids? Huh! *Anybody* can do it!" Not so to my colleagues in CDGM. To many of them I was against jobs for the needy, and in favor of absurdly unnecessary nuances and abilities—"unnecessary," because not understood in relation to freedom goals.

I was for experimentation with *new careers* for the poor: entry into opportunity not based on previous education and training—but *careers*, which implies the *acquisition* of all sorts of high caliber training. This, I thought, was much more important than merely a policy of new *jobs* for the poor, though that itself should not be sneezed at. As poverty is defined in terms of money, no solution can realistically be effected without including income. But it was careers, career progression, and development for trainees, resource teachers, area teacher guides, and all other members of the staffs of all other divisions that intrigued and concerned me.

During the second grant, nothing came of my personnel standards. The ruiners continued to teach with the inspirers. This added to our customary community cacophony. I was the culprit, because, as Mrs. S put it: "You likes some to teach bad, and you stamps it with approval, because you pays them the same, no matter what they does."

Mr. Oscar Lott of Manpower Evaluation and Development Institute was an older gentleman who had been in education and personnel work for many years. He responded to CDGM's unique efforts and character as did so many of our consultants: with warm affection, imaginative protectiveness, and a desire to make his part of the whole a special thing, too. As the spring wore on, I felt increasingly that Mr. Lott was more concerned with a vigorous, aggressive, and fast-moving program of career development and training than were any CDGM planners. New careers for the poor was no longer a priority in CDGM, though paychecks for the poor remained a very prominent topic of warfare.

Problems regarding the pay scale for resource teachers were perhaps the most debilitating and demoralizing our division had. While I'd been in Washington for three weeks between the first summer's grant and the first fall's volunteer interim, and he was holding the fort alone, John had worked out a pay scale for resource teachers which offered more money for *early childhood* experience. When I returned, he'd asked me to write a description of courses, experiences, merit, etc., that should "count" for moving up on the pay scale. I'd done so immediately. John and I had spent considerable time on it. We wanted it to reward for superior performance, not for superior past luck: opportunities, degrees, etc. But at grant-signing time, OEO didn't want to let us do this until Mr. Lott had set up the personnel plan.

Meanwhile, resource teachers were restless and angry at me. We had an all-day statewide resource teacher meeting in Moman's warehouse to discuss the pay scale, and to set up local committees responsible for coming up with local preferences for a system. Hundreds of people at the meeting voted to have ATGs rate those who felt they had special "qualifications" if they mailed these to them. I persuaded all but the most deeply suspicious that this was not my decision to make. It was up to John, the board, and OEO. I promised that very soon a decision would be relayed through me to them. Results would appear on their paychecks. None did during the entire spring and summer. Therefore, sitting on my limb out there, I was the object of much rage. Whether it was OEO, the board, or John who balked at making a decision, I was never able to ascertain. John was too busy to tell me.

In any event, a cheated and betrayed feeling soured many resource teachers, many of whom I'd never met, on me. This rendered other more positive responses to our educational ideas negative. Some of our offerings were readily accepted, of course, but we felt that others had been demagnetized—had lost their potential power to attract. It wasn't that people were "just working for money." It was a matter of the relative magnetic power of a cluster of ideas.

Educational ideas had high appeal until circumstances beyond our control contaminated me and Mary. Therefore, any ideas emanating from us were contaminated. By contrast, the idea of resenting us had more appeal and magnetic power to attract than the idea of working cooperatively with us. We had been moved from the side of the allies to the Devious Deceitful Mean White Lady list. This, in turn, affected some of the trainee teachers' attitudes, though they as well had in many cases not met us. But you don't have to meet a witch to know her powers and fear her.

Those who knew us and liked us intuitively had no trouble being simultaneously suspicious of us. Anybody who knows anything about witches knows they are often disguised as fairy princesses. They come bearing persimmons, pomegranates, rare perfumes, rubies, emeralds, and evil enchantments. Witches cast spells and turn people to stone. They destroy the lives of fancy-free knights and beautiful maidens. The reverse can be true too. Those accustomed to being kept in stone casts, by evil circumstances, can be painfully disoriented if their psychic structures are disrupted by the chaotic anticoagulant of sudden "freedom." To many people I was the Wicked Witch of the North.

Along the same line as the impact visit idea--that is, along the line of crash emergency measures to give remedial help to the most dreary or most excellently susceptible center staffs--Mary and I each held workshops; not quite of the small, intimate seminar recommended size. Each of us, as the lone leader, had around five hundred in our groups each session.

My first mass workshop was one for resource teachers to discuss the pay scale. The day before, we built many varieties of shelves and containers, painted them, and arranged them in attractive, convenient classroom setups, full of our general supplies, toys, and equipment. The invitation to resource teachers urged people to bring special things they and their children had made. By the time all the teachers had sauntered in and got seated, the usually tomblike, windowless warehouse in which we met looked as exciting as a state teachers' convention. We planned time for each person to wander around the warehouse, observing, asking questions, sharing what she had done with others, and taking notes. We had a general discussion that gave any interested party an opportunity to talk about whatever she wanted to discuss.

Here and there a resource teacher was able to express her hostility toward us, overcome it, and proceed: "When I first heard of you and all your suggestions, Polly, I thought you were one of *those*. So I watched you, but didn't obey you. One day I thought, oh well, might as well try a few of those things. She'll never know, so it's not really following her. Our basement was flooded with water. We mopped this water up. Before, we had had the children very crowded upstairs because the basement water was up to their ankles. Then we made large white curtains. It took six hours to make the curtains. The whole time I was sewing, I was saying to myself I don't see why Polly says we should make curtains. When we hung the curtains and the drab walls had clean ironed white streams of cloth I began to see why. Cheeriness is happiness, and that is what Polly had in mind for our children. Then of course next to the lovely curtains the walls looked even more drab, so we painted the walls. It took five hours to paint them a bright green. I told myself I would not be telling Polly of these things. We covered the two low tables in our storage room with yellow oilcloth. It was a storage room. We had taken out old broken tables, chairs, and unused lumber. We made stuffed toys, crates with wallpaper for shelves and other things such as flannel boards. We supplied mats we quilted for the children to sit on the floor. Polly, you know a funny thing? By the end of that time, when the children came, I was no longer thinking of you, I was taking pride, as if I thought of these things myself! Then I said to the others, you know we can take what she gives, even if we don't want to take what whites give. They give poison that keeps us from getting up and deciding things, but she is giving keys so we can accept and unlock things for ourselves. I believe the other thing that turned my mind from my ways was when you stayed at my house and slept in the bed with my daughter. I thought then that maybe I was mistaken about your reasoning. In the spring when you looked so sick, I even felt sorry for you. You could have stayed home in Washington and had your rich husband take care of you, and here you were helping us. I decided from then on to appraise an individual before resenting."

My second workshop was offered on four successive days at Mount Beulah instead of in the warehouse, the latter being totally windowless, depressingly dank, dark, etc. This time I invited one fourth of the total number of resource teachers and one fourth of the ATGs, each of the four days. The ATGs were assistant group leaders. The theme was children's language and reading readiness. We opened with Joe Harrison and his guitar doing freedom songs. As one more clue to the changing times, the singing annoyed most teachers. They wanted to dispense with this "waste of time" and get down to business. Our atmosphere was workmanlike now, not spiritual. We kept up our resource teacher "correspondence course," too. Almost every week we mailed in a new weekly lesson plan for the Sound Table Game. (See Appendix F for a sample week-long lesson plan.) We mailed details of "How To Use Your Public Library," specifics of "How To Take a Trip," and so on. Whenever we mailed anything, we sent copies to each member of each area staff. We tried hard to establish good relations with them.

Meanwhile, Mary held a colossally large workshop for trainees in Tougaloo. This one also ran for four days, and had one-fourth of our trainees each day. This was approximately three hundred people per day in one room. Mary had planned ahead with ATGs. They were group leaders. Mary reported that some ATGs "contributed magnificently," but over-all she was disappointed at their half-heartedness.

Mary thought the workshop wasn't worth what it cost. I thought anything was worth gas money until we could hold adequately staffed, adequately small workshops in communities. Indisputably, the latter was what was needed. Yet, in the meantime, I was sure a great deal from our emergency efforts was rubbing off on the staff. Our center standards were rising up, up, quietly, like the tide.

We preferred, of course, smaller workshops in the communities themselves. We hoped to be done with the need for these wild sessions and in shape for the better kind in a few months. But we had to wait till ATGs gained strength, more teachers returned from the OEO eight-week university Head Start courses, and we had more of a staff than merely Mary and I before we could really count on big things happening in community workshops. Still, even at this point, we promoted the development of regular area workshops. Every week in ATG workshop, we asked ATGs if they had met with other members of their teams that week to talk over mutual business, problems, plans, etc. They rarely had.

There was a great deal of jealousy, rivalry, quarreling, and going behind backs in area offices. "Well," we urged, "if you aren't ready yet to work in teams in your areas, at least let's get some area teachers' meetings rolling." Either Mary or I accompanied the ATG from each area to one such meeting, till we had covered all sixteen areas, and had had in each a showing and discussion of our film *A Chance for Change*. These were night meetings for all interested adults in the area. They were quite successful. Then we planned with ATGs that each of them would schedule an all-day workshop where the teacher from the area who had attended the OEO eight-week Head Start teaching course on a college campus would lead the program, to share in any form she wanted whatever she wanted to from her experience. These sixteen meetings were almost all very constructive and popular too. The ATG was in charge. Mary and I weren't present. We were working on weaning.

Two experienced ATGs held a workshop in Jackson for resource teachers new to our program. They did an admirable job, from planning whom to invite, to planning and carrying through a schedule. The team gave a report to ATG workshop on "Hints of How to Plan a Successful Workshop." Just before I left for Washington, I started something I hoped would become important during the summer. This was special workshops for advanced centers: those which had overcome initial handicaps unusually well, had achieved some kind of routine preschool status, and seemed to have staff capable of going much more deeply into the work. We planned to have a team of Pacific Oaks experts as consultants. I'd spent weeks arranging for them, but unfortunately, at the last minute, they had to cancel. We worked on discipline. We produced a manual which we duplicated and mailed to all other centers. Unfortunately, this idea of advanced center workshops was dropped. New people in the teacher development and program for children division during the summer thought it undemocratic and unkind to acknowledge publicly that some teachers and centers were better than others. We had a bit of a split on that. I believed in all they believed. But I also believed in acknowledging merit and capitalizing on the motivation power intrinsic in a situation where peers who've had no more than equal opportunity, but who have *achieved something superior through effort alone,* are given the reward of further opportunity. And there is no greater motivation to others than to see "their own make good." When those in the position of sponsor act as though all they see is mediocrity, it seems to me that they are breeding mediocrity all the more intensely.

The heart of Mary's and my work continued to be working with the area teacher guides toward taking over the educational leadership of their people. We all had mixed feelings about how to conduct workshop. We wanted to be lax and loose and always have time for actual problems weighing on the mind of the ATGs who were on the battlefield, while Mary and I were more and more in the business office. Yet we wanted to progress in a sensible order with child development concepts, content areas of an early childhood education program, etc. During the launching period, neither Mary nor I, nor an ATG committee, made advance plans for our weekly 10 A.M. to 4 P.M. workshops. We came together, quite gratefully, out of our respective frays, and tried to unsnarl messes through sympathetic analysis and sensible collective recommendations.

We usually began with half an hour of business announcements, collection of information we had agreed on together last time, and planning of information to be brought in next time. From then until after late lunch, which most of us carried and munched with coffee we brewed in our warehouse suite, we examined homemade things we had brought in, gossiped, discussed major problems, and hurried each other along so we could get to something substantive in the afternoon.

There was so much to think about before we could get to children. The business office needed to make up an in-kind contribution statement. It needed ATGs to bring in a list of every hour they worked free since last August, and what they did. The personnel people wanted to know to whom ATGs handed in their applications. The area administrators asked that we talk about what centers needed to do before they opened. Don't let them open just because ATGs checked them out and rated them educationally ready. They have to have bank accounts, applications in and OK's on all workers, etc. Remember not to do your AA's work. Discussion defining his work: But what do the COs do different from us? Aren't we supposed to visit parents? Discussion defining the role of the CO: There is much overlap with the ATG.

We reassigned a few centers when several ATGs seemed too heavily burdened and others had far fewer than their share of eight centers. This took a while. We had to discuss it and prod till the ATGs thought of reasons and procedures for making the changes. Mary and I prodded, but didn't make decisions. We found replacements for an ATG who switched to CO work, for one who had a baby, and for one with insufficient centers to make her area qualify for an ATG.

We needed to know the ATGs' schedules. Where would each of them be between Wednesdays when we worked together in Tougaloo? If we needed to reach them—about a visitor coming and needing hostessing in an area, or about a center that called in with an emergency need, or about a sudden statewide meeting, or with a message for a far-flung center—where could each ATG be found? We waited patiently while ATGs, not in the habit of organizing themselves so closely, juggled and rejuggled till each had a schedule that suited her somewhat, wrote it down for herself, and made us a copy.

We needed to know the opening and closing dates of any center that volunteered during the interim, and names of any out-of-state workers in centers. (There turned out to be only two in all our hundreds of centers: Marilyn Lowen who was back working in midstate centers after a long absence during which she studied excellent nursery schools and worked in the SNCC office in Atlanta; and Pat Spalding, a very able and adaptable young lady from the North, who was working in a Holly Springs center.)

We needed to know budgeted and actual units of children in each center. Area staff had to work out reallocations where a center had many more children than budgeted for, and another center had unfilled but budgeted units. The problem was usually the former. I felt strongly that our teacher development and program for children department, *with other departments working to support us,* should help communities deal with extra enrolled children. We should not turn them down, but aid communities in *offering* them something, rather than just smiling benignly and cramming them into already crowded centers. Here, again, was the relativity problem. In contrast to early educators I was unduly lenient in my view of what we could welcome in quality and consider as a great improvement in a child's experience. But in contrast to CDGMians, I was very fussy and strict about high quality program, ratio of children to adults, facilities, etc. Though John had by that time hired a "facilities consultant," it seemed to Mary and me that neither he nor the board took that sort of thing very seriously.

Mr. Dickert, a very earnest retired plumbing contractor from Wisconsin, didn't feel that he was taken seriously either. He felt that there was only one thing wrong with our Head Start facilities: poverty. He said that perhaps 60 percent of the center buildings were worth less than $2,500, and that in most of the cases in which he recommended renovations, the cost of the repairs would be greater than the cost of the building itself. Mr. Dickert felt that experience in big city housing projects had taught us that if we picked people up and put them in modern facilities they didn't "appreciate it." He didn't favor popping our centers into prefabs, trailers, or buildings outside of their communities, but thought money and materials should be made available for them to participate in the improvement or construction of their own facilities. He did, however, feel that certain immediate improvements should be made, pending more permanent solutions.

He sent bulletins to John and temporary Deputy Director Martin Cohn from time to time, making modest recommendations such as: "Center has open gas flame heaters, should be fenced in so clothing and/or others can not catch fire." But everybody at the top was busy with bigger headaches. Mr. Dickert's inspections resulted in slow and sporadic repairs and rennovations, accompanied by a great deal of resentful resistance.

I was anxious to continue our summer efforts to coordinate with whites wherever possible; not to let them seep and wiggle into control, but to coordinate with them, and to include them under controlled conditions. We asked ATGs to collect information from each center as to goods and services asked for, and received or refused from whites in its community, and to urge communities to try. How many white children are enrolled, and what efforts had been made to tempt them, we wanted to know.

We were still having trouble interesting community people in using libraries for the children, and in taking children on trips. We discussed logistical and psychological details of these problems. Jesse Paris, director of the area administration division, and his full-time consultant Sam Sanderson from New York, explained to ATGs about time and activity sheets, car logs, gas reimbursement forms, and so forth. We worked out a better system for information spreading and retrieval, and selection and transportation processes, in case we were honored by OEO with more places at the eight-week Head Start teachers' courses on campuses. We discussed ways of keeping records and notes and filing them and sending us copies for the teacher development and program for children central files.

Much time was spent on problems originating in centers and in uncertain ATGs. Some committees were firing teachers before they put in their first day of work because they were pregnant. Now how could teachers get *that* pregnant between last week, when they were hired, and this week, the ATGs speculated. The committee must have known she was pregnant. Was it fair to fire someone when no circumstances had changed?

Some centers hadn't got their letters from Jesse Paris authorizing them to open. This was making teachers mad at ATGs. What to do? We talked over and over about the benefits the ATG would reap for herself and her center if she would communicate with her AA; if she would work cooperatively with him. Some church deacons wouldn't let center teachers display the children's work or feel at home in the kitchen. We had the authority to do what in these situations? We were paying rent, right? One chairman told the teachers they would have to hold school outside for a week because he would be using the rooms he had rented them for Bible School. Was that a violation of the facilities contract? The AA should take care of it? Yes, but the AA agrees with the chairman, and we don't. Do we have to accept the ridiculous decision of the AA? When we find a terrible teacher, should we put *her* need for an opportunity to develop a new career or the need of the children for a kind and good teacher first?

The supplies weren't getting distributed the way they should have been. Didn't we work out a system for AAs to rent station wagons with CDGM funds and carry everything to centers? What happened to the drop-shipping idea? Why doesn't John insist that AAs do their work? The ATGs thought he was afraid to antagonize them. Some teachers came back from the eight-week OEO sponsored courses and sat on what they had learned. Did Mary and I think they were hoarding power, or had they been too dumb to absorb anything? What should we do next time to make sure we got high returns from teachers allowed the privilege of going? How could we give guts to committees, fearful of hurting feelings or firing relatives, in getting grim teachers to do better? Some trainees were better than some more highly paid resource teachers. ATGs wanted to know how to teach committees what to do about that.

By late spring we had to admit that one of the ATGs (one whom we had had to "accept" without solid and multiple recommendations because no one knew anyone excellent in that area) wasn't working out. In fairness to children and teachers in the area, she should be replaced with someone capable of serving as a pipeline: transmitting messages, concepts, techniques, and stimulation from communities to central, from central to communities, and from area to area. Mary had worked extensively and personally with her to no avail. We'd been patient with her in every instance, and had tried to tap all sides of her.

I'd discussed with her the possibility of her trading places with one of the teachers in her area. Then she would still have a productive place in the CDGM program. I'd even written this to her. But she remained silent, even when it was her day to preside over trainee workshop, except when she said "yes ma'm." She was the only isolate in the ATG group. Infinitely complex networks of friendships and enmities had sprung up among the ATGs, but this older woman stood alone. When I finally had a terminal discussion with her, and cemented it with a final thank-you letter, she went to the board in a rage.

At the same time OEO had clamped down on "nepotism." One ATG, Frances Alexander, or her husband had to go because of this. She went. Bad feeling increased. We hired two new half-time ATGs in extra heavy areas. Musically gifted ATG Valentine Blue decided to become a rotating music specialist ATG. Under great pressure from other members of that particular area staff, I agreed to hire someone new to CDGM. I felt badly about this, because I felt strongly that ATG positions should be promotions for excellent resource teachers, or even trainees. It was not only fairer, but it was a practice more likely to produce the most helpful area teacher guide we could find to serve developing teachers in centers. The removal of several old-time ATGs was interpreted as Polly axing her friends. You can't trust white people. The addition of several new people introduced an abrasive element into our intimate group. Emotionally, all wasn't well with us.

On the substantive side we did many things, too. At the March 9 ATG workshop we showed a film about the Los Nietos preschool program in California. We stressed apearance of the classroom, many activities going on at the same time, informality, what the teachers were doing, and the application of things we saw in the film to our centers.

On March 16 we visited the elite white Broadmoor Baptist Nursery School. The director took us on a tour and explained highlights of a nine-class nursery and kindergarten program. ATGs enjoyed a massive children's art show currently on display in the Broadmoor meeting room. They were incredulous that little children could do such lovely work and in so many mediums.

The same day we showed *A Chance at the Beginning*, a film showing Dr. Deutsch's preschool program in New York. In the discussion we featured teaching through each event of the day: language at music time, counting at refreshment time, etc. We encouraged ATGs to itemize what and how the teacher in the film was teaching as she played with the children.

On March 23 we discussed what ATGs had noticed when they had made exchange visits to each other's areas during the week. We had a special joint workshop of community organizers and ATGs two days later. We tried to tie together the duties and goals of the two. Community organizers seemed very resentful of any emphasis on the preschool part of CDGM. Somehow, someone, somewhere, had failed to promote the fact that this was what Head Start was all about, and that we were, in effect, "getting away with" anything else.

That afternoon was only the third time in six months I had been able, with all my tedious long-distance phoning and endless letter-writing, to scare up a nursery education consultant. The first had been Claudia Lewis, and the second Flemmie Kittrell from Howard University. She stayed two days and told the ATGs that white church women would help them if they asked. She also urged ATGs to involve parents. The third lady was Jean Kunz from the early education department at the University of Maryland. In her friendly direct way she helped ATGs make up jokes and spontaneous songs with children, and showed how one can teach and chat while going about the little things that small children go about.

On April 1 John Mudd conducted a combined ATG-CO-AA workshop to discuss the deeper meanings of CDGM. Children weren't mentioned. More and more the Head Start aspect of CDGM was becoming an eccentric appendage to the ever more bureaucratic business side, and all the ever angier other elements.

On April 6 Mary Emmons made games to teach concepts of *big* and *little* to children. The nurse, Mrs. Mason, discussed what teachers could do about the medical program. She showed ATGs how to make play nurses' caps, examination instruments, etc. At the April 14 ATG workshop we showed the film *Phonovisual in Action,* and discussed the difference between teaching the alphabet and phonics, and why. On April 20 we played the Sound Table game. We showed the Vassar College nursery school film and talked about how our centers compared.

On May 7 we were lucky enough to get the spirited Miss Fan Brooke from the University of Georgia. She pretended the ATGs were children, and ran them through an excellent six-hour sample nursery school day. ATGs were crazy about her. She didn't "beat around the bush, teach, preach, tell rules, and give us lists of things that're important," as one of them explained. "She was jus' a lively lady you could see loved children. Her eyes sparkled and she leaped around. She didn't have to tell you anything to do, she jus' *did* it." ATGs also appreciated the packet of duplicated ideas in all program areas that Miss Brooke distributed. The second most popular workshop among the ATGs was on June 23, when Miss Judy Phillips of Peabody College showed slides and lectured on attitudes and activities of teachers in that Head Start. She emphasized purposeful, individual, sequential teaching. However, several ATGs commented that they saw the Peabody program as very condescending—backed by a philosophy that it's possible to redeem the deficient children.

Thinking that seeing is believing, and believing is a better kind of learning than is memorizing, I had budgeted an out-of-state air trip for each ATG to visit a quality nursery program. I had a lot of trouble arranging these visits with overloaded schools of excellence. Due to scheduling difficulties, some ATGs never got their trips. Those who did grew a great deal. Lavaree Jones and Clarice Coney went to New York to visit the Bank Street and Grand Street educational programs. Frances Alexander, Lillie Ayers, Ella Hubbard, and Valentine Blue visited the National Child Research Center and Greenacres in Washington, D.C. When they returned, they wrote reports on their findings, and were featured at workshops in which they shared them.

I couldn't clearly see how we could spare any ATGs during the spring launching period, so they could attend the OEO eight-week university Head Start courses. They were the pipes between the crude rich oil and the refinery. But by summer surely we could find substitute ATGs from among our more sensitive and able resource teachers. Then we could part with most of the ATGs. We would save places at the best universities for them. Because they were the most advanced educators in our program, we felt that they would benefit most from the subtler qualities which better courses might offer and less good universities would be likely to overlook.

Again, this plan didn't entirely materialize, but some ATGs were able to enjoy the opportunity. Gaynette Flowers, Dorothy Noble, Anna Ashley, and Flora Brooks attended a six week course at Peabody College. They enjoyed it, but came home parroting enough clichés and using enough jargon to distress us. They seemed to have picked up more coating than content.

This is the greatest danger in education for all people at all levels. It's a danger that increases in direct proportion to how eager a person is to be a good student. One of the greatest challenges we teachers face, is avoiding it.

Lillie Ayers and Carrie Davis, amused by the challenge, were among the first Negroes to attend Ole Miss: They went to the eight-week course for Head Start teachers. They learned a lot and liked their teachers, but found it funny that though CDGM was the biggest Head Start in the state, and was enjoying a national reputation as well, their teachers took them to observe only in unremarkable public school Head Starts. Furthermore, our people felt that they were strenuously discouraged from discussing their CDGM experiences. Lavaree Jones attended an eight-week course for Head Start directors at the Bank Street College of Education. Hattie Saffold enrolled in a one-week course for preschool teachers at the University of Southern Mississippi. She was excited by the agenda full of excellent consultants.

Mary Emmons, I, and the ATGs talked over all our workshop plans together. Agenda emerged accordingly. While we were never in conflict on what we were doing at any given time, we were all unsure and ambivalent. In retrospect Mary felt that we should have done much more toward helping ATGs become good nursery teachers and spent less time on helping them deal with problems of educational administration. She also thought ATGs weren't given enough say in planning our programs, and that some should have been promoted earlier to the central office. In retrospect I remained unsure. I agreed with her, yet thought it unavoidable to have dealt with many administrative problems unless we were going to abandon the idea of trying to develop area teacher guides *as teaching supervisors* from the start.

We could have taken the more traditional approach and prepared teachers first, promoting them eventually to administrative studies and jobs. Given the choice, I vastly preferred our experiment. The traditional method would of course "work." I wanted to know if *our* method could succeed. If it could, and could be disseminated, it would be of great significance to education generally. The price one pays for doing one thing is not doing another. So, logically, devoting a sizable piece of each weekly workshop to field programs left us too little time to devote as much as we should to quality preschool teaching. I agreed, also, that ATGs should plan their own workshops, and should eventually, in the near future, not just be *included* in the Central Staff or the teacher development and program for children division, but should *be* it. However, I saw the whole program in longer range terms than Mary did. I thought ATGs needed to see some possibilities, films, contrasts, consultants, etc., for a few brief spring months, before they took more planning responsibility in the summer and in following grants. It's hard to plan in maximally useful ways, if one has extremely limited horizons. My desire was to widen ATGs horizons first and then turn them loose to fly.

I was equally interested in widening Mary's and my horizons. One can get in a rut. Policy planners wearing provincial and traditional blinders are a disaster. I was eager to make sure that both of us attended workshops and whatnot at exciting places whenever possible.

We heard of what promised to be a mind-shaking week-long session with Dr. Caleb Gattegno in New York. On the morning that I was to leave for this workshop, with two ATGs who looked forward to the adventure as much as I did, I was quite ill. Mary volunteered to go in my place. The workshop shook Mary's mind all right, but also any shrinking certainties she may have had. She was young, confused by all bewildering hurry and hostility around us, and impressionable in the field of early education. Dr. Gattegno was mature, sure of himself and his educational beliefs, and had the hypnotic power to persuade that so many mystics do.

Mary returned from New York in a dreamlike dazzlement of new realization of the powers within people, and a noticeably heightened discontent that we weren't doing enough about it. This took the form of feeling that it was I who didn't care enough about structuring CDGM so people could develop. What I felt to be her nonspecific, negative attitude toward everything I had done or was doing in CDGM served to increase *my* unhappiness along the same lines. I *knew* we weren't doing enough, but felt so hemmed in by constantly curtailing circumstances within the organization. I had at least had the security of thinking that Mary and I were united in trying to keep developmental considerations uppermost.

We were obviously very different kinds of personalities. She was quiet, impersonal, practical, and rational. She was utterly capable. She wasn't given to introspection. I, of course, was ebullient, did better at getting a spirit awakened in people than in helping them in practical ways, accomplished more through relationship than through details, and was more intuitive and mystical than rational. I was capable, but not with the business department, which annoyed Mary. I was inclined to ponder and to talk too much about the swarming ponderings. Nevertheless, I thought we worked well together. Rather like Jack Sprat and his wife, our shortcomings complemented each other. Now I felt abandoned even by her. Somehow, it seemed to me, in some never-named way, I, too, had become, in her eyes, a deterrent to Doing Good.

I was program division director. Mary was program division deputy director. Though far less than is customary, I was following the usual procedure for such a staffing pattern. The director concentrates on long-range and over-all policy planning and the development of special projects. The deputy director does almost all the overseeing of daily administration. Whether because of pressures wearing her down combined with her new excitement about Dr. Gattegno's convictions, or because of inexperience with distinctions between the role of directors and deputy directors (she was twenty-two years old and had never worked in an office or large organization), she began more and more to feel that I had a vision, and that I operated in terms of my vision, rather than in practical immediate terms she understood. In this observation she was entirely right. The more she and incoming others urged that we develop this or that known method or part of the project to the detriment of teaching an experimental attitude and to the detriment of the even growth of the whole, the more I feared that CDGM would sink in a swamp of ordinary emphases and definable details, and would lose the essence of what those of us who created it had been trying to do.

This, Mary began to feel, was my instinctive tendency to cling to control. It was. Perhaps wrongly, and definitely uncomfortably in our new context, I was very consciously and always more tensely trying to keep the project moving in its original direction, until it could keep itself rolling that way. I yearned to go home to my normal happy life in the daily more alluring North. That kind of project in that kind of state left something to be desired for those nonfanatics who like more in their lives than work. As Mary moved toward focusing on the achievement of particular tasks, I, in response, moved toward the maintenance of what it was all about.

An example of this was our reading program. Mary, after her New York trip, was all for Dr. Cattegno's Words-in-Color reading method. As earlier, I was anxious to see CDGM develop a total reading program, essentially new, while including the best of the best. I was as ardent a believer in Dr. Gattegno's faith in inner powers as Dr. Gattegno was, but didn't share Mary's growing feeling that buying Words-in-Color materials for all our people would necessarily help us release individual potential. Dr. Gattegno came to Mississippi. I questioned him relentlessly as to *how* he would advise us to proceed *in our context.* His answers were emotionally convincing but intellectually elliptical. What emerged was that if Dr. Gattegno himself, with the extraordinary magnetism he undeniably had, could work with each of our four thousand teachers personally, marvelous wonders would result. But he couldn't come for many months. And even then, he would be able to work with only a limited number of manageably small groups. We could joyfully fit his work into our whole reading project, but we *did* need a whole reading project.

During that period the reading project was giving me much grief. More teachers were using more children's literature more skillfully. More teachers were playing the Sound Table game, the Sylvia Ashton-Warner Word Elicitation game, and were labeling items in their classrooms. But the Bridge Readers were to have been the core of our reading program, and they were almost at a standstill. By late spring I'd collected enough material for thirteen or fourteen books, but no one else seemed very interested in the project. In my off hours (midnight till dawn) I sometimes worked at putting material from the children together and trying to pull it into artistic shape. However, both my energy and support for the project from those above me were too limited. I became discouraged. None of these or any others were printed during the next year. Only one book was printed by CDGM. It was a lovely book that Lucia, who came later, did. However, it wasn't a Bridge Reader, because it ignored one of our biggest points: large block letters for easy reading. Lucia's book, *The Hike,* was done in beautiful spidery semiscript. I'd also started writing an easy-to-read digest of leading preschool methods. It pointed out the essence of their differences, and emphasized their similarities.

When we'd got our second OEO grant, John Mudd had hired a talented young man named Richard Murphy to work exclusively on developing a reading program. As Mary and I were quite busy with so many parts of the children's program, I postponed the digest, and came to count more and more heavily on Dick to come up with an over-all reading plan, collected and revised from existing methods, or invented by himself, with ready-to-go materials for an immediate beginning. It was my understanding from John, that Dick was not only going to prepare a learning-to-read system for our children, based on folklore and their own conversations, but was also going to develop a reading program for our *teachers,* stemming from his revisions of our Newsletters, Blue Book, and other material of interest to them as preschool teachers. I was excited about this. It would be one of the first adult literacy programs in the world, having an appropriate vocational base from the first to the last word.

Dick started to revise a book of toy-making patterns I'd been working on from material collected at centers, to which our new Administrative Assistant Mary Ann Ware (formerly John's secretary) had added.

We asked Dick to see if he could do anything with a similar book of songs we were making. Both projects petered out. Dick did a lot of research and had a lot of ideas, but little emerged. A year lated he devised the beginning stages of some interesting reading-readiness material for use with children, but it wasn't widely used in CDGM. Dick was having his own difficulties getting recognized in busy CDGM.

I felt guilty about neglecting the reading project. However, increasing Central Staff criticism and apathy toward it affected me adversely. The more people sniped at me about what *I was* doing with it, the more I observed what the snipers were *not* doing about it; the more I felt the onerous number of crushing, screaming, nagging obligations Mary and I had; the more I thought about Dick having solely reading to be responsible for; and the more frustrated I became at the apparent shift of CDGM policy planners from innovative program efforts to institutional and political concerns, the more I withdrew from the whole developmental arena. I would do what I could still do in nonconflict segments of the foundation laying, and leave. Probably, I thought, I was just becoming too tired to take all the emotional turmoil, disheartening disdain, and bureaucratic red tape that was nowadays necessary to do anything worthwhile. I was behaving far from my best.

My diary reminds me of another possible reason for my decline:

". . . I didn't think at the time [late April] that my accident affected me in any way, but it must've more than I thought. Though at the time I wasn't at all afraid, I now find that I panic at high speeds on rural highways—something of a handicap, since the major portion of my days and nights must be spent at high speeds on rural highways. I keep reliving that feeling of hurtling through darkness; flying past that mammoth live oak tree and missing it (judging by the tire tracks found later) by eight inches; plunging into that freezing creek; and dully wondering (a) how to save the poor peoples' job applications in the back seat, and (b) how to get out before the car filled with water and I drowned endless miles east of nowhere. The 2 A.M., the hitchhiking home alone, the headache, aren't lingering memories—just that fearful isolated hurtling nowhere through nothing. Probably because it represents my feeling about the possibility of doing good as much as because of the event itself."

Sometimes the program division's disappointments were caused by factors outside CDGM. These were easier to tolerate. One of my launching goals was to establish an unusual audio-visual program of some kind. I had hoped to re-establish the photography trainee project from the first summer, so local people, under the guidance of skilled photographers, could learn to take pictures of center life which we would use in teacher development work and in public relations as slides, film-strips, sets of mounted enlargements (so far, all we had done was make a set of fifty beautiful mounted color enlargements of center program ideas to display to teachers), and illustrations for the Bridge Readers. I'd hoped to be able to fit a creative audiovisual expert into the budget so local people could begin making slides and filmstrips of use to them in community development work; and of course, to purchase good film strips, slides, and story records for the children.

My interest in this had been given a great boost one day in the winter when Dr. Sandy Kravitz, director of the OEO Demonstration Program, had called me at home to outline a proposal to bring a Children's Caravan to Mississippi. He told me that a man named Dr. Morton Schindel had a contract with OEO to outfit a fleet of brightly repainted red and white retired school buses as traveling movie theatres. They were heated, air-conditioned, filled wth steps instead of seats, carpeted in red, and could seat thirty children at a time. OEO would give CDGM two of these buses, and would finance almost everything related to the project. We were to send ten local people to Dr. Schindel's headquarters in Weston Woods, Connecticut, for a three-week training course.

Some would learn to be advance men to travel to CDGM communities ahead of the caravans to set up schedules and facilities. Some would learn to service and set up the audiovisual equipment and to care for the mechanics of the buses. Each bus had its own generator for an independent power source. This was a footnote of great concern to us, as we weren't sure what kind of cooperation we could get from the Mississippi electric power company for a project in Negro communities. A third group would learn how to use the materials on the buses in the most educational manner. Each bus would have a staff of three people. Each caravan would carry beautiful films and filmstrips made from the literature most appropriate to CDGM's clientele of all ages. Each caravan would carry a movie screen, loudspeaker, record player, etc. Buses would also come equipped with outdoor screen and arrangements for larger audiences.

We were to provide an audiovisual director to assure that the mobile movie theaters were booked morning, afternoon, and night, except when moving on to the next town. The director was also to see that the project was used creatively, to work out follow-up, and to help communities plan what materials they wanted to make to enrich existing materials. Books could be left behind in centers. The team could stay and help teachers make their children's literature and audiovisual program richer. There would be extra projectors and an accompanying central library for warm-up and follow-up purposes. We were also to provide salaries for the bus crew.

The Children's Caravan was planned to fit into existing poverty programs, especially Head Start. OEO was planning to give caravans to the Appalachian Volunteers and to a ten-county project sponsored by Tuskegee in Alabama. I'd heard of Dr. Schindel. He had been producing high quality films from childrens' books for many years. He had won awards, and was widely acknowledged in advanced educational circles to be an outstanding person in the field. Many of the films the caravans would carry had won prizes in American and foreign film festivals. This was a fantastic opportunity, and both Mary and I were thrilled.

We saw a possible side effect that increased our excitement. If the advance men for the Children's Caravan announced the imminent arrival of these rural rarities in white communities as well as in black, and if we parked them in borderline neighborhoods, we might, for once, have something wonderful enough to tempt out hard-to-reach poor whites. The project might serve as an opener for some kind of contact.

Mary allowed herself the luxury of turning her back on her work and going all the way to Weston Woods to work out specifics. I allowed myself the luxury of taking a day off to escort Dr. and Mrs. Schindel around the communities for a preliminary impression. We advertised for an audiovisual director, and got some promising responses. Then Mr. Shriver decided that, to quote the assistant who broke the news to me, "CDGM has too much." The Children's Caravan project was canceled. We worked some more, now to see if Ken Dean's Mississippi Human Relations Council, an active "cautious liberal" group, would satisfy Mr. Shriver as a noncontroversial vehicle for the project. We did lots of conferencing and proposal writing. The decision remained *no.* I wasn't even angry. By then I was acclimated. I just chalked the experience up to one more example of the curious contradiction that while OEO accused us of not caring about the children, only about politics, it seemed always to be *OEO* that acted in relation to political factors, even when it deprived children. Ah, people, what paradoxical animals we are!

We were forever mailing things. We sent packets of letters to resource teachers, which they could, if they wished, distribute to their families, urging them to go to their centers and help. We wrote letters to ATGs whenever they missed workshop, catching them up on what we had done. We mailed packets of such brochures as James Hymes' "Three to Six: Your Child Starts School," the Mississippi Day Care Department's pamphlets to parents on what to look for in nursery schools and kindergartens, and OEO Head Start booklets. Whatever we mailed to ATGs, chairmen, or resource teachers, which was folders full every month, we mailed to other members of each area staff so they would be up-to-date on what we were doing in our division.

I worried that the board of directors, largely composed of poor people to whom early education was quite foreign, was not being consistently and sophisticatedly exposed to and "educated" about early education. Yet it controlled our program. The board spent nearly all its time and energy on an avalanche of administrative and political problems—usually on crises. We couldn't afford or find consultants to advise the board on educational affairs, as we did on administrative matters. John felt that the board had too much else to do to meet with me, or central, area, or local members of the teacher development and program for children division staff about our purposes and problems. Board members often said that thinking about these things "wasn't important," because that, at least, was one area of the program in which there was no calamity; all was going well.

My feeling was that the board wouldn't have thought this, had they known more about quality education. I felt it was incumbent upon me and John to share with them some of our higher horizons, so their aspirations for the children's educational experiences could rise. There is no doubt whatsoever that the board was overwhelmed with work and concerns. However, there was always doubt in my mind about the wisdom of concentrating with such determination on board members' development in terms of ability to run an organization, and neglect, month in and month out, to help them develop knowledge and judgment regarding the *content* of the organization they were learning to run so competently. On this, John and I deeply disagreed. I thought, with OEO critics, that the educational part of CDGM was, under John, and in sharp contrast to Tom Levin's CDGM, very much the stepchild.

As a result of this situation the best I could do was write reports to the board at regular intervals: detailed, informative, opinionated reports, which went as much into the philosophy of each of our plans and accomplishments as into the facts. The first such report was sent to each board member and to John in February—when we received the second grant. It was a detailed outline of my "launching" and "quality building" ideas. The second report, delivered March 11, was an explanation of our philosophy of who should teach. The April 17 report listed our achievements, major problems, and what we hoped to emphasize and do by June. The June 30 report brought the board up to date on recent events in our part of the program, and laid out explicit plans for the summer, when I would be in Washington. According to various members of the board, these reports were neither read nor discussed in meetings. It was my belief that had John done more with the board in the educational arena, many later problems with OEO regarding the quality of the program, overcrowding, etc., could have been avoided.

There were other efforts; other areas of tension and dissension. I was for pushing parent involvement in the actual children's program. Parents taught. Parents were on committees. Parents were in on policy decisions. Fine. Outstanding. Basic to our success. Yet anyone who worked in the communities could see that many, many parents were still *sending their children* to the center. They weren't in on it. I thought we should, through board letters to chairmen and through area staff teams, almost insist, at least over minor resistance, that any child attending the center must, except in the most extraordinary circumstances, have a family member willing to be scheduled at regular intervals by the resource teachers and trainees, to serve as a volunteer teacher, or cook, or toy-maker, or social service worker, *while* the children were in session, so he or she could get some of the feeling of a "freedom program." This would have helped solve our excess children problem. It would have increased the impetus we were providing parents in learning about educational possibilities and pushing public schools toward improvement. It would have given a spark to more older brothers or sisters, or fathers, or mothers, or whoever participated from the child's family.

Those to whom I presented this view welcomed volunteer parents, but hesitated to stress any personal view: such as that parents should participate in Head Start classrooms. I wasn't for requirements, either. But I think leaders should make available, clearly, their opinions on important topics, and shouldn't defect from sharing well-grounded conclusions. The board didn't write to chairmen on this matter. In many communities there was far less involvement than CDGM liked to admit; some of it inevitable; some correctable, had we concentrated on it.

Our division and the ATGs were severely curtailed in what we could have done about this neglected problem, because the COs felt that parents were their property. We, too, thought it their prerogative to head work done with parents. However, they did nothing about urging parents into classrooms. When, I've always wondered, is failure to fulfill obligations on the part of one group legitimately an invitation for another concerned group to cross territorial boundaries and do the undone task? We didn't know. We feared to be called worse names than we already were being called, so we did nothing. "It's *their* job," we said. Always, anywhere, evidently, an acceptable excuse.

Lack of men in each center was something that troubled me a lot too. Not only do research and common sense agree that virile men in leadership roles are essential to changing aspiration patterns in victimized and particularly matriarchal families, but my own experience and question-asking in CDGM had revealed that almost without exception, strong CDGM men had had an influential strong man in their early lives! Both strong men working constructively, and strong men working destructively, had had strong males in their backgrounds. Listen, for example, to Reverend James McCree, from the start a vital member of CDGM's board of directors: "Nobody's going to tell me what to do—not the system, not a white man, not FDP, not COFO or CDGM, and not a black man, either. I do what I think is right. I don't like to be threatened.

"I learned long ago that it's possible to stand up and hold out for who you are. I was the baby of my family. Had four sisters and seven brothers. My mother died when I was a baby. One night the Klan sent my father a letter saying they were going to whip my brother because my brother was working for a Klansman who didn't pay him enough, and he had said so.

"The Klansmen came around that night to get the boy. Dad went out instead—with his shotgun. He said, 'Anything you got to say to him, you just say to me and my friend here.' The Klansmen laughed nervously, said they were just having a little fun, just wanted to scare the boy a little, and retreated.

"I grew up knowing it was possible to stand up against whites—or against anything."

Reverend James McCree went on to a long string of darings and defiances. A white beat him up in Quitman because, as a twelve-year-old, he dared to use a white men's room. He worked for an insurance company and traveled for business, education, and pleasure, "because I didn't care who wanted me to, I wanted to see things." At the insurance company he supervised eight white men. "I didn't care who liked it, I was better at the job than them, and someone who needed the Negro customers I could get was willing to hire me." When he was older, and back in Quitman, Mississippi, a white man called him an SOB—a crazy black SOB. McCree said, " 'One of us is going to die!' He said he'd kill me for talking like that. I said, 'Try; I'll kill you first.' He ran.

"I lived in Laurel. Lots of people didn't like me. I wouldn't use their back doors. If I couldn't sit in the living room, I didn't go in. They said I acted like a nigger raised up North. I didn't act like a Mississippi nigger. I was uppity. I didn't care what they said. I've never been accountable to anyone but me."

He was ordained as a minister. He got into civil rights work early. His congregation was fearful, and objected. He cooperated with the NAACP in the beginning, helping with voter registration, but thought procedures of long courtroom fights were too slow. He advocated a more militant approach. Direct action. "They started to put Interstate 59 through our part of town. They cut us off from getting in and out. I stirred up the people and met with City Council to protest. I went to City Hall to see the street commissioner. He told me I was a troublemaker, doing no good. I should go away. I said, 'I didn't come to see you anyway, I came to see the top men—you're nothing but a hired hand.' I got people to go with me to see the mayor. The mayor told the commissioner to go speak to the people. The commissioner said, 'How are you, boys.' I said to him, 'There are no boys here, commissioner, only well-grown older men.' We got the street the way we wanted it. Through this, the people learned that if they would unite their forces, they could accomplish something."

In 1964, now in Canton, he allowed a Freedom School to house itself in his church. He and a few friends were the first to let whites stay in their homes. His brother's house was bombed. Other houses nearby were bombed.

"My congregation was scared to death. I told them you can't be good Christians if you're not good citizens, and good citizens live by their convictions. Some members of the congregation came to my house and told me I couldn't continue in civil rights. I said to them, 'I will believe and belong where I want. I will continue my meetings. I will continue voter registration, and insisting that our part of town be like their part of town. I will also continue being your preacher. If you're finished, please leave, I have to watch TV now.' "

One night at a mass meeting, police circled. "I told them they could circle all they wanted, but they were not to set one foot on our property unless they wanted to leave their guns outside and join our meeting. They didn't bother us.

"We got a lot of threatening phone calls at the church. I said to the whites, 'Go ahead and destroy our Methodist Church if you like, but if you do, keep in mind that I will not rebuild; I will bring my entire congregation to *your* Methodist Church. They didn't bother us. And my congregation kept coming. They kept contributing to our work. They kept praying. Of course, there was a big drop in attendance, and in my income, which dropped from a hundred and fifty dollars a week to nine dollars a week at one point, but others came to our meetings, more courageous ones. Lots of people still hate me. Some call me a Tom, some call me a Black Nationalist; I couldn't care less. I do what I do. Whites respect me. They know they can't push me around."

For this kind of reason, I was anxious for CDGM, again through the director, board, and area teams, to stress the importance of each community committee considering the active young men in their areas as teaching candidates, and trying, where possible, to hire at least one in each center. I thought that because of the familylike relationships our children had with their whole community, a young man of this kind, although not their father, would serve the purpose almost as well as that type of father, which most of them didn't have. At least it would have been an improvement over surrounding the children with more community-dominating, home-dominating, and now center-dominating women. Nobody claimed to feel otherwise, but CDGM leadership was too busy, and nothing consistent was done about it.

Through the morass of special projects, special problems, and the details of immense daily operational administration, the weightiest matter on my mind in preparation for pulling myself out was how to bring varied, stimulating, sensitive people to CDGM to work next to the local people. Until we had more such people actually (but temporarily) in centers to serve as spurs and samples, and until we had more such people available (but *not* at supervisory levels keeping people dependent) in areas to do team teaching with ATGs, we weren't going to be able to keep up what seemed to me to be our diminishing rate of progress. Courses, correspondence, and crash workshops had carried us an amazingly long way, but personal contact and personal influence had always been a need. Now summertime was coming, and with it a whole world of personnel possibilities not in the picture during the school year.

When the second grant had been signed in February, Jule Sugarman had written into it approximately double the number of resource teacher positions we had expected. He did this because he was worried about our untrained teachers. He wanted to ascertain that we would have enough immediately able people in each unit. But budgeting positions and finding able early educators in Mississippi (or anywhere) are two different matters. With Jule's intention and Mississippi's scarcity as motivation, John and I had made a decision that, as we realized only later, had not been ours to make. We had decided not to announce these extra positions for additional open community committee hiring to fill exclusively with more poor people.

Presumably, committees had already done their best to fill CDGM teaching positions with the most promising people they had. We had in mind saving these positions till summer. Then Mississippi public school teachers would be on vacation and the more appropriate could surely offer many things to temporarily assist our learning teachers. Then Mississippi Negro college students would be needing summer jobs to enable them to finance future years in college, and we might be able to intrigue some of the more open-minded with our concepts of education—an act which might influence them throughout their future public school teaching careers. Then we might do our bit to help race relations in the state by enticing Mississippi *white* college students—of whom we as yet had none, and who were sometimes more liberal than their parents—into taking a trial summer plunge into integration by working with us. And then we could follow the precedents of the 1964 COFO summer and the 1965 CDGM summer by bringing in suitable out-of-state specialists, teachers, and college students to keep up healthy (and new in Mississippi) intercommunication between groups and colors.

There was increasing feeling in and around CDGM against "experts." But how do you train in meaningful ways without trainers? This plan would avoid the issue of experts, but would bring in semi-enriching staff. People were afraid of being dominated. This would circumvent that problem too. The extra workers wouldn't have been around for initiating or even for reopening, and they wouldn't be around come autumn. Clearly, and more so if we stressed the point, they would *have* to see themselves as temporary and noncentral in holding up our extraordinarily awkward edifice.

John and I should've taken our idea to the board for approval. John took scads of things to the board for approval; but, in the opinion of many observers, not always the most important things. I shouldn't have lifted a finger toward implementing the idea until the board had spoken officially. Frankly, largely because of the boredom the board had previously exhibited toward educational aspects of the program, neither of us thought of it. Which doesn't excuse us. The road to hell is paved with . . . I did, however, discuss these thoughts with Social Service Division Director Sam Howze and Area Administration Division Director Jesse Paris. I listened long to their reactions. There were none of note, except friendly, amused acquiescence and the admonition to "get students with special interests, not specialists."

I also discussed the idea of summer enrichment people with ATGs, three times during February, March, and April workshops. I emphasized the point that those hired by community committees to work *in* centers would be under the *jurisdiction* of community committees, as were all other center employees. If summer people didn't work out, they could be dismissed. I emphasized another point, one about which ATGs expressed some feelings of insecurity: Extra people hired for the summer by Central Staff, as roving Central Staff or temporary area staff helpers, would be *temporary* and *teammates*. They would give more on-the-job, on-the-spot aid in the field than Mary and I could manage to give. They would *not* be supervisors of ATGs. ATGs said little, asked a few questions, talked about the plan a bit, and didn't seem too interested one way or the other. They agreed to discuss the idea with their area staff teammates, and relay back responses so we could tell how the wind was blowing before doing anything definite.

Being as insensitive to hidden innuendos (*i.e.*, silence) as many professionals are in their dealings with the poor, I saw no significant dissent. So I asked John for permission to go ahead with recruiting and screening from each of the above-outlined categories. On a first-come-first-serve basis, community committees could hire a candidate who suited them. Hopefully, this would work out to one white per center to help us meet our neglected obligation to OEO to try to integrate. Centers could have other summer workers, many of whom were predicted to be Negroes, if their committees so desired. No center would be forced to take a person from this pool. And of course no assignments would be made. John rather reluctantly agreed that I should undertake this project. I knew that many poor people *were* primarily concerned with effective education for the children, and with constructive rapid reform in all areas of their lives. Not realizing that the balance of pressures on them and the degree of turmoil within them had shifted as severely as it had, I mistakenly thought that John, Mary, *et al.*, would support community people in keeping progress in these directions uppermost in all of CDGM's actions. So commenced my solo flight into what soon emerged as CDGM's most infamous, internal catastrophe up to that time.

Meanwhile, as a routine compliance to OEO regulations for teacher recruitment, John's assistant Dave Flemming had placed ads for volunteers and teachers. ("Formal training or teaching credentials are not necessary. We can train teachers, but we cannot train people to love and enjoy noisy, active children.") in a number of local newspapers. The returns began to pour in just at this time. It turned out that no one had been assigned to deal with responses, and that no one cared to do it. Therefore it was agreed that Dave would reply to inquiries with packets of materials about CDGM, and I would then follow up with further correspondence, screening, etc., of those who persisted. Thus I found myself coping with the 457 people answering the three ads run in the Jackson *Clarion-Ledger*, the 143 people who had read the Jackson *Daily News*, the 335 people responding to ads in the Greenville Delta *Democrat Times*, the 214 people answering announcements in the Gulfport-Biloxi *Daily Herald*, the 84 people answering the *Commercial Appeal*, the 117 people responding to the McComb *Enterprise Journal*, the 132 folks who had read the Holly Springs *South Reporter*, the 114 people picked up through the Meridian *Star*, and the 22 people inquiring because of ads run in the Vicksburg *Evening and Sun Post*.

Also as a matter of routine OEO required efforts to advertise widely for capable teachers and helpers. I had, in February, studied lists of colleges at the public library, compiled a list of those that sounded appropriate, composed a two-page description of CDGM's special features and specifications for the kind of assistance we needed, written a cover letter, and sent the material to placement offices at every college and junior college, black and white, *in* Mississippi, and to eighty-two out-of-state colleges known for good departments in areas relevant to CDGM's needs. At this very period this project began to "pay off," too; if one could call it that. According to the most accurate count we could get, not counting the 1,618 newspaper respondents, approximately 3,500 college students wrote to us—to me, as immediately became clear. We really didn't have a personnel officer, and everyone consulted felt that I was the logical person to handle the situation.

To add fat to the fire, another talent-scouting project I'd been engaged in since the unfunded autumn began to yield results. I had thought that perhaps some of the nine colleges in the country which operated on the nonresident work-term plan might be interested in sending us some students to work in Centers. I'd spent quite a bit of time on the phone and writing back and forth to Mrs. Dorothy Scott at Antioch, Mr. Cary Smith at Goddard, Mr. John Hamilton at Wilberforce, Mr. Hugh Allen at Beloit, etc., with only one resulting worker. She was a lovely girl from Antioch named Mary Dettweiler, whom I had happily met at the train station and driven to Hollandale in the Delta, which had requested such a person. Suddenly, some of these schools had students available, and intensified correspondence about individuals.

On April 25 I sent a memo to John's second assistant, Abron Wells, responsible for administrative matters, describing our plans and asking how many positions were available and at what salaries.

I never received a reply to this memo. No one seemed to know how many jobs were empty. But CDGM was a leaky sieve and a den of intrigue that spring, and regardless of what *I* didn't know on the subject, the Freedom Democratic Party (FDP) had lots of information about it. The next day Lawrence Guyot, FDP chairman, and Mrs. Annie Devine, FDP Health and Welfare chairman, sent a letter to CDGM committee chairmen "strongly recommending" that they hire Mississippi college students to fill CDGM's "200 jobs." FDP felt that this would "have the effect of increasing and broadening" their strength in Mississippi.

I was somewhat skeptical of FDP's abrupt interest in CDGM. Its scattered volunteers had seemed to CDGMians to be engaged in various sabotage campaigns in our communities prior to this letter. I was interested in FDP's view of CDGM's educational goal as providing Negro children with "order, stability, and . . . training." I would have thought we were working, at a different age level, toward FDP's own freedom goals.

I seriously doubted that the kind of refunding support we would need to force OEO's hand if it came to another showdown would come from two hundred Negro Mississippi college students, rather than from well-connected Northern students and their powerful senators, etc. Nor did I think we could afford to turn our backs on talents offered by out-of-state students, as Mississippi institutions didn't specialize in the kinds of experience we needed. But I smiled to myself that at last I had pleased FDP; finally, after having been considered the bourgeois enemy of the people for a year by many volunteers, I had inadvertently managed to come up with a common desire. (Alas, as I soon learned, FDP's CDGM informants had given FDP to believe that in-state students would be hired over my dead body—that I was trying to "sneak in" exclusively out-of-staters. My purpose? To "take jobs" from poor people because in my lofty, aristocratic manner, I considered them incompetent! I soon became more the enemy than ever.)

But at the time I was too frantic, scurrying and crawling around the floor of my office and bedroom at home sorting stacks of categories of correspondence, to know what was happening in the outer—or under, depending upon one's point of view—world. When out-of-state candidates returned the applications we sent them and seemed serious, I phoned them at their respective colleges, and interviewed them for ten to twenty minutes apiece. I was trying to get a feeling of their personality and motivation, and trying to give them the breathless, overwhelming, poor-people-governed nature of CDGM. Of course I failed at both. People's true natures and inadequacies don't always come through on the phone. People pick out of one's communication that which they *can* hear, after their own unconscious screening mechanisms reject the rest of what you have said.

We didn't do telephone interviews with in-state applicants, but sent them a letter thanking them for their responses and inviting them to an ATG workshop where our film, *Chance for Change,* would be shown and our program discussed.

The letter to in-staters enclosed a two-page listing of our center names and the counties in which they were located and explained: "The CHILD DEVELOPMENT GROUP does not have any Centers in Jackson. We have Centers in 30 counties from the Delta to the Gulfcoast. Please check ANY PLACE ON THE LIST IN WHICH YOU *COULD* WORK, and return the list to us."

The movie was announced and shown again on Monday, May 16, at 7 P.M., Tuesday, May 17, at 7 P.M., Wednesday, May 18, at 10 A.M., Thursday, May 19, at 7 P.M., and Friday, May 20, at 7 P.M. We tried to be quite flexible and conscientious in hopes that we could lure Mississippi whites and Negro college students into our "Communist" lair. But after reading the address of Moman's Warehouse (an all Negro community) and discovering that we had no job openings in Jackson itself, our list of in-state applicants dwindled appreciably.

The nearly five thousand inquirers with whom I'd been communicating and about whom I'd been keeping records, were now down to about one thousand serious applicants. I typed master lists with applicants' names, addresses, phone numbers, choices of assignments should these specific communities want them, and reasons why communities might find each candidate desirable. I got little help on this. The number of staff members in the teacher development and program for children division's central office was now at an all-time peak, but this only meant that we now had, besides Mary and myself, an administrative assistant, a secretary, a half-useful clerk, and a clerk who shortly was dismissed for utter incompetency. (And *that,* in view of CDGM's standards of "qualified," was wondrously incompetent.) Mary was totally occupied with all our other projects. She was also extremely ambivalent about using out-of-state workers for the summer. So we agreed that this one "small" segment of our work would be handled by me.

Mrs. Carolyn Stevens, the administrative assistant Mary had hired in March, was extremely ambivalent about everything. To add to her misery, we had unintentionally miscast her. It soon turned out that in spite of her initial excitement about the job, she hated all the harassing details related to being the administrative assistant in a hair-raising wrestling division such as this, and she did admirably well, though she felt I was tryng to get rid of her, when I urged her to transfer to the less-active, less-white social service division. Meanwhile, she was wretched and angry, and while Mary and I had many long, long sessions with her trying to work out tasks, general responsibilities, and working relationships she could tolerate, she refused to have anything to do with the summer hiring program.

Our first and only secretary, Lorrie Tremper, who joined CDGM from FDP in April, frequently expressed her dim opinions of CDGM as a whole (a sellout to deceive the poor), and of our division in specific (run by white girls). She had little use for whites who had come to Mississippi to work. (Lorrie was a white who had come to Mississippi to work.) So I did the master lists myself.

Because of this absurd understaffing, caused both by our overzealousness in wanting a foolishly low overhead, sensibly bottom-heavy organization and by lack of capable applicants earlier, I hoped to hire several of the most promising summer applicants for our office. They could each be responsible for a section of our division's work, and could help ATGs, either by working on all educational problems in several areas, or by working on several "subjects" in all areas. We had had a few vacant professional positions since the start of the second grant, but no one had made any specific suggestions as to who should fill them.

My situation was becoming desperate. How long could I go on *offering* jobs to eager-to-get-settled candidates, and yet not *promising* jobs? Anxious applicants called daily, by the dozens, wanting a decision. Were they accepted or not? Most of the college students, out-of-staters as well as local people, needed summer incomes, and had to seek other employment if we were not going to decide soon. Some of the cream of the crop had already withdrawn. So, on April 30, after getting John's permission "if the board agrees," I sent a "proposal" to the board sketching John's and my thinking about enrichment summer staff. In it I requested permission to promise jobs, pool-style. To make definite commitments to students from each specified group.

Reverend James McCree, chairman of the CDGM board and leader of the Movement poor black faction in the organization, said the plan was "all right." The board was very busy with urgent administrative concerns, he told me. I should just go on ahead with this. No one had time to bother with a written reply. Just be sure not to assign people to centers, he said. Taking his word turned out to be a grave error. I should've been smart enough to know that in many past instances Reverend McCree had, for his own personal and political reasons, said one thing to Central Staff, and another to community people with whom he had a lot of influence. I should have been self-protective enough to refuse to do anything further without written authority. I should have been astute enough to know that simply having a good plan and going about it in a reasonable way, communicating actions throughout, is not enough. One must cope with the climate. I should have known that the chief issue currently concerning Reverend James McCree and many others wasn't enriching our educational program, but white vs. black power. I say these things not bitterly, but with the clarity of rejudgment that retrospect lends any scene. I blundered obliviously onward.

To those who didn't seem right enough for us to give precious salaries I wrote: "Due to the tremendous response we have received from our ads and placement office notices, we unfortunately do not have enough jobs to go around. I wish we could offer you a job, because I am sure you would be a big help to our program, but we just simply do not have more positions available now.

"We welcome your help if you can give us volunteer time. We cannot pay transportation expenses or salaries, but we can always use talent and dedication. Please let us know if you would like to help us in this way."

And to the others, oh impending doom, after more conversations and correspondence to ascertain which of their credits and experiences John's and my formula allowed us to count in finding the correct niche on the still pending salary scale (the same scale by which our own trainees and resource teachers were to be retroactively paid if whoever was holding the thing up ever ratified it, and after filling in the blanks as befitted each case, I wrote, oh ill-chosen decision: "We are very glad that you will be with us this summer. We will expect you around———. Your salary will be———. You will be receiving more specific information in about two weeks. See you soon!"

In my diary I wrote: ". . . and Al called at 3 this morning to say the Bolton Center burned down. He asked if I could collect toys, materials, etc., and get them out there in the morning: they want to hold classes outside, today, if possible. . . ."

CHAPTER 36

THE APPROACH OF THE BLACK PANTHERS

"Move over, or we'll move on over you"

. . . After a few steps in the darkness you will see strangers gathered around a fire; come close, and listen, for they are talking of the destiny they will mete out to [you]. . . . They will see you, perhaps, but they will go on talking among themselves, without even lowering their voices. This indifference strikes home: their fathers, shadowy creatures, *your* creatures, were but dead souls; you it was who allowed them glimpses of light, to you only did they dare speak, and you did not bother to reply to such zombies. Their sons ignore you; a fire warms them and sheds light around them, and you have not lit it. Now, at a respectful distance, it is you who will feel furtive, nightbound and perished with cold. Turn and turn about; in these shadows from whence a new dawn will break, it is you who are the zombies.[34]

For while we were busy moving with the myths of the mother country, capturing the left-outs and helping them catapult into the capitalist system, bringing a nice kind of neocolonialism to a black Mississippi still living in medieval days, complete with midwives, superstitions, taboos, and tribal chieftains, and inadvertently paving the way for the bourgeois settlers and overseers who certainly soon would follow in our pioneering footsteps; while we were piously scurrying about doing these things, the sons of the slaves were building their bonfire bigger and bigger. Big enough now, that suddenly ravenously furious flames leapt over to where we were, ferocious enough to destroy us. These sons *did* ignore us. We *did* feel furtive; fat and sleek and smug in contrast to their hard, hating, hurting, black desperation. Now and then one of them, still not having conquered feelings of friendship and memories of warm relationship with us altogether, would slip secretly, ashamedly,

[34] Fanon, Frantz, *The Wretched of the Earth.* New York: Grove Press, Inc., 1963. From Jean-Paul Sartre's Introduction.

the TRUTH. Nobody don't sympathize with us, baby, and we can't wait for nobody. Move on over or, we're gonna move on over you. That's it, doll, just it, period, america and Europe are ending their reign.

I: Well, if America and Europe are in such a state of decadence, decrepitude, and imminent disaster, don't we have to work harder to stave off the end? I mean, the end of the whole human race?

HE: Maybe *you* do, honey. You're interested in the whole Goddamn human race. We don't really care what you do. We're only interested in Black folks.

I: Yeah, I understand that. You've made that point abundantly clear, but if there *is* no human race, because we all blunder into blowing ourselves up with nuclear weapons, then what black folks will be left for you to be interested in? Don't you have to concern yourselves with *people*, mankind, with a corner of yourselves?

HE: You know what I answer to that: We care about Blacks only. If Blacks can't make it this time, God Bless the destruction of the whole phony mealy-mouthing human race. Maybe the time's up for people anyway.

I: You guys are vindictive enough to prefer total extermination than more procrastination.

HE: You're brilliant tonight.

I: You make no distinctions between "bad whites" and "good whites."

HE: Of course not. We've been around watching long enough to know there *are* no good whites.

I: Tom Levin is no different from the Grand Dragon Wizard, or whatever he calls himself?

HE: That's right.

I: I know you think that. I'm not arguing with you, but can you explain it to me? I know you think I'm dense, but it doesn't make sense to me.

HE: Tom's worse than the Klan Wizard. All of you, you're much more dangerous. Because if you admit the TRUTH, you know that whites have a propensity for prejudice. It's just in the normal nature of the white man. He can't help it. History has proven it. It's a congenital racial weakness. He oversimplifies everything, generalizes, categorizes. Some whites want to do good, cure poverty, rescue the poor Black bastard and all that, but you're all still categorizing. The man running the Poverty Program; he isn't dealing with me, ______________, an individual.

He's CURING THE ILLS OF ALL US IGNORANT NIGGERS, in capital letters, in a category. Then, this white weakness is accentuated by the problem of personal personality development. I mean, each kid gets made to feel inferior by his superior white middle-class parents, so he has to take it out on somebody, so the nameless nigger is the scapegoat. Each white is a victim of the racial weakness toward prejudice, and also a mirror of his group's attitude toward it. Huh? Oh, yeah, sure, the liberals, too. When all the words are washed away, look where they live. Look what they don't give. Bitter? Not me! I don't give a Goddamn about them: the beautiful self-righteous liberals! They're just the same as the rest of the middle-class whites except more of them are Jews and they have an additional opportunity for superiority because they enjoy looking down on typical middle-classians *as well as* on the dear deprived colored folks, for whom they do a little guilt duty.

I: That's what us whites in CDGM are doing too, right? I mean, we're doing our guilt duty more intensively, and maybe more usefully, but we're still feeling superior and motivated by guilt? There's no place in your system for the belief that maybe some people care a lot about fairness and justice, right?

HE: You look good, baby, but you're motivated just like everybody else. You're striving to feel good. Satisfied. Unguilty. It's just that you have a more refined conscience, you, John, Tom, Mary, all your crowd; you just settle for less in the way of appeasement to your own consciences. Your standards of what's decent are a little more developed, so you drive yourselves harder, you're more self-sacrificing. But that's not because you believe in fairness and justice; shit on fairness and justice, don't give me that goody-goody crap; you're motivated by having to tell yourself you are working for those things so you can stand yourself and sleep at night.

You girls'll sleep with Black men, and you'll all work for very little (between working for glorious salaries, of course), and you'll take a lot of beatings from us niggers, but it's all part of you trying to get on the right side—the winning side. You're smarter than some, so you *know* what color folks are the winning side of the soon-future. You wanna be on it, don't you? But, baby, *it's too late!* You can court us to hell with all your beautiful generosity and willingness to be kicked in the teeth, but you're like all of them: you're working to improve your image of yourself; working to keep your familiar world, only improve it a little. Well, it ain't improvable. We have to start all over with a right approach. You can't build on a rotten foundation, and that's what america, the white man's world, is.

I: Hasn't OEO helped then? Assuming what you say is true; but regardless of motivation. Wouldn't you say then that for whatever reason of weakness or Machiavellianism, or whatever you will, that OEO has helped by solidifying war-torn Negro ranks? By inadvertently posing as the enemy and accidentally getting you all furious and together?

HE: No. Definitely not. CDGM employed many people and paid out large sums of money in salaries, rent, and supplies for the Head Start Centers, etc. Because Black people were in such desperate need for money, We accepted it, without too many questions asked. Now We're not as angry. We're not as violent. whitey is safer. We're not as uncompromising and some of us even think We're not as poor. And that's exactly what Lynchum B. Johnson intended when he created the Poverty Program. How can anyone who's not angry, hostile, violent and uncompromising do the things that're necessary to liberate the Black people from america's strangle hold? We've been had again.

They tell us the reason We're in poverty is that We're dumb niggers, and if we will submit ourselves to a white head shrinker named Tom Levin, and a white lady who calls herself an "expert" in education named Polly Greenberg, and a rich white boy from the Philadelphia suburbs named John Mudd who wants to study us niggers so he can get his

Ph.D. from Harvard, We won't be poor anymore. Mudd came to Mississippi in a big expensive automobile to work with a lady named Marian White. She used to work for us. Now she works for him. He says he doesn't want money, but he gets $250 a week while the poor people don't. But he cares deeply about them. Why are Levin and Lynchum B. as bad as klansmen? They aren't, they're worse. Lynchum is a born, bred, and thoroughly seasoned southern cracker who's been around us niggers all his life and knows how to handle us. With pacification and diversion. George and Lurleen are shrewd and vicious. They use the direct gestapo method. So is Lynchum, but he knows how to deal with his darkies more successfully. For one thing, he distracted us with fighting over integration: the privilege to learn that We were no good till the white missionaries tamed us, and that we're still at the bottom of the white man's wonderful ladder. Only now We are sitting next to white children instead of sitting next to all Black children. What's the difference? Either way We learned We're rotten. But the trick worked. We fought about *that,* integration, for years, and that took up the energy We might have used sooner for our Revolution.

Lots of us ignorant niggers have fallen for all this: especially the Poverty Program. They don't understand. It isn't changing anything, except for the worse—quieting the burning baby so his screams won't save him from death. How're you going to improve a worm-ridden putrid maggot-writhing pot of food by adding vitamins? How're you gonna revive a stinking corpse by sprinkling perfume on it? There's only one answer, and it isn't pretty.

I: Would you be willing to tell me about it?

HE: No. That's Black business. But you can see what comes first: unveil your fraudulent do-good programs. Unmask the cast of lying characters. Drive you out of here. Then we can talk to poor people.

I: About . . . ?

HE: About. You can sweat about that one.

I: I think the Poverty Program has done a great deal of good: It's got a great many young, strong Negroes to the frustrated, end-of-the-line boiling point you're at.

HE: We would've gotten there anyway. The Poverty Program has pacified. It just makes us more work to agitate people again like they were when they were in the Movement.

I: The Poverty Program *is* expanding the understanding and compassion of many whites; people who were "decent" before, but it just seemed so remote from them; nothing they could do about it, personally. But that's irrelevant, isn't it?

HE: Utterly. We're not interested in the size of whitey's heart. We'll take what's ours, and let the Lord take care of the soul.

I: According to your philosophy, all you guys, I mean, solutions will never come for blacks through any amount or any speed of white dedication to change.

HE: Correct.

I: So the more serious and credible some of us are in our efforts, the more we distract people from what they really "should" do?

HE: That's right. The more people believe you, the more evil you are. A person like you, that poor folks like, love even, and they feel you care *really*, you are indescribably terrible. The harm you do can't be expressed. You may deter people for decades. Except, of course, We won't let you.

I: But you talk all the time about poor people participating in the democratic process; in decision making. They *like* CDGM. You think it's ethical to take it away from them? Smash it up? Poison them against anyone trying to get them on their feet so they can run it?

HE: We *used* to talk that way when we were naïve and trusted our glorious system of government; that it meant well. Now We don't say those things. Not till a later stage. You haven't been listening. Now we say, Lots of times it's right to lie for an honest end, or postpone for eventual greater good.

I: So then it's OK to tell people totalitarianly "what's good for them" because they don't know, and you know, and you're right.

HE: [a great grin].

I: How do you know you're right?

HE: History tells us.

I: I'm not as sure as you are that one group alone, solely, exclusively one group, is privy to the ultimate secrets of the universe.

HE: Don't you sometimes in some areas know more than other people?

I: Yes.

HE: In this area. Blackness, we know more than whites. And more than black folks who haven't had a chance to think it through. They'll all agree with us when We get through with them.

I: Brain-washing is acceptable?

HE: That's all *you* do; those Area Teacher Guides, you just stuff their mouths with words so they echo you; black bodies, white brains. You don't even mind if they talk like they resent you; you're proud that your little puppets can talk all by themselves. "It's good for them to express their feelings." No matter which way they think or what they decide, you've cast your spell over them, you can explain it; I told you, you're a much more dangerous bitch than a whole lot of these silly little white girls running around down here—because you're a master psychologist. And you're sexy. All the men are drawn under *that* spell. And you're a mother. All the women in the communities are under *that* spell. And you're not too conventional to scare them off like A WHITE LADY would, but then, you're not a beatnik like these other chicks either, so they feel a rapport with you.

You should leave. You're leaving wreckage in your wake. We'll have to hurt lots of black folks to get you out of their systems. And, baby, We'll have to hurt *you*. We'll have to beat the magic out of you, expose you as human, and WHITE, just another WHITEY, before We can fix it so you won't be able to use your sorceress skills anymore.

I: I know you'll do that. I believe you.

HE: So why don't you go? We don't want you here.

I: Because while I agree with everything you say in one way of thinking, I can see that, yes, I don't reject that, but on the other hand, I can see another side, so I get confused, and I don't see it as simply, or to be picturesque, I don't see it in as black and white terms as you do. That is, I understand that I might be innocently doing evil, but I'm not sure *you* aren't—also for theoretically good reasons. Probably social "progress" is a matter of each faction doing it's own kind of evil for it's own wicked motivations till we batter it out and something better emerges. I don't see it as "the good guys" and "the bad guys." You ex-Movement types are the feudal Lords down here, and you don't like anybody messing with your natives. That's part of the truth, too. You have a vested interest in seeing that the serfs stay as is, shackled by their own inadequacies and need to follow the leader.

HE: You don't know anything about Black people, you have no business saying anything.

I: There again, I agree that I, we whites, have no business interfering now in black business when we've screwed up for so long, but there're two sides to that too: Being black gives *you* a certain kinship and subtlety of communication, but it doesn't ordain you with supreme knowledge of all things—black people are black, and the nature of that is your domain. But they're also human, and other people here and there throughout the centuries have given *that* a little thought: speculations and agitations on the nature of being a human being is the "property" of poets and philosophers and historians and psychologists and writers and biologists and all sorts of people. I agree that it's presumptuous for whites to "know" all about what's good for Negroes, but doesn't it occur to you that it's kind of presumptuous for *you* to declare that you and yours and *only* you and yours, a select segment of radical you and yourses, are qualified to comment authoritatively on such a complicated and huge subject as humanness? Don't you thing its incumbent on all of us to have a little humility?

HE: Humility is the enemy of violent action. Niggers have always had humility. Now we need violent action to shock whitey out of his smugness.

I: Coming back to your Revolution, don't you need skilled people to lead it?

HE: A few. We have them. Mostly we need thousands of *angry* people. Those We have too. We're working on readiness. Sooner or later the right leader will appear: a man who is original and dazzling and defiant and full of reckless determination to ignite the readiness and craving into flames to burn your Goddamn world down. We can wait for that; for him. We're good at waiting.

I: So the fact that CDGM is trying to get people committed to risk being leaders is also irrelevant?

HE: Right.

I: Am I right in thinking that you all don't care much if people grow?

HE: You're right, you're right. Growing can come later. First is force. We have to get our people out of prison first.

I: If whites were trying to help do that, would you let them?

HE: No. You can't give people freedom.

I: Then each one has to work it through personally?

HE: Yeah.

I: Well, that's what CDGM is trying to do. Help people figure what they want and how they'll get it.

HE: There isn't time.

I: Is it a valid goal?

HE: Nothing's valid if it's whites interfering with Blacks.

I: Are *you* helping people stand up and think?

HE: whites can't. They make Blacks think in crooked circles.

I: But I asked you are *you* trying to get people to think?

HE: We're too busy.

I: Doing what?

HE: [*laugh*]

I: Seriously, going along with the idea that the only way to solve racial inequality in this country is to *do* it, push, shock, act, etc., accepting that, because much as I hate to think it, I s'pose it's true, so assuming that, then what're you guys doing about it? I should think the logical thing to do would be to make a comprehensive plan and go at it from all angles—*all* angles.

It helps a little if more kids get better education, if only so they can read radical literature and see the issues as you do. It helps if more people begin to *think, think, think*, because if you're right, if you *are* right, then with reading and thinking, most Negroes will see it your way. It helps if you work to get all services from health agencies. How can undernourished, sick people carry out as effective a Revolution as they could after you got them in good health? Use libraries, learn how to understand white politics and learn to maneuver triumphantly through them for your *own* goals? Learn to make ammunition and be excellent fighters, if you will, I don't care what, but it seems that unless you do lots of things to combat apathy, fearfulness, etc., you are not going to get very far, whatever your goal or technique.

I don't understand how blowing up everything can get you anywhere. And just on the straight Revolution level: Have you a "military" plan? You've got a somewhat formidable foe. Are you acquiring weapons? Mapping strategy? How will you achieve *your* goal, never mind anyone else's goal, if you're all the time smoking pot and drinking beer and sitting around in these all-night hate-white soul sessions?"

HE: The Urban League, the NAACP, all those fucked-up organizations, *they* stress self-improvement, and the masses haven't even heard of them. We don't need trained minds, just people who believe in the TRUTH. Our doctrines give more power than any amount of knowledge. Knowledge creates questions, uncertainty. Faith creates certainty. Baby, don't bother to worry about it. We'll take care of our own.

I: I wish to God I could believe that. I wish I could see that you're trying to get rid of us so you could *take over* CDGM, instead of getting rid of us so you can eliminate CDGM.

HE: There's your orientation showing through again! Her holiness, CDGM. We don't want it, dead or alive. We have a better way. You'll see.

I: When?

HE: When the time is ripe.

I: I wish I could see how you are ripening it.

HE: We don't have to. whitey is doing that for us with his sullen refusal to be human.

I: So ideally, what are whites supposed to do? If I stay out of the race problem arena, I'm a racist, selfish, etc. If I get in in conventional ways, I'm an ignorant worthless do-gooder. If I try to work *with* blacks in determining what they need and want and in serving as a catalyst for them to do it themselves, I'm dangerous and evil. No matter which of the three I do, I'm a phony who doesn't practice what she preaches, I'm salving my conscience, and I'm to blame for the sins of all my ancestors (who, incidentally, cared a lot and did a lot in these directions, too). You Jacobin blacks have renounced and denounced all problems having to do with whites, but are you saying I, as a white, am obliged to sever any feeling of responsibility I might have toward all problems having to do with suffering human beings, fairness, justice, etc.?

HE: Chick, I don't give a shit *what* you do. We're interested only in us.

I: We just don't even begin thinking in the same place, ________. I believe that all people are born with enormous potential. It's blank potential. It's psychic energy that can be developed into complicated patterns of priorities, choices, hierarchies, complementary designs, etc., to achieve what's best for that individual's growth toward ultimate fulfillment of all his innate capacities, another way of saying *real* satisfaction, pride, and joy—with the least harm done to others along the way.

Or that same mass of neither good nor bad potential can be blocked, distorted, twisted, etc., till it's self-destructiveness, general destructiveness, failure, bitterness, waste, and all that. I can't believe you that one race or another lacks this mass of potential.

But I also believe that if a group of any sort, in this case a black group, has systematically been deprived of all the opportunity and encouragement that lets the potential grow in *good* directions, then we have to self-consciously concentrate on compensatory arrangements to provide these opportunities and encouragements.

But my goal is the eventual evolution of all human beings, as a biological species, toward something close to "God's image," or whatever you want to call it—toward man's highest aspirations for his species throughout history. And I *do* believe in self-improvement, self-discipline; not in the Booker T. sense of suffer in silence, turn the other cheek, etc., and not in the sense that everyone else should turn their backs or step on you while you're improving and developing self-discipline, but I don't see how anybody's goals are going to be reached through tolerating weakness and laziness and negativeness in themselves. I mean politicians, professionals, parents, whites, blacks, *everyone* improve.

You say whites, even "good" whites, categorize Negroes. Well, what are *you* doing? Certainly you're categorizing them. Why can't we build individuals?

HE: You forget that individuals aren't as important or as powerful as the generative germinating strength of an *idea,* and an anger. You worry about numerical strength and organizational forms. Social upheaval comes from forces that are invisible. It comes from mass movement, provoked by pain, not by organizations with elaborate policies, programs, and procedures. We aren't concerned with individuals. We'll work relentlessly against you.

We're for a rejection of self. We're creating a new corporate identity. You whites call us "hate-mongering," "deplorable reverse-racists," "creating a bad image for Blacks just when the race picture is improving"; We've gotta do that now, nothing else worked. Our job isn't to fit into whitey's CDGM and lead the sheep toward whitey's absorption goal—it's to be sinister, to stir the masses! You say we aren't a program, we're just an accommodation to american racism, a response to anguish. Swell. Call it want you want, whitey, it's an important indicator of what's coming your way.

I: I didn't say that. The race picture, basically, *isn't* improving, and I *can* see the value of applied anger. But I don't *see* the constructive application of collective anger. I see instead the rapid growth of a new set of dictators. I see an urge to wipe out, not to create something better.

HE: All your sociologists and politicians have failed to accomplish anything through reason. Now it's our turn to do it through rage. It's valuable to burn the ambassador's limousine and urinate on Lynchum B.'s portrait, and stone the embassies, and slaughter white cheats stealing from Blacks in our neighborhoods. We've got a glue much more cohesive than your "information." We've got the cement of hatred. And we've got an ever-present enemy to goad us together: whitey.

I: Alright, alright, I never disagreed with that. But the white man is *still* ahead in the skills and tools of being on top. Why not work toward equalizing that? I don't see that smashing, slaughtering, rioting is enough. Sure it's a beginning, but what else? What actual good does it do anybody? What's the goal?

HE: We're getting there. The Red Chinese, the Africans, us, We're being bound closer and closer by the actions of whites. whitey can't survive another war. We'll reach our final cohesion when Russia and america go at it, and We'll defeat both. We don't have to do anything, whitey is doing it all for us as his rotten soul sinks in spiritual decadence and he nervously awaits the end of "civilization" as he likes it. The blue-eyed white devils lack the moral strength and courage to cast off their arrogance, and revive their jaded consciences.

They try to hide their record and to buy us off. Niggers don't need to read to know that. They *know*. We give solidarity to lonely people. Rehabilitation to wrecks from the underworld. Faith to those whom Christianity has disillusioned, charisma to those Christianity has crushed. We give accurate Black history instead of the stuff whitey has given us about our worthless selves.

We give Black folks courage to be themselves instead of the callous crushing whitey gives us; toothbrushes, the policeman-is-your-friend, slick hair, clean clothes and all. Your schools teach black equality and practice segregation. We practice separation and teach Black Supremacy. We're finished agreeing with our adversaries about what our goals should be so We'll become inconspicuous. We're finished being ingratiating,

> cringing sycophants, clowns to amuse the master, flatterers to sooth the master. We're finished making sneaky little forays against whitey to get a tiny bit of petty revenge.
>
> We're finished with CDGM's kind of colonialism. You don't think We're hard workers? It depends what you conceive the work to be. If the work is to get rid of the new colonialist We're doing it. You first. As I said, We've learned a lot from the MauMaus. We're going to do you like the MauMau's did to their victims: each man was expected to strike at the victim. The important thing wasn't to have him dead, it was for each man to take credit for a personal part in the killing–it was a collective "we" building act. Why don't you go home?

"Why don't I go home? Why don't I go home?" [my diary asks]. "Because though a handful of blacks preach hate, and hate is real, true, and something worthy of being preached, and because though they say 'we must do it ourselves,' and of course each person must, still, they dwell exclusively on one thing. We *can't* concentrate exclusively on one thing. One thing isn't real. When we insist on bending every thought and action toward one idea, it becomes unreal. Forcing all things to one idea distorts so many things that what was true is no longer true because it isn't in a true context, a context of what is; it stands alone, isolated. One bit of truth in isolation is a lie.

"I may go, of course I *will* go in a short or shorter time anyway, would've anyway, short or shorter being the only flexible factor, but why I haven't so far is that I don't believe life has spit up her centuries' old secrets of what it's all about and how to proceed to master it to a few young black men—anymore than it ever did to millions of others. I don't believe that they and they alone have divined the essence and solved all human problems. Conceited as it would be perceived to be by the Turks, I do believe there's still room for the rest of us in the search.

"But there it is. The fundamental difference between us that makes engagement together futile. I am searching; they are waging war. Both worthy aims, but incompatible.

"I don't know what to do. I never know what to do, but usually there's a current that kind of pushes us into doing what seems most sensible or meaningful at each moment, or season, or job choice-point, but now, more than ever in my life, I don't know what to do.

"I came here full of excitement about our experiment; full of excitement about discovering the dramatic features of a culture more or less new to me, that might hide the secret of how we can strengthen what is strong instead of ignoring it, and thus build better roads for people. But now I've seen too much. I'm constantly confronted with evidence that man's society isn't a congenial place for man. I don't think it's a racket; I just don't think it's a possible framework for most of mankind to survive in.

"I don't feel capable, anymore, of soaking myself in a useful project, and sustaining my confidence in it by not having time to look at surrounding reality. Surrounding reality is impossible, I think. What's the use of struggling with a manageable corner if the whole is impossible?

"No doubt those public servants who've developed calloused sensitivities can do more good, in the long run, than I can. Because their hardened softness gives them endurance, whereas my inability to exclude reality, by toughening and blindering it, gives me only a writhing, retching spirit, that makes me physically nauseous; an ominous feeling of anxiety that keeps me from sleeping at night with its sudden flashes of terror; a nasty looking red rash of repressed misery rambling up and down my arms; an exhaustion of compassion that makes me snap at people; and a generally disintegrated internal system of values and reference points.

"The young Turks are inconsistent, lazy, and sound like a recording of the books they drink in, but of course they're partially right. And what should we whites do?

"John and Mary seem to be reacting to this inhuman pressure toward facing our obsolescent selves and our untenable roles by becoming black. They no longer seem to be judging what we should do as CDGM's leadership in terms of community people's wishes or needs, or in terms of OEO's intentions regarding Head Start, or in terms of Tom's balance of these two divergent things, but exclusively in terms of what the rebels will think and "allow." Mary says she thinks it's very risky for me to plan to write a CDGM book, because *"they"* will never forgive me. I'm to judge what *I* should do solely in terms of what this subgroup thinks? They're not weak, they're just so sensitive to the truth in the Turks' views, and so sympathetic to their understandable anger, that they're losing touch with other criteria for judging our actions. It's their virtues that are causing them to forget what this project is supposed to be, and to guide it that way. It's their honest respect for needs that clash with their own that are causing them to substitute the value judgments of others for their own. It's their humility and democratic spirits that are causing them to stand by while the Turks tear this experiment of ours to bloody shreds. And I do believe it's their need to be accepted, too, by those with whom they've come to identify so strongly. It's torture to be white here. So they are becoming black.

"But I can't. So probably John and Mary will remain productive while I collapse; probably their greater flexibility is healthier than my psychic rigidity; probably their new identities will serve them adequately while my loss of identity will drive me insane. But I'm white. White. And white I'll remain. So I have to be honest in terms of that fact.

"The Turks may be right about what *they* have to do. But destruction isn't *my* goal, and hatred isn't *my* talent. I may well be working for the devil, but I'm me, and my métier is experimentation toward greater human growth and development; destroying the white world I'll have to leave for others, though it may be the more worthwhile of the two efforts. This context is no longer suitable for my approach, so I'll do it somewhere else. Maybe it's best for CDGM to become a snarling panther. I can't attempt to decide that. But *I'm* not a panther, and I can't stand either to pretend I am, or to try to work while being mangled by his marauding fangs.

"I'm weak? Yes. But I'll be weak in Washington from now on. There, at least, if I make it through the shock of re-entry, my weakness won't kill me. I'll be called insensitive, I'll be called controlling, yes, and also rigid, she refuses to learn, OK, and the bad true things, but where is the line between blowing with the wind (very flexible!) and hanging on to the string of the principle, even when the wicked wind is lashing in the silent skies, the skies that are impervious to principles and weaknesses, warriers and searchers alike?"

The truth is that whatever whites do, we *are* the victims: of our own race's refusal to give anything but hypocrisy and promises; of the vehement reaction of angry blacks who have given us many warnings. We have waited, and waited, and waited. What are we victims waiting for? It is as Martin Luther King wrote in 1963:

> . . . a submerged social group, propelled by a burning need for justice, lifting itself with sudden swiftness, moving with determination and a majestic scorn for risk and danger, [which] created an uprising so powerful that it shook a huge society from its comfortable base.
>
> Never in American history had a group seized the streets, the squares, the sacrosanct business thoroughfares and the marbled halls of government to protest and proclaim the unendurability of their oppression. Had room-sized machines turned human, burst from the plants that housed them and stalked the land in revolt, the nation could not have been more amazed. Undeniably, the Negro had been an object of sympathy and wore the scars of deep grievances, but the nation had come to count on him as a creature who could quietly endure, silently suffer and patiently wait. He was well trained in service and, whatever the provocation, he neither pushed back nor spoke back.
>
> Just as lightning makes no sound until it strikes, the Negro Revolution generated quietly. But when it struck, the revealing flash of its power and the impact of its sincerity and fervor displayed a force of frightening intensity. Three hundred years of humiliation, abuse and deprivation cannot be expected to find a voice in a whisper. The storm clouds did not release a "gentle rain from heaven," but a whirlwind, which has not yet spent its force or attained its full momentum.[35]

But not all Negroes involved in CDGM felt as the panther contingent felt. If we were listening to "the people," we had to *listen,* at least, to *all*

[35] King, Martin Luther, Jr., *Why We Can't Wait.* New York: Harper & Row, 1963, pp. 2–3.

of them. Sunflower County, where there were many CDGM centers the first summer, was the home of Senator Eastland. He reportedly said that CDGM would be re-funded in his county only over his dead body. Though OEO denied any connection between the good senator's sentiments and its own actions, it did *not* (coincidentally, of course) re-fund CDGM centers in Sunflower County when it re-funded the rest of CDGM.

When I had designed the ATG system, I'd asked Cora Flemming from Indianola to be an ATG. After CDGM got its second grant, and Sunflower didn't, I rarely saw Cora. The following is her account of how she, as one of the "puppets" the Panthers alleged I sought and spoon-fed with white lies, carried on during the next fundless year: "We ate all the black-eyed peas and hog jaw anyone else in the South did at midnight New Year's Eve, and I guess it did bring us *some* luck: We haven't got beat up by the police yet this year, and we haven't all died off yet from conditions here. And best of all, each year we convince one more white we're human. . . .

We had a successful CDGM program. During the unfunded winter, we thought we would be refunded too, along with the other CDGM counties, and we never stopped working.

"We had eighty-two volunteer staff members in Indianola alone. We had four hundred kids enrolled, but could only manage to pick up about two hundred fifty-five each day. We operated Indianola Community center, the Duchess Day Care, Shriver's Progress, and Johnson's Opportunity. Ruleville had another hundred sixty-eight kids.

"When we asked parents who had never helped us out to help, they said, 'Oh, sure, I didn't understand.' Then they'd give us a jar of fruit they'd put up, or some meat from their hog. We had community meetings once a week, and staff meetings also.

"Of course, since I was an ATG, I came to workshop every week, and that kept my hopes up. Polly had so much pep and hope, and we were doing so much in workshop at Beulah, you just *couldn't* think you were finished. The resource teachers from here came to November workshop; this kept their spirits up, too.

"By Christmas, we began to think maybe a CAP board existed in Sunflower County, organized by whites behind our backs. We couldn't say how long it had been in existence, as we were not told of it. CAPS, OEO says, are supposed to be widely advertised to the community, and everyone who wants is supposed to be in them, but *we* learned of this through CDGM, who had been told by OEO, that there was a CAP here that was 'almost ready to be funded.' We heard through CDGM who heard through OEO in Atlanta, that we would probably have to 'cooperate' with that, and not be in CDGM any more.

"So we searched out the CAP board members in our county. No one would tell us who they were, *if* they were, anything. When we finally began to find out, it turned out all the board members were white except some picked Negro school teachers, and one farmer. You know how much teachers represent us! They all said they didn't have any idea how they got on the board. They either were such white men's Negroes that they were afraid to talk to us, their own people, or else such puppets that they actually *didn't* know how they got on it. We couldn't get any sense out of them. They had no ideas about program, of even what CAP and Head Start *was* according to OEO guidelines, they didn't know anything about freedom; all they knew was money, money, money—they all explained that to us. But we tried to work with them. If that's what OEO wanted us to do, we'd try.

"Next, according to OEO guidelines, we followed all the correct procedures. We sent a committee of us to visit the chairman of the CAP board, Mr. Allen. We asked could we combine the two programs, as ours was already functioning, and we'd had experience. He said definitely not, this was to be a *new* program, the right kind. We asked if theirs would be integrated. He said definitely not. He's a planter, an enemy of the people, if you go by his past record. We have two kinds of whites up here: worse and worser. He's one of the second kind. We asked why hadn't there been a public meeting. He said he'd meet with two or three of us, but he didn't want no public nigger meeting. We asked how was his board organized—were there elections? He said, 'I don't know myself.' Later we asked again, and he said, 'I told the nigger leaders to organize themselves, and this is what they came up with.'

"Then, since he refused to let us combine, we asked him to sign our delegate agency proposal, to work under them, if we had to, instead of with CDGM, if we had to. He said he couldn't sign it till he'd read it. When he read it, he said, 'This is good. We haven't got a proposal yet. And we haven't got any idea how OEO wants us to write one. We can just copy this and add to it.' Bryce Alexander was there, too. He was chief of police when the library demonstrators were arrested and the lady's house burned down and the child's arm was broken. He had a national record for brutality; personally. But now he had resigned from that, and had been named our Community Action Program director! Because he cared so much about us.

"Mr. Allen might have signed our proposal, he looked like he might, but Mr. Alexander signaled to him not to. He wanted to arrange something first. Something where the CAP board handled all the money and hiring, and we could baby sit the children, like we Negro women have *always* baby sat those white folks' children. They wouldn't even sign the proposal to show they'd *received* it. So we left, and took it with us, and sent it to him registered so he'd have to sign for it. They didn't want us in with them, even *under* them, because they're so weak and ignorant of all this, and we're so dedicated and informed that when we're next to them, they look like idiots.

"After that, according to OEO guidelines, the CAP board was supposed to let us know their decision on our application for delegate agency within fifteen days. They didn't think enough of us to do that. They finally told CDGM in Jackson, 'No,' and CDGM had to tell *us*, right across the street from where they were in the first place! Right across the street, their life-long neighbors in Indianola. They thought we weren't smart enough for them to talk to directly.

"Next, after we had over and over asked Mr. Allen to have public meetings, they hired a Negro teacher to run their new Head Start, and he came to one of our regular CDGM area meetings of about two hundred people, and invited us to a CAP meeting. This was the first in all that time we got ourselves even invited to!

"When we got there, there was only Allen, Alexander, and one more man! We said, 'Where are the others? Where are the Negro board members?' They said the Negroes didn't know about the meeting. We said, 'How can they not *know* about their own board meeting? Don't you notify your board members when they're supposed to have a meeting? Besides,' we said, 'that's not true, because we told them ourselves we'd been invited to come and meet with them tonight.' Then Allen said, well, he'd told them to stay at home. We got mad. We said, 'Are they little kids or something? You say stay home and they say yes sir and stay home?' Allen answered, 'We thought you would feel freer.' I said, 'That's great! Are you trying to tell me that you thought we'd feel freer talking to white planters and police chiefs famous for trying to kill us, than we would feel with members of our own race?'

"Then Alexander said he had written CDGM a letter rejecting our delegate agency proposal on the grounds that Sunflower County School Board had run a successful Head Start the first summer of Head Start, and didn't need any 'help' from us now.

"All through our visit Allen kept using the word 'nigger.' We kept interrupting him, and asking him not to. Then he would turn red, and a minute later forget, and use it again. We asked him how had Alexander gotten hired to be director? Allen said he'd been brought before the board and approved. We asked how come Alexander suddenly had so much interest in eradicating poverty, when last month all he wanted was to eradicate the poor? Allen said, 'I'll speak for him, he's been converted, he's a changed man!'

"Meanwhile, a solid hand-picked Negro 'advisory committee' was sitting there. According to OEO guidelines. We asked one of these Negro men what kind of advice he gave this board. We got the idea that the kind of advice *he* gave was silent advice, because he answered so low we couldn't hardly hear him. I told him as an advisor, he was supposed to be on top of that board, telling them what was right to do. With the scaredest look I ever saw, he said, 'Oh, no, Cora, you got it wrong!' (Later he came 'round to my house and told me our group has bad morals, that's why we shouldn't be running a children's program. I told him, 'Don't you dare ever tell me one more word about bad morals! If you do, I'll tear up your church and all your fine saintly deacons and I'll tear up your school and all your fine upstanding teachers, and I'll tear up your white people. We colored women know more about *their* morals than their wives do!)

"At the same meeting, I asked Mr. Alexander, 'Please may we see *your* proposal, since you have rejected ours? That must mean that yours is better.' He said we would have to go to Atlanta or Washington to see it, and anyway, just to take his word, they have accepted everything in it. I said I didn't see why we should have to go that far to see a proposal we were supposed to have been part of planning. Surely he had one on file? He said he couldn't let me see it without the consent of his board! Those people think they can tell Negroes anything, and we're too dumb to know our rights!

"Frank Glover from CDGM Central Staff was with us that time. He said he had the right to help people who weren't getting their rights. I guess the CAP people reported this to OEO, because the next week OEO sent a telegram to CDGM saying its *own* grant would be cut off if any more staff members went into Sunflower County!

"Then Mr. Allen invited us to a public meeting at City Hall for next week. We received an open verbal invitation. Their assistant director canvassed us on the day of the meeting and told us to be sure not to forget.

"We all met, about thirty of us, and were standing on the sidewalk in front of City Hall, where the meeting was supposed to be at 7:30 P.M. Police in crash helmets started peeping out windows and doors. A few people went in, but someone told them rudely to 'get up and get out' till the board members came in and got seated; the chairs were reserved for them. The police carried billies and blackjacks that they kept twirling. They told us if they wanted us, they'd send for us. Others kept their hands ready on their pistols. A few of our people went in when they saw the board members go in, but a policeman who had been shifting his pistol from side to side quickly drew it on him and told him to get out. Then police blocked the door and told us to 'stay where we belonged.'

"Since we'd come for an invitation, not a lynching, we 'decided' to leave. A policeman ordered me to drive my car forward—backward—forward—he told me to take a drivers' test right there! He was just showing his power; anything, however silly, to embarrass me. I was so scared my knees were knocking. We quickly decided to have our own emergency meeting at our church. I was so upset, I got lost going to my own church in that tiny town!

"Police and auxiliary police kept cruising and circling, talking to each other on two-way radios. They had circled our houses like that before the meeting, too, trying to scare us from going, like they did the year before when they thought we might be coming to City Hall to ask that our streets be paved.

"At our church that night, a white newspaperman showed up. He said he'd been called to City Hall to cover a story about 'a bunch of niggers outside.' He didn't see us when he got there, so he asked them, 'Where are they?' They told him, 'In niggertown sayin' their prayers.' So he came to our church. He told us he was raised poor, picking cotton in the hills. He said all white people haven't had such an easy time as we might think. He said he has sympathy, and Negroes must stick together if they want to get anywhere. We were all awfully shook up. We sang freedom songs to calm us. He joined in!

"When I finally got home that night, the police circled my house for hours and hours, and the only thing I could think to do was call the office in Jackson, and see if there were any CDGM people in so late to give me strength. Polly was there . . ."

[My diary tells that story: "Tonight I was working at the office at about eleven P.M., when Cora called, voice trembling, sounding terrified. She said her house was surrounded by furious police. . . . She kept saying, 'Make me laugh, take my mind off it.' My automatic reaction was to want to call the police! God, what a crazy world! Once I'd dispensed with that idea, and had gotten used to the idea that *there was nothing I could do,* so many miles and so many hours away from her, I thought, well, better do like the lady says: make her laugh.

"I suggested that we send telegrams at once to VIPs in Washington, such as Katzenbach, Senator Javits . . . etc. They should know about little details of the day in Mississippi. So for an hour, we amused ourselves long distance by composing telegrams, some of which Cora actually sent. Our favorite was meant for Mr. Shriver: 'Tonight in Sunflower County, Mississippi, poverty stricken people who were invited to public CAP meeting in City Hall to plan programs to lift them from poverty, were driven from meeting by police wielding blackjacks and wearing riot helmets. Request clarification: Is this consistent with CAP guidelines concerning maximum feasible participation of the poor?' "]

Cora's account continues, "So, as I was saying, what happened next. Oh, yes, OEO sent two people right in to investigate this. Usually they've sent us white Southerners who are entirely sympathetic with the CAP. This time it was Mr. Zierdon. He was very fair. The CAP people tried their usual trick, buying off troublemakers. They offered me a job. But none of us with any responsibility, you see, just *me,* the ringleader, a hushmouth job so I'd feel I owed them something, and I'd get out of the way. The OEO men told us they knew it was a rotten CAP board, and not to believe these people, OEO wasn't accepting it as it was. They told us to go on and get more people, keep working, prove we have poor people participating.

"So we went out and recruited Morehead, Inverness, Drew, Sunflower

City, Rome, and Blaine. The center in Morehead City opened in May. It had two hundred thirty-six children. It's a little hard for the people to run a school that size with no money, but where there's a will, there's a way. They serve sandwiches, milk, and cookies when it's warm. But when it's cold, they cook in a home and carry hot dinner in every day.

"A man came by that center before the regular Friday night PTA meeting, and said he was told another man had set a bomb at the meeting place, and said he would hate to see so many nice people get killed. So our men armed themselves, hid in the fields around the church: all that. Most people at the meeting didn't know anything was unusual, it all went so smooth, but we knew our men were out there protecting us.

"Sunflower City opened with a hundred children, Inverness with one hundred and fifteen, Blaine with forty-five, Rome with sixty, and Doddsville with sixty, and Drew with a hundred five.

"We went to quite an effort to staff these many schools with no salaries or food money—the schools meant quite a little bit to us. You can understand that we weren't pleased when Mr. Zierdon came back again, this time bringing a Southern white lady, Mrs. Martha McKaye from OEO, who tried to take five of *our own centers* from us and make us *give* them to the CAP. There the children would be trained in the usual public school way to suit the white world. They would fire all our volunteer teachers who had taught for *nothing* all these cold, hopeless months, and hire their own 'better qualified' people, teachers, to replace us. Did CAP create these schools? Use their buildings? Take life and death chances? Work for nothing for a year? Did CAP do *anything* except come around now when it thought we were dead to pick our bones?

"We had begun to call ourselves the Associated Communities of Sunflower County. I told Mrs. McKaye, 'Not on your life, not on history, will I sign away the rights and toil of my people. We've worked too hard. If they want to sign away their rights, let *them*, but don't look to me to lead them into the devil's arms. I don't sell my people.' Mrs. McKaye was angry. She threw down the thing she had been wanting me to sign, and she said, 'I don't give a dern what is said, we're going to fund the people with the most participation.' Whatever that meant! I thought she meant the people with the most senators. Well, I was mad too—felt like hitting her right in her damn mouth. I thought, 'How dare the government raise our hopes so high, and lie to us about if we work hard, and then throw us down like this? They say we're lazy and don't care, and we work so hard to prove different to them, and look what that government does to us now?

"We had one thousand one hundred thirty-four signatures for us, and CAP had absolutely no participation outside of the 'owners' of it, as you might call it. Then why did Mrs. McKaye say they had more participation? Because she knew CAP could never come over to us if we were funded; they would quit. Yet we would have to run to them if they were funded. They didn't want to fund both because of all this cooperation thing they're after. So she thought she was arranging a clever thing politically. Never mind fairness, learning opportunities, all that, just so she could fix up a good deal for OEO and get credit for being a big fixer and go home and brag about her expert job.

"We opened this area for the Poverty Program. The whites didn't have anything to do with it. The rich blacks didn't have anything to do with it. *We* did, the poor people, and we don't see how it's fair to take this from us no matter what the guidelines say about cooperating. OEO turns down our proposal to be with CDGM, our proposal to be a delegate agency of this CAP, everything. They say we will be accepted on the CAP board, if we want to be, and that we are stubborn and ugly. They don't know one darn thing about it! The day I'm accepted by Bryce Alexander and his crowd, that's the day I'll know the devil got me good!

"We want to work with whites, but decent people, like CDGM whites and others we've known. And *with* them, not be their servants. We don't want OEO or any other 'friend of the poor' to force us back into slavery under our own well-known murdering whites.

"We intend to run our centers as long as the kids need us, even if OEO *never* decides we deserve money. You know where else the devil is? Right in the corner of our own CDGM AA and CO workshops! Some of those young men want to crack up CDGM and our Association just as bad as the CAP kinds do. Well, the community people don't, believe me!"

Through scarcity of skill, bureaucracy of style, and every kind of commotion and undercurrent, Negroes in and "descended" from CDGM were struggling for autonomy. Some saw success as demolishing, some saw it as establishing, but in either case, autonomy was the aim.

I found this memo on my office desk: ". . . P.S.: Did anyone tell you? New Hope Center mysteriously burned down yesterday. McComb area famous for that sort of thing. Are going to try to get tent donated from Delta Ministry. Rainy season may make it impossible to hold classes every day, but people are optimistic. . . ."

CHAPTER 37

COLLISION

WE ALL SAW CDGM as much more than a self-contained project. We saw it as a catalyst and jumping off point for many other kinds of human development projects. In the middle of May, Jack Wiersma, John, Marian, and I were preparing a proposal for a grand experiment in literacy and vocational training, combining research and demonstration. I was the person doing the most policy planning and implementation in the children's and teachers' programs *within* CDGM. I was the greatest promoter of new *careers* for the poor. I had the greatest amount of contact with educators in and out of the state, but John and Marian were primarily concerned in all they did with the "renovation" of the entire state of Mississippi. They had far more vision, concern, skill, and contacts than I did in this area. They were in perpetual discussion with national experts and local whites too by this time, in fields relative to all aspects of economic, political, and legal change.

Marian, especially, had a significant say in nearly every project being contemplated by any group, that pertained to interracial or Negro development. She was only twenty-seven years old, and already had a distinguished record, including having been named in 1965 by *Mademoiselle* magazine one of the four most exciting young women in America. She was the first Negro woman admitted to practice law in Mississippi.

As a cooperating attorney with the NAACP Legal Defense and Educational Fund, Marian, at this time, had more than one hundred cases involving harassment and violence pending, and was pressing for school suits.

While a student at Spelman College in Atlanta, Marian had been a member of the student group that coordinated all civil rights demonstrations in Atlanta. She had been arrested in 1960 for taking part in a sit-in. She was an early participant in the Northern Movement and the Student Nonviolent Coordinating Committee, of which she was also on the executive committee. She had been named a Merrill Scholar in recognition of her first-place standing in her college class. This had allowed her to spend her junior year at the universities of Geneva and Paris. While abroad, she had been chosen to take part in the Lisle Fellowship's second U.S.-U.S.S.R. Student Exchange, and make a study-tour of East Germany, Poland, Czechoslovakia, spending six weeks in Soviet Russia.

Home again, she graduated as valedictorian from Spelman. In 1962, while attending Yale University Law School on a John Hay Whitney Fellowship, she was selected to spend two months on the Ivory Coast of West Africa as a participant in the "Operation Crossroads Africa" pilot project of the Peace Corps. In addition to her astonishingly heavy work load, Marian served as perhaps the most important member of CDGM's board of directors, a member of the board of directors of the Citizens Crusade Against Poverty, and as a member of the Commission of the Delta Ministry of the National Council of Churches. She was a constant customer of Delta Airlines; she spent almost as much of her time here, there, and everywhere, planning and coordinating for Mississippi, as she did in the state. In the spring of 1966 she had just returned from a three-month Ford Foundation study grant in England and Israel.

No significant long-lasting improvements could be made in Mississippi without taking action to help a large number of desperately unemployed and seriously underemployed families. So John and Marian were very interested in this vocational educational project we were currently developing. Jack was involved because he was John's consultant for major off-shoot projects. I was included, I guess, because at that time I was still in the policy planning group of CDGM and its possible offspring, and because I was still CDGM's chief "writer."

After much planning, I was told to lock myself up for a weekend, and write a preliminary vocational proposal, which we would all carry up to the Ford Foundation. The grantee would be Mary Holmes Junior College. The National Board of Missions, its sponsor, was interested in strengthening it, and making it a leader of federal and foundation programs for educational and social development in the state. The Board of Missions would create a new board of directors. This board would oversee our vocational project. It would consist of three leaders from the National Board of Missions, three outstanding white Mississippi leaders (we had three individuals in mind), and three outstanding Negro Mississippi leaders (these we had identified, too). There would also be an advisory board made up of active, hard-working substantial people of both races. This group would be divided into working committees. We knew that, socially speaking, centuries had gone by in Mississippi since the early 1960s. We felt that the time was ripe for an interracial project like this. A national organization called Trust would provide business, scientific, and technical assistance. The General Learning Corporation would provide management services and management training. Ernst and Ernst would audit the project. All parties had agreed.

As we described it, the project would have a number of important features. Poor families would participate in planning each phase of the program from the beginning. We would have a group of staff members whose task was to negotiate with light industries, in an effort to work out their needs and fears and succeed in attracting them to Mississippi. Literacy, vocational, and world-of-work materials and approaches would be collected, revised, and invented. Poor people would be trained in leadership, administration, and in knowledge of the many services, agencies, programs, projects, and materials in the state not known to them, so that *they*, in phase two of the project, could train other poor families in these critical areas. As families passed out of phase one, approximately four months after funding, other families would replace them, so that a continuing upward flow could commence.

Phase two called for the establishment of some small light industry parks, balanced with agriculture and enriched by small businesses (such as movie theaters, laundromats, etc.) owned by poor families moving into the parks for training. People would move up through job clusters, the more advanced of which would be planned by the industries we hoped to bring into the program. People would teach the cluster they had just mastered to those following them. We wanted to work with about fifty families on a large Delta plantation (several were available to us with the full cooperation of the owners), about two-hundred families in an urban poverty area, and about two-hundred more families "out of context" at a place such as the unused Greenville Air Base.

On Monday, May 16, after we had completed an all morning conference and elegant lunch with Ford people in New York, and while John and I were still at Ford using its phones to tie off a few loose ends of business, we received word from CDGM that "all hell had broken loose" over the out-of-state people involved in my summer hiring project. At their weekly workshop, furious area administrators, highly-heated by the mood of the panthers, had made the statement that: "Jesse Paris is to take responsibility for the AA's and is not to be bought off. He is to support the AA's motion as passed . . ." and had unanimously passed a motion: "That the Director of Field Operations [Jesse] take the necessary steps to prevent the people committed to work for CDGM for the summer from being assigned until such time to hold Area Staff meetings and Community meetings to come up with what the people want."

They had called a statewide meeting for all community chairmen for Thursday, May 19. The written statement of these accomplishments, read to us on the phone, concluded: "All department heads are invited to attend."

John and I were terribly upset. One reaction was of joy that at last, at last, after all our hitherto fruitless urging, the area administrators, who tended to see themselves more as errand boys for Central Staff than as heads of areas and initiators were following the advice given in the Old Testament: "Put not your trust in princes." They were calling the tune! "the princes" *could* attend *their* meeting! Allelujah! We were making progress toward local autonomy.

But we had other reactions, too. If all the keen, teeming antiwhite feelings mounting in the state were funneling into one tornadolike cone over the out-of-state matter, surely I would be slaughtered. Regardless of my intentions, I would never come out of this politically alive as far as CDGM's inner life was concerned. As one of CDGM's humorists quipped later in the week, after John and I had hurried home: "The whole hysterical new nationwide black/white thing that's been silently building, is taking the form, here, of a head-on collision between the dedicated Aces of Spades and the dedicated Queen of Hearts. Right or wrong, she'll hang."

John and I were both unhappy that we'd allowed me to make the decision to bring whites or anyone into the state or into CDGM, without having gone through the kinds of procedures we ourselves advocated. True, I had kept ATGs, area staff members, and the board informed of what I was doing. There had been no secrecy. I'd listened for responses. But this, of course, is public-school-style communication. I *told* them, and asked for approval. *I didn't ask first.*

We were unhappy, too, that it seemed some people were aching for a white lynching, and weren't interested in understanding the facts of what I had actually done (which turned out to be greatly distorted: for example during the following months it was never mentioned that I had been recruiting *in-state* people as well as out-of-state, and *black* as well as white, *and that the vast majority of responses were from in-state black*). Nor were the accusers interested in understanding my intentions (which were almost unanimously assumed and widely advertised to have been to insult the ability of in-state Negroes, and to dominate them with white out-of-staters). It was the young Turks who were instigating this revolution, and a few of their girl friends. Having themselves been brought up in typical matriarchal Negro homes, they "knew" that women always run men, and they "knew" that I ran John. Logically, then, as one of them explained to me a year later: "If we got rid of you, John would fold up. He's scared of us niggers. We could make him do anything we wanted if you weren't there; you ain't scared of niggers."

Some of our consultants felt that I was chosen as the victim instead of John or Mary, because: "You were much more visible. He was always closeted away with visiting dignitaries and us consultants and his ledgers and the board, and you were always in communities, signing letters to communities, heading up what they saw. No one thought Mary had much power; they were after a symbol of power. You *were* powerful at that time, but also they attributed more power to you than you had."

"You were weaker—a girl. They said they hated John and you, but they needed him. He had powerful connections and contacts. He controlled the financial side. They could understand that. They were scared of it. You controlled the program content side. That they didn't understand. They didn't know they needed it. They figured they could do without you, so you could be the one sacrificed to show they meant business about whites in control."

"The old story: black men and white women in the South. What'd' you expect when they find one that won't have them literally lynched for 'raping' her? They'll do her good, turn the tables, get revenge for all the centuries of white woman injustice, watch her writhe. Besides, they all have it in for you for not sleeping with them. They think you think you're too good for them. The black men and white women in the South syndrome again."

"John doesn't make people as mad as you do till they have a chance to reflect on it later. You get all excited and say what you think; express your opinions. He appears more submissive. He's coy, shields himself better, plays it cooler. He's less direct and honest than you, and it works better. In fact, he's very determined and unyielding about what he thinks and does. It's the appearance of humility that makes the difference in how people react at the moment."

An area administrator, one of the few that were friendly to me in more than a "how are you today" way, offered his opinion of the cause of the AA's anger: "Most of us felt incapable when we looked at you. You were so competent, so fair, such a politician in the communities. We felt it was what we should be doing. It was sort of irrational: kind of a rage at ourselves for not being able to do like you did. Kind of a feeling that if we didn't have to look at you, we would like our own performance better. And lots of AAs used the excuse that *you* were doing it, that you *didn't want* them to do it, for an excuse or a crutch to cover the fact that they *couldn't* do it."

Jesse Paris, as director of the AA's field operations division, was in a terrible position too. He had never been trusted by his area administrators, the large majority of whom were angry at him, as one of them named Charles Hamberlin explained: "Because he doesn't jive, he doesn't think on his own, he doesn't make decisions, he doesn't follow through and stick up for the AAs like Polly does for the ATGs. Lots of us are jealous of the ATGs for having Polly to get them everything they need, so persuasive. We wanted to test Jesse; put him on the spot and see if he would come through for us against the powers that be."

Jesse admitted that he had known about my plan for months, and didn't argue now about *why* Program wanted some out-of-staters. But, under all this pressure, he was newly questioning *how* we had gone about all this: without consulting communities first.

John quickly sent a very fair letter to community committees, which neither supported my actions nor condemned them, but which clarified the problem confronting us all: It announced an emergency meeting of community committee chairmen and Area Staff members for May 19.

This meeting was more positive than any of us had dared hope. The danger we had anticipated was that Negro non-Mississippi non-CDGMians—dedicated to the destruction of CDGM because it was their greatest rival in communities in terms of their own dominance as opinion leaders, and because it represented "black and white together," which had come to be the antithesis of what they now strove for, and who always circulated subterraneanly in and out of CDGM's affairs—would try to blast CDGM apart. In fact, many people had secret meetings that week in which they planned tactics for so doing. However, community people weren't interested, and kept the discussion on the track. A number of valid points were raised by community people. They took turns coming before the huge audience at the Masonic Temple to take the mike:

Bringing out-of-state whites in for three months isn't real integration. There are local whites willing to work now in 1966; we should try to get them.

We appreciate what whites have given us in the past, but it's time now for us to practice getting along without them. This is *our* problem. Besides, lots of out-of-staters come in, enthusiastically do a lot of things, and then pull out, leaving us just where we were before.

Though it wasn't stated that I had been recruiting and interviewing *many* local whites, and that we were trying to screen out whites who *couldn't* leave skills behind them, it was wonderful that local people were feeling strong enough to think these things.

There were a handful of people who didn't yet feel ready to do without whites: It was whites that got things going in this state. If it weren't for them, we wouldn't have so many registered voters. If it weren't for them, we wouldn't have had CDGM in the first place. If it weren't for them, we'd never have gotten funded again last February.

But this view was booed—another sign of growing autonomy. A year ago people would have clapped and cheered.

There were a handful of people who denied that whites had *ever* made a contribution to Mississippi: Outsiders didn't change Mississippi. It was the black people of Mississippi that changed Mississippi.

This opinion was greeted with silence each time it was offered. People knew what they had done. They also knew who had encouraged them to do it—who had been their allies in the extraordinary effort.

Many other points were made, showing a mixture of new courage to make decisions, defensiveness, lack of understanding of OEO's Head Start, lack of familiarity with quality nursery education, and a kind of common sense to which, when we relayed it, OEO turned a deaf ear:

We are overenrolled already. We have many poor people volunteering.

Why can't we pay them instead of hiring anybody else? It isn't fair to bring in new people, and still not pay these who've worked so hard.

If this program is meant to alleviate poverty in Mississippi, let's spend the money on poor Mississippians. The point of OEO is jobs for the poor. Those students aren't poor. They should come for a slight subsistence sum. Why do they have to come here? Aren't there poverty programs and jobs in their own states?

What can they do that we can't do? We can do everything as well as anyone else.

We need experience. Don't give it to those who already *have* experience.

We don't have enough money for supplies and food. Let's not hire anybody else, let's spend the money on supplies and food.

Let's go to OEO and ask for more money.

Still others were in favor of the out-of-state idea, and made suggestions similar to the program department's:

Some of the children go to integrated schools. It's been easier for those who had been to our integrated Head Start centers. We want a white or two. They should be welcome if they want to come. We did it together before; we can do it together now too.

It should be left to each community to decide. Central Staff should supply the communities with information about what is available—social workers, music or art specialists, etc.—and then communities should decide if they want one, and which one.

* * *

"Dear Polly, I'm slipping you this note at this meeting to say, we WANT ONE. Our community thinks its good for our children to play with nice whites. Removes fear. Please don't tell . . . [the area administrator]. He would HAVE OUR HEAD. But if there's any way you can bring us one bring us. We apologize for the ungreatful attitude of some peoples we are GREATFUL to our friends what color they may be they didn't choose it. . . . God decides the color and only the devil picks on it."

* * *

It was concluded that John's original decision to allow me to go ahead with this on my own and my choice of a system were arbitrary. It was moved that *all* applications, including out-of-state, be given to the area administrators. They would take them to communities, and communities would tell central office what they had decided. I amended the motion to say that *all* applications, including *in-state*, since most of them *were* more poor Negroes, be handled in areas.

I also begged area offices and communities to write to applicants. I had a vision of all these thousands of eager people being forgotten in the area office shuffle. Efficient paper work was not one of their outstanding virtues. If I was having trouble keeping every applicant straight and up-to-date, I wasn't confident that inexperienced administrators could do it. Also, it seemed obvious that they had no intention of doing anything but chucking the applications in the wastebasket. This didn't seem fair to the applicants. I felt no obligation to hire them, except the fifty-seven to whom I'd already made commitments. These fifty-seven, unfortunately, were almost all out-of-state students. We had made the first of our contemplated commitments into a pool from which communities could hire them, because they were withdrawing to take other jobs.

In-state students had fewer job choices. They were putting less pressure on us to decide. We had planned to make promises to an equal number of them next, but had been interrupted.

The AAs wanted me to cancel commitments made. I felt that though they were right about my wrongness in undertaking this project myself, and though I would cooperate fully in making no *more* commitments, I couldn't decently renege on promises personally made; promises which I had been verbally authorized to make by both project director and chairman of the board. And I *did* feel an obligation to treat turned down applicants with courtesy: not to force them to pay the price of our internal struggle.

The motion was passed as amended. Mary helped me spend the next week, literally day and night (going home at 7 A.M. to fix my kids breakfast, take them to school, and return at 9 A.M. to start up again) sorting applications by area and status, summarizing pertinent information to be stapled on the application as a cover sheet, and stapling special yellow flyers on some saying in large magic marker: "MISSISSIPPI COLLEGE STUDENT. PLEASE NOTE: THIS PERSON IS ANXIOUS TO HEAR FROM US, AND CAN WORK IN MORE THAN ONE AREA. WE WILL CONTACT YOU TO SEE IF YOU CAN PLACE HIM. IF YOU CAN'T, WE WILL TRANSFER HIS APPLICATION TO ANOTHER AREA."

We kept records detailing the whereabouts of each applicant's applications. We sent each applicant a letter explaining the hiring system and telling him whom to contact regarding the fate of his application. We made endless follow-up phone calls to each area office to determine which applications to rotate to another area. We Xeroxed hundreds of copies of a letter saying, "Sorry, no jobs left, but we need your volunteer service badly," and mailed batches to each area office for them to mail to rejects. However, as we had anticipated, almost no applicants were notified of anything.

I was very angry at this display of "concern" for the poor shown by area staff members, and disgusted at the thought of the image of arrogance and inefficiency this would give us in and out of the state, when we had worked so hard on the opposite. I was sickened to think how much time I'd wasted all spring on this abortive project. And most of all, while I could understand and appreciate the CO and AA's charge that some communities felt intimidated by me and thought that, no matter what I said to the contrary, they *had* to hire a white person, I was furious that CDGM's leadership was allowing, as an "improvement" to my possible overinfluence, the nihilist group to run roughshod over communities, refusing to let them see applications in many cases, and circuit riding to make speeches *against even considering* applications. Two wrongs don't make a right. I acknowledged the error of my procedure. But for CDGM's policy makers to replace Central Staff overinfluence by area staff level petty dictatorship, seemed to me, at the time, an all-time high in our growing problem: white cowardice in the face of black power; popularity-seeking, over wise, but unloved leadership toward democratic processes. Probably I was wrong. John managed to save CDGM from drowning. Perhaps the temporary setting aside of idealism was the only way he could have achieved that excellent and intricately achieved fact.

A handful of out-of-state students long-expected through the earlier nonresident term college project arrived. I'd been prohibited from going ahead with the immediate workshop and placing of them in communities that I had planned and promised them, so they landed in the office, bag, baggage, and white faces. This inflamed the situation even more. The longer they hung around, in lay away, as it were, helping with a thousand and one clerical chores no one else had time to handle, the greater grew the rumors of the floods of foreigners I allegedly was bringing in. We called the controversial committed fifty-seven students and told them the situation. A few, therefore, decided not to come. We continued to arrange for the staggered arrivals by bus, train, and plane of those who wanted to take their chances with us.

One bleak, gray, wet, windy, muddy Mississippi March Monday morning I had passed Marilyn Lowen on the dining room steps at Mount Beulah, and had asked her if she would like to be in charge of planning and carrying out all the details of a five-day workshop for temporary summer staff. During her few weeks with the living arts program the first summer, and also in her work as roving resource teacher in Panola and Tallahatchie counties since she'd returned to CDGM after the second grant began, she had demonstrated an unusual sensitivity to community feelings and an understanding of early education that was rare in CDGM. She seemed to me to be the only person we had who could sensitize newcomers to the nuances of nonpoor imports working *with* the poor, and to the kinds of aims we had for CDGM children and teachers. Besides, I had been wanting to work her into a more central position. She was too talented to be used only in a small area of the state and of the total program. Marilyn agreed to take on this large project.

But now the workshop had to be put off, so out-of-state students fell into our festering situation, without adequate provisions having been completed for their initiation and distribution. I had promised that we would have housing for them for their orientation days in Jackson, at no more than fifteen dollars a week. Now, of course, hostility was such that no one would put them up. Between the students and me, we got hotel bills paid, but with anger on both parts. They, too, stewed around the office in completely legitimate distress, and in considerable anger at me.

I had many letters from communities on file, such as this one. Some had been received during the winter, and others during this crisis period: "Dear Pollie, And the other part of the community I have call you the Second time and I get no answer, now i am writing you to let you no that the Hudsonvill center Staff would like to have you too Send the Hudsonvill Center a Resource Teacher I thank that would be best. Johnnie Gatewood"

It was obvious that no one else was going to do anything about seeing that communities could meet and consider the students we had committed. The "auctioning" of students we had planned to have at the postponed workshop, following the precedent of the preceding summer, could not occur. Therefore, I called communities from which someone had contacted me in writing or verbally regarding their desire to have an out-of-state summer worker, and made appointments to bring carloads of students for interviews. I took four or five such groups of students to six or eight CDGM communities. We talked, and I urged the community committees to think it over, and notify me; not to decide while we were still sitting there. This was construed by enraged AA's, CO's, and some of the students themselves, as me "forcing" out-of-staters on people, though it resulted in only a handful of hirings, and a greater number of rejects.

The area teacher guides were between the devil and the deep blue sea during this period. A few took strong positions on one side or the other. Most of them reacted with inertia and silence toward me and toward their area staff teammates. Their mixed loyalties caused them to be immobile, because they were, like wary cats, poised to pounce forward or backward, as soon as circumstances indicated to them which was the feasible direction.

Gaynette Flowers later told me: "AAs didn't like us ATGs because if there was any information available from OEO or central, we ran to the people with it, and tried to make sure people understood their choices. AAs, a lot of them at least, didn't want people to know they could unelect chairmen and board members, and could control them to do right, because some AAs had things just the way they wanted them. There were quite a few organized, self-appointed chairmen's cliques. They told me, 'You just don't know Polly like I do. She's sending out this information to get people fighting.' I said, 'No, she wants people to have information.' I said, 'If you want a puppet on a string, I need out today.' I felt like I was between two stone walls, with these people threatening to fire me all the time for trying to get information to people, and Polly saying to develop a good children's program, even if we had to go against some community politicking and slick stuff. How could I do anything if I was fired? But what was the point of clinging to the job if I couldn't do it right? I was a little bit daunted for a few months, but then I decided, job or no job . . ."

Tension between me, Mary, and the ATGs came to a head at the Mary Holmes workshop. During the spring D. I. Horn, president of Mary Holmes, and Marvin Matteson, Mary Holmes business manager, had secured a U.S. Office of Education College Work-Study Program grant of $73,332. The purpose of the program was to provide a summer opportunity for 180 Mary Holmes students to earn money to help defray their college expenses. Marv and Dave Flemming worked out arrangements for these students to work in CDGM centers. Work-Study funds would pay the students, except for 10 percent of their wages, which CDGM would pay. Negro students from Alabama, Florida, Georgia, Tennessee, and Mississippi, many of them from economically and socially deprived backgrounds and few with skills appropriate to our enormous need for specialties, arrived to prepare for this program on the MHJC campus at the end of May. Dave asked me and Mary to carry on an intensive four-day workshop for them.

Mary and I spent several of our regular Wednesday ATG workshop sessions planning with ATGs. We hoped that they would plan, set up, and run this workshop. Dave arranged for a truck to pick up enough supplies and materials at our warehouse in Tougaloo so that ATGs could simulate Head Start classrooms at Mary Holmes. He sent letters to communities notifying them of these additional "free" summer workers. He coordinated community housing and placement for each student with Marv Matteson. By various means most ATGs, much of our tiny teacher development and program for children staff, and local people from a number of centers straggled up to Mary Holmes from all around the state, on the evening of Tuesday, May 31, or the morning of June 1.

The workshop was well organized, full of content, and satisfied Mary Holmes coordinators. However, we thought it quite poor, because in many cases we didn't feel we had really reached the students. Also because it marked another collision point: this time between ATGs and central teacher development and program for children. On the first morning I explained Head Start in general, CDGM in specific, showed *A Chance for Change*, and led a film discussion stressing the differences between CDGM and public school programs the students might have experienced, communities doing things for themselves, and what roles the students could see for themselves in CDGM. After lunch, students filled out forms giving their first, second, and third choices of centers to work in, and their special interests or skills. Jesse Paris talked about

CDGM's administrative structure, and outlined jobs for some students as area office aides. Mr. Dickert discussed building repair and renovation needs, and suggested that some students work as facilities aides. Jesse Harris, an AA who was a community development specialist, discussed CDGM's position relative to the earlier Freedom Movement. Carolyn Stevens, administrative assistant in the teacher development and program for children division, discussed the similarity between CDGM's goals for children and FDP's goals for adults. Joe Harrison, one of our two roving resource teachers for community music, led the singing of slave and freedom songs, and talked about pride in one's heritage. Throughout, many of the Work-Study students seemed bored. Many slipped out, and an MHJC faculty member suggested that we lock the door.

The evening session went even less well. Jesse Harris started an unscheduled civil rights discussion with some students, just before scheduled activities. Also, a fact which we hadn't been told in advance, a dance had been planned for the students, and they were eager to put in their time with us and get to the more meaningful business of dancing. Nevertheless, some students enjoyed making puppets and smocks to take to centers, building such things for children as tin can stilts, an easel, and the beginnings of a sandbox, with lumber and other workshop materials we had provided, and painting pictures with children's paints. Most students seemed to us timid and reluctant, but appeared to open up as the evening progressed, and to get the idea that a children's program is a relaxed, informal, fun program.

On the second day I led a discussion of activities for children in the centers. Few seemed interested in activities for children in centers. In the afternoon ATGs put on "good and bad teaching" skits depicting nap time, playground time, greeting the children in the morning, and free play time. They split into small groups to do this, and led discussions after each brief skit, focusing on the students' own experiences with children. After the skits, student groups rotated through rooms the ATGs had set up as reasonable facsimiles of center classrooms. ATGs explained uses of materials and activities revolving around what students saw. The ATGs did this rather more lifelessly than usual. I left at noon, as prearranged, to get back to our other projects, and Mary took over.

Of the evening session Mary wrote: "Great participation by most students. Shifted emphasis in evening program from producing games, etc., to more experimenting on part of students. Some built wonderful . . . Doris and Marilyn worked in art room, Lucia in building, Lynn in puppets . . . ATGs helped out in each room but not really actively.

"I tried to talk with different groups of students about place or use in center of things they were doing.

"Many kids were totally involved—really went wild about these experiences which it appeared they had never before had—dough, paint, etc."

Mary and I were continuously learning that regardless of how much learner experimentation and learning through inquiry and discovery we included in our training programs, *more* worked very much better.

But we had still not begun to solve the problem of how much and *how* to use people with experience in early education. The more gifted people we had working with our learners, the more inspired and creative the learners became. Yet the more "experts" we used, the more resentful the learners became, too. Which result outweighed which?

Doris was the outstanding resource teacher from the first summer, featured in CDGM's film *Chance for Change.* She had been able to give us only two or three days of consulting time every couple of months during the year, as she was fully occupied as the art director for the Poor People's Corporation. She was marvelous, and was resented less than others because of her extensive freedom work background, her long duration in the state, and her color.

Lucia Clapps and Lynn Lazar were new additions to our staff. Lynn was a college student acquired through my spring efforts. I hired her to be a summer roving Central Staff person to help ATGs and centers where invited. While it was impossible to judge a person's ability or personality by phone, Lynn's was the kind of background I was hunting for in the college student

Lucia had been recommended by Christopher Jencks, a fellow at the Institute for Policy Studies in Washington, who had recently visited us for a few days, and had written a piece about Mississippi history for the April 16, 1966, *New Republic*, including a long discussion of CDGM's role; he called CDGM the "residual legatee" of the movement.

We had paid Lucia's way to pay us a visit in late April. She sounded like, and proved to be, an outstanding person to help us with our problem of promoting educational quality. She came to work in May. The Mary Holmes workshop was one of her first appearances before the ATGs. In spite of her youth, friendly informal graciousness, giftedness, and creativity, Lucia immediately became a glittering example of our unsolved problem regarding "experts."

Shortly after I left the workshop, the ATGs erupted in rage at Mary, who was reduced to tears. ATG Valentine Blue later explained her feelings: "I was a ringleader in that MHJC thing. It was ignited by Lucia. Every single thing any of us placed anywhere in the sample classrooms, she came around behind us and moved. She never said anything to us, discussing the different ways we would do it. She just undid each thing we had done. We had never seen her before, she was new to us—we had just heard about her. And after we had been setting up empty classrooms for months, she came in and rearranged everything. Then the thing that really made me mad was she said, 'OK, I guess you can knock off now'; like we *worked* for her.

"Then Mary stood up there in front of us and gave us all these directions. It made me *so* angry—it was impulse, that's all it was, to see *her* standing up there, and me the same age, and the other ATGs older than her, and *her* giving the directions.

"We told some of those who always thought everything you and Mary did was so wonderful, that *they* had a mouth, and they could open it to disagree. It wasn't that I *dis*agreed with you, but I thought they should know they *could*. And I told Lucia, 'Let's just have a cooling off period between us, let's just cut off communications till I feel I can accept your apology. Right now I can't accept it. Didn't you know we had any feelings?' And several months later, I *did* go and tell her I was ready to accept her apologies.

"Lots of the ATGs kept saying we shouldn't do Mary like that. Reverend Martin said, 'We would never have been allowed into this field if it weren't for Mary and Polly. They are so patient with us, and they fight for our right to get into this work. We shouldn't treat them like this.' What we did to Mary wasn't fair. I realize that now. But I told the others, 'Sometimes the way to get something done that we want done and that we *should* learn to speak up and do, is just to go ahead and hurt someone's feelings if necessary.' It only lasts a week or so, and then you say, 'Yes, I meant that, but you're still my friend, and I didn't mean everything else, only *that!*' "

It's highly doubtful that Lucia was as tactless as many ATGs reported her to have been—or that Mary stood up there and gave directions. Yet the essence of the affair was as Valentine's views implied: Why has everything in our lives conspired to create a situation in which *we* have to be learners, and whites of the same age are *able* to lead? We really *were* striving for local individuals to achieve autonomy. So we had to try to salve our hurt feelings with the realization that when people first begin to be able to express their true feelings, and to stop depending upon "parental" figures for guidance, and to take the bull by the horns, they do it in primitive ways. We aren't surprised or shocked at the belligerence, anger language, and tantrums of two year olds and teen-agers. But when the struggle for personal independence, which we take in stride at these critical developmental stages, is suppressed by circumstances beyond the control of the individual, and is released later, we tend to react with outrage instead of with insight. The pain and strain of the season were severe for us. But they were unbearably greater for those fighting lifetimes of emotional habit—for those emerging into real maturity.

The remainder of the MHJC workshop went along without incident; and without much effect on anybody.

In spite of its weaknesses, this workshop was a landmark for us. It was the first time that MHJC had become involved in any way in developing any CDGM content area. We hoped it would be a precedent.

* * *

A trainee teacher, who whispered to me, "I lied on the application to get the job; actually, I didn't complete ninth grade: it was second grade," slipped me this "report": "We have no picks. We use new ideals every day. This program is great hope to the community. We have some that wont turn their thumb loose. We have some that falls out on the floor and wallers. One loves to kick and bite and cant be found. He bites himself till he bleeds. We talk to them and reason. We busy them till incorporate children become corporate. All of them are becoming sweet under the starlight appearance of our fine teachers. Many children hover over the playground when school turns out for the day.

"One girl wouldn't talk to no one. I taken her under a sweet gum tree and talk and talk till my voice rusty. Then from then on she bring candy peanuts gum and other signals of fond to me and her equals. There is a boy who is a mental. He burst out laughing at no reason. He burst out crying also. He cling onto a old rag.

"As you see, we coup with each of the childrens in a manner compatable with being a individual free beloved child of God."

* * *

Partially as a result of the tensions created by the out-of-state and the ATG collisions, which put her in an extremely difficult position, Mary was more distressed with me and down on me than ever. Her silence and lack of support conveyed her feelings to newcomers in teacher development and program for children. At best, they wouldn't have felt comfortable coming into the disastrous situation we offered them at that period. Strained relations were strained further by our different perceptions of priorities. The newcomers wanted to feel their way in communities; to observe, and make decisions as to how they could best use themselves later. Mary was just beginning to feel sure of herself, and wanted to be free of me. I, on the verge of departing for the summer or for good, wanted to leave as tight a plan as possible for the summer "quality building" phase, which I had envisioned would follow the now completed spring "launching" period.

To me, "later" was too late for people to decide how to help CDGM. We had needed help for too long already. We needed to use people immediately. There were only four or five of them anyway. They would only be available for a few months. We had more than 120 centers to help. We had excellent ATGs to help. We had repeated meetings and individual discussions, in which I begged each person in our division to consider what she would like to do—work on a "subject" in as many places as possible? Work on general development in one or two areas? or what? I urged them to consult ATGs, communities being considered. I pressured them to decide, to make schedules, etc., so we could get an overview of what each community would be getting, and to make sure that our offerings were made equally everywhere.

My staff tended to be specialists and purists. They resented the idea of spreading themselves thin, giving crash help, and other working styles appropriate to CDGM's vast and urgent needs. They liked to be thorough and deliberate. They resented my emphasis on the total picture, and thought I favored shallowness of quality. They tended to be very in dependent people and resented my attempts to "pin them down." We wound up with plans, many of which were carried through in my absence; but not without a collision of spirits that resulted in serious barriers preventing communication.

Jackie Shearer thought it would be interesting to hold area workshops in storytelling, reading to children, and bookmaking. With a great many interruptions, this is what she spent the summer doing. Lynn worked on general development at centers that were claimed by the ATGs to be in dire need. Lucia and a friend of hers named Frances Hawkins, who was from Educational Services Inc., and who came to Mississippi as a CDGM consultant for two weeks, worked on encouraging creativity, especially in science, at a number of centers. Mrs. Draine—a former member of Mississippi's poorest Negro echelon, and presently a primary grades teacher in Jackson as well as a Movement woman, whom we hoped would be able, and more important, *willing*, to play a key role in teacher development and program for children during a third grant and after my departure from CDGM—worked in the office in Mary's former job, while Mary took my job for the summer. Mrs. Draine also did inspirational work in some centers. Doris continued to contribute another two or three days a month to specific centers.

Marilyn had been wanting to do music and movement workshops. She would consult ATGs and community centers, make a schedule of those responding affirmatively, and hold approximately fifteen workshops (one per area) of half a day for all resource teachers in that area, with about a dozen of their liveliest children. Part of each session would be a discussion of simple instruments and how to make them. Marilyn's workshops were a great success. She also planned a creative film making project, and made one of the filmstrips involved. Marilyn was angry at me for suggesting that she work in four Panola and Tallahatchie centers, which after she came and had started working in them, were not refunded by OEO, and which John explicitly told me she could work in anyway, as long as she was a roving resource teacher, and was based in an authorized center. Paycheck problems resulted. Being in on the fact that an employee doesn't get paid as promised is, understandably, the surest way to obtain that employee's dislike.

From June 20 to 23 Marilyn *did* run the workshop for summer students that I had delegated to her. It was a unique orientation. To me it was a brilliant and beautiful job of presenting and involving students in the painful and complicated realities of what they were getting into. However, for those preferring the pretty to the real, it was a shocking violation of *how it should be.* It brought OEO down on our heads once again. Evidently OEO was not yet aware of black consciousness as a new national passion to be reckoned with.

On the first morning I welcomed the students. John Mudd spoke on the history and structure of CDGM and stressed that people in CDGM communities are used to being manipulated—that the students should think about how to get information to people so that they could accept *or reject* it. John used Christopher Jencks's piece called "Accommodating Whites" from *New Republic* and Project Head Start brochures from OEO, as resource material. Sam Howze, director of CDGM's social service department, discussed how community people feel about white students. Sam emphasized that mistakes had been made in the past by temporary workers coming into communities with few skills, making big promises and launching big plans, and then leaving, with a wake of still unskilled, very disappointed, and resentful people left behind them.

After lunch ATG Lavaree Jones discussed her own experiences teaching with CDGM, and the goals of CDGM's Head Start program. Don Jackson of the CDGM social service department, and Bob Fletcher, both of whom were Negroes with many years experience with the problems of whites in the civil rights movement, read and discussed the "Atlanta Position Paper on the Role of Whites in Organizing in the Black Community." The paper deals with whether whites can contribute anything but a reinforcement of dependency habits now, in the new Negro struggle for autonomy. Marilyn felt that it was only fair to expose the summer students as soon as possible to a sensitive and thorough explanation of the roots of Negro ambivalence and the controversy regarding whites in the Negro community resulting from it.

Following this discussion, Dr. Alvin Poussaint, Southern director of the Medical Committee for Human Rights, presented and led discussion of his paper, "The Stresses of the White Female Worker in the Civil Rights Movement in the South." As a psychiatrist he had had a great deal of experience with white women who come from a middle-class environment and first encounter the problems of coming to live in an all-Negro lower-class environment. Dr. Poussaint was able to bring out into the open some frequently ignored or "politely" covered over insights about the "emotionally shattering crossfire of racial tensions, fears, and hatreds that have been nurtured for centuries. Whatever their prior strengths and good intentions, few are able to cope with the personal tensions generated by this crossfire." The whole afternoon session was in keeping with Peace Corps training, which always gives its volunteers an intensive orientation to the customs, language, problems, and feelings of the culture in which they will be working. This is intended to reduce the degree of disorientation or culture-shock experienced by most people when they first live in a cross-cultural situation which has none of their accustomed values.

On the second day the out-of-state students were divided into five groups, each with the leadership of a person from teacher development and program for children. Equipped with a detailed and well-thought-out observation sheet, each group spent a day visiting one of the centers CDGM classified as "outstanding."

The third day of Orientation began with a three-hour discussion of what the students had seen the day before, and how they thought they might fit into it. In the afternoon a woman from the Mississippi Welfare Department Day Care Division discussed state standards for running day care programs. A child psychologist from Peabody talked about deprived children and showed slides. Marv Hoffman, a psychologist from the first summer who had just returned to CDGM in June to strengthen and coordinate the social service division, talked about working with the children as they are, rather than as "deprived children." Materials to be purchased by the students were passed out: *Teacher,* by Sylvia Ashton-Warner (also used with out-of-staters by Tom Levin the first summer), and several packets from Bank Street College of Education. Free materials were also distributed: Head Start booklets from OEO, pamphlets on day care from the Mississippi State Department of Welfare, and a field observations paper Marilyn had written. In the evening Dan Safran, a consultant newly working with area administrators and community organizers, led one of his wonderful role-playing sessions, based on problems raised the first day. Mary showed and led a discussion of our film, *Chance for Change.*

The fourth and final day of the orientation was devoted to intensive small group work on various aspects of a preschool program: free play, group time, reading readiness, and art, primarily. Each group was led by a staff member of teacher development and program for children. Art materials, books, play equipment, records, etc., were used. In the afternoon, Joe Harrison, one of our two roving community music specialists, sang many songs of Afro-American origin, and discussed something of the heritage of slave songs and spirituals. Marilyn played some records that she had ordered for centers, and taught circle dances and movement exercises.

Most of the students were extremely upset by Marilyn's workshop. Some returned home to the North. She and I had planned that she would conduct several follow-up workshops to help students with problems as they arose on location. Unfortunately, due to tangles with the business office when I was no longer in the state, Marilyn was unable to do this. This was a further frustration to the students, who were right that I had assured them of frequent opportunities to work through difficulties with CDGM Central Staff. Marilyn did hold one subsequent workshop, and sent a fascinating confidential questionnaire to each student. Though she kept her promise about "Confidential," and refused to share the answers with teacher development and program for children staff, other sources revealed that those students who "worked out," gained a great deal—they felt that perhaps they grew more than they had ever grown in an equally short period. The students who left, and some of the students who stayed, were disgusted with me for what appeared to them to be extreme dishonesty on my part. And well it might have appeared.

The next of CDGM's multiple collisions of the season occurred in July. For some time John Mudd, at the suggestion of management consultant Jack Wiersma, had been discussing with General Electric, the possibility of GE supplying CDGM with badly needed administrative support services. General Electric was being considered because it not only offered such service, but had offices in Mississippi. Plans were fairly well under way, but the CDGM board had as yet made no decision, when a number of CDGM Central Staff members took violent exception to the proposed arrangement.[36]

On July 15 Hunter Morey wrote an open letter to the CDGM board. Hunter was deputy field operations division director under Jesse Paris. He was a white Movement graduate who had come to CDGM during the second grant. Hunter was primarily responsible for the unmentioned thousands of things that went *right* each day in CDGM's vast administrative setup. He was a quiet, modest, efficient, and cooperative aide to Jesse, who was learning, and needed this kind of excellent support. Hunter wrote a letter expressing displeasure at the possibility of GE having major involvement with CDGM because of price-fixing resulting in convictions and jail terms for several top GE officials; alleged international racism by GE in its involvement in apartheid conditions of South Africa; alleged antiunionism; and a history of heavy support of the right wing. Hunter suggested that the panel of GE people John proposed to hire be questioned thoroughly on these matters.

Don Jackson and others in the social service division circulated a petition. Don was a student prior to his employment with CDGM just after the second grant began. He had attended Lincoln University, Altus Junior College, and Williams College. Don had had three years of community organization experience with NAACP and CORE. He had organized tenant groups, tutorial programs, job reference services, civic actions. He had developed OEO financed programs in Chester, Pennsylvania. Don, like almost every intelligent, socially aware Negro in CDGM, appeared to be experiencing sincere and severe conflict concerning "which way to go." The petition protested further contemplation of contract-signing with GE on the same grounds as Hunter's, plus:

> GE has a history of racially discriminatory hiring and promotion practices in the North and South, GE has no significant number of Black People in managerial positions . . .

[36] The following is merely a documentation of positions and passions in CDGM, and does not necessarily reflect either the author's opinion or the facts about GE.

GE personnel have shown disrespect for some CDGM employees . . .

GE has an outlook of economic and racial exploitation that goes against CDGM's goals of economic, social and educational progress for poor Negroes in Mississippi,

GE works hand-in-glove with Eastland, Stennis and Russell to get military contracts from the Federal Government regardless of GE's racist policies;

AND CONSIDERING THAT:

Certain CDGM officials have begun preliminary steps to involve GE in CDGM without prior consultation with or information to CDGM employees or community people,

Certain CDGM officials and consultants have shown a disrespect and disregard for the sentiments of Staff and Community People against GE involvement in CDGM,

Certain CDGM officials have allowed a crisis to develop within our organization concerning this problem;

Because of the above mentioned reasons, sentiments, and facts, we have committed ourselves to refuse to cooperate with GE or with CDGM if certain CDGM officials in the name of CDGM make a contract with or have any transactions with GE.

Further, if necessary, this non-cooperation will take the form of direct action protest against the institution CDGM. . . .

The COs added another petition to the plethora of petitions. This one demanded that CDGM immediately recruit a native Negro Mississippian for the vacant position of deputy director, and that only firms that hire Negroes be used in CDGM training projects.

On July 18, seven Central Staff members were selected to attend a meeting of the CDGM Board Personnel Committee with GE. Hunter was one of these representatives. He wrote an open letter to CDGM Staff on his perceptions of what happened, which was that GE people insulted CDGMians, behaved in an authoritarian manner and either refused to discuss or defended GE's questionable past.

John had done what I had done in the out-of-state affair. Due to the people's need for professional assistance, not to domineering motives, and due to lack of suggestion or help from other quarters, not a wish to slip something over on people, he had proposed the best thing he knew. He had neither done it secretly nor in bad faith. The fact *that he had acted* made people furious.

The third vital function of whites in CDGM was becoming clear during this struggle-for-autonomy period in CDGM's quick growth. We had served our purpose, or nearly so, as originators, organizers, catalysts, connections to the outer world, etc. We had served our role as trainers. We could no longer be useful in a training capacity as staff members, because prominent CDGM Negroes could no more accept white-originated programs than they could white people—a healthy sign.

Our skills were still needed, but in the less controlling and threatening role of consultants. But our third vital function was just now being fully realized and utilized. We were unconsciously serving as spears and spurs to the motivation of "the apathetic poor." Middle and top level Negroes, who had previously been unable to move themselves to deep involvement in top decisions, were, through angry feelings of competitiveness with us, suddenly feeling hot enough to leap up and act—*against*, maybe, but *act!* They often leaped before they looked, but at last, they leaped! We were very useful, if not happy, as the mock enemy with which Negroes with potential high-level leadership capacities could practice fighting white power with appropriate white man's techniques: scheming, manipulation, articulateness, counterproposals; perseverance until a goal is reached. One of the answers to the question we kept asking ourselves in anxiety and self-torture, "Why am I here if I am so hated?"—was becoming clear. "I'm serving a useful purpose as the simulated enemy. I'm a honing stone for Negroes to sharpen their skills. I'm the safe one, the ever-guiltier one, who won't leave, though I'm trampled, while my coming-of-age companions practice separation and independence on/from me."

John responded immediately, with grace and sincerity, as always. The central and constant theme of his work in CDGM was to urge involvement. He sent a five-page memo to CDGM Central Staff, detailing our urgent needs for help: preparing a document in progress since late May, and already fifty pages long, showing budget revisions to justify remaining grant fund expenses after August 31; preparing routinely required monthly reports of a statistical analysis of finance and program; writing final financial and program reports for OEO at the conclusion of the current grant; designing and implementing a management report system so CDGM could begin collecting and analyzing enough data to enable divisions to anticipate problems and plan; analyzing statistical data provided by the CDGM accounting system and IBM machines regarding expenses, in order to get cost comparisons, estimates of funds which would remain in August, etc.; preparing information for the questioning to be expected from the GAO (Government Accounting Organization), so we could inform them about the quality of our facilities and efforts to improve them, cost of rental cars and transportation for children, number and quality of teaching personnel, efforts to integrate, etc.; because OEO said that our next application could include only the present number of children in the current counties, and it had actually included thirty thousand children, and because OEO said in counties where CAP boards exist we had to work with them jointly or in delegate agency capacity, it would now be necessary to develop sixteen different budgets for each CAP county, make a breakdown of the proposed budget into present counties with or without CAP programs and new counties with or without CAP, and reassess the training budget in light of these restrictions; developing concrete proposals and finding funds for the training institutes we were working on—teacher training, community organization training, public health training, administrative training, and communications and dissemination training.

John's memo to the staff then explained that he had consulted with each division director, who said our present staff couldn't accomplish all these complex tasks. So John began searching for short-term specialized help to help with these pressing obligations until August 31. The search led to GE. The CDGM board of directors had insisted that CDGM have the veto power over the five GE individuals who would be with us, that there be orientation sessions for GE personnel, that GE specialists make every effort to give CDGM staff on-the-job training, rather than just do the jobs themselves, and that when CDGM personnel could do the work themselves, the GE project could be terminated. Other alternatives had been considered, but no company, individual, union, poverty program, industry, or accounting firm, except Ernst and Ernst, had submitted a proposal, as had GE.

John's memo ended: "Communication and productive work between peoples of differing backgrounds, between professionals and nonprofessionals, between Negro and White, between those who participate in institutions whose fundamental purposes are vastly different—all present profound problems. CDGM has specific, and immense duties to fulfill for the communities. It cannot accomplish these without added assistance and it must deal with institutions which have the resources that it needs. And it is a sad reality that the Orientation of the individuals that have the required skills is likely to be very similar, whether the organizational experience has been in industry, unions, government, or universities.

"I must make recommendations to answer these needs at the meeting of the Board of Directors on Thursday evening, July 21st.

"ALL INTERESTED STAFF ARE REQUESTED TO SUBMIT PLANS TO FULFILL CDGM'S RESPONSIBILITIES.

"These plans should be presented to the Division Director's meeting in writing if possible at 3:00 on Thursday afternoon for review and coordination before presentation to the Board of Directors."

Hunter Morey was later felt by OEO officials and investigators to have been irresponsible against management. On the contrary, Hunter was for Negroes learning how to *be* management, precisely because he considered management so important, and Movement-orientated Negroes so poor at it. On July 20 Hunter wrote an open letter to the CDGM staff urging that the anti-GE protesters do more than protest: "SUBJECT: WHERE WE STAND NOW. We have raised many important issues which CDGM, as all elements of our society, must grapple with and change: race, training and development, orientation and progress toward social change. CDGM has the extra burden of growing out of and being one of the main institutional expressions of the hopes of the civil rights movement, the poor Negro community of Mississippi. We must never violate the trust of this community.

"Our position as staff gives us peculiar responsibilities. We must not only raise issues, we must follow them through. This is the hard part. Take administration. In the Movement we have the problem of volunteers and whites running the Movement offices because hardly anyone is willing to come out of the field to work administratively. Even though the job of administration is to merely facilitate the program, if administration is not done properly, there is no program. If there is no money, for example, there is no program. The unglamorous, day to day work must be done and will be done, if not by us, then by people we consider worse. With CDGM now, we must follow through and make sure that we back our professed values with action.

"Our Board of Directors is about to deal with GE. We called for alternatives—so we must be willing to work to find them—both for now and for the long range and next grant (give names to Mat King). We raised the question of present staff potential—which we can illustrate and prove by increased productivity. Each division has great, uncompleted tasks—involving evaluation, supervision, follow through, and carrying out of assigned jobs. The degree to which we can come up with relevant reports and tabulations and analysis of our present operations and projected future possibilities is the degree to which GE or any other outside group is not needed. . . .

"Some of the follow through, I believe, must take the form of greater community among the staff and local people. We hardly talk to each other in our various departments, let alone among all the staff. Mr. Wells, Hoffman, and I, among others, are attempting to arrange for seminars, weekly staff meetings and weekend activities. Our administrators must get a greater feel from the communities. Our Board should be informed continuously. Just as many people feel it is not the best thing to do to leave Mississippi because it is bad, so it is not the best thing to do to leave or attempt to destroy CDGM because it has substantial problems. We must stick with it and make it good, because so many people's hopes rest with us."

In terms of growth stages, courage to object and raise hell comes before ability to take positive corrective and alternative action. In the GE case, as in so many other instances involving central CDGM needs, the angry protesters left the work of suggesting new leads and lengthily investigating them to a few. Marv Hoffman, who had taken my place as John's right hand since I had left CDGM on June 27, and several others bore the brunt of it. In the week following the flurry of memos, many possibilities were actively explored, including the North Carolina Fund, Ralph Showalter's Social Development Corporation, fifteen individuals, the Episcopal Church, the United Auto Workers, the United

Packinghouse Workers, the Jerald Corporation, the American Friends Service Committee, the Industrial Union Department of the AFL-CIO Inland Steel, the Office of the Mayor of New York, Xerox Corporation, Federal Electric, the Education and Research Development Corporation, J. B. Blayton, the School of Business Administration at Atlanta University, the School of Business Administration of Indiana University, the National Association of Intergroup Relations, officials, and others.

The picket line threat caused quite a stir. Arverna Adams, a local Negro who had graduated from Tougaloo College, gone on to Harvard graduate school, and come to help Marv Hoffman temporarily, wrote an open letter to everybody. She took the liberty of criticizing picket proponents for not keeping informed of the status of GE-CDGM relations, presupposing the Board's denial and rejection of staff's recent relevant recommendations, picketing without reason, and failing to unveil some hidden reasons for this apparently irrational behavior. Ann Mallett, secretary to the Board of Directors, also objected to the picketing performance in an open letter. Her objections were that picket organizers were acting anonymously, (no names of initiators or anything) autonomously (no staff discussions, just secret clique decisions), and without prior recourse to regular channels. Her letter included this sentence:

"Since I am a white southerner, I doubt anyone will give any dignity to my arguments, or even listen to my position, but as a human being with a certain amount of pride and respect of myself, I feel it is important to me that I state my position . . ."

John had selected a group of staff to consider this matter and advise him on it. The group wrote:

GE BEING RETAINED UNDER PRESENT TERMS (QUESTION)

ADVANTAGES

Technical competence
Immediate availability
Familiarity with CDGM
Flexible contract allowed (Dissent)
Ability to meet end of grant needs
Possible help in getting additional or new funding
Possible political rewards
Make CDGM director happy

DISADVANTAGES

Unwholesome office relationship
Bad publicity for CDGM due to GE's history
Present pressure from FDP, SNCC against CDGM if contract is signed
Possible danger from GE meddling with CDGM operations and policies
GE tradition is opposed to CDGM position:
  a. We shouldn't give GE money
  b. GE is a bad model
Tension between GE and CDGM would be unproductive
Possible danger of GE dominating CDGM
Pressure to find resources good for

immediate CDGM goals would be reduced
Too little analyzing of other resources, easy way out of crisis
Create distrust of CDGM by communities
Create distrust of CDGM by staff

EVALUATION

1. Definite no (3 votes)
   Community and staff feeling would prevent GE from doing the job and thereby could endanger refunding; contract with GE could endanger CDGM's effectiveness in community.
2. Mild no (2 votes)
   Pressure of CDGM's administrative and management obligations to the community and to OEO may *or* may not require a contract which has serious and obvious disadvantages
3. Can't say (1 vote)
   We possess too little information to decide.

A CO summed up his feelings on this issue by saying: "We're closer to the freedom fence now in CDGM than we've ever been. But whites are still management. If you ain't tore down the fence yet, or jumped over it, you're still on the wrong side of it, right?"

On August 1, John wrote to the staff: "After considering the quality and availability of the services and personnel which various groups would be prepared to offer CDGM at this time, the Board of Directors decided at its meeting on Sunday, July 31, to conclude a contract for necessary support services with the firm of Klein and Saks, subject to the approval of OEO. . . .

"The firm of Klein & Saks has performed management consulting services for numerous foreign governments including many in Latin America and Liberia; The Agency for International Development; the Economic Development Agency of the Department of Commerce; the Visiting Nurses Association; international social services organizations; and the World Council of Churches—in addition to many industrial concerns. . . ."

We had, as yet, not collided anew with OEO, but a collision appeared imminent. During the summer the OEO inspection office began rumbling with rumors that it "knew" CDGM was a front group for a black power organization. I received a call from a high-level inspection office man, which began, "Hello Polly, now listen, don't deny it, we *know*, we've had inspectors down there and we *know* —— and —— are Black Nationalists, so just admit it." After expressing my pleasure at hearing my friend again, and my opinion of his sense of scientific inquiry and method of examining evidence before making a judgment which might cost the poor people millions of dollars, we talked. Not only did he "know" that these two ambivalent and uncertain individuals were Black Nationalists, a term which he refused to attempt to define, but he also knew in the best Joe McCarthy manner that this made all thirty-thousand other CDGMians accomplices in the "crime."

On July 22 Frank Sloane, the Atlanta regional OEO director, a white South Carolina lawyer and White House appointee, wrote to CDGM demanding a report answering certain of his suspicions. One of these was the issue of blackness. CDGM leadership suspended many more important activities to engage in a large and sober research project, and wrote a reply including the fact that sixty-one white staff members worked in forty-one centers; and that twenty-six of these were out-of-staters, twenty-one were local whites, and fourteen were one or the other, it wasn't known which. We had seven white children enrolled. The report then itemized attempts made to integrate our program. But even after reading pages and pages and more pages [like those below] of pathetically ingenious attempts on the part of the poor to woo a little integration out of their white communities, OEO people managed to appear to remain unmoved:

SHARKEY AND ISSAQUENA COUNTIES	Filter: No integration. When a notice was posted in the Post Office announcing Head Start and asking everyone to come, regardless of race, the post master received so many threats and harassing calls that he has removed the announcement. A large part of the surrounding population are plantation owners who are very much opposed to Head Start. People are afraid to ask. Six local whites signed a refunding petition in one community, and the grocer gives vegetables. Valewood: The center was burned last year and this is still fresh in people's minds.
WASHINGTON COUNTY	Greenville Recruiting: They announced at public meetings and to the press that the program was for all children—no matter the race—but the press did not print this information for CDGM as it did for the county Head Start program. Had some applicants for summer jobs from local whites, some young teachers just out of college. Many went to work with county Head Starts because they could earn between $125 and $150. We only pay $75. Donations of toys and materials.
MADISON COUNTY	Canton area staff went to employment agency and to STAR placement office. Both said they would refer people. No results.
MADISON, LEAKE, OR/AND ATTALA COUNTIES	Letters were sent to whites in Ofahoma to come and fill out applications. None came.
NESHOBA	Philadelphia: Center staff and committee were afraid to canvass

COUNTY	due to racial tension in the area. . . . Whites very hostile in this area.
LOWNES COUNTY	Columbus: Was one out of state teacher, but received so many bomb threats she left.
JONES COUNTY	Central: Some were enrolled, but the parents were harassed and were afraid to send their children to the center . . . No integration. Morning Star: Promises were made but later broken. We have even offered jobs to white parents hoping to get their children and maybe their neighbor's children into the center.
JASPER OR CLARKE COUNTIES	Beaver Meadow: Center contacted local school principal and welfare department to try to find local white teachers to integrate staff but was told that they wouldn't work. Enterprise: They invited local business men to visit the center. . . . The out-of-state white worker has received threats when walking about town and attending church.
JASPER OR CLARKE	Mt. Zion: The committee here contacted some local whites to serve on an advisory committee, but failed to get anyone. They canvassed for children and offered jobs to both races, but only Negroes accepted. Two out-of-state men were hired as RTs, but they were threatened and finally left. The Negro family that they first lived with was forced to move out of their house.
CLAY COUNTY	West Point: Staff and committee have made many contacts. They invited all white schools to come and visit the center. They encouraged city and county superintendents to encourage people to come. They canvassed in white neighborhoods, but they were not successful in getting children to come. A few local whites visited and volunteered including a Catholic priest and a doctor who held a medical workshop.
EATON (FORREST COUNTY)	Local white woman applied and hired as Roving Teacher. She quit and was replaced by out-of-state white. Twelve white children were enrolled at the beginning, but none of them showed up. Two parents of these children asked for jobs, received them, but didn't come.
FORREST	In the spring of 1966 Vernon Dahmer was murdered here.
JACKSON COUNTY	1st Baptist: Two white children were enrolled but then dropped out because of pressure from neighborhood. Union Baptist: One local white was working but because her paycheck was late from CDGM, she quit. Gautier: They do receive boxes and crates from white store owners. Three Rivers: . . . Have visited the Board of Supervisors for references. . . .

BOLTON HINES COUNTY

No integration of the staff or children of this center. Before the center opened, the center staff and committee was forced into an unofficial agreement with mayor (they were renting an old school building from county) that there would be no white people working at the center. This center was later burned to the ground.

RANKIN COUNTY

True Vine: Center is integrated by a Hawaiian. After she arrived some local whites came to the house where she was living and threatened the owner.

WARREN COUNTY

Vicksburg: Welfare had a white specialist who worked in this center, but left because work was too much. Social Security office was too busy to help Local School system; said they had no time to dedicate to Head Start.

HOLMES COUNTY

Second Pilgrim's Rest: Before we could really make any definite efforts to involve the white people in our center, we were harassed by many of the white citizens of our town. They tried to burn our church down where we first started, until we had our center built, while having a staff meeting, some of them rode by and fired shots at us. We even had ads in the newspaper trying to involve them. Despite this, they burned crosses at our homes and threatened a great number of people. We were afraid most of the time, and didn't know what to expect from them any of the time.

Virgie Saffold of First Pilgrim's Rest made this report: We have four white families in our community. We do not know any way of getting up to them. They have blocked the roads and have thrown shot-guns on us. We have to go ten miles out of our way to get home. How can we get up to them when they hold shot-guns in our faces?

Longbranch: We have not tried to get any local whites. We were afraid that they would start bombing and firing at our homes and center. We had an ad in the paper, but know no other way to contact them. Our lives have been threatened, crosses have been burned at our homes, and police dogs have been put on us. We don't know how to ask them, except to put another ad in the paper.

PIKE AND AMITE COUNTIES

Area staff here distributed leaflets in both the white and Negro communities announcing the Head Start programs . . . were not very successful. . . .

WALTHALL COUNTY

The people in the Walthall County area have been threatened and the New Hope Center was burned during this program.

"FIRE DESTROYS HOUSE USED FOR HEAD START CLASSES Tylertown, Mississippi (Special)—A small frame house which was being used for Head Start classes north of here was burned to the ground Friday night, Walthall County Sheriff J. C. Knippers said today.

Knippers said he had not ruled out the possibility of arson. . . ."

An Atlanta office OEO official who had a great deal to do with CDGM told me: "One trouble is CDGM has never been assigned to one person. We handle it committee-style. No one is responsible. Every time something comes up, they call a meeting, and everyone listens for everyone else's feelings, and we all get time to decide which way to duck.

"Another trouble is John Mudd's superior attitude. He acts like he and his are all-perfect, and OEO is a shark tank. When I have to work with him, I get my guts torn out. I come staggering back feeling that I am the enemy of the poor. One day after I was with John, I looked in the mirror, and I saw a fin sprouting on my back. CDGM would fare better if John took us into his confidence. He treats us like dirt. Who reacts his best that way?"

A central figure in the OEO inspection office told us on the telephone: "Mudd is defiant and defensive. We evaluate CDGM by the same standards we use in any Head Start project anywhere in the United States. No one in CDGM gives a God-damn about Head Start; it's just one big employment program. A good many of your centers are custodial; purely custodial. Other projects have problems with us, but they don't resort to yellow journalism! We find a power struggle inside CDGM! Maybe you're unaware of it, but it's there! We aren't funding things like that. We didn't find that CDGM in any way affected the agencies and institutions around it.

"As far as I'm concerned, our major criticism of CDGM is that it doesn't seem to be an agency or an organization as much as it's some kind of a damn concept. It's supposed to be a school for small children, yet it seems to be a community project involving much more than that. That may be great, but we are only funding Head Start here."

* * *

Page One, OEO pamphlet "Project Head Start Parents"—the opening line of this booklet says: "The Child Development Center is both a concept and a community facility."

CHAPTER 38

JOHN MUDD

Swimming upstream with stiffened resolution: Management Training Project; Transolve; including poor people in proposal writing; a constitution for a decentralized CDGM; a community college

IT WOULD HAVE been easy for John to drown, as I was doing—or to join the howling storm, as he sometimes appeared on the verge of doing. But in a manner that seemed infuriatingly obstinate to many OEO officials and seemed admirably persevering to many CDGMians, John persisted toward his goal of providing opportunities for poor people to gain greater and greater understanding and "ownership" of themselves and their organization. John was too numbed and overwhelmed to try to justify his actions. His stance was rather like that of Martin Luther at the Diet of Worms: "Here I stand: I can do no otherwise."

During the spring John was distressed that the area administrators were so leaderless and somehow so outside the real point of CDGM. They were, in some cases, authoritarian about performing their functions. In other cases they were so laissez-faire and vague that their functions weren't performed adequately. Only a few were real administrative and spiritual leaders for their areas, which was neither surprising nor shameful nor an oversight in a program intended to give new career opportunities to poor people. We had the poor people in administrative positions. Having achieved this, John had already achieved more toward new careers for the poor than almost any other Head Start director. However, it was now urgently time for something more: management training for these more than sixteen individuals. So far they had had help only from Jesse Paris, who was learning himself, and consultant Sam Sanderson, whose specialty was hand-holding and providing a much-needed outlet for ventilation.

Consultant Jack Wiersma suggested to John that a Washington, D.C., consulting firm headed by Kenneth G. Olson undertake such a program from May to August. Mr. Olson secured the services of Messrs. Secundy, Martinson, and Safran, who flew into Mississippi from the East at intervals to conduct workshops. Bob Secundy was a business and financial analyst. John Martinson was an independent consultant in the field of information retrieval and communication systems. He had had experience relating to the training of subprofessionals in the U.S. Office of Education, National Institutes of Health, National Science Foundation, and OEO projects. Dan Safran had done undergraduate work in anthropology, and had graduated from the Bryn Mawr School of Social Work. He had organized fair housing groups and a neighborhood house for the American Friends Service Committee, had consulted on Head Starts in Kentucky, North Carolina, South Carolina, Georgia, and Alabama the previous summer, and currently worked in Washington as Director of Training at the United Planning Organization. It was Dan who wrote the ideas of starting with the *AA's* problems and helping them become trainers in their own areas into the otherwise traditional Olson proposal.

One of the local poor people serving as an area administrator at the time, said: "When Safran showed up was the first time we really began to understand what our job could be. Up till then we were just messenger boys to central administration. I don't know if they meant it that way, or we just didn't know how to wring more water from the job. Dan Safran helped us become somebodies in CDGM. The first thing Safran did was he got *us* to make a list of our management problems. Man, we had plenty, too! I mean, he didn't start teaching us some course way out on cloud nine, he had *us* state the problems so *we could teach ourselves* a course in how to solve them.

"See, one thing, we had to work with center coordinators, but they didn't know how to do anything, any of these administrative things, and we had no control over them. Safran thought if we became more sensitive to their needs, we could help them better, and that would help us, see, because their mistakes were keeping us in a tizzy. I know, I talked to Safran a lot. He thought we could learn best by teaching others. That's why he didn't lecture us, he helped us design what we would do with center coordinators and secretaries. See, one thing the ATGs always had over us, what gave them the advantage, was they had somebody to teach, and they had Polly to fight for them. Jesse Paris was supposed to be our Polly, but he didn't know anything either, and his past behavior didn't make him too admired, and he was weak—he always agreed with the last person he spoke to—he wouldn't stand up for us. Safran was our Polly. We took to trusting him. He wasn't like all the other white consultants. He didn't stay at fancy hotels. He stayed in the Negro community."

In the first three workshops, AAs evolved a problem-solving approach. By Workshop IV and V on June 13 and 16 AAs were ready to begin Phase II of their training: acquiring specific management skills. They focused on the applications process strategies for involving their community constituents without dominating them, and varied approaches to CDGM's goal of further decentralization for the next grant, expected to begin at the end of the summer. We had made a major move toward decentralization, toward greater leadership in each community, in the second grant with the area staff system. But we had a long way to go to eliminate the need for any central office—to be able to have sixteen autonomous areas, staffed exclusively by poor people.

Dan was dealing with two of the central difficulties in CDGM here. First, many area administrators were highly ambivalent about whether they wanted their constituents, and even each other, to develop decision-making powers (freedom) or not (the thought of capable constituents was a great threat to their own insecure roles). An example of this was a man who listened to Dan's whole discussion of the reasons for learning problem solving instead of simply "answers," and then said, "Yeah, but what if they make the wrong decisions?"

The second problem was to what degree was inadequate performance of AAs caused by lack of skill, in spite of full will to perform well? And to what degree was inadequate performance caused by ambivalence about wanting to take on so much responsibility? If the former was the situation, then skill training was all that was needed. But if, as is the case with people who have learned not to try to be leaders, individuals had very mixed feelings and many guilt feelings when they stood above their fellow community people, then working the ambivalence through was required before any amount of skill training could be used fully.

The June 20 workshop dealt with problems of organizational structure. CDGM's organizational chart as well as those of other organizations were considered. Participants discussed reasons for using this or that structure. AAs discussed ways of maintaining flexibility, yet making sure that various functions and operations within the organization were facilitated and problems were analyzed. The final workshop in Phase II began with the questions: What is planning? Why plan? How do you follow up your plans? Do you ever have to change your plan of action? What is long-range planning? Dan Safran helped AAs establish work priorities, find the easiest method for doing the best work in the least amount of time, and apply the problem-solving method to office operations.

Phase III of the Management Training Project, ending on August 22, included six sessions on "the future." AAs played a management game in which they themselves exercised administrative responsibilities, made and justified decisions. They developed organizational structures for Head Start programs of five hundred to fifteen hundred children by selecting from a list of job titles and descriptions those they felt to be suitable personnel for CDGM, and filling in blank organizational charts. They then worked on how to make a cost-item breakdown, how to estimate costs by comparing one program with similar or neighboring programs, how to compare a previous year's expenses with estimated current needs, and how to analyze OEO guidelines for items under consideration. They were enthusiastic and understood the principles involved very well, but had the trouble one would expect with mathematical computations. They practiced decision-making on transactions similar to tasks they encountered in their CDGM AA roles.

They practiced recognizing and coping with the many problems of personnel management. The "management game" that was used when dealing with personnel problems included giving each participant a series of ten cases involving personnel problems, with a space below each for the participant to write his solution. Guidelines for good personnel administration were also given to each AA. Supposedly the answers to the problems presented could be arrived at by applying the rules stated in the guidelines. Discussion followed, in which solutions were compared and judged by the group. The cases were artfully invented by John Martinson from real-life CDGM situations. Dan emphasized creative management as well as technical management. He was perhaps the most excellent trainer I'd ever seen in action.

In this area revolving around people AAs had greater difficulty and were more defensive about criticisms of their ideas than when problems surrounding the management of designs, materials, and money were involved.

In his final report on the series of workshops, Dan described some of the conditions that had made work difficult, such as the large size of the trainee group, inadequacy of facilities, substantial demands on the participants' time by their jobs ("daily and during the sessions"), reticence of some members, insufferable heat in the warehouse where training took place, continued interruptions from other wandering-through nonparticipants as they went about their other kinds of business in the building, and finally, the great variety of educational and work experience of participants that made uniformity in the instruction offered, in providing analogies, examples, and in fulfilling expectations, impossible.

These things didn't daunt Dan; they led him to use the problem-solving technique. Dan was very excited by the results of this program. He came to CDGM with great faith in the abilities and further potentials of the poor. He left with even greater faith. His only disappointment was that he had intended to write a training manual geared to this kind of group, for use in other programs. Mr. Olson and Mr. Safran didn't see eye to eye on this. In spite of Dan's exertions and offer to do it on a volunteer basis, the "training manual" Mr. Olson authorized turned out to be merely summaries and excerpts of tapes from the workshops. This caused us all to comment that there are all kinds of people in the popular poverty business lately, and for all kinds of reasons. The

Management Training Project was perhaps unnecessarily expensive, but seemed to be of some or much benefit to all participants.

John's second major spring and summer 1966 project designed to promote growth toward community people's autonomy was one called Transolve. Afterward John's only question about Transolve was the cost. He wondered if it couldn't have been done less expensively. But about the project's effectiveness none of us had any doubts. Transolve, Inc., was a Boston firm co-owned by two psychologists with extensive experience in leadership training: George Land and Herbert Sonthoff. Along with his other consulting contributions, Jack Wiersma introduced John to this firm, which specialized in the systematic development of creative problem-solving in leaders (or potential leaders) of industry, institutions, and others highly appropriate to CDGM's philosophy and needs.

One of John Mudd's most striking qualities was his extraordinarily good judgment in screening out hordes of people who wanted to "help" but who would have molded CDGM into traditional shapes, had they been given the authority to work with us, and conversely, to choose unusual groups to give us critically needed skills. Transolve's proposal to conduct an employee development program for CDGM, submitted April 11, 1966, was the result of a preliminary study that made it possible for Dr. Land and Dr. Sonthoff to devise a training program uniquely suitable for us. The unusual thing about the Transolve people wasn't that they could write a delightful proposal, studded with all the stunning, currently stylish words, like "innovative" and "creativity" and "sensitivity"—*they could do what they said they would do.*

George Land found that Central Staff and community personnel alike showed a low level of sensitivity toward and understanding of human relationships, presumably due to lack of experience in understanding group dynamics. This caused him to conclude that high emphasis should be placed on cases and problems involving the recognition of human relations problems and *action* on these problems.

He felt that many people revealed lack of familiarity with fundamental administrative concepts, and sometimes unfamiliarity even with administrative language. His proposal included strong emphasis on concepts of administration and the application of these concepts to the daily work of the area administrators and community organizers who would participate in the training project. Because the organizational structure of CDGM continually underwent such sudden and extensive growth, George recommended much stress on problems and cases dealing with administrative problems occasioned by change and growth. Training should emphasize skills as well as the skill of coping with an unusual degree of flexibility and constantly appearing new circumstances.

He suggested that a sizable amount of workshop time be devoted to cases and problems leading to the appraisal of the proper function of each of the area staff's many responsibilities. They had to be leaders and administrators of an area team. They had to be diplomats and decision-making catalysts to committees and communities. They had to be shrewd negotiators and public relations drum beaters with other agencies and divisions, inside and outside CDGM. They had to be working partners with Central Staff members, and also their representatives in communities that never saw Central Staff members.

Communications were dreadful between diversified divisions and geographical locations. George proposed working in all areas of communications to create a smoother flow of information in all directions concerning the clarification of aims, objectives, procedures, ideas, etc. Transolve intended to foster in each member of the group greater insight into himself and into his impact on other people; to develop an attitude of self-confidence in each participant and faith in his own ideas; to stimulate open-mindedness to the ideas of many area employees; and to provide methods with which the area staff could be leaders in developing creative problem-solving skills in center employees.

Transolve used many valuable case histories as core material. These were prepared by Dr. Land and Dr. Sonthoff. Material was factually correct, but identities were disguised.

The Transolve method included the use of worksheets. These were not instructions in how to do something, but detailed road-map type instructions of how to *think*. They detailed processes of piling up alternatives in fact-finding, problem-finding, idea-finding, solution-finding, and acceptance-finding. The worksheets also provided *practice* in stretching the individual's imagination at every stage. As is the case with every other skill, practice produced vastly improved performance in the majority of cases. Dr. Land's observations and impressions end with the statement: "*Negligible motivational or acceptance problem for the course.* Observations have suggested that there will be little or no problem in securing the interest and participation of various staff members in the intensive workshop proposed. We have been impressed with the singular dedication these people have for their work, their enthusiasm in discussing their problems and needs, and their conviction as to the benefit of CDGM activities. We have also noted that many staff members are accustomed to speaking openly and easily with each other—a fact which should contribute to the high degree of participation necessary for these workshops."

Transolve was enormously popular with ecstatic area teams that were selected to participate. A community organizer and Transolve participant said of the program: "Transolve was just great. We need more. It's a strange program. It's not explainable what happens. At first you feel you're not nuthin'. Then it uplifts you, gets you seeing your blocks and how to get around them till you feel as creative as anybody in the world. You begin with seventeen problems, and you begin systematically just peeling them off. As you do this, you force your mind to decide what's *most* important and how you're going to do it. You begin to face your downfalls, upgrades, how the other person feels even if you may not agree with it, and to *really* listen, interpret what they did say instead of repeating what we wish they had said, so to speak. You sort out your feelings and deal with your anger. I didn't know how confused I'd been till all my confusion began to come out and I could sort myself out and learn to cope with some of me. I learned how to lead meetings, get people back on the subject: I learned how to *do* Transolve with others. *I* trained classes—I saw people beginning to feel they were somebody, and I knew it was my skills helping my people! It was the first useful training I ever got. If we could do more of this at the local level, a lot of poor people would be mighty different. Freer."

If this lady's account of her life from its beginning to the point at which Transolve intercepted it is not a saga of rags to riches, it is, more importantly, an amazing story of inner growth. She was born thirty-odd years before on a Mississippi plantation. She moved many times from Mississippi to Tennessee to Arkansas with one or the other or both parents, as they looked for work and better working conditions. Somehow they managed to keep her in school till the eighth grade. By then, though she loved school, she felt she had to go to work to support her desperately poor mother.

"I picked cotton and worked for the white people. I got married and went to Florida; we were migrant workers. My husband worked three months out of the year. He picked tomatoes. I didn't make much money because I didn't know how to pick tomatoes, but I learned how to pick tomatoes. Then I heard that there was work at the tomato canning factory. There I learned the art of how to *peel* tomatoes; hit it a certain way at the same time you keep your eyes on the belt so you could catch a warm scalded tomato, because they're easier to peel that way. I started to make twenty dollars a week. It was by the big water bucket full they paid, twenty-five cents a bucket. The faster I learned to use my reflexes, eye, hand, feel, the more I made. Finally I made eighty dollars a week. I figured, 'Whatever you do, do it better. It pays!' I washed and ironed, and whenever the white lady would leave home, I'd sit down with her baby and read.

"Then I had children. When they was getting to school age, we wanted to stop this seasonal work so they could go to school, so we came back here to Missoula, Mississippi, where my husband was raised up, because his mother had died and left this acre of land here. I came here in 1962, and I took one look at this dead place, Oh, *Lord*, was it dead! And I said to my husband, Harry, 'Ooh, Harry, I got to get out of *here!*' Anything there was to do, though, I did it. I always did want training. They started up some extension classes. First we was making pound cakes. Now I been making pound cakes for years, child, I know all there is about pound cakes. But when you ain't got no eggs and all those flavorings, you just can't make no pound cakes. Anyway, pound cakes wasn't the central problem in my life, as I saw it. Then we started to work on sewing dresses. But I kept hearing all these important things going on in the world, and I just got bored to death sewing on them dresses. So next we was making jewelry boxes. We was supposed to buy this macaroni and then run on out and buy some glue. I said to my husband, 'Harry,' I said, 'I'm going to *cook* this macaroni, and shit on that box!'

"Next thing I hear five hundred civil rights workers is coming to Mississippi. My friend said, 'Lord, honey, they wouldn't come *here*. Nobody comes here!' But one day we saw these young boys come walking into town. I said, 'Now who's *that?* It must be them!' They didn't even walk the same. We couldn't even understand what they was saying, they talked so funny. It sounded funny to us. We never had heard anybody talk except us. Ain't that funny? Now I can understand anybody.

"We were used to Negroes with a college education to expect us to get all set up for them, so we got in a strain, jumped up, trying to wipe up, fix up, run out, and cook up a fine dinner.

"I've seen so many changes here, though, you wouldn't believe it was possible. First came the Negro and white SNCC volunteers. I told those white folks, 'Don't *you* come here, you come later, it's too dangerous for you still.' So they did. If it wasn't for them civil rights workers, I don't know where we'd've been. They really got us rolling. We just wouldn't believe the way they were comin' in, eating what we ate, beans and peas, just talking to us little people, and were interested in *our* lives. They just didn't come in with some message—they came in to get to know *us*. I mean, they didn't want nuthin' from us. They wanted to know what *we* wanted.

"The first important thing I ever did, I began working on voter registration with SNCC that summer. We had never heard of NAACP or any of these other groups. I tried to register three times myself before I finally made it. This is famous —— County, you know! I was even a delegate to Atlantic City for FDP. I was also a project director for COFO in —— and —— Counties. If there was ever anything sensible to do in this stupid town, you could count on me to volunteer.

"In 1965 Delta Ministry began talking about forming something, some CDGM thing, so I began organizing for that. I helped formulate local committees, tried to get people willing to teach. Nobody was willing, because anything new sounded like civil rights to them. That's natural. There hadn't been anything new in this Godforsaken place for several centuries till SNCC. I didn't apply for a CDGM job myself. I was still getting thirty-six dollars from SNCC every other week; when they had it. And I felt looser, freer, that way. CDGM was a federal program—I wasn't sure I could do much good restricted like you had to be. I had other things to do. Like in 1965 a bunch of us put in a suit to desegregate the schools in this county. I was the organizer of that.

"It was rough! Ooh, it *was* rough! One night Marian came up here and those people followed her; you know who I mean. We were *so* scared. But Marian, she just lay down on that sofa and went to sleep! Harry and me stood out there all night in those beans. Harry had a quart beer and I had a great big old butcher knife—oh, Lord, we were scared to death. All *night* we stood out in that garden in those beans trying to drink that beer to calm our nerves. Only one quart wasn't nearly enough.

"The only time I can rest is when I'm out of this state. When I'm layin' in that bed here, I just keep thinkin' alla these things I'm doing to these here white folks and what they might do in return, and I just get scared to deather!

"One thing I figured out through this Movement—I get stronger in Christ everyday. I'm doing the work He started. He said go with the people, help better their condition. And if people say politics and the church don't mix, just look at Jesus. Jesus is a big political figure. I got it right here. I reads all there is to read half the night. Now, I do wrong; I do wrong every day, just like other people. But you have to think, what *is* wrong? It's when you put The Man ahead of Christ's work, that's what it is. We just must make people see how this work, all these things, *is* God. We need to pray and *do*. We done prayed so long most of us has forgot what we're prayin' *for*. We been sayin', 'Lord, will you save us? Lord, will you deliver us?' Now here come these people and these programs that *can* save us and deliver us, and we find it *hard* to get these people out. They don't understand God is hearing the prayers, and Christ is coming and working through man, through me, through each of us, to help us deliver us. Jesus didn't just pray. He acted too. Never forget that.

"Some people say, 'We just want to go out on Saturday night and drink corn liquor and cut and gamble. Well, you got to understand, you got to strike out at someone, and it surely can't be the man who's really keeping you down. I don't know how long it's gonna be that poor folks is gonna go around gettin' each other and letting all these officials get them. But personally, I think the poor in this country has a lotta guts to still be sane after all the pressures they've gone through—and a lotta something to have a mind left after it all. They get it somewhere, and it ain't in school! I can understand the gamblers and drinkers better than I can the ones that lays down and rests when they ain't scuffled a muscle.

"One thing CDGM has done for folks—everybody thinks he's creative, everybody says he can do everything. I charge Polly with that. She told everybody, 'You don't have to have a high school diploma, you just have to try.' She talked about trying and training, not about all kinds of credentials. She said that from one end of the state to the other, and the funny part was, people were ripe to hear that. Somewhere in them they had believed that all along, so people *moved.* Now we've got people so up and full of it, they're angry at all these OEO guidelines that are anxious to see if all these teachers have all these qualifications. That comes next, all that training and sorting everybody out, but first we've got to get these people *into* everything, and CDGM has done that. It's wonderful how people have come alive!

"Oh, we still have people trying to run this program like a church; a deacon or somebody passing down orders and everybody agreeing to everything. And we have more arguing people now than we *ever* had. Some of the arguing is bad—it's about silly things. But to my way of thinking it's wonderful that they're all stirred up, coming out; now you can get two thousand people to a meeting where you was doing well before if you could get two. Only one thing they'd *all* come out to before was a funeral. Once you get all these people out, it can lead to all kinds of action.

"Some people keep saying we should have unity. They think the hassling we have now in these communities is awful. They wants it all smooth and fine. They like it better when everybody is scared to death all the time they're working that somebody'll snatch their money out from under them. I thought we'd have a shooting-do over who will be chairman, where it used to be you couldn't get no one! But it was quiet then, and 'peaceful,' and we sure did have unity. That's good? Hah! You tell me that lively fighting is bad? Hell, it's fantastic! They see the powers working now, and they want to be part of it. Before, they couldn't ever even *see* the powers, and they certainly couldn't dream to be part of them. Now, they quit the committees and they say, 'If things don't be like I like, I just won't mess with this mess no more.' We've still got a mess as long as we've got all this wrassling and tassling, but they're *beginning:* asking questions, being inquisitive, fussing, misunderstanding, getting it all wrong, making a big rigamarole: but it's started, you hear me?

"The conversations in this town are different. I never saw people so interested in elections. And they talk about what the governor said last night, and why their child was behind on his report card, and who should we vote for, and why are our schools so backward and nasty, and where are all these training programs we're supposed to be getting; where all they used to say was that mother wit was enough. There's still gossip, true, but that's *all* there used to be, and now it's not the focus. The focus now is education. They fight about hiring and how to spend the money, but they're making decisions. This is the first program here where poor people made these decisions. This is the first time people have made their own decisions about their own children in their own structure, instead of shrugging their shoulders and sending them out to somebody else. They quit the committees, but then they get on another one! Do you see the importance of that? If they get mad, they don't quit altogether, they make *another* way. Alternatives. Trying. People just seem to act crazy, quitting, starting up new things, attacking each other, coming to me to tell me the dirt about each other. I tell 'em, 'Why don't you go over there and tell the chairman? If you can't face her, how in the world are you going to face that lady in the courthouse?'

"After while I asked what do the community organizers do for CDGM? It was outlined to me. I thought I could be of service doing that. I thought, 'You have to come and go with these organizations; sometimes work next to them—sometimes *in* them. Now's the time for me to get *in* CDGM.' I worked with parents and community committees explaining federal programs that would benefit Head Start children and older children. I learned a lot about federal agencies, doing this.

"So I done my best as a CDGM community organizer, to get people going. There's no set pattern for a organizer. One day you're holdin' a prayer meetin', and next day you're at a dance. Then you might be havin' a beer with the boys at the cafe. You got to be where the people be, to get in, get started talking. You may not be so interested in that chicken out there that they're talkin' 'bout in that house up the road a piece, but you just better *get* interested in the blasted chicken, because it's the most joyful feeling in the world to go out there and talk with people and get communicating. OEO don't understand this, that's why they get all upset about what the COs are doing.

"I'm moving, honey, and thanks a lot to Transolve. In Transolve I got selected to go to Cambridge, Massachusetts, for intensive training. After I come back, I was a trainer. I trained about seven hundred people: parents, committees, area staff, even central. All this Transolving helped me understand a lot about CDGM.

"In these other poverty programs I been looking at, you don't just *talk* to these big people like Polly and John. You have to go through secretaries and assistant secretaries and super secretaries. But we just grab John by the collar and holler at him and curse him out because we know he *cares*—him and Polly, you can let them have an earful, and not fear, you know they're trying to straighten it out better. Maybe we look madder than in most programs, but I believe it's just we're all honester in CDGM.

"Some of us black folks are so tied up in mistrust and looking up to whites and all, that it's just in our blood. Even me, I feel so mixed up and confused because I was brought up under all this, and I have these scars too. These scars are so hard to heal. They keep opening up again when things happen like the 1954 desegregation cases, and then I turn my head thirteen years later and I see all these same segregated Negro and white schools. The scars open up again and I get sore when these federal officials come down here and talk to these lying white and local officials and just take what they say and go flying home again. Then the scars open again when you look at the school lunch program. It's supposed to be for poor children, hungry children. But you have to go through one agency after another to even get two or three free lunches out of them. They guard those lunches like you was taking food from *their* mouth, and then the rest of your children still go hungry, and you stand there and explain why their brother got fed and they didn't. Justice. Love your country. Teachers is fair and good. Admire and respect them, Johnny!

"In CDGM they just couldn't get all the powers to the poor at once, so in the beginning you still had some white people with these administrative powers. We have to find a way that we just don't scream about whites getting all the positions. But we have to use all these federal programs because we need them. There isn't enough money to help us with our huge problems anywhere else, and we have to make sure these programs work like CDGM does to make sure these Negroes is getting the training so they are getting ready to get into these administrative positions. CDGM didn't do everything, but it was the first one even trying to do the right things.

"Then you get some black people coming around here saying, 'BLACK POWER!' and I'm supposed to forget those CRs who got us moving and John and Polly, and I'm supposed to drop everything and run around yelling, 'BLACK POWER! BLACK POWER!'—why, God, where would we be without the whites who helped us see? The thing that causes a lot of our problems is we don't have too many people who sit down for a minute by the side of the road and think about what's good and what's bad about each of these programs. Now, take SNCC. There aren't too many people can sit down and talk sensible about SNCC. Some say it's all bad and what did it really do? And others say it's the only real thing, CDGM is just a million-dollar paycheck. If anything's wrong, *everything* must be wrong. Or if anything's right, don't risk it by questioning, everything must be right. Life ain't like that chile —there's Jesus and the Devil all mixed together in each thing you look at.

"Talking about what Polly should do, well, chile, she'll just have to set down and study her heart and weigh things. If she doesn't think she was wrong to help start CDGM, then she should go start another good project. She knows more now than she did before because she's banged her head three or four times. She know now how tangled up we are, and when it begins to come out, it comes out all crooked. Some people will take it all out on one white person, because that's the only white person they can reach—or the only one they dare. Polly learned, it's new for these people to sit around and rumble and mumble underground against somebody. Used to be only underground mumbling they would've mumbled was, 'Shhhh! Don't get into that, it's white! She's white! Shhhh!' So someday maybe they'll kick up at the real problems instead of at some person came to help them. Even now it's boiling near the top, even leaking at the edges; sometime soon they'll learn what to mumble at.

"Nowadays I'm doin' all kinds of other things to bring change: and for all this, all I get for salary is bills. Know anyone has my type job open, that pays? Thanks to Transolve, I don't know where I'll be next—watch me fly, honey chile!"

Transolve staff reported: "The trainees . . . in the opinion of the Transolve Instructors, worked harder than the usual group encountered in business or higher education. . . . The group saw that what it had learned was a way to realize the ultimate objective of the Head Start program. . . . Transolve believes that at least two-thirds of the group demonstrated superior competence in conducting . . . [their own] systematic problem-solving training programs, and all trainees will become more competent with more practice."

The Management Training Project and Transolve were two programs John thought very important. He put a great deal of time into planning and coordinating both. But consultants carried them through. Involving poor people in thrashing out the additions, revisions, alterations, and amount of decentralization in CDGM that they really wanted and felt they could handle, and putting all this into proposal form for a third grant from OEO, was John's own personal baby. He managed to get some help from Coleman Miller, recently imported and installed CDGM associate deputy director for community program, from others in the community organization division, and from several of our consultants, but it was John's passionate belief in the task, perseverance, endurance, and skill that wheedled the poor into becoming ever more involved in the central problems of CDGM.

Agonizing ambivalences entangle the poor when they're faced with tasks of putting feelings into formats, protests into positive actions—actually, actively *committing* themselves to a personal part in social institutions from which they've been excluded for so long that they've developed antagonisms toward them. Only those viscerally familiar with this can anticipate the agility with which John had to swim and duck and dive and do every kind of leadership gymnastic to induce people to participate and progress in his proposal-writing project. As many do-gooders have discovered, apathy is an antidote to unmanageable psychological pain, just as unconsciousness is a blessing to those in acute physical pain. After people have been systematically, institutionally spurned for centuries, a spurning attitude grows in *them,* self-defensively, and is passed on from generation to generation. They *don't want* to join that, or anything resembling that, which has historically refused them admittance—even though they see it may benefit them. An ATG explained it perfectly:

"We're smart. We adapt. That's why we've survived. If they won't let us, we learn first to unwant to; then to *not* want to; then to want *not* to. Then suddenly they *will* let us. They want us. And something in us wants to want to. But we've trained ourselves to want *not* to. So then you feel like a cat ready to pounce ahead or leap back all with the same muscles in the same minute. Then you feel angry because going two ways at once, you don't go no place."

The apathetic were apathetic, while either mouthing the usual empty words about how wonderful it was to join in this endeavor, or absenting themselves altogether from working sessions. The angry were angry, and worked either belligerently in meetings or underground in communities to convince others that the whole ordeal was one more phony plot of Mudd's to put something over on the ignorant and the innocent.

Essentially, one issue ran through all the informal impromtu gatherings and major proposal-planning meetings during the spring and summer months of 1966. Another ATG summarized it to me: "We don't want central and the board to run our business. But it's a lot of responsibility we don't even know all the details of what are, to run something this big, and do we really want to work that hard and learn that much, and maybe fall on our face to *really* do it all the way ourself without John and them? Area staffs have goofed up a lot and bossed people and lost things and not known enough with the responsibility they do have. Are we ready to take on more? If area staffs run a whole bunch of separate CDGM Head Starts with no central, we'll lose our national contacts and our safety in numbers. But we'll be autonomous. That's what we say we want: no central.

"But do we know how to follow all the OEO regulations? That would be part of our responsibility then, no interpreters. And do we know when and where you can insist to OEO that they're wrong and win what you know that's right? It's scary to think of doing all this without our white friends.

"And we say we don't want central to choose area staff members next time. We want community people to elect their own bosses. Yet we area staff people have not done so hot, we're just learning, a lot of community people resent our new power. Prob'ly they won't elect us. They'll elect their friends. Then nobody in the leadership will know *anything* about how CDGM works and what it stands for, and everything we've got'll collapse. If we risk going autonomous, the gains could be great; but we also risk losing *everything*.

"We say we want to be in on everything. But who's in the Milner Building till the cock crows every night sweating and planning? I'll tell you who it *ain't:* it ain't us . . . it's John and that group, and those who are willing to work when nobody else shows up to do what's gotta be done by tomorrow morning. So here it is, in a nutshell: Some of us think it's a wild and foolish idea. Some of us thinks it's a further step in the direction we've been marching anyhow. Freedom ain't as easy as I used to think before I met up with CDGM."

One of John Mudd's most significant techniques for promoting maximum participation of the poor in CDGM as a total institution was to spend a great deal of time preparing people. He wanted them to understand what decisions would soon be coming up, and what points they might consider in their local community meetings, before mass meetings were scheduled to be held. People were confused enough by the intricacies and complexities of policy decisions and parliamentary procedures. They would have withdrawn into helpless and frustrated acceptance of whatever happened had John not had the extraordinary patience he did in helping them democratically deal with such questions in advance.

A much-publicized statewide meeting to consider a new Head Start program was scheduled for June 18 at the Masonic Temple on Lynch Street in Jackson. Before the meeting a list of problems predicted to arise and be discussed, with suggestions and reasons for and against them, was sent to communities. Space was included on the form under each of eleven items for each community to write its opinions about what it thought would be the best policy for CDGM to adopt concerning each of the points. The document began by reminding community people that our grant was slated to end on August 31, and that OEO expected a proposal by July 1, if we wanted the program to be renewed on September 1. It started by stating:

Some people may feel:
–the program should not continue
–their area should apply to OEO for its own Head Start
–the communities should continue to work with CDGM, but the area office should do many things that the central staff does now,
–CDGM should continue to operate in the same way.

EVERYONE IN THE COMMUNITIES SHOULD SAY
WHAT HE THINKS AND SEND REPRESENTATIVES
TO THE STATEWIDE MEETING WHO WILL EXPRESS
THEIR IDEAS FOR EVERYONE TO HEAR.

It then went on to present eleven problems the proposal had to deal with, and outlined reasons for and against each one. John didn't try to sell and persuade people—he tried to help them think. The problems were all those pertaining to any level of project design. "Answers" weren't always what the documents' author thought. For example:

THE FEDERAL GOVERNMENT REQUIRES THAT ALL PEOPLE BE CONSIDERED FOR EMPLOYMENT WITHOUT REGARD TO RACE, RELIGION, CREED, OR PLACE OF NATIONAL ORIGIN. OEO ALSO ASKS IF THERE IS ANY REASON WHY ANY HEAD-START CENTER WILL NOT BE INTEGRATED.

How Would Your Community Answer This Question?

FOR

We should make *every effort* to integrate our centers. We are working for an integrated society. Having white children and white staff in the centers helps the children overcome their fears of whites and makes them able to grow up facing up to a white society.

AGAINST

We are working for an integrated society. We are working to improve ourselves and our position. Our first responsibility is to our own community and to our own children. Whites who want to participate in our program should be treated fairly without discrimination; however, *no special effort* to bring whites into the program should be made.

On the appointed Saturday representatives of fifty-four currently funded centers and forty-five now unfunded centers came together for an all-day discussion of what decisions needed making, when, by whom, and by what procedures. Approximately 550 people attended the meeting. There were "old" people from Isaac Chapel and North West Durant, and Tchula, and the Sidon center, and from Mount Olive and True Light. There were people from Pilgrim Home and Mount Carmel, from Valley View, Ofahoma, Philadelphia, Meridian, Mount Zion, St. John, and Pink Hill. There were representatives from New Hope and Mother Goose and Triumph and Osyka and many more. There were "new" people, many of them operating schools without funds, others organized and planning to open if funded, from the Morning Star Annex in Tutwiler and from Waterford, Sardis, and Pickens, from both North Lexington and South Lexington centers, from Kings, and Grange, and Hazelhurst, from Northeast Newton and West Preston, and Shady Grove, and Pleasant Grove and Pleasant Ridge, from Fernwood and Tylertown, and the State Line center, and Chinagrove, and Escatawpa, and Ocean Springs, and from the Soso center in Soso and from the Buckatunna center in Buckatunna, and many, many more—more and more and more people wanting to work for a brighter future. The preparedness forms that were turned in indicated that the number of children applying to be in CDGM Head Start for the next grant would be 6,487, and the number from new centers wishing to join CDGM would be an additional 6,175.

As was customary at mass CDGM meetings, the first matter on the agenda was the manner in which the meeting in session should be conducted. People rightly resented being railroaded through someone else's prearranged agenda. It was unanimously passed that this meeting should be chaired by a community chairman, not by John or some other Central or area staff member. Speakers must raise their hands for recognition and limit their words to three minutes, and the chairman must call upon any person desiring to speak, regardless of his faction or fame for causing friction.

By the end of the day the group had agreed by unanimous vote to this statement: "CDGM at all levels should be run by elected representatives of the people. The people should give these representatives the power to speak and act for them. Each community would hold elections to choose a committee. These community committees would hold elections for an area council. The area council would then hold elections for a statewide board of CDGM."

This fact and the following points were duplicated and distributed on the spot to those in attendance, and through the mail to stay-at-homes: "For example, this would mean that we would have a way to elect an Area Council. This Area Council would then have the power to decide what responsibilities the area will take. This way, whatever the Area Council decides should represent the way people in that area feel.

"2. There are a lot of details about these elections and about what rules the whole organization should have. These should be written down in a Constitution. (CDGM does not have a Constitution right now). The group decided that we couldn't write a Constitution at the meeting. Instead, each Area should have a meeting this week to choose one representative to be on a committee. This committee would meet next weekend to work on the Constitution. Meeting dates were set for each Area.

"3. At the same Area Meeting, another representative will be elected to work on the new proposal. They would bring specific suggestions from their Area that people want to see included in the new proposal. This group of Area representatives will meet next Saturday and Sunday in Jackson."

The Constitution was written. In eleven articles, a number of sections, and very professional sounding language, the Constitution enumerated the responsibilities and limitations of power of community committees, area councils, the state board of directors, and Central Staff. It was in complete accordance with OEO regulations and both state and federal laws. It also included procedures for amendments and for ratification. The Constitution was sent to a number of liberal lawyers for suggestions, but wasn't ratified during the second grant.

Coleman Miller prepared an eight-page easy-to-read document for communities, called "So You Want to Write a Proposal—O.K. Let's Go." In a few well-chosen words Coleman gave instructions on how to think and what to think about when you are trying to write a proposal.

His valuable guidelines began by advising community people to focus on the problem, show a new or different way of solving the problem, spell out what you plan to do about it very clearly, and include information on such matters as personnel, housing, transportation, etc. Fully outline the procedures you intend to follow. Explain "who gets what and how much?": salaries, wages (full or part-time), fringe benefits, consultants, materials and supplies, travel, communication, training, insurance, rent, and reservations—Coleman assumed that just telling community people that they were welcome to contribute to proposal-producing wasn't enough. His outline included suggestions about how many copies to make, on what kind of paper, that double-spaced typing with large margins would be best, and to send the proposal by registered mail. He wound up with:

A FEW OTHER ITEMS TO THINK ABOUT:
1. Have you read the Bill if you are going for a Federal program?
2. Do you have a nonprofit organization that will sponsor the project?
3. If you need more help, where can you get the help?
4. How far will you go in negotiating?
5. Is this project just your idea? . . .

Of course, in spite of Coleman's efforts, many community meetings, area meetings, impromptu and scheduled statewide meetings, central office bull-sessions and formal meetings open to all, letters, memos, invitations, phone calls, and great emphasis on the part of John, few people did anything more tangible toward preparing a proposal than protest that they were tired of white people writing their proposals for them. The situation could not accurately be summarized by simply saying, "Well then, that's what they want—actions speak louder than words." A more apropos explanation was given by a poor man in Pascagoula, who said, "Habit speaks louder than intentions. We *want* to do all these things, but something in us makes us not."

The last CDGM project in which I was involved before leaving for the summer, on June 27, was writing the teacher development and program for children section of the third grant proposal. Because of the great growth toward autonomy CDGMians had achieved, proposal designers were able to write a proposal specifying structures, procedures, and jobs that were closer to the original ideals of Tom Levin and Art Thomas's CDGM than had been feasible before. Elected area councils were to serve as the decision-making body for each area. This was a more "real" stage of Tom's initially conceived Neighborhood Councils, which had caused such turmoil the first summer, and had functioned in a scattered, sporadic, and abortive fashion in spite of John's concern about them during the second grant. Communities seemed more ready to actually implement this than they had yet been.

The board of directors had been composed primarily of poor people and almost exclusively of Negroes since Art and Tom had designed it. Further elections and additions of professionals interested in social development had been promoted and had occurred during John's regime. Now it was to be reconstituted and made more genuinely representative of the people's will, a fact made possible because the people were much more sophisticated about representation and leadership. The board would be made up of the presidents of the area councils, who would, in turn, elect five to ten other people to the board from among relevant professional and service fields.

There was to be a new office of evaluation, directly responsible to the board. The staff and consultants of this office were to provide reports and recommendations about the quality and standards of all aspects of the CDGM programs, and were to certify those areas that wished to be altogether autonomous. This would be a giant step toward Art and Tom's most fundamental goal: for Negroes to be on top of their own project. It was planned that senior staff in this evaluation office would be "graduates" of other positions in CDGM. The time had come when whites could no longer "evaluate" and regulate blacks in CDGM. Consultants to help evaluate would be selected by blacks. Tom and Art's initial concept that "mature" and more skilled communities could break off from CDGM, and raw newcomers could take their places, was going to be implemented through the "spin-off" process. If an area was deemed by the evaluation office to have reached an acceptable level of ability in managing its own program, administration, and all other aspects of its operation, it could begin its own project.

Perhaps the most important innovation described in the third grant proposal was the implementation of Tom's Poor People's College plans. New careers for the poor *within* the framework of CDGM seemed to have reached about the end of its workability, as Tom had predicted it would. People needed and wanted much more training than could be squeezed in on the job, or than frantic, insufficiently trained senior staff members could provide. And the vast ambivalence toward authority figures that people had always had, and were increasingly able to bring out into the open, made it next to impossible for "management" to train "employees." Whether or not CDGM Central Staff leaders looked at themselves as management, or desired others to look at them that way, or took active steps to change this perception, the fact remained that community people saw it that way. People wishing to give help can't define what help is. It can only be defined by those being or not being helped. Help isn't a matter of what's offered, essentially. It's a question of what's wanted, absorbed, and transformed into those qualities that can help a person become creative in terms of becoming able to solve his own problems better than before.

John asked me to write a proposal for a Teacher Development Institute, which would be part of the Community College we were planning. Part of my proposal appeared in the CDGM grant proposal:

The development of new programs, such as Teacher Development Institutes in Mississippi . . . will be necessary. The purpose of the Teacher Development Institute will be to blend the best that is known about training "sub-professionals" with the needs of this particular experimental project in an innovative model program for underdeveloped areas everywhere. . . .

The basic and biggest program will be to offer six-week Teacher Development courses to CDGM Resource Teachers (first) and Trainees. All candidates for such an Institute will be referred by CDGM Central Staff's Training Program Co-Ordinator or by the semi-autonomous Area Projects. If there is adequate funding and competent personnel, courses can be offered to non-CDGM teachers from OEO funded Head-Starts in Mississippi also.

The course will include three days a week of practice teaching in a sample classroom from 8–1, two afternoon hours three days a week of seminar on teaching, which will include discussions of what was seen and done in the morning, analysis of the tape recordings made in the morning, case studies, child development theory, and methods and materials with regular staff or specialist consultants, appropriate films, etc. The same three days will include a two-hour reading improvement course, and a daily group therapy session. On the other two days of the week, the student teachers will work in their own centers, practicing what they are working on at the Institute. Institute staff will work with them in their centers. This part of the course will take four weeks. Teachers will work in their centers for seven weeks, and will return for a final two weeks of solid five-day-a-week work. The basic course is planned this way because we find that our teachers learn most effectively through real practice and through help in applying the "ideal" to the "real" situation in which they work. We find that most of our teachers can barely read, so reading must be a critical part of the course. Personality problems are our other biggest problems, so we need to build in good therapy. The purpose of the return after seven weeks in the field is to reinforce, see how much back-sliding occurs and correct it, and to give a certificate THAT DOES NOT JUST SAY THE CLASSROOM WORK WAS ACCOMPLISHED, BUT SAYS SOMETHING MORE MEANINGFUL—THAT THE ACCOMPLISHMENTS ARE SHOWING UP IN THE CENTER. No certificate will be given unless the new learnings get into the center's daily life, regardless of how well the student teacher does in the demonstration center, the seminars, or in other phases of the Institute's program. The goal is not a good student; it is a better practicing teacher.

The demonstration class head-teacher will also be the seminar teacher for the student. Other staff will handle other courses. The classroom teacher will have no more than fifteen student teachers for the basic course. She will work with these fifteen in their centers as well as at the Institute. We find that the relationship developed between our teachers and teacher development staff is the chief factor governing successful or unsuccessful training.

The Institute will also offer a small program to teachers able to attend for a full year. Hopefully, they will receive college credit for this and will engage in the basic program above, plus many extra classes in related college level subjects. We feel that this program is essential if we are developing new careers for the poor, because no matter how good they are, our teachers will not be hired by others in the future unless they have some kind of 'official' credentials.

The Institute will have a materials development staff as well as a teacher teaching staff. This staff will develop films, materials for teachers, materials for children, and materials for other groups (such as hiring committees, parents, Area Staff) as needed and requested.

There will be another section which will be responsive to needs as stated by CDGM's Central Staff Children's Program Division for short courses, orientations, field assistance, etc., for below average centers, for committees who need broader concepts and more knowledge about Head-Start, for Area Councils trying to go independent, for parents, for centers wanting to develop special projects, and for the Area Teacher Guide in each area to continue her growth. These programs, of varying length and depth, will be tailored individually.

There will be a Research section in the Institute which will study and develop new careers.

Careful evaluations will constantly be made to see if the training is helping to build quality in the centers. The reports will be sent to the student teacher, the committees that hired the teacher (only hired teachers in OEO funded centers will be taken at the Institute unless arrangements are made for the Institute also to take hired teachers at non-CDGM Head-Starts), the Area Council, the CDGM Central Staff Training Co-ordinator, and the CDGM Program Inspection Office.

My proposal for a restructuring of the children's program division of CDGM reflected the strong wish of the ATGs and other community people not to have outsiders "control" their operation, and to make possible the further promotion of talented local people. I was to move either into consulting and support services on a personal services contract with CDGM and not be a CDGM staff member, or into a staff position at the new separate Teacher Development Institute, or exclusively work on a biography of CDGM and not be involved in CDGM or its offshoot projects at all. Mary Emmons said she was planning to do the same thing as soon as CDGM got a third grant. John wanted to head up the institute, which would train community program workers, and Marv Hoffman, who returned to CDGM from Tougaloo College in June, would also work in the Community Programs Institute.

Therefore, I proposed a staffing pattern for the children's program division, which I thought graduates of our ATG program could handle. Pearl Draine, our wonderful new local discovery, seemed to be the person with the judgment, stamina, and potential to head the program inspection and evaluation work. Training and development would be done at the institute. With these two functions, plus materials development and research on other programs removed from the teacher development and program for children division, remaining positions were administrative in nature. We could break my job and Mary's into parts that ATGs could manage.

One ATG could move into my job. She would work out policies and plans with a new CDGM director and with other division heads on Central Staff. She could be helped by a skilled administrator. Another ATG could be supply officer. She could select and explain the uses of quality preschool equipment and materials, and could plan and promote community equipment-making projects. A third ATG could be a training program coordinator. She would not need to be able to offer training courses, but would announce courses at the institute, recruit and screen for the institute, and be responsible for dissemination of training in centers. A fourth ATG could be communications officer. She would handle the extraordinary number of local staff problems, requests for information, letters, phone calls, etc. I had discussed individual jobs with our most capable ATGs, and they were very enthusiastic. Mrs. Draine was anxious to try the evaluation job.

Other parts of the proposal relating to the children's program were a summary of what we had accomplished during the second grant, and a section by me on our philosophy of who should teach and why. There was a long discussion of our daily program, which was almost exactly copied from the program description I had written for the second proposal.

The grant application also moved forward on my pet passion: community demonstration centers. To date we had used the twenty or so outstanding centers for other teachers to visit. We had one special center operating at the time of proposal-writing. In the spring I had called Mrs. Lena Gitter, a consultant and lecturer for the American Montessori Society, to see if she could come to Mississippi and help us. Mrs. Gitter had an outstanding reputation for extracting the essence of the Montessori method, and establishing it in non-Montessori preschools.

To my utter joy, Mrs. Gitter had said she could spend almost a solid six weeks with us during the summer. She had come in June, and I had taken her to discuss a possible special workshop center with some of the Gulf Coast CDGM staff. During July and part of August Mrs. Gitter did beautiful work with many CDGM teachers. They prepared lesson plans, made samples for use in centers, demonstrated Montessori materials and techniques that were inexpensively adaptable to our circumstances, did a great deal with children's art, and transformed the First Baptist center into a lovely demonstration center, which teachers from a wide area visited. Mrs. Gitter later put out a glowing report, illustrated with photographs she had taken, called "Montessori in Mississippi."

Some of the summer teacher development and program for children staff had had serious doubts about the wisdom of mixing Montessori with CDGM. I had felt that the two situations had much in common.

The Montessori philosophy originally began with rare emphasis on the inner wealth of children living in poverty and difficult social conditions, and with strong emphasis on nonprofessional teachers who were thus not paralyzed by the pedagogic prejudices so many teachers impose on freedom-needing children. Montessori also stresses neatness and order, the beauties of nature, respect for the practical tasks required in life, and an open-ended educational program tailored to the pace of each individual child. Above all it features an educational philosophy that puts primary value on the development of a positive self-concept in each child, which is carried through in an educational program quite free of a middle-class bias. While it's true that many of the externals of Montessori, such as expensive and rigidly prescribed equipment, an unbending sequence of tasks, and a de-emphasis of language development wouldn't have been desirable in CDGM centers, it seemed to me that these peripheral accompaniments seen in many Montessori schools are neither the essence of what Montessori has to contribute to present educational problem-solving, nor the features practiced in the best Montessori schools themselves. It's sad to lose the benefit of something because of professional quarrels over facets of it that can be modified.

Mrs. Gitter later wrote in support of CDGM: ". . . The Child Development program in Moss Point and the other CDGM centers which I visited is without a doubt one of the most creative and progressive I have seen in my many years of early childhood education experience. . . . From my personal observation CDGM is doing an excellent job. It's program could stand comparison with any in the country—and remember, they are working under difficult circumstances."

Mrs. Gitter's work resulted in a remarkable diffusion of creative teaching throughout the entire area. Teachers who had been involved in it also related much more positively to CDGM written material after this dramatic first-hand experience. We hoped that the demonstration centers planned for the third grant would be as successful.

The proposal included a brief history of CDGM and highlighted its chief accomplishments. It presented the Constitution, and many letters and views of poor people. Of course the bulk of it was budget. Perhaps the most interesting sections were those on the theory and reality of Community Action Programs in Mississippi. These were largely thought out and written by Marv and John.

At the time of proposal-writing, there were twenty-eight CAP boards in Mississippi, with fifty-three others in formative stages. The proposal expressed agreement with OEO's basic concept of a community action program, but enumerated three preconditions CDGM felt must exist before the OEO approach could work: (a) various groups from conflicting backgrounds first have to agree on goals and methods to some extent before planning and implementing together is possible; (b) the poor must have enough strength and skill to participate in a real way;

(c) imaginative plans for breaking into the cycle of perpetually recurring poverty have to be built in—new leadership roles, new careers for the poor, etc.

The proposal stated that these preconditions were present in very few Community Action agencies in Mississippi. Few were responsive to the groups for whom the poverty program was invented. Marv and John then wrote an eloquent explanation. It was much like the eloquent explanations Tom had repeatedly written two and a half years before for CDGM and many times thereafter for other poor-people-participation projects in which he was subsequently involved.

This report spoke of the need for *parallel* OEO projects—one project for the concerned communities of the *non*outcasts, and one project for the outcasts almost exclusively. Consensus *can* be achieved between the two groups—at least enough to work with—but only through separate processes in which respect for each other's work is allowed to grow, competitiveness sharpens the ability of both, and discussion devoid of overtones of authority and fear can occur. Through these processes, the preconditions necessary for consolidation into one effective poverty program, consistent with the rules and intents of the Congress, can be established.

Marv Hoffman wrote a section on a Community Workers' and Community Leaders' Training Institute. Like the Teacher Development Institute, we saw this as part of an eventual Community College for the poor. It was a part of the whole that we thought we could muster up the capability to implement within a few months.

As part of an intensive training and support effort designed to prepare nonprofessional community people to assume as many of the roles in CDGM as possible, we are proposing a Community Workers' and Community Leaders' Training Institute. This Institute will be funded outside of regular Head-Start funds, although it might organize eight-week courses at the standard Head-Start tuition cost. Approaches have been made to the Southern Regional Council, the Citizens Crusade Against Poverty, and contacts are planned with other private foundations, as well as with other offices of OEO.

In essence the program is designed to provide its students with the skills and information necessary to assist communities in their efforts to overcome decades of fragmentation and lack of cohesion in order to create a structured community capable of defining and acting on problems in an autonomous, independent manner. The failure to achieve this goal is a repeat of the first post-Reconstruction experience. When outside supports are removed, as they are already beginning to be, there will be a sliding back into a state of powerlessness and renewed dependency unless internal operating situations are created. The Negro community now needs the ability and the knowledgeability to work out programs of self help and self-organization.

A. *The Training Program: Structure*

The Leadership Training Institute will be a centrally located residential training center which will provide training programs for whatever community or statewide groups—CDGM, economic coops, voter leagues, etc.—choose to request them. Special emphasis will be given to CDGM area staff (Community Program Workers) and CDGM community committees.

The training program for Community Program workers would bring together approximately fifteen trainees for a three-week period in the residential center. This initial three-week period would be followed by three-day sessions every month, and week-long returns every three months—a total of sixty-six training days.

The training program itself would be run by the permanent center staff and faculty with heavy support from consultants who would be hired on the basis of the specific skills which are needed by the trainee. The faculty of the Institute would consist of five people who would serve as both resident teachers in the Institute and as field supervisor-consultants. These two functions would be carried out on a rotating basis, such that at all times after the initial three-week training period there would be at least three faculty members in the field serving as supervisors.

B. *The Training Program: Content*

The content of the training program would consist of:

1. Relevant information and background—e.g., federal programs, CAP structure, basic political science, economics and sociology.
2. Examination of problems of group organization and structure in general and groups in the Negro community in particular.
3. Training in the use of techniques for dealing with community problems centering around organizational decision-making and representation. These techniques would include the use of role-playing, the case study approach, group problem-solving techniques, sensitivity training, etc.

(All of these techniques have been used successfully with area level staff in CDGM.) . . .

C. *Information and Research: A Support Service for Community Workers*

In order to deal effectively with specific problems, there must be provision for the collection, analysis, translation, and dissemination of information by competent professionals and/or nonprofessionals who will be providing a support service for local community leaders and those engaged in training them.

This service would be performed by a research and rewrite specialist and his staff who will be connected with the Training Institute staff. This team would prepare information and materials requested by the Community Program Workers and their supervisors as the need arises in their projects. The information and research staff would also be responsible for preparing necessary materials for the training course itself.

The proposal described the responsibilities and functions of the Community Program worker. He was to do what the CO was theoretically to do in the second grant, but was never given enough training to be able to do, through no fault of anybody's. Mary Holmes Junior College, owned and operated by the Board of National Missions of the United Presbyterian Church in the USA, was again to be the grantee. The theme stressed and discussed throughout the proposal was decentralization. Though CDGM had made no deliberate effort to expand by way of encouraging new communities to join it, local communities all over Mississippi selected committees and registered children.

When the proposal was submitted to OEO on July 7, 1966, it requested 41 million dollars for thirty thousand children in forty-four counties. This was less than 20 percent of the eligible children in the state. On July 14 the proposal was returned by the Atlanta regional office of OEO. On July 16 Mr. Sugarman and other OEO officials met with CDGM leadership in Jackson to explain the reasons for the rejection. CDGM could not be funded for more children than had been provided for in its previous program, and the level of funding could not exceed 2 percent above the existing 5.6-million-dollar grant. No expansion into new counties could be allowed. On July 22 Regional Director Sloan wrote to Mr. Horn, president of Mary Holmes, to inform him that OEO had been receiving reports of serious administrative problems in CDGM. Though CDGM requested details at once, they were not forthcoming. On August 19 Mr. Sloan wired CDGM, instructing it to cease all center operations by September 15. CDGM submitted a severely cut application for a full-year program to OEO on August 29.

The submission of the revised proposal followed a public hearing, called by the CDGM board for August 13 in Jackson. This was done in accordance with OEO CAP Memo #32. Memo #32, issued in March, 1966, specified that every organization's new proposals should be announced and discussed publicly with the people to be involved—or in this case, excluded. Public hearings were to be announced at least ten days ahead of time, by formal notice to newspapers and radio and TV stations, etc. A month later, OEO said it wouldn't enforce the public hearings rule. The CDGM board felt that people in Mississippi weren't getting enough information about community action programs. The board felt that if CDGM set a precedent for exchanging information with other poverty agencies, OEO might encourage or require others, operating almost secretly, to do the same.

This was the first such public hearing in the state of Mississippi. John sent a letter of invitation to each Community Action agency, and each member of the congressional delegation, as well as to other relevant officials. At least a dozen letters were sent to OEO officials announcing the meeting. Telegrams were sent to Mr. Sloan and State Poverty Program coordinator, Mr. Fraley. Two thousand people attended the hearing. Needless to say, few of the above-mentioned people appeared in the crowds.

Almost unanimously the poor people insisted that if *their* particular community was to be even partially served, the 41 million dollars was necessary. Board members struggled to explain the limited funds available to OEO. The President had said that major resources were going into Vietnam. It was unthinkable to raise taxes—and so forth.

The board spent the ten days following the meeting agonizing over whom to drop from the application, and by what criteria. After being strenuously battered and pressured by intense conflicting pressures, the board decided to limit the program to four and five-year-olds—which meant cutting out our threes and our older children who had never attended school and were eligible by OEO proclamation—and to centers that had operated under funded CDGM previously.

The only additions, which would increase the size of the project just 10 percent over the present number of children attending, would be those communities that *had been operating* Child Development centers under the name of CDGM *without any funds at any time.* The board felt that the dedication demonstrated by these communities, and the overwhelming sacrifices they had made, couldn't be ignored. The August 29 version of the application represented almost a slashing in half of the first application in July. It requested 21 million dollars to serve 13,500 children.

Most board and staff members were deeply depressed. Part of the problem was gloom at the prospect of another interminable squabble with OEO, another fundless winter for desperate Mississippians, and another endless cycle of newspaper attacks and counterattacks. A deeper concern was that thousands of little black children wouldn't be served, even if the grant did get approved.

CHAPTER 39

THROUGH THE LOOKING GLASS

Coordinating with community action programs

OEO DIDN'T GIVE the impression of putting maximum pressure on the State Poverty Program coordinator, the state health cmmissioner, the state director of welfare, the state school superintendent, or local Community Action agencies and other county and crosscounty poverty projects, or county health clinics, or county welfare departments, or county school systems, to initiate relations with CDGM. But it *did* insist forcefully that CDGM make extensive and sincere efforts to cooperate with the above-mentioned groups. OEO didn't recognize CDGM's friendly gestures toward cooperation unless these gestures resulted in workable, tangible, coordinated projects. Thinking these things through with OEO made some of us feel a little like Alice, about to take the plunge into the rabbit hole where sequences, sizes, events, and personalities took the most astonishing turns, or through the looking glass, where everything was backward.

Tom, of course, had made many attempts to establish contact with relevant white officials during his tenure as CDGM director. John had continued the policy of trying to build bridges. In January, 1966, a month before CDGM had maneuvered its second grant out of OEO's angrily clenched fists, CDGM Central Staff had made telephone contacts with ten Community Action agencies; those that existed in CDGM counties. Seven of the ten responded with some degree of willingness to continue communications. These were: Southwest Mississippi Opportunity, Inc. (in CDGM counties Pike and Amite); Jackson County Civic Action Committee (some CDGM Gulf Coast centers); Forrest-Stone Opportunity, Inc. (CDGM Hattiesburg area centers); Central Mississippi, Inc. (including the Holmes and neighboring counties area); Bolivar County Community Action Program, Inc.; Mid-State Opportunities, Inc. (counties in the Panola-Tallahatchie area); Leake County officials who were interested in forming a CAP, Sunflower County Progress, Inc., and

Greenville-Washington County Economic Commission refused to discuss any possible cooperation or coordination in any phase of planning or programming.

In January and at all times thereafter OEO made it difficult for CDGM to work with Community Action agencies by failing to notify CDGM about the existence, status, funding, etc., of these CAPs. The serious impediment OEO thus created was called to the attention of appropriate OEO officials at high and low levels, in Atlanta and in Washington, in writing and in conversation, repeatedly. The answer usually was a statement, after a lapse of a week or two, to the effect that CDGM was "refusing" to cooperate with other poverty program agencies in the state, and in this regard was exhibiting its usual arrogance. Only once did CDGM receive official notice of the funding of a new program, and this wasn't a CAP, but merely another independent Head Start program.

Meanwhile, Central and area staff members, as well as local people in communities, continued to act in accordance with the special grant conditions insisted upon by OEO at the time of the second grant in February, 1966: they continuously made advances to other projects.

In February a CDGM staff worker first approached Central Mississippi, Inc. (CMI), to get information about it. The meeting was an informal one with a Negro CMI board member. He couldn't answer any of the questions about CMI's plans that he was asked. CDGM had another informal meeting with another CMI board member. The meeting was satisfactory, in that the board member's attitude toward CDGM was positive. In March CDGM Area Staff members attended four meetings involving this CAP. They made information about the Community Action Program, unknown to others present, available to everybody.

In April CDGM staff attended and participated in three Holmes County Advisory Committee meetings. This Committee was part of the CMI. They felt that discussions went reasonably well, though one white member did insist that CMI would make all decisions about programs regardless of community feelings, on the grounds that they "knew more about these things." In May CDGM representatives met with the CAP advisory board to discuss the program. It became clear that certain members of the advisory board and of the over-all CMI board weren't given certain information until it became general knowledge. Coincidentally, these members were Negro, and this information regarded major thinking. In June some CDGM people met with advisory board members one by one to discuss CMI's willfully segregated program, CMI hiring practices, salaries of CMI employees, and to explain CDGM. In July a CDGMian met twice with a CMI board member to discuss present and future poverty programs. The board member explained that CMI didn't attempt to inform communities until decisions had been made, because it "confused" them.

In August CDGM had contact with the advisory board and with six CAP board members. John sent four communications to CMI during late July and early August. CDGM attended two CAP meetings to inform people about the program, as it was felt that CMI had failed to do so. The CDGM community organizer for this area visited two CAP Head Start centers, and invited CAP personnel to visit CDGM centers. There were no return visits made, to the knowledge of local teachers.

Beginning in May, CDGM area staff played a significant role in the reorganization of an appointed and nonrepresentative board of directors in the Southwest Mississippi Opportunity, Inc. (SMO). Four former CDGM people (the community organizers, two center chairmen, and the brother of the area administrator) became SMO board members. They were instrumental in getting information out to the communities. SMO board meetings were at that time closed to the public. For example, on May 28, when sixty to seventy residents in counties served by this CAP went to a CAP meeting in the Amite County Courthouse, the sheriff locked the door. John wrote to SMO four times during the summer regarding possible kinds of coordination.

Until fall, when other factors intervened, SMO didn't seem extremely enthusiastic about working with CDGM. Nevertheless, two CDGM workers visited the executive director and appeared that evening at the SMO board meeting. SMO's deputy director visited CDGM's area office in August. Later in August two CDGM workers again attended the SMO board meeting. SMO decided that it preferred the Head Start run by the McComb public school system to CDGM's Head Start. (The McComb public school system refused to sign the school desegregation compliance to receive federal funds.) In September CDGM personnel attended a CAP meeting.

It was hard for CDGM people to get in touch with Prairie Opportunity, Inc. It had a staff director, but no programs. There was for some time a board. Appointed board members, according to the bylaws of the organization and as told to the CDGM community organizer during one of several contacts, were to elect all other board members. Though John sent three letters and a telegram to Prairie Opportunities, he received a reply to only one communication. Extensive cooperation with this CAP agency was made difficult by the research necessary to determine whether or not it existed. OEO had given it program development money, and hoped something would come of it.

Pearl River Valley, Inc. (PVO), was in Walthall County, a CDGM county. Though the PVO executive director did agree to let the CDGM community organizer visit him twice, he exhibited a superior and sarcastic attitude. No one from PVO made any attempt at any time to see CDGM's Central Staff or board. Two CDGM community people were on the PVO advisory board in Walthall County, but weren't contacted after they were elected in regard to meetings, activities, or indeed, at all.

When the community organizer asked about this, the executive director responded with an interrogation as to why he wanted to know. Pearl River Valley rejected offers to work together in some manner.

Several members of CDGM's Central Staff, working on instructional materials, arranged to visit the adult literacy program in Jackson called STAR. Later, when CDGM had a few days of the internationally known Dr. Caleb Gattegno, and wanted to see how his materials worked with adults, a visit was planned in which Dr. Gattegno would teach a demonstration class, free of charge, using STAR students. Many phone calls, letters, messages, and people were involved in arranging this. Local administrative and teaching staff at STAR watched, discussed what they had seen, and seemed very enthusiastic. Senior staff, though located nearby, declined to attend or comment or initiate further contact. It had been hoped that similar interests might bring STAR and CDGM closer together, as nothing else had been able to do.

In May the CDGM area administrator and the assistant community organizer went to visit the executive director of the Jackson County Civic Action Committee (JCCAC). He was out. They talked with several other people in the CAP, and were told that it was unlikely that the CAP would be willing to work with CDGM. Because the CDGM team could get no satisfactory answers to carry back to the community people concerning the purpose and activities of the Jackson County Civic Action Committee, they invited a JCCAC staff member to a meeting to discuss these topics. The gentleman said he or a representative would come, but both failed to do so. In June the CDGM area teacher guide and community organizer were invited to a CAP meeting. From that point on, their relationships with JCCAC were limited to contact with Negro members of JCCAC. They called whites in the organization many times. They were always out of the office. Each time they left messages asking the people to call back. They never did.

In July a Negro involved in JCCAC responded to an invitation to describe the organization's activities and did. Community people were pleased to get this information. The program had been in effect for eleven months, and they hadn't previously been able to find out anything about either its intentions or its actions. Though area staff continued to attempt to contact JCCAC officials regarding a date for a public meeting, and the officials continued to ignore the calls, two officials *did* go to see John in Jackson. JCCAC neither obligated itself to cooperate with CDGM, nor did it refuse to do so. A second area level meeting was made possible by the surprise appearance of several area and Central Staff members, who went to JCCAC, and having given up on the possibility of being able to make an appointment, "just walked in and talked." However, throughout, CDGM area staff stayed in touch with several of the CAP board members. In September community people asked their area staff to help them petition JCCAC for a public hearing. The petition was ignored.

Research revealed that though this was an OEO sanctioned agency, there was a preponderance of whites, a handful of relatively insignificant Negroes (no Negroes representing the poor, or even representing relevant subject areas, such as education), and several people widely believed to be closely associated with the Klan. Of seven staff persons, three were Negro and four were white. Whites occupied all the high administrative positions, and earned salaries almost twice that earned by Negro staff members. The assistant director, selected over the wishes of the four Negro board members, was charged, but not convicted, with embezzling school funds, and was instrumental in helping whites create a private school system to avoid integration.

Community people in the area wrote to OEO a number of times. They protested the appointed board, which operated secretly. Area staff in this jurisdiction felt frustrated and not very fruitful in their attempts to fulfill CDGM's special grant condition regarding making "all efforts to establish a working relation with the CAP."

In a similar manner, and with similar degrees of "success," CDGM tried to work things out with the Community Service Association, Forrest-Stone Opportunity, Inc., and the Mid-Delta Education Association. The Bolivar County situation was a striking case in point.

Its history began in March, 1965, when people interested in the pending CDGM program, then being organized by Tom, tried to enlist the participation of white and Negro middle-class citizens of the county. These were individuals who had previously not been implicated in any kind of projects for social progress. This first meeting was considered a resounding failure by CDGMians. Influential citizens insisted on control of any program, and refused to make their facilities available on any other terms. In June a formal announcement of a Bolivar County Community Action agency appeared in the newspapers. CDGM poor people in the area were not aware of how this was organized, or who was responsible for the announced board members, or where the meetings had been held. Many of the names were those of people at the March meeting, who knew CDGM leaders and had refused to work with them as equals.

CDGM operated centers in Bolivar County during the summer of 1965. In November a Mr. Don Wiley, previously an employee of the Cleveland, Mississippi, Chamber of Commerce, was hired as director of the CAP agency. He had been invited by CDGM community people to visit one of their centers during the summer. After taking his new job, he made no effort to contact experienced CDGM people in his county, though he knew their names and how to reach them, and was aware of their extreme interest in the poverty program.

During August and September, 1965, many poor Negroes in Bolivar

County had communicated with OEO in order to express their feelings about specific board members being considered. OEO had responded by giving its approval to the board in September, and asking for the addition of four more members. The board of the CAP agency then advertised in the Bolivar *Commercial* for recommendations of board members. Few semiliterate Negroes in the country subscribed to this local paper, so they didn't write in their suggestions. Then CDGM Negroes discovered that except for these recommendations from "residents of the target area," CAP agency board members would be approved by the County Board of Supervisors. Poor people definitely did not feel that the board of supervisors, whom they were forbidden to join the rest of the community in electing due to the fact that they were prohibited from voting, had an outstanding record of "prior concern with poverty."

All fall and winter unfunded CDGM staff and concerned community people were holding weekly community meetings to spread information about federal programs, about CDGM, and specifically, to investigate this CAP agency. On January 19, 1966, community people held their first countywide meetings, and invited Mr. Wiley and the CAP agency board members to present their plans for their own competing Head Start. From October on, the Bolivar County group had passed out information about their proposed Head Start through the school system. It hadn't consulted CDGM Head Start people, or sent delegates to their weekly meetings. At the January 19 meeting, more than four hundred poor people drafted a resolution rejecting the Bolivar County CAP agency's Head Start. They said they had successfully run their own Head Start for their own children, and intended to continue to control it. They would happily welcome help.

After this the CAP made active attempts to hold meetings in places acceptable and accessible to poor Negroes in the county. It feared their lack of support. In February, when CDGM and OEO were entering final negotiations for the second CDGM grant, it was decided by CDGM leaders in Bolivar, John Mudd, and OEO officials, that CDGM should submit a proposal to the CAP for delegate agency status. It was also agreed that the CAP would be granted fifteen days to respond to this proposal, and that if it didn't agree to it, OEO would fund CDGM as a single-purpose agency in Bolivar County within the fifteen days following the CAP's negative decision. Local CDGM people submitted their proposal as planned, and requested a meeting with CDGM Central Staff, board, Bolivar constitutents, and the entire CAP board to discuss the proposed arrangement.

The meeting took place in the courthouse on March 7. Hundreds of poor people were present. They described CDGM's system in detail, and what it meant to them. They described the volunteer Head Start program they had been running by themselves for thirteen hundred children during the past three months while the bickering continued. The CAP board chairman said the board would not hesitate to reply to these people's proposal immediately. However, the next day, when local CDGM representatives went to the CAP office to get the final answer, they were told that no formal reply was ready. Neither were CAP personnel able to produce a copy of their *own* Head Start proposal, which the representatives requested. CDGM community people thought it strange that with a large number of poverty projects available to it as a multipurpose CAP, the only one they seemed determined to rush through was a Head Start: coincidentally (?) the only one community people were running already.

In late March, John Mudd and OEO were still writing back and forth about Bolivar. CDGM urged OEO to fund the Bolivar CAP *and* CDGM. An OEO official replied that he would never fund CDGM in opposition to the CAP's wishes. Another said that OEO does not solve a community's problems for it, and that the poor people should calm down and be more cooperative.

A poor man from Bolivar said that OEO was "backin' up fast as a crawfish." According to reliable sources Mr. Sloane, head of the Atlanta OEO office, took the position that CDGM should leave this CAP alone so white Bolivar County leaders could get off their soap boxes, drop their rigid positions, calm down, and become willing to compromise.

It was now April. A CAP board member said that "his group" had had two hundred years experience in administering programs, and couldn't "trust" all these "new people."

Eventually OEO funded Bolivar County CDGM centers with local CDGM leadership, minus CDGM central, as a delegate agency of the CAP called Association of Communities of Bolivar County (ACBC). GE did their auditing and accounting work with them. A key member of ACBC and former Movement initiator in Mississippi, said: "We would have nothing if it weren't for the fact that we had CDGM. That gave us a little power. But this isn't CDGM; it's close, but no cigar. It's a poverty program without the main features—they do everything they can to keep us from growing strong and skillful. But it's better than nothing. Maybe that's all America's ready to give us black folks yet."

The only exception to the general CAP situation was the excellent working arrangement CDGM developed with Mid-State Opportunities. CDGM had had centers in Panola and Tallahatchie Counties. These weren't refunded by OEO in the second CDGM grant, because of the existence of the Mid-State CAP agency in that location. The CAP board agreed that CDGM could be a delegate agency, operating with almost total freedom under Mid-State, and could continue to operate its centers. OEO funded the program for just under $200,000, but the governor vetoed the arrangement.

CDGM didn't appeal the decision through procedures outlined in

CAP Memo number nine, but instead worked out the Associated Communities of Panola and Tallahatchie counties, a delegate agency headed by a former CDGM area staff member. This new organization was the delegate agency of Mid-State. CDGM wasn't in the picture, except insofar as it initially offered technical and management information and educational consultants (I organized a workshop for teachers, for example), at the request of the CAP and the delegate agency. The director of Mid-State visited the CDGM office from time to time. He invited me to discuss CDGM's approach with his board, which I did. Relations between the two organizations were cordial. The director of Mid-State and I had been close personal friends prior to the friendship of the two organizations.

CDGM people took an active part in helping establish Community Action Program agencies where there were none. This responsibility was not part of the grant conditions, but many CDGM workers enjoyed working as catalysts to get sluggish or fearful communities moving. They tried in Sunflower County. In Issaquena County Mrs. Unida Blackwell and a member of the CDGM board of directors worked hard to establish the South Delta Economic Opportunities, Inc. OEO had stated that the East Mississippi Opportunities Program in Lauderdale County wouldn't be funded, because the board wasn't correctly constituted. It wasn't a representative board, and the CAP had not completed CAP form number three. CDGM area staff actively participated in reorganizing the board. They attended meetings with OEO officials and CAP people. The CDGM area administrator was selected to be a member of a new representative steering committee, which led to the more effective structuring of the CAP. Two CDGM Central Staff members attended a meeting of two hundred Negroes, who were holding elections for representatives to the South Central Mississippi Opportunities in Copiah County. CDGM area staff people and a board member took a leading part in reorganizing the Harrison County Civic Action Committee.

John wrote to such other poverty programs in the state as the Sophia Sutton Mission Assembly; Lift, Inc., in Tupelo; Northwest Mission Development Association, Inc.; Yazoo Community Action, Inc.; Father Sweeney Memorial School in Pass Christian; North Mississippi Economic Development Corporation; the Singing River Educational Association; etc., requesting information, sending material relevant to CDGM, etc. Copies were always sent to OEO and the state poverty program coordinator, Martin Fraley.

Because of these tediously documented repetitiously relentless, relentless, relentless efforts to "cooperate" with Mississippi CAPs, CDGM found it hard to graciously accept OEO's continuing charges that CDGM was remiss in this duty. Yet in fairness to OEO, it must be admitted that a majority of observers and participants *in* CDGM felt that this community organization and social service division *was* our weakest; that John was very unclear in his thinking and actions toward the community organization and social services aspects of our program, and that this was a severe handicap to workers in that division. Many people said that this was all part and parcel of John's inability to delegate and stick to a clear division of labor. They sensed that this was his favorite section of the program; the one in which he most wished to be included. He found it hard to relinquish. Yet, much as he hated it, administration and Northern politics took all his time. He couldn't do the social service division justice. For the whole first half of the second grant he didn't have a division director on whom he could count. Frank Glover, who stepped into the void and worked terribly hard in the winter and early spring, was not a community organizer, and besides, by now he had left Mississippi.

John brought CO Sam Howze in from the field in Holmes County to take on many of the division director's duties when recruiting still hadn't produced a director by late spring. Sam had always had his mind on other things, and couldn't do any of the massive, concerted things that needed to be done. Sam's philosophy of community organization was that a building built on a weak foundation will crumble. He was still promoting in 1966 a mode of community organizing that meant something meaningful in Mississippi in 1964, but was now not enough. He urged organizers to take the tiny, tedious steps of talking lengthily with families on front porches, holding mass meetings in churches regularly even if there was little content, and really getting to know their small number of families intimately.

Sam didn't set his thirty-two community organizers (twice as much field staff as we had in the teacher development and program for children division) to researching their areas. Observers thought they should have been gathering a great deal of information about resources, obstacles, structures, and possibilities, as well as knowing the gross and obvious needs of Negroes.

The COs needed guidance in this. They needed help focusing on what to find out, and why and how, and they needed a well-organized schedule guiding them on *when*. They needed guidance in how to be enablers in communities: how to get community people divided into committees to do the above things, how to turn infighting in communities toward problem-solving, how to build strong area councils. Sam said there was time for all this later. But in fact Mississippi wasn't standing still in terms of internal politics and development. Unless Sam guided the COs into creating strong CDGM-style structures, white power would soon wipe out decentralized CDGM groups. Sam didn't give his workers much concrete help in how to establish cooperatives, credit unions, etc. He seemed to think the children's program more or less a frill, annoyingly attached to CDGM, so he didn't give COs aid in working with parents on child development, becoming a force in centers, becoming a force in public education, libraries, health clinics, and so forth. He did little about investigating CAPs. This was done later, under new personnel.

Because CDGM had sent COs into deep waters and had subsequently stranded them, they were, most of them, bitter. They tended to do a perfunctory job of errands, and then fabricate paranoid fantasies, about what was being done to them by Central Staff. While we assumed that COs were trying to create simple but profound changes in communities, in fact their frustrations and restless cravings "to do something" were causing them to withdraw into childlike retaliation, negative acts toward Central Staff—and very little else.

Many people questioned John's wisdom in putting up with Sam as long as he did. Some explained John's patience by noting his tendency to give everybody ten chances. How could he be *sure* that Sam, who was extremely intelligent and immersed in Negro problems, wouldn't take hold? Others felt as an OEO official did, when he commented, "John is a scared white boy riding a raging black panther, and he's afraid to crack the whip." Sam was, eventually, relieved of his duties.

Meanwhile, John *was* recruiting strenuously for someone to head this division. People with the flexibility, versatility, stamina, and commitment to take on this job were few, and happily occupied elsewhere. John felt some relief and some anxiety when he discovered Coleman Miller, who came to visit, and came to work. But from the first Coleman was very unpopular with the CO office and field staff. His fist-banging style and seemingly opportunistic approach angered the soul-searchers. The former tended not to be too insightful and subtle; the latter, not too effective or energetic, and the combination was quite combustible. Coleman did get the COs working on medical examinations for children in August, and did some work trying to excite community people about proposal and Constitution writing. But he didn't seem to have an over-all strategy or belief.

On June 24 Fred Mangrum came to work as a roving CO. He was a community organizer in Washington, D.C. He had spent a year with SNCC in Tallahatchie County, and had just completed a week of independent work in Sunflower County, because he had met Cora Flemming [an ATG] in Washington, and was very impressed with her. Fred *wasn't* very impressed with what he saw in CDGM's social service division: mis-selected individuals (many with personalities too weak to withstand all the pressures and yet remain strong leaders) who had had little or no experiences with CDGM before the first interim period, poor people leadership and absence of training, inadequate role definition, great frustration from lack of a firm stance regarding them on John's part, and great frustration from the OEO-white community situations they continually encountered. Fred headed up CAP research and negotiation work for the rest of the summer.

During the last week of June, Marv Hoffman, John's close friend from

Tougaloo days, had joined the social service devision. Marv had left CDGM in the middle of its first summer under Tom, and since had had little or nothing to do with it. He had "vigorously dissuaded" John from taking the directorship when the latter was trying to decide whether or not to get mixed up in CDGM at all, and he had been an understanding friend from time to time, when John would suddenly appear with CDGM problems. Marv's arrival at CDGM was a very strengthening factor to both John and the organization.

Marv came the same week that I left, and a wave of anger once again passed through Central Staff and the board of directors. At the time when there was such emphasis on putting CDGM's top positions into black hands, John had placed a white at the top of the previously Negro-led (Sam, Coleman, Fred) social service division. Furthermore, when there was a great deal of discontent about John's need for a white in-group to support him, he had brought a close friend into this very group. Few people looked at the facts that Marv's work was first-rate in a division where most of the work could hardly be called that, and that Marv was highly regarded by those poor people with whom he had contact in communities. They murmured for months that maybe *this* was why John had kept saying he couldn't find a capable black social service division director. Maybe he had been saving this choice position for his friend, who would not be free of his teaching duties at Tougaloo College till June.

During this summer, the summer of 1966, Paul J. Cotter of Senator Stennis's staff again came around investigating. The Jackson *Clarion-Ledger* carried the usual headlines: "Stennis Would Halt Funds to CDGM," "State CDG Gave Food to Marchers," "Probers Say U. S. Figure $170, 'Child Development' Project Cost $450 Per Child More." The good senator's charges caused OEO to panic. They sent missionaries "to bring back alive any embryonic black panthers they might find on CDGM territory,"[37] as Andy Kopkind so aptly phrased the thing. If this were wallpaper instead of a book, I could just write, *repeat.* One gets weary.

Yet we did know, in spite of our fatigue, that OEO was having untenable troubles too. It had become, as Andy expressed it, "something close to a Department for Fulfilling the American Dream; the Ministry of Hope,"[38] charged with solving all of America's ills. It was being widely and systematically attacked for not having "succeeded yet." As if someone should have made an announcement one day, after OEO had been in existence for a year, that now there was suddenly no more class hostility, racial segregation, powerlessness of the poor—that now

[37] Kopkind, Andrew, "How Do You Fight It?" The *New Republic,* September 3, 1966.

[38] Kopkind, Andrew, "America's War on Poverty," *New Statesman,* March 11, 1966.

it was time to celebrate with firecrackers ". . . and funny hats and people kissing each other in Times Square."[39]

I had left CDGM on June 27 and had spent six weeks in Washington starting this book, working on further details of the Teacher Development Institute (TDI) proposal, and intermittently flying down to Mississippi as a consultant. By late August my children and I had moved back to Mississippi again: the children to go back to school, and I to continue the above three projects on the fringes of CDGM.

We were feeling very optimistic about the Community College. In September I called and wrote to foundations. We needed funds to start something small as soon as possible. I contacted the big foundations that had enough money to help: Ford, Carnegie, and Rockefeller. I contacted some smaller foundations with a reputation for projects involving a little innovation and risk: Field, Merrill, New World, New York, Stern, Norman, and the Southern Education Fund. I spoke to OEO about funding parts of it out of their eight-week Head Start training course money, and to the U. S. Office of Education about funding remaining portions of it as a pilot project. There was much interest in many quarters, and no cash forthcoming.

I called literally hundreds of possible candidates, looking for faculty for TDI; or when people couldn't actually move to Mississippi, for TDI consultants. At the same time I tried to get consultants to help CDGM immediately. With little luck, I tried to interest educators at Mississippi's Millsaps and at Jackson State College to plan with us. I spoke with people at the Massachusetts Department of Mental Health, the University of Pittsburgh's Child Study Center, the Merrill-Palmer Institute, and the University of Delaware preschool department, Sarah Lawrence College, the Vassar College special program, University of Georgia, Tulane University, the Harvard preschool faculty, the University of Chicago, Peabody, and Pacific Oaks. I spoke to individuals in programs from Bank St. to Watts, and individuals recommended by other individuals. OEO, of course, could neither offer nor suggest anything positive.

I was successful in getting a few days of wonderful help that month from B. J. Seabury, director of the National Child Research Center in Washington; Nancy Curry, associate director of Child Development at the University of Pittsburgh and head of the Arsenal Family and Children's Center; and Norma Canner, a noted movement specialist from Massachusetts. Marilyn Lowen's efforts at the telephone produced a week's time from a wonderful child development person from Harlem, Miss Jerri Wilson. But most people were busy. The best people logically are. At most, they could come "later." Later our funds would again have vanished. Those who came, were as enthusistic as Miss Nancy Curry,

[39] *Ibid.*

who wrote in a letter: ". . . It was with mixed feelings that I left C.D.G.M. and Jackson, Mississippi, yesterday. The indignation, disgust and horror that I felt in seeing first hand the conditions under which Mississippi Negroes must endure were counter-balanced by the feelings of deep humility, heartfelt admiration, and boundless respect on seeing the accomplishments of all those I met involved in C.D.G.M.

"Many of the things you are doing I could not have believed possible —teachers recruited from the poorest people in the community, supervisors like the A.T.G.'s expressing child development principles in articulate, meaningful terminology after only a year's training experience, and classrooms reflecting real parental commitment and involvement. To see the philosophy of education based on the worthwhileness and dignity of the human personality operating on a practical level, not just for children but also adults, is the most exciting part of your project to me. I salute the courage with which you face the daily almost unsurmountable tasks.

"Please thank your Area Teacher Guides and the staffs of the Valewood and Glen Allen Schools for their warm reception. I have rarely, if ever, talked with such articulate, perceptive, and deeply committed people. The rest of the country can and must learn from the Child Development Group of Mississippi if the 'War on Poverty' is to be won. . . ."

PART VII

Doing Good

SEPTEMBER 30, 1966–JANUARY, 1967;
ACCORDING TO WHOM? IS IT POSSIBLE?

CHAPTER 40

GOLD AND GARBAGE FALL ON MYSTIFIED MISSISSIPPI

ON FRIDAY, SEPTEMBER 30, 1966, the front page of the Jackson *Daily News* ("Mississippi's Greatest Newspaper"), carried the headline: "12 MAN BOARD REPLACES CDGM . . ." The article went on to explain:

> The controversial Child Development Group of Mississippi—chief recipient of federal antipoverty funds in this state—will be replaced next month by a 12-man board of white and Negro leaders set up recently under the personal supervision of antipoverty director Sargent Shriver. . . .
>
> The new board, headed by industrialist Owen Cooper of Yazoo City and Negro leader Aaron Henry of Clarksdale, is scheduled to take over the programs now operated by CDGM and expand into 60 other Mississippi counties. . . .
>
> Meanwhile from Washington, Sen. John C. Stennis, D-Miss., a CDGM critic said:
>
> "I have been working toward turning this project over to local responsible people where it should be and should have been all the time . . .
>
> "I fully expect the CDGM group to be replaced. . . ."
>
> It was also revealed that the CDGM funds have been extended until Oct. 15 to give the new board time to set up its operation. . . .
>
> The new board was apparently formed without the knowledge of CDGM officials and is already under attack from some civil rights groups around the state because it does not include any poor people. . . .

My diary of Wednesday, September 28, 1966, two days earlier says: ". . . one of my white Mississippi politician friends from a bad part of the state called yesterday to say he hears all sorts of rumors about OEO working behind CDGM's back to form some kind of more conservative Board to 'take over' (?) CDGM Centers and get rid of our whole Central Staff: us agitators. He said he had been approached, and knows of others OEO has asked to be in on this. He said, 'I hate to see them do a thing like this with your group. Every honest white person in Mississippi knows what you people have done for the Negroes that we couldn't stick our necks out to do. I'll do anything I can to help you. The first thing I did, was to refuse to be on a board to eliminate you all.'

"OEO must be doing something secret, so many rumors are coming in from white Miss. friends."

And there was this in *New Republic* this month by Andy [Kopkind], beginning:

> Older readers may remember the War on Poverty, which was fought briefly and sporadically on several fronts during the mid-1960's. One of the most furious battles was also one of the last: the campaign to save the Child Development Group of Mississippi from politics, parsimony, racism, and bureaucracy.

And ending:

> Sargent Shriver has apparently retired for the moment to consider the possibilities of surrender. His aides recommend total restructure: "Safe" new Negro and white directors, elimination of community action functions, and a tightly controlled new management. A few people inside and outside OEO are planning to fight for CDGM, but the situation at this point is bleak. "What can you do," the ex-OEO staffer asked, "when practically the whole mechanism of government has gone into getting the goods on CDGM, and killing it?" By way of an answer, a present poverty program official said, "Shriver has apparently made a basic decision not to refund, and we have to accept it. They have all the cards and we don't have any. How do you fight it?"

" '*How can you fight it?*': the call of the spineless of the world. This I believe. But I find it incredible that OEO shrewd politicians are contemplating something as crude and heavy-handed as to manipulate *to this extent* behind the scenes under the banner of 'community involvement.' Politically, how could they dare? Pressure us cripplingly, yes. Insist on restrictions based on anxiety alone, of course. But murder us without discussion? I suppose anything can happen."

* * *

My diary for Thursday, September 29, the next day, reports that John and Marian had just received a leak: "a charter for a takeover group was signed by Governor Johnson on September 13. Board members known. *Three rich white Mississippians!* We've been in touch with OEO daily lately; with high officials. They've never mentioned this. Can it be that they are this dishonest?"

* * *

Friday's diary, September 30, the day of the headline, describes subsequent events and reactions to them. After receiving the leak, John had sent someone over to pick up the charter of the takeover group. There was one. It was called "Mississippi Action for Progress." It was supposed to take over *CDGM* centers lock, stock, and barrel and human beings.

It was OEO-style community action at its most dramatic. The charter had been signed and approved by Governor Paul B. Johnson and the Secretary of State; as good a guarantee that the new thing wouldn't be freedom-oriented as could have been achieved.

We were told that a White House staff member negotiated this. There seemed to be much corroboration. Certain surprising facts appeared in the MAP charter; odd things for OEO to have *admitted* preferring to CDGM things, though not at all odd for them to have preferred politically. For example: After naming the three rich white men, there was a statement saying: "The incorporators shall constitute the original board of directors. Said directors are further authorized and empowered to name additional directors as they, in their discretion, may determine."

Then it said a purpose was: "To consult with and coordinate its activities with the Governor of the State of Mississippi or his designee or such Commission which may be subsequently established by the Governor, or the Legislature of Mississippi to accomplish the purposes and goals for which this corporation is established."

The charter included the statement: "This corporation shall not be required to make publication of its charter."

All the words sounded good, including the proudly put forth first purpose of this corporation, which was "to eliminate the paradox of poverty." Whatever that substitute for programmatic content may have meant, it all sounded good until we remembered things like *another* commission in charge of Mississippi's "social development" during this decade—the Sovereignty Commission, which gave state funds to the White Citizens' Council. Or until we remembered statements of this governor's, like the one during one of his 1963 campaign speeches, in which he defined the NAACP as "Niggers, alligators, apes, coons, and possums."

OEO's logic fascinated us: It called CDGM a "monopoly" and said it must break it up. Then OEO created a *bigger* monopoly (approximately ninety counties contemplated, instead of CDGM's approximately thirty). OEO said it needed to turn our project over to "responsible" people. So it grabbed it from those who had funded and operated it out of their (literal) pockets of poverty and served it, all developed, on a stolen silver platter to those who refused to help us or even recognize us during our first year and a half struggles. OEO proposed to take it from a poor elected board and give it to a nonpoor nonelected board. This was the reverse of what OEO was harping on elsewhere. Variety is the spice of life. Consistency is the hobgoblin of little minds, and all that. We thought this action politically brilliant: Shriver couldn't come out and kill his most famous, most excellent project. Neither could he, for reasons of political precariousness, tolerate a controversial or successful project. So: flash! genius! Castrate CDGM while claiming to improve it. Take its power, take care of its little children. Who in the liberal

North would protest, as long as the little children were getting taken care of? Everyone was too far away to comprehend this unlikely one-more-Mississippi-human-rights-murder, especially with OEO putting out insinuating stories about us and smiling stories about itself. It could easily hide its blood-stained hands with a "benevolent parent of deviant off-spring" public relations camouflage campaign. OEO, we thought, could no doubt skate through with haste and grace.

Another OEO assumption in evidence here seemed to be that rich people are more local than poor people. We imagined that MAP would have some out-of-state talent on its professional staff, too. According to our calculations we had 2,272 employees, 2,112 on local center staff, 80 in area offices, and 62 in central office. This was 80 percent local Mississippians on central staff; 99 percent in local centers, and 100 percent in area offices. Decision making involved 945 local poor on 121 committees, and 17 on the board of directors.

We thought it a rather funny joke that OEO had decided to disband CDGM before its own investigation staff filed its own report of the findings on our operation. Was this, we wondered, a decision based on facts? Or was it facts (selected and distorted) to enshroud and dignify a premade decision?

Even OEO couldn't have planned to handle this lynching so gauchely. We thought Senator Stennis's office must have leaked this to the press to freeze Shriver's alternatives; to keep him from reneging or killing CDGM as he had done year before. This could be the senator's way of forcing action.

* * *

September 30, 1966, CDGM Press Release: For Immediate Release

The CDGM Board of Directors and the Director John Mudd today made public the following statement:

The formation of the 12-man group, Action for Progress in Mississippi, supposedly to replace the Child Development Group of Mississippi, indicates both a shocking violation of the Office of Economic Opportunity's stated commitment to involvement of the poor in anti-poverty programs and a flagrant disregard of CDGM's own legitimacy and competence in operating a Head Start Project.

If Sargent Shriver personally supervised the establishment of this group, then he did so in defiance of his own policy. As recently as three weeks ago on September 9, Mr. Shriver stated in an OEO memorandum whose purpose was "to reaffirm . . . the necessity of including the poor in all our activities" that: "It has become clearer than ever in the past months that the poverty program must stake its existence on that same ideal upon which our nation gambled from the outset: Democracy. . . . The word must go out—and it must go out unmistakably—that token participation [of the poor] is unacceptable. . . ."

* * *

We were deeply distressed about those Negroes who we thought sold out before they found out. They hadn't seen any proof from OEO that

CDGM had done all these terrible things. (Neither had CDGM. OEO hadn't had the courtesy to send us formal charges yet. This was sensible. As they were not about to negotiate with us, why tell us accusations and allow us to answer, thus risking publicity on the fact that we were right?)

Dr. Owens, president of Tougaloo College, was listed in the paper as a MAP board member. He denied it. He said on the phone that he was offered the position by the conveners of the group, but that he never accepted it. He also refused to make a public statement in behalf of a fair hearing for CDGM. We couldn't stand the need to refuse either (a) to endorse CDGM as having done good and being capable of doing continuing good, or minimally (b) to support the idea that we get a fair hearing before being silently wiped out.

Another Negro was much more important in this catastrophe: Aaron Henry. Wooing and winning him was the key that made it possible for OEO to get away with MAP. Aaron was a long-time symbol of the new-world Negro in Mississippi. Shriver knew that liberals in the North, seeing Aaron's name on a list of board members for MAP (picked and controlled by the three chartering whites), would automatically believe MAP to be the good-guy group. Shriver could assume that Northerners wouldn't know that there were two categories of groups for progress in Mississippi that season. The first group was almost all Negro, with some civil rights workers and radical reformers in it. This group stood for utmost feasible degree of protest and program. Unhindered by waiting for whites or cautious Negroes, who couldn't go too fast, rock the boat, take big risks, etc., this group was disliked by more careful Negroes. They didn't consider it made up of Immediate Constitutionalists, as we did, but thought it radical.

Aaron Henry used to be the leader for this rapid-reform group.

The second group working for progress in Mississippi was composed of emerging white moderates and more middle-class-oriented, too-much-to-lose-to-go-fast Negroes. They were enough socially concerned to be for some risks; they were conservative doing good Negroes. This group included NAACP. NAACP was headed by Mr. Aaron Henry.

For two years, Aaron Henry had been the leader of the cautious moderate group, not of the rapid-reform group.

Therefore, taking CDGM from the rapid-reformers and giving it to the conservative reformers (Aaron Henry) was a social step backward, *not* as it would look to Northerners, because it was integrated in Mississippi, and included well-known moderates in Mississippi and Aaron (falsely believed to represent the most radical group) a step forward.

Aaron represented the group that wanted as much progress as possible without antagonizing too many of the reactionaries who dominated Mississippi, and without losing too much of its membership, which was minute. Aaron's group, MAP-type people, based its thinking on the principle that during the last century whites neglected their duty to take care of Negroes, to uplift them. Progress, therefore, required negligent whites, the traditional fathers of society, to start their tardy uplifting. Negroes in good shape believe they should be paternalistic too. Other sectors of this MAP-type group act out of fear of the violence they know they'd have to undergo if they didn't "appease" the angry colored folks. They see they are getting by-passed by new leadership in the state, and don't want to find themselves left out in the cold. They are the leaders, they feel, so they must hurry to catch up with their followers.

We talked a lot about why Aaron Henry did what he did. He had never been part of CDGM, but appeared to be an ally. Why didn't he at least call us before committing himself to the other side? Was it because he didn't control CDGM and felt he could control at least the Negro component of MAP? Evidently he sincerely believed it was progress to sit with whites at long last, a la his dream. Evidently he sincerely believed NAACP was a more appropriate vehicle than SNCC-FDP-DM-CDGM for progress. He was badly informed about CDGM and believed the OEO rumor-type charges. He sincerely seemed to believe CDGM was dead and he was "saving the children of Mississippi." However, all this didn't explain why he didn't check first with John instead of joining the stealthy, the underground, the assassins.

Aaron Henry issued a press release justifying his cooperation with OEO. It sounded great, but overlooked the central question: Why didn't he check with CDGM to see if we had done all these things we were charged with? To see if we considered us dead and were going to lie down and give up, or if he could help us fight this injustice?

September 30, "D Day," was busy. John threw everyone into action at once; everyone from board members and visiting VIPs, and from director to mail clerk, sat at John's big table to start stuffing envelopes to communities. Information sheets had been written and run off during the afternoon, just after we read the headline.

Jule Sugarman called to say he wanted to come down immediately with Ted Berry, director of OEO's community action program, to "straighten things out." Jule wanted to meet privately with the board.

John said there had been quite enough private meetings lately, and he would telephone-poll our board to see if members could make it from their homes all around the state on such short notice, but that he was pretty sure they would want a public hearing, and would not agree to a private one. He was right. Board members who could be reached said they wanted an open meeting a week from Saturday for all those in the state, in and out of CDGM, who were interested. They said Shriver's staff would be welcome. Sugarman and Berry said they were catching a plane in a minute, and would be right down. They were told no one at CDGM would be available to talk with them on those terms; that we needed time to collect the facts, contact MAP board members regarding their intentions, etc. (Mr. Sugarman and Mr. Berry were scheduled to come to a meeting with our board the week before the blow, to talk about the new grant, but had to cancel because the Poverty Bill was defeated by voice vote. Its defenders were not on hand when it came up, and the OEO officials had to stay in Washington to clean up the catastrophe.)

On October 2 some visitors from the New York Foundation asked John and me if we were organizing poor people to fight for CDGM. John answered that the issue was not one organization or another, or defending the organization. The issue was whether or not poor people were to be allowed to make key decisions. Some CDGM poor people might prefer MAP. The point was not loyalty to CDGM, but loyalty to the principle of honesty and respect, rather than yielding to sneakiness and manipulation.

CDGM staff, board, and friends mobilized at once to notify friends and allies around the nation of our newest crisis. We had a good cause and good connections. People came instantly to our support.

Newsmen swarmed. I took CBS-TV men to the Richmond Grove Center. The visit was used nationwide on the six o'clock news a few days later.

The Jackson *Clarion-Ledger* of October 2 ran this report:

REUTHER PROTESTS BI-RACIAL BOARD

Creation of a new bi-racial group to replace the controversial Child Development Group of Mississippi is being assailed by the Citizens Crusade Against Poverty as an "arbitrary, high-handed political move."

"It can only arouse suspicion that the 12,000 children in the 121 Head Start centers operated in 28 counties across the state are being made the pawn in a political power play," CCAP executive director Richard W. Boone said here Saturday.

CCAP ALARMED

The CCAP, whose chairman is labor leader Walter Reuther, is alarmed by the Jackson *Daily News* report that the CDGM will be replaced in October by a twelve-man board called Action for Progress in Mississippi, chartered by Gov. Paul Johnson. Boone added:

"This report is a matter of great concern to the CCAP which last year supported the Child Development Group's request for anti-poverty funds and currently, at the CDGM's request, has appointed a distinguished citizens' board of inquiry to make a full and independent analysis of the program operated by the CDGM and compare it with other anti-poverty programs in the state. Members of this board of inquiry have just returned from Mississippi."

Boone charged that the new set-up was rushed forward to "discredit" that board's report in advance.

He called upon the Johnson administration and anti-poverty chief Sargent Shriver to "clarify" their positions about the Mississippi group.

John, and Dave Emmons—Mary's husband, who had been a very helpful public relations and press release man during our first unfunded crisis and who again took time off from his thesis studies to help now—and Marv Hoffman put out another release October 2. Board members ratified these things before they became official statements "issued by the CDGM Board of Directors and Director John Mudd":

> We believe that a full, frank, intelligent, and public discussion of all issues surrounding the refunding of CDGM is imperative. On Friday, September 30, CDGM requested Mr. Sargent Shriver, Director of the Office of Economic Opportunity, or his representatives, to attend a public meeting in Jackson on Saturday, October 8, to insure that the thousands of impoverished throughout the state who are affected by this program will have the fullest opportunity to participate in those decisions having significant influence on their future lives.
>
> After the clandestine formation of an alternative organization (M-A-P), reported in recent days, further private meetings with OEO officials would merely perpetuate and deepen the intense distrust which thousands of CDGM participants and supporters in communities throughout the state of Mississippi feel toward those who would manipulate the future of *their* program in secrecy. We feel that OEO officials must explain their shocking actions aimed at subverting a successful program to *all* the people most affected by the project.
>
> We have also extended an invitation to those individuals identified with the so-called Board of MAP to attend the public meeting on October 8 with the hope that all persons who wish to lend their assistance and energies in promoting the most effective means for overcoming the causes of poverty in the state will be present to discuss their ideas with those impoverished Mississippians and their elected representatives who have already successfully entered the battle to break the cycle of poverty throughout Mississippi.

Only two of the many MAP board members took the trouble to reply to the telegrams of invitation sent them by the poor they were so concerned about. One was Aaron Henry, who felt himself in rather more than a gentle vise. Not one came to the meeting to reveal their intentions to CDGM (MAP?) constituents. As one MAP key board member explained to a CDGMian who called upon him to discuss matters of mutual concern: "Aw, hell, we don't need all those damn meetings—democracy works best when two men who know what they're doing meet in a backroom and talk things over."

My diary of October 3 reports: "Several CDGM people went to Greenwood last night to co-ordinate with Delta Ministry, FDP, etc, ldrshp. Has rarely ever happened before, in spite of OEO's insinuations and allegations!

"Ironic: we never did what they charged us with till they drove us into death rattles, which finally made FDP et al. sympathetic for almost the first time in an organizational way. Aaron thinks he represents Negro feeling in Miss., but wow is he in trouble with thousands of articulate CDGM-type Negroes! They are absolutely livid with rage at him. Won't listen to any reasonable discussion about his possible motives. As far as they are concerned, he's a quisling. Horrible to have a split within like this. We've all avoided it meticulously and scrupulously for a year and a half. The division was there, but we didn't let it become a public schism. One more fractionalizing of the civil rights mvmnt.

"A community lady at the Greenwood meeting said MAP is OEO's 'new plantation system.' Splendid phrase. Expect we'll hear more of it! . . . ."

On October 3, 1966, this press release was issued by the CDGM board and John Mudd:

> It is our understanding the OEO will today publicly release allegations against CDGM which it has had neither the courtesy or goodwill to reveal to us at any point during the last seven months. We consider this as shocking a move as their secretive formation of an alternative board of directors to CDGM.
>
> (1) At every point during this project we have requested OEO to provide us with criticism against our competency and suggestions to correct any faults. They have at no time offered either.
>
> (2) CDGM's current management system was designed in a co-operative effort by CDGM staff, Ernst and Ernst, a respected local accounting firm, OEO consultants and management employees. All of these parties agreed to the workability of the system and, during the early days of this project, referred to it as a model for poverty agencies.
>
> Thus any indictment of CDGM's competence is a self-indictment of OEO. More important, the release of charges by OEO at this late date, given their past silence and lack of criticism, is in fact a bald political move to destroy a nationally acclaimed program.

Finally, on October 3, OEO sent the famous audit report. It was dated September 15; *two days after the chartering of MAP*; clear proof that MAP was formed to eliminate CDGM for political reasons, not because of legitimate and insoluble faults administratively. OEO had a press conference *before* CDGM board members had received copies of the charges against *CDGM*. At the conference officials distributed anti-CDGM literature to reporters. A newsman laughed in OEO officials' red faces, and mocked them for accusing "a victim" publicly before "having the nerve" to do so privately. He outlined the various political deals OEO had made behind CDGM's hard-working back. At this conference an OEO spokesman made the first official direct statement we had heard, that CDGM was not going to be refunded. The newsman said he thought it most "professional, ethical, and symbolic of OEO's deep concern for 'helping' CDGM, it's best project, to tell the world before you tell CDGM leadership."

The Jackson *Daily News* headline for October 3, 1966, was: "CDGM REFUSED FEDERAL MONEY. OEO TURNS DOWN $20.3 MILLION BID."

And from my diary come the following comments: ". . . state AFL–CIO director Claude Ramsey infuriated by labor's exclusion from MAP board. We had approached him to be on our expanded board. A brave man in this state: unions being about as popular as castor oil.

"Father Law, important Catholic, angry at Catholic exclusion from MAP board. STAR is the huge Catholic poverty project in Miss. Evidently MAP is conceived as the Protestant group, to balance the federal fund gift-giving.

"——— from a very poor spot in Forrest County said, 'I ain't so worried that OEO ain't read its own guidelines, but what gits me, it don't seem they's read *God's* guidelines. You can't blame 'em for bein' dumb: they're just a bunch of federal jerks: but you cin blame 'em for bein' a bunch of dirty, dishonest politicians playin' with us little people. I sure am tired of them as the big "I," and us as the little "you."'

" . . . Funny thing to notice: CDGM has become, to many people, what OEO originally was: an ideal. Many OEO originals, big and little, (Conway, Boone, Caprio, Cahn, Morris, Walls, me) who had deep commitment to developing and protecting *OEO*, have left it behind and gone on to develop something *more* ideal, and are helping CDGM develop and protect its image.

"Somebody in CDGM office today suggested changing OEO's name from OEO (Office of Economic Opportunity) to SPONGE (Society for the Prevention of Negroes Getting Everything).

"A poor man on CDGM's Board said, 'Who d'you s'pose gave OEO the idea that whenever they want to know what Negroes in Mississippi think, they should just call up one man in a drugstore?' (reference to Aaron Henry, who owns the 4th St. Pharmacy in Clarksdale).

"Two hard-to-reconcile statements: a legislature friend told me at breakfast today that the only thing he doesn't like about CDGM is the way it's 'mongrelizing' the races. Too damn much integration. And an OEO friend said on the phone an hour later that the only thing he doesn't like about CDGM is the way it's breeding black power. Ah, la, we are guilty either of too much or too little integration, I forget which, but surely we *must* be guilty of something! Otherwise, why would OEO be corraling CDGM into a box canyon and pouring acid on our heads? Answer: we are guilty of believing in citizenship. OEO believes in it ardently; but not in too much for politically 'inconvenient' people."

* * *

"Oct. 4. More drama today, Wash. Star ran a front page piece called, 'OEO Charged With Spying on Poverty Project in South.'"

The Office of Economic Opportunity has been accused of ordering six temporary employees—college students here—to disguise themselves as civil rights workers to investigate an anti-poverty project in Mississippi.

The allegation was disclosed shortly after OEO announced yesterday that it would no longer finance the project in question—a statewide program long opposed by Sen. John C. Stennis, D-Miss. - - -

My diary from October 4 continues: "Mbrs. of Citizens' Crusade Against Poverty's Board of Inquiry, set up to investigate (and clear?) CDGM, are still swarming around the state on several-day 'inspection' tours. They're talking to non-CDGM white-Mississippi oriented Community Action agencies funded by OEO, the Human Relations Council (several people on it friendly, many more silently antagonistic: very few have ever had anything to do with us, being as how we're controversial); church dignitaries of many faiths, labor, etc. Seem pretty thorough. Are planning to write a report. Not colored by the kinds of political pressures many feel Shriver's 'reports' are colored by.

"This is probably excellent in-state PR for CDGM—no matter what position they take, members of this Board of Inquiry are spreading honest info. about CDGM. So many Mississippians are mis-informed about us, of course, thanks to the Hederman press. (Own both papers, that duly daily cover all this scandal; on the front page, usually.)

"This seems to be good "involvement' for the Board of Inquiry members too. CDGM *is* an ideal, a nationally held 'concept' in certain circles. These people seem warmed and glowing to be 'a part' of us. It's fantastic how many people we never heard of have heard of CDGM. And not only that, but its fantastic how many people who've never been in Miss. are now claiming to have practically *created* CDGM! Involvement of the poor isn't the only necessary ingredient for social development!

"CCAP issued a release today in Dick Boone's name . . ."

. . . I am shocked but not surprised by the announcement of the Office of Economic Opportunity that the Child Development Group would not be refunded. It has been apparent for some time now that the Office of Economic Opportunity and the Administration have joined with Senators Stennis and Eastland to launch a "New Plantation Policy" of which the poor of Mississippi are the chief victims.

The Administration and the Office of Economic Opportunity must take full responsibility for what can only be considered a crass political sell out of the poor to the very forces which have fought to keep them in bondage for so long.

The news that a new 12-man group—Action for Progress in Mississippi—will take over the CDGM program fits into this policy completely. . . .

While the Child Development Group of Mississippi program has had its growing pains, its administration has been vouched for by both the distinguished accounting firm of Ernst and Ernst and the management firm of Klein and Saks. The accounting system was developed in close cooperation with OEO. Of course no program run by poor people can be expected to run perfectly. But the distorted nature of the charges against CDGM only underscore the cynically political nature of the decision. OEO officials approved the spending of $35,000 for a film about CDGM which is being distributed nationally as a teacher training film for developing more pre-school programs.

As part and parcel of the "New Plantation Policy" of the OEO in Mississippi has been an unparalleled Federal investigation of the CDGM programs. Thousands upon thousands of taxpayers' dollars have been spent looking into a program that has won the plaudits of experts around the Nation, and which was described by Sargent Shriver himself as "a success in fulfilling the purpose of the program, which is what Congress asked us to do." These investigatory methods have often been extremely questionable.

There has been no corresponding investigation of community action programs in Mississippi which by any fair standard must be judged some of the worst in the Nation.

The people of Mississippi are deeply disturbed by this "poor be damned" policy, and they will be coming together in Jackson next Saturday at a mass meeting to let their feelings be known. At this meeting the people of Mississippi will decide what action they will take to preserve this vital program. . . . The Citizens' Crusade Against Poverty wishes to reiterate its four-point program on CDGM:

(1) The Federal Government should refund the Child Development Group of Mississippi;
(2) That OEO can work with the present CDGM board to improve the program;
(3) That the CDGM should consider expanding its Board to include other segments of the community which could contribute to the program.
(4) OEO must reform local community action programs in Mississippi so that they will gain the confidence of the thousands of poor people in the State. Only then should there be any move to merge CDGM groups with CAP programs.

* * *

Owen Brooks, acting director of the Delta Ministry since Art Thomas was plucked from his excellent leadership of this initially creative organization by the church strategists and powers that be, issued a public statement beginning: "The arbitrary decision to kill off the Child Development Group of Mississippi and replace it with a hand-picked board is producing a wave of bitterness and cynicism among the poor people of Mississippi" and ending: "When you destroy hope, you are sowing the seeds of bitterness and hatred. And the men of power are doing that; they are trampling a dream."

* * *

On October 4, 1966, the Jackson *Daily News*, outstanding in the newspaper world for its scornful contempt for facts, had a page one story headed "CDGM Promised Private Grant." It began:

The controversial Child Development Group of Mississippi was officially dead today but the director of the organization said today that the group has received a private grant that will permit it to continue operation.

John H. Mudd said that CDGM has been notified that it will receive a grant from the Field Foundation. He said that he did not yet know the amount of the grant or final details. . . .

This is the *Daily News*'s version of the fact that the poor people's community college we had long been planning entirely separately from CDGM got a $20,000 grant for planning and trying a pilot economic development institute. This wasn't a penny for CDGM to maintain a central office, area staff, or Child Development centers.

The Jackson *Clarion-Ledger* also had a front page article. After approximately 258 words in two columns on the front page about OEO's and Senator Stennis's attacks and lacerations, and about another 474 words in a two-column continuation on page 14, the article *finally* acknowledged that CDGM's accounting system had been praised by the international accounting firm of Ernst and Ernst (hired as CDGM's regular accountants last winter at Mr. Shriver's insistence), by OEO's accounting department, by the U.S. government's General Accounting Office, and by an investigator representing Senator Stennis from the Senate Appropriations Committee.

The New York Times also had something on October 4. It was a story by Joseph Loftus which revealed the judgment of the author, as most "factual" newspaper pieces do, as to what's important. The article discussed exclusively OEO's actions and the makeup of MAP. It was evidently not significant to the writer that OEO had done a massive frame-up and Kafkaesque distortion job on its number one model project in the country. Mr. Loftus didn't consider it relevant to state one word of CDGM's replies! In fact, as we frantically worked, he referred to us with that cold-as-clay word "was": CDGM's sponsor "was" Mary Holmes Junior College with the effect of reinforcing the idea that CDGM was guilty and OEO was merciful. Mr. Loftus gratuitously tossed in the sentence, "No criminal charges are being made." He also reported that: "The politically delicate task of setting up a new body is handled by Harry C. McPherson, Jr., a special council to the President and . . . ." With "friends" like this, the whole shocking thing could well have been smoothed over and hidden from the concerned public.

On October 5 the *Clarion-Ledger* said:

FDP ATTACKS CDGM CUTOFF

A civil rights geared political party Tuesday threatened demonstrations across Mississippi if a head start agency loses federal financial support. . . .

Lawrence Guyot, chairman of the predominately Negro Freedom Democratic Party, said his organization wants the disbanding of the New Action for Progress in Mississippi Board, a biracial group that apparently will inherit the CDGM's head start programs.

The party said it considers the formation of the new group a "high-handed colonial act" designed to control the Negro vote and to strengthen the national Democratic Party organization in Mississippi. . . .

It's possible to manipulate the Negro vote in a regime where whites are fair and decent, like the MAP board whites, whereas it's not possible if whites are cruel and Klan-type, because Negroes don't fall for them, hate them, don't allow themselves to be hoodwinked or bribed into voting "suitably," as one of my Mississippi politician friends calls it.

The Washington *Post* also had an article on October 5. It stressed John Mudd's assertions of innocence first. *What facts* are put *where* in a story makes such a difference in the impression the "reporting" creates. The author also said CDGM was "brought into being by officials of the United Presbyterian Church and the National Council of Churches." Of course, the only person there who brought CDGM into being was the remarkable Art Thomas, who is never mentioned. Maybe the churches didn't think it politically desirable to give him credit. Like Tom Levin, he was "erased," a technique all big, powerful organizations use for dealing with those they have finished using.

The *Post* article mentioned that OEO said we spent $654,000 which we accounted for inadequately or irregularly; that OEO said we paid $104,000 to consultants and that unsupported or supporting invoices were inadequate; and that OEO said we paid $64,000 in salaries in excess of OEO guidelines.

Almost every penny of these apparent peculiarities could be explained convincingly. The fact that all receipts, reports, facts, etc., were not in *yet*, only meant that our records were not absolutely up to date because we operated daily and it was a fluid situation. It didn't mean we spent anything "illicitly" or illegally. Our salaries were those *we* judged appropriate until OEO came out with some salary guidelines March 17. These said no one could earn more than 20 percent more than he had earned on his last job. This was inappropriate in the case of college students who didn't *have* a last job, or cheated poor people whose last job paid three dollars a day. Were we to cheat and enslave them too? But we did put OEO salary guidelines into effect at once. Anything OEO found wrong with our salaries predated March 17.

The Jackson *Daily News*, page one, Thursday, October 6, 1966, carried this:

MAP BOARD TO PASS UP CDGM RALLY

A spokesman for the newly formed Mississippi Action for Progress board, scheduled to become the chief recipient of antipoverty funds in Mississippi, said today that members of the board will not attend a mass meeting of the Child Development Group of Mississippi the MAP is replacing.

Newspaper Editor Hodding Carter III of Greenville, one of the incorporators of MAP and a member of the 12-man board, said that none of the board members will be on hand for the meeting to be held Saturday at 10 A.M. on the Jackson State College campus.

Meanwhile, John H. Mudd, executive director of CDGM, said that a crowd of 10,000 is expected at the meeting, being held to discuss the future of CDGM. . . .

Mudd said that the meeting here Saturday "will not be a demonstration, but a peaceful and orderly gathering of our friends and supporters from across the state. The meeting is intended to provide them with the opportunity of expressing their resolve about CDGM's future and their opinions about the formation of the so-called Mississippi Action for Progress group."

And the Jackson *Daily News* of October 6, 1966, ran this editorial:

It is a common practice for the latter day first class citizens to employ blackmail to try to get what they demand. Either give them what they ask or they will start a demonstration or one of those now-famous street riots. . . .

. . . the same attitude is being taken in Mississippi by street walkers who claim they will demonstrate or touch off a riot somewhere in the state if the Child Development Group of Mississippi doesn't get $21 million Head Start grant. . . .

These are serious irregularities and rather than staging demonstrations and riots some of those responsible for the CDGM irregularities might well find themselves en route to a Federal Prison.

At any rate, the American public is fed up with blackmail of riots from the Black Power element.

My diary for the same day says: ". . . and of course would never consider having any kind of rowdy affair. We've all been working night and day to notify community people of Sat. rally: imp't. that people continue to be able to discuss, decide, etc., even in these days of checker games on the part of the big boys in Wash.

"I've been taking time out from the book to do 'volunteer fireman' chores—call every liberal newspaper in DC, NY etc., to invite them to the rally, etc. Adam Giffard is coming to it to shoot some fresh footage.

"The educational-documentary film I discussed so much with NET in NY earlier has evolved into not using *Chance for Change* pure, but into using a lot of excerpts of it, and some from the other film the Giffards and I made called *Struggle for Ourselves*, plus a *new* script written by our sharp-tongued daring supporter Andy Kopkind, and this new rally material taken Sat. by Adam. It will be a one hour show and will be shown on over a hundred NET stations around the country, if they subscribe to it.

"NY Times had another article: Reuther indignant at OEO. I wonder if this CDGM affair is causing union splits. I wonder what Mr. Meaney thinks. Reuther plans to see Shriver about us Friday."

The Jackson *Clarion-Ledger*, Friday, October 7, 1966, said:

. . . CDGM said [of the MAP Board], "The board has extremely close ties to the National Democratic Party.

"Two members of the board are contributors to Lyndon Johnson's 'President's Club.' "

The group named Leroy Percy of Greenville and Charles Young of Meridian.

"Carter is state co-chairman of the 'Young Demoncrats,'" CDGM said. "Douglas Wynn, a Greenville Lawyer, mentioned in various newspapers as a major behind-the-scenes organizer of MAP, is another 'President's Club' contributor and a member of the state Democratic party's executive committee."

CDGM said also that MAP had no representative of labor, charging that member Owen Cooper, president of Mississippi Chemical Corp. in Yazoo City, was anti-labor.

. . . The CDGM said Percy and Oscar Carr of Clarksdale owned plantations where Negroes have worked for $3 a day or less. . . .

OEO refused to attend the proposed Saturday rally. Ted Berry sent a telegram to John, including the statements: "since you have refused our invitation to a conference, please be advised that CDGM must take full responsibility for any misunderstanding and misinterpretations given to the people, of OEO's desire to make Head Start available to all the children of Mississippi. . . ."

Subsequent talks with OEO officials involved in this week of CDGM's hysterical history, reveal that undoubtedly most officials who took this view, sincerely believed that *CDGM* was not as concerned with making "Head Start available to all the children of Mississippi" as *they* were. It's probably only possible for decent people to be destructive if they deceive themselves into thinking they're not.

Meanwhile, MAP was moving ahead. MAP applied, finally, for a poverty program grant. MAP planned to add seven people "from the target area" to the eleven "safe" Negroes and whites already on board. With this balance, thought CDGM, things could be kept well under control. Owen Cooper made a public announcement saying that the primary purpose of the new antipoverty board was to help communities around the state develop a working program. That, thought CDGM, is why MAP has to destroy extraordinarily well-working programs which communities around the state now have in connection with CDGM.

During this same strange week other interesting events emanating from OEO policy-planning offices were occurring in the hinterlands of Mississippi. In mid-September OEO had sent a task force into Mississippi to help CDGM implement its February grant condition, which said that in areas where both Community Action Programs and CDGM Head Starts were operating, the two must try to work together. Bob Moore headed this task force.

Bob stressed that Mr. Shriver or somebody had made a judgment about whether or not to fund CDGM, why, how much, where, etc., and that his mission was simply to provide a vehicle so that the grant condition could be implemented and so that Head Starts could operate.

Bob insisted that it wasn't his job to make a study of CDGM. He said he didn't pretend to know everything about CDGM. He didn't know everything about MAP, either. Bob appeared to be very irritated that CDGM people seemed to think he should be confronting "all kinds of issues." During the MAP-CDGM crisis week, before our statewide rally, reports of how task force teams assigned to the nine CDGM-CAP overlap areas were proceding and succeeding filtered into our office. Mrs. Anna Ashley, our mature and inspiring ATG in the area, was heartsick. Someone called on the phone: "I'm from Pike County, so I can only tell you about Pike County," said the upset community person on the telephone, "but some terrible things are going on down here! There's been these two men from the OEO task force down here? They came to help us work things out with the white CAP here? So we'd all be fairly treated?

"We've known there was a CAP here for some time. We know OEO says cooperate. But we weren't going to give in without trying to stay with CDGM—*quitting* isn't cooperating.

"John Mudd had writ to this CAP. It's called Southwest Mississippi Opportunity, Inc. [SMO] He asked about cooperating. They answered to hell with us . . ."

That answer, dated August 15, 1966, from Miss Kathleen O'Fallon, executive director of Southwest Mississippi Opportunity, Inc., to John Mudd said in part:

> . . . A thorough study of the CDGM Program in Amite and Pike Counties was made and representatives of CDGM were invited and discussed the program. A study of other Head Start Programs operating in the area (including one program in the neighboring State of Louisiana) was made and presented to the Board of Directors.
>
> These studies clearly place the CDGM Program in an unfavorable position in the areas of local participation and representation in the planning, control and evaluation; in comparable cost; and in the area of coordinating its activities with all local state and federal agencies and programs as a concerted attack on the conditions contributing to poverty.
>
> Therefore, the Board of Directors of Southwest Mississippi Opportunity, Inc., has directed its staff to immediately undertake the planning, and prepare a Head Start proposal for Amite, Pike and Wilkinson Counties, to submit same to OEO and to notify CDGM and OEO of the disapproval of the proposal indicated in the attached CAP Form 46. . . .

The voice on the telephone continued: ". . . The first we knew of this task force was these two men, Mr. Collins and Mr. Bradford. They walked into the CDGM area office here, and said they had come to try to get CDGM and CAP together. But from that moment on, the only thing they talked good about, was the white CAP. They downgraded us and ignored us. We were only poor people, and couldn't understand all this, so they'd help us get 'what was good for us.' Mr. Bradford said, 'I come that you might have life, and have it more abundantly.' He thought because he was an educated Negro, he could say anything to us, and we should believe it. We all felt he was lying and *knew* he was lying.

"The task force presented the outline of a proposal to our CDGM area council. They said they would think about it, and tell Mr. Collins and Mr. Bradford later. Sunday night, after the rally, they said the task force told them, 'Sign on the line *now! Don't go to the rally!*'

"Our area council was very weak. We had had a lot of trouble with CDGM in this area all along. We complained to central all the time asking for help. We aren't too happy with John Mudd, much as we like him and CDGM, because we kept asking them to send people down to help us straighten things out, and he kept answering or mostly sending messages by other people that we should settle things for ourselves. We couldn't. We had some of our people practicing some pretty crooked practices. They controlled others through fear of losing paychecks—things like that. People thought the crooked ones had more power than they did—were afraid to get rid of them.

"So later that night after the area council meeting, the task force people went to see this one man on the council they thought was wavering. He was a man we never trusted. He was mad at CDGM for never hiring him, because we didn't want him, because we didn't trust him. He just liked to feel important. Here he saw his chance. The task force told him to sign this agreement signing all our Head Starts over to SMO. They said we could work out the details later. So he signed it!

"We heard about it on the air! We were shocked! We ran around checking. Did he verbally agree? Was it binding? Could we get out of it? One weak man didn't represent *us! We* had built CDGM, not him!

"Then we heard OEO had given SMO seven hundred thousand dollars to take over our centers. We were supposed to run this *under* them. Hah! How long would *we* last? We asked how this could be, so fast. Nobody gets grants like that in one day from OEO!—without even a written proposal! Mr. Collins said he got authorization from Washington by 'telephonic transmission,' whatever that is!

"We asked Mr. Collins, 'Why are you so tooth and toenail for this arrangement here, when there are so many other counties that don't have *any* poverty program?' He kept saying, 'This is your last chance to get anything. OEO won't refund you as CDGM. This is your last chance. Don't be stubborn.' We knew the real answer, though. SMO had thirty thousand dollars already to get started, and they couldn't attract any parents and children. So they had to steal ours or fold up. Then they would lose face. So they just had to sham this over. We told the task force people what we thought of them. They had control over this. They could've worked this out right. They were weak. They didn't try to understand. They didn't care. They just wanted to get credit for a quick maneuver with their bosses in Washington. We told them, 'We understand this: first you take away our authority to make decisions, and next you'll let the CAP decide us right out of our jobs.' We said, 'CAP was began wrong, it was built wrong, and it'll *stay* wrong until we change it. Now you've made us sign away our position to try to change it.'

"We're coming to the rally. We'll be there! We want to know what's happening. Is CDGM dead? Everywhere? Is it here for us? Can't we at least get some bargaining power? I think it's too late for us. This whole poverty war down here is a tight fight with a short stick! I can't believe OEO truly believes they're doing good!"

This apparently wasn't an isolated instance of OEO-style "doing good." On October 7 CDGM issued another press release to A.M. and P.M. papers:

CDGM Director John Mudd today charged that "the apparent funding of two Head Start programs in CDGM areas (Lafayette and Marshall Counties, and Jackson County) announced today by the Office of Economic Opportunity, involved the crass manipulation of people by OEO officials in a hurried attempt to buy off Mississippi communities and keep them from attending CDGM's state-wide meeting Saturday.

"In the last three days," he said, "members of the OEO task force in Mississippi have attempted to establish instant Head Start programs with deceptive promises and veiled threats in total disregard of OEO's own guidelines."

Mudd pointed out that "task force personnel have insisted CDGM is dead, when in fact that is still an open question. They have told CDGM persons in Pike County, for example, not to attend the Saturday meeting and begged them to sign proposals under pressure without careful and broadly based deliberation. In other areas, they have announced grants without receiving, let alone reviewing Head Start applications.

"This treatment of people as things is even more shocking and unconstructive than the distorted accusations OEO officials have raised against CDGM's competence in management," he commented. "Largely irrelevant and untrue, the accusations were made," Mudd said, "to create the illusion of poor management for what was essentially a political decision against refunding CDGM." . . .

On page one, the Jackson *Clarion-Ledger,* Saturday, October 8, 1966, said:

. . . A newly-formed Gulf Coast organization announced Friday it has been assured it will be the only federally-funded Head Start project in Jackson County.

Edward B. Wright, Jr., secretary of the Jackson County Citizens for Child Development, said his organization expects to complete details of a program to be submitted to the OEO within the next 30 days.

Almost $2 million was approved Friday for two Mississippi Head Start projects, the first since the Child Development Group of Mississippi fell by the wayside when the OEO refused its plea for funds to continue operation of centers because of alleged mismanagement irregularities.

An OEO spokesman in Washington said $1.2 million was approved for a project in Marshall and Lafayette Counties and $713,000 for one in Pike, Amite and Wilkinson Counties.

OEO director Sargent Shriver said both will provide education for pre-school children plus nutritional, health and social services for them and their families.

The larger grant will be administered by Rust College at Holly Springs for 600 pre-school children in eight centers manned by 50 teachers and 160 non-professional workers. Jacob U. Gordon is the director. Funding is for 12 months of operation.

The Southwest Child Development Council with headquarters in Woodville will administer the eight-month, three-county project. The OEO said there will be 14 centers in Pike County, three in Amite and nine in Wilkinson to care for 935 children, most of them utilizing centers established by the CDGM. . . .

An assistant to CAP Director Ted Berry at OEO, said there was no connection between the fact that Rust College is a Negro Methodist school, and that Ted Berry is a leading Negro Methodist layman.

* * *

"The thing I can't stand about CDGM, especially John Mudd," complained a senior OEO official in a voice expressing injured feelings, "is that they don't trust us."

* * *

Ring around the rosey,
A pocket full of posies,
Tisha! Tasha!
We all fall down!

* * *

From the Saturday, October 8, 1966 Jackson *Clarion-Ledger*, Tom Ethridge's "Mississippi Notebook," "Hash for Saturday, Bits & Briefs" came this:

In the Old South of Reconstruction days, home folks who cooperated with the Carpetbagger regime were known as "Scalawags."

In conquered France during World War II, those who played footsie with the German occupation were branded as "Collaborationists."

In Norway, then everywhere, turncoats became known as "Quislings." Today, as rampant federalism uses force to impose its whims, Mississippi seems to have quite a few Scalawag, Collaborationist, and/or Quisling types, abetting the "Revolution"—by any name you may prefer to call them.

These new manifestations will fail—as others have failed—because unfair, un-natural and un-reasonable movements can never overcome public Sentiment which is the basis of truly democratic society.

And in the same paper on the same day appeared the headline "PRESBYTERIAN GROUP HITS SUSPENSION."

My diary reports: "The day before MAP Board was announced there was an antipoverty conference at the Benbow: STAR, CDGM, JKSN. H-S [Jackson Head Start], Mid-State Opportunities, CAPs, Task Force. Marian asked if Task Force was here because of Stennis's pressure on OEO. Head of Task Force said he doubted if Stennis even knew Task Force was in state. Everyone fell off their chairs laughing. One member of the Task Force said it was all he could do not to tell his leader to stop lying.

"Martin Luther King spoke lengthily to Randolph Blackwell. King was tragically uninformed about CDGM. Had been to see Berry a month before. Evidently Berry told King we were black power through and through. King was astonished to learn that our director was white, lots of white staff, some white board members. Rumor has it he thought he could have persuaded Aaron not to go MAP if he had been better informed.

"Rally was today. Tremendous! Many thousands all day at Jackson State College. Started with Joe Harrison leading singing.

"Then Fannie Lou Hamer (which meant commitment of FDP top level, weren't sure we'd get that) in one of her funniest, bitterest speeches delivered in that melodious contralto voice and marvelous comic manner of hers: 'Really glad to see y'all out here today. That's one thing the man didn't expect! You know, there's a sign that says we'd rather fight than switch. We're gonna fight for the principle, and we're gonna sing, "Go Tell it on the Mountain" . . . we ain't gonna let no Uncle Toms or Nervous Nellies turn us round . . . National Association for the Advancement of Aaron Henry . . . The only way we can win is, winners don't quit.'

"Guyot spoke for FDP too. Great for us, even though FDP's motivation, many think, is to grab the show and gain a little of the power they don't have—think they are happy to see CDGM hit below the belt and crying for help—plays into their hands—have an office with a phone and a handful of people—no action—dying organization—think they think might be their rebirth—

"Rev. McCree spoke, of course, with his usual power to hold and move an audience: '. . . They had led us to believe if we sent in a revised proposal, that we would be funded without any problem. Then all of a sudden we saw the allegations in the newspaper. . . . We want people to know that OEO may be divided, but we people here in Mississippi are not divided. We want them to know that we are not going to be divided by the political tricks and manipulations that they have used. We are still going to be here, and we are *still* going to be here . . . There have been talk going around the state that CDGM is dead, but when I see all these people, I *know* CDGM is not dead. CDGM is still alive and by the help of God, and with the help of your people, CDGM is going to *remain* alive. . . . We have been used before. We have been misused. We have been manipulated. We have had things rammed down our throat that we didn't want. But we want to show today . . . and not only today, but tomorrow and other days, that we ain' gonna be sold no more.

"'Most of you know about the so-called MAP Board. Most of you know this Board was formed. All of you people were completely ignored. You and your communities that have banded together to have a Head Start program in '65 were completely ignored. And if these so-called people [are so interested in the] welfare of the poor of Mississippi and so interested in our kids . . . why didn't they come forward when we were seeking an answer, when we were . . . asking for help . . . they stayed in the background. Now we have a program operating. When they see that we have a program which the Director of OEO, Sargent Shriver, says was one of the best programs in the country, then a deal is made. . . .

"'I think Shriver has relinquished his power to Senator Stennis, and Senator Stennis is now, in fact, the Director of OEO. . . . We are not going to be sold one by one . . .'

"Marian talked eloquently about why don't OEO people check the CAPs in Mississippi? We follow the guidelines, they don't, *we* are considered the rotten program. She listed all the powerful good groups behind us . . .

"A telegram was read from Martin Luther King.

"Unida talked about the new plantation system—I think she was the one who made up the phrase earlier in the week. . . .

"Ed King [Movement hero, chaplain at Tougaloo College, white Mississippian] talked: '. . . . Two years ago I stood [with] two men—Medgar Evers and Aaron Henry. Mississippi has killed Medgar Evers, and Mississippi had tricked Aaron Henry . . .'

"Dick Boone came. Gave a brief statement about CCAP and the Committee of Inquiry . . . '. . . you must remember that you have support at the national level . . . You have a program, and probably one of the most important poverty programs, and you got it by working together. You will only save it by sticking together.'

"American Federation of Teachers supported us. . . . Reps. at rally. Some seemed to be union organizers. We'd thought of forming all our teachers into an AFL teachers' union, which would have been very dramatic politically but lots of people were against it because it wouldn't have been a move that grew out of the poor people's understanding and choice. National press present . . . Tom [Levin] came for this momentous occasion . . ."

Community people talked extensively, got together in small groups and caucused, planned, ended up with eleven resolutions. These were duplicated and distributed at once:

1. We resolve that the people of Mississippi will completely support the CDGM Board and its structure and issue a vote of no-confidence for the new MAP Board.
2. We resolve that we will boycott the MAP Board and all CAP Boards not responsive to the poor in favor of CDGM.
3. We resolve that we will support no board that will not fully involve the poor people and which are not chosen by the poor people of Mississippi.
4. We resolve that we will operate our centers on a volunteer basis wherever feasible and will attempt to raise funds in our local communities and accept no support from MAP or undemocratic CAP Boards.
5. We resolve that CDGM employees will refuse any employment or cooperation with MAP; that we will fight the forces against CDGM and against the independence of poor people in Mississippi until victory is won.
6. We resolve that we will ask the Citizens' Crusade Against Poverty and the Committee of Inquiry to help set up national support groups to raise money to help the poor people and CDGM maintain their centers.
7. We resolve that we will boycott and picket those leaders whose actions do not follow the desires of the people and that we will support only those people who support us.
8. We resolve that we will send a petition to the national NAACP requesting that all local NAACP people currently supporting MAP withdraw their support and support CDGM and the poor people of Mississippi.
9. We resolve that we request Congressman Adam Clayton Powell to investigate CAP Boards in Mississippi and the Atlanta Regional Office of OEO to determine whether or not OEO guidelines are being followed and whether or not programs involve and help the poor people of Mississippi.
10. We resolve that we request the Equal Opportunities Employment Commission to investigate the hiring policies and practices of the Mississippi Chemical Corporation, headed by Owen Cooper.
11. We resolve that we will immediately request a public hearing of the poor in Washington, D.C., where CDGM and other poor people can defend their program and express their feelings to the nation.

Governor Paul B. Johnson, on October 10, 1966, issued the following press release:

Not since the days when Mississippi was occupied by scalawags after the War between the States have we been subjected to such an obnoxious group of people as those who operated the Child Development Group of Mississippi. . . .

* * *

Sing a song of sixpence,
A pocket full of rye;
Four and twenty blackbirds
Baked in a pie.
When the pie was opened
The birds began to sing;
Wasn't that a dainty dish
To set before the King?

* * *

In an October 11, 1966, OEO Public Affairs release, superbly titled "OEO Builds Community Action in Mississippi," we learned with no great astonishment, that NAACP was playing it cool and cautious politically once again. John A. Morsell had sent a telegram to Mr. Shriver saying that his organization regretted that CDGM was not refundable, but that "we join our leadership in that state in welcoming the decision to continue vital work of providing educational opportunity . . ." In other words, NAACP, not unnaturally, welcomed OEO's decision to "take" the action, the power, and the prestige in Mississippi from the rapid reformers, and "give" them to the more conservative civil rights workers, who had not been able to get popular themselves.

A cruelly maligned official in the OEO public affairs office defensively, pompously, sputtered about his innocence and integrity, and mailed me an authorized document, saying: ". . . In Mississippi as elsewhere, OEO is interested only in creating projects helpful to the poor and free of political control. For more than two years OEO has successfully accomplished that objective, and it will not tolerate political domination of Head Start or other OEO programs in Mississippi or in other states or localities. . . ." I wondered how they could sleep at night.

In contrast to statements from Mr. Shriver, Mr. Berry, Mr. Sugarman, and the task force members in Mississippi, an OEO memorandum for Congressional Relations, dated October 13, 1966, baldly commented: ". . . It has been made clear that OEO is ready to consider an application from any qualified applicant at any time. Theodore Berry, CAP Director, had emphasized that 'the door is always open' to any group, including CDGM, if it presents a program application. But, OEO has made it clear, as well, that it cannot lawfully refund any group which has failed to "demonstrate that it is qualified to administer the funds and programs in the proposed grant. . . ."'"

And my diary comments: ". . . As Oct. 15 was the date of the termination of Federal assistance to CDGM, and OEO won't pay the rent anymore, the few remaining CDGM Central people moved cartons of materials from the files, on-going crisis work, and a pathetic little vase of dried field flowers and grasses, to a plaster-cracked, paintless, walk-up at 507½ N. Farish St.; in with FDP. No phones, no furniture, no heat. Saw somebody typing with gloves on, on a battered borrowed typewriter, balanced on boards stretched across two cartons of John's junk.

Lois [Lois Rogers: the white former legal secretary who had come from California the fall before and been the office manager ever since for CDGM] is absolutely fantastic. She is always efficient, calm, concerned about everyone's feelings and work-needs . . . lives in a Negro apartment building with CDGM Negro staff, joins in all the soul sessions . . . she never takes any credit or talks about herself, but during the year I've managed to ferret out the fact that she was the child of a very poor white family herself, suffered . . . strove to 'better herself' . . . quietly does a magnificent job of discovering potential office talent in local poor, training them. It's always fascinating to see who comes through in times of crisis. . . .

"CDGM changed its name today, and its structure, along with most of the Central Staff. Now it's the Friends of the Children of Mississippi. They hope this will give them a broader base and greater scope to attack their A-Number-One problem: how to exist.

"The show must go on. Defiled and disbanded do-gooders band together in desecrated quarters. Grimey, grim, friendless; the story of doing good the world over . . ."

The story of CDGM seems to me to be a fairy tale, complete with all the blood, magic, shining beauty, and repeated themes characteristic of fairy tales. It's a simple narrative dealing with such supernatural beings as fairies, magicians, and dragons who are typically of folk origin and are written or told about for the amusement of children. It's also a more sophisticated narrative, containing supernatural or obviously improbable events, scenes, persons; and having a whimsical, satirical, and moralistic character. A fairy tale, like certain facets of CDGM's history, is an improbable, incredible, or lying story, a story designed to delude or mislead.

CHAPTER 41

BY THE PEOPLE, OR BUY THE PEOPLE?

ON OCTOBER 11 MAP received a three-million-dollar grant from OEO. According to the October 12 Jackson *Clarion-Ledger:* "Shriver said . . . no federal program in Mississippi has ever been under the direction of such an outstanding board of white and Negro leaders." MAP got right to work. One of the sections included in its territory was Clarke County; a county in which CDGM had been strong. One day in the late winter, when I had not been working for CDGM for more than six months, I drove down to see how my friends were feeling and doing.

Fourteen men and women had gathered together in Mrs. —'s living room. Included in the group were the extraordinary area staff. There was Garlee Johnson, thc community organizer. She had worked for thirty dollars a week in the kitchen at the colored school. Her husband was a janitor at a bank. She had a teacher's license, which she had acquired upon completing the eighth grade. She had a wonderful way with community people. Garlee said of herself, "There's three things I'm not: a hypocrite, a liar, and a Judas."

There was Mamie Jones, a vastly competent woman. She was area administrator. There was center chairman and brave leader Reverend Killingsworth, who was nicknamed "the wildman."

And there was Carrie Davis, the remarkable ATG in Clarke County. She was the oldest of nine children, born at home. She herself had her first baby at home. She had washed clothes for a living, and later was a presser in a laundry at thirty cents an hour, a cafeteria waitress 4 A.M. to 2 P.M., six days a week, at fourteen dollars a week, a domestic for eight dollars a week if she just cleaned, and twelve dollars a week if she stayed to cook dinner. Her husband was a laborer in the Midwest, whom she missed acutely, and went to visit whenever possible.

Carrie was the moving spirit in Clarke County CDGM. She had extraordinary energy, an astonishing range of emotions, an impassioned commitment to "doing good," and a lovable way of expressing what she thought in no uncertain terms. People called her Joan of Arc. The following is an edited composite of many things that were said at that meeting of fourteen. Much background discussion and repetition has been omitted, but that which is here is as it was spoken. It's not guaranteed to be in chronological order or "true"; it is the "truth," as perceived and recounted by this group:

"The first we knew about MAP, we read in the paper about MAP. We thought we were gone ducks. We thought, oops! There we go, back to the cotton patch!

"We asked CDGM, what's this, a mistake? Where did this 'board' come from? *We* didn't elect them? What's wrong with our elected CDGM board? CDGM said, we're not dead yet! Find out what the people want and let us know."

"We canvassed our communities to see what did they want. They wanted CDGM. Parents did. We read in the paper that one thousand one hundred and five children were already in MAP in Clarke County. We couldn't understand this. We didn't know who they were, or where anybody got this number from—the more we canvassed, the more we couldn't find *any body* who had a child in MAP. Most had never even heard of it.

"Some of us went to see Mr. Smith, the head MAP man in Jackson. [Hazel Brannon Smith's husband] We asked where did he get these children? He said it's just *budgeted* children. We asked how were they going to pick their children? We have many more than one thousand, one hundred and five: Who will be left out? Mr. Smith throwed his hands up over his head and laid back and said, that's what I don't know. That's where the ones working out there are going to have their headaches. I said to Mr. Smith, this trouble won't even get as far as their heads to make them ache. The whole thing don't set well on our *stomachs,* and it won't work. You can't take this child, and skip over there and take that child, and leave out my child in the middle. He said five-year-olds only. I felt like that wasn't fair to our four and three year olds who've been attending."

"I asked Mr. Smith could we see the MAP proposal. They said they didn't have a proposal. They would send down a committee to show us. They had a committee preparing something. *They* were! What about *us?*"

"They said they were having *two* advisory boards: skilled and unskilled. I said to Mrs. —, 'Righto, Smithio: The skilled advisory board is the people who ain't never seen a Head Start or a preschool before, and they'll rule the roost, run the show, and teach the tots.' The *unskilled* advisory board, I told Mrs. —, is us experienced in preschool teaching and community work, and we'll say *yassir,* obey the dictates, and wipes the babies' bottoms."

"We asked about teacher qualifications and salary. He said trainees have to have twelfth grade education. Oops! We thought—there goes lots of our teachers! What about resources? He said they would have to have at least two years of college. We asked would they recognize our ATG CDGM training. He said *no.* We said who will hire? He said they will have some people to do that, maybe he would. They didn't even ask us with two years Head Start experience who *we* recommended! Some new whites would do it! I don't see this catering to white people. They just pops their fingers, and everybody jumps—or crawls, I should say."

"How did MAP get into the county if we feel like this? Easy, one of our CDGM chairman from . . . *invited* MAP in. All that man talked about the whole time anyway was money, money, money! He told us outright ahead of time, he was going to catch the first thing going through with money, even if it was the hind end of a running dog. That chairman and a preacher told us they had to get their building paid for, and they didn't care how they did it. It was all government money, anyway, they said.

"When we heard about this, our area staff called an area meeting to get ourselves together. Did we want to protest MAP or go with it? We had two more area meetings. We talked. Each center met separate, too, and talked, to tell the information and see what should we do. Last February when we got our second CDGM grant, a CAP tried to come in here. They came around to us. But they wouldn't agree to be integrated, and we wouldn't agree to be segregated. They submitted a proposal to OEO, but OEO didn't pass it. So now we thought, well, CDGM has opened our eyes to all these strings and things, and we've learned how to pull them, and we kept CAP out because it wasn't right, and we'll keep MAP out, because it isn't any righter.

"We did these things on our own, led by our ATG, CO, AA; our area staff and several others. There were no CDGM centrals down here. As poverty people, we told MAP direct, we don't think their program accommodates us. Each time we sent a delegation to see MAP, they told us something different. It was because they didn't know what they were doing. That thing didn't have a head or a tail. Truth is, CDGM *little* people had more information and federal know-how than MAP *leadership* people. They're so pathetic I hafta feel sorry for them.

"They had nothing to offer, and they knew that, and they knew *we* knew that. So they just kept telling us about qualified Negroes. We said, 'Oh Jesus, are they qualified!' Some of our Negroes have had a few years and a few dollars more opportunity than us, and are they qualified! To rip us down the back and keep their foot on our neck like they like to have it. These Negroes, they've always scorned us in the Movement, in CDGM, they wear us ragged; now they are telling us, 'See? We have money and you don't.'

"Here's how MAP was set up here, and what kind of people's on it. Like last August, we wrote a proposal about some demands we wanted like street lights and some considerations for the people. We had a march one Saturday in Shubuta; we wanted the mayor and these people to pay us some attention. So a lot of highway patrols from all around nearby went in there and beat up a lot of people. Then Mayor Busby, who Owen Cooper appointed for MAP, who then in turn appointed himself for chairman of it, Mayor Busby made charges that CDGM was responsible for this protest!"

"CDGM was *not* responsible, the community was. It's just they blame everything on CDGM and its outsiders because, when the chips are down, they *still* don't believe we can do anything for ourselves. We all were marching very orderly. As we attempted to stop at the town hall, about twenty-five highway patrolmen, they just came rushing out with billies, black jacks, and they bursted heads, faces, tore a little boy's ear near off, went for eyes; you should've seen Reverend Killingsworth: He looked like a butchered hog, head, knee, shoulder, eye, fractured rib . . . you could sum up what they did just to say they made us more determined. We got so hot we started perking like coffee pots! The FBI took a lot of notes. John Sumerall and Reverend Killingsworth filed suit against the Mississippi Highway Patrol with the help of the President's Committee. It was their idea—for violation of their rights. We didn't most of us have time to go to the hospital. We Negroes have work to do! Now here's my point: If Mayor Busby takes a position like that on a point like this, do we want him as chairman of our poverty program? Have mercy, Jesus!"

"Then Mr. Busby appointed three white men and three Uncle Toms. All these Toms are our school teachers. All but one Negro on this board, we invited much earlier to sit on our CDGM advisory board, but they all refused. One didn't even dare reply! Three others answered they couldn't do it, 'due to the condition.' That condition was the principal, who had to go ask the superintendent, who pretended he never heard of CDGM. He was full of Santa Claus. The age-old favorite 'technique' these whites use to keep us ignorant is to play ignorant themselves. Then no one can accuse them of being mean.

"Some people'll tell you, well, what have you got against teachers and all them? If they want to help, now, why not *let* them? Because you can't *trust* them. Look at a man's record. Then decide if you can count on him in a pinch. If not, who wants him? This one colored lady on the MAP board said, 'What was wrong with CDGM last year was they ran around hiring all the trash'; *she* should represent *me?*

"But Busby, he told a group, 'I was informed that I could go ahead and appoint my board and get my schools going anyway I wished.' That's not the way CDGM started! Maybe if you can't do no better, and you want real bad to start *some* poverty *something,* maybe that's the way you have to do it. But you don't take what we've done and do like that, and call it *better,* and we all should grin and be *so* grateful for all their help! When CDGM started, a few started it, but they pushed and pushed for us to elect and say and come. Mr. Sugarman told that man there, 'Well, MAP is making a few mistakes, and CDGM made a few mistakes, too.' Sure did! But it didn't never make the mistake of purposely holding secret meetings and keeping us excluded! The difference between MAP and CDGM is this: CDGM says, 'Come on, come on, what's keeping you back?' And MAP says, 'Go 'way, go 'way, what the hell do *you* want?'"

"Another difference of MAP and CDGM is what they stood for in the past. CDGM people, before they got into this, they were Movement people or professionals and you might say 'radical' professionals up North. MAP people, before this, I don't say they were Klansmen, but I say they sat silent and *watched* the Klansmen—I don't say those top boys like Hodding Carter did that, but at local levels of MAP, like here.

"That's right! One night at six P.M. we heard of a MAP meeting going to be held near the Courthouse at seven! It was secret. We weren't supposed to know. One MAP meeting, I don't remember if it was the first or second we heard of, we went. We walked in. They whispered and whispered. Made us feel right at home, that did! Then someone of our group said, 'Maybe we're not wanted.' I said, 'It'll only take me a minute to find out,' and I asked the Negro principal they had selected to 'represent' us. He said, 'just a minute, I'll ask the mayor if this is a public meeting.' He *had to ask a white man if people could even sit down!* Sure, MAP will work with us; just so long as they control us even to the degree of if we can sit down! When somebody kept asking to see their proposal, somebody handed a sheet of any old anythings, and said, 'Here's the proposal!' Oh, Lord! How they'll lie to the colored! Just *anything* to keep us shut up; like throwing cornmush at the puppies to make 'em hush! But we *know* more than to take that now. CDGM showed us how to call Washington, get the right one, get the right message: We won't take this stuff no more!

"So the mayor said, 'Yeah, it's public, tell them to go set in the library. We'll send for them when we are ready.' He didn't even have the 'equality' to tell that man who asked; he told the Negro principal to tell that man. We walked down the hall to the library, and to our surprise, we found a whole room full of CDGM people. We talked and we set for an hour and a half! They never did come for us! They had their meeting privately! A private public meeting. When they're ready for us, is after they've cooked up their crooked deals. A lady says she overheard the mayor say, 'If I have to work with niggers on MAP, I'll quit it.' One of the Negro board members told us later the mayor said, '*You* tell that bunch anything you want—I'm not talking with colored people.'

"One of those first meetings, I think it *was* the first, we outnumbered the people who didn't want us. They told us we couldn't add other people to their board, because they wanted the 'right' people. We said, 'Well, we're sorry if we're in your way.' They said, 'We're not ready for you yet; we're still setting up the board.' I told him, 'You're supposed to hold public meetings of white and colored and *then* elect a board—that's OEO guidelines.' He said, 'We're not working for OEO, we're working for Mississippi.' I said to myself, 'Man, you sure are: *white* man's Mississippi.' To him I said, 'OEO is funding MAP.' He said nothing. One person asked the mayor, 'Why does MAP lie to us? Why do you all keep telling us CDGM is dead, and if we want jobs, we better go MAP? You know you've only got seven teaching jobs, way less than we have now, and you aren't planning to give them to us.' Then we excused ourselves.

"And when he thought we were all gone, I heard the mayor say, 'Those are just CDGM people. Don't worry about them—we won't have them working in our program anyway.'

"A few of us optimistic ones kept thinking, well, maybe MAP just don't know what CDGM really *is*—what we've accomplished—what we're doin' *now*. So they would asplain to them. Tell them, since our second CDGM grant ended, we've been running our centers volunteer again: Stonewall's open; Quitman was open for three weeks and then they got thrown out of the church because they couldn't pay their rent, but they later reopened in the Church of God; Vossburg, St. Peters, and East Barnett were open, but in December they closed because the gas had given out and it was too cold; Beaver Meadow never closed; Enterprise is open volunteer; Shady Grove in Heidelberg started up in May and are still going, and they never were *included* in our grant; Shubuta was open, shut, open again; there's another new one at Spring Hill, name of De Soto, they've been operating since June without ever being part of funded CDGM, too; and another new one is organized called Silver Spree, but they haven't started running quite yet; and the St. Mary Community Center . . . (but they didn't care nuthin' about our experience. They erase us. We just ain't there, baby.)

"Yes, the St. Mary Community Center. This man, Mr. Jesse Allen, he decided Shubuta was too crowded, and a lot of their children was from Quitman anyhow, so he decided to build a community center. He was a CDGM driver, and he got tired driving his neighbors' children fifty-five miles, so he decided to put a center closer. He went to FHA to see about financing for it. They said he had to have nine other people as an association. Then they said we couldn't have a Head Start in it, because then the rent would be paid by government money, and they couldn't give us government money to get us *more* government money. Nothing education could go in it, or if we did, we would have to repay the FHA money immediately.

"So we went to a building man in town. We have a few decent people here. He said he would give us the materials on three-year credit. We told him if Head Start didn't come in here, we'd make sure he wouldn't get stuck with that building—we'd hold parties and things and functions and raise money and pay him back for his kindness.

"So by now Mr. Allen has the well down, running hot and cold water, we're overheading it now, we wired it, we have to put the cut-offs in and the partitions and three face bowls and two commodes. We have six classrooms twelve by twelve, an office, a hall, a kitchen, and a dining room. It's a block building. We leveled the ground off. Then we cut a form for a foundation. We got a man to come lay the blocks. Rafters next. Then we sheeted it, and put a top on it; shingles. We'll be ready to open school maybe next week.

"We had *so* much trouble getting anyone to work for CDGM in the beginning. They just blew their mouth about us. Gradually, we built up to what we've got. The ones on the MAP board are the one were tearin' us up before. But no center has quit for MAP, even though they've got the funds and we don't, and it's been months like that. We believe in praisin' the bridge that brought us across—and MAP warn't it. A few people have gone MAP—we should have a law never to let them back in CDGM. Loyal to where the grass is greenest. One of these is a sanctified lady. I don't see how a person can be a preacher's assistant, Christified to the bottom of her soul, and do her people like that. She calls it religion; I dunno, it sure ain't *my* religion! God said, 'What you do to a little one, you do to me.' What's *she* doing to the little ones? Selling um back into slavery."

"MAP had another 'public meeting' and they elected and appointed each other ever' which way. Mysteriously, mostly teachers were 'elected.' The ones wouldn't put up the white civil rights kids a few years ago, or the white CDGM kids later. The ones kept sayin' all fall, 'Oh, honey, CDGM's dead, quit raisin' sand and a big ruckamurrow, and join the money wagon.'

"Well, they got the money, but we got the children. We won't let MAP in this county, we just won't."

"We're going to fight it on all fronts. We're fighting to get help from the FBI, for instance. I asked an FBI once, 'Why don't you offer us a little protection, instead of just writing notes?' And he said, 'The FBI is not authorized to offer protection; we are an investigatory organization.' and I said, 'Aw, hell, man, *we* know how to *write;* what we need is protection,' We'll push 'em.

"'And we'll worship where we please,' said Reverend Killingsworth. Did you hear about when I went to a white church in Quitman to *worship?* You can't hardly beat that reason for going to church. I was accompanied by six persons. They went to worship, too. After having been there for about nineteen minutes, just when I was about to be happy, the devil popped up.

"Men began getting up all over the church, hollering, saying curse words. They asked us what we were here for. I said, 'For the same reason I hope you're here for—to worship.' I motioned to them that their minister was still standing, speaking his message. They shouted louder. They began swinging on us.

"I realized I would have to practice my religion actively. I swung back. Soon, one dozen men were on the floor. I could do three at a time: an uppercut, a bolo, and ten with a foot.

"A man from town stopped the fight. He is a well-to-do businessman. He told them they were acting like heathenry out of the jungle to treat visitors to their church that way. He said, 'The sign outside says *welcome,* so they have as much right here as you do.' He said this to six hundred persons in that church! Courage!

"The minister said, 'I never thought of living to see the day when people couldn't worship without being jumped. You should all recognize that most of the people acting in this shameful way are *leaders* of this church. You should *act* like leaders. When Christ came and died for man, he didn't die for the black man, the white man, the red man—he died for all mankind.'

"I said, 'Freedom, brother!' Then the sheriff came. The fight started all over again. I had to put twenty men on the floor that time. The men said to the businessman that they wouldn't go to any church that was going to let niggers in. The man said, 'That's all right, in fact, it would've been better if you hadn't come *today.*' Then the twenty said they weren't going to *support* such a church. The businessman said, 'That's all right, too, if that's how you feel. I can certainly support it myself.'

"This is what we're working for. More colored like us. More whites like this. There are many. They'll actually come out and shake hands with you on the street if they don't think anybody's looking.

"I have recruited white families. One morning I went to call on a family I'd spoken to casually before, during the five years I'd been a preacher in the area. They'd always been fairly friendly; not an extra amount, just *fairly friendly.* The house is about four doors from our center. It's very rundown. The mother is the only one who works. She works in the mill. They have two children of Head Start age.

"I said to them that this is a program for *children.* It's a poverty program for *poor* people, both for children and workers. We need another trainee teacher right now, I said, and I gave the amount of the salary. I also said we would like very much for it to be a person of the white race from this community; not from the outside.

"The man called his older daughter to the door and told her what I'd said. She said, 'It's true I need a job, but I'd starve before I'd work with old niggers.' I said, 'We're *not* the old niggers. Anybody, even a white person, could be the old nigger; scared, bowing to the man; but we are the new Negroes, trying to change things. For *all* of us.'

"A preacher's job is more than in the pulpit. I teach my people how to live an eternal life, but I must help them live as citizens on this earth, too. I think God let this thing ride so long because we were afraid to face it. I'm trying now. I can see a change. CDGM has brought many changes in all areas of life. But MAP is to capture us again, and that we cannot let happen!"

"The difference between MAP and CDGM is, if you give a man a fish, you've fed him for a day. If you teach him *how* to fish, you've fed him for a lifetime."

CHAPTER 42

THE GAMES PEOPLE PLAY

THROUGH THE WINTER the OEO-CAP-MAP-CDGM controversy raged in liberal circles around the country. Nick von Hoffman wrote in the Washington *Post* on October 9, 1966, about some of the "black frontlash" OEO was getting from CDGM constituents:

> . . . Today another high OEO official, Theodore Berry, accused the pre-school administrators of building a 'highly centralized program, a gigantic monopoly. They are trying to build an empire.'
>
> At the same time Berry said Child Development was guilty of excessive decentralization which, he argued, had resulted in inefficient handling of funds and the hiring of unqualified personnel. Berry added he saw no contradiction in the two indictments. . . .
>
> While OEO and Child Development were tugging each other the Washington poverty headquarters has made pre-school grants totaling almost $2 million to other groups in the state.
>
> In so doing OEO, which has not had a reputation for speed heretofore, has probably set a track record for grant approval, 48 hours in one case and no more than 4 days in another after receipt of the application.
>
> "It's not a quick pitch," Berry explained, but an attempt to maintain the "continuity of the program."
>
> However Boone remarked here, "It's evident that they are trying to give the money away so quickly they will have none or very little left for CDGM."

A few days later, Nick wrote another piece in the *Post*, headlined "Manna from OEO Falls on Mississippi."

> Poverty gold is falling over Mississippi.
>
> Nearly $12 million of it has been dropped on the State by Sargent Shriver and his Office of Economic Opportunity in five hasty and hectic days of philanthropy.
>
> In at least one case the recipients got their money before they had signed an application for it. . . .

So anxious was Washington to get the green stuff off its hands that Jule Sugarman, national Headstart Director, dispatched a representative from his office to Holly Springs with orders to draw up preliminary plans and a budget within 18 hours. The resulting budget is more than $600 per child over the recommended OEO maximum figures. . . .

The Rust College situation has a second shadow over it. The college's board chairman, W. Astor Kirk, is a Shriver employe. Reached in his Austin, Texas, office where he is OEO's Deputy Regional Director, Kirk appeared to be backing from Washington's largesse. "I don't know what the decision of the Board will be on the grant" Kirk declared. "We meet on Oct. 26 and we'll decide whether or not to take it then."

College President Smith indicated something like abashed confusion: "We're sorry we got caught by a situation we weren't aware of. We weren't aware of all these political undercurrents."

A $700,000 money missile was landed on top of a group called Southwest Mississippi Opportunities. . . .

The biggest stake in the OEO Klondike belongs to Mississippi Action for Progress. . . .

One of the local residents with Mississippi Action describes its genesis as follows:

"OEO got in touch with us. We didn't seek them out. That was in August. Their theme was always that the decision not to refund Child Development had been made. It was Sugarman and Berry . . . . who did the talking. Their whole thesis was for us to hustle it. They presured us to make an announcement. They sent down two people from Washington to draw up our application.

There still wasn't any board. We got together a rush-through charter. Most of it was copied from another organization's. . . ."

Had MAP not been organized to extinguish CDGM, we ourselves would have been most enthusiastic about MAP. It *did* represent, as *The New York Times* of October 13, 1966, pointed out, a miracle in Mississippi:

. . . Champions of Action for Progress describe it as a "blue ribbon" group of white and Negro leaders. . . .

Action for Progress is the first state-recognized organization bringing together moderate and liberally inclined white business and civic leaders of the state and Negro leaders. . . .

Gov. Paul B. Johnson, who is committed to a campaign pledge that he will never appoint a state biracial commission, has nonetheless endorsed the board and approved its incorporation charter.

That white leaders in Mississippi would sit down with widely known Negro integration leaders was unthinkable in the recent past. "It's still difficult to get people who have a lot to lose even at this stage of the game to do it," said a key figure in the group.

But the reaction in still-segregationist Mississippi to the new group has been unbelievable.

"I've only had one nasty letter," said Mr. Cooper, the chairman of the group, and "otherwise I have had nothing but a favorable reaction."

The fact that MAP indeed had *not* had much negative reaction from Mississippians meant three things to CDGMians. First, that people make choices between alternatives, not in a vacuum. And having taken the position of extremity in regard to social change that Mississippians considered CDGM to have taken for the past two years, we had paved the way for Mississippi's citizens to consider anything competitive but less "radical" a tolerable thing. Second, when the federal government wishes to use its tempting money and great influence to move people in local communities toward more rapid progress than they, without this push, would be capable of, it *succeeds*. What a shame decision-makers in government so rarely use this power for progress that they possess. Third, the ease with which MAP had slipped in Mississippi's back door and had been accepted by the governor meant to us that agreements had been made in its inner circles that it wouldn't rock the boat. Had MAP been created parallel to CDGM, in non-CDGM counties we would have felt that it *was*, truly, *progress*. As it was, we felt that it represented social steps backward. In amusing noncontrast to one of Mr. Berry's criticisms of CDGM, MAP, too, planned to have its headquarters, lawyers, accounting firm, etc., located in Jackson, and also intended to operate local projects in many counties.

The New York Times of October 14, 1966, said:

> The Citizens' Crusade Against Poverty withdrew today as a combatant in the fight to get new Head Start funds for the Child Development Group of Mississippi.
>
> At the same time, Senator Jacob K. Javits, Republican, of New York, entered the controversy with a request that Sargent Shriver . . . hold a public hearing on his decision to terminate the group.
>
> Walter P. Reuther is chairman of the poverty crusade, a private organization financed by the United Automobile Workers, of which he is president; the Ford Foundation, and others. . . .
>
> Mr. Reuther said that the board of inquiry of the Citizens' Crusade "found that the reasons given by the O.E.O. for refusing to continue the funding of C.D.G.M. were completely unjustified. . . ."

My diary for this period comments: ". . . in the beginning of this, CCAP seemed cock-sure that they could crack this thing easily. Now members of CCAP's Committee of Inquiry seem nervous about infuriating Shriver. He reportedly has called most members of this Committee *personally* and lengthily tried to induce them to get off it. Embarrassed. Sees himself as the master good-guy, and in this scene he finds himself cast as the villain. . . . gave an excellent report on us, but after Sarge's call, buckled, withdrew it. . . . said Shriver is fighting like a rat in the corner of a cage, and is making a fool of himself, flushing, raising his voice; not his usual cool cucumber self. Committee doesn't want to make public report on CDGM 'vindicating' us till a delegation of them has gone to see Shriver quietly. Reasoning: if the main charge against OEO is that they didn't give us due process, *we* must not be guilty of the same in 'retaliating.' Very gentlemanly and sensible. Also, I think Committee is scared of the open split in the CR groups that this has caused. Maybe MAP wouldn't have been funded so soon and so positively if Committees had been more strenuous.

"So much stuff is flying. . . . The whole thing has gone off on two tangents: political and esoteric. There's more lore and myth these days (on both sides) than love and progress, which incidentally, seem to be lost in the political shuffle. Berry offered our Board to meet it in Atlanta; our Board said no because that place is symbolic of everything wrong; Berry said we won't talk to OEO; our Board wants to go to DC; can't unless Berry authorizes the expense; won't; they say that Roy Wilkins (NAACP) saved Berry from Shriver when the latter was after his head, and that therefore Berry owed Wilkins a favor, and that therefore Berry had to give Wilkins-NAACP more power in Mississippi, *i.e.*, MAP, Aaron Henry, etc.; Marian is making . . . mad because they don't think she should deal with Javits because he's a Republican (!); they say Reuther is mad because MAP is a slap in the face of Labor; maybe Clarke will join Javits to make it bi-partisan; Javits might invite CDGM Board to Wash. for public hearing if OEO won't; Javits wants to see Berry; it would be hard for Berry to refuse to see a 'good Senator' . . . and the NCC-Board of Missions church strategists? What makes their sparks fly and their eyes sparkle? What's more challenging, and how do you untangle it, the pure and/or the power?

"Ah, God, what does all this manipulating and maneuvering and focusing on the image instead of on the internal truths have to do with *people*, and their growth and development? I'm not a bit politically naive—I *know* it's necessary. I'm just politically disgusted and bored. When will people stop playing these games, peripheral to all that's important? Just think what it would have been worth if OEO had put all this unflagging energy into building and improving CDGM? And if our 'friends' were interested in any part of CDGM except emerging from their various enterprises at times of political crisis to take credit for being the knights on white horses? It's fantastic, the number of people and organizations that never *saw* CDGM that are now claiming the dead body, wanting to deliver the funeral oration, get a free ride into heaven on the tail of our dragon.

"Have talked to lots of Task Force, Atlanta, and DC-OEO people. Break down into primarily two groups: the blues and the grays—the Civil War isn't over yet in the government, either. Then both groups break down further, in a most confusing way: the stars and bars set breaks into the icy isolationists; who condemn all but themselves, and into the reactionary-but-gentlemanly group, which sounds bad but is actually an effective force toward 'the good.' Meanwhile, the Yankees break out into two groups: those within the ranks who are on 'our side' and do their level best to use their influence, leak to our allies, etc.; and the liberal-but-weak who are shams. When the name of the game is CDGM, we're the greatest. When MAP is the rage, well, there it is. (They say the Georgetown Warriors are wearing buttons saying: 'I've been in Mississippi for one day—will you invite me to your cocktail party?')

"The predominant opinion of most in every group is that 'lower eschlon' workers mustn't question the 'insight and authority' of their superiors. When you are an employee, to be a thinking citizen is of less value than is to avoid being 'insubordinate.'

"There are also a few on the 'other side' who sincerely have a different opinion of 'what is best': the application of 'good' to practical realities of life is sticky.

Included in the sincere group seemed to be many of the whites involved in MAP. When Hodding Carter III, editor of the Greenville *Delta Democrat Times* in Greenville, Mississippi, protested in a letter to the Washington *Post* (October 17, 1966) that MAP's intentions were being distorted, I felt sympathetic. I think MAPians don't really understand that the Negro problem *is* a Negro problem, as well as a white problem; and that ending discrimination, and even beginning some helpful programs, won't alter the fact that many Negroes are afflicted with an unwillingness to compete, an unwillingness to cope, a desire to use the "inferiority" that we've bred into them as a crutch; and that *Negro-ego development* programs like CDGM must parallel *integrated antidiscrimination and doing-good* programs if anything real is going to happen. Sincerity is not enough. Yet I'm sure it's true that the intentions of those MAP people like Mr. Carter, who *are* sincere, are being distorted.

Mr. Carter also said, as "proof" that MAP formers were motivated by concern rather than politics: "If anyone knows anything about Mississippi politics . . . he must know that service on a biracial committee of this sort would automatically destroy any white man's political ambitions in Mississippi." This, of course, while true in 1964, was *not* true in 1966. And the fact that this balance had tipped was to the credit of CDGM, as well as to the White House. If they wanted to keep their ascendancy in 1966, white Mississippi leaders were forced to recognize that the povery program *was* wanted by "influential" Mississippi citizens, and *was*, demonstrably, possible *without* white Mississippi leaders (witness CDGM). Therefore, they were forced to be leaders in the poverty program. And certainly the White House had helped to make this so.

For it was as James Ridgeway explains it in the October 15, 1966, issues of *The New Republic:*

. . . The White House was instrumental in setting up the board [of MAP]. The President is anxious to paste together a loyalist Democratic party in Mississippi in time for next year's gubernatorial election, and the CDGM program has been sacrificed to this end.

Harry McPherson, Jr., special counsel of the President, negotiated the deal. About a month ago, he called Douglas Wynn, a Greenville, Mississippi, lawyer who is a personal friend of the President's. Following this conversation, Wynn got two 'moderate' Democrats to agree to be members of the new board. Owen Cooper, president of the Mississippi Chemical Corporation, agreed to be co-chairman. Leroy Percy, chairman of Mississippi Chemical, would be a board member. Both Wynn and Percy are members of the President's Club. Cooper is considered to be a possible "moderate" candidate for governor of Mississippi next year.

The White House called Roy Wilkins, head of the NAACP, who in turn got in touch with Aaron Henry, a one-time Mississippi radical who has turned moderate; Henry agreed to be the other co-chairman. The board draws heavily from young moderate Democrats and older men who have remained loyal to the national party. . . .

With encouragement and support like this, it doesn't seem likely that white Mississippians on the MAP board were "automatically destroying" their political chances. Indeed, the reverse seems somewhat more than likely.

I noted in my diary: ". . . Mrs. — in C— said today, 'OEO thinks the answer to friction is put two fighting dogs in a sack and dip 'em in the cold river—when they come out, they'll never fight again. OEO don't know; that ain't the road to human development, it just works 'cause they scare us shitless.'

"Tom Levin says, 'Confrontation is the key to change.' I think MAP is meant by OEO to be pacification to the Mississippi 'New' Democrats, and I think, speaking of pacification, that there's a line somewhere in Moby Dick about, 'Woe unto him who tries to pour oil on the waters, when God has brewed them into a gale' . . ."

On Sunday, October 16, the Washington *Post* carried an editorial called, "Question of Credibility":

The chief victim of Mr. Sargent Shriver's current maneuvering in Mississippi is Mr. Sargent Shriver himself. His office of Economic Opportunity is currently trying anxiously to close the very conspicuous gap between its high-minded press releases and its coarsely unjust abandonment of the Child Development Group of Mississippi. The OEO has made a variety of charges against the Child Development Group, but none of them is wholly convincing. All of them suggest that the OEO is moving rapidly away from the great purposes that Mr. Shriver himself set in its early days.

One must assume that some of the Federal money has been lost, or strayed. But the Mississippi case bears comparison with the history of HARYOU-ACT in Harlem, which lost track of very large sums of money. But HARYOU-ACT continues to get heavy Federal grants. OEO is able to distinguish between the two examples, but it is a narrow and lawyerish distinction that only raises further doubt in a disinterested mind. The Child Development Group is operating almost as an underground, in a part of the country where in recent and fresh memory people have been killed for doing approximately what the poverty workers are doing. If their relationships with the white community are not as warm as OEO would like, it is at least understandable. In Harlem the OEO has deliberately subsidized open and purposeful examples of black nationalism.

The Child Development Group is run mostly by Mississippi Negroes for local Negro children. It is a highly creative, loosely organized, and by no means unsuccessful departure in unorthodox educational techniques. It has made substantial progress where there was very little upon which to build. If OEO persists in its error, and refuses further funds to this courageous and highly useful movement for these insufficient reasons, it will be guilty of an inexplicable injustice. The OEO could very properly give funds to other kindergarten and community action projects in Mississippi beside the Child Development Group, which claims no monopoly. But it cannot break off all support to the Child Development Group, without tarnishing its own credit and credibility throughout the Nation.

And on October 19, 1966, *The Christian Science Monitor* said:

R. Sargent Shriver . . . has gotten himself into a tangle.

The more he squirms to get out, the knottier it becomes.

It started when he cut off poverty funds for the Child Development Group of Mississippi . . .

This wouldn't have been troublesome in itself, except for one thing: Earlier, Mr. Shriver had held up this program as a model for Head Start programs all over the country. . . .

Marchers began arriving to protest the decision.

Urban specialists of the Episcopal and United Presbyterian Churches and the United Church of Christ interrupted a meeting in Chicago to fly to Washington to picket the poverty headquarters.

Now, the Republicans are pointing out that the new program, called the Mississippi Action for Progress (MAP), includes as directors two members of President Johnson's $1,000 a head President's club. . . .

The Republicans are careful not to come to CDCM's defense, But they do capitalize on the general lack of credibility in Mr. Shriver's moves. "It is evident," charge GOP congressmen Albert H. Quie and Charles E. Goddell, "that once again poverty is enmeshed in politics. . . ."

It was during this protest that the House Appropriations Committee voted to cut OEO's funds for next year below the President's budget figure of $1.75 billion. The Appropriations Committee voted only $1.563 billion—just about last year's level.

OEO officials lay this cut directly to the furor caused by the cutoff of funds. Some say they wish they had never heard of CDGM. . . .

. . . "Don't they realize this jeopardizes the whole program?" asked one official, referring to the demonstrators.

"OEO should have thought about that a long time ago," said a CCAP spokesman. "They shouldn't have trumped up the charges—allowing no hearings, and give CDGM no chance to defend themselves. . . ."

. . . Whatever success MAP may have in the future, it won't easily remove the impression that Mr. Shriver backs away when the political pressures get heavy.

It only lends credence to his critics who charge that once again—as he has done in the past over programs in Syracuse, N.Y., and in Cleveland—Mr. Shriver has retreated.

It makes his own staff wonder if every time a program really reaches the poor, begins to stir their motivations, and ultimately involves them meaningfully in the process of protesting against conditions which perpetuate poverty—the man who speaks so eloquently for this kind of involvement will shy away from the ultimate consequences.

The urban church specialists, a group of sophisticated activists, social action ministers, had been having a routine meeting in Chicago. The subject of whether or not to help CDGM in some tangible way arose in a morning session. It kept recurring. Though many in the group were eager to do something, it seems clear that Bob Spike of the University of Chicago Divinity School, an ardent friend of CDGM, was responsible for consolidating feeling into immediate action. The group finally gave up on its regular agenda, and concentrated on the problem of whether picketing OEO in CDGM's behalf would constitute paternalism and uninvited intervention with the concerns of the poor, or whether it would be support welcomed by the CDGM board.

A call was made to CDGM. The ministers received assurance that CDGM would be delighted to be joined by the ministers as it itself picketed OEO. While the ministers continued debating, one member slipped out and made reservations for everybody to fly to Washington. The vote authorizing the trip wasn't actually taken until evening. When approximately eighty ministers arrived in Washington and found that CDGM poor people weren't yet there, they were disappointed. They picketed by themselves, went to talk to Mr. Bookbinder because Mr. Shriver couldn't see them, and were eventually joined in picketing by some CDGM board members, who had been tied up with other relevant matters, and by carloads of people from Mississippi communities, who had raised cash to come for the occasion.

This demonstration was followed next day by one of the more festive looking picket lines that has ever decorated D.C. A group of more than thirty Radcliffe and Wellesley-type women, one pushing a baby carriage, several with babies strapped to their backs, and many accompanied by cheerful little children, picketed OEO Headquarters. From time to time a mother dropped out of line to sit on the curb and feed a hungry child. This enterprise had been organized by John Mudd's sister-in-law Marion Mudd, and my cousin Joan Weiss. Both were Bethesda housewives, and both had organized the housing arrangements for the Children's Crusade to Washington the previous winter. When they called friends to participate in this odd picketing, many of whom had been participants the winter before in the Children's Crusade, they had varying degrees of luck with people who were excited and eager "to *do* something," and people who said they didn't like to picket. Reasons ranged from principle, to possible bad weather and the baby's health, to involvement with other activities and engagements, to the fact that it might not be a becoming role for respectable ladies.

Three members of the group worked up their courage and went inside "to see Mr. Shriver." They were sure he wouldn't see them, and weren't surprised to be told that an interview would be impossible, as Mr. Shriver was testifying at the hearings on the Hill. However, though they replied, "Nonsense," and acted as if they fully expected to see a high level official of one sort or another, they were incredulous to learn that Mr. Edgar May, head of the OEO inspection office, would see them at once. "We couldn't believe they would take time out for *us*," said one of the ladies. When Mr. May appeared, the ladies were still further astonished to discover that he was very upset by their presence; that he seemed, indeed, quite nervous with them. He protested his dedication to the cause, repeated frequently that this was the kind of concern he had devoted his life to, and seemed to the ladies quite distressed that *they* were questioning *his* sincerity. The more the ladies realized how nervous they were making Mr. May, the more they pressed their advantage. Finally, one of them said she felt that he was obviously not the decision-maker in the CDGM situation, and was consequently not the right person for them to talk to on the subject. They said, if you please, we will see Mr. Sugarman. Their amazement rose still further when Mr. May picked up the phone and made them an appointment to see Mr. Sugarman at once.

Joan Weiss, carrying her apple-crunching crawler, Danny, and two other women, went to see Jule Sugarman. Joan later said: "I was surprised that they spoke to us. I was amazed that they seemed so afraid of us. They seemed to feel that we were their natural allies, so much like their wives and ladies they met at cocktail parties. So they kept trying to justify their actions to us. They seemed quite defensive. We had felt we didn't have any power, yet we seemed able to upset them deeply."

The success of both the Preachers' Picket and the Mothers' March seems to have been that both brought home to decent people inside OEO the significance of the CDGM situation. Many, until these straws that broke the screen of statistics thrown up by OEO senior staff, hadn't really grasped it before. Restlessness within the walls of OEO increased from this time on, until it reached its height about ten days later.

* * *

It had all gotten quite far from the heart of Dixie:

Negro Child: Who's your grandmother?
White Teacher: Mrs. Jordon.
Child: Who's your mother?
Teacher: Mrs. Miller.
Child: Is Mrs. Jordon colored?
Teacher: No, she's white too.
Child: Is Mrs. Miller colored?
Teacher: No, she's white too.
Child: And *you're* white. I see how it is. I'm gonna git me a white grandmother too!
Teacher: But you don't need one. You're colored. That's fine: which would you rather have me call you: colored, black, or Negro?
Child: I'd rather have you call me white.

* * *

On October 19, a full page ten-thousand-dollar CDGM support ad beginning, "SAY IT ISN'T SO, SARGENT SHRIVER," ran in *The New York Times.* It was signed by the National Citizens Committee for the Child Development Program in Mississippi, an ad hoc committee. This group had been organized by individuals in CCAP and the Board of Missions. Panel members were A. Philip Randolph, president of the Brotherhood of Sleeping Car Porters; Dr. Robert W. Spike, Divinity School, University of Chicago; Paul Anthony, executive director of the Southern Regional Council, Inc.; Philip Bernstein, director of the Council of Jewish Federations and Welfare Funds; Dr. Kenneth B. Clark, City College of New York; Francis Coe, Board of Education, Memphis, Tennessee; Eli Cohen, executive secretary of the National Committee on Employment of Youth; Clarence Coleman, director, Southern Regional Office of the National Urban League, Inc., Atlanta, Georgia; Robert Coles, research psychiatrist at Harvard University; Ralph Helstein, president of the United Packing House, Food and Allied Workers, Chicago, Illinois; Dr. Vivian W. Henderson, president of Clark College in Atlanta, Georgia; John P. Nelson, Jr., attorney, New Orleans, Louisiana; and Judge Justine Wise Polier, Family Court, New York City. It carried the signatures of one hundred and sixty other religious, educational, labor, and civil rights leaders from every part of the nation.

Reliable sources reported that Mr. Shriver was genuinely hurt by this ad. He apparently felt that though it was par for the course for Republicans and conservatives of every kind to have always been against his poverty program, it was appalling that now its supporters and allies were becoming so outspokenly critical, too. Said a nationally distinguished "liberal": "Political positions aren't static. They keep shifting depending on who else and what other groups are taking what position at which period. Sure, Sarge had his neck way out in the beginning—speaking for the poor, and activating them. He got it from all kinds of status quo groups. But when the poor began to *move,* and when liberal groups began to gain experience in this new do-it-yourself approach to doing good, Shriver stayed where he had been in the beginning. And that left him at the tail end of the snake. That's what progress is all about: In each new era, we criticize what we settled for as the best we could do in the past era. That's what conservative means: Some want to preserve that past era. Sarge seems to want to preserve the era in which the rich and noble did great things for the needy. He doesn't really believe in this new way. Or, if he believes in it, he isn't willing to risk standing for it politically. Otherwise, he would welcome our help in bolstering him against the segregationists, et al."

As quoted in the Jackson *Clarion-Ledger* on October 19, 1966, Mr. Shriver commented that he was: ". . . shocked to find some clergymen resorting to character assassination tactics to protest an administrative decision." We reflected briefly on some of the things that had been done to the characters of Tom Levin, many top Peace Corps staff members, and many senior members of OEO's staff by Mr. Shriver and his *in* group. We didn't shed many tears over his plight now.

The Washington *Post* on October 24, 1966, said:

> OEO in Decline. The high spirits and sense of mission are rapidly leaking out of the Office of Economic Opportunity. Its long, trying struggle this year to get even an inadequate budget has badly eroded its assurance. In the imbroglio over the Child Development Group of Mississippi, the OEO gives evidence of having badly lost its bearings. The diagnosis is clear. The OEO has been given a responsibility beyond the political strength of any independent federal agency.
>
> The President has a choice of two remedies. He can fold the OEO into one of the large Departments of Cabinet rank, presumably the Department of Housing and Urban Development. Or he can extend once again to his embattled creation the strength and prestige that flows from direct and personal presidential leadership and concern.
>
> The Office of Economic Opportunity and its administrator, Mr. Shriver, deserve to be judged generously. They were given 1.5 per cent of the Federal budget and told to solve two centuries' accumulation of social evil with it. Now the Education Act has largely given school reform to another agency; employment training turns out to be unimaginably expensive; the low-cost housing efforts are crippled by high interest rates.
>
> A black mood of hopelessness hangs over the OEO, obscuring the very great achievements of this remarkable war on poverty over its two years. The idea that poor people should participate in social policy is now so widely accepted that it has become all but a legally enforceable right. It has spread beyond the Federal operations to private social agencies, schools, hospitals and even political parties. Strong new lines of communication are now open

between the slums and the men, who, from another world, govern them. The Head Start pre-schools have generated an astonishing wave of public interest in early education, and throughout the country local school systems are establishing their own kindergartens. In many cities, the community action centers have begun a decentralization of social services that is decades overdue. In Washington, at least, the juvenile delinquency figures have dropped a bit for the first time in years.

This progress has historic importance in the record of the Johnson Administration. The question now is how President Johnson intends to maintain it. The savage bullying of the agency by Congress, and the reduction of its unexpectedly small budget request, can only foreshadow a long decline if the President does not intervene.

To put the community action programs into the Department of Housing would give them a measure of institutional protection (and it would be good for that stodgy Department). But the high purposes of the Economic Opportunities Act might be even better assured if the President were now to take stock, publicly, of these two years' performance, and personally set the direction for the coming year. The need for presidential power here is great. The opportunities still contained in the Act are even greater.

Finally, after weeks of offers, counteroffers, refusals, and renegotiations regarding meeting place and conditions, on Monday, October 24, Sargent Shriver and the CDGM board of directors met in Atlanta. Many OEO staff members representing various aspects of the organization were there. Many people went in behalf of CDGM, among them Joseph Rauh, Jr. (National vice chairman of Americans for Democratic Action) as special Counsel, Robert Barrie of the National Board of Missions, Bob Patricelli of Senator Javits' staff, Ralph Caprio of CCAP, and Martin Luther King. People argued about qualified teachers. They argued about Mary Holmes College's lack of relationship to CDGM, and its responsibilities as grantee. They argued about CDGM's responsibility to broaden its board representations. They quarreled about two well-qualified people whose applications weren't given consideration in Pascagoula. They argued about my summer hiring mess (why vacancies? what happened to all the applicants?) and the procedure of community committee hiring. The area teacher guides' qualifications for being supervisors were discussed. Mary Emmons' age was a bone of contention. They argued about CDGM's efforts, lack of efforts, to cooperate with CAPs. Each group talked about the other group doing something to show confidence "in the enemy." "Lift the fog off CDGM's head so it can get whites on the board." On the whole, CDGM was put, as usual, on the defensive. Each instrument in each orchestra played its familiar tune, and the result was the predictable continuation of a cacophonic affair. [Quotes are from tapes of the meeting.]

Mr. Shriver spoke of the many OEO people who had been sent to Mississippi to "help" CDGM, of the extreme amounts of time OEO had devoted to CDGM in every way. He added an opinion, in which after being the CDGM person primarily working on the problem for a year and a half, I heartily concurred: "I think it's something of a criticism of the liberal community of America that they are very anxious to make speeches in one place, but very unlikely to come down and give you people any sort of a hand, except for a consultant who comes through and says everything is great."

Mr. Shriver told Reverend King that the meeting was a private one, and asked him to leave, but first asked him to make a statement. Reverend King spoke strongly in favor of CDGM, and left.

Someone said of all the mismanagement allegations against CDGM that he didn't know all the truths involved, but he *did* know that where there's smoke there's a fire. Somebody representing CDGM replied, "Not always—as in the Joe McCarthy days, often where there's smoke, there's a smoke machine." Mr. Shriver mentioned maybe five million dollars for CDGM, but made no commitments. A local board member said, "Five million dollars would be slow death." And I recorded in my diary: "came home from Atlanta seething with angry frustration.——said he found the OEO people so utterly impenetrable, intransigent, and insensitive that at one point he had to walk out for a minute to regain his composure.——said Joe Rauh was furious at OEO's conduct——said Mr. Shriver kept walking in and out of the meeting, as if it was quite inconsequential in his life. On the other hand——said John smirks in such a superior and self-righteous manner that it makes him sick to his stomach, and contaminates CDGM as far as he is concerned.

"I wasn't there. I'm not in CDGM anymore. But CDGM has become public property, nationally. It's no longer just a search of ours, or a continuation and transition of the movement toward federal programs, or an organization. It's become a concept. An ideal. So there or not there, everyone 'has a right' to measure himself according to it.

"In my opinion, and of course it would be an intolerable one to CDGM leadership so I'll confine it to 'the diary of an ex-,' Sargent Shriver is just as 'right' as John is. John's purpose (*i.e.*, Tom's-my-Art's-everybody-who planned-or-plans-CDGM's purpose) is one thing. Mr. Shriver's, over the dead bodies of many irate Congressmen, is quite another. Though there are overlapping areas between a rapid reform Negro development project and a moderate all-facets-of-the-community project, there are obviously parallel and not necessarily incompatible ideas. This was clear during the first CDGM summer, and has been clear ever since. We need OEO to exist. OEO needs us as a model, as an example of *some* of the best that was in the original OEO design. The dialogue needs to continue. But it doesn't seem to me that Mr. Shriver is swerving from *his* initial position any more than John is. I think Mr. Shriver has done an enormous GOOD THING in pulling off OEO and a nationwide upheaval as effectively as he has. And it is predictable but lamentable that he will come out a villain. . . ."

The Atlanta meeting was reported the next day by the Washington *Star,* Washington *Post, The New York Times,* etc. When I thought how hard we used to try to get any of them to write anything about us, I laughed.

In Washington, on the same day that the Atlanta meeting was held, there was an internal uprising inside OEO concerning CDGM. I don't know of any previous case in which federal employees took official "sides" and demanded that their superiors explain themselves. It seemed a historic event. This, too, was well covered by the press.

Now that CDGM had become so popular a topic with the press, all manner of surprising things were printed. Evans and Novak began their "Inside Report" in the Washington *Post* on October 26 with this enjoyable concoction:

> The real and widely misunderstood reason why poverty czar Sargent Shriver cut off Federal funds to the Child Development Group of Mississippi (CDGM) can be found in the double life of a young man named R. Hunter Morey.
>
> Morey is a key policymaker for CDGM. . . . But simultaneously, he has been a leading activist in the Mississippi Freedom Democratic Party and its parent organization, the Student Nonviolent Coordinating Committee (SNCC). . . .

We thought that a pretty funny federal charge, and a delightful image to picture: "SNCCers in sneakers infiltrate nursery schools on tip toe." R. Hunter Morey, "the monster," said several months later, when I asked him if he could tell me a little about himself and what brought him to Mississippi: "I grew up in a snobby little suburb named Evanston, Illinois. I was very active in the Congregational Church. There was a minister there who was the only single influence in my life who created a crack in my Evanston way of life—like he showed me his modern art collection, which was a pretty left wing thing in Evanston at that time.

"I went to Princeton and found that it was a right-wing rich-boy place, too.

"In March, 1960, just after the sit-ins started, the Student Christian Association [at Princeton] invited Martin Luther King to speak. I thought that was extremely hypocritical, because I felt that these students weren't interested in confrontation with themselves, in involvement, in honesty—they just wanted to do the fashionable thing and look relevant. So I wrote a letter to the student paper at Princeton saying, 'If you're serious, join me at one o'clock in front of Woolworth's, and we'll picket in sympathy with those picketing in the South. We'll start something real here.' It worked. This was my first activism. It threw me into the racial realities.

"By 1962 I felt that the Young People's Socialist League that I was in was so ideologically sophisticated but so pragmatically irrelevant that I was determined to go South, where I felt I *could* be relevant. From then on, many routine facts of life struck me with their hypocrisy. I analyzed the situation and came to the conclusion that Mississippi is the worst state racially, the poorest economically, and being in the Bible Belt, is the most primitive religiously. I thought it had the greatest potential for change, so I came.

"In 1964 I was the COFO legal coordinator. I helped recruit groups of lawyers for Mississippi. I went to the National Lawyers Guild in Detroit, to the President's Committee in Philadelphia, to LCDC in New York, etc. The INC Fund [Legal Defense and Education Fund of the NAACP], of course, was already here. We developed an eminent national legal advisory board. I divided the cases fairly between all these lawyers' groups.

"My work in the Movement taught me that there was a great need for Movement administrators. We weren't efficient; we could be more effective. I came into CDGM as an administrator—to learn, to do my best to promote the kind of society fit for humans."

Accusations and answers flew like machine gun fire in Vietnam.

Charge—CDGM last year misspent $500,000 which was forgiven by OEO.

Reply—The allegation last fall that government investigations, initiated by Senator Stennis, had uncovered $500,000 of mismanaged funds were proven wide of the mark by more than $485,000. The funds in dispute finally amounted to approximately $14,000—or less than 1% of CDGM's budget—none of which involved the intentional misuse of funds, fraud, or payment for political activity. The $14,000 was not "forgiven," but was reimbursed to OEO through a privately raised escrow fund.

Charge—CDGM's cost per child is $627.50, $450 more than OEO's estimated national cost figure of $170.

Reply—CDGM's cost per child is in fact lower than OEO's estimated national cost figure. On the basis of a 25 week $5,644,000 program for 12,000 children, CDGM's cost per child per week is actually $19. (It would be even less if the anticipated grant surplus at the end of the program were taken into account.)

The OEO estimate is for a seven week program and reduces to a cost per child per week figure of $24.

The allegation is in error on simple mathematical grounds: $627.50 and $170 are not immediately comparable figures because they refer to different time periods.

The $170 figure, which assumed that Head Start facilities would be donated by public school systems contrary to much later practice, was also estimated in April, 1965, before any programs were operating. The figure has been revised upward twice since then.

Charge—There is a "significant relationship" between CDGM and the militant "Black Power" movement.

Reply—The evidence presented is hardly sufficient to warrant let alone prove the charge. The charge is only possible by the strained use of guilt by association: The actions of a few individuals are tied to prominent events and then assumed to speak for the more than 30,000 citizens of Mississippi associated with CDGM. Evidence that would be inadmissible in court is being presented in our trial by the press.

Charge—The CDGM board met with SNCC Director Stokely Carmichael several times prior to the Meredith March.

Reply—The CDGM board has *never* met with Stokely Carmichael at any time. Several board members, as individuals on their own time, did meet him and other march leaders while the march was in their community. This activity or any other which is legal should not be an issue of propriety or lawfulness subject to government inquiry, as Senator Stennis seems to make it. On this point Sargent Shriver has been quite explicit. Testifying last fall before a Senate appropriations subcommittee hearing, at which Senator Stennis was present, Mr. Shriver said: "The impression . . . has been created that something un-American has been going on here (in CDGM), because somebody when they are not working in the child development center, has participated in some civil rights activity. . . .

So far as I am concerned, I didn't know that there was something un-American or illegal about participating on your own time in activities of that type. Frankly, I have done this on my own time. . . ."

A poor lady from Canton explained her personal experience regarding participating on her own time in activities of a questionable type: "The OEO inspector told me why did I mess with Black Power. I'll tell you how it was.

"I came home to Canton after my CDGM working hours. The Meredith marchers were marching and chanting on the school grounds across from my house. The whole town had turned out for it. I walked over there with my baby in my arms. I stood on the edge of the crowd. There was no bad-acting—the crowd was praying. Then they started a slow chant, 'Pitch the tent, pitch the tent.' As they were chanting, a tent was slowly being pulled up. Everything was very quiet. Too quiet. Like the weird purple calm before a tornado. It scared me, so I began gathering the children and bringing them back to my porch. There were dozens of them.

"I heard something pop. A dull explosion. More, one right after the other. I thought someone in the crowd had firecrackers. And everybody had guns, so I didn't know what to think. About fifty policemen had been standing there watching. Suddenly, without warning, they rushed at all us women and children shooting tear gas! They had machine guns on trucks! Suddenly, I saw this smoke rise. I'd never seen that before, not like that. I heard somebody scream, 'Oh, God, they're going to kill us all!'

"Somebody threw something to a lady. She didn't know what it was; she caught it. Her daughter suddenly yelled, 'drop that! Get down! Drop down! I seen tear gas before, they're throwing it, run!' Her daughter pulled her down in a tackle, and screamed, 'Mama, crawl, crawl, don't rub your eyes Mama, crawl!'

"She couldn't crawl. It had bursted into her eyes. She was overcome. She just lay in the field on her face. She thought she was dying. The skin on her face was all burned off. Her eyes was paining her terrible, and she was blinded, and her chest burned like fire for weeks after. Her daughter drug her to a car, somebody's, with keys in it, she didn't know whose till later, and drove her to the hospital in Jackson. On the way she said she saw a white man way up in a hind window, smiling, and holding up a sign that said, 'Good luck, you poor creature of God.'

"Everybody started running and screaming. I saw this white girl from New York getting dragged, and her husband crying, 'Somebody help her, help her, my wife is blind!' He asked me, could he bring her in my house? I said, 'Of course! Of course! Bring her on in!' They put her to bed. People, many people, hundreds of people, were suddenly running across the school grounds to my door, trying to escape. 'Of course! Of course!' I cried to them all, 'Come in, hurry, come in! My God, help us!'

"The wind was blowing from the South, and blowing it right into the house. We were all choking. Someone opened all the windows to get air. That was worse, I ran and slammed them all shut. Somebody called, 'Soak all your towels! Soak the sheets and pillow cases! Hold them across your face!' We had everything sloshing in water, dripping, trying to breathe water instead of that poison. Somebody shouted, 'Let all the faucets run! The water will absorb the gas!' We had inches of water all over the floor, flooding, like a lake, before anybody noticed a little thing like that.

"Then a lady screamed, 'Oh, my God, something's wrong with your little boy! He's having convulsions! Help, someone, save this child, he's dying!' My only son! I grabbed him and rushed out of my house with him in my arms—I ran, just ran, anywhere, out, away from the gas, away from the screaming women and children and the men cursing in my house—I ran to the back fence, but before I got there, I stepped on a man, all kinds of people were out there, lying, crawling all over each other in my back yard.

"The man I stepped on, he grabbed my leg, held hold of me, I said, 'Let go, man! Let go, my baby is terribly sick! I have to get him away from here!' He said, 'Lady, give him to me! I just got back from Vietnam, I know what to do for him.' Then he pulled my son out my arms and pushed him head first down into the mud; started ramming his face in the mud, just scrubbing it and digging it into the mud. He told me, 'Lady, do that yourself, you'll be able to breathe!' I did, and in a minute, I realized we were both breathing better.

"In a minute, I was able to jump and start running toward the house. The man said, 'Lady, are you crazy? Where are you going?' I said, 'I have to get back in there, my other children are in there, other people's children are in there, they're just as sick and blind as this one!'

"We tried to get the victims to the hospital, took them to Canton hospital, but they wouldn't treat the victims, so we rushed them to University Hospital in Jackson, forty-five minutes away. Later I kept sending out for food, and making gallons and gallons of coffee for those poor people, all night. Later I was faced with the bills; but at the time, my only thought was God, these suffering people!"

Much was made of nepotism in CDGM communities. When analyzed, it seemed that the excitement largely revolved around a petition, bearing the names of more than one hundred workers and community residents, accusing CDGM's Richmond Grove center of nepotistic control by two families. The petition, responsible for nationwide reverberations, repercussions, attacks, and counterattacks, was examined carefully, and was found to be of doubtful validity. Of the signatures on it 20 percent belonged to children. Seventy-five belonged to persons outside the community in question. Fifty percent of the names were signed by a total of eight persons. Four names occurred twice, and four people whose names appeared insisted they'd never signed it. The petition was initiated and circulated by a nearby resident who had never liked CDGM, after her daughter was fired by legitimate procedures and for legitimate reasons from the center staff.

In spite of this, the center *was* operated by two families. The tiny community had been founded by two families, whose members had so intermarried and been so limited in mobility, that as the lady said: "Nepotism? First tell me what it is, and then I'll tell you if we got it. —Oh, that's it? You mean we done something wrong to run a school if her sister-in-law is my sister-in-law because her brother is married to my husband's sister, and my cousin's wife is also Mrs. —'s sister and is also my sister-in-law's cousin and my sister-in-law's husband is F's husband's cousin? Well, durnit, who woulda guessed *that* was our crime?"

Columnist Carl Rowan read the General Accounting Office's (GAO) sixty-eight page, eighteen-item "secret" report to OEO on CDGM, and concluded that, "either GAO is woefully inept at digging out the truth or CDGM has been given the sharp end of a rusty knife."

The cases of 'nepotism' are laughably piddling. If they justify OEO's cutting off $5.6 million, then Congress is justified in impeaching President Johnson for having the Bundy brothers, the Moyers brothers or the Rostow brothers on the government payroll simultaneously.

Fiscal irregularities? The practices in some CDGM units were a scream. If Mary wanted off Tuesday, she got Cousin Sally to work. The time card showed Mary present, so Mary was paid. Then Mary paid Cousin Sally. A lot of those poor kids in Mississippi didn't have the word as to how much these short ends bother the big city auditors—although they resort to much more devious tactics in Washington just to keep the bookkeeping "simple."[40]

CDGM had in its arsenal a powerful weapon, which it *kept* in the arsenal and didn't use. It could have turned out to be a precedent-setting piece of brilliance, or a dangerous boomerang. It was a lawsuit against OEO for denial of due process. Jean Cahn, a former OEO staff lawyer, and wife of Mr. Shriver's speech writer, Edgar Cahn, thought of this idea. She wrote a brief charging OEO with failing to notify CDGM of charges against it, giving it a chance to rebut the charges, or present a case in its own behalf.

The brief stated that there were mitigating circumstances (hostility from Mississippi establishment, Klan, etc.); that the past year demonstrated CDGM's desire to improve itself through work with consultants and through constant revisions of itself; that CDGM had a singular degree of democratic structure, symbolic status; and that certain charges, if true, supported the conclusion that CDGM was, in fact, carrying out the spirit and letter of the poverty program; that other specific charges involved gross and patent distortion and inflation; that certain charges were so vague as to be incomprehensible or unanswerable; that other charges were simply untrue, because they took place before the grant year; that certain charges condemned CDGM for putting into practice the very procedures, and utilizing the very contractual forms and accounting methods designed and approved by OEO; that certain charges of violation of OEO regulations omitted the vital information that CDGM had notified OEO of these violations *itself*, and had requested waivers or exemptions, to which OEO had never given either negative or affirmative answers; that there still remained, after this process of elimination, a small number of charges which were true, but which were correctable and inconsequential in terms of the total program; and finally, that OEO had subjected CDGM to far different standards of scrutiny than those it used in projects that were politically safer—projects in which OEO explicitly refused to take notice of blatant violations, segregationist practices, mismanagement, nepotism, and corruption.

The brief was sent around to a number of distinguished lawyers for expert opinion. They recommended holding it, because, as it was an unprecedented case, it would first have to go to the federal district judge, who would rule on whether or not CDGM could do it. The judge might say *no*. This would be a great setback for CDGM. Also, even if the judge gave it the green light, the case might be "on the agenda," and "coming up," for months. Thus Mr. Shriver would have a legitimate excuse for stalling on refunding, or even for spending all his money on other proj-

[40] Rowan, Carl T., Washington, D.C., *The Evening Star*, November 9, 1966.

ects such as MAP, which would make the refunding of CDGM an absolute impossibility.

It was certainly the end of an era in Mississippi. The closed society had been cracked by the end of the summer of 1964, though all that remained of the Movement army were a few "remnant bands" of relatively ineffective SNCC and FDP workers. And now CDGM, which had picked up the Movement spirit and individuals and had carried them through a transitional period into the Age of Federal Programs, appeared to be nearing its end.

Leslie Dunbar, former executive director of the Southern Regional Council and presently executive director of the Field Foundation, said in a talk on November 3, 1966, at Stiles College, Yale University: "Just as every tree has its own best season and its own finest fruit, so CDGM might fairly be called the finest fruit of the student movement. . . . there is probably no comparably large and important endeavor in this country . . . that is, as is CDGM, controlled and led by Negroes plus white youth. Everywhere now we weep and worry at what we fearfully apprehend to be the progressive withdrawal of Negroes and youth from the bonds of general society. So we then, through our government, repudiate and knock down their one big vote of confidence, the one biggest thing we entrusted to them. Machiavelli would have marveled at such statesmanship. . . ."

Under Art Thomas's skillful leadership, the Delta Ministry had continued to function productively through these difficult transitional two years. Now J. Edward Carothers, associate secretary of the national division of the Board of Methodist Missions, was promising twelve irate Methodist superintendents in Mississippi "sweeping changes" in the Delta Ministry's leadership and operations.

In a telegram to the Mississippi Methodist Bishops, Carothers said: "It is my openly expressed personal view that these changes in method and procedure have been overdue for some time. . . .

"There is no adequate way for me to express to you the sweeping nature of these changes. . . .

"We greatly respect and admire the heroic manner in which the people of your area confront the heart breaking needs of our time and together with all of you we pray for the methods and procedures that will bring us all together to do God's will in Christian ways. . . ."

The most significant change was the removal of Art Thomas from the directorship of the Delta Ministry. Art had left the Delta Ministry, the CDGM board of directors, of which he was such a vital part, and the South, in the summer. In the silent and humble way so characteristic of him, he made no accusations.

Tom Levin later wrote of Art: "Arthur Thomas is a saint. Thieves have St. Dismas, workers St. Joseph and mothers St. Monica; the poor people of Mississippi had St. Art Thomas and St. Bob Moses. But

Art was a missionary saint. He brought dedication, warmth, creativity and a superb tactical acumen gained from sophistication in a world larger than Mississippi. As an outside saint he accrued the enmity of indigenous acolyte saints. I hope history will blur the human frailties of all of us involved in Mississippi. If that happens Art's Movement detractors will be canonized alongside Art as saints of Mississippi black kids. Most certainly there would have been no CDGM without Art Thomas. May his name be ever hallowed."

Had it not been for the sustained efforts of key figures in eminent elements of the liberal community, CDGM wouldn't have continued to have whatever leverage it had. We owed a great deal to Dick Boone at CCAP, who decided that if CCAP was to be valuable, it would need to fight for what it had been created to represent; and to Ralph Caprio, who arranged who would do what, when, to keep the issues burning; and to that remarkable, quick-thinking, hard-headed invisible man-of-the-hour, Bryant George, at the Board of Presbyterian Missions; and to Dr. Kenneth G. Neigh, general secretary of the Board of National Missions of the United Presbyterian Church, who committed his powerful organization to take a risk, obligate funds, and to stand for something; and to such people as Morris Abram, Truman Douglas, and Joe Rauh.

There were continuous conferences, consultations, documents, delegations, letters to editors, negotiations, magazine articles, professional journal articles, newspaper articles ranging from a plea in the official publication of the American Federation of Teachers for donations to keep the multitude of volunteer centers open, to a denunciation of CDGM in *Barrons.* There were alignments, splits, realignments, intrigues, high level encounters, and broken appointments; checks, balances, threats, and implications. It *was* community involvement—of the nation's distinguished *liberal* community. With few exceptions, they had neither been in Mississippi, nor met the poor people they were defending. The issues reflected in CDGM had escalated. CDGM had become a symbol.

Leadership of the Board of Missions and the National Council of Churches arranged for Vice President Humphrey to speak to the General Assembly of the National Council of Churches in Florida in early December, and to meet privately with a few individuals in his hotel room afterwards in order to focus his attention on CDGM. They presented their case eloquently, and outlined its implications. The Vice President hadn't known much about the matter. He left the session with tears in his eyes. After three intensive days of discussion between officials of CDGM, MHJC, and OEO, ending on December 16, an "agreement in principle" was reached, CDGM would continue sponsorship of a nineteen-county Head Start in Mississippi.

Though at the end of December OEO reversed itself and declared that CDGM would *not* be funded to operate in five of the agreed upon counties, on January 30, 1967, a grant for $4,927,100 for a full year program in fourteen counties was signed.

The five forgotten counties and an additional county agreed to retain the name Friends of the Children of Mississippi, and to continue the operation of volunteer centers, and the battle for funds—both at staggering odds. To get the grant, CDGM made many compromises—some in fact, some only on paper. MHJC would have many more powers over CDGM, and would "maintain continuous surveillance" over its operation. CDGM's board would be enlarged, and would guarantee that at least 30 percent white membership would be achieved. CDGM would add new administrative personnel to its Central Staff. Sargent Shriver said, "We regard this as an important step forward in Mississippi's War on Poverty." In an unrelated statement printed in the Washington *Post*, Saul Alinsky accused OEO of "zoo-keeper mentality," in the hope of keeping the caged animals quiet.

CDGM, and what it represented, had won the battle but lost the war.

CHAPTER 43

AIN'T NO HIDIN' PLACE DOWN THERE

THIS HAS BEEN a biography only of the beginning of CDGM, because there doesn't seem to be much more of note or new to put in a biography about it. CDGM survived and performed in a somewhat similar way to that already described; with small improvements—though increasingly more unsmilingly, despondently, and bureaucratically throughout the third grant, which expired in December, 1967. At the opening of 1968 CDGM found itself mobilizing to fight for a fourth grant. Only by then the fire had gone out of it. What could it do? The Green Amendment gave Head Start to Community Action Programs and the governor's control. President Johnson had cut 25 million dollars out of the Head Start budget nationally, so he could put more money into Northern ghettos before voting time. Seven million dollars was cut from Head Start in Mississippi alone.

The kaleidoscopic thing that Tom had kindled had become well ordered by OEO nonentities. The creativity had somewhere, slowly, seeped out of CDGM. The many experimental elements had become as many mere routines. The discussion and the dialogue of departures from the norm had dwindled to the level of dull, diluted, and diffuse declarations, put forth by discussants who hadn't the smallest notion of the deep significance of the subjects on which they spoke. Oblations had obliterated our outcries, and our omniverous overreaching orientation. Our peppery and pandemonious pageant had been replaced by a perfunctory, pallid paltriness. No longer was CDGM the subject of national panegyrics. Thanks to the strenuous efforts of OEO politicians and parvenus (the latter of which wielded powers way beyond them—negative powers, at least—there's no evidence that they were authorized to do anything positive, and those who did were deviants), CDGM had lost its splendid Pegasus qualities. It had achieved a nearly perfect parochial point of view. Like most institutions, it had developed cancer of the courage. OEO had stripped Joseph of his coat of many colors. Though it was still without a doubt the best big project going in the state, CDGM had become parenthetic to progress in Mississippi.

And therein lay the paradoxical secret of its success. The Freedom Movement during the summer of 1964 had "cracked the pillars of the closed society." And CDGM, during the years 1965–1967 had hastened to slither its foot in the crack; had served as a catalyst for all kinds of crucial consequences. OEO high mucky-mucks and heavyweights with their welter of harum-scarum activity and glacé of gibberish had effectively curdled CDGM's convictions into something relatively gelatinous. But its gemmiparousness OEO couldn't curtail. OEO could evict the heteroclitic heresiarchs—or rather, cause conditions conducive to their volitional evacuation. Thus it could straighten our hyperbolas to nestle neatly into guidelines and ledgers. But it couldn't stifle CDGM's afterlife in the minds of men all over the country who had learned many things from the grand experiment, and in the hearts of poor people in Mississippi—for "as he thinketh in his heart, so is he."

CDGM as a coursing creative enterprise was in chains, but CDGM as a testament to the talents and tenuosity of the poor endured as a national monument. One by one the "outsiders" left, leaving CDGM in the hands of local black leadership. I left in June, 1966. For another six months I helped sporadically as a friend. John Mudd left in the summer of 1967, shrouded in the same cloud of suspicious hostility that had mantled me at the end. Marv Hoffman left at the end of that winter. (John and Marv moved to New York to write a book about the project. John married Lucia Clapps, whom he had met during her short stay in the teacher development and program for children department. Marv and his wife had a baby. I returned to Washington, a restless "rebel without a cause.") There were no parades when I left CDGM—no parties, testimonials, demonstrations of gratitude, or good-bye letters from the board. But there was Pearl Draine serving in my stead as director of teacher development and program for children. To me, it was the ultimate of all rewards, to turn my job over to a local Negro after only one year!

Pearl was born in rural Holmes County. She was a middle child among nine children. The family was very poor. The children slept four in a bed. They ate sparely, mostly what was raised on the farm. For a special treat, when their daddy sold a bale of cotton, he would buy two apples and cut them up to share with the nine children and his wife. In addition to being a farmer, her daddy was a deacon in the Holiness Church. Her mother was one of the church mothers. Pearl never had enough of anything, and always wanted more. Her father would call the children around him and console them by saying that things would be getting better—that there would be a time when the family would have all it needed—that God would make a way. Many times, when things got really rough, the father would pray with the family for more food and clothing, for a good crop, and that the children would grow up without disgrace; without having illegitimate children, without being jailbirds.

The family was flooded with white salesmen who would walk up to Pearl's mother, whose name was Cora, saying, "Annie, whatchoo want today?" or to her father, whose name was George, saying, "Uncle, whatchoo want?" The parents would remind the salesmen of their correct names and ask them please to leave. The family traveled in an ox wagon. They cut wood and sold cords of firewood on weekends to whites. The whites wanted to set the price on the wood, or offered old clothing in trade. Pearl's father let people know that *he* set the price on his wood, and they could either buy it or not. Often he went home without having made a sale, rather than be pushed around. The family sold corn. One day Pearl saw a white man come to buy a bushel of corn, and ask how he was going to get it in his car. Pearl's mother told him he could pick it up and put it in the car. The man asked what was the matter with George? The mother replied that nothing was wrong with him, but that he wasn't going to lift the bushel. The man did it for himself; but he never came back for any more.

An antique dealer came around and insisted on having some of the family's antique pots, fire irons, etc. The parents said *no*. The dealer told his helper to pick up the things and take them. Pearl's Mama said nothing, but she turned, went inside, and returned, still silent, holding a .22. The dealer left without the antiques. Incidents like these made a strong impression on little Pearl. One day when she and the other children were in elementary school, their white neighbors stormed into the school demanding that "George's nigger kids" get the family's cows, which had strayed onto their property. Pearl's brothers and sisters attempted to obey. Pearl told them not to do anything for people who spoke to them in those tones. The whites, in response, offered to kill the cows. Pearl told them to go ahead if they had to, but if they did, to be sure not to waste them—to eat them—if they were that hungry she wouldn't want to keep the meat from them. The whites retreated. Later in the day the white man went to see Pearl's father and told him decently that his cows were out. The father offered to pay for any damage they had done, and drove them home at once.

The mother urged each child to attend each day of elementary school. The family wasn't able to send Pearl to high school, so she picked cotton, made nine dollars clear, and enabled herself to enroll in Saints Junior College high school nearby. She took a job in the kitchen at the school. She earned eleven dollars a week. Later, she became the president's personal maid. At the school she took a course in beauty culture, and on the side, made enough change in the beauty business to allow her to finish high school.

In 1945 she went to Jackson State College with thirty-five dollars from her beauty work, and all her clothing in a fruit jar box tied with a string. After taking the bus to Jackson, she couldn't afford the cross-town bus to college, so she walked the many miles. Then she couldn't afford a proper place to stay, so for the first college quarter, she slept on a rooming house floor in exchange for doing chores. She worked from four till midnight in a Negro-owned restaurant to make ends meet. She found that the point constantly pressed by Jackson State faculty was not to fail. During her four years there, she never heard an issue of importance to Negroes discussed. Nor did any faculty member indirectly inspire her to fight the system.

Upon graduation she joined the Jackson school system, and taught elementary grades for seventeen years. She soon learned that the school supervisor's interviews and questionnaires were designed to let Negroes know they had a place, and a place to stay in, if they wished to remain with the system. Membership in the NAACP wasn't tolerated. So much emphasis was put on this that Pearl decided that anything the Southern white man hated so much must be good for her. She was an early NAACP joiner. She was also an early member of the Human Relations Council. Her motive seems to have been modest self-improvement; she was never a troublemaker, but seemed to many who knew her a quite conventional middle-class-oriented lady. In the same vein she went to Indiana University, stayed three and a half years, and got first a master's degree in elementary education, and then *another* in special education.

Yet, with all the talents, wisdom, experience, and degrees she developed, Pearl Draine didn't develop self-confidence. She was a Negro. She lived in Mississippi. When she first walked into the CDGM office and I told her I would be happy to talk with her, or Carolyn (our administrative assistant) could talk with her, she construed this to mean that I didn't care one way or the other about her. She later decided it meant I respected Carolyn's (black) judgment, and would go along with Carolyn's decision regarding hiring her for teacher development and program for children central staff. Still later, when she was in my position and found herself appearing the same way to other Negroes, she laughed. In the early CDGM meetings she attended, she felt that I went, went, went, and that what I said had weight, weight, weight. Finally she began to speak up. To her astonishment, everyone, naturally, listened and used her suggestions. During the summer I was in Washington, Mrs. Draine was acting deputy director of teacher development and program for children—Mary Emmons was acting director. Mrs. Draine felt very much alone.

She and I had talked extensively about whether she would be interested in leaving the school system and taking on the job proposed in the third grant: chief of the teacher development and program for children inspection office. But though she heard me, and didn't think I was lying, she was so used to the South, so incredulous that *she* would ever be considered for such a position, so used to a world in which things are said, just as a formality, and not meant, that she continued to hesitate and feel very insecure. None of my extolling and concrete offers convinced her that we all thought extremely highly of her work.

During the MAP crisis we didn't have a grant, and we didn't want to lose Pearl Draine. So John wrote her a letter outlining a number of jobs she could do if we didn't get a grant, or until we got a grant, guaranteeing her the job of head of the inspection office when we did, and guaranteeing her a salary of $700 a month, up to the amount of $6,300, grant or no grant. He would be sure the money to back the promise was somehow scraped together. On the basis of the letter, Mrs. Draine wrote to the Jackson Board of Education, asking leave for a year. (Her contract said she could take off a year for study after five years of teaching, and she had never done so.) She received a brief letter telling her that the board had met and had denied the request. She was also told that she had thereby forfeited her contract.

Mrs. Draine took on her new responsibilities. These turned out to be my former job, because the positions I'd planned (director of the program inspection office, and a split version of the director of teacher development and program for children position, tailored so promoted ATGs could handle it) hadn't panned out when OEO and CDGM had negotiated the third grant contract. But Pearl took on the new responsibilities with such a devastating degree of role-shock that we feared she would collapse altogether. She couldn't eat or sleep, shook as if palsied, and expressed constant uncertainty about whether or not she was competent to do the job with which she was entrusted.

No matter how encouraging and trusting John and Mary were, every time she made a mistake she wondered if she had made it because she was a Negro, or if she would have made it anyway if she had been white. She didn't associate with white staff members after hours, because she just didn't feel that she matched the image of "executives" she had in her mind; and they *did.* She couldn't feel comfortable with them socially, regardless of how informally and warmly they accepted and invited her. She felt she couldn't get all the work done. She also couldn't believe us when we said we hadn't ever been able to get all the work done either. She didn't know how to use the dictaphone, and was afraid to ask me one day when I was around as a consultant, because she thought I'd *feel* (not act but *feel*) superior, or at least that *she* would feel that I would feel superior. When I told her that I'd never in my life used a dictaphone either, she exploded into laughter, saying that that's a perfect example of a basic problem Negroes have. She had assumed that of course I'd been born with a dictaphone in my hand.

She got terribly upset about writing anything. She knew so deeply and passionately what she wanted to say about *real* things. But terminology kept creeping into her way, making everything sound glib to her as it came echoing back off the paper. She felt that she didn't know any of CDGM's "real bosses" in Atlanta and in Washington, and that she might listen to the wrong person, or mix up all the permissions and procedures. She had faith in her own judgment, but *not* faith that she understood all the guidelines and *not* faith that *OEO* people had faith in her judgment, or even that *John* had faith in her judgment.

Mrs. Draine felt a wall with John. She knew he welcomed criticism, begged for openness, meant it, but only when she was ten words from tears could she blurt out what she wanted to say. She felt swallowed up by John, entirely stumped by his perceptive, unpredictably provocative replies—overwhelmed by his full to overflowing mind—a mind she deeply admired. She thought distrust (including the distrust she herself felt) was disgraceful. She hated hunting for racial misinterpretations. But she had learned as a child to respect superiors and to distrust whites.

She had never managed a budget. She knew no one expected perfection of her. But *she* expected perfection of herself, nonetheless. She felt sure that everybody knew more about everything than she did. She evaded making statements for fear of criticism. Slowly, she began to learn that everyone was learning. She began to see that we felt more secure *not* because we knew more, but because we felt more familiar with the kind of risk one has to take to learn.

The change of pace nearly drove her to drink. There was no time to buy her family's groceries, no time to get to church, and the phone rang all night with friends who wanted jobs and CDGMians wanting decisions. She worried that her wardrobe wouldn't be suitable for her new executive position. Her husband, a self-employed refrigerator technician, was realistically afraid that she wouldn't ever get another job after going CDGM. If that happened, how would they keep the four children paid for whom they at that time had in college? It bugged her blue that, though she had a position that should have been rewarding to her, the fact was that she missed the human rewards of personal service and closeness with her children, other children, other people, *more* than she felt the rewards of "doing good" on such a vast and impersonal scale. She had traded being a big fish in a little pool for being a little fish in a big pool. She had traded her secure position of esteem in the colored community for a precarious position in the backbiting undercutting throat-slicing world of the ambitious.

She protected herself in ways that I never had. For instance, she never took action till she had authorization in writing. And she knew some things I'd never know *ever*—and neither would the armies of dogooders like me descending suddenly on the poor all over the country to emancipate them. She knew the anguishing pain of change. She *knew* why more poor people don't flock to change. It's too desperately disruptive for all but the strongest, such as Pearl Draine, to risk. By some miracle, many people must have been that strong, because many people, through CDGM, risked all they had. And Pearl knew why some of the people who *do* become conscious, who do become able to allow themselves to examine and release their feelings, develop overwhelming, imperturbable, impenetrable, apparently irrational hatred for whites. Raised aspirations reveal what whites have prevented people from aspiring to before, and raise rage as well. Increased intimacy with whites removes the need to be sullenly, apathetically angry at everything, and provides a direct target—a personal target, whose previously illusive mystery and genius has vanished, as its human vulnerabilities, vanities and vulgarities, wiles and ways, hypocrisies and high-handedness emerge through contact. This clarification of truth, and resulting retaliatory attitudes, OEO couldn't stop.

Nor could OEO contracept CDGM's offspring, which were many and sturdy. For in the joust, some worthwhile jetsam had jostled loose, and was growing into things of value.

After the MAP battle, strategists at the Board of Missions decided that they would remain strong supporters of CDGM, but would resign themselves to a CDGM suffering from hardening of the arteries. They would put their major investment into new projects made possible by new moods, directly attributable to what CDGM had accomplished. The first of these was to be the one John and I had worked on so extensively with Mr. Robert Barrie—the Community College as an extension of MHJC. In preparation for a renovation of Mary Holmes, a new president, Donovan E. Smucker, white, had been installed. The fourth CDGM proposal to OEO described a Community College. (Nothing had come of the Community College plans we had put in the third proposal.) Now preliminary feelers seemed to indicate that the Field and the Ford foundations might fund it jointly. The TransCentury consulting firm in Washington had agreed to find faculty for it.

Essentially the ideas for the Community College were those Tom had put forth in his first position paper on it two years before, and those Marv, John, and I had developed. While much had been lost in the way of particular and innovative ideas for medical and other special projects between Tom's cup and MHJC's lip, we felt that this watered down reality would be a great improvement over a full-strength *non*reality.

Planners of Mary Holmes's growth into a precedent-setting institution of higher education tailored to the special needs of the poor also were planning a "Poor People's College" at Mount Beulah. This had long been Art Thomas's dream: to make Mount Beulah into more than a sparsely and sporadically used conference center—to make it into a center for community education of the kind wanted and needed by poor Negroes in Mississippi. At the end of 1967, this idea hadn't been developed as thoroughly as had the CEE idea, but it looked very likely.

Mary Holmes was on the move in many ways. It had applied to the

U.S. Office of Education for Title III funds under the Higher Education Act of 1956, with which to initiate a general upgrading program in conjunction with five colleges (Smith, Amherst, Mount Holyoke and Hampshire Colleges, the University of Massachusetts, and Mississippi State University), and with Klein and Saks, the consulting firm with which CDGM had finally contracted for management support services after the GE crisis. MHJC hoped to add a third year soon, and from there to grow into a four year college. It was still a junior college. It was also anticipating the addition of an Antioch-Wilberforce style nonresident work term program. How much of the raised aspirations and increased actions of the policy-planners who controlled MHJC were influenced by CDGM can't, of course, be ascertained. Its planners were ambitious men. Nevertheless, some CDGM fallout must have been in effect, for nothing had been happening along these lines before the advent of CDGM and its association with MHJC, and nothing as massive was happening even in 1967, at most of the other Board of Missions controlled small Southern Negro colleges.

Certainly MHJC had been upgrading itself without the boost CDGM may have given it. In 1958 it still had a high school department. In 1959 it had dropped it. In 1959 it had only sixty-seven students, while in 1967 it had 357 students. (The faculty still stood at eighteen.) Yet there was no evidence that MHJC was expanding into community education in 1965, when CDGM formed a connection with it; nor was there any such evidence throughout the first two years of CDGM's life. So it seems logical that at least the new climate in Mississippi—caused to a large extent by CDGM, if by nothing more direct than our mission-with-a-vision discussions with key Board of Missions people—played some part in the exciting new directions MHJC was choosing to take.

Reliable spokesmen for the National Council of Churches say that as a result of NCC's intervention in behalf of CDGM, NCC won OEO's respect, and achieved access to its ear.

An institution that was an even more direct descendant of CDGM, in fact, an out-and-out offshoot of it, was MACE. Even its name, Mississippi Action for Community Education, was a revival of Tom's original title for CDGM itself. MACE was developed by John Mudd, Marv Hoffman, and many strong local poor people who were instrumental, too, in the instigation and implementation of CDGM in communities. When MACE began to require full-time attention in the winter of 1966–1967, Dave Emmons (Mary's husband and a long-time sounding board and cynical kibitzer who, in the manner of an aloof, analytic graduate student, regularly shredded CDGM's cast of characters and proudly claimed accomplishments to keep us from becoming smug) took primary responsibility. When MACE began to come of age in the winter of 1967–1968, Ed Brown was hired as director. Ed had been the Citizens' Crusade Against Poverty's talented staff member assigned to work with

CDGM in Mississippi during the MAP crisis. He had formerly, also, been a SNCC worker in the state.

MACE's first money, $25,000, came from Merrill during the month that MAP was formed and CDGM was, according to the obituaries, "dead." This was program development money. By December, 1967, the Ford Foundation had pledged $142,000 to MACE. It was to be matched seven to ten from other sources. Negotiations indicated that the other sources would probably be the Merrill, Field, Johnson, and Interfaith Church Groups for Community Development Foundations. The money was to last a year. There was an understanding that more might be available for a second year through Ford's grant to the Citizens' Crusade for various leadership training projects.

Because MACE was Dave's "own" project, he regarded it with none of the vindictiveness with which he appeared to deal with "our" CDGM. The large role that territorial traits play in the dealings of even the most sincere and sophisticated do-gooders is truly amazing. Under Dave's intelligent and sensitive direction, MACE developed exciting plans for training twenty poor people in community organization intensively for a year. It would also train many other local leaders in various special short programs. MACE would focus on seven counties—Bolivar, Sunflower, Holmes, Madison, Issaquena, Sharkey, and Grenada—all of them early Movement and original CDGM counties, except Grenada. Its philosophy and approach were those of CDGM. The two major differences were: (a) MACE chose to work deeply and to a high degree of sophistication with a small group, rather than more superficially with a huge group, and (b) MACE wasn't aiming at building its own base through the establishment of local projects or branches, but planned to devote itself to strengthen and promote cooperation between existing local organizations so that they might "pursue and protect their mutual interests and meet their common needs."

The fact that Tom had seen the need for seizing the moment and seizing the scene when he created CDGM, and had therefore created it instantly and massively, made it possible now for follow-up projects to develop more slowly and on a smaller scale. Had CDGM not reserved the stage and enraptured two audiences (poor local and Northern liberal), the other projects could never have gotten started. The Movement had petered out, and the establishment was ready to re-entrench; to roam the state seeking vengeance. But Tom, maneuvering around resistant remaining Movement die-hards as well as around the establishment, had had the political brilliance to grab the gap and fill it with germinating happenings. Fruits of this were now appearing.

For many months MACE operated out of the Friends of the Children of Mississippi's office, performing its almost year-and-a-half program development functions there. In January, 1968, MACE was on the verge of beginning its program.

Friends of the Children of Mississippi (FCM) was neither born of CDGM, as was the Community College, nor a new twig of it gone independent like MACE. It was more or less the remains of CDGM, which sprouted out on its own from the sawed off mother stump. This sometimes happens in the jungle. Originally, October, 15, 1966, the day federal assistance to CDGM was terminated, FCM was just another name and another form of organization of duties and a relocation of office for CDGM. John remained director. Marv was his right hand man. Mary Emmons was in teacher development and program for children, and Lois Rogers still managed the office.

And so it was until January 18, 1967, when representatives of five CDGM counties, which OEO had failed to fund, went to Jackson to discuss their response to OEO's deceitful action. OEO had made "an agreement in principle" with CDGM on December 16, 1966, to fund *nineteen* counties. By December 28, OEO had reversed itself. It announced that CDGM would be allowed to operate in five of the agreed-upon counties—Clarke, Wayne, Neshoba, Humphrey, and Leflore. These five counties plus Greene, which had never been officially CDGM, but which had operated volunteer centers for months, decided to band together as an independent group. They would keep the name Friends of the Children of Mississippi. Their purpose was to continue offering volunteer Head Start programs to thousands of children, and to fight for reinclusion in the CDGM program, or delegate agency status, or some other form of support from OEO. When CDGM was "given" its third grant, it moved to its fourth location. This was the Vincent Building on Capital Street in Jackson. Housing had been bad for morale at the Milner Building. It was many times worse here. John now had a penthouse suite. It had been a private drinking club and was still decorated accordingly. He and his secretaries were on the thickly carpeted floor alone. Other departments were separated from each other by elevators and beliefs.

FCM stayed at the rickety old CDGM office at 507½ North Farish Street. The few members of Central Staff who had hung on during *this* unfunded interim period now left for the Vincent Building. FCM would have been left stranded without coordination, Central Staff, or office, had it not been for Fred Mangrum and Dave Flemming. Fred was the former Howard student and SNCC worker who had worked on CAPS and community organization with CDGM since coming to CDGM half a year before. He left CDGM, probably for the same reason so many of its "new frontiersmen" were leaving: Its growth potential was gone. Fred became director of Friends. Dave Flemming was the Delta Ministry volunteer who had been temporary CDGM Medical Coordinator during the first unfunded interim, and John's administrative assistant ever since. These two young men, both in their twenties, were the only nonlocal people, the only nonpoor people, and Dave was the only white, in FCM.

Though the FCM program was largely a defensive and subsistence level program, it was also a shining example of the essence of the spirit that had been CDGM. In March, 1967, MAP, which local people said was going so far as to bribe families to send their children to its centers, had only four hundred children in FCM territory. *FCM had nearly two thousand children in 130 classes in twenty-eight centers!* This represented an *increase* of CDGM poor people's spirit and determination to "do it ourselves." When communities twice, each time for six-month periods, ran CDGM volunteer centers, they had only the choice of operating Head Starts or having no Head Starts. FCM communities, however, had a third choice: They were actually *sacrificing* the toys, the medical program, and all the other features that a funded Head Start has above what an unfunded Head Start has, because MAP was there, operating. Some poor people were also sacrificing high paid jobs. MAP frequently tried to pick off, by hiring, the FCM poor leaders. Few went; none of the old-time CDGM loyalists. Eleven months later, in February, 1968, FCM was still going strong. It still had 1,600 children in centers!

For nine of the eleven months FCM had been negotiating with MAP for delegate agency status, or later, for a merger. MAP evidently couldn't tolerate even the admission that FCM existed as an organization—that it was something real enough to be capable of being a delegate or of merging—because it wouldn't agree to anything short of total capitulation and total control by MAP. FCM communities refused to do this. They preferred the flimsy financing on which they were limping along to a return to the traditional system.

When CDGM had been refunded, its board had agreed to give Fred and Dave each twenty-five dollars a week "salary" to see what they could do about getting FCM counties reincluded. Communities got nothing, but ran centers, regardless. In March the Field Foundation had given FCM $75,000 to last till July 1. That meant that the director and Dave were raised to glorious salaries of forty dollars a week. And the 435 local employees and the thirteen county-level poor people employees and the five others helping in the Jackson office were raised from nothing to twenty-five dollars a week for two weeks a month—the other two weeks of each month they worked free. Field refunded the tenuous operation on July 1: $300,000 for a year. In order to make it on that sum, all employees received $15 dollars a week three weeks out of every four, and volunteered the rest of the time. Children were fed hot dinners and in some cases breakfast for one dollar a week per child. Official funds were expanded slightly by donations from church groups, students, and individuals around the country. CCAP continued to back Friends strenuously, but not financially.

MAP itself, in an illegitimate sort of way, was a result of CDGM. In spite of the sins of those who conceived it, and in spite of its own bumbling, bungling amateurishness and occasional crass and gross errors in comprehending either early education or the concept of community action, it *did* deal with a total of ten thousand children at one time or another during its first year. And it *did* draw some white and more conservative Negro Mississippians into cautiously touching the hot potato of race relations, social development, change, and so forth. After Hazel Brannon Smith's husband ceased being MAP's director, CDGM's Helen Bass Williams took the job. Under her influence MAP changed some from its original aristocratic approach.

CDGM strongly influenced a newly established Mississippi Head Start Training Coordinating Council. All Head Starts in the state were represented. Its purpose was to plan training primarily for supervisory personnel. Mary Emmons and Pearl Draine had executive positions in this organization. CDGM philosophy was often presented at meetings. A bit of it may have filtered into "white" Head Starts. Or it may not have. But at least earlier enemies interacted.

Certainly CDGM had an effect on the majority of CAPs in Mississippi. There were only one or two when CDGM started. There were many in the winter of 1968. Though a number of them went into business for other reasons, many sprung up for fear CDGM would organize everything. Mr. Rex McRaney, a close personal friend, former member of the Mississippi House of Representatives, associated with the state government since that time, and at one time the governor-appointed director of the Mississippi Game and Fish Commission (an important post in sports-oriented Mississippi), was the organizer and director of the first chartered poverty program project in the state. This was Mid-State Opportunities, Inc., one of the largest CAP agencies in Mississippi.

Rex said: "You have to have lived in Mississippi before and after CDGM to realize the good it did our state. No one likes to give up authority. So CDGM caused many people in leadership positions to rethink; Who was going to lead? It stimulated them to action so that their influence wouldn't be lessened. The fact that Mississippi's leaders began to think in different ways from the way they have traditionally thought is for the betterment of the whole state.

"In 1954, when the school desegregation act came along, the lines were set: black here, white there. It wasn't a matter of race as much as one of custom. OEO caused the customs to change quickly. You had to have black and white leadership sitting down together on the same Board to get a grant. The state badly needed this grant money as a stopgap to keep the economy going after the 35 percent cotton allotment reduction which began to be phased in in 1965. OEO was the first government program to fund 'association.' And CDGM was a great stimulant to OEO's poverty program in Mississippi."

If CDGM had influence in a general way in promoting white Mississippi's acceptance of the War on Poverty, it had far greater specific influence on CAPs operating in its counties. And it had a still greater influence in those places where it served as a staging ground for feeding community people into delegate agency status to some of these CAPs: Panola-Tallahatchie, Sunflower, Bolivar, McComb, Forest, and Holmes, for example. Unfortunately, in most cases OEO forced former CDGMians into relationships with local whites before they were ready to hold their own.

Consequently, the local poor did well, but much less well than they could have done, would have, *should* have done, with readiness and support. There was only one instance in which an OEO task force team tried to communicate with elements other than those in the establishment, ascertained what these elements needed and wanted, *and gave them sufficient support in negotiating with their Community Action Program agencies so that a credibly well-rounded agency resulted.* This was the team working in a six-county CAP area in central Mississippi. The area included one of CDGM's and the Movement's best developed counties: Holmes.

Holmes County had many advantages. In the thirties the government had broken up some bankrupt plantations and sold off pieces to Negroes. Many Negroes, now, were small independent farmers. In the early 1960's Freedom workers had found strong responsive people here, and had concentrated forces in the county. Intensive, in-depth work had carried people's courage and strength and skills in community organization a long way. Many communities in Holmes County had created centers CDGM's first summer. More opened up during the second CDGM grant. CDGM also concentrated its energies in Holmes. It was less than two hours from Mount Beulah and Jackson. There were magnificent people there, like the beautiful woman I asked to be our ATG: Hattie Belle Saffold. Unlike in other counties, the Movement continued to maintain resident workers in Holmes. Not only were workers there for a continuous long time, but they were the Movement's highest caliber workers: Mike Kenney and Henri Lorenzi and Henri's wife, for instance.

Members of this unique OEO task force team were Peter Mickelsen and Jim McCartney. In contrast to some of their colleagues, Peter and Jim weren't afraid to think, feel, judge, and act in accordance with common sense and conviction. Though they were respectful and loyal to the organization they worked for, it was to its *essence* they were responsive, not to its eloquent, vacant words alone.

Peter said of his experience in the Holmes County area: "I feel that all government people and agents who go into a community to work, no matter what that specific community situation may be, always identify with the establishment, whether they want to or not, because they don't know how to meet and talk with other groups. Yet there are other forces in each community too, and these are the ones it's difficult to understand and cope with.

"What made our work unique was that we *did* identify with these other forces. We knew about them because we asked. We even asked the mayor who the troublemakers were and went to see them. We asked Delta Ministry and civil rights groups. When I went down there, I had barely heard of CDGM, and had no opinion about it. But I met CDGM community people in a few weeks time. I immediately realized that this was the only true community action in Mississippi projects at that time.

"Our mandate was to make it possible for low income people to have an effective voice in policy-making, decision-making, and a large amount of control in all parts of programs affecting them. When I came in, the civil rights groups and CDGM had done the ground work. People were ready to go out on their own—out from under the thumb of CDGM headquarters in Jackson.

"Another reason for the effectiveness of our work was that we were there for a long time—Jim and I worked for three solid months in the Holmes County area. By the end of that time we had put together a strong delegate agency, the Milton Olive Memorial Program for Children (former CDGM buildings, centers, people, and children), and in addition had left the community with a completely revamped and viable Community Action agency.

"As government agents, Jim and I could not have accomplished what we were able to accomplish there if it hadn't been for the prior and continuing work of CDGM and other civil rights forces, such as FDP, with such people as Henri Lorenzi. As far as I'm concerned, civil rights and the War on Poverty are one and the same thing."

Jim McCartney added: "If OEO had realized that you can't achieve real community action two days a week, or over the telephone, and had used the long-term and team approach in more places, it would probably have ended up with good Community Action agencies and good delegate agency arrangements, in which poor people were important, all over the country. As it is, with one thousand and fifty CAPs in the country, it's hard to find the level of grassroots involvement that I saw in this situation and in several others in Mississippi in more than a handful of agencies."

Perhaps it's partly a problem of OEO's inability to *realize* that you can't achieve community action the way they go about it. I tend to think the greater problem by far is that no one much, including OEO, *wants* to achieve community action in which poor people are important.

CDGM accomplished other things—the dialogue it carried on with many foundations attracted some of them into the state for the first time, and drew others into more daring involvement than that in which they had hitherto allowed themselves to indulge. CDGM was the Citizens' Crusade's first test case and chance to prove itself a leader in support of the poor, even in tense political situations. Surely one of the most important things CDGM did for Mississippi, for the South, was to provide an arena for emerging new-style Southern white leaders.

After the second grant CDGM added several white Mississippians to its board of directors. The Reverend Jimmy Jones was one of these. He was a young Methodist chaplain at Ole Miss, born and bred in the Delta town of Leland, Mississippi. He later became chairman of the board. In contrast to many in CDGM, Jimmy Jones *was* concerned with the deepest implications of the thing: "The thing that drew me to CDGM was that it seemed to be a mechanism that had actually succeeded in giving people a sense of worth. Any program that can *really* do *that* is something to look at twice. CDGM wasn't a 'step' in progress. Progress doesn't have to happen step by step, logically, in sequence. It can occur in flashes and lurches. CDGM was one of these.

"Some of us are in the position of wheeling and dealing and making decisions for other people, but it's only right if it's to free other people to get into the decision-making as fast as possible. It's no success to substitute 'good' people for 'bad' people making the 'right' decisions for others. It's so easy for us to buy our way out of our guilt by 'giving' people something. Giving is far more complicated than that, and so is caring.

"A most important question to me is *how* do I care? I care. I do. I gave the poor a turkey at Thanksgiving. That's not the answer. *I* care that we take our responsibility to be sure that people are given a chance to take *their* responsibility to participate in making decisions about everything that concerns them.

"In the last analysis, no individual has to be a victim of anything. Each of us makes a decision. I can decide to be a victim (What can I do? I'm only one person), or I can decide to make the only possible *other* decision (I'm the greatest! I *can* do!). Part of reality is what *is*, the limitations. But part is what I want it to be.

"History doesn't just make itself. Somebody gets an idea from the mesh he's in, and he moves out alone with his idea and he educates himself and others and forms a model that's back down in the mesh; but it's *new*. The perpetual revolution is what I see as the essence of life. The job will never be done by people who do something and then sit back down and never do anything else—or people who never do anything at all. I call them the living dead. An idea is like any living thing: the minute it's birthed, it's on its way to death. We have to keep on with the birthing process—creating, creating, learning, experimenting. . . .

"Some people work out in the twilight zone between the no longer and the not yet—where you don't know, but you venture. It's no better out there than it is in the world of the PhDs and the ordinary people who know all the answers and live by all the rules. But that's where you've decided to be, and maybe you'll find out something you didn't know.

"The point of the New Testament to me is that this cat Jesus just walked into life and he *lived* it—he really *lived* it, even when Pilate told him, 'I'm going to take your life.' Jesus said, 'Mm-mm; you're not taking it—I'm going to *give* my life.' He even made that decision. He *felt*, he *chose*, he *lived*.

"What's the role of the white man in all this? The tragedy of race relations today, the way we've made them, is that we have to begin answering this question negatively. The role *isn't* to avoid the issue and stay off in a world of our own, floating, failing to tangle with issues, wandering around wondering what God wants us to do. The answer *isn't* to run things for people, nit-picking here and there, pulling a tick off our social problems, slapping at gnats, while the dog runs round and round the room spreading more. How do you get to people's gizzards? And the answer *isn't* to hang around in the Negro communities apologizing and agonizing. The role is to help change the model we've got that perpetuates the dehumanization of both races. It's to intrude upon everyone's illusions.

"It's as significant to have shown up white in this world as it is to have shown up black. It's a gift to be what you are. Certainly, we don't like what the past has been. But the only live option I see is to look to the future—what can we do *now*? Our role is to work together and deal with the problems. This brings about personhood and does away with some of the physiological problems.

"OEO's paperwork is so immense, and OEO is so short of staff, that it just hasn't sent in enough people who can explode the minds of the whites to enable *them* to act as catalysts in resolving the problems of the state; or to explode the minds of blacks to solve their problems. This is one of those limits and realities that we fear to tamper with. *Why* can't the OEO have enough, and good enough, staff, to do what we've learned has to be done humanly?

"I've always wondered if the upper echelon of government could possibly know what's going on. It seems to me that the only way you can find out how to construct one of these programs is to get out there and listen. You can't know or imagine without listening in each situation. The minute you stop considering the human element your program gets stale. You have to keep involved with the human things and keep working with change, the constant changes that human beings bring to something, or you lose the creative edge.

"Is the race to the moon the answer to the unrest on earth? Certainly I'm inquisitive, I want to know what goes on in the furthest galaxy. I don't know, maybe the answer to our human problems here *does* lie on the moon. But I tend to think it lies in making a few budget cuts in some of the agencies' budgets and putting a little more effort, staff, money, ideas, experimentation into solving people's problems here on earth."

Certainly our civilization's death wish is evident in the example of the

CDGM story—from our personal and professional and political territorial possessiveness and fighting instincts, to our monstrous dread of being whole sole unduplicated individuals; from our great insistence on technical proficiency to our terrible avoidance of pondering the goal, the substance, the why of existence. But maybe, also, CDGM symbolizes our better side.

In his book *The Free Men,* John Ehle comments that few people up to now have really expected that we could achieve in our society what our political saints envisioned for it, as few men have believed we could fulfill our spiritual expectations. He says that America is still young and unfinished,

> And the call which we hear is our own call from our own people, new pioneers in a way, not of the wilderness roads, not of the clearing of land and the building of cities and factories, but of the other effort we have been making in this country from the first, the companion effort to build here a society in which democracy can exist without vulgarity, and all men can fulfill the best that is in them as free and productive citizens.

I think, really, the significance of CDGM can best be considered in terms of that distinguished biologist Conrad Lorenz's thinking. In his book *On Aggression* he makes the point that perhaps we are wasting time in worrying about "the missing link" between ape and human. Probably the point is that the human being *is* the link between the ape of the past and the *humane* being of the future. With this as a frame of reference, I think the success and value of CDGM, or any other specific project, situation, or individual action can be judged. Is it an effort to make the society and the country which we have created more fit for humane living? And if it is, to what extent does it try to apply the scientific spirit of the search, problem-solving, trial, error, discovery, and proof to the personal and social problems of man?

These aren't matters auditors, administrators, and experts alone are fit to judge. Each of us is qualified, obligated in fact, to ask. Perhaps the answers are negative. Perhaps it's too late to worry about the society, the country, and the general population. Perhaps the best we can do now, alone, those who can, is to develop inwardly toward the universal spirit of being—of life, of good—and forget about the others.

But if we ask and the answers are positive, then should we withdraw into the luxury of living only for the sake of our own souls, or should we stick with these actions that are a bit of the battle of human evolution? What better is there than that? As yet, to be sure, "the dove has found no resting place for the sole of her foot." But we can work and pray that the "drums are bigger than the drummers when the drumbeat starts. . . ."[41]

[41] Stembridge, Jane, *I Play Flute.* HJK Publishing Co., 1966, p. 58.

APPENDIX A

Background 1964: the Political Context into Which CDGM Came: the "Loyal" Democrats, the Freedom Democrats, and the "Reform" Democrats

CDGM had political reality with which to deal. In Mississippi, in the spring of 1965, there was one political party: the Democratic party. There were two would-be parties: the Reform Democrats, which hopefully would be made up of a growing coalition of labor, moderates, NAACP middle-class Negroes, and college students; and the Freedom Democratic party, already consisting of poor Negroes, Movement activists, and backed by Northern liberals.

In order to understand what happened to CDGM a few months after its birth, it's helpful to understand that there was at this point no Reform Democratic party. There was only the shadowy beginning of one. The White House Administration had a strong interest in developing such a party. Reform Democrats would back the national Democratic party, whereas the traditional "loyal" Democratic party in the state was almost three-quarters Goldwater fans. The liberals representing potential membership for the Reform Democratic party were in no way involved in poor communities at this time. Though eventually they hoped to move in this direction, indeed would *have* to move in this direction if they wanted to gain substantial support, in the spring of 1965 they were still struggling to gain a toehold on college campuses and in cautiously liberal circles.

One possible part of the Reform Democratic party was a new group of about thirteen hundred individuals in their twenties and thirties called the Young Democratic Club of Mississippi. The group had begun recently on college campuses. Membership was drawn largely from cities, and Mississippi is primarily rural. But it was a sprout of hope in the spring after the cold spell of the closed society, which had lasted until the end of 1964.

On the other hand, the Freedom Democratic party worked in poor Negro communities. It was the only forceful group concerned with political, civic, and all other kinds of development in these communities. President Johnson's Administration knew this, and was afraid of it. There was no chance of forming the moderate Reform Democrat party in Mississippi, which would be of far greater use to the Administration than was the existing Democratic "Goldwater" party, if the FDP got too powerful. It would scare off the moderates, who were having a hard enough time coming out of hiding as it was, and would leave them nowhere to go except to the traditional party.

During CDGM's organizational days, in fact during his entire tenure at CDGM, Tom Levin never talked directly with the leadership of the Freedom Democratic party. OEO was in such terror that CDGM was "political," and one of the tightropes Tom had to walk was the one that was above governmental reproach, yet beneath the distinctions OEO made between things that were legitimate for the poor to concern themselves with in a community action program, and things that were illegitimate for the poor to concern themselves with in a community action program; a distinction made complicated by the fact that they were all the same things.

FDP proved to be intimately connected with the CDGM story, because according to OEO, the two organizations were too closely related, and according to FDP spokesmen, the two organizations were not at all related, and because it was hard to distinguish between the goals and constituency of FDP and CDGM.

There was an emerging Reform Democratic party on which the Administration was pinning hopes. The political squeeze CDGM shortly got into was intimately related to that fact. There was also a context created by FDP out of which CDGM mushroomed. This explains the accusations that soon were made about overlappings, and undercuttings that occurred.

The Mississippi Freedom Democratic party was officially established at a meeting in Jackson in April, 1964—one year before the establishment of CDGM.[42] It was part of the COFO Summer Project. The Mississippi FDP followed the laws of Mississippi regulating political parties, insofar as it was allowed to do so. In a brilliant move, FDP delegates went to the Democratic National Convention of 1964 in Atlantic City, and requested to be seated instead of the traditional, regular Mississippi Democratic party.

The issue FDP presented was, "whether the National Democratic Party takes its place with the oppressed Negroes of Mississippi or their white oppressors, with those loyal to the National Democratic Party or those who have spewed hatred upon President Kennedy and President Johnson and the principles to which they dedicated their lives. In the final analysis, the issue is one of principle: whether the National Democratic party, the greatest political instrument for human progress in the history of our nation, shall walk backward with the bigoted power structure of Mississippi or stride ahead with those who would build the State and the Nation in the image of the Democratic Party's greatest leaders—Thomas Jefferson, Andrew Jackson, and Franklin D. Roosevelt."

While the traditional Mississippi delegation arrived at the convention in cars bearing Goldwater bumper stickers, and openly voiced themselves during recess and prior to the convention being called to order as favoring the candidacy of Senator Goldwater, the Freedom delegation came "as bona fide Democrats who have the interests, welfare and success of the Democratic Party at Heart." The Mississippi FDP openly and proudly identified itself with the basic programs and principles of the national Democratic party, including full employment, collective bargaining, food stamp programs,

[42] All quotes and facts about MFDP are from "Brief Submitted by the Mississippi Freedom Democratic Party" by Joseph L. Rauh, Jr. Further documentation of quotations can be found in this brief, printed in pamphlet form and available through Mr. Rauh's office in Washington, D.C.

Medicare, civil rights, reapportionment, job retraining, an antipoverty-program, United Nations, foreign aid, and the Peace Corps. The Mississippi FDP came representing a *functioning* political organization, and for this reason, as well as others, claimed it had no counterpart anywhere in the South.

The "traditional" Mississippi Democratic party, on the other hand, couldn't be considered "bona fide Democrats." The campaign literature for Governor Paul B. Johnson, a radical by comparison with his predecessor Ross Barnett, made such statements as: "Our Mississippi Democratic party is entirely independent and free of the influence of domination of any national party," and "The Mississippi Democratic party, which long ago separated itself from the national Democratic party, and which has fought everything both national parties stand for. . . ." The state convention called for a repeal of the Civil Rights Act of 1964, which it asserted was "a naked grasp for extreme and unconstitutional federal power" and "a betrayal of the American people." It also favored "getting the United States out of the United Nations, and the United Nations out of the United States." Johnson said that point one in his program would be 'to spearhead an all-out effort to secure cooperation from other governors and leaders to get the Kennedys out of the White House" ("small wonder, too, since he had already referred to them as 'dimwits' "). Governor Ross Barnett was also a "loyal Democrat." He called President Johnson a "counterfeit confederate who resigned from the South and may one day soon resign from the white race as well. . . ." And Congressman John Bell Williams, the 'friend of the Administration' who said, "Kennedy is the most predatory Chief Executive of all times. If we don't stop him and his brother Bobby, human liberty will disappear from this nation and the face of the earth."

This "traditional" Mississippi Democratic party ran the state of Mississippi. It controlled the legislative, executive, and judicial branches of the state government. At this time all forty-nine senators and all but one of the 122 representatives were Democrats. There was no noticeable Republican party, and there was no third party until FDP came on the scene. "As Governor Johnson said in his keynote to the 'traditional' state convention, the Mississippi Democratic Party 'holds all but a handful of the elective and appointive offices, from constable to governor . . . for the past 89 years, [it] is the framework, or the structure, through which Mississippians maintain political unity, and operate self-government.'" The major subject on which Mississippians thus maintained political unity was the "sacred principle of segregation," and its necessary relative: preventing Negro voting.

The statutes of Mississippi provided that "No person shall be eligible to participate in any primary election unless he . . . is in accord with the statement of the principles of the party holding such primary . . ." and one of those principles that was a prerequisite to participation in Mississippi Democratic affairs was: "We believe in separation of the races in all phases of our society. It is our belief that the separation of the races is necessary for the peace and tranquility of all the people of Mississippi and the continuing good relationship which has existed over the years." Thus, in order to have a part in the political life and government of Mississippi, one must believe in, and promise to support, segregation, and violation of the federal law! "A Negro's mere belief in his own dignity and the United States Constitution makes him ineligible to participate in the political processes of Mississippi."

When FDP was formed, only 6.7 percent of the 435,000 Negroes in the state, age twenty-one or over, were registered to vote. Though Negroes represented 40 percent of the population, all voter registrars were white. Professor Russell H. Barrett of the University of Mississippi said in a speech: "First, the whole pattern of voting requirements and in the registration form is calculated to make the process appear to the voter to be a hopelessly formidable one. The pattern is supposed to bristle with complexities which culminate in the publication of the would-be voter's name in the local newspaper for two weeks. A major purpose of all this is to so overwhelm the voter that he will not have the audacity even to attempt registration. Behind this approach is supposed to be—and all too often is—a collection of fears that someone will challenge the voter's moral character, that he may be prosecuted for perjury, or that he may be subjected to economic or other pressures if he attempts to register. . . .

"A second important point is that the law provides no clear and meaningful standards for its highly general requirements. These now familiar generalities require the voter to be able to explain any section of the constitution, to describe the obligations of citizenship, and to demonstrate to the circuit clerk that he is a good moral character. It is clear that those requirements were stated vaguely for one simple reason, to permit the registrar to apply different standards to different people. . . ."

If a Negro did overcome all these obstacles, he found that the purpose of running his name and address in the newspaper for two weeks was to allow ample time for economic pressure to be applied. He lost his job, his credit, sometimes his home.

Negroes have risked more than economic survival when they registered to vote. Lamar Smith was shot to death on a courthouse lawn for urging others to vote, and a grand jury refused to indict the three men who were charged with the slaying (1955). Herbert Lee's 1961 murder was ruled a "justifiable homicide," though he was shot to death for being active in voter-registration activities by a member of the Mississippi State Legislature. Louis Allen, a witness in the Lee killing, was shot to death in 1964, and local authorities said they were not "able" to come up with any clues as to who did it. In 1962 on the day she went to the country courthouse to register, Mrs. Fannie Lou Hamer, vice chairman of the Freedom Democratic party at the 1964 convention, was fired from the plantation job she had held for eighteen years and was told by the plantation owner that she had to leave if she didn't withdraw her registration application. An unidentified person fired a rifle through the window of a home and seriously wounded Marylene Burkes and Vivian Hillet because the grandparents were active in voter registration. The sheriff and two deputies assaulted and drove three Negroes from the Rankin County Courthouse before they completed their voter registration forms (1963). And in Philadelphia, in 1964, three students were murdered because they were part of a registration drive.

FDP workers were exhausted in the spring of 1965 when CDGM was conceived. They were trying to recover from their massive voter registration drive. They were very much against diverting what was left of the energies of their staff from voter registration. Their delegation had not been seated at the Convention. The FDP people refused a compromise offered to them, and left the convention. Whether they should have been so idealistic or not is still a controversial issue. In any event the incident was significant in national Democratic party-Mississippi politics. The FDP were not optimistic about the chances of an Administration-sponsored Head Start being "with" their cause and free from the Mississippi power structure's cause. They did not trust this new group coming into their territory.

The fact that Tom Levin insisted from the beginning that CDGM was a federally financed community education program with guidelines to follow and was not going to be involved in partisan politics further increased local FDP workers' suspicion. Tom's refusal to be deferential to FDP leadership, or even to work in a partnership arrangement with it, infuriated many key FDP people. At no time did CDGM officially use its government-paid-for facilities or personnel for activities directly related to any political party, including FDP.

Johnson of Johnson and Boswell fame once said that even if there are two apples on the apple tree, it is fair, reasonable, and accurate to say that there are no apples on the apple tree this year. If one or two violations of policy could be proven relevant to the subject, it didn't negate the fact that the policy, written and spoken, was to avoid political activity of a partisan nature, nor did it negate the fact that over three thousand people connected with CDGM, acting over a period of hundreds of days, didn't violate the policy; in fact, bent over backward to honor it, even when it appeared absurdly arbitrary. There was little or no political or administrative overlap, but there was human overlap. Joan Bowman, CDGM historian, in her unpublished book touches on this occasional overlap because of the similarity of the causes we were all working for, and because of the tendency of human beings to be considerate of each other:

> To those involved there seemed something unnatural about a distinction between the FDP and a government program. Arguments for remaining detached from the demonstrations in the interest of a "government program" appeared weak when set up alongside the moral energy of Negroes going to jail for civil rights . . . arguments against offering government resources to the Freedom Democratic Party seemed academic, as if they had nothing to do with the realities of working and living in Mississippi.
>
> . . . it was common practice in the communities to share resources. Automobiles have always been a premium in poor communities. Vital to civil rights work is the ability to transport people to meetings, to be able to deliver food and clothing and run errands, to canvass in rural neighborhoods, to travel across the state cheaply. Even to get away for a glass of beer or some companionship requires an automobile. The CDGM staff always had access to automobiles and to federal money for gasoline to run them. . . . When we made our rounds on CDGM business and found that by driving over to Belzoni and picking up a woman for a meeting we might further the efforts of a local committee, or by driving a few miles out of the way to run an errand for a harassed SNCC worker, in the name of common decency, who could refuse?

One of Tom Levin's toughest tasks was to prevent "common decency" from taking precedence over government regulations in the behavior of his staff.

Yet when OEO officials later insinuated that we were so similar to FDP that they couldn't tell where one organization left off and the other began, how were we to explain? Would we vigorously deny that we, too, were in favor of "full employment, collective bargaining, food stamp programs, Medicare, civil rights, reapportionment, job retraining, an antipoverty program, United Nations, foreign aid, the Peace Corps," and other principles and programs for which FDP and the national Democratic party stood? Would we vehemently assert that we were in complete accord with the state of Mississippi's policies of rigorous segregation in spite of the Civil Rights law, and that we strenuously repudiated FDP's suspect suggestion that all citizens have the right to vote? FDP didn't represent politics alone, as a party might in the North. It represented all civic efforts for Negroes.

The Child Development Group had Child Development centers in Liberty, Mississippi, where Lee was killed, and in Ruleville, where Mrs. Hamer lost her job, and where the young ladies were wounded because their grandparents were active in voter registration, and in Rankin County, where the sheriff drove off the would-be voters, and in many, many other places where violence and retaliation had come to those who moved toward liberation.

In many communities in which CDGM was active, the individuals with enough awareness, initiative, influence, daring, and diligence to mobilize members of their poverty-stricken and psychicly-stricken neighborhood into making an *educational* program for the purpose of breaking a major barrier between their people and a better life, were the *same* individuals with enough awareness, initiative, influence, daring, and diligence to mobilize the members of their neighborhoods into making a political program for the purpose of breaking a barrier between their people and a better life. However, regardless of how active a handful of leaders, or an individual leader, from a poor community may be, any group with experience in making sincere and imaginative efforts to "involve the poor" in a project "for them," knows that it is impossible to "get them to participate" unless they themselves want to participate.

In the case of CDGM, as in the case of Birmingham,

> In this time and circumstance, no leader or set of leaders could have acted as ringmasters, whipping a whole race out of purring contentment into leonine courage and action. If such credit is to be given to any single group, it might well go to the segregationists, who, with their callous and cynical code, helped to arouse and ignite the righteous wrath of the Negro.[43]

Poor people responded to the possibility of CDGM so positively because it was a piece of the "new world" package of which they had recently become aware. The new world package was wrapped in a refreshingly, strengtheningly new picture of Southern Negroes:

[43] King, Martin Luther, Jr., *Why We Can't Wait*. New York: Harper & Row, 1963, p. 144.

> A man's valuation of himself is derived and sustained by his reading of other people's assessment cf him, and at all times in a person's life there are some "other people" whom he regards as the most authoritative assessors. . . . With some notable variations, [Negroes] adopted the social values and standards of the dominant white society. For generations, Negro Southerners had no sustained insight into white society beyond their own neighborhood, and they consequently shaped their self-portrait through the terms of local opinion. The past three or four decades have been a time, even for rural Negroes, of awareness of a larger universe of values and authoritative opinions, and increasingly they have tended to disregard local definitions in preference for more favorable nation-wide and world-wide judgments of their worth. . . . The grand generalities of American democracy seeped into their consciousness. . . . And always, Negroes were accompanied by a few stereotypes which sprang easily into the minds of white persons, even those a Negro might regard as friends, and displaced the actual Negro person they knew—or thought they knew. The stereotypes were and are the damning judgments of white society on Negro identity. What is happening today is that Negroes are disowning the stereotypes, the white man's creations, are refusing any longer to acknowledge themselves to *be* what the white man said they were.[44]

Television, newspapers, magazines, and books for the few who read books, and above all, civil rights workers of all sorts, including FDP workers, were the harbingers of "the new image." They were the new "other people" whose authoritative assessments of Negro worth was being substituted for the old condemning ones. Poor people responded to CDGM because, thanks to this infiltration of a new image and a new world concept, they were beginning to believe that they were *entitled* to government funds, to education for their children, to jobs for themselves, to plan for their own lives, and that they were *capable* of instigating and carrying on a program.

It may have been clear to the government which details belonged in this or that department, agency, or organization, but to the poor Negroes, there were only two divisions: those individuals and institutions that, through threats, violence, or manipulation, attempted to keep them out and down, and those individuals and institutions that, through inclusion in policy-making, training, and participatory democracy, attempted, however imperfectly, to let them go in and up, if they wished. CDGM and FDP were different organizations with different functions and procedures, but they were both part of the new world package, and thus shared many views, aims, and constituents.

As in most other American communities, middle-class or otherwise, when a new civic improvement project is being considered and launched, it is local civic leaders who consider and launch it. Undoubtedly there were some active Democrats and even, maybe, Republicans in community action projects and antipoverty programs around the country. While they focused, one hoped, primarily on the projects they were running, it couldn't be said that their

[44] Dunbar, Leslie W., "The Changing Mind of the South," in Leiserson, Avery, ed., *The American South in the 1960's*. New York: Frederick A. Praeger, Inc., 1964, pp. 9–11.

political party membership was entirely irrelevant. The same was true in CDGM regarding FDP.

The historians may make up their own facts to prove the hidden "influence" FDP had over CDGM, but the unpopular and unfortunate truth that lay at the bottom of this matter was that CDGM was a powerful program with much to offer people that was visible and tangible on a day-to-day basis, while FDP was a weakly staffed, underfunded program that was, except in a few cases, sporadic, and which, except in a few cases, offered principles and eventualities that were vitally important, but did not have much for the here and now.

From its inception, CDGM appealed to a much wider group than did FDP. First, CDGM provided the first structure in the state that organized people on a day-to-day basis in a nonprovincial manner around issues of statewide significance. FDP had outposts in many of the same communities, but workers were often cut off from maximum impact because only a handful of people worked regularly. Others participated only occasionally when they attended mass meetings or undertook a specific brief assignment. A great percentage of the steady work was done by imported staff. Freedom Schools the summer before involved people daily, but often the people were children. The involvement was of a provincial kind—each community unto itself. The over-all statewide connection was not for community people, it was for out-of-state and professional staff workers.

CDGM was a multicounty coalition, on which daily activities depended. CDGM had three additional attractions which tempted poor people out of isolation and into a league: jobs with money, where money made a huge difference; a *service*, not a political program, which brought immediate tangible benefits, and because it was both apolitical and for children, attracted people across political and religious lines; it brought an aura of protection and respectability because of its federal backing, so it seemed safe to more than just those daring enough to participate in FDP.

In communities where FDP was a success, CDGM could be seen as an extension of the services it was beginning to bring, and thus as a great boost to the lagging FDP. In communities where there was no FDP, CDGM was the introduction of services and organization. To discuss FDP's relationship to CDGM was less relevant than to discuss CDGM's relationship to FDP: The question was whether CDGM bled FDP of its political vitality—because poor people were more concerned about immediate jobs and rallying to do something for the children, and because staff workers in some cases switched to CDGM—or whether CDGM boosted FDP, which was dying as an organization, but whose *cause* CDGM picked up and carried quite a distance forward.

APPENDIX B

Background 1964: the Delta Ministry and CDGM's Relation to It

The Delta Ministry believed that working for love and justice, traditional goals of the churches, is only meaningful when new concepts of ministry and new action methods, which are responsive to today's revolutionary situation, are adopted and invented. The Delta Ministry started with specific incidents that arose in the lives of individuals. It tried to see them through from roots to real solution. It was a group that was willing to work shoulder to shoulder and brain to brain with people—not for them or on them. It helped them fight through their problems, one by heavily burdensome one, as they cropped up and came to a festering head. The strength people gained from discovering that social institutions and warm white individuals could be on their side can't be overestimated. Program accomplishments were important, but psychological accomplishments were more important.

The "presence" of the Delta Ministry also affected the white community. Ministers, businessmen, and civic leaders rejected most of the consistent efforts Delta Ministry workers made to interpret their work and to work through and with the power structure. Yet at the rate that they attacked Delta Ministry with newspaper blasts and occasional shotgun blasts, the moderates among them were able to come out from hiding and do many decent and moderate things which they have wanted to do before, but were under too much fire to dare to do. The Delta Ministry served as a "lightning rod" to catch some of the bitter criticism always showered lavishly on those who moved in Mississippi. The Delta Ministry became the presence on the far end of the continuum that runs between racist reactionaries and social reformers. Then the Mississippi moderates, who used to be regarded by their state-mates as radical reds and who could do nothing for fear it would further exaggerate this wild-eyed image, found themselves regarded as the only group ready and able to save the sovereign state from deadly dangerous outside agitators, in this case a bunch of mild-mannered ministers.

Besides being an invaluable "presence" representing dignity and decency for each person in a state which was, for black people, a barbarically brutal police state using all the well-known terrorist tactics, the Delta Ministry engaged in a wide variety of excellent programs. Because of its philosophy that "a ministry of service to relieve suffering" and "a ministry of community development" in today's Mississippi must, to be really meaningful, get into basic issues of voting, education, jobs, and politics, the Delta Ministry was usually in hot water with cool white Mississippians and cautious segments of sponsoring churches elsewhere.

The Delta Ministry was fifteen paid people, many of them ministers, over three hundred out-of-state volunteers who came to live and work in Mississippi, and a group of local Negro volunteers who worked for fifteen dollars a week, all led by the remarkable Art Thomas. Always with a particular need as a beginning, the Delta Ministry had, in its short life, established four project centers in various parts of the state, as well as sponsored individual Freedom Corps volunteers in isolated communities, and run a conference and training center called Mount Beulah on the campus of a former Negro junior college in the middle of Mississippi.

The thirty-five acre oasis with thirteen buildings on it quickly came to be known as the "Freedom Headquarters" of the state—with varying degrees of enthusiasm, but with equal amounts of excitement, from different elements of the population. At first Mount Beulah was the only place in the state in which large interracial groups of the poor could meet in complete freedom and open discussion. This was spiritually important as well as logistically valuable. Mount Beulah was made available for conferences by the Freedom Democratic party, the Southern Christian Leadership Conference, the Southern Students Organizing Committee, CORE, the national convention of the Episcopal Society for Cultural and Racial Unity, and other groups, which were in 1964 still excluded from "the closed society." Since then, such groups have become only bristlingly tolerated in the more urban places.

The Delta Ministry sponsored and housed many such training and orientation sessions as crafts training for the Poor People's Corporation (a self-help crafts corporation which made and sold clothing, leathercraft, jewelry, etc., and marketed them in the North), briefings for Hattiesburg high school students who were becoming involved in social change projects, a program of the Presbyterian Church in which Southern teen-agers spent a year in the North, headquarters for Northern clergy active in demonstrations against the state legislature, weekend retreats and citizenship workshops for Natchez youth escaping from the tensions of the demonstrations there, programs for the Freedom Corps (a group of young Mississippians learning how to do voter registration and community organizing), several series of educational and economics conferences sponsored by the Delta Ministry and CORE, orientations for fresh Delta Ministry volunteers. It had also conducted citizenship workshops all over the state to help newly enfranchised people become thoughtful, informed voters and skillful leaders, and provided full facilities for all of CDGM's headquarters and training operations for the first year.

Delta Ministry played a big role in registering twenty thousand voters. It brought to national attention the dismal dilemma of Delta plantation workers.

Delta Ministry used Mount Beulah as an island of peace in the middle of angry seas for persons in deep distress. There was the mother of a Negro convict who killed a state trooper. Although she had not been involved in the crime in any way, she was continually harassed by the police. There was another woman with lots of children who came to this way-station because she was afraid. The week before, her son had been shot and killed, and the week before that her husband had been shot and killed—both for talking about voting, or one for talking about voting and the other for being his son. Mount Beulah fed people and let them live. These things alone are bountiful blessings to some people. After six weeks at bleak, wintery, muddy drab, overcrowded Mount Beulah, a poor man said "Bless them, the Lord bless them, they give us food and a roof. What more does a person need?" Not an uncommon aspiration level for a Southern Negro.

Mount Beulah served as a displaced persons camp for hundreds of men, women, and children. People made plans for self-government, attended classes in literacy and citizenship, and began learning how to take their lives in their own hands. The Delta Ministry did more for people than assisting them in material ways. Each encounter that Delta Ministry workers had with any person made that person respect himself a little more and gave him courage to be self-determining.

Delta Ministry distributed tons of food, clothing, and books to ten thousand families in the Delta. Distribution, largely of things sent from church groups in the North, was done through local community committees.

Delta Ministry also supported local employment committees fighting job discrimination in a number of cities, sometimes in the courts, sometimes in the picket lines. And it supported a doctor and four nurses in a program of community organization for health improvement.

They housed the Freedom Information Service, which provided simple literature and a relevant information library for the Freedom Movement of Missississippi. They joined local leaders in door-to-door canvassing to urge hundreds of frightened Negro parents to take advantage of desegregated schools. Without this program, many would have been frightened by the white community's silent pressure, and would not have responded.

CDGM could not have existed had it not been for the foundation laid by the Delta Ministry, through Art Thomas, its extraordinary director for almost two years.

APPENDIX C

First Summer Application Form; a Reflection of CDGM's Values

Our application forms for the first summer reflected some of our values, and were therefore not the same forms as those used by the Mississippi School System.

9. Briefly outline employment experience including name and address of present employer:
10. Briefly outline your educational experience:
11. Describe the community activity in which you have participated:
12. Briefly outline the civil rights activities in which you have been involved:
13. List some political, social and community groups in which you have been active:
14. Have you been in the South? Where and When?
15. List name, address and telephone contacts for reference and/or aid:
    A. Parents/guardian/Other Family:
    B.
    C.

Please answer the following questions briefly, concisely, and honestly. This way you can help CDGM evaluate the most appropriate assignment for staff.

1. Why do you want to work with the program?
2. What problems might you have working with a rural community?
3. How do you feel you will adjust to rural housing, sanitation, food, etc.?
4. How do you think you will work in loosely structured situations?
5. Do you prefer to work on your own or under supervision? Why?
6. Discuss your leadership abilities.
7. What do you like to do best with children? Adults?
8. What do you like to do least with children? Adults?

(If necessary, use back of sheet to complete your answers.)

We also sent a suggested reading list of books to applicants, thirteen of which were in the field of preschool education and reading readiness.

APPENDIX D

Sample Weekly Lesson Plan for Sound Table Game

This was the way we showed people how to work out the scheme the first summer. However actual centrally designed lesson plans like this weren't developed until the following spring, 1966.

Sound Table
LESSON 1

The sound we are studying with the children is "p-p." This is the lesson plan for one whole week. We don't care about the *name* of the letter, "*pee,*" we care about the *sound* it makes, "p-p-p," like the beginning sound of "pig."

At Staff Meeting Time Friday

First, you need a special table, your sound table, painted or covered with a very bright color to attract the children's attention. Nothing should *ever* be put on the sound table except items starting with the sound you are studying.

Make a letter P, four inches high, straight and round and neat, with black, on white. Copy, draw, or trace a large pig next to it. Make sure it looks like a pig. Copy one from a library book or above if necessary. Fasten this to the wall eight inches above your table. Collect five or six objects that start with the sound "p-p-p." (For example, popsicle, package, popcorn, pillow, pinecone, pill, peaches, pudding, paint, pen, pencil, paper, pig, plate, potato chips, peanut, peas, pickle, pail.) Be sure to choose things the children will know. Put things where there is no chance of making a mistake, there is only one name it could be called. Be sure one of your objects is something to eat.

First Day, Monday

Smile and be friendly, no matter what else you do. Take a group of about seven or eight children to your sound table. Trace the letter with your finger as if you were writing it. Tell the children that every time they see this mark in their whole life, it will always say "p-p-p," like "pig"! Do *not* call it "pee," call it "p-p-p, like pig." Ask the children if they can help make that noise, "p-p-p like pig"! Let them do it again and again until all are joining in. Each time the teacher says it too. Then tell the children that every single thing on this table starts with the same sound, "p-p-p," like the way "pig" starts, "p-p-p."

Pick up each item. Lift it up as you call its name. After each item say "p-p-p." Then let the children call each item's name *with* you as you lift it up. If any child wants to name one or more items alone, *lifting each as he names it,* let him. Then do the whole game again.

Give each child something to eat off the sound table, saying "p-p-p" and the name of the food as you give it to each child. Tell the children that you will be playing this game again tomorrow. Tell them you still need their help to find more things that start like "pig, p-p-p." (Not "pee," don't say "pee.")

Staff Meeting Time, Monday

Place some objects around the room, and find those there already that start "p-p." Be sure you know where at least seven or eight are.

Second Day, Tuesday

Do the whole lesson again, from beginning to end, exactly as you did it yesterday. When you are finished with everything, tell the children you are going hunting for things to go on your sound table, things that start like "pig, p-p-p."

Take the group slowly walking around the room with you. Ask them if "toys" begin "p-p-p," then say, "No, *toys,* t-t-t, that's *not* the same as p-p-p pig." Let's look till we find something. Walk around till you have found all the things starting "p-p-p." Let each child carry an item back to the table. Name the items you have found. Name them again as you ask each child to place his object on the table. Give each child something to eat, *off the table,* that starts with the sound "p-p-p." Tell them you will play again tomorrow.

Staff Meeting Time, Tuesday

Buy or find *pink* and *purple* chalk, crayons, or paint. Also some paper. Put both on the sound table.

Third Day, Wednesday

Do everything you did Monday, starting with tracing the letter and naming each item and letting the children answer. Then tell them this color is "purple." Ask everyone to say "purple" with you. Then ask each child to say "purple." Ask what color it is (hold up the purple chalk, crayon, or paint). Let them all say "purple." Do the same thing with "pink." Then hold up the paper, and say "paper." Tell them everybody's going to make a "purple and pink picture on the paper." Say "p-p-p, *p*urple, *p*ink, *p*icture, *p*aper." Get them to say "I'm going to make a pink and purple picture on a paper" along with you. Tell them they can make anything they want and you will hang it up over the sound table. When each child is finished, tell him he made a "pink and purple picture, p-p-p, like pig, like this," and write a big straight "P" on the bottom corner of his picture. Then hang it up. Give each child his food off the sound table that starts "p-p-p." Make sure he understands you are giving it to him because it starts "p-p."

Staff Meeting, Wednesday

Collect and make things that will make a good noisy "p-p-parade" tomorrow with the children. Rhythm instruments, "*pans* and *pots*" to beat with spoons, two pot lids to clap together, two pieces of wood, jingle bells on a bracelet he can wear on his wrist, paper plates with coke tops fastened to the edges with string through a hole, etc.

Fourth Day, Thursday

Do everything all over again like Monday. Then tell the children you're going to have a "*p*arade, p-p-p parade." Give each a noisemaker. Line them up, gently. Laugh, all these things are play. If you have a marching record, play it, if you play the piano play a march. If not, just lead the parade, lifting your knees high and stepping sharply. Do this till most of your group (never more than eight children) do it and have fun. Make up a song about "pig's parade, p-p-p pig is having a p-p-parade"! Take the children back to the table and give them their "p-p-p" food. Ask the children if they can bring something tomorrow from home that starts "p-p-p, like pig" for your sound table.

Staff Meeting, Thursday

Trace your large letter "P" on separate squares of paper, one for each child in your group. Use black and white. Trace your pig next to the "p" on the same square of paper, so each child will have one. Get sandpaper and make exactly the same letter, the same size, out of sandpaper. Cut it out, one for each child. Get Elmer's Glue. Cut out old magazine pictures of things starting "p." Make a "book" for each child, with empty pages.

Fifth Day, Friday

Ask if any child brought something starting "p-p-p like pig." If anyone did, say the name of the object, and put it on the sound table. Hug the child, show everyone you are very proud. If a child brings something, but it doesn't start the right way, say the name of it, explain why it is different from "p-p," and say, "We will talk about that sound another time, bring this back then, but today we only want things that start like "pig, p-p-p." Trace your "p-p" again, name each object on the table again. Give each child his book and let him glue in his "p" sign, his sandpaper "p," and his picture cut from a magazine starting "p-p-p." Let each child trace over his "p" with his finger while you watch. Then let him draw a page full of them, as big as he wants. Collect the books. Tell the children "*p*lay, *p*-play, starts like pig, now we will run and *p*lay."

After school, take a large piece of paper. Take your "p" sign, with the pig, off the wall, and paste it in the top left corner of this paper. You are beginning a "sound chart."

APPENDIX E

Final Readiness Report: Is This Center Ready to Offer a Good Program for Children?

Name of Center________________________________

Where is it?________________________________

Name of Area Teacher Guide________________________________

Name of Other Members of Area Team Present Today____________

Date________________________

Was the meeting held in the Center? List staff members absent by name and position.

Is the building large enough for the number of children budgeted to play freely? Is each classroom large enough for children to move around and play in it?

Is the heat good? Are heaters safe from children?

Is there any sharp glass, nails, sharp corners, holes, broken steps or any other danger in the building or on the grounds?

Is the floor free from splinters and things to catch feet and trip on?

Each person on the staff must have a health card or a written statement proving that he tried and was refused one.

Is there a fence or some kind of rope arrangement to keep children from darting into the road?

What are the exact arrangements for serving food and drinks, including water, if the proper kitchen is not yet ready?

Each child must have a separate drinking container unless it is washed with some soap and water between uses.

Is there a place for the children to go to the bathroom?

There must be a bowl of water with disinfectant in it near the bathroom unless there is a wash bowl with running water.

Do the classrooms look like the community has worked hard to prepare an interesting and pretty place for children to play and work?

- —Is there a science area, labeled, with library books and homemade books in it?
- —Is there an art area, labeled, with places to work and places to keep things?
- —Is there a place with each child's name on it for him to keep his things and feel at home?

—Is there a number games table with games on it?
—Are there at least some tables and things to sit on?

DOES THE PLACE LOOK ATTRACTIVE, BRIGHT? GAY? FRESH?

—Are there many kinds of toys (dress up? store? doll house? blocks? stuffed animals and dolls? trucks, airplanes, cars?)

Does the playground look exciting and bright? Is there enough equipment for the units budgeted?
—At least one swing for every two units?
—A large sandpile with scoops, dishes, spoons, buckets?
—Something to climb on for each two units (ladders, climbing bars, jungle gyms, etc.?)
—Are there barrels, tires, boards, steps, and other kinds of fun outdoor play equipment?
—One seesaw for every two units?

IF ANY OF THE PLAYGROUND EQUIPMENT IS BROKEN, NOW IS THE TIME TO FIX IT.

Has the resource teacher attended orientation? If any have not, take their names, and plan an orientation in your area for them before opening.
Has the resource teacher read her material from orientation thoroughly?
Has every trainee worked with her resource teachers in discussing the printed material, including the newsletters?

NO PERSON MAY BEGIN WORK UNTIL HE HAS READ ALL THE MATERIAL AND KNOWS WHAT CDGM IS.

APPENDIX F

Report Form ATGs Devised to Help Them See Important Things at Centers

REPORT TO HELP THE AREA TEACHER GUIDE SEE THE IMPORTANT THINGS AT EACH OF HER CENTERS AND TO HELP US PLAN HOW TO HELP EACH CENTER BETTER

NAME OF CENTER______________________________

TOWN______________________________

YOUR AREA NUMBER AND YOUR OWN NAME______________________________

DATE OF THIS VISIT______________________________

SECTION ONE

It is very important for the Center to be a peaceful happy place for children. These questions are to help us know if anything is wrong with the *happiness* in this Center. Please use names in your report, don't just list problems without telling us WHO, so we can help that person.

STAFF AND STAFF

1. Are staff members fighting? Who is fighting? Why? What do you think we could do to help? Please tell us enough in your answer so we can help?

CHAIRMAN AND COMMITTEE

2. Is the chairman at this Center reading letters to the whole committee? Does the committee think and talk about the program for children? The activities? Does the chairman help the staff run a good program? Does the staff get along with the chairman? Are there any problems between the teachers and chairman or committee? What can we do to help? Have you talked to the AA about these problems so he can help too? Has this committee used its best common sense and judgment in hiring teachers? Could they find anyone better? Are you helping the committee understand their responsibility to choose people who need a job and people who are good with children? Are the part-time workers good with children too? If not, can you help the committee with this? If the chairman is employed at the Center as a teacher, is she doing both jobs well?

(She is not allowed to do any work while the children are there except work directly with them.)

TEACHERS AND PARENTS

3. Are the teachers working closely with parents and community people? Do parents take turns coming in to watch and help work with the children? Are there after-school meetings for parents to see each activity area and learn what their children are doing at the Center? Are refreshments served? Are there evening meetings where everyone talks about reading readiness, number understandings, reading to children, taking children to the library? On trips? Talk to children at home? Ask them questions about what they are doing and what they think? What are teachers helping parents do for children at home? Are people helping make rag dolls? Bring in dress-up clothes? Build playgrounds? Build shelves and tables and benches or chairs? Make curtains? This is a *community* school. What can we do to help the community act on this idea?

TEACHERS AND PARENTS

4. Is the teacher a *helping* person? Is each teacher gentle and kind and friendly to the children? Are we putting the government's money to good use and encouraging the children and admiring their play and work? Is there any teacher that the children dislike or are afraid of? Is there any teacher that just stands or sits around and does not work and talk with the children *all the time whatever they are doing?* Are there any indifferent teachers? Bored teachers? Teachers who are not enjoying the children? Is there a teacher who helps *too much* and does everything *for* the child instead of patiently showing him how to do it for himself? (Do teachers show children how to comb their hair? Do their buttons? Tie their shoes? Clean up toys? Scrub the table? Wash and dry their hands? Hang up coats and smocks? Set the table? Stir and mix paint and dough? Peel carrots? Be gentle with books? Set the table for lunch? Carry their own chairs? Spread their own rest mats and put them away when finished?) Does each teacher help each of the children in her group including the shy ones and the wild ones? Is there any teacher who uses harsh or frightening discipline? Is there any teacher who doesn't seem able to control children? How can we help teachers with these problems?

SECTION TWO

It is very important for the Center to be a *learning* place. People in Mississippi have not had opportunities to learn as much as they could. Our job is to bring the best in educational ideas and practices to the Centers. These questions are to help us know if there is anything we can do to help improve *learning experiences* for children. We know Centers are not doing all these things. We know they are not doing them perfectly (whatever that is!).

These questions are so we can plan how to help and what to help with. Please think about the ideas in your notebook when answering these questions.

GROUP COZY TIME

1. Is there some kind of circle time or together time at this Center where each child is personally welcomed by name and made to feel wanted and important? Do they talk about what they did yesterday? Do they plan and talk about what they will do today at this time? Does the teacher ask the child questions about something? A trip? Who is in his family? What he thinks about the Center? Lightning? Dogs? Do they sing? Do they sing songs with the child's name in? Do they take attendance? Does the child have a card with his name to put in a special place at this time? Is there a friendly feeling at this group time, or does it seem just like something to get done with? Is the teacher talking a lot? Is it interesting? Can each child see and hear?

OUTDOOR PLAY

2. Is there a half hour or hour of outdoor time? Do teachers play with children at this time? Does the teacher notice fights and help children fairly work them out? Does the teacher help each child get a turn if he wants one? Does she know what each child is playing? Does she talk with each child as he plays? Does she ask him questions and admire what he can do? Does the teacher help children count things at this time? Is the playground well equipped? If the playground could use more equipment, have you discussed this at staff meeting? Have you talked about it at a community meeting? Have you talked to the AA about greater help in building a playground from community people?

FREE CHOICE TIME

3. Is the room set up to encourage free choice time? Are there separate activity areas all around the room? If they don't all fit in one room, are children allowed to go from room to room as they wish at free choice time so they can really choose whatever they want when they want? Are shelves painted or covered brightly and freshly? Are teachers acting as hostesses in each area? Do any teachers need help in understanding what they need to do at free choice time? Are teachers moving around talking with children at free choice? Are teachers noticing floating children and helping them get busy? Are teachers helping the child who "quits" because his work or play is too hard? Does each teacher help the child solve the problem and continue until he is finished to his satisfaction? If you see teachers who need help, write their names so we can help them with this to make the program richer for children. Do you see a science table? Dress up and house-play corner? Scrubbing table? Story

corner where books are attractive? Is there a little rug or quilt near it for children to sit on? Is there a teacher there to invite children in groups of two or three to cuddle up and hear a story? Who is helping with the puzzles? Is she enjoying it? Who is helping and enjoying the blocks? Is there painting going on daily at this time? Dough daily? Have parents made trucks, airplanes, dolls, and other toys for boys and girls? Do teachers show children how to keep sets and puzzles together and tops on magic markers when they are not in use? Are children learning to take care of toys? To use them new ways? Do teachers help children make friends and play together? Do teachers help "problem" children at this time so they learn to have more fun and get along with others better? Do teachers respect children? Do they give them time to finish their work before they put toys away? Do children help put the things they were using away? Do they sing and talk while cleaning up? Is it a happy educational time too?

MEAL TIME

4. What is dinner time like? Do children help set tables? Do they serve themselves from bowls on each table? Do teachers sit with children and talk with them at dinner time? Do they teach good eating habits and talk about the food? Do they make a game of learning table manners? Do children clear the table themselves and wash it up? Do children sweep?

NAP TIME

5. What is rest time like? Are there enough quilts or mats so children are not too crowded? Are sleepers put where they can sleep and the restless ones put where they can get up after twenty minutes? Do teachers play quiet records or sing at rest time? Are teachers angry and threatening or gentle?

TRIPS

6. Does this Center take trips? Do teachers take small groups of children on talking walks in the neighborhood? Do they notice everything around them? Do a few children go with a teacher to the store to get supplies and groceries? Do they talk about the money (counting, subtracting, adding) and what they will buy and what they will do with it? Does each teacher take her children to the library *often* wherever there is a library available? Has the Center been to the zoo? Fire house? Post office? When they go, do they talk about it first in small groups so *every* child understands what is happening? Have they been to the doctor? Do they talk a lot about this to make it educational as well as medical? Do they talk about the trips later and the next day? Does each child get a chance to tell about what he saw? Does the teacher make a wall chart or book of his words? Does she read it to him every day? Is it on the story shelf where he can get it at free

choice time? Can you help your Center show the children more of the world?

STORY READING EACH DAY

7. Is there planned story time once or twice each day? Do the teachers get books from you? From the library? Do they make books? Do they sound like they have practiced the story the afternoon before so they read with interest, expression, and smoothness? Are the children comfortable at story time? Can each child hear? No more than seven children should be read to at once. Does story time follow an active kind of play? Are they using good books the children can understand? Do children like story time? Are you practicing reading stories at staff meeting and demonstrating how to do it well?
8. Are there clear labels, large, on things in the room? Do the teachers play word matching games with children each day where the child has a twin label and finds the one in the room that it matches? Is this boring? Fun? Is the teacher lively and interested in these games? Does each child get a turn? Does the teacher act friendly and helpful if the child gets it wrong? Does she help him get it right?
9. Do teachers use their other reading readiness games? Is there a time each day to play these games with seven or fewer children? At staff meeting, do you help teachers make copies of games and understand how to teach with them? Do you explain this at community meetings? Are teachers helping parents use games like this at home?
10. Is there a sound table in the room? Is there a sound lesson each day? Is it fun? Are children bringing in interesting things for the sound table? Are they doing activities that start with the sound they are studying? (Parade if they are studying "p," ball games if they are studying "b," etc.) Are teachers preparing each sound lesson the day before?

WORD CARD GAME

11. Does each teacher play the game of getting each child to give a word for his word card daily? Do they talk about his word? Does he have a place to keep all his words so they collect and he doesn't lose them? Do these words go home each night and come back each day?

NUMBERS DAILY

12. Is there a time each day for planned number games? Are Centers making and using many number games? Are children learning to *understand* numbers, not just to read and write and count them? Is there a number table with interesting games on it? Do teachers teach at this table daily? Is there a hostess at this table at free choice time?

ART DAILY

13. Is there an art time each day? Are teachers helping children do many different kinds of things in art?

MUSIC DAILY 14. How is music time? Do they sing Freedom songs, folk songs, children's songs, exercise songs? Do they play musical games? Is the phonograph going at free choice time? Do children listen to records for a few minutes at music time? Do they make up songs and parts of songs? Do they play or hear instruments? Do they dance? Do they act out animals and the wind and skip and jump and do other rhythm things at music time?

SPECIAL 15. If there is something special at this Center you think others should have a chance to learn about, describe it here. Have someone write it for the newsletter and *sign their name, job, and Center,* But also make a note of it here yourself. Is this a Center we should show visitors from out-of-state? Is it one of your best? Is this all-around a weak Center that needs extra help? Should we take our own teachers from other Centers to visit this Center? Why, to see what especially?

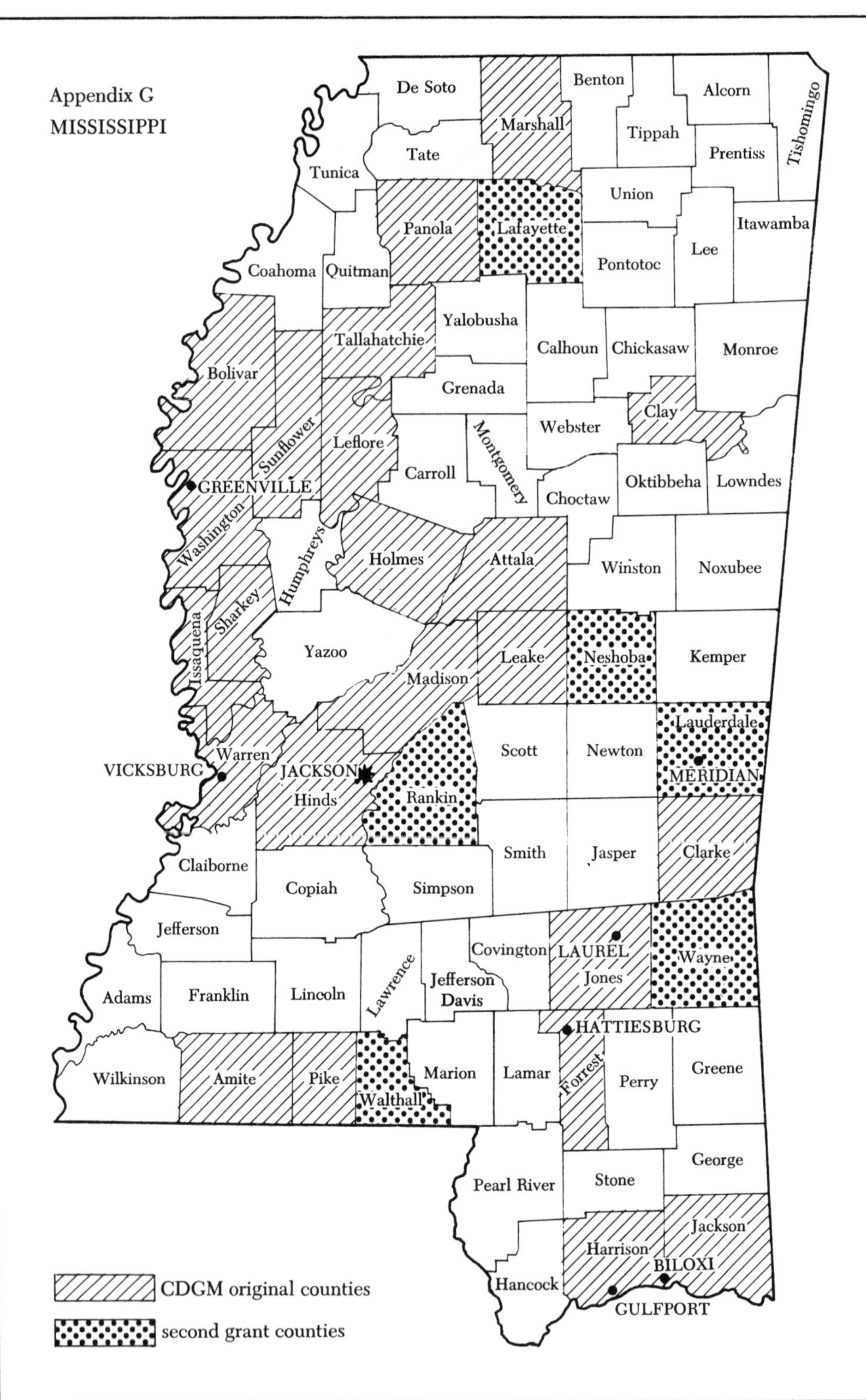

Appendix G
MISSISSIPPI
De Soto
Marshall
Benton
Alcorn
Tishomingo
Tate
Tippah
Prentiss
Tunica
Union
Panola
Lafayette
Itawamba
Lee
Coahoma
Quitman
Pontotoc
Yalobusha
Tallahatchie
Calhoun
Chickasaw
Monroe
Bolivar
Grenada
Clay
Sunflower
Leflore
Webster
Montgomery
Carroll
Oktibbeha
Lowndes
GREENVILLE
Choctaw
Washington
Humphreys
Holmes
Attala
Winston
Noxubee
Sharkey
Issaquena
Yazoo
Leake
Neshoba
Kemper
Madison
Lauderdale
Warren
Scott
Newton
VICKSBURG
JACKSON
MERIDIAN
Hinds
Rankin
Smith
Jasper
Clarke
Claiborne
Copiah
Simpson
Jefferson
Covington
LAUREL
Wayne
Jones
Adams
Franklin
Lincoln
Lawrence
Jefferson Davis
HATTIESBURG
Wilkinson
Amite
Pike
Marion
Lamar
Forrest
Perry
Greene
Walthall
George
Pearl River
Stone
Jackson
Harrison
BILOXI
Hancock
GULFPORT
CDGM original counties
second grant counties

References

Allport, Gordon W. *The Nature of Prejudice* (Reading, Mass., Addison-Wesley Publishing Company, Inc., 1954). A scholarly work on how prejudice operates on both sides.

Ashton-Warner, Sylvia. *Teacher* (New York, Simon and Schuster, Inc., 1963). Education involves excitement, creativity, relevance, to the life of the educatee.

Baldwin, James. *Go Tell It on the Mountain* (New York, The Dial Press, Inc., 1952). A glimpse of a family in the black ghetto.

Brown, Claud. *Manchild in the Promised Land* (New York, The Macmillan Company, 1965). The autobiography of a Northern urban ghetto Negro.

Bruner, Jerome S. *On Knowing* (Cambridge, Mass., The Belknap Press of Harvard University Press, 1962). An esoteric essay on learning theory and the common sense of how people learn.

Camus, Albert. *The Plague,* tr. Stuart Gilbert (New York, Alfred A. Knopf, Inc., 1948). A way of seeing life.

Camus, Albert. *The Rebel,* tr. Anthony Bower (New York, Alfred A. Knopf, Inc., 1956). A way of seeing life.

Ehle, John. *The Free Men* (New York, Harper & Row, Publishers, 1965). A depth study of nonviolence in North Carolina and how it affected all parts of the community.

Erickson, Erik H. *Childhood and Society* (New York, W. W. Norton & Company, Inc., 1950). A person "becomes" in a context.

Fanon, Frantz. *The Wretched of the Earth* (New York, Grove Press, Inc., 1963). There are black rebels elsewhere, too.

Farmer, James. *Freedom—When?* (New York, Random House, Inc., 1965). How and why CORE got started.

Fromm, Erich. *Man for Himself* (New York, Holt, Rinehart and Winston, Inc., 1947). What do we mean by a mature man?

Goodman, Paul, *Growing Up Absurd* (New York, Random House, Inc., 1956). What society and education do to potentially reasonable people.

Hansberry, Lorraine. *The Movement* (New York, Simon and Schuster, Inc., 1964). A beautiful and shocking picture book.

Hentoff, Nat. *Our Children Are Dying* (New York, The Viking Press, Inc.,). A description of a public school in New York City, the principal of which has a philosophy of nurturing living children, instead of letting them become lost and crushed people.

King, Martin Luther, Jr. *Why We Can't Wait* (New York, Harper and Row, Publishers, 1963). Feelings and facts involved in the nonviolent era.

Lincoln, Eric D. *The Black Muslims in America* (Boston, The Beacon Press, 1961). The history and explanation of one Black Power group.

Lorenz, Konrad. *On Aggression* (New York, Harcourt, Brace & World, Inc., 1963). Fascinating studies of aggression in animals by a biologist, with implications for man.

The Autobiography of Malcolm X (New York, Grove Press, Inc., 1964). Representative of much that many Black Power people feel.

Pearl, Arthur, and Riessman, Frank. *New Careers for the Poor* (New York, The Free Press, 1965). Theory and examples.

Silberman, Charles E. *Crisis in Black and White* (New York, Random House, Inc., 1964). A gripping study of the crisis and some causes.

Silver, James W. *The Closed Society*, enlarged edition (New York, Harcourt, Brace & World, Inc., 1963). Recent Mississippi before the "freedom summer," by a white Mississippian who welcomed change.

Styron, William. *The Confessions of Nat Turner* (New York, Random House, Inc., 1967). A novel.

Sutherland, Elizabeth, ed. *Letters from Mississippi* (New York, McGraw-Hill, Inc., 1965). Touching letters from Northern civil rights workers involved in the "freedom summer"—what it all meant to them.

Zinn, Howard. *The Southern Mystique* (New York, Alfred A. Knopf, Inc., 1964). Why the South can change.

FILM

Chance for Change (New York, Contemporary Films). A thirty-eight-minute black and white film about CDGM.

RECORD ALBUM

Head Start in Mississippi (Asch Recordings, #701). Community people and children sing in CDGM. A set of two long-playing records with printed words of songs.

INDEX: *Selected Topics*

BLACK POOR PEOPLE

CDGM PEOPLE

CONSULTANTS AND TEMPORARY STAFF FROM OUT OF STATE

EDUCATION
(also see film *Chance for Change*, McGraw Films, NY)

FREEDOM MOVEMENT

GOVERNMENT AGENCIES AND POLITICIANS

HARASSMENT OF CDGM

OFFICE OF ECONOMIC OPPORTUNITY

PRESS

RACE

WHITE HOUSE

NOTE: The following section of this book was not in the original 1969 edition; the index does not include the new pages.

BOOK THREE:

Assessment

(longitudinal)

After Words (1990)

PART VIII

Social Progress Occurs Inch by Inch, One by One (If Individuals Work at It)

1965–1990: CHILDREARING, EDUCATION, ECONOMICS, POLITICS—IT'S ALL ENTWINED, IT'S ALL THE CHILD'S ENVIRONMENT; "PROVIDING AN OPTIMAL ENVIRONMENT FOR THE LOW-INCOME MINORITY CHILD'S DEVELOPMENT" MEANS DEALING WITH ALL THIS RACISM, CLASSISM, AND POLITICKING WHEREVER WE ARE; IT MEANS HAVING GREAT PATIENCE; IT MEANS (TO QUOTE FORMER FARMER AND CDGM AREA TEACHER GUIDE HATTIE SAFFOLD, WHO IS NOW, THANKS TO HEAD START, A PUBLIC SCHOOL KINDERGARTEN TEACHER), "KEEPING ON KEEPING ON."

When I was a small girl, following the end of any anecdote or daily trivia tale my father would tell, I would inadvertently—but inevitably—annoy him by asking (with intense and very sincere interest), "What happened after that?"

My daddy died during the two-year time that his flock of beloved little stair-step granddaughters and I were living in Mississippi working first with CDGM and then on this Slippery Shoes book. Ed Brown, now Executive Director of the Voter Education Project, was at my house that morning; and Marian Wright came to call that sad Sunday, carrying a lovely bouquet of flowers. This caused my four-year-old Liza—we called her Biffie in those days, nowadays she's a public health policy professional—to urge that we send flowers to our Gramma in Wisconsin, "because she will be so unhappy, and flowers make you smile." Then Liza's face clouded; a disappointing thought had occurred. "Oh, no, we can't mail her flowers," she said. "Flowers would rot in the mail." Suddenly, sunshine filled her face and, inspired with a grand idea, she added, "But we could send seeds so Gramma can grow flowers!"

So my dad doesn't know what happened after 1966. Well, what's happened with Head Start since the sixties is quite amazing. We surely did plant seeds and some wondrous flowers have grown! Especially in CDGM, the most remarkable Head Start ever because poor people operated it for their own children and for the children of their own communities. In these "after words," I'll touch lightly upon a handful of highlights.

In 1990, Head Start celebrated its 25th anniversary; a quarter of a century has slipped by since CDGM's—and the national Head Start program's—first chaotic summer, the summer of 1965.

In its first twenty five years, Head Start has chalked up an incredible record of achievement. It has won widespread support from Head Starters' parents, public school people who receive children who have come in and up through Head Start, and policy makers who realize that Head Start is a sound investment because children who enter school healthy, full-bellied, having had a happy taste of learning through friendships, play, projects, simple excursions, and parental example of involvement in personal growth do better in school, hence in later life. Included, too, in Head Start's corps of supporters are the National Governors' Association, the Committee on Economic Development, the National Conference of State Legislatures, the Children's Defense Fund (which has—under the extraordinary leadership of Marian Wright Edelman—more than once led successful efforts to save Head Start's life), and the National Head Start Association.

The National Head Start Association (NHSA) is a membership organization representing the parents, staff, directors and friends of Head Start programs across the country. NSHA was launched in 1983 (and FYI, its present Vice President, Arvern Moore, started with Head Start when Head Start started—he started with CDGM in Holly Springs, Mississippi). In the fall of 1989, NHSA convened a panel of distinguished advisors to examine what has made Head Start such a smashing success and how the program should be expanded and improved. Everyone interested in Head Start's future needs to read this report. Whether or not we agree with all specifics, we must get involved by writing to congress-people in Head Start's behalf.

For innumerable poor families and eleven million young children in and far beyond Mississippi, Head Start has been a miracle program. As a woman in Tallahatchie County told me in 1990, "In our family, Head Start (CDGM) planted lots of seeds. Miracle seeds."

CHAPTER 44

UNHEALTHY, LESS UNHEALTHY, LESS UNHEALTHY—

Inching toward a bottom line basic: good health

HEAD START WAS designed (in the fall of 1964) with a "health first" focus. For this reason, a *physician*, Dr.Robert E. Cooke, was selected by Poverty Program Tsar R. Sargent Shriver as chairman of a Head Start Planning Committee; and a *pediatrician* with a wealth of background in mental health, social services, and early childhood education, Dr. Julius B. Richmond, was named National Head Start Director.

Dr. Richmond convinced the American Academy of Pediatrics, whose physicians usually treat only private patients, to become much more active in the health problems of low-income children. This was valuable indeed because, according to Dr. Reginald Lourie, the psychiatrist on the Planning Committee who several years later designed Head Start's wonderful Parent Child Centers, the statistics on the number of unknown and untreated health problems that were uncovered could have become a national scandal, had they been publicized.

Gertrude Hunter, M.D., first Health Services Coordinator for the national Head Start program, who is both black and female, says,

"We found large numbers of children who had never seen a doctor. The health system thought it had everything under control. It was unaware of all the families that had never come near it. Some of us knew about poverty. I kept after Head Start decision makers on this subject. Most of them weren't too pleased."

Health is basic to any person's ability to learn optimally in school and afterwards; take advantage of growth opportunities throughout life; get, hold, and do a good job on the job; be a good parent; be a positive participant in America's democratic way of life; and enjoy the blessings that this country can, when it chooses to (which is not, in most cases, to poor people) offer.

Today, for low-income children, Head Start is the leading health care system in the United States. According to the January 1990 Project Head Start Statistical Fact Sheet: In 1985–86, ninety-nine percent of the children enrolled ninety days or more completed medical screening including all of the appropriate tests, and ninety-eight percent of those identified as *needing* treatment *received* treatment. Ninety-eight percent of the children enrolled ninety days or more completed dental examinations, and ninety-six percent of those *needing* dental treatment *received* dental treatment. Ninety-eight percent of the children had completed all of the required immunizations or were up-to-date on them.

While we take justifiable pride in these accomplishments, we must simultaneously sober ourselves with awareness of the appalling fact that four out of five preschool children eligible for Head Start are prevented from enrolling due to lack of Congressional funding for slots. This means that eighty percent of the children who should be benefitting from the nation's number one health program are *not*. They are *not* ensured immunizations; nutritious food; medical, mental health, and dental screening exams; and treatment as needed, although some percent of them may be taken care of via other routes. Furthermore, millions more children who are three, two, one, or younger, who, with their families, could benefit immeasurably from infant/toddler, parent/child Head Start services, are not provided for in the dollar allocation Head Start is given. We must also remind ourselves that we are a backward nation and have as yet no system of national health insurance *for all of us.*

Today, Head Start's two thousand Health Coordinators, a great many of them former Head Start parents, are confronted with the same problems of coordinating health and mental health services for each center, and for each child, and of reaching hard-, harder-, and hardest-to-reach family members and enlisting them as managers of their children's participation in their communities' health system and—where appropriate—mental health system, that have *always* confronted them in Head Start. But today, Health Coordinators *also* are faced with some confounding *new* problems: HIV-infected children, large numbers of children born afflicted with cocaine- or alcohol-addicted mothers and with resulting fetal cocaine or alcohol syndrome, and other such vicious equal opportunity destroyers. These situations and conditions handicap children right from the start.

One of President Lyndon Johnson's, Sargent Shriver's, and Jule Sugarman's original objectives for Head Start was to get it to the poorest of the poor—to the three hundred poorest counties in the country. Jules Sugarman, in particular, who had had considerable experience with federal grant programs, was determined that the sophisticated cities and counties surrounding major metropolises not gobble up all the grant money "as usual" before out-of-the-way rural ne'er-do-well counties even heard of Head Start. A number of the three hundred poorest counties in the United States were—and still *are*—in Mississippi. Moreover, Mississippi was—and still *is*—the poorest *state* in the United States. To its credit, in this case the government stuck to its guns, and for many years, in spite of constant complaints from powerful states and municipalities which claimed that they weren't getting their fair share, Mississippi got more money for Head Start than any other state, as well it should have; it needed it most.

The health situation for Mississippi's black children is still grim. Too many children are not adequately nourished because of poverty. Over seventy percent of the state's children qualify for free and reduced school lunches; but their younger-than-five siblings are not *in* school and may not *get* lunch. A Mississippi family qualifying for food stamps may receive an amount less than two-thirds of the national average. Mississippi leads the nation in teen pregnancy with black youth affected more than white, and Mississippi is second only to Washington, D.C., in its unmarried mother birth rate. Since the sixties, some progress has been made in infant mortality, but Mississippi still ranks first in the nation, and black babies are almost twice as likely as white babies to die before their first birthday. Mississippi still ranks fiftieth in physicians per hundred thousand persons. But thanks to Head Start, other federal, state and local efforts, some innovative private projects, and above all, thanks to many of the Magnolia State's dedicated African American physicians, there has been—inch by inch, one by one, great improvement during the past quarter century.

Review the earlier chapter in this book, "Medical and Social Services Programs: CDGM vs. Mississippi," and note the difference reflected below.

Says the Reverend Ed King (see pp. 205 and 622), Associate Professor in the School of Health Related Professions of the University of Mississippi Medical Center,

"The State Public Health Department has done an excellent job in health, mental health, and social services. The leadership is still white, but these are caring, dedicated people. As more black physicians get degrees in public health, we'll begin to see blacks in higher places. There isn't the racism and classism there was in the health department in the sixties. There *is* racism and classism—but no more than you find in other states." Ed King teaches the sociology of health care, and medical ethics.

Ed King is a wonder of wonders for a number of reasons.

First, he is one of that rare breed, like Hazel Brannon Smith—native white Mississippians who began, in the 1950s and 1960s, to realize the wrongness of racial segregation and white supremacy, *to speak out*, to refuse to be run out of Mississippi, *and to continue to speak out* in spite of boycotts and bombings. That was an era when leaders who spoke or wrote about the immorality and illegality of white sovereignty were forced to leave the state; leaders like the pastor of the largest Methodist church in Mississippi, or Jim Silver who was chairman of the history department at Ole Miss and author of *The Closed Society.* That era saw the temporary collapse of the white moderate sector, a collapse that lasted into the 1970s. In response to the 1954 U.S. Supreme Court school desegregation decision, racist extremists took over. White moderates at the universities, at leadership levels of every denomination, in the press, and in politics (U.S. Congressman Frank Smith, for example) were silenced or run out of the South (Representative Smith lost his seat in Congress). Ed King, on the other hand, a Vicksburg born Mississippian, participated in the sit-ins.

Secondly, Ed became deeply involved in the Freedom Democratic Party, a political party of black people and others devoted to the principle of civil rights for blacks as well as whites. (For information about the Freedom Democratic

Party—FDP—look in the index under the category heading Freedom Movement.) Ed had attended a private white Mississippi college, Millsaps College, in the 1950s. He then left the state and went to Boston University for divinity degrees, and on to Harvard for another degree in sociology and religion. In the process, he had learned a thing or two about interracialism. When Ed returned to Mississippi and saw what was going on he quickly became convinced that black people could only escape the incredible conditions in which they lived if they and their allies took matters into their own hands and began working assertively for change.

Thirdly, in the eyes of a beholder of Mississippi in the 1960s, Ed King is a wonder of wonders because with a background like that, he is a tenured faculty person at the University of Mississippi. About the health scene Ed adds,

"Aaron Shirley and James Anderson are black pediatricians who have been very involved in starting several health clinics for the black community." They are also very involved in Democratic politics. Dr. Shirley was an early director of MAP. Ed says, "These are very demoralizing times for Mississippi's public health people, though. They've made many gains, and they set realistic goals for a good rate of continuing improvements, but with the federal and state cutbacks in funding, there just isn't money to continue the rate of progress we had expected. For instance, T.B. had been gotten under control and now it's coming back. We don't want to back down the ladder we've been climbing rung by rung. It's a very bad sign, a statement of willingness to neglect the basics, when a society allows an old problem that's been successfully beaten to recur. I guess there is so little concern in this country about improving poor people's health because doing it won't result in a profit for anyone."

As taxpayers, why do any of us tolerate cutting back funding for fundamental health care anywhere in America?

As to the state's dedicated black physicians, here is one example of inch by inch, one by one.

Robert Smith, M.D., who was instrumental in CDGM's health program (he is referred to but not named on page 184 of this book) has been a major hero. Robert Smith went to elementary school in a four-room segregated school for black children in rural Mississippi. Until the year before he was ready to go to high school at the end of the 1940's, there *wasn't* one for people of his color in the county. Fortunately for him, a high school, complete with second-hand school bus, opened in Utica. He and about one hundred other students who lived scattered all over the entire county attended. Robert bounced along country dirt roads—rode seventy five miles a day to get some secondary education. He and fewer than a dozen classmates continued to college and graduated, Robert Smith from Tougaloo College in Tougaloo, Mississippi, founded in 1869 by the American Missionary Association—whose mission was emphatically *human freedom* on the five hundred acre site of a former plantation.

Smith had already decided to become a doctor. At the time—the early 1950s—

Tougaloo, still unaccredited back then, was the only college open to blacks in Mississippi that offered a definitive premed program.

Today, although less than one percent of all the African American students who go to college in Mississippi go to Tougaloo, twenty eight percent of Mississippi's black dentists, forty percent of its black physicians, and fifty percent of its black attorneys have received their bachelor's degrees from Tougaloo College, which has about one thousand students at any one time, a dapper and eloquent president named Adib A. Shakir, a "first lady"—Annette Shakir—with a doctorate in education and a professional life of her own, and a powerful spirit of African American pride. In 1957, Tougaloo was among the first Negro colleges in the South to be fully accredited by the Southern Association of Colleges and Schools. Tougaloo College boasts many remarkable graduates including, to name but a few, John Milton Wesley (Fannie Lou Hamer's godson and a poet who received his graduate training at Yale University), Ollye Brown Shirley (regional director of the Children's Television Workship and Chair of the Jackson School Board), Walter Turnbull (founder and director of the internationally acclaimed Harlem Boys' Choir), Ed Blackman (representative in the Mississippi State Legislature), Dr. Walter Washington (president of Mississippi's Alcorn State University), Dr. Joffre Whisenton (former president of Southern University in Baton Rouge, Louisiana), and the Honorable Reuben Anderson (a Mississippi Supreme Court justice). Tougaloo College and its remarkable faculty are a prime example of how social progress occurs *if we work at it;* it occurs person by person, student by student, one by one.

Tougaloo and Brown University have long had a mutually enriching exchange program; you may recall (page 32 of *Slippery Shoes*) that Dr. Owens was, in the spring of 1965 when CDGM was desperately seeking an institution of higher education to serve as the recipient of the federal Head Start grant, the *acting* president of Tougaloo College, and was apprehensive about rocking the boat in which Tougaloo and Brown University were newly sitting together by getting more involved in civil rights than Tougaloo already was. It's fairly clear why Tougaloo College, rather than Mary Holmes Junior College, was Arthur Thomas's first choice for CDGM's token Head Start grant recipient.

In 1957, after graduating from Tougaloo, Robert Smith who refers to Tougaloo as "an oasis," went on to Howard University School of Medicine in Washington, D.C., where he was the only person accepted from Tougaloo's class of twenty five premed students. (Both Howard Medical School and Meharry Medical School in central Tennessee accepted Tougaloo premed students throughout the years when other medical schools were not open to black students; Meharry took many more than did Howard. Beginning in the 1940s, other medical schools, Northwestern and Tufts early among them, began admitting black students. [The May 1989 issue of *Money Magazine* identified Tougaloo College as the least expensive school in the United States that sends fifty percent of its graduates to graduate and professional schools, probably because from the day they get there, Tougaloo students are encouraged to think about grad school.] Many doctors, dentists, and other health professionals, regardless of where they train, return to Mississippi to serve their people, generally for very little money compared to what they could earn elsewhere.)

Robert Smith did his internship at Cook County Hospital in Chicago, where he was one of five out of 1,000 house staff. To his amazement, here in the nonsegregated North, there were no black doctors in any of fifty-two area hospitals, and only five black doctors had privileges at hospitals other than the predominantly black Providence Hospital. He and a small group of other black interns, residents, and young doctors campaigned to win equal privileges with white doctors, a movement which became nationwide.

When young Dr. Smith returned to Mississippi in 1962, he found himself in the midst of the flaming civil rights movement. James Meredith was attempting to enter Ole Miss, the entirely white state university; the Sovereignty Commission (whose sealed archives, by the way, are now, after all these years of secrecy, open to the public) was engaged in its infamous activities (the unsealed papers reveal that the Sovereignty Commission was doing even more deviltry than we thought!); and other events chronicled in this book were going on. Robert Smith went to work first for the Mississippi State Hospital, and then for Baptist Hospital, where he was allowed to function only in the segregated "green annex." Although in the early 1960s there were about eight-hundred thousand black people in Mississippi, there were only twenty-five Black M.D.s. White doctors treated black patients, but they had two waiting rooms, and one was considerably more of a *waiting* room than the other.

Robert Smith was a founding member of the Medical Committee for Civil Rights, which used nonviolent methods to secure membership in the American Medical Association for minority physicians in order that they could get hospital privileges. Angered over the tragic assassination of Medgar Evers, Smith answered a call to help organize a Medical Committee for *Human* Rights. The first organizational meeting was held in Smith's office. At that meeting, he met Tom Levin, from whom the call had come. Dr. Smith became a founding member of MCHR, initiated by Tom Levin, to provide medical care for poor people and civil rights workers alike—to serve as the medical wing of the civil rights movement. (The impetus for Tom to start organizing the Medical Committee for Human Rights, which led to his call to Robert Smith, was a call *he* received from Aaron Henry in Clarksdale, Mississippi, the day after the three disappeared in Philadelphia, Mississippi, and were feared dead; Aaron urged Tom to get *M.D.s* to Mississippi. The idea was that they could help keep civil rights workers from bleeding to death, and, because Klansmen were less likely to kill with media material M.D.s standing by, would make workers feel more secure.) Dr. Smith has been instrumental in establishing community health centers around the state of Mississippi, is founder and director of the Mississippi Family Health Center, and is chief of staff of Hinds County General Hospital.

Dr. Smith says, "It did not surprise me at all that Tom Levin came back the next summer to organize CDGM. CDGM was the first program since slavery that granted black people some power. Many four- and five-year olds had never seen a doctor. College students I see *now* got treatment and dental care in Head Start.

Head Start is a remarkable program, and CDGM was a remarkable Head Start.''

Intelligent assessment of a program like Head Start's (and CDGM's) health component takes into account much more than specifics such as how many children got shots. How has this program facilitated and accelerated progressive and positive trends already ongoing in the low-income family or community, we must ask? To what extent has this program, we need to inquire, activated people in their own behalf, or added more impetus or more individuals to the effort, or given greater stature and resources to people and institutions that were already making significant contributions to community improvement? No program for poor children can reasonably be evaluated as a separate entity, although that is almost always the way these programs *are* evaluated. A new health, education, or other human service program doesn't start in a vacuum. It's dropped (or, far better, it sprouts, as did CDGM) in a community with a past, present, and future. As part of assessing any program for low-income children and their families, we should investigate how helpful the program is perceived to be (or to have been), especially as a step toward the *next* step, whatever that is.

From Herb Doctor Seth Ballard, Sr., of Pocahantas, Mississipi, trained by an ancient slave in the use of making salves, potions, teas, and tonics from roots, flowers, barks, and lotions; to Dr. Sidney D. Redmond, son of Ebeneezer, Mississippi, slaves and sharecroppers, who made his way to and through Rust College in Holly Springs, Meharry, and Harvard Medical School—then back to practice in Jackson; and to all the dedicated African American medical and health professionals who have *been* there when few white specialists were, we owe gratitude. The trends we've been touching upon continue in the 1990s: Many Tougaloo College graduates continue to go into medicine—to go out of state to medical school and to return to practice in Mississippi. And the physicians get better and better. One recent example is Carl Reddix, M.D., a Tougaloo chemistry major and graduate who went to Tufts University School of Medicine and Harvard University's School of Public Health. After a stint as Chief Resident at Johns Hopkins's Department of Obstetrics and Gynecology, Dr. Reddix returned to Jackson. As this brief introduction to medical training for Mississippi indicates, in spite of major health problems, especially for poor people, especially for poor black people, Mississippi is on the right track. This is as true in dentistry and nursing as it is with regard to physicians. Progress is also apparent in several troublesome health related areas such as the teen birth rate and births to unmarried women (who often *are* teenagers).

An interesting aspect of this subject that must certainly be included in a ''since the sixties after word'' about the health universe in Mississippi is the extraordinary role African American *pharmacists* played in the Civil Rights movement. These men dispensed a lot more than medicine. Pharmacies used to be one of the few businesses blacks owned. (Funeral parlors were another.) In the 1940s, '50s, and '60s many black pharmacists owned their *own* pharmacies; now, although there are fifty black pharmacists in the state, only twelve of them own their own establishments, probably in part because white-owned drugstores now hire black pharmacists.

An example of the pharmacist/civil rights connection is the case of Dr. Fielder. The drugstore of Dr. Alvin Fielder, Sr. of Meridian, a 1933 graduate of the Meharry Medical School's pharmacy program and a founder of the Mississippi Pharmaceutical Society, was the usual meeting spot for martyr Medgar Evers, murdered "for the cause" in 1963, and northern civil rights lawyers. Dr. Fielder also rented an apartment to the soon-to-be-slain civil rights workers James Earl Chaney, Andy Goodman, and Mickey Schwerner when no one else in war zone Meridian dared to. Pharmacists cashed out-of-state checks for civil rights workers when no one else would, and posted bail for them when they were (routinely) incarcerated for crimes such as "reckless walking" (read "voter registration").

Dr. Aaron E. Henry, owner of the Fourth Street Drug Store in Clarksdale, is, of course, famous far and wide for his decades of work with the Democratic Party and the NAACP. Aaron is president of the Mississippi State Conference of NAACP and a member of the national NAACP board of directors. He is also the majority stockholder in WLBT, Mississippi's largest television station. My, oh my, how times do change!

As has been shown, CDGM was forever being charged with a sin called "civil rights involvement." Is it possible to meaningfully assess Head Start's health component without examining how successfully it has influenced policymakers at local, state, and federal levels to become more active in behalf of better health care for minority and nonminority poor people?

Even at Head Start headquarters, officials had no idea how little health care America's poor children were getting. During its first summer, Head Start rarely paid for children to be treated. Only due to ardent advocacy from all sides was this policy altered. Dr. Richmond. National Head Start Director, says he knew the situation, but was afraid that if all children who needed it were treaated at Head Start's expense, the budget for every program component would be spent on health alone. However, we can all learn from aroused poor people who won't take no for an answer. When he heard that this book was going to be re-issued, Bob Clampitt, first Deputy Director, then Acting Director, Office of Inspection and Special Projects at OEO wrote to me. Among other things, Bob (with whom I had worked closely when I was an OEO staff person myself) said

> I remember your dedication in finding progressive Head Start sponsors in the Southeastern U.S. at a time when conservatives were trying to co-opt the program. I remember very well that it was you who alerted me to some key issues in the Head Start program—especially our failure to include medical treatment . . .CDGM was a truly innovative and pioneering program involving "maximum feasible participation" of the poor as few progams have. Indeed, the extraordinary and extensive role played by the Mississippi people who were served by CDGM in every aspect of its planning and implementation gave it an almost unique character among OEO's funded programs.

Head Start now fills teeth and fits eyeglasses, and that is a great contribution. But increasing awareness of gaps, lacks, low quality, and insultingly inferior service in the health care system is needed too. And even awareness, left at that, will not do. It isn't enough.

Pressuring the multiple aspects of the health care system to close gaps through collaborative coordination, to create whatever is required to eliminate lacks, to provide high quality care and respectful, responsive service is *also* needed. Awareness is virtually useless if it fails to lead to action. Is it accurate to say that such involvement is not political? When we educate the allocators of funds in our communities, states and nation about the unmet general and specialized needs of low-income children and their families, and when we strongly, ceaselessly encourage them to take action, we are lobbying. Lobbying is a vital part of our country's political process. The American Medical Association lobbies. The cigarette companies lobby. The pharmaceutical and health insurance companies lobby. The industries that dangerously pollute our air, water, and earth lobby. Why should it be considered any *more* political to lobby for poor people's health rights? "Civil rights" means "the rights of citizens." Among these rights, the right to adequate preventive and curative health care seems one of the most basic and essential.

Activating local, state, and national level shapers and makers of laws, and allocators of funds, means engaging in advocacy work with legislators, other politicos, and candidates for elected office. It means engaging in a right given to us by our forefathers, the right to vote for those who will best represent us in areas that concern us and on issues to which we are committed. Therefore, intelligent assessment of Head Start's health component necessitates looking at how well Head Start educates people about health issues and about how to use the political process to promote outcomes deemed desirable. This includes promoting voting (one way or another).

Intelligent assessment of Head Start's Health component includes examining how successful it has been in activating the American Academy of Pediatrics, the American Public Health Association, the American Dental Association, the American Nursing Association, the American Psychological Association, the American Psychiatric Association, et. al. at local, state, and federal levels to donate appropriate services to Head Start, but also to participate in the political process in an effort to improve the health care system America provides (or doesn't provide) for its low-income citizens. Dr. Julius B. Richmond, first national Head Start Director, worked hard to involve these groups. Regrettably, much less has been accomplished along these lines in more recent years.

Intelligent assessment of Head Start's health component must include measurement of increased activity in the medical world regarding the renovation of medical schools to better aquaint their faculty and students with daily life as poor people experience it, including working with family members in their homes, their communities, and their homeless shelters, and to better acquaint their faculty and students with health care as poor people *deserve* to experience it.

CDGM's health coordinators gave people information about the whereabouts of ordinary and specialized health services (to the extent that there were any of either), and about their health rights. In many cases, people didn't have this knowledge. Knowledge is power. Part of "empowering parents"—a popular phrase these days—is ensuring that they have knowledge of (1) "the system's" offerings, (2) how to operate the system as well as is possible for an outsider, and

(3) *how to protest most effectively when adequate services don't exist.* CDGM health coordinators gave people courage and kept them company so they could confront the system when it didn't graciously offer its services in the first place. This, health personnel seldom do when poor people are the clientele. The problem isn't confined to Mississippi. While there are innumerable health professionals who exemplify the ideal, most low-income people have loads of anecdotes about atrocities (emotional, intellectual, and even physical) committed by the health care system.

Because, as the story of Robert Smith, M.D., shows, health care is part of a bigger educational and political picture, significant assessment of Head Start's health component has to investigate the extent to which it offers its two thousand Health Coordinators *training in organizing the Head Start community (parents, staff, and friends) around health issues.* Because the health scene for poor people is pocked with so much ugliness, an urgent effort Head Start can make to help its constituency is to train health activists who are well informed about

- how the health care system works at local, state, and federal levels;
- how to link up with an influence more members of the AAP and the APHA, and other relevant health-related organizations; and
- how to lobby political candidates and officeholders.

Head Start has always been committed to the concept of "upward bound" and "new careers" opportunities for the poor. (See New Careers heading in index category "Poor Black People.") A new career called Health Advocate would be a useful addition to the universe of allied health professionals. The closest we come is the public health nurse, but she is hampered from being a one hundred percent poor family's advocate because she can only refer within the limited sphere of what's available in the public health care system, and without rocking the health establishment's boat too much; the hospital ombudsman (but you have to be hospitalized to use him); the medical social worker (rarely available to everyday young children from average low-income families); and Head Start social service coordinators. Social service coordinators can focus on Head Start families' needs, but they also have to recruit children for Head Start, have dozens of other duties, and have absurdly large "case loads." Health Coordinators who chose to participate in an Associate of Arts degree program—Health Advocate Associate—structured as is the national Child Development Associate credentialing program, could remain in this new career with Head Start or another employer, or could continue developing their careers—go on to nursing, physician's assistant, dental, medical, public health, college or graduate school programs.

Perhaps, if we work at it, progress can be brought about faster than inch by inch.

CHAPTER 45

CLIMBING THE ECONOMIC LADDER RUNG BY RUNG

Head Start—part of a multi-pronged anti-poverty program

IF IT IS to live up to its original intention of offering poor families opportunities, a way up and out of the various suffocations and frustrations which enshroud many family members, Head Start must keep uppermost its tradition of offering an educational and employment "hand up."

One of the earliest memos in Head Start's archives of which I have a copy—you recall that I was an Office of Economic Opportunity staff member at the time that Head Start was invented—emphasizes the major role that opportunity for parents to participate in the program, and opportunity for parents to have paid jobs in the program, were to play.

CDGM, of course, reserved *all* the classroom teaching jobs, *all* the social service coordinator jobs, *all* the health coordinator jobs, *all* the administration, custodial, transportation, and cook jobs—in other words, *all* center and area level jobs and most central staff jobs, for parents and their peers. There are many people in poor neighborhoods and rural areas who are in good enough health and mental health to work, although there are certainly some who aren't. This is as true today in urban ghettos as it was in the 1960s in rural areas. *Many people need only opportunity.*

Nationwide, Head Start has had an excellent track record with regard to encouraging people to become involved in the program as volunteers and paid employees, and to become involved in literacy, adult education, job training, community college, and college programs. Although some grantees don't adhere to this important cornerstone of the Head Start philosophy, and *many* don't do as well as they might, educational opportunities and new careers for the poor continue to be core Head Start concepts. The most effective and permanent way to help "the children of poverty" is to enable their parents to learn and earn themselves into the middleclass *if they want to*—that is, to allow the children to become "the children of the middleclass." It's a plus if the jobs that enable people to learn and earn are meaningful jobs, new *careers*, for example careers as specialists in human services for poor people.

Any evaluation of Head Start, and of the present proliferation of programs for low-income young children that are alleged to be "Head Start-like," must include examining and weighing how well each program is enabling its families to clamber out of poverty, leading their children toward lives of greater opportunity.

If it is to live up to its initial "economic opportunity" intent, Head Start and its communities must ensure that easy-to-reach, ready-to-go (or *almost* ready-to-go) parents who are in excellent or fairly good shape physically and mentally, and who lack only opportunities or awareness of them, get connected to volunteer roles and then to

- paid jobs in the program (in classroom, kitchen, custodial, health or social services, family support, transportation, administration, or other aspects of the program) *with on-the-job training and career ladders* where applicable, permitting people, if capable, to earn credentials and eligibility for further advancement in or outside of the Head Start system,
- continuing education (learn to read, complete a G.E.D., get technical training, earn an A.A. degree at an area community college, earn a four-year degree, etc.) through vigorous, gap-closing collaboration between Head Start and other programs and institutions, and, if necessary, guidance in subsequent job finding through community networks,
- ancillary services, as needed, so people who are willing and able to work *can* (health care, child care, transportation),
- or just help in locating a job if employment *opportunities* are the problem rather than lack of *employability.*

That there are a small percent of "unredeemable" families whose children we surely should "rescue," and that there are an even smaller number of abandoned children who *have* no families—children who are certainly society's responsibility to care for as therapeutically as possible—is not an excuse for us to fail to make every effort to offer every child's family whatever supports our sophisticated human services system has in the way of a hand up.

When reminded that such support systems cost money, Marian Edelman, our very own CDGM Board member Marian Wright Edelman, reknown children's crusader and founding President of the Children's Defense Fund in Washington, D.C., usually says, "There ain't no cheap grace. One way or another the taxpayer will pay. If you don't like crime and welfare, pay up front,it's less expensive and more humane. There are no shortcuts. We're just going step-by-step up the stairs."

Any evaluation of Head Start, to be meaningful, must include an examination of the hundreds upon hundreds of happy stories, success stories that abound in any up-to-par Head Start program that's been around for a while.

With respect to CDGM, the Child Development Group of Mississippi, every time we turn around we run into multi-generational success stories like the one that follows:

Alean M. Adams and her husband were very active in civic affairs even before

Head Start (CDGM) came to their state. Mr. Adams was a leader in the local NAACP group. In this connection, the couple joined in the early sixties effort to open the University of Mississippi to black people. The Adams' part in the project was to risk their lives by marching with James Meredith, the man who integrated Ole Miss, and to use their home as a headquarters for marchers. They also helped bail civil rights workers out of jail, fed them, though food for the family was in short supply, and ran a Freedom School in their house.

"I raised my children in community meetings. There are just things you do because they need to be done," says Mrs. Adams. "My mother fed everybody, too. Her pot was always full. There were always neighbors' hungry children playing around, and she would pour more water in the peas and say, 'It will be enough to go around, the Lord will provide'; and it always *did* go 'round—the Lord always *did* provide.

"She and my father were sharecroppers. They got married when they were seventeen. My father's parents died young so he and my mother raised his six siblings along with their *own* six, starting when they were teenagers. My mother never knew her parents. Her grandparents raised her. My mother has a low self image; I think it's partly because she never knew her parents and she doesn't read well. She's very, very patient. She finds the best in everyone. My father was a very hard worker.

"Like my husband. My husband has always worked to support all these things I did in the community and at church. (My church is 142 years old. It was organized by eleven slaves.) My husband is a mechanic. He fixed the bus that carried people from our area to the famous March on Washington. The summer after we had the Freedom School, we opened the first Head Start center (CDGM) in Rankin County. I had several of my children in Head Start. When I started working there in 1965, I had completed 11th grade. I went to STAR and got a G.E.D. Then I went to TIECE [the Tougaloo Institute for Early Childhood Education, a Child Development Associate type program for mature women started by CDGM in 1967 at Mary Holmes Junior College—a number of years before the *national* CDA program was developed. After the two year degree, I attended Tougaloo College and got a master's in elementary education. I couldn't have done all this if my husband hadn't been working. For a while, two of my daughters were at Tougaloo at the same time I was. Chemistry was *so* hard, I told my husband I thought I might drop out. Then one of my daughters wrote a paper saying that I was her inspiration. I *couldn't* drop out! I've been teaching public school for twelve years now.

"After they changed our Head Start from CDGM to a different grantee, parent involvement in the program and in the community wasn't wanted. They told the whole group of us to stop. But you have to do this work—in the family, church, school and community, to improve opportunities for your children.

"Things in Mississippi are much better for black people now, we worked and worked at it, and we're still working. Progress is a family thing, lots of people are involved over the generations. One thing that has helped a lot in so many ways—health, economics, education—is Head Start. Head Start is a program to help the whole family improve itself. I was in on Head Start (CDGM, the Pisgah center) from the beginning."

By any conventional early childhood educator's standards, Pisgah, and almost all of the dozens of other CDGM Head Start centers, were not good. Certainly they were not "developmentally appropriate." But the Head Start experience for children and families can't accurately be assessed by measuring only (or even mainly) what goes on in the classroom. *Head Start, and other social programs, have to be looked at in terms of how they fit into a family's and community's ongoing life—its ecology—in terms of what additional opportunities they offer and whether or not this is the maximum feasible opportunity they could offer.* The reason most Head Start programs are average is that most do not offer families maximum feasible opportunity for the development of each member. Growing up in a family full of people who are getting on with their lives and making the most of them, motivates children more than does a set of "teaching strategies" in a classroom.

Mrs. Adam's little Head Start daughter Laurie is now a dentist, a Meharry graduate, living very near where she grew up. "This week we're examining seventy-two children at our community's Head Start Center," Laurie says, bringing our story full circle.

"It brings up strange memories, feelings I haven't thought about for a long time. How did I go from being a Head Start child to being a dentist treating Head Start children? It doesn't just begin somewhere like fourth grade or in college. It starts at the beginning and adds up.

"My father's confident, outgoing personality had a lot to do with it; *I'm* that way, combined with my mother's commitment. They were both always involved in everything. It influences a child. I remember one night when I was little, people coming to my house from all over the community carrying guns, piling guns up—people were preparing just in case because of something scary going on, something to do with my grandfather. They were brave. It made an impression on me. I remember, I was very small, five hundred civil rights workers gathering for a march in our front yard—white people, hippies from the east coast, people from Jamaica and Howard University—seemed like my mother was feeding all five hundred. Her pot was always full. It's not just the lessons you learn in school, it's the people around you, what they do, how they live their lives. My parents always explained to us that if you respect people, even if they're the janitor, if you be humble and friendly, those people will probably respect you and be nice, too—*most* people, anyway. This was one of the blessings my parents gave me. My father always taught us to respect the wisdom of elder people, especially. I try to always keep this positive mind. You never know what child is listening, who might be downhearted that day and your words are the words that sustain that person through another day.

"When Head Start [CDGM] began in our community, my mother was right in there, she taught there, and she enrolled two of us at the Pisgah Center. I always felt that I was Ms. Flossie's pet. I *know* I was. She thought I could do *anything,* so I thought so too. I remember when Valentine Blue [see pages 391, 403, 448, 475, 489, 490, and 542] took a group of us to Tougaloo College, twenty minutes away, for a little trip. I thought I was a million miles from home. (And then years later I *attended* Tougaloo as a college student!)

"After Head Start, my parents took us to the white public school. We were the only black family. I was in first grade. I had a very supportive teacher in the white school, I didn't have a bad experience. There *were* some mean teachers, but my teacher was very nice. I think I was her pet. I'm sure she made all the difference; the kind of person this one woman was. Always having someone believe I was special, believe I could do it, that's what made *me* always believe I was special and believe I could do it. Each one of these people influenced me. I always knew, whatever I was going to do, I was going to succeed at it.

"One summer when I was about twenty, my mother volunteered me to do the summer food program. For $60 a *month* I took care of the children from nine to one, picked up the milk, cooked for them and served their lunch, cleaned, drove them home. . . .Why am I doing all *this* for people? I wondered. My mother just sort of eased me into it. My mother brought hundreds of welfare children home over the years and fed them and they stayed overnight. I always thought, well, why do I have to sleep with *this* child?

"It took me a while to understand why my parents did all that. In white school, I had to be neutral.

"After college I was a teacher for a while, but it wasn't for me. I had already met my future husband; he always said, 'Don't be so nonchalant, everybody doesn't have the opportunities you do, be compassionate.'

"When I went to Nashville to Meharry, he moved up too, and we got married. I don't know where I got this wonderful man from. Another blessing. A lot of black women when they look around for a husband they find men with AIDS, and in prison. . . it's a blessing. (I got quite involved with AIDS work in Nashville. That's *another* area where you see a lot of bias.)

"When my husband and I got married—we have two little children now—our mothers *knew* each other. *His* mother was a Head Start [CDGM] teacher, too. My *husband* went to Head Start, too, Richmond Grove [another CDGM center]. His mother raised eleven children and nine of them graduated from Tougaloo College. She did, too; she went to the TIECE teacher education program there."

One by one, rung by rung!

Economic development in Mississippi's black communities has fared badly, but there is *real* progress. There's more improvement in education and job availability than in ownership of business, i.e., than in economic *power.* Obviously, one major obstacle has been (and continues to be) cutbacks in, and hamstringing of, vital aspects of pertinent federal programs targeted at economic development in the black sector. These impairments of programs created and initiated by Democratic administrations (Kennedy and Johnson), impairments instigated and executed by two decades of almost continuous Republican administrations (Nixon, Ford, Reagan, and Bush), have severely handicapped the growth of black business. To some of us it seems quite ironic that the very leaders who constantly decry "handouts" to the poor consistently refuse to promote sufficient numbers of adequately extensive and intensive *self-help* programs—literacy, job training, financial aid for higher education, small business loans, and all the other approaches to lending a "hand *up*" that our society has invented and perfected to enable individuals and families to struggle to their feet—to self-sufficiency and satisfaction. On the plus side, thousands of jobs established by 1960s anti-poverty programs still exist with career ladders. They are in health, legal services, social services, Head Start, and elsewhere. Head Start alone employs thousands of Mississippians, the majority of them black.

Leo Turner, a leader of poor black Mississippi community people and one-time CDGM board member, advises, "If you want economic development in our communities, at least vote for candidates who *claim* they want it *and have a history of working for it.* Understand that money and politics go hand in hand at every level. If you don't vote, or if you don't vote for the right candidate, you can't influence what you'll get. A public official who doesn't have the will to pull the trigger sure ain't gonna hit nuthin'. We have to vote for the people who are at least pulling in the right direction."

Another thoughtful leader in low-income black Mississippi, Emma Sanders, pessimistically but correctly points out a second truth:

"The white establishment doesn't care if we *do* elect blacks at low levels because they can easily block them at *higher* levels. When the white establishment *does* care, but can't prevent the fact that a black will be elected, they manipulate *which* black and get themselves a conservative—someone they can control. We have to work to get the right people elected and then to higher and higher levels. You can't help a poor child in any real way without changing the political and economic environment the child lives in."

Thelma Barnes, who, in the 1960s, worked for the Delta Ministry in Greenville, Mississippi, organized all the CDGM community committees in Washington County, and served on CDGM's overall Board of Directors, explains (in 1989) yet another impediment to economic development:

"Integration in Mississippi has had a negative impact in one big respect: We've gotten carried away with going to places we'd never been *allowed* in before—white stores, restaurants, cleaners, businesses, the Holiday Inn—we used to stay at our *own* places when we traveled. So money paid to blacks doesn't get spent in the black community. Black people are buying *white.* Ironically, there used to be more black business than there is *now.* Some of us will have to get smart and support black business, and develop black business.

"CDGM tried to start black co-ops and small businesses. CDGM understood the importance of income *independent* of white people to form a base for social change activities. You can't bite the hand that feeds you, or how would you eat? So you have to be able to feed yourself free of the white hand. In the 1960s, people understood the importance of this, but the understanding isn't strong now."

Thelma credits Art Thomas with "helping me go beyond my administrative duties in the Delta Ministry's Greenville office and go out to organize people. He saw abilities in me I didn't know I had. I didn't know too much about him other than that he was a United Methodist minister, but without him, there would have been no CDGM. Nobody would have known about the Head Start program, or that we could get it for our communities' children and organize it ourselves."

Thelma Barnes still lives in Greenville, Mississippi, and does community work for the United Methodist church.

"Another current problem about jobs for black Mississippians," Ms. Barnes adds, "is the white-owned temporary employment agencies. There are a *lot* of them. I think they may be working with white employers; people are hired as temporaries and are let go before they ever achieve better jobs and seniority.

"Another thing the employers do is hire lots of part-time people so they aren't legally required to pay benefits.

"Something else that's a *big* problem is the fact that if people want to work, and go off Aid to Families with Dependent Children to a minimum wage job, they lose Medicaid. They can't *afford* doctor bills for the whole family on minimum wage, so they're worse off than they were before! The majority of people *want* to work. I'm not saying all, but the *majority* do. Take a pen and paper and you'll see they can't *afford* to work."

It *is* easy to understand why people prefer a glittering supermarket with its glorious galaxy of goods to a dark, dusty hole-in-the-wall store with little to offer. So the latter, instead of increasingly thriving over the years as black patrons get paid more, gradually go out of business. These stores, like the black-owned pharmacies we've spoken of, were a critical core of the civil rights movement. Without them and some of the black churches, there would have been no place for people to gather, become informed about their rights, meet their Northern allies, exchange information, make plans, *take action.* The famous Giles grocery, for example, that Church Street institution in Indianola that serviced its impoverished Sunflower County community for forty-two years and ten months until Mrs. Giles closed it during the last days of 1988, was a place for brave people as well as for penny-saving shoppers.

"In 1946," says Mrs. Giles, we opened it with the name Giles Pennysavers Store because my husband Oscar said, 'Live and let live.' We served farm laborers from the nearby Gerrard Plantation. We didn't want to rob them. We were farm workers ourselves before we opened the grocery. Ours was one of the first black stores in Indianola. Our friends and neighbors patronized us. At that time the Indianola High School—for black children—had no cafeteria, so every day I made piles of sandwiches to sell them. We didn't want to rob the *children* either. Children we served came back years later from Memphis and Chicago to show *their* children their 'store'."

The "Giles Gro." sign on the boarded-over storefront windows was a familiar sight to CDGM folk. The windows were boarded because, on May 1, 1965, while couriers (civil rights workers, Delta Ministry volunteers, and black community people) were carrying the word about organizing this new Head Start/CDGM thing, night-riders fire-bombed Giles Gro. Two Molotov cocktails, as they were called, were thrown into the store. The reason? Oscar Giles, a leader of the Mississippi Freedom Democratic Party (FDP) in Sunflower County, often led marches around the Sunflower County Courthouse and Public Library protesting the fact that black people were prohibited from entering either. "He was always interested in us voting," Mrs. Giles explains. "He was very involved. He thought it was a right for all Americans." Oscar and Alice Giles were involved in organizing CDGM Head Start centers in Indianola.

"My husband was a CDGM organizer. I was director of the CDGM Head Start Center. We organized a parent club. We organized them to take our children and file a lawsuit to get our children in white Indianola High School. The parent club we set up, we raised money and drove our kids to the white schools. Our children didn't get in, but others did later.

"May 1, 1965 was my birthday," says Alice Giles (who was 70 on May 1, 1990). "For my birthday, while we were sleeping, they burned up everything we had in the store. Our neighbors helped us get the children and the flames out. We fixed it right back up. They canceled our insurance, though, after we were bombed, so we didn't have that. They never caught whoever bombed us, so we thought it best just to keep boarded up. When I closed the store in 1988 after Oscar died, it was those same boards on the windows.

"Another interference with economic development in Mississippi's black communities," explains the Reverend Harry J. Bowie, president and chief executive officer of the Delta Foundation, Inc., a nonprofit community development corporation in Greenville, started in 1969 as an outgrowth of the civil rights movement, "is that whereas many white people pass their businesses on to their children, most black people who *can* send their children away to college and on to better opportunities." Harry Bowie was already an ordained episcopal priest when he went to Mississippi as a summer worker for the National Council of Churches during Freedom Summer (1964). He had only been back home in New Jersey for a month when some bombings in McComb, Mississippi caused community people to request that he return. He did; so far *that* trip has lasted twenty six years. Harry is an organizer. He has organized day care, transportation, legal services, and health projects, as well as a number of significant economic development projects.

The Gileses are a perfect example of a family that encourages its children to go out of state to find opportunity. Alice Giles says, "I always told my son he could be whatever he wants to be. When he was coming up, the only thing he could do was go out and chop cotton. We sent him to everything we heard of, every opportunity, Rust College summer programs, Tennessee State summer programs, white collar and necktie jobs. . . . Then he attended Tennessee State and Meharry Medical School. Now he's a physician in Louisville, Kentucky."

There may not be as many black-owned businesses as one might wish for, but there are significantly more black professionals.

There are many more jobs of *all* kinds for black people in Mississippi now in the 1990s than there were in the '60s, but they "didn't come naturally." Hattie Saffold (see pages 179, 394, 491, 669–670), former CDGM Area Teacher Guide and star of the film we made (see p. 415) at her Second Pilgrim's Rest Head Start center, "Chance for Change," is now a public school kindergarten teacher near where she has always lived. She explains:

"We worked hard for these jobs here in the Delta, in Holmes County. It worries me that these young people today take it for granted. They don't understand that they have to work and work to keep it up and get it better.

"Progress is something you have to keep on keeping working on. There's no end you get to and then you lay down. Seems like there's always the next step to go—putting in electricity, getting in a phone or an indoor bathroom—the next right to fight for, or the next opportunity to let somebody who doesn't know about it know about it. You just have to keep on keeping on, reaching and preaching and teaching. I tell my co-workers and my kindergarten children all about where our people have come from in this county—in this state—and in this nation. I tell them, you can do it, you have to *work* for it and be whatever you want to be, you've got it in you and you've got the *right.* But nothing will happen if you don't go after it.

"Before CDGM came in 1965, my husband Mr. Saffold and I were farmers. CDGM brought the first jobs other than farming or being maids into this rural community in Holmes County. We raised some cotton, some corn, vegetables, a few hogs, cows, chickens. My mother and father were farmers. We lived near them. For survival, we had to work on plantations, too, chopping cotton for about $3 a day in that hot, hot sun, or picking—$2 for a hundred [pounds of cotton. It takes over half a day to accomplish this, so this *also* paid $3 a day]. When our children were small, I'd drop them off up the road at my mother's, but when they got a little bigger, they'd come along and work too. We needed every dollar. How much were most people in other places earning in 1963 and '64? We were getting about $45 a week for the full-time work of two adults and a bunch of kids, and it was seasonal. After a while, Mr. Saffold went to work where they cut logs into boards, the sawmill. We didn't have a car, so he rode his bike about five miles to work before and after a hard working day. The children and I kept the farm going.

"In 1963, I think it was 1963, or 1964, three young people came into Holmes County from a northern university—a woman named Ann, Henry Lorenz, and Mike Kenny. They were white. This is how *all* of this got started. They started trying to get us to come to meetings. They came door to door and started telling us about our rights. They said did we know we were full citizens of the United States of America and we had a right to vote? No, we didn't know that. My mind started traveling—I said to people, 'Well, if these white people who don't even *live* here know we have a right to vote, why don't these white folks right here in

Durant know we do? And if they *do* know, why don't they let *us* know? Why don't they enlighten us about our rights?' We were getting tired of life as we had always been living it, as we were living it right as they spoke.

"So some of us bold ones, just a few, we went to one of their meetings. Mr. and Mrs. Glover went and Jesse Williams, Hubbard Ellis and his wife, my mother, and Albert Patterson and his wife. I was kind of skeptical. I said, 'Well, Lord, I don't know where I'm going, but it can't be much worse than this.' Henry and Mike and Ann, these were just three college students, but they changed our lives. They encouraged us to register to vote. That's what they had come down here to the county for. They told us, 'Yes, you *will* get a lot of threats and trouble from the local whites. They won't want you to do this, but it's your *right,* and things won't ever get better if you don't take a stand. If you want things to change, they said, you're going to have to sacrifice your time, you're going to have to put your whole heart and mind into this. No one can change your life for you, only *you* can bring about this change.' They gave us courage. They stood behind us. They gave us information and a lot of good laughs. They stayed in our community and were good friends to us.

"Besides registering our people to vote—we did that, we went door to door and got people to dare to register—we went to Washington, and one of the projects we did was about some new jobs coming into the county.

"It was 1963 or '64. Some white people had come around asking us to sign petitions to get some factories in, some plants with jobs. So a lot of us signed the petitions. Then the plants came in and they wouldn't let us work in them. So when we went up to Washington for the March on Washington and we made groups to go to the different agencies, I said I wanted to go in the Labor Department group.

"Some of us, Ms. Glover was there, you know Ms. Glover, she was very active in CDGM at Second Pilgrim's Rest, we went to see Mr. P. T. Williams at the Labor Department. He asked, 'Well, have you *applied* to work at the new coat plant to make coats?' We looked at each other and we realized and we said, 'Well, no, we haven't actually *applied* but they won't *take* applications from Negroes, we are *afraid* to go over there.'

Mr. P. T. Williams said, 'Well, when you go back, you all go to that plant and keep your voice very nice and ask to please fill out applications. Then if they won't let you, walk away right straight to a phone and call me. I can't do anything without evidence,' he said. 'And sitting up here in Washington, D.C., I can't know what's going on in Durant, Mississippi, unless you *tell* me, now can I?'

"So we went to the plant and we walked up to a side door. They said, 'Hattie, you're going to have to be our spokeperson' 'Me?' I said, 'Well, O.K., I'm always asked to be the spokeperson, so that's O.K. with me.' A huge white dude opened the door, *huge!* He said, 'What you want, niggers?' We remembered what Mr. Williams said, and we spoke *so* politely: 'We would like to fill out job applications, may we come in?' 'Hell, no,' he shouted. 'We ain't havin' no niggers work here!' (White folks like this dude worked in the factories and at home hired black maids!) 'Well, then could you bring some applications to the door?' we asked.

'Hell, no,' he shouted. I said, 'Now I remember a while back we was asked to sign petitions to get 200 jobs into the area, and I'm wondering if my name was worthy *then,* is my name worthy *now* to sign a job application?' He said, 'Hell, no! We ain't havin' no niggers workin' *here!'* We questioned him very nice for about half an hour, brought him out, got him to say all these things. We introduced ourselves and asked his name. Then we thanked him and ran straight to the phone to call Mr. P. T. Williams at the Labor Department in Washington, D.C.

"In three days, that huge white dude was fired. Ads were out. After they learned our story, people weren't afraid anymore, they came pouring out from *everywhere,* Tchula, Kosciusko, *all* directions. Within two weeks, lots of black people were working there. Now in 1990 it's changed to an electrical plant and the *majority* of the workers are black. Shortly after, several more plants located in the area. Most workers are black. Some whites quit because they don't want to work side by side with black people, so that opens up more jobs for us. Then the black people who've been there a while know how to work the machines and do the job, so some whites wanting to start work there *won't* because they won't work under a black.

"Now black people work everywhere around here. *Everybody* in the food store is black, even the cashiers, even the manager. It's white owned, though, we know that, but it's jobs. We've even gotten the banks to hire a black here and there, not too many, but a few. When I go into the bank, I always go straight to the black person and do all my business through that person to show I have confidence.

"CDGM came along at just the right time. Because of my movement work where the workers enlightened me on what I had a right to do, I couldn't get jobs. CDGM gave many people a job to start with. From there, for many of us, one thing has led to another, in Head Start and on to other things.

"It was one of Henry Lorenz's and Mike Kenny's and Ann's meetings that I first heard of the CDGM Head Start idea. The meeting was at Old Pilgrim's Rest. Four or five people came together from four or five communities. Henry started talking about someone had called them from the Delta Ministers and told them we could set up something for our own young children. 'You would have to do all the work,' they said; 'collect children's names door to door of people who would be willing to allow their children to come out to a center, although the whites might fight us for making our own program for our own children. You would have to allow your church to be used for this program, and repair it, or build a building. You would have to do all this volunteer. But if many, many communities all over the county, Holmes County, and all over the state get together and *cooperate,* we think we can get money from the federal government for jobs as teachers and others in this brand new Head Start program. The Delta Ministers are working on this with a lady in Washington' [me, Polly G.].

"After this meeting, my husband Mr. Eugene Saffold and I were talking and I said, 'This is a great idea!' He said, 'You'll never be able to do this, you'll never be able to get all these people organized, they'll be scared, they won't go along with it, and fix up a building—you won't be able to do it.' But my mind was traveling and I thought, We've got to do something to bring opportunity to these children.

"And I thought, A lot of people are without jobs because of their movement activities, meaning registering to vote and trying to open up jobs at the plant for black people like for white people. This would be jobs so they can make a better life for their children. Mr. Patterson said, 'Well, Hattie, if you're going to do this, I'll help you. I think it's a grand idea.'

"You bring about change one person at a time. It was just a few of us. We went door to door talking to our people. It was one by one. I said, 'Yes, you will get in trouble with whites for getting involved in this program for children. They won't want you to do this. But it's your right to do this for your child. Things won't ever get better if you don't take a stand. If you want things to change for your child, you're going to have to sacrifice your time and help us get this Head Start together, and you're going to have to put your heart and soul into it. We have to realize, ain't nobody gonna change our life but us. Only us can bring about a better life for our children. You'll have to get involved *volunteer.* But if all of us in this community come together and cooperate with other communities where movement workers are helping, we think we can get money from Washington for food and toys and medical for the children.'

"I had four older brothers and my father and mother. My father and mother, both, always supported me in all that I did. They never disencouraged me. My mother went to meetings with me and my father stood up for me with people who disagreed. So Mr. and Mrs. Glover said we could use their land and build a Head Start community center there. So we did.

"Then I started going down to Mt. Beulah once a week to work with all of you all, and you, Polly, I guess because you were the *children's* program person, and so you were looking for people who loved children and who were bold and confident and willing to work to make life better for our children, asked me to be an Area Teacher Guide to work with eight centers up here in Holmes County besides our own here at Second Pilgrim's Rest. I always credit you with me being where I am today, Polly, a public school kindergarten teacher.

"At first we rode down to orientation at Mt. Beulah together. Then you gave me a CDGM current model Dart Dodge car. It was so I could come several hours drive to Mt. Beulah and go to each of my centers each week. At first I'd get in that car and I'd say, 'Oh, Lord, I don't know where I'm going.' I was scared to death. I would start off down my road and I'd pass five or six trucks with young white guys sitting on the hoods holding guns across their lap. Sometimes they'd take out their privates and try to pee on me as I passed. I was afraid they'd get me in some dead end road, so my goal was to learn all those little roads around there and remember *never* to go on those ones with no way out. It was the poor and middle-class whites that did these things, but we always thought the owners were behind it, too.

"That first CDGM Head Start summer, people like that attempted to burn our church down *twice.* The first time, I'd taken my children by my Mom's and we went to Durant and stayed a few hours. It was night, and we were on the way home. When we tilted the hill we saw a blaze. We had always had an arrangement that if any of us were in trouble we would lean on the horn until the others heard and had come. So we blowed and blowed and our husbands came and we got the fire out. I don't know how—no running water and they had soaked rags and sacks in gasoline—you know how quick *that* goes. I guess the Lord was just in our favor. Then the second time was when we were building the new center near the Glovers' house. Adam and Fran [the talented filmmakers Tom Levin had hired so we could make a documentary film for staff training and public relations in the North] were staying in our community, up there, for six weeks. They were *sleeping* in it to guard it from the Klan. They went to town to get a sandwich, and when they came up that same hill they saw that church blazing again. They ran and stomped it out. This time those young white men had nerve enough to go *in* our church and pile up soaked rags and run a soaked rope out the door and lit it from the outside.

"This is how it was all that first Head Start summer. One day we had gone to Mrs. Glover's house to get something for the Head Start that the children needed. We heard a truck coming, tearing up the road real fast like they do when they're planning to shoot at you. So we jumped down in the ditch and lay low down in there till the truck flew past, and then popped up real quick to see who it was. It was [name's] truck with two white guys in front and one in back shooting. But when they shot at the community center, our husbands were there waiting for them and shot back. It was always the same people defended our property and our rights, Mr. Williams, Mr. Glover, Mr. Saffold...

"You remember when I came home from one of your teacher workshops and we couldn't find our children? We couldn't find them anywhere. Finally, they came scrambling out from under the beds. We had always trained them, 'If anybody comes by here shooting when we're away, drop to the floor, stay low, stay away from the windows and doors.' The way we gradually got all this shooting stopped was standing up for our rights and not being afraid. And we'd shoot right back. I myself don't do much aiming, but I can shoot pretty good."

The story of Hattie Saffold's economic, political, personal, educational, and professional development continues in the education chapter on p. 000. It should be clear to the reader by now that it's quite difficult and altogether arbitrary to separate these categories (that only academia departmentalizes) in order to state definitively, "This is relevant to Head Start, this is not."

Harry Bowie, whose work focuses on economic development for black Mississippians, says growth of minority-owned business is "pitifully small, but a very important beginning; it's progress, we're moving in the right direction. But we aren't seeing nearly *enough* progress." The Reverend Bowie says that some of the minority-owned business that there *is* represents incoming Asian people: "They have dark skin, but they aren't American blacks." Harry says *franchise* businesses are growing—auto dealerships, McDonalds, 7-Elevens; the security business is growing—more and more night watchmen and guards are needed as crime rises in Mississippi, just as it's rising everywhere else in the

U.S.A.; and in urban areas service businesses, such as janitorial services and janitorial supplies, are starting up. Four or five small garment manufacturers like the one in which Hattie Saffold and her group triumphed in winning jobs for black people, have come into the state, including a plant that makes blue jeans for J. C. Penney.

About ten small black-owned manufacturing businesses have begun, each employing twenty to one hundred fifty workers: the Electro National Corporation makes electric and mechanical parts; Port Gibson Electric makes wire harnessing for General Electric; Griffin Lamp makes headlights, tail light reflectors, and side mirrors for trucks; Mound Bayou Cycle makes bicycles and tricycles; one plant makes precision parts; there's a catfish processing plant; and there are some construction companies. One black-owned construction company employs fifty people and does $4 million worth of business a year. There are several black-owned insurance companies, and a few of them have as many as twenty-five agents. The Woodcutters Association has enabled blacks to move up from the lowest jobs to being loggers—the men who haul the huge trees. But to be a logger, a person has to have $50,000 for a cab, another $75,000 for a loader, $60,000 for a skidder, and a $20,000 flatbed. A black *woman* owns an electrical and mechanical auto parts manufacturing plant employing about eighty-four people—this plant has contracts with Ford Motor and Chrysler.

The Reverend Rims Barber, a white minister who came to Mississippi in 1964 says,

"Many of the people who are business entrepreneurs are the same people who were active in the movement—and *they* are the same people who were active in organizing and running CDGM and they are also the people who filed school desegregation lawsuits district by district by district—progress inches along. It's better. We have a long way to go, but it's much better."

Rims went to Mississippi when the National Council of Churches put out a plea for ministers to volunteer to help in community service work, community organization, and other social change activities relating to race and rights. He became intrigued. He decided to go back again in 1965 for a year as a Delta Ministry volunteer. His year isn't up yet.

In 1971, the woman who soon became Mrs. Rims Barber arrived in Mississippi. Until she married Rims, she lived in Starkville and worked on an Appalachian Regional Commission grant doing day care. After she moved to Jackson, Judy worked for a year in a Rankin County community health program, and for another year in an American Friends Service Committee project. Since 1979, she has been with the State Health Department; Judy Barber is the Director of Social Services for the state. These days this department has seventy five social workers.

In 1976, Rims went to the Jackson Children's Defense Fund office, opened several years earlier by Marian Wright Edelman, to work on the rights of special needs children in school systems. This became all around child advocacy regarding school rights. Rims did this for thirteen years, until the office was closed in 1989. Now, as Director of the severely underfunded Mississippi Human Services Coalition, which serves as an informal "freedom information" and "supportive escort'' service for black Mississippians engaged in educational and diverse other opportunity development activities, Rims continues to do the same work.

One by one and two by two; individuals make a difference in society's inch by inch progress toward peace, freedom, and equity for all. Projects alone cannot reasonably be evaluated. How, together, they total a whole approach, or build one upon the other, must be looked at too.

Rims reflects upon what CDGM meant to Mississippi:

''Assess the significance of CDGM in the long run? I view it as a critical turning point in the state. If you don't institutionalize change, it disappears without a trace. The movement had accomplished an incredible amount, but was unable to deliver anything more concrete than the vote. That's kind of abstract. The movement was falling apart. Rivals were fighting for leadership roles in SNCC. The first principle of community organizing is that people have to win goodies at the end of their effort. SNCC didn't get this concept. You can't go on and on stirring up people about rights they deserve. They want something real. CDGM offered an opportunity to get organized, fix up your own buildings, provide an educational program for your own community's kids, learn to do one of a number of jobs, earn serious money (the first in your life), link up with adult literacy and G.E.D. and other opportunities, link up with other communities, work as a team, work together for a better life. CDGM provided the first chance people had to form a network—it provided cars, telephones, information, Washington contacts. . .Then anything could be done.''

If anyone knows the depths of CDGM's dismal fiscal woes, so might be disposed to say that CDGM was a disaster, it's David C. Rice. In 1967, Rice, a Northerner, employed by IBM's World Trade Corporation at the time, was recruited by an Urban League ''black talent'' searcher for the Board of Missions of the Presbyterian Church, which sought a black financial manager to go to Mississippi on a temporary basis as CDGM's Director of Finance. The church (the National Board of Missions of the United Presbyterian Church, U.S.A.), the government (Sargent Shriver and President Johnson), labor (The Citizens Crusade Against Poverty), the NAACP Legal Defense and Education Fund, Inc. (Marian Wright Edelman), and all of CDGM's other mighty Northern allies wanted to keep quantities of money in Mississippi to provide opportunity for black people, but President Johnson's War on poverty was under increasing siege from all sides and Senator Stennis was almost unassuageable. Dave was to work under John Mudd, CDGM's Executive Director, to clear up the financial chaos. But Dave Rice does not think CDGM was a disaster; in fact, he thinks quite the contrary.

''CDGM was definitely a great success,'' Dave says in 1990. Rice was one of IBM's few chosen people; black people, chosen carefully, treated so well, Dave says, that it was hard to leave. He never meant to leave. But as the national effort to recruit financial rescuers for CDGM escalated, so did pressure on Dave to go to Mississippi. Finally, a well-placed person asked IBM's *president* if Rice could be lent—sent to Mississippi on loan for six months. The response was, Oh, sure, that could easily be arranged. Dave, at the time in his twenties, was mildly interested. His family thought he must be insane. A black businessman voluntarily moving to Mississippi? This was not a SNCC worker, willing to risk all for a cause, or a fanatic as were some Northern volunteers; Dave was "a financial type." Dave agreed to go to Mississippi to have a look. He became *more* interested. Why not? he said to himself; I'm young, I've never done anything really meaningful, and it's only for six months.

Minus his family, Dave arrived (1967) in CDGM's sweltering summer cotton fields, attired in his IBM uniform—dark suit, white shirt, conservative tie—and he wore it every eighteen-hour day for three months. Gradually, he changed his look. He became more involved. "How could I help it?" CDGM's power, the power of an obviously right "movement," transformed him as it did almost everyone who seriously participated in it.

Dave says, "CDGM *was* for little children. It was a wonderful thing for little children. *Thousands* of little children. But it was a lot more than that. For the first time, poor black people in Mississippi had some money in their pockets. Not much, but more than they'd ever had before. This created change. For the first time, they were able to start small businesses. CDGM bought groceries and whatever else it needed for all those centers from local black vendors whenever possible. I always got good prices. I made the Head Start money we had go as far as I could. What was best for children came first. But CDGM brought more than a health and education program for children and an economic change to people. It also brought a change of atmosphere. Poor black people felt a sense of hope for real change in their situation. I went to Mississippi to do something for children but soon began to realize that there was more to it. You had to affect education, economics, and politics to do any real good."

The six months were up. Dave asked IBM if extending his leave of absence for a second six months could be considered. This request was quickly granted. At the end of the *second* six months, CDGM centers were without funding again, and again the poorest people in the United States were funding and operating their own Head Start centers. Dave, still Director of Finance, ever more deeply involved in CDGM (which, though dismembered and reduced to fewer counties, was still called CDGM), requested another leave of absence. IBM took a while to reply. It granted Dave's wish, but this time reluctantly. One request led to another, until after two years Rice stopped asking, left IBM, and stayed in Mississippi—for a total of nine years.

After a year and a half as Financial Director, Dave became Deputy Director. He served in this role for a year and a half, too. After three years in Mississippi, he became Chief Executive Officer, which he remained for four years. He also became Chairman of the Hinds County Democratic Party and a founding member of the Delta Foundation.

Dave says, "No question about it, CDGM and all its descendants—CDGM centers and people now under other grantees and names—have made a great contribution to Mississippi economically, educationally, and politically. SNCC never understood that. Ed Brown is a former SNCC person and Citizens Crusade Against Poverty staff member, he is very well informed about black people's situation in Mississippi; I don't know what he would say about CDGM now, looking back, assessing its value."

Former SNCC activist Ed Brown, Executive Director of the Voter Education Project in Atlanta (a community organizer with a long, long history of working for social change in black Mississippi and a low key but lifelong devotion to the subject) says, "CDGM was one of the big incremental changes in Mississippi's historical process. By providing people with a financial base—all those hundreds of jobs—it completely undermined the system of intimidation and violence—"Don't vote, or I'll fire you and see that my friend cuts off your credit at his store so you can't buy food or clothes." It was that system of fear and keeping people in peonage that stifled their initiative and prevented them from registering to vote or working for any kind of change. CDGM created the first cash economy Mississippi black people ever had. For the first time, they had a little money, they didn't *need* the white man's credit that kept them enslaved to him. They could spend their money wherever they pleased. That's why CDGM embodied revolutionary potential. That's why the establishment fought it."

"Oh, yes, it's much better," the Reverend Bowie agrees, "though as I said, we have a long way to go."

Northern industry has come to Mississippi, as to the South in general, but usually in predominantly white areas. This is the case in all Southern states. White areas tend to have better schools, more cultural amenities, infrastructure, etc., *and are less likely to unionize.* In Mississippi, industry has emerged in the northeast, down the east side, across the gulf coast, and in Jackson. (See the map of Mississippi on p. 698.) There's a big difference between urban and rural areas. Hattie and her neighbors are happy about their success in making jobs accessible to themselves in the 1960s, but in truth, only labor-intensive, minimum wage jobs came to the black belt where Hattie lives, and many of them, the Reverend Bowie points out, have moved on down to Mexico, where people can be exploited for even *less* money.

In general, Mississippi's economy is changing, but not improving. The state's agricultural base is eroding; it lost 88,000 farms in the period between 1960 and 1984. Direct farm sector employment accounts for only three percent of all employment. The state's average weekly earnings for labor and manufacturing activities in 1985 was $293, compared to a Southeastern average of $345 and a United States average of $386. In 1988, Mississippi's unemployment rate was 8.4 percent, compared to the national average of 5.4 percent. The black unemployment rate was 14.7 percent (Bureau of Labor Statistics). Economic conditions threaten Mississippi's viability as a place to live and work. While the Southeast as a whole gained substantial population, Mississippi led the region in out-migration between 1975 and 1987. Almost all of the adult children of almost all my Area Teacher Guide friends from CDGM days, for example, are living and working out of the state.

One place where black people are doing *much* better job-wise is in school system, county, and state-level positions. Jackson's new school superintendent, for example, is black.

Head Start evaluation specialists spent many years and millions of dollars measuring young children's intelligence (I.Q.) gains. Head Start was never conceptualized by War on Poverty planners as an I.Q. raising program, or even as a predominantly educational program at all, though everybody wanted—and still wants—Head Start classroom experiences to be as good as possible *without sacrificing other equally or more important aspects of the total project.* Moreover, there is no evidence that the I.Q.s of "successful" people are several points higher than the I.Qs of "unsuccessful" people. The entire I.Q. measuring era in Head Start's history illustrates a problem: The academic community should be encouraged to participate in social programs, but should not be given final decision making authority. Scholars have their own agendas and reward systems. Social change is not at the top of the agenda, and actualizing it is not the reward that moving up the academic career ladder is.

Had evaluators spent many years and millions of dollars measuring how many jobs Head Start, directly and indirectly, has opened to poor people who are climbing the economic ladder, especially to poor and formerly poor minority people in Mississippi and in the nation, they would probably have learned more of value about Head Start's contributions to a war against poverty. At one point, ten percent of the new jobs in Mississippi were provided by Head Start.

A longstanding and cherished goal of the national Head Start program is the practice of providing job opportunities for parents. Thirty-five percent of all present Head Start staff are parents, and a good number of them have risen to positions of national prominence. CDA training has been an important avenue of early childhood education career development. The opportunity for a poor person to get a meaningful paid job with upward bound possibilities (probably by leaving Head Start and becoming employed elsewhere in a setting that pays better) is, perhaps, the most critical link between poverty and a way out of it. Yet for a program considered to be an anti-poverty program to pay as badly as Head Start does for staff who have been with it for a while and who are doing the job well, should cause some serious concern.

The National Head Start Association has recently done a comprehensive salary study of the salary structure across all components. Ray Collins of Collins Management Consulting, Inc., analyzed the data and wrote the final report. It was published in the NHSA Journal, Vol. IX, Number 2, Fall 1990.

The report reveals that Head Start and public school teachers in the same community, working the same number of days a year, earn grossly unequal salaries. Head Start teachers' average salaries are less than two-thirds of the beginning salaries of their counterparts who teach kindergarten or first grade. Compared with earlier such studies, it's evident that the gap is widening. The average salary of Head Start teachers in the country is $11,859. (In Mississippi it's $7,863, or only thirty-eight percent of public school starting levels.) The NHSA/Collins report shows that starting salaries for other Head Start staff are significantly lower than staff salaries for comparable jobs in public schools or other community agencies:

Home Visitor = fifty-four percent

Education Coordinator = fifty-four percent
Head Start Director = fifty-eight percent
Social Services Coordinator = fifty-nine percent
Parent Involvement Coordinator = sixty-one percent
Health Coordinator = sixty-two percent

A concern is heard in certain quarters that if salaries become too high, and credentialing requirements as well, Head Start staff will absorb the professional orthodoxies of the early childhood education club, including its penchant for putting preciousness over priorities (for example, focus on building cognitive skills in children rather than on building leadership and job skills in parents). There is concern that if salaries are too high and benefits are good, staff will burn out but settle in until retirement time, and Head Start will lose the kind of gung ho true believers who give it much of the remarkable spirit it has. Although this is a legitimate worry, and although offering an opportunity for a parent to enter a meaningful, paid career is the critical point, keeping employees forever on poverty wages does not appear to be the best answer.

Because Head Start is above all an anti-poverty program, probably evaluators should also note its economic aspect. For instance, in the case of Mississippi, according to the Regional office and the Governor's office, Head Start has brought a billion dollars to the state. It seems myopic that a billion dollars has slipped past evaluators' eyes without causing a blink.

CHAPTER 46

EDUCATION: A HANDICAPPING DEPRIVATION, OR AN ESSENTIAL PART OF ELEVATION

Seeking (equal) educational opportunity, individual by individual, lawsuit by lawsuit

ALTHOUGH IT'S MUCH more as well, Head Start is, in part, an education program—an *early childhood* education program. (In fact, eighty percent of all paid Head Start personnel work in educational roles.) And high quality education is one of the keys to freedom. Our CDGM centers of twenty-five years ago suffered the same ills that large numbers of currently operating Head Starts all over the country suffer in the 1990s. Other types of programs for young children—day care, preschool, kindergarten—have exactly the same problems; any on-site staff development specialist or validator for accreditation by the National Association for the Education of Young Children in Washington, D.C., can verify this.

One problem is *formality.* Many teachers remember the schools they went to. What they're remembering is the higher grades where students sit at desks and write with pencils. Teachers give instructions and instruction. Children are supposed to sit and soak it up. This is especially so in places that didn't have kindergarten when today's Head Start staff members were five-year-olds, or didn't have high quality kindergarten. They can't accurately remember what a good kindergarten program feels like because they never experienced one—full of move-around, free-choice, child-directed *play* enriched with interesting props; children's conversations; teachers' appreciative comments and remarks that expand upon the children's activity without pushing or pulling it in any way; joint child-adult democratic-style planning; and special teacher-prepared *projects,* such as an abundance of simple outings, cooking, discovery science, music and movement, and lots of story reading. Many teachers of young children do not have a child development and *early* childhood education background. Many who *do* were trained in elementary education departments that tacked kindergarten onto their lower ends. These teachers have never grasped or have never been *taught* true *early* childhood education, *which is based on an understanding of how children develop* physically, emotionally, socially, and intellectually. Many teachers tend to think they're doing nothing if children "just" play. So children are seated and given papers and pencils. But there's a good reason not to teach this way: Like the rest of us, children learn more effectively if they are encouraged to take a more active part in learning; if they are encouraged to plan, take initiative, decide, choose. . . . And, as with adults the very best projects emerge and evolve out of what children are spontaneously engaged in. If our goal is to offer children the best possible educational foundation, we shouldn't ignore all evidence regarding how they best learn.

In CDGM's staff development work with the Area Teacher Guides (ATGs) I focused on helping people think through the characteristics they value in adults and want to develop in children. This went a long way toward teachers' realization that encouraging children to cooperate, plan, work independently, care for each other, express themselves articulately and comfortably, develop strong interests, and make decisions are what wise adults consider the core curriculum for kindergarten and younger groups. (See pp. 387–389.) *The core curriculum in high quality early childhood education is character development.* CDGM centers never approached well-done play and projects programs, but we moved away from a seated academic approach and had a great many interesting and educational things going on. (See listings under EDUCATION in index, especially the listing beginning *early education,* and these items: *arts; facilities, equipment, materials and supplies,* pp. 127–136, 418–419, 580; *freedom,* pp. 79–80, 694–695; *games; music; number work; reading and language; science; trips.*)

A second problem in many 1990s Head Starts and other programs for young children in Mississippi and everywhere else, a problem CDGM had as well, is *transitions.* Teachers don't know how to move children smoothly from one activity right into the next, or to fill the few gaps that are occasionally still unavoidable (even if teachers develop better transitions skills) with hearty singing, a well-told tale, an engrossing beautifully illustrated storybook, or a game to sharpen minds, such as "I'm Thinking of Something Red." The CDGM ATGs and I practiced flowing easily from one thing to another, and improvizing gap-filling activities. Teachers could see how much richer the educational program was without so many gaping, time-wasting holes in it. *They wanted educational excellence for the children of their communities more than any professionals and policy makers in the world could possibly want it.* Many changed their teaching ways.

With a program that better reflected children's lively bodies, inquisitive minds, sociability, and love of talking, and that featured few seemingly endless stretches of time in which children are expected to sit vacantly and wait, "*discipline problems,*" a third category of problems that plague many children's programs nationwide, largely evaporated in CDGM.

The discipline problems that remained—mainly children hurting each other, each other's projects, or each other's feelings—lessened when the ATGs and I thoroughly discussed the importance of getting along as adults—of not tolerating exploitative bullies, of not being victims—and shared ideas for helping children learn how to state their needs and feelings in words, and to negotiate, so that they could learn young not to be exploiters or victims. Most people who work with two-, three-, four-, and five-year-olds, and with children in the early grades, don't do any better in this dimension of their work than untrained CDGMians did. In fact, *large numbers of CDGM teachers excelled in helping children learn not to be bullies and not to be victims because it had deep meaning for them.* Adults, like children, learn most eagerly and effectively that which is meaningful and urgently important to them.

A fourth common problem is adults' failure to develop *authentic relationships* with children. Teachers tend to role play and "teach." When the Area Teacher Guides and I shared our conviction that *children are more strongly and permanently influenced by adults who stand up for what they believe in, and who encourage each child to be all he or she can be, than they are by any number of cleverly constructed "lessons,"* CDGM teachers loosened up, made friends with children, and spent more time being real with them—doing things, going places, and discussing with children *their* issues and ideas. Many CDGM people said they hadn't realized what good examples they are for children; that it wasn't necessary to play the part of someone called "teacher." In general, Head Start staff appears to do better with regard to forming genuine friendships with children than do teachers in all but the best programs of other types, although any generalization has its exceptions.

A fifth serious flaw, endemic to primary-grade programs as well as programs for younger children, is that while *language development* is considered critically important to children's later ability to learn to read—thus to learn whatever else the school has to offer—and although *children best learn language*

1. by hearing people talk all around them,
2. by talking and being listened to, and
3. by being included by adults in frequent conversation,

many teachers prefer that children be quiet! Teachers aren't usually taught how to have conversations with young children.

In CDGM I spent considerable time encouraging Area Teacher Guides to encourage Head Start center teachers to chat with children. We *practiced* initiating, participating in, and extending conversations with five-year-olds, at first a foolish-sounding use of time to most of our teaching parents—e.g. teachers. (See pp. 165–166.) Teachers of young children could help them develop effective language better if in institutions of higher education they were taught less (or nothing) about the technicalities and mechanics of how a child learns language, and more (a *lot* more) about the practicalities of conversing naturally with little children. Listening to children and talking *with* (instead of *at*) them is closely related to developing authentic relationships with them.

A strong tendency to avoid honest exploration and defusing of *race and class tensions and prejudices,* hushing children and glossing over the issues in an effort to be proper, is a sixth deficiency frequently found in children's programs. CDGM couldn't have been accused of that! We don't learn to love one another and to live together constructively by pretending "we're all friends," any more than we do by attacking one another. Exposure to diversity, becoming familiar and comfortable with other people's ways, openly discussing differences, misunderstandings, fears, and angers helps, hard as it may be. This complicated human relations area is one in which most teachers and parents can profit from discussion with skilled group leaders. Head Start has been a national leader in multicultural, bilingual education and is beginning to emphasize anti-bias curriculum, too.[46]

In the sixties, confronting bias toward children with handicaps and special needs was not a subject to which the early childhood education field paid attention. However, Head Start has been a leader in this arena, as in so many others. CDGM included many mentally retarded and other special needs children. Since 1972 Head Start has been pioneering in mainstreaming children with disabilities, and in diversity education pertaining to people with special problems, so all children in the group can become unbiased. In the 1988–89 program year, over thirteen percent of Head Start's enrollment consisted of children with disabilities (mental retardation, health impairments, visual handicaps, hearing impairments, emotional disturbances, speech and language impairments, orthopedic handicaps, and learning disabilities). Head Start was the first federally funded program for special needs children, and remains the largest. In Mississippi, Head Start is helping the public schools mainstream children with special needs.

In the sixties, gender bias was not a subject either. It's interesting to note, that the leaders of the anti-masculinist movement, that is the women who shaped the feminist movement of the 1970's, emerged from the civil rights movement in the South. Either intentionally or unintentionally, most programs for young children still promote a great deal of gender bias.

Family diversity may not be much greater than it used to be among low-income families, but now, as then, the average teacher, even the average early childhood teacher, speaks of families in a manner that indicates insensitivity to each child in her group.

And homophobia is a prejudice as yet unconfronted in any type of educational program, including early childhood programs of all varieties.

All across the country, a seventh and very grave problem in most preschools, Head Starts, kindergartens, and primary classrooms with large numbers of low-income children is getting an optimal balance of

- *play and projects*—important because, as almost a century of experimentation in the classroom and research have overwhelmingly shown, it's through this medium that young children learn most and best
- *and literacy education*—important because children from homes in which reading and writing are not everyday, matter-of-fact occurrences that weave through all the events of daily family living are at a severe disadvantage

[46]In this regard, I highly recommend Derman-Sparks, Louise, and the A.B.C. Task Force, *Anti-Bias Curriculum: Tools for Empowering Young Children.* Washington, D.C.: NAEYC, 1989.

when they arrive in public school, where success in the program depends upon a vast amount of previous, almost invisible education common to children from typical middle-class homes *unless early childhood education programs focus on enriching all play and all projects with reading readiness skills, dictating, writing, reading, and quality children's literature.*

I learned well the lesson taught me by poor parents during July of 1965. Although I am today, and was for many years before we ever invented CDGM, a devout believer in (and product of) the enriched play and projects approach to educating young children, I'm also convinced that *programs for children who do not come from literacy-rich homes need to provide an enormous amount of guided opportunity for children's "emerging" literacy knowledge to emerge.* When teachers make a steady effort to enrich all play and all projects with literacy experiences they significantly contribute to the probability that low-income and English (or standard English) as a second language children will do well in elementary school and therefore thereafter.

Poor parents, and many teachers who work with their children, are right: These children do not automatically understand why print is important, and how letters and sounds relate to it. The majority of the children do *not* learn to read easily and well. They need a vast amount of experience in seeing labels, charts, messages, notes, lists, etc. made for everything that happens during their child care or school day and interrelated in some creatively naturalized way into everything they play. It's the responsibility of educators to let parents and coworkers understand how this promotes later academic success.

Poor parents, and many teachers who work with their children, are right: These children need to learn how to recognize and form most letters of the alphabet, and the *names* of the letters, and that the letters are all there are, there aren't any more, it's manageable. Children need to learn how to read and write these letters, and the sounds they make (phonics), and that they will be easily able to read and write later, "when you're old enough." This is an empowering, confidence-building understanding for children to have. It's greatly preferable to the helpless, bewildered feeling they often have when they encounter the public school beginning reading program. Teachers should integrate experiences with writing and naming letters and the sounds they make into the wide variety of daily play and projects and scribbling and drawing activities that have traditionally been a part of nursery education and progressive education currently called "developmentally appropriate" education. This is a term chosen by the National Association for the Education of Young Children to identify and promote the learning through enriched play and projects philosophy. It's educators' responsibility to let parents and coworkers understand how this makes more likely later academic success than other philosophies and methods. (For information about the curriculum I developed for CDGM to integrate the learning of letters and their sounds into a play and projects program, see footnote 48.)

Because many children see no connection between what they do, feel, and think in their everyday lives and the writing and reading with which they are saturated in their school world, it's important that teachers take dictation—later, help children *themselves* write—about dreams and all sorts of experiences they have had outside the classroom. Children's ideas, knowledge, fantasies, creativity, families' ways of life all are legitimized when teachers feature them and help children make it all into books for their friends to read. (This used to be called the language experience approach, and is currently called the whole language approach, but by either name it has the same effects: *showing respect for individual children,* and *helping children relate positively to books.*) The same principle applies when parents and teachers tell stories from their personal lives—perhaps even write *these,* too, into books for their children.

Poor parents are right: Their children do not dearly love books; they are probably not destined for lives enriched with extensive informational and recreational reading. So it becomes incumbent upon early childhood educators to fill their classrooms with deliciously tempting high quality children's literature. Not junk books, but books with beautiful illustrations, marvelous language, and themes centering on issues important to young children, such as being loved and accepted as they individually and imperfectly are, being able to count on adults to care for them, the rewards of curiosity and independence, the thrill of achievement in a meaningful, self-chosen endeavor. (For a better notion of the reading readiness program I developed and encouraged Area Teacher Guides to encourage teachers to implement in CDGM, see Chapter 13.) In the sixties, there was very little high quality literature featuring the culture of African Americans, or other American minority groups. This remains a problem.[47]

Many early childhood educators, including Head Start educators, adhere fairly rigidly to one of two beliefs:

1) They believe that play and projects are of great educational value for children seven years old and younger—or at least five and younger—and oppose "academics," including helping children learn to recognize and write the alphabet and grasp phonics; or

2) They believe it's important for children to be readied for the reading- and writing-based elementary school they will shortly be plunged into and oppose play and projects except as recess, "rewards" ("when you finish your work, you can. . ."), and "enrichments."

I agree with both and neither adamant camp; I'm unalterably committed to a third alternative, which incorporates generous amounts of each. I'm committed to this approach for *all* young children, but have been convinced by poor parents and by working with their children in education settings (Head Start, day care, preschool, and the early grades in public school) for many years that anything less for children from homes not heavy in reading and writing and reading *to* children seriously impairs one of their freedoms, reading. These are two common camps and where I stand:

• Children *do* learn best through play and projects, so we waste their time

[47]For further information contact the Council on Interracial Books for Children, 1841 Broadway, New York, N.Y. 10023.

and turn them off to school when we insist that they sit and do paperwork *at all* prior to age three; more than perhaps once or twice a week for a few minutes when they're three, possibly five minutes a day when they are four, and no more than fifteen or thirty minutes or so a day when they're five. (Sitting and working with papers should certainly be an option though; some children enjoy it.) But I've learned that I teach *all the literacy skills taught in "skill and drill" style programs more effectively when I weave them informally into play and projects, most of which children freely choose.* Thousands of teachers prefer this approach because they see it's the most effective approach. And I've had great success in staff development work helping other teachers teach "academic" skills through play and projects and fall in love with this way of working with "whole children," as did CDGM's Area Teacher Guides in the sixties. Often a child asks a question; the teacher teaches by answering it. Some children *don't* ask literacy-related questions; the teacher initiates a literacy-related suggestion.

• Children from illiterate, semiliterate, and low-literacy homes *do* need to be taught the readiness-for-reading facts (books are fabulous friends and fun, we read from top to bottom and left to right, writing is part of everyday life) and mechanics (to recognize, form, and know the sounds made by the letters in the alphabet). *Children from literate and high-literacy homes learn all this indirectly or explicitly from their parents and siblings.* It's classist and arrogant to insist that what's not needed by some children (because they have already been given it) is not needed by *any* children, many of whom will fall by the wayside in the early grades if we don't give it to them). But the most effective way to teach this reading readiness knowledge and these critically important skills is by consciously and conscientiously weaving them throughout all play and projects children choose from a classroom richly prepared by hard-working teachers. *It's the teaching method that matters.* A child learns better when he or she bumps into a *need,* a *reason* to know or know how, and the adult *responds* helpfully, individually.

Children learn much by osmosis. Not everything that is learned is taught. They learn invisibly and unconsciously. Children pick up much of what's going on around them, especially if their peers are enjoying it. Children learn informally from their peers. They acquire interests, make personally meaningful discoveries, apply their discoveries to new situations, and thus reinforce them. Therefore it's important for a teacher of children from low-literacy homes to prepare and present on an invitational basis—as an optional activity to which children are invited and in which they are in no way expected to participate—fun "reading readiness," "literacy" "lessons." Some children love them, especially girls. Other children learn the same "lesson" in their own way, in their own time, because it's "in the air." Ensuring that one teacher carries on this thread of the total program, while another spontaneously enriches whatever children are choosing to do is part of achieving a high quality comprehensive literacy-rich early childhood education program for children from low-literacy or standard English as a second language homes.[48]

ATGs and I tried hard to help CDGM's hundreds of teachers to do this. I worked with ATGs one by one. They worked with the people teaching in Head Start centers one by one. The National Association for the Education of Young Children accredits programs for young children one by one. The Child Development Associate Program credentials teachers one by one. Progress in achieving quality education for young children comes one teacher and one program at a time.

* * * * * * * * * * * *

Here is a clear analysis of how and why the two philosophies/methods of education (academically enriched play and projects; seated, paper and pencil programs) differ. Both prepare young children for school. But which is more compatible with the kind of character Head Start and other children's programs are trying to develop?[49]

1. The first early childhood education philosophy is play and projects enriched with math, science, writing, reading, and human relations skills

The child is believed to be an active learner who learns best when she

• moves at will, becomes involved in something, usually with other children (purposefulness and creative thinking are encouraged),

• makes *major* choices—chooses among a variety of worthwhile "live" activities ("live" meaning that the child is not choosing only among worksheets),

• initiates and "does" within a richly prepared indoor and outdoor environment (initiative is encouraged),

• discovers, dismantles, reassembles,

• discusses with friends and grown-ups,

• grapples with challenges (some of which she inadvertently stumbles into, and some of which she consciously sets out to conquer),

• constructs understandings, each at her own rate of intellectual development,

• plans and collaborates with friends and adults,

• solves problems she runs into (not problems that are concocted out of context and set before her in bite-sized portions of a "problem solving curriculum"),

• *creates* concepts and *re*creates or elaborates upon them as she learns something new that seems true but doesn't mesh with what she thought she knew,

[48]My *Bridge-to-Reading Comprehensive, Integrated, All-Subject, All-Day, All-Year Early Childhood Education Curriculum for Three/Seven-Year-Olds* was designed in 1965–66 to accomplish this, refined in 1970–71, and updated in 1986. It was first published by General Learning Corporation, and then by The Growth Program. It will be reissued in 1991.

[49]A version of this segment first appeared as an article by Greenberg, Polly in the Jan., 1990 issue of Young Children, NAEYC, Washington, D.C.

• works with an interesting, intuitive, endorsing adult who mingles with children as they play and work, and in informal interest groups, skill groups, and social groups—all of them often mini-groups,

• evaluates her own work and behavior with peer and adult participation,

• feels rewarded by the satisfaction of a job well done (intrinsic reward),

• experiences spontaneous encounters with learning as her mind meets interesting or puzzling things that capture her attention and intrigue her, which always include things related to what adults and older children do, hence generally include pretending to read books by two or three years of age; writing letters and numerals while playing and drawing somewhere between ages three and seven (typically beginning by four or five years old); and guess-spelling, asking how to spell words, and real reading at five, six, or seven, if not sooner.

All of this is believed to be best learned through enriched free play and teacher-designed, teacher-guided projects usually planned so they expand upon what the child has freely elected to do. Sophisticated guidance and enrichment intended to ensure that opportunities to develop creativity, imagination, generous amounts of concepts relating to math, science, social studies, language, and literacy, as well as opportunities to learn in all the arts, grow out of or are interplanted in a **naturalized** manner throughout what the child has become absorbed in. Teachers, parents, the community; and supervisors, consultants, and teacher educators connected in one way or another with the program determine what should be included in the curriculum, but it isn't believed that there is a fixed body of knowledge that children should "master."

Teachers assess children's progress by

• *observing* them,

• *recording and keeping* anecdotal notes about anything of particular interest or very typical emotionally, socially, physically, intellectually, academically, aesthetically, or otherwise,

• *identifying* special needs in any of these areas, and following up or referring as needed,

• *collecting and keeping* samples and photos of their activities; and

• *sharing* extensively in the information- and opinion-gathering process with the child's parent(s) and other staff.

This philosophy believes not *only* in preparing the environment for excellent play, but *also* that for the child to have **optimal** learning opportunities, adults (parents or teachers) need to **enrich** the play, **plan** projects, and **teach** children many things somewhat in the same way that one **naturalizes** plants. You carefully arrange your purposeful additions to the landscape here and there and all around in the midst of what's happening there naturally so that to a person stumbling into it, all seems relaxed and natural. We **naturalize** "subjects" and "skills" and the conventional knowledge that we expect children to learn, throughout the children's learning environments (home, school, community).

This naturalizing means that "subjects" are integrated, but more than this: It means that children learn "subject" area "skills" and "subskills" and facts in meaningful contexts, sometimes in thematic, teacher guided projects—**as**

need for these skills crops up in activities a child has eagerly elected to involve himself in.

Intellectual learning is fostered, but is not given priority over physical, social, and emotional learning. Academics may be informally included in the array of learnings occurring, **but learning is never narrowed to "mere" academics.** Developmentally appropriate program people strongly believe that children are capable of learning and should learn when three, four, and five years of age, but resist the idea of *limiting* learning to academics only.

Children have opportunities at school (as they do at home in moderately literate families) to learn letters and sounds and a great deal more that goes into easy early reading, but they learn most of it one child at a time during sociable playing, drawing, and talking times with friends. Children learn

- as they experiment and discover, or
- as a need for the new knowledge comes up **for an individual** in his play and projects, or
- as children's observant teachers purposefully expand upon what a child (or small group) is doing to include literacy experiences, or
- when adults are reading stories to children and conversing about them, or
- when an adult is engaged in an activity and children are invited to join in if they wish.

In the case of children who don't get all this at home, which includes most Head Start children, it becomes a critical part of the school's obligation to do a large amount of low-key, home-style literacy, math, and science education of this kind.

Children have opportunities to figure out mathematical relationships as they play and work with objects and people, to count, to make graphs, to classify and weigh things, to learn liquid and linear measurement, more and less, bigger and smaller, adding on and taking away, how to recognize numerals—**but all as it comes up in their play and projects,** or as their teachers **extend these play and project activities to include such experiences.** In math learning, understanding (mastering) the basics (the principles involved) should precede memorizing the details (skills and facts).

For children to learn optimally this way, teachers must be given

- **training in**
  - — child development, and *more* child development, all of it from a practical perspective,
  - — observing individual children, including the art and science of taking pertinent notes,
  - — working informally as equal people with all parents,
  - — working with specialists as needed in assessing and assisting children and families with special needs,
  - — recognizing moments when one can connect with a child to develop trust and friendship, from which learning grows (a sophisticated skill),
  - — creating a complex, stimulating, ever-fresh yet predictable and manageable learning environment including a variety of interlinked learning centers,

— recognizing moments when a child or group of children could learn something new—a new idea, an approach to solving a problem, a new fact, a new skill,
— Interjecting thought-provoking comments and queries without interrupting or interfering (a skill that many expert teachers believe intuitive teachers do better than non-intuitive teachers, no matter how well trained),
— helping children with the intricacies and nuances of having and being friends,
— helping children discipline **themselves** (develop inner controls); and
— helping each child feel good about himself or herself throughout all this.

• **authority to use their**
— intuition,
— judgment,
— knowledge,
— materials, and
— resources

in making the moment into a learning encounter—possibly one that can be expanded into a week-long or six-week-long project with depth, dimensions, aspects, and angles "covering" in a web-like way learning in many "subject" areas, totaling educational excellence. (In all honesty, we need to note that a great number of teacher education programs purporting to believe in this general approach to early education do *not* give students a thorough grounding in these things, nor do many work places give teachers the freedoms and support necessary for them to fully use their sensitivities and skills.)

Currently, this "developmentally appropriate" philosophy is being strongly promoted by all national education associations that have published position statements on early childhood education. Among them are the National Association of Elementary School Principals, the Association for Supervision and Curriculum Development, and the National Association of State Boards of Education. The reason all these leaders are forcefully advocating this kind of educational experience for three-, four-, and five-year-olds—and even for six- and seven-year-olds—is that a wealth of recent research confirms and corroborates what most expert practitioners have been explaining, writing, and teaching for a hundred years: **This is the most effective way to educate young children. It works best in the long run, and with any luck, life *is* longer than five or six years, so there's no need for five-year-olds to know everything they will need to know throughout their school and later years.**

2. The second early childhood education philosophy is the academic preschool/kindergarden/first grade

The child is believed to learn best when he

• sits still, pays attention to the teacher who is "instructing," or does assigned, often paper-and-pencil, seatwork (receptivity is praised),

• makes *minor* choices—which color paper he wants for making a patterned craft item (it's expected that he *will* make the craft item; not to do so usually isn't an option),

• obeys and follows directions in the classroom (compliance is rewarded with compliments),

• initiates and "does" only during a brief free play period, at recess, and on his own time at home in a home environment (that *may* be loaded with learning opportunities, and *may* offer an adult to assist the child in interpreting and expanding the learning his mind comes upon; or *may* be an environment in which learning opportunities are starkly limited and in which an adult is not available to promote spontaneous learning),

• discovers, but on a narrowly restricted scale—discovers the right answer from among several possible answers on a workbook page,

• discusses, but in a formal, teacher-led, tightly topic-related format; children have little chance to learn through informal conversation with one another while in the classroom,

• experiences few intellectual challenges to grapple with and construct understandings from—his own rate of intellectual development may or may not be recognized, but is seldom honored and responded to in the curriculum that confronts him,

• goes along with plans his teacher has made—teachers and children do very little planning *together*; children are expected to tolerate their circumstances good-naturedly,

• solves only prefabricated, packaged problems out of purchased curriculum, if (officially) any; even social problems are usually "solved" for him because the teacher, focused as she is on the academic curriculum she must "cover," doesn't have time to help the child see and test behavioral alternatives, so she tells him the rule and possibly puts him in "the time-out chair to think about it"; very little assertiveness is "allowed,"

• memorizes facts (may create some concepts), waits to be told whether he has gotten them "right" or "wrong," tries again (often guessing, because if the answer was wrong, maybe this answer will be right), doesn't develop *evidence* that he's right or wrong,

• works with an almost-always-right adult who approves of him when he's right and disapproves when he is wrong, usually in "instructional" settings, rarely in small interest or social groupings,

• awaits, passively, adult evaluation and praise (extrinsic reward) rather than judging for himself whether or not his work is good and his behavior helpful,

• experiences reprimands and restraining procedures when he spontaneously encounters something that captures his attention and intrigues him but does not happen to be on the worksheets he has been assigned or in the lesson he's supposed to be attending to.

In this broad category and philosophy of education, the schedule includes play periods, but they're brief and are seen as a break for "rest and recreation." Projects and some of the arts are scheduled, but are offered as "enrichment": play and projects are important but peripheral activities, not the core curriculum. The core curriculum is a tightly structured sequence of splinter skills, presented to the child through a strictly structured sequence of instructional steps. These educators believe that all of this is best learned through short periods of separated subject instruction, intended to give the child the necessities for *later* learning *earlier.* This minimizes the importance of the child's *present* age and stage.

It's believed that there is a fixed body of knowledge that four-year-olds need to master. Adults either

• don't realize how much more easily children learn abstract academic subskills *later,* say at six or seven, or

• believe that learning must be unpleasant to be effective, or

• are unaware that *the same abstract academic* subskills can be taught as the need arises in contexts meaningful to this age group.

Children's progress is assessed with tests, so there's heavy emphasis on mastery. The degree of children's measurable "performance" in academic tasks is what's valued. Children are positively "reinforced" (given stars, smiles, etc.) for absorbing, at least for the moment, as much memorized information in the form of abstract symbols (letters, shapes) as they reasonably can. Adults control most of the use of space, time, and materials in all early childhood programs in that they arrange and manage all of it, set behavioral standards, and so on. But in the academic preschool there is little if any emphasis on children using most of the space most of the time *in their way.*

This broad category of programs and philosophies features

• direct instruction,
• teacher as minute-by-minute schedule planner,
• emphasis on
  — the subskills involved in reading and math,
  — symbols representing things (letters, numerals) instead of on examining and exploring the things themselves *first*, and
  — conventional knowledge such as days of the week, colors, courtesies, and so on,

• curriculum **prepared outside the classroom—purchased by the program and "covered" by the "teacher"** (in contrast to curriculum created by the teacher, or purchased curricular materials that provide a sound philosophy, a framework to preclude a piecemeal, mishmash bunch of activities, and many time-saving specifics, but also encourage and enhance teacher creativity and familiarity with the local community),

• "child as the recipient of lessons,"
• "sooner is better,"
• "learning through a limitless supply of paper-and-pencil worksheets,"
• emphasis on mastery and testing,
• "operant conditioning,"
• "rewards" as "reinforcement" for "right answers," and
• authoritarian management.

Developing genuine self-esteem may be more important than anything else an early childhood teacher can accomplish with the children she's in charge of. The presence of high self-esteem correlates with school success, therefore it's a very important thing for children to learn at this age. (Moreover, low self-esteem correlates with all sorts of serious problems, such as dropping out of school, teen-age pregnancy, alcohol and drug abuse, delinquency and crime, teen-age depression, and teen-age suicide. If she thought about it, no educator would want to risk contributing to any child's low self-esteem.

Self-esteem is generated in children in large part through the process of frequently meeting and mastering **meaningful** new challenges. A key concept here is **meaningful.** If we expect a young child to master tasks that are meaningless to her *as an individual*, she has little satisfaction or feeling of self-worth in doing the chore, even if she succeeds. Hence we are not fostering maximum feasible positive self-esteem, which *should* be one of our chief goals.

Becoming competent in a wide variety of ways enhances self-esteem. Learning enhances self-esteem. But learning trivia and splintered sub-skills is not the most meaningful, or the most valuable for later learning.

Sad to say, in assessing Head Start's classroom component over the past twenty-five years, we see that much of the original spirit of enriching children's lives with games, outings, songs, visitors, stories, and all sorts of events including a great deal of casual conversation, has been sacrificed to make room for "seat-work." This unfortunate trend is evident in many children's educational programs, not just Head Start. We can hope the tide is turning, and, one by one, can strive to make it turn. As we assess each Head Start program, and Project Head Start as a whole, we must keep in mind the fact that Head Start has its roots in the struggle for social justice, so every effort should be made to help children encounter opportunities, not merely shapes, letters, colors, and numbers.

* * * * * * * * * * * *

CDGM Area Teacher Guide Hattie Saffold's story since the end of the era SLIPPERY SHOES documents is one of thousands of examples of the educational path upon which Head Start has gotten so many people without much promise in their futures started or fast forwarded. The path to personal and economic progress. Here is the continuation of Hattie's account of her life after the period she described (on pages 729–733), as she moved from field hand to public school kindergarten teacher, trustingly putting one foot above the other on the rungs of the ladder CDGM offered. And then, after that, taking advantage of other ladders up from poverty.

The stories of Hattie Saffold, Alean Adams, and so many other former CDGMians beautifully illustrate the African proverb, "stumbling blocks can be carved into stepping stones."

"The first CDGM summer, CDGM opened my eyes to many many things. I don't just believe it did, I *know* it did. Polly kept getting us to talk about treating children with respect if we want them to respect themselves. Of course that's right, we just hadn't thought about it.

"Polly gave me that new Dodge rental car. That was during the first CDGM summer when Tom was still there. We had a white resource person from the North, Noni. I'd be driving that new white car with white Noni sitting on the front seat right next to me. White people in Holmes county weren't used to seeing 'niggers' driving around like that. They didn't even allow us in Durant. And later, when we *were* allowed, if a white person came walking along the sidewalk, we stepped off, that's the way it was, our parents trained us like that so we wouldn't get hurt. They didn't like it. They wouldn't sell us groceries for our Head Start center. One day someone went and told my dad that Ms. White up at the store said she was going to get a gun and kill me if I didn't quit riding around so high and mighty with that white girl in that white car. My dad told the person who told him that message, 'If anyone is planning to kill my Hattie, she better have a plane ticket out of Mississippi in her pocket first, because I'll go after her and kill *her*.' My dad always stood up for me. That's the way you have to do those people, you have to stand up to them, all they know is tough.

"Then that lady, Ms. White, she got a job at the movie theatre. She let the word be known, 'That Hattie Saffold better not try to come into this movie house.' So the very day I heard that word, I said to the folks, 'Hey, how 'bout we all go see a movie?' We got a good laugh out of that. We went there. John Mudd or someone like that had called the F.B.I. in Greenville, and they had visited this Ms. White. They told her to let up on me or they'd get on her case. So me and the folks went and saw a movie. Every time we did something like that I got more braver and more braver and more braver.

"So Polly said, 'You'll need this car to go to the Pickens Center and your other seven centers, that's why CDGM is loaning you this rental car. How could you get to all those rural centers without a car? And to Beulah every Wednesday for our all day workshop together? You'll need to go to Pickens and pass on to them what I pass on to you, so we'll meet the Head Start educational standards and they won't cut us off.' 'Drive to Pickens!' I said to myself, 'Lord, I ain't ever been to Pickens. Why, that's eleven, twelve miles away!'

"I said to Polly, 'I can't drive to Pickens. I know I can't get that far.' Polly said, 'Of course you can drive to Pickens. I'll make you a map. The people at Pickens center need you. They need you to help them develop this Head Start program to help them develop the children.' I was ashamed to say any more, but I was so afraid. I got in that new little white car and off I went. I said to myself, 'Lord, I don't know where I'm going, but I know I can count on you to help me get there.' I got there. Then I laughed and laughed. My mind was traveling fast, and I said to myself, 'Well! If I can go to Pickens, I can go anywhere I want to!'

"Next it was the Jackson public library. Polly said to go in there and check out some children's books. Any children's books, just because none of us black people had ever been in there, and she said, 'They won't hurt you, they're *librarians*, not Klansmen. And it's your right. You have a right to get books out of there for the Head Start children,' I said, 'I can't go in there.' Polly, she said, 'Of course you can go in there, Hattie. I'll sit out in front and wait for you.' I said to myself, 'Lord what won't that woman think of next!; But I went in. I took books. They didn't even bother me at all. Ever since I go to the library and take out books.

"Then, in 1965 or '66, Polly insisted that as an Area Teacher Guide I had to go to the University of Southern Mississippi and take a course. I said I couldn't possibly take a college course. I couldn't pass. And a *white* college! She said, 'Of course you can take a course. You'll prob'ly pass the course, but even if you flunk the course, who cares, you'll learn a lot, and you'll learn that all this we're talking about all day every Wednesday, how to work with young children, is the correct early childhood way they teach teachers in college. It will give you confidence as a teacher to know that. We're teaching young children the best way,' she said, 'treat them with love and encouragement and respect, play and talk with them, take them places, read them stories, help them tell and you write their *own* stories. . .'

"I got three credits and a certificate. I kept going back there to Southern Mississippi in Hattiesburg every summer for seven summers. Each summer I got three more credits.

"Then I thought, 'Well, we have a college right here in the county, Saints Junior College in Lexington, so I'll take some courses there. I went and I went and I went. I got an A.A. degree. Then I thought, 'Well, if I've gone this far, I might as well go farther.'

"So I went down to Tougaloo College, to the TIECE program, the Tougaloo Institute of Early Childhood Education. And there I discovered that nothing I'd taken at Saints counted. So I started over and got another A.A. degree at Tougaloo. In early childhood education. Then I decided, well, I might as well go on and go all the way, so I'll just keep on keeping on and get me a four year teaching degree. I had to take some at Jackson State, some at Mississippi Valley State, and some at Mississippi State.

"Since 1986, I've been teaching kindergarten in a county public school. I have thirty-two children. One child in the school is white, a special ed child. The child is in my class part of the day. The special ed teacher is white. There's one white first grade teacher, not local. Our principal is wonderful. He's always telling me how well I work with parents. He encourages me to get involved whenever there are tense situations. When the supervisors come, they like my learning centers. I help the other kindergarten teachers any way I can to set up their centers and let the children move around and choose and do. I belong to the Mississippi Association for Children Under Six, MACUS. The way Polly said to do it in CDGM, that's the way it's done in early childhood education.

"At a teachers' meeting one day, each person was asked to tell a little about themself, their background, their family—when I finished telling about where I've come up from and about each of my children, I sat back and I said, 'My, I really *do* have some things to be proud about don't I? One daughter went to the University of Illinois at Champagne-Urbana, and is married to an air force man and lives in the Washington, D.C. suburbs. Another daughter is a business teacher in Memphis and does some real estate work. I have another daughter in Memphis; she was with the IRS, now she's managing at a plant. Two of my daughters and a son are in Oklahoma: One of them works for a lawyer, the other for Oklahoma City, and my son is self-employed.'

"Oh, my yes, we've made a lot of progress! In CDGM days, my family didn't have an indoor bathroom or a phone. Look where I am now!"

* * * * * * * * * * * *

Hattie Saffold is happy about the amazing progress in Holmes County, and she surely should be. But she's right, too, to worry about complacency. Because in spite of all the progress in the education of Holmes County black children, during the (typical) 1989–90 school year, 4,262 black children were enrolled in the Holmes County public schools, and *one white child* (the special needs child in Hattie's class of whom she spoke). The county school superintendent is black. Four of the five school board members are black. *In short, instead of integrating their schools, Holmes County white people gave the entire system to black people.*

In Bolivar County, the population consists of two black people for each white person; we would expect to see in public school classrooms two black children for every white child. But in the county's six school districts, the racial breakdown looks like this:

District	Black children	White children
Bolivar #1 (West Bolivar)	14,002	168
Bolivar #2	333	7
Bolivar #3	1,057	14 (six of whom are special ed)
Bolivar #4 (Cleveland)	3,223	1,506
Bolivar #5 (Shaw)	918	73
Bolivar #6 (Mound Bayou)	1,274	1

Even in Jackson, a big city, a place of better educated people, a place with a population that's fifty percent black and fifty percent white, in the same school year just mentioned, there were 26,000 black children in the public schools, and 7,000 white children.

The Reverend Rims Barber comments caustically,

"It's not just getting kindergarten. Yes, since 1986 we've had it statewide and full-day. But in many of the classrooms, the first day children learn to sit down and shut up. The second day's lesson is color inside the lines. The third day is hold your water until lunch time. If you achieve all this, you can go work in the chicken plucking factory for the rest of your life. There, amidst the blood, stench, and squawks, you'll make good minimum wage money, and you'll be able to pay the rent on your shack, which on welfare you can't.''

And then there is that federal fiasco, the Follow Through program. If Head Start is our nation's pride, Follow Through is our nation's disgrace. Designed at the same time that Head Start was designed, but not activated until a little later, Follow Through was supposed to support Head Start graduates through the transition into kindergarten and the early grades. It was intended to ensure that children's gains in confidence, in the joy of learning, and in their families' abundant participation in the educational process were maintained through those dangerous grades in which many low-income children are allowed to fail to learn to read.

The Follow Through program got off to a great start. Many excellent educational models were developed. There were model Follow Through programs in a number of schools, many of them very good. But developing models is merely the opening act. After that comes political organizing and advocacy until the rest of the scenes are seen. Follow Through programs should be in every school that regularly receives Head Start graduates. A handful of programs in the entire United States just won't do. Unfortunately, although advocates, led by the Children's Defense Fund, succeeded, when OEO was eliminated, in preventing the placement of Head Start in the Department of Education, and secured it in the more supportive Department of Health and Human Services, they did not fight to the finish for Follow Through. Unfortunately, it *is* in the Department of Education, which doesn't appear to give two hoots about it. It has languished ever since. Luckily, recent official evaluators making recommendations regarding Head Start graduates' continuing education, have emphasized continuing support for children after they enter kindergarten and the primary grades.

Margrit Garner, a long-time Tougalooian specializing in services for children, says with disgust, ''They play yo-yo with the children. Help them up in Head Start, let them down in the public school.'' Probably many good-hearted Americans are unaware of what children who are at a disadvantage in our public schools need to boost them through to success. Or naively believe that the children are getting what they need. The same cannot be said about the federal government. All pertinent legislators and administrators are well aware of what's needed.

''Yes,'' says a woman from Wayne county Mississippi. ''And they are well aware that they can get away with whatever they want where *we* are concerned. They prefer military build-ups to letting little black children have a chance. They know a powerful secret: The public will not speak up and stand up for the children. The Republicans can do whatever they want. They do just enough to make their conscience feel good. Follow Through? Oh sure, *we* have it. Huh!

In sixteen schools in the whole country? That isn't having a Follow Through program. That's having a way for rich people not to have to feel guilty."

Many matters remain to be resolved before education for Mississippi's black children becomes excellent. Black leaders, their many allies (the relentless Reverend Rims Barber among them), and their liaison groups (the Lawyers' Committee, NAACP Legal Defense and Education Fund, Inc., etc.) are vigilant and active in the ongoing struggle to improve the quality of education. Many of the long-term leaders of positive social change in education, as in so many other arenas, are people who participated in the movement and in CDGM in the 1960s, for example Henry Kirksey (see pages 50, 158, 170, 276, 293) and Bennie Thompson.

A major issue in 1990 was "the equity issue." "To us," says Rims, "Equity means 'the same.' " Most of the funding for Mississippi's public schools comes from the state on the basis of average daily attendance. The amount per child is equal across the state. School districts can add to the state-given minimum, but rich and poor districts, defined and taxed according to property value, vary widely in their ability to do so. The amount a poor district is able to raise and what an economically well-off district can raise ranged (in 1990, for example) from $175 per child to $1,750 per child! (In 1990, one poor district asked families please to send their children's toilet paper to school with them.) The richer districts can pay higher salaries, so they can hire better teachers and *more* teachers (to keep class size sensible.) The better off high schools can offer the full array of courses required for the college-bound track. This affects SAT scores, thus future opportunities.

With regard to education for black people, Mississippi's state government may have been a large part of the problem in the late 1960s, but in the late 1970s, well before the much heralded *Nation at Risk* report (in tandem with other factors) galvanized most states into a reform mode, Mississippi began a grand campaign to improve its school system. Although the focus has not been on blacks, they have benefited like everyone else. As they say in African coastal villages, when the tide comes in, all boats float higher. However, the educational system in Mississippi, as in most of the United States, still does not provide a way for "at-risk" black children to overcome the educationally and economically disadvantaged circumstances in which history has stranded them. Forty percent of today's first graders, ten percent more than the national average, will drop out before graduating from high school. According to the NAACP Legal Defense and Education Fund, Inc., in 1986 the Mississippi Department of Education identified thirty-five school districts with dropout rates of at least fifty percent. Of twenty-four districts where the dropout rate was between fifty and sixty percent, eighteen had black student populations of more than fifty percent; of the remaining eleven districts, where the dropout rate was sixty percent or greater, nine had fifty percent or more black students.

Like most of the states that later launched a great deal of school improvement rhetoric, and some degree of actual school improvement, Mississippi emphasizes student memorization of millions of mini-facts and fragmented skills—the type of drill and kill learning that can be measured with relentless "achievement" testing (and causes thousands of children to drop out). To graduate from high school, recent Mississippi law requires people to pass the FLE (Functional Literacy Exam, which looks for an eighth grade reading level). However, again like most other states, Mississippi has neglected to improve the appropriateness and excellence of the education provided to each individual child; the "group teach and constantly test" approach so popular in every state is like throwing "students" in the ocean to swim or sink, in contrast to the "individualized educational excellence" approach, which insists on educating each person by any and all means possible, ensuring that she or he learns a great deal of value, whether or not it's readily measurable by means of nationally standardized tests. Head Start in Mississippi and in all other states has gone along with this unfortunate trend: focusing on the boring mechanics of learning instead of on the excitement of learning valuable information (with all necessary skills learned along the way as needed).

Mississippi's Education Reform Act of 1982 reinstated compulsory school attendance, which, as explained in earlier pages, was wiped out in a bygone era to avoid requiring people to send children to integrated schools. It required that kindergartens be developed in every school district. It mandated a teacher's aide in every K–3 classroom. It established required school accreditation standards for the first time in Mississippi history. In 1988, the state legislature authorized an average increase of $3,800 in teachers' salaries, bringing Mississippi's teaching salaries up from 49th place in the 50 states to 34th place; quite a difference!

In 1985, the Board of Trustees of the Institutions of Higher Learning (the state college board) ruled that all young people applying to state colleges had to have taken the academic curriculum in contrast to the general program. However, not all districts offer all necessary courses each semester, and not all districts counsel students *into* the academic track. (For example, in Bolivar County—District #4—while almost eighty percent of all white high schoolers are in the academic track, less than twenty-five percent of the black students are.)

In 1990, fewer than one-fifth of Mississippi's black high schoolers are taking the courses that could prepare them for any but dead-end jobs. Over 700,000 adult Mississippians lack a high school diploma. In fact, a third of the state's adult population—400,000 people—have less than eight years of schooling. Mississippi ranks 45th among the 50 states on literacy level. (However, Mississippi is making what Children's Defense Fund defines as adequate progress in increasing the percent of students who do graduate from high school.) Families are being informed by black leaders and their liaison groups of the importance of urging their children into the academic fast track. According to studies done by the NAACP Legal Defense and Education Fund, Inc., forty-five percent of Mississippi's high school graduates are black, and in 1989 only twenty-four percent of them (compared to thirty-eight-point-six for whites) completed the academic core curriculum. Though more black students than before are taking the core, the rate has gone up only slowly in the past few years. *If families are unaware of the lasting effects of high school tracking, and also lack confidence in their children's academic proficiency, an unfortunate turn may be taken at this fork in the road of life.*

Furthermore, even when black high schoolers as well as white are in the "IHL" track (the track intended to get people accepted by "Institutions of Higher Learning"), the quality of the (separate) courses they take may be very unequal. For example, in Bolivar (districts) #5, #3, and #2, ninety percent of all students are low-income black people. But in #5, the scores of students who took the academic core in the widely used American College Testing Programs are much higher than scores of students in #3 and #2 *who also took the core.*

Moreover, there's a strong incentive for black teens to attend Mississippi's *black* colleges, which are educationally inferior, not its (so-called integrated) white colleges: The minimum ACT score required for admittance into Mississippi Valley is 10; for Alcorn and Jackson it's 13; and for the five white colleges it's 15 (Ole Miss, the University of Southern Mississippi, Delta State, Mississippi State U, and Mississippi University for Women.) The black community and its allies, including the U.S. Department of Justice, have a lawsuit underway charging the State of Mississippi with operating a racially separate system of public higher education in violation of the Constitution and the Civil Rights Act of 1964.

Like all significant social change affecting families, serious improvement in Mississippi's educationally inequitable school and higher education system *has* come and *will* come as a result of the efforts of older students, parents, (a high percentage of them former Head Start parents—specifically CDGM parents), child advocates, and community leaders.

The Adams family is typical of many Mississippi black families, especially CDGM families. In Adams vs. Rankin county, John and Alean won the right for their children to go to school where they chose to. One year, Mississippi announced freedom of choice for first graders (only). The Adams' had a first grade son. They didn't want him to go to white school without his siblings. They sued for the right for children of any age to go to white school if they so chose. Alean says, "We had to go to court many times, to meetings and more meetings, to Biloxi. . . Finally we won. We led the way and other families followed." All over the state people had to sue to go to the school of their choice.

An essential element to evaluate when assessing Head Start is the extent to which parents continue to be a vital force for positive educational change with regard to meeting the needs of low-income and minority children in their public elementary and secondary schools, and in the area's public colleges. How many parents are active champions for these children? Is there an ever-swelling group of parents, expanded every year as a new wave graduates from Head Start? How well have parents been trained to understand and deal with issues of extreme importance to the success of their children, such as the urgent need to eliminate achievement tests upon entrance to kindergarten given to enable school personnel to label children "failures" before they begin, thus freeing the system from feeling accountable for educating these children "equally"? Do parents *stay* involved as agitating advocates until their children graduate from college with honors?

Social change toward a more just society comes one step at a time as a result of the actions of families like the Adams family. And like the Ayers family: It's 1990. I'm on my way to visit former CDGM Area Teacher Guide Lily Ayers, a lovely person; I've always loved her. From Jackson, I drive past Yazoo City, past another hour-and-a-half of absolutely flat, dusty Delta, empty, completely empty, except for an occasional gray shack, fancy tractor, or dead armadillo on the straight unswerving highway. Lily still lives on the same corner in a back alley of Glen Allen that she and Jake, a star member of CDGM's Board of Directors and a star human being, lived on twenty-five years ago when first we met. [For more about Lily and Jake Ayers, see index.]

However, the *house* isn't the same: two days before Christmas 1985, the home in which the Ayers' had raised the twins and their other seven children burned to the ground—something about the gas line. Poor people get burned out at a much higher rate than others do. The Lord has always watched over Lily, though, she feels, because she so deeply believes He is good. In this instance, Jake and Lily had bought new fire insurance just two months before the fire—three times as much as they had had for less money than they'd paid before. A man had come around selling it. So they were able to buy a $17,000 modular home, have it hauled a hundred miles and put high up on blocks, and buy all new carpeting and furniture. It looks very nice now, every item store bought, appearing to be smack out of a Sears show window. Every *old* item, the relics of two long rich lives, was incinerated.

The *home* is not the same, either, not only because of lost treasures from a family's lifetime, and not only because all but the baby, now 18, have moved on and away from Glen Allen to get jobs and live their lives (a sad aspect of growing older in an area of great job scarcity is that your adult children and grandchildren are likely to live far away), but, more importantly, because four months after the arrival of the new home, right in front of Lily's eyes, Jake, age 66, dropped dead of a heart attack. "I'm all right," Lily says, but one senses that she isn't. Lily and Jake were remarkably close. "He's always right here with me," she sighs. She spends more and more time in church. The lights are on in Lily's eyes, but the impression is that she's only half home, that her soul is halfway to heaven with her beloved husband.

Even though Jake Ayers has passed on to the far side, he's still fighting to bring better education to black people. When their own Head Start children became school aged, Jake and Lily bravely sent them to the *white* public school. Inch by inch, child by child. When it came time for Jake's kids to go to college, he discovered how much less money Mississippi's three traditionally black institutions—Alcorn, Mississippi Valley, and Jackson State—receive than do the five historically *white* colleges. "He wanted them to go to black colleges, but he wanted them to be *good* colleges,'' Lily explains. So Jake filed a law suit.

Lily has her eight dispersed sons, who, she says, all look like Jake, and *their* children, and her daughter the teacher in Chicago. Lily still does social services for the Washington County Head Start, as she has since 1975: ''I help people get housing, transportation to the doctor, and other services. The welfare people are much, much better than they used to be. They learned from Head Start how it's supposed to be done. Many of the welfare workers used to *work* in Head Start. The schools are much better, too, but way below where they should be. In this area, Washington County, the whites all went off to private school in the beginning, but many couldn't afford it, and have come back. We have public kindergarten now, and a full-year program for four-year-olds in the one Glen Allen school. The kindergarten, classes for four-year-olds, and Head Start, they all have activity centers set up for the children for the inspectors' sake, but the children stay seated and learn how to use pencils the right way. Parents love it, it's much better than when we were coming up, but it isn't the way CDGM said—children playing, moving freely, making choices.

''The only higher education I've gotten was through CDGM: You, Polly, had me at the eight-week early childhood education training at Ole Miss—*me* at Ole Miss, and that was only three years after Meredith integrated it!—and I went to many more places, too.

''There aren't a lot of new jobs, but *some*, because white employers hire black people now to work along with whites, and there's been the CAP agency for many years, making jobs to help folks get some of what they need.''

There may be many changes for the better, but steep-banked open drainage ditches still crowd Lily's ill-paved street, the tiny houses still huddle together on the wrong side of town, and a neighboring white man with whom I checked directions said, ''Oh you mean niggerville.''

''We don't have to say, 'Yessir' and 'No ma'am' anymore,'' Lily continues, ''though some people continue to do it. We can speak up about our side of things now, and we are heard. At least to some extent. Politically it's much better. We have twenty black people in the legislature. No matter what they do there it's good. It's good for the white people just to see black people every day dressed up and in important places having their say. But most of them *do* do good things for us. I've always thought that Robert Clark from our second district here was very good. And Mike Espy, our congressman in Washington, D.C. is too, very good. [See chapter 47 for more about the political picture regarding elected black officials.]

''Jake's lawsuit to make Mississippi's black colleges equal to the white colleges? Al Chambliss at Legal Services in Oxford is the lawyer handling it. You can call him.''

Attorney Alvin O. Chambliss, Jr. of North Mississippi Rural Legal Services has been working on the inequities of Mississippi's system of higher education for over twenty years, ever since he graduated from Howard University Law School and returned to his native state. (Before that, in 1966–67 when I lived in Mississippi, Al, at the time a recent graduate of Jackson State, was employed by CDGM's social service department. He worked out of Jackson all over the state.)

Late in 1990, Al excitedly explained the Ayers case to me:

"As I see it, the Ayers case is a watershed case. Last month, in September 1990, the Fifth Circuit Court of Appeals in New Orleans ruled *against* equal opportunity for the races! *Against* equalizing funding for the black and the white institutions of higher education in Mississippi! This means that the Court is saying, in effect, 'Forget the U.S. Supreme Court's Brown v. Board of Education decision. Forget affirmative action. Let's go back to 1896, Plessey v. Ferguson, when separate and unequal was declared OK.'

"Never in the history of the Fifth Circuit Court has there *ever* been a black judge, not one, not ever; could that be a Court that considers black people's needs and rights as much as it considers whites?"

Fourteen judges voted on the Ayers case, nine against and five for it. Two of the judges didn't vote; one of the two, Judge Clark, disqualified himself—maybe because, in 1962, he was the attorney representing Mississippi Governor Ross Barnett when the governor stood barring a doorway, proclaiming all the way to President Kennedy's White House and Robert Kennedy's Justice Department that James Meredith, a black man, would never be permitted to enroll at Ole Miss, nor would any other black person ever be admitted.

Attorney Chambliss continues:

"The Brown v. Board of Education decision in 1954 was about doing away with a dual school system, which in my mind means kindergarten through college. Here we have the Fifth Circuit Court, which decides cases for an entire section of the United States where a high percentage of the people are black, in effect saying, 'We have fulfilled our obligation: A long time ago, the Court ruled that white schools must take qualified black students. Students can choose which university to go to. Choose! When Ole Miss has bleachers with seats for 50,000 and Mississippi Valley has a cowpen to play in? When Southern Mississippi has millions of volumes in its library, and Jackson State has a small percent of that? Choose! What kind of choice is that? Many black students have to go to college near where they live or they can't go to college at all, and they should have available to them a *good* college, a public college equally as good as another public college, as good as any or all colleges in the public system of higher education in the state. Isn't that what equal opportunity means? This recent court decision is nothing but a legalization of apartheid.

"The week after James Meredith was admitted to Ole Miss in 1962, the powers that be came up with the ACT score of 15 that you had to have to be admitted to Ole Miss; this at a time when black people were averaging 7 and whites were averaging 16! What is that except a way of formalizing and determining where whites will 'freely choose' to go, and where blacks will 'freely choose' to go? How could black children make higher scores when they are given such inferior education?

"Simply declaring a school or college desegregated and saying, 'No more discrimination allowed.' 'We don't discriminate against any race.' Is that enough? Is that all there is to it? One hundred years of *serious* underfunding for the black colleges, then with no major new funding, they are suddenly declared equal? How *could* they *possiby* be equal? In fact, the Board of Trustees of the Institutions of Higher Learning made these institutions even *less* equal; they made three (white ones) *comprehensive* (major) institutions, and five others (black) *regional* (minor) institutions. Then they even have an *excuse* to invest much more in certain universities!

"The University of Mississippi has been going since 1840, and it has always been a school for white people, even though, since the sixties, some black people attend. In 1984, nine black students testified that their fellow students taunted them, threw dead black cats in their windows, things like that. In 1984, Hawkins became the first black cheerleader at Ole Miss. After he refused to wave the rebel flag at the first game, four thousand people marched on his house—he would have been killed—the national media covered it—in *1984!* Ole Miss is not a choice for most black students who want a college education.

"I have been involved in this business of equalizing institutions of higher education for over twenty years. I could see that the education I myself was getting at Jackson State was not as good as it should have been. A number of us at Jackson and at other colleges were concerned about it. In 1970, we formed the Black Mississippians Council for Higher Education. Some of the founders were Aaron Henry, Ed Brown, Bennie Thompson, Rims Barber, Jake Ayers [pages 212, 262, 428, 431–432], Ike Madison, Margaret Walker Alexander, Robert Walker (the first black mayor of Vicksburg), Ed Bishop (the first black mayor of Corinth), Johnny Walls and his wife Dorothy Walls—The Charles Hayes Foundation paid for us to research the problem of separate and unequal. We were involved in the Adams v. Richardson case, when Secretary Richardson of the U.S. Department of Education said that Mississippi isn't making a reasonable effort to do the law—we have been working on this for a very long time, you have to keep working on these things, progress doesn't take place overnight."

In 1971, this group pointed out to the governor that there were thirteen white people on the state's Institutions of Higher Learning Board of Trustees, *and no blacks*. Of 514 public officials and decision makers with a voice in making policy affecting black colleges, *only six were black*. There were and are also sixteen junior colleges in the state, *and no black people are in policy making positions*. In 1990, all aspects of the situation remain the same. But, as the African proverb says, " A pound of patience is worth a bushel of brains," and many black leaders in Mississippi, bless them, have both.

* * * * * * * * * * * *

When assessing the worth of a human services/social change project, the question of descendants must be investigated. Did the project have any? Were they of value? Do they still exist, and if so, are they still worthwhile? CDGM not only has alive and thriving Head Start center and staff descendants, but also a number of spin-off descendants that continue to do good.

Of all the projects in whose origination I've been significantly involved, one of the ones of which I'm most fond and proud is Tougaloo College's TIECE program, mentioned by former CDGM Area Teacher Guides Lavoree Jones and Hattie Saffold as the program through which they earned A.A. degrees and CDA credentials. An A.A. degree is a two year Associate of Arts college degree; a CDA credential is a nationally recognized Child Development Associate credential given by the Council for Early Childhood Professional Recognition. The CDA program represents an effort on the part of the federal government and the child care profession (particularly the National Association for the Education of Young Children) to prepare qualified Head Start staff and staff for other early childhood education programs. The Child Development Associate credential is largely based on individual competency, although CDA candidates are expected to have taken some courses somewhere in subjects such as child development, curriculum planning for early childhood education, and so on. The courses are supposed to be tailored to the needs of those taking them—often mature and wise people like Lavoree or Hattie. The CDA plan for training, assessing, and credentialing child care staff was created in 1971 by the federal government's Office of Child Development—now the Administration for Children, Youth and Families (part of the Department of Health and Human Services). Three, four, five, and six years *before* 1971, we CDGMians were working on such a program; first Tom Levin, Art Thomas, Marv Hoffman, and I, then John Mudd and I, and many other people after that. Tougaloo's TIECE program (the Tougaloo Institute for Early Childhood Education), which has by 1990 graduated 250 Child Development Associates, is a direct descendant of the Area Teacher Guide staff development program that I devised. The transition started in 1965. (See pages 174–177.)

TIECE descended from CDGM's teacher development program in this manner: Art Thomas had ideas about a "Poor People's College" (see pages 663–665). Ideas of a "Community Education Extension"—a new community college—first appeared in written form in Tom Levin's 1965 position paper to OEO about what CDGM and all its special projects were to be. (The pre-CDA program is briefly sketched in this book on pages 320, 474–551.) These were the same ideas that John Mudd, Marv Hoffman and I developed soon after (pages 576–579, 582–583). This was the Teacher Development Institute (TDI) for which, in the summer of 1966, I was night and day trying to acquire foundation funds (page 597). This is the program that the Field Foundation funded in October, 1966 through Mary Holmes Junior College; the Community Education Extension. For a while it was the Mississippi Institute for Early Childhood Education (MIECE). It then m oved to Tougaloo and became TIECE.

Another part of our Poor People's College was funded by the Merrill and Ford Foundations, still using Tom's original name for it; this was Mississippi Action for Community Education (MACE), managed by Dave Emmons and Ed Brown.

* * * * * * * * * * * *

In the "speaking of progress" department, I eagerly record this entry: On April 21, 1990 I attended an extraordinary event in Jackson, Mississippi. Twenty-five years ago I would have sworn it could never happen. At the Ramada Inn Coliseum Hotel, a remarkable Conference was held entitled "Educating the Black Child: Mississippi."

The first thing that struck me as remarkable was this gathering of black educators in the sort of hotel where twenty-five years "Negroes" who entered risked being the center of serious scenes, even if the people in question were one or two in number, and were well-dressed middle-class people. Here were hundreds of black people, most of them referring to themselves and the children they teach as African Americans.

The second thing that struck me as remarkable was that hundreds of middle-class black people were attending a conference featuring, among many other speakers, the Director of the Division of Policy and Information of the NAACP Legal Defense and Education Fund. Very, very few middle-class black people in the sixties dared have anything to do with NAACP, which was equated by white Mississippians with the Communist Party. It was poor people who had nothing to lose—except, ironically, their lives—who dared to join and deal with NAACP. Equally stunning to me was the esteemed luncheon speaker's enormously forceful call to the audience to develop dormant or nonexistant African American pride in themselves and in the children in their classrooms. The extemporaneous and impassioned presentation was delivered in the manner of a Southern black preacher's sermon, full of dedication, rhythmic cadences, and ardent, heart-felt audience responses. The speaker was Asa G. Hilliard III, a well-known specialist in the study of psychological test validity in cross cultural usage and early childhood education, among other things. The speech sounded exactly like the overwhelmingly moving orations we heard so many of in the civil rights world of Mississippi's sixties. Rarely, very, *very* rarely, did a middle-class black person dare attend in those days, and the reasons were real. Teachers who did, usually learned that for various mysterious reasons their contracts were not being renewed.

The third thing that seemed mind bogglingly non-sixties was the presence of most of the Jackson public school system's handful of high-up white officials.

The Conference presenters (to a person whose perspective was that of a sixties civil rights worker, and who was doing a Rip van Winkle return to Mississippi after a quarter century absence) were a positively astonishing group, almost all of them African American. It was not the high level of distinctions each speaker had that was astonishing, but rather the fact that black people of such stature in this particular state could now, in 1990, participate openly, without bomb threats and flying bullets, in a happening flagrantly billed as "a blueprint for action" to improve the achievement of "African American" children in Mississippi from Head Start to high school.

The Mississippi Committee on Educating the Black Child, sponsors of the

Conference, was created in 1988 in Atlanta, Georgia. Its mission is to focus on all obstacles between the black child and educational excellence. The Committee is a coalition of concerned educators and citizens, who are asking themselves, parents, teachers, administrators, students, community members, and policy makers, "What can we do in our roles to improve the education of African American children? What will I do next week, month, year, the rest of my life to help African American children?" The Committee is an outgrowth of The National Conference on Educating Black Children convened in 1986 by the Honorable Augustus Hawkins, Chairman, House Committee on Education and Labor.

I could scarcely believe my ears when, at the Conference, the Blackburn Junior High School Choir of the Jackson public schools sang the freedom song we had defiantly sung so many times in terrifying tight spots in the sixties, "Don't You Let Nobody Turn You Round."

I could scarcely believe my eyes when I saw before me on the podium Alyce Clarke, the first black woman elected to the Mississippi House of Representatives. She has been an instructor of employment skills at the Opportunities Industrialization Center. She has been director of nutrition and WIC services for the Jackson-Hinds Comprehensive Health Center, created by Dr. Aaron Shirley; a member of the Mississippi Association of Community Health Centers Nutrition Society; and a member of the Board of Directors of Mississippi's Food Network. Representative Clarke is a member of the Mayor's Advisory Committee, the Board of Directors of United Way, Hinds Federation of Democratic Women, Hinds County Executive Democratic Committee, Southeastern Educational Improvement Laboratories, and the National Women's Political Caucus.

I could scarcely believe my eyes when I saw before me on the podium Alice Harden, the first black woman to serve in the Mississippi State *Senate*. She was a public school teacher and teacher educator for fourteen years, and President of the Mississippi Association of Educators. She is the Democratic National Committeewoman from Mississippi and Past President of the Hinds County Federation of Democratic Women. Senator Harden serves on these committees in the Mississippi State Senate: Education, Elections, Municipalities, Business and Financial Institutions, Public Utilities, Public Property, Corrections, Joint Legislative Committee on Reapportionment and Congressional Redistricting.

And my teeth, genuine as they are, nearly jumped out of my mouth when the Honorable Mike Espy arrived on stage, Mike Espy, the first black Congessman Mississippi has elected to the United States Congress since Reconstruction.

CHAPTER 47

SEEKING POLITICAL REPRESENTATION, VOTE BY VOTE, CANDIDATE BY CANDIDATE: AN AMERICAN RIGHT, NOT A VIRULENT BLIGHT

Head Start—services, yes, but how much "empowerment"?

MIKE ESPY is the first black Congressman elected from Mississippi since Reconstruction, and won a landslide victory in his November 8, 1988 re-election to the Second Congressional District seat. Congressman Espy carried all of the twenty two counties in his district and received sixty six percent of the total votes. The second congressional district covers most of the western half of Mississippi, and is one of the nation's poorest districts, which is why Congressman Espy's appointments to the House Budget Committee and House Agriculture Committee have been important.

Congressman Espy was one of a few freshmen members of Congress to pass a major piece of legislation in the 100th Congress, the Lower Mississippi River Valley Delta Development Act, a blueprint for economic development in a seven-state area including Mississippi, Arkansas and Louisiana. Espy introduced and passed National Catfish Day, which gained worldwide attention to the catfish industry. This industry employs some seventeen thousand or more people in the second district. Unfortunately, most of the better jobs in the industry are held by whites, and as you would expect, the low-paid, hazardous jobs are filled by unskilled blacks. Many of the congressman's constituents don't feel that he pays much attention to this issue. He is seen by many as being a little too close to the producers.

Congressman Espy sits on the House Select Committee on Hunger and chairs the committee's Domestic Task Force on Hunger. He serves on three subcommittees of the Agriculture Committee: subcommittees on Cotton, Rice, and Sugar; Conservation, Credit and Rural Development; and Domestic Marketing, Consumer Relations, and Nutrition. Congressman Espy was chosen by the House Democratic Leadership as an At-Large Whip for the 101st Congress. He was also elected vice president of the 1986 House Democratic Class and chairman of the House Democratic Freshman Class Budget Task Force.

An Espy backer who has followed his performance carefully says, "He votes eighty-five percent right according to Washington liberals, but he doesn't do enough for the folks back home. He doesn't care enough what *we* need and think. His eyes are on some other, bigger prize. But right now he's all we've got, so we'll keep on working for him till we get someone who will represent us better.''

Mike Espy is one black person, but in Washington he has the power of many more through the Congressional Black Caucus. Furthermore, there will soon be additional black representatives from Mississippi and from other states.

At the Educating the Black Child Conference, Mike Espy said to the well-dressed black middle-class audience, ''There is nothing sadder than being all dressed up and having no place to go. . . .We need to interest our kids in reading books instead of buying Reeboks. We need to interest them in getting grades, not getting Guccis. . . .Cars are convenient, but it doesn't matter what you ride in as long as you take someone with you. . . .Every day in this country, three thousand black children drop out of school. . . .Our president [Bush] says he wants to be the education president. There's a big difference between rhetoric and reality. . . .Unless teachers learn how to use democratic practices in their classrooms, children will continue to grow up just being an audience.'' Congressman Espy's message was clear as a school bell. It was, although he didn't say it, the message of the old African proverb: If you don't know where you're going, any road will get you there.

Quality education is entirely wrapped in politics. If parents and educators don't participate in electing officials at all levels who will work for quality education, and don't advocate for quality education with these officials once elected, parents' dreams and teachers' efforts will be hampered by unhelpful policies and requirements, and by too-small budgets.

One black congressman from an entire state? So what is that worth? For one thing, it's better to have someone in Washington watching out for your interests than *no one*. Secondly, one drop at a time makes an empty bucket fuller.

In 1970, there were only ten black elected officials at the federal level (congressmen or senators). In 1990, there are twenty-four. Slow progress in securing representation for the various interests of America's diverse black population, to be sure, but progress nonetheless. Especially because these representatives created the Congressional Black Caucus; twenty-four voices, especially when in harmony, which Caucus members' voices usually are, speak louder than one.

Of course Espy is a member of the Congressional Black Caucus on Capitol Hill. The CBC was created soon after the War on Poverty ended and President Nixon's reign of nonaction began. Some powerful people, many of whom had been actively involved in the civil rights movement (Shirley Chisholm of Brooklyn, William Clay of St. Louis, John Conyers and Charles Diggs of Detroit, and Ron Dellums from Berkeley, for instance) organized the Caucus. For twenty years, its goal has been to watch out for and promote black Americans' general well-being through legislation. Among the CBC's greatest achievements was leading the 1981 effort to extend the Voting Rights Act of 1965, after which black representation in Congress doubled. This was the reason that right-wing Republicans didn't like it.

Making life better for poor children and their families depends in large part upon what laws and appropriations state and federal legislators make available to—or deny—people, thus powerfully influencing service delivery agencies' incentives, attitudes, options, and behaviors. Therefore, part of evaluating any program intended to help low-income families and their children get on their feet must be to evaluate the program's voter registration and education efforts and successes. Almost always, this is overlooked by evaluation "experts," designers and implementers of Head Start, Community Action Agencies, and indeed *all* human service programs. Retroactively, CDGM should be awarded an A+. Among Head Start bureaucrats in Washington, there have always been some who understood this "political awakening" aspect of the program. Urging every Head Start employee and parent to vote isn't heresy, nor is it partisan politics; it's just common sense.

The political picture for black Mississippians is much, much better. Twenty black people in the Mississippi state legislature, two in the State Senate, and a U.S. Congressman, too!

Five months after my children and I completed our two full years of living in Mississippi, in November 1967, the first black person since Reconstruction was elected to the *state* legislature. Inch by inch, one by one. He lives in Holmes County (Hattie Saffold's county). He was supported by most movement and CDGM families in the second district, and all their relatives, plus the many people whose votes he won through exhausting campaigning.

Robert Clark was born on a cornshuck bed. His grandfather was a slave near Jackson, freed after the Civil War. In 1875, before absolute racial segregation set in for a century or so, he was at a meeting of whites and blacks that erupted into the Clinton Massacre; political disputes exploded into gunfire, and men of both colors were killed. In angry response, white men from nearby Jackson, Vicksburg, and Bolton rushed to Clinton and lynched large numbers of people. Robert Clark's grandfather escaped only because a white friend dragged him into the woods and pretended to shoot him, leaving him to make his terrified way through darkness and swamps to Ebenezer, where he settled.

Years after he had started serving in the state legislature, Robert Clark still lived in his simple house in Ebenezer (originally named Bucksnort, Mississippi), where, a young widower, he parented his two school-age boys. When in 1967 Clark first arrived in the Mississippi House chamber, no one would sit beside him until, one evening, the respected newsman Bill Minor, a white, sat at his table. Even after that, however, the House Speaker refused to acknowledge Robert Clark when he stood to make a statement or a motion. After eight years of isolation in the legislature, throughout which this mild-mannered, politically effective moderate man made slow progress in winning respect from some of his white colleagues, Clark was joined by three more elected black representatives (1975); by 1979 there were seventeen. Robert Clark was a member of the Public Health and Welfare Committee, and the Appropriations Committee. By 1982, he was chairman of the House Education Committee for the state of Mississippi. (He had been a teacher, and had a masters' degree from Michigan State University.) Consistently, Clark worked to bring compulsory education to a state that still didn't have it; as mentioned earlier, compulsory education has just recently been reinstated. Inch by inch, issue by issue.

Twice, Robert Clark ran for a seat in the U.S. House of Representatives. Both times he lost his race (*due* to race), but his campaigns helped the cause; Clark lost in 1982 and 1984, but in 1986, Espy won.

In 1982, Clark's campaign manager was long-time movement man Ed Brown (see index). Both times Clark's press secretary—just to show how times, even in the delta, change—was Melany Neilson, a young white woman from Lexington, Mississippi, an Ole Miss graduate,[50] the daughter of a former planter turned local lawyer, then city judge—Judge Neilson. Judge Neilson said on local TV that Robert Clark was a fine upstanding Christian man. For this, the judge was socially ostracized. The Jackson *Clarion-Ledger* endorsed Clark! Hazel Brannon Smith, editor of the Lexington *Advertiser* (see pages 000), supported Clark. In the 1950s when Ms. Smith had criticized the white sheriff for shooting a black man without provocation, she had suffered economic reprisals, a libel suit, and threats against her life. In the late 1960s and 1970s, she had led a group of pragmatists, newly visible across the state, who repeatedly said: Black people are not going back to Africa. White people are not going back to Europe. Blacks are a large percentage of our state's population. They *are* going to vote. And they aren't going to vote for folks who castrate or kill their kin.

Although Clark was actively supported by Walter Fauntroy (Chairman of the Congressional Black Caucus); Washington, D.C.'s later notorious Mayor Marion Barry (who is *from* Itta Bena, Mississippi); House Speaker Tip O'Neill, Senator Edward Kennedy, the Governor of Mississippi, Senator Eastland and Senator Stennis, he lost, narrowly, to Webb Franklin, a man whose slogan was "He's one of us." Franklin's campaign was riddled with racist rhetoric and race-baiting. He was supported by the White Citizen's Council, the National Rifle Association, and the American Medical Association. The traditional lack of black voting and a heavy white turnout to ward off this gentle threat to the white supremacist system defeated Robert Clark.

Clark's opponent in his second (1984) campaign called himself "a cotton boll" (cotton bolls are white) and Robert Clark "a lump of coal." He talked a lot of red, white, and blue, too. His slogan was "Barrett before it's too late." Jesse Jackson stumped for Clark. Fans had banners reading "Hands that picked cotton now pick presidents."

By 1990, twenty-five years after Head Start and CDGM started, there were twenty black people in the Mississippi House of Representatives, one of them (but only *one*) a woman, and two blacks in the State Senate.

[50]Melany has written a fascinating little book showing the evolving racial understanding of a white plantation owner's daughter: *Even Mississippi,* Tuscaloosa, University of Alabama Press, 1989.

Racism exists not only in Mississippi. It's deeply ingrained in America's history and always lurks just beneath the surface. The resurgence of dramatic racist incidents in recent times serves to remind us of this. The widening gap between blacks and whites in educational levels nationally, and the rapidly swelling population of urban black people straitjacketed by poverty and all its devastating ills underscore the pervasiveness of racism. If we cared *enough* we would elect leaders and prepare professionals who would make available the legal, financial, and technical resources to all but eliminate these problems. Instead we prepare more papers saying that it's all too complicated, and recommending caution and a handful of tiny model projects. There is no doubt that blacks have made substantial progress since World War II. But an approach to progress so slow that one third of a people is still shackled by bonds created in slave days after fifty years of sporadic, half-hearted national effort must be considered "gradualist" to the extreme.

In 1990, thirty-three percent of Mississippi's voting age population is black, but only thirteen and a half percent of its elected officials are. Yet twenty representatives is much better than the traditional number—none.

Of the twenty, twelve, including Robert Clark, the one woman—Alyce Clarke, and Charles Shepphard, a former CDGM man, had 100 percent voting records on issues of priority concern to the black community: for example, capital improvements for schools, computers for learning, the school failure prevention program, early childhood programs, literacy and parenting programs, a teenage pregnancy reduction program, an alliance for families to get better parent involvement, equity funding for school districts, early intervention for infants and toddlers, child care licensing, allowing AFDC payments to be made to two-parent families where the main breadwinner is unemployed, and expanded Medicaid to include all children younger than six in families with incomes below 133 percent of poverty (about $1,200 per month for a family of three).

Besides the twelve black representatives with 100 percent positive voting records, four more, including Aaron Henry, had 90 percent or above voting records, and one voted 86 percent of the time for bills and amendments that would benefit the black community.

In addition to black votes, nine *white* members of the Mississippi House voted 100 percent on these issues, and thirteen whites voted above 80 percent positive. Inch by inch, ally by ally, vote by vote. There's a way to go, though: Nine whites vote right from a black perspective, but in the state legislature there are an additional one hundred sixty-five whites who don't. And then there were the three black representatives who voted *against* the best interests of their people most of the time. The devil has slippery shoes. And times haven't changed totally: Tommy Horne from Meridian is still being elected to the House, and in 1964 he was a member of the KKK Clavern that plotted the triple murder of Schwerner, Chaney, and Goodman.

Positive social change comes inch by inch if it comes at all, and it only comes at all if individuals in *every* walk of life, individuals of *every* race take risks *wherever they are*, in ivory towers or cotton fields, to *make* it happen. But if people work for progress it *does* occur. Even in formerly murderous Meridian, Mississippi:

At about 9 p.m. on June 16, 1964, Beatrice and Bud Cole (in 1989, 83 and 86 years old) were pulled from their car in the driveway of their church, Mt. Zion. Bud was brutally beaten by Klansmen. Beatrice was knocked to her knees, where she stayed and prayed. A few hours later, from their home, they saw flames lighting the night sky. Five days later, on June 21, three voting rights activists, James Earl Chaney, an eighteen-year-old black youth from Meridian; Andrew Goodman, a twenty-year-old sophomore at Queens College, and Michael Schwerner, a twenty-four-year-old New Yorker, drove into Philadelphia, Mississippi, to look into the burning of Mt. Zion Church. That night they were murdered. Compare that with this:

In June of 1989, thirteen Greyhound busloads of people from Philadelphia, *Pennsylvania* and Philadelphia's Mayor W. Wilson Goode, *and Mississippi's Governor Ray Mabus,* plus other high-ranking Mississippi officials, gathered at Mt. Zion Methodist Church to erect a marker like other markers put up by Mississippi's Department of Archives and History. The marker reads:

FREEDOM SUMMER MURDERS. On June 21, 1964, voting rights activists James Earl Chaney, Andrew Goodman and Michael Schwerner, who had come here to investigate the burning of Mt. Zion Church, were murdered. Victims of a Klan conspiracy, their deaths provoked national outrage and led to the first successful Federal prosecution of a Civil Rights case in Mississippi.

James Farmer, founder and former national director of the Congress of Racial Equality (C.O.R.E.), organizer of the Freedom Riders who traveled through the South—being beaten at every stop with the tacit or open approval of local officials and police—to test a 1960 U.S. Supreme Court decision that declared segregation of interstate bus terminals unconstitutional, spoke. He said a nation that forgets its martyrs has lost its soul. He said they died in an effort to help us all learn to get along, *all* Americans. "Getting along," I said to a friend, "sounds like a pretty worthy goal, but wouldn't it be easier to achieve if there was a little more health care, economic, educational, and political equity? Doesn't legitimate furious resentment on the part of the have-nots interfere substantially with the good will needed to get along? Isn't it a little odd for us to have—and vehemently hang onto—control of all resources and privileges, while preaching at people who have little except the short end of the stick that they should get along with us?" "Yes," the CDGM friend said. "Now they talk about 'race relations' and 'getting along.' In the sixties, and in CDGM, we were talking about social change."

"The people with the power to create social change don't *want* social change. They want 'better race relations.' The situation in Mississippi is *not* better, although for many *individuals* things are much better," says Owen Brooks. Owen was Director of the Delta Ministry for twenty years following Art Thomas's departure to run a Model Cities program in Trenton, New Jersey.

Art had asked Owen to come to Mississippi in the sixties because of his background in progressive politics. Owen is Congressman Mike Espy's Field Representative in the Greenville and Yazoo City offices. Owen continues,

"There's no single force that prevents progress. In a way, it's the whole capitalist system. It's people's greed, it's classism, it's racism.

I have lived to see great loss since the era of active community change in the sixties. If we had just kept going at the same pace! We control nothing. We have no real power. We do not make decisions about things that effect our lives.

"We need hope. CDGM was an agent of hope. It gave people a way to engage with the system, do something practical for their children, become political activists. After CDGM, lots of CDGM people ran for political office. Board member Clarence Hall ran for the Board of Supervisors. Thelma Barnes ran for office. Sarah Johnson became the first black person on the Greenville city council, Ernest White was elected to the Belzoni city council—there are lots more. Bennie Thompson, movement man, Tougaloo grad, and CDGMian, is Hinds County Supervisor—a political heavy in the state. He got a HUD grant, built housing and a new city hall with a day care center. In response to an uncontrollable fire and black complaints, he put water mains on the black side of town big enough to carry sufficient water to put out fires, and bought a new fire engine that would start.

"We need vision. We do not elect visionaries to public office. The might and power of a *few* elect a president of the United States. The *people* don't elect the president, money elects the president. Money elects officials at all levels most of the time. Then they don't do enough for the folks back home. They're on the way up. The people's needs are almost always left out.

"We need to struggle. The struggle goes on. We try not to make the same mistakes too often. We've got to vote, but then we've got to keep after these thieves and thugs and make them accountable.

"We need to trust in the Lord."

Most of the elected black officials in this country are liberals. A few are conservatives. Black liberals believe it's possible to work with *some* white people. Generally, they support racial integration and joint efforts. Black liberals organized the NAACP (originally the Niagara Movement). The famous A. Philip Randolph was a black liberal, as was Martin Luther King. Marian Wright Edelman and Jesse Jackson are black liberals. People with this point of view sharply criticize the government's complacency about the squalor and lack of opportunity that enshroud many black people, and involve themselves in progressive social action of one sort or another—economic, political, educational, public policy, civic, etc. People with this social change orientation are sometimes called *reconstructionists.* In the DEVIL book and elsewhere, I've called them, be they black or white, *rapid reformers.*

Some black people, including political leaders, are conservatives. They practice a protective sort of psychological denial. They see no racial discrimination, so see no need for government intervention via guarantees of equal opportunity.

As far as they're concerned, poor people are personally to blame or individually unfortunate. They see no unfair forces at work that cumulatively keep some people down. Almost all of the black people in the Reagan and Bush administrations are conservative accommodationists.

Internalization of "the master's" perspective is a common human response to permanent or long-term political, economic, educational, and psychological oppression. We see it in many blacks, women, and other minorities. Accommodation, as it's called, is a reasonable way to survive, with as little trouble as possible, what appear to be unalterably repressive unequal life conditions. For many African American slaves, conditions were truly inhuman, and accepting—accommodating to—the situation was the sole way to survive. (Even so, some brave slaves fought back. Those who did usually died.)

Times have changed, at least in this country. Political, economic, educational, and psychological conditions are no longer unalterable. It's hard to respect educated blacks (and whites who've never had the same reasons to be politically apathetic) who don't join their brothers and sisters in an effort to create a more democratic society.

A very large number of black Americans believe that white people are incapable of behaving acceptably regarding rights for racial minorities, black people in particular. They see a great deal of incontrovertible evidence that this is true. They believe that whites are incorrigible. They want nothing to do with us. They do not favor integration. It appears that at times of heightened racial tensions, like the 1960s, this feeling increases. There have always been black separatists in this country. Although most don't participate in the formal political process, some do, and have always had leaders and spokesmen. For example, names like Marcus Garvey, the Reverend George Stallings, Jr., and Louis Farrakhan, Nation of Islam leader, may sound familiar.

The hardest of these three perspectives to have, it seems to me from knowing my friends, is the liberal perspective. Andy Kopkind, who now writes for the *Nation* magazine (see pages 000) explains:

> Black liberals have to deal with two truths that can make you crazy. The truths are incompatible; this divide affects every generation. On the one hand, they know how extreme and sometimes how subtle and how deeply institutionalized white racism is, and that total integration is impossible. On the other hand, they know that the alternative—separate development—black nationalism—won't work either. Blacks have to deal with white power. Working with both these truths at the same time could make you schizophrenic.

SNCC was a mixture of black separatists, black liberals, and whites who agreed that separatism (with allies of any color assisting) was best for a while so people could get out from under whites and experience themselves as decision-makers, but that the ultimate goal was to work as a team of equally empowered people. It was this mixture within one group that caused so much combustible anger. Much of it was directed at the whites by those who felt, not without reason, that when dealing with the Feds, to quote a well-known African proverb, "the more you stir the mess, the more it stinks."

In 1964, twenty nine thousand Mississippi black people were registered voters, a great many of them thanks to NAACP, the Delta Ministry, and SNCC. This was the year before the Voting Rights Act. Only about three hundred blacks held elected office in the *nation*. In 1966, one year after the Voting Rights Act and during the height of CDGM, one hundred seventy five thousand black Mississippians were registered to vote. Promised federal protection and personally encouraged by CDGM and its predecessor and liaison groups, black Mississippians registered to vote at a rate nearly 700 percent that of two years earlier. In 1968, still during CDGM days, Mississippi boasted two hundred fifty-one thousand black voters. Ed Brown says,

"These numbers embodied revolutionary potential. It was a social revolution with immense political implications. It had a lot to do with people changing their view of themselves, and that had a lot to do with CDGM."

Twenty years laters, in 1988, Mississippi could claim four hundred eighty-eight thousand, two hundred and fifty-one black registered voters.

Andy Kopkind comments, "SNCC's wing of the civil rights movement never had a clear and final goal. After helping people win legal and political enfranchisement, then what? In many Mississippi counties, CDGM was the next thing on the continuum. It delivered economic, political, and educational power."

In 1970, the distinguished black social psychologist Kenneth B. Clark (husband of Mamie Clark, a member of the original Head Start Steering Committee) and others founded the Joint Center for Political and Economic Studies to help ease blacks' transition from civil rights protesters to participants in mainstream politics. The following appears in the Joint Center's 20th Anniversary report (p. 6):

> The successes of the civil rights movement are indisputable. In the 1950s and 1960s, organizations and individuals waged an unrelenting assault on segregation, disenfranchisement, and other legally sanctioned forms of inequality and shattered the edifice of white supremacy. New laws, effective enforcement, Supreme Court decisions, and the growth of a national consensus against racial inequality helped to change the legal status of black Americans. Many members of the black community were already poised to take advantage of the new educational and employment opportunities, and they soon became part of an expanding black middle class.
>
> The political landscape, too, was changing, mainly because of passage in 1965 of the Voting Rights Act. Assured of federal protection, thousands of black citizens across the South voted for the first time. This upsurge of political activity gave rise to a new presence—the black elected official.

Political journalist Kopkind continues, "The main achievements of the civil rights movement, and CDGM was a phase of it, were breaking the back of the Southern white racist Democrats (there is a two-party system in Mississippi and in the whole South now); and empowering northern liberal congressmen and senators. Serious congressional reform resulted from taking much of the power from the Southern white racist Democrats. Northern liberals took over the power vacuum. Since the civil rights movement, Democrats can't be elected anywhere in the country without the black vote.''

The power was taken from the Southern white racist Democrats by enabling blacks to vote in sufficient numbers that those who wanted to continue in office had to make significant concessions, first via covert operations (see page 818), then through ceasing their racist rhetoric, and eventually by representing their black as well as their white constituents. And anyone wishing to be newly elected had to have—or appear to have—a ''new South'' viewpoint.

* * * * * * * * * * * *

In assessing CDGM, and, in fact, the whole Head Start program, a vitally important but typically ignored question to investigate is: To what degree and how effectively have parents, staff, and all persons who participate(d) in it at *any* level and in *any* role from cooks and custodians to CAP Directors and school principals, become politicized? One reason that this question is ignored by Head Start evaluators is that they represent only *one* of Head Start's parents—the *scholarly* parent, not the *political activist* parent. Here, it's necessary to step back and consider a bit of Head Start history.

In 1964, it was with great political effort and with strong political reason that a new War on Poverty agency—the Office of Economic Opportunity (OEO)—was established *as a freestanding federal agency.* Although existing federal agencies, such as the Department of Labor, fought bitter battles to get War on Poverty programs relevant to their subject to administer (DOL, for example, wanted Job Corps), War on Poverty strategists knew that to spur slow and stiff bureaucracies into greater compliance with poor people's needs and to glue together splintered, gap-separated services, the new programs would have to be housed in a new federal agency focused not on a subject like ''health'' or ''education'' for everyone, but on *assisting people in escaping from poverty.* Had this approach not been taken, War on Poverty programs, including the Community Action Program, Job Corps, Neighborhood Health Services, Legal Services, VISTA Volunteers, Head Start, and the others, would have been so delayed, diluted, and diminished as to have been unrecognizably, ineffectively weak.

The Community Action Program (CAP) in particular, intended to be the core of the war, had to be created outside the ''system'' because its primary purpose was to organize interested poor people and encourage them to elect representatives *of their choice* to CAP boards, and then to stimulate from traditional agencies appropriate service delivery—including the *coordination* of disparate services—and including appropriate *collaboration* with poor ''clients.'' CAP was designed before OEO existed (see page 812).

• to bring poor people leaders into the human services and political system as an empowered political entity to shake it all up and make it more respectful and responsive,
• to bring poor people leaders into the system so they could have an opportunity to develop the skills and sophistication necessary to achieve the political clout that many other interest groups have,
• to bring a reservoir of new voters to the sponsoring Democratic party; it was expected that they would be grateful, therefore loyal.

Not all creators of the CAP program cared equally about all three of these agendas but in general they agreed.

Dick Boone, Sargent Shriver's Director of Policy Planning and Development at OEO, and one of the conceptualizers of the Community Action Program, explains, "The education, health, and social welfare institutions were set in traditional molds. They were far from accomplishing the goal of providing all that people needed and were unwilling to coordinate with each other, or to collaborate with their 'clients.' " The agencies weren't even attempting the goal of helping adults develop in any or all of a variety of ways; not even to learn to navigate—or better yet, to manipulate—"the system" to get it to provide required services such as decent health care and education for their children.

The Community Action Agency in any city or county that had one was intentionally funded directly from the federal government, from the Office of Economic Opportunity. Federal funds usually go to states, and from there to localities—their ultimate destinations are determined more by political popularities and pressures than by equity or need. The purpose of this unique direct funding arrangement was to empower the leaders poor people selected from among themselves to be CAP board members, and their professional allies on community action agency staffs.

Dave Hackett, another original CAP strategist, points out, "If the funds had traveled the usual route they certainly never would have gotten to poor people who were organized and full of lots of legitimate demands and protests. We wanted to provide the financial resources required to get established politicians to pay attention to these voices."

A primary purpose of a Community Action Agency was meant to be to put political pressure on established agencies and institutions to cause them to become more accountable to their low-income constituencies. Another primary purpose, Dick Boone adds, "was to offer opportunities to people so they could participate as key players in planning and operating their own programs." As Sargent Shriver's Director of Policy Planning and Development at the Office of Economic Opportunity, Dick was the major advocate of "maximum feasible participation of the poor." Indeed it was he, in an earlier incarnation, who got the famous phrase written into the Economic Opportunity Act law.

Within OEO, in late 1964, Head Start was designed—*under the Community Action Program.* From the outset, Head Start was a maverick. Unlike CAP, it was to be a direct service delivery program. In this regard it was similar to Job Corps. The services Head Start was to deliver, as we all know, were health, early childhood education kinds of experiences such as play, outings, stories, etc., social services for families, and parent education. The comprehensive services emphasis and the belief that teaching parents how to be better parents was an important ingredient of the Head Start Program came from the interdisciplinary Advisory Committee, of which Sargent Shriver appointed the chairman, pediatrician Robert Cooke, and from the National Head Start Director Shriver appointed a little later, Dr. Julius B. Richmond, also a pediatrician—and from a few of the other committee members who, like Cooke, had been involved with Sargent and Eunice Shriver in Kennedy Foundation work.

Sargent Shriver was unarguably Head Start's primary parent. But Head Start had *two* parents. Because CAP people, most of whom were devout believers in maximum feasible participation of the poor and the importance of providing varied and plentiful opportunities to people poised to benefit from them, did the staff work for Sargent Shriver, they wrote into the Head Start plan requirements for heavy parent participation at every program level—on the local governing board, in program planning, as volunteers, and in paid jobs throughout the program.

Dick Boone and several other CAP people drafted the first official personnel plan for Head Start: It called for "3,400 professionals, 12,000 full- and part-time volunteers, and 5,000 paid non-professionals—largely parents." It was also several CAP people, including Jule Sugarman, who made up the list of suggested Advisory Committee members, other than the Kennedy Foundation mental retardation specialists whom Sargent Shriver had named.

Head Start would not have had its remarkable parents-as-employees-leaders-and-activists emphasis had only the Kennedy Foundation people Shriver selected, and the other scholars and leaders added mainly by Jule Sugarman, been making decisions. They had much of value to offer, of course, but neither awareness nor understanding of the importance to poor children's development of seeing their parents (their *real*, extremely powerful, life-long role models) participate in personal growth, program development and problem solving, and related political advocacy to the maximum feasible degree. These research oriented scholars and physicians obviously were not dedicated social change specialists, successful grass roots program entrepreneurs, or experts experienced in providing meaningful jobs and "new careers for the poor." Their primary interest was not in developing families and communities. They were child development "interventionists," and representatives of other fields put on the Advisory Committee as political window dressing.

It was the marriage of

- Community Action Program theoreticians' dedication to the principle of multiple opportunities and to maximum feasible participation requirements for poor parents and their peers, with social change as the goal, and
- human services theoreticians' skilled and scholarly knowledge of comprehensive services for children, with intervening positively in children's lives and educating parents about parenting as the goal that made Head Start a maverick.

And a political survivor.

Community Action people were nervous about Head Start's "service delivery" orientation. How much would the poor really be allowed to plan, decide, and advocate (agitate) for their children before the powers that be—the mayors, et al.—decided that their boats were being rocked too vigorously, their moats were being crossed too successfully, and their castles stormed; before they declared that Head Start people were, quote, "too political"?

And academics, professionals, and bureaucrats were nervous about Head Start's activist orientation.

During the national Head Start program's first few months of existence, the Child Development Group of Mississippi inadvertently served as the test case to define where the boundaries were to be for all Head Starts in the country, for at least the next quarter century—perhaps forever more. The extent to which

- maximum feasible opportunities for the poor and
- maximum feasible participation of the poor in securing needed services and a brighter future for their own children were to be permitted were determined by the government in the case of CDGM v. OEO. You know the story.

But you may not know this fascinating fact: It was at the end of the dramatic CDGM saga that the schism between these two factions within OEO ended. Services advocates "won," and official Head Start history was purged of its community activist origins. Dick Boone and all early documents with a vigorous "maximum feasible participation of the poor" emphasis disappeared from both stage and page (although the papers, at least, are in the archives). Sargent Shriver, who was frightened of maximum feasible participation of the poor because of its probable political volatility, and the Kennedy Foundation (for mental retardation research) scholars and doctors, who had scarcely heard of this core CAP concept, didn't understand it, and mildly disliked the potentially messy idea, were soon seen (because so they portrayed themselves) as the founders of Head Start. It's doubtful that the scholars and doctors ever knew they represented only half of Head Start's heritage and parentage, so thoroughly did Sargent Shriver, a remarkably intuitive and politically adept leader, delete the "maximum feasible participation of the poor" mandate—and its leading proponent, Dick Boone—from history. (War on Poverty battlefields were littered with the bodies of those who displeased "Sarge"; this was by no means a unique situation. See page 40.) The Poverty Tsar had his reasons.

Sargent Shriver had never been a fan of maximum feasible participation of the poor. That was his brother-in-law Bob Kennedy's cause. Sargent Shriver came from a family with a long tradition of progressive public service. Shriver inspired many leaders and everyday citizens to become more active in doing good. He was probably the world's leading advocate of volunteerism. But he did not talk about empowering the poor. The idea of doing something for young children living in poverty before they started school in the fall of 1965 was entirely Sargent Shriver's idea; it was certainly not the idea of outside scholars or doctors. OEO senior staff, a group of men which included the Director or Acting Director of each OEO program (Job Corps, Community Action, etc.) loved the concept when Shriver (who had been informally picking the brains of friends, his family's physician, famous political and media people, and a few distinguished developmental psychologists) tossed the notion to them at a staff meeting in late October, 1964. Staff viewed the proposed project primarily as a health assessment, immunizations, hot lunch and enrichment program, and a way of minimizing the culture shock the children of poverty experience when they enter the middle class world of the school. Dick Boone and other staff, including me, brainstormed and explored the idea of a large scale program for young children. For the first time, several early childhood educators were briefly consulted. In November, Sargent Shriver asked Jule Sugarman, who had been helping CAP in key ways, to administer Head Start into reality, which Jule, a public administrator beyond compare, did in record time. Sargent Shriver removed the community action facet of Head Start's origins and intentions from history because it wasn't something *he* believed was so important, it wasn't *his* contribution to the marvelous program, and it was the most politically unpalatable aspect of the War on Poverty. Efforts to politically empower people of a socioeconomic class the establishment experiences as threatening had to be exorcised from Head Start in hopes that the more innocent, traditional, donor/donee services aspects would not be torpedoed.

Dick Boone was deleted because he went over to the enemy—Citizens Crusade Against Poverty—and mounted against OEO an attack by politically powerful liberal groups to *counter* the attack by Mississippi white supremacists that was forcing OEO to shut down CDGM. Dick Boone was deleted from OEO/Head Start history because he was Bob Kennedy's representative. Boone stood for "maximum feasible participation of the poor."

* * * * * * * * * * * *

In 1990, a quarter of a century later, Tom Levin, evicted creator of CDGM, suddenly received a document from Mississippi's Governor Ray Mabus, a "commendation" thanking him for being "the founder and first official director of CDGM. Dr. Levin created this plan in hopes that certain social changes would occur in rural Mississippi. Dr. Levin was concerned for human dignity, powerlessness and the perpetuation of a second class citizenship," said the commendation. After recovering from his astonishment at receiving this astounding document, Tom, who still lives in New York, wrote to me; I still live in Washington, D.C.:

"I was taken aback when I opened the mail in January and found the commendation from Mississippi's Governor Mabus. How could this happen? The 1960s established the ferocity of white resistance to shared power. What changed?

"CDGM preached and taught the poor blacks of Mississippi that they could successfully run their own programs. Malcolm X said, 'Chickens come home to roost.' The poor black Mississippians who organized and ran CDGM communities used their success to become a political force in the state that must be reckoned with. Scholars a quarter of a century later who are studying Mississippi sixties history and the War on Poverty understand that CDGM was more than a Head Start program. CDGM was a significant turning point economically, politically, educationally, attitudinally, and psychologically for black people, especially poor black people. This is the social change goal that interested me, not Head Start per se.

"Who did it? If you look back over hundreds of years of human history, no one's name stands out, or even is known. Yet there are individuals who have a memorable role in the stream of human endeavor that makes history. Everyone recognizes that there are magical moments in individual life, in community life, in politics. And it is at these moments of collective concern when one person says the words, does the deeds, carries out the commands that are emanating from the larger body of people all around, that events of historical significance occur.

"It was no mystery what Mississippi's poor black people wanted in the mid-1960s, they could not have made it more clear: food, housing, jobs, education for their children and health care, as well as hope, equality, opportunity, and respect. All we did was carry them the word of a way in which they could actualize these yearnings, and bring the necessary technical assistance to make it happen. It was this alliance of black aspiration and the resources we provided that made CDGM work.

"SNCC certainly could not have brought Head Start to the communities. SNCC workers railed against government regulations and interference, and understandably so. The government had been the enemy of the civil rights movement. SNCC vehemently opposed co-opting people by 'buying them' with federal money. SNCC leaders did not understand organizing communities around their yearnings for a better life for black children even after we got CDGM going.

"Several of Mississippi's school superintendents applied for Head Start funds in the spring of 1965, but they certainly were not interested in developing political leadership in poor black communities. The notion of a network of black communities eager to work on voter registration, jobs and new careers for black people, and economic freedom from the plantation system was abhorent to them.

"Nor is it conceivable that Mississippi's black middle class would have considered creating among Head Start staff and parents relentless advocates for poor black children and families. Some black middle class groups did sponsor Head Start programs, but not activist programs. The middle class was primarily interested in consolidating its own developing economic and political power. It was leery of an educational and power system based in poor black communities.

"There could not have been stranger standard bearers for the aspirations of Mississippi's poor black people at that historical moment of political vacuum after the exhilaration and enormous success of the 1964 Freedom Summer. Polly Greenberg, Tom Levin, and Art Thomas were not Mississippians or even Southerners. None of us were poor, none of us were black, and you, Polly, did not even have movement credentials. The strangeness of the combination, these speakers of the words, these instigators of the action, these writers of the dream, was a miracle of the moment. The trajectories of our three widely different lives, skills and goals intersected at the point where poor black Mississippians' most fervent desires lay—palpable success and a brighter future for a new generation of black people, their children.

"CDGM instantly took on a life of its own. Community people were ready to work incredibly hard to make their dreams of freedom come true. SNCC and Delta Ministry workers had earned great trust in the communities as a result of the civil rights summer of 1964. This trust provided well-oiled wheels on which to roll in the new opportunity that Head Start offered. In tiny unheard-of Mississippi communities, people understood that Head Start offered, through arduous work and difficult organizing on their part, an opportunity to provide a new education program for their own young children, jobs for themselves and others in their communities, and a chance to function as leaders. Art Thomas and I understood that the history of SNCC and Delta Ministry volunteers' dedicated efforts and strong organizing skills provided a base for a Head Start program on which to build community power. *You* and I understood that there is no more effective way to ''motivate'' young children than to create situations where, throughout the day, they see, hear, and feel their parents developing *themselves* and developing programs for *them*.

''How we three were to function within CDGM becomes understandable only when we look at where each of us was coming from in March of 1965 when Art and I first met you.

''You were working as OEO staff with Dick Boone at the Community Action Program in War on Poverty headquarters in Washington, your 'home town.' You were imbued with the CAP core concept: maximum feasible participation of the poor. You worked for Jule Sugarman, and shared his belief that there are good people in every community who know how to provide adequately for young children if given guidance and resources. Further, you know how to make a marriage of the community action concept and the kind of child development oriented educational program that your profession has always advocated—and make it work.

''Head Start was not just a design concept to you, but a viable administrative and program entity. OEO charged you with getting the new Head Start program to every county in the Southeastern states. Your job as Senior Program Analyst was to get as many applications as possible to OEO's processors. President Johnson was to announce Head Start grants in May, 1965 in the White House Rose Garden.

''There was intense pressure on you from Sargent Shriver's Office of Inspection (Bill Haddad, Bob Clampitt, etc.) to discourage segregationist applicants and locate integrationist ''new South'' groups. People today would have a hard time believing how the Mississippi school superintendents responded to the news of Head Start. It meant summer jobs for their teachers and a chance to clean up 'the dirty little darkies' before school started in September. When your telesearch finally located me and I invited you to what turned out to be a historic meeting in my office in New York with Art Thomas, we were planning a handful of freedom school style daycare centers for civil rights workers' children for the 1965 summer.

''I had been especially interested in Mississippi politics since the previous summer, when we organized a medical arm for the movement, the Medical Committee for Human Rights. I had worked closely with SNCC and the Reverend Arthur Thomas, Director of the Delta Ministry.

''In the mid-1960s, black Mississippians were in a position of pivotal importance because of the upcoming Democratic elections in the South which would challenge the Dixiecrat machine. President Johnson, a brilliant tactical politician, understood that a political party's power comes through patronage. The OEO War on Poverty programs were the way to create political machines loyal to the National Democratic Party among the politically voiceless, politically unorganized black people, previously unavailable to the Party. The Mississippi voter registration campaign of 1964 simply alerted the Democratic party to the size of the pot and the taste of victory.

''Neither Art Thomas nor I had heard of soon-to-be-launched Project Head Start. It had just been invented by Sargent Shriver, Dick Boone, and Jule Sugarman in your Washington OEO offices. My initial reluctance gave way to excitement as you talked about Head Start's proposed comprehensiveness, including early childhood education, health care and food, jobs and decision-making roles for parents and other poor folk. I began to realize what I am sure President Johnson was the *first* to realize: Head Start was the high card that the Mississippi Dixiecrats could not trump. Head Start was the program within OEO that had the greatest potential for politically organizing Mississippi while avoiding flack as a pork barrel. While Head Start had obvious political advantages for Democrats all over the country, I was thinking about Mississippians, and the chance this presented for fundamental social change.

''Besides Mom and apple pie, Americans best love little children. Historically, we are a people who accept and prize aspirations for our children. I immediately understood the political potency of the high card. When you stressed that the governor of Mississippi had threatened to veto any Head Start grants in his state unless they came through his people, but that OEO had a way around the veto, my ears perked up. You said that institutions of higher education could be grantees and were exempt from the veto. Listening to you, I believed that with your help, OEO could be induced to fund a poor people oriented Head Start, perhaps the only one in the country.

"Art Thomas saw his ministry as dedicated to the powerless. He was as politically idealistic as I. He was convinced that his job as Delta Ministry Director was to fully involve poor black people in the decision-making process. He wanted community people to vote for representatives from among themselves to run each local community Head Start center. Art suspected that Head Start could be the vehicle for organizing poor people into an effective political force. Once they were organized for Head Start, he reasoned, they could work simultaneously toward *any* of their social and political goals.

"Working with Art to open the black communities to the new Medical Community for Human Rights in the summer of 1964 had given me credentials in the eyes of the community people. If Art said I could be trusted, they trusted me. An amazing thing about Art was that he had the respect of field hands and professionals at one and the same time. I had a busy psychoanalytic practice in New York City, but my early background was in organizing. My father was a union man. I was a freelance union organizer in New York City when I was fifteen, and I remained active thereafter in human and civil rights causes. I believe that only when individuals organize and begin to experience the responsibilities of power can they develop effective leadership skills and create real social change.

"It was your relentless pleas, your persistent insistence over the phone during the two weeks following our meeting that led to initial steps that developed a momentum that could not be halted. I responded to your entreaties and dashed off a four page "modest proposal" for a five-center, one hundred child experimental preschool program. Art contacted the many poor communities to which he had access and in which he was trusted. He advised these communities to elect committees and send representatives to a statewide Head Start organizing meeting if they were interested. Every time Art called me, he mentioned more communities that wanted to be involved. I grew more and more excited.

"While Art contacted the communities, I attended a SNCC statewide planning meeting in Waveland, Mississippi. I knew no black community project in Mississippi could survive without, at the very least, the tolerance of SNCC's leaders. I was not a 'member' of SNCC, but my work in organizing the Medical Committee for Human Rights, and the many group and individual counseling sessions I had held with SNCC volunteers during and after the summer of 1964, made me familiar to, though ambivalently respected by SNCC leadership. My dilemma was to avoid SNCC opposition to a government project and keep SNCC minimally friendly to it, without arousing OEO's suspicion and ire. I wanted to neutralize SNCC so we could promote the community development possibilities of Head Start (which *said* it was dedicated to them), yet avoid any direct connection with or public endorsement from SNCC, an organization of social change agents the government hated. Politics in SNCC were baroque and convoluted, but Bob Moses trusted me enough to remain neutral. Frank Smith was devoutly anti-government and hostile until, in a private discussion, I offered him a community organizing position with our project. This was probably my most effective, as well as my most disastrous ploy in establishing CDGM. In the end, many SNCC workers joined us, some of them bringing courage, energy, and dedication as well as experience. Others were primarily dissidents and rebels.

"Meanwhile, at OEO you had succeeded in arousing considerable receptivity to our extraordinary coalition and its proposal. At the meeting you later arranged in D.C. (but were not at), I remember the unexpectedly warm reception from Jule Sugarman. Jule called the Citizens Crusade Against Poverty and on the spot arranged a $5,000 development grant so a group of us could get together to write a proposal for a large Head Start.

"From then on, it was frenetic going. Through your advocacy inside OEO, and the work of Art's people and several of the more positive SNCC representatives in more and more Mississippi communities, the modest initial proposal was rapidly expanding into a proposal for an extended statewide network, eventually including 64 communities, 12,000 children, and 1,100 poor people employees for the summer of 1965.

"Ultimately, the final piece that ensured CDGM's success was that you agreed to leave the government—to quit OEO—and come to work for CDGM. Art and I knew all about the movement, but nothing at all about nursery schools, kindergartens, staff development, or the educational standards required for the new Head Start program. Having you in Mississippi, we were starting a huge experimental early childhood education program with the top expert in the whole country about how to combine the OEO Community Action Program "maximum feasible participation of the poor" concept with Head Start's comprehensive services focus. You were the only early childhood educator who worked with OEO's Community Action Program so understood Dick Boone's message about the importance of maximum feasible participation of the poor in the delivery of their own services. To this day, most early childhood educators do not understand that. *And* you *also* worked in OEO Head Start headquarters and understood that Head Start was aiming at traditional quality early childhood education objectives—developing confident, autonomous people who can plan and work cooperatively together.

"You saw the compatibility of this approach and movement philosophy. You believed strongly in helping each child, parent, and community person involved in the education program in growing *from where they were* to where they wanted to be. You knew Head Start's intent, the process and content expected in the children's program, and the minimum standards that would be tolerated by the early childhood educators who would be monitoring classroom aspects of CDGM's program. Everyone in CDGM knew and expected that they had to do the children's program the way Polly Greenberg said because she was the only Head Start person in the entire project. We would lose our funding if we didn't do the children's program the way Head Start wanted it, and what that was only Polly knew.

"To many SNCC people, Polly was the person who represented the power of the government to buy out the people. There are others who still hold to the myth that you were simply an idealistic early childhood educator. Nonsense!

"The ideas that became the Child Development Group of Mississippi came from outside; from a child development professional, a professional psychologist, and a professional community organizer. What made CDGM work was the profound mutual respect we three had for each other, and the vigorous, aroused communities that knew *they* were CDGM.

"Polly, thanks for the memories."

In 1990, twenty-five years after the fact, I got a "commendation" too. But it wasn't from Mississippi's governor. It was from Mississippi's poor black people. And it wasn't called a commendation. It was called a proclamation. I had received a notice from my neighborhood Washington, D.C. post office that it had a package for me to pick up. When I got there and opened it, I saw a framed document beneath a heap of smashed glass. The shocked joy that rushed over me as I read this out-of-the-blue "proclamation" caused tears to flow down my face. In the contemptuous tones to which most white patrons of seventy-two percent black "Chocolate City's" almost entirely black-staffed municipal services are often addressed, a postal clerk bristling with hostility sneered,

"You don't have to *cry,* miss. Just fill out this form and new glass can be purchased for the picture in the package."

"No, no," I stammered, tears streaming down my cheeks, "it's not the broken glass. I worked in Mississippi black communities for a few years during the civil rights times in the sixties, and read this!"

First this postal clerk, then all the others who were summoned by the first one, gathered and read over my shoulders. While a long line of increasingly irate white customers waited, one by one the postal clerks put an arm around me, shook my hand, or joined me in crying. The manager, a man known for his refusal to make eye contact and his all-around sullen, stony style with white folks, gazed straight into my reddening green eyes and said,

"Just see what one person can mean! What would happen to the world if each person did what he could to make it better?"

I've never received a more wonderful gift of any kind—the quarter century delay only ripened the sweetness—or job performance "evaluation" than the one on page 787 from my superior at CDGM, Board President Reverend James McRee, and from former Area Teacher Guide (and organizer—"president"—of a CDGM reunion several decades after its dissolution) Lavaree Jones.

* * * * * * * * * * * *

After its dismemberment by the government, many CDGM people and programs remained alive and thriving for many years, although participants unanimously report that the philosophy rapidly (to quote a community person still employed by one of the take-over groups) "went downhill." Typical comments from people *still* employed in Head Start are these:

"They didn't want parents in the middle any more. They keep them on the edges. We are supposed to 'train' parents how to help instruct their children, not have them decide and do things in every element of the project and in the community to better it for children."

"Head Start since CDGM wants people to deny our history. They want us to 'forget all that and teach children in readiness for school', that's how they tell us to do. Well let me tell you, black children do not do as well when their parents and teachers fail to tell them their brave history in slavery and rising out of the ashes afterwards and the heroism of civil rights relatives among them, and the reality of racism and classism and how to deal with it. Nowadays, the Head Start honchos here in Mississippi want a curriculum unit on Martin Luther King in January and national sports heroes' pictures on a bulletin board, but nothing close and inspiring. They say, 'teach black history and culture,' but they mean out of a can, not out of real life in familiar families and communities. Our raw, fiery history has been cooked and cooled and distanced to far away dates and historical figures.

"I have nothing against traditional black names in American history, but

Child Development Group of Mississippi
Community Education Extension Proclamation

Whereas, it has been 25 years since CDGM was created and formed an Association with Ms. Polly Greenberg, who being inspired by GOD, showered her special gifts, attitudes, and foresight to carry out HIS will by creating opportunities for the poor to change their lives from slavery and discrimination to justice and self-sufficiency; and

Whereas, she greatly impressed our nation's leaders in Washington, D.C. and provided a most vocal voice in maintaining the struggle Mississippians faced in the 60's; and

Whereas, opportunities provided by CDGM and guided by Polly for many to receive educational enrichment through traveling to other states experiencing different lifestyles and values was like the fulfillment of a dream. To know her is to love her. There is no substitute for the way she gleened information and gave it in layman's terms to be mastered by the unlearned parent and community volunteers and;

Whereas, she, having love for young children regardless of creed or color, created an environment where learning was fun, combining what one learns innately with his/her home lifestyles, and building on to that the formation of concepts in developing the person as a whole; and

Whereas, she instructed, inspired, encouraged, supported, labored without pay, fighting the power forces, managing with four small children under inadequate living conditions, giving of herself, her body and mind, mapping strategies to keep hope alive for Mississippi's parents and their children; and

Whereas, Polly can be described as a mentor and friend to the world as she still dedicated her life and time to the creation of and development of educational learning materials, enhancing and emphasizing why we should appreciate black history; for what we do for ourselves in our own community must portray a sense of identity and self-love. It is the essence and prerequisite to doing anything of value; and

Whereas, in giving admiration and appreciation to Polly for documenting our lives, our work, our hopes, our continuing dreams in "The Devil Has Slippery Shoes."

Now Therefore, be it resolved that we, the grassroots representatives who hold the key of progress through CDGM and what it represented for all the social, economical, educational and political advancement of the people of Mississippi, do on this the ______________________________ day of ______________________________ in the year of Our Lord one thousand nine hundred and ninety and in accordance with our desire to do honor to this great lady, do publicly proclaim her: Our Guiding Light, Our Heroine of the 60's and 80's; in whose path we still walk to bridge the path to the future.

Signed by:

Rev. James F. McRee
Past Chairman, CDGM

Lavaree Jones
President

why not *also* Amzie Moore, the hero responsible for inviting Bob Moses into Mississippi? Bob Moses moved around the state in a *dangerous, dangerous* time and awakened people to their rights. Many black college students at Rust, Tougaloo, Jackson State and all the colleges were leaders in SNCC and participated in getting Head Start—CDGM—into *our* people's control, not the school superintendent's control. A lot of the groundwork for change was laid by NAACP and those folks in the 1930s, '40s, and '50s. Then Moore, Moses, and them. The groundwork was done. The hymns were sung. The prayers were prayed. The martyrs were murdered. Then we noticed that the Mississippi Democratic delegation to national politics had no blacks in it. The idea of organizing the Freedom Democratic Party—FDP—was to bring this out in the open. We held mock elections. Fannie Lou Hamer went to the Democratic convention, made a speech, got on national T.V. Then home town heroes organized Head Start. It's all of a piece. There's a whole lot more to do. *This* is the black history and culture we want to see Head Start—and the public schools, too—teach.

"What about Aaron Henry? He had been in the absolutely segregated armed services. President Harry Truman desegregated them. Being in the desegregated military is where a lot of these Southern blacks and Southern whites got their eyes pried open to another way besides the Jim Crow they growed up with. Aaron Henry went to President Kennedy, and he asked him to desegregate the American Legion, too. I don't speak perfect, but I know some things Head Start and elementary school people don't. What about Connie Slaughter, Connie Slaughter Harvey? She's a Tougaloo graduate and the Assistant Secretary of State for Elections! And Jake Ayers' niece Cynthia was a delegate for Jesse Jackson, what about that?

We have in 1990 thirty-four black mayors. Our children need to know this. We have Earl Lucas, Mayor of Mound Bayou. We have Unita Blackwell, daughter of migrant sharecroppers, Mayor of Mayersville since 1976. Unita is President of the Mississippi Conference of Black Mayors, Chair of the Black Mayors' Women's Caucus, and Second Vice-President of the *National* Conference of Black Mayors. I think Unita must have been a gifted child. Even without what they call opportunities, she's got where she's got.

"Unita *is* the law in a town where they arrested her and jailed her every day for thirty days because she had the nerve to file lawsuits against just about every agency in the state. Fannie Lou Hamer was her mentor. Whites beat Mrs. Hamer so bad she nearly died. But Unita wasn't scared off—instead, she was a key organizer of the Freedom Democratic Party. Unita Blackwell has a master's degree now. She has been all over the world.

"What does seeing as powerful and beautiful a black woman as Unita Blackwell in a leadership position do for black children? Well, what does it do for their parents? What does it do for black people in a small Southern town? In Mississippi? In the South? In the United States? In the world? Well, what does it do for you?

"The head of our Head Start says all this is 'political'. White history is not political. Black history *is* political. Can you explain that Polly? These Head Starts today refuse to let our children learn recent history. It's critically unlike CDGM. CDGM was a mess in many ways, but it taught positive black pride. And where black children's education is concerned, that is as basic as the ABCs."

"The educational goal for Head Start now is to press children into shape for the white establishment designed and dominated school system, which is designed to let black children get only so far. The limits are set by providing only low quality education so the black person can't get too far. The educational goal for children in CDGM was to create free, independent individuals who were prepared to deal with the school system, but who were *also* prepared to be creative and to take a stand against what's wrong in this country.

"In the Freedom schools before CDGM, we were taught African history. The peoples and tribes in Africa had much in common. They had kingdoms, wealth, knowledge. We were hoping to get teachers to teach that in CDGM; CDGM wanted it. Our history does not begin with George Washington Carver and others you might read about. We had a powerful civilization. Our children need to know about this. They will never learn it in the white dominated Head Starts and public schools in Mississippi—maybe not in this whole nation. We may need private schools for African American children for a while, till kids know enough about their proud heritage to teach it to their children and future generations."

"Preachers are no longer the lead men in black Mississippi. They're still important, but nowadays elected officials are more important. During CDGM days, we fought the power of the bullet with the power of the ballot. The teachers were parents, so they dedicated their lives to improving opportunities for their children. Many Head Start teachers today are selfish and complacent. They need to rededicate their lives to the children's betterment. But how can we expect that to happen in a climate where the Director of this multi-county Head Start says, 'All that is history. We have to do it the way Washington wants it done. And what Washington wants done is to prepare children for the school system.'"

"You see, Polly, what it is, is we black people raise our children different than you white people do. All the families in these little communities of poor people band together and share in the parenting of the children. We've been doing that since slave days, when we *had* to because they would sell children's parents. When you see these children whose parents are parents solely by reason of having accomplished *one* parenting function—procreating—maybe the parent is in prison or on drugs or a drunkard—some children don't come from 'families', they come from disaster areas—and these children who live in rickety, paint-thirsty shacks way way out wherever—you see, what we in CDGM did was we were parents taking care of our community's children. We mothered them and fathered them first, and then we exposed them. These other Head Start teachers, well, many of them are comfortable; they don't have that heartfelt concern—

some do, but there aren't enough parents. They're teachers, teaching at the children. There's nobody keeping their eye on the door, shutting out the devil to protect these little children."

"The philosophy of who is best for *our* children is dramatically different. They insist on credentials over character. CDGM said character first, then gradually get your credentials. You can't develop character in someone who doesn't have it like you can give courses and develop credentials. Real role models for children are seeing people they respect and love doing right, learning, earning, pulling up the children to a higher level of life. To these Head Start leaders today, role models are people children don't even identify with, but who have the right degree. I can't agree."

"We have a large number of Head Start grantees in Mississippi. Many of them used to be CDGM. The buildings look better. The teachers look more like teachers and have more credentials. Compared to Head Starts in other states we're OK, and of course it's a great opportunity for the children. But compared to CDGM with Tom Levin's ideas spouting every hour, our Head Starts now are brain dead. We appreciated the connections you people knew and connected us to. We appreciated the skills you all taught us to do. Our rate of learning was thrilling, and it was super for the kids to see and sense, it motivated them. You can't think black and white *only,* although it is in a way good to have black Mississippi middle class leaders instead of Northern white middle class leaders; but it's the creative ideas and great personal growth I miss."

As has been said (764-765) one aspect of a Head Start or other human services or social change project that must be considered when assessing it is its spin-offs and descendents, and CDGM has a great many that are still alivc and thriving.

During the dismemberment, as you know, the biggest chunk of CDGM—twenty eight counties—was given to MAP. Former CDGM Board President, the Reverend James McRee, one of the very few black Mississippians on the Board to vote against allowing CDGM to be taken from the poor communities, said (1989):

"I was increasingly shocked and disgusted as I realized the extent of the political motivation and machination behind everything the government does, and all of it is dominated by a determination to keep power in the hands of certain white people and the black people they name. This is as true of the liberals as it is of the racists; none of them are about to relinquish power to the little people whose lives are at stake. CDGM's first leaders, Tom, Art and Polly with the Area Teacher Guides, were different in that respect. They were trying to transfer knowledge, contacts and skills to leaders in poor communities.

"Jule Sugarman, Dr. Julius Richmond, Senator Robert Kennedy, they all told me *personally*—because in CDGM little people talked directly to people like that—they all told me that Senator Stennis was the menace. They couldn't risk losing the entire Head Start program nationwide—maybe all the War on Poverty programs—to save CDGM. They said they had to surrender this one battle.

"Senator Stennis preferred that MAP be organized with Owen Cooper, a wealthy white man from Yazoo City, as chair of the board. They put progressive *middle class* blacks on the board—Aaron Henry, Charles Young, and Reverend R.F. T. Smith. This is a major way that white people maintain control. They hand pick their blacks. They can count on them not to go against the ruling groups too much; they have too much to lose. Poor people are more bold about creating social change. And with every successful experience they have in going up against the system to get their rights, they get more bold. Success is emboldening. Success is contagious, too, others join.

"Mine was a ministry ministering to the poor. When I first heard of Head Start (CDGM), what interested me about it was that it sounded like something the poor and *their* representatives—representatives that *they* selected that represented *them*—could control. My motivation for change in Mississippi had gotten a great boost when I fought for my country in World War II and wasn't even allowed to vote! In 1964, I had a Freedom school in the church I pastored. There was a lot of opposition from the black middle class within my congregation. I used to tell them time and time again that I hoped and prayed to God that He was not seeing a new black middle class growing up that was just as heartless and ruthless to the poor as the people who blacks have been struggling against all these years.

"Head Start in Mississippi today appears to be run by black people, but it isn't. It's run by these middle class black people I'm talking about who owe everything they've got to whites. They want children to go to class and go home, with some extra services on the side. No change. No social change."

Sunflower and Bolivar counties ended up going with their area (establishment controlled) Community Action Agency. Some CDGMians are with them still, including several Area Teacher Guides, who have continued all these years to offer leadership toward CDGM-style early childhood education in a part of the country not bubbling over with early childhood expertise. Some CDGM counties simply refused to go with MAP (Mississippi Action for Progress)—Humphries, Wayne and two other adjacent counties—and OEO backed down. Feeling politically powerful is a big part of being politically powerful. These counties formed the group called Friends of the Children of Mississippi (FCM). Fred Mangrum was made FCM's director and the Field Foundation funded it. Field's $17,000 kept FCM alive until the federal government picked it up again and gave it a standard Head Start grant. Marvin Hogan, a black Mississippian, who had started with Head Start when Head Start started—he was Health Coordinator with Aaron Henry's Coahoma Head Start in 1965—became, in 1966, FCM's Executive Director; in 1990, Marvin is *still* FCM's Executive Director. Although Friends of the Children of Mississippi has been cut back, it's still funded for eight million four hundred thousand dollars, still pays a staff of five hundred and forty, and still serves three thousand children at any one time. CDGM's giant descendent can't be overlooked when we assess CDGM's legacy.

In 1990, CDGM people and their Head Start programs live on in many parts of the state, though they function under various names and auspices. This is true from the northernmost part of Mississippi to the southernmost on the Gulf coast.

For example, CDGM's Newell Chapel center, organized in Marshall county by the Robinson family, is still directed by Nola Robinson, who in the beginning was a teacher there. The center is now housed in a new building in nearby Byhalia. Newell Chapel is now known as the Whitaker Center. It's one of the twenty-one operated by the Institute for Community Services (ICS). In fact, in 1965, Nola Robinson was Angela Moore's Head Start teacher. Angela is now a physician in Texas, and chair of the natural sciences department at Wiley College. Since 1967, ICS's Executive Director has been Angela's father, an original CDGMian, currently Vice President of the National Head Start Association, Arvern Moore. (In the CDGM break up, Marshall and Lafayette counties were given to Rust College to run. For four years, Diane Trister Dodge, whom I had hired to help CDGM's educational component develop, and who is well-known nationwide both for her expert on-the-job staff development work, and as a member of the Governing Board of the National Association for the Education of Young Children, was this two county Head Start's Education Director.)

Former Area Teacher Guide Wilma Backstrom explains (1990) that in the Hattiesburg vicinity, CDGM centers "went through some changes, with ATG Earline Beard fighting for what's right in early childhood education all the way, until she died in the 1980s. The director didn't understand, wanted the children to act like high school students, but we knew from Polly how to do curriculum and teaching with *young* children. We worked on the director, and after quite a bit of pressure from the Head Start Regional Office, he began to get the idea.

"Our Head Start grantee now is PACE. Last year we became a High Scope project. Would you believe? They tell us all the same things Polly did twenty five years ago about each child making his own plans and decisions, and all the valuable things children learn through play. . . I've known it was true all along. I took courses at the University of Southern Mississippi in Hattiesburg—curriculum, child development, things like that—I got my Child Development Associate credential. They teach you all this, too. It's the way to help children develop to their fullest, and that was always the CDGM goal. It *still* isn't the goal of the power structure and the school system's Head Starts, even though they say the words. Actions speak louder than words. But the real difference is that CDGM gave power to the people. It wasn't just about children."

Mary Holmes Junior College was allowed to retain a big chunk of CDGM—fourteen counties, seventy-two centers, five thousand children, and a budget of as much as eight million dollars, another fact that has to be counted in a CDGM assessment. However, OEO insisted that

• Six hundred and forty thousand dollars, which OEO denied had been accounted for in proper government accounting style, was to be repaid;

• Mary Holmes, which had never been more than two words to CDGMians, was to control—first OEO gave it people to do the controlling, and then gave it control;

• "Procedures" were "to be instituted"—one of the procedures was that this truncated CDGM was not to call itself CDGM. The people begged and bullied to be allowed to call their Head Start CDGM: "It means something very special to us—it's a magic word meaning we are in charge for the first time in our history—they gave us a way to work magic beyond what we ever dreamed." But no, the name CDGM was a dirty word, not to be used.

The new name was the Community Education Extension (CEE) of Mary Holmes Junior College. People continued to call their program CDGM for some five years, but finally succumbed to CEE.

It was CDGM's loyal friend, the National Board of Missions of the United Presbyterian Church, U.S.A., that saved the day. The Presbyterians did a nationwide search and found Herman (Tex) Wilson to direct the payback. Tex documented all but forty thousand dollars, and the Presbyterians paid that to OEO. Ken Neigh, head of the National Board at the time, chuckles and says (in 1990), "I doubt that anyone ever stole a penny. Poor people were learning accounting. OEO was trying to dismantle the project." Tex, who became CEE's Executive Director, was a perfect choice. He was a Harvard lawyer. For five years, he had been with the Justice Department. He had been the head of an OEO Regional Legal Services office; Legal Services was another War on Poverty program. He had been on the staff of the Kerner Commission, put together by President Johnson to investigate the big city riots. And he was black.

In assessing the success of CDGM, or a Head Start, or any social change project, we have to look at what effect it had on the individuals who participated in it. What has become of them, what have they contributed to bettering the world since, one by one, and what influence do they feel the project had on their later contributions? Many poor children's advocates would say that CDGM was worth a great deal if its only contribution had been motivating Marian Wright Edelman to initiate the Children's Defense Fund some years later. She says that it was her years in Mississippi, especially her experience trying to get further funding for CDGM, that gave her the CDF idea. But CDGM changed the understanding of many, many people involved in education and other human services work, all kinds of people, including John Mudd, including myself. Simply stated, I'm a different person because of my CDGM years, and that fact colors all my work and my way of living as well.

"CDGM changed my life, too," says Clarece Coney. When a large segment of CDGM became CEE, and her title changed to Field Supervisor, Area Teacher Guide Clarece Coney (pages 401-406) continued working with Head Start teachers in the same capacity as she had from the outset.

"I stayed till 1974, then I went with the public schools. Dave Rice was the CEE Director. He followed Tex Wilson. It was the CDGM spirit. I just kept on doing what we Area Teacher Guides did with you, Polly, trying to inspire parents and teachers to create great kids. I do positive thinking. I try to encourage others to do it too.

"You start teaching positive thinking with children in the family, church, school, and community. My mother gave it to me. I tried to give it to my children, from there on it's up to them. I believe it worked. My first daughter has a master's degree and works in California. The second daughter is an investigator for the Equal Opportunity Commission; she also has a master's degree. My third daughter has a college degree and is in corrections, she's a parole officer in Jackson. My fourth daughter was the youngest person ever to get a law degree from Howard University. My baby daughter is at Tougaloo College, and my young son is at Jackson State. My oldest son is at Louisiana State getting a master's in architecture and landscaping. Part of what has helped my children is the positive thinking I gave them, and part is the example of their mother. They see me do it; so they think, yes, I can do well, too. I try to express this enthusiasm and confidence in *all* the children and parents I come in contact with. I say, 'Go on, do it!'

"I developed my thirst for learning in CDGM. It was running around all over the place with you, Polly, I got the idea I could go places, like we did together. I'll never forget the first time I flew on an airplane. I was an ATG and you arranged for me to fly over to Atlanta to meet with Mr. Sargent Shriver about getting another Head Start grant. I had an A.A. degree in sociology at the time. Then you sent me and Lavoree flying off to New York City to preview the film you wrote, "Change for Change," and to attend a Bank Street College of Education course in early childhood education. I was raised poor, but I took a look at how the other half lived on these trips and in these places, and I said, 'Hmmmm, I could do that. That looks better to me, I think I'll just do it that way.'

"So I kept on taking courses and going to school. First I got a four year degree in early childhood education at Jackson State. But I kept on at Alcorn, Mississippi State U., U.S.M., and Ole Miss. I attended school around the edges until 1975. I got lots of degrees, including a master's in special ed and my psychometrics qualifications. I test public school children. I've been with the public schools for sixteen years now. The truth is that I learned more during CDGM than at any other time in my life. I learned an attitude that I can do whatever I want to do, so I did. So I do. Now it's travel. I just love it! I'm always flying in from somewhere else, somewhere new."

CDGM seems to have been a turning point or the highpoint in many lives. In February, 1989, my home phone in Washington, D.C. rang one evening, and it was one-time CDGM Area Teacher Guide Lavaree Jones.

"I'm planning a CDGM/CEE 25th reunion," she said casually—as casually as if there had been no twenty-three year gap since our last chat. "I'm the President. We'd like you to come. Do you have Tom's number in New York?" (Luckily, *I've* had the same number for a hundred years, or I might never have heard about the Reunion, which, as it turned out, was one of the highlights in my life.) Lavoree had managed single handedly to talk Jackson State University's Institute for the Study of History, Life, and Culture of Black People into sponsoring the three day event, and Tougaloo College into housing it. (The Institute for the Study of History, Life, and Culture of Black People was established and directed until her retirement by Professor Margaret Walker Alexander, author of nine books.) Lavaree had organized a Reunion Committee. CDGM's finance man Bill Sanders was on the Committee's Finance Committee, his wife, Emma, was on the Research Committee, and former ATG Clarece Coney (who flew in from a Carribbean cruise half way through the three day happening) was Vice President. Lavoree had gotten a grant, and contributions from many people, including a good-sized gift from novelist Alice Walker, Margaret's sister. Much of the "history" presented at the Reunion was invented to increase self pride, or garbled by the limited glimpse of the whole available to whichever individual participant was speaking, but then the same can be said for the history of the national Head Start program itself.

A story about Head Start in Mississippi and its CDGM origins appeared on the front page of the Sunday, July 2, 1989 Jackson Clarion-Ledger, which had a quarter century before been so pugilistically inclined toward CDGM.

The experience of one little Head Start child was poignantly portrayed by the journalist. Her mother hadn't allowed her to start school at six, but in 1965, a Head Start teacher convinced the woman to let her daughter attend Head Start. The seven-year-old and her seven siblings had never had more than one meal a day, a meal, usually, of beans, rice, corn bread, and bologna. Little Grace eagerly awaited each mid-day dinner at Head Start, and Head Start was where she received the first Christmas gifts she had ever gotten, toys and clothes. Twice in her life, the now grown girl reports, she did the unheard of in her family: she graduated high school, then she graduated college. The Head Start, of course, was a CDGM first summer center, Pickens #1, one of Area Teacher Guide Hattie Saffold's seven centers. And the child was Grace Simmons, the Clarion-Ledger staff writer who authored the front page story.

* * * * * * * * * * * *

When assessing rapid reform projects whose avowed priority goal is social change, we must take into consideration the fact that these projects frequently have far less financial support than other kinds of projects—projects less threatening to the power structure because they propose to give fish rather than to teach fishing. Few of the thousands of charitable foundations deliciously described in fat directories (inaccessible to the poor)—few meaning perhaps four or five—support poor people sponsored social change projects. The few who do give grants to grassroots projects usually require people without typists, typewriters, or dimes for the copier to jump through proposal writing hoops and then to submit ten copies with a recently audited annual financial report and a list of liberal elite board members. What would social change projects achieve if they were well-funded? The case of CDGM gives us a clue!

With few exceptions, the support of the liberal foundations—even the handful of progressive foundations dedicated to "social change"—goes to Certain People on the approved circuit and those they recommend. (If for any reason—including professional competitiveness, as well as the never-stated wish to keep silent rapid reformist views that threaten the teak-tabled board room inner sanctums—members of the liberal elite frown upon a grant applicant, the applicant almost always is denied funding by the entire league of allied foundations, regardless of the merit of his proposed project, his qualifications, and his track record of successfully completing high quality work.) Certain people's model projects are funded—and their next project and their next project and their next project. The Certain People are not poor people; they are self-appointed spokesmen for poor people. Certain People get generous support for report and book research and writing, so they can hire assistants to do most of the work for them, and can take time off from their fast track jobs—without losing them—to work on the project themselves. Both the projects and the books done by Certain People are given dissemination and publicity grants and cash awards, enabling their principle authors to travel, prepare papers, present at symposiums and conferences, etc. The same Certain People and their disciples are nearly always the beneficiaries of opportunities to become "the" spokespeople for The Poor, The Black Child, Family Involvement in Education, or whatever is "in" in the foundation world. When their jobs evaporate—due, say, to a gap between fundings of their projects, the death of the "project leader", or an election that displaces them—they can count on quickly arranged "parachute grants" to keep them afloat till their normal sources of income resume. The result of all this is a tapestry of intellectually incestuous theories about what's best for the poor. Conversely, starved of resources, rapid reformists and the poor they organize and work collaboratively with are effectively almost silenced. Only small gurgles can be heard from this stream; it will never be given enough support to become a dangerously swollen force.

Of course, as with radio, TV, and book publishing, far and away the highest percent of people whose voices are supported by foundations, liberal as well as conservative, are white males. Research amply documents this. The primary route to foundation grant, media, or publication access for women and minorities is to be the disciples, wives, or select minority pets of Certain People. If one is not on the network, gaining the support of the liberal elite is indeed a feat. And rapid reformists are rarely (with notable exceptions) on the network. The reason is obvious—they want *real* social change, which would obviate the elite.

In spite of this general scene, CDGM was extraordinarily fortunate in winning small financial and large political support from several progressive foundations and several national organizations; very likely because it was so enormously politically visible. When foundations or institutions *do* help grassroots or social change projects, frequently the impetus comes from one person who is able to persuade several key people—people either already on this path, so working with the project is another step forward for them in their own efforts, or people who see supporting the project as a feather in the cap of their own professional futures. Because their motive was political, not philanthropic, only *cloaked* in the mantle of philanthropy, when the latter group talks and writes about the project later, one hears of *its* role, but not of the grassroots *people's* role, or of the project's key players, or even of the key *ideas* intentionally exemplified in the project. There are many of this sort of mentions of CDGM.

Everyone wants to take credit for something famous and successful, however minor, peripheral, or even oppositional their role may at the time have been.

An example of the former situation—a situation in which the crucial role that can be played by progressive *individuals* who are ready for the next step on the road they are travelling when the project happens to crop up in their path—is the Presbyterians' role in assisting CDGM.

One of the groups that played a major role in "restructuring" CDGM (as the kill was euphemistically called) and in picking up the pieces was said to be the National Council of Churches. It wasn't the National Council of Churches. It was, specifically, the National Board of Missions of the United Presbyterian Church, U.S.A., one of the few progressive parts of the National Council of Churches. It had been a friend of CDGM since the outset.

The National Council of Churches had been established a generation before as a confederation of thirty-three Protestant denominations. It included almost all Protestant denominations except the Southern Baptists. The National Council of Churches had the appearance of having more influence than it really had, but several groups within *were* powerful, and used their powers in CDGM's behalf. Of the denominations, the most helpful to civil rights efforts everywhere were the Presbyterians, the United Church of Christ, the Episcopalians, and the Methodists. One by one, the denominations decided which way to go. NCC served as headquarters; it housed all these groups in New York City at 475 Riverside Drive. Just before the origination of CDGM, the NCC had gone through a major reorganization, resulting in the creation of three large divisions within the overall umbrella organization. These divisions were:

- Overseas Activities
- Christian Education, and
- Christian Life and Mission.

Within the division of Christian Life and Mission, were the Commission on Race and Religion, created in 1963 under the courageous leadership of J. Irwin Miller, and headed by Bob Spike; and the Delta Ministry, headed by Art Thomas. The Director of the Christian Life and Mission division was the progressive and determined John Regier. Regier had been at the National Council of Churches for fifteen years, and was a great advocate and protector of its civil rights activities.

The Commission on Race and Religion was created because of pressure from John Lewis, National Chairman of the Student Nonviolent Coordinating Committee (SNCC), and other black leaders who wanted the NCC to take a moral stand and do something in the South. Kenneth Clark and James Baldwin, and with them Harry Belafonte, Lena Horne, and Andy Young, had gone to Robert F. Kennedy and said, in essence, The cities are burning, you've got to do something. R.F.K. had not yet awakened to the injustice and immorality of the race situation in this country. He responded as if the problem was merely a matter of controlling riots. He said that he didn't have enough police to quell them all. After this, the group, including Regier, convened at a Harlem YMCA—and stayed till five a.m. The result of the all night meeting was the establishment of the Commission on Race and Religion. It was not created by a huge, amorphous institution, the National Council of Churches, it was created by individuals, black and white, individuals, one by one. Out of the Commission on Race and Religion grew the Delta Ministry.

"We pulled off a real coup to get funding for the Delta Ministry," laughs John Regier (1990). "We asked the World Council of Churches to give us money for missionary work in an underdeveloped area of the world—Mississippi. Officials were shocked! They hadn't realized there *was* such a spot in the wealthy United States."

John Regier and others had wanted a black director for the Delta Ministry. But at the time, black church leadership was largely Republican and conservative, Regier says. He says, "The black church was the Safe Place. Neither the black pastors nor their people wanted to take the risk of becoming too involved in civil rights. There were exceptions, of course, but civil rights leadership came mainly from the NAACP Legal Defense Fund." Bob Spike and Bruce Hanson, Spike's special assistant, came up with Art Thomas, a young methodist pastor. Says Regier,

"We made him Acting Director. In his own way, Art was a genius. By 1964 and early 1965 when Art came to us with the CDGM idea, we were experiencing some counter forces within our division. J. Irwin Miller's term was up. He had been replaced by Bishop Reuben Miller. *This* Miller didn't feel comfortable with our progressive projects. There were some significant efforts to stop what we were doing with the Delta Ministry. The Episcopal Bishop in Mississippi was putting serious pressure on Reuben Miller. The Mississippi Bishop was overruled at the national level."

After I called Tom with word of the new Head Start program, and Tom invited me to meet with him, Art, and several others to outline the program to them, and we completed the meeting, Art went to his superior, John Regier, with the information and our idea. During the next few weeks, Art Thomas, John Regier and Bruce Hanson discussed which church-run institution of higher education in Mississippi would be the best one to commandeer as grantee, if it was decided to go forward with this wild scheme (CDGM). Tom Levin recalls, "Art worked night and day and every angle to get the church people to back this."

"We decided to go along with Art. We wanted Tougaloo College, of course," says Regier. "It was United Church of Christ. We had had a long history with it. It was very daring. But George Owens, the Acting President, was scared, and with good reason—they'd had some recent shootings with F.B.I. men standing around watching in their characteristic way."

Of the NCC's thirty-three denominations, the National Board of Missions of the United Presbyterian Church, U.S.A., headed by Kenneth Neigh was the most active in civil rights activities. David Ramage was Neigh's Associate Director, and Bryant George was his assistant. Bruce Hanson and Bryant George came up with the idea of Mary Holmes Junior College as the ideal grantee to serve as a pass-through for CDGM—a fund-eligible, governor's-veto-proof front for us. It was in Westpoint, Mississippi, hours away from where Art proposed to locate CDGM's headquarters at Mount Beulah, but it was in Mississippi—and it was operated by the Presbyterians. Art's quick trip to Westpoint to twist Mary Holmes President D.I. Horne's arm has been described (page 33) but here are a few more funny details, some of them told to me by Ken Neigh, some by Julius Richmond, and some by Frank Keppel (a former boss of mine):

While Art was camped in Mr. Horne's outer office waiting for him to consult and consider, Bryant George was on the phone with him, urging him to comply, and Julius B. Richmond, national Head Start director, was on the phone in Washington with the U.S. Commissioner of Education, Frank Keppel, asking for a definitive definition of "an institution of higher education." "Is MHJC one?" Dr. Richmond inquired, and added, "It's an unaccredited junior college." Commissioner Keppel immediately asked an Office of Education attorney for a legal definition of an institution of higher education. Very shortly thereafter, Keppel called Richmond back with the answer everyone wanted to hear: MHJC *is* an institution of higher education, thus is eligible for this Head Start grant. An institution of higher education is any institution from which any graduate ever was accepted into a yet *higher* level educational institution; and there was, once, an MHJC graduate who went on in another college in Atlanta. CDGM was born because, one by one, individuals caused it to be.

* * * * * * * * * * * *

When it died, CDGM was not alone. Several groups were instrumental in helping to dismember it and mop up the mess. Each of these liberal groups saw what it was doing as "saving" the situation—salvaging most of CDGM's Head Start programs for the children, and salvaging many positions and salaries for poor people in contrast to giving the majority of them to middle class people as was and is done in most Head Starts. And in a sense, to a degree, this perception was accurate. The following observations are true, too...

CDGM was a test case illustrating how far the powerful elite liberal establishment is willing to go in relinquishing its role as savior and manager of the poor. The answer was: Not very far. One of the most unique of Tom Levin's concepts in designing CDGM was the self-elimination of the status-holding liberal project creator, generalist and professional. We were all to view ourselves as catalysts, conceptualizers, emotional support, technical assistants—*temporary*. The difference between liberal intellectuals as initiators or as management in perpetuity is immense. The difference between liberals and professionals as management or as hired technical assistants (*who can be dismissed*) is immense.

Social commentator Andy Kopkind explains:

"What happened at the end of CDGM's first summer *always* happens when it begins to look like people are on the verge of achieving real change in their battle for political and economic status. They come under the gun from the opposition that's threatened by the impending change. In CDGM, it was Senator Stennis and those types, but there is always enormous opposition from people who will fight to keep the power and elite status they have.

"Then, the story always goes, the liberals step in and 'save the people'; the liberal saviors are members of an elite, too—an entrepreneurial policy elite. In CDGM, it was the AFL-CIO's Walter Reuther, the Board of Presbyterian Missions part of the National Council of Churches, Hubert Humphrey, John Brademas, Al Lowenstein, the Kennedys and the Kennedy-connected civil rights lawyers led by Marian Wright (Edelman). But it wouldn't matter who, it's always the people who are tied to all kinds of resources and power and are wonderfully articulate and literate that step in to 'save the poor'—who have been successfully, proudly, running their own project, and are now under attack. In CDGM's case, it was a huge, statewide comprehensive project, with significant national ramifications.

"'But the price you pay for us bailing you out,' say the elite liberals, many of whom are Old Boys and Girls from the ivy league, 'is that we will need to control the project for you.' (What they *mean,* though maybe not all of them consciously know it, is, 'We will need to protect our status as liberal intellectuals and the power our social class has in the world.')

"Liberal leaders genuinely want to do good. They're always in search of victims who are, *indeed* truly in need of rescue. They want to provide services and programs. That's one of the things Head Start is all about, and it's a very popular program with liberals. As long as the poor are 'totin' dat barge, and haulin' dat bale' or are enrolled in some sort of self-improvement effort, the liberals have strong empathy for them. But if the downtrodden become convinced that they can take care of themselves—that they at least want to *try* to take control of managing their own rescue projects and no longer feel like victims passively awaiting rescue by others, if the victims become actively antagonistic toward their oppressors and their would-be rescuers *alike,* which is inevitable—liberals flee in droves.

"The liberal intelligentsia (most of it white but with a few prized black stars) gets its power from being able to serve as a broker between the politically powerless and the powerful. These public policy people in the human services professions, universities, foundations, government, can talk a certain currently 'in' jargon. They can say and write the right words and be heard and understood. Their role is to carry the message from the powerless and translate it into proposal language and fundable terminology; then to carry some services back to the powerless, leaving them just as powerless. What's in it for the *really* powerful liberal elite who *control* these resources is a way to do good without actually having to deal with politically messy poor people directly, and a new loyal constituency. The liberal elite brokers deliver to the powerful politicians and to their political party another group of loyal (because deeply appreciative) followers, e.g. dependents.

"In a real struggle, when people begin to speak out for themselves, the brokers are threatened with role obliteration, thus with finding themselves powerless. If they are not permitted by the down-and-out to serve as translaters and bearers of urgently needed services and resources, they cannot deliver a grateful constituency to those in control of 'the system', so they themselves are powerless. They have no role. That's why liberal social planners and their spokespeople are always in search of victims who need their assistance. And even if they haven't been seriously involved in a project, but have merely been supportive by-standers or board members, they always rush in when they see poor people fighting for control of their own schools or social action projects to mediate and master-mind the sell-out. (Only of course they see it as salvaging the situation; they try their best to make the victims of the take-over they are engineering see it that way, too.) It isn't solely the conservative opposition that always quashes poor people bids for power. The liberal elite has just as much to lose.

"In CDGM, the prize that was delivered by the liberal intermediaries was the vote of Mississippi's poor black population (which was grateful that its multi-county Head Start programs had been 'saved') to the moderate part of the Democratic party. This was the straw that broke the back of the traditional segregationist Democrats, who had controlled the state for almost a century.

"After it's all over, and poor people are properly battened down in their place again, the saviors are always generously rewarded. Today, the deliverers aren't doing too badly. It's understandable; they knew that their careers didn't lie with the Fannie Lou Hamers and Hattie Saffolds in the red dirt counties of Mississippi. You have to have reliable connections to power, wealth, and the elites to do good in the only terms that the liberals have come to accept. They need their Georgetown connections and suburban lifestyles. They rationalize that as the only route to significant achievement in the circumscribed world of public policy.

"Radicals and radical projects, even if short-lived *always* promote progress. They create space for moderate liberal leaders and followers to move into. Radicals move the front lines farther forward, and therefore do significant good, too. But they don't get the plums and status that the liberal elite saviors of the poor get.

"It's very depressing. The world's population is predominantly poor people of color—one color or another. On a daily basis, people are desperate, struggling for a bite to eat, struggling to keep a shack over them. There are a whole lot of liberals who have given up. The problems seem too immense. People are struggling to survive and change their lives toward some little kind of empowerment, and liberals are talking about 'conflict resolution.' Poor people who are fighting for the smallest degree of political power understand powerlessness and power incredibly well. Liberals don't have any understanding of the dynamics of power. People who have privilege don't see it. Figure merges imperceptibly with ground. Masters understand nothing about their servants, they don't need to. But servants understand *everything* about their masters—they *have to* to survive. Social change comes from people who urgently need a change in their lives. Liberal policy leaders do not need a change in their lives. They live very, very comfortably. They have the best of everything—career mobility, unlimited access, unchallenged legitimacy, and of course the creature comforts that come with all that. They are always looking for a trend they can lead. Every five years, there is a new set of trendy words. But while the liberal elite meet and talk and write about poverty and this theory or that, the poor still stay just as desperately poor in this country and in most other countries. Especially the third world, which is most of the world.

"The legendary British journalist Claude Cockburn once asked an editor of *The Times* of London who decides the paper's policy. 'It's decided,' the editor replied, 'by a committee—that never meets.' In the same way, there is no conspiracy to keep power from the poor. But somehow, a 'committee that never meets' manages to maintain control of all important positions and resources."

The devil has slippery shoes.

An indicator that Andy's analysis is right is the fact that liberal intellectuals interested in the poor like to think about "service delivery" "models". Conceptualizing solving the probems of poor people this way, has obvious advantages for the conceptualizers. Service *delivery* implies that all the action is with the establishment, which (after making all necessary decisions) *delivers* something to passive *recipients* (people benefitting from one or another social service are actually often called recipients!). A *model* gives the impression of being a small, carefully crafted, ideal thing. Focus is not on training massive numbers of people and obtaining massive amounts of funding (think federal) so massive replication will be ensured and excellent. Emphasis is on the details of the model—researching them, refining them, writing and meeting about them. . .Conversely and conveniently, focus is not on strategizing how to actualize the offering of all needed services to all who could use them. The word *replication,* as used by the creators of models, means merely creating a manageable number of additional model programs.

For a century, America—through its private philanthropists, religious institutions, voluntary sector, local and state actions, direct and indirect federal activities, academics and intelligensia—has been making a wide variety of anti-poverty efforts. These include efforts to give poor families a hand up instead of a hand out. The former approach is recommended by all who are knowledgeable about our welfare system, and is most recently reflected in the Family Support Act of 1988. Many efforts have been made to "intervene" in the lives of poor children in hopes of putting them on the path to a brighter future.

By now, we should know a few things, which if we are sincere about significant social change we will act upon; some of them are highlighted below in no particular order:

1.) First, the problem is not a dearth of excellent models, demonstrations, and theories for any aspect of anything we might be trying to do in the way of helping poor children and their families. An abundance of excellent approaches exists. The function of scholars is to find out, so it goes without saying the scholars will always tell us that enough is not yet known for widespread replication. (Actually, this is *exactly* what they said in the last months of 1964 and the first months of 1965 when Head Start was being conceptualized—in fact, rumor had it at the time that a man who these days takes major credit for being "the father of Head Start" threatened to resign from the Advisory Committee if Head Start was implemented as a huge program right from the outset; fortunately, Lyndon Johnson, Sargent Shriver, and Jule Sugarman ignored all their cautious advisors.) But for poverty warriors, a need for more knowledge is not the main problem. The function of trend-setting liberal intellectuals is to think and to show one another that they are on the cutting edge intellectually, so they always focus on ideas over actions. For poverty warriors, a need for new ideas to circulate to members of the inner circle and then beyond, isn't the issue.

The problem is creating and mobilizing enough focus, understanding, conviction, concern, optimism, energy, and will on the part of the public to cause it to elect and pressure progressive leaders to make monies available for large scale initiatives—for example, to make available universal Head Start, including parent/child and infant/toddler programs for all who would benefit from them, and follow through programs extending throughout high school for all who would benefit from *them.* Our problem is securing funding for intensive, comprehensive social services for all members of all families who need them in order to become positively functioning citizens and parents; we always seem to celebrate and settle for absurdly small incremental improvements. Our problem is making whatever changes are needed in relevant laws so services can be offered conveniently and coherently, and need not, due to appalling scarcity, have to be hidden in a bewildering assortment of bureaucratic and geographical ways to keep access, therefore cost, down. Our problem is to make available to all who would benefit the hundreds of *other* poverty alleviation and eradication programs we have, through a century of trial and error, evolved, among them good wages and benefits, health and mental health prevention and treatment services, and affordable housing. Simply put, our problem is putting our money where our mouths and models are.

2.) Secondly, we should know by now that because significant social change does not come from us, it comes, as Andy explains, from the fed-up poor who finally begin to feel they deserve more of the American way of life. Therefore, liberals and rapid reformers who are serious about wanting to promote better lives for low-income children must promote social change, and if we are serious about wanting to promote social change; we need to work toward raising poor people's expectations and awareness of how "the system" works—e.g., to inform and activate the poor in their own behalf. As a former poverty warrior said, "In the sixties, we *did* this, and scared everyone shitless."

The problem is that because job training without jobs, help in locating housing without income to pay the rent, and similar frustrations make people furious and prone to riot, over-throwing their well-intentioned advocates and guides as they go, gung ho liberal leaders learned their lesson in the sixties; first they backed down from community *action* to far safer community *development,* and then they narrowed their efforts much further and kept them contained within classroom walls, literally or figuratively speaking. For a quarter of a century, liberals allowed the War on Poverty to be dubbed a failure and to be ignored, not because it didn't work, but because it was so successful in activating poor people that liberal leaders' positions as gurus of the poor were endangered. How will we generate professional courage in our retreated leaders and in their successors? That is our problem.

3.) Thirdly, we know by now—and have known for many decades—that most middle class white teachers—with glorious exceptions—are not very successful teaching low-income minority preschool and primary children. The school failure statistics testify to our failure. We also know—and have known for many decades—that parents' influence on their young children's (low? high?) self-esteem, mental health, underlying directions, motivations, aspirations, and self-imposed limitations is much more profound and permanent than is the influence of schools and other social institutions or individuals. Although in borderline cases, where there are enough strengths and positive factors to build upon, all or any of the latter may push the child over the hump into "success", a basic fact of child development is that families—particularly parents—are basic.

Long ago and ever since, psychoanalytic practice and theory have proven this. Parents' deep, perhaps unspoken—even unconscious—beliefs are contagious to young children. Children unwittingly act them out. This includes the dual beliefs, held by many poor minority families, that it's fruitless, and moreover disloyal, to try to succeed in the white middle class world. We in the child development field are also familiar with the modeling theory of socialization, which tells us that children grow to feel they can influence their own destinies when they interact regularly with "significant others" (read "parents" or parent substitutes) who *themselves* feel able to influence their environments, shape their own lives, and significantly effect the lives of their children. Cultural reproduction theory illuminates the ways in which parents—sometimes consciously, sometimes unconsciously—train their children to fit into the socioeconomic class the adults find themselves in. We have learned, too, about learned helplessness.

Is there any doubt among the experts that the children of college graduates are more likely to be college graduates than are the children of high school graduates or dropouts? That the children of parents who participate actively in all levels of their children's school careers are more likely to do well in school than are the children of parents who remain completely disengaged from the schools? That the parents of low-income minority children are unlikely to engage deeply in their children's schools?

So we should know that giving poor parents

- focused opportunities
- minimal guidelines
- ample resources

to provide early childhood education and daycare programs—Head Start educare programs—for their own children is, psychologically and sociologically speaking, a brilliant idea. Tom Levin had a brilliant idea; the idea was his and no one's but his. And "the model" CDGM—would be easy to replicate.

We're talking about enabling poor parents to start and operate their own programs for young children, just as an earlier generation of mothers nationwide—including me—started and operated cooperative nursery schools—yet another "model." Only we were middle class and didnt't need to be paid, whereas poor parents *do.*

The problem is how can we get our profession—the early childhood profession—to let go, give up control, shift to a new role, become paid technical assistants to funded, "new careerist," low-income parents? This would be so hard. Giving up power, even the small amount of power our laughably low status field gives us, is so hard. It would be a measure of our maturity and degree of dedication to the principle of permitting trampled people to stagger to their feet and lead their little children to better lives if we could *help* instead of dominate.

4.) Fourthly, because a child's parents and *their* peers are a greater influence on her than are "programs," we should know by now that the problem is not tinkering with program quality within classroom walls; focusing on the family is the wisest way to go. Indeed we *do* know this—a flurry of family resource and support projects proves that we do.

If the goal is to create brighter futures for poor children, the best place to "intervene"—or at least, a place where we need to intervene simultaneously while offering high quality health and other services to the children, and funding so families can operate and improve early childhood education programs themselves while earning and learning—is in the *parents'* lives, by providing whatever is necessary to enable parents (or those serving in their places) to scramble to their feet and clamber out of poverty and take charge of improving their children's lives and future chances. Children will probably be impressed and motivated by their parent's effort.

The crux of our problem here is not lack of know-how regarding ways to offer family members a hand up in any needed dimension. We have a variety of expert health, mental health, and social services specialists and model programs. We know how to provide excellent and respectfully "delivered" health care, psychiatric services, counselling, job training, job placement and support during a transition period. We know how to provide transportation, one of the services most mentioned by poor people as a lack preventing them from being able to take advantage of job training and job opportunities. Day care for their young children is another. We know how to provide high quality day care. Head Start has understood from the outset the importance of health, social and mental health services, and has always included them. But they are the weak sister components of the overall Head Start program, as they are the weak sister services in this entire society. Everybody knows that their county has a school system, and where each of the schools is located. Few people know that their county has a mental health and a social services system, and where each of the separate services is located. Why all these helping services are so scarce and so little understood by the public is one of the major problems facing poverty fighters.

The problem is that it is the way it is because most of the people who know best how to help people out of poverty are the very people with a vested interest in having a nation full of poor people to help, to study, and to write about. If poverty were to be eliminated, they would have to change their professions and areas of specialization, with accompanying loss of the status they now enjoy. Because this is true, professionals and related intellectuals mildly protest drastic underfunding—and mildly protest the two tons of paperwork required of each "client"—surely a deterrant for semi-literate, already overwhelmed people in need—and mildly protest our system of splintering services and burying them all over the country in an obscure bureaucratic maze shimmering with false "lights at the end of the tunnel" and harboring hordes of hidden deadends. But we never protest vehemently enough to change the system. Splintering services may work against fully helping a poor person in need, but is advantageous to each group of specialists. Each group is ensured a funding stream. Interest group members need only look *up* to the source of their money. There is no need to bother looking sidewards and coordinating with those in related special services groups; in fact, these groups are bitter rivals for money given by the federal government to the states as block grants for each state to allocate within itself. For the federal government—the White House and the Congress—perennially faced with the thankless task of dividing insufficient funds among underfunded special interest groups—there is an advantage, too; kept separate, human service advocates fight each other for funds, whereas were they united, they would fight for funds now given to non-human services (such as highways) and inhuman services (such as bombing the children of Vietnam, Panama, and other countries), for which fortunes are always immediately available.

The problem is that, although liberals may cause poor people less pain and enable more individuals to slip the shackles of poverty and escape than conservatives who vote against most booster and bootstrap efforts, liberals only work to alleviate and remediate poverty, not to create the fundamental changes in our society required to eliminate it.

5.) Fifth, we should know by now—because they've been telling us long enough and loud enough—that for many minority groups the problem is not what ingenious new methods and materials white educators should lay on minority children.

The problem is, as has just been said, to get us white educators to step graciously aside from almost complete control of the controls, to offer technical assistance, if it's wanted, thus freeing minority children to see their own people running their educational programs, at least in the early years. Black people, for example, whose focus is on building high confidence, motivation, and aspiration in African American children generally agree that definite steps must be built into childrearing and education at all levels to counteract erased or negatively conveyed facts and impressions about their race and its place seeping subtly and banging blatantly at the children from all angles in this overwhelmingly European-American-dominant society. Whereas dominant culture children—white children from European backgrounds—are constantly being taught and running into validations of their heritage and customs, African American, Jewish American, Asian American, Native American, Hispanic American, Arab American, and all other minority children are just as constantly experiencing the omission and distortion of *theirs.* Especially black children.

White European Americans assume that young children should be cared for "by their own kind." The liberals among them want, also, regular exposure to people of other colors, religions, ethnicity, etc., to ensure diversity (a synonym for reality). They want a healthy measure of minority children, parents, and teachers in their children's programs. Rarely do whites with choice select predominantly black preschools or public schools. Rarely do Protestant families place their children in Hebrew schools, certainly not for more than a few preschool years if at all. Many black parents want what white parents want—for young children to be surrounded by their own culture before being saturated in someone else's. Many African American parents want their children's classrooms to reflect a preponderance of African American art, dance, music (including spirituals, work songs, and freedom songs), literature, story telling, drama (including Black English Vernacular—BEV), prayers, proverbs, history, customs, and all the rest of what, cumulatively, is called culture. These parents, who do not represent *all* black parents, do not have the goal of making their children into white people. This means that some minority parents favor a certain amount of separatism, at least in the early years, to get children off to a proud start. They believe this to be part of personal empowerment, thus part of social change. The schools might be better or worse, but they would be theirs.

* * * * * * * * * * * *

Dick Boone, the War on Poverty official under whom the national Project Head Start program was initially developed, says (1990),

"If in the War on Poverty and in Head Start two principle goals were to reach the children of the poor with valuable services and to achieve maximum feasible participation of the poor in helping themselves, CDGM must be judged the best program that OEO supported. CDGM was the best embodiment of these two principles in the country."

In 1965, as now, there were people who believed that poor people need to be helped by the provision of appropriate services. If possible, these people believed, the services should be comprehensive, coordinated, intensive, offered to all members of families as needed, and offered in a family and community context by trusted persons; these are not new ideas, they've been implemented on a small scale since Settlement House days. Some people still believe these things.

But this approach to poverty leaves the poor out of the political loop, still politically disempowered, still at the mercy of those in power for whatever crumbs the passionately committed and the moderately well-intentioned can scrounge and squeeze into the seemingly always insufficient budget after all powerful interest groups get their chunks of it. This approach to poverty is a continuation of the age-old donor/donee system, a modern day version of *noblesse oblige.* It does nothing to confront and to alter racism and classism in America, two roots of poverty, by changing the political balance of power so those who manage the nation's monies must heed the needs of the down and out, which they need not heed today.

In 1965, there were people who believed that *poor people need and deserve ownership of their own programs and services,* and every opportunity to learn to work the system that any mover and shaker has. If possible, these people believed, the services should be comprehensive, coordinated, intensive, offered to all members of families as needed, and offered in a family and community context by trusted persons *from among themselves, hired by elected representatives from among themselves;* and by trusted technical assistance people *also hired by the "recipients" of the services and by their peers.*

"For poverty to be significantly reduced," says Dick Boone, "the political equation has to change."

Says Tom Levin, "Some people still believe this." I among them.

ABOUT THE AUTHOR, BEFORE CDGM

In the early 1960s, I was a staff person at the Department of Education (then called the U.S. Office of Education). I worked for Francis A.J. (Fritz) Ianni in the Developmental Activities Program of the Cooperative Research Bureau. (Ever since, Fritz Ianni, an anthropologist, has been at Columbia Teachers College. I liked working for an anthropologist; cultural anthropology had been a major interest of mine in college.) This program gave "by invitation only" grants to "underdeveloped areas of education" (inner cities, rural areas, Southern "negro" colleges, and early childhood education, especially for low-income minority children). Francis Keppel, on leave as Dean of the Harvard School of Education, was U.S. Commissioner of Education; John F. Kennedy was President of the United States; Robert F. Kennedy was U.S. Attorney General; and black leaders everywhere (as well as their white allies) were insisting upon equal opportunity for their people in all aspects of life in this democracy.[51]

Because crime, poverty, and civil rights issues seemed to be more entwined and complicated than had previously been thought by the Kennedy brothers, President Kennedy created the President's Committee on Juvenile Delinquency, and named Attorney General Robert Kennedy its Chairman. With the help of two distinguished sociologists, Lloyd Ohlin and Richard Cloward, Robert Kennedy, in charge of crime-fighting for our country, came to understand apathy, juvenile delinquency, crime, and many other ramifications of poverty as lack of opportunity. Robert Kennedy grew increasingly convinced that innumerable poor people, particularly young people, particularly young minority people, become disillusioned, resigned to small futures, and drop out (of school, of the struggle to "succeed"), or turn this energy, leadership skill, and entrepreneurism to (sometimes brave, sometimes clever) underworld endeavors because, due to the inferior educations they have received, the biases they confront in our society, and the lack of contacts and networks that are their lot, struggle as they may, few are likely to make it (past nasty minimum wage jobs) regardless of what they do.

[51]For brilliantly researched and written background on the American race situation during and somewhat prior to this period, read Taylor Branch's book *Parting the Waters, America in the King Years 1954–63.* 1988. New York, Simon and Schuster.

The President's Committee on Juvenile Delinquency (PCJD) was housed across the hall from the Attorney General's office in the U.S. Justice Department. It had been put together by a talented young public administrator named Jule Sugarman, and was run by Bob Kennedy's best friend from prep school days—when the two were seventeen years old—David L. Hackett. It was the bright, dedicated, multi-talented PCJD team members who discovered— through their work in ghetto neighborhoods from coast to coast, through the guidance of their ever curious Executive Director Dave Hackett, and through consultation with a number of poor people in many cities—that if human services and other self-improvement efforts are to be effective to a maximum feasible extent, poor people must be encouraged to participate to the maximum feasible extent in designing and directing them. Like anyone else, a poor person wants to feel a meaningful degree of "ownership" of circumstances and institutions (such as schools, human services, and jobs) affecting her or him. If essentially disempowered people are merely "recipients" of programs and services, they feel alienated from them and oppressed by them. PCJD devoted itself to the dissemination of this principle.

Because it had little money of its own, the President's Committee on Juvenile Delinquency's carefully thought out strategy was to work *through progressive people in as many federal agencies as possible to build maximum feasible participation of the poor into all pertinent programs*. Commissioner of Education Frank Keppel was very cooperative. I was one of his progressive people, although a junior staff member. Therefore, I was one of the few USOE staffers who worked with several PCJD staff members—primarily junior staff members, "Bobby's guerillas," as the group was affectionately called.

Years later, I asked Stan Salett, one of the group and even younger than I (I had already been married for twelve years, divorced, and the mother of four children for some time—after Mississippi I had a fifth daughter, Gwen) how it was that we got to do such thrilling things when we were not important people, though appropriately credentialed. "We were there. We were able. We were willing," Stan replied. Since those days, I've learned over and over that this is the way the world works. Incredible opportunities often await those who are in the right place at the right time, are able, and are willing. (Like most *contemporary* young women at policy levels in early childhood education, I got a head start on professional opportunities by being the bright dedicated disciple of a male academician, prominently positioned in a prestigious university psychology department. I was one of George Goethal's girls. George was at Harvard's School of Social Relations.)

Because I am the daughter of a pioneering progressive educator who devoted her seventy year professional life to social change work—to projects addressing the eradication of poverty, injustice, prejudice, and war through child development, education and political action—it was natural that I became an instant convert to the conviction that **poor people must organize, make major decisions in, operate, and staff programs intended to "help" them, with (of course, it seemed to me) the same degree of technical assistance from "experts" that is available to others who design and administer programs.**

The early 1960s were years of

- national affluence,
- optimism among liberals that problems standing as barriers between *reality* for many poor and minority Americans and "the American dream" were soluable,
- rising unrest on the part of black leaders who were insisting that equal opportunity be provided to everyone regardless of race, religion, or color, and
- increasing guilt in liberal intellectual circles about the obviously "inferior" and "few and far between" opportunities available to black people compared to those available to white people.

In response to this swelling national feeling that "something must be done," the President's economic advisors and the President himself were looking at their options.

During the spring of 1964, shortly after President Kennedy was assassinated, the War on Poverty, originally suggested by his economic advisors, was being planned by representatives of each federal agency and a select group of outside consultants named by the agency heads. The confederation was called the President's Task Force Against Poverty. It functioned under the direction of R. Sargent Shriver, appointed Poverty Tsar by newly installed President Lyndon B. Johnson. Though many thought Robert Kennedy the obvious man for the job, President Johnson did *not* select him to head the poverty program. He couldn't stand him. For some time, LBJ and RFK had been intense political enemies. (This was well-known by all who worked on Capitol Hill, were close friends with those who did, or who were insiders of the secretarial and special assistant sort.) President Johnson, however, *did* capitalize on John F. Kennedy's great popularity with the public; Sargent Shriver was the slain president's sister's husband.

Working under Wade Robinson, who was one of Commissioner Keppel's representatives associated with the President's Task Force Against Poverty—the group planning a brand new federal agency to be named the Office of Economic Opportunity, and planning, at the same time, OEO's many soon-to be programs—I was privileged to participate on the fringes of Job Corps design.

When the Congressional appropriation made funds available to *launch* the new Office of Economic Opportunity (War on Poverty headquarters for all components of the poverty program—Job Corps, the Community Action Program, VISTA Volunteers, etc. for the entire nation), Wade, and I as his special assistant, were transferred to it—to OEO. Sargent Shriver made Wade Robinson Acting Director of Job Corps. (Wade was another one who hit the dust hard because he politically displeased the Poverty Tsar.)

When Sargent Shriver and his senior staff—about two dozen men—decided to start a comprehensive, multiservice program for children on the verge of entering school, Wade assigned me the task of writing a position paper about the idea "for Sarge." (I was an early childhood educator. I had taught poor and black children in a variety of settings. No other early childhood educator yet worked at OEO.) I wrote the requested paper. In the government, "white" papers are written by the dozen every week; I had been asked to write a good many of them in my years at the U.S. Office of Education. However, this particular paper—dated Oct. 31, 1964—is the first paper in Project Head Start archives.

Head Start was initially conceptualized by OEO's senior staff—men representing all components of the poverty program and its administration—some of them conservative administrators, some of them social change theoreticians, some of them progressive liberals and a number of them good friends of mine—as a response to Sargent Shriver's growing feeling that the War on Poverty should do something for poor *children*. It was doing something for every *other* age group. Sargent Shriver and his wife Eunice, primarily Eunice, were at the time deeply involved in the Kennedy Foundation, which they had established to research mental retardation. (A Kennedy sister was mentally retarded.) In the early 1960s, developmental psychologists were just discovering the devastating results that poverty (lack of opportunity in all dimensions) usually has on optimal human development. They, and Sargent Shriver, were particularly interested in I.Q. boosting.

Another critical reason for the creation of Head Start was a political reason pertaining to gaining popularity for the overall War on Poverty—e.g., for the Democratic Party, which was out to get the new black vote that history was about to produce. Sargent Shriver was extremely worried that there would be no visible War on Poverty programs by the summer of 1965 to show the hostile press, a press ever ready to "expose" federal "failures." From the moment the Economic Opportunity Act was passed and made into law two months before, there were many reporters and Congressional Representatives ready to shred its as yet unborn efforts. When Sargent Shriver took the Head Start idea to President Johnson, the president immediately recognized what a brilliant move its creation would be; no one hates little children.

Sargent Shriver's senior staff and their assistants (including me) were working day and (literally) night to get the components of this new White House program that were named in the enabling legislation organized and operative; all at the same time, VISTA Volunteers, Job Corps, and the Community Action Program were being developed by staff and outside specialists hired as consultants, each with an advisory board to provide status for the project in its specialty area (youth specialists, social workers, etc.).

The Community Action Program had inherited 17 ongoing model programs from the President's Committee on Juvenile Delinquency. A few of them contained components for young children. CAP was working on many more programs. However, CAP leaders, most of whom had come to OEO from PCJD, knew that **if community action programs are to effectively help poor people improve their own lives by using newly available resources and technical assistance, time must be allowed for able poor people—opinion leaders among their peers—to surface, and begin the arduous task of planning their own programs. Laidback but strong support from community organizers is essential, and is usually required for a rather long time until people unused to planning flounder and fail, and a percent of them struggle and succeed. Programs intended to help poor people improve themselves are most effective when they are self improve-**

ment programs. Programs of this kind cannot be planned hurriedly, nor can they be planned primarily by scholars, human services professionals and politicians, though all groups have much to offer, and must be included.

Richard W. Boone, a member of the earlier President's Committee for Juvenile Delinquency staff, and the person most responsible for writing the keystone concept "maximum feasible participation of the poor" into law, was Sargent Shriver's Director of Policy and Development for the Office of Economic Opportunity. Dick Boone and the Community Action staff knew that they would not have much to show the media in a mere eight months. Dick's boss, Sargent Shriver, was concerned about the political viability of the War on Poverty; teenage dropouts, many from minority populations—the kind of people Job Corps was being created to serve—are not popular in our society. To fly politically, the War on Poverty would have to serve constituencies perceived as "the deserving poor." What clientele would better fit the bill than young children from economically impoverished families?

Head Start was in part invented as a temporizing measure to put something appealing on the table while what Dick Boone and the Community Action staff (and the Job Corps staff as well) considered to be the *real* poverty program—the war being mounted in a sincere effort to break the cycle of poverty—was whipped into shape. Head Start, first conceived of as a health program (nourishing food, immunizations, and health screening) plus a variety of generally enriching experiences and excursions for children who would enter school for the first time in the fall of 1965, was also, everyone enthusiastically agreed, a great way of *really* readying children for their imminent encounter with the middle class world of school systems.

Based on his own admiration for the man's uniquely creative abilities in public administration, and on the enthusiastic recommendations of David L. Hackett, former Executive Director of the President's Committee on Juvenile Delinquency, Dick Boone, brought Jule Sugarman in from the State Department to serve as administrative head of Head Start during its launch year. Jule had been a key consultant to CAP for some time; actually, he had designed its organizational aspects. Dick Boone remembers (1990):

"As Jule and I and other staff developed the Head Start concept, we became increasingly convinced that this would be a unique opportunity to reach children, often in desperate need, with multiple services. Equally important, it would be an opportunity to reach their families to *truly* involve them in planning programs for their own children, and in on-the-job training in a variety of human services. The education, health, and social welfare institutions were set in traditional molds. They were far from accomplishing the goal of providing all that the children needed, were unwilling to coordinate and collaborate, and weren't even *attempting* the goal of offering *parents* opportunities for all-around development."

A memorandum drafted by Dick to Sargent Shriver in December, 1964, the subject of which was "PROJECT HEAD START—A PROGRAM FOR DISADVANTAGED CHILDREN BEFORE THEY ENTER SCHOOL," outlines Head Start, much as we know it today, stressing, in a section entitled "Project Head Start: A First Step," that "it will reach into. . .communities which

—Show concrete evidence that parents want and will participate in the programs. . .

—Need help most

—Head Start will use the talents of
3,400 professionals
12,000 full- and part-time volunteers
5,000 paid non-professionals—largely parents"

I.Q. boosting was the last thing on the minds of Dick Boone and his staff.

An Advisory Panel of interdisciplinary specialists was quickly put together, chiefly by Jule Sugarman, except for several people put on by Sargent Shriver because they were connected to the Kennedy Foundation, and greatly respected by "Sarge". It met a record eight times in six weeks to add depth and prestige to the new program. Many other specialists were flown in for the day for consultation. Dick Boone, Stan Salett, Sandy Kravitz and I chaired these one day meetings. Head Start was flung together with historic speed by the remarkable Jule Sugarman. Sargent Shriver found the perfect national Head Start Director, Dr. Julius B. Richmond, a pediatrician with a long history of involvement in early childhood education and social services for the young children of low-income families, plus impeccable academic credentials. Dr. Richmond came down from Syracuse each week during Head Start's first year-and-a-half.

Eventually the Head Start program was administered out of the federal government's regional offices, as it is today. But in the beginning we had only regional individuals, all of us working in one huge room at OEO headquarters. Because I was on staff first, when the moment came for OEO administrators to create seven Senior Program Analyst positions, one for each region of the country, I was given first choice, and chose the Southeastern Region, consisting of seven states.

The Southeastern Region interested me most because I had been sitting in the bleachers watching the civil rights movement swell in the South throughout the thirteen years that Jack Greenberg of the NAACP Legal Defense and Education Fund, Inc. had been my brother-in-law, and the husband of one of my best friends. In addition to having frequently listened from the sidelines while Jack's colleagues engaged in animated dinner table and living room discussions of their hair raising adventures in the segregated, Klan infested Southern states, I had taken a course with Jack at N.Y.U. entitled, "Legal Approach to Human Relations," and later in the 1950s had written my masters degree thesis at the University of Delaware on racial desegregation in Delaware's public schools—in 1954, Jack had argued and won the Delaware school desegregation case in the U.S. Supreme Court.

Prior to that I had done an extensive special project at Sarah Lawrence College on "the history and culture of the American black family" with History of American Society professor Bert Lowenberg and Cultural Anthropology professor Irv Goldman. This was an aspect of my "major"—parent/child psychology and early childhood education (progressive education) as avenues of social change. I took a ton of social science and depth psychology.

Because of my mother's background, deep caring, and life work, I had grown up in the midst of concerns highly relevant to my later work with Head Start and CDGM.

My mother's grandmother attended a Quaker boarding school in Downingtown, Pennsylvania that—in the basement—ran an underground railway station for escaping slaves. It was this great grandmother's responsibility—she was sixteen at the time—to watch the younger children every night while the teachers cooked and planned with the freedom seekers. As an adult, this great grandmother was a member of the group that founded the Ethical Culture Society originated by Felix Adler, a former rabbi. The goal of this (largely Jewish) group of people was to focus on leading ethical lives and to do good without religious rituals, robes, and other trappings. They were liberals actively involved in bettering their communities. The great grandmother founded and participated in guiding New York City's Christie Street settlement house. The Ethical Culture Society founded and sponsored a number of social change oriented projects, including the Hudson Guild (another settlement house, one in which my grandmother was actively involved); the Ethical Culture School (started to provide opportunity to working class children); and the Encampment for Citizenship.

In 1946, my grandmother, Alice Pollitzer, was a co-founder of the Encampment which is headquartered in Berkeley, CA, and still operates its six-week summer program for sixteen-to-nineteen-year-old youth from diverse ethnic, religious, racial, economic, and geographic backgrounds. For forty-five years, this program, long supported by Eleanor Roosevelt, has been developing social responsibility, leadership skills, and critical thinking through in-depth exposure to current social issues and emphasis on active citizen participation. Among its graduates are Ada Deer, the Native American Rights activist who played a central role in restoring reservation status for the Menominee Indians, and Eleanor Holmes Norton, Washington D.C.'s new Congressional Delegate.

My mother's mother, Alice Pollitzer, was a member of the first class to graduate from Barnard College. She married a physician who became heavily involved with New York City Public Health Department work, especially visiting impoverished families whose children needed treatment for typhoid fever. (He had some frail-looking, bird-like Southern lady sisters who were among the first people in Charleston, South Carolina—long before the sixties—to insist on racially integrating everything they did.) My mother's mother and her husband sent their daughters—my mother and aunt Honi—to the Ethical Culture School, which featured a "discovery style," "developmentally appropriate" program, and educational excellence.

My aunt, Honi Weiss, with a masters from the New School for Social

Research, was a social worker in a Harlem public school; a leading board member and fund-raiser for the (model) Wiltwyck School for (delinquent) Boys for many decades; and an active board member or significant contributor to many progressive and/or race related causes. Her husband, Louis Weiss, was part of a well-known liberal New York law firm. He was Marshall Field's lawyer and played a key part in creating P.M. newspaper and the Field Foundation.

Like her mother and sister a Barnard graduate, my mother Margaret Pollitzer, was active in the peace movement during the World War I era, and a life-long student of how parents and educators create war- or peace-making psychologies in young children. For a few years, she lived at the famous Henry Street settlement house. Settlement houses were the original one-stop "multi-service" plus "resource and referral" centers, where poor families lived, learned, planned and earned with dedicated, trusted middle class liberal and rapid reformist professional people who strongly wanted to be helpful in developing parents and children. Some were benevolent dictators of the social services and health orthodoxies of their times; some were political activists advocating the eradication of specific roots of poverty and the empowerment of poor people. The mix of service "deliverers" and community organizers was probably about what it is today.

For many years, my mother was co-director of a well-known (still operating) school established to experiment with and demonstrate the philosophies and practices of Freud, Jung, Adler, and Dewey. The school started with the (nine-to-three p.m.) two-year-old group, and went through high school. Walden School's goal was to develop people who could live cooperatively and constructively in a democracy. All her life my mother was interested in cultural anthropology, history, and politics. She was a big international traveller and had a very global view of the world. In 1929, on a solo trip to the Soviet Union to check out the extraordinary social change underway, she met the fellow American—a journalist—who became her husband and my father, Lindsay Hoben.

My father's father, Allan Hoben, was a Baptist minister, faculty person at the liberal University of Chicago, and college president. He was an early convert to and proponent of the concept of family planning information and services for all, to increase the probability that all children would be wanted and well cared for. My father later became the liberal Editor-in-Chief of a leading liberal newspaper, the Milwaukee Journal. The two organizations to which he made substantial contributions throughout his lifetime were Planned Parenthood International and the Urban League.

My mother contributed annually all her adult life to these and many other social change concerned organizations, including the United Negro College Fund (she knew all about Tougaloo College long before I'd ever heard of it); NAACP (she knew all about Aaron Henry long before I'd ever heard of him); a Mississippi sharecropper relief fund; Myles' Horton's Highlander Folk School where Rosa Parks learned the passive resistance skills that made her so famous in the Montgomery Bus Boycott later led by the Reverend Martin Luther King, and where a song that Mrs. Myles Horton—Zylphia Horton—had taught Pete

Seeger—"We Shall Overcome"—became the theme song of the freedom movement.

My mother taught elementary education and supervized students who practice taught largely in inner city schools. She was an active professional on the board of a big city family service agency whose clients were usually multi-problem, low-income people.

Professionally, I've seldom done anything original. Usually, I just walk in my mother's footsteps, carrying on family traditions. So it's no wonder that at OEO/Head Start, in February 1965, I chose the Southeast Region.

Sargent Shriver's office contacted top officials directly to announce the new national Head Start program. I sent telegrams to the people in charge of social services, health, and education in each county in the Southeastern states further explaining and encouraging them to apply for Head Start (and had a copy of each telegram sent to OEO for the files). Many of them did. I phoned every progressive and grassroots group in the South that I could think of, starting, of course, with my mother's friend Myles Horton. Myles came to see me in Washington to learn about Head Start.[52] A handful of assistants were brought on board to help each regional individual. Then Jule Sugarman came up with the idea of borrowing government interns—he had *been* one—to serve as runners to help us spread the word of Head Start across the United States and into all its hidden crevices. We regional individuals also flew around on airplanes and dashed to and fro in our rental cars. I made many trips to many parts of each of "my" states. Applications piled up. The piles grew so tall they tipped over. We filled cartons and more cartons and more cartons, and processed and processed and processed. One stop on the assembly line was where the budget was checked. At another stop, a group checked compliance with the (at least token) racial integration requirement. When applications reached the Community Action shop, plans for participation of poor people themselves in various levels of the proposed Head Start program were examined. Hundreds of District of Columbia substitute teachers were hired, apparently overnight, to help move the applications along our conveyor belt toward funding.

Mississippi was the problem. The Governor had said that War on Poverty programs were not going to enter his state. Actually, however, I *was* getting some. I met with a white state legislator in Yazoo City. I went to Corinth with a bright young white man named Troy Norris. There were a handful of white school superintendents. It was puzzling. How did these people dare defy the Governor? And none of them seemed the least bit defiant. They all seemed super establishment. The most puzzling of all was an applicant named Rex MacRaney who came to see me in Washington about a project called Mid-State Opportunities. He was a nice, mild man, and an attorney. He had been a Mississippi Game and Fish Commissioner. He invited me to Mississippi to help develop

[52]Two books about the Hortons' remarkable Highlander Center can be ordered from Highlander in New Market, TN, 37820. The first is called *We Make the Road by Walking*; the second is *Highlander Folk School, a History of its Major Programs, 1932–1961.*

the Mid-State Opportunities project. I went. Rex was (and is) a heavy drinker. We talked a lot and became friends.

Gradually that spring, gleaning clues from many sources, I got the picture. Governor Johnson, Senator Stennis, and Senator Eastland were all powerful and all talked tough racist talk, but they were not all the same. Senator Eastland understood that social change was coming. He wanted it kept under the establishment's control, of course, but he realized that the lid could not be kept on the boiling over black situation much longer. He also knew that something had to be done about the increasing poverty being caused by his state's loss of agriculture and lack of industry to replace it. From Rex's friends, I heard what was alleged to be the Senator's perspective: "We'll give the niggers half, but not the top half." (In my more cynical moments, I believe that this is the bottom line feeling of all us white folks, even the elite liberals who lead in progressive public policy planning.) All of the applicants for Head Start in Mississippi, I came to believe, were Senator Eastland's "safe" people. (Troy Norris, for example, was Alabama Senator Sparkman's nephew.) Better them than the integrationists, or—worse yet—the civil rights workers, or, God forbid, "the niggers" *themselves.*

Recently, Rex has said in public what he often used to tell me in private—that Senator Eastland always had the state police follow me around Mississippi's dark night, long distance highways as I went (before CDGM, when I still worked for OEO) from (white) applicant to (white) applicant developing Head Start proposals for submission to Washington. "He didn't want anything to happen to a girl from Sargent Shriver's office. It wouldn't have looked good in the newspapers," Rex has confided.

There was one applicant that didn't fit this mold, but I didn't work with him. He was the *only* Mississippi applicant I didn't work with. This was Aaron Henry in Clarksdale. Sandford Kravitz, Director of Research, Development and Training for the Community Action Program, was sent to Mississippi to develop a very large Head Start program with Aaron. Sandy remembers Rex MacRaney being there. He didn't know why. Later, Rex explained to me that he was keeping an eye on the development of this major "new South" political project backed by the moderate Democrats in Washington as part of eliminating the segregationist Democrats. Senator Eastland sent Rex to report on happenings as they occured. (Later, Congressman John Brademas, Sargent Shriver, and others visited Aaron's Head Start. It was the moderate Democrats to whom a large part of CDGM was given—to MAP. Aaron Henry was a MAP board member.)

According to Rex MacRaney, it went like this: In the spring of 1965, Senator Eastland phoned and said, "Boy, you come on down to Dodgeville." That was where Senator Eastland lived. When Rex got there, Governor Paul Johnson was sitting with the Senator. The Senator knew Rex because Rex's father had owned the cotton gin and the mill in Eastland's county, thus was an important constitutent. Therefore, Rex had been chosen to introduce the Senator when he was the graduation speaker at Rex's high school. Senator Eastland had been appointed to fill Senator Bilbo's seat when he died; Eastland was appointed by Governor Paul Johnson's *father* when *he* was governor. The Senator had seen the black vote coming, and had seen that Rex had "good relations" with blacks as he worked side by side with them in the mill and then in World War II.

"He courted me. He made me feel good. We were drinking buddies. He wanted me to lead the newly voting blacks his direction," Rex explained to me over drinks in the sixties and again in 1990. "And I knew young Paul Johnson" [the man who was governor of Mississippi during CDGM's early years, and who was sitting in Eastland's mansion in Dodgeville when Eastland summoned Rex to come] "because we were in Hawaii together in World War II.

"When I got down there to Dodgeville, the Senator said, 'Son, Aaron Henry's trying to start a War on Poverty program over in Clarksdale. We'll let him do it, but he isn't going to get the whole pie. I want *you* to start a CAP in *our* counties, Rex. The plantation owners need heavy machinery operators, so put in for a few million for that among other things.' So I developed Mid-State Opportunities in Panola, Quitman, Tunica, Grenada, Tallahatchie, Lafayette, Calhoun, and LeFlore counties. I went to see you in Washington about Head Start money, and carried messages from the Senator and the Governor to people in the highest offices in OEO. We got a lot of money and trained heavy equipment operators, had literacy training, we built two hundred houses, we had Head Start. . .The Senator and Governor 'assigned' me to keep an eye on Aaron Henry's poverty program. I had been in World War II and seen something of the world. I knew change was coming. We needed to be on top of it."

"Did the Senator 'assign' you to keep an eye on CDGM and its millions through me?" I asked in 1990. Rex grinned and ordered another drink.

INDEX

(to new 1990 pages only, pages 707–819)

POLLY GREENBERG was centrally involved in CDGM from its conception early in 1965 and was in fact instrumental in initiating it, *first* as the staff person at the Office of Economic Opportunity responsible for introducing PROJECT HEAD START into the seven Southeastern states and bringing applications back to Washington, D.C.; *then* as one of three people who dreamed up this *particular* HEAD START—planned, operated, and staffed by thousands of poor black Mississippians; *next* (having resigned from the federal government) as DIRECTOR OF TEACHER DEVELOPMENT AND PROGRAM FOR CHILDREN for the 12,000-child CDGM project itself in rural Mississippi; also as initiator and writer/editor of CDGM's newsletter, created as community support (emotional) and northern support (political), as well as script writer of CDGM's immensely moving film "Chance for Change"; and *finally* as researcher/interviewer/author of SLIPPERY SHOES and its 1990 updating section, which in itself is an exciting addition to the literature on how social programs should be assessed.

POLLY GREENBERG deeply believes that, to a greater or lesser degree, low-income parents, whether minority or not, always feel alienated from—or oppressed by—programs "provided" *for* them. Usually, the result of "delivering" services to "recipients," be they parents' children in child care settings and schools, or in the health care system, or welfare "recipients," is far less parental support of "the system" and its offerings than is in children's best interest. This so-called apathy is often combined with dependency or resentment.